Commissioners of National Education in I

Commissioners of National Education in Ireland : forty-first report, 1874, with appendices

Commissioners of National Education in I

Commissioners of National Education in Ireland : forty-first report, 1874, with appendices

ISBN/EAN: 9783741104589

Manufactured in Europe, USA, Canada, Australia, Japa

Cover: Foto ©ninafisch / pixelio.de

Manufactured and distributed by brebook publishing software (www.brebook.com)

Commissioners of National Education in I

Commissioners of National Education in Ireland : forty-first report, 1874, with appendices

THE

FORTY-FIRST REPORT

OF THE

COMMISSIONERS

OF

NATIONAL EDUCATION

IN IRELAND,

(FOR THE YEAR 1874).

Presented to both Houses of Parliament by Command of Her Majesty.

DUBLIN:
PRINTED BY ALEXANDER THOM, 87 & 88, ABBEY-STREET,
FOR HER MAJESTY'S STATIONERY OFFICE.

1875.

[C.—1226.] *Price 3d.*

THE

FORTY-FIRST REPORT

OF THE

COMMISSIONERS OF NATIONAL EDUCATION IN IRELAND,

(FOR THE YEAR 1874).

TO HIS GRACE JAMES DUKE OF ABERCORN, K.G.,

LORD LIEUTENANT-GENERAL AND GENERAL GOVERNOR OF IRELAND.

May it please your Grace,

I.—1. We, the Commissioners of National Education in Ireland, submit to your Excellency this our Forty-first Report.

2. On the 31st of December, 1874, we had 7,257 schools in operation, which, compared with 1873, was an increase of 97. *Increase of Schools.*

3. The number of individual pupils on rolls who made any attendance at our schools between 1st of January and 31st of December, 1874, was 1,006,511, which, compared with 1873, was an increase of 31,815. *Increase in number on rolls.*

4. The average daily attendance of pupils for the year 1874 was 395,390, which, compared with 1873, was an increase of 22,019. *Increase in average attendance.*

5. On a recent occasion, in reply to an inquiry from your Grace in reference to the irregularity in the attendance of pupils at Irish National Schools, we stated:— *Improvement in quality of attendance.*

"This is a subject which from year to year has occupied the serious attention of the Board. The Commissioners regret the disproportion which exists in their schools between the average attendance and the number on the rolls. The habit, and, in a vast proportion of cases, the necessity of the Irish farmer to make his children, however young, take part in the spring and harvest operations of the farm, have much to say to this unfortunate result; and when it is remembered that there are in the country upwards of 300,000 holdings, the value of each of which does not exceed £8, it cannot be a matter of surprise that this habit or necessity of bringing into requisition the labour of the children causes great periodical reductions in the attendance at the schools.

"The Commissioners have endeavoured, as the only remedy at their command, to make the schools as attractive to the children and their parents as possible, and the liberality of Parliament in awarding grants for payments for results during the last three years has proved to be a salutary stimulus in this direction. The Commissioners in their last Report had the satisfaction of informing His Grace that, whilst there was an increase in the number of individual pupils actually attending the schools in 1873, as compared with 1873, of only 14,363, the *average daily attendance* had increased by 17,550, thus indicating a decided improvement in the regularity of the children's attendance."

6. Taking into consideration the fact that during the year 1874, scarlatina and other infectious diseases were epidemic in numerous parts of Ireland, and that in consequence the attendance of the children was seriously interrupted, we feel very great satisfaction in referring to the increase of 31,815 in the number on the rolls, and especially to that of 22,019 in the average attendance, showing as these numbers do, not only a gratifying augmentation in the number of our pupils, but a continuing improvement from year to year in the *quality* of their attendance.

Number of schools in operation, and children on rolls from 1833 to 1874.

7. The following Table exhibits the number of National Schools in operation, together with the number of children on the rolls, as specified in our several Reports, to the 31st of December, 1874:—

No. and Date of Report.	No. of Schools in operation.	No. of Children on the Rolls for	
No. 1, 31st December, 1833,	789	[illegible]	107,042
No. 2, 31st March, 1835,	1,106	,,	145,521
No. 3, do. 1836,	1,181	,,	153,707
No. 4, do. 1837,	1,300	,,	166,929
No. 5, do. 1838,	1,384	,,	169,548
No. 6, 31st December, 1839,	1,581	,,	192,971
No. 7, do. 1840,	1,978	,,	232,560
No. 8, do. 1841,	2,337	,,	281,849
No. 9, do. 1842,	2,721	,,	319,792
No. 10, do. 1843,	2,912	,,	355,320
No. 11, do. 1844,	3,153	,,	395,550
No. 12, do. 1845,	3,426	,,	432,844
No. 13, do. 1846,	3,637	,,	456,410
No. 14, do. 1847,	3,825	,,	402,632
No. 15, do. 1848,	4,109	,,	507,469
No. 16, do. 1849,	4,321	,,	480,623
No. 17, do. 1850,	4,547	,,	511,239
No. 18, do. 1851,	4,704	,,	520,401
No. 19, do. 1852,	4,875	,,	544,604
No. 20, do. 1853,	5,023	,,	550,631
No. 21, do. 1854,	5,178	,,	551,110
No. 22, do. 1855,	5,124	,,	535,905
No. 23, do. 1856,	5,245	31 Dec.,	560,134
No. 24, do. 1857,	5,337	[illegible]	776,473
No. 25, do. 1858,	5,408	,,	803,610
No. 26, do. 1859,	5,496	,,	806,510
No. 27, do. 1860,	5,632	,,	804,000
No. 28, do. 1861,	5,830	,,	803,364
No. 29, do. 1862,	6,010	,,	812,527
No. 30, do. 1863,	6,163	,,	840,569
No. 31, do. 1864,	6,263	,,	870,401
No. 32, do. 1865,	6,372	,,	922,084
No. 33, do. 1866,	6,453	,,	910,819
No. 34, do. 1867,	6,520	,,	913,198
No. 35, do. 1868,	6,586	,,	918,344
No. 36, do. 1869,	6,707	,,	941,289
No. 37, do. 1870,	6,806	,,	950,999
No. 38, do. 1871,	6,914	,,	972,006
No. 39, do. 1872,	7,050	,,	960,434
No. 40, do. 1873,	7,160	,,	974,696
No. 41, do. 1874,	7,257	,,	1,006,511

8. The number of applications for grants to new schools in the year 1874 was 221. To 166 of these we gave the required assistance, either as grants for building, or grants of requisites and in aid of salaries. The remaining 55 applications were rejected for various reasons, of which official records are kept. Applications for grants to new schools.

9. The annexed Tabular Return of the 166 Schools added to our list during the Year 1874 (viz., 145 schools in operation, and 21 building grants), shows the Number in each Province, with the Nature of the Aid Granted. New schools.

Provinces.	Requisites, and in aid of Salary.	Towards Building and Furnishing Schools.	Total.
Ulster, . .	69	7	76
Munster, . .	29	11	40
Leinster, . .	22	–	22
Connaught, .	25	3	28
Total, . .	145	21	166

10. Forty-one vested schools, towards the erection of which grants had been previously made, were opened for the reception of pupils during the year. The names of these schools are given in the Appendix. Vested schools opened, &c.

11. One suspended school was re-opened during the year. Suspended School re-opened.

12. During the year 85 schools were struck off the rolls, chiefly for want of sufficient attendance, and 5 schools were placed on the suspended list. Schools struck off and placed on suspended list.

13. The number of schools on the "suspended list" at the close of the year was 77. Suspended schools are from time to time re-opened, when the causes for their suspension cease. Suspended schools.

14. At the termination of the year 1874, we had on our list 2,096 vested schools. The number vested in trustees was 1,186; the number vested in our Board (including 146 assigned) was 815; the number for which we held bonds for the observance of our rules was 95—total, 2,096. Of this total number, 137 schools, to which building grants are outstanding, are not yet in operation. Vested schools.

15. The number of non-vested schools in connexion with us on the 31st of December, 1874, was 5,356. Number non-vested.

16. The following is the distribution of schools in operation according to the several provinces, showing the numbers for which Operation Schools and attendance.

returns have been received. The pupils on rolls and in attendance, and the averages for each school are as follows:—

Provinces.	Total Operating Schools.	Total No. of Schools from which returns have been received.	Total No. of Pupils actually attending School during the year ended 31st Dec., 1874.	Average daily attendance for year ending 31st December, 1874.
Ulster, . . .	2,737	2,634	356,013	132,457
Munster, . . .	1,813	1,779	268,095	120,328
Leinster, . . .	1,558	1,510	206,508	83,476
Connaught, . . .	1,150	1,100	173,292	59,135
Total, . .	7,257	7,022	1,006,311	395,396
Average per School,	—	—	143·1	56·2

Religion of Managers of New Schools.

17. The following Table shows the Number of the new schools under Managers of each religious denomination—distinguishing clerical from lay:—

Religious Denominations.	Clerical.		Lay.		Total.	
	No. of Managers.	No. of Schools.	No. of Managers.	No. of Schools.	No. of Managers.	No. of Schools.
R.C.,*	60	75	3	3	63	78
E.C.,*	40	43	22	28	63	71
Pres.,*	11	11	1	1	12	12
Others,*	2	2	1	1	3	3
Total, . .	113	131	27	33	140	164

The remaining 2 schools are Poor Law Union Schools, under official management.

A considerable number of the managers accounted for in this return, especially in the case of the clerical managers, are persons who at the time of the award of the new grants had several other National Schools under their management.

Total Managers on Rolls.

18. The following Table shows that on the 31st of December, 1874, there were 1,889 clerical and 999 lay managers.

RETURN I.—NUMBERS of INDIVIDUAL MANAGERS of NATIONAL SCHOOLS, classified according to RELIGIOUS DENOMINATIONS, LAY and CLERICAL.

CLERICAL MANAGERS:		LAY MANAGERS:	
R.C., ...	1,252	R.C., ...	204
E.C., ...	261	E.C., ...	369
Pres., ...	328	Pres., ...	176
Other Denominations,	48	Others, ...	43
		Official, ...	207
Total, . .	1,889	Total, . .	999

* Throughout this Report "R.C." denotes Roman Catholics; "E.C.," members of the late Established Church; "Pres.," Presbyterians, and "Others," persons of other persuasions.

RETURN II.—NUMBER of NATIONAL SCHOOLS, classified according to RELIGIOUS DENOMINATIONS of MANAGERS, and distinguishing the latter into LAY and CLERICAL.

SCHOOLS UNDER CLERICAL MANAGERS:		SCHOOLS UNDER LAY MANAGERS:	
R.C. . .	4,741	R.C. . . .	209
E.C. . .	390	E.C. . . .	741
Pres. . .	588	Pres. . . .	725
Others, . .	63	Others. . . .	69
		Official, . . .	373
Total, . .	5,782	Total, . .	1,006

NOTE.—Return II. is exclusive of a few schools under joint management, which cannot be classified under the headings of the Return.

19. We have received from the managers a return of the religious denominations of the pupils in attendance in 1874, from which it appears that— Religious Denominations of Pupils.

79·6 per cent. are R.C.
11· per cent. Presb.
8·6 per cent. E.C.
·8 per cent. others.

The details in counties and provinces will be found in the Appendix.

20. The following Table shows the per-centage of Schools exhibiting a mixed attendance of Roman Catholic and Protestant Pupils, for each year from 1867 to 1874:— Schools with mixed Religious attendance.

	1867.	1868.	1869.	1870.	1871.	1872.	1873.	1874.
Ulster, . .	63·9	63·2	63·5	62·6	60·1	60·0	70·1	78·7
Munster, . .	40·5	40·1	40·3	40·5	39·5	40·3	41·5	41·4
Leinster, . .	48·0	48·3	46·9	46·7	46·6	48·0	49·6	51·4
Connaught, .	50·5	48·9	47·5	49·6	45·8	47·8	47·9	48·1
Total, .	59·9	59·3	58·6	59·8	57·1	58·1	59·4	58·0

21. In the Appendix will be found tables exhibiting details of the attendance at mixed schools, and also at schools where the attendance is unmixed.

22. The number of District and Minor Model Schools in operation at the end of the year was 26—this number is exclusive of the Model Schools in the Metropolitan District. The Results' examinations, of which a special tabulation is set forth in the Appendix, fully show that these Schools continue to maintain their high character. Model Schools.

23. The total number of pupils on the rolls of the Model Schools for the year ended the 31st of December, 1874, was 19,012, and the average daily attendance for the same period, 8,619. The numbers for the year 1873 were 18,951 on rolls, and 8,654 in average daily attendance.

County.	Number.	Name of School.	Religious Denominations.				Total.	Average Daily Attendance.
			E.C.	R.C.	Pres.	Other Persuasions.		
Dublin,	1	Metropolitan:						
"		Marlborough-st.,	1,419	2,400	369	201	4,442	1,687
"		Inchicore,	175	370	6	–	551	235
"		West Dublin,	65	711	20	3	799	375
Antrim,	2	Belfast,	749	84	1,478	197	2,488	1,116
"	3	Ballymena,	78	16	281	43	418	211
Armagh,	4	Newry,	236	65	230	50	581	263
Cavan,	5	Bailieborough,	137	280	134	–	551	260
Down,	6	Newtownards,	39	7	480	77	603	227
Fermanagh,	7	Enniskillen,	276	14	43	64	397	107
Londonderry,	8	Coleraine,	77	11	244	42	374	163
"	9	Londonderry,	224	15	390	66	695	300
Cork,	10	Dunmanway,	26	550	–	11	587	269
"	11	Cork,	488	188	47	96	819	401
Limerick,	12	Limerick,	250	114	42	64	470	238
Tipperary,	13	Clonmel,	95	214	16	2	327	143
Waterford,	14	Waterford,	146	168	36	64	414	166
Kildare,	15	Athy,	128	9	68	6	211	110
Kilkenny,	16	Kilkenny,	206	38	27	9	280	135
Meath,	17	Trim,	72	180	1	5	258	117
Wexford,	18	Enniscorthy,	96	17	24	11	148	75
Galway,	19	Galway,	99	61	61	32	243	116
Sligo,	20	Sligo,	170	25	88	117	400	214
Antrim,	21	Ballymoney (Minor),	60	11	346	11	428	233
"	22	Carrickfergus,	113	5	268	69	456	244
Armagh,	23	Lurgan,	338	46	200	57	641	347
Monaghan,	24	Monaghan,	220	18	169	10	417	227
Tyrone,	25	Omagh,	241	14	175	63	493	227
"	26	N.-T.-Stewart,	76	–	164	3	243	126
King's,	27	Parsonstown,	148	81	11	21	261	129
		Total,	6,454	5,744	5,427	1,387	19,012	8,619
		Percentage,	34·	30·2	28·5	7·3	100	–

Number trained. 24. We trained during the year in the Marlborough-street Training Establishment, and supported at the public expense 288 persons, of whom 105 were males and 183 females; 136 of these were either Principal or Assistant Teachers of National Schools; the remaining 102 were chiefly ex-pupil teachers or monitors of Model Schools, ex-monitors or distinguished pupils of National Schools. 108 were R.C.; 67 were Pres.; 54 were E.C.; and 9 were of other persuasions. The total number trained from the commencement of our proceedings to the 31st of December, 1874, is 9,503.

Training departments. 25. The establishments in which the Teachers attending at our Training Institution are boarded and lodged, continue to be efficiently conducted. The inmates have been distinguished, as heretofore, for the general correctness of their conduct, for order and discipline, for the exercise of kindly feeling towards each other, and for the careful observance of their religious duties.

26. We had in our service at the end of the year 1874, 7,038 Principal Teachers, 2,901 Assistants, and 204 Junior Literary and Industrial Assistants, making, in the whole, 10,148, of whom 8,514 were trained in our Normal Establishment. We also had in our service, at the same period, 310 Workmistresses. The Conductors of Convent Schools paid by capitation are not included in this return. Number of Teachers.

27. The number of teachers in the several classes was as follows:—

Class.	Principals.		Assistants.		Junior Assistants.	Workmistresses, &c.
	Males.	Females.	Males.	Females.		
1¹ . .	129	89	10	13	.	.
1² . .	449	230	27	48	.	.
2¹ . .	976	580	23	149	.	.
2² . .	825	378	43	207	.	.
3¹ . .	1,586	781	240	930	.	.
3² . .	748	380	306	889	.	.
Total, .	4,413	2,625	660	2,241	204	310
	7,038		2,901			

The scale of salaries of teachers is as follows:—

	Males.	Females.
First class—First division, . . .	£52 a year,	£43 a year.
" Second division, . .	38 "	30 "
Second class, ...	30 "	24 "
Third class, ...	24 "	20 "
Assistants, ...	24 "	20 "

28. The total amount of salaries, premiums, gratuities, and results fees paid by us in the twelve months ended the 31st December, 1874, to the Principal Teachers, Assistants, Monitors, and Workmistresses in National Schools—including the Central and other Model Schools, and the payments to Organizing Teachers—was £448,860 16s. 6d. This sum includes £5,127 10s. 11d., school fees, apportioned to Teachers in Model Schools. Total amount of salaries, gratuities, &c., paid in 1874.

29. The following table shows, in counties and provinces, the amount of local emoluments received in aid of salaries of teachers of National Schools (excluding Workhouse Schools, Prison Local emoluments of Teachers.

Schools, and Lunatic Asylum Schools), during the year 1874, with the average for each school, and for each pupil in average daily attendance.

Provinces and Counties.	Payments by Pupils.			Subscriptions, &c.			Total.			No. of Schools.	No. of Pupils.	Average per School.			Average per Pupil.	
	£	s.	d.	£	s.	d.	£	s.	d.			£	s.	d.	s.	d.
Ulster:																
Antrim,	8,190	16	1	1,062	13	1	9,253	11	2	516	30,023	18	13	3½	6	3½
Armagh,	1,719	12	8	927	11	1	2,647	3	7	272	12,461	9	14	6½	4	3¼
Cavan,	813	6	11	315	0	0	1,128	6	11	256	11,685	4	7	11½	2	6½
Donegal,	1,348	7	3	648	1	0	2,036	8	3	347	13,340	5	15	7½	2	10½
Down,	5,037	15	6	1,137	5	4	6,174	1	10	302	21,226	13	11	0½	5	8½
Fermanagh,	923	11	8	346	4	10	[illegible]	3	3	137	5,752	7	3	11	3	7½
Londonderry,	1,929	17	8	2,033	7	3½	3,963	4	6	333	11,624	11	18	10	6	9½
Monaghan,	799	11	4	463	10	0	1,263	1	4	163	8,393	7	17	11½	3	1½
Tyrone,	1,691	13	3	616	7	0	2,311	0	3	321	13,973	7	13	9	3	6
Total,	21,582	6	6	7,616	9	5	29,201	1	3	2,496	127,674	11	13	8	4	6½
Munster:																
Clare,	1,911	4	6	105	0	0	2,016	4	6	207	12,316	9	14	9½	3	2½
Cork,	[illegible]	15	1	1,101	10	1	[illegible]	5	2	673	45,171	[illegible]	5	4	2	7
Kerry,	2,363	7	2	353	4	4	2,716	11	6	288	20,071	9	8	9½	2	7
Limerick,	3,274	11	8	461	5	0	3,735	16	8	230	16,039	16	16	7½	4	7½
Tipperary,	3,035	19	4	503	3	4	3,539	3	8	278	14,107	12	12	10½	4	5½
Waterford,	1,275	8	1	538	13	8	1,814	1	1	118	8,473	14	9	0½	4	11½
Total,	18,723	3	4	3,251	14	9	21,977	18	1	1,789	117,325	12	13	0½	3	8½
Leinster:																
Carlow,	384	3	5	94	3	8	478	6	11	62	3,308	7	14	3½	3	10
Dublin,	3,529	18	5	1,059	3	10	4,589	14	8	219	10,516	22	10	10½	5	9
Kildare,	775	6	11	174	7	6	949	14	5	101	5,221	9	8	0½	3	7½
Kilkenny,	1,183	12	5	391	11	11	1,576	3	4	172	8,673	7	18	10½	3	1½
King's,	793	8	4	150	10	1	950	18	0	101	4,914	9	6	10½	3	10½
Longford,	301	7	4	139	15	11	441	7	3	118	4,673	4	14	1½	1	10½
Louth,	444	7	10	257	7	0	701	14	10	112	5,172	8	13	11½	3	3½
Meath,	726	8	4	549	18	1	1,276	6	5	164	8,723	7	14	7½	3	9½
Queen's,	543	8	8	339	9	0	882	3	8	98	4,535	8	5	0½	3	6½
Westmeath,	590	6	8	136	9	10	726	16	6	124	5,657	5	17	2½	2	6½
Wexford,	910	11	9	174	19	3	1,115	11	0	148	7,156	7	9	8½	3	1½
Wicklow,	727	8	1	378	6	5	1,102	13	8	98	4,976	11	19	1½	4	5½
Total,	11,318	17	4	3,983	17	0	15,232	15	1	1,477	81,232	10	6	6½	3	0
Connaught:																
Galway,	1,361	16	4	322	19	0	1,684	8	4	277	13,816	6	4	3½	2	5½
Leitrim,	426	1	6	295	3	0	721	4	6	185	8,838	3	18	0½	1	8½
Mayo,	1,211	17	1	458	9	6	1,670	6	7	278	15,382	6	0	4½	2	2½
Roscommon,	861	13	2	174	18	8	1,036	11	10	285	10,621	5	9	1½	1	11½
Sligo,	868	12	2	138	17	5	1,007	9	7	146	7,510	7	3	11	2	6½
Total,	4,730	1	0	1,390	18	7	6,120	0	4	1,070	56,171	5	14	4½	2	2½
Grand Total,	57,355	2	11	16,116	11	10	73,531	11	9	6,074*	382,283	16	13	11½	3	10

This return shows an increase as compared with the previous year of £8,888 18s. 2d. in the school fees of the pupils, and of £1,240 16s. 5d. in the local subscriptions.

* This amount does not include £6,436 8s. 10d., the value, estimated by the managers, of free residences and gardens for the teachers. The actual value of the local emoluments was £79,967 17s. 7d., which would give an average of £11 18s. 8½d. per school. The disparity between the averages in this table and those in paragraph 33 is mainly due to the circumstance that these averages relate to schools—i.e., to the emoluments of principals and assistants combined, whereas the averages in paragraph 33 relate to principal teachers only.

80. The total amount received by the teaching staff of the schools in connexion with our Board for the year 1874, appears to have been £517,283 0s. 4d., 14·2 per cent. of this sum having been locally provided, and 85·8 per cent. derived from the funds placed at our disposal by the State. Total amount received by teaching staff.

81. When recently invited by your Grace to express our views on the question of the great disproportion which exists between the contribution of the State and of the localities towards the support of schools, we directed our Secretaries to state:— Disproportion between State and local aid.

"The Commissioners direct us to say that they see no mode of substantially increasing the amount of the local contributions, except by the levy of a rate; but, upon the expediency of adopting that course, the Board do not think it to be within their province to tender any advice."

82. In reply to your Grace's recent inquiry as to our views on the important question of the inadequacy of the remuneration of the National teachers, we instructed our secretaries to state— Inadequacy of the pay of the Teachers.

"The Commissioners, when considering this question, took occasion to review the salaries awarded by the Board to the National Teachers at the different periods of a change in the scale of payment since the institution of the National system, and they have directed us to append to this letter an abstract of the salaries granted at each of those successive periods. [See Appendix.]

"The Commissioners also have made minute inquiry to ascertain the incomes from all sources at present derived by the principal teachers for services rendered in conducting National schools, excluding private tuitions, Science and Art payments, and other emoluments earned out of school hours, and have found that, on the average, those incomes are as follows:—

Class of Teachers.	[illegible]	Average Incomes of Principal Teachers.											
		Class Salary, and Good Service Salary.			Results Fees, Gratuities, &c., from Board.			Local Contributions.			Total.		
		£	s.	d.	£	s.	d.	£	s.	d.	£	s.	d.
Males.													
First of First Class, .	93	61	6	1	26	8	10	29	2	11	116	17	10
Second of First Class,	338	44	5	8	20	14	11	18	7	0	83	7	7
Second Class, . .	1,263	33	6	1	17	6	10	12	7	6	62	2	4
Third Class, . .	1,916	24	15	6	11	11	8	7	6	3	43	13	6
Average of all Classes,	.	30	3	11	14	16	11	10	13	7	55	14	5
Females.													
First of First Class, .	50	48	14	9	25	10	6	18	17	9	93	2	5
Second of First Class,	226	35	7	5	19	15	6	14	2	2	69	5	3
Second Class, . .	629	24	18	2	14	18	5	8	4	3	48	0	10
Third Class, . .	623	21	2	5	10	19	0	5	10	3	37	11	8
Average of all Classes,	.	25	4	11	14	2	6	6	6	2	45	12	9

"The Commissioners look with some satisfaction to the result of their inquiry, so far as it exhibits the condition of the First Class Teachers, not only in regard to the personal salaries from the Board enjoyed by these teachers, and the substantial quota of results fees earned by them, but also in respect to the amount of local contributions which they command. The Commissioners, however, desire it to be borne in mind that the teachers of the First Class are a very small proportion of the whole body of the teachers, that they have charge of the largest and best schools, and that, for obvious reasons, it is desirable to be able to point to the comparatively high pecuniary result of their labours as a stimulus to the teachers of the other classes.

"The Commissioners are of opinion that having regard to the high qualifications and valuable services of the First Class Teachers, their pay, as a matter of justice and policy, ought to be still further, to a moderate degree, increased; and that the remuneration of the Second and Third Class Teachers, whether it be compared with the importance of their services, or with the earnings of persons of corresponding acquirements in other employments, is still inadequate.

"They are of opinion that if, in addition to the provisional grant for payments for results, which next year, if the grant be renewed, will amount to at least £120,000, there were an additional grant of a like sum, viz.: £120,000 (also to be expended in payments for results), the incomes of the National teachers would then be placed on a satisfactory footing.

"We are, therefore, directed to state that the Commissioners recommend a renewal, as a permanent arrangement, of the provisional grant for results, viz.: for 1875–76, £120,000; and that they further recommend that an additional grant of £120,000 should also be made, to be applied to the same purpose, making the total for payments for results in 1875–76, £240,000.

"The average incomes of the different classes of principal teachers would then, it is estimated, be as follows:—

Class.	Males.				Females.			
	No. in Class.	Average Income.			No. in Class.	Average Income.		
		£	s.	d.		£	s.	d.
First of First Class,	93	140	17	3	59	116	12	6
Second of First Class,	346	102	13	8	236	87	7	3
Second Class,	1,963	78	8	9	829	69	2	10
Third Class,	1,018	64	15	10	823	48	2	7
Average income of all Classes.	–	69	15	5	–	50	0	8

Pensions.

35. In reference to the question of providing a scheme of pensions for old and disabled teachers, we recently informed your Grace—

"That we are of opinion that a scheme might be advantageously established on some such basis as that of the Post Office system of annuities, calculated on the principle of the 'Money Returnable' Tables in the Post Office Regulations, and that the State should contribute some proportion of the premium annually payable by the teachers.

"If the Government adopt this suggestion, the Commissioners will submit a statement in detail as to the means of carrying it out."

34. On the question of the want of suitable residences for teachers, we, last year, recommended that grants should be made for the erection of such residences in connexion with vested schools. Since then, in reply to an inquiry upon the general subject, we instructed our secretaries to state to your Grace— Teachers' Residences.

"The Commissioners have already expressed for the information of the Government, their views upon this important subject as far as they relate to vested schools.

"They have again considered the question in its bearings on the non-vested schools, and they have arrived at the conclusion that the wisest course would be to adopt a modification of the recommendations of Lord Powis's Commission, which suggested that loans under the Land Improvement Act should be authorized for providing teachers' residences. The provisions of the Glebe Loan Act might also, in the opinion of the Commissioners, be usefully applied to any measure which may be framed on this subject.

"The Commissioners are further of opinion that *half* the annual instalment payable to the Board of Works under the provisions of these Acts, ought to be paid by the National Board, provided such moiety should not exceed the sum of £5.

"It is estimated that a suitable residence could be erected for £200. The annual instalment at five per cent. for thirty-five years to be paid to the Board of Works for a loan of that amount would be £10.

"The proposal of the Commissioners is to pay £5 of this instalment yearly, so long as the house is *bonâ fide* used as the residence of the principal teacher of a non-vested National school, the teacher or local authorities of the school paying the other half.

"The plans of the houses should, of course, be subject to the approval of the Commissioners, and also of the Board of Works. Questions as to the tenure, occupancy, &c., would be matters of detail easily settled by the Commissioners and by the Board of Works."

35. During the year 1874-5 there were 681 persons newly appointed as Teachers in National Schools. We have received returns from 53 of the 60 School Districts, relative to the antecedents of 540 of the New Teachers. New Teachers.

Pupil Teachers,	From Model Schools,	43	70
Paid Monitors,		21	
Pupils only,		12	
Paid Monitors,	From Ordinary Schools,	231	414
Pupils only,		183	
Paid Monitors,	From Convent Schools,	35	50
Pupils only,		15	
			540

Only a few of the new teachers were trained in the Establishment in Dublin. But owing to the operation of the monitorial system in the ordinary schools, and to the pupil-teacherships in the model schools, 61·2 per cent. of the new teachers whose antecedents have been ascertained had received some preparation of a technical character for their office.

Number of Teachers who have been withdrawn from the service.

86. We have thought it desirable to ascertain and report for the information of your Grace the number of teachers who have permanently been withdrawn from the service within the year. Our return refers only to the 55 school districts above referred to.

The number of teachers in these districts who were withdrawn from the service during the year 1874 was 528. Of these 186 had been trained at the Central Training Institution, Dublin, at the public expense.

The causes of withdrawal were as follows:—

Causes of Withdrawal.	Trained.	Untrained.	Total.
Resigned to enter the Civil Service, . .	5	33	38
" for Domestic Duties (marriage, &c.),	23	51	74
" " Commercial Pursuits, &c., .	6	15	21
" " Collegiate or Religious vocation,	3	17	20
" on account of age, ill-health, &c.,	13	11	24
" on receiving Retiring Gratuities, .	37	31	68
" to teach in schools not in connexion with the Board, ...	12	10	22
" Emigrated, ...	22	41	63
Dismissed, ...	10	70	80
Died, ...	27	30	57
Resigned for other pursuits than foregoing, .	9	18	27
Destinations unknown, ...	13	15	28
Totals, ...	186	342	528

Retiring Gratuities.

87. We publish in the Appendix the names of the Teachers who withdrew during the year from the office of Teacher, through old age or infirmity, on receiving retiring gratuities.

Paid Monitors.

88. The number of Paid Monitors in our service in Ordinary National Schools was 4,612: First Class, 354; Second Class, 3,671; and Third Class, 587; showing a total increase of 694 over the staff of Monitors recognised at the close of 1873.

39. The following Table shows the number of Monitors, Male and Female, of each grade in each year of service:—

Year of Service.	First Class.		Second Class.		Third Class.	
	Males.	Females.	Males.	Females.	Males.	Females.
1st year, . .	35	147	535	845	164	130
2nd „ . .	13	134	418	731	106	120
3rd „ . .	2	23	206	429	26	32
4th „ . .	.	.	149	338	.	.
Total, .	50	304	1,328	2,343	296	291
	354		3,671		587	
	4,612					

For Paid Monitors the term of service in each class is *three* years, and the scale of salaries is—

	Third Class Monitors.	Second Class Monitors.	First Class Monitors.	
			Males.	Females.
	£	£	£	£
For first year, .	4	6	14	12
„ second year, .	4	8	17	15
„ third year, .	4	10	20	18

40. The following Table shows the classification of 608,675 of the pupils on the rolls for the *last quarter* of the year 1874. Literary classification of pupils.

Provinces.	Number of Children on the Rolls during the last quarter of the year 1874, with their Proficiency, as indicated by classes.							
	Infants.	Class I.	Class II.	Class III.	Class IV.	Class V.	Class VI.	Total.
Ulster, . .	68,760	63,600	53,512	44,373	31,873	17,902	2,735	282,446
Munster, .	48,465	45,374	41,246	35,340	28,290	20,873	4,478	224,573
Leinster, .	40,657	38,084	32,866	25,085	17,363	10,289	1,675	166,316
Connaught, .	28,407	34,482	28,464	21,169	13,700	7,158	933	134,330
Total, .	186,290	181,658	157,010	126,170	90,930	56,222	9,819	608,675
Per-centage, .	23·	22·3	19·5	15·0	11·2	7·	1·8	.
					19·4			

41. The striking discrepancy between the average attendance and the number of children on the rolls requires explanation. The figures, as shown in paragraphs 3 and 4, are 1,006,511 on the rolls, and 395,390 in average attendance.

In our annual return of the number on the rolls every child who has attended school upon any one day in the year is counted; this method was adopted in the year 1857 and has been since continued, the object being to ascertain the number of children in the country who, in the course of the year, had been attending our schools, whether for a short period only or regularly throughout the year. We have it under our consideration whether this method should not be altered, as the result must be to show a greater number on the rolls than the actual number of individual pupils, inasmuch as the same child attending different schools at different periods would be reckoned several times—casual or chance scholars are also reckoned—and, therefore, so long as that mode of calculation is adopted the divergence between the number on the rolls and the average attendance must necessarily be very great.

In England, on the contrary, the number on the rolls represents only the number on the rolls on the last day of the month preceding the annual examination, not counting any child who had left school during the year. In the English schools the name of a child is not allowed to be kept on the roll for more than a fortnight after the child ceases to attend, unless in case of sickness. Even those who are thus kept on for a fortnight's grace are struck off in the annual return.

Hence, as the English return represents only the number on the roll on the last day of the month preceding the examination, and as our return includes all who had attended at any time, even for a day, during the year, the returns do not furnish any data upon which a relative comparison of the success of the children in passing can be made, and any comparison based upon those numbers must mislead.

Great misapprehension has arisen from not attending to this distinction.

For instance, the Royal Commissioners of Primary Education in Ireland state that in the year 1867 the number who passed in reading *represents* only 18·6 per cent., and in writing 7·8 of the number on the rolls, which is quite true. The number of pupils who passed in reading in that year was 170,291, but the number of those who were examined in reading was 243,235, and it is between these two numbers that the comparison should be made, which would show that 70 per cent. had passed.

For the same year the number examined in writing in our schools was 130,781, of whom 71,824, or 55 per cent., passed.

Comparisons unfavourable to the National education system in Ireland, as contrasted with the system in England, have been erroneously made from not attending to the distinction we have pointed out as to the different mode adopted in each country of calculating the numbers on the rolls. These numbers mean an entirely different thing in each country and cannot be made a common standard of comparison. In order to form a just estimate of the comparative proficiency of the pupils, we must take the per-centage of those who pass on the number examined, or on the average attendance, not on the number on the rolls, which does not represent the same thing in the two countries.

We subjoin a table showing the per-centages of the number of scholars examined in the following years in England and Ireland, who passed in reading, writing, and arithmetic:—

Years.	Ireland.			England.		
	Reading.	Writing.	Arithmetic.	Reading.	Writing.	Arithmetic.
1872, . .	87·6	88·0	71·3	86·6	82·3	72·2
1873, . .	87·7	83·8	70·4	86·6	81·6	72·1
1874, . .	86·8	86·7	69·0	88·3	80·5	70·9

For the year 1874 the per-centage of the number of children presented for examination in Irish National Schools who passed without failure in reading, writing, *and* arithmetic was 62·7. In England, according to the returns just published, the corresponding per-centage was 50·2.

42. In the year ended the 31st March, 1874, we awarded a sum of £101,620 6*s.* 11*d.* in payments for results. The amount paid for results in the year ended the 31st of March, 1875, was £117,931 0*s.* 7*d.*, which was an increase of £16,310 13*s.* 8*d.* on the previous year. Results.

Exclusive of Poor Law Union, Evening, Industrial schools, &c., details of which will be found in the Appendix, there were 6,730 schools examined for results in the 12 months ended 31st March, 1875.

The number of pupils at these schools who had made the 90 attendances of four hours each, which our regulations require to qualify pupils for examination, and who were present and examined on the days of the results examinations, was 397,206.

The average attendance at these schools was 369,088, which gives a centesimal proportion of 107·4 of the numbers examined to the number in average daily attendance.

In the Appendix will be found tables of the details of the examinations. Here we give the per-centages of passes to the number of pupils examined in—

Reading, . .	86·9	Grammar, . .	55·3
Spelling, . .	75·1	Geography, . .	54·4
Writing, . .	86·7	Agriculture, . .	41·1
Arithmetic, . .	60·	Needlework, . .	91·8

43. Since the year 1855 we have, with very gratifying success, encouraged instruction, as extra branches, in singing, drawing, and the mathematical and physical sciences, by a system of gratuities for satisfactory answering in these subjects; and recently we have added classics and French, and also, for girls, the Extra Subjects.

use of the sewing machine, and the higher branches of needlework. The scale of results' fees now payable for extra branches and a detailed statement of the answering last year will be found in the Appendix.

The programme of examinations for our schools will be found appended to this Report.

44. The National System of Education has been now in operation for forty-four years, and we may be fairly required to show what has been the general progress of education during that period.

Notwithstanding the opposition which the system has had to encounter, and the time necessarily required before its benefits could be fully appreciated by the people at large, we find in the Tables of the Census of 1871 returns which show a marked, progressive, and steady improvement in the education of the people.

The returns of 1871, 1861, 1851, and 1841 (1841 being the year of the earliest educational census of Ireland) are given in the following Table.

PROPORTION per cent. of the POPULATION, Five years old and upwards, who could NEITHER READ NOR WRITE, in each Province, County, City, &c., in Ireland, at the Census periods of 1841, 1851, 1861, and 1871.

Provinces, Counties, Cities, &c.	Percentage of Population, 5 years old and upwards, who could neither Read nor Write,			
	In 1841.	In 1851.	In 1861.	In 1871.
IRELAND.	[illegible]	46·8	[illegible]	33·4
PROVINCES.				
LEINSTER.	44·5	[illegible]	31·1	27·9
MUNSTER.	60·5	48·6	46·1	[illegible]
ULSTER.	40·6	35·2	[illegible]	26·4
CONNAUGHT.	72·1	64·3	57·1	48·3
LEINSTER.				
Carlow County.	[illegible]	36·1	[illegible]	[illegible]
Drogheda (Co. of the Town).	46·4	37·7	[illegible]	14·7
Dublin City.	18·3	14·9	[illegible]	10·3
" County.	34·9	[illegible]	[illegible]	15·4
Kildare	41·9	34·7	30·6	25·9
Kilkenny City.	40·7	37·3	34·9	30·5
" County.	41·3	46·6	34·5	28·4
King's "	57·3	43·1	34·5	[illegible]
Longford "	51·3	45·9	[illegible]	[illegible]
Louth "	61·1	[illegible]	45·0	25·7
Meath "	54·5	47·5	37·5	32·1
Queen's "	41·6	[illegible]	[illegible]	[illegible]
Westmeath "	47·1	41·4	38·1	31·0
Wexford "	41·3	[illegible]	35·5	31·7
Wicklow "	41·3	45·1	32·4	28·1
MUNSTER.				
Clare County.	67·3	[illegible]	[illegible]	37·7
Cork City.	35·6	35·7	32·1	27·4
" County.	66·5	[illegible]	[illegible]	47·7
MUNSTER—con.				
Kerry County.	79·4	64·3	[illegible]	[illegible]
Limerick City.	42·1	37·6	33·2	29·4
" County.	[illegible]	61·7	[illegible]	[illegible]
Tipperary "	61·0	44·7	36·6	29·9
Waterford City.	38·3	31·5	34·5	27·1
" County.	79·4	[illegible]	54·6	[illegible]
ULSTER.				
Antrim County.	[illegible]	20·3	18·6	15·4
Armagh "	47·6	39·1	34·3	30·4
Belfast Town.	27·2	20·4	17·4	15·7
Carrickfergus (Co. of the Town).	18·5	11·7	8·7	11·3
Cavan County.	61·6	45·9	33·6	[illegible]
Donegal "	61·7	61·3	53·1	46·9
Down "	37·3	[illegible]	[illegible]	18·5
Fermanagh "	44·6	36·6	31·5	27·6
Londonderry Co. and City.	39·4	30·6	24·3	[illegible]
Monaghan County.	51·3	43·0	34·7	[illegible]
Tyrone "	46·9	[illegible]	[illegible]	[illegible]
CONNAUGHT.				
Galway County (including the Co. of the Town).	78·0	70·1	62·9	54·5
Leitrim County.	57·3	52·8	41·1	[illegible]
Mayo "	79·8	72·1	66·9	57·4
Roscommon "	69·6	58·9	47·1	39·9
Sligo "	65·7	53·9	48·9	42·1

In our report for 1863 we referred with satisfaction to the evidence afforded by the Census returns of 1861, that the proportion of the uneducated in the population had been considerably diminishing.

In the returns for 1871, showing as they do, a decrease from 38·7 per cent. in 1861 to 33·4 in 1871, and from 53·7 per cent. in 1841 to 33·4 in 1871, we again recognise most gratifying evidence of the steady disappearance of illiteracy.

The Census Commissioners begin the enumeration of the illiterate with those of five years of age. Such a standard is manifestly too exacting. In Great Britain no educational census of the people has ever been taken; but even in Continental countries where such enumerations are made, the expectations of statesmen have never led them to look to five years of age as the initial period for those who should read or write. At five years old scarcely any of the children of the poor and very few of the children of the rich would be found to be able to read or write.

Were we to seek an illustration of the illiteracy of 1871 from that portion of the population for whose education the National system might, to a certain degree, be held responsible, we should turn to the Census tables of those between the ages of fifteen and twenty, viz., of those who might have attended our schools between the year 1861, when two-thirds of the children in the country were on the rolls of our schools, and the year 1871, when three-fourths of the children in the country were on our rolls. These tables show that the per-centage of persons between fifteen and twenty who could neither read nor write was only 17·5. In 1861 the per-centage of illiteracy for those who were 15 and under 20 was 27·8, which shows a vast improvement for the decade of years ending with 1871.

In view of these facts it can, we trust, be affirmed that the National system has produced satisfactory results.

45. The total number of School Farms in connexion with us on the 31st December, 1874, was 195—of which 21 were School Farms of the First Class under the exclusive management of our Board, and 11 were School Farms of the First Class under local management. Of the remaining number, 137 were ordinary School Farms, and 26 were School Gardens. *Agricultural School Farms.*

Very important measures are at present under consideration in reference to the agricultural department, especially with a view of reducing the number of large farms which are managed and entirely supported by the State, and of developing agricultural instruction in the ordinary National schools.

In the year 1874, 12,981 pupils of the ordinary and agricultural schools obtained passes in the examinations upon agriculture, and earned results fees for their proficiency in this subject for their teachers.

46. The amount received for books, school requisites, and apparatus, sold at reduced prices to National Schools in the year 1874, was £23,851 2s. 5*d.* The number of orders was 14,548; and the average amount of each order, £1 12s. 1½*d.* *Sale Stock Requisites.*

Free Stock Requisites.

47. The value of the grants of requisites and apparatus given as Free Stock to National Schools in 1874, was £2,829 11s. 5d. The number of grants was 583, the particulars of which are annexed.

			£	s.	d.
218	Grants to	Ordinary National Schools,	1,011	0	6
72	„	Model Schools,	383	16	5
91	„	Pupil-teachers and Monitors,	252	11	6
18	„	Classes of Teachers in Training, &c.,	637	13	10
97	„	Schools under Organization,	351	14	3
31	„	Agricultural Schools,	88	4	1
33	Grants of	Music Requisites,	33	0	0
23	„	Drawing Requisites,	71	10	10
Total, 583			£2,829	11	5

48. We have to express our regret at the loss by death within the year of a member of our Board, J. A. Dease, esq., D.L. Sir Dominic J. Corrigan, Bart., M.D., and the Honorable Jenico Preston were appointed during the year to seats on the Board.

49. We publish a full statement of our receipts and expenditure for the twelve months ending the 31st March, 1875.

50. We submit this, as our Report for the past year, to your Excellency, and in testimony thereof have caused our Corporate Seal to be hereunto affixed, this First day of June, One Thousand Eight Hundred and Seventy-five.

SEAL.

(Signed)

JAMES KELLY,
WM. HOMAN NEWELL, } *Secretaries.*

NAMES OF THE COMMISSIONERS

OF

NATIONAL EDUCATION IN IRELAND,

ACCORDING TO THE DATES OF THEIR RESPECTIVE APPOINTMENTS.

Rev. Dr. Henry, President, Queen's College, Belfast.
His Grace The Duke of Leinster.
James Gibson, Esq., Q.C.
Right Hon. Mountifort Longfield.
Right Hon. the Lord O'Hagan.
Right Hon. Lord Chief Justice, Common Pleas (Monahan).
Right Hon. Mr. Justice Lawson.
John Lentaigne, Esq., C.B.
John O'Hagan, Esq., Q.C.
Right Hon. Mr. Justice Fitzgerald.
James William Murland, Esq.
Right Hon. Mr. Justice Morris.
Rev. Charles L. Morell.
Rev. John H. Jellett, F.T.C.D.
Most Rev. Marcus G. Beresford, Archbishop of Armagh and Primate of all Ireland.
Right Hon. Viscount Monck, G.C.M.G.
Patrick Joseph Keenan, Esq., C.B., Resident Commissioner.
Sir Dominic J. Corrigan, Bart.
Hon. Jenico Preston.

One vacancy by the recent death of Mr. Waldron.

PROGRAMME of INSTRUCTION and EXAMINATION for NATIONAL SCHOOLS, and SCALE of RESULTS FEES.

INFANTS.

Fee, 3*s*.—1. *Over 4 and under 6 years of age*—To know the letters of the alphabet, and to spell and read words of two letters.

Fee, 3*s*.—2. *Six years and under 7 years of age*—To read and spell to the end of Second Section of First Book.

FIRST CLASS.

1. READING.—*Fee*, 2*s*.—To read correctly lessons in the latter half of the First Book.

2. SPELLING.—*Fee*, 1*s*.—(*a*.) To spell correctly the words arranged in columns at the head of the lessons in the First Book.

(*b*.) To spell phrases or short sentences *selected from the lessons in First Book*.

3. WRITING.—*Fee*, 1*s*.—To transcribe on slate any short sentence from the latter half of the First Book.

4. ARITHMETIC.—*Fee*, 1*s*.—(*a*.) To read and set down numbers up to, *and including*, three places of figures.

(*b*.) To know the Addition Table.

(*c*.) To add on slate or blackboard three numbers, each not exceeding two places of figures.

SECOND CLASS.

1. READING.—*Fee*, 2*s*.—(*a*.) To read correctly, and with due attention to pauses, the lessons in Second Book. (*b*.) To answer simple questions on the meanings of words, the subject matter of the lessons, and to point out on the map places therein referred to. (*c*.) To repeat at least four of the pieces of poetry correctly.

2. SPELLING.—*Fee*, 1*s*.—(*a*.) To spell orally the words arranged in columns at the head of the lessons in Second Book. (*b*.) To spell phrases or short sentences *selected from the lessons in Second Book*.

3. WRITING.—*Fee*, 1*s*.—(*a*.) To transcribe on paper with correct spelling any short sentence in Second Book to page 16. (*b*.) To exhibit in copy-books at least sixty pages of the *elementary numbers* of any approved series of copy-books, *written on sixty different days* since the preceding annual inspection; each page to be dated.

4. ARITHMETIC.—*Fee*, 3*s*.—(*a*.) To read and set down any number up to, and including, four places of figures. (*b*.) To know the Addition and *Subtraction* Tables. (*c*.) To work on slate questions in Simple Addition of not more than five addends of three places each, and easy questions in Simple Subtraction.

5. NEEDLEWORK.—*Fee*, 6*d*.—To know how to hem, *or* to do plain knitting.

THIRD CLASS.

1. READING.—*Fee*, 2*s*. 6*d*.—(*a*.) To read with ease and correctness the lessons of the Third Book. (*b*.) To be fairly acquainted with the meanings of words and the subject-matter of these lessons. (*c*.) To repeat correctly five of the pieces of poetry contained in Third Book.

2. SPELLING.—*Fee*, 1*s*.—(*a*.) To write from dictation on slate an easy sentence from the first half of Third Book. (*b*.) To spell correctly the words arranged in columns at the head of the lessons.

3. WRITING.—*Fee*, 1*s*. 6*d*.—(*a*) To transcribe on paper with correct spelling, any four lines from the first half of Third Book. (*b*.) To exhibit in copy-books at least *ninety* pages in round hand or elementary small hand, written on *ninety different days* since the preceding annual inspection—*each page to be signed and dated by the pupil*.

4. ARITHMETIC.—*Fee*, 2*s*. 6*d*.—(*a*.) To read and set down any number up to, *and including*, six places of figures. (*b*.) To know the Multiplication and Pence Tables. (*c*.) To work on slate or paper sums in all the Simple Rules, and also sums in Addition of Money not exceeding five addends.

5. GRAMMAR.—*Fee*, 6*d*.—To be well acquainted with the definitions of the Parts of Speech, and to distinguish the Parts of Speech in an ordinary sentence.

6. GEOGRAPHY.—*Fee*, 1*s*.—To know the outlines and leading features of the Map of the World.

7. NEEDLEWORK (GIRLS).—*Fee*, 1*s*.—To know how to hem *and* to do plain knitting.

FOURTH CLASS.

1. READING.—*Fee*, 2*s*. 6*d*.—(*a*.) To read with ease and correctness the lessons of the Fourth Book. (*b*.) To be acquainted with the meanings of words, and the subject-matter of the lessons. (*c*.) To repeat six of the pieces of poetry in Fourth Book correctly.

2. SPELLING.—*Fee*, 1*s*.—(*a*.) To write from dictation on paper a passage of six or seven lines selected from the Third Book. (*b*.) To spell correctly the words arranged in columns at the head of the lessons.

3. WRITING.—*Fee*, 1*s*. 6*d*.—(*a*.) To transcribe on paper, with correct spelling and punctuation, any six lines selected from the Third Book. (*b*.) To exhibit in copy-books at least ninety pages in fair small hand, *written* on *ninety different days* since the preceding annual inspection—each page to be signed and dated by the pupil, and *to be kept neat and free from blots*.

4. ARITHMETIC.—*Fee*, 2*s*. 6*d*.—(*a*.) To know Numeration and Notation *well*, and all the *more useful* arithmetical tables. (*b*.) To perform *mentally* easy exercises in Addition and Subtraction; and to work on slate or paper, *accurately and speedily*, a sum of seven lines in Addition of Money. (*c*.) To work on paper questions in all the Compound Rules and Reduction.

5. GRAMMAR.—*Fee*, 1*s*.—(*a*.) To be well acquainted with the definitions of the Parts of Speech, and to distinguish the Parts of Speech readily and intelligently in any ordinary sentence. (*b*.) To be well acquainted with the gender, number, and cases of nouns and pronouns, the comparison of adjectives, and the moods, tenses, &c., of verbs.

6. GEOGRAPHY.—*Fee*, 1*s*.—(*a*.) To know the ordinary geographical definitions. (*b*.) To be acquainted with the Maps of the World, Europe, and Ireland.

7. AGRICULTURE (BOYS).—*Fee*, 2*s*.—To answer intelligently on the subject-matter of the lessons in Part III. (CROPS) of the Agricultural Class Book.

8. NEEDLEWORK (GIRLS).—*Fee*, 2*s*.—To exhibit fair proficiency in hemming, stitching, and top-sewing, and in plain knitting.

Fifth Class.—First Stage.

1. Reading.—*Fee*, 2s. 6d.—(a.) To read with fluency, correctness, and intelligence the first 200 pages of the Fifth Book of Lessons. (b.) To answer intelligently on the subject-matter of the lessons read. (c.) To repeat correctly six of the poetical pieces in the prescribed portion of the Fifth Book.

2. Spelling.—*Fee*, 1s.—(a.) To write from dictation, on paper, with correct spelling, an ordinary passage of *six or seven* lines from the Fourth Book. (b.) To spell ordinary words and phrases selected from the prescribed portion of the Fifth Book.

3. Writing.—*Fee*, 1s. 6d.—(a.) To write a neat legible hand with ease and freedom. (b.) To exhibit in suitable books ninety pages of well-written school exercises, executed *on ninety different days* since the preceding annual inspection—each page to be signed and dated by the pupil.

4. Arithmetic.—*Fee*, 2s. 6d.—(a.) To know the numeration and notation of Decimals, and *all the arithmetical tables* in the Board's First Book of Arithmetic, and to be able to write out on paper any of the latter in correct form. (b.) To perform simple arithmetical questions *mentally*, and to work on slate or paper, *accurately and speedily*, a sum of ten lines of Addition of Money. (c.) To work neatly, on paper, questions in simple Proportion and Practice.

5. Grammar.—*Fee*, 1s. 6d.—(a.) To be well acquainted with Orthography and Etymology. (b.) To parse simple sentences.

6. Geography.—*Fee*, 1s. 6d.—(a.) To understand Longitude, Latitude, Zones, &c. (b.) To know the *Maps* of the Continents.

7.—Agriculture (Boys).—*Fee*, 2s. 6d.—To answer intelligently on the subject-matter of the lessons in Parts III. and IV. of the Agricultural Class Book.

8. Needlework (Girls).—*Fee*, 2s. 6d.—To be proficient in sewing and knitting.

Fifth Class.—Second Stage.

1. Reading.—*Fee*, 2s. 6d.—(a.) To read with fluency, correctness, and intelligence the Fifth Book of Lessons. (b.) To answer intelligently on the subject-matter of the lessons. (c.) To repeat correctly six of the poetical pieces in the Fifth Book.

2. Spelling.—*Fee*, 1s.—(a.) To write from dictation, on paper, with correct spelling, an ordinary passage of *six or seven* lines from the Fifth Book. (b.) To spell ordinary words and phrases selected from the Fifth Book or the Girls' Reading Book.

3. Writing.—*Fee*, 1s. 6d.—(a.) To write a neat legible hand with ease and freedom. (b.) To exhibit in suitable books ninety pages of well-written school exercises, executed *on ninety different days* since the preceding annual inspection—each page to be signed and dated by the pupil—*and at least thirty of these exercises to be letters on simple subjects.*

4. Arithmetic.—*Fee*, 2s. 6d.—(a.) To know the numeration and notation of Decimals, and *all the arithmetical tables*, and to be able to write out on paper any of the latter in correct form. (b.) To perform simple arithmetical questions *mentally*, and to work on slate or paper, *accurately and speedily*, a sum of ten lines of Addition of Money. (c.) To work neatly, on paper, questions in simple and Compound Proportion, Practice, and easy questions in Vulgar Fractions and Decimals.

5. Grammar.—*Fee*, 1s. 6d.—(a.) To be well acquainted with Orthography and Etymology. (b.) To know the *principal* Latin roots, prefixes, &c. (c.) To parse simple sentences.

6. GEOGRAPHY.—*Fee*, 1s. 6d.—(*a.*) To understand Longitude, Latitude, Zones, &c. (*b.*) To know the *Maps* of the Continents. (*c.*) To be acquainted with the geography of the British Empire.

7. AGRICULTURE (BOYS).—*Fee*, 2s. 6d.—To answer intelligently on the subject-matter of the lessons in Parts III. and IV. of the Agricultural Class Book.

8. NEEDLEWORK (GIRLS).—*Fee*, 2s. 6d.—To be proficient in sewing and knitting, and in cutting out any simple article of dress.

SIXTH CLASS.

[N.B.—Pupils presented for the *first time* will not be examined in Reading, Spelling, or the repetition of Poetry beyond the first 200 pages of the Sixth Book.]

1. READING.—*Fee*, 3s. 6d.—(*a.*) To read the Sixth Book with fluency, correctness, and intelligence, and to answer intelligently on the subject-matter of the lessons. (*b.*) To repeat correctly six of the pieces of poetry in the Sixth Book.

2. SPELLING.—*Fee*, 1s.—To write on paper in a free legible hand, and with correct spelling and punctuation, *a paragraph of six or seven lines* dictated from the Sixth Book.

3. WRITING.—*Fee*, 2s.—(*a.*) To exhibit in suitable books ninety pages of *school exercises*, written in a good hand on *ninety different days* since the preceding annual inspection—at least thirty of them to consist of examples of Cash, Personal, and Real Accounts, comprising the first three sets of Book-keeping, the principles of which must be understood. *Each exercise, as in the preceding classes, to be signed and dated by the pupil.* (*b.*) Specimens of ornamental Penmanship may be included amongst the exercises.

4. ARITHMETIC, &c.—*Fee*, 3s.—(*a.*) To be expert in mental calculation. (*b.*) To perform *accurately and speedily*, on slate or paper, a sum of twelve lines in Addition of Money. (*c.*) To work neatly on paper, questions in any rule of arithmetic (including, *for boys only*, Involution and Evolution).

5. GRAMMAR.—*Fee*, 1s. 6d.—(*a.*) To parse prose and poetry correctly. (*b.*) To be acquainted with the principal roots, prefixes, and affixes employed in the formation of English derivatives. (*c.*) To write, with correct grammar and composition, a simple letter on any subject suggested by Inspector.

6. GEOGRAPHY.—*Fee*, 1s. 6d.—(*a.*) To be acquainted with the elements of mathematical and physical Geography. (*b.*) To draw *from memory* an outline map of Ireland. (*c.*) To know the geography of the Continents and of the British Empire.

7. AGRICULTURE (BOYS).—*Fee*, 3s.—To answer intelligently on the subject-matter of the lessons in Parts I., III., and IV. of the Agricultural Class Book.

8. NEEDLEWORK (GIRLS).—*Fee*, 3s.—(*a.*) To be able to cut out any article of *females'* apparel. (*b.*) To exhibit satisfactory proficiency in the different branches of plain sewing and knitting.

N.B.—The Lesson Books referred to in this revised Programme are the NEW Books as recently arranged to meet the requirements of the Results Examinations. Thus, the Lesson Book for 2nd class is the new Second Book which comprises the lessons to page 160 of the former Second Book;—that for 3rd class is the new Third Book, which comprises the lessons from page 160 to end of *former* Second Book, and those to page 60 of former Third Book. The new Fourth Book comprises only the lessons from page 60 to end of former Third Book. The new Fifth Book is the former Fourth Book, and the new Sixth Book is the former Fifth Book.

Subjects.	Classes.								
	Infants.	First Class.	Second Class.	Third Class.	Fourth Class.	Fifth Class, First Stage.	Fifth Class, Second Stage.	Sixth Class, First Stage.	Sixth Class, Second Stage.
	s. d.	s. d.	s. d.	s. d.	s. d.	s. d.	s. d.	s. d.	s. d.
Reading,	–	2 0	2 0	2 6	2 6	2 6	2 6	2 6	2 6
Spelling,	–	1 0	1 0	1 0	1 0	1 0	1 0	1 6	1 6
Writing,	–	1 0	1 6	1 6	1 6	1 6	1 6	2 0	2 0
Arithmetic,	–	1 0	2 0	2 6	2 6	2 6	2 6	3 0	3 0
Grammar,	–	–	–	0 6	1 0	1 6	1 6	1 0	1 0
Geography,	–	–	–	1 0	1 0	1 6	1 6	1 6	1 6
Agriculture,	–	–	–	–	2 0	2 6	2 6	3 0	3 0
Needlework,	–	–	0 6	1 6	2 0	2 6	2 6	3 0	3 0
Maximum value, Male National Schools,	3 0	5 0	6 6	9 0	11 6	13 0	13 0	14 6	14 6
Maximum value in Female National Schools,	3 0	5 0	6 6	10 6	11 6	13 0	13 0	14 6	14 6
Extras (inside or outside School hours):									
Singing,	–	–	1 0	2 0	2 0	2 6	2 6	3 0	3 0
Drawing,	–	–	–	2 0	2 0	2 6	2 6	3 0	3 0
Other approved extra subjects (each),	–	–	–	–	–	5 0	5 0	5 0	5 0
Classics (outside School hours):									
Greek,	–	–	–	–	–	10 0	10 0	10 0	10 0
Latin,	–	–	–	–	–	10 0	10 0	10 0	10 0
French,	–	–	–	–	–	5 0	5 0	5 0	5 0

NOTES.

(*a*.) No results fee can be paid in respect of any pupil whose attendance at the school during the year ended on the last day of the month preceding the annual examination shall be less than ninety days.

(*b*.) No pupil may be presented for examination in a higher class than that in which he is enrolled. (This rule applies equally to pupils under seven years of age, and to those above that age.)

(*c*.) The same results fees as in day schools are obtainable in an evening school for every branch taught in the latter; but an attendance on FORTY-FIVE evenings will be accepted as qualifying an evening school pupil for admission to examination for results. *Under no circumstances should a day school pupil be presented for examination in an evening school.*

(*d*.) A written exercise signed and dated by the pupil, must be presented for every attendance for which credit is claimed in an evening school.

(*e*.) Pupils *above* four and *under* seven years of age, who make the necessary minimum number of attendances in the year, may be presented for inspection as infants. *Individual* examination of such pupils may be dispensed with in those schools ONLY in which there is *bonâ fide* provision made for the systematic training of infants.

(*f*.) In a thoroughly organized infants' school, with a separate staff, and in a separate room, a fee of 4s. per pupil may be paid.

(*g*.) (After the results examinations of the current financial year 1874–5, no fee shall be paid in an infant school for any pupil presented in a class higher than second.)

(*h*.) Only *one fee for each subject* can be paid for a pupil in any class, no matter how long the pupil may remain in the class, except in the case of *infants*, and of the fifth class (in which a pupil may be paid for twice, viz., once in each stage), and of *sixth* class pupils. Any pupil in first, second, third, or fourth class who earns for the teacher fees for reading, writing, *and* arithmetic, cannot again earn a fee for any subject in the same class. But if the pupil fails in any of these three subjects, he may be presented a second time in the same class, and earn fees in the subjects in which he failed previously, subject to conditions specified in notes (*i*) and (*l*).

(*i.*) *Under no circumstances* can a pupil be presented for examination for results fees more than twice in the same class, except in the case of the *fifth* and *sixth* classes, and in that of *infants*.

(*j.*) Should a pupil be presented for examination for results oftener than once in the sixth class, such pupil, to entitle the teacher to *any* results fees, must—(*a.*) *If a boy*, exhibit proficiency in *three* books of Euclid; or in algebra, up to and including quadratic equations; or in plane trigonometry; or in navigation; or in one of the physical sciences; or in some other approved extra branch: (*b.*) *If a girl*, exhibit proficiency in "cutting out" as taught in the Board's Manual of Needlework; or in the use of the sewing machine; *or* in the cooking of plain food: or in the management of poultry and other domestic animals; *or* in physical geography; or in some other approved extra branch. (N.B.—Payment can be made only once for the same pupil for proficiency in the use of the sewing machine.)

(*k.*) In cases, however, where it is found necessary by the Inspector, to hold a results examination at a date less than eleven months after the date of the termination of the last results year, teachers will be allowed to present pupils again in the same class in which they passed at the previous examination, subject to conditions specified in notes (*i*) and (*l*). This privilege will not however extend to the presentation of pupils again in the *same stage* of fifth or sixth class.

(*l.*) No pupil of seven years of age or above who has been enrolled for a year in any class can be presented in a lower class than that in which he is enrolled; and under no circumstances can a pupil be presented in a lower class than that next below the class in which he is enrolled.

(*m.*) Results fees cannot be paid for needlework in a *female* school in which there is a workmistress paid by the Board.

(*n.*) The attendance of paid monitors must be marked on a separate roll, and included in the average daily attendance in all schools; but they are not to be reckoned as pupils for capitation payments, or (except in the case of third class monitors,) to be presented for examination as pupils at the results examination in subjects that form part of their prescribed school course.

(*o.*) First and second class monitors may however be presented for results examinations in Classics or French, or in a science branch not included in any part of their prescribed course of instruction. Only two such subjects will be allowed to be taken in any one year.

(*p.*) Third class monitors presented for results examinations, are subject to the same rules as ordinary pupils.

Extra subjects:—

(*q.*) No fee will be paid for any pupil for whose proficiency in the same subject grants are made by the Department of Science and Art.

(*r.*) A fee of five shillings will be paid for every pupil in the fifth or sixth class, who, *having passed in reading, spelling, writing,* AND *arithmetic*, shall exhibit satisfactory proficiency in geometry (*First Book of Euclid* or *Mensuration of Surfaces* for fifth class, *and First and Second Books of Euclid* AND *Mensuration of Surfaces* for sixth class), algebra (*Elementary Rules* for fifth class, *Elementary Rules and Simple Equations* for sixth class), one of the physical sciences, navigation, or other *approved* extra branch.

The regulations of the Commissioners enable teachers to earn results fees under each of the following heads :—

I. Vocal Music and Drawing.

II. Classics and French.

III. Geometry, Algebra, or other approved branch of science.

Provided that :—No fees shall be paid for more than two extra subjects, besides vocal music and drawing, in the same class to the same teacher. This limitation does not however extend to classics.

Vocal Music and Drawing.

I. Results fees will be paid according to the following scale :—(*a.*) Vocal Music—For pupils presented in second class, a fee of one shilling and sixpence for each pass. (*b.*) Vocal Music and Drawing—For pupils presented in third or higher classes, fees equal to that paid for arithmetic in the class.

II. No fee will be paid for any pupil who is not a member of a regularly constituted class for instruction in the theory and practice of vocal music, or of a regularly constituted drawing class, in operation in the school.

III. No fee for vocal music or drawing will be paid for any pupil who does not pass in reading, and at least two of the other ordinary subjects of instruction (viz., spelling, writing, arithmetic.)

IV. The following is the minimum proficiency upon which pupils will be allowed to pass in the different classes :—

Vocal Music.—Programme.

Second and Third Classes.—(*a.*) To name the notes on the clef, and to sing the natural scale. (*b.*) To sing with precision, in unison, any six approved school songs.

Fourth and Fifth Classes.—(*a.*) To define satisfactorily the various intervals in the diatonic scale. (*b.*) To read accurately any ordinary piece in common time. (*c.*) To join in at least three harmonized pieces.

Sixth Class.—(*a.*) To exhibit a fair knowledge of the theory of the subject. (*b.*) To transpose an easy passage from one key to another. (*c.*) To take first and second parts in at least three harmonized pieces.

Note 1.—No fees will be paid for pupils in second or third classes unless the pupils of the higher classes show a satisfactory proficiency.

2.—As pupils advance from class to class, they must exhibit a knowledge of at least two new songs in each class.

3.—If the Tonic Sol Fa system be pursued in any school, a programme of proficiency for each class must be submitted for the approval of the Board before the class can be presented for examination for results fees.

Drawing.—Programme.

Third and Fourth Classes.—(*a.*) Free-hand drawing from the flat on paper, such as simple arrangements of straight lines, forming either simple familiar objects, or geometrical designs, or easy curved line ornament.

Fifth Class.—(*a.*) Free-hand drawing, of a more advanced character, such as simple ornament, curved lines, or (*b.*) Easy practical geometry.

Sixth Class.—(*a.*) Free-hand drawing, of a still more advanced character, from the flat on paper, such as advanced ornament, higher practical geometry, or elementary drawing from objects in outline. (*b.*) Free-hand drawing from the model and from shaded examples.

Note.—If a pupil be presented a second year in sixth class, he may exhibit drawings from examples of landscape, figures, or animals, or shading from the model, perspective, and water-colours. The proficiency must in all cases be satisfactory to entitle the pupil to a pass. Specimens of drawings to be forwarded by the Inspector to the Education Office with his report.

Classics and French.

The Commissioners of National Education have sanctioned the payment of results fees for Latin, Greek, and French, upon the following conditions:—

I. If these subjects be taught by a recognized National teacher, he must devote at least four hours per day, on five days in the week, to instruction in the ordinary English subjects.

II. Pupils learning Classics or French must also receive instruction for at least twenty hours weekly in the ordinary branches taught in the school.

III. Instruction in Classics and French, when given by the recognized National teacher, must be given out of the ordinary school hours; but pupils, who have passed *once* in the *sixth* class, may be allowed to devote a portion of these hours to the *study* of their Classical or French lessons, provided that the routine business of the school be not interfered with.

IV. No pupil may be presented for examination in these branches who has not reached at least the *fifth* class.

V. No payment can be made for any pupil who has not made the necessary number of attendances; or for any pupil who fails to pass in *reading, spelling, writing,* and *arithmetic.*

VI. The course will extend over a period of three years; and a pupil can be presented only once for examination on the course for each year.

VII. For every pupil fulfilling the foregoing conditions who passes a satisfactory examination on the course prescribed for his year on the following programme, results-fees will be awarded to the teacher:—In Latin, 10s.; in Greek, 10s.; in French, 5s.

VIII. Payment of results fees for Classics or French will not debar a teacher from payment for two other approved extra branches, exclusive of vocal music and drawing.

Classics and French—Programme.

Latin.—*First Year.*—Grammar, including syntax, Latin Delectus, or any similar elementary book. *Second Year.*—Two books of Cæsar, or two books of Virgil, or the Jugurtha of Sallust, or any approved course of equal difficulty. *Third Year.*—Not less than 500 lines of Ovid, Horace, or Juvenal, or of the Georgics of Virgil, *and* any book of Livy. An easy passage of at least twenty lines from the Third Book of Lessons to be translated into Latin prose.

Greek.—*First Year.*—Grammar, to the end of the regular verbs. *Second Year.*—Grammar, including syntax, Greek Delectus, and one book of Xenophon, either the Anabasis or the Cyropædia. *Third Year.*—Two books of the Iliad and a book of Herodotus.

French.—*First Year.*—Grammar, not including syntax, with twenty pages of a French vocabulary, or of an easy phrase-book. *Second Year.*—Grammar, including syntax, with twenty additional pages of a phrase-book, and translation of two books of Telemachus, or Charles XII., or Chambaud's "Fables Choisies," edited by Du Gué. *Third Year.*—The Athalie of Racine, or any approved book of French poetry. Translation of an easy passage of English into French. Fair correctness of pronunciation.

Notes (1).—The elementary books used during the first year must be approved by the Inspector.

(2.)—Other books may be substituted for those prescribed for second and third years; but the sanction of the Commissioners for the change must be previously obtained.

Scientific Branches.

A fee of 5s. will be paid for every pupil in fifth or sixth class who having passed in Reading, Spelling, Writing, and Arithmetic, shall exhibit satisfactory proficiency in Geometry, Algebra, or other approved extra branch.

The several branches of science for which results payments may be claimed are thus classified:—

I. Mathematical Science, comprising—1. Geometry and Mensuration. 2. Algebra. 3. Plane Trigonometry. *4. Navigation.

II. Mechanical Science, comprising—1. Mechanics. 2. Hydrostatics and Pneumatics. *3. Heat and the Steam Engine.

III. Physical Science, comprising—1. Physical Geography (*advanced course*). 2. Magnetism and Electricity. 3. Light and Sound. 4. Botany and Vegetable Physiology. *5. Zoology and Animal Physiology. *6. Inorganic Chemistry. *7. Geology.

The whole course of Physical Geography is required in one examination to constitute an extra branch, inasmuch as an elementary knowledge of the subject forms part of the regular programme for sixth class.

As regards Geometry and Algebra the course will extend to three examinations; for the other branches there will be two examinations, one elementary, the other more advanced.

It is strongly recommended that the pupils should have passed at least one examination in Geometry, and one in Algebra, before engaging in any of the other branches.

GEOMETRY AND MENSURATION.

The entire course will be comprised in three examinations, as follows:—the first year's examination may take place while the pupil is in fifth class—

FIRST EXAMINATION.—Euclid, Book I. Mensuration, area of rectilineal figures.

SECOND EXAMINATION.—(*In addition to above*)—Euclid, Book II. Mensuration; circle—ellipse—zone—surfaces of the principal solids.

THIRD EXAMINATION.—(*In addition to above*)—Euclid, Books III. and IV., with the first eight propositions of Book VI. Mensuration, solidity of prism, cylinder, cone, and sphere—artificer's work—a general knowledge of the principles of land surveying.

ALGEBRA.

The entire course will be comprised in three examinations—the first may take place while the pupil is in fifth class:—

FIRST EXAMINATION.—Definitions—simple rules—computation of algebraic expressions—easy simple equations.

SECOND EXAMINATION.—(*In addition to above*)—Simple equations, and problems producing them—simultaneous equations—algebraic fractions—involution and evolution—theory of integer indices—ratio and proportion.

THIRD EXAMINATION.—(*In addition to above*)—Quadratic equations, and problems producing them—theory of fractional and negative indices—surds—arithmetical and geometrical progression—binomial theorem with integer indices.

PLANE TRIGONOMETRY.

Two examinations will embrace the course in this branch:—

FIRST EXAMINATION.—Definitions—measurement of angles—trigonometrical functions—logarithms—use of logarithmic tables—formulæ for the solution of right-angled triangles—heights.

* The subjects marked with an asterisk are to be taken by pupils in the sixth class only.

SECOND EXAMINATION.—(*In addition to above.*)—Four fundamental formulæ, with the more useful formulæ deduced from them—oblique-angled triangles—application to distances—description and use of theodolite and vernier.

NAVIGATION.

The course will comprise two examinations :—

FIRST EXAMINATION.—General knowledge of "Mathematical Geography"—rhumb line—difference of latitude—departure—course—correction of courses—plane sailing—middle latitude sailing—mariner's compass—variation—deviation—leeway.

SECOND EXAMINATION.—(*In addition to above.*)—Mercator's sailing—Mercator's projection and chart—the great principle of the chart, and in what its value consists—to determine a ship's place on the chart from her latitude and longitude, and *vice versâ*—to find the course and distance between two places on the chart—to compute a day's run—great circle sailing—oblique sailing.

(This subject should be preceded by a course of plane trigonometry, and it should be taught only after a pupil has reached the sixth class.)

MECHANICS.

FIRST EXAMINATION.—Matter—different states—laws of matter—natural forces—properties of bodies—momentum—equilibrium—action and re-action—composition and resolution of forces—lever, different kinds of—human arm as a lever—pulley—relation of P to W in lever and pulley—centre of gravity—toy figure explained—conditions to be satisfied by a balance—delicacy of balance—how obtained—double weighing.

SECOND EXAMINATION.—(*In addition to above.*)—Absolute unit of force—unit of work and horse power—systems of pulleys—wheel and axle—inclined plane—wedge—screw—relation of P to W in each—laws of motion—accelerated motion—laws of falling bodies—water hammer—feather and penny experiment—Attwood's machine—pendulum—terrestrial gravitation and the causes which modify it.

HYDROSTATICS AND PNEUMATICS.

FIRST EXAMINATION.—Pressure of non-elastic fluids—laws of pressure—bursting of rocks by pressure of small quantity of liquid. Hydrostatic paradox—Bramah's press—pressure of air—Magdeburg hemispheres—tumbler and card experiment—elasticity—air gun—barometer—construction of—specific gravity of solids—liquids—gases, how determined—pumps—suction pump—force pump—air pump—conveyance of water across valleys—syphon.

SECOND EXAMINATION.—(*In addition to above*).—Expansion of gases—Boyle and Marriotte's law—pressure supported by a body immersed in a liquid—hydrostatic balance—specific gravity bottle—Nicholson's hydrometer—conditions of equilibrium of floating bodies—Cartesian diver—swimming—capillary phenomena—endosmose and exosmose—Torricellian vacuum—determination of heights by the barometer—aneroid barometer—balloons—parachute.

LIGHT AND SOUND.

FIRST EXAMINATION.—(1.) LIGHT.—Undulating and emission theory—how objects are seen—intensity of light—law of inverse squares—velocity of light, how determined—shadows and penumbræ—laws of reflection—mirrors—formation of images by plane mirrors—use of concave mirrors in lighthouses—analysis of light—photometers.

(2.) Sound.—Sound waves, nature of them—density and elasticity of air, how affected by heat—velocity of sound through air, how determined—calculation of distance by light and sound—velocity of sound through water.—law of inverse squares as applied to sound—reflection of sound—echo—whispering galleries.

Second Examination.—(*In addition to above*).—(1.) Light.—Kaleidoscope—concave spherical mirrors—meaning of term axis—principal focus—centre of mirror—refraction of light, illustrations of—different kinds of lenses—course of a ray of light through a converging and a diverging lens—optical structure of the eye and the condition of distinct vision—use of spectacles—solar spectrum—rainbow—stereoscope—magic lantern.

(2.) Sound.—Structure of the ear—difference between music and noise—musical notes—pitch and intensity—various methods of producing musical sounds—laws of vibrations of strings and use of sound boards—laws of vibration of columns of air in pipes—ear trumpet—speaking trumpet.

Heat and the Steam Engine.

First Examination.—1. Heat.—Theories as to the nature of heat—effects of heat—radiation—convection—conduction—good and bad conductors—metallic surfaces—when to be bright and when rough—absorption and transmission of heat—thermometers, how constructed—determination of the fixed points—expansion of solids—compensation pendulums—maximum density of water—freezing of deep and shallow water—salt and fresh water—vapour—dew—clouds.

2. Steam Engine.—Properties of steam—how produced—unit of heat—history of steam engine—Savary's engine—Newcomen's engine—difference between high and low pressure engines—horse-power.

Second Examination.—(*In addition to above*).—1. Heat.—Differential thermometers—maximum and minimum thermometers—expansion of solids—of liquids—of gases—ventilation of mines and buildings—specific heat—how illustrated by experiment—latent heat and sensible heat—trace the successive effects of heat applied to ice below the freezing point till converted into steam—cooling effects of evaporation—how exemplified in different regions on the earth's surface—effects of specific heat of water on climate—freezing mixtures.

2. Steam Engine.—Watts' single acting engine—oscillating engine—fly-wheel—parallel motion—eccentric—governor—propulsion of vessels by means of (1) paddlewheel—(2) screw—computation of the horse-power of an engine.

Physical Geography.

Full Course.—One Examination.—Form of the earth—motions—magnitude and measurement—distribution of land and water—zones—climates—temperatures—mountains—table lands—plains—deserts—rivers—lakes—tides and currents—atmosphere, its properties and uses—reflection—refraction—evaporation—clouds—rain—dew—hail—winds, three kinds of—hurricanes—cyclones—typhoons—hot winds—distribution of plants and animals—relation of horizontal and vertical distribution—different races of men and how distributed.

Magnetism and Electricity.

First Examination.—1. *Magnetism.*—Natural and artificial magnets—magnetic poles—theories of magnetism—magnetic induction—coercive force—explain experiments with iron filings, and with broken magnet,

2. *Frictional Electricity.*—History and general nature of—development by friction—electrical machines—conductors and non-conductors—two kinds of electricity, and how related to each other—Franklin's discovery.

3. *Dynamical Electricity.*—History of—different names for—Voltaic couple—explanation of action—origin of currents—simple experiments to show the existence of electric currents—Volta's pile.

Second Examination.—(*In addition to above*).—1. *Magnetism.*—Mariner's compass—terrestrial magnetism; inclination—declination—magnetic intensity—magnetic equator and poles—magnetisation—magnetic battery.

2. *Frictional Electricity.*—Best insulators—distribution of electricity—tendency to accumulate on corners and points, and to escape from them—induction—condensers—description of the Leyden jar as a condenser—electroscopes—thunder and lightning—lightning conductors.

3. *Dynamical Electricity.*—Different methods of originating the voltaic current—Smee's battery—galvanometer—electric telegraph—chemical effects of the current—decomposition of water by the current.

Vegetable Physiology and Botany.

First Examination.—General structure of a flowering plant—distinction between flowering and flowerless plants—ascending and descending axis—functions of the several parts—root—stem—leaf—stipules—inflorescence—germination of bean—grain of wheat—three great classes of plants, with the characters of each—description of daisy, pea, primrose, and lily.

Second Examination.—(*In addition to above*).—Vascular and cellular plants—various tissues of plants—various forms of root, stem, leaf, inflorescence, flower, fruit—cohesion, adhesion, and suppression of various parts of the flower—characters of ranunculaceæ—cruciferæ—leguminosæ—rosaceæ—umbelliferæ—labiatæ. Description and classification of the following plants:—Wheat; clover; rice; Indian corn; turnip; rhubarb; cucumber. Description of the following vegetable products, with the names and classification of the plants which yield them:—Opium—cotton—mustard—sugar—chocolate—tea—coffee—starch—jute—flax—cinnamon—pepper—galls—quinine.

Animal Physiology and Zoology.

First Examination.—*Animal Physiology.*—(*a.*) General build of the human body—human skeleton—names and position of the principal bones—composition of bone. (*b.*) Circulation of the blood—the heart and blood vessels—course of the circulation—valves of the heart—aorta—composition of the blood. (*c.*) Respiration—changes in the blood—venous blood—arterial blood—the lungs and their appendages—changes in respired air—mechanical movements of respiration—animal heat.

Zoology.—Characteristic differences between plants and animals—divisions of the animal kingdom—classes of the vertebrates.

Second Examination.—(*In addition to above.*)—*Animal Physiology.*—Digestion—mastication—teeth—the pharynx—stomach—intestines—secretion and excretion—liver—pancreas—the skin and its functions—the senses—organs of the senses—structure and movements of the eye ball—structure of the ear—animal mechanics.

Zoology.—A complete knowledge of the characteristic features of the sub-kingdoms, and classes of the animal kingdom—modification of the vertebrate skeleton in birds, reptiles, amphibia, and fishes—general nature of the skeleton or hard parts in the several groups of invertebrate animals—general form and nature of the organs of digestion, circulation, and respiration in the various classes of animals.

Inorganic Chemistry.

First Examination.—Matter—simple and compound—divisions of elementary bodies—symbols and atomic weights of the ordinary elementary bodies—to know the properties and mode of obtaining oxygen, hydrogen, and nitrogen—to know the chief properties and composition of water, air, ammonia, carbonic acid, muriatic acid, nitric acid, potash, and soda; and to give the chemical symbols for each—to understand the laws of chemical combination—allotropic modifications of elementary bodies—chemical affinity or force.

Second Examination.—(*In addition to above.*)—To understand the terms of chemical nomenclature and the use of the several prefixes and affixes employed—atomic weights and combining proportions—acids—alkalies—oxides—salts. To know the symbols and combining proportions of oxygen, hydrogen, nitrogen, chlorine, carbon, phosphorus, sulphur, silicon, iron, lead, mercury, sodium, potassium, calcium. To know the principal oxides, acids, and salts formed by the combination of these elements—to explain the ordinary experiments with oxygen, hydrogen, and chlorine.

Geology.

First Examination.—(*a.*) Classes of rocks, aqueous, igneous, and metamorphic rocks—mode of formation of each—origin and composition of siliceous, argillaceous, calcareous, and carboniferous rocks—to be able to refer a specimen to its proper class. (*b.*) Agencies at work in *wasting* the land, and how they act—air—frost—ice—rain—rivers—the sea. (*c.*) Movement of the earth's crust—central heat—volcanoes and earthquakes—mountain chains—anticlinal and synclinal curves—faults—dip and strike of strata. (*d.*) Definitions of common geological terms.

Second Examination.—(*In addition to above.*)—(*a.*) Palæozoic rocks—names and order of the chief sub-divisions of this group—their distribution in the British Islands—leading fossils in the various groups. (*b.*) Coal—its nature, origin, and distribution—its position in the stratified series—ores of metals found in palæozoic rocks, and their mode of occurrence—probable origin of lodes. (*c.*) Mesozoic rocks—names and order of the chief members of this group—their distribution in the British Islands—principal fossils in the various groups—origin of chalk, rock salt, and gypsum. (*d.*) Cainozoic rocks—sub-divisions—distribution in British Islands—principal fossils—nature, origin, and distribution of the boulder clay or glacial drift—bone caves, and their contents—fossils of the drift.

ACCOUNTS

OF THE

PARLIAMENTARY GRANT, AND CASH RECEIPTS AND PAYMENTS

BY

THE COMMISSIONERS

OF

NATIONAL EDUCATION, IRELAND,

FROM

1ST APRIL, 1874, TO THE 31ST MARCH, 1875.

		£ s. d.	£ s. d.
1.	OFFICE: Salaries and Wages,		10 3 6
1.	INSPECTION: Salaries,		81 13 9
2.	Do., Travelling Allowances, &c.,		1,028 0 3
2.	NORMAL ESTABLISHMENT: Male Teachers' Training Department,		3 19 3
[illegible]	Do., Female ditto,		8 4 6
1.	MODEL SCHOOLS: Central Model School Department,		4 10 3
5.	DISTRICT MODEL SCHOOLS,		13 8 9
6.	MINOR MODEL SCHOOLS,		1 10 5
1.	NATIONAL SCHOOLS: Principal and Assistant Teachers,		34 6 6
1.	Do., Monitors,		5 16 8
[illegible]	Do., Training Monitors, &c.,		6 8 6
[illegible]	Do., Retiring Gratuities,		36 10 1
	(For sundry Repayments in aid of above Sub-heads of the Vote.)		
	EXCHEQUER EXTRA RECEIPTS: SCHOOL FEES received from PUPILS attending the following MODEL SCHOOLS. (The Salaries of Principal and Assistant Teachers of Model Schools are supplemented by a sum of £4,000 or thereabouts, being about four-fifths of the Fees received from Pupils attending these Schools. The balance of the Fees—about £1,000—is payable to H. M. Exchequer):—		
	CENTRAL MODEL SCHOOL, Co. DUBLIN,	1,217 7 4	
	WEST DUBLIN MODEL SCHOOL, Co. DUBLIN,	237 19 8	
	INCHICORE MODEL SCHOOL, Co. DUBLIN,	124 15 5	
	ATHY MODEL SCHOOL, Co. KILDARE,	84 5 6	
	BAILIEBOROUGH MODEL SCHOOL, Co. CAVAN,	148 10 1	
	Carried forward . £	1,810 9 2	681,252 7 9

PAYMENTS by the COMMISSIONERS of NATIONAL EDUCATION, to 31st March, 1875.

DISCHARGE.

Sched.		£	s.	d.
A.	OFFICE IN DUBLIN:			
1.	Salaries and Wages, ...			
2.	Travelling Expenses, ...			
3.	Legal Expenses, ...			
4.	Police, ...			
5.	Rent, ...			
6.	Rates and Taxes, ...			
7.	Incidental Expenses, ...			
B.	INSPECTION:			
1.	Salaries, ...			
2.	Travelling and Personal Allowances, &c., ...			
C.	NORMAL ESTABLISHMENT:			
1.	Salaries, Professors, &c., ...			
2.	MALE TEACHERS' TRAINING DEPARTMENT:			
	Salaries, &c., Superintendents, &c., . . .	£416	14	10
	Maintenance, &c., Teachers under Training,	1,728	2	11
	General Expenditure, ...	182	8	7
3.	FEMALE TEACHERS' TRAINING DEPARTMENT:			
	Salaries, &c., Superintendents, &c., . . .	£304	0	0
	Maintenance, &c., Teachers under Training,	1,091	17	6
	General Expenditure, ...	380	3	1
4.	TRAINING DEPARTMENTS:			
	Miscellaneous Expenditure, ...			

MODEL SCHOOLS.

Sched.		£	s.	d.
D.				
1.	CENTRAL MODEL SCHOOL:			
	Salaries and Allowances—Teachers, Pupil-Teachers, and Monitors, ...	£5,129	11	5
	General Expenditure, ...	81	17	10

CHARGE.	£	s.	d.	£	s.	d.
Brought forward, . .	1,810	9	3	[illegible]	7	3
Amount of School Fees—*continued.*						
Ballymena Model School, Co. Antrim, . .	164	3	10			
Belfast Model School, Co. Antrim, . . .	781	1	5			
Clonmel Model School, Co. Tipperary, . .	[illegible]	6	8			
Coleraine Model School, Co. Londonderry, .	161	18	9			
Cork Model School, Co. Cork, ...	[illegible]	19	0			
Dunmanway Model School, Co. Cork, . . .	96	15	10			
Enniscorthy Model School, Co. Wexford, . .	81	19	11			
Enniskillen Model School, Co. Fermanagh,	167	14	7			
Galway Model School, Co. Galway, . . .	[illegible]	9	10			
Kilkenny Model School, Co. Kilkenny, . .	191	9	1			
Limerick Model School, Co. Limerick, . .	187	4	6			
Londonderry Model School, Co. Londonderry, . .	[illegible]	13	9			
Carried forward, . £	[illegible]	6	6	[illegible]	7	3

and Disbursements—*continued.*

	DISCHARGE.		£ s. d.	£ s. d.
	Brought forward, . .		1,583 4 6	70,[illegible]
Schd. D 4.	Ballymena District Model School:			
	Salaries and Allowances—Teachers, Pupil-Teachers, and Monitors, ...	£916 16 4		
	General Expenditure, ...	49 16 10		
			96[illegible] 7 3	
	Belfast District Model School:			
	Salaries and Allowances—Teachers, Pupil-Teachers, and Monitors, ...	£3,683 7 8		
	General Expenditure, ...	250 16 6		
			3,934 4 2	
	Clonmel District Model School:			
	Salaries and Allowances—Teachers, Pupil-Teachers, and Monitors, ...	£571 18 6		
	General Expenditure, ...	60 10 10		
			[illegible] 4 4	
	Coleraine District Model School:			
	Salaries and Allowances—Teachers, Pupil-Teachers, and Monitors, ...	£813 16 2		
	General Expenditure, ...	58 18 9		
			[illegible] 12 11	
	Cork District Model School:			
	Salaries and Allowances—Teachers, Pupil-Teachers, and Monitors, . . .	£1,578 8 2		
	General Expenditure, ...	134 4 10		
			1,71[illegible]	
	Dunmanway District Model School:			
	Salaries and Allowances—Teachers, Pupil-Teachers, and Monitors, ...	£678 18 8		
	General Expenditure, ...	63 [illegible]		
			742 [illegible]	
	Enniscorthy District Model School:			
	Salaries and Allowances—Teachers, Pupil-Teachers, and Monitors, ...	£828 17 1		
	General Expenditure, ...	40 17 7		
			869 14 8	
	Enniskillen District Model School:			
	Salaries and Allowances—Teachers, Pupil-Teachers, and Monitors, ...	£891 13 6		
	General Expenditure, ...	123 18 4		
			1,015 11 10	
	Galway District Model School:			
	Salaries and Allowances—Teachers, Pupil-Teachers, and Monitors, ...	£700 8 10		
	General Expenditure, ...	81 6 9		
			781 15 7	
	Kilkenny District Model School:			
	Salaries and Allowances—Teachers, Pupil-Teachers, and Monitors, ...	£604 2 1		
	General Expenditure, ...	118 8 3		
			722 10 4	
	Limerick District Model School:			
	Salaries and Allowances—Teachers, Pupil-Teachers, and Monitors, ...	£894 1 10		
	General Expenditure, ...	137 4 11		
			1,031 6 9	
	Londonderry District Model School:			
	Salaries and Allowances—Teachers, Pupil-Teachers, and Monitors, . . .	£1,324 1 4		
	General Expenditure, ...	169 9 11		
			1,493 11 3	
	Carried forward, . £		15,[illegible]	70,[illegible]

ACCOUNT of RECEIPTS

	CHARGE.	£ s. d.	£ s. d.
	Brought forward, . .	4,463 6 6	581,243 7 2
	ACCOUNT OF SCHOOL FEES—*continued.*		
	NEWRY MODEL SCHOOL, Co. DOWN, ...	206 17 4	
	NEWTOWNARDS MODEL SCHOOL, Co. DOWN, . .	183 16 4	
	SLIGO MODEL SCHOOL, Co. SLIGO, ...	203 12 6	
	TRIM MODEL SCHOOL, Co. MEATH, ...	54 1 11	
	WATERFORD MODEL SCHOOL, Co. WATERFORD, .	150 4 7	
	BALLYMONEY MODEL SCHOOL, Co. ANTRIM, . .	159 14 0	
	CARRICKFERGUS MODEL SCHOOL, Co. ANTRIM, .	174 7 5	
	LURGAN MODEL SCHOOL, Co. ARMAGH, . . .	158 9 8	
	MONAGHAN MODEL SCHOOL, Co. MONAGHAN, . .	149 3 0	
	NEWTOWNSTEWART MODEL SCHOOL, Co. TYRONE, .	79 7 8	
	OMAGH MODEL SCHOOL, Co. TYRONE, . . .	170 8 1	
	PARSONSTOWN MODEL SCHOOL, KING'S COUNTY, .	116 10 6	
			6,330 5 0
	Carried forward, . £	—	587,573 12 2

and DISBURSEMENTS—*continued.*

	DISCHARGE.		£ s. d.	£ s. d.
	Brought forward, . . .		15,879 19 5	70,570 3 6
Sched. D 5.	NEWRY DISTRICT MODEL SCHOOL:			
	Salaries and Allowances—Teachers, Pupil-Teachers, and Monitors, ...	£[illegible] 10 6		
	General Expenditure, ...	69 15 4		
			570 5 10	
	NEWTOWNARDS DISTRICT MODEL SCHOOL:			
	Salaries and Allowances—Teachers, Pupil-Teachers, and Monitors, ...	£1,357 8 3		
	General Expenditure, ...	85 10 5		
			1,443 17 8	
	SLIGO DISTRICT MODEL SCHOOL:			
	Salaries and Allowances—Teachers, Pupil-Teachers, and Monitors, ...	£842 9 9		
	General Expenditure, ...	83 10 10		
			925 0 7	
	TUAM DISTRICT MODEL SCHOOL:			
	Salaries and Allowances—Teachers, Pupil-Teachers, and Monitors, ...	£610 18 5		
	General Expenditure, ...	58 1 9		
			669 0 2	
	WATERFORD DISTRICT MODEL SCHOOL:			
	Salaries and Allowances—Teachers, Pupil-Teachers, and Monitors, ...	£757 4 4		
	General Expenditure, ...	86 10 11		
			844 [illegible]	
				20,759 6 3
D 6.	MINOR MODEL SCHOOLS.			
	BALLYMONEY MINOR MODEL SCHOOL:			
	Salaries and Allowances—Teachers, Pupil-Teachers, and Monitors, ...	£774 6 7		
	General Expenditure, ...	29 15 3		
			804 1 10	
	CARRICKFERGUS MINOR MODEL SCHOOL:			
	Salaries and Allowances—Teachers and Monitors, ...	£621 1 9		
	General Expenditure, ...	74 2 11		
			695 4 8	
	LURGAN MINOR MODEL SCHOOL:			
	Salaries and Allowances—Teachers, Pupil-Teachers, and Monitors.	£1,177 7 8		
	General Expenditure, ...	[illegible] 2 8		
			1,[illegible] 9 0	
	MONAGHAN MINOR MODEL SCHOOL:			
	Salaries and Allowances—Teachers and Monitors, ...	£669 9 5		
	General Expenditure, ...	34 0 0		
			703 8 5	
	NEWTOWNSTEWART MINOR MODEL SCHOOL:			
	Salaries and Allowances—Teachers, Pupil-Teachers, and Monitors, ...	£455 18 4		
	General Expenditure, ...	22 12 7		
			478 6 11	
	OMAGH MINOR MODEL SCHOOL:			
	Salaries and Allowances—Teachers, Pupil-Teachers, and Monitors, ...	£512 7 10		
	General Expenditure, ...	63 11 6		
			575 19 4	
	PARSONSTOWN MINOR MODEL SCHOOL:			
	Salaries and Allowances—Teachers, Pupil-Teachers, and Monitors, ...	£587 6 9		
	General Expenditure, ...	36 16 2		
			623 2 11	
				5,[illegible] 6 7
	Carried forward, . . £		—	[illegible]85 10 6

ACCOUNT of RECEIPTS

Subhd.	CHARGE.	£ s. d.	£ s. d.
	Brought forward, . .	—	387,373 12 2
F.	AGRICULTURAL ESTABLISHMENTS.		
	RECEIPTS FOR SALES OF FARM PRODUCE, &c., FROM FARMS UNDER THE MANAGEMENT OF THE BOARD:—		
3	ALBERT MODEL FARM AND GARDEN, GLASNEVIN, CO. DUBLIN, ...	5,104 19 10	
4	ATHY SCHOOL FARM, CO. KILDARE, ...	594 12 7	
	BAILIEBOROUGH SCHOOL FARM, CO. CAVAN, . .	242 13 10	
	BALLYMONEY SCHOOL FARM, CO. ANTRIM, . . .	394 14 9	
	BATH SCHOOL FARM, CO. MONAGHAN, . . .	230 6 9	
	BELFAST (ULSTER) SCHOOL FARM, CO. ANTRIM, . .	912 2 2	
	DERRYCASTLE SCHOOL FARM, CO. TIPPERARY, . . .	91 1 10	
	Carried forward, . . £	[illegible] 11 9	387,373 12 2

and DISBURSEMENTS—*continued.*

Sched.	DISCHARGE.		£ s. d.	£ s. d.
	Brought forward, . .		—	96,283 18 1
D.	MODEL SCHOOLS:			
7	Miscellaneous Expenditure, ...		—	276 17 6
	Retiring Gratuities, ...		—	373 14 6
E.	NATIONAL SCHOOLS, &c.:			
1	Principal and Assistant Teachers, ...		339,827 0 7	
2	Workmistresses, ...		3,523 10 10	
3	Good Service Salaries, ...		3,072 14 3	
4	Monitors, ...		32,479 0 2	
5	Training, Monitors, &c., ...		5,030 15 10	
6	Travelling Expenses, Teachers and Monitors for Examination,		739 13 8	
7	Gratuities to Teachers of Workhouse Schools, ...		334 19 6	
8	Organizing Teachers, ...		827 11 5	
9	Retiring Gratuities, ...		6,139 12 3	
10	Navigation Teachers, &c., ...		128 0 0	
11	Maritime Schools, Meals, &c., ...		30 0 0	
12	National Schools—Incidental Expenditure, ...		45 13 7	
				414,073 11 3
F.	AGRICULTURAL ESTABLISHMENTS:			
1	General Superintendence and Inspection, ...		—	1,579 3 0
2	ALBERT AGRICULTURAL TRAINING DEPARTMENT:			
	Salaries and Wages, ...		402 12 11	
	Maintenance of Agricultural Pupils, &c., ...		1,317 14 9	
	General Expenditure, ...		350 3 8	
				2,170 11 4
3	ALBERT MODEL FARM AND GARDEN, CO. DUBLIN:			
	Purchase of Live Stock, Seeds, Implements, and General Farm Expenses, &c., ...		—	2,347 19 0
4	AGRICULTURAL SCHOOLS.			
	ATHY MODEL AGRICULTURAL SCHOOL:			
	Salary, &c., of Agriculturist, and Maintenance of Resident Agricultural Pupils, &c.,	£181 12 0		
	Purchase of Live Stock, &c., and General Farm Expenses, ...	617 8 6		
			799 0 6	
	BAILIEBOROUGH MODEL AGRICULTURAL SCHOOL:			
	Salary, &c., of Agriculturist, and Maintenance of Resident Agricultural Pupils, &c.,	£144 0 1		
	Purchase of Live Stock, &c., and General Farm Expenses, ...	196 11 2		
			340 11 3	
	BALLYMONEY MODEL AGRICULTURAL SCHOOL:			
	Salary, &c., of Agriculturist, and Maintenance of Resident Agricultural Pupils, &c.,	£149 3 1		
	Purchase of Live Stock and General Farm Expenses, ...	184 13 11		
			333 16 0	
	[illegible] MODEL AGRICULTURAL SCHOOL:			
	Salary of Agriculturist, ...	£41 17 9		
	Purchase of Live Stock and General Farm Expenses, ...	189 13 5		
			231 11 5	
	BELFAST (ULSTER) AGRICULTURAL SCHOOL:			
	Salary, &c., of Agriculturist, and Maintenance of Resident Agricultural Pupils, .	£209 11 2		
	Purchase of Live Stock and General Expenditure connected with the Literary and Agricultural Departments, ...	1,136 18 10		
			1,346 10 0	
	[illegible] MODEL AGRICULTURAL SCHOOL:			
	Salary of Agriculturist, ...	£31 10 0		
	Purchase of Live Stock and General Farm Expenses, ...	84 16 0		
			116 6 0	
	Carried forward, . . £		3,179 1 2	518,112 17 0

ACCOUNT OF RECEIPTS

Sched.	CHARGE.	£ s. d.	£ s. d.
	Brought forward, . . .	5,560 11 9	387,873 13 2
	RECEIPTS FOR SALES—*continued.*		
F 4.	DUNMANWAY SCHOOL FARM, Co. CORK, ...	143 11 2	
	FARRAHY SCHOOL FARM, Co. CORK, ...	69 18 1	
	GLANDORE SCHOOL FARM, Co. CORK, ...	129 11 0	
	GORMANSTOWN SCHOOL FARM, Co. TIPPERARY, . .	291 19 11	
	KILKENNY SCHOOL FARM, Co. KILKENNY, . . .	873 11 0	
	KYLE PARK SCHOOL FARM, Co. TIPPERARY, . . .	16 0 6	
	LEITRIM SCHOOL FARM, Co. LEITRIM, ...	29 8 7	
	LIMERICK SCHOOL FARM, Co. LIMERICK, . . .	539 8 7	
	MOUNT TRENCHARD SCHOOL FARM, Co. LIMERICK . .	21 0 0	
	MUNSTER SCHOOL FARM, Co. CORK, ...	684 3 2	
	TEMPLEDOUGLAS SCHOOL FARM, Co. DONEGAL, . .	63 18 4	
	TERVOE SCHOOL FARM, Co. LIMERICK, ...	68 0 7	
	Carried forward, ... £	8497, 18 10	387,873 13 2

and DISBURSEMENTS—*continued.*

Sched.	DISCHARGE.		£ s. d.	£ s. d.
	Brought forward, . . .		6,179 1 9	518,412 17 9
F 4.	DUNMANWAY MODEL AGRICULTURAL SCHOOL:			
	Salary, &c., of Agriculturist, and Maintenance of Resident Agricultural Pupils, .	£75 19 4		
	Purchase of Live Stock and General Farm Expenses, ...	146 19 10		
			222 18 2	
	ENNISKILLEN MODEL AGRICULTURAL SCHOOL:			
	Salaries, ...	£[illegible] 0 0		
	General Expenditure, ...	9 14 3		
			82 16 3	
	FARRAHY MODEL AGRICULTURAL SCHOOL:			
	Salary, &c., of Agriculturist, . . .	£47 17 4		
	Purchase of Live Stock and General Farm Expenses, ...	64 2 10		
			112 0 2	
	GLANDORE MODEL AGRICULTURAL SCHOOL:			
	Salary of Agriculturist, ...	£31 8 1		
	Purchase of Live Stock and General Farm Expenses, ...	137 10 7		
			168 18 8	
	GORMANSTOWN MODEL AGRICULTURAL SCHOOL:			
	Salaries, &c., of Literary and Agricultural Departments, ...	£[illegible] 2 5		
	Purchase of Live Stock and General Farm Expenses.	619 8 3		
			849 10 8	
	KILKENNY MODEL AGRICULTURAL SCHOOL:			
	Salary, &c., of Agriculturist, and Maintenance of Resident Agricultural Pupils, . .	£390 16 0		
	Purchase of Live Stock and General Expenditure connected with the Literary and Agricultural Departments, ...	331 18 7		
			722 14 7	
	KYLE PARK MODEL AGRICULTURAL SCHOOL:			
	Salary of Agriculturist, ...	£[illegible] 10 0		
	Rent, ...	35 10 0		
			67 0 0	
	LEITRIM MODEL AGRICULTURAL SCHOOL:			
	Purchase of Live Stock and General Farm Expenses, ...	. . .	162 12 11	
	LIMERICK MODEL AGRICULTURAL SCHOOL:			
	Salaries and Allowances, Agricultural Department, and Maintenance of Resident Literary and Agricultural Pupils, ...	£[illegible] 19 11		
	Purchase of Live Stock and General Expenditure connected with the Literary and Agricultural Departments, ...	486 6 4		
			1,169 6 3	
	MOUNT TRENCHARD MODEL AGRICULTURAL SCHOOL:			
	Salary of Agriculturist, ...		7 10 0	
	MUNSTER MODEL AGRICULTURAL SCHOOL:			
	Salaries, &c., of Agriculturists, and Maintenance of Resident Agricultural Pupils, &c., .	£[illegible] 6 0		
	Purchase of Live Stock and General Expenditure connected with Literary and Agricultural Departments, ...	484 9 10		
			1,151 16 10	
	TEMPLEDOUGLAS MODEL AGRICULTURAL SCHOOL:			
	Salaries—Literary and Agricultural Departments, ...	£37 12 11		
	Purchase of Live Stock and General Farm Expenses, ...	115 16 6		
			153 9 5	
	TREVOR MODEL AGRICULTURAL SCHOOL:			
	Purchase of Live Stock and General Farm Expenses, ...	. . .	75 10 10	
	Carried forward, . . . £		7,249 5 11	518,412 17 9

ACCOUNT of RECEIPTS

Sched.	CHARGE.	£ s. d.	£ s. d.
	Brought forward, . . .	8,497 16 10	[illegible],573 [illegible] [illegible]
	RECEIVED FOR SALES—*continued.*		
F 4.	WOODSTOCK SCHOOL FARM, CO. KILKENNY, . . .	6 14 6	8,[illegible] 13 10
	EXCHEQUER EXTRA RECEIPTS, payable to H. M. Exchequer: Amount received for Books, School Requisites, and Apparatus sold to the National Schools in Ireland, at reduced prices, during the twelve months ended 31st March, 1875, . .	—	23,210 6 7
	Do., Miscellaneous, ...	—	1,1[illegible] 18 4
	PRIVATE CONTRIBUTION FUND, being dividends on Legacies and Donations invested in Government Securities, . .	—	[illegible] 0 9
	INCOME TAX DUTY: For Amount of Income Tax for the Establishment, being deductions under the head of Salaries, &c., ...	—	474 9 4
	SUNDRY REPAYMENTS IN AID OF GENERAL ACCOUNT VOTE 1873–4, ...	—	53 6 1
			£ [illegible] 0 1

and Disbursements—*continued.*

	DISCHARGE.	£ s. d.	£ s. d.
	Brought forward, . .	7,740 5 11	518,412 17 0
Sched. P 8.	Woodstock Model Agricultural School: Allowance to Agriculturist and Wages to an Industrial Class, &c.,	50 10 6	
	Dunlewy Model Agricultural School: Salary, &c., of Agriculturist, and General Expenditure, .	20 0 0	
	Agricultural Schools under Local Management, . . .	933 1 3	
	General Expenditure, ...	18 10 0	8,747 7 0
G.	Book and School Apparatus Department:		
1.	Book Porters' Wages, ...	800 12 8	
2.	Contractors for Paper, Printing, and Binding of National School Books; and for Maps, Apparatus, and School Requisites, purchased from Publishers, ...	46,031 3 3	46,831 15 11
H.	Poundage on Post Office Orders, ...	—	3,317 7 10
			576,480 8 5
	Exchequer Extra Receipts:		
	Amount paid over to the Exchequer for Books and Requisites,	—	22,234 1 8
	Do. for Model School Fees, ...	—	1,033 10 1
	Do. Miscellaneous, ...	—	834 9 11
	Do. Do., refunded to Treasury, . .	—	1 0 0
	Private Contribution Fund, ...	—	123 0 0
	Commissioners of Income Tax: Payments of Deductions for Income Tax under the head of Salaries and Allowances, ...	—	462 10 7
	Parliamentary Grant, 1873-4: Savings surrendered, ...	—	8,902 15 6
			611,046 11 6
	Balance on the 31st March, 1873, ...	—	10,083 8 7
	JAMES CLARIDGE, *Accountant.*	£	621,130 0 1

JAMES KELLY, } *Secretaries.*
WM. HOMAN NEWELL, }

Education Office, Dublin 1873

DUBLIN: Printed by ALEXANDER THOM, 87 & 88, Abbey-street,
For Her Majesty's Stationery Office.

APPENDIX

TO THE

FORTY-FIRST REPORT

OF THE

COMMISSIONERS

OF

NATIONAL EDUCATION

IN IRELAND,

(FOR THE YEAR 1874).

Presented to both Houses of Parliament by Command of Her Majesty.

DUBLIN:
PRINTED BY ALEXANDER THOM, 87 & 88, ABBEY-STREET,
PRINTER TO THE QUEEN'S MOST EXCELLENT MAJESTY.
FOR HER MAJESTY'S STATIONERY OFFICE.

1876.

[C.—1228. I.] *Price 1s. 6d.*

CONTENTS.

APPENDIX A.

APPENDIX B.

APPENDIX C.

List of Schools in operation on 31st December, 1874, by Provinces and Counties:

APPENDIX TO FORTY-FIRST REPORT

OF

COMMISSIONERS OF NATIONAL EDUCATION IN IRELAND

(1874).

APPENDIX A.

I.—TABLE showing the Classification of 808,675 of the Pupils on the Rolls for the *last quarter* of the year 1874.

Provinces and Counties.	Infants.	Class I.	Class II.	Class III.	Class IV.	Class V.	Class VI.	Total.
ULSTER.								
Antrim,	18,169	14,360	13,844	10,957	7,464	3,945	867	69,036
Armagh,	6,748	6,563	5,168	3,927	2,628	1,583	250	26,855
Cavan,	5,260	5,573	5,063	4,294	2,818	1,635	231	24,870
Donegal,	7,327	7,890	6,442	4,743	3,140	1,763	247	31,792
Down,	11,809	9,187	8,069	6,430	4,864	3,100	450	43,889
Fermanagh,	2,591	2,908	2,864	2,036	1,458	792	61	12,335
Londonderry,	5,938	5,171	4,384	3,940	3,147	1,958	345	25,091
Monaghan,	4,255	4,417	4,036	3,114	2,293	1,113	199	19,447
Tyrone,	6,745	6,837	6,063	4,892	3,450	2,043	388	30,413
Total,	68,700	62,880	55,512	44,375	31,273	17,602	2,738	283,448
MUNSTER.								
Clare,	5,230	4,950	4,606	4,392	3,680	2,311	498	25,927
Cork,	19,070	17,286	15,490	18,208	10,318	8,069	1,371	84,739
Kerry,	8,005	6,848	7,344	6,337	4,864	3,550	840	39,804
Limerick,	6,432	5,546	5,125	4,635	4,000	3,367	1,287	30,314
Tipperary,	6,657	6,109	5,970	5,231	4,065	2,646	498	31,486
Waterford,	2,862	2,901	2,455	1,796	1,443	697	173	12,425
Total,	48,465	45,374	41,248	36,549	28,390	20,673	4,473	224,573
LEINSTER.								
Carlow,	1,576	1,629	1,456	1,120	791	417	62	7,051
Dublin,	11,861	8,070	6,732	5,226	3,457	2,052	539	38,617
Kildare,	2,469	2,629	2,255	1,492	1,070	527	65	10,307
Kilkenny,	4,916	3,834	3,067	2,616	1,887	1,351	214	17,507
King's,	2,302	2,339	2,101	1,360	1,039	568	103	10,052
Longford,	2,393	2,311	2,271	1,765	1,252	791	103	11,036
Louth,	2,456	2,794	2,397	1,849	1,150	394	32	11,022
Meath,	2,941	3,079	2,618	2,279	1,770	1,074	116	13,677
Queen's,	2,383	2,307	2,177	1,642	1,115	578	118	10,294
Westmeath,	2,571	2,510	2,474	1,898	1,513	812	121	11,900
Wexford,	3,311	3,726	2,774	2,134	1,432	863	110	14,340
Wicklow,	2,078	2,016	2,124	1,346	1,004	676	69	10,113
Total,	40,637	38,894	32,366	25,083	17,560	10,289	1,675	168,316
CONNAUGHT.								
Galway,	6,808	8,409	6,763	4,754	3,182	1,446	282	32,749
Leitrim,	4,155	4,432	4,421	3,339	2,093	1,069	76	19,499
Mayo,	8,660	10,293	7,998	5,970	3,523	1,846	244	38,524
Roscommon,	4,690	6,276	5,525	4,161	2,871	1,565	310	25,394
Sligo,	3,994	4,062	3,774	3,081	2,037	1,314	141	18,263
Total,	28,407	34,462	28,481	21,149	13,700	7,158	933	134,339
Grand Total,	184,269	181,634	157,610	126,178	90,929	56,222	9,819	808,675

B

II.—Table showing the Religious Denominations of the Pupils on the Rolls ... Attendance of Roman Catholics

Provinces and Counties.	Total No. of Schools.	Under Protestant Teachers.						Under ...	
		No. of Schools.	R.C.	E.C.	Pres.	Others.	Total.	No. of Schools.	R.C.
Ulster.									
Antrim, . .	276	293	4,988	11,850	33,602	1,039	53,089	62	10,498
Armagh, . .	168	101	2,222	7,170	4,251	813	14,495	56	9,615
Cavan, . .	136	37	846	1,119	567	76	2,597	167	19,035
Donegal, . .	293	106	4,175	2,860	3,488	273	10,785	156	18,248
Down, . .	287	194	8,836	7,297	17,201	830	33,644	87	10,808
Fermanagh, . .	127	87	764	3,451	144	168	8,527	86	7,974
Londonderry, .	226	134	3,484	4,198	9,359	376	17,417	67	7,358
Monaghan, . .	149	49	1,636	1,710	2,029	30	5,438	97	14,281
Tyrone, . .	283	130	2,983	6,153	5,780	859	14,328	118	14,863
Total, . .	2,078	1,084	24,167	45,910	76,230	4,777	149,933	833	112,794
Munster.									
Clare, . .	88	1	3	35	–	–	40	81	11,726
Cork, . .	287	27	146	1,556	180	71	1,963	225	66,224
Kerry, . .	117	1	24	22	–	–	46	116	20,223
Limerick, . .	91	1	1	35	13	3	52	89	14,835
Tipperary, . .	149	6	256	121	74	1	452	143	16,974
Waterford, . .	41	–	–	–	–	–	–	88	5,267
Total, . .	736	35	429	1,772	277	75	2,553	692	105,709
Leinster.									
Carlow, . .	85	9	14	104	–	–	118	32	5,918
Dublin, . .	108	12	266	664	165	35	1,129	78	11,387
Kildare, . .	54	8	66	79	5	12	162	50	7,128
Kilkenny, . .	74	8	142	105	9	2	254	69	7,880
King's, . .	67	1	8	49	–	–	57	65	6,809
Longford, . .	64	6	91	342	43	–	456	63	7,618
Louth, . .	47	4	282	69	56	–	407	45	5,227
Meath, . .	102	2	62	46	56	–	164	97	9,740
Queen's, . .	56	4	34	184	–	9	220	52	6,557
Westmeath, . .	58	–	–	–	–	–	–	56	7,061
Wexford, . .	70	1	6	45	6	5	59	69	7,824
Wicklow, . .	55	4	788	189	–	–	275	50	6,252
Total, . .	758	47	1,070	1,834	349	54	3,316	711	97,811
Connaught.									
Galway, . .	104	9	164	43	8	–	210	190	18,871
Leitrim, . .	124	14	874	352	–	10	1,260	110	14,619
Mayo, . .	116	5	105	230	120	–	455	111	22,807
Roscommon, . .	80	3	209	82	5	–	296	77	11,890
Sligo, . .	105	5	128	246	105	78	557	99	15,884
Total, . .	529	29	1,180	1,878	243	88	3,784	497	83,036
Grand Total,	4,121	1,191	26,614	48,779	77,999	4,994	157,586	2,533	409,143

of the 4,121 Schools from which Returns have been received, exhibiting a Mixed and Protestants, for the year 1874.

Roman Catholic Teachers.				Under Protestant and Roman Catholic Teachers.						Provinces and Counties.
E.C.	Pres.	Others.	Total.	No. of Schools.	R.C.	E.C.	Pres.	Others.	Total.	
										Ulster.
348	846	18	11,658	16	1,183	1,279	2,311	248	5,021	Antrim.
743	271	9	10,841	9	537	812	584	164	2,105	Armagh.
1,167	215	2	20,533	7	701	147	179	1	1,101	Cavan.
1,346	819	21	20,645	1	61	37	1	14	109	Donegal.
1,187	1,147	73	13,283	6	567	194	769	78	1,589	Down.
2,710	57	24	10,263	4	71	343	48	64	510	Fermanagh.
539	1,126	27	9,284	5	167	731	328	79	915	Londonderry.
849	629	3	13,011	3	132	140	138	8	434	Monaghan.
2,062	1,338	54	10,477	5	675	1,286	238	67	2,351	Tyrone.
11,940	6,096	[illegible]	120,018	56	3,710	[illegible]	4,763	700	13,703	
										Munster.
234	21	15	11,606	-	-	-	-	-	-	Clare.
931	53	44	37,304	3	279	406	48	90	820	Cork.
384	7	2	21,835	-	-	-	-	-	-	Kerry.
409	34	62	15,442	1	96	69	13	18	140	Limerick.
127	57	9	17,595	-	-	-	-	-	-	Tipperary.
182	26	16	3,181	2	130	118	27	42	318	Waterford.
2,777	176	133	108,766	6	434	704	88	130	1,384	
										Leinster.
117	-	-	4,633	1	150	4	-	-	154	Carlow.
907	64	37	11,940	18	4,111	1,571	344	184	6,840	Dublin.
214	80	3	7,289	1	8	46	39	8	71	Kildare.
237	2	1	8,261	2	34	160	10	7	209	Kilkenny.
360	18	2	7,296	3	61	140	11	50	261	King's.
233	21	8	7,806	-	-	-	-	-	-	Longford.
181	83	3	8,459	-	-	-	-	-	-	Louth.
384	28	5	10,155	3	163	67	1	2	233	Meath.
253	14	-	8,784	-	-	-	-	-	-	Queen's.
213	30	-	7,396	-	-	-	-	-	-	Westmeath.
219	30	10	8,143	-	-	-	-	-	-	Wexford.
265	6	11	6,334	2	231	45	-	-	276	Wicklow.

Appendix A.

Average number of Protestant and Roman Catholic pupils in mixed schools.

MIXED SCHOOLS.

III.—The following tables show the *average* and also the total number of Roman Catholic and Protestant Pupils in each of the MIXED Schools, according to Provinces, in 1874, for which returns have been received.

A.—Under ROMAN CATHOLIC Teachers exclusively.

Provinces.	Mixed Schools.	Roman Catholic Pupils.	Protestant Pupils.
Ulster, . . .	933	120·8	19·3
Munster, . . .	092	154·3	4·4
Leinster, . . .	711	125·2	5·
Connaught, . .	497	165·2	5·7

A.—Under ROMAN CATHOLIC Teachers exclusively.

No. of Schools.	Roman Catholic Pupils.	Protestant Pupils.	Average per School.	
			Roman Catholics.	Protestants.
2,833	389,143	27,599	137·3	9·7

B.—Under PROTESTANT Teachers exclusively.

Provinces.	Mixed Schools.	Roman Catholic Pupils.	Protestant Pupils.
Ulster, . . .	1,084	23·2	115·2
Munster, . . .	36	11·9	69·
Leinster, . . .	42	26·1	52·8
Connaught, . .	29	40·0	55·3

B.—Under PROTESTANT Teachers exclusively.

No. of Schools.	Roman Catholic Pupils.	Protestant Pupils.	Average per School.	
			Roman Catholics.	Protestants.
1,191	26,814	130,873	22·5	109·8

C.—Under ROMAN CATHOLIC and PROTESTANT Teachers conjointly.

Provinces.	Mixed Schools.	Roman Catholic Pupils.	Protestant Pupils.
Ulster, . . .	56	66·7	161·7
Munster, . . .	6	54·2	118·7
Leinster, . . .	30	159·1	89·
Connaught, . .	5	17·6	99·6

C.—Under ROMAN CATHOLIC and PROTESTANT Teachers conjointly.

No. of Schools.	Roman Catholic Pupils.	Protestant Pupils.	Average per School.	
			Roman Catholics.	Protestants.
97	9,002	12,977	92·8	133·7

IV.—Religious Denominations of Pupils on Rolls of Unmixed Schools for year ended 31st December, 1874.

Provinces and Counties.	Total Number of Schools.	Under Roman Catholic Teachers. Number of Schools.	Under Roman Catholic Teachers. No. of Pupils. R. C.	Under Protestant Teachers. No. of Schools.	Under Protestant Teachers. No. of Pupils—Protestants. R. C.	Pres.	Others.	Total.
Ulster.								
Antrim,*	139	29	8,270	110	4,808	13,904	471	18,875
Armagh,	42	25	6,119	18	869	706	150	1,725
Cavan,	65	53	6,055	33	800	100	27	927
Donegal,	93	83	8,707	9	308	311	4	623
Down,	109	21	3,629	88	2,792	7,695	179	10,658
Fermanagh,	11	5	778	6	442	13	9	464
Londonderry,*	52	15	2,630	37	384	1,196	81	1,611
Monaghan,	19	11	1,931	8	484	245	10	749
Tyrone,*	44	30	3,877	14	733	594	87	1,414
Total,	553	273	43,036	280	10,880	24,728	1,308	36,854
Munster.								
Clare,	133	133	20,073	–	–	–	–	–
Cork,	383	361	61,051	22	1,218	62	319	1,599
Kerry,	175	169	28,311	6	286	12	31	329
Limerick,	135	130	22,540	3	172	18	20	210
Tipperary,	140	139	21,479	1	36	–	–	36
Waterford,	77	77	9,811	–	–	–	–	–
Total,	1,043	1,011	164,880	39	1,739	112	263	2,114
Leinster.								
Carlow,	28	27	4,179	1	60	–	–	60
Dublin,	137	133	37,063	4	144	68	66	278
Kildare,	51	48	3,724	3	188	15	–	203
Kilkenny,	103	101	13,040	9	120	4	–	124
King's,	38	35	5,463	3	179	12	17	208
Longford,	39	37	5,533	2	75	13	–	88
Louth,	49	46	8,177	3	119	93	6	218
Meath,	68	63	6,623	5	213	11	–	224
Queen's,	43	38	5,457	5	805	10	20	835
Westmeath,	71	67	7,296	4	306	11	20	337
Wexford,	78	78	10,128	–	–	–	–	–
Wicklow,	41	40	5,603	1	26	–	10	36
Total,	736	703	114,303	33	1,681	234	139	2,054
Connaught.								
Galway,	177	176	25,003	1	13	25	16	54
Leitrim,	63	54	7,193	8	500	62	54	616
Mayo,	168	165	32,137	1	43	–	5	48
Roscommon,	137	137	19,817	–	–	–	–	–
Sligo,	38	39	8,950	–	–	–	–	–
Total,	571	561	90,102	10	562	87	75	724
Grand Total,	2,903	2,548	412,019	355	14,862	25,159	1,785	41,826

* In Antrim there is one school with an attendance of [illegible] Protestant pupils; in Londonderry one school with an attendance of [illegible] Protestant pupils; in Tyrone two schools with an attendance of [illegible] Protestant pupils; under teaching staffs of Protestants and Roman Catholics.

Appendix A.

Religious denominations of pupils on rolls.

V.—Religious Denominations of 1,050,772* Pupils on the Rolls.

Provinces and Counties.	Religious Denominations.				Total Number of Pupils returned for Year ended Dec. 31, 1874.
	Roman Catholic.	Presbyterian.	Established Church.	Other Persuasions.	
Ulster:					
Antrim, . . .	24,729	50,703	17,602	3,005	96,040
Armagh, . . .	18,417	5,825	9,003	1,136	34,981
Cavan, . . .	26,419	1,158	8,266	100	30,943
Donegal, . . .	32,152	4,519	4,744	351	41,766
Down, . . .	18,377	26,812	11,890	1,163	57,742
Fermanagh, . .	9,584	263	5,468	985	15,880
Londonderry, . .	13,779	12,291	5,411	536	32,017
Monaghan, . .	18,092	3,078	3,211	50	24,431
Tyrone, . . .	22,147	8,094	8,829	579	39,049
Total, . . .	188,696	112,743	69,525	7,185	378,149
Munster:					
Clare, . . .	31,800	24	272	2	32,098
Cork, . . .	101,402	355	4,228	425	106,410
Kerry, . . .	47,357	19	702	83	48,311
Limerick, . . .	37,502	80	705	103	38,390
Tipperary, . . .	38,692	112	784	10	39,598
Waterford, . . .	15,208	63	801	58	15,630
Total, . . .	272,161	653	6,992	631	280,437
Leinster:					
Carlow, . . .	8,201	.	368	.	8,569
Dublin, . . .	32,625	839	2,886	247	36,598
Kildare, . . .	12,916	88	328	17	13,349
Kilkenny, . . .	21,196	33	630	10	21,869
King's, . . .	12,480	38	716	40	13,274
Longford, . . .	13,327	78	670	8	13,083
Louth, . . .	13,686	184	372	9	14,261
Meath, . . .	16,590	95	709	7	17,401
Queen's, . . .	12,048	24	715	22	12,809
Westmeath, . . .	14,377	41	419	20	14,857
Wexford, . . .	17,044	36	334	13	18,397
Wicklow, . . .	12,325	6	475	91	12,797
Total, . . .	207,766	1,292	8,762	494	218,324
Connaught:					
Galway, . . .	42,080	121	494	48	42,743
Leitrim, . . .	22,288	78	2,040	67	24,473
Mayo, . . .	55,049	169	719	11	55,948
Roscommon, . . .	32,025	29	405	.	32,459
Sligo, . . .	21,923	183	991	142	23,219
Total, . . .	173,365	580	4,649	268	178,862
Ulster, . . .	183,690	112,743	69,525	7,185	373,149
Munster, . . .	272,161	653	6,992	631	280,437
Leinster, . . .	207,766	1,292	8,762	494	218,324
Connaught, . . .	173,365	580	4,649	269	178,862
Ireland, . . .	837,008	115,268	89,928	8,578	1,050,772
Per-centage, . . .	79·0	11·	8·6	·8	100·

* The numbers included in this return the 41,701 pupils who had ceased to [illegible] in the last quarter of 1873, but whose names were not struck off the rolls until the first quarter of 1874.

APPENDIX B.

Appendix B.
Results.

I.—Tabulations regarding Examinations of Pupils on Results System.

We submit the results ascertained through individual examination of the pupils of National Schools by the Inspectors at their annual inspection under the new scheme :—

I.—(*a*.) The total number of distinct schools, ordinary and model, examined for Results within the twelve months ended 31st March, 1875, by the Inspectors, and for which we have been able to tabulate the following particulars, was 6,730.

This number does not include Poor Law Union, Gaol, Lunatic Asylum, Evening, or Industrial Schools, which we refer to elsewhere.

(*b*). Number of pupils on School Rolls on last day of month preceding inspection :—

Males, 351,934; Females, 367,002; Total, 718,936.

(*c*.) Number who had made 90 attendances or over, within the Results year, and were present and examined on day of inspection for Results Fees :—

Males, 197,406; Females, 199,800; Total, 397,206.
Percentage to number on Rolls, . . . 55·2

(*d*.) The average daily attendance for twelve months ending last day of month immediately preceding the Results examinations in their respective schools was—

Males, 183,201; Females, 186,487; Total, 369,688.

We find, therefore, that the centesimal proportion of number examined to the average daily attendance was 107·4.

(*e*.) The following figures will show the numbers of pupils examined, and who, having passed in reading, writing, and arithmetic, were promoted at the Results examinations :—

(Model and Ordinary Schools combined.)

Grades.	Number Examined.	Number Promoted.	Percentage Promoted.
Infants, ...	71,239	28,595*	40·1*
First Class, . . .	88,010	50,333	57·1
Second Class, . . .	65,146	43,859	65·6
Third Class, . . .	73,753	47,255	64·0
Fourth Class, . . .	47,697	29,082	61·0
Fifth Class (1st division),	23,450	15,769	67·2
Fifth Class (2nd stage), .	5,636	4,459	79·0
Sixth Class, . . .	2,346	1,707	72·7

* Infants are not necessarily promoted into First class, after satisfactory answering, until they reach seven years of age, which accounts for the smallness of the above numbers.

(*f*.) Percentage of pupils examined in each class to the total number examined in all the classes:—

Percentage in Infants' grade,	18·0	Class V. (1st stage),	6·0
Class I.,	22·1	Class V. (2nd stage),	1·4
Class II.,	21·4	Class VI.,	·8
Class III.,	16·5		
Class IV.,	13·0		100·

GENERAL ABSTRACT OF ANSWERING.

(*g*.) Of the total number of infants (71,939) who had attended 90 days within the year and were examined by the Inspectors, passes were assigned to 61,933.*

Percentage of infants who gained passes to total number examined, ... 86·9

(*h*.)

Classes.	No. of Pupils examined for Results Fees in subject.	No. of Passes assigned for answering in subject.	Percentage of Passes to No. of Pupils examined in Class.
Reading.			
Class I.,	88,010	72,579	82·5
" II.,	85,146	71,347	83·7
" III.,	73,752	65,333	88·6
" IV.,	47,627	44,032	92·4
" V^1.,	23,450	22,369	95·3
" V^2.,	5,636	5,485	97·4
" VI.,	2,346	2,187	93·0
Total,	325,967	283,137	86·8
Spelling.			
Class I.,	88,010	66,531	75·5
" II.,	85,146	59,735	69·6
" III.,	73,752	56,048	75·9
" IV.,	47,627	36,516	76·6
" V^1.,	23,450	20,401	84·9
" V^2.,	5,636	5,477	97·1
" VI.,	2,346	2,070	88·2
Total,	325,967	245,790	75·4
Writing.			
Class I.,	88,010	68,222	77·5
" II.,	85,146	71,191	83·6
" III.,	73,752	67,099	90·9
" IV.,	47,627	44,112	92·6
" V^1.,	23,450	22,378	95·4
" V^2.,	5,636	5,436	96·4
" VI.,	2,346	2,150	91·6
Total,	325,967	280,577	86·7
Arithmetic.			
Class I.,	88,010	56,628	64·3
" II.,	85,146	63,772	74·8
" III.,	73,752	50,904	69·0
" IV.,	47,627	30,813	64·6
" V^1.,	23,450	16,387	69·8
" V^2.,	5,636	4,530	80·3
" VI.,	2,346	1,720	73·2
Total,	325,967	224,851	69·0

Classes.	No. of Pupils examined for Results Fees in subject.	No. of Passes assigned for answering in subject.	Percentage of Passes to No. of Pupils examined in Class.
Grammar.			
Class III.,	73,752	34,942	47·4
" IV.,	47,627	25,719	54·0
" V^1.,	23,450	14,927	63·6
" V^2.,	5,636	4,256	75·5
" VI.,	2,349	1,718	73·1
Total,	152,814	84,572	55·3
Geography.			
Class III.,	73,752	39,961	54·1
" IV.,	47,627	24,334	51·1
" V^1.,	23,450	13,377	57·0
" V^2.,	5,636	3,936	69·8
" VI.,	2,349	1,550	65·9
Total,	152,814	83,160	54·4
Agriculture.			
Class IV.,	17,825	6,211	34·8
" V^1.,	10,013	4,341	43·3
" V^2.,	2,659	1,589	60·0
" VI.,	1,092	650	59·5
Total,	31,589	12,991	41·1
Needlework.			
Class II.,	38,018	33,125	87·1
" III.,	34,679	33,103	95·4
" IV.,	22,336	20,866	93·5
" V^1.,	10,738	10,058	93·7
" V^2.,	2,407	2,295	95·3
" VI.,	1,049	951	90·6
Total,	109,224	100,198	91·8

* The proficiency of an infant is marked by a single pass.

Appendix B.

(*i.*) Extra Subjects.

The number of pupils presented for examination in extra subjects was comparatively small. The payment of fees was subject to the following regulations:—

A fee of five shillings will be paid for every pupil in the fifth or sixth class, who, *having passed in reading, spelling, writing,* and *arithmetic,* shall exhibit satisfactory proficiency in geometry (*First Book of Euclid* or *Mensuration of Surfaces* for fifth class, *and First and Second Books of Euclid* and *Mensuration of Surfaces* for sixth class), algebra (*Elementary Rules* for fifth class; *Elementary Rules and Simple Equations* for sixth class), one of the physical sciences, navigation or other *approved* extra branch; and a fee equal to that paid for arithmetic for any pupil *in the third or higher classes* who, *having passed* in reading and in *any two* of the other three subjects, shall exhibit satisfactory proficiency in any system of vocal music, or any system of drawing;—provided however;—

(*a*). That no fees shall be paid for more than two extra subjects in the same class to the same teacher; and

(*b*). That no fees shall be paid for any pupil for whose proficiency in the same subject grants are made by the Department of Science and Art.

The numbers examined, and results, were as follows:—

Extra Subjects.—(Model and Ordinary Schools conjoined).

Subjects.	2nd Class.		3rd Class.		4th Class.	
	No. Examined.	No. of Passes.	No. Examined.	No. of Passes.	No. Examined.	No. of Passes.
Singing,	11,008	7,296	12,701	8,783	9,655	6,129
Drawing,	—	—	5,808	3,607	5,587	3,616

Subjects.	No. of Schools.	5th Class.		6th Class.		Total.	
		No. Examined.	No. of Passes.	No. Examined.	No. of Passes.	No. Examined.	No. of Passes.
Singing—*continued*,	963	5,067	4,510	563	445	33,628	27,106
Drawing—*continued*,	591	4,411	3,637	532	429	16,582	10,623
Geometry and Mensuration,	48	476	291	702	644	1,178	783
Mensuration,	600	3,013	1,856	—	—	6,013	1,685
Geometry,	648	2,719	1,172	83	66	7,809	1,528
Algebra,	682	2,781	1,610	858	637	6,640	1,067
Trigonometry,	41	5	2	—	—	5	2
Mathematical and Physical Geography,	1	7	9	—	—	7	9
Physical Geography,	40	169	72	123	81	287	154
Navigation,	1	1	1	6	4	7	5
Mechanics,	5	190	75	86	64	265	129
Hydrostatics,	5	81	58	48	46	120	103
Light and Sound,	2	12	11	1	1	13	12
Magnetism and Electricity,	8	72	38	24	14	96	53
Animal Physiology,	3	56	20	13	7	89	27
Geology,	1	42	28	6	1	45	37
Botany,	1	67	77	·	·	67	77
Physical Science (branch not specified),	2	86	20	14	11	50	40
Latin,	83	78	53	106	80	183	128
Greek,	14	93	0	52	63	80	63
French,	51	221	180	101	81	332	311
Sewing Machine,	90	503	350	219	158	732	510
Cutting Out,	5	5	3	1	4	9	7
Machine and Drafting,	3	104	72	9	1	118	73
Cookery,	6	29	8	12	5	64	18
Management of Poultry,	10	50	28	14	0	64	31

Appendix B. Results—Model Schools.

II.—Model, Workhouse, Evening, and Industrial Schools.

1. Model Schools.

The total number of Model Schools examined for results within the twelve months ended 31st March, 1875, was 93.

This number is exclusive of Evening Model Schools.

Number of pupils on School Rolls on last day of month preceding inspection :—

Males, 6,710 ; Females, 5,138 ; Total, 11,848.

Number who had made 90 attendances, or over, within the results year, and were present and examined on day of inspection for results fees :—

Males, 4,233 ; Females, 3,365 ; Total, 7,598.
Percentage to number on Rolls, . . 64·1.

The average daily attendance for 12 months ending last day of month immediately preceding the results examination in the respective schools, was :—

Males, 4,770; Females, 3,711 ; Total, 8,481.
Centesimal proportion of number examined to the average daily attendance was . . . 89·5

The following figures will show the number of pupils examined, and the number promoted at the results examinations :—

Grades.	Number Examined.	Number Promoted.	Percentage Promoted.
Infants, . . .	746	227	30·4
First Class, . . .	742	510	68·7
Second Class, . .	1,178	867	73·6
Third Class, . . .	1,444	1,063	73·6
Fourth Class, . .	1,470	1,061	72·1
Fifth Class (1st grade),	1,105	809	73·2
Fifth Class (2nd grade),	585	500	85·4
Sixth Class, . . .	328	274	83·5

Percentage of pupils examined in each class to the total number examined in all the classes :—

Percentage in Infants' grade, . . . 9·8
Class I., ... 9·8
Class II., ... 15·5
Class III., ... 19·
Class IV., ... 19·3
Class V. (1st stage), ... 14·5
Class V. (2nd stage), ... 7·7
Class VI., ... 4·3

General Abstract of Answering.

Of the total number of infants (746) who had attended 90 days within the year, and were examined by the Inspectors, passes were assigned to 701.

Per-centage of infants who gained passes to total number examined, ... 93·9

Appendix B. — Results — Model Schools.

Subject.	No. of Pupils examined in subject.	No. of Passes assigned in subject.	Percentage of Passes to No. of Pupils examined in Class.	Subject.	No. of Pupils examined in subject.	No. of Passes assigned in subject.	Percentage of Passes to No. of Pupils examined in Class.
Reading.				**Grammar.**			
Class I.,	743	631	85·	Class III.,	1,444	690	62·1
" II.,	1,178	962	81·9	" IV.,	1,479	1,029	69·8
" III.,	1,444	1,279	88·5	" V., 1st stage,	1,165	911	78·6
" IV.,	1,479	1,351	91·6	" V., 2nd do.,	585	473	80·6
" V., 1st stage,	1,165	1,019	94·9	" VI.,	329	288	87·5
" V., 2nd do.,	585	546	93·9	Total,	4,993	3,459	79·7
" VI.,	329	317	96·8				
Total,	6,852	6,175	90·1				
Spelling.				**Geography.**			
Class I.,	743	587	79·1	Class III.,	1,444	863	59·6
" II.,	1,178	871	73·9	" IV.,	1,479	1,064	71·7
" III.,	1,444	1,105	76·5	" V., 1st stage,	1,165	898	76·9
" IV.,	1,479	1,228	82·9	" V., 2nd do.,	585	470	80·3
" V., 1st stage,	1,165	1,069	91·3	" VI.,	329	281	85·6
" V., 2nd do.,	585	549	93·8	Total,	4,852	3,628	73·7
" VI.,	329	318	95·4				
Total,	6,852	5,654	82·5				
Writing.				**Agriculture.**			
Class I.,	743	626	84·3	Class IV.,	639	329	51·5
" II.,	1,178	1,034	87·7	" V., 1st stage,	434	290	66·4
" III.,	1,444	1,316	91·1	" V., 2nd do.,	299	290	97·5
" IV.,	1,470	1,396	94·9	" VI.,	94	63	69·3
" V., 1st stage,	1,165	1,087	93·3	Total,	1,458	969	66·
" V., 2nd do.,	585	571	97·6				
" VI.,	329	316	96·3				
Total,	6,852	6,346	92·6				
Arithmetic.				**Needlework.**			
Class I.,	743	584	78·7	Class II.,	357	306	85·7
" II.,	1,178	949	80·6	" III.,	414	350	84·6
" III.,	1,444	1,127	78·	" IV.,	467	359	89·7
" IV.,	1,479	1,219	82·9	" V., 1st stage,	503	438	89·7
" V., 1st stage,	1,165	839	75·9	" V., 2nd do.,	329	396	97·3
" V., 2nd do.,	585	517	88·3	" VI.,	173	156	90·1
" VI.,	329	278	84·7				
Total,	6,852	5,515	80·5	Total,	3,479	2,165	85·7

Extra Subjects.

The numbers examined, and results, were as follows :—

Subjects.	2nd Class.		3rd Class.		4th Class.	
	No. Examined.	No. of Passes.	No. Examined.	No. of Passes.	No. Examined.	No. of Passes.
Singing,	830	817	437	329	514	383
Drawing,	—	—	591	281	550	349

EXTRA SUBJECTS—*continued.*

SUBJECTS.	No. of Schools.	5th Class.		6th Class.		TOTAL.	
		No. Examined.	No. of Passes.	No. Examined.	No. of Passes.	No. Examined.	No. of Passes.
Singing—*continued*,	34	617	646	111	92	1,000	1,238
Drawing—*continued*,	85	680	469	150	120	1,866	1,213
Geometry and Mensuration,	8	140	102	88	56	232	158
Mensuration,	6	104	60	–	–	104	60
Geometry,	22	287	181	–	–	287	131
Algebra,	22	380	207	106	72	483	279
Physical Geography,	9	48	34	70	41	118	65
Mechanics,	3	168	72	18	8	186	80
Hydrostatics,	3	24	14	17	10	41	24
Magnetism and Electricity,	1	9	2	9	5	18	7
Animal Physiology,	1	22	17	9	9	31	26
Geology,	1	42	26	–	–	42	26
Botany,	1	87	77	8	8	95	85
Physical Science,	2	36	29	14	11	50	40
Latin,	4	13	9	34	19	47	28
Greek,	1	–	–	3	1	3	1
French,	17	86	43	23	10	109	58
Sewing Machine,	16	144	70	102	71	246	141
Machine and Drafting,	1	104	72	9	1	113	73
Management of Poultry,	3	21	6	4	4	25	10

The numbers examined in the foregoing Table do not include pupils of Model Schools whose teachers elect (under specified conditions) to be paid an annual gratuity instead of results-fees.

Appendix B.

Workhouse Schools.

2.—WORKHOUSE SCHOOLS.

The total number of Workhouse Schools examined for results within the twelve months ended 31st March, 1875, was 152.

Number of pupils on school Rolls on last day of month preceding inspection:—

Males, 4,426; Females, 3,858; Total, 8,284.

Number who had made 90 attendances or over within the Results year, and were present and examined on day of inspection:—

Males, 2,726; Females, 2,330; Total, 5,066.

Percentage to number on Rolls, ... 61·

The average daily attendance for 12 months ending last day of month immediately preceding the results examinations in the respective schools was—

Males, 3,492; Females, 3,231; Total, 6,723.

Centesimal proportion of number examined to the average daily attendance was 75·3.

The following table shows the number of pupils examined, and the number promoted at the results examinations:—

CLASSES.	Number Examined.	Number Promoted.	Percentage Promoted.
Infants,	1,184	388	32·8
First Class,	1,263	698	55·2
Second Class,	1,083	754	69·6
Third Class,	835	541	64·7
Fourth Class,	495	299	60·4
Fifth Class (1st grade),	185	105	56·7
Fifth Class (2nd grade),	6	2	33·3
Sixth Class,	5	3	60·0

Appendix A. Reports—Workhouse Schools.

Per-centage of pupils examined in each class to the total number examined in all the classes:—

Per-centage in Infants' grade,	23·4
Class I.,	25·
Class II.,	21·4
Class III.,	10·8
Class IV.,	9·3
Class V.,	3·8
Class VI.,	·1

GENERAL ABSTRACT OF ANSWERING.

Of the total number of infants (1,164) who had attended 90 days within the year, and were examined by the Inspectors, passes were assigned to 850.

Per-centage of infants who gained passes to total number examined, ... 71·8

Subject.	No. of Pupils examined in subject.	No. of Passes assigned in subject.	Per-centage of Passes to No. of Pupils examined in Class.
READING.			
Class I.,	1,203	1,090	90·7
" II.,	1,065	937	88·0
" III.,	835	781	93·5
" IV.,	495	467	94·3
" V., 1st stage,	185	174	94·
" V., 2nd do.,	6	4	66·
" VI.,	5	4	80·
Total,	3,672	3,397	87·6
SPELLING.			
Class I.,	1,263	934	73·9
" II.,	1,063	807	74·8
" III.,	835	698	83·2
" IV.,	495	419	87·3
" V., 1st stage,	185	180	97·3
" V., 2nd do.,	6	4	66·
" VI.,	5	3	60·
Total,	3,672	3,035	78·4
WRITING.			
Class I.,	1,273	971	76·3
" II.,	1,063	879	82·4
" III.,	835	811	97·1
" IV.,	495	478	96·5
" V., 1st stage,	185	181	97·8
" V., 2nd do.,	6	4	66·
" VI.,	5	2	40·
Total,	3,672	3,438	89·4
ARITHMETIC.			
Class I.,	1,263	819	64·8
" II.,	1,063	833	78·3
" III.,	835	558	66·8
" IV.,	495	333	67·5
" V., 1st stage,	185	109	59·
" V., 2nd do.,	6	2	33·3
" VI.,	5	2	40·
Total,	3,672	2,630	67·9

Subject.	No. of Pupils examined in subject.	No. of Passes assigned in subject.	Per-centage of Passes to No. of Pupils examined in Class.
GRAMMAR.			
Class III.,	835	440	52·6
" IV.,	495	303	61·
" V., 1st stage,	185	121	65·4
" V., 2nd do.,	6	2	33·3
" VI.,	5	2	40·
Total,	1,526	867	56·8
GEOGRAPHY.			
Class III.,	835	550	65·8
" IV.,	495	325	65·6
" V., 1st stage,	185	118	63·8
" V., 2nd do.,	6	3	50·
" VI.,	5	2	40·
Total,	1,526	998	65·4
AGRICULTURE.			
Class IV.,	171	65	38·0
" V., 1st stage,	64	23	35·9
" V., 2nd do.,	3	2	66·6
" VI.,	3	–	–
Total,	241	90	38·5
NEEDLEWORK.			
Class II.,	422	371	87·9
" III.,	349	325	93·1
" IV.,	188	176	93·6
" V., 1st stage,	73	72	98·7
" V., 2nd do.,	–	–	–
" VI.,	1	1	100·
Total,	1,033	943	91·1

Appendix B.

Workhouse Schools.

EXTRA SUBJECTS.

The numbers examined, and results, were as follows :—

Subjects.	No. of Schools.	2nd Class. No. Examined.	2nd Class. No. of Passes.	3rd Class. No. Examined.	3rd Class. No. of Passes.	4th Class. No. Examined.	4th Class. No. of Passes.	5th Class. No. Examined.	5th Class. No. of Passes.	6th Class. No. Examined.	6th Class. No. of Passes.
Singing, . .	4	33	31	18	14	8	–	11	7	–	–
Drawing, . .	6	–	–	9	8	14	7	1	1	–	–
Instrumental Music.	1	–	–	–	–	–	–	6	2	–	–
Mensuration, .	2	–	–	–	–	–	–	9	4	–	–
Geometry, . .	1	–	–	–	–	–	–	6	9	1	1
Algebra, . .	1	–	–	–	–	–	–	3	1	1	1
Latin, . .	1	–	–	–	–	–	–	1	1	–	–
Greek, . .	1	–	–	–	–	–	–	1	1	–	–
French, . .	1	–	–	–	–	–	–	1	1	–	–

Evening Schools.

3.—EVENING SCHOOLS.

The total number of evening schools examined for results within the twelve months ended 31st March, 1875, was 138.

Number of pupils on school rolls on last day of month preceding inspection :—

Males, 6,544 ; Females, 3,799 ; Total, 10,343.

Number who had made 90 attendances or over within the results year, and were present and examined on day of inspection for results fees :—

Males, 2,730 ; Females, 1,520 ; Total, 4,250.

Per-centage to number on Rolls, . . . 41·

The average daily attendance for twelve months ending last day of month immediately preceding the results examinations in the respective schools was—

Males, 3,307 ; Females, 1,832 ; Total, 5,139.

Centesimal proportion of number examined to the average daily attendance was 82·7.

The following table shows the numbers of pupils examined and the numbers promoted at the results examinations :—

Classes.	Number Examined.	Number Promoted.	Per-centage Promoted.
First Class, ...	606	364	60·
Second Class, ...	1,148	800	70·4
Third Class, ...	1,206	776	63·9
Fourth Class, ...	846	455	53·6
Fifth Class (1st stage), . .	368	249	67·6
Fifth Class (2nd stage), . .	68	52	76·4
Sixth Class, ...	4	4	100·0

Per-centage of pupils examined in each class to the total number examined in all classes :—

Class I., ... 14·3
Class II., ... 27·0
Class III., ... 28·4
Class IV., ... 19·9
Class V. (1st stage), ... 8·7
Class V. (2nd stage), ... 1·6
Class VI., ... ·1

Appendix B.

Results—Evening Schools.

Subject.	No. of Pupils examined in subject.	No. of Passes obtained in subject.	Percentage of Passes to No. of Pupils examined in Class.	Subject.	No. of Pupils examined in subject.	No. of Passes obtained in subject.	Percentage of Passes to No. of Pupils examined in Class.
Reading.				**Grammar.**			
Class I.,	608	508	83·6	Class III.,	1,208	148	12·2
" II.,	1,148	984	85·7	" IV.,	843	187	22·1
" III.,	1,208	1,036	85·9	" V., 1st stage,	368	87	23·6
" IV.,	848	782	92·2	" V., 2nd do.,	68	33	48·5
" V., 1st stage,	368	343	93·2	" VI.,	4	1	25·
" V., 2nd do.,	68	68	100·	Total,	2,491	456	18·3
" VI.,	4	4	100·				
Total,	4,250	3,730	87·8				
Spelling.				**Geography.**			
Class I.,	608	464	76·3	Class III.,	1,208	160	13·2
" II.,	1,148	778	67·8	" IV.,	843	158	18·7
" III.,	1,208	816	67·5	" V., 1st stage,	368	59	16·
" IV.,	848	618	72·9	" V., 2nd do.,	68	20	29·4
" V., 1st stage,	368	307	83·4	" VI.,	4	–	–
" V., 2nd do.,	68	64	94·1	Total,	2,491	397	15·9
" VI.,	4	4	100·				
Total,	4,250	3,044	71·6				
Writing.				**Agriculture.**			
Class I.,	608	491	81·				
" II.,	1,148	1,010	88·				
" III.,	1,208	1,108	91·8	Class IV.,	171	66	38·6
" IV.,	843	787	93·3	" V., 1st stage,	108	50	48·
" V., 1st stage,	368	351	95·3	" V., 2nd do.,	28	12	42·8
" V., 2nd do.,	68	68	100·	" VI.,	3	–	–
" VI.,	4	4	100·	Total,	304	128	42·1
Total,	4,250	3,817	87·7				
Arithmetic.				**Needlework.**			
Class I.,	608	457	75·4				
" II.,	1,147	893	77·7	Class II.,	316	299	94·5
" III.,	1,208	783	64·2	" III.,	247	233	94·3
" IV.,	843	458	54·8	" IV.,	200	187	93·5
" V., 1st stage,	368	233	63·6	" V., 1st stage,	53	52	98·1
" V., 2nd do.,	68	50	73·5	" V., 2nd do.,	6	6	100·
" VI.,	4	4	100·	" VI.,	–	–	–
Total,	4,250	2,885	69·6	Total,	822	777	94·5

EXTRA SUBJECTS.

The numbers examined and results were as follows:—

Subjects.	No. of Schools.	2nd Class.		3rd Class.		4th Class.		5th Class.		6th Class.	
		No. Examined.	No. of Passes.	No. Examined.	No. of Passes.	No. Examined.	No. of Passes.	No. Examined.	No. of Passes.	No. Examined.	No. of Passes.
Singing,	11	283	162	180	129	182	89	50	39	1	–
Drawing,	8	–	–	108	66	77	44	60	30	–	–
Algebra,	6	–	–	–	–	–	–	50	29	–	–
Mensuration,	10	–	–	–	–	–	–	66	33	–	–
Sewing Machine,	3	–	–	–	–	–	–	23	16	–	–
Geometry and Mensuration,	1	–	–	–	–	–	–	6	5	–	–
Geometry,	1	–	–	–	–	–	–	6	1	–	–
Greek,	1	–	–	–	–	–	–	1	1	–	–
Latin,	1	–	–	–	–	–	–	1	1	–	–
Magnetism and Electricity.	1	–	–	–	–	–	–	14	9	–	–

Appendix B.

Results—Industrial Schools.

4.—Industrial Schools.

The total number of Industrial Schools examined for results within the twelve months ended 31st March, 1875, was 22.

Number of pupils on school rolls on last day of month preceding inspection :—

Males, 195 ; Females, 1,370 ; Total, 1,565.

Number who had made 90 attendances or over within the results year, and were present and examined on day of inspection for results fees :—

Males, 164 ; Females, 1,115 ; Total, 1,279.

Per-centage to number on Rolls, . . 81·7

The average daily attendance for twelve months ending last day of month immediately preceding the results examination in their respective schools was :—

Males, 179 ; Females, 1,218 ; Total, 1,397.

Centesimal proportion of number examined to the average daily attendance was 91·5.

The following figures will show the numbers of pupils examined, and the numbers promoted at the results examinations :—

Classes.	Number Examined.	Number Promoted.	Per-centage Promoted.
Infants, ...	30	15	50·
First Class, ...	210	138	65·7
Second Class, ...	342	222	64·9
Third Class, ...	371	254	68·4
Fourth Class, ...	238	123	51·6
Fifth Class (1st stage), . .	85	40	47·
Fifth Class (2nd stage), . .	1	1	100·
Sixth Class, ...	2	2	100·

Per-centage of pupils examined in each class to the total number examined in all the classes :—

Per-centage in infants' grade, . .	2·4
Class I., ...	16·4
Class II., ...	26·7
Class III., ...	29·
Class IV., ...	18·6
Class V., } Class VI., }	6·9

General Abstract of Answering.

Of the total number of infants (30) who had attended 90 days within the year, and were examined by the Inspectors, passes were assigned to 25.

Per-centage of infants who gained passes to total number examined, . . . 83·3

Appendix B. — *Results — Industrial Schools.*

Subject.	No. of Pupils examined in subject.	No. of Passes obtained in subject.	Percentage of Passes to No. of Pupils examined in Class.	Subject.	No. of Pupils examined in subject.	No. of Passes obtained in subject.	Percentage of Passes to No. of Pupils examined in Class.
READING.				GRAMMAR.			
Class I., . .	210	171	81·4				
„ II., . .	343	285	83·3	Class III., . .	371	189	50·9
„ III., . .	371	329	88·6	„ IV., . .	238	158	66·3
„ IV., . .	238	233	97·9	„ V., 1st stage	85	64	75·3
„ V., 1st stage	85	77	90·6	„ V., 2nd do.,	1	–	–
„ V., 2nd do.,	1	1	100·	„ VI., . .	2	2	100·
„ VI., . .	2	2	100·	Total, . .	697	413	59·2
Total, . .	1,249	1,098	87·9				
SPELLING.				GEOGRAPHY.			
Class I., . .	210	154	73·3				
„ II., . .	343	229	66·8				
„ III., . .	371	293	78·9	Class III., . .	371	215	57·9
„ IV., . .	238	204	85·7	„ IV., . .	238	124	52·1
„ V., 1st stage	85	71	83·5	„ V., 1st stage	85	54	63·5
„ V., 2nd do.,	1	1	100·	„ V., 2nd do.,	1	1	100·
„ VI., . .	2	2	100·	„ VI., . .	2	2	100·
Total, . .	1,249	953	76·2	Total, . .	697	396	56·8
WRITING.							
Class I., . .	210	165	78·5				
„ II., . .	343	291	85·	AGRICULTURE.			
„ III., . .	371	331	89·2				
„ IV., . .	238	230	96·6	Class V., 1st stage,	2	1	50·
„ V., 1st stage	85	78	91·7				
„ V., 2nd do.,	1	1	100·	Total, . .	2	1	50·
„ VI., . .	2	2	100·				
Total, . .	1,249	1,098	87·9				
ARITHMETIC.				NEEDLEWORK.			
Class I., . .	210	141	67·1				
„ II., . .	343	234	68·2	Class II., . .	289	255	88·
„ III., . .	371	240	64·6	„ III., . .	339	322	94·9
„ IV., . .	238	125	52·5	„ IV., . .	216	214	99·
„ V., 1st stage	85	40	47·	„ V., 1st stage	78	75	91·5
„ V., 2nd do.,	1	1	100·	„ V., 2nd do.,	1	1	100·
„ VI., . .	2	2	100·	„ VI., . .	2	2	100·
Total, . .	1,249	783	62·6	Total, . .	925	883	94·3

EXTRA SUBJECTS.

The numbers examined and results were as follows :—

Subjects.	No. of Schools.	2nd Class.		3rd Class.		4th Class.		5th Class.		6th Class.	
		No. Examined.	No. of Passes.	No. Examined.	No. of Passes.	No. Examined.	No. of Passes.	No. Examined.	No. of Passes.	No. Examined.	No. of Passes.
Singing, . .	12	95	79	129	108	109	78	82	80	2	2
Drawing, . .	7	–	–	61	25	73	47	18	13	1	1
Sewing Machine,	1	–	–	–	–	–	–	4	4	1	1
Geometry, . .	1	–	–	–	–	–	–	2	1	–	–

[illegible] the beginning

[illegible]	[illegible]							[illegible]					
	[illegible]			[illegible]		[illegible]		[illegible]			[illegible]		[illegible]	
	[illegible]	[illegible]	[illegible]	[illegible]	[illegible]	[illegible]	[illegible]	[illegible]	[illegible]	[illegible]	[illegible]	[illegible]	[illegible]	[illegible]
	d.	d.	d.	d.	d.	d.	d.	d.	d.	d.	d.	d.	d.	d.
[illegible]	[illegible]	[illegible]	[illegible]	[illegible]	[illegible]	[illegible]	[illegible]	[illegible]	[illegible]	[illegible]	[illegible]	[illegible]	[illegible]
[illegible]	[illegible]	[illegible]	[illegible]	[illegible]	[illegible]	[illegible]	[illegible]	[illegible]	[illegible]	[illegible]	[illegible]	[illegible]	[illegible]
[illegible]	[illegible]	[illegible]	[illegible]	[illegible]	[illegible]	[illegible]	[illegible]	[illegible]	[illegible]	[illegible]	[illegible]	[illegible]	[illegible]
[illegible]	[illegible]	[illegible]	[illegible]	[illegible]	[illegible]	[illegible]	[illegible]	[illegible]	[illegible]	[illegible]	[illegible]	[illegible]	[illegible]
[illegible]	[illegible]	[illegible]	[illegible]	[illegible]	[illegible]	[illegible]	[illegible]	[illegible]	[illegible]	[illegible]	[illegible]	[illegible]	[illegible]
[illegible]	[illegible]	[illegible]	[illegible]	[illegible]	[illegible]	[illegible]	[illegible]	[illegible]	[illegible]	[illegible]	[illegible]	[illegible]	[illegible]
[illegible]	[illegible]	[illegible]	[illegible]	[illegible]	[illegible]	[illegible]	[illegible]	[illegible]	[illegible]	[illegible]	[illegible]	[illegible]	[illegible]
[illegible]	[illegible]	[illegible]	[illegible]	[illegible]	[illegible]	[illegible]	[illegible]	[illegible]	[illegible]	[illegible]	[illegible]	[illegible]	[illegible]
[illegible]	[illegible]	[illegible]	[illegible]	[illegible]	[illegible]	[illegible]	[illegible]	[illegible]	[illegible]	[illegible]	[illegible]	[illegible]	[illegible]
[illegible]	[illegible]	[illegible]	[illegible]	[illegible]	[illegible]	[illegible]	[illegible]	[illegible]	[illegible]	[illegible]	[illegible]	[illegible]	[illegible]

[illegible]

IV.—List of Seventy-two Teachers awarded Retiring Gratuities during the year ended 31st March, 1875.

Appendix B.

Teacher.	Roll No.	School.	County.	Dist.
1. S. M'Intyre,	10044	Cranagh Hill,	Derry,	3
2. W. M'Cormick,	8419	Caddy,	"	15
3. H. Grant,	6463	Killowen,	Down,	19
4. B. Lynch,	7764	Greaghdulagh,	Cavan,	21
5. M. Connolly,	1938	Killycarran,	Monaghan,	18
6. A. O'Reilly,	8368	Drumcrow,	Cavan,	23
7. T. M'Elgun,	1004	Ballinasloe, m.	Galway,	35
8. J. Barrett,	5281	Abbey, f.	Kildare,	37
9. L. Martin,	10978	Meenglass,	Donegal,	8
10. C. M'Connell,	1167	Glenone, f.	Derry,	0
11. S. Skilling,	8874	Mill-street,	Down,	10
12. A. English,	6124	Portadown, (2)	Armagh,	16
13. M. Meany,	4108	Clintstown,	Kilkenny,	47
14. D. M'Kinney,	2787	Tiroony,	Tyrone,	6
15. J. Brown,	9469	Kilbeary, m.	Tipperary,	66
16. E. Brown,	9689	Do., f.	"	26
17. P. Coyne,	6297	Shanbough,	Kilkenny,	43
18. P. Coghlan,	8440	Skibbereen, (1)	Cork,	58
19. S. Whiteside,	1778	Knockaleen, f.	Monaghan,	18
20. W. Walsh,	10011	Lettermore,	Galway,	61
21. H. Parker,	1108	Ballywilliam,	Cork,	48
22. J. Murray,	5865	Carrickmannon,	Down,	10
23. P. M'Evoy,	208	Borrameen,	"	17
24. J. Curtin,	7063	Lough,	Tipperary,	43
25. M. Feeny,	1568	Ballinalee,	Longford,	23
26. D. Scully,	2803	Banteer, m.	Cork,	56
27. S. Manning,	6963	Belfast, Model Infant,	Antrim,	8
28. E. Boden,	8948	Milltown, m.	Cavan,	29
29. T. Mulhall,	918	Killenard, m.	Queen's,	41
30. M. Ryan,	6583	Emly, m.	Tipperary,	14
31. M. Connolly,	7532	Ballydehob, m.	Cork,	59
32. C. Byrne,	10285	Rahoon,	Galway,	84
33. J. O'Beirne,	7959	Cavanreagh,	Tyrone,	14
34. J. Graham,	4583	Kennagh,	Cavan,	24
35. M. Moore,	9100	Newbridge, f.	Kildare,	44
36. M. Hackett,	2354	Glenmoney, m.	Clare,	48
37. J. Davis,	2951	Lisleevane,	Cork,	59
38. F. M'Cambridge,	6171	Ballycastle,	Antrim,	8
39. F. Kennelly,	7009	Killerk,	Clare,	15
40. M. Garthan,	6780	Leitrim, f.	Leitrim,	23
41. M. Hearns,	1805	Levitstown,	Kildare,	44
42. E. Lennon,	6787	Drumsberry,	Armagh,	18
43. T. Brady,	7971	Drumcrompie,	Cavan,	24
44. T. Sarlich,	1277	Boolymbane,	Kerry,	54
45. J. Edmiston,	6283	Culmore, m.	Derry,	2
46. J. Wallace,	8403	Trimslinagh,	"	7
47. M. Murphy,	7059	Lady's Island,	Wexford,	50
48. M. Shea,	8601	Balleen,	Kilkenny,	47
49. J. M'Caw,	2673	Townsend, S.	Antrim,	9
50. J. M'Donnell,	7007	Croagh, m.	Limerick,	43
51. H. Fennelly,	8195	Knockrainey,	"	16
52. M. Monahan,	9937	Granagh, m.	"	63
53. P. Heaman,	11008	Glen,	Donegal,	1
54. T. Lacy,	6973	Kill, m.	Kildare,	27
55. L. Doyle,	7474	Macreddin, m.	Wicklow,	40
56. W. Thompson,	6768	Ballintaylor,	Waterford,	18
57. J. Scanlan,	7817	Glengurt, m.	Limerick,	53
58. J. Wilson,	2589	Crinlyframe,	Antrim,	9
59. A. M'Cann,	8497	Johnstownbridge, m.	Kildare,	37
60. L. Cowell,	870	Leighlinbridge, m.	Carlow,	69
61. M. Ryan,	6063	Kilkenny Model, f.	Kilkenny,	47
62. T. O'Reilly,	8786	Shanagolden, m.	Limerick,	53
63. P. Byrne,	4605	Derrylinn,	Cavan,	24

LIST of SEVENTY-TWO TEACHERS awarded Retiring Gratuities during the year ended 31st March, 1875—*continued.*

Teacher.	Roll No.	School.		County.	Dist.
64. L. Doran,	796	Freshford,	m.	Kilkenny,	47
65. T. Finn,	6445	Ballyquin,		Kerry,	54
66. I. Murphy,	1398	Rathcormack,		Cork,	56
67. A. Cassidy,	9271	Lisdrumchor,		Armagh,	16
68. B. Reilly,	6080	Belturbet,	m.	Cavan,	23
69. B. M'Donagh,	5807	St. Brigid's,	m.	Clare,	40
70. M. M'Donagh,	6304	Toomore,		Mayo,	21
71. Thomas Gibson,	8903	Clongorey,	m.	Kildare,	37
72. L. Brennan,	3914	Cloonfane,	m.	Mayo,	31

V.—LIST of THIRTY-NINE BUILDING CASES brought into operation during the year 1874.

County.	District No.	Parish.	Roll No.	School.	
ULSTER.					
Donegal,	1	Conwall,	10778	Tremkeel.	
"	5	Inishkeel,	10673	Drumnacrush.	
"	7	Killymard,	10558	Lackrum.	
"	7	Lackernagh,	10527	Acres,	f.
"	3	Lower Moville,	10754	Carrowbleg.	
Monaghan,	18	Clontibret,	10645	Bilready.	
"	"	Muckno,	10878	Anaglaive.	
MUNSTER.					
Clare,	45	Kilballyowen,	10318	Kilbaha,	m.
"	"	Do.	10319	Do.	f.
"	"	Kilfiddane,	10320	Effernan.	
"	43	Kilkeedy,	10768	Boston.	
Cork,	58	Ballymoney,	10739	Ballinacarriga,	m.
"	"	Do.	10740	Do.	f.
"	"	Kilbrittain,	10090	Barran.	
Kerry,	54	Ballyheige,	10403	Glenderry,	m.
"	"	Do.	10404	Do.	f.
"	57	Dromod,	10603	Kilmakerin.	
"	"	Glanarought,	10664	Drinagh.	
"	"	Kilcummin,	10339	Turreencahill.	
"	54	Killury,	10545	Rathmorrell,	m.
"	"	Do.	10546	Do.	f.
"	55	Knockanure,	10775	Knockanure,	m.
"	"	Do.	10776	Do.	f.
"	54	Lispole,	10182	Minard Castle.	
"	51	Lisltoo,	10535	Lisdoo,	m.
"	"	Do.	10536	Do.	f.
Limerick,	46	Galbally and Emly,	10731	Knockcarron,	m.
"	"		10732	Do.	f.
"	52	Killagholehane,	9657	Broadford,	m.
"	"	Do.	9658	Do.	f.
"	"	Kilfergus,	10534	Glin,	inft.
Tipperary,	56	Ballygibbon,	10066	Glenahilty.	
CONNAUGHT.					
Galway,	34	Gorumna,	10688	Gortmore,	m.
"	42	Killogilleen,	10675	Ballymanagh.	
"	34	Moyrus,	10591	Ardmore.	
Roscommon,	37	Kilglass,	10636	Tully,	m.
"	"	Do.	10637	Do.	f.
Sligo,	29	Kilfree,	10654	Mullaghroe,	m.
"	"	Do.	10655	Do.	f.

VI.—TABLE showing the Number of Vested School-houses in each County and Province, with the Number of separate Schools held in those Houses.

Appendix B. Vested schools, in counties and provinces.

Counties and Provinces.	No. of School-houses Vested. Leased to Commissioners.	Assigned to Commissioners.	Leased to Trustees.	Secured by Bond.	Total.	No. of Separate Schools held in Vested Houses. Leased to Commissioners.	Assigned to Commissioners.	Leased to Trustees.	Secured by Bond.	Total.
ULSTER:										
Antrim,	18	8	27	3	56	62	10	35	8	[illegible]
Armagh,	5	.	17	2	23	14	.	19	4	[illegible]
Cavan,	4	5	23	.	[illegible]	7	10	39	.	56
Donegal,	42	7	49	2	100	48	7	57	2	114
Down,	9	2	25	5	41	17	3	36	7	63
Fermanagh,	9	7	19	7	42	11	7	23	7	48
Londonderry,	11	8	21	.	38	17	4	34	.	55
Monaghan,	10	.	24	2	36	12	.	33	2	47
Tyrone,	28	12	33	5	78	34	15	38	6	93
Total,	139	44	236	25	444	192	55	311	61	589
MUNSTER:										
Clare,	31	9	28	.	68	83	17	59	.	159
Cork,	42	8	95	9	158	75	10	132	14	231
Kerry,	59	6	79	7	151	97	11	114	7	229
Limerick,	18	3	27	.	48	33	6	48	.	88
Tipperary,	14	1	34	8	57	23	1	50	4	79
Waterford,	4	5	8	1	18	7	8	15	2	32
Total,	158	30	281	20	490	318	53	468	27	798
LEINSTER:										
Carlow,	.	.	14	5	19	.	.	22	8	30
Dublin,	8	1	18	1	33	29	3	24	2	44
Kildare,	2	.	15	2	19	5	.	23	4	33
Kilkenny,	8	.	14	1	23	11	.	24	1	36
King's,	7	.	10	.	17	10	.	15	.	25
Longford,	1	.	12	1	14	2	.	22	3	27
Louth,	.	1	14	2	17	.	2	28	8	38
Meath,	5	.	25	4	32	7	.	45	6	58
Queen's,	4	1	7	1	13	7	2	11	1	21
Westmeath,	.	.	19	.	19	.	.	35	.	35
Wexford,	5	.	10	.	15	9	.	17	.	26
Wicklow,	6	.	4	6	16	7	.	5	4	16
Total,	42	8	157	19	221	64	6	271	33	394
CONNAUGHT:										
Galway,	39	4	36	.	79	45	8	55	.	108
Leitrim,	4	8	18	2	27	6	4	22	2	34
Mayo,	45	10	16	.	71	56	12	24	.	92
Roscommon,	16	2	15	.	33	24	4	23	.	50
Sligo,	3	3	14	1	21	7	4	21	1	33
Total,	98	31	101	3	234	137	32	144	4	317
Grand Total,	438	89	775	67	1,379	659	146	1,186	96	2,094

VII.—List of Agricultural Schools in connexion with Board on 31st December, 1874.

1.—21 First-class Agricultural Schools under exclusive Management of Board.

Note.—Schools marked with an asterisk are under Mr. Boyle's inspection. The others are inspected by Mr. Brogan.

No.	County.	Roll No.	School.	Post Town.	Area of Farm. A.	R.	P.	District No.
1	Antrim,	4787	Ballymoney,	Ballymoney,	22	2	2	6
2	Ditto,	6967	Ulster (Belfast),	Belfast,	108	1	25	9
3	Cavan,	5627	Bailieborough,	Bailieborough,	48	0	15	24
4	Cork,	1272	Glandore,*	Leap,	94	3	0	59
5	Ditto,	3226	Farrahy,*	Kildorrery,	48	3	8	58
6	Ditto,	5626	Dunmanway,*	Dunmanway,	12	0	8	55
7	Ditto,	6730	Munster (Cork),*	Cork,	128	3	17	60
8	Donegal,	6968	Templedouglas,	Letterkenny,	20	0	0	1
9	Ditto,	4702	Dunlewey,	Dunlewey,	15	0	0	1
10	Dublin,	—	Albert Training Institution,	Glasnevin,	178	3	24	80
11	Kildare,	6289	Athy,	Athy,	61	0	28	46
12	Kilkenny,	3251	Woodstock,	Inistioge,	8	2	35	48
13	Ditto,	6961	Kilkenny,	Kilkenny,	78	0	34	47
14	Leitrim,	1125	Leitrim,	Leitrim,	15	0	0	22
15	Limerick,	5643	Mount Trenchard,*	Foynes, Shanagolden,	30	0	0	57
16	Ditto,	5364	Tervoe,*	Clarina, Limerick,	23	2	21	51
17	Ditto,	6969	Limerick,*	Limerick,	76	3	8	51
18	Monaghan,	4888	Rath,	Drumfield, Castleblayney,	42	2	0	21
19	Tipperary,	3694	Kyle Park,	Borrisokane,	10	0	2	36
20	Ditto,	5474	Derrycastle,*	Killaloe,	18	1	22	51
21	Ditto,	5618	Garrymorestown,*	Ardfinnan, Clonmel,	67	2	33	53

2.—11 First-class Agricultural Schools under Local Management.

No.	County.	Roll No.	School.	Post Town.	Area of Farm. A.	R.	P.	District No.
1	Antrim,	3434	Larne,	Larne,	7	0	23	6
2	Carlow,	5363	Garryhill,	Bagnalstown,	11	2	16	53
3	Clare,	5186	Cahersherkin,*	Ennistymon,	20	0	0	42
4	Ditto,	3378	Ballybank,*	Broadford,	16	0	0	51
5	Ditto,	2488	Feakle,*	Feakle,	14	2	16	43
6	Fermanagh,	2561	Carrick,	Lisbellaw, Enniskillen,	25	0	0	13
7	Kilkenny,	6189	Piltown,*	Piltown,	6	1	20	58
8	Meath,	6392	Woodpark,	Kells,	15	0	0	29
9	Monaghan,	378	Corraghlin,	Glenagima,	16	0	0	19
10	Roscommon,	5783	Clonard,	Lecarrow, Athlone,	30	2	20	27
11	Waterford,	1710	Glengarra,*	Lismore,	29	0	0	48

3.—26 School Gardens.†

No.	County.	Roll No.	School.	Post Town.	Area of Garden. A.	R.	P.	District No.
1	Armagh,	7290	Derryvaghan,	Markethill,	0	1	0	16
2	Ditto,	9271	Lisdrumchor,	Ditto,	0	1	0	16
3	Ditto,	1478	Markethill,	Ditto,	0	2	0	16
4	Ditto,	4634	Ballylane,	Ditto,	0	2	0	16
5	Donegal,	9716	Glenmaquin,	Manorcunningham,	0	1	0	1
6	Ditto,	2932	Donegal,	Donegal,	0	0	0	5
7	Ditto,	5299	Convoy,	Raphoe,	0	1	0	1
8	Ditto,	7157	Drumnaviah,	Stranorlar,	0	1	10	6
9	Dublin,	4292	Glasnevin,	Glasnevin,	1	2	19	30
10	Fermanagh,	4423	Ballindarragh,	Lisnaskea,	0	1	10	13
11	Ditto,	9971	Enniskillen,	Enniskillen,	3	0	0	12
12	King's,	824	Rahan,	Tullamore,	0	1	0	41
13	Londonderry,	6223	Ballyronan,	Magherafelt,	0	2	0	7
14	Longford,	858	Longford,	Longford,	0	1	35	29
15	Mayo,	1971	Ballaghaderreen,	Ballaghaderreen,	0	1	0	31
16	Ditto,	5937	Prizon,	Balla, Ballyglass,	0	1	0	29
17	Roscommon,	4109	Loughglynn,	Loughglynn, Frenchpark,	0	2	27	21
18	Sligo,	9791	Rathscanlan,	Ballymote,	0	1	10	21
19	Ditto,	1347	Camphill,	Collooney,	0	1	16	12
20	Tipperary,	10167	Cahir,*	Cahir,	0	0	0	33
21	Tyrone,	5957	Clare,	Castlederg,	0	2	10	5
22	Ditto,	8131	Moy,	Moy,	0	2	0	15
23	Ditto,	10023	Killyman,	Ditto,	0	1	0	15
24	Ditto,	7180	Stewartstown,	Stewartstown,	0	1	0	15
25	Ditto,	6796	Drummond,	Moy,	1	0	0	15
26	Wexford,	4479	Carrickbyrne,	Adamstown,	0	1	15	40

4.—137 Ordinary-Agricultural Schools under Local Management.

No.	County.	Roll No.	School.	Post Town.	Area of Garden. A.	R.	P.	District No.
1	Antrim,	6061	Ballycarry,	Ballycarry,	7	0	38	8
2	Armagh,	4509	Poyntzpass,	Poyntzpass,	2	0	10	16
3	Ditto,	4371	Tassagh,	Ditto,	7	0	0	16
4	Ditto,	4325	Drumbanagher,	Ditto,	1	0	0	19
5	Ditto,	10311	Brackley,	Markethill,	1	0	0	19
6	Ditto,	8311	Lisnadill,	Armagh,	7	0	39	16
7	Cavan,	4943	Drung,	Drung, Ballyhaise,	11	1	35	22
8	Ditto,	6837	Termon,	Killinkere, Virginia,	25	3	35	24
9	Ditto,	6713	Carrowleigh,	Glangevlin, Dowra,	12	2	0	31
10	Ditto,	4824	Tullyconnor,	Ditto,	15	0	0	31
11	Ditto,	4319	Kilcogy,	Granard,	4	1	39	29
13	Ditto,	6957	Mounragh,	Blacklion,	14	0	0	13
13	Ditto,	7773	Kilmaleck,	Kilmaleck,	8	2	25	23
14	Ditto,	6766	Barran,	Blacklion,	35	0	0	13
15	Ditto,	5359	Mountallen,	Dowra, Carrick-on-Shan.	3	1	0	13
16	Ditto,	7142	Derrycarrick,	Cootehill,	1	3	0	29
17	Ditto,	1182	Garvah,	Glangevlin, Dowra,	17	0	0	31
18	Clare,	5133	O'Callaghan's Mills,*	O'Callaghan's Mills,	1	2	0	47
19	Ditto,	148	Partean,*	Limerick,	2	1	7	41
20	Ditto,	6783	Tubber,	Tubber, Gort,	16	3	33	43
21	Ditto,	2379	Ballinruan,*	Crusheen, Ennis,	6	2	1	42
22	Ditto,	6378	Moveen,*	Carrigaholt,	11	1	11	45
23	Ditto,	3480	Drumandoora,*	Gort,	35	0	0	42
24	Ditto,	7798	Tullycrine,*	Kilrush,	6	2	35	44
25	Ditto,	6241	Scropul,*	Miltown Malbay,	3	0	0	45

† The school gardens are all under local management, with the exception of that at Glasnevin, which is under the exclusive management of the Board.

4.—137 Ordinary Agricultural Schools under Local Management—con.

No.	County.	Roll No.	School.	Post Town.	Area of Farm. A.	R.	P.	[illegible]
26	Cork,	5700	Cloghroe,*	Rosscarbery,	5	0	0	59
27	Ditto,	3131	Kildinan,*	Rathcormack, Fermoy,	7	0	32	56
28	Ditto,	6293	Freemount,*	Milford, Charleville,	9	0	0	55
29	Ditto,	4453	Newmarket,*	Newmarket, Kanturk,	16	1	29	55
30	Ditto,	4935	Ballyhass,*	Castletown, Mallow,	16	0	0	55
31	Ditto,	10498	Curra,*	Leap,	1	0	0	59
32	Ditto,	8768	Shandrum,*	Dunmanway,	1	2	0	55
33	Ditto,	8567	Adrigole,*	Adrigole, Castletown,	12	0	0	55
34	Donegal,	3363	Balleighan,	Manorcunningham, Strabane,	80	2	0	1
35	Ditto,	5069	Carradoan,	Rathmullen, Rathmelton,	6	2	0	1
36	Ditto,	6571	Arranmore Island,	Burton Port, Letterkenny,	4	0	0	1
37	Ditto,	6349	Croveeny,	Rathmullen,	5	0	0	1
38	Ditto,	5874	Coolmore,	Rossnowlagh, Ballyshannon	13	2	0	5
39	Ditto,	4809	Keadue,	Burton Port, Letterkenny,	8	0	0	1
40	Ditto,	1735	Killybegs,	Killybegs,	3	2	20	5
41	Ditto,	4418	Carrickboy,	Ballyshannon,	2	2	0	5
42	Ditto,	8829	Harvestmore,	Donegal,	4	0	0	5
43	Ditto,	2175	Knock,	Stranorlar,	2	0	0	6
44	Down,	6591	Hill Hall,	Lisburn,	1	2	29	17
45	Fermanagh,	3784	Crieve,	Fivemiletown,	15	2	16	15
46	Ditto,	6789	Lack,	Lack, Kesh,	5	0	0	15
47	Galway,	1645	Kilcurra,	Kilcurra,	19	0	0	47
48	Ditto,	4216	Castlehacket,	Castlehacket, Tuam,	13	0	0	39
49	Ditto,	8284	Esker, No. 2,	Banagher,	8	2	29	39
50	Ditto,	8953	Williamstown,	Williamstown, Ballymoe,	8	0	0	42
51	Ditto,	7107	Carraghmore,	Kilserrig,	6	0	30	33
52	Ditto,	8942	Cloonkeenkerrill,	Menlough, Mount Bellew,	28	0	0	35
53	Ditto,	10480	Killimor,	Caltra, Ballinasloe,	3	1	0	35
54	Ditto,	4025	Toberroe,	Creggs,	4	2	0	27
55	Ditto,	6702	Creggs,	Ditto,	3	0	0	27
56	Kerry,	7813	Derreendarragh,*	Kenmare,	4	0	0	57
57	Ditto,	6891	Lansdowne,*	Ditto,	7	0	0	53
58	Ditto,	8231	Sneem,*	Sneem,	6	0	0	57
59	Ditto,	8348	Ballinskelligs,*	Cahersiveen,	11	0	0	57
60	Kildare,	2284	Twomileshouse,	Naas,	4	0	17	37
61	Ditto,	1713	Clane,	Clane, Naas,	3	1	13	37
62	Ditto,	7230	Eadestown,	Rathmore, Naas,	3	1	39	37
63	Kilkenny,	4881	Ballygiass,*	Piltown,	8	3	24	55
64	Ditto,	6183	Whitechurch,*	Carrick-on-Suir,	8	0	15	55
65	Ditto,	6918	Clonmore,*	Piltown,	5	1	0	53
66	Leitrim,	5850	Kilmore,	Drumkeeran,	4	0	0	12
67	Ditto,	10609	Cornmacahle,	Dowra,	19	2	0	31
68	Ditto,	5294	Askill,	Ballyshannon,	29	0	0	5
69	Ditto,	8079	Tullydevnan,	Drumkeeran,	8	0	0	12
70	Ditto,	8431	Cloonmark,	Dromod,	11	1	0	29
71	Ditto,	8463	Lisconaghill,	Dromkeeran,	5	2	0	12
72	Limerick,	4167	Kilfinnane,*	Bruree,	10	0	0	59
73	Ditto,	7229	Banogue,*	Croom,	8	0	0	61
74	Ditto,	9306	Croom,*	Ditto,	1	0	29	61
75	Longford,	5559	Rathcline,	Lanesborough,	7	0	0	27
76	Ditto,	1438	Cloonagh,	Killashee, Longford,	19	0	0	29
77	Ditto,	7877	Stonepark,	Longford,	2	1	29	29
78	Mayo,	4592	Carragarra,	Knockmore, Ballina,	9	0	0	29
79	Ditto,	1412	Doonmaile,	Bunninadden, Ballymote,	1	2	19	21
80	Ditto,	1058	Brusna,	Ballaghaderreen,	4	1	0	21
81	Ditto,	7327	Rooskey,	Ditto,	8	2	0	21
82	Ditto,	6120	Lahinch,	Hollymount,	9	0	0	32
83	Ditto,	2239	Cloughans,	Knockmore, Ballina,	4	2	0	29
84	Ditto,	7756	Derrinacartha,	Ballaghaderreen,	2	0	32	21
85	Ditto,	8239	Lismolake,	Ballina,	1	0	0	29
86	Ditto,	7619	Cloonta,	Carrowcastle, Ballaghaderreen,	4	0	0	21
87	Ditto,	6943	Bekan,	Ballyhaunis,	1	2	10	32
88	Ditto,	10286	Turlough,	Swinford,	23	0	0	29
89	Ditto,	3949	Culkilla,	Kiltimagh,	1	0	0	21
90	Ditto,	8942	Kilmovee, No. 1,	Kilmovee, Ballaghaderreen,	6	0	0	21
91	Ditto,	6708	Callow,	Foxford,	1	0	0	21

4.—137 Ordinary Agricultural Schools under Local Management—*con.*

No.	County.	Roll No.	School.	Post Town.	Area of Farm. A.	R.	P.	Detailed No.
92	Mayo,	6761	Brackloon,	Swinford,	1	2	29	21
93	Meath,	556	Ratoath,	Ratoath,	7	3	20	37
94	Ditto,	2797	Kilcloon,	Maynooth,	2	0	0	37
95	Monaghan,	8113	Drumlusty,	Carrickmacross,	13	2	17	24
96	Ditto,	8501	Ballymackney,	Ditto,	16	1	11	24
97	Ditto,	8111	Broomfield,	Broomfield, Castleblayney,	9	1	0	24
98	Ditto,	8459	Ashburton,	Cremartin,	5	0	0	24
99	Ditto,	6821	Corravoo,	Monaghan,	11	0	22	10
100	Ditto,	8630	Drumhillagh,	Smithboro', Monaghan,	1	0	0	18
101	Ditto,	10430	Drumaloony,	Monaghan,	1	1	0	18
102	Queen's,	6555	Rath,	Ballybrittas,	2	1	0	41
103	Ditto,	1812	Arles,	Ballickmoyler,	3	1	0	44
104	Roscommon,	1807	Cornafulla,	Athlone,	13	0	11	25
105	Ditto,	7292	Ballymurray,	Ballymurray,	29	0	0	27
106	Ditto,	8405	Ballyvoneen,	Ballyfarnan, Ballinameen,	5	1	7	27
107	Ditto,	7897	Shass,	Rooskey, Dromod,	11	0	0	17
108	Ditto,	7863	Mountallen,	Keadue, Ballyfarnan,	4	2	16	23
109	Ditto,	9169	Ballyfeeny,	Strokestown,	12	0	0	27
110	Ditto,	10216	North Yard,	Ditto,	5	0	0	27
111	Sligo,	1213	Unsragh,	Ballyfarnan, Carrick-on-Shannon,	1	0	28	23
112	Ditto,	6464	Carry,	Ballaghy, Swinford,	4	0	4	21
113	Ditto,	9659	Doonflin,	Skreen, Sligo,	5	0	0	20
114	Ditto,	8623	Powellsboro',	Tubbercurry,	2	2	18	21
115	Ditto,	4106	Kilrusheighter,	Dromore West,	13	0	0	20
116	Ditto,	7761	Bunnacranagh,	Bellaghy, Swinford,	3	2	0	21
117	Ditto,	9086	Culfadda,	Ballymote,	15	0	0	21
118	Ditto,	7923	Carrowcrory,	Sligo,	4	3	22	19
119	Ditto,	1093	Banada,	Aclare, Tubbercurry,	1	2	20	21
120	Ditto,	7909	Quigabar,	[illegible]	2	2	[illegible]	20
121	Ditto,	2536	Cloonloogh,	Boyle,	4	0	0	23
122	Ditto,	4809	Cloonacool,	Cloonacool, Tubbercurry,	5	0	0	21
123	Ditto,	9229	Bunninadden,	Bunninadden, Ballymote,	20	0	0	21
124	Ditto,	10473	Coolavin,	Ballaghaderreen,	5	2	29	22
125	Ditto,	3136	Ballincurra,	Beltra, Ballisodare,	11	0	0	13
126	Ditto,	3455	Carrowneden,	Dromard, Ballisodare,	11	0	0	13
127	Tyrone,	10963	Termon,	Carrickmore, Omagh,	4	0	0	18
128	Ditto,	10176	Benburb,	Benburb, Moy,	1	2	19	13
129	Ditto,	1337	Ballymacor,	Dunnamanagh,	54	0	0	6
130	Ditto,	2738	Drummakan,	Castlecaulfield,	19	2	23	15
131	Ditto,	6438	Castlederg (Edward's),	Castlederg,	1	0	0	6
132	Ditto,	9784	Parkanaur,	Castlecaulfield, Dungannon,	2	0	20	15
133	Ditto,	10203	Newmills,	Coal Island,	5	1	25	13
134	Waterford,	1233	Grange,*	Ardmore,	2	0	0	43
135	Ditto,	8446	Ballysaggart,*	Lismore,	12	0	0	46
136	Westmeath,	631	Ballinvally,	Castletowndelvin,	6	2	0	33
137	Wicklow,	7012	Annacarter,	Roundwood,	5	2	20	41

APPENDIX C.—LIST of SCHOOLS in OPERATION on 31st December, 1874;

List of Schools in operation on the

ULSTER—

COUNTY OF ANTRIM—

NOTE.—In the column headed "*Vested or Non-Vested*," the letters V.T. denote Schools *Vested in Trustees*; V.T.B. those *Vested* by *Board* namely. Schools not having any of these letters are "*Non-Vested*." Religious R.C., Roman Catholic; Pres., Presbyterian;

Number.	Roll Number of School.	Parish.	District.	School.	Religious Denomination of Managers or Correspondents: Clerical.	Lay.	Number and Religious Denomination of Teachers: Principals.	Assistants.	Attendance for the Year. Total number of Pupils on Rolls within the Year 1874: Males.	Fem.	Total.	Average Daily Attendance for the Year 1874.
1	7804	Aghagallon,	11	Derrymore,	–	R.C.	R.C.	–	49	35	84	29
2	7858	Do.	–	Derrynaseer, m.	R.C.	–	R.C.	–	78	–	78	30
3	10007	Do.	–	Do. f.	R.C.	–	R.C.	–	–	68	68	21
4	8408	Aghalee,	–	Aghalee,	Diss.	–	R.C.	–	58	23	81	38
5	6618	Ahoghill,	4	Ballymena District Model, m.	Com.	N.E.	Pres.	R.C.	157	–	157	80
6	6022	Do.	–	Do. f.	Com.	N.E.	Pres.	E.C.	–	178	178	96
7	[illegible]	Do.	–	Do. i.	Com.	N.E.	E.C.	E.C.	45	38	83	46
8	[illegible]	Do.	7	Killygarvin,	R.C.	–	R.C.	R.C.	83	78	161	60
				Do. evg.	–	–	R.C.	–	43	26	69	27
9	[illegible]	Do.	4	Leymore,	–	R.C.	Pres.	–	39	30	69	29
10	[illegible]	Do.	7	Gortgole,	R.C.	–	R.C.	R.C.	64	49	113	61
11	1927	Do.	4	Aughterclooney,	R.C.	–	R.C.	–	77	64	141	42
12	2070	Do.	–	Glenhugh,	Pres.	–	Pres.	–	78	76	152	61
13	2576	Do.	–	Cullybackey, m.	Pres.	–	Pres.	Pres.	161	–	161	66
				Do. evg.	–	–	Pres.	–	93	10	103	24
14	[illegible]	Do.	–	Do. f.	Pres.	–	Pres.	Pres.	–	153	153	64
15	[illegible]	Do.	–	Moyasset,	–	Pres.	Pres.	–	71	38	109	54
16	7721	Do.	7	Upper Largy,	Pres.	–	Pres.	–	71	48	116	59
17	3074	Do.	4	Tullaghgarley,	–	Pres.	Pres.	Pres.	86	49	134	61
				Do. evg.	–	–	Pres.	–	30	34	69	32
18	3307	Do.	–	Carndsey,	Pres.	–	Pres.	Pres.	83	63	146	69
19	[illegible]	Do.	–	Scald,	Pres.	–	Pres.	Pres.	117	62	179	64
20	[illegible]	Do.	4	Ballymacilrough,	Pres.	–	R.C.	–	74	32	106	45
21	[illegible]	Do.	7	Gortfad,	–	Pres.	Pres.	–	35	23	58	40
22	[illegible]	Do.	–	Aughnacleagh,	–	Pres.	Pres.	–	61	48	100	60
23	[illegible]	Do.	–	Tullynahinnion,	–	Pres.	Pres.	–	57	31	88	32
24	4093	Do.	–	Garvaghy, West,	–	Pres.	Pres.	–	61	62	113	37
25	6331	Do.	4	Ballylig,	Pres.	–	Pres.	–	43	37	80	26
26	6423	Do.	7	Lisrodden,	–	Pres.	Pres.	Pres.	71	53	124	48
27	6640	Do.	4	Galgorm, m.	–	Pres.	Pres.	–	96	–	96	43
28	7746	Do.	–	Do. f.	–	Pres.	Diss.	Pres.	–	134	134	65
29	[illegible]	Do.	7	Portglenone,*	–	Pres.	–	–	–	–	–	–
30	8090	Do.	–	Moboy,	–	Pres.	R.C.	Pres.	89	70	159	39
31	6114	Do.	–	Garvaghy, East,	Pres.	–	Pres.	–	69	49	118	48
32	6419	Do.	4	Leam,	Pres.	–	Pres.	Pres.	88	84	172	67
33	6414	Do.	–	Bridge End,	–	Pres.	Pres.	–	77	48	125	49
34	6731	Do.	–	Ahoghill, m.	R.C.	–	R.C.	–	106	–	106	38
35	6732	Do.	–	Do. f.	R.C.	–	E.C.	Pres.	–	128	128	57
36	6063	Do.	–	Do. i.	E.C.	–	Pres.	–	157	169	326	121
37	[illegible]	Do.	–	Tullygrawley,	–	Pres.	Pres.	–	82	78	160	62
38	8057	Do.	–	Tenniban,	–	Pres.	Pres.	Pres.	127	103	230	70
39	8394	Do.	–	Gracehill, f.	–	Diss.	Diss.	–	–	61	61	28
40	2367	Antrim,	–	Cranagh,	–	Pres.	Pres.	–	63	49	112	44
41	2764	Do.	8	Antrim, m.	R.C.	–	R.C.	–	86	–	96	36
42	[illegible]	Do.	–	Do. f.	R.C.	–	R.C.	–	–	75	75	27
43	6314	Do.	–	Do. Workhouse,	P.L.	Gds.	E.C. / Pres.	–	60	59	109	60
44	[illegible]	Do.	–	Mill-row, m.	Pres.	–	Pres.	–	49	8	57	30
45	4671	Do.	–	Do. f.	Pres.	–	Pres.	–	–	61	61	22
46	4072	Do.	–	Lady-hill,	Pres.	–	Pres.	–	79	31	110	45
47	5440	Do.	–	Rash,	Pres.	–	Pres.	–	39	16	50	24
48	[illegible]	Do.	–	High-street,	Pres.	–	Pres.	Pres.	102	66	108	61
49	1	Ardclinis,	8	Glenariff,	R.C.	–	R.C.	–	36	33	69	24

a Including value of Free Garden.

b Including value of Free Residence.

with SUMMARIES in COUNTIES and PROVINCES.

31st December, 1874.—Province of ULSTER.

2,684 Schools.

330 Schools.

those with additional security of Bond; V.C., those Vested in Commissioners; A., Assigned to Commissioners; and B. [illegible] denominations of Managers and Teachers are expressed thus—E.C., the late Established Church; [illegible] other Protestant Dissenters, Dis.

Amount paid for Books, Requisites, and Apparatus at Reduced Prices.	Aid granted by the Board during the Year 1874. In Free Stock of Books, Requisites, and Apparatus.	In Salaries, Premiums, and other Gratuities.	Results Fees, Financial Year.	Amount of Local Emoluments received in Aid of Teacher's Salary. School Fees.	Subscriptions, Endowments, &c.	Total Local Aid.	Vested or Non-Vested.	Number.
£ s. d.	£ s. d.	£ s. d.	£ s. d.	£ s. d.	£ s. d.	£ s. d.		
1 13 1	—	24 0 0	5 15 0	7 16 6	5 0 0	*12 16 6		1
1 1 6	—	32 0 0	7 7 0	9 8 0	—	9 8 0		2
—	—	20 0 0	6 5 0	7 18 0	—	7 18 0		3
5 10 7	—	21 10 0	8 16 6	7 5 0	6 0 0	13 5 0		4
33 10 1	5 12 3						V.C.	5
13 0 4	10 5 1	708 5 6	69 1 3	125 12 0	—	125 12 9		6
—	—							7
8 0 6	—	68 0 0	16 18 6	8 6 4	—	3 8 0	V.V.	8
—	—		9 11 6	0 5 0	—	0 5 0		
0 14 6	—	24 0 0	4 13 6	4 8 0	—	4 8 0		9
1 4 9	—	36 0 0	11 4 0	5 17 4	—	2 17 4	V.S.	10
2 13 1	—	31 0 0	0 10 0	4 15 0	—	4 15 0	V.V.	11
1 10 1	—	51 12 4	11 1 0	8 19 9	—	8 19 9		12
4 5 7	—	43 19 4	22 19 6	17 11 11	—	17 11 11		13
—	—		9 1 6	3 1 8	—	3 1 8		
6 5 8	—	52 10 0	51 0 0	16 19 1	—	16 16 1		14
1 8 5	—	35 0 0	8 17 6	5 6 6	—	5 6 6		15
2 11 5	—	24 0 0	10 11 6	6 15 6	—	6 15 6		16
3 15 0	—	47 0 0	16 17 0	5 19 9	—	6 14 9		17
—	—		0 18 0	3 5 0	—	3 5 0		
3 11 8	—	50 10 0	16 17 6	8 6 6	—	8 5 6		18
4 0 8	—	16 0 0	18 9 0	15 14 10	—	16 14 10		19
2 4 0	—	20 0 0	18 17 0	7 5 0	—	7 5 0		20
1 6 3	—	30 16 8	12 18 6	7 14 6	—	7 14 6		21
—	—	31 10 0	14 0 6	18 1 6	—	19 1 6		22
1 1 8	—	30 0 0	10 18 0	4 2 6	2 0 0	6 2 6		23
3 0 3	—	24 0 0	11 18 6	11 12 6	—	11 12 6		24
0 12 11	—	34 0 0	8 13 0	4 10 4	2 11 0	7 4 4		25
3 10 2	—	30 0 0	23 17 0	13 11 0	—	18 11 0		26
1 7 4	—	40 0 0	10 18 6	7 17 9	10 0 0	17 17 9		27
4 1 4	—	58 16 8	13 0 6	7 15 10	10 0 0	17 15 10		28
—	—	—	—	—	—	—		29
1 11 7	—	44 0 0	6 7 6	7 11 2	—	7 11 2		30
3 1 8	—	30 0 0	16 8 0	11 1 11	—	11 3 11		31
6 0 1	—	57 0 0	21 7 6	18 6 9	—	18 6 9		32
6 4 2	—	30 3 4	19 8 6	8 18 0	—	8 18 0		33
4 16 11	—	23 6 8	11 18 6	10 3 9	0 15 0	16 18 9		34
2 10 9	4 3 3	45 0 0	23 19 0	12 18 8	10 10 0	23 9 8		35
4 14 1	—	60 16 4	18 15 0	0 1 0	15 17 0	16 15 0		36
3 1 11	—	27 0 0	0 10 6	10 10 0	—	10 10 0		37
4 1 5	—	60 6 0	21 3 6	20 4 6	—	20 4 6	V.C.	38
4 17 11	—	20 0 0	5 8 0	5 1 9	6 0 0	11 1 0		39
3 11 0	—	37 17 0	9 6 6	8 14 9	—	8 15 9		40
8 16 1	—	37 18 0	19 5 6	16 4 8	—	16 1 8	V.V.	41
—	—	29 0 0	6 10 0	5 16 4	—	8 15 4	V.P.D.	42
8 6 4	—	8 0 0	—	—	—	—		43
4 18 0	—	18 15 4	2 5 0	1 9 0	—	1 9 0		44
4 0 0	—	30 10 0	10 14 6	9 18 0	—	8 18 0		45
4 11 2	—	67 0 0	10 3 6	11 18 8	—	11 18 8		46
—	—	29 0 0	6 0 6	9 0 6	—	9 0 6		47
2 9 4	—	08 16 8	18 15 3	47 0 0	—	47 0 0		48
8 0 4	—	20 0 0	3 1 6	0 4 0	—	0 4 0		49

* Imperative.

List of Schools in operation on the 31st December, 1874.—

Number.	Roll Number of School.	Parish.	District.	School.	Religious Denomination of Managers or Correspondents: Clerical.	Lay.	Religious Denomination of Teachers: Principals.	Assistants.	Attendance for the Year. Total number of Pupils on Rolls within the Year 1874: Males.	Fem.	Total.	Average Daily Attendance for the Year.
50	4437	Ardclinis,	4	Point of Garron,	-	E.C.	R.C.	-	53	15	68	35
51	[illegible]	Do.	-	Carnlough, m.	-	R.C.	Pres.	-	85	-	85	38
52	[illegible]	Do.	-	Do. f.	-	E.C.	E.C.	-	-	63	63	34
53	[illegible]	Do.	-	Waterfoot, i.	R.C.	-	R.C.	-	78	63	141	49
54	[illegible]	Armoy,	8	Breen, m.	R.C.	-	R.C.	-	74	-	74	25
55	[illegible]	Do.	-	Do. f.	R.C.	-	R.C.	-	-	74	74	30
56	[illegible]	Do.	-	Mullaghduff,	Pres.	-	Pres.	-	45	45	90	17
57	[illegible]	Do.	-	Armoy, m.	-	Pres.	Pres.	-	88	-	88	33
58	[illegible]	Do.	-	Do. f.	-	Pres.	Pres.	-	-	130	130	43
59	[illegible]	Ballinderry,	11	Killedragh,	E.C.	-	E.C.	E.C.	60	70	130	48
60	[illegible]	Do.	-	Legatirriff,	Diss.	-	Pres.	-	49	30	79	31
61	11107	Do.	-	Ballymacravan,	E.C.	-	E.C.	-	38	49	87	30
62	[illegible]	Do.	-	Tullyballydonald,	E.C.	-	E.C.	-	37	36	73	35
63	10944	Do.	-	Upper Ballinderry,	E.C.	-	E.C.	E.C.	97	75	172	67
64	11050	Do.	-	Lower do.	E.C.	-	E.C.	-	38	33	71	32
65	27	Ballintoy,	8	Cloghcorr,	-	E.C.	E.C.	-	68	36	104	48
66	[illegible]	Do.	-	Croaghbeg,	Pres.	-	Pres.	-	68	63	131	60
67	8376	Do.	-	Prolusk,	Pres.	-	Pres.	-	71	69	140	52
68	11678	Do.	-	Ballinlea,	R.C.	-	R.C.	-	43	67	110	50
69	8	Ballyclug,	6	Craigbilly,	E.C.	-	E.C.	E.C.	141	105	246	83
70	[illegible]	Do.	-	Moorfields,	-	E.C.	Pres.	-	73	84	158	47
71	4104	Do.	-	Harryville, No. 1, m.	Pres.	-	Pres.	-	138	-	138	48
72	7074	Do.	-	Do. No. 2, m.	E.C.	-	E.C.	-	94	-	94	31
73	7057	Do.	-	Do. No. 1, f.	E.C.	-	E.C.	-	-	61	61	35
				Do.* evg.	E.C.	-	-	-	-	-	-	-
74	9301	Do.	-	Do. No. 2, f.	Pres.	-	Pres.	Pres.	-	210	210	84
75	10177	Do.	-	Do. i.	E.C.	-	E.C.	-	38	33	71	35
76	10672	Ballycor,	8	Ballyeaston, m.	Pres.	-	Pres.	-	97	-	97	34
77	[illegible]	Do.	-	Do. f.	Pres.	-	Pres.	Pres.	-	150	150	73
78	[illegible]	Do.	-	Ballyboley,	Diss.	-	Pres.	Pres.	73	63	134	66
79	22	Raloo,	-	Tildarg,	Pres.	-	Pres.	-	66	50	116	44
80	17	Ballylinny,	-	Bruslee,	Pres.	-	Pres.	Pres.	67	48	115	37
81	18	Do.	-	Palentine,	-	Pres.	Pres.	-	61	47	108	40
82	109	Do.	-	Ballyhimmy,	-	Pres.	E.C.	-	48	38	78	33
83	[illegible]	Do.	-	Carntall,	-	Pres.	Pres.	Pres.	61	51	102	40
84	[illegible]	Do.	-	Lisnalinchy,	Pres.	-	Pres.	-	47	43	90	30
85	[illegible]	Do.	-	Mossley, day	-	Pres.	Pres.	Pres.	125	109	234	107
				Do. evg.	-	Pres.	Pres.	Pres.	64	43	107	49
86	[illegible]	Ballymoney,	3	Garry,	Pres.	-	Pres.	-	38	39	77	33
87	[illegible]	Do.	-	Seacon,	Pres.	-	Pres.	-	67	44	111	45
88	[illegible]	Do.	-	Ballymoney, m.	E.C.	-	E.C.	-	91	-	91	48
89	[illegible]	Do.	-	Do. f.	E.C.	-	E.C.	-	-	105	105	40
90	[illegible]	Do.	-	Do. Minor Model, m.	Com.	N.E.	Pres.	E.C.	178	-	178	103
91	[illegible]	Do.	-	Do. f.	Com.	N.E.	E.C.	Pres.	-	134	134	65
92	[illegible]	Do.	-	Do. i.	Com.	N.E.	E.C.	-	67	50	116	55
93	[illegible]	Do.	-	Do. Workhouse,	P.L.	Gds.	Pres. / E.C.	-	25	22	48	38
94	[illegible]	Do.	-	Kirkhill,	Pres.	-	Pres.	-	28	25	53	19
95	[illegible]	Do.	-	Cabbra,	Pres.	-	Pres.	-	33	75	98	33
96	[illegible]	Do.	-	Garryduff,	Pres.	-	Diss.	-	63	60	123	41
97	[illegible]	Do.	-	Landhead,	Pres.	-	Pres.	-	70	43	113	33
98	[illegible]	Do.	-	Stranocum,	-	E.C.	Pres.	-	79	35	114	35
99	[illegible]	Do.	-	Ontragh,	-	Pres.	Pres.	-	-	-	-	-
100	[illegible]	Do.	-	Wesley-place,	Diss.	-	Diss.	Diss.	88	90	158	67
101	[illegible]	Do.	-	Balnamore,	-	E.C.	Pres.	Diss.	75	77	153	61
102	[illegible]	Do.	-	Roseyards,	Pres.	-	Pres.	-	35	44	79	35
103	[illegible]	Do.	-	Falligan,	Pres.	-	Pres.	-	43	28	71	25
104	[illegible]	Ballynure,	9	Killgavanahane,	-	Pres.	Pres.	-	30	35	61	19
105	[illegible]	Do.	-	Ballylagan,	Diss.	-	Diss.	-	50	61	111	44
106	[illegible]	Do.	-	Ballymacary,	-	Pres.	Diss.	-	67	33	88	33
107	[illegible]	Do.	-	Ballyvale, m.	Pres.	-	Pres.	-	73	-	73	32
108	7550	Do.	-	Do. f.	Pres.	-	Pres.	-	-	60	60	42

a Including value of Free Garden. b Including value of Free Residence.

Province of Ulster: County of Antrim—*continued.*

Amount paid for Books, Requisites, and Apparatus, at Reduced Prices.	Aid granted by the Board during the Year 1874. — In Free grants of Books, Requisites, and Apparatus.	In Salaries, Premiums, and other Gratuities.	Results Fees, Financial Year.	Amount of Local Emoluments received in Aid of Teacher's Salary. — School Fees.	Subscriptions, Endowments, &c.	Total Local Aid.	Vested or Non-vested.	Number.
£ s. d.	£ s. d.	£ s. d.	£ s. d.	£ s. d.	£ s. d.	£ s. d.		
—	—	24 0 0	6 8 8	0 10 0	10 10 0	*11 0 0	V.C.	50
8 18 9	—	68 15 8	10 17 0	5 8 8	10 0 0	15 8 8	V.C.	51
1 10 4	—	33 0 0	8 14 0	2 14 1	10 0 0	12 14 1	V.C.	52
3 6 9	—	25 0 0	0 11 0	3 2 0	—	3 2 0		53
2 5 6	—	24 0 0	5 7 0	8 18 8	1 0 0	9 18 8	V.T.	54
1 8 7	—	30 0 0	5 18 0	3 11 8	—	3 11 8	V.T.	55
2 4 8	—	30 0 0	1 8 8	2 8 6	—	2 8 6		56
5 4 7	—	24 10 0	9 10 0	7 8 5	—	7 8 5		57
8 10 9	—	48 3 4	15 3 0	9 16 3	—	9 16 3		58
8 11 6	—	44 0 0	8 19 1	7 0 6	—	7 0 6		59
8 18 4	2 11 6	33 15 0	5 9 6	8 8 8	—	8 8 8		60
1 10 10	4 10 0	19 10 0	7 18 0	10 7 10	5 0 0	15 7 10		61
—	—	24 0 0	6 16 4	5 14 6	—	5 14 6		62
10 0 11	—	50 0 0	29 8 5	21 10 2	11 0 0	*32 10 2		63
2 13 6	4 10 0	13 15 7	7 18 5	4 8 0	10 10 0	b14 18 0		64
4 6 1	—	24 0 0	15 7 6	7 4 8	—	7 4 8	V.T.	65
1 10 10	—	28 10 0	6 9 6	7 10 6	—	7 10 6		66
4 10 0	—	30 0 0	6 18 0	5 0 0	4 0 0	10 0 0		67
1 15 1	4 10 0	10 13 4	4 4 0	5 18 2	5 0 0	10 18 2		68
2 15 7	—	30 8 8	13 16 5	2 0 8	9 10 0	11 10 8	V.T.	69
4 15 11	—	30 10 0	14 1 0	8 4 0	—	8 4 0		70
2 6 4	—	38 5 9	7 14 0	5 18 8	—	5 18 8		71
1 5 9	—	23 0 0	4 8 0	1 7 1	—	1 7 1		72
—	—	50 0 0	6 14 0	2 16 11	6 0 0	b8 16 11		73
9 11 7	—	54 0 0	35 6 0	20 18 4	—	20 18 4		74
8 10 0	—	30 0 0	8 11 5	1 13 5	—	1 13 5		75
1 13 8	—	57 0 0	6 9 0	10 0 1	—	10 0 1	V.T.	76
8 19 0	—	42 10 8	21 0 0	11 18 6	8 0 0	19 18 6	V.T.	77
9 1 3	—	35 0 0	17 18 0	6 8 1	—	6 8 1		78
2 12 6	—	24 0 0	14 19 0	6 18 0	—	6 18 0		79
7 12 9	—	44 0 0	21 11 0	17 18 11	—	17 18 11		80
8 8 8	—	17 0 0	11 9 6	7 0 0	—	7 0 0		81
—	—	20 0 0	5 14 8	8 0 0	1 11 6	9 11 6		82
1 14 0	—	35 0 0	10 18 7	9 17 0	—	9 17 0		83
—	—	28 0 0	8 8 8	4 1 1	1 11 6	5 12 7		84
19 8 11	—	122 10 0	64 8 6	69 4 6	20 0 0	89 4 6		85
—	—		31 13 0	11 5 6	—	11 5 6		
9 9 6	—	24 0 0	8 4 0	6 2 9	—	6 2 9		86
3 10 0	—	25 0 0	18 4 5	10 0 0	—	10 0 0		87
—	—	35 16 8	11 1 0	12 8 5	—	12 8 5		88
5 5 8	—	36 0 0	10 18 6	7 16 6	—	7 16 6		89
30 17 1	8 15 0	697 18 6	101 13 0	105 5 10	—	105 5 10	V.C.	90
—	—						V.C.	91
—	—						V.C.	92
8 4 6	—	—	—	—	—	—		93
1 12 6	—	30 10 0	4 17 6	4 14 0	—	4 14 0	V.	94
4 0 1	—	22 0 0	3 18 6	4 7 0	—	4 7 0		95
2 14 4	—	32 0 0	5 10 0	1 19 10	—	1 19 10		96
2 13 3	—	24 0 0	6 4 6	4 6 6	—	4 6 6		97
8 8 5	—	30 6 8	7 8 0	5 14 3	1 0 0	6 14 3		98
1 8 10	—	24 0 0	6 7 0	—	—	—		99
8 10 0	—	56 18 4	16 9 0	12 14 8	18 0 0	*30 14 8		100
1 16 6	—	22 0 0	10 19 5	15 0 1	10 0 0	25 0 1		101
—	—	24 0 0	10 14 6	7 1 6	—	7 1 6		102
8 17 6	—	24 0 0	7 18 0	14 18 5	10 0 0	24 18 5		103
—	—	30 0 0	6 0 6	8 1 0	—	8 1 0	V.T.	104
6 1 1	—	33 0 0	18 6 0	6 2 6	—	6 2 6		105
1 8 6	—	21 16 0	5 0 5	4 18 1	—	4 18 1		106
2 14 4	—	24 0 0	8 8 0	8 0 1	—	8 0 1		107
2 1 4	—	45 8 4	29 10 0	6 12 6	—	6 12 6		108

* Closed half quarter. b Including value of Free Residence.

List of Schools in operation on the 31st December, 1874.—

Number.	Roll Number of School.	Parish.	District.	School.	Religious Denomination of Manager or Correspondent: Clerical.	Lay.	Number and Religious Denomination of Teachers: Principals.	Assistants.	Attendance for the Year. Total Number of Pupils on Rolls within the Year 1874: Males.	Fem.	Total.	Average Daily Attendance for the Year.
109	7712	Ballymore,	9	Ballygowan,	Diss.	–	Pres.	–	40	41	90	39
110	8366	Do.	–	[illegible], m.	Diss.	–	Diss.	–	93	–	93	39
111	5675	Do.	–	Do. f.	Diss.	–	Pres.	–	–	56	56	29
112	34	Ballyscullion Grange,	6	Taylorstown, South,	–	Diss.	R.C.	–	58	73	131	57
113	4609	Do.	–	Do. North, day	Pres.	–	Pres.	Pres.	119	117	236	72
				Do. evg.	Pres.	–	Pres.	–	25	90	115	39
114	1961	Do.	–	Millquarter,	R.C.	–	R.C.	R.C.	129	101	230	94
115	6250	Do.	–	[illegible],	–	R.C.	Pres.	–	37	61	98	61
116	8858	Ballywillin,	8	Portrush, No. 1,	R.C.	–	R.C.	–	29	30	59	30
117	9102	Do.	–	Do. No. 2,	Pres.	–	Pres.	Pres.	91	53	144	71
118	11092	Do.	–	Church-street, m.	R.C.	–	R.C.	–	74	–	74	32
119	9360	Billy,	–	Carnmoon,	–	Pres.	Diss.	–	85	62	147	67
120	2812	Do.	–	[illegible],	Pres.	–	Pres.	–	53	49	102	38
121	2042	Do.	–	Bushmills, m.	Pres.	–	Pres.	–	118	–	118	61
122	3042	Do.	–	Do. f.	Pres.	–	Pres.	Pres.	–	130	130	56
123	3681	Do.	–	[illegible],	Pres.	–	Pres.	–	40	42	82	39
124	8914	Do.	–	Moycraig,	–	Pres.	Pres.	–	75	47	122	54
125	8947	Do.	–	Mosside,	Pres.	–	Pres.	Pres.	81	145	226	67
126	8337	Do.	–	[illegible],	Pres.	–	Pres.	–	23	70	93	39
127	9769	Do.	–	Billy, f.	R.C.	–	R.C.	–	40	58	98	62
128	11137	Do.	–	Liscolman,	–	Pres.	Diss.	–	30	31	76	35
129	1327	Do.	–	Ballyallaght,	Pres.	–	Pres.	–	50	53	103	31
130	10871	Blaris,	11	Castle-st. (Lisburn) Convent,	–	R.C.	Nuns.		–	130	130	39
131	4259	Do.	–	Lisburn, m.	R.C.	–	R.C.	R.C.	100	–	100	72
132	4924	Do.	–	Do. f.	R.C.	–	R.C.	–	–	90	90	35
133	6781	Blaris,	11	Do. Workhouse,	P.L.	Gds.	1 Pres. 1 R.C.	–	43	43	86	47
134	10624	Do.	–	Do. Ragged,	–	Diss.	Pres.	Pres.	73	61	134	48
135	10811	Do.	–	Railway-street, f.	Pres.	–	Pres.	a Pres.	–	–	b –	–
136	5027	Do.	–	Market-square, m.	Pres.	–	Pres.	R.C. Pres.	164	–	161	94
137	8286	Do.	–	Do. f. day	Pres.	–	Pres.	Pres.	–	123	123	61
				Do. evg.	Pres.	–	Pres.	Pres.	54	23	77	27
138	10734	Do.	–	Railway-street, m.	Pres.	–	Pres.	a Pres.	318	–	310	148
				Do. b evg.	Pres.	–	Pres.	–	–	–	–	–
139	1979	Camlin,	–	Crumlin,	Pres.	–	Pres.	–	39	46	69	37
140	4652	Do.	–	Glenavy,	–	Pres.	Pres.	Pres.	69	55	124	50
141	24	Carncastle,	8	Carncastle, No. 1,	Pres.	–	Pres.	R.C.	48	55	103	41
142	6585	Do.	–	Do. No. 2,	Pres.	–	Pres.	–	29	51	80	39
143	22147	Do.	–	Ballygilbert,	Pres.	–	R.C.	Pres.	60	43	103	57
144	23	Carnmoney,	–	Carnmoney, No. 1,	R.C.	–	R.C.	Pres.	84	57	141	65
145	26	Do.	–	Do. No. 2,	Pres.	–	Pres.	Pres.	90	65	155	78
146	27	Do.	–	Whitehouse, m.	–	Pres.	Pres.	Pres.	168	–	168	64
147	2232	Do.	–	Do. f.	–	Pres.	Pres.	R.C.	–	148	149	58
148	7560	Do.	–	Do. i.	–	Pres.	Pres.	Pres. R.C.	163	103	266	98
149	10184	Do.	–	Do. Lower, m.	R.C.	–	R.C.	–	67	–	67	44
150	10185	Do.	–	Do. f.	–	–	R.C.	–	–	67	67	30
151	8846	Do.	–	Ballycraigy, m.	Pres.	–	Pres.	–	60	54	114	48
152	2049	Do.	–	White Abbey, m. day	–	Pres.	R.C.	a Pres.	318	–	318	114
				Do. a evg.	–	–	–	–	–	–	–	–
153	2950	Do.	–	Do. f. day	–	Pres.	Pres.	Pres.	–	248	248	106
				Do. a evg.	–	–	–	–	–	–	–	–
154	4564	Do.	–	Monkstown,	Pres.	–	Pres.	Pres.	140	110	250	100
155	37	Carrickfergus,	–	Carrickfergus,	Pres.	–	Pres.	Pres.	91	128	219	76
156	10632	Do.	–	Do. f.	R.C.	–	R.C.	–	–	92	92	62
157	10634	Do.	–	Do. i.	R.C.	–	R.C.	R.C.	88	83	171	80
158	7752	Do.	–	Do. Minor Model, m.	Com.	N.E.	Pres.	1 R.C. 1 E.C.	180	–	180	99
159	7754	Do.	–	Do. f.	Com.	N.E.	R.C.	Pres.	–	120	120	65
160	7755	Do.	–	Do. i.	Com.	N.E.	R.C.	a Pres.	92	74	166	80

a Including value of Free Residence.

b Returns not available.

Province of Ulster: County of Antrim—*continued.*

Amount paid for Books, Requisites, and Apparatus, at Reduced Prices.	Aid granted by the Board during the Year 1874. In Free Stock of Books, Requisites, and Apparatus.	In Salaries, Premiums, and other Gratuities.	Results Fees, Financial Year.	Amount of Local Endowments received in aid of Teacher's Salary. School Fees.	Subscriptions, Endowments, &c.	Total Local Aid.	Vested or Non-Vested.	Number.
£ s. d.	£ s. d.	£ s. d.	£ s. d.	£ s. d.	£ s. d.	£ s. d.		
3 6 1	—	21 0 0	12 4 0	4 4 0	—	4 4 0		109
2 19 1	—	29 18 8	0 14 0	5 10 10	—	5 10 10		110
0 0 6	—	21 0 0	6 19 6	2 19 8	—	6 19 8		111
1 11 4	—	47 8 4	7 17 8	8 13 6	—	8 13 6		112
10 8 0	4 1 9	61 8 10	20 15 0	10 2 0	—	10 2 0		113
—	—		7 15 8	0 19 0	—	0 19 0		
0 5 6	—	44 6 0	24 12 6	10 17 4	—	10 17 4		114
1 8 4	—	30 0 0	0 16 6	4 1 9	—	4 1 9		115
6 6 0	—	24 10 6	9 6 6	8 14 3	9 7 1	17 1 4		116
11 11 1	—	60 0 0	24 14 0	30 0 0	10 0 0	40 0 0		117
3 0 5	4 0 0	16 0 0	6 8 0	0 17 6	16 0 0	*16 17 6		118
5 12 8	—	25 19 10	11 9 0	8 8 7	—	8 8 7	v.v.	119
1 6 0	—	24 0 0	4 15 8	8 3 6	—	0 3 0	v.v.	120
0 6 8	—	57 10 0	17 10 6	21 14 5	—	21 14 5	a.	121
2 0 6	—	56 10 0	18 18 6	19 6 7	—	10 6 7	a.	122
1 7 6	—	16 18 4	2 15 0	—	—	—		123
4 17 11	—	56 8 0	4 0 0	3 8 4	—	3 8 4		124
9 19 10	—	52 6 0	18 10 6	8 19 10	—	8 19 10		125
1 8 7	—	22 0 6	4 17 0	2 19 0	—	2 19 0		126
5 7 6	1 0 0	20 3 4	3 0 0	2 10 0	2 0 0	*4 10 0		127
8 0 6	4 0 0	20 0 0	5 7 6	4 15 0	—	4 15 0		128
6 0 11	—	20 8 0	8 15 0	7 8 6	—	7 3 6		129
7 4 5	—	19 13 0	6 0 0	—	—	—		130
9 12 5	—	53 10 0	18 17 0	26 19 3	5 0 0	*31 19 3	v.v.	131
1 8 9	—	24 0 0	0 10 0	4 0 1	4 11 8	*8 11 9	v.v.	132
4 8 7	—	7 0 0	—	—	—	..		133
1 0 3	—	43 16 11	0 1 6	—	34 0 0	*34 0 0		134
0 18 11	—	71 10 0	20 1 0	—	—	—		135
16 4 6	—	115 0 0	43 18 0	43 13 6	—	43 13 6		136
2 13 6	—	71 8 4	22 19 6	21 13 8	—	21 13 8		137
			2 11 0	7 3 8	—	7 3 8		
17 1 11	—	109 6 6	05 11 6	48 0 0	3 0 0	48 0 0		138
—	—	—	4 16 8	—	—	—		
8 7 7	—	23 6 4	8 15 8	8 10 8	8 0 0	13 18 5		139
8 14 6	—	65 16 6	25 0 0	8 0 10	13 4 0	*31 10 10		140
2 19 1	—	80 0 0	16 12 0	6 6 4	8 15 0	9 1 6		141
0 16 6	—	30 16 4	14 13 0	6 12 11	—	5 10 11		142
—	—	45 0 0	25 17 6	11 4 1	—	11 5 1		143
3 2 1	1 0 0	00 10 0	14 0 0	15 13 11	4 0 0	*10 13 11		144
4 3 6	—	81 0 0	25 12 0	28 1 3	2 8 0	34 6 8		145
3 13 9	—	87 0 0	27 10 0	63 4 5	67 14 0	100 18 6		146
—	—	51 3 4	18 18 0	13 7 1	—	13 7 1		147
—	—	73 15 0	16 16 0	16 15 11	—	16 16 11		148
6 1 0	—	30 0 0	6 16 0	22 10 1	—	22 16 1		149
1 6 0	—	20 0 0	6 11 6	5 10 6	8 0 0	5 10 6		150
2 17 8	—	85 0 0	12 17 6	15 8 10	—	15 8 10		151
0 7 4	—	98 7 10	60 9 6	20 13 0	—	20 18 0		152
6 10 2	—	75 0 7	86 17 6	83 17 6	—	83 17 6		153
8 17 8	—	70 8 9	44 16 8	20 14 11	—	22 16 11		154
4 17 11	—	71 10 0	21 1 5	16 7 6	—	15 7 3	a.	155
7 16 5	—	22 10 0	6 19 0	7 2 8	—	7 2 8		156
1 5 6	—	62 16 6	8 9 5	6 14 2	—	6 14 2		157
15 10 0	17 10 6	648 12 6	90 0 0	137 4 4	—	167 4 4	v.c.	158
11 0 0	—						v.c.	159
6 5 6	—						v.c.	160

* Closed.

List of Schools in operation on the 31st December, 1874.—

Number.	Roll Number of School.	Parish.	District.	School.	Religious Denomination of Manager or Correspondent: Clerical	Lay.	Number and Religious Denomination of Teachers: Principals.	Assistants.	Attendances for the Year: Total number of Pupils on Rolls within the Year 1874: Male.	Fem.	Total.	Average Daily Attendance for the Year 1874.
161	26	Carrickfergus,	5	Duncrew,	Pres.	–	Pres.	–	31	25	56	37
162	31	Do.	–	Loughmourne, No. 1,	Pres.	–	Pres.	Pres.	35	41	80	33
163	1225	Do.	–	Alden,	Pres.	–	Pres.	Pres.	88	59	147	67
164	5542	Do.	–	Trooper's-lane,	Pres.	–	Pres.	–	33	60	93	34
165	6514	Do.	–	Woodburne,	–	Pres.	Pres.	Pres.	87	93	180	69
166	7120	Do.	–	Minorca-place, day	R.C.	–	R.C.	–	182	–	182	30
				Do. evg.	–	–	R.C.	–	96	–	90	23
167	10540	Do.	–	Do. f.	R.C.	–	R.C.	R.C.	72	140	212	95
168	7600	Do.	–	Joymount, day	Pres.	–	Pres.	Pres.	81	59	140	58
				Do. evg.	–	–	Pres.	–	54	30	84	20
169	8264	Do.	–	Barnhills,	–	R.C.	Diss.	Diss.	91	94	185	68
170	9148	Do.	–	Bella Tober,	Pres.	–	Pres.	–	83	50	133	61
171	9417	Do.	–	Upper Woodburne, No. 1,	Pres.	–	–	–	–	–	–	–
172	9572	Do.	–	Do. No. 2,	R.C.	–	Pres.	–	34	35	69	30
173	10578	Do.	–	Eden,	R.C.	–	R.C.	–	25	42	68	27
174	1737	Do.	–	Straidnahanna,	Pres.	–	Pres.	–	45	41	86	38
175	40	Connor,	4	Upper Tannybrack,	–	Pres.	Pres.	Pres.	97	110	212	78
176	2679	Do.	–	Whappstown,	–	Pres.	R.C.	–	52	48	100	70
177	5503	Do.	–	Connor,	Pres.	–	Pres.	Pres.	39	123	162	81
178	2257	Do.	–	Tardree,	–	Pres.	Pres.	Pres.	87	72	159	65
179	2290	Do.	–	Tullynamullan,	Pres.	–	Pres.	Pres.	114	100	214	83
180	2651	Do.	–	Kells,	–	Pres.	Pres.	–	92	72	164	52
181	10178	Do.	–	Bellee,	Pres.	–	Pres.	Pres.	80	68	148	67
182	10803	Do.	–	Lisnamurrican,	Pres.	–	Pres.	–	52	55	107	42
183	8146	Do.	–	Crosshill,	–	Pres.	Pres.	Pres.	74	82	160	61
184	8311	Do.	–	Maxwell's Walls,	Pres.	–	Pres.	Pres.	94	61	155	65
185	8417	Do.	–	Slaght,	Pres.	–	Pres.	Pres.	83	61	144	57
186	4664	Craigs,	–	Craigs,	–	Pres.	Pres.	Pres.	70	91	161	46
187	11843	Do.	–	Do. Parochial,	R.C.	–	R.C.	R.C.	85	71	156	53
188	1229	Culfeightrin,	3	Glenshesk,	R.C.	–	R.C.	–	40	33	73	27
189	1353	Do.	–	Ballyvoy, m.	–	Pres.	R.C.		95	–	95	54
190	1787	Do.	–	Do. f.	–	Pres.	R.C.	–	–	96	90	58
191	2803	Do.	–	Craigfad,	R.C.	–	R.C.	–	61	65	126	54
192	5175	Do.	–	Ballyucan,	–	R.C.	R.C.	–	79	35	114	53
193	8142	Do.	–	Culramoney,	R.C.	–	R.C.	–	75	71	146	53
194	10618	Derryaghy,	11	Stonyford,	–	Pres.	R.C.	R.C.	81	64	145	57
195	8615	Do.	–	Ballymacward,	R.C.	–	R.C.	R.C.	40	68	108	32
196	10738	Do.	–	Rocky Hill,	–	R.C.	Pres.	–	42	39	81	27
197	9557	Derrykeighan,	6	Tullybane,	Pres.	–	Pres.	–	50	35	85	58
198	8612	Do.	–	Knockanboy,	Pres.	–	Pres.	–	29	33	62	31
199	4948	Do.	–	Derrykeighan,	Pres.	–	Pres.	–	70	56	100	50
200	9816	Do.	–	Dervock,	R.C.	–	R.C.	–	16	30	46	16
201	10922	Do.	–	Upper Dervock,	–	R.C.	Pres.	R.C.	79	65	144	64
202	43	Grange of Doagh,	5	Ballyclare, m.	–	Pres.	Pres.	–	85	20	105	44
203	8158	Do.	–	Do. f.	–	Pres.	Pres.	–	17	84	101	53
204	276	Do.	–	Do. No. 2,	–	Pres.	Pres.	Pres.	95	107	202	98
205	8190	Do.	–	Coggrey Mill,	–	R.C.	R.C.	–	64	109	173	60
				Do. b evg.	–	–	–	–	–	–	–	–
206	7736	Do.	–	Doagh, m.	–	Pres.	Pres.	Pres.	180	62	180	57
207	5562	Donegore,	–	Dunnymaggy,	Pres.	–	Pres.	–	58	40	98	50
208	7557	Do.	–	Donegore,	Pres.	–	Pres.	–	58	47	99	50
209	9108	Do.	–	Parkgate,	Pres.	–	Pres.	–	85	56	141	47
210	39	Drummaul,	4	Tannaghmore,	R.C.	–	R.C.	R.C.	75	74	149	49
211	41	Do.	–	Magheralane,	R.C.	–	R.C.	–	53	20	75	33
212	42	Do.	–	Randalstown, m.	R.C.	–	R.C.	–	84	–	84	39
213	6928	Do.	–	Do. f.	R.C.	–	R.C.	–	–	93	91	45
214	9778	Do.	–	Do. No. 2,	Pres.	–	Pres.	R.C.	120	56	179	90
215	42	Do.	–	Ferinflough,	R.C.	–	R.C.	–	60	59	139	55
216	3742	Do.	–	Seymour's-bridge,	–	Pres.	Diss.	–	67	67	114	39
217	1200	Do.	–	Ballydunmaul,	–	Pres.	Pres.	Pres.	72	53	125	56
218	2935	Do.	–	Muckamore,	Pres.	–	Pres.	Pres.	67	56	123	44
219	8147	Do.	–	Terrygowan, day	–	Pres.	Pres.	Diss.	90	74	165	64
				Do. evg.	–	–	Pres.	–	49	15	64	29

a Including value of Free Residence.

b Closed.

Province of Ulster: County of Antrim—*continued.*

Amount paid for Books, Requisites, and Apparatus, at Reduced Prices.	Aid granted by the Board during the Year 1874. In Free Stock of Books, Requisites, and Apparatus.	In Salaries, Premiums, and other Gratuities.	Results Fees, Financial Year.	Amount of Local Emoluments received in Aid of Teacher's Salary. School Fees.	Subscriptions, Endowments, &c.	Total Local Aid.	Vested or Non-Vested.	Number.
£ s. d.	£ s. d.	£ s. d.	£ s. d.	£ s. d.	£ s. d.	£ s. d.		
0 19 5	—	30 0 0	8 8 0	1 15 9	—	1 15 8		161
1 8 0	—	41 0 0	9 9 0	8 8 4	—	3 8 4		162
4 18 4	—	44 0 0	18 4 0	13 18 8	—	12 15 8	V.P.	163
8 10 1	—	33 8 8	5 8 6	3 9 0	—	3 9 0		164
3 0 2	—	85 8 4	23 8 8	10 0 0	3 10 0	*13 10 0		165
4 8 2	—	45 10 0	11 18 0	8 0 8	—	8 0 8		166
			3 8 0	3 11 8	—	8 11 8		
8 17 0	—	40 0 0	14 8 4	9 15 8	—	0 18 8		167
—	—	35 0 0	8 8 0	19 14 3	—	19 14 3		168
			8 7 0	6 4 3	—	8 4 3		
1 17 11	—	47 3 4	7 8 6	7 7 11	—	7 7 11		169
5 19 11	—	26 0 0	13 7 0	9 9 10	—	8 8 10		170
—	—	—	—	—	—	—		171
1 14 7	1 0 0	30 0 0	8 9 0	1 18 9	—	1 12 0		172
1 8 0	—	30 0 0	10 18 8	7 7 5	3 10 0	*18 17 5		173
8 18 1	—	35 0 0	7 8 8	4 8 10	—	4 8 10		174
9 18 8	—	51 10 0	17 15 0	10 0 0	7 10 0	*17 10 0		175
8 10 10	—	34 0 0	8 10 0	4 14 5	2 0 0	6 14 5		176
9 14 5	—	71 10 8	18 4 0	7 8 1	3 8 8	10 12 9		177
0 19 7	—	38 0 0	15 10 0	5 15 6	—	5 15 6		178
4 19 9	—	50 15 8	19 9 6	16 17 6	—	16 17 6		179
4 1 0	—	30 0 0	18 19 6	10 5 0	—	10 5 6		180
6 8 0	—	44 0 0	10 8 0	9 0 11	—	0 0 11		181
8 8 8	—	54 0 0	10 5 8	3 5 0	—	3 5 0		182
3 15 8	—	46 0 0	24 16 0	8 7 8	—	8 7 8		183
8 8 10	—	32 0 0	22 7 0	8 8 6	5 6 8	*13 15 3		184
4 8 8	—	57 10 0	14 8 0	15 16 8	—	15 16 8		185
4 8 11	—	38 0 0	13 7 0	11 13 10	—	11 13 10	V.P.	186
7 8 8	—	62 13 4	15 8 6	7 19 9	14 0 0	*22 19 9		187
1 8 1	—	24 0 0	8 17 0	4 19 4	0 3 9	43 1 10	V.P.	188
—	—	30 0 0	10 8 0	6 0 0	—	*6 0 0	A.	189
5 3 10	—	22 0 0	4 19 5	6 15 3	—	6 15 3	A.	190
4 15 6	—	31 13 4	5 4 0	5 9 2	—	5 9 2		191
—	—	21 0 0	—	2 8 6	8 8 8	5 0 8		192
6 4 11	1 0 0	30 0 0	6 11 6	5 8 8	4 0 0	9 8 8		193
1 10 7	—	64 0 0	61 10 0	16 18 1	8 0 0	*18 18 1		194
—	—	64 18 8	7 14 0	6 10 0	—	6 10 0		195
3 10 4	—	24 0 0	6 6 6	4 8 8	10 0 0	*14 8 8		196
8 11 4	—	23 0 0	4 8 0	—	—	—		197
1 14 4	—	30 0 0	6 6 0	9 8 9	—	9 8 9		198
1 9 8	—	24 0 0	8 1 0	5 3 0	—	5 3 0		199
—	—	30 0 0	8 8 0	1 5 7	5 0 0	6 5 7		200
6 5 9	—	57 8 8	27 18 0	8 7 8	25 0 0	33 7 8		201
8 15 8	—	35 0 0	7 19 0	15 0 8	—	15 0 8		202
1 8 8	—	30 8 0	6 6 8	7 18 9	—	7 18 0		203
8 0 0	—	35 6 8	25 8 0	25 0 7	—	25 0 7		204
9 15 8	—	44 0 0	12 1 8	3 0 1	4 0 0	*7 0 1		205
—	—	—	—	—	—	—		
6 1 1	—	58 10 8	10 18 6	18 14 11	—	18 14 11	V.C.	206
3 14 10	—	24 0 0	4 2 4	8 14 8	—	8 14 8		207
4 2 8	—	35 0 0	8 18 0	8 17 7	—	8 17 7		208
8 11 8	—	39 15 0	16 4 0	14 8 8	—	14 8 8		209
8 3 0	—	32 0 0	13 15 6	15 7 11	—	15 7 11	V.P.	210
9 16 7	—	30 0 0	10 7 0	8 10 3	—	8 10 3		211
2 4 4	—	45 18 4	8 0 0	8 18 8	—	8 18 8		212
8 11 5	—	22 8 0	16 18 0	8 5 1	—	8 5 1		213
15 8 7	—	32 8 4	48 8 5	45 8 8	—	45 8 0		214
1 8 8	—	30 0 0	6 19 0	8 1 11	—	8 1 11	V.C.	215
—	—	33 16 8	18 18 6	9 14 6	—	9 14 6		216
8 0 8	—	38 1 8	18 8 0	8 13 0	—	8 13 0		217
2 19 1	—	30 8 5	18 15 5	7 4 0	1 5 0	8 9 0		218
	—		25 8 6	10 10 10	—	10 10 10		219
7 8 8	—	34 0 0	6 7 6	0 19 0	—	0 19 0		

Including value of Free Residence and Garden.

* Including value of Free Garden.

List of Schools in operation on the 31st December, 1874.—

Number.	Roll Number of School.	Parish.	District.	School.	Religious Denomination of Manager or Correspondent: Clerical.	Religious Denomination of Manager or Correspondent: Lay.	Number and Religious Denominations of Teachers: Principals.	Number and Religious Denominations of Teachers: Assistants.	Attendances for the Year. Total number of Pupils on Rolls within the Year 1874: Males.	Fem.	Total.	Average Daily Attendance for the Year 1874.
220	6160	Drumaul,	4	Caddy, . . day.	–	Pres.	Pres.	–	60	71	131	46
				Do. . . evg.	–	–	Pres.	–	31	24	55	62
221	6032	Do.	–	Groggan, . . day.	Pres.	–	Pres.	–	77	59	130	55
				Do.[a] . . evg.	–	–	–	–	–	–	–	–
222	47	Drumbeg,	9	Dunmurry, . . m.	–	Pres.	Pres.	Pres.	174	–	174	80
223	4714	Do.	–	Do., . . f.	–	Pres.	Pres.	Pres.	–	142	142	57
224	6418	Do.	–	Ballyfinaghy,	R.C.	–	R.C.	–	43	66	109	62
225	44	Dunaghy,	6	Glenravel,	R.C.	–	R.C.	R.C.	129	127	256	79
226	4144	Do.	–	Ballylessy,	Pres.	–	Pres.	–	50	31	81	30
227	4025	Do.	–	Caraboy,	Pres.	–	Pres.	–	69	50	119	48
228	7822	Do.	–	Tullaghans,	Pres.	–	Pres.	Pres.	104	76	180	65
229	9219	Do.	–	Lisnavallaghan,	Pres.	–	Pres.	–	92	74	166	45
230	9522	Do.	–	Killyree,	–	Pres.	Pres.	Pres.	73	87	160	65
231	10526	Do.	–	Dunaghy, parochial,	E.C.	–	E.C.	–	65	46	111	43
232	7699	Grange of Dundermot,	–	Frocess,	Pres.	–	Pres.	Pres.	71	76	147	56
233	49	Duneane,	–	Moneynick,	R.C.	–	R.C.	R.C.	76	92	168	78
234	1632	Do.	–	Creggan,	R.C.	–	R.C.	R.C.	63	45	108	54
235	10745	Do.	–	Gallagh,	R.C.	–	R.C.	R.C.	87	82	169	64
236	6420	Do.	–	Ballynamullan,	R.C.	–	R.C.	R.C.	83	67	150	62
237	7032	Do.	–	Duneane,	Pres.	–	Pres.	–	37	27	64	22
238	8113	Do.	–	Do. parochial,	E.C.	–	E.C.	–	50	43	93	39
239	8073	Do.	–	Staffordstown, . day,	Pres.	–	Pres.	–	41	32	73	33
				Do.[a] . . evg.	–	–	–	–	–	–	–	–
240	11009	Do.	–	Mulorn,	R.C.	–	R.C.	R.C.	59	50	111	48
241	2331	Dunluce,	8	Ballytober,	Pres.	–	Pres.	Pres.	98	69	167	56
242	2864	Do.	–	Kilmoyle,	–	E.C.	Pres.	–	51	61	112	58
243	3022	Do.	–	Seneirl,	Pres.	–	Pres.	Pres.	88	67	155	47
244	6917	Do.	–	Ballyhome,	Pres.	–	Pres.	–	58	69	127	53
245	7588	Do.	–	Ballymagarry,	Pres.	–	Pres.	–	29	45	74	30
246	10201	Do.	–	Dunluce,	E.C.	–	E.C.	E.C.	77	73	150	46
247	1088	Finvoy,	7	Dunloy, . . m.	R.C.	–	R.C.	–	119	–	119	57
248	11151	Do.	–	Do. . . f.	R.C.	–	R.C.	–	–	118	118	60
249	4282	Do.	–	Caldanagh,	E.C.	–	Pres.	–	91	70	161	62
250	6277	Do.	–	Eden,	Pres.	–	Pres.	–	64	64	108	57
251	6583	Do.	–	Carrowreagh,	Pres.	–	Pres.	–	41	51	92	30
252	10148	Do.	–	Lisheegan,	Pres.	–	Pres.	–	80	57	137	55
253	10201	Do.	–	Tow,	–	E.C.	Pres.	E.C.	70	75	151	58
254	2578	Glenavy,	11	Ballymacricket, m.	E.C.	–	E.C.	–	77	–	77	58
255	7671	Do.	–	Do. . . f.	E.C.	–	E.C.	–	–	91	91	22
256	10965	Do.	–	Sandholes,	–	E.C.	E.C.	–	40	53	93	32
257	2578	Glenwhirry,	6	Clatteryknowes,	–	Pres.	Pres.	–	44	44	88	30
258	11076	Do.	–	Craigs,	–	Pres.	Pres.	–	67	49	116	44
259	4507	Do.	–	Lowtown,	–	Pres.	Pres.	–	51	56	107	44
260	55	Glynn,	5	Glynn Village,	–	E.C.	Pres.	Pres.	50	70	120	67
261	81	Do.	–	Mounthill,	Pres.	–	Pres.	–	38	44	82	35
262	62	Do.	–	Mullaghsandall,	Pres.	–	Pres.	Pres.	102	92	194	70
263	10810	Hannahstown,	9	Hannahstown,	R.C.	–	R.C.	R.C.	73	67	140	61
264	60	Inver,	5	Ballysnod,	Pres.	–	Pres.	Pres.	81	57	138	64
265	8531	Inver,	–	Larne and Inver,	Pres.	–	Two {Pres. R.C.}		164	90	253	108
266	1042	Island Magee,	–	Mullaghboy,	Pres.	–	Pres.	–	52	41	93	34
267	2137	Do.	–	Mullaghdubh,	Pres.	–	Pres.	Pres.	101	75	176	65
268	8202	Do.	–	Brownsbay,	Pres.	–	Pres.	–	63	38	101	39
269	7613	Do.	–	Lower Kilcoan, f.	Pres.	–	Pres.	Pres.	–	114	114	56
270	8812	Do.	–	Ballymoney, No. 2,	Diss.	–	Diss.	Diss.	66	45	111	51
271	9073	Kilbride,	6	Ballyvoy,	–	Pres.	Pres.	–	73	35	108	39
272	4054	Do.	–	Kilbride,	Pres.	–	Pres.	–	78	52	130	47
273	4170	Do.	–	Newmill,	–	Pres.	Pres.	–	37	33	70	23
274	6219	Killagan,	4	Drumadoon,	R.C.	–	Pres.	–	66	76	142	62
275	61	Killead,	11	Carmavy,[a]	Pres.	–	–	–	–	–	–	–
276	62	Do.	–	Straidhavern,	Pres.	–	Pres.	–	42	40	82	31
277	64	Do.	–	Ballyquillan,[a]	R.C.	–	–	–	–	–	–	–

[a] Closed. [b] Including value of Free Residence. [c] Including value of Free Residence and Garden.

Province of Ulster: County of Antrim—*continued.*

Amount paid for Books, Requisites, and Apparatus at reduced Prices.	Aid granted by the Board during the Year 1874. In Free Stock of Books, Requisites, and Apparatus.	In Salaries, Premiums, and other Gratuities.	Results Fees, Financial Year.	Amount of Local Emoluments received in Aid of Teacher's Salary. School Fees.	Subscriptions, Endowments, &c.	Total Local Aid.	Vested or Non-Vested.	Number.
£ s. d.	£ s. d.	£ s. d.	£ s. d.	£ s. d.	£ s. d.	£ s. d.		
} 6 19 3	—	44 16 4	{ 21 16 5	7 18 5	—	7 13 5		[illegible]
			0 5 0	0 14 0	—	0 14 0		
9 14 9	—	27 11 8	4 18 0	1 17 0	—	1 17 0		[illegible]
—	—	—	—	—	—	—		
5 13 8	—	62 16 8	25 7 0	17 19 5	—	17 17 5		[illegible]
6 8 6	—	62 0 0	16 7 0	7 9 6	5 0 0	b 12 9 6		[illegible]
2 14 0	—	44 10 0	20 8 0	14 3 0	—	14 3 0		[illegible]
8 10 10	—	44 0 0	10 18 6	18 5 9	—	18 5 9	[illegible]	[illegible]
1 11 0	—	14 0 0	4 9 0	5 8 0	—	5 8 0		[illegible]
2 7 4	—	40 0 0	10 11 0	6 3 4	—	6 3 4		[illegible]
0 1 8	—	51 10 0	16 11 0	9 18 9	—	9 18 9		[illegible]
9 13 0	—	24 0 0	5 10 6	8 10 2	—	8 10 2		[illegible]
8 12 10	—	64 0 0	21 11 6	16 14 7	—	16 14 7		[illegible]
—	—	—	11 18 0	8 17 2	9 10 0	* 18 7 2		231
6 4 8	—	63 10 0	16 6 0	0 0 11	—	0 0 11		[illegible]
6 17 5	—	62 3 4	18 14 0	5 10 0	—	5 10 0		[illegible]
1 18 7	—	62 0 0	23 6 0	6 6 11	—	6 6 11	[illegible]	[illegible]
1 14 6	—	48 10 0	21 0 0	3 15 6	—	3 15 6		[illegible]
1 6 4	—	41 10 0	12 12 0	4 2 6	—	4 2 6		[illegible]
8 6 0	—	19 11 8	4 18 6	6 9 0	—	6 9 0		[illegible]
1 7 11	—	30 0 0	7 18 6	1 16 10	2 0 0	b 3 16 10		[illegible]
1 8 3	—	27 10 0	6 14 6	1 6 0	—	1 6 0		[illegible]
—	—	—	—	—	—	—		
8 10 10	—	37 11 6	10 1 3	2 1 1	—	2 1 1		[illegible]
0 11 9	—	61 8 4	18 18 0	6 12 8	19 14 9	* 27 6 5		[illegible]
0 7 6	—	20 0 0	11 3 0	6 0 0	—	6 0 0		[illegible]
5 16 11	—	65 6 4	18 18 0	6 10 0	—	6 10 0	[illegible]	[illegible]
3 7 6	—	24 0 0	7 4 0	6 18 6	—	6 18 6	[illegible]	[illegible]
—	—	25 6 0	8 18 0	8 11 5	—	8 11 5		[illegible]
6 1 7	—	40 0 0	9 2 0	8 0 0	13 0 0	21 0 0		[illegible]
0 8 1	—	15 9 3	11 11 6	4 0 10	—	4 0 10		[illegible]
8 8 7	4 16 0	10 0 0	9 2 6	4 6 0	—	4 6 0		[illegible]
1 5 8	—	24 0 0	6 7 0	8 17 6	—	8 17 6		[illegible]
3 3 1	—	20 0 0	18 8 0	6 13 10	—	6 13 10		[illegible]
1 6 2	—	60 0 0	13 16 6	4 11 8	7 0 0	* 11 11 8		[illegible]
2 6 0	—	24 0 0	11 10 0	4 12 0	10 0 0	14 12 0		[illegible]
8 12 0	—	44 0 0	17 2 0	0 4 6	6 2 6	a 6 7 0		[illegible]
7 19 0	—	61 6 0	11 11 0	7 10 1	—	7 10 1		[illegible]
8 11 4	—	20 0 0	7 7 0	6 4 8	—	6 4 8		[illegible]
8 10 1	—	26 13 4	10 2 6	0 17 8	10 0 0	b 10 17 8		[illegible]
1 18 11	—	19 10 0	3 3 0	6 0 2	—	6 0 2		[illegible]
5 1 7	4 10 0	19 10 0	11 3 0	6 0 4	—	6 0 4		[illegible]
4 11 0	—	24 0 0	13 13 0	9 0 0	—	9 0 0		[illegible]
6 10 6	—	57 10 0	19 14 6	18 17 11	—	18 17 11		[illegible]
—	—	24 0 0	7 7 0	5 0 0	3 0 0	8 0 0		[illegible]
6 11 2	—	35 10 0	25 0 0	16 0 0	5 0 0	16 0 0		[illegible]
6 11 0	—	66 18 6	26 10 0	24 9 0	—	24 9 0		[illegible]
4 16 10	—	52 0 0	26 18 0	12 14 0	—	12 14 0		[illegible]
8 6 6	—	90 16 10	26 17 6	63 16 10	—	63 16 10		[illegible]
1 11 10	—	48 0 0	10 0 0	10 18 0	—	10 18 0		[illegible]
2 8 2	—	63 16 4	27 16 0	24 4 2	—	24 4 2		[illegible]
8 14 0	—	57 6 4	6 1 0	22 0 0	—	22 0 0		[illegible]
6 17 2	—	64 0 0	22 11 0	16 0 6	—	16 0 6		[illegible]
8 1 11	—	50 10 0	20 6 6	18 14 6	9 0 0	b 27 14 6		[illegible]
1 16 6	—	28 6 6	0 1 6	6 16 0	—	6 16 0		[illegible]
10 12 11	—	28 0 0	11 7 0	0 12 8	—	0 12 8		[illegible]
8 2 10	—	24 0 0	5 8 6	5 8 7	—	5 8 7		[illegible]
1 6 10	—	6 10 0	—	9 4 6	—	9 4 6		[illegible]
—	—	—	—	—	—	—		[illegible]
2 9 11	—	24 0 0	6 0 6	6 8 7	—	3 [illegible] 1		[illegible]
0 18 9	—	—	—	—	—	—		277

a Including value of Free Garden. * Inoperative.

List of Schools in operation on the 31st December, 1874.—

Number.	Roll Number of School.	Parish.	District.	School.	Religious Denomination of Manager or Correspondents: Clerical.	Lay.	Number and Religious Denomination of Teachers: Principals.	Assistants.	Attendance for the Year: Total number of Pupils on Rolls within the Year 1874: Males.	Fem.	Total.	Average Daily Attendance for Year 1874.
278	1948	Killead,	11	Gortnagallon,	–	Pres.	R.C.	–	38	28	66	26
279	5792	Do.	–	Ballyrobin,	–	Pres.	Pres.	Pres.	63	56	119	44
280	6252	Do.	–	Mount Cariage,	–	E.C.	Pres.	Pres.	89	63	152	71
281	8816	Do.	–	Diamond,	–	Pres.	Pres.	–	37	28	65	29
282	8496	Do.	–	Killead,	Pres.	–	Pres.	–	34	26	60	19
283	10942	Do.	–	Loanends,[b]	Pres.	–	Pres.	–	–	–	–	–
284	11119	Do.	–	Seacash,	E.C.	–	E.C.	–	30	21	51	20
285	8178	Grange of Killyglen,	6	Killyglen,	Pres.	–	Pres.	Pres.	53	57	110	42
286	8608	Kilraghts,	5	Ganaby,	Pres.	–	Pres.	–	19	65	84	37
287	5218	Do.	–	Ballymacquillan,	Pres.	–	Pres.	Pres.	72	70	142	51
288	17606	Do.	–	Kilraughts,	Pres.	–	Pres.	–	43	44	87	33
289	1843	Kilroot,	6	Kilroot, day,	–	E.C.	Pres.	Pres.	88	95	183	54
				Do. evg.,	–	–	–	–	53	23	76	27
290	56	Kilwaughter,	–	Craiginorne,	Pres.	–	Pres.	Pres.	67	59	126	50
291	55	Do.	–	Kilwaughter, m.	Pres.	–	Pres.	–	116	–	116	45
292	7779	Do.	–	Do. f.	Pres.	–	Pres.	–	–	101	101	40
293	7677	Do.	–	Mullaghsandal,	E.C.	–	E.C.	–	54	48	102	38
294	66	Kirkinriola,	4	Clinty,	–	E.C.	Pres.	Pres.	73	71	144	60
295	2276	Do.	–	Monaghan,	Pres.	–	Pres.	–	44	67	111	24
296	2046	Do.	–	Parade,	Pres.	–	Pres.	–	86	55	141	49
297	[illegible]	Do.	–	Craigywarren, Upper,	–	Pres.	Pres.	–	37	51	88	33
298	[illegible]	Do.	–	Guy's, m.	Pres.	–	Pres.	Pres.	229	–	229	119
299	7707	Do.	–	Do. f.	–	Pres.	Pres.	Pres.	–	108	108	44
300	[illegible]	Do.	–	Do. i.	–	Pres.	Pres.	Pres.	110	151	261	91
301	[illegible]	Do.	–	Carnlea,	Pres.	–	Pres.	Pres.	119	103	222	60
302	[illegible]	Do.	–	Castlestreet,	Dis.	–	Dis.	–	83	44	126	19
303	[illegible]	Do.	–	Ballymena, f.	R.C.	–	R.C.	–	–	118	118	53
304	6542	Do.	–	Do. Workhouse,	P.L.	Gds.	Pres. / Pres.	–	65	101	166	77
305	[illegible]	Larne,	6	Larne 1st (Glass Agr.	Pres.	–	Pres.	Pres.	148	–	148	70
306	[illegible]	Do.	–	Do. f.	Pres.	–	Pres.	–	–	73	73	27
307	[illegible]	Do.	–	Do. i.	Pres.	–	R.C.	–	47	37	84	36
308	[illegible]	Do.	–	Do. No. 2,	Pres.	–	Pres.	Pres.	45	88	133	60
309	[illegible]	Do.	–	Do. Workhouse,[a]	P.L.	Gds.	–	–	–	–	–	–
310	[illegible]	Do.	–	North End, Larne, m.	R.C.	–	R.C.	R.C.	116	–	116	67
311	[illegible]	Do.	–	Do. f.	R.C.	–	R.C.	R.C.	–	132	132	69
312	[illegible]	Layd,	4	Kilmore,	R.C.	–	R.C.	–	29	37	66	27
313	[illegible]	Do.	–	Cushendall, m.	R.C.	–	R.C.	–	161	–	161	63
314	[illegible]	Do.	–	Do. f.	R.C.	–	R.C.	–	–	169	169	68
315	[illegible]	Do.	–	Knocknacarry, m.	R.C.	–	R.C.	–	143	–	143	41
316	[illegible]	Do.	–	Do. f.	R.C.	–	R.C.	–	–	107	107	33
317	[illegible]	Do.	–	Glenaan,	R.C.	–	R.C.	–	89	51	140	36
318	78	Loughguile,	3	Magherahoney,	R.C.	–	R.C.	–	[illegible]	63	94	26
319	77	Do.	–	Carroweeris,	–	Pres.	R.C.	–	68	56	124	32
320	[illegible]	Do.	–	Loughguile, m.	R.C.	–	R.C.	–	111	–	111	39
321	[illegible]	Do.	–	Do. f.	R.C.	–	R.C.	–	–	123	123	50
322	[illegible]	Do.	–	[illegible]	Pres.	–	Pres.	–	52	19	71	27
323	[illegible]	Do.	–	[illegible]	Pres.	–	Pres.	–	84	36	120	44
324	[illegible]	Do.	–	[illegible]	Pres.	–	Pres.	Pres.	97	68	165	47
325	7597	Do.	–	Ballypersagh,	Pres.	–	Pres.	–	59	54	113	37
326	[illegible]	Do.	–	Ballyweaney,	Pres.	–	Pres.	–	69	51	120	35
327	[illegible]	Do.	–	Corkey,	–	R.C.	R.C.	R.C.	73	61	134	44
328	78	Magheragall,	11	Ballycarrickmaddy,	–	Pres.	Pres.	Pres.	90	61	151	61
329	1914	Do.	–	Sheepwalk,	–	Dis.	E.C.	–	63	46	109	34
330	10419	Do.	–	Mullaghcarton,	–	Dis.	E.C.	–	34	50	84	36
331	60	Magheramesk,	–	Maghaberry,	–	E.C.	Pres.	–	67	36	103	36
332	6782	Muckamore, Grange of,	9	Oldstone,	Pres.	–	Pres.	–	22	28	50	25
333	10269	Do.	–	Muckamore,	Pres.	–	Pres.	–	40	68	108	47
334	[illegible]	Newtown Crommelin,	4	Newtown Crommelin,	Pres.	–	Pres.	–	93	78	171	49
335	9049	Grange of Nilteen,	9	[illegible]	Pres.	–	Pres.	Pres.	83	78	161	70

a Including value of Free Residence.

b Returns not available.

Province of Ulster : County of Antrim—*continued.*

Amount paid for Books, Requisites, and Apparatus at Reduced Prices.	Aid granted by the Board during the Year 1874. In Free Stock of Books, Requisites, and Apparatus.	In Salaries, Premiums, and other Gratuities.	Results Fees, Financial Year.	Amount of Local Endowments received in Aid of Teacher's Salary. School Fees.	Subscriptions, Endowments, &c.	Total Local Aid.	Vested or Non-Vested.	Number.
£ s. d.	£ s. d.	£ s. d.	£ s. d.	£ s. d.	£ s. d.	£ s. d.		
1 6 8	—	21 0 0	6 11 0	9 5 1	—	9 5 1		278
1 7 10	—	77 6 4	11 6 6	8 18 8	20 0 0	28 18 8		279
7 0 0	—	93 10 0	25 4 0	11 18 0	6 0 0	[a] 20 12 0		280
1 0 4	—	26 0 0	0 0 6	8 10 1	6 0 0	[a] 14 10 1		281
0 12 0	—	24 0 0	8 4 6	6 1 9	—	6 1 9		282
—	—	24 5 0	22 16 0	—	—	—		283
1 5 3	4 0 0	19 6 8	8 9 0	8 18 4	10 0 0	18 18 4		284
10 9 8	—	55 0 0	8 18 2	8 18 8	8 0 0	16 18 8		285
1 9 7	—	24 0 0	8 16 6	10 6 0	—	10 6 0		286
4 7 8	—	44 0 0	15 2 6	9 19 0	—	9 19 9		287
1 16 11	—	20 0 0	8 6 6	10 0 0	—	10 0 0		288
—	—	72 11 4	27 16 0	17 19 6	—	17 19 6	A.	289
7 4 10	—		16 1 0	4 1 6	—	4 1 5		
6 14 6	—	47 0 0	9 7 6	12 18 0	—	12 18 0		290
1 5 5	—	24 0 0	6 4 6	5 0 0	2 0 0	7 0 0		291
4 12 10	—	24 0 0	8 0 8	8 17 0	2 0 0	10 17 0	V.T.	292
0 10 2	—	31 0 0	4 2 6	2 12 0	—	2 12 0		293
5 10 0	—	33 6 4	16 3 6	6 12 0	—	6 12 0		294
5 0 10	—	30 15 6	7 16 0	6 5 6	—	6 5 6		295
2 0 11	2 6 7	35 0 0	11 19 0	6 11 5	—	6 11 5		296
2 6 2	—	20 0 0	7 14 6	6 16 0	—	6 10 6		297
15 10 0	—	67 18 4	43 6 0	—	46 10 0	[a] 46 10 0		298
6 0 7	—	10 0 0	17 11 0	—	30 18 0	[a] 30 18 0		299
0 11 4	—	75 0 0	16 2 0	—	25 0 0	[a] 25 0 0		300
—	—	60 0 0	13 17 0	9 0 5	—	9 0 5		301
5 6 6	—	40 13 4	4 11 0	7 6 0	22 0 0	[a] 30 0 0		302
2 18 0	1 0 0	30 0 0	6 10 6	1 0 5	—	1 0 5		303
2 16 11	—	7 0 0	—	—	—	—		304
6 1 11	—	83 16 8	24 17 0	24 17 6	7 0 0	[a] 31 17 6	V.S.	305
3 19 0	—	55 10 0	14 18 0	10 7 6	7 0 0	[a] 17 7 6	V.T.	306
2 10 0	—	82 18 6	7 19 0	4 0 4	6 0 0	[a] 10 0 4	V.T.	307
1 0 0	—	47 13 4	8 17 6	0 16 2	—	0 16 2		308
6 15 3	—	9 0 0	—	—	—	—		309
0 2 7	—	60 0 8	18 17 6	16 12 9	—	16 12 9		310
4 6 5	—	43 10 0	22 16 0	11 8 4	—	11 8 4		311
1 10 0	—	20 0 0	2 14 6	2 18 0	—	2 18 0	A.	312
1 5 6	—	24 0 0	5 14 3	4 10 0	—	4 10 0		313
5 6 5	—	22 10 0	10 10 0	1 19 7	—	1 19 7		314
1 9 0	—	45 13 4	3 16 0	3 6 1	—	3 6 1	V.G.	315
1 6 0	—	20 0 0	7 1 0	6 6 0	—	6 6 0	V.C.	316
1 6 4	—	25 0 0	11 1 0	6 17 7	—	6 17 7		317
2 16 2	—	17 0 6	4 6 6	0 6 2	—	0 6 2		318
1 10 6	—	21 0 0	4 12 6	6 6 6	—	6 6 6		319
1 10 3	—	54 6 8	5 19 0	6 6 0	—	6 6 0	V.T.	320
6 1 7	—	49 6 8	5 6 6	6 15 0	6 0 0	12 15 0	V.T.	321
2 0 9	—	24 0 0	3 14 0	6 0 6	—	6 0 6		322
2 0 4	—	59 0 0	16 7 6	12 6 0	4 0 0	[b] 16 6 0		323
2 12 0	—	50 18 4	6 9 0	15 0 0	—	15 0 0		324
2 9 6	—	30 0 0	6 14 6	9 4 6	—	9 4 6		325
—	—	24 0 0	6 4 6	6 11 6	—	6 11 6		326
2 18 4	—	44 0 0	10 11 6	5 10 6	—	5 10 6		327
6 11 1	—	46 0 0	19 18 6	22 18 6	—	22 18 6		328
3 15 6	—	50 0 0	6 15 0	7 10 0	—	7 10 0		329
1 7 5	—	21 15 0	9 10 6	7 12 4	—	7 12 4		330
2 11 1	—	23 0 0	7 18 11	5 3 1	—	5 3 1		331
2 10 2	—	20 0 0	5 8 0	1 9 7	—	1 9 7		332
5 4 10	—	24 0 0	18 5 0	10 18 8	—	10 18 8		333
5 6 5	—	22 0 0	10 14 8	10 10 10	—	10 10 10		334
1 16 1	—	29 0 0	25 11 6	12 10 0	—	12 10 0		335

[a] No Return.

[b] Including value of Free Residence and Garden.

List of Schools in operation on the 31st December 1874.—

Number.	Roll Number of School.	Parish.	District.	School.	Religious Denominations of Managers or Correspondents. Clerical.	Lay.	Principal and Religious Denominations of Teachers. Principals.	Assistants.	Attendance for the Year. Total number of Pupils on Rolls within the Year 1874. Males.	Females.	Total.	Average attendance
336	4030	Grange of Nilteen,	9	Islandbane,	Pres.	–	Pres.	–	43	56	99	20
337	5996	Do.	–	Dunadry,	–	Pres.	Pres.	–	57	83	76	45
338	6316	Portglenone,	1	Cunnaughliggor,	Pres.	–	Pres.	–	71	45	116	46
339	2501	Rasavas,	4	Burkna,	Pres.	–	Pres.	–	107	88	195	61
340	2933	Do.	–	Rasavas,	Pres.	–	Pres.	–	88	82	148	68
341	5568	Do.	–	Lisnamurrikin,	Pres.	–	Pres.	Pres.	113	114	226	76
342	8768	Do.	–	Broughshane, m.	Pres.	–	Pres.	–	135	20	155	41
343	8078	Do.	–	Do. f.	Pres.	–	Pres.	Pres.	–	164	164	80
344	2968	Do.	–	Upper Buckna,	Pres.	–	Pres.	–	76	70	146	44
345	63	Raloo,	5	Tureagh,	Pres.	–	Pres.	Pres.	78	74	152	56
346	65	Do.	–	Ballyvallagh,	Pres.	–	Pres.	Diss.	68	61	120	53
347	66	Do.	–	Loughmourne, No. 2,	Pres.	–	Pres.	–	41	34	75	33
348	8261	Do.	–	Ballyrickardmore,	Pres.	–	Pres.	–	51	46	97	46
349	8264	Do.	–	Ballyrickardbeg,[a]	Pres.	–	–	–	–	–	–	–
350	7378	Do.	–	Glenoe,	–	Pres.	R.C.	Pres.	77	87	164	70
351	1042	Rasharkin,	8	Moyarget,	–	R.C.	R.C.	–	67	28	95	35
352	8462	Do.	–	Cloghanmurray,	–	R.C.	Pres.	–	57	46	103	35
353	8915	Do.	–	Ballycastle, m.	R.C.	–	R.C.	–	119	–	119	56
354	8934	Do.	–	Do. f.	R.C.	–	R.C.	–	–	128	128	45
355	3657	Do.	–	Do. Workhouse,	P.L.	Gds.	Pres.	–	20	21	41	19
356	2942	Do.	–	Ramoan,	R.C.	–	R.C.	–	83	80	163	42
357	8315	Rasharkin,	7	Dunminning,	–	R.C.	Pres.	–	73	65	148	52
358	2388	Do.	–	Ballymaconnelly,	Pres.	–	Pres.	–	86	60	146	47
359	8091	Do.	–	Dromore,	Pres.	–	Pres.	–	44	56	100	31
360	8624	Do.	–	Rasharkin,	Pres.	–	Pres.	–	89	68	156	55
361	4686	Do.	–	Carclinty,	–	Pres.	Pres.	–	59	76	135	41
362	7406	Do.	–	Tamlaght,	R.C.	–	R.C.	R.C.	68	56	125	49
363	7804	Do.	–	Bellaghy,	–	Pres.	Pres.	Pres.	105	118	223	84
364	8141	Do.	–	Crankybracken,	–	Pres.	Pres.	–	79	75	155	60
365	3628	Rashee,	6	Ballyeaston,	–	Pres.	Pres.	–	61	86	147	35
366	6876	Rathlin,	3	Rathlin Island, m.	–	R.C.	Pres.	–	37	56	93	33
367	6182	Do.	–	Do.[a] f.	–	R.C.	–	–	–	–	–	–
368	6946	Shankill,	8	Belfast Dist. Model, m. day,	Com.	N.S.	Pres.	3 Pres. 1 R.C. 3 Diss. 1 E.C.	1,036	–	1,036	538
				Do.[a] evg.	–	–	–	–	–	–	–	–
369	6954	Do.	–	Do. f.	Com.	N.S.	E.C.	1 R.C. 1 E.C. 2 Diss. 2 Pres.	–	603	603	301
370	6960	Do.	–	Do. i.	Com.	N.S.	E.C.	1 R.C. 1 Pres. 1 E.C.	230	173	403	162
371	6967	Do.	–	Do. 1st Class Agr.[a]	Com.	N.S.	–	–	–	–	–	–
372	8548	Do.	–	Do. Workhouse,	P.L.	Gds.	6 Pres.	4 Pres. 1 R.C.	392	273	665	329
373	7036	Do.	8	Crumlin-rd. Conv. f. day,	–	R.C.	Nuns.		–	626	626	341
				Do. evg.	–	R.C.	Nuns.		–	514	514	164
374	9036	Do.	8	Hamilton-st. Conv. day,	–	R.C.	Nuns.		83	453	536	228
				Do. evg.	–	–	Nuns.		–	186	186	60
375	16	Do.	–	Upper Falls,	–	R.C.	R.C.	R.C.	107	63	160	34
376	14	Do.	6	Lagmall, No. 1,	Pres.	–	Pres.	Pres.	81	75	156	77
				Do. evg.	Pres.	–	Pres.	–	84	–	84	35
377	62	Do.	–	Highstown,	Pres.	–	Pres.	Pres.	53	65	118	44
378	1824	Do.	–	Edenderry,	–	Pres.	Pres.	Pres.	207	123	330	118
379	2592	Do.	8	Fountain-street, f.	Pres.	–	Pres.	Diss.	–	175	175	63
380	2675	Do.	–	Townsend-street,	Pres.	–	2 Pres.	Pres. E.C.	148	130	278	109
381	9770	Do.	8	Cavehill Railway,	–	Pres.	Pres.	–	48	46	89	50
382	9221	Do.	8	Eliza-street, m. day,	R.C.	–	R.C.	3 R.C.	411	–	411	194
				Do. evg.	R.C.	–	R.C.	–	94	–	94	27
383	9627	Do.	8	North River,	Pres.	–	Pres.	Pres.	80	46	87	34
384	9091	Do.	8	Victoria-place, day,	Pres.	–	2 Pres.	1 R.C. 1 Pres. 1 Pres.	403	243	646	259
				Do. evg.	–	–	2 Pres.	Pres.	174	80	254	49

[a] No return.

[b] Including value of Free Residence and Garden.

[c] Including value of Free Residence.

Province of Ulster: County of Antrim—*continued.*

Amount paid for Books, Requisites, and Apparatus, at Reduced Prices.	Aid granted by the Board during the Year 1874: In Free Stock of Books, Requisites, and Apparatus.	In Salaries, Premiums, and other Emoluments.	Results Fees, Practical Fees.	Amount of Local Emoluments received in Aid of Teacher's Salary: School Fees.	Subscriptions, Endowments, &c.	Total Local Aid.	Vested or Non-Vested.	Number.
£ s. d.	£ s. d.	£ s. d.	£ s. d.	£ s. d.	£ s. d.	£ s. d.		
9 9 11	—	21 0 0	4 19 6	8 1 0	—	8 1 0		336
0 14 6	—	80 0 0	6 8 8	5 0 0	—	5 0 0		337
8 12 10	—	24 0 0	14 6 6	10 10 11	—	10 16 11		338
6 2 6	—	46 18 4	12 0 4	6 8 9	—	6 8 0		339
1 7 10	—	39 8 4	8 14 8	10 4 7	—	10 4 9		340
4 10 1	—	49 0 0	15 9 9	18 14 0	—	18 14 0		341
2 12 6	—	37 8 4	8 10 6	5 16 2	—	5 16 2		342
10 8 8	—	35 0 0	23 4 8	11 15 0	—	11 14 0		343
8 0 0	—	24 16 8	13 3 0	5 9 11	—	5 9 11		344
5 10 5	—	53 10 0	6 19 0	6 18 4	—	6 18 4		345
0 8 0	—	44 0 0	11 17 8	7 8 10	—	7 8 10		346
2 17 0	—	24 0 0	4 6 8	1 4 0	—	1 4 0		347
3 16 8	—	44 0 0	10 17 0	6 12 6	—	6 12 6	A.	348
1 10 4	—	30 15 0	5 11 0	—	—	—		349
14 1 0	—	44 0 0	28 12 0	11 14 6	—	11 14 6		350
1 1 8	—	80 0 0	8 10 6	8 15 0	—	8 15 0		351
8 15 0	—	80 0 0	6 10 0	7 8 8	6 0 0	b13 6 8		352
1 5 0	—	22 13 4	7 13 0	10 19 3	—	10 19 3		353
8 17 0	—	26 0 0	10 10 0	4 15 8	1 0 0	5 15 8		354
3 18 0	—	—	—	—	—	—		355
6 0 1	—	29 5 0	10 6 0	12 10 4	10 7 0	22 6 4		356
9 8 0	—	32 0 0	13 17 6	14 18 10	—	14 18 10		357
1 6 8	—	21 0 0	11 1 0	7 2 4	—	7 2 4		358
1 12 6	—	34 0 0	5 17 6	4 8 4	—	4 8 4		359
8 8 0	—	31 0 0	7 13 0	4 8 9	—	4 8 9		360
8 9 9	—	21 0 0	13 0 0	7 11 9	—	7 11 0		361
1 12 0	—	46 0 0	0 18 0	2 16 7	—	2 16 7		362
4 18 10	—	44 0 0	18 10 0	11 17 0	—	11 17 0		363
1 19 9	—	21 0 0	14 8 8	4 0 0	—	4 0 0	V.A.	364
2 0 8	—	24 0 0	19 10 0	10 9 4	—	10 9 4	V.E.	365
3 6 4	—	21 0 0	2 10 0	0 14 0	7 0 0	*7 14 0		366
—	—	—	—	—	—	—		367
126 0 0	—						V.G.	368
		2800 18 10	544 14 1	700 17 6	—	700 17 6		
43 0 0	44 5 6						V.G.	369
—	24 15 6						V.C.	370
82 1 7	—	158 16 3	—	—	—	—	V.G.	371
51 10 3	—	11 0 0	—	—	—	—		372
			69 16 0	62 14 0	—	62 14 0		
16 7 10	—	170 6 6	16 8 6	9 17 0	—	0 17 0		373
			24 1 6	41 17 6	—	41 17 0		
11 4 6	—	116 17 4	—	0 8 6	—	0 8 0		374
11 8 2	4 2 2	80 18 6	28 2 0	30 10 1	25 0 0	b55 10 1		375
			18 2 0	84 16 11	2 0 0	*86 16 11	V.E.	
2 17 0	—	68 10 0	10 0 6	18 14 0	—	14 14 0		376
2 10 6	—	44 0 0	12 6 6	10 17 2	—	10 17 2		377
5 4 1	—	98 15 7	24 0 6	48 2 6	10 0 0	58 2 6	A.	378
15 8 0	—	61 0 0	33 17 0	15 0 0	16 0 0	*31 0 0		379
10 14 9	—	160 16 6	56 1 9	62 1 6	—	62 1 6		380
8 5 4	—	40 18 4	10 8 0	11 14 11	—	11 14 11	V.E.	381
			33 18 6	43 19 0	—	43 19 0		
19 15 6	—	122 18 4	7 16 0	7 8 11	—	7 8 11		382
9 0 6	—	45 10 0	8 18 0	15 8 6	—	15 8 6		383
			149 0 0	109 1 7	—	109 1 7		
87 6 2	—	273 17 9	16 15 0	12 10 0	—	12 10 0		384

d Closed last quarter of the year.

* Returns not available.

List of Schools in operation on the 31st December, 1874.—

Number.	Roll Number of School.	Parish.	District.	School.	Religious Denomination of Manager or Correspondent. Clerical.	Lay.	Number and Religious Denomination of Teachers. Principals.	Assistants.	Attendance for the Year. Total number of Pupils on Rolls within the Year 1874. Males.	Fem.	Total.	Average Daily Attendance for the Year 1874.
385	[illegible]	Shankill, . .	6	Kent-street,* . .	Pres.	–	–	–	–	–	–	–
386	[illegible]	Do. . .	–	Frederick-st., No. 1, or Lancasterian Industrial, f.	–	Pres.	Pres.	3 Pres.	84	189	[illegible]	127
387	8777	Do. . .	–	Frederick-street, .	Diss.	–	[illegible]	Diss. R.C. Pres.	247	187	434	163
388	8017	Do. . .	–	Do. No. 2,	–	Pres.	Pres.	3 Pres.	157	150	307	91
389	5785	Do. . .	–	Seamen's Friend Society, . . m.	–	Pres.	Pres.	–	118	–	118	83
390	5194	Do. . .	–	Do. . . f.	–	Pres.	Pres.	2 Pres.	–	271	271	79
391	8519	Do. . .	–	Do. . . i.	–	Pres.	Pres.	Pres.	83	110	193	49
392	6817	Do. . .	6	Conway-street, day,	Pres.	–	2 Pres.	3 Pres.	482	291	773	176
				Do. . . evg.	–	–	Pres.	Pres.	157	107	264	91
393	6894	Do. . .	–	Fountain-lane, i.	Pres.	–	Pres.	R.C. Pres.	130	303	[illegible]	107
394	8402	Do. . .	6	Oldpark, . . .	–	Pres.	Pres.	2 Pres.	164	109	273	87
395	6031	Do. . .	–	Earl-street, m. day,	R.C.	–	R.C.	R.C.	188	–	188	71
				Do. . . evg.	–	–	R.C.	–	83	57	140	24
396	[illegible]	Do. . .	–	Do. . . f.	R.C.	–	R.C.	2 R.C.	–	107	107	38
397	8149	Do. . .	–	Do. . . i.	R.C.	–	R.C.	2 R.C.	173	218	391	130
398	[illegible]	Do. . .	6	Chapel-lane, m. day,	R.C.	–	R.C.	4 R.C.	317	–	317	83
				Do. . . evg.	–	–	R.C.	–	153	–	153	65
399	6096	Do. . .	–	Do. . f. day,	R.C.	–	R.C.	3 R.C.	45	344	389	118
				Do. . . evg.	–	–	R.C.	4 R.C.	–	180	180	66
400	[illegible]	Do. . .	–	Alexander-street, f. day,	R.C.	–	R.C.	4 R.C.	–	731	731	224
				Do. . . evg.	–	–	R.C.	3 R.C.	–	265	265	46
401	7840	Do. . .	–	Milford-street, i.	R.C.	–	R.C.	3 R.C.	243	191	434	165
402	7819	Do. . .	6	Wolf-hill, . day,	R.C.	–	R.C.	R.C.	116	101	217	71
				Do. . . evg.	R.C.	–	R.C.	R.C.	67	73	140	55
403	[illegible]	Do. . .	–	Stanhope-st., m. day,	Pres.	–	R.C.	R.C.	177	–	177	58
				Do.* . . evg.	–	–	–	–	–	–	–	–
404	8186	Do. . .	–	Do. . f. day,	Pres.	–	Pres.	Pres.	–	153	153	61
				Do. . . evg.	–	–	Pres.	–	–	109	109	19
405	[illegible]	Do. . .	–	Do. . . i.	Pres.	–	[illegible]	Diss. R.C.	[illegible]	116	[illegible]	86
406	7123	Do. . .	–	Eglinton-street, .	Pres.	–	[illegible]	Pres. R.C.	[illegible]	310	[illegible]	170
407	[illegible]	Do. . .	–	Union-place, . day.	Pres.	–	Pres.	Pres.	189	74	263	80
				Do.* . . evg.	–	–	–	–	–	–	–	–
408	[illegible]	Do. . .	6	Fisherwick-place, day.	–	Pres.	[illegible]	Pres. R.C.	[illegible]	205	[illegible]	169
				Do. . . evg.	–	–	Pres.	–	–	169	169	23
409	7632	Do. . .	–	Do. . . i.	–	Pres.	Pres.	2 Pres.	150	196	341	103
410	7736	Do. . .	–	Malone, . .	Pres.	–	Pres.	–	80	77	157	45
411	7381	Do. . .	6	North Thomas-st.	Pres.	–	Pres.	Pres.	157	83	240	56
412	8124	Do. . .	–	Do. . . i.	Pres.	–	Pres.	Pres.	108	158	266	81
413	[illegible]	Do. . .	–	Lodge Mill, . day,	–	R.C.	Pres.	Pres.	[illegible]	[illegible]	174	55
				Do. . . evg.	–	–	Pres.	–	118	7	125	33
414	6086	Do. . .	6	Springfield, . .	–	Pres.	R.C.	R.C.	75	106	181	36
415	8121	Do. . .	6	Nelson-street, .	Pres.	–	Pres.	–	73	53	126	55
416	[illegible]	Do. . .	–	Do. . . i.	Pres.	–	Pres.	–	111	108	219	53
417	[illegible]	Do. . .	6	Linen-hall-street, day,	Pres.	–	[illegible]	Pres. R.C.	[illegible]	153	[illegible]	109
				Do. . . evg.	–	–	Pres. R.C.	–	169	–	169	44
418	8316	Do. . .	6	Loguniel, No. 2, .	Diss.	–	[illegible]	R.C. Diss.	145	155	300	74
419	[illegible]	Do. . .	–	Old Lodge-rd., m. day,	Pres.	–	Pres.	Pres.	240	–	240	90
				Do. . . evg.	–	–	Pres.	–	228	–	228	41
420	[illegible]	Do. . .	–	Do. . f. day,	Pres.	–	b Pres.	–	–	197	197	53
				Do.* . . evg.	–	–	–	–	–	–	–	–
421	[illegible]	Do. . .	–	Do. . . i.	Pres.	–	b Pres.	Pres. Diss.	146	154	300	86

* Closed temporarily.

b Including value of Free Residence.

Province of Ulster: County of Antrim—*continued*.

Amount paid for Books, Requisites, and Apparatus at Reduced Prices.	Aid granted by the Board during the Year 1874. In Free Stock of Books, Requisites, and Apparatus.	In Salaries, Premiums, and other Gratuities.	Results Fees, Financial Year.	Amount of Local Emoluments received in Aid of Teacher's Salary. School Fees.	Subscriptions, Endowments, &c.	Total Local Aid.	Vested or Non-Vested.	Number.
£ s. d.	£ s. d.	£ s. d.	£ s. d.	£ s. d.	£ s. d.	£ s. d.		
—	—	10 16 6	—	—	—	—		385
6 9 0	—	—	86 17 6	20 0 0	23 0 0	[a] 43 0 0		386
19 11 0	—	148 0 0	66 14 6	36 1 7	—	38 1 7		387
1 10 6	—	68 10 0	21 6 0	10 18 10	—	10 18 10		388
3 15 8	—	48 10 0	4 18 0	9 1 8	10 0 0	19 1 8		389
1 17 7	—	88 10 8	66 2 6	23 0 5	9 0 0	32 0 5		390
0 10 8	—	47 10 0	9 8 6	6 5 2	5 0 0	11 5 2		391
11 14 10	—	166 8 4	37 2 0	30 8 8	—	30 8 8		392
			26 18 0	10 11 4	—	10 11 4		
1 18 4	—	63 8 4	26 17 0	—	10 0 0	10 0 0		393
9 17 10	—	70 8 4	20 16 6	52 10 0	12 0 0	64 10 0		394
7 8 6	—	65 0 0	14 13 0	23 8 10	—	23 8 10		395
			8 14 6	6 16 6	—	6 14 6		
5 16 6	—	84 8 8	23 1 0	17 3 9	—	17 1 9		396
8 0 8	—	36 7 0	11 11 0	21 9 5	—	21 0 5		397
8 17 0	—	78 0 0	15 11 6	15 18 5	—	15 15 8		398
			11 14 6	5 8 7	—	5 9 7		
6 4 10	—	118 11 8	32 8 6	10 16 8	—	19 10 8		399
			17 14 6	6 3 5	—	6 8 8		
11 0 11	—	204 15 0	44 6 0	55 18 7	—	63 18 7		400
			37 6 6	14 8 1	—	14 8 1		
8 18 4	—	100 5 0	28 5 8	19 17 2	—	18 17 8		401
5 4 8	—	63 10 0	20 12 0	8 8 4	—	8 8 4		402
			16 0 0	5 16 8	—	5 16 8		
0 15 4	—	55 10 0	7 8 8	11 5 1	8 0 0	19 5 1		403
7 0 4	—	82 0 8	20 4 0	21 19 4	10 0 0	31 19 4		404
			0 7 6	8 16 8	—	8 16 8		
9 18 0	—	64 0 0	14 11 0	14 18 4	6 0 0	20 18 4		405
93 5 1	—	187 13 4	78 1 8	108 10 1	—	108 10 1		406
1 8 10	—	57 10 0	11 10 0	17 12 8	—	17 12 8		407
			78 0 0	81 18 8	25 0 0	106 18 8		408
18 4 11	—	166 10 0	—	0 17 4	—	0 17 4		
4 0 1	8 0 0	70 0 0	13 15 0	26 6 1	8 0 0	27 6 1		409
0 18 8	—	90 11 8	8 14 0	7 15 10	—	7 15 10		410
1 10 0	—	61 16 8	6 19 0	13 7 11	—	13 7 11		411
1 14 8	—	86 13 4	17 12 6	20 0 1	—	20 0 1		412
4 12 9	—	65 16 8	18 11 8	81 11 9	9 0 0	[b] 90 11 9		413
			11 9 6	7 18 10	—	7 18 10		
7 12 10	—	65 18 11	26 8 8	84 8 0	10 0 0	94 8 0		414
2 12 8	—	—	8 1 6	8 1 1	—	8 1 1		415
2 11 7	—	—	7 10 8	7 14 0	—	7 14 0		416
34 8 5	—	212 8 8	115 16 0	121 16 8	—	121 16 8		417
			18 10 6	18 6 8	—	18 6 8		
8 4 4	—	83 15 9	86 9 8	62 0 0	—	62 0 0		418
2 15 0	—	59 0 0	28 16 0	29 17 10	—	29 17 10		419
			15 9 0	7 17 7	—	7 17 7		
—	—	45 0 0	15 12 0	18 10 8	—	18 10 8		420
—	—	87 8 4	19 6 6	18 8 7	—	18 8 7		421

[a] Closed.

[b] Inoperative.

List of Schools in operation on the 31st December, 1874.—

Number.	Roll Number of School.	Parish.	District.	School.	Religious Denomination of Managers or Correspondents. Clerical.	Lay.	Number and Religious Denomination of Teachers. Principals.	Assistants.	Attendance for the Year. Total number of Pupils on Rolls within the Year 1874. Males.	Females.	Total.	Average Daily Attendance for the Year 1874.
422	8412	Shankill, . .	9	Campbell's-row, .	–	R.C.	Pres.	2 Pres. 2 R.C.	289	300	[illegible]	180
423	10631	Do. . .	–	Milford Mills, . .	–	R.C.	Pres.	Pres. R.C.	290	239	529	81
424	10816	Do. . .	9	Carrie, . . m.	–	Pres.	Pres.	Pres.	170	–	170	63
425	10819	Do. . .	–	Do. . . f.	–	Pres.	Pres.	–	–	121	121	40
426	10820	Do. . .	–	Do. . . i.	–	Pres.	Pres.	Pres.	84	100	184	73
427	8712	Do. . .	–	York-street, No. 1,	Diss.	–	Pres.	Diss.	110	90	200	80
428	8725	Do. . .	–	Do. No. 2, m.	Pres.	–	Pres.	Pres.	163	–	163	71
429	8738	Do. . .	–	Do. . f. day,	Pres.	–	Pres.	2 Pres.	–	183	183	74
				Do. . . evg.	–	–	Pres.	Pres.	–	171	171	59
430	8721	Do. . .	9	Brown-street, m. day,	Pres.	–	Pres.	2 Pres. 1 Diss.	618	–	618	180
				Do. . . evg.	–	–	Pres.	2 Pres. 2 Diss.	300	181	480	146
431	8722	Do. . .	–	Do. . . f.	Pres.	–	Pres.	R.C. Pres.	–	277	277	70
432	8723	Do. . .	–	Do. . . i.	Pres.	–	Pres.	Pres.	177	230	407	116
433	8744	Do. . .	9	Falls-road, . .	Diss.	–	Diss.	2 Diss.	128	115	243	82
434	8804	Do. . .	8	Wolfhill Mill, . day,	–	Pres.	Pres.	R.C. Pres.	163	170	331	181
				Do.[b] . . evg.	–	–	–	–	–	–	–	–
435	8815	Do. . .	9	Harveston-place, f. day,	R.C.	–	R.C.	4 R.C.	16	225	241	99
				Do. . . evg.	–	–	R.C.	–	–	81	81	24
436	8820	Do. . .	–	Dunmore, . m.	Pres.	–	Pres.	Pres.	180	–	180	69
437	8836	Do. . .	–	Do. . . f.	Pres.	–	Pres.	Pres.	–	101	101	50
438	8977	Do. . .	–	Do. . . i.	Pres.	–	Pres.	Pres.	88	71	159	64
439	8990	Do. . .	–	Great George's-st., day,	Pres.	–	Pres.	3 Pres.	274	229	503	178
				Do. . . evg.	–	–	Pres.	–	163	22	185	53
440	9016	Do. . .	–	Hemsworth-street, m. day,	Pres.	–	Pres.	Pres.	273	230	503	128
				Do. . . evg.	–	–	Pres.	Pres.	290	–	290	96
441	9019	Do. . .	–	Do. . . f.	Pres.	–	Pres.	2 Pres.	–	293	293	79
442	9020	Do. . .	–	Do. . . i.	Pres.	–	Pres.	2 Pres.	58	77	135	63
443	10737	Do. . .	9	Blackstaff-road, .	Pres.	–	Pres.	2 Pres.	263	203	466	101
444	9024	Do. . .	–	Hutchinson-street, .	Diss.	–	Diss.	2 Diss.	175	135	310	115
445	9074	Do. . .	–	Linfield, . . .	Pres.	–	2 Pres.	4 Pres.	399	278	673	69
446	9513	Do. . .	–	Do. . . i.	Pres.	–	Pres.	2 Pres.	195	246	441	152
447	9129	Do. . .	8	Crumlin-road, No. 2,	R.C.	–	R.C.	–	58	20	78	46
448	10508	Do. . .	–	St. Matthew's, . .	R.C.	–	R.C.	Pres.	110	93	203	66
				Do. . . evg.	R.C.	–	R.C.	–	47	22	69	29
449	9155	Do. . .	9	Welsh-street, . .	Pres.	–	Pres.	R.C. 2 Pres.	190	128	318	99
450	9166	Do. . .	–	Do. . . i.	Pres.	–	Pres.	Pres.	74	78	150	67
451	9173	Do. . .	–	Malvern-street,[b] m.	R.C.	–	–	–	–	–	–	–
452	9174	Do. . .	–	Do. . . f.	R.C.	–	R.C.	–	53	61	104	34
453	9285	Do. . .	–	Academy-street, m.	Pres.	–	Pres.	–	105	–	105	32
454	9366	Do. . .	–	Do. . . f.	Pres.	–	Pres.	–	–	150	150	61
455	9403	Do. . .	9	Ashmore-street, day,	–	Pres.	Pres.	2 R.C. 7 Pres. 2 Diss. 1 Meth.	291	177	468	193
				Do. . . evg.	–	–	Pres.	Pres. Diss.	171	102	273	60
456	9404	Do. . .	–	Do. . . i.	–	Pres.	Pres.	R.C. Diss.	186	217	403	137
457	9179	Do. . .	–	Shankill-road, . i.	Pres.	–	Pres.	Pres.	122	107	229	90
458	9718	Do. . .	–	Milford-street, m. day,	R.C.	–	2 R.C.	3 R.C.	367	–	367	142
				Do. . . evg.	–	–	R.C.	–	179	–	179	31
459	9723	Do. . .	–	Wesley-place, . .	Diss.	–	Diss.	3 Diss.	204	200	404	120
460	9767	Do. . .	–	Lawnview-street, . .	–	R.C.	Pres.	4 R.C.	196	299	495	109
461	9778	Do. . .	–	St. George's, . .	R.C.	–	R.C.	6 R.C.	146	119	265	119
462	9779	Do. . .	8	Fountain-square,[b] day,	–	Pres.	–	–	–	–	–	–
				Do.[b] . . evg.	–	–	–	–	–	–	–	–

[b] Including also of Pres. Buildings.

Province of Ulster: County of Antrim—*continued.*

Amount paid for Books, Requisites, and Apparatus at Reduced Prices.	Aid granted by the Board during the Year 1874: In Free Stock of Books, Requisites, and Apparatus.	In Salaries, Premiums, and other Gratuities.	Results Fees, Financial Year.	Amount of Local Contributions received in Aid of Teacher's Salary: School Fees.	Subscriptions, Endowments, &c.	Total Local Aid.	Vested or Non-Vested.	Number.
£ s. d.	£ s. d.	£ s. d.	£ s. d.	£ s. d.	£ s. d.	£ s. d.		
6 9 2	—	159 0 0	28 1 0	1 14 9	60 18 0	62 7 9		422
5 13 9	—	65 10 0	18 16 6	4 1 6	60 19 10	67 4 9		423
17 0 3	—	66 16 8	16 19 8	23 15 8	—	23 15 8		424
1 8 9	—	40 3 4	15 5 6	19 5 5	—	10 5 6		425
—	—	58 18 0	14 0 0	18 18 0	—	18 18 0		426
2 11 8	—	56 8 8	7 14 6	11 0 0	—	11 0 0		427
5 13 6	—	90 13 4	20 8 6	29 8 6	—	29 0 0		428
10 9 8	—	60 0 0	23 13 0	50 18 0	—	50 18 0		429
			11 10 6	8 16 8	—	8 16 8		
23 17 7	—	246 8 8	71 16 0	65 8 0	10 0 0	*65 8 0		430
			36 8 6	32 8 1	—	32 8 1		
6 6 10	—	80 0 0	18 1 8	29 8 8	7 0 0	36 8 8		431
4 9 1	—	68 13 4	24 6 0	22 12 0	4 0 0	26 12 0		432
19 8 1	—	84 0 0	15 8 8	10 14 0	—	19 14 0		433
13 0 11	—	157 0 8	61 8 6	44 10 0	—	44 10 0		434
			—	—	—	—		
1 5 3	—	75 10 0	11 10 6	12 9 8	—	12 9 8		435
			4 17 0	8 15 4	—	8 15 4		
7 17 7	—	61 10 0	26 3 0	30 5 11	—	30 5 11		436
2 14 5	—	87 0 0	28 1 0	26 8 3	—	26 8 3		437
1 4 11	—	64 0 0	11 16 0	18 3 0	—	13 8 4		438
10 2 6	—	164 18 4	41 12 0	87 16 8	—	87 15 8		439
			4 15 9	3 16 9	—	8 18 0		
6 8 7	—	68 15 0	10 3 0	36 11 10	—	36 11 10		440
			9 4 0	12 13 4	—	12 18 4		
6 4 7	—	64 0 0	13 15 0	18 14 10	—	18 14 10		441
1 18 6	—	75 0 0	21 3 0	8 10 4	—	8 10 4		442
8 14 1	5 0 0	71 8 10	16 6 5	30 15 3	—	30 15 3		443
1 8 0	—	67 15 8	16 0 8	17 18 9	—	17 18 0		444
—	—	114 12 2	17 12 0	27 16 7	—	27 16 7		445
7 18 6	—	87 6 4	27 11 0	28 0 11	—	28 0 11		446
11 14 4	—	—	6 18 0	—	—	—		447
6 12 4	—	68 14 4	24 7 0	17 11 10	—	17 11 10		448
			8 6 0	5 16 0	—	8 15 0		
8 16 7	—	65 10 6	20 8 6	25 11 11	—	25 11 11		449
2 18 5	—	55 0 0	17 12 0	15 15 6	—	15 15 0		450
—	—	—	—	—	—	—		451
—	—	20 0 0	3 11 0	8 16 1	—	8 16 1		452
1 8 10	—	24 0 0	1 5 0	3 19 0	—	3 19 6		453
1 7 6	—	28 10 0	3 8 0	5 13 8	—	5 13 8		454
21 11 8	—	221 8 8	169 8 0	110 1 9	7 0 0	117 1 9		455
			40 4 0	81 1 9	—	81 1 9		
2 3 11	—	78 11 8	22 3 0	22 8 10	—	22 8 10		456
3 8 6	—	40 0 0	11 18 6	10 7 4	—	10 7 4		457
16 2 4	—	64 0 0	23 5 8	44 18 0	—	44 18 0		458
			4 11 6	7 6 6	—	7 8 6		
61 7 8	—	74 9 4	21 18 0	32 0 8	—	33 0 8		459
61 8 6	—	78 8 4	30 12 6	30 12 6	—	30 12 8		460
9 17 1	—	83 3 4	45 6 0	35 6 1	8 0 0	43 6 1		461
—	—	—	—	—	—	—		462

* Closed.

List of Schools in operation on the 31st December, 1874.—

No.	Roll Number of School.	Parish.	District.	School.	Religious Denomination of Manager or Correspondent: Clerical.	Lay.	Number and Religious Denomination of Teachers: Principals.	Assistants.	Attendance for the Year: Total number of Pupils on Rolls within the Year 1874: Males.	Fem.	Total.	Average Daily Attendance for the Year 1874.
463	9778	Shankill, . .	8	Trench-street, day.	–	Pres.	2 Diss.	Diss.	331	186	517	130
				Do. . . evg.	–	–	2 Diss.	–	110	54	164	48
464	10276	Do. . .	9	Porter's, . . m.	–	Diss.	Pres.	1 Pres. 1 R.C.	236	–	236	109
465	10277	Do. . .	–	Do. . . f.	–	Diss.	Pres.	2 Pres. 1 R.C.	–	205	205	120
466	9765	Do. . .	8	St. Ann's Parochial, m.	–	R.C.	–	–	–	–	–	–
				Do.[a] . . evg.	–	–	–	–	–	–	–	–
467	9766	Do. . .	–	Do.[a] . f. day.	–	R.C.	–	–	–	–	–	–
				Do.[a] . . evg.	–	–	–	–	–	–	–	–
468	9791	Do. . .	–	Trinity Church, m.	R.C.	–	R.C.	R.C.	179	–	179	61
469	9792	Do. . .	–	Do. . . i.	R.C.	–	R.C.	R.C. Pres.	130	149	279	[illegible]
470	[illegible]	Do. . .	–	Do. . . f.	R.C.	–	R.C.	Pres.	–	163	163	[illegible]
471	[illegible]	Do. . .	–	Hardinge-st., m. day.	R.C.	–	R.C.	2 R.C.	343	–	343	139
				Do. . . evg.	R.C.	–	R.C.	–	96	–	96	25
472	[illegible]	Do. . .	–	Do. . . f.	R.C.	–	R.C.	2 R.C.	108	309	417	97
473	10342	Do. . .	9	Rowland, . .	–	Pres.	Pres.	R.C.	76	39	115	31
				Do.[a] . . evg.	–	–	–	–	–	–	–	–
474	10346	Do. . .	–	St. Catherine's Convent	–	Nuns.	R.C.	–	–	1046	1046	387
475	9056	Do. . .	–	Conway-st. No. 2, m. day.	R.C.	–	R.C.	R.C.	360	–	360	[illegible]
				Do. . . evg.	R.C.	–	R.C.	–	63	–	63	18
476	[illegible]	Do. . .	–	Do. No. 2, f. day.	R.C.	–	R.C.	3 R.C.	30	291	321	66
				Do. . . evg.	R.C.	–	R.C.	–	–	[illegible]	[illegible]	22
477	10394	Do. . .	–	Andersonstown, .	Diss.	–	Diss.	–	34	[illegible]	96	[illegible]
478	9714	Do. . .	–	Northumberland-st., m.	Pres.	–	Pres.	2 Pres.	217	–	217	[illegible]
479	[illegible]	Do. . .	–	Do. . . f.	Pres.	–	Pres.	3 Pres.	–	239	239	103
480	[illegible]	Do. . .	–	Do. . . i.	Pres.	–	Pres.	2 Pres.	161	177	338	160
481	[illegible]	Do. . .	8	Clifton-street, . .	Pres.	–	Pres.	4 Pres.	128	160	288	116
482	[illegible]	Do. . .	–	St. Paul's, . m.	R.C.	–	R.C.	R.C.	234	–	234	75
483	10581	Do. . .	–	Do. . . f.	R.C.	–	R.C.	R.C.	–	335	335	90
484	10075	Do. . .	–	Crumlin-road, m. day.	Pres.	–	Pres.	4 Pres.	409	–	409	100
				Do.[a] . . evg.	–	–	–	–	–	–	–	–
485	10084	Do. . .	8	Townsend-street, i.	Pres.	–	Pres.	Pres.	111	98	209	70
486	10769	Do. . .	9	M'Crea's Mill, .	–	R.C.	R.C.	R.C.	109	219	328	61
487	11143	Do. . .	8	Albion-street, . .	Pres.	–	Pres.	3 Pres.	265	170	435	164
488	11142	Do. . .	–	Do. . . i.	Pres.	–	Pres.	Pres.	91	118	209	[illegible]
489	10274	Do. . .	–	M'Quiston, . . m.	Pres.	–	Pres.	4 Pres.	324	–	328	136
				Do. . . evg.	–	–	Pres.	–	203	49	251	41
490	[illegible]	Do. . .	–	Do. . . f.	Pres.	–	Pres.	4 Pres.	–	339	339	181
491	[illegible]	Do. . .	8	Crumlin-road, No. 3, f.	Pres.	–	Pres.	3 Pres.	–	346	346	140
				Do.[a] . . evg.	–	–	Pres.	–	–	–	–	–
492	[illegible]	Do. . .	–	Holycross, . m.	R.C.	–	R.C.	R.C.	247	–	247	107
				Do.[a] . . evg.	R.C.	–	–	–	–	–	–	–
493	[illegible]	Do. . .	–	Do. . . f.	R.C.	–	R.C.	R.C.	–	219	219	73
				Do. . . evg.	–	–	R.C.	R.C.	–	131	131	[illegible]
494	[illegible]	Do. . .	8	Hercules-place, m.	R.C.	–	R.C.	R.C.	196	–	196	[illegible]
				Do. . . evg.	R.C.	–	R.C.	–	[illegible]	–	[illegible]	[illegible]
495	11919	Do. . .	–	May-street, . m.	R.C.	–	R.C.	–	150	–	150	41
496	10742	Do. . .	–	Do. . . f.	R.C.	–	R.C.	R.C.	–	169	169	[illegible]
497	10807	Do. . .	–	Argyle-place, . .	Pres.	–	Pres.	3 Pres.	[illegible]	[illegible]	301	107
				Do. . . evg.	–	–	Pres.	Pres.	102	30	132	37
498	10[illegible]	Do. . .	–	Do. . . i.	Pres.	–	2 Pres.	3 Pres.	226	226	452	137
499	10482	Do. . .	8	Jennymount, . .	–	R.C.	Pres.	1 R.C. 1 Diss. 1 Pres.	181	209	390	184
500	11160	Do. . .	9	Linfield Mill, . .	–	R.C.	Pres.	3 Pres. 1 R.C.	171	248	419	112
				Do. . . evg.	–	–	Pres.	–	80	86	166	44
501	2014	Shankill, . .	4	Mullinderam, . .	Pres.	–	Pres.	–	48	45	93	[illegible]
502	[illegible]	Do. . .	–	Little Ballymacarn, .	Pres.	–	Pres.	Pres.	73	71	144	[illegible]
503	[illegible]	Do. . .	–	Killygore, . .	Pres.	–	Pres.	–	101	83	184	[illegible]
504	2910	Do. . .	8	Lower Kilcairn, m.	Pres.	–	Pres.	–	103	–	103	[illegible]
505	[illegible]	Do. . .	4	Braidujle, . .	–	Pres.	Pres.	–	53	54	107	43

[a] Closed.

[b] Including value of Free Residence.

Province of Ulster: County of Antrim—*continued.*

Amount paid for Books, Requisites, and Apparatus at Reduced Prices.	Aid granted by the Board during the Year 1874: In Free Stock of Books, Requisites, and Apparatus.	In Salaries, Premiums, and other Gratuities.	Results Fees, Financial Year.	Amount of Local Emoluments received in Aid of Teacher's Salary: School Fees.	Subscriptions, Endowments, &c.	Total Local Aid.	Vested or Non-Vested.	Number.
£ s. d.	£ s. d.	£ s. d.	£ s. d.	£ s. d.	£ s. d.	£ s. d.		
7 6 6	—	105 11 6	66 1 0	44 3 11	—	44 6 11		463
			16 7 6	7 16 9	—	7 16 9		
5 1 6	2 10 0	91 18 11	37 10 6	34 0 6	—	31 0 6		464
15 11 6	2 10 0	105 16 8	37 13 0	33 15 10	—	33 15 10		465
—	—	—	—	—	—	—		466
—	—	—	—	—	—	—		
—	—	—	—	—	—	—		467
—	—	—	—	—	—	—		
6 16 6	—	65 13 4	29 14 0	21 13 6	—	21 13 6		468
6 16 9	—	74 10 0	28 16 0	23 11 8	—	23 11 8		469
5 2 0	—	60 15 7	17 14 0	10 17 1	—	10 17 1		470
6 6 8	8 15 0	61 0 0	24 9 6	20 8 5	—	20 8 6		471
			2 1 6	6 16 0	—	6 15 8		
6 10 6	—	65 0 0	16 10 0	15 4 6	—	15 4 6		472
4 18 1	—	48 10 0	18 10 0	30 0 0	15 0 0	b 45 0 0		473
			—	—	—	—		
7 3 10	—	71 9 4	21 18 6	19 18 0	—	19 16 0		474
4 6 8	—	66 6 4	27 8 6	23 3 6	—	23 3 6		475
			5 0 6	2 16 6	—	2 13 6		
4 6 9	—	77 10 0	27 10 6	55 2 1	—	25 2 1		476
			18 4 0	3 3 4	—	3 3 4		
1 6 8	—	29 8 0	6 16 0	10 16 0	6 0 0	16 10 0		477
5 16 8	—	41 3 3	63 9 0	55 16 8	—	55 16 8		478
6 1 0	6 2 0	124 15 0	64 15 6	45 15 0	—	45 15 0		479
1 18 7	—	95 18 4	81 17 0	63 13 8	—	63 13 8		480
6 18 6	—	107 0 6	61 18 6	66 5 0	—	66 5 0		481
2 6 8	—	84 10 0	15 9 6	10 8 6	—	10 8 6		482
6 1 4	—	60 5 4	19 16 6	29 14 6	—	29 14 6		483
16 16 5	—	101 6 6	58 15 0	67 16 7	—	67 16 7		484
			—	—	—	—		
1 6 11	—	75 10 0	17 18 0	23 18 6	—	23 18 6		485
4 5 7	—	44 10 0	8 12 0	29 16 10	16 0 0	45 16 10		486
10 14 6	—	141 6 6	46 11 1	50 16 8	—	50 16 8		487
1 18 5	—	46 0 0	19 14 6	11 11 7	—	11 11 7		488
16 17 4	—	193 11 6	42 11 6	57 6 6	—	57 6 6		489
			10 7 0	10 8 7	—	10 8 7		
8 16 6	3 0 0	187 0 0	45 11 0	50 6 8	—	50 6 8		490
9 1 0	1 0 0	136 16 4	64 11 0	63 1 11	—	63 1 11		491
			4 6 0	—	—	—		
7 6 6	—	96 0 0	27 8 6	86 7 1	—	34 7 1		492
			1 15 0	—	—	—		
—	—	61 6 4	14 18 6	36 9 10	—	36 9 10		493
			2 10 6	5 12 7	—	5 18 7		
—	—	60 2 4	10 0 6	16 10 6	—	16 10 6		494
			5 15 0	6 15 0	—	5 10 0		
1 10 9	—	30 0 0	6 5 0	15 6 8	—	15 6 3		495
3 6 0	6 0 0	41 18 4	10 6 6	31 6 0	—	31 6 0		496
17 9 4	—	72 1 7	36 6 6	40 6 6	—	40 6 6		497
			6 5 6	9 14 1	—	9 14 1		
5 15 1	—	80 0 0	26 5 0	28 9 7	—	28 9 7		498
6 14 11	—	108 10 0	35 4 6	30 0 0	10 0 0	40 0 0		499
17 1 1	7 0 0	46 6 8	21 9 8	43 16 6	—	43 16 6		500
			2 18 6	6 1 0	—	6 1 0		
—	—	95 0 0	16 3 0	4 0 0	—	4 0 0		501
5 0 6	—	51 10 0	14 16 0	6 18 6	—	6 18 6		502
1 10 6	—	39 6 0	18 0 6	6 9 6	—	6 9 6		503
4 17 11	—	87 16 0	19 16 6	16 9 8	—	16 6 3		504
2 16 6	—	35 0 0	10 4 1	9 0 7	2 10 0	11 10 7		505

b Returns not available.

List of Schools in operation on the 31st December, 1874.—

Number.	Roll Number of School.	Parish.	District.	School.	Religious Denomination of Manager or Correspondent: Clerical.	Lay.	Number and Religious Denomination of Teachers: Principals.	Assistants.	Attendance for the Year: Total number of Pupils on Rolls within the Year 1874: Males.	Fem.	Total.	Average daily Attendance for Year 1874.
506	2633	Skerry,	4	Loughcannally,	Pres.	–	Pres.	–	60	48	108	57
507	7284	Do.	–	Cloughwater,	Pres.	–	Pres.	–	63	23	86	35
508	7630	Do.	–	Correen,	Pres.	–	Pres.	–	40	46	86	37
509	9062	Do.	–	Braid,	R.C.	–	R.C.	R.C.	110	82	192	56
510	93	Templemoran,	5	Whinlygap,	Pres.	–	Pres.	–	54	25	79	38
511	5613	Do.	–	Ballycarry,	Pres.	–	Pres.	Pres.	81	73	154	61
512	6291	Do.	–	Do. Agricultural m.	Pres.	–	Pres.	–	64	32	96	57
513	7911	Do.	–	Ballyhill, No. 1,	Pres.	–	R.C.	–	80	11	40	31
514	7940	Do.	–	Do. No. 2,	–	R.C.	Pres.	Pres.	38	67	105	53
515	93	Templepatrick,	9	Lylehill,	Pres.	–	Pres.	Pres.	44	40	84	35
516	95	Do.	–	Ballyrobert,	Pres.	–	R.C.	R.C.	63	70	133	43
517	98	Do.	6	Molusk, m.	–	Pres.	Pres.	–	111	–	111	44
518	6190	Do.	–	Do. f.	–	Pres.	Pres.	Pres.	61	55	116	50
519	2007	Do.	8	Rickamore,	–	R.C.	Pres.	–	75	40	115	49
520	6231	Do.	–	Roughfort,	–	Pres.	Pres.	–	63	40	103	42
521	8014	Do.	–	Templepatrick,	Pres.	–	Pres.	–	77	67	144	41
522	93	Tickmacrevan,	4	Feystown,	R.C.	–	R.C.	–	63	64	127	41
523	1759	Do.	–	Knocknataken,	–	R.C.	Pres.	–	56	50	106	40
524	2861	Do.	–	Carnalbanagh,	–	R.C.	Pres.	–	74	64	138	47
525	8241	Do.	–	Aughagash,	–	R.C.	Pres.	–	73	60	141	44
526	4552	Do.	–	Glenarm, m.	–	R.C.	R.C.	–	96	–	96	32
527	4822	Do.	–	Do. f.	–	R.C.	R.C.	–	–	104	104	45
528	8172	Do.	–	Do. i.	–	R.C.	Pres.	Pres.	60	91	151	73
529	8754	Do.	–	Longfield,	–	R.C.	Pres.	–	36	45	83	32
530	11084	Do.	–	Harphall, m.	R.C.	–	R.C.	–	101	–	101	38
531	10971	Do.	–	Do. f.	R.C.	–	R.C.	–	–	121	121	40
532	5806	Tullyrusk,	11	Dundrod, m.	Pres.	–	Pres.	Pres.	80	100	180	65
				Total for County Antrim, 532,					48970	47070	96,040	35,400

COUNTY OF

1	101	Armagh,	16	Armagh, m.	R.C.	–	R.C.	–	145	–	145	60
			–	Do. inf.	–	–	R.C.	–	101	–	101	48
2	102	Do.	–	Do. f.	R.C.	–	R.C.	R.C.	–	213	213	74
3	10416	Do.	–	Do. Workhouse,	P.L.	Gdn.	R.C.	R.C.	38	37	75	65
4	4317	Do.	–	Grangemore,	–	Pres.	Pres.	–	69	25	94	55
5	6782	Do.	–	Gosford-place,	Pres.	–	Pres.	Pres.	117	80	200	69
6	6822	Do.	–	Ballynahone,	Pres.	–	R.C.	–	80	60	140	44
7	10572	Do.	–	Callan-street, i.	R.C.	–	R.C.	–	40	52	89	40
8	9379	Do.	–	Abbey-street, m.	–	Dis.	Dis.	–	116	–	116	56
9	9552	Do.	–	Do. f.	–	Dis.	Dis.	Dis.	–	120	120	58
10	10420	Do.	–	Banbrook,	R.C.	–	R.C.	R.C.	80	69	179	89
11	[illegible]	Do.	–	Mount St. Catherine Convent, f.	–	R.C.	Nuns.		37	277	314	163
12	10578	Do.	–	Mall, f.	R.C.	–	R.C.	–	–	103	103	43
13	10574	Do.	–	Do. i.	R.C.	–	R.C.	–	51	44	95	39
14	10579	Do.	–	Do. m.	R.C.	–	R.C.	–	122	–	122	67
15	4156	Ballymore,	–	Old Clare, m.	Pres.	–	Pres.	–	63	–	63	31
16	4402	Do.	–	Do. f.	Pres.	–	Pres.	–	–	73	73	35
17	8732	Do.	–	Cushenny,	Pres.	–	Pres.	–	47	49	96	38
18	4271	Do.	–	Tannyokey Ordinary Agricultural, m.	–	R.C.	Pres.	–	130	–	130	60
19	4272	Do.	–	Do. f.	–	R.C.	Pres.	–	–	119	119	50
20	4960	Do.	–	Poyntzpass, m.	–	R.C.	R.C.	–	83	–	83	45
21	4961	Do.	–	Do. f.	–	R.C.	R.C.	–	25	86	111	47
22	5051	Do.	–	Tanderagee, No. 2,	R.C.	–	R.C.	R.C.	68	49	116	44
				Do. inf.	–	–	R.C.	R.C.	63	28	91	33
23	6409	Do.	–	Do. m.	–	R.C.	R.C.	R.C.	130	–	130	61
24	8404	Do.	–	Do. f.	–	R.C.	Pres.	–	–	119	119	45

a Including value of Free Garden. b Including value of Free Residence and Garden.

Province of Ulster: County of Antrim—*continued.*

Amount paid for Books, Requisites, and Apparatus, at Reduced Prices.	Aid granted by the Board during the Year 1874. In Free Stock of Books, Requisites, and Apparatus.	In Salaries, Premiums, and other Gratuities.	Results Fees, Financial Year.	Amount of Local Endowments received in Aid of Teacher's Salary. School Fees.	Subscriptions, Endowments, &c.	Total Local Aid.	Vested or Non-Vested.	Number.
£ s. d.	£ s. d.	£ s. d.	£ s. d.	£ s. d.	£ s. d.	£ s. d.		
3 2 6	—	24 0 0	10 8 6	4 18 0	—	4 18 0		506
1 4 11	—	24 0 0	3 16 6	6 4 9	—	6 4 9		507
8 16 0	—	20 0 0	8 8 0	2 10 0	—	2 10 8		508
0 18 8	—	46 0 0	15 10 6	9 17 11	—	0 17 11		509
8 10 1	—	30 0 0	14 14 6	7 13 7	—	7 13 7		510
7 16 0	—	74 3 4	16 3 7	18 10 3	2 17 4	16 7 6		511
6 8 5	—	40 3 4	10 0 0	11 17 8	5 8 10	*17 8 6		512
1 7 8	—	16 0 6	—	2 14 7	—	2 14 7	V.G.	513
5 10 3	—	44 0 0	18 12 0	8 16 9	—	8 16 9	V.C.	514
5 10 11	—	67 15 0	18 1 6	15 8 10	—	15 8 10	N.	515
3 19 3	—	60 0 0	22 19 0	17 16 1	6 0 0	23 16 1		516
8 2 1	—	87 0 0	18 2 6	14 17 0	—	14 17 0		517
3 13 9	—	40 0 0	15 13 6	10 19 0	—	10 18 0		518
6 0 5	—	48 0 8	28 4 6	20 14 8	11 10 0	*32 4 8		519
6 14 7	—	20 10 0	17 7 0	16 17 7	—	16 17 7		520
4 19 2	—	18 6 8	13 19 6	9 0 2	—	9 0 2		521
4 4 10	—	31 10 0	9 18 6	8 8 4	—	8 8 4	V.T.	522
8 8 6	—	88 0 0	12 10 0	0 8 6	10 0 0	18 8 6		523
3 16 2	—	40 6 8	15 18 6	9 0 4	8 0 0	17 0 4		524
1 0 11	—	24 6 6	10 1 8	4 9 2	6 0 0	10 9 2		525
8 3 3	—	81 0 0	19 7 8	10 8 4	9 8 6	19 6 10		526
1 5 11	—	33 6 8	24 1 0	0 18 0	10 0 0	19 18 0		527
1 5 6	—	54 0 6	11 8 0	8 6 8	10 0 0	18 6 8		528
2 14 11	—	23 6 8	8 18 6	5 4 5	5 0 0	10 4 5		529
1 15 1	—	86 0 0	11 5 0	6 18 1	5 2 11	*12 18 0		530
2 0 5	—	40 0 0	18 7 0	7 17 10	4 11 8	*13 9 1		531
6 15 8	—	70 5 0	45 11 6	24 5 4	—	24 5 4	V.C.	532
2,673 10 5	198 0 6	10,247 3 5	6,087 3 9	6,491 16 1	1,298 7 8	8,789 5 0		

ARMAGH—225 Schools.

Amount paid for Books, &c.	Free Stock	Salaries, &c.	Results Fees	School Fees	Subscriptions, &c.	Total Local Aid	Vested or Non-Vested	Number
4 8 10	—	44 10 0	18 19 0	6 3 5	—	6 9 8	V.T.	1
			11 9 6	6 9 6	—	6 8 0		
0 0 0	—	78 18 4	19 13 6	6 3 7	—	6 8 7	V.T.	2
5 3 1	—	—	—	—	—	—		3
3 18 4	6 8 6	67 10 0	14 16 0	2 0 7	12 0 0	*17 0 7		4
8 0 0	—	90 18 8	21 4 6	60 0 0	—	60 0 0		5
1 6 0	—	80 7 6	6 6 6	2 0 0	—	2 0 0		6
—	—	26 0 0	6 11 6	0 4 0	10 0 0	10 4 0		7
18 14 9	—	42 1 8	14 9 0	16 17 8	30 10 0	49 7 8		8
4 14 6	—	55 0 0	20 6 6	24 12 0	—	24 12 0		9
1 13 10	—	40 8 0	6 11 0	6 9 4	—	6 9 4		10
8 7 8	—	62 10 0	41 11 0	5 0 0	—	5 0 0		11
2 7 8	1 0 0	31 11 6	13 11 6	6 0 0	14 0 0	*20 0 0		12
0 15 2	—	26 0 0	5 5 0	6 10 0	—	6 10 0		13
7 3 10	—	43 10 0	15 9 6	15 17 0	37 0 0	*52 17 0		14
8 11 10	—	24 0 0	8 3 0	1 1 3	11 0 0	*12 1 3		15
3 2 7	—	24 6 0	6 8 6	0 12 0	11 0 0	*11 12 0		16
1 11 10	—	24 0 0	6 11 0	3 6 0	2 0 0	5 6 0		17
6 14 1	—	66 10 0	29 10 6	15 19 1	20 10 0	*36 9 1		18
5 10 8	—	61 1 8	22 6 6	16 0 11	18 0 0	*38 0 11		19
2 0 7	—	64 10 0	25 0 0	6 10 0	19 10 0	*25 0 0		20
4 9 5	—	60 0 0	19 18 6	4 10 0	10 0 0	14 10 0		21
6 7 5	—	68 0 6	15 8 6	6 10 11	—	6 10 11		22
			6 17 0	4 13 0	—	4 13 0		
1 15 4	—	64 0 0	16 10 0	12 6 7	37 16 0	*50 11 7		23
1 13 1	—	25 0 0	18 17 0	9 19 8	17 18 0	*26 12 8		24

* Including value of Free Residence.

List of Schools in operation on the 31st December, 1874.—

Parish.		District.	School.		Religious Denomination of Manager or Correspondent. Clerical.	Lay.	Number and Religious Denominations of Teachers. Principals.	Assistants.	Attendance for the Year. Total number of Pupils on Rolls within the Year 1874. Males.	Fem.	Total.	Average Daily Attendance.
Ballymore,	.	16	Tandragee,	f.	–	E.C.	E.C.	E.C.	80	83	163	65
Do.	.	–	Acton,	f.	–	E.C.	E.C.	–	51	57	108	44
Do.	.	–	Poyntzpass,	day,	R.C.	–	R.C.	R.C.	52	59	111	56
			Do.	evg.	–	–	R.C.	–	59	18	77	25
Do.	.	–	Clare,	.	E.C.	–	R.C.	–	25	24	49	15
Do.	.	–	Drumnaleg,	.	R.C.	–	R.C.	–	90	68	158	61
Ballymyre,	.	–	Knockavannon,	.	R.C.	–	R.C.	–	32	31	63	22
Balleek,	.	–	Carrickgalogly,	.	R.C.	–	–	–	–	–	–	–
Creggan,	.	16	Dorsey,	.	R.C.	–	R.C.	R.C.	97	90	187	63
Do.	.	–	Tullyvallen,	.	Pres.	–	Pres.	–	66	51	117	43
Do.	.	–	Cullyhanna,	.	R.C.	–	R.C.	R.C.	58	58	116	41
Do.	.	–	Creggan duff,	.	R.C.	–	R.C.	–	59	44	103	39
Do.	.	–	Crossmaglen,	m.	R.C.	–	R.C.	R.C.	224	–	224	97
Do.	.	–	Do.	f.	R.C.	–	R.C.	R.C.	–	174	174	63
Do.	.	–	Ballynaclosha,	.	R.C.	–	R.C.	–	110	78	188	62
Do.	.	–	Annaghmare,	.	R.C.	–	R.C.	R.C.	100	108	208	70
Do.	.	–	Clonalig,	.	R.C.	–	R.C.	–	91	98	189	49
Do.	.	–	Glassdrummond,	.	R.C.	–	R.C.	R.C.	194	161	355	105
Do.	.	–	Creggan,	f.	R.C.	–	R.C.	–	61	70	131	36
Clonfeacle,	.	16	Blackwatertown,	m.	R.C.	–	R.C.	–	132	–	132	53
Do.	.	–	Do.	f.	R.C.	–	R.C.	–	–	128	128	46
Do.	.	12	Tullyroan,	day,	Dis.	–	Dis.	Dis.	128	94	222	79
			Do.	evg.	–	–	Dis.	–	66	–	66	50
Drumcree,	.	16	Richmount,	.	–	E.C.	Pres.	–	96	83	179	57
Do.	.	–	Breagh,	.	–	E.C.	E.C.	–	67	62	129	57
Do.	.	–	Maghery,	.	–	E.C.	E.C.	R.C.	92	88	180	50
Do.	.	–	Portadown, No. 1,	m.	R.C.	–	R.C.	R.C.	198	–	198	71
Do.	.	–	Do. No. 1,	f. day,	R.C.	–	R.C.	R.C.	–	170	170	64
			Do.	evg.	–	–	R.C.	–	–	83	83	31
Do.	.	–	Do. No. 2,	m.	–	E.C.	Pres.	R.C.	189	–	189	50
Do.	.	–	Do.	f.	–	E.C.	E.C.	Dis.	134	94	228	78
Do.	.	–	Do. No. 2,	f. day,	–	E.C.	Pres.	E.C.	–	176	176	85
			Do.	evg.	–	–	Pres.	E.C.	104	98	202	45
Do.	.	–	[illegible],	.	R.C.	–	R.C.	R.C.	182	74	256	64
Do.	.	–	Thomas-street,	.	Dis.	–	Dis.	Dis.	168	93	261	70
Do.	.	–	Do.	f.	Dis.	–	Dis.	Dis.	104	100	204	58
Do.	.	–	Corcrain,	.	R.C.	–	R.C.	R.C.	180	65	216	84
Do.	.	–	Derrykeeran,	.	Dis.	–	E.C.	–	58	60	118	64
Do.	.	–	Killmoriarty,	.	R.C.	–	E.C.	–	67	80	147	48
Do.	.	–	Derryanvey,	.	R.C.	–	Pres.	–	63	58	121	46
Do.	.	–	Curran-street,	.	–	Pres.	Pres.	–	53	65	118	38
Do.	.	–	Drumnagoon,	.	R.C.	–	E.C.	–	59	50	115	39
Derrynoose,	.	–	Lislea,	.	Pres.	–	Pres.	–	56	45	101	45
Do.	.	–	Derrynoose,	m.	R.C.	–	R.C.	R.C.	183	–	183	69
Do.	.	–	Do.	f.	R.C.	–	R.C.	R.C.	–	167	167	53
Do.	.	–	Madden,	.	R.C.	–	R.C.	R.C.	94	109	203	58
Do.	.	–	Temple,	.	–	Pres.	Pres.	–	39	30	69	29
Do.	.	–	Drumhillery,	.	R.C.	–	R.C.	R.C.	87	96	183	60

Province of Ulster: County of Armagh—*continued.*

Amount paid for Books, Requisites, and Apparatus, at Reduced Prices.	Aid granted by the Board during the Year 1874.			Amount of Local Emoluments received in Aid of Teacher's Salary.			Vested or Non-Vested.	Number.
	In Free Stock of Books, Requisites, and Apparatus.	In Salaries, Premiums, and other Gratuities.	Results Fees, Financial Year.	School Fees.	Subscriptions, Endowments, &c.	Total Local Aid.		
£ s. d.	£ s. d.	£ s. d.	£ s. d.	£ s. d.	£ s. d.	£ s. d.		
0 0 7	—	41 0 0	5 13 6	6 5 6	21 13 0	*26 18 6		25
6 10 6	—	20 0 0	14 18 0	—	16 0 0	16 0 0		26
1 5 4	—	49 0 0	21 8 6	6 17 11	—	6 17 11	v.	27
			5 16 0	1 18 0	—	1 18 0		
0 15 7	—	20 10 0	4 5 8	1 14 0	9 0 0	*3 14 0		28
1 15 0	—	27 10 0	5 13 6	1 8 9	14 0 0	15 8 9		29
1 0 0	—	80 0 0	6 8 8	2 0 0	20 8 4	*23 8 4		30
—	—	24 0 0	4 8 0	—	—	—		31
6 3 7	—	48 10 0	15 8 6	7 0 8	—	7 0 8		32
2 17 8	—	24 0 0	15 7 0	4 1 0	—	4 1 0		33
—	—	22 0 0	11 8 8	—	—	—		34
2 10 6	—	24 0 0	5 4 0	0 16 0	—	0 16 0		35
2 13 11	—	57 0 0	22 3 5	3 11 8	0 5 0	*3 16 8	V.C.	36
2 14 5	—	67 10 0	6 0 6	2 11 7	0 10 0	*3 1 7	V.C.	37
5 15 0	—	34 10 0	—	5 0 6	—	5 0 6		38
9 3 8	—	71 10 0	19 13 6	1 18 6	—	1 18 6		39
1 12 8	—	83 0 0	10 0 0	4 7 8	—	4 7 8		40
4 9 1	—	72 0 0	14 10 0	5 10 0	—	5 10 0		41
1 11 6	—	20 0 8	14 2 6	4 10 10	—	4 10 10		42
—	—	67 10 8	22 16 6	4 18 4	—	4 18 4		43
—	—	49 10 0	23 1 6	4 1 6	—	4 1 6		44
10 10 2	—	63 16 8	25 4 0	8 8 11	17 10 0	*26 18 11		45
			5 16 6	3 11 0	—	3 11 0		
6 4 8	—	40 16 8	15 0 0	6 6 2	10 0 0	d14 6 2		46
9 10 0	—	25 10 0	10 0 6	5 2 6	9 0 0	d14 2 6		47
1 16 6	—	38 0 0	17 10 0	6 0 0	12 0 0	d17 0 0		48
8 7 1	—	61 0 0	22 5 6	13 3 0	—	13 3 0		49
0 18 6	—	57 16 4	17 16 0	6 10 3	—	6 10 3		50
			3 0 6	0 5 3	—	0 5 3		
1 18 8	—	96 3 6	27 7 6	30 11 7	17 0 0	*47 11 7		51
1 8 10	—	56 8 4	14 8 0	6 6 1	13 0 0	*19 6 1		52
8 4 7	—	80 16 4	20 19 0	18 1 6	15 0 0	*33 1 6		53
			7 8 0	7 16 10	—	7 16 10		
8 14 4	—	52 8 4	18 0 0	4 18 4	1 0 0	*6 18 4		54
6 1 8	1 0 0	57 18 4	28 8 0	20 0 0	—	20 0 0		55
5 16 1	—	40 0 0	9 4 0	15 1 10	—	15 1 10		56
2 0 8	8 16 0	45 0 0	16 11 0	4 9 0	—	4 9 0		57
1 5 8	—	30 16 0	7 7 0	4 10 0	4 0 0	8 10 0		58
1 16 0	—	86 0 0	11 18 8	6 10 10	22 12 0	*16 2 10		59
8 2 8	11 9 3	29 13 4	18 17 0	10 5 11	6 10 0	*15 15 11		60
1 13 0	—	24 13 4	3 4 8	1 1 1	—	1 1 1		61
—	—	24 10 0	4 19 0	1 8 5	5 0 0	d6 8 5		62
1 6 2	4 16 8	81 0 0	18 10 0	1 8 8	—	1 8 8	V.C.	63
6 0 6	6 13 6	75 2 6	20 19 6	0 10 0	—	0 10 0		64
8 18 0	4 7 9	70 0 0	24 9 0	2 12 6	1 0 0	*3 12 6		65
4 5 5	—	65 16 4	20 6 0	8 5 0	—	8 5 0		66
—	5 2 2	57 14 8	5 2 11	—	—	—	V.C.	67
8 5 6	—	60 10 0	16 6 0	6 7 6	1 0 0	*4 7 6		68
8 8 8	—	55 8 0	24 7 6	—	—	—		69
			61 15 6	4 1 7	—	4 1 7		
1 16 7	—	24 0 0	13 8 0	6 1 0	2 0 0	*10 1 0		70
1 19 8	—	25 10 0	15 17 6	8 0 0	—	8 0 0		71
8 8 9	—	44 8 4	17 4 0	1 5 0	—	1 5 0		72
8 2 4	—	24 0 0	8 14 0	6 3 6	1 0 0	7 3 6		73
6 0 3	—	67 7 6	67 3 0	8 16 0	20 0 0	d28 16 0		74
9 16 2	—	45 5 0	16 19 0	9 18 6	5 10 0	d15 8 6		75
1 15 6	—	24 0 0	7 19 0	8 18 0	—	8 18 0	V.T.	76
8 9 4	—	20 0 0	8 3 0	3 17 6	—	3 17 6	V.T.	77
1 6 8	—	66 0 0	16 7 5	6 19 0	1 0 0	*7 19 0		78
4 10 10	—	45 0 0	23 2 6	18 19 4	—	18 19 4		79
8 1 3	—	36 0 0	10 7 0	4 7 11	0 10 0	4 17 11		80
2 5 7	—	34 0 0	6 16 0	4 8 4	6 10 0	*10 18 4		81
1 12 8	—	48 0 0	15 8 0	3 10 5	—	3 10 5		82
—	—	21 6 8	5 16 0	0 6 0	3 10 0	*3 15 0		83

* Including value of Free Garden.

d Including value of Free Residence and Garden.

List of Schools in operation on the 31st December, 1874.—

Number.	Roll Number of School.	Parish.	District.	School.	Religious Denomination of Manager or Correspondent: Clerical.	Lay.	Number and Religious Denomination of Teachers: Principals.	Assistants.	Attendance for the Year: Total number of Pupils on Rolls within the Year: Males.	Females.	Total.	Average Daily Attendance for Year.
84	165	Grange,	16	Brownlow's Grange, m.	–	R.C.	R.C.	–	87	–	87	48
85	1021	Do.	–	Do. f.	–	R.C.	R.C.	R.C.	14	109	123	57
86	10711	Do.	–	Grange, m.	R.C.	–	R.C.	–	51	46	97	53
87	4134	Jonesborough,	17	Jonesborough, m.	R.C.	–	R.C.	R.C.	271	–	271	71
88	418	Do.	–	Do. f.	R.C.	–	R.C.	R.C.	–	284	284	56
89	112	Killevy,	–	Cloghoge, m.	R.C.	–	R.C.	–	209	–	209	60
90	6458	Do.	–	Do. f.	R.C.	–	R.C.	R.C.	–	123	123	43
91	4324	Do.	–	Drumintee Agricultural, m.	–	R.C.	R.C.	–	58	47	105	47
92	472	Do.	–	Drumilly,	R.C.	–	–	–	122	85	209	60
93	6296	Do.	–	Bessbrook, m.	–	Diss.	Diss.	R.C.	254	–	254	60
				Do. evg.	–	Diss.	Diss.	R.C.	116	–	116	41
94	6251	Do.	–	Do. f.	–	Diss.	Pres.	R.C.	–	281	281	61
				Do. evg.	–	Diss.	Pres.	–	–	161	161	15
95	6806	Do.	–	Do. inf.	–	Diss.	Diss.	Pres. R.C.	167	168	335	114
96	115	Do.	–	Lislea, m.	R.C.	–	R.C.	R.C.	225	–	225	73
97	6758	Do.	–	Do. f.	R.C.	–	R.C.	–	–	164	164	60
98	116	Do.	–	Lisnacumman,	R.C.	–	R.C.	R.C.	75	67	142	61
99	10671	Do.	–	Adavoyle,[c]	R.C.	–	–	–	–	–	–	–
100	1854	Do.	–	Camlough,[c] m.	R.C.	–	–	–	–	–	–	–
101	8707	Do.	–	Do. f.	R.C.	–	R.C.	–	–	131	131	57
102	10702	Do.	–	Mackernakelly,[c]	R.C.	–	–	–	–	–	–	–
103	4739	Do.	–	Killeen, m.	R.C.	–	R.C.	–	214	–	214	30
104	4760	Do.	–	Do. f.	R.C.	–	R.C.	R.C.	–	226	226	67
105	10191	Do.	–	Craignamore,	–	Diss.	Diss.	–	58	46	96	46
106	6394	Do.	–	Ballintlea, m.	R.C.	–	R.C.	R.C.	190	–	190	60
107	3610	Do.	–	Do. f.	R.C.	–	R.C.	R.C.	–	164	164	60
108	10616	Do.	–	Mullaghglass,	–	R.C.	R.C.	–	71	83	154	52
109	10298	Do.	–	Newry Workhouse,	P.L.	Glds.	R.C. Pres.	R.C.	80	93	173	74
110	10972	Do.	–	Corinshego,	–	R.C.	Pres.	–	77	63	167	63
111	121	Kilmore,	18	Ballinahinch, m.	Pres.	–	Pres.	–	90	30	120	49
112	122	Do.	–	Do.[c] f.	Pres.	–	–	–	–	–	–	–
113	4557	Do.	–	Ballyrath,	R.C.	–	R.C.	R.C.	108	92	160	60
114	10294	Do.	–	Ballyloughan,	R.C.	–	R.C.	–	43	67	110	43
115	7141	Do.	–	Aghory,	Pres.	–	Pres.	–	84	54	138	51
116	10000	Do.	–	Ballintaggart,	R.C.	–	R.C.	R.C.	76	63	139	48
117	[illegible]	Do.	–	Mullavilly,	R.C.	–	R.C.	–	41	42	83	67
118	10501	Do.	–	Mullahead,	R.C.	–	R.C.	–	42	45	87	57
119	10312	Do.	–	Derryhale,	R.C.	–	R.C.	–	36	48	78	30
120	11061	Do.	–	Rockfield,	R.C.	–	R.C.	R.C.	96	78	184	61
121	2773	Keady,	–	Keady, m.	Pres.	–	Pres.	–	75	–	75	23
122	6428	Do.	–	Do. f.	Pres.	–	Pres.	–	16	64	79	34
123	2071	Do.	–	Aughnagurgan,	Pres.	–	Pres.	–	80	86	161	48
124	4824	Do.	–	Carrickawillin,	Pres.	–	Pres.	–	30	39	76	31
125	7181	Do.	–	Crossmore Keady, m.	R.C.	–	R.C.	R.C.	220	10	230	61
				Do. evg.	R.C.	–	R.C.	R.C.	156	22	178	68
126	11697	Do.	–	Carnagh,	–	R.C.	Pres.	–	45	46	91	37
127	7047	Do.	–	Darkley, m.	–	Pres.	Pres.	R.C.	147	–	147	60
				Do. evg.	–	Pres.	Pres. R.C.	Pres. R.C.	100	76	176	60
128	6640	Do.	–	Do. f.	–	Pres.	Pres.	R.C.	–	148	148	63
129	8301	Do.	–	Hermitage,[c]	R.C.	–	–	–	–	–	–	–
130	6722	Do.	–	Granemore,	R.C.	–	R.C.	R.C.	134	113	247	66
131	6931	Do.	–	Clay,	–	R.C.	R.C.	–	63	49	112	50
				Do.[c] evg.	–	R.C.	–	–	–	–	–	–
132	10607	Do.	–	Keady Parish,	R.C.	–	R.C.	–	82	41	123	47
133	4256	Kilclooney,	–	Cladymore,	Pres.	–	R.C.	R.C.	74	68	142	50
134	446	Do.	–	Ballylane,	Pres.	–	Pres.	Pres.	61	49	109	41
135	10611	Do.	–	Brackley,	R.C.	–	R.C.	–	96	61	157	66
136	1161	Do.	–	Clady,	R.C.	–	R.C.	R.C.	81	106	186	55
137	10682	Do.	–	Cladybeg,	R.C.	–	R.C.	–	67	61	128	42
138	12480	Loughgilly,	–	Tullyvoughan,[c] m.	Pres.	–	–	–	–	–	–	–

[a] Including value of Free Residence. [b] Including value of Free Residence and Garden. [c] Inoperative.

Province of Ulster: County of Armagh—*continued.*

Amount paid for Books, Requisites, and Apparatus at Reduced Prices.	Aid granted by the Board during the Year 1874. In Free Stock of Books, Requisites, and Apparatus.	In Salaries, Premiums, and other Gratuities.	Results Fees, Financial Year.	Amount of Local Endowments received in Aid of Teacher's Salary. School Fees.	Subscriptions, Endowments, &c.	Total Local Aid.	Vested or Non-Vested.	Number.
£ s. d.	£ s. d.	£ s. d.	£ s. d.	£ s. d.	£ s. d.	£ s. d.		
2 1 6	—	67 10 0	14 10 0	1 16 6	12 0 0	a 15 16 9		84
1 6 0	—	67 10 0	21 18 0	1 16 6	9 0 0	a 3 16 6		85
2 18 2	—	30 10 0	10 6 6	6 10 4	5 0 0	11 10 4		86
3 1 6	—	61 10 0	11 18 0	6 6 1	9 0 0	b 14 6 1	V.T.	87
1 15 10	—	40 0 0	8 10 6	2 14 9	6 12 0	a 8 6 9	V.T.	88
2 7 3	—	42 16 4	15 11 6	6 11 5	6 10 0	b 16 1 6		89
1 5 0	—	40 0 0	14 18 0	2 15 7	3 0 0	6 15 7		90
1 17 5	—	97 0 0	18 4 0	5 5 0	26 0 0	b 31 5 0		91
—	—	90 0 0	28 6 0	7 0 0	—	6 0 0	V.G.	92
16 4 0	—	} 55 0 0	{ 24 0 0	12 8 8	45 0 0	58 6 8		93
—	—		9 9 0	10 4 9	10 0 0	a 20 4 6		
9 8 7	—	} 62 2 9	{ 38 7 0	15 13 6	39 0 0	a 73 15 9		94
—	—		5 15 0	3 8 4	—	3 8 4		
2 2 1	—	65 1 11	28 14 0	20 9 9	18 5 6	47 16 9		95
6 18 9	—	69 16 8	30 10 6	14 15 9	—	14 15 0	D.	96
1 6 3	—	86 19 1	16 18 8	6 7 5	—	6 7 5	D.	97
4 19 10	—	30 0 0	16 18 0	9 9 8	—	9 9 8		98
2 18 5	—	—	7 17 8	—	—	—		99
—	—	84 0 0	—	—	—	—	V.T.	100
1 19 11	—	84 0 0	8 2 6	8 11 5	—	8 11 5	V.T.	101
—	—	—	—	—	—	—		102
—	—	20 0 0	2 6 4	4 18 1	2 0 0	a 6 19 1	V.G.	103
—	—	40 0 0	7 5 6	8 1 0	1 9 0	b 6 1 0	V.G.	104
6 6 6	—	30 0 0	6 18 0	11 0 0	10 14 2	21 14 2		105
1 0 0	—	45 9 0	18 16 6	6 5 6	9 10 0	a 6 15 6	V.G.	106
2 6 4	—	44 0 0	9 11 0	1 9 0	—	1 9 0		107
4 4 9	—	64 10 0	11 18 6	9 4 11	21 0 0	b 30 4 11		108
2 2 9	—	—	—	—	—	—		109
2 3 10	—	61 18 6	5 6 0	7 10 0	10 0 0	17 10 0		110
1 16 5	—	93 0 0	22 18 8	10 0 0	—	10 0 0		111
—	—	—	—	—	—	—		112
1 12 3	—	78 9 9	24 15 8	5 0 0	—	5 0 0		113
1 9 3	—	24 10 0	10 11 6	2 10 0	8 0 0	8 10 0		114
1 4 11	—	48 0 0	11 8 0	6 16 7	2 0 0	a 7 16 7		115
4 2 0	—	88 0 0	4 10 0	6 8 4	22 0 0	b 29 8 4		116
—	—	95 0 0	6 15 0	—	5 0 0	a 5 0 0		117
4 5 0	—	51 10 0	0 19 0	2 4 0	4 10 0	a 6 14 0		118
—	—	30 10 0	8 8 6	1 16 2	5 15 6	b 7 18 2		119
2 12 8	3 15 6	47 10 0	17 6 0	2 14 5	5 10 0	a 8 4 5		120
2 2 4	—	80 12 4	8 15 0	—	—	—		121
3 13 5	—	65 10 0	14 5 6	14 15 2	—	14 15 2		122
6 3 10	5 18 6	30 16 0	7 8 6	5 0 0	—	5 0 0	V.T.	123
1 6 6	—	120 0 0	8 10 0	2 15 6	1 0 0	6 15 6		124
0 11 3	—	} 110 10 0	{ 66 11 8	4 7 8	—	4 7 8		125
—	—		61 18 0	—	—	—		
2 1 0	4 10 0	16 12 4	9 8 0	2 1 0	—	2 1 0		126
6 6 6	—	} 94 6 6	{ 83 10 0	42 18 0	—	42 18 0		127
—	—		6 6 6	6 0 0	—	6 0 0		
6 15 6	—	56 3 4	69 18 0	15 0 0	15 0 0	30 0 0		128
—	—	—	—	—	—	—		129
2 18 11	—	47 16 8	35 18 6	18 4 9	—	18 4 0		130
0 13 3	—	24 0 0	6 9 6	1 15 11	8 0 0	9 15 11		131
2 15 9	4 16 8	68 0 0	11 11 6	4 18 0	17 10 0	b 22 8 0		132
8 16 2	—	30 0 0	35 12 0	14 8 9	5 0 0	19 8 9		133
1 0 7	—	57 6 8	16 15 0	7 0 0	12 0 0	b 19 0 0		134
8 19 8	—	41 10 0	14 17 6	7 0 0	17 0 3	b 24 0 3		135
—	—	52 10 0	17 8 0	2 8 9	—	2 8 9		136
2 0 3	—	84 15 0	19 14 0	6 18 4	8 10 0	b 15 8 4		137
—	—	—	—	—	—	—		138

d No Returns.

a Including value of Free Cards.

List of Schools in operation on the 31st December, 1874.—

Number	Roll Number of School	Parish.	District.	School.	Religious Denomination of Managers or Correspondents: Clerical	Lay.	Number and Religious Denomination of Teachers: Principals.	Assistants.	Attendance for the Year. Total number of Pupils on rolls within the Year 1874: Males.	Fem.	Total.	[illegible]
139	6221	Loughgilly,	16	Derrycughan, f.	Pres.	–	Pres.	Pres.	68	58	124	43
140	11029	Do.	–	Kingsmills,	Pres.	–	Pres.	–	60	54	114	36
141	8441	Kildarton,	–	Collone,	–	R.C.	Pres.	Pres.	94	116	210	71
142	6618	Killyman,	15	Clonmore,	R.C.	–	R.C.	–	57	57	114	46
143	6318	Knockmenackly,	11	Moyraverty,	Pres.	–	Pres.	–	58	47	105	47
144	132	Lisnadill,	16	Foley,	–	R.C.	R.C.	R.C.	181	145	326	80
145	2315	Do.	–	Drumgaw,	–	Pres.	R.C.	–	37	[illegible]	65	[illegible]
146	8437	Do.	–	Ballenan,	–	R.C.	Pres.	Pres.	101	61	162	70
147	7311	Do.	–	Lisnadill,	R.C.	–	R.C.	–	38	40	78	36
148	6636	Do.	–	Drumsloe,	R.C.	–	R.C.	–	41	30	71	30
149	8702	Do.	–	Millford,	–	Pres.	Pres.	Pres.	114	98	212	62
				Do. evg.	–	Pres.	Pres.	–	41	36	80	25
150	9260	Do.	–	Ennislare, c	–	R.C.	–	–	–	–	–	–
151	9676	Do.	–	Scotchan,	Pres.	–	Pres.	–	36	35	71	33
152	10798	Do.	–	Lisdoo (2),	R.C.	–	R.C.	–	41	46	87	34
153	2966	Loughgall,	–	Ware Lands,	–	R.C.	Pres.	–	56	45	101	28
154	2904	Do.	–	Aughanlig,	R.C.	–	R.C.	–	73	55	127	37
155	6487	Do.	–	Loughgall,	R.C.	–	R.C.	R.C.	75	68	143	56
156	10478	Do.	16	Charlemont,	R.C.	–	R.C.	R.C.	64	45	109	33
				Do. evg.	R.C.	–	R.C.	–	80	–	80	28
157	8506	Do.	16	Ballytyrone,	–	R.C.	R.C.	–	58	48	106	12
158	9623	Do.	–	Hockley,	–	R.C.	R.C.	R.C.	71	58	129	58
159	10187	Do.	–	Ardress,	–	R.C.	R.C.	–	87	44	131	53
160	11181	Do.	–	Kinnego, c	–	Diss.	Diss.	–	–	–	–	–
161	8448	Loughgilly,	–	Tullyherron,	R.C.	–	R.C.	R.C.	75	54	129	67
162	6252	Do.	–	Belleek, m.	R.C.	–	R.C.	–	161	–	161	40
163	6253	Do.	–	Do. f.	R.C.	–	R.C.	–	–	120	120	48
164	7880	Do.	–	Ballymoyer,	R.C.	–	R.C.	R.C.	98	68	166	85
165	8711	Do.	–	Lisnawanshaw,	Pres.	–	–	Pres.	66	53	119	60
166	9478	Mullaghbrack,	–	Markethill, m.	–	R.C.	Pres.	–	92	–	92	47
167	8174	Do.	–	Do. f.	–	R.C.	Pres.	Pres.	80	110	190	60
168	8848	Do.	–	Greenkeys, c	Pres.	–	–	–	–	–	–	–
169	6487	Do.	–	Cockhillbeg,	R.C.	–	R.C.	R.C.	68	74	142	69
170	9381	Do.	–	Tassaghmore, No. 2.	R.C.	–	R.C.	–	45	24	68	28
171	11903	Do.	–	Ballymorey, b	R.C.	–	R.C.	–	–	–	–	–
172	10719	Montiaghs,	11	Ardmore,	–	R.C.	R.C.	–	23	17	40	35
173	4256	Do.	–	Derrytrasna,	R.C.	–	R.C.	R.C.	112	71	183	60
				Do. evg.	R.C.	–	R.C.	–	60	33	93	30
174	10277	Do.	–	Bellville,	Pres.	–	Pres.	–	30	17	47	10
175	1107	Newtownhamilton,	16	Mullaghduff, m.	–	R.C.	Pres.	–	110	–	110	41
176	6088	Do.	–	Do. f.	–	R.C.	Pres.	–	–	59	59	41
177	1102	Do.	–	Tullyvallen,	–	R.C.	R.C.	R.C.	126	117	243	64
178	6792	Do.	–	Cortamlet,	–	R.C.	Pres.	Pres.	81	117	198	74
179	4280	Do.	–	Newtownhamilton,	R.C.	R.C.	R.C.	R.C.	86	70	156	66
180	6160	Do.	–	Skerriff,	Pres.	–	Pres.	–	50	45	95	33
181	11176	Do.	–	Townsend,	Pres.	–	Pres.	Pres.	98	40	138	72
182	6592	Do.	–	Carrickrovaddy,	R.C.	–	R.C.	–	71	95	166	35
183	8456	Do.	–	Camly Mountboy,	R.C.	–	R.C.	–	46	38	84	28
184	5824	Newry,	18	Newry Dis. Mod. m.	Com.	N.R.	Pres.	R.C.	209	–	208	93
185	4626	Do.	–	Do. f.	Com.	N.R.	R.C.	Pres.	–	240	240	114
186	5829	Do.	–	Do. i.	Com.	N.R.	R.C.	–	61	68	131	56
187	7208	Do.	–	Convent-st. Convent, f.	R.C.	–	R.C.	–	108	448	540	208
188	137	Shankill,	11	Tannaghmore,	–	R.C.	R.C.	R.C.	61	54	118	45
189	1897	Do.	–	Dougher, m.	R.C.	–	R.C.	R.C.	228	–	228	85
190	8994	Do.	–	Lurgan, m.	Pres.	–	Pres.	Pres.	162	–	162	71
191	6297	Do.	–	Do. f.	Pres.	–	Pres.	Pres.	–	115	115	49
192	6840	Do.	–	Lurgan Model, m.	Com.	N.R.	R.C.	1 R.C., 1 Pres., 1 Diss., 1 R.C.	270	–	270	106
				Do. b evg.	Com.	N.R.	R.C.	–	68	–	68	10
193	6841	Do.	–	Do. f.	Com.	N.R.	R.C.	1 Pres., 1 R.C.	–	108	108	60
194	6842	Do.	–	Do. i.	Com.	N.R.	Pres.	1 R.C., 1 R.C.	98	46	143	91

a Including value of Free Residence and Garden.
b Including value of Free Garden.
f School in charge of Assistant during last quarter of year.
c School in charge of unrecognised Teacher.

Province of Ulster: County of Armagh—*continued.*

Amount paid for Books, Requisites, and Apparatus at Reduced Prices. (£ s. d.)	Aid granted by the Board during the Year 1874. In Free Stock of Books, Requisites, and Apparatus. (£ s. d.)	In Salaries, Premiums, and other Gratuities. (£ s. d.)	Results Fees, Financial Year. (£ s. d.)	Amount of Local Emoluments received in Aid of Teacher's Salary. School Fees. (£ s. d.)	Subscriptions, Endowments, &c. (£ s. d.)	Total Local Aid. (£ s. d.)	Vested or Non-Vested.	Number.
4 4 0	3 5 0	24 5 8	17 18 0	7 7 8	9 12 0	a17 2 8		139
8 18 6	—	24 0 0	10 10 0	6 0 0	—	6 0 0		140
7 14 10	—	31 0 0	21 8 0	—	2 0 0	a2 0 0		141
2 14 2	—	23 6 8	15 16 0	6 0 0	20 10 0	b26 10 0		142
1 16 3	—	26 18 8	10 2 6	4 11 8	—	4 11 8		143
8 8 8	—	78 18 8	28 0 0	4 18 10	10 0 0	a14 18 10		144
—	—	30 0 0	3 18 0	—	2 0 0	2 0 0	V.E.	145
5 3 8	—	38 8 4	29 9 0	6 8 0	37 0 0	a43 8 0		146
1 5 3	—	29 0 0	6 6 0	—	14 9 8	a14 9 8		147
—	—	22 0 0	6 16 0	0 1 9	—	0 1 9		148
0 2 6	—	106 3 4	84 18 0	10 9 1	35 0 0	44 9 1		149
—	—	—	10 17 6	6 13 10	—	6 13 10		
—	—	29 0 0	10 0 6	—	—	—		150
3 8 4	—	45 5 4	16 1 6	3 10 0	1 13 0	a5 3 0		151
1 18 1	5 0 6	30 0 0	9 8 6	1 7 6	1 0 0	a2 7 6		152
1 14 7	—	21 0 0	6 8 6	2 14 8	14 0 0	a16 14 8	V.E.	153
0 10 1	—	50 16 6	8 6 0	8 8 8	10 10 0	a18 18 8	V.E.	154
5 8 0	—	23 18 8	24 14 9	7 13 2	2 0 0	a9 13 2		155
1 9 3	—	41 0 0	16 6 6	4 14 8	13 10 0	a18 4 8		156
—	—		3 6 6	2 4 6	—	2 4 6		
3 5 2	—	10 10 3	16 4 8	4 16 8	17 0 6	a21 16 8		157
4 12 2	—	47 10 0	13 4 0	4 11 7	23 10 0	a28 1 7		158
1 8 3	—	24 0 0	6 14 0	2 14 8	14 0 0	a16 14 8		159
1 8 3	4 0 0	18 0 0	7 8 6	—	—	—		160
8 17 7	1 17 6	64 8 4	21 9 0	15 5 0	—	15 5 0		161
1 8 6	—	24 0 0	7 18 0	1 8 6	—	1 8 6		162
2 10 6	—	26 3 4	16 1 6	8 0 0	—	8 0 0		163
2 19 10	—	40 16 8	22 11 0	2 18 0	—	8 18 0		164
8 19 9	—	73 3 4	29 3 0	8 0 0	4 10 0	a12 10 0		165
—	—	77 0 0	14 18 0	13 4 1	6 10 0	a19 14 1	V.T.	166
4 14 10	—	78 10 8	23 19 6	15 3 0	5 0 0	20 3 0	V.T.	167
—	—	—	—	—	—	—	V.E.	168
3 1 5	—	35 0 0	27 9 0	5 2 6	5 0 0	10 2 0		169
1 10 5	—	24 0 0	9 8 5	3 0 11	4 0 0	a7 0 11		170
1 10 6	—	26 1 8	14 11 0	—	—	—		171
9 10 8	1 0 0	—	—	0 14 6	18 0 0	18 14 6		172
5 15 0	—	75 15 0	30 18 0	18 11 3	—	18 11 3		173
—	—		5 10 0	1 18 0	—	1 18 0		
—	—	23 0 0	9 16 0	1 18 0	10 0 0	11 18 0		174
6 3 7	—	49 15 0	16 8 0	2 8 0	1 0 0	b3 8 0		175
—	—	28 18 4	14 14 8	—	—	—		176
3 8 4	—	60 0 0	17 18 0	0 10 0	4 0 0	a4 10 0		177
4 10 5	—	58 0 0	66 5 0	1 19 6	—	1 19 6		178
0 18 6	—	64 3 4	28 17 0	6 16 0	—	6 16 0		179
3 19 11	—	21 0 0	7 0 6	1 8 6	—	1 4 6		180
5 18 6	5 0 8	11 6 8	19 15 6	8 0 0	—	8 0 0		181
1 15 8	—	24 0 0	11 4 6	3 0 0	—	3 0 0		182
0 9 7	—	24 0 0	5 2 0	3 5 0	2 0 0	a4 5 0		183
29 0 0	9 6 6	320 15 11	100 9 9	143 16 9	—	143 16 0	V.C.	184
6 16 9	—							185
—	—							186
18 11 2	—	100 12 10	45 18 0	26 8 1	—	29 8 1		187
3 8 4	—	60 0 0	17 7 8	14 9 6	5 0 0	19 9 6		188
0 5 8	—	114 8 8	31 18 0	20 0 0	0 0 0	26 0 0	E.	189
6 2 2	4 2 8	61 0 0	30 14 0	21 9 6	—	21 9 6		190
—	—	50 8 4	12 12 0	12 0 0	—	12 0 0		191
37 11 1	6 15 4						V.C.	192
—	—	773 6 7	148 0 0	180 15 6	—	189 15 6	V.C.	193
20 19 3	5 14 3						V.C.	194
—	—							

a Closed for portion of year. b Returns not available. c Including value of Free Residence. d Returns not up to date. e Closed during last quarter.

List of Schools in operation on the 31st December, 1874.—

Number.	Roll Number of School.	Parish.	District.	School.	Religious Denomination of Managers or Correspondents: Clergy.	Lay.	Teachers and Religious Denomination of Teachers: Principals.	Assistants.	Attendance for the Year: Total Number of Pupils on Rolls within the Year 1874: Males.	Females.	Total.	Average Number daily in Attendance for the Year.
195	6719	Shankill,	11	Edward-st. Conv. f.	R.C.	–	Nuns.		121	419	540	217
				Do. evg.	R.C.	–	Nuns.		–	236	236	56
196	9202	Do.	–	Hillcrest, Lurgan,[c]	Pres.	–	–	–	–	–	–	–
197	4567	Do.	–	Halftown,	R.C.	–	R.C.	R.C.	68	69	137	65
198	8779	Do.	–	Queen-street,	Pres.	–	Pres.	Pres.	124	109	233	94
199	6825	Do.	–	Knocknashane,	Pres.	–	Pres.	–	58	46	104	56
200	10411	Do.	–	Tullygally,	–	R.C.	R.C.	–	64	51	115	48
201	1747	Seagoe,	–	Aghacommon, m.	R.C.	–	R.C.	–	110	–	110	40
				Do. evg.	R.C.	–	R.C.	–	75	–	75	20
202	6204	Do.	–	Do. f.	R.C.	–	R.C.	–	–	107	107	35
203	6365	Do.	–	Edenderry,	Pres.	–	Pres.	3 Pres. 1 R.C.	331	281	612	300
				Do. evg.	Pres.	–	Pres.	–	103	22	125	37
204	6391	Do.	–	Ballinacor,	–	R.C.	Pres.	R.C.	95	86	181	61
205	9002	Do.	–	Turmoyra,	Pres.	–	Pres.	–	62	35	97	39
206	11149	Do.	–	Seagoe,[a]	R.C.	–	Pres.	–	–	–	–	–
207	9524	Do.	–	Keara,	Diss.	–	Diss.	–	71	40	111	34
				Do.[a] evg.	Diss.	–	–	–	–	–	–	–
208	11032	Do.	–	Silverwood,	R.C.	–	R.C.	R.C.	116	58	174	65
209	2337	Tartaraghan,	15	Maghery,	R.C.	–	R.C.	R.C.	66	39	105	60
210	6164	Do.	–	English, (1),	R.C.	–	R.C.	R.C.	67	64	131	63
211	8910	Do.	–	Do. (2),	Diss.	–	Diss.	–	74	44	124	31
212	8202	Do.	–	Clonmore,	–	Diss.	Pres.	–	119	108	228	78
213	8273	Do.	–	Tartaraghan,	Pres.	–	Pres.	Pres.	105	77	182	48
214	9946	Do.	–	Derryinver,[a]	Diss.	–	–	–	–	–	–	–
215	10680	Do.	–	Derryland,	R.C.	–	R.C.	–	100	31	131	41
216	4022	Tynan,	16	Middletown, m.	R.C.	–	R.C.	–	101	–	101	37
217	5816	Do.	–	Do. f.	R.C.	–	R.C.	–	–	134	134	39
218	8912	Do.	–	Mullyloughan,	R.C.	–	R.C.	–	64	46	100	38
219	9734	Do.	–	Listrany,	Pres.	–	Pres.	–	20	34	54	20
220	10345	Do.	–	Drumsallilary,	–	R.C.	R.C.	–	63	43	106	42
221	10469	Do.	–	Liss,	R.C.	–	R.C.	R.C.	101	79	180	63
222	9877	Tartaraghan,	16	Cranagill,	–	Diss.	R.C.	Pres.	101	11	112	50
				Do. evg.	–	Diss.	R.C.	–	115	81	196	63
223	10051	Do.	–	Milltown,	R.C.	–	R.C.	–	80	86	84	84
224	10282	Do.	–	Tartaraghan, No. 2,	R.C.	–	R.C.	R.C.	99	74	173	78
				Do. evg.	R.C.	–	R.C.	–	66	7	73	73
225	10724	Upper Creggan,	16	Glassdrummond,[a]	R.C.	–	R.C.	–	–	–	–	–
		Total for County Armagh, 225,							18283	16701	34,981	13028

COUNTY OF

1	136	Annagh,	23	Drumhaney,	R.C.	–	R.C.	R.C.	80	48	128	53
2	1520	Do.	–	Shercock, m.	R.C.	–	R.C.	–	109	–	109	39
3	1483	Do.	–	Do. f.	R.C.	–	R.C.	–	–	84	84	25
4	1467	Do.	–	Kevlagh,	R.C.	–	R.C.	R.C.	80	90	170	54
5	2775	Do.	–	Kilnaleck,	–	R.C.	R.C.	–	80	73	153	53
6	9060	Do.	–	Belturbet,[d] m.	R.C.	–	–	–	–	–	–	–
7	10477	Do.	–	Castle Saunderson,	R.C.	–	R.C.	–	40	38	78	31
8	10429	Do.	–	Belturbet Convent, f.	R.C.	–	Nuns	–	57	231	288	99
9	10780	Do.	–	Drumaloor,	R.C.	–	R.C.	–	76	46	122	54
10	11117	Do.	–	Cloverhill,	–	R.C.	R.C.	R.C.	54	50	104	32
11	157	Annagelliff,	–	Coolboyogue, m.	R.C.	–	R.C.	–	92	44	136	39
12	1034	Do.	–	Pullamore, m.	R.C.	–	R.C.	–	70	–	70	22
13	2304	Do.	–	Do. f.	R.C.	–	R.C.	–	–	68	68	25
14	3450	Do.	–	Cavan Workhouse,	P.L.	Gds.	R.C.	R.C.	51	53	104	57
15	5249	Do.	–	Curlurgan,	–	R.C.	R.C.	–	54	25	79	30
16	8453	Do.	–	Cratnagy, m.	R.C.	–	R.C.	–	69	–	69	23
17	8596	Do.	–	Do. f.	R.C.	–	R.C.	–	–	73	73	35

[a] Returns not available. [b] Including value of Free Residence. [c] Inoperative. [d] Including value of Free Garden.

Province of ULSTER: County of ARMAGH—*continued.*

Amount paid for Books, Requisites, and Apparatus at Reduced Prices.	Aid granted by the Board during the Year 1874. In Free Grants of Books, Requisites, and Apparatus.	In Salaries, Premiums, and other Gratuities.	Result Fees, Financial Year.	Amount of Local Emoluments received in Aid of Teacher's Salary. School Fees.	Subscriptions, Endowments, &c.	Total Local Aid.	Vested or Non-Vested.	Number.
£ s. d.	£ s. d.	£ s. d.	£ s. d.	£ s. d.	£ s. d.	£ s. d.		
16 10 11	—	110 6 0	25 0 0	27 18 1	—	27 18 4		195
—	—	—	6 8 0	1 19 9	—	1 19 9		
4 6 10	—	62 13 4	16 17 6	—	—	—		196
4 7 4	6 7 9	64 0 0	11 8 6	11 13 6	—	11 15 6		197
4 1 6	—	67 2 8	16 6 4	—	5 0 0	5 0 6		198
1 7 9	—	29 8 4	12 4 6	6 13 5	—	6 13 9		199
2 17 11	—	27 18 4	12 17 6	5 13 3	5 0 0	10 18 6		200
1 8 3	—	44 10 0	18 2 6	10 14 0	2 0 0	12 14 0		201
—	—	—	2 11 0	2 8 8	—	2 9 9		
1 1 0	—	29 10 6	8 6 0	3 18 4	1 0 6	4 18 6		202
15 6 8	—	182 15 0	74 18 0	48 0 8	—	48 0 8		203
—	—	—	8 11 0	5 11 2	—	5 11 2		
6 18 4	—	47 0 0	20 5 0	7 0 4	10 15 0	22 15 4		204
1 6 6	—	58 0 5	6 7 0	5 3 10	—	5 3 10		205
1 14 1	4 10 0	5 0 0	—	—	—	—		206
2 17 6	—	32 0 0	6 5 0	4 16 0	10 10 0	b 15 6 0		207
—	—	—	—	—	—	—		
—	5 10 0	40 7 1	14 1 0	13 1 10	—	13 1 10		208
0 10 0	—	33 0 0	0 7 0	6 12 0	2 0 0	b 4 12 0	V.T.	209
1 6 0	—	60 15 0	11 0 0	0 6 0	1 6 0	b 1 12 0		210
0 11 6	—	21 0 4	—	5 0 0	7 0 0	11 0 0		211
0 1 9	—	40 18 3	15 18 6	4 17 11	12 6 4	d 17 0 3		212
1 13 0	—	45 10 6	19 8 0	7 0 8	4 0 0	b 11 0 8		213
—	—	5 0 0	—	—	—	—		214
4 6 10	—	24 15 0	11 5 6	3 10 6	5 0 0	8 10 5		215
8 18 9	—	23 0 0	0 9 0	1 19 9	—	1 12 9		216
1 6 11	—	33 12 4	13 17 6	2 17 0	—	2 17 0		217
1 5 3	—	26 13 4	12 8 0	0 0 0	—	0 6 0		218
—	4 5 8	19 11 6	0 15 0	1 0 6	5 0 0	6 0 6		219
6 0 6	—	80 6 0	16 17 0	—	16 0 0	c 16 0 0		220
4 18 10	—	64 15 4	18 7 6	0 13 6	1 10 0	c 2 3 0		221
0 15 6	—	} 63 0 0	{ 18 0 6	8 10 0	—	8 10 0		222
—	—		8 7 0	7 18 6	7 10 0	b 15 2 6		
1 0 0	—	24 0 0	—	5 5 0	2 0 0	4 5 0		223
5 0 0	—	} 47 10 0	{ 21 0 0	1 10 0	8 0 0	c 2 10 0		224
—	—		—	3 0 0	—	3 0 0		
1 11 7	—	25 0 0	—	—	—	—		225
648 19 10	114 10 11	10,097 15 8	3,707 14 0	1,749 13 6	1,244 4 5	2,993 18 11		

CAVAN—260 Schools.

Amount paid for Books, Requisites, and Apparatus at Reduced Prices.	In Free Grants of Books, Requisites, and Apparatus.	In Salaries, Premiums, and other Gratuities.	Result Fees, Financial Year.	School Fees.	Subscriptions, Endowments, &c.	Total Local Aid.	Vested or Non-Vested.	Number.
1 6 8	—	60 0 0	16 8 0	5 19 6	—	5 10 6		1
2 15 9	—	52 0 0	11 2 6	6 3 8	—	6 3 6	V.T.	2
0 1 6	—	30 0 0	4 13 0	1 4 8	—	1 4 8	V.T.	3
2 17 9	—	48 0 0	14 9 6	4 6 6	—	4 6 6	V.T.	4
0 14 11	—	24 0 6	6 19 0	2 6 9	—	2 5 8	V.T.	5
1 17 1	—	33 0 0	5 5 4	—	—	—		6
5 16 7	—	24 0 0	0 0 0	6 0 0	0 0 0	h 18 0 0		7
4 2 11	—	42 6 0	24 7 0	5 1 6	—	5 1 6		8
3 16 7	—	24 0 0	7 2 0	6 9 6	4 0 0	d 11 6 6		9
10 8 1	4 10 6	32 6 8	23 5 6	1 17 6	22 0 0	b 23 17 6		10
—	—	27 5 0	6 2 0	2 16 0	—	2 16 0	V.T.	11
5 1 6	—	24 0 0	12 2 0	3 4 10	1 0 0	f 3 4 10	V.T.	12
1 12 4	—	24 0 0	11 12 6	1 8 5	2 0 0	f 3 8 5	V.T.	13
4 6 4	—	1 10 0	—	—	—	—		14
2 15 5	—	30 0 0	5 5 6	0 14 1	4 0 0	b 4 14 1	A.	15
3 0 0	—	30 0 0	12 4 6	3 15 10	—	3 15 10		16
1 13 0	—	30 0 0	5 2 6	1 15 4	—	1 15 4		17

a Closed. b Including value of Free Residence and Garden. c Closed last quarter; no returns.

List of Schools in operation on the 31st December, 1874.—

Number.	Roll Number of School.	Parish.	District.	School.	Religious Denomination of Managers or Correspondents: Clerical.	Lay.	Teachers and Religious Denomination of Teachers: Principals.	Assistants.	Attendance for the Year: Total number of Pupils on Rolls within the Year 1874: Males.	Fem.	Total.	Average daily attendance.
18	10184	Annagelliffe,	23	Drumcrave,	R.C.	–	R.C.	–	73	46	119	60
19	187	Ballymachugh,	–	Ballymarry, m.	R.C.	–	R.C.	–	100	–	100	46
20	181	Do.	–	Do. f.	R.C.	–	R.C.	–	–	69	69	30
21	135	Do.	–	Carrick, m.	R.C.	–	R.C.	–	97	–	97	51
22	189	Do.	–	Do. f.	R.C.	–	R.C.	–	–	65	65	29
23	3780	Bailieborough,	24	Dromcarrow,[b]	Pres.	–	–	–	–	–	–	–
24	4991	Do.	–	Cronkmbastin,	–	R.C.	R.C.	–	90	93	183	49
25	5540	Do.	–	Lear,	Pres.	–	Pres.	Pres.	102	80	182	65
26	7971	Do.	–	Drummonapick,	R.C.	–	R.C.	–	51	25	76	33
27	8039	Do.	–	Lisball,	–	R.C.	Pres.	R.C.	69	60	129	16
28	8794	Do.	–	Bailieborough, m.	R.C.	–	R.C.	–	79	–	79	28
29	9621	Do.	–	Do. District Model, m.	Com.	N.E.	Pres.	R.C.	206	–	206	111
30	9629	Do.	–	Do. do. f.	Com.	N.E.	–	R.C.	–	251	251	124
31	8511	Do.	–	Do. do. i.	Com.	N.E.	R.C.	–	48	53	101	44
32	10084	Do.	–	Do. No. 2, f.	R.C.	–	R.C.	–	–	101	101	37
33	8412	Do.	–	Do. Workhouse,	P.L.	Gds.	R.C.	–	32	38	70	55
34	10189	Do.	–	Lisgar,[c]	Pres.	–	–	–	–	–	–	–
35	7365	Ballintemple,	23	Drumkey, m.	R.C.	–	R.C.	–	143	–	143	56
36	7505	Do.	–	Do. f.	R.C.	–	R.C.	–	–	134	134	60
37	7350	Do.	–	Drumalrada, m.	–	R.C.	R.C.	–	67	–	67	32
38	7367	Do.	–	Do. f.	–	R.C.	R.C.	–	–	73	73	35
39	7723	Do.	–	Aughaloora, m.	R.C.	–	R.C.	–	125	–	125	43
40	7129	Do.	–	Do. f.	R.C.	–	R.C.	–	–	97	97	31
41	7990	Do.	–	Coolkeeva,	R.C.	–	R.C.	–	69	37	106	48
42	8904	Do.	–	Lurganlanny, m.	R.C.	–	R.C.	–	163	–	163	56
43	0006	Do.	–	Do. f.	R.C.	–	R.C.	–	–	111	111	36
44	153	Castletara,	–	Ballyhaise, m.	R.C.	–	R.C.	–	87	–	87	37
45	154	Do.	–	Do. f.	R.C.	–	R.C.	–	–	100	100	30
46	3710	Do.	–	Castletara, m.	R.C.	–	R.C.	–	84	–	84	31
47	4039	Do.	–	Do. f.	R.C.	–	R.C.	–	–	73	73	30
48	8920	Do.	–	Corratubber,	R.C.	–	R.C.	–	37	47	84	34
49	10308	Do.	–	Drumsharrid,	R.C.	–	R.C.	–	80	69	149	50
50	11034	Do.	–	Ballyhaise,	R.C.	–	R.C.	–	44	65	109	37
51	5174	Castlerahan,	–	Castlerahan, m.	R.C.	–	R.C.	–	93	–	93	28
52	5175	Do.	–	Do. f.	R.C.	–	R.C.	–	–	83	83	31
53	7108	Do.	–	Loskan,	R.C.	–	R.C.	–	133	–	133	55
54	8158	Do.	–	Ballyjamesduff, m.	R.C.	–	R.C.	–	117	–	117	57
55	10175	Do.	–	Do. Convent, f.	R.C.	–	Nuns	–	–	160	160	77
56	8218	Do.	–	Mullaghmore,	R.C.	–	R.C.	–	106	77	183	67
57	8867	Do.	–	Barony Robinson, m.	R.C.	–	R.C.	–	88	–	88	34
58	8698	Do.	–	Do. f.	R.C.	–	R.C.	–	–	83	83	33
59	10797	Do.	–	Killdallagh,	R.C.	–	R.C.	–	25	16	41	19
60	9635	Do.	–	Garrirune,	R.C.	–	R.C.	R.C.	94	63	157	56
61	1356	Crosserlough,	–	Kilnaleck, m.	–	R.C.	R.C.	–	109	–	109	53
62	1482	Do.	–	Do. f.	–	R.C.	R.C.	R.C.	52	117	169	70
63	2717	Do.	–	Callow,	R.C.	–	R.C.	R.C.	144	116	260	89
64	2713	Do.	–	Lackerry, m.	–	R.C.	R.C.	–	143	–	143	61
65	2748	Do.	–	Do. f.	–	R.C.	R.C.	–	–	128	128	43
66	6460	Do.	–	Drumakilly, m.	R.C.	–	R.C.	–	166	–	166	63
67	6451	Do.	–	Do. f.	R.C.	–	R.C.	R.C.	–	129	129	54
68	6637	Do.	–	Drumcora, m.	R.C.	–	R.C.	–	117	–	117	49
69	7087	Do.	–	Do. f.	R.C.	–	R.C.	–	–	131	131	58
70	6469	Do.	–	Banana,	R.C.	–	R.C.	R.C.	54	57	111	38
71	10492	Do.	–	Aughareeney,	R.C.	–	R.C.	–	67	69	136	39
72	134	Drumlane,	–	Derravona,	R.C.	–	R.C.	–	45	31	76	37
73	1169	Do.	–	Stagball, m.	R.C.	–	R.C.	–	150	–	150	45
74	7777	Do.	–	Do. f.	R.C.	–	R.C.	–	–	74	74	27
75	4250	Do.	–	Drumheel, [illegible]	R.C.	–	R.C.	–	70	68	138	31
76	6750	Do.	–	Greaghrahan,	R.C.	–	R.C.	R.C.	60	80	140	40
77	0831	Do.	–	Ashgrove,	R.C.	–	R.C.	–	36	45	81	26
78	7774	Do.	–	Corrasloe,	R.C.	–	R.C.	–	43	57	100	37
79	8085	Do.	–	Milltown, m.	R.C.	–	R.C.	–	87	–	87	18

[a] Including value of Free Residence and Garden. [b] No Teacher. [c] Inoperative.

Province of ULSTER: County of CAVAN—*continued.*

Amount paid for Books, Requisites, and Apparatus, at Reduced Prices.	Aid granted by the Board during the Year 1874. In Free Stock of Books, Requisites, and Apparatus.	In Salaries, Premiums, and other Gratuities.	Results Fees, Financial Year.	Amount of Local Contributions received in Aid of Teacher's Salary. School Fees.	Subscriptions, Endowments, &c.	Total Local Aid.	Vested or Non-Vested.	Number.
£ s. d.	£ s. d.	£ s. d.	£ s. d.	£ s. d.	£ s. d.	£ s. d.		
3 10 4	—	24 0 0	6 3 2	4 7 2	—	4 7 2		18
1 9 4	—	30 0 0	12 6 0	6 6 6	—	6 0 6		19
2 6 1	—	24 0 0	11 0 6	3 0 5	—	3 0 5		20
1 16 8	—	75 0 0	6 4 0	1 10 0	2 0 0	*3 10 0	V.T.	21
1 17 10	—	30 0 0	6 4 0	2 10 6	—	2 10 6	V.T.	22
—	—	—	—	—	—	—		23
2 13 8	—	26 0 0	16 0 0	3 11 0	—	3 11 0		24
7 14 6	—	118 3 0	24 5 0	7 1 0	—	7 1 0		25
1 12 4	—	30 0 0	5 18 0	1 10 6	—	1 10 0		26
3 4 0	—	50 0 0	13 6 6	4 10 0	4 0 0	8 10 0	V.C.	27
—	—	24 0 0	3 14 6	3 15 6	—	3 15 6		28
37 7 0	1 11 0	757 13 10	159 16 4	97 19 3	—	97 19 3	V.T.	29
—	—							30
—	—							31
2 0 11	—	24 0 0	4 17 6	0 10 0	—	0 10 0		32
2 18 3	—	—	—	—	—	—		33
—	—	—	—	—	—	—		34
1 15 5	—	28 10 0	16 16 6	3 1 0	—	3 1 0		35
0 16 2	—	28 13 4	16 16 0	1 17 0	—	1 17 0		36
3 3 0	—	21 0 0	4 3 0	0 11 0	—	0 11 0		37
1 0 6	—	20 0 0	6 7 0	0 16 0	—	0 16 0		38
2 14 4	—	22 10 0	7 5 6	1 1 6	—	1 1 6		39
1 0 4	—	20 0 0	8 0 6	1 4 6	—	1 4 6		40
3 5 4	—	24 0 0	7 3 6	0 10 0	—	0 10 0		41
3 1 5	—	27 0 0	13 6 6	1 10 0	—	1 10 6		42
1 0 2	—	21 0 0	6 4 0	1 7 6	—	1 7 6		43
2 5 1	—	39 15 0	11 17 6	4 18 6	—	4 18 6	V.T.	44
1 15 9	—	30 0 0	7 9 0	8 3 10	—	8 3 10	V.T.	45
4 6 6	—	24 0 0	4 0 6	3 19 0	—	3 19 0		46
—	—	20 0 0	0 17 0	2 11 6	—	2 11 6		47
2 0 7	—	20 0 0	7 4 6	4 7 6	—	4 7 6		48
2 3 4	—	20 0 0	8 13 8	0 6 4	—	0 6 4		49
3 18 3	—	38 0 0	14 16 0	0 7 0	20 0 0	*20 7 0		50
2 18 9	—	31 0 0	6 13 6	1 11 6	—	1 11 6		51
2 18 3	—	30 0 0	12 17 6	3 17 6	—	3 17 6		52
3 10 2	—	20 0 0	16 13 0	3 0 6	—	3 0 6		53
6 1 4	—	31 0 0	13 11 0	7 6 6	—	7 6 6		54
5 10 7	—	39 11 0	21 16 0	7 8 8	—	7 8 8		55
3 6 8	—	44 0 0	9 4 6	1 8 0	—	1 8 0		56
0 12 2	—	34 6 0	9 19 0	1 10 0	—	1 10 0		57
1 14 0	—	28 10 0	7 7 0	3 6 0	—	3 6 0		58
0 13 3	—	12 10 0	4 6 0	—	—	—		59
4 4 6	—	30 0 0	14 1 6	2 10 0	1 10 0	*4 0 0		60
2 13 1	1 0 0	41 16 8	14 2 0	4 11 0	1 10 0	*6 1 0	V.T.	61
3 0 7	—	42 0 0	0 18 0	3 10 0	—	3 17 0	V.T.	62
3 15 1	—	44 6 0	15 4 6	6 0 6	—	6 0 6		63
3 17 3	—	57 6 8	14 1 0	6 3 0	1 10 0	*7 13 0		64
5 6 6	—	40 10 0	16 14 6	6 11 6	1 10 0	*8 1 6		65
3 6 9	—	30 13 4	7 7 6	4 14 6	—	4 14 6		66
1 18 6	—	30 0 0	12 17 10	8 3 0	—	8 3 0		67
6 9 1	—	28 0 0	10 16 6	5 17 0	—	5 17 0		68
2 14 2	—	24 0 0	12 3 0	8 13 0	—	8 13 0		69
—	—	41 16 8	5 1 6	0 10 6	—	0 10 6		70
1 10 0	—	20 0 0	6 19 2	2 6 6	—	2 6 6		71
0 14 0	—	24 0 0	7 3 6	0 16 11	—	0 16 11	V.T.	72
6 6 7	—	32 0 0	16 11 0	7 6 10	—	7 6 10		73
2 19 7	—	60 0 0	7 7 0	8 0 7	—	8 0 7		74
2 3 2	—	54 0 0	12 5 3	3 14 4	—	3 14 4		75
1 15 0	—	35 0 0	6 3 6	3 4 0	—	3 4 0		76
1 6 1	—	30 0 0	7 19 0	0 11 10	—	0 11 10		77
1 0 6	—	30 10 0	6 16 0	1 10 3	—	1 10 6		78
1 13 7	—	30 0 0	—	0 18 6	—	0 18 6	V.T.	79

* Including value of Free Residence. * Including value of Free Garden.

List of Schools in operation on the 31st December, 1874.—

Number.	Roll Number of School.	Parish.	District.	School.	Religious Denomination of Managers or Correspondent: Clerical.	Lay.	Number and Religious Denomination of Teachers: Principals.	Assistants.	Attendance for the Year: Total number of Pupils on Rolls within the Year 1874: Males.	Fem.	Total.	Average Daily Attendance for Year 1874.
80	6919	Drumlane,	23	Milkern, f.	R.C.	–	R.C.	–	–	77	77	31
81	1858	Drumgoon,	24	Dernakesh, m.	R.C.	–	R.C.	–	94	–	91	13
82	1954	Do.	–	Do. f.	R.C.	–	R.C.	–	–	94	94	27
83	1357	Do.	–	Cootehill, m.	R.C.	R.C.	R.C.	–	200	–	200	73
84	1809	Do.	–	Do. f.	R.C.	R.C.	R.C.	R.C.	–	125	125	67
85	3844	Do.	–	Do. Workhouse,	P.L.	Gds.	R.C.	–	39	26	65	33
86	9299	Do.	–	Cohaw, m.	R.C.	–	R.C.	–	63	–	63	29
87	9130	Do.	–	Do.[a] f.	R.C.	–	–	–	–	–	–	–
88	4185	Do.	–	Drumanan,	R.C.	–	Pres.	–	68	47	115	41
89	4303	Do.	–	Knappagh,	–	R.C.	R.C.	R.C.	94	119	213	64
90	4632	Do.	–	Killyclaare,	Pres.	–	R.C.	–	39	39	89	34
91	10354	Do.	–	Tullyienkine,	R.C.	–	R.C.	–	65	56	117	37
92	153	Drumkeenan,	23	Loughaerydaff, m.	R.C.	–	R.C.	–	153	–	158	51
93	154	Do.	–	Do. f.	R.C.	–	R.C.	R.C.	–	169	169	84
94	10237	Do.	–	Mynagh,	R.C.	–	R.C.	–	49	53	101	38
95	6322	Do.	–	Cloncoose, f.	R.C.	–	R.C.	–	98	89	187	43
96	6819	Do.	–	Killoggy, m.	R.C.	–	R.C.	–	178	–	178	63
97	6813	Do.	–	Do. f.	R.C.	–	R.C.	–	–	189	189	45
98	9507	Do.	–	Clonooney,	R.C.	–	R.C.	–	78	73	151	58
99	1343	Denn,	–	Crossakeys,	–	R.C.	R.C.	R.C.	103	57	160	77
100	7023	Do.	–	Denn, m.	R.C.	–	R.C.	–	61	–	61	33
101	7838	Do.	–	Do. f.	R.C.	–	R.C.	–	–	60	60	25
102	7930	Do.	–	Lackan, f.	R.C.	–	R.C.	–	–	118	119	43
103	8488	Do.	–	Corraneary,	R.C.	–	R.C.	–	28	36	64	19
104	10197	Do.	–	Bruskey, m.	R.C.	–	R.C.	–	63	–	63	30
105	10198	Do.	–	Do. f.	R.C.	–	R.C.	–	–	69	69	33
106	10482	Do.	–	Drumavaddy, m.	R.C.	–	R.C.	–	160	–	160	59
107	10483	Do.	–	Do. f.	R.C.	–	R.C.	–	–	117	117	43
108	6921	Drumgever,	24	Cootehill, No. 2, m.	Pres.	–	Pres.	–	85	–	85	41
109	9282	Do.	–	Do. f.	Pres.	–	Pres.	–	–	79	79	34
110	4912	Drung,	23	Drung Ord. Agricul.	R.C.	–	R.C.	–	78	–	78	25
111	5481	Do.	–	Do. f.	R.C.	–	R.C.	–	–	87	87	31
112	7226	Do.	–	Leppan,	R.C.	–	R.C.	–	49	53	94	32
113	8298	Do.	–	Cornahill, m.	–	R.C.	R.C.	–	94	–	94	21
114	8271	Do.	–	Do. f.	–	R.C.	R.C.	–	–	79	79	30
115	8973	Do.	–	Lisboduff, m.	R.C.	–	R.C.	–	137	–	137	40
116	8961	Do.	–	Do. f.	R.C.	–	R.C.	–	–	107	107	32
117	9826	Do.	–	Maghera,	R.C.	–	R.C.	–	87	71	158	54
118	10542	Do.	–	Drung,	R.C.	–	R.C.	–	48	47	95	28
119	7021	Drumgood,	20	Lanyloe,	–	R.C.	R.C.	–	49	32	81	32
120	9724	Drummully,	21	Ardmeave,	R.C.	–	R.C.	R.C.	69	48	117	30
121	1632	Enniskeen,	24	Kilmengully, m.	R.C.	–	R.C.	–	109	–	109	39
122	8845	Do.	–	Do. f.	R.C.	–	R.C.	–	–	117	117	35
123	4591	Do.	–	Northlands,	–	R.C.	R.C.	R.C.	168	146	304	87
124	7760	Do.	–	Lisier,	R.C.	–	R.C.	–	109	90	199	44
125	8161	Do.	–	Kingscourt, m.	R.C.	–	R.C.	R.C.	178	–	178	39
126	8165	Do.	–	Do. f.	R.C.	–	R.C.	R.C.	–	183	183	66
127	10062	Do.	–	Do. No. 2, m.	–	R.C.	Pres.	–	81	–	81	[illegible]
128	10184	Do.	–	Do. f.	–	R.C.	Pres.	–	–	80	80	33
129	147	Killdrumsherdan,	23	Kill,	R.C.	–	R.C.	R.C.	105	95	200	60
130	7162	Do.	–	Dunmerick,	R.C.	–	Pres.	Pres.	97	67	164	70
131	7990	Do.	–	Carnunan,	R.C.	–	R.C.	–	79	63	142	49
132	8488	Do.	–	Drumnatrade,	R.C.	–	R.C.	–	88	77	165	65
133	8447	Do.	–	Ashfield,	R.C.	–	Pres.	–	58	48	104	31
134	8648	Do.	–	Tullyvin, f.	R.C.	–	R.C.	–	39	44	83	21
135	1141	Killsallen,	20	Killsallen, m.	R.C.	–	R.C.	–	64	–	64	27
136	5090	Do.	–	Do. f.	R.C.	–	R.C.	–	–	70	70	25
137	2571	Do.	–	Killygorman, m.	R.C.	–	R.C.	–	81	–	81	28
138	8047	Do.	–	Do. f.	R.C.	–	R.C.	–	–	87	87	28
139	1288	Kilmore,	25	Ballymagh, m.	R.C.	–	R.C.	R.C.	148	–	148	67
140	9768	Do.	–	Do. f.	R.C.	–	R.C.	R.C.	–	155	155	60
141	8098	Do.	–	Drumcor,	R.C.	–	R.C.	–	57	61	118	33
142	8287	Do.	–	Drumerow,	R.C.	–	R.C.	R.C.	73	86	159	32

[a] Including value of Free Residence and Garden. [b] Excluding value of Free Residence.

Province of Ulster : County of Cavan—*continued.*

Amount paid for Books, Requisites, and Apparatus at Reduced Prices.	Aid granted by the Board during the Year 1874. In Free Stock of Books, Requisites, and Apparatus.	In Salaries, Premiums, and other Gratuities.	Results Fees, Personal Fees.	Amount of Local Emoluments received in Aid of Teacher's Salary. School Fees.	Subscriptions, Endowments, &c.	Total Local Aid.	Vested or Non-Vested.	Number.
£ s. d.	£ s. d.	£ s. d.	£ s. d.	£ s. d.	£ s. d.	£ s. d.		
4 18 11	—	16 18 4	4 5 0	1 0 0	—	1 0 0	V.T.	80
1 5 5	—	44 0 0	9 14 6	—	—	—	V.T.	81
—	—	21 0 0	6 5 5	1 9 0	—	1 9 0	V.T.	82
10 17 10	—	37 0 0	25 3 6	9 8 1	6 0 0	a 15 8 1	V.T.	83
0 14 1	—	64 0 0	89 8 8	10 3 10	4 0 0	b 14 12 10	V.T.	84
1 2 9	—	—	—	—	—	—		85
3 4 2	—	24 0 0	8 12 0	3 0 0	—	3 0 0	V.T.	86
—	—	—	8 4 8	—	—	—	V.T.	87
4 16 11	—	30 0 0	11 14 6	5 5 1	1 10 0	a 6 15 1		88
6 7 8	—	60 0 0	11 15 6	—	6 0 0	6 5 6		89
1 6 0	—	24 0 0	6 0 0	2 1 0	—	2 1 0		90
—	—	20 0 0	5 7 0	0 16 8	1 5 0	a 2 1 8		91
8 17 11	—	27 10 0	14 10 0	3 0 0	—	3 0 0	V.T.	92
3 11 11	—	47 10 0	14 0 6	1 7 6	—	1 7 6	V.T.	93
2 9 0	—	20 0 0	9 2 6	1 12 6	—	1 12 6		94
2 7 0	—	30 0 0	6 2 0	0 10 0	4 10 0	5 0 0		95
1 6 0	—	35 0 0	4 16 0	1 18 0	18 13 6	a 20 6 6		96
4 17 6	—	28 6 8	9 15 0	0 1 6	—	0 7 0		97
5 0 8	—	53 0 0	10 16 7	2 10 0	—	2 10 0		98
5 4 8	—	77 13 4	23 9 5	5 15 2	—	5 15 2		99
0 12 8	—	24 0 0	5 16 0	1 19 4	—	1 19 4		100
1 12 0	—	20 0 0	5 18 0	0 1 0	—	0 1 0		101
1 7 8	—	20 0 0	10 6 7	5 6 6	—	5 6 6		102
2 18 5	—	20 0 0	0 [illegible] 6	1 14 10	3 10 0	5 4 10		103
1 7 11	—	30 0 6	11 0 6	1 12 0	—	1 12 0		104
1 4 6	—	35 0 0	10 5 6	1 12 6	—	1 12 6		105
2 17 0	—	61 0 0	11 17 0	2 3 6	—	2 3 6		106
5 16 1	—	22 10 0	12 3 0	3 15 0	—	3 15 0		107
2 12 6	—	44 6 8	17 1 6	7 6 8	4 0 0	b 11 6 8		108
4 12 8	—	31 6 8	19 12 0	4 16 11	—	4 16 11		109
137 10 0	—	25 0 0	0 6 8	3 0 4	—	3 0 4		110
1 16 8	—	20 0 0	6 6 8	0 16 0	—	0 16 0		111
1 10 0	—	17 13 4	8 15 9	0 10 0	—	0 10 0		112
0 8 0	—	30 0 0	6 18 5	1 7 6	—	1 7 6		113
6 7 4	—	20 0 0	4 17 5	0 11 0	—	0 11 0		114
1 0 10	—	30 5 4	10 10 8	1 18 6	—	1 18 6		115
2 16 6	—	20 0 0	9 11 0	8 10 6	—	8 10 6		116
2 10 7	—	30 10 0	13 15 0	—	10 0 0	b 10 0 0		117
3 5 8	—	20 0 0	5 6 0	0 10 6	1 10 0	a 3 0 6		118
1 5 8	—	28 14 0	4 1 0	1 11 7	—	1 11 7		119
1 10 8	—	38 0 0	18 15 0	1 4 0	—	1 4 0		120
1 10 4	—	24 0 0	5 18 0	2 1 0	—	2 1 0	A.	121
3 7 5	—	30 0 0	6 0 0	3 16 6	—	3 16 6	A.	122
6 8 5	—	74 18 11	18 8 6	6 16 6	—	6 18 0		123
6 6 3	—	24 0 0	11 17 6	6 9 10	—	6 9 10		124
2 1 3	—	60 0 0	25 6 0	6 6 6	—	0 6 6		125
1 7 2	—	52 6 4	31 6 0	5 5 6	—	5 5 0		126
1 14 6	—	30 0 0	8 6 0	5 16 7	11 10 0	a 17 6 7		127
1 7 1	—	35 0 0	12 8 0	7 7 10	17 10 0	a 24 17 10		128
1 17 5	—	50 0 0	15 10 0	1 4 6	—	1 4 6		129
5 16 11	—	54 0 0	28 0 6	6 15 0	10 0 0	a 16 15 6		130
4 15 1	—	52 6 8	10 18 6	5 12 5	—	5 12 6		131
2 12 3	—	22 6 8	0 15 0	2 1 6	—	2 1 6		132
1 18 0	—	38 0 0	7 8 0	5 17 0	5 0 0	a 8 17 0		133
—	—	30 0 0	4 9 0	2 2 11	—	2 2 11		134
1 15 2	—	24 0 0	8 7 6	2 18 6	—	2 15 6		135
0 15 0	—	30 0 0	7 10 0	2 0 0	—	2 0 0		136
0 16 2	—	18 0 0	6 15 6	1 0 0	—	1 0 0	V.T.	137
0 19 2	—	24 0 0	8 17 8	0 18 8	—	0 18 8	V.T.	138
4 15 7	—	56 0 0	17 17 0	0 8 11	—	0 8 11	A.	139
7 11 6	—	73 0 0	20 6 6	4 2 6	—	4 2 6	A.	140
2 18 1	4 0 0	15 0 0	1 8 1	—	—	—		141
1 8 5	—	80 0 0	4 17 0	8 0 0	—	3 0 0		142

a Inoperative.

b Including value of Free Garden.

List of Schools in operation on the 31st December, 1874.—

No.	Roll Number of School.	Parish.	District.	School.		Religious Denomination of Manager or Correspondent. Clerical.	Lay.	Number and Religious Denomination of Teachers. Principals.	Assistants.	Total number of Pupils on Rolls within the Year 1874. Males.	Fem.	Total.	Average Daily Attendance for the Year.
145	[illegible]	Kilmore,	22	Crumlevery,		–	R.C.	R.C.	–	19	33	52	22
146	9211	Killeagh,	19	Cmalebawn,		R.C.	–	R.C.	–	49	51	98	40
147	3337	Do.	–	Gubeverty,		R.C.	–	R.C.	–	49	43	92	55
148	3501	Do.	–	Kiltiff,		R.C.	–	R.C.	–	45	43	88	47
149	[illegible]	Do.	–	Monaghanhal,		R.C.	–	R.C.	–	56	59	115	44
150	[illegible]	Do.	–	Gortahill,		R.C.	–	R.C.	–	34	30	69	22
151	4564	Do.	–	Tullinacrossyle,		R.C.	–	R.C.	–	41	42	84	33
152	4788	Do.	–	Toher,		R.C.	–	R.C.	R.C.	70	77	147	60
153	7554	Do.	–	Mossaville,		R.C.	–	R.C.	–	63	45	108	57
154	[illegible]	Do.	–	Derran,		R.C.	–	R.C.	–	53	51	104	42
155	6997	Do.	–	Mouragh,		R.C.	–	R.C.	–	55	45	100	54
156	7481	Do.	–	Carrickmagrew,		R.C.	–	R.C.	–	59	43	81	30
157	[illegible]	Do.	–	Coragan,		R.C.	–	R.C.	–	55	59	64	30
158	4730	Killinkere,	21	Finlescraugh,	m.	–	R.C.	R.C.	–	91	–	91	37
159	3731	Do.	–	Do.	f.	–	R.C.	R.C.	–	–	79	79	37
160	4811	Do.	–	Derryhum,		R.C.	–	R.C.	–	59	37	93	33
161	1947	Do.	–	Killinkere,	m.	R.C.	–	R.C.	–	129	–	129	39
162	8116	Do.	–	Do.	f.	R.C.	–	R.C.	–	–	134	134	61
163	4094	Do.	–	Carrickgorman,		Pres.	–	Pres.	–	39	23	61	33
164	9316	Do.	–	Largamore,		R.C.	–	R.C.	R.C.	79	70	149	46
165	[illegible]	Do.	–	Termon Ord. Agricul.		R.C.	–	R.C.	R.C.	182	115	301	97
166	[illegible]	Knockbride,	–	Dagliera,		R.C.	–	R.C.	R.C.	104	89	173	73
167	[illegible]	Do.	–	Rosaubride,		R.C.	–	R.C.	R.C.	78	101	179	56
168	3711	Do.	–	Corlaoycanrel,		R.C.	–	R.C.	–	78	49	119	47
169	[illegible]	Do.	–	Cullies,		–	R.C.	R.C.	R.C.	93	58	151	60
170	[illegible]	Do.	–	Corcenary,		Pres.	–	Pres.	–	41	31	72	30
171	[illegible]	Do.	–	Bambiere,		–	R.C.	R.C.	–	31	35	67	30
172	[illegible]	Do.	–	Tonyfugle,		R.C.	–	R.C.	–	88	51	147	46
173	[illegible]	Do.	–	Latney,		–	Pres.	Pres.	–	63	48	110	44
174	[illegible]	Do.	–	Turlad,		R.C.	–	R.C.	–	75	69	144	60
175	[illegible]	Do.	–	Derrylavaugh,		–	R.C.	Pres.	R.C.	79	84	164	84
176	[illegible]	Do.	–	Kilmaterum,		–	R.C.	Pres.	–	40	44	84	30
177	10518	Do.	–	Three Carragins,		R.C.	–	R.C.	R.C.	68	125	194	50
178	11137	Do.	–	Tonnyduff,		R.C.	–	R.C.	–	59	–	59	14
179	141	Killeshandra,	31	Gortinnary,		Pres.	–	R.C.	–	37	39	76	37
180	[illegible]	Do.	–	Arva,	m.	R.C.	–	R.C.	–	191	–	191	59
181	[illegible]	Do.	–	Do.	f.	R.C.	–	R.C.	R.C.	–	152	152	69
182	[illegible]	Do.	–	Killeshandra,*	m.	R.C.	–	–	–	–	–	–	–
183	[illegible]	Do.	–	Do.	f.	R.C.	–	R.C.	–	55	104	159	[illegible]
184	[illegible]	Do.	–	Drumkeeran,		Pres.	–	Pres.	–	65	47	102	61
185	[illegible]	Do.	–	Coolaygrallen,		Diss.	–	Diss.	–	90	44	134	43
186	[illegible]	Do.	–	Derinagrnas,	f.	R.C.	–	R.C.	–	37	53	89	32
187	[illegible]	Do.	–	Cordin,		R.C.	–	R.C.	R.C.	100	56	156	61
188	[illegible]	Do.	–	Corlesna,	m.	R.C.	–	R.C.	–	134	–	134	37
189	[illegible]	Do.	–	Do.	f.	R.C.	–	R.C.	–	–	148	148	61
190	[illegible]	Do.	–	Killeshandra,		R.C.	–	R.C.	–	55	45	100	47
191	[illegible]	Kinawley,	–	Swanlinbar,	f.	R.C.	–	R.C.	–	33	70	103	31
192	[illegible]	Do.	–	Derryvrail,		R.C.	–	R.C.	–	37	22	59	24
193	[illegible]	Do.	–	Commons,		R.C.	–	R.C.	–	64	45	109	33
194	[illegible]	Do.	–	Drugh,	m.	R.C.	–	R.C.	–	116	–	116	41
195	[illegible]	Do.	–	Do.	f.	R.C.	–	R.C.	–	–	93	93	30
196	[illegible]	Kilbride,	23	Dungummin,	m.	R.C.	–	R.C.	R.C.	89	72	161	78
197	[illegible]	Do.	–	Garryvallagh,	f.	R.C.	–	R.C.	–	–	119	119	40
198	[illegible]	Do.	–	Do.	m.	R.C.	–	R.C.	–	103	–	103	65
199	[illegible]	Kilmainhamwood,	24	Ballynamanny,		R.C.	–	R.C.	–	45	53	98	38
200	147	Lurgan,	–	Coppanagh,	m.	R.C.	–	R.C.	–	68	–	68	27
201	[illegible]	Do.	–	Do.	f.	R.C.	–	R.C.	–	–	78	78	35
202	161	Do.	23	Lavey,	m.	R.C.	–	R.C.	–	64	–	64	29
203	[illegible]	Do.	–	Do.	f.	R.C.	–	R.C.	–	–	66	66	29
204	[illegible]	Do.	24	Virginia,	m.	R.C.	–	R.C.	R.C.	249	–	249	73
205	[illegible]	Do.	–	Do.	f.	R.C.	–	R.C.	R.C.	–	149	149	44
206	[illegible]	Do.	–	Ballanis,		Pres.	–	Pres.	R.C.	93	84	177	17
207	4371	Loughan,	–	Loughnaneer,		R.C.	–	R.C.	R.C.	176	141	317	[illegible]

* Including value of Free Residence and Garden.

b Including value of Free Garden.

Province of Ulster: County of Cavan—*continued.*

Amount paid for Books, Requisites, and Apparatus, at Reduced Prices.	Aid granted by the Board during the Year 1874.			Amount of Local Emoluments received in Aid of Teacher's Salary.			Vested or Non-Vested.	Number.
	In Free Stock of Books, Requisites, and Apparatus.	In Salaries, Premiums, and other Gratuities.	Results Fees, Financial Year.	School Fees.	Subscriptions, Endowments, &c.	Total Local Aid.		
£ s. d.	£ s. d.	£ s. d.	£ s. d.	£ s. d.	£ s. d.	£ s. d.		
2 2 0	—	20 0 0	9 3 6	—	28 0 0	a 28 0 0		143
—	—	29 10 0	12 13 0	0 4 0	—	0 4 0		144
0 17 11	—	24 0 0	15 14 6	—	—	—		145
1 11 10	—	24 10 0	6 18 0	1 2 6	—	1 9 0		146
9 10 11	9 11 11	37 15 7	19 5 6	—	—	—		147
1 5 8	3 0 8	24 0 0	—	—	—	—		148
1 4 3	—	24 16 0	12 2 6	—	—	—		149
1 6 1	—	44 0 0	21 10 0	1 9 0	—	1 9 0		150
—	—	56 0 0	19 0 0	—	1 0 0	b 1 0 0		151
5 1 10	—	29 16 8	16 16 8	—	5 10 0	b 6 10 0		152
2 5 10	2 14 0	41 0 8	15 16 8	0 3 0	14 0 0	b 14 3 0		153
1 6 1	—	24 0 0	11 7 0	—	—	—		154
0 12 1	8 5 0	24 0 0	18 2 0	—	1 10 0	1 10 0		155
1 18 7	—	62 0 0	7 8 0	8 8 0	7 0 0	a 0 8 0		156
0 10 2	—	30 0 0	10 19 0	1 6 0	6 10 0	a 7 16 0		157
—	—	21 0 0	3 0 0	1 0 0	—	1 0 0		158
2 16 10	—	21 0 0	6 19 6	1 7 3	—	1 7 3		159
4 8 10	—	37 4 8	17 6 6	0 7 0	—	0 7 0		160
0 10 2	—	21 0 0	8 5 0	2 0 0	—	2 0 0		161
1 8 8	—	44 0 0	9 18 6	1 5 0	—	1 5 0		162
10 19 11	—	51 1 8	40 14 0	1 18 0	—	1 18 0		163
3 11 6	—	49 10 0	43 9 0	0 7 6	—	0 7 6		164
4 0 8	—	41 13 4	24 1 6	0 18 3	—	0 18 3		165
1 16 0	—	24 0 0	10 0 0	1 11 6	—	1 11 6		166
5 16 8	—	35 18 4	19 19 0	—	18 0 0	18 0 0		167
1 10 10	—	60 0 0	11 19 0	8 16 6	—	8 16 6		168
—	—	20 0 0	10 18 6	—	16 0 0	16 0 0		169
2 4 11	—	24 0 0	8 9 9	1 10 0	—	1 10 0		170
1 5 0	—	30 0 0	12 11 8	0 4 0	—	0 4 0		171
8 10 6	—	26 0 0	16 14 8	—	—	—		172
4 11 8	—	51 0 0	19 18 8	0 18 9	11 0 0	b 11 18 9		173
4 13 11	—	64 0 0	13 3 8	6 0 8	8 10 0	8 10 8		174
5 1 7	—	56 3 4	22 3 0	2 8 0	2 0 0	4 8 0		175
1 7 6	4 10 0	16 18 4	10 6 8	1 0 10	—	a 1 0 10		176
0 17 2	—	24 0 0	9 15 8	4 10 0	—	4 10 0	V.T.	177
6 19 0	—	30 0 0	24 16 0	12 5 0	—	18 5 0		178
7 17 0	—	64 10 0	28 4 0	9 6 6	—	9 6 6		179
—	—	—	—	—	—	—		180
2 5 6	—	20 0 0	8 7 8	4 10 8	—	4 16 8		181
2 2 4	—	24 0 0	7 19 8	4 6 0	—	4 6 0		182
8 9 2	—	21 10 0	18 5 0	5 6 10	11 0 0	16 6 10		183
0 9 0	—	20 0 0	7 0 8	1 7 6	—	1 7 6	V.T.	184
3 19 10	—	30 13 4	19 6 8	4 10 6	—	4 10 6	V.T.	185
1 15 5	—	24 0 0	1 8 1	4 5 9	—	4 5 9		186
4 4 0	—	27 9 8	16 17 0	4 18 0	—	4 15 0		187
6 17 11	—	56 18 8	13 18 9	5 8 0	29 0 0	a 34 8 0		188
1 17 5	—	24 0 0	17 7 0	—	18 10 0	b 18 10 0		189
0 7 0	—	24 0 0	4 4 0	1 10 0	—	1 10 0		190
2 12 5	—	24 0 0	6 19 6	2 17 0	—	2 17 0		191
1 5 8	—	24 0 6	16 13 8	4 3 0	—	4 3 0		192
0 11 7	—	35 8 4	18 12 8	2 2 0	—	2 2 0		193
4 18 10	—	49 0 0	17 4 8	2 17 8	—	2 17 8		194
2 3 10	—	27 10 0	12 15 0	2 8 0	—	2 8 0		195
2 6 6	—	22 6 8	8 6 0	8 1 0	—	8 1 0		196
1 10 8	—	30 0 0	7 10 8	0 17 0	—	0 17 0		197
1 7 6	—	30 0 0	10 8 0	0 0 0	12 0 0	a 12 0 0	V.T.	198
1 0 0	—	20 0 0	0 12 0	2 11 6	2 0 0	b 4 11 6	V.T.	199
1 5 8	—	21 0 0	3 12 6	1 8 6	—	1 8 6	V.T.	200
0 14 0	—	26 0 0	2 1 6	8 0 0	—	8 0 0	V.T.	201
4 2 6	—	66 10 0	21 14 6	2 5 9	—	2 5 9	V.C.	202
5 0 5	—	50 0 0	18 0 0	10 4 1	—	10 4 1	V.C.	203
4 8 3	—	35 10 0	16 15 0	0 0 9	—	0 0 9		204
7 8 1	—	58 10 0	33 9 9	5 17 6	8 0 0	10 17 6		205

a Including value of Free Residence.

b Inoperative.

List of Schools in operation on the 31st December, 1874.—

Number.	Roll Number of School.	Parish.	District.	School.		Religious Denomination of Manager or Correspondent: Clerical.	Lay.	Number and Religious Denomination of Teachers: Principals.	Assistants.	Attendance for the Year: Total number of Pupils on Rolls within the Year 1874: Male.	Fem.	Total.	Average Daily Attendance for the Year 1874.
[illegible]	8614	Lurgan,	22	Clifferna,	m.	R.C.	–	R.C.	–	196	–	196	41
[illegible]	9106	Do.	–	Do.	f.	R.C.	–	R.C.	–	–	95	95	36
[illegible]	[illegible]	Do.	–	Callfield,		R.C.	–	R.C.	–	67	49	116	45
[illegible]	[illegible]	Do.	–	Carrickallen,	m.	R.C.	–	R.C.	–	104	–	104	46
210	[illegible]	Do.	–	Do.	f.	R.C.	–	R.C.	–	–	105	105	47
211	[illegible]	Do.	–	Lurgan,	m.	R.C.	–	R.C.	–	85	–	85	[illegible]
[illegible]	[illegible]	Do.	–	Do.	f.	R.C.	–	R.C.	–	–	119	119	[illegible]
[illegible]	[illegible]	Do.	–	Ravenswood,		–	R.C.	R.C.	–	54	[illegible]	[illegible]	[illegible]
[illegible]	[illegible]	Do.	–	Tierlahood,		R.C.	–	R.C.	–	64	68	132	64
[illegible]	[illegible]	Do.	–	Drakell,		R.C.	–	R.C.	–	69	69	137	[illegible]
[illegible]	[illegible]	Lavey,	–	Drumaveigh,		R.C.	–	R.C.	R.C.	96	79	175	58
[illegible]	[illegible]	Do.	–	Corraboe,	m.	R.C.	–	R.C.	–	130	–	130	55
[illegible]	[illegible]	Do.	–	Do.	f.	R.C.	–	R.C.	–	–	108	108	[illegible]
[illegible]	[illegible]	Do.	–	Kneeshnagillah,	m.	R.C.	–	R.C.	–	120	–	120	53
[illegible]	[illegible]	Do.	–	Do.	f.	R.C.	–	R.C.	–	–	162	162	65
221	[illegible]	Mullagh,	24	Killinar,		–	R.C.	R.C.	–	87	84	171	65
[illegible]	[illegible]	Do.	–	Raffony,		–	R.C.	R.C.	R.C.	96	95	191	59
[illegible]	[illegible]	Do.	–	Dean,		–	R.C.	R.C.	R.C.	66	95	161	45
[illegible]	7201	Do.	–	Mullagh,[b]	m.	R.C.	–	–	–	–	–	–	–
[illegible]	[illegible]	Do.	–	Do.	f.	R.C.	–	R.C.	–	–	109	109	41
[illegible]	7801	Do.	–	Greaghrnagh,		R.C.	–	R.C.	R.C.	86	74	160	62
[illegible]	[illegible]	Munterconnaught,	29	Knocktemple,	m.	R.C.	–	R.C.	–	137	–	137	66
[illegible]	[illegible]	Do.	–	Do.	f.	R.C.	–	R.C.	–	–	126	126	48
[illegible]	[illegible]	Do.	–	Ballyderran,	m.	R.C.	–	R.C.	–	96	–	96	[illegible]
[illegible]	[illegible]	Do.	–	Do.	f.	R.C.	–	R.C.	–	–	90	90	39
231	[illegible]	Do.	–	Ryefield,		R.C.	–	R.C.	–	36	28	64	[illegible]
[illegible]	[illegible]	[illegible]	24	Leaha,		R.C.	–	R.C.	–	60	56	116	[illegible]
[illegible]	[illegible]	Do.	–	Glenlack,		Pres.	–	Pres.	–	40	45	85	31
[illegible]	6175	Do.	–	Nalagh,		R.C.	–	R.C.	–	66	51	117	43
[illegible]	5780	Do.	–	Shercock,	m.	R.C.	–	R.C.	–	116	–	116	41
[illegible]	[illegible]	Do.	–	Do.	f.	R.C.	–	R.C.	–	–	118	118	41
[illegible]	[illegible]	Do.	–	Dunish,[c]		R.C.	–	R.C.	–	81	98	179	64
[illegible]	4711	Scrabby,	29	Scrabby,	m.	R.C.	–	R.C.	–	107	–	107	41
[illegible]	[illegible]	Do.	–	Do.	f.	R.C.	–	R.C.	–	–	103	103	[illegible]
[illegible]	[illegible]	Do.	–	Carratober,		R.C.	–	R.C.	–	75	80	155	[illegible]
241	[illegible]	Templeport,	31	Garvoll,		R.C.	–	R.C.	–	94	[illegible]	108	36
[illegible]	[illegible]	Do.	–	Currin,		R.C.	–	R.C.	R.C.	51	48	[illegible]	49
[illegible]	[illegible]	Do.	–	Bawnboy,		R.C.	–	R.C.	–	57	60	117	41
244	[illegible]	Do.	–	Do. Workhouse,		P.L.	Gds.	R.C.	R.C.	34	24	[illegible]	10
[illegible]	[illegible]	Do.	–	Tullybrack,	m.	R.C.	–	R.C.	–	[illegible]	–	[illegible]	31
246	4141	Do.	–	Do.	f.	R.C.	–	R.C.	–	–	54	[illegible]	25
247	[illegible]	Do.	–	Drumalcher,		R.C.	–	R.C.	–	51	91	182	33
[illegible]	[illegible]	Do.	–	Tonymore,	m.	R.C.	–	R.C.	–	94	–	[illegible]	[illegible]
[illegible]	[illegible]	Do.	–	Do.	f.	R.C.	–	R.C.	–	–	73	73	31
[illegible]	[illegible]	Do.	–	Tullynacross,		R.C.	–	R.C.	R.C.	75	[illegible]	155	[illegible]
251	[illegible]	Do.	–	Derrynanagh,		R.C.	–	R.C.	R.C.	69	78	137	56
[illegible]	[illegible]	Do.	–	Ardara,		R.C.	–	R.C.	R.C.	[illegible]	[illegible]	149	[illegible]
[illegible]	[illegible]	Do.	–	Cappragh,		R.C.	–	R.C.	–	[illegible]	60	103	[illegible]
254	[illegible]	Do.	–	Tirenahan,		R.C.	–	R.C.	–	54	34	[illegible]	[illegible]
[illegible]	[illegible]	Do.	–	Legnatraghta,		R.C.	–	R.C.	–	54	38	74	[illegible]
[illegible]	[illegible]	Do.	–	Mauleagh,		–	R.C.	R.C.	–	45	42	87	40
257	[illegible]	Do.	–	Drumbrucklis,		R.C.	–	R.C.	R.C.	42	45	[illegible]	[illegible]
[illegible]	[illegible]	Do.	–	Altachullion,		R.C.	–	R.C.	R.C.	[illegible]	75	148	[illegible]
[illegible]	[illegible]	Do.	–	Tullycasson Ord. Agr.		R.C.	–	R.C.	–	70	57	127	[illegible]
260	[illegible]	Do.	–	Corraleigh Ord. Agr.		–	R.C.	R.C.	–	35	19	[illegible]	[illegible]
261	[illegible]	Do.	–	Killyvra,		–	R.C.	R.C.	–	31	[illegible]	81	[illegible]
[illegible]	10681	Do.	–	Crea,		R.C.	–	R.C.	–	[illegible]	[illegible]	70	[illegible]
[illegible]	[illegible]	Tomregan,	–	Ballyconnell,	m.	R.C.	–	R.C.	–	139	–	139	[illegible]
[illegible]	[illegible]	Do.	–	Do.	f.	R.C.	–	R.C.	R.C.	–	90	[illegible]	[illegible]
[illegible]	8492	Urney,	23	Cavan Convent,	f.	R.C.	–	Nuns.		–	507	507	194
[illegible]	10062	Virginia,	24	Headford,		R.C.	–	R.C.	–	59	56	75	[illegible]
		Total for County Cavan, 266,								15782	16176	30,945	11237

[a] Including value of Free Garden. [b] No returns. [c] Including value of Free Residence.

Province of Ulster: County of Cavan—*continued.*

Amount paid for Books, Requisites, and Apparatus, of Compact Funds.	Aid granted by the Board during the Year 1874. In Free Stock of Books, Requisites, and Apparatus.	In Salaries, Premiums, and other Gratuities.	Results Fees, Financial Year.	Amount of Local Endowments received in Aid of Teacher's Salary. School Fees.	Subscriptions, Endowments, &c.	Total Local Aid.	Vested or Non-Vested.	Number.
£ s. d.	£ s. d.	£ s. d.	£ s. d.	£ s. d.	£ s. d.	£ s. d.		
2 14 2	—	41 8 8	14 7 0	5 2 0	—	5 2 0		206
3 4 1	—	20 0 0	16 14 0	4 2 0	—	4 2 0		207
5 6 10	—	36 18 4	15 2 0	2 10 6	—	2 10 6		208
2 10 8	—	31 0 0	14 18 0	4 18 8	—	4 18 8		209
4 10 3	—	20 0 0	4 18 0	4 8 0	—	4 8 0		210
1 6 0	—	34 0 0	10 18 6	6 7 8	—	6 7 8		211
2 15 10	—	22 10 0	16 10 6	3 2 8	—	3 2 8		212
1 6 0	—	24 0 0	4 6 6	1 1 0	10 0 0	11 1 0		213
5 1 7	—	22 0 0	16 9 0	6 4 0	—	6 4 0		214
1 7 6	—	22 0 8	7 8 6	1 9 6	—	1 9 6		215
4 13 4	—	66 8 4	15 2 6	4 4 6	—	4 4 6		216
6 19 11	—	50 10 0	14 14 6	6 12 0	0 5 0	*6 17 0		217
1 14 6	—	23 0 0	12 10 6	4 4 0	—	4 4 0		218
2 8 8	—	60 0 0	15 18 0	4 11 0	—	4 11 6		219
2 19 8	—	41 18 8	20 10 6	4 2 0	—	4 2 0		220
2 16 10	—	46 0 0	14 18 6	7 4 0	—	7 4 0	A.	221
3 11 8	—	44 0 0	13 6 6	6 5 6	—	6 5 0		222
2 0 1	—	62 0 0	7 6 0	—	—	—		223
1 7 6	—	—	—	—	—	—		224
2 1 6	—	24 0 0	—	1 14 6	—	1 14 6		225
4 10 4	—	44 0 0	12 18 6	2 17 11	—	2 17 11		226
6 2 7	—	41 10 0	22 6 0	4 0 0	—	4 0 0		227
2 16 8	—	31 0 0	20 4 0	3 17 0	—	3 17 0		228
2 11 11	—	37 18 4	18 19 6	0 19 6	—	0 18 6		229
—	—	20 0 0	11 11 6	0 13 0	—	0 13 0		230
3 0 6	—	24 0 0	20 6 0	8 10 0	16 0 0	*24 10 0		231
3 7 11	—	22 0 0	14 16 0	6 7 0	—	6 7 0	V.T.	232
1 0 8	—	24 0 0	7 6 0	4 0 0	6 0 0	10 0 0		233
1 10 6	—	34 1 8	11 18 0	0 11 0	6 0 0	6 11 0		234
6 6 9	—	41 1 8	16 1 0	0 14 6	6 0 0	6 14 6		235
1 16 6	—	41 6 0	14 11 0	0 8 0	—	0 8 0		236
1 6 6	—	56 6 6	16 10 0	2 10 6	6 0 0	8 10 6		237
1 16 10	—	24 10 0	16 17 6	2 3 0	—	2 3 0		238
1 16 0	—	20 10 0	16 6 0	3 5 6	—	3 5 6		239
1 16 8	—	25 10 0	16 14 0	0 16 0	—	0 16 0		240
—	—	20 0 0	6 16 6	0 14 0	—	0 14 0		241
1 7 10	—	42 0 0	—	3 18 2	1 10 0	*5 8 2		242
3 7 6	—	20 0 0	8 10 6	0 19 6	—	0 19 6		243
3 16 5	—	2 10 0	—	—	—	—		244
1 1 0	—	8 0 0	5 7 6	1 1 0	0 10 0	*1 11 0	V.T.	245
1 1 4	—	20 0 0	8 18 0	1 15 6	—	1 15 6	V.T.	246
6 1 1	—	40 0 0	11 11 6	2 9 6	1 10 0	*3 19 6	V.T.	247
1 4 3	—	30 0 0	6 6 6	—	—	—		248
2 1 2	—	20 0 0	8 17 0	—	—	—		249
8 1 11	—	44 0 0	14 5 0	1 19 6	—	1 19 6		250
5 12 1	—	46 0 0	18 18 6	6 0 0	—	6 0 0		251
2 14 6	—	41 0 0	18 6 0	2 10 0	—	2 10 0		252
0 17 11	—	20 0 0	9 14 6	—	—	—		253
1 10 7	—	28 16 8	17 18 0	0 10 6	2 0 0	*2 10 6		254
3 1 10	—	21 0 0	6 17 0	0 19 6	—	0 19 6		255
2 10 6	—	24 0 0	7 1 6	1 5 6	12 0 0	*13 5 6		256
2 6 8	—	24 0 0	10 5 6	—	—	—		257
3 3 6	—	28 0 0	28 18 0	1 9 6	—	1 9 6		258
1 11 0	—	30 18 4	10 18 6	1 0 0	8 0 0	*9 0 0		259
—	—	37 0 0	18 8 0	0 7 6	13 10 6	*13 18 0		260
1 8 2	—	24 0 0	18 6 6	1 0 0	12 0 0	*13 0 0		261
—	—	24 0 0	7 17 0	0 8 4	8 0 0	8 8 4		262
3 6 7	—	61 10 0	67 9 6	4 8 6	—	4 8 6		263
6 18 11	—	27 10 0	15 4 6	4 0 0	—	4 0 0		264
0 11 6	—	61 17 8	35 8 0	12 8 4	—	12 8 4		265
6 7 6	8 8 2	10 16 8	—	1 18 10	60 0 0	*61 18 10		266
751 6 6	38 5 1	2,148 16 10	2,670 11 8	813 6 11	637 14 0	1,451 0 11		

* Manager dead; returns certified by teacher. * Including value of Free Residence and Garden.

List of Schools in operation on the 31st December, 1871.—

COUNTY OF

Number.	Roll Number of School.	Parish.	District.	School.	Religious Denomination of Manager or Correspondent. Clerical.	Lay.	Religious Denomination of Teachers. Principals.	Assistants.	Attendance for the Year. Total number of Pupils on Rolls within the Year 1871. Males.	Fem.	Total.	Average Daily Attendance.
1	6118	All Saints,	6	Gorewoods,	–	Pres.	Pres.	–	61	54	115	45
2	5578	Do.	–	Newtowncunningham,	Pres.	–	Pres.	–	96	52	148	69
3	9128	Do.	–	Do. 1.	R.C.	–	R.C.	–	17	23	40	15
4	11192	Do.	–	Do. No. 2,	R.C.	–	R.C.	–	95	75	170	63
5	6716	Aughnish,	1	Kilmacrenan,	R.C.	–	R.C.	–	41	38	79	34
6	8312	Do.	–	Rampton, Robertson's,	R.C.	–	R.C.	–	60	48	108	35
7	10878	Do.	–	Ramelton,	R.C.	–	R.C.	R.C.	75	84	159	45
8	8464	Aghanunshin,	–	Woodland,	R.C.	–	R.C.	–	68	39	107	37
9	10220	Do.	–	Aghanunshin,	R.C.	–	R.C.	–	28	16	44	10
10	6030	Burt,	4	Carrowreagh, b	Pres.	–	Pres.	–	–	–	–	–
11	2080	Do.	–	Burt, No. 1,	R.C.	–	R.C.	–	40	33	73	28
12	10027	Do.	–	Do. 2,	Pres.	–	Pres.	–	14	40	54	21
13	8577	Do.	–	Carrowen,	–	R.C.	Pres.	–	27	48	69	33
14	10104	Balkeire,	6	Lackbins,	R.C.	–	R.C.	–	43	60	103	47
15	105	Culdaff,	2	Ballycharry,	R.C.	–	R.C.	–	64	77	141	44
16	158	Do.	–	Bocan, m.	R.C.	–	R.C.	–	123	–	123	57
17	8593	Do.	–	Do. f.	R.C.	–	R.C.	–	–	123	123	54
18	161	Do.	–	Carrowmore,	R.C.	–	R.C.	R.C.	80	70	150	56
19	9181	Do.	–	Drimarm,	R.C.	–	R.C.	–	83	74	157	42
20	1237	Clonmany,	–	Gaddyduff, m.	R.C.	–	R.C.	–	191	–	191	54
21	8415	Do.	–	Do. f.	R.C.	–	R.C.	–	–	142	142	54
22	1902	Do.	–	Rashenny,	–	R.C.	R.C.	–	–	110	110	38
23	1670	Do.	–	Belize,	R.C.	–	R.C.	–	91	81	172	38
24	1907	Do.	–	Tirnaslige,	R.C.	–	R.C.	R.C.	116	100	224	80
25	8285	Do.	–	Cross Connell,	R.C.	–	R.C.	R.C.	112	91	203	60
26	1022	Convoy,	1	Roundpath,	R.C.	–	R.C.	–	49	47	96	32
27	3597	Do.	–	Lisnalsk,	R.C.	–	R.C.	–	42	59	101	30
28	8426	Do.	–	Carradowy,	Pres.	–	Pres.	–	33	28	57	26
29	8014	Do.	–	Drumkeen,	R.C.	–	R.C.	–	58	60	114	48
30	9125	Do.	–	Aghaveagh,	–	R.C.	R.C.	R.C.	79	69	148	57
31	5294	Do.	–	Convoy Sch. Garden,	Pres.	–	Pres.	Pres.	49	38	80	24
32	11111	Do.	–	Cloghroe, c	–	R.C.	Pres.	–	–	–	–	–
33	2147	Clondavaddog,	–	Ballymichael,	–	R.C.	R.C.	–	62	47	109	31
34	8454	Do.	–	Drumfad,	Pres.	–	Pres.	–	22	24	48	21
35	8492	Do.	–	Doaghbeg,	–	R.C.	R.C.	–	60	44	104	48
36	7375	Do.	–	Glenvar,	R.C.	–	R.C.	–	112	84	196	44
37	9259	Do.	–	Ballyhoorisky, b	R.C.	R.C.	–	–	–	–	–	–
38	9063	Do.	–	Ballyhalloo,	R.C.	–	R.C.	–	81	65	146	57
39	9607	Do.	–	Rosnakill,	R.C.	–	R.C.	–	102	89	201	67
40	11182	Clondahorky,	–	Tamney Robertson,	R.C.	–	R.C.	–	40	21	61	23
41	10058	Clondahorky,	–	Cashelagh,	–	R.C.	R.C.	–	83	76	114	38
42	6701	Do.	–	Dunfanaghy,	–	R.C.	R.C.	R.C.	116	82	198	72
43	8492	Do.	–	Do.	R.C.	–	R.C.	R.C.	80	142	222	98
44	8857	Do.	–	Do. Workhouse,	P.L.	Gds.	R.C.	–	7	3	10	4
45	8452	Do.	–	Kilmacroddan,	–	R.C.	R.C.	–	95	64	149	60
46	11163	Do.	–	Ballymore a	–	R.C.	R.C.	–	–	–	–	–
47	10441	Clondavaddog,	–	Ballyhar,	R.C.	–	R.C.	–	117	94	211	63
48	10528	Do.	–	Fanad,	R.C.	–	R.C.	R.C.	77	51	128	48
49	10900	Do.	–	Cashel, (2)	R.C.	–	R.C.	–	101	64	165	58
50	1230	Conwal,	–	Letterkenny, m.	R.C.	–	R.C.	R.C.	–	–	–	–
51	2236	Do.	–	Do. f.	R.C.	–	R.C.	–	–	108	108	48
52	8342	Do.	–	Do. No. 2,	Pres.	–	Pres.	R.C.	108	60	178	60
53	8975	Do.	–	Do. Workhouse,	P.L.	Gds.	–	–	14	16	30	20
54	9764	Do.	–	Ballifree,	R.C.	–	R.C.	–	69	54	123	35
55	2056	Do.	–	Glencar,	R.C.	–	R.C.	–	39	32	70	25
56	9034	Do.	–	Letterkenny, 1.	R.C.	–	R.C.	R.C.	79	112	191	88
57	4467	Do.	–	Trentagh,	–	R.C.	Pres.	–	67	74	141	43
58	9861	Do.	–	Killierin,	–	R.C.	Pres.	–	44	42	86	38
59	10232	Do.	–	Kirkmeady,	R.C.	–	R.C.	–	48	45	93	41
60	9653	Do.	6	Lough Eske,	R.C.	–	R.C.	–	66	56	122	38
61	9763	Do.	1	Heathrlauge,	R.C.	–	R.C.	–	68	69	137	37
62	8825	Do.	–	Meenatahany, b	R.C.	–	–	–	–	–	–	–

a Including value of Free Residence and Garden. b Closed. c Including value of Free Garden.

Province of Ulster: County of Donegal.

DONEGAL.—[illegible] Schools.

Amount paid for Books, Requisites, and Apparatus, at Reduced Prices.	Aid granted by the Board during the Year 1874. In Free Stock of Books, Requisites, and Apparatus.	In Salaries, Premiums, and other Gratuities.	Results Fees, Financial Year.	Amount of Local Emoluments received in Aid of Teacher's Salary. School Fees.	Subscriptions, Endowments, &c.	Total Local Aid.	Vested or Non-Vested.	Number.
£ s. d.	£ s. d.	£ s. d.	£ s. d.	£ s. d.	£ s. d.	£ s. d.		
2 15 6	—	26 0 0	12 10 6	0 0 8	1 10 0	10 10 0		1
5 9 7	—	35 6 8	12 16 8	13 7 8	—	18 7 6		2
0 18 2	—	20 0 0	5 12 6	2 8 8	—	2 8 8		3
1 15 8	7 0 0	14 12 4	—	5 15 6	—	5 10 9		4
1 13 10	—	24 0 0	5 6 0	3 0 9	—	8 0 0		5
—	—	23 10 0	6 8 6	1 9 0	18 0 0	*18 0 0		6
8 6 10	—	30 10 0	13 12 0	6 8 0	—	6 0 0		7
0 10 5	—	24 0 0	4 17 0	4 7 10	—	4 7 10	V.C.	8
—	—	28 0 0	5 11 0	1 17 6	11 1 6	12 16 0		9
1 6 0	—	18 0 0	—	—	—	—		10
0 10 4	—	30 0 0	4 1 0	1 17 8	—	*1 17 8		11
1 5 6	—	28 0 0	16 16 0	12 0 0	3 0 0	15 0 0		12
1 16 11	—	20 0 0	18 18 6	19 17 6	10 0 0	29 17 6	V.C.	13
2 6 6	—	24 5 0	11 11 6	6 2 6	11 7 0	*16 8 0		14
1 11 9	—	29 8 4	8 19 6	5 16 8	—	5 18 8		15
3 8 6	—	28 8 4	11 6 0	5 16 0	—	5 16 0	N.	16
1 16 3	—	26 10 0	10 8 0	3 4 0	—	3 4 0		17
—	—	44 10 0	15 8 6	0 5 0	—	0 5 0	V.V.	18
6 5 4	—	28 0 0	6 1 6	1 16 11	—	1 16 11	V.V.	19
9 0 0	—	24 0 0	6 6 6	5 11 9	0 6 0	*5 18 9		20
2 10 3	—	20 0 0	4 10 0	2 0 1	0 5 0	*2 5 1		21
0 19 11	—	24 0 0	6 0 6	1 18 10	4 15 0	*6 11 10	V.V.	22
0 10 6	—	24 0 0	0 8 6	1 0 0	—	1 0 0	V.N.	23
1 15 0	—	57 6 8	10 18 0	8 8 11	—	8 8 11	V.V.	24
2 16 6	—	50 5 4	4 10 8	6 6 7	0 10 0	6 16 7		25
1 15 6	—	21 16 0	4 17 8	1 18 6	—	1 16 6		26
1 6 3	—	20 8 0	8 8 8	—	—	—		27
1 17 0	—	16 0 0	6 7 0	1 10 0	1 0 0	2 16 0		28
5 9 3	—	28 10 0	8 19 6	3 11 8	—	8 11 6		29
1 16 0	—	40 18 4	20 15 6	7 14 8	6 0 0	*15 14 8		30
1 14 11	—	40 0 0	11 0 0	8 0 0	7 5 11	*18 5 11		31
1 6 6	4 0 0	16 0 0	4 0 0	—	—	—		32
—	—	20 0 0	15 8 0	1 9 6	8 0 0	*9 8 6		33
1 7 1	—	24 0 0	11 11 0	4 8 8	—	4 8 8		34
1 11 4	—	24 0 0	14 19 0	8 4 10	—	8 4 10		35
1 5 3	—	26 0 0	9 5 6	1 11 4	—	1 11 4		36
—	—	—	—	—	—	—		37
4 12 0	—	24 0 0	18 5 0	5 6 1	—	6 6 1		38
3 16 6	—	74 0 0	15 6 8	6 17 8	—	5 17 8		39
1 10 0	4 0 0	7 10 0	—	5 0 0	18 1 8	*23 1 8		40
2 4 4	—	80 0 0	6 16 6	6 10 0	10 0 0	*16 10 0		41
17 6 1	—	71 13 4	28 1 6	8 4 8	20 0 0	*28 4 8		42
1 6 8	—	51 6 6	22 6 0	1 13 0	—	1 13 0	V.V.	43
—	—	—	—	—	—	—		44
3 17 2	—	30 0 0	5 4 0	0 2 0	8 3 0	8 5 0		45
1 7 8	4 10 0	—	—	—	—	—		46
5 16 11	—	28 0 0	19 16 6	8 14 0	—	9 14 8		47
2 8 10	—	24 0 0	10 16 0	2 0 0	—	2 0 0		48
5 8 10	—	28 0 0	12 5 6	6 9 6	2 10 0	*4 19 6		49
9 12 10	—	47 0 0	28 18 0	24 15 4	—	24 13 4	V.N.	50
1 15 9	—	46 6 4	19 1 6	4 16 3	—	4 19 3	V.N.	51
6 16 4	—	61 0 0	40 16 0	41 0 7	—	41 0 7		52
2 14 8	—	3 10 0	—	—	—	—		53
1 5 0	—	20 0 0	10 8 8	1 10 0	—	1 10 0		54
—	—	24 0 0	6 6 0	0 7 0	2 2 0	3 0 0	V.V.	55
8 10 6	—	30 0 0	17 18 0	7 17 8	12 0 0	19 17 6		56
1 16 9	—	24 0 0	6 19 0	1 19 0	4 0 0	6 16 0		57
1 6 6	—	27 16 0	4 14 6	1 0 0	—	1 0 0		58
—	—	20 0 0	11 11 0	0 6 6	—	0 6 6		59
2 12 6	—	38 0 0	7 18 6	0 16 4	12 0 0	12 16 4		60
2 8 6	—	21 0 0	6 15 0	1 0 0	—	1 0 0		61
—	—	—	—	—	—	—		62

§ Including value of Free Residence.

* Returns not available.

List of Schools in operation on the 31st December, 1874.—

Number.	Roll Number of School.	Parish.	District.	School.	Religious Denomination of Manager or Correspondent: Clerical.	Lay.	Number and Religious Denomination of Teachers: Principals.	Assistants.	Attendance for the Year. Total number of Pupils on Rolls within the Year 1874: Males.	Fem.	Total.	Average Daily Attendance for the Year 1874.
63	0418	Conwal,	5	Balleghenny,	R.C.	–	R.C.	–	47	63	110	30
64	2471	Do.	–	Meenaniele,	R.C.	–	R.C.	–	42	43	85	25
65	6738	Do.	–	Ards,	Pres.	–	Pres.	–	27	26	53	21
66	8963	Do.	–	Templedouglas 1st Class Agricultural,	Com.	N.E.	R.C.	R.C.	124	123	247	43
67	10776	Do.	–	Treankeel,	R.C.	–	R.C.	–	37	67	104	48
68	162	Clonleigh,	6	Murlog,	R.C.	–	R.C.	–	61	50	101	33
69	163	Do.	–	Clogfin,[a]	R.C.	–	R.C.	–	–	–	–	–
70	166	Do.	–	Ballylennon,	R.C.	–	R.C.	–	68	30	98	35
71	11123	Do.	–	Lifford, f.	R.C.	–	R.C.	–	–	60	60	27
72	1237	Do.	–	Porthall,	R.C.	–	R.C.	–	65	51	116	47
73	6284	Do.	–	Illinabrack,	E.C.	–	E.C.	–	33	64	[illegible]	34
74	169	Clonca,	2	Aghaclay,	R.C.	–	R.C.	–	113	80	193	43
75	165	Do.	–	Maliabreal,	R.C.	–	R.C.	–	110	97	207	60
76	1728	Do.	–	Carthkinny,	R.C.	–	R.C.	–	57	76	133	33
77	8867	Do.	–	Malin,	–	E.C.	E.C.	E.C.	71	40	117	50
78	6516	Do.	–	Keenagh,	–	R.C.	Pres.	–	47	59	118	43
79	7038	Do.	–	Urblereagh,	–	E.C.	R.C.	–	118	72	185	55
80	7324	Do.	–	Gorey,	–	E.C.	R.C.	–	33	65	98	30
81	10408	Culdaff,	–	Falmore,	E.C.	–	R.C.	–	94	40	110	30
82	176	Donagh,	–	St. Patrick's, m.	R.C.	–	R.C.	–	187	–	187	41
83	10626	Do.	–	Do. Convent,	R.C.	–	Nuns	–	–	273	273	68
84	171	Do.	–	Craigtown,	R.C.	–	R.C.	–	86	94	180	27
85	1228	Do.	–	Glenmakin,	R.C.	–	R.C.	–	114	79	193	44
86	2033	Do.	–	Glentogher,	R.C.	–	R.C.	–	74	70	144	41
87	8388	Do.	–	Inishowen Workh.	P.L.	Gds.	R.C.	–	18	19	37	10
88	8971	Do.	–	Carrowreagh,	Dis.	–	R.C.	–	45	28	73	27
89	1363	Donaghmore,	6	Carricker,	–	R.C.	R.C.	–	57	67	124	31
90	1620	Do.	–	Cooladawson,	R.C.	–	R.C.	–	30	33	73	30
91	1930	Do.	–	Drumnamurphy,	Pres.	–	Pres.	–	40	50	90	30
92	1934	Do.	–	Castlefin,	R.C.	–	R.C.	R.C.	97	164	261	81
93	2860	Do.	–	Do. (2),	Dis.	–	R.C.	–	63	34	97	33
94	2471	Do.	–	Crossroads, No. 2,	R.C.	–	R.C.	–	45	43	88	33
95	2473	Do.	–	Knock,	–	E.C.	R.C.	–	64	48	100	34
96	3191	Do.	–	Dreenan,	R.C.	–	R.C.	–	33	50	83	31
97	4036	Do.	–	Carnowen,	Pres.	–	Pres.	–	42	61	93	33
98	4422	Do.	–	Glencolly,	R.C.	–	R.C.	R.C.	103	70	173	57
99	6183	Do.	–	Donaghmore, No. 2,	Pres.	–	Pres.	–	55	61	116	31
100	10227	Do.	–	Meenglass,	–	R.C.	R.C.	–	33	24	57	20
101	7157	Donoughmore,	–	Drumarisk,	–	E.C.	R.C.	–	63	53	116	46
102	7427	Do.	–	Sessiagh O'Neill,	R.C.	–	R.C.	–	67	69	116	41
103	1550	Donegal,	6	Laghaway,	Pres.	–	Pres.	–	110	90	213	56
104	4801	Do.	–	Drumnahoul,	–	E.C.	Pres.	–	30	41	80	21
105	9549	Do.	–	Barnesmore, m.	R.C.	–	R.C.	–	134	–	134	52
106	9661	Do.	–	Do. f.	R.C.	–	R.C.	–	–	152	152	50
107	9289	Do.	–	Donegal, No. 2, f.	R.C.	–	R.C.	–	50	123	181	63
108	4513	Do.	–	Do. Workhouse,	P.L.	Gds.	Dis.	–	23	21	44	12
109	10823	Do.	–	Spearstown,	Dis.	–	Dis.	Dis.	91	79	170	38
110	10724	Do.	–	Hawk, m.	R.C.	–	R.C.	–	101	–	101	38
111	1577	Desertegney,	2	Meenagh,	R.C.	–	R.C.	R.C.	140	90	245	55
112	2613	Drumhome,	5	Ballintra, m.	R.C.	–	R.C.	–	66	–	66	26
113	8499	Do.	–	Do. f.	R.C.	–	R.C.	–	–	94	94	32
114	3675	Do.	–	Ballymagroarty,	–	E.C.	R.C.	–	61	63	123	37
115	6193	Do.	–	Tullynaught,	–	E.C.	Pres.	–	38	31	69	20
116	8400	Do.	–	Ballydermot,	–	E.C.	R.C.	–	42	41	83	31
117	8437	Do.	–	Ballymacahillew,	R.C.	–	R.C.	–	40	30	79	30
118	6150	Do.	–	Laghey,	R.C.	–	R.C.	–	87	72	169	35
119	9743	Do.	–	Golard,	–	E.C.	E.C.	–	35	30	74	25
120	172	Fahan, Lower,	2	Cockhill,	R.C.	–	R.C.	R.C.	193	145	338	67
121	1672	Do.	–	Drumfries,	R.C.	–	R.C.	R.C.	78	65	143	58
122	1671	Do.	–	Lower Illies,	R.C.	–	R.C.	–	115	108	223	43
123	2407	Do.	–	Ballymagarraghy, m.	R.C.	–	R.C.	–	100	–	100	35
124	2406	Do.	–	Do. f.	R.C.	–	R.C.	–	–	53	53	31

[a] Returns not available.

[b] Including value of Free Buildings and Garden.

Province of Ulster: County of Donegal—*continued.*

Amount paid for Books, Requisites, and Apparatus, at Reduced Prices.	Aid granted by the Board during the Year 1874. In Free Stock of Books, Requisites, and Apparatus.	In Salaries, Premiums, and other Gratuities.	Results Fees, Financial Year.	Amount of Local Emoluments received in Aid of Teacher's Salary. School Fees.	Subscriptions, Endowments, &c.	Total Local Aid.	Vested or Non-Vested.	Number.
£ s. d.	£ s. d.	£ s. d.	£ s. d.	£ s. d.	£ s. d.	£ s. d.		
—	—	22 18 4	1 10 0	1 10 0	—	1 10 0		63
0 7 11	—	24 0 0	1 16 6	0 12 5	—	0 12 5		64
1 16 2	—	20 0 0	5 14 6	1 16 0	—	1 16 0		65
1 18 9	0 1 0	48 12 8	1 16 6	0 14 0	—	0 14 0	V.C.	66
1 17 9	6 0 0	12 0 0	12 1 0	3 0 3	—	3 0 3	V.T.	67
1 11 8	—	24 0 0	0 7 6	0 7 6	—	0 7 6	V.T.	68
3 1 7	—	21 0 0	6 12 6	—	—	—	V.T.	69
3 8 11	—	24 0 0	5 7 6	1 13 6	—	1 13 6	V.T.	70
3 0 0	4 0 0	8 6 8	—	—	14 0 0	14 0 0		71
1 7 4	—	23 3 4	18 10 6	6 0 0	—	6 0 0	V.T.	72
0 8 10	—	37 6 8	10 6 6	6 18 10	31 0 0	b 37 18 10		73
3 10 10	—	20 10 0	3 5 0	3 4 7	—	3 4 7		74
1 7 11	—	40 0 0	6 15 0	1 17 6	—	1 17 6	V.T.	75
1 8 5	—	50 0 0	3 16 0	4 9 7	—	4 9 7		76
2 6 8	—	64 15 0	18 4 0	4 0 0	3 0 0	* 7 0 0		77
1 5 9	—	32 10 0	11 8 0	4 5 0	—	4 5 0		78
8 15 1	—	31 0 0	13 12 6	6 18 0	—	6 18 0	V.C.	79
1 4 0	—	10 0 0	7 8 0	2 0 0	—	2 0 0		80
3 10 7	—	25 18 8	7 10 0	3 3 8	—	3 3 8		81
1 7 6	—	27 10 0	7 4 0	5 17 7	—	5 17 7		82
6 4 8	—	30 12 0	16 10 6	9 8 3	—	9 8 3		83
—	—	36 0 0	—	8 3 0	—	8 3 0	V.T.	84
3 0 8	—	28 10 0	0 8 6	8 15 6	—	8 15 6	V.T.	85
9 13 1	—	24 0 0	18 0 6	3 6 9	—	3 6 9	V.T.	86
5 8 10	—	1 10 0	—	—	—	—		87
1 6 8	—	32 0 0	8 7 0	6 8 8	23 0 0	* 29 8 8		88
5 0 5	—	38 10 0	20 6 0	—	2 0 0	2 0 0	V.T.	89
—	—	21 0 0	8 10 0	3 2 6	0 5 0	3 7 6	V.T.	90
8 12 11	—	20 0 0	9 10 6	6 6 8	9 0 0	15 6 8		91
11 6 7	—	52 10 0	35 0 0	6 6 6	—	6 6 6		92
2 9 6	—	24 0 0	7 10 6	4 15 6	—	4 15 6		93
2 8 0	—	24 0 0	11 14 0	0 1 6	—	0 1 6		94
8 1 1	—	41 13 4	18 16 6	0 11 0	6 0 0	6 11 0		95
2 8 6	—	23 5 0	3 12 0	0 14 0	—	0 14 0		96
5 8 0	—	33 0 0	10 8 6	0 17 8	—	0 17 8		97
4 17 7	—	54 18 4	28 3 6	0 10 0	—	0 10 0	V.C.	98
—	—	27 0 0	7 17 6	6 8 0	12 0 0	* 18 8 0		99
3 15 8	—	19 0 0	8 18 0	1 6 9	2 10 0	* 3 16 9		100
1 4 7	—	25 13 4	7 8 6	4 4 0	—	4 4 0	V.C.	101
6 0 9	—	61 6 8	18 6 0	8 10 0	—	8 10 0		102
1 7 8	—	40 10 0	18 9 0	3 18 0	—	3 18 0		103
0 18 6	—	39 0 0	6 1 6	1 11 0	3 0 0	* 4 11 0		104
2 18 0	—	66 16 0	18 18 6	2 15 6	4 10 0	* 6 5 6	V.T.	105
3 14 0	—	28 0 0	22 10 6	2 5 0	—	2 5 0	V.T.	106
9 7 7	—	53 10 0	26 1 0	5 5 3	—	5 5 3		107
3 11 1	—	—	—	—	—	—		108
4 1 10	—	58 0 0	37 8 6	4 0 11	26 0 0	* 30 0 11		109
1 6 0	—	22 0 0	6 8 0	4 0 8	—	4 0 8		110
1 5 0	—	43 0 0	18 14 6	3 17 0	—	3 17 0	V.T.	111
1 7 2	—	57 0 0	6 11 0	6 15 6	—	6 15 6		112
1 18 7	—	28 0 0	10 19 0	2 11 0	—	2 11 0		113
1 6 1	—	48 0 0	8 15 6	2 11 6	—	2 11 6	A.	114
—	—	60 0 0	6 16 6	3 3 0	10 10 0	14 13 0		115
1 8 8	—	25 10 0	11 6 0	3 15 0	5 0 0	8 15 0		116
1 5 8	—	24 0 0	7 19 6	4 18 6	9 0 0	13 18 6		117
—	—	24 0 0	9 12 0	6 10 0	—	6 10 0		118
1 11 8	—	20 0 0	6 17 0	6 15 0	—	6 15 0		119
7 9 11	—	54 6 7	37 8 0	13 4 4	—	13 4 4		120
2 17 3	—	73 13 4	12 4 0	20 18 0	1 0 0	21 18 0		121
2 6 9	—	28 0 0	8 14 6	0 3 0	—	0 3 0	V.T.	122
1 8 9	—	38 0 0	10 18 0	4 14 8	1 0 0	* 5 14 8	V.T.	123
1 16 4	—	25 0 0	5 18 6	5 12 9	—	5 12 9	V.T.	124

* Including value of Free Residence. b Including value of Free Garden.

List of Schools in operation on the 31st December, 1874.—

Number.	Roll Number of School.	Parish.	District.	School.	Religious Denomination of Manager or Correspondent. Clerical.	Lay.	Teacher and Religious Denomination of Teachers. Principals.	Assistants.	Attendance for the Year. Total number of Pupils on Rolls within the Year 1874. Males.	Fem.	Total.	Average daily attendance for the Year 1874.
125	8160	Fahan, Lower,	2	Tullydish,	R.C.	–	R.C.	–	65	57	122	55
126	6275	Do.	–	Buncrana,	Pres.	–	Pres.	–	79	48	127	58
127	1172	Fahan, Upper,	–	Ballymagan,	R.C.	Pres.	Pres.	–	56	41	97	35
128	6005	Do.	–	Carnshanagh,	–	Pres.	R.C.	–	44	26	70	34
129	1585	Do.	–	Crislagh or Tooban Ordinary Agricul.	R.C.	–	R.C.	–	73	70	143	44
130	6069	Gartan,	1	Church hill,	–	R.C.	R.C.	–	20	23	43	14
131	11202	Do.	–	Drumnalough,	R.C.	–	R.C.	–	31	30	61	20
132	11077	Do.	–	Lisnaseta,	R.C.	–	R.C.	–	38	40	78	28
133	6105	Glencolumbkille,	4	Meenaneary,	R.C.	–	R.C.	–	40	55	95	30
134	7841	Do.	–	Carrick,	R.C.	–	R.C.	–	82	97	179	77
135	7051	Do.	–	Teelin,	R.C.	–	R.C.	R.C.	109	98	207	103
136	10642	Do.	–	Cashel,	R.C.	–	R.C.	R.C.	128	94	222	81
137	7692	Do.	–	Malinbeg,	R.C.	–	R.C.	R.C.	43	44	80	46
138	6458	Do.	–	Meenacross,	–	R.C.	R.C.	–	58	40	97	42
139	9535	Do.	–	Straleeny,	R.C.	–	R.C.	–	25	37	62	39
140	9744	Do.	–	Malinmore,	R.C.	–	R.C.	–	65	39	104	34
141	10267	Do.	–	Glencolumbkille,	–	R.C.	Pres.	–	13	22	30	16
142	1754	Inishkeel,	–	Mullinamore,	R.C.	–	R.C.	–	85	66	152	50
143	2302	Do.	–	Glenties,	–	R.C.	R.C.	–	92	45	135	44
144	10170	Do.	–	Do. f.	R.C.	–	R.C.	–	–	130	130	47
145	10675	Do.	–	Drumnacrosh,	R.C.	–	R.C.	R.C.	163	62	225	74
146	7114	Do.	–	Glenties Workhouse,	P.L.	Gds.	R.C.	–	18	16	30	18
147	2651	Do.	–	Cronaghboy, m.	R.C.	–	R.C.	–	67	50	117	36
148	10284	Do.	–	Kentlemagh,	–	Pres.	R.C.	–	65	33	98	30
149	7771	Do.	–	Drumbeghill,	R.C.	–	R.C.	–	41	41	75	31
150	8548	Do.	–	Brackey,	R.C.	–	R.C.	–	76	34	110	40
151	10128	Do.	–	Gruffy,	R.C.	–	R.C.	–	61	32	93	31
152	4360	Do.	–	Bough,	R.C.	–	R.C.	–	38	46	94	43
153	4562	Do.	–	Clooney,	R.C.	–	R.C.	–	35	48	77	30
154	8108	Do.	–	Ballinamore,	–	R.C.	R.C.	–	63	44	107	32
155	6328	Do.	–	Tullymore,	R.C.	–	R.C.	–	45	20	65	30
156	8731	Do.	–	Shallogans,	R.C.	–	R.C.	–	30	15	45	28
157	7480	Do.	–	Loughyinacorragh,	R.C.	–	R.C.	–	32	28	60	23
158	7532	Do.	–	Kilkenny,	R.C.	–	R.C.	–	65	59	124	38
159	10166	Do.	–	Glenleighan,	R.C.	–	R.C.	–	44	27	75	26
160	10434	Do.	2	Laurielugga,	R.C.	–	R.C.	–	54	32	86	30
161	8079	Do.	6	Kilclooney,	R.C.	–	R.C.	–	78	41	119	37
162	8769	Do.	–	Loughrospoint,	Diss.	–	Diss.	–	43	20	63	23
163	8901	Do.	–	Edeninfagh,	R.C.	–	R.C.	–	40	25	65	21
164	10631	Do.	–	Derryloughan,	R.C.	–	R.C.	–	62	43	105	42
165	9562	Inver,	–	Drumbarron,	–	R.C.	R.C.	R.C.	90	60	150	49
166	8977	Do.	–	Drumaha,	–	R.C.	R.C.	R.C.	119	65	184	65
167	[illegible]	Do.	–	Letterilly,	R.C.	–	R.C.	R.C.	134	97	231	75
168	[illegible]	Do.	–	Meenacahan,	R.C.	–	R.C.	R.C.	66	85	151	60
169	[illegible]	Do.	–	Glenmagh, m.	R.C.	–	R.C.	–	141	–	141	48
170	[illegible]	Do.	–	Do. f.	R.C.	–	R.C.	–	–	151	151	59
171	8653	Do.	–	Legan,	R.C.	–	R.C.	–	68	44	112	45
172	7415	Do.	–	Drumnabeck,	R.C.	–	R.C.	–	67	76	143	40
173	11082	Do.	–	Letterbrock,	R.C.	–	R.C.	–	100	85	185	67
174	7640	Do.	–	Kealoge,	R.C.	–	R.C.	R.C.	105	78	183	57
175	9993	Inch,	2	Inch,	R.C.	–	Pres.	–	45	49	94	35
176	8457	Inishmacsaint,	3	Drumnagrough,	–	R.C.	R.C.	–	51	39	90	33
177	8429	Do.	–	Bundoran, m.	R.C.	–	R.C.	–	101	–	101	37
178	4033	Do.	–	Do. f.	R.C.	–	R.C.	–	–	73	73	30
179	4418	Do.	–	Carrickboy, m.	R.C.	–	R.C.	–	120	–	120	64
180	4419	Do.	–	Do. f.	R.C.	–	R.C.	–	89	54	43	25
181	9291	Do.	–	Dunmuckrum,	R.C.	–	R.C.	–	81	63	65	19
182	8768	Do.	–	Ardfarna,	R.C.	–	R.C.	–	47	38	85	30
183	7345	Do.	–	Loughill,	R.C.	–	R.C.	–	33	46	79	24
184	9277	Do.	–	Rock of Bundoran,a	–	–	–	–	–	–	–	–
185	4152	Do.	–	Ballyshannon Works,	P.L.	Gds.	E.C.	–	36	31	67	22
186	10801	Do.	–	Magheracar Convent,	R.C.	–	None	–	72	125	107	70

a Including value of Free Residence.

b Including value of Free Residence and Garden.

Province of Ulster: County of Donegal—*continued.*

Amount paid for Books, Requisites, and Apparatus, at Reduced Prices.	Aid granted by the Board during the Year 1874. In Free Grants of Books, Requisites, and Apparatus.	In Salaries, Premiums, and other Gratuities.	Results Fees, Financial Year.	Amount of Local Emoluments received in Aid of Teacher's Salary. School Fees.	Subscriptions, Endowments, &c.	Total Local Aid.	Vested or Non-Vested.	Number.
£ s. d.	£ s. d.	£ s. d.	£ s. d.	£ s. d.	£ s. d.	£ s. d.		
2 10 7	—	24 0 0	15 2 0	2 11 1	—	2 11 1	V.E.	125
8 5 2	—	44 0 0	23 1 0	16 1 10	7 15 0	23 16 10		126
1 12 5	—	31 0 0	11 16 0	7 14 2	—	7 14 2		127
3 0 8	—	16 10 4	9 15 8	6 12 8	—	6 12 8		128
5 7 7	—	24 0 0	16 3 6	0 10 0	8 0 0	*8 10 0	V.E.	129
1 8 11	—	20 0 0	8 15 6	1 10 0	—	1 10 0		130
1 6 7	—	20 0 0	8 19 6	0 8 8	—	0 8 8		131
2 3 6	4 10 0	14 0 0	7 14 6	1 1 9	—	1 1 9		132
—	—	24 0 0	3 7 0	2 9 6	—	2 9 6		133
2 1 8	—	50 13 4	23 12 8	—	—	—		134
4 7 10	5 0 0	122 2 8	53 8 0	—	—	—		135
3 18 5	—	63 18 8	67 12 8	0 6 0	—	0 6 0		136
4 0 8	—	40 8 6	16 4 0	—	—	—		137
1 17 1	—	24 0 0	6 11 0	—	—	—		138
1 5 8	—	22 0 0	6 8 0	—	—	—		139
3 1 11	—	25 8 0	7 6 6	1 4 2	—	1 4 2		140
—	—	20 0 0	2 7 6	—	16 1 6	b16 1 6		141
2 10 2	—	106 12 4	16 6 0	—	—	—	V.C.	142
1 17 4	—	51 13 4	9 4 0	6 2 9	—	6 2 9		143
4 17 6	—	67 0 0	16 15 0	8 8 10	12 10 0	18 18 10	V.C.	144
4 15 11	5 10 0	43 16 8	64 16 6	13 11 5	—	13 11 5	V.C.	145
3 4 7	—	—	—	—	—	—		146
2 11 8	—	22 0 0	10 6 8	0 1 9	—	0 1 0		147
1 11 11	—	21 0 0	7 0 0	2 5 0	6 0 0	*8 5 0		148
1 7 10	—	20 0 0	10 7 0	0 2 5	—	0 2 5		149
0 8 0	—	23 0 0	13 6 0	—	—	—		150
1 5 2	—	21 0 0	6 4 0	8 13 3	—	8 16 8		151
1 6 3	—	24 0 0	19 16 0	—	—	—		152
—	—	21 0 0	9 13 0	—	—	—		153
1 7 8	—	22 5 0	8 9 6	1 6 0	—	1 6 0	V.C.	154
1 16 0	—	21 0 0	11 4 0	—	—	—		155
0 13 6	—	20 0 0	4 6 6	1 0 5	—	1 0 5		156
0 8 0	—	24 0 0	6 9 0	0 5 0	—	0 6 0		157
1 19 1	—	22 10 0	22 1 0	3 4 0	—	3 4 0		158
—	—	21 0 0	0 4 0	—	—	—	V.C.	159
—	—	24 0 0	0 12 0	1 2 11	—	1 2 11	V.C.	160
1 6 7	—	43 18 4	14 12 0	0 7 4	—	0 7 4	V.C.	161
1 11 2	—	24 0 0	6 15 6	—	6 0 0	6 0 0		162
1 7 6	—	16 0 0	1 19 6	1 18 8	—	1 12 6		163
2 7 11	—	24 0 0	12 0 6	7 4 2	—	7 4 2	V.C.	164
2 15 7	—	41 0 6	11 7 0	4 14 0	—	4 14 0	V.C.	165
4 6 0	—	78 5 4	23 3 6	9 6 6	2 0 0	a11 6 6	V.V.	166
2 12 10	—	102 10 0	26 6 0	—	—	—	V.C.	167
6 6 5	—	51 14 5	17 11 6	2 0 4	—	2 0 4	V.C.	168
2 14 9	—	63 0 0	14 16 0	7 19 2	—	7 19 2	V.C.	169
5 5 4	—	25 8 8	13 5 6	5 15 1	—	5 15 1	V.C.	170
1 6 1	—	23 0 0	15 10 6	1 12 9	—	1 12 9		171
2 10 10	—	25 0 0	17 18 0	0 18 10	—	0 18 10		172
5 9 2	5 0 0	23 0 0	14 19 0	1 3 7	—	1 3 7		173
1 10 6	—	61 0 0	9 7 6	3 7 1	—	3 7 1		174
1 18 9	—	30 8 6	16 15 0	9 18 10	6 0 0	15 18 10		175
—	—	23 0 0	6 11 0	—	—	—		176
2 9 10	—	24 0 0	9 10 0	2 11 8	—	2 11 0		177
2 6 8	—	23 0 0	10 8 0	1 5 8	—	1 5 0		178
—	1 5 0	61 8 0	15 14 0	8 14 8	—	8 16 8	V.C.	179
1 6 3	—	10 0 0	3 18 6	0 0 1	—	0 8 1	V.C.	180
0 15 6	—	20 0 0	2 8 6	—	—	—		181
1 15 6	—	24 0 0	11 18 6	0 18 0	—	0 18 0		182
2 6 11	—	24 0 0	5 7 0	0 15 6	—	0 15 0		183
0 11 8	—	—	—	—	—	—		184
4 15 6	—	—	—	—	—	—		185
8 0 3	—	35 6 0	21 6 0	—	—	—		186

* Including value of Free Garden.

a Closed.

List of Schools in operation on the 31st December, 1874,—

Number.	Roll Number of School.	Parish.	District.	School.	Religious Denomination of Manager or Correspondent: Clerical.	Lay.	Religious Denomination of Teachers: Principals.	Assistants.	Attendance for the Year. Total number of Pupils on Rolls within the Year, Males.	Fem.	Total.	Average daily Attendance for Year.
187	10072	Kilbarron,	6	Tullymore,	R.C.	–	R.C.	–	49	45	87	58
188	10595	Do.	–	Mulhanahan,	Pres.	–	R.C.	–	27	34	61	32
189	1240	Kilcar,	–	Kevenaghan,	R.C.	–	R.C.	2 R.C.	129	120	249	108
190	2405	Do.	–	Shalvey,	R.C.	–	R.C.	–	51	40	91	29
191	3074	Do.	–	Crgulah,	R.C.	–	R.C.	R.C.	111	60	180	44
192	3169	Do.	–	Crove,	R.C.	–	R.C.	–	35	29	57	21
193	5841	Do.	–	Muckross,	R.C.	–	R.C.	–	71	47	118	46
194	6878	Do.	–	Straleel,	R.C.	–	R.C.	–	30	40	70	33
195	10780	Do.	–	Roxborough,[a]	–	–	–	–	–	–	–	–
196	1350	Killaghtee,	–	Crough,	R.C.	–	R.C.	R.C.	106	103	209	63
197	1351	Do.	–	Castletown,	R.C.	–	R.C.	R.C.	74	69	143	46
198	4033	Do.	–	Bruckless,	–	R.C.	R.C.	–	83	80	163	80
199	7363	Do.	–	Ballyotherland,	–	R.C.	R.C.	–	60	28	88	36
200	9044	Do.	–	Killaghtee,	R.C.	–	R.C.	R.C.	56	50	106	36
201	10760	Do.	–	Drumkeenly,	Diss.	–	R.C.	–	19	55	74	37
202	1804	Kilteevoge,	1	Cloghan,	–	R.C.	R.C.	–	42	21	63	27
203	5582	Do.	–	Letterbrick,	R.C.	–	R.C.	–	70	73	153	47
204	6198	Do.	–	Gortnacorn,	R.C.	–	R.C.	–	85	50	135	41
205	9698	Do.	–	Welshtown,	R.C.	–	R.C.	–	68	80	148	40
206	7580	Do.	–	Ardlahes,	R.C.	–	R.C.	–	76	55	131	45
207	8708	Do.	–	Altnapaste,	E.C.	–	Pres.	–	43	17	60	32
208	1671	Kilmacrenan,	–	Glenvreaganamagh,	–	R.C.	R.C.	–	127	100	227	67
209	1533	Do.	–	Carbel,	–	R.C.	R.C.	–	130	57	187	43
210	1658	Do.	–	Letter,	Pres.	–	Pres.	–	41	47	88	30
211	3522	Do.	–	Kilmacrenan,	–	R.C.	R.C.	–	53	60	113	34
212	8715	Do.	–	Loughnalustry,	R.C.	–	Pres.	–	55	58	113	35
213	6978	Do.	–	Cranford,[a]	–	R.C.	R.C.	–	77	53	130	36
214	6845	Do.	–	Currin,	R.C.	–	R.C.	–	103	103	206	34
215	8451	Do.	–	Kilmacrenan,	R.C.	–	R.C.	–	62	69	131	45
216	10808	Do.	–	Portlean,	R.C.	–	R.C.	–	16	36	51	21
217	1651	Killybegs, Upper,	6	Fintra,	R.C.	–	R.C.	–	85	55	140	55
218	1738	Do.	–	Killybegs,	R.C.	–	R.C.	R.C.	148	126	274	100
219	8095	Do.	–	Meenavally,	R.C.	–	R.C.	–	91	80	161	43
220	8105	Do.	–	Murray, m.	–	R.C.	R.C.	–	92	–	92	40
221	8524	Do.	–	Do. f.	–	R.C.	Pres.	–	–	102	102	45
222	5727	Do.	–	Ardara,	Diss.	–	Diss.	–	30	60	136	34
223	1785	Killybegs, Lower,	–	Do. m.	R.C.	–	R.C.	–	100	80	130	39
224	3187	Do.	–	Do. f.	R.C.	–	R.C.	–	49	57	118	31
225	5547	Do.	–	Gorgamore,	R.C.	–	R.C.	–	28	20	48	24
226	7454	Do.	–	Lochanall,	R.C.	–	R.C.	–	41	27	68	20
227	8317	Do.	–	Meenalmadat,	–	R.C.	R.C.	–	97	42	139	33
228	7787	Do.	–	Garrowart,	R.C.	–	R.C.	–	34	48	70	23
229	8470	Killybegs,	–	Roshin,	R.C.	–	R.C.	–	55	40	101	42
230	2303	Killymard,	–	Donegal, m.	–	R.C.	Pres.	–	123	–	123	48
231	2833	Do.	–	Do. f.	–	R.C.	Pres.	Pres.	–	116	114	50
232	2834	Do.	–	Ballydevitt,	R.C.	–	R.C.	–	84	61	145	40
233	9507	Do.	–	Drumagna,	–	R.C.	R.C.	–	45	38	78	26
234	10556	Do.	–	Lackagan,	–	[illegible] R.C.	R.C.	–	38	34	72	21
235	3184	Kilbarron,	–	Creevy,	R.C.	–	R.C.	–	64	28	92	43
236	4128	Do.	–	Ballyshannon, m.	R.C.	–	R.C.	–	128	–	130	45
237	4471	Do.	–	Do. f.	R.C.	–	R.C.	–	14	59	73	29
238	7525	Do.	–	Do. (3) Conv., f.	R.C.	–	Nuns		–	102	102	71
239	8674	Do.	–	Coolmore,	R.C.	–	R.C.	–	68	66	134	38
240	5578	Do.	–	Cashelard,	R.C.	–	R.C.	–	35	24	59	24
241	7283	Do.	–	Doobelin,	R.C.	–	R.C.	–	44	51	95	29
242	10922	Do.	–	Carrickanahorna,	Diss.	–	R.C.	–	64	46	110	44
243	8722	Do.	–	Bahey,	R.C.	–	R.C.	–	59	62	121	39
244	10092	Do.	–	Killarron,	–	R.C.	R.C.	–	48	20	68	23
245	8018	Do.	–	Rockfield,	R.C.	–	R.C.	–	49	56	105	33
246	10826	Do.	–	Cliftere,	–	R.C.	R.C.	–	48	31	79	33
247	9206	Do.	–	Cliff,[a]	–	–	–	–	–	–	–	–
248	6849	Killygarvan,	1	Creevary,	–	R.C.	R.C.	–	74	66	139	39

[a] Closed. [b] Including value of Free Garden. [c] Including value of Free Residence and Garden.

Province of ULSTER: County of DONEGAL—*continued.*

Amount paid for Books, Requisites, and Apparatus, at Reduced Prices.	Aid granted by the Board during the Year 1874. In Free Stock of Books, Requisites, and Apparatus.	In Salaries, Premiums, and other Gratuities.	Results Fees, Financial Year.	Amount of Local Emoluments received in Aid of Teacher's Salary. School Fees.	Subscriptions, Endowments, &c.	Total Local Aid.	Vested or Non-Vested.	Number.
£ s. d.	£ s. d.	£ s. d.	£ s. d.	£ s. d.	£ s. d.	£ s. d.		
1 16 6	—	24 0 0	0 12 0	5 14 2	—	5 14 2		187
5 8 2	—	22 18 4	11 7 6	15 0 0	4 0 0	19 0 0		188
1 5 6	—	122 3 4	26 18 6	0 8 0	—	0 8 0	V.T.	189
0 15 6	—	24 0 0	6 5 0	—	—	—	V.T.	190
8 17 1	—	42 0 0	23 11 6	—	—	—		191
0 15 2	—	63 16 0	1 14 6	—	—	—		192
3 5 0	—	53 5 6	21 10 6	0 16 0	—	0 10 0		193
1 10 11	—	24 0 0	0 15 6	—	—	—		194
—	—	8 0 0	—	—	—	—		195
6 11 0	—	104 10 0	21 6 0	11 2 3	—	11 2 3	V.T.	196
4 9 6	—	65 18 4	27 7 6	7 9 6	0 10 0	b 7 19 6	V.T.	197
6 1 0	—	85 10 0	29 16 6	13 14 0	4 5 0	a 17 19 0		198
—	—	62 0 0	10 9 6	0 14 10	—	0 14 10	V.C.	199
8 0 6	—	60 6 5	22 8 0	2 18 6	16 1 6	a 19 0 0		200
2 15 7	—	20 0 0	11 1 6	20 0 0	8 11 4	28 11 4		201
1 8 2	—	24 0 0	5 5 6	1 5 0	7 0 0	a 8 5 0	V.T.	202
1 5 8	—	67 10 0	18 3 6	—	—	—		203
8 6 10	—	67 0 0	11 18 0	4 0 6	—	4 0 6		204
0 10 8	—	39 0 0	23 10 0	2 9 0	—	2 9 0		205
1 12 1	—	68 0 0	0 12 6	1 17 6	—	1 17 6		206
1 12 4	—	80 0 0	18 4 6	2 6 0	4 0 0	6 6 0		207
—	—	24 0 0	20 16 0	6 10 11	—	6 10 11	V.C.	208
2 11 6	—	65 8 4	6 15 6	5 18 9	1 15 0	7 8 9		209
0 10 3	—	24 0 0	5 9 0	2 0 0	—	2 0 0		210
—	—	27 8 4	10 1 6	2 0 1	—	2 0 1		211
0 6 10	—	24 0 0	2 16 6	5 0 0	—	5 0 0		212
—	—	4 0 0	—	1 13 4	—	1 13 4		213
6 5 6	—	37 5 0	6 0 6	5 3 4	—	5 3 4		214
4 4 2	—	68 8 4	6 16 0	2 10 0	11 1 4	13 11 4		215
1 9 0	—	20 0 0	5 5 0	1 10 0	2 0 0	3 10 0		216
1 11 1	—	49 6 8	0 8 0	—	—	—	V.T.	217
—	—	103 12 4	27 18 0	10 0 6	4 0 0	a 14 0 6	V.T.	218
3 17 2	—	80 10 0	18 5 6	5 3 6	—	5 3 6		219
3 5 9	—	71 0 0	11 16 0	7 12 2	25 0 0	a 32 12 2		220
2 11 6	—	35 6 2	13 10 0	7 0 10	20 0 0	b [illegible] 0 10		221
1 19 0	—	28 1 8	10 2 0	—	—	—		222
1 5 7	—	47 0 0	13 9 0	—	6 0 0	a 6 0 0	V.T.	223
9 17 2	—	37 6 8	7 8 0	—	—	—		224
1 0 0	—	13 6 8	4 11 0	—	—	—		225
0 11 2	—	24 0 0	11 6 0	—	—	—		226
1 6 1	—	60 10 0	8 0 0	1 14 6	5 12 0	b 7 6 6		227
—	—	20 0 0	5 2 6	—	4 0 0	b 4 0 0		228
—	—	57 10 0	12 0 6	—	—	—		229
—	—	50 13 0	12 6 6	1 10 0	12 10 0	b 14 0 0	V.T.	230
—	—	37 1 1	17 16 0	1 10 0	11 0 0	a 12 10 0	V.T.	231
1 15 1	—	30 13 4	12 0 0	4 3 7	—	4 3 7		232
2 16 5	—	63 0 0	9 16 0	2 10 0	10 0 0	12 10 0		233
1 15 9	4 10 0	14 3 4	6 10 0	5 0 0	—	6 0 0	V.C.	234
1 0 10	—	35 0 0	6 14 0	3 14 0	—	3 14 0	A.	235
6 9 4	—	56 6 4	6 2 0	12 0 6	—	12 0 6	V.C.	236
1 15 10	—	20 0 0	6 7 0	1 14 6	—	1 14 6	V.C.	237
4 7 3	—	57 18 4	24 1 0	8 9 11	—	8 9 11		238
3 16 0	—	58 6 2	19 14 6	12 0 0	—	12 0 0	V.C.	239
0 9 0	—	24 0 0	4 12 6	1 10 0	—	1 10 0	V.C.	240
0 10 9	—	24 0 0	1 6 6	0 5 0	—	0 5 0		241
1 6 0	—	20 0 0	12 15 0	3 0 0	8 0 0	11 0 0		242
—	—	62 6 4	16 8 0	—	—	—	V.C.	243
4 18 1	—	27 16 6	9 4 6	3 9 6	6 7 0	9 16 6		244
1 13 7	—	22 6 6	7 11 6	2 10 0	—	2 10 0		245
0 17 6	—	23 0 0	6 8 0	4 19 6	5 0 0	a 9 19 6		246
—	—	—	—	—	—	—		247
6 16 4	—	50 15 0	7 8 8	3 10 0	15 0 0	18 10 0		248

a Including value of Free Residence.

b Temporary.

List of Schools in operation on the 31st December, 1874.—

Number.	Roll Number of School.	Parish.	District.	School.	Religious Denomination of Patron or Correspondent. Clerical.	Lay.	Number and Religious Denominations of Teachers. Principals.	Assistants.	Attendances for the Year. Total number of Pupils on Rolls during the Year 1874. Males.	Fem.	Total.	Average Daily Attendance for the Year 1874.
[illegible]	[illegible]	Killygarvan,	1	Rathmullan (Robertson),	R.C.	–	Pres.	–	43	35	78	39
[illegible]	[illegible]	Do.	–	Do. l.	–	R.C.	Pres.	–	19	22	41	25
[illegible]	[illegible]	Do.	–	Rathmullan,	R.C.	–	R.C.	–	41	50	90	35
[illegible]	[illegible]	Do.	–	Carradoan Ord. Agr.	–	R.C.	Pres.	–	74	72	146	52
[illegible]	[illegible]	Killea,	2	Carrigans, f.	R.C.	–	R.C.	–	31	53	84	50
[illegible]	[illegible]	Leck,	1	Knockbrack,	R.C.	–	R.C.	–	48	74	122	29
[illegible]	[illegible]	Do.	–	Gortyvady,	Pres.	–	Pres.	–	38	27	65	26
[illegible]	[illegible]	Do.	–	Drumlodge,	–	E.C.	R.C.	–	30	33	63	17
[illegible]	[illegible]	Lettermacaward,	–	Aaron, f.	–	R.C.	R.C.	–	–	93	93	34
[illegible]	[illegible]	Do.	–	Doory,	R.C.	–	R.C.	R.C.	59	77	136	41
[illegible]	[illegible]	Do.	–	Boyoughter,	R.C.	–	R.C.	–	77	40	117	45
[illegible]	[illegible]	Do.	–	Dunmory,[a]	R.C.	–	R.C.	–	–	–	–	–
[illegible]	[illegible]	Do.	–	Meenagowan,	R.C.	–	R.C.	–	46	34	80	35
[illegible]	[illegible]	Muff,	2	Clonelly,	R.C.	–	R.C.	–	57	59	116	31
[illegible]	[illegible]	Do.	–	Tara,	R.C.	–	R.C.	–	53	76	129	64
[illegible]	[illegible]	Do.	–	Threetrees,	Pres.	–	Pres.	–	11	64	79	22
[illegible]	[illegible]	Do.	–	Muff,	–	R.C.	Pres.	R.C.	84	76	160	61
[illegible]	[illegible]	Do.	–	Carnamoyle,	Pres.	–	Diss.	–	41	18	61	19
[illegible]	[illegible]	Mevagh,	1	Aghadachor,	R.C.	–	R.C.	–	68	48	116	37
[illegible]	[illegible]	Do.	–	Manor Vaughan,	–	R.C.	R.C.	–	92	82	174	47
[illegible]	[illegible]	Do.	–	Derrylamman,	–	R.C.	R.C.	–	70	69	139	67
[illegible]	[illegible]	Do.	–	Mevagh,	R.C.	–	R.C.	–	42	42	84	32
[illegible]	[illegible]	Do.	–	Bohanny,	R.C.	–	R.C.	–	160	[illegible]	[illegible]	33
[illegible]	[illegible]	Do.	–	Glen,	R.C.	–	R.C.	–	118	91	209	48
[illegible]	[illegible]	Moville, Upper,	2	Drung,	R.C.	–	R.C.	–	80	66	146	37
[illegible]	[illegible]	Do.	–	Ballyratten,	R.C.	–	R.C.	–	38	35	73	29
[illegible]	[illegible]	Do.	–	Cabry,	R.C.	–	R.C.	–	33	37	70	25
[illegible]	[illegible]	Do.	–	Tirroran,	R.C.	–	–	–	50	28	78	17
[illegible]	[illegible]	Do.	–	Tullynavin,	R.C.	–	R.C.	–	45	45	90	38
[illegible]	[illegible]	Do.	–	Whitecastle,	Diss.	–	Diss.	–	31	32	63	28
[illegible]	[illegible]	Do.	–	Calry,	R.C.	–	R.C.	–	45	29	74	28
[illegible]	[illegible]	Moville, Lower,	–	Culkeeny,	R.C.	–	R.C.	–	85	32	117	38
[illegible]	[illegible]	Do.	–	Glenagivny,	R.C.	–	R.C.	–	75	46	121	38
[illegible]	[illegible]	Do.	–	Shrove,	R.C.	–	R.C.	–	68	71	139	55
[illegible]	[illegible]	Do.	–	Moville,	R.C.	–	R.C.	–	51	30	81	45
[illegible]	[illegible]	Do.	–	Do. No. 2, m.	R.C.	–	R.C.	–	131	–	131	56
[illegible]	[illegible]	Do.	–	Do. Convent, f.	R.C.	–	R.C.	–	–	145	145	64
[illegible]	[illegible]	Do.	–	Drumaweir,	R.C.	–	R.C.	–	96	63	159	39
[illegible]	[illegible]	Do.	–	Carrowtrasna,	R.C.	–	R.C.	–	69	50	119	46
[illegible]	[illegible]	Do.	–	Greencastle,	R.C.	–	R.C.	–	55	47	102	48
[illegible]	[illegible]	Raphoe,	6	Ramkey,	R.C.	–	R.C.	R.C.	77	45	122	45
[illegible]	[illegible]	Do.	1	Glenmaquin,	R.C.	–	R.C.	–	94	62	68	30
[illegible]	[illegible]	Do.	6	Do.	Pres.	–	Pres.	–	33	34	67	30
[illegible]	[illegible]	Do.	–	Raphoe, No. 1,	R.C.	–	R.C.	–	67	62	129	43
[illegible]	[illegible]	Do.	–	Do. No. 2,	Pres.	–	Pres.	Pres.	107	64	171	78
[illegible]	[illegible]	Do.	–	Robertson Parish,	R.C.	–	R.C.	R.C.	103	79	182	75
[illegible]	[illegible]	Raymunterdoney,	1	Ballyten,	R.C.	–	R.C.[b]	–	159	108	267	38
[illegible]	[illegible]	Do.	–	Myragh Ord. Agri.	–	R.C.	R.C.	–	32	36	68	28
[illegible]	[illegible]	Raymoghy,	–	Errity,	Pres.	–	Pres.	–	41	36	77	35
[illegible]	[illegible]	Do.	–	Ballyoughan Ord. Agri.	–	Pres.	Pres.	–	70	34	104	47
[illegible]	[illegible]	Stranorlar,	–	Dunish,	R.C.	–	R.C.	–	50	45	95	31
[illegible]	[illegible]	Do.	–	Stranorlar, m.	R.C.	–	R.C.	–	118	–	118	56
[illegible]	[illegible]	Do.	–	Do. f.	R.C.	–	R.C.	–	–	141	141	66
[illegible]	[illegible]	Do.	–	Do. No. 2,	Diss.	–	Diss.	–	80	7	87	15
[illegible]	[illegible]	Do.	–	Meenlaney,	R.C.	–	R.C.	–	30	43	73	33
[illegible]	[illegible]	Do.	–	Meencorrigan,	R.C.	–	R.C.	–	67	45	112	37
[illegible]	[illegible]	Do.	–	Ballybofey,	R.C.	–	R.C.	–	56	63	119	47
[illegible]	[illegible]	Do.	–	Cappry,	–	R.C.	R.C.	–	49	42	91	41
[illegible]	[illegible]	Tullaghobegly,	–	Derryhenny,	R.C.	–	R.C.	R.C.	181	72	253	61
[illegible]	[illegible]	Do.	–	Gortahork,	R.C.	–	R.C.	–	126	107	233	53
[illegible]	[illegible]	Do.	–	Cashelnagore,	R.C.	–	R.C.	–	69	64	133	39
310	[illegible]	Do.	–	Gola,	R.C.	–	R.C.	–	81	16	97	19
311	[illegible]	Do.	–	Knockastoller,	R.C.	–	R.C.	–	102	54	156	35

[a] Including value of Free Garden.

[b] Including value of Free Residence and Garden.

Province of Ulster: County of Donegal—*continued.*

Amount paid for Books, Requisites, and Apparatus at Reduced Prices.	Aid granted by the Board during the Year 1874. In Free Stock of Books, Requisites, and Apparatus.	In Salaries, Premiums, and other Gratuities.	Results Fees, Financial Year.	Amount of Local Emoluments received in Aid of Teacher's Salary. School Fees.	Subscriptions, Endowments, &c.	Total Local Aid.	Vested or Non-Vested.	Number.
£ s. d.	£ s. d.	£ s. d.	£ s. d.	£ s. d.	£ s. d.	£ s. d.		
1 13 6	—	16 13 4	6 14 6	4 0 0	10 1 4	a 20 1 4		449
0 7 3	—	20 0 0	8 0 0	3 0 4	1 0 0	4 0 4		450
0 5 5	—	26 10 0	11 13 0	4 10 8	—	4 16 8		451
1 15 8	—	30 0 0	6 11 6	1 12 6	23 8 6	b 25 0 11		452
3 17 6	—	20 0 0	10 3 8	4 7 8	13 0 0	a 17 7 8		453
1 6 0	—	20 0 0	11 8 0	0 10 0	—	0 10 0		454
0 10 10	—	18 0 0	1 12 6	0 17 0	5 0 0	5 17 0		455
2 6 5	4 0 0	—	—	0 12 0	8 0 0	a 8 12 0		456
4 13 3	5 0 0	14 0 0	9 12 6	0 7 0	—	0 7 0	V.C.	457
2 3 1	—	51 0 0	16 6 6	—	—	—		458
0 10 8	—	26 0 0	11 1 0	—	—	—		459
1 6 10	—	29 10 0	14 0 0	—	—	—		460
3 11 8	4 10 0	24 0 0	4 0 0	—	—	—		461
2 4 11	—	24 0 0	7 16 0	2 14 7	1 0 0	a 3 14 7	V.V.	462
2 19 6	—	21 0 0	11 14 6	2 19 6	3 0 0	5 19 0	V.V.	463
1 0 2	—	24 0 0	10 5 0	3 15 10	4 0 2	b 7 5 0		464
6 11 1	—	77 8 0	45 18 6	22 16 5	5 0 0	27 16 5		465
1 7 6	—	16 18 4	1 7 0	1 16 2	—	1 16 2	V.C.	466
1 5 3	—	24 0 0	6 11 0	8 5 6	—	8 5 6	A.	467
1 16 6	—	23 0 0	18 8 6	2 0 0	6 0 0	8 0 0		468
1 16 5	—	21 0 0	3 8 6	1 3 0	—	1 3 0		469
2 17 5	4 10 0	15 0 6	4 8 0	3 3 0	—	3 3 0		470
—	—	10 13 4	4 13 0	0 10 5	—	0 10 5		471
3 8 11	—	31 4 6	7 2 0	0 10 0	—	0 10 0		472
1 9 4	—	22 0 0	4 13 6	2 9 0	3 10 0	6 19 0		473
1 17 1	4 2 3	24 0 0	11 0 6	4 11 0	5 0 0	9 11 0	V.V.	474
1 6 0	—	20 0 0	6 5 0	1 6 0	10 0 0	11 6 0		475
0 12 10	—	12 0 0	4 13 4	1 0 0	4 0 0	5 0 0		476
2 0 5	—	20 0 0	6 14 6	1 17 11	8 0 0	9 17 11	V.C.	477
1 4 6	—	20 10 0	6 16 0	4 15 0	17 0 0	b 21 15 0		478
1 0 11	—	24 0 0	4 13 6	3 13 11	—	3 13 11		479
2 16 8	—	21 0 0	5 19 0	3 17 4	—	3 17 4		480
1 0 0	6 10 0	61 0 0	4 0 0	1 4 0	—	1 4 0		481
2 16 8	—	45 6 8	20 4 8	12 5 3	6 0 0	a 18 5 8		482
3 17 5	—	29 16 0	14 3 0	0 0 0	8 0 0	8 0 0	A.	483
3 8 0	—	68 0 0	13 14 6	14 6 7	—	14 6 7		484
4 8 0	—	20 18 0	24 16 0	18 10 2	—	18 10 2		485
1 6 9	—	25 0 0	10 16 0	6 13 0	—	6 13 0		486
1 16 5	5 0 0	—	—	1 16 4	3 10 0	4 6 4	V.C.	487
2 13 2	—	24 0 0	17 8 0	12 17 4	14 0 0	a 26 17 4		488
0 10 8	—	58 0 0	19 7 0	6 10 6	—	6 10 6	V.V.	489
0 4 0	—	81 15 4	6 10 0	—	—	—		490
2 10 6	—	32 15 0	13 0 0	4 0 8	5 6 0	a 9 15 6		491
1 10 6	—	43 10 0	12 5 6	3 2 4	—	a 3 2 4		492
0 8 1	—	91 10 0	29 12 6	21 6 4	—	21 6 4		493
2 6 0	—	46 0 0	21 1 8	4 6 2	15 1 6	b 19 9 6		494
1 8 11	—	24 0 0	—	1 15 11	—	1 15 11	V.V.	495
1 18 8	—	21 0 0	7 6 0	—	16 0 0	a 13 0 0		496
3 15 4	—	22 0 0	10 0 0	6 3 6	5 0 0	a 11 3 6		497
2 2 8	—	22 10 0	14 17 0	6 19 0	5 0 0	11 19 0		498
4 0 1	—	33 16 8	6 6 0	1 8 8	2 0 0	a 3 8 8	V.V.	499
6 0 0	—	56 10 0	18 4 0	6 4 1	—	6 4 1		500
0 9 1	—	37 0 0	17 8 0	3 12 11	—	3 12 11		501
1 6 1	4 0 0	7 0 0	—	2 17 0	41 0 0	b 43 17 0		502
1 7 4	—	20 0 0	4 3 6	0 10 0	—	0 10 0		503
1 10 4	—	24 0 0	7 12 0	1 6 0	—	1 6 0	V.C.	504
4 0 11	—	41 18 6	10 11 0	4 6 11	—	4 6 11		505
2 1 3	6 10 0	12 6 8	—	1 1 6	2 0 0	a 3 1 6		506
1 6 8	—	20 0 0	8 8 0	—	—	—	A.	507
3 3 6	—	51 16 8	7 17 8	—	—	—	B.	508
0 15 0	—	26 0 0	4 1 0	0 7 7	—	0 7 7	A.	509
—	—	20 0 0	8 0 6	—	—	—	V.C.	510
1 12 11	—	41 0 0	6 17 0	2 11 0	—	2 11 0	V.C.	511

a Including value of Free Residence.

b No Returns.

List of Schools in operation on the 31st December, 1874.—

Number.	Roll Number of School.	Parish.	District.	School.	Religious Denomination of Manager or Correspondent. Clerical.	Lay.	Number and Religious Denominations of Teachers. Principals.	Assistants.	Attendance for the Year. Total number of Pupils on Rolls within the Year 1874. Males.	Fem.	Total.	Average Daily Attendance for the Year 1874.
312	4741	Tullaghobegly,	1	Dore,	R.C.	–	R.C.	–	51	47	98	22
313	11204	Templecrone,	–	Derrylammy,	R.C.	–	R.C.	–	45	49	94	24
314	3042	Tullaghobegly,	–	Meenacladdy,	–	R.C.	R.C.	–	63	48	111	46
315	8154	Do.	–	Tory Island,	–	R.C.	R.C.	–	18	31	49	24
316	6166	Do.	–	Bunaninver,	R.C.	–	R.C.	–	98	54	152	55
317	10916	Do.	–	Derryconnor,	R.C.	–	R.C.	–	91	68	159	31
318	4766	Do.	–	Bunbeg, 1st Class Agr.	R.C.	–	R.C.	–	48	38	86	24
319	2407	Tullyaughnish,	–	Ramelton, m.	Pres.	–	Pres.	–	85	–	85	[illegible]
320	8561	Do.	–	Do. f.	Pres.	–	Pres.	Pres.	–	115	115	50
321	4917	Do.	–	Croghan,	Pres.	–	R.C.	–	21	46	67	18
322	4904	Do.	–	Bridge End,	R.C.	–	R.C.	–	40	41	81	27
323	9446	Do.	–	Kerrykeel, or Carrowkeel,	–	E.C.	Pres.	–	71	64	135	36
324	7464	Do.	–	Brown Knowe,	–	E.C.	Pres.	–	98	63	161	51
325	10744	Do.	–	Glenalla,	–	E.C.	E.C.	–	59	51	110	35
326	5189	Templecrone,	–	Dungloe, m.	R.C.	–	R.C.	–	125	–	125	43
327	6617	Do.	–	Do. f.	R.C.	–	R.C.	–	14	101	115	45
328	4739	Do.	–	Rosbine,	R.C.	–	R.C.	–	74	50	124	44
329	4809	Do.	–	Keadue,	R.C.	–	R.C.	R.C.	98	61	159	45
330	9794	Do.	–	Inishkeeragh,[a]	–	R.C.	–	–	–	–	–	–
331	5472	Do.	–	Meenmore,	R.C.	–	R.C.	R.C.	105	65	170	55
332	8478	Do.	–	Owey Island,	R.C.	–	R.C.	–	20	18	38	20
333	10542	Do.	–	Letterenagh,[a]	R.C.	–	–	–	–	–	–	–
334	10575	Do.	9	Sheriff's Mountain,	R.C.	–	R.C.	–	40	43	83	30
335	10617	Do.	1	Meenacross,	R.C.	–	R.C.	R.C.	75	62	137	61
336	10715	Do.	–	Tulighena,	R.C.	–	R.C.	–	71	62	133	42
337	10716	Do.	–	Meenatotan,	R.C.	–	R.C.	–	36	19	55	29
338	2278	Do.	–	Acres,	R.C.	–	R.C.	–	125	–	125	40
339	8460	Do.	–	Rutland,	R.C.	–	R.C.	–	30	16	46	20
340	8732	Do.	–	Belcruit,	R.C.	–	R.C.	–	90	71	161	43
341	10910	Do.	–	Rannafast,	R.C.	–	R.C.	–	46	34	80	35
342	6809	Do.	–	Inishfree,	R.C.	–	R.C.	–	26	25	51	28
343	10211	Do.	–	Loughanure,	R.C.	–	R.C.	–	52	40	92	29
344	6861	Do.	–	Annagry,	R.C.	–	R.C.	–	94	30	124	47
345	10271	Do.	–	Cruit Island,	R.C.	–	R.C.	–	60	23	83	35
346	6751	Do.	–	Mullaghduff,	R.C.	–	R.C.	–	81	30	111	35
347	8571	Do.	–	Arranmore Ord. Agrl.	–	R.C.	R.C.	–	75	41	116	45
348	6908	Taughboyne,	6	St. Johnston,	Pres.	–	Pres.	–	40	25	65	27
349	7143	Do.	–	Monreagh,	Pres.	–	Pres.	Pres.	77	48	125	54
350	8104	Do.	–	Castletown,	R.C.	–	R.C.	–	73	51	124	53
351	8738	Do.	–	Anlagh,	R.C.	–	Pres.	–	71	64	135	49
352	9035	Do.	–	Drumbar,	R.C.	–	R.C.	R.C.	96	72	168	55
353	10640	Do.	–	Craigadooish,	R.C.	–	R.C.	–	63	50	113	40
354	9416	Do.	–	Taughboyne,	R.C.	–	R.C.	–	33	57	90	41
355	7185	Templecarn,	5	Gortnessy,	Pres.	–	Pres.	–	70	37	107	42
356	10183	Do.	–	Pettigo, m.	R.C.	–	R.C.	–	81	–	81	15
357	10182	Do.	–	Do. f.	R.C.	–	R.C.	–	–	97	97	43
358	10257	Do.	–	Lettercran,	R.C.	–	R.C.	–	74	78	152	41
359	7979	Tullyfern,	1	Glenaddely,	R.C.	–	Pres.	–	45	51	96	19
360	9774	Do.	–	Milford, f.	–	R.C.	R.C.	–	–	101	101	35
361	10594	Do.	–	Do.	–	Pres.	Pres.	–	103	–	103	42
362	4879	Do.	–	Do. Workhouse,	P.L.	Gds.	Pres.	–	11	20	31	16
363	9440	Do.	–	Ballyarr,	R.C.	–	R.C.	–	43	34	77	23
364	10717	Do.	–	Tullyboy,	R.C.	–	R.C.	–	49	30	79	24
365	7246	Urney,	6	Alt, No. 1,	R.C.	–	R.C.	R.C.	61	88	149	63
366	8291	Do.	–	Do. No. 2,	Pres.	–	Pres.	–	45	35	80	39
		Total for County Donegal, 366,							22303	19463	41,766	[illegible]

a Including value of Free Residence and Garden.

b Including value of Free Garden.

Province of ULSTER: County of DONEGAL—*continued.*

Amount paid for Books, Requisites, and Apparatus, at Reduced Prices.	Aid granted by the Board during the Year 1874. In Free Stock of Books, Requisites, and Apparatus.	In Salaries, Premiums, and other Gratuities.	Results Fees, Financial Year.	Amount of Local Endowments received in Aid of Teacher's Salary. School Fees.	Subscriptions, Endowments, &c.	Total Local Aid.	Vested or Non-Vested.	Number.
£ s. d.	£ s. d.	£ s. d.	£ s. d.	£ s. d.	£ s. d.	£ s. d.		
1 5 9	—	24 0 0	3 8 6	—	—	—	V.C.	912
1 15 6	—	4 0 0	—	—	—	—		913
—	—	27 0 0	18 0 6	—	—	—	V.C.	914
—	—	20 0 0	1 11 5	—	—	—	V.C.	915
1 16 6	—	24 0 0	6 15 6	—	—	—	V.C.	916
—	—	20 0 0	1 19 0	0 2 0	—	0 2 6		917
1 8 6	—	72 7 6	4 14 5	—	6 0 0	*6 0 6	V.C.	918
2 18 0	—	40 0 0	11 8 0	5 18 8	1 0 0	*6 18 8		919
7 2 7	—	65 13 4	19 8 0	14 18 0	—	14 18 0		920
0 10 11	—	20 0 0	4 6 0	1 17 1	2 0 0	*3 17 1		921
1 6 11	—	26 0 0	11 6 0	6 2 7	—	6 2 7		922
1 5 3	—	24 0 0	6 0 0	3 7 10	0 10 0	*3 17 10	V.C.	923
9 0 8	—	27 10 0	10 14 0	3 14 8	—	3 14 8		924
8 6 6	—	28 1 0	10 8 6	6 10 11	6 10 0	*12 0 11		925
2 17 7	—	64 0 0	18 0 0	1 13 0	—	1 13 0		926
2 0 10	—	93 3 4	12 17 6	0 10 0	—	0 10 0		927
1 8 3	—	30 15 0	6 17 0	—	0 10 0	*0 10 0	V.C.	928
1 7 0	—	40 0 0	7 3 6	1 0 6	—	1 0 0		929
—	—	9 0 0	—	—	—	—		930
6 6 11	—	97 3 4	17 16 6	—	—	—		931
0 9 8	—	20 0 0	6 3 6	—	—	—		932
—	—	—	—	—	—	—		933
1 19 5	—	26 0 0	3 8 6	0 18 7	5 0 0	5 18 7		934
0 18 7	—	35 18 0	12 18 0	—	—	—		935
4 16 8	—	33 10 0	6 18 6	—	—	—		936
—	—	21 6 6	10 4 6	—	—	—		937
2 8 7	—	24 0 0	16 18 0	0 18 6	—	0 13 6		938
—	—	24 0 0	6 4 0	1 15 0	1 5 0	3 0 0		939
4 1 8	—	45 0 0	20 12 0	—	—	—	V.C.	940
1 5 3	—	24 0 0	7 13 6	—	—	—		941
—	—	20 0 0	4 18 0	—	—	—		942
0 18 6	—	27 0 0	10 0 6	—	—	—		943
0 15 7	—	31 0 8	12 18 0	1 0 0	—	1 0 0		944
0 18 0	—	24 0 0	8 5 6	—	—	—		945
0 10 0	—	24 0 0	4 8 6	—	—	—		946
8 17 6	0 16 0	50 15 6	11 10 0	—	—	—		947
1 6 6	—	33 6 8	8 18 6	12 0 0	3 0 0	*15 0 0		948
—	—	68 8 4	23 1 0	17 10 0	3 0 0	*20 10 0		949
3 3 0	—	42 13 4	17 1 0	6 8 0	5 0 0	*11 8 0		950
—	—	48 10 0	16 2 6	7 7 0	4 0 0	*11 7 0		951
1 11 8	—	47 0 0	16 6 0	7 6 6	2 16 0	*9 15 6		952
—	—	24 16 0	10 17 6	6 6 0	3 10 0	*9 16 0		953
1 14 4	—	25 0 0	0 9 0	8 14 3	13 13 6	*22 7 9		954
6 0 0	—	37 13 4	16 6 6	12 6 1	4 0 0	*16 6 1		955
3 6 10	—	21 0 0	13 6 6	3 2 7	23 0 0	*26 2 7		956
9 1 6	—	30 10 0	12 8 0	4 8 1	10 0 0	14 8 1		957
0 8 8	—	24 0 0	11 6 0	1 5 0	18 0 0	19 5 0		958
1 6 6	—	10 0 0	4 11 0	0 11 8	—	0 11 8		959
1 15 8	—	24 0 0	6 14 7	21 11 10	6 0 0	*27 11 10		960
7 1 5	—	41 3 4	17 18 0	11 18 4	15 0 0	26 18 4	V.T.	961
5 0 3	—	1 10 0	—	—	—	—		962
1 12 6	—	26 6 8	6 0 6	1 10 0	11 0 0	*15 10 0		963
1 5 0	—	22 10 0	5 8 8	2 8 6	—	2 8 9		964
5 13 7	—	30 15 0	18 10 0	2 14 10	—	2 14 10	V.T.	965
3 1 6	—	24 0 0	6 1 0	3 18 0	—	3 18 0		966
794 17 9	96 7 9	11,880 8 6	2,684 15 6	1,219 7 2	249 15 8	[illegible] 8 9		

* Including value of Free Residence. § Closed.

List of Schools in operation on the 31st December, 1874.—

COUNTY OF

Number.	Roll Number of School.	Parish.	District.	School.	Religious Denomination of Patrons or Correspondents. Clerical.	Lay.	Number and Religious Denomination of Teachers. Principals.	Assistants.	Attendance for the Year. Total number of Pupils on Rolls within the Year 1874. Males.	Fem.	Total.	Average Daily Attendance for the Year 1874.
1	8862	Annaclone,	17	Ballynafern,	Pres.	–	Pres.	–	40	20	60	29
2	7015	Do.	–	Annaclone,	Pres.	–	Pres.	–	34	35	69	23
3	9718	Do.	–	Monteith,	R.C.	–	R.C.	–	67	43	105	51
4	167	Aghaderg,	19	Loughbrickland, No. 1,	R.C.	–	R.C.	R.C.	73	71	144	67
5	7778	Do.	–	Do. No. 2,	Pres.	–	Pres.	Pres.	86	65	151	65
6	2270	Do.	–	Ballyvarty,[a] m.	R.C.	–	–	–	–	–	–	–
7	2271	Do.	–	Do. f.	R.C.	–	R.C.	R.C.	63	78	141	61
8	2624	Do.	–	Meenan,[a]	Pres.	–	–	–	–	–	–	–
9	4571	Do.	–	Glaskerbeg,	R.C.	–	R.C.	R.C.	90	61	153	53
10	[illegible]	Do.	–	Glaskermore,	Pres.	–	Pres.	–	75	56	131	56
11	7601	Do.	–	Brague,	Pres.	–	Pres.	–	19	41	60	25
12	8454	Annahilt,	17	Cluntagh,	Pres.	–	Pres.	–	64	42	106	46
13	8647	Do.	–	Annahilt, m.	Pres.	–	Pres.	–	115	–	115	47
14	8694	Do.	–	Do. f.	Pres.	–	Pres.	–	–	94	94	42
15	9022	Do.	–	Ballykeel, Loughaghery,	Pres.	–	Pres.	Pres.	103	93	196	56
16	7042	Ardquin,	20	Ardquin,	R.C.	–	Pres.	–	46	33	77	31
17	10039	Ardglass,	11	Ardglass, No. 2,	Pres.	–	Pres.	–	38	35	73	23
18	8011	Do.	–	Do.[c] m.	R.C.	–	–	–	–	–	–	–
19	8812	Do.	–	Do. f.	R.C.	–	R.C.	–	41	50	91	53
20	8411	Ardkeen,	19	Kirkistown,	–	R.C.	R.C.	Pres.	63	53	116	53
21	1894	Ballee,	11	Ballee, m.	Pres.	–	Pres.	–	34	–	34	22
22	6113	Do.	–	Do. f.	Pres.	–	Pres.	–	–	60	60	27
23	2174	Do.	–	Ballycruttle,	R.C.	–	R.C.	R.C.	80	69	149	61
24	11767	Ballymacarrett,	10	Ballymacarrett-road,	R.C.	–	Pres.	[1]R.C.	209	285	594	187
25	10025	Do.	–	Short-strand, m.	R.C.	–	R.C.	[1]R.C.	246	–	246	161
26	10266	Do.	–	Do. f.	R.C.	–	R.C.	R.C.	–	316	316	96
27	4815	Bangor,	9	Conlig, No. 1,	–	Pres.	Pres.	Pres.	63	77	139	73
28	2779	Do.	–	Cotton,	Pres.	–	Pres.	Pres.	63	47	110	65
29	4344	Do.	–	Groomsport,	Pres.	–	Pres.	Pres.	68	63	131	71
30	5011	Do.	–	Bangor, m.	Pres.	–	Pres.	Pres.	175	–	175	76
31	5012	Do.	–	Do. f.	Pres.	–	Pres.	–	–	164	164	71
32	3653	Do.	–	Ballyvallagh,	–	R.C.	Pres.	E.C.	16	53	69	33
33	4028	Do.	–	Ballymaconnell,	–	R.C.	Pres.	Pres.	82	97	189	66
34	6611	Do.	–	Ballyvester,	–	R.C.	Pres.	Pres.	64	51	115	36
35	4754	Do.	–	Copeland Island,[a]	–	–	–	–	–	–	–	–
36	2162	Ballyroney,	17	Aughnavallog,	Pres.	–	Pres.	–	62	38	90	30
37	11025	Ballyhalbert,	10	Portavogie,	E.C.	–	E.C.	E.C. / Unc.	113	109	222	112
38	7878	Ballyphilip,	9	Ballyphilip, m.	R.C.	–	R.C.	[2]R.C.	173	–	173	82
39	4348	Do.	–	Do. f.	R.C.	–	R.C.	[3]R.C.	–	186	187	84
40	10904	Do.	–	Do., parish,	–	R.C.	R.C.	–	25	71	96	36
41	3641	Do.	–	Portaferry, No. 2, m.	Pres.	–	Pres.	Pres.	99	60	156	64
42	11138	Do.	–	Ballyphilip, No. 2, m.	E.C.	–	Pres.	–	78	–	78	31
43	8742	Bright,	17	Bright,[a] m.	–	R.C.	–	–	–	–	–	–
44	8744	Do.	–	Do. f.	–	E.C.	R.C.	–	86	68	84	43
45	10924	Do.	–	Rossglass,[a]	R.C.	–	–	–	–	–	–	–
46	10898	Do.	–	Legamaddy, m.	R.C.	–	R.C.	R.C.	77	68	145	47
47	11341	Blaris,	20	Lurganure,	–	E.C.	R.C.	[3]E.C.	152	121	273	101
48	[illegible]	Ballywalter,	10	Ballyfrenis,	–	R.C.	Pres.	–	33	15	48	24
49	10617	Do.	–	Ballywalter, f.	–	E.C.	Pres.	–	42	29	71	34
50	7045	Ballytrustan,	–	Kearney,[a]	Pres.	–	–	–	–	–	–	–
51	7281	Ballyculter,	11	Strangford,	–	E.C.	R.C.	–	41	51	92	44
52	192	Clonallan,	20	Mayobridge, m.	R.C.	–	R.C.	R.C.	178	–	178	68
53	[illegible]	Do.	–	Do. f.	R.C.	–	R.C.	R.C.	2	170	177	82
54	1256	Do.	–	Carrick, m.	R.C.	–	R.C.	–	158	–	158	48
55	[illegible]	Do.	–	Do. f.	R.C.	–	R.C.	–	–	132	132	56
56	3176	Do.	–	Warrenpoint, m.	R.C.	–	R.C.	–	153	–	153	55
57	3431	Do.	–	Do. f.	R.C.	–	R.C.	–	–	180	186	80
58	3748	Do.	–	Clontafleece,	–	E.C.	Diss.	R.C.	172	88	260	74
59	10611	Do.	19	Burren,	–	E.C.	E.C.	–	42	46	88	36
60	192	Comber,	10	Tullygarvan,	Pres.	–	Pres.	–	47	60	107	32
61	1698	Do.	–	Crossnacreevy,	–	Pres.	Pres.	–	44	52	96	29

[a] Inoperative. [b] Including value of Free Residence and Garden. [c] Closed last Quarter; no Returns.

Province of Ulster: County of Down.

DOWN.—416 Schools.

Amount paid for Books, Requisites, and Apparatus at Reduced Prices.	Aid granted by the Board during the Year 1874. To Free Stock of Books, Requisites, and Apparatus.	In Salaries, Premiums, and other Gratuities.	Results Fees, Financial Year.	Amount of Local Emoluments received in Aid of Teacher's Salary. School Fees.	Subscriptions, Endowments, &c.	Total Local Aid.	Vested or Non-Vested.	Number.
£ s. d.	£ s. d.	£ s. d.	£ s. d.	£ s. d.	£ s. d.	£ s. d.		
1 6 5	—	24 9 0	4 13 6	5 8 0	—	5 8 0		1
1 5 1	—	20 0 0	8 19 0	4 10 0	—	4 10 6		2
1 16 7	—	21 0 0	8 6 0	6 12 0	—	5 19 0		3
7 15 8	—	64 9 6	16 19 0	8 0 4	—	8 0 4	V.P.	4
1 5 7	—	64 8 8	23 19 6	26 9 6	—	26 6 0		5
—	—	—	—	—	—	—	V.P.	6
6 9 0	—	40 5 6	18 2 0	4 7 6	—	4 7 6	V.P.	7
1 8 0	—	—	1 2 6	—	—	—		8
9 18 2	—	22 6 0	12 14 0	0 17 6	—	0 17 6		9
4 9 6	—	12 13 4	9 8 0	16 4 8	—	16 4 8		10
1 15 1	—	20 6 0	7 17 0	2 11 0	—	2 11 0		11
9 16 6	—	24 0 6	10 12 6	15 6 2	—	15 6 8		12
5 0 1	—	26 10 0	21 11 6	—	22 0 0	b 23 8 6		13
6 1 6	—	22 15 0	16 17 0	—	10 0 0	10 0 0		14
4 1 1	1 6 0	59 19 6	12 4 0	13 10 3	—	13 10 3		15
4 15 0	—	24 0 0	8 10 8	0 6 10	16 0 0	17 6 10		16
9 16 1	—	20 0 0	8 14 6	5 0 3	1 0 0	6 0 3		17
—	—	21 0 0	—	—	—	—	V.P.	18
4 4 6	—	28 10 0	7 4 6	4 3 9	—	4 3 9	V.P.	19
1 17 7	—	44 0 0	7 11 0	5 13 3	—	5 13 3		20
—	—	22 6 6	3 4 6	0 17 5	7 0 6	b 16 17 5		21
8 5 2	—	20 8 0	6 0 6	10 11 10	—	10 11 10		22
4 16 2	—	52 13 4	20 11 6	9 14 0	1 17 6	11 14 6	V.P.	23
7 19 7	—	80 3 4	23 10 0	30 16 11	—	30 16 11		24
15 4 7	—	70 6 6	28 6 6	29 14 1	12 0 0	a 41 14 1		25
5 12 0	—	24 10 0	23 12 0	22 5 4	—	22 5 4		26
4 6 0	—	61 18 8	21 4 0	14 0 6	—	14 0 6		27
5 7 0	—	54 3 4	14 19 0	10 19 0	—	16 19 0	V.P.	28
10 6 9	—	70 5 0	61 18 0	32 13 9	8 12 0	a 41 6 0		29
6 3 4	—	80 8 4	16 16 4	22 18 6	—	24 18 6		30
8 0 11	—	70 6 0	35 15 0	26 0 0	—	26 0 0		31
7 4 7	—	70 13 4	23 1 6	15 8 4	27 17 6	a 43 5 10		32
5 5 1	—	64 16 8	17 6 6	10 10 3	6 16 0	a 16 6 3		33
7 7 7	—	103 16 8	17 9 0	27 7 10	14 18 0	32 0 10		34
—	—	—	—	—	—	—		35
3 6 7	—	21 0 0	7 2 6	6 7 2	—	6 7 2		36
9 5 10	5 0 6	52 3 4	29 9 6	8 14 2	21 5 0	a 29 19 2		37
5 19 0	—	121 6 8	60 15 0	22 6 4	—	22 6 4		38
4 3 11	—	70 0 0	60 18 6	10 4 0	—	10 4 0		39
2 17 8	—	91 0 8	9 9 0	8 15 5	10 0 0	18 15 5		40
16 13 10	—	90 10 0	50 4 6	23 0 6	10 0 0	33 0 6		41
1 10 8	4 0 6	16 9 8	9 10 0	5 18 6	16 5 0	a 21 18 5		42
—	—	—	—	—	—	—	V.P.	43
9 18 1	—	28 0 0	14 6 6	8 0 0	—	8 0 0	V.P.	44
—	—	18 0 0	4 8 0	—	—	—		45
5 11 11	—	22 0 0	14 4 0	5 13 4	—	5 13 4		46
4 6 8	8 6 0	87 6 8	28 8 6	29 1 8	10 0 0	39 1 8		47
—	—	24 6 6	8 16 0	8 11 10	6 8 0	a 6 14 10		48
—	—	29 13 4	6 15 9	0 5 0	6 0 0	11 5 6		49
1 17 0	—	27 10 0	10 17 0	—	—	—		50
6 8 0	—	64 6 8	30 3 6	8 0 8	26 10 6	b 23 10 8		51
1 18 8	—	46 0 0	18 7 6	12 6 8½	—	12 6 8½	V.P.	52
7 16 8	—	80 16 4	24 1 6	10 10 2	—	10 10 2	V.P.	53
3 0 6	—	29 0 0	11 8 0	6 5 0	—	6 5 0	V.P.	54
1 7 6	—	20 0 0	6 3 0	4 8 1	—	4 8 1	V.P.	55
8 5 8	—	59 6 6	31 18 6	9 6 4	—	9 6 4		56
2 2 10	—	85 0 5	15 8 6	9 0 6	1 0 0	10 9 6		57
1 5 6	—	91 8 4	22 19 0	9 10 6	18 0 0	a 28 15 0		58
8 6 0	4 10 0	24 0 0	6 6 6	6 18 6	37 10 0	b 34 5 6		59
3 2 6	—	20 10 6	6 1 6	3 11 6	—	5 11 5		60
3 6 6	—	28 0 6	7 5 6	5 10 6	—	5 10 6		61

a Including value of Free Residence.

* No Return.

List of Schools in operation on the 31st December, 1874.—

Number.	Roll Number of School.	Parish.	District.	School.	Religious Denomination of Manager or Correspondent: Clerical.	Lay.	Religious Denomination of Teachers: Principals.	Assistants.	Attendance for the Year. Total number of Pupils on Rolls within the Year: Males.	Females.	Total.	Average daily attendance.
62	13607	Comber,	10	Ballymaleddy,	–	Pres.	Pres.	Pres.	48	43	91	31
63	4694	Do.	–	Comber, m.	Pres.	–	Diss.	–	97	–	97	40
64	10486	Do.	–	Do. f.	Pres.	–	Pres.	–	–	60	60	37
65	14407	Do.	–	Do. i.	Pres.	–	Pres.	–	48	19	67	36
66	5473	Do.	–	Moneyreagh,	Diss.	–	Diss.	Diss.	73	80	153	62
67	5934	Do.	–	Magherascouse,	Pres.	–	Pres.	Pres.	90	80	170	61
68	6876	Do.	–	Ballystockart,	Pres.	–	E.C.	–	74	49	123	35
69	7720	Do.	–	Ballymaglaff, c	–	–	–	–	–	–	–	–
70	8109	Do.	–	Smyth's, Comber,	Pres.	–	Pres.	1Pres.	93	70	163	74
71	10410	Do.	–	Mill-street, Comber,	–	Pres.	Pres.	3Pres.	131	186	317	188
72	10354	Do.	–	Killynether,	Pres.	–	Pres.	–	33	43	76	34
73	8691	Do.	–	Castlereagh, c evg.	–	–	–	–	–	–	–	–
74	1242	Clonduff,	17	Clonduff, or Kinghill, m.	–	R.C.	R.C.	–	80	–	80	30
75	1463	Do.	–	Do. f.	–	R.C.	R.C.	–	–	87	87	33
76	7304	Do.	19	Ballygorianmore, day,	–	R.C.	R.C.	R.C.	61	41	102	43
				Do. c evg.	–	–	–	–	–	–	–	–
77	7465	Do.	–	Ballymaghery, m.	R.C.	–	R.C.	R.C.	204	4	208	58
78	7492	Do.	–	Do. f.	R.C.	–	R.C.	R.C.	–	170	170	83
79	7306	Do.	17	Cabra, m.	–	R.C.	R.C.	–	84	–	84	30
80	7503	Do.	–	Do. f.	–	R.C.	R.C.	–	–	77	77	39
81	7724	Do.	19	Tamary,	–	R.C.	R.C.	–	44	27	71	30
82	104	Dromore,	11	Tullymacnous, m.	–	Pres.	R.C.	–	58	–	58	28
83	300	Do.	–	Dromore, No. 1, m.	Pres.	–	Pres.	–	83	–	83	41
84	301	Do.	–	Do. f.	Pres.	–	Pres.	Pres.	–	88	88	40
85	3464	Do.	–	Do. No. 2, day.	R.C.	–	R.C.	–	183	–	183	71
				Do. evg.	R.C.	–	R.C.	–	61	43	104	30
86	9117	Do.	–	Do. No. 2, f.	R.C.	–	R.C.	R.C.	–	110	110	66
				Do. evg.	R.C.	–	R.C.	–	–	78	78	25
87	4087	Do.	–	Do. No. 3,	Pres.	–	Pres.	Pres.	93	70	171	51
88	10290	Do.	–	Do. Parochial,	R.C.	–	R.C.	R.C.	81	68	149	52
89	7728	Do.	–	Dromlough, No. 1,	Pres.	–	Pres.	Pres.	53	70	123	67
90	8757	Do.	17	Do.	–	Pres.	Diss.	–	69	38	107	40
91	3710	Do.	11	Ashfield,	–	Pres.	E.C.	–	14	68	82	37
92	4041	Do.	–	Bannamanagh,	Pres.	–	Pres.	–	57	40	97	46
93	4007	Do.	–	Skeogh,	–	Pres.	Pres.	R.C.	103	67	170	55
94	5943	Do.	–	Ballykeel, No. 2,	–	Pres.	R.C.	–	78	65	143	65
95	5806	Do.	–	Ballyvicknacally,	Pres.	–	Diss.	Pres.	83	56	149	50
96	6621	Do.	–	Tullyglush,	Pres.	–	Pres.	Pres.	67	53	110	34
97	7746	Do.	–	Ballymacormick,	Pres.	–	Diss.	–	63	40	103	30
98	10271	Do.	–	Killyminnan or Mound Ida,	–	E.C.	Pres.	–	82	81	163	39
99	10799	Do.	–	Magherabeg,	–	E.C.	E.C.	–	57	45	102	38
100	903	Drumgath,	17	Barnmeen,	R.C.	–	R.C.	–	54	54	108	41
101	8153	Do.	–	Lurganconlane,	R.C.	–	R.C.	R.C.	56	80	136	67
102	5810	Do.	–	Rathfriland, m. day,	R.C.	–	R.C.	R.C.	147	–	147	31
				Do. evg.	R.C.	–	R.C.	–	60	–	60	24
103	6617	Do.	–	Do. f.	R.C.	–	R.C.	–	0	118	123	57
104	8177	Do.	–	Newry-street, Rathfriland, m.	–	Pres.	Pres.	Pres.	183	–	183	43
105	8448	Do.	–	Do. f.	–	Pres.	Pres.	Pres.	–	186	186	53
106	876	Drumgooland,	–	Magheramayo, m.	R.C.	–	R.C.	–	109	–	109	41
107	7807	Do.	–	Do. f.	R.C.	–	R.C.	–	–	140	140	42
108	1868	Do.	–	Legananny,	R.C.	–	R.C.	R.C.	81	69	150	48
109	1970	Do.	–	Dunmore,	R.C.	–	R.C.	R.C.	100	78	178	57
110	7881	Do.	–	Leitrim,	–	E.C.	R.C.	Pres.	94	64	158	30
111	8742	Do.	–	Drumlee,	Pres.	–	Pres.	–	37	47	84	37
112	10227	Do.	–	Ballymacaratney,	Pres.	–	Pres.	–	64	44	108	48
113	10805	Do.	–	Drumadonnell,	E.C.	–	E.C.	–	82	65	147	33
114	219	Drumbo,	–	Carryduff,	–	Pres.	Pres.	Pres.	58	66	125	42
115	2041	Do.	–	Carr,	–	Pres.	Pres.	Pres.	87	79	166	57
116	2561	Do.	–	Drumbo,	–	E.C.	Pres.	Pres.	86	81	167	62
117	2612	Do.	–	Lessans,	Pres.	–	Pres.	–	54	31	85	41
118	4013	Do.	–	Purdysburn, m.	E.C.	–	E.C.	–	104	–	104	34

a Including value of Free Residence. b Closed. c Closed; no return.

Province of Ulster: County of Down—*continued.*

Amount paid for Books, Requisites, and Apparatus at Reduced Prices.	Aid granted by the Board during the Year 1874. In Free Stock of Books, Requisites, and Apparatus.	In Salaries, Premiums, and other Gratuities.	Results Fees, Financial Year.	Amount of Local Emoluments received in Aid of Teacher's Salary. School Fees.	Subscriptions, Endowments, &c.	Total Local Aid.	Vested or Non-Vested.	Number.
£ s. d.	£ s. d.	£ s. d.	£ s. d.	£ s. d.	£ s. d.	£ s. d.		
5 17 2	—	48 16 6	5 7 0	6 15 0	—	6 15 6	R.	62
3 4 6	—	45 13 4	18 17 0	20 0 0	—	20 0 0		63
9 0 1	—	31 16 6	21 7 0	18 1 10	—	19 1 10		64
—	—	25 2 8	0 8 0	7 8 3	—	7 6 3		65
4 9 9	—	41 0 0	18 10 8	18 0 0	8 0 0	a21 0 0		66
8 12 10	—	45 10 0	9 16 0	5 11 8	—	5 11 8		67
5 13 0	—	88 18 4	14 15 6	11 10 0	—	11 10 0		68
—	—	3 0 0	—	—	—	—		69
15 12 3	3 3 0	74 0 0	19 13 0	27 0 0	—	27 0 0		70
11 12 6	—	103 8 4	46 14 6	40 18 6	—	40 18 6		71
0 17 0	—	12 0 0	6 1 6	6 0 0	—	6 0 0		72
—	—	10 18 0	—	—	—	—		73
1 6 7	—	24 0 0	3 6 6	1 0 6	—	1 0 6	V.C.	74
—	—	24 0 0	3 17 6	2 1 6	—	2 1 6	V.C.	75
6 15 8	—	27 6 8	9 6 6	6 8 8	18 8 4	a18 15 10		76
2 1 4	—	81 16 8	0 9 6	2 15 11	—	2 15 11		77
3 15 1	—	46 10 0	9 4 2	4 8 0	—	4 3 0		78
—	—	24 0 0	3 12 6	2 12 4	—	2 12 4		79
—	—	24 0 0	3 17 11	1 3 11	—	1 3 11		80
9 5 4	—	24 0 0	1 12 6	3 11 8	0 0 0	a11 11 8		81
4 15 0	—	45 0 0	14 2 0	8 1 9	—	8 1 9		82
4 10 1	—	79 0 0	18 6 6	21 6 4	4 0 0	a25 6 4	V.C.	83
6 15 8	—	62 13 4	17 2 0	17 1 0	—	17 1 0	V.C.	84
5 4 6	—	43 16 6	11 19 0	17 2 8	—	17 2 6		85
			0 6 6	3 6 4	—	3 0 4		
4 5 4	—	51 10 0	20 5 0	10 11 8	—	18 11 8		86
			2 8 6	0 0 0	—	6 0 9		
8 8 9	—	33 10 0	27 13 0	23 10 3	—	23 10 3		87
7 6 1	—	63 10 0	23 8 6	10 18 4	7 1 0	a17 19 4		88
4 8 0	—	58 10 0	29 18 0	16 0 0	1 0 0	a17 0 6		89
6 10 4	—	84 0 8	15 8 8	20 16 8	—	20 16 8		90
3 1 0	—	41 17 6	12 8 6	18 18 4	4 0 0	a18 18 4	A.	91
4 13 4	—	80 13 4	20 14 0	13 7 4	—	13 7 4		92
4 8 10	—	44 0 0	10 18 0	10 10 0	—	10 10 0		93
5 6 5	—	24 0 0	24 11 6	10 18 8	1 0 0	a11 18 8		94
3 18 7	—	44 0 0	21 6 0	11 10 0	2 0 0	13 10 10		95
3 11 4	—	44 0 0	24 9 0	14 12 6	6 10 0	a18 8 6		96
1 6 10	—	24 0 0	6 5 6	9 5 7	—	9 5 7		97
0 15 2	—	24 0 0	4 17 6	4 11 0	—	4 16 0		98
8 8 10	5 0 0	50 0 0	6 18 0	4 0 0	5 0 0	a6 0 0		99
2 4 0	—	91 16 4	5 11 6	4 4 11	—	4 4 11		100
2 15 4	—	85 10 0	21 8 6	0 8 6	—	9 8 5		101
			7 15 6	2 15 6	—	2 15 6	V.C.	102
2 6 6	—	79 10 0	10 1 6	1 3 6	—	1 3 6		
8 5 9	—	94 5 4	17 2 0	2 10 1	—	2 10 1	V.C.	103
6 11 8	—	69 18 4	8 2 0	8 8 5	—	8 8 8		104
1 14 9	—	70 8 4	15 9 6	10 8 5	—	10 8 8		105
4 11 9	—	30 0 0	0 10 6	4 8 8	0 10 0	a4 18 8		106
5 2 1	—	63 15 0	15 0 6	8 14 11	—	8 14 11		107
—	—	58 0 0	10 7 0	6 0 0	—	6 0 0		108
7 1 6	—	71 18 8	18 18 0	8 10 8	—	8 10 8		109
3 2 11	—	78 18 6	17 1 0	11 8 0	11 0 0	22 8 0		110
1 6 6	—	83 10 0	11 0 0	6 18 0	—	6 18 0		111
6 19 5	—	24 0 0	10 17 0	4 0 1	—	4 0 1		112
1 10 0	—	24 0 0	4 7 6	8 10 0	1 6 0	a9 16 0		113
2 10 5	—	44 0 0	9 6 0	7 10 9	—	7 10 9		114
5 14 6	—	61 0 0	21 0 6	15 10 8	1 0 0	a16 10 8		115
4 6 7	—	92 0 0	20 17 6	20 11 1	—	20 11 1		116
—	—	88 0 0	10 10 6	6 9 7	—	6 9 7		117
8 14 10	—	87 8 8	6 10 6	12 0 0	17 0 0	a29 0 0		118

a Including value of Free Garden. b Including value of Free Residence and Garden.

List of Schools in operation on the 31st December, 1874—

Number.	Roll Number of School.	Parish.	District.	School.	Religious Denominations of Managers or Correspondents. Clerical.	Lay.	Religious Denominations of Teachers. Principals.	Assistants.	Attendance for the Year. Total number of Pupils on Rolls within the Year 1874. Males.	Fem.	Total.	Average daily Attendance for the Year.
119	4848	Drumbo,	17	Purdysburn, f.	R.C.	-	R.C.	-	-	60	60	31
120	4810	Do.	-	Clogher,	Pres.	-	Pres.	-	39	17	56	19
121	4581	Do.	-	Carryduff,	Pres.	-	Pres.	-	50	40	90	31
122	6722	Do.	-	Ballymaconaghy,	-	Pres.	Pres.	Pres.	58	58	116	49
123	7900	Do.	-	Legacurry,	Pres.	-	Pres.	Pres.	77	46	123	60
124	11191	Do.	-	Ballylesson,	R.C.	-	R.C.	-	19	25	44	28
125	9697	Do.	-	Milltown,	-	R.C.	Pres.	-	35	50	85	27
126	10724	Do.	-	Clontonacally,	Pres.	-	Pres.	-	41	61	102	31
127	1241	Drumballyroney,	-	Magheral,	R.C.	-	R.C.	R.C.	79	65	144	44
128	2595	Do.	-	Edentrevy,	-	Pres.	Pres.	-	95	12	107	40
129	9094	Do.	-	Hardale,	Pres.	-	Pres.	-	51	47	98	22
130	2075	Do.	-	Ballybrick,	-	Pres.	R.C.	-	30	38	68	27
131	6546	Do.	-	Clonkelt,	Pres.	-	Pres.	-	77	55	119	37
132	10845	Do.	-	Ballyroney, day.	Pres.	-	Pres.	R.C. / Pres.	119	139	258	70
				Do. evg.	-	-	-	-	-	-	-	-
133	7708	Do.	-	Moneyslane,	-	Pres.	Pres.	Pres.	61	109	170	46
134	9084	Do.	-	Annahlochigo,	-	R.C.	Pres.	-	69	54	121	45
135	9185	Do.	-	Drumdrevagh,	-	Pres.	R.C.	Pres.	72	70	142	40
136	1634	Down,	-	Downpatrick, m.	-	R.C.	Pres.	Pres.	148	-	148	64
137	1525	Do.	-	Do. f.	-	R.C.	Pres.	-	-	60	60	25
138	9724	Do.	-	Do. i.	Pres.	-	R.C.	Pres.	63	61	124	34
139	10870	Do.	-	Do. Workhouse.	P.L.	G.	Pres. / R.C.	-	60	58	118	48
140	2673	Do.	-	Rossconor,	R.C.	-	R.C.	R.C.	98	65	163	69
141	6323	Do.	-	Infirmary-lane,	Pres.	-	Pres.	Pres.	40	108	148	64
142	9429	Do.	-	Saul-street, m.	R.C.	-	R.C.	2 R.C.	180	-	180	62
143	10248	Do.	-	Do. Convent, f.	-	R.C.	Nuns	-	-	850	850	181
144	2311	Donaghadee,	10	Killachy,	Pres.	-	Pres.	-	43	60	103	41
145	2619	Do.	-	Millisle,	Pres.	-	Pres.	Pres.	78	88	166	78
146	2941	Do.	-	Herdstown,	-	R.C.	Pres.	-	41	57	98	47
147	8695	Do.	-	Granges,	Pres.	-	Pres.	Pres.	63	49	111	48
148	6656	Do.	-	Ballyferris,	Pres.	-	Pres.	-	60	60	120	41
149	9057	Do.	-	Donaghadee, m.	Pres.	-	Pres.	2 Pres.	109	-	160	91
150	9595	Do.	-	Do. f.	Pres.	-	Pres.	R.C.	-	180	186	64
151	8288	Do.	-	Do. No. 2,	Diss.	-	Diss.	Diss.	85	84	179	54
152	8763	Do.	-	Do. No. 3,	Pres.	-	Pres.	Pres.	78	70	158	56
153	5032	Do.	-	Ballyhaskin,	Pres.	-	Pres.	-	53	45	97	48
154	9497	Do.	-	Carrowdore,	-	R.C.	Pres.	R.C. / Pres.	80	78	158	61
155	9901	Drumbeg,	17	Hill Hall,	R.C.	-	R.C.	2 Pres.	102	94	196	78
156	10888	Dromore,	-	Mountalban,	R.C.	-	R.C.	R.C.	75	74	140	60
157	6661	Do.	-	Finnis, m.	R.C.	-	R.C.	-	80	-	80	36
158	4874	Do.	-	Do. f.	R.C.	-	R.C.	-	-	63	63	23
159	4049	Do.	-	Artana,	-	Pres.	Pres.	-	93	67	110	46
160	6151	Do.	-	Guiness,	R.C.	-	R.C.	R.C.	80	78	108	53
161	6176	Do.	-	Oranabe,	-	Pres.	Pres.	Pres.	128	90	218	55
162	7146	Do.	-	Moydalgan,	-	Pres.	R.C.	-	57	43	100	27
163	7845	Do.	-	Magherahamlet,	-	Pres.	Pres.	Pres.	104	72	176	56
164	9245	Do.	-	Dreenan,	Diss.	-	Pres.	-	49	28	77	34
165	1627	Donaghmore,	19	Barr,	R.C.	-	R.C.	-	58	43	101	46
166	2521	Do.	-	Four Towns,	Pres.	-	Pres.	-	38	32	70	27
167	5128	Do.	-	Derrycraw, m.	R.C.	-	R.C.	-	69	-	69	26
168	5465	Do.	-	Do. f.	R.C.	-	R.C.	-	-	68	68	21
169	8448	Do.	-	Donaghmore,	Pres.	-	Pres.	Pres.	79	60	139	49
170	8731	Do.	-	Tullymore,	Pres.	-	Diss.	-	54	30	90	27
171	2900	Dunsfort,	17	Ballyclock, m.	R.C.	-	R.C.	-	94	-	94	32
172	2803	Do.	-	Do. f.	R.C.	-	R.C.	-	-	67	67	30
173	3072	Donaghcloney,	11	Donaghcloney,	Pres.	-	Pres.	Pres.	67	73	158	58
174	6508	Do.	-	Fortescue,	Pres.	-	Pres.	Pres.	52	60	112	78
175	8626	Do.	-	Waringstown,	Pres.	-	Pres.	Pres.	88	61	188	51
176	8704	Do.	-	Corcreany,	Pres.	-	Pres.	Pres.	84	70	169	61
177	8890	Do.	-	Banoge,	-	R.C.	Diss.	Pres.	110	98	201	63
				Do. evg.	-	-	-	-	-	-	-	-

a Including value of Free Residence.

b Including value of Free Residence and Garden.

Province of Ulster: County of Down—*continued.*

Amount paid for Books, Requisites, and Apparatus, at Reduced Prices.			Aid granted by the Board during the Year 1874. In Free Stock of Books, Requisites, and Apparatus.			In Salaries, Premiums, and other Gratuities.			Results Fees, Financial Year.			Amount of Local Emoluments received in Aid of Teacher's Salary. School Fees.			Subscriptions, Endowments, &c.			Total Local Aid.			Vested or Non-Vested.	Number.
£	s.	d.	£	s.	d.	£	s.	d.	£	s.	d.	£	s.	d.	£	s.	d.	£	s.	d.		
11	0	2		—		18	0	0	8	11	6	5	0	9	10	0	0	a 15	0	9		119
1	15	10		—		24	0	0	4	8	0	0	18	8		—		0	18	8		120
3	7	9		—		48	0	0	7	14	0	8	15	0		—		8	15	0		121
4	8	5		—		60	0	0	21	17	0	16	0	0	7	0	0	b 23	0	0		122
4	9	2		—		45	10	0	15	11	8	19	6	2		—		19	6	2		123
1	7	6	4	10	0	15	0	0	7	16	0	5	6	10	15	0	0	a 20	6	10		124
	—			—		20	0	0	8	16	6	6	5	3		—		6	5	3		125
1	8	6		—		54	0	0	14	2	8	14	18	2	15	0	0	29	18	2		126
2	2	8		—		48	15	0	18	0	0	8	18	6		—		8	18	6	V.T.	127
1	10	11		—		24	0	0	7	14	6	3	0	0	6	0	0	b 9	0	0		128
1	16	8		—		20	0	0	6	0	0	1	6	0	5	0	0	a 6	6	0		129
2	1	9		—		24	0	0	8	10	6	5	16	9		—		5	16	9		130
3	8	2		—		24	0	0	6	11	0	8	17	8		—		8	17	8		131
4	18	5		—		77	10	0	10	10	0	16	0	0		—		16	0	0		132
6	1	0		—		45	16	4	18	9	0	7	2	0		—		7	2	0		133
4	8	9		—		32	0	0	12	0	0	8	14	10	18	0	0	a 19	14	10		134
8	17	7		—		61	8	8	7	10	6	2	10	0		—		2	10	0		135
8	16	8		—		58	0	0	18	9	8	53	13	4		—		53	13	4		136
8	19	7		—		20	0	0	8	14	0	6	2	8		—		6	2	8		137
1	14	10		—		22	0	0	8	8	0	6	14	9		—		6	14	9		138
7	1	10		—		8	0	0		—			—			—			—			139
8	0	8		—		68	3	4	19	0	8	10	16	7		—		10	16	7	[illegible]	140
8	2	9		—		64	17	10	18	15	6	0	0	8		—		0	0	8		141
5	13	9		—		100	10	0	32	17	6	19	0	0	4	0	0	23	0	0		142
6	18	11		—		60	14	0	27	4	0	11	8	4		—		11	8	4		143
6	8	4		—		72	8	4	30	8	8	11	11	0	6	0	8	a 14	11	8		144
11	9	5		—		61	4	2	28	18	8	81	15	4	5	0	0	86	15	4		145
	—			—		25	0	0	12	7	8	12	15	6		—		12	15	6		146
2	2	0		—		44	0	0	9	0	0	11	19	4		—		11	19	4		147
8	4	4		—		87	18	4	8	7	0	14	8	6		—		14	8	6		148
9	8	11		—		129	11	8	44	0	6	50	8	6		—		50	8	6	V.C.	149
8	19	10		—		58	6	0	37	7	6	29	6	8		—		29	6	8	V.C.	150
6	19	7		—		62	6	8	10	12	6	24	7	10	6	15	0	31	2	10		151
	—			—		50	6	6	0	4	8	14	10	0		—		14	10	0		152
8	6	6		—		58	18	4	21	7	0	18	17	11		—		18	17	11		153
8	8	1		—		78	13	4	27	0	0	18	6	2		—		18	6	2		154
4	19	9		—		74	0	0	27	8	8	21	1	6	11	3	7	b 32	5	1		155
2	13	4		—		68	18	4	19	1	8	9	18	4	1	10	0	b 11	8	4	V.T.	156
8	8	2		—		31	0	0		—		8	8	0	1	10	0	9	18	0		157
9	12	1		—		30	10	0	4	0	0	0	18	7	1	10	0	2	8	7		158
8	1	0		—		24	0	0	14	12	8	8	12	2		—		8	12	2		159
8	4	7		—		44	0	0	18	8	0	8	9	8		—		8	9	8		160
8	5	0		—		87	0	0	20	0	6	8	17	8	8	0	0	10	17	8		161
2	8	8		—		94	10	0	4	17	0	0	8	0	1	10	0	b 1	18	0		162
4	12	9		—		52	0	0	18	17	6	9	3	6		—		9	3	6		163
8	10	8		—		24	0	0	8	9	0	9	1	0		—		9	1	0		164
1	18	4		—		24	0	0	10	8	0	8	8	8		—		8	8	8	V.T.	165
0	14	10		—		20	0	0	6	10	8	2	10	0		—		2	10	0		166
2	8	9	0	1	0	24	0	0	9	18	0	9	9	8		—		9	9	8		167
8	16	0		—		28	0	0	7	17	6	5	9	2	2	0	0	b 7	9	2		168
8	6	5		—		69	10	0	10	9	0	6	8	8	4	0	0	a 10	8	8		169
1	6	5		—		52	5	0	4	18	0	4	10	0	2	10	0	7	0	0		170
2	17	11		—		24	0	0	20	9	0	11	0	6		—		11	0	6	V.T.	171
8	1	8		—		30	0	0	13	0	6	6	9	7		—		6	9	7	V.T.	172
7	19	8		—		104	8	4	32	2	0	20	8	8		—		20	8	8		173
8	14	10		—		64	8	4	27	0	0	21	0	0	3	0	0	a 24	0	0		174
8	2	0		—		82	10	0	20	12	0	12	8	8	7	0	0	a 19	8	8		175
8	8	0		—		54	16	8	20	7	6	21	14	9	15	0	0	a 36	14	9		176
4	1	11		—		69	10	0	23	18	6	16	8	1		—		16	8	1		177

a Closed. b Inoperative.

List of Schools in operation on the 31st December, 1874.—

Number.	Roll Number of School.	Parish.	District.	School.	Religious Denomination of Manager or Correspondent: Clerical.	Lay.	Number and Religious Denomination of Teachers: Principals.	Assistants.	Attendance for the Year. Total number of Pupils on Rolls within the Year 1874: Males.	Fem.	Total.	Average Daily Attendance for the Year.
178	4290	Dundonald,	16	Dundonald, m.	Pres.	–	Pres.	–	106	–	106	44
179	4291	Do.	–	Do. f.	Pres.	–	Pres.	–	–	117	117	49
180	7366	Do.	–	Ballymiscaw,	Pres.	–	Pres.	Pres.	80	76	156	61
181	214	Grey Abbey,	–	Tullycavey,	–	Diss.	Pres.	Pres.	71	52	123	36
182	6704	Do.	–	Grey Abbey,	–	E.C.	E.C.	E.C.	96	78	174	44
183	6705	Do.	–	Do. i.	–	E.C.	Pres.	–	70	71	141	34
184	6151	Do.	–	Ballyboley,	Pres.	–	Pres.	Pres.	95	65	150	61
185	9523	Garvaghy,	17	Castlevennan,	–	Pres.	Pres.	–	39	47	86	27
186	9750	Do.	–	Carnew,	–	Pres.	Pres.	Pres.	64	89	153	64
187	8187	Do.	–	Shanrod,	R.C.	–	R.C.	R.C.	78	70	148	54
188	6377	Do.	–	Tullyorier,	R.C.	–	R.C.	–	45	35	80	23
189	216	Holywood,	16	Creighton's Green,	Pres.	–	Pres.	–	30	52	82	33
190	6134	Do.	–	Belmont, m.	Pres.	–	Pres.	E.C.	180	–	180	66
191	9724	Do.	–	Do. f.	Pres.	–	Pres.	–	–	116	116	49
192	8895	Do.	–	Holywood, m.	Pres.	–	Pres.	E.C. Pres.	204	–	204	96
193	8896	Do.	–	Do. f.	Pres.	–	E.C.	Pres.	–	197	197	64
194	4887	Do.	–	Do. i.	Pres.	–	Pres.	2 Pres.	88	70	158	60
195	6250	Do.	–	Do. Par. m.	E.C.	–	E.C.	–	78	–	78	62
196	8378	Do.	–	Do. Par. f.	E.C.	–	E.C.	Pres.	50	125	180	72
197	7298	Do.	–	Knocknagoney,	Pres.	–	Pres.	–	54	39	93	41
198	8576	Do.	–	[illegible], day,	–	Pres.	Pres.	2 Pres.	210	261	471	165
				Do. evg.	–	–	Pres.	Pres.	134	74	208	36
199	10215	Do.	–	Strand-street, m.	R.C.	–	R.C.	–	82	–	82	22
200	10216	Do.	–	Do. f.	R.C.	–	R.C.	–	33	80	113	42
201	2359	Hillsborough,	11	Ballykeel, Artifinny,	Pres.	–	Pres.	–	41	73	118	40
202	2360	Do.	–	Do. Ednagonnell,	Pres.	–	Pres.	–	62	43	105	41
203	7376	Do.	–	Hillsborough,	Pres.	–	Pres.	–	58	40	98	46
204	7734	Do.	–	Reilly's Trench,	R.C.	–	R.C.	–	57	44	101	30
205	8026	Do.	–	Edenagrilla,	Pres.	–	Pres.	–	56	55	111	32
206	263	Inishargy,	16	Kircubbin,	Pres.	–	Pres.	2 Pres.	104	85	189	109
207	11184	Do.	–	Ballycranbeg, m.	R.C.	–	R.C.	–	56	–	56	33
208	11185	Do.	–	Do. f.	R.C.	–	R.C.	R.C.	17	81	98	40
209	7071	Do.	–	Glastry,	Pres.	–	R.C.	–	59	47	96	37
210	10831	Do.	–	Tubber-na-Carrig,	E.C.	–	Pres.	2 E.C.	81	82	163	62
211	9440	Inch,	17	Rann,	–	Pres.	R.C.	–	48	31	79	38
212	2031	Do.	–	Ballygally,	Pres.	–	Pres.	E.C.	79	61	140	62
213	221	Kilkeel,	19	Moneydarra,	R.C.	–	R.C.	–	90	60	150	40
214	2401	Do.	–	Dunavan, m.	R.C.	–	R.C.	–	116	–	116	54
215	2402	Do.	–	Do. f.	R.C.	–	R.C.	R.C.	–	197	197	81
				Do. evg.	–	–	R.C.	–	–	61	61	34
216	2285	Do.	–	Grange, m.	R.C.	–	R.C.	–	148	–	148	67
217	2899	Do.	–	Do. f.	R.C.	–	R.C.	–	–	126	126	46
218	6846	Do.	–	Kilkeel,	Pres.	–	Pres.	Pres.	88	66	154	39
219	6831	Do.	–	Ballymartin,	R.C.	–	R.C.	–	61	74	135	50
220	9406	Do.	–	Annalong, m.	Pres.	–	Pres.	–	63	–	63	37
				Do. evg.	–	–	Pres.	–	41	7	48	27
221	4618	Do.	–	Do. f.	Pres.	–	Pres.	–	–	106	106	36
222	11042	Do.	–	Ballymageough,	–	E.C.	Pres.	–	112	97	209	84
223	7910	Do.	–	Glassdrummond,	R.C.	–	R.C.	–	69	57	126	35
224	10780	Do.	–	Lisnacree,	Pres.	–	Pres.	–	61	66	127	21
225	222	Killinchy,	10	Ardmillan,	–	Pres.	Pres.	Pres.	49	44	93	47
226	223	Do.	–	Ballymacashen,	–	Pres.	Pres.	Pres.	68	57	125	51
227	2510	Do.	–	Tullycore,	–	R.C.	Pres.	2 Pres.	104	81	185	65
228	2234	Do.	–	Ballyalgan,	Pres.	–	Pres.	–	73	50	123	45
229	5137	Do.	–	Barnamaghery,	–	Pres.	Pres.	–	51	52	103	42
230	5652	Do.	–	Carrickmannon,	–	R.C.	R.C.	2 R.C.	128	116	250	77
231	6034	Do.	–	Raffrey,	–	R.C.	Pres.	–	43	57	100	40
232	9483	Do.	–	Drumreagh,	Pres.	–	2 Pres.	–	40	26	66	29
233	227	Kilmegan,	17	Aughlisnafin,	R.C.	–	R.C.	–	44	58	102	38
				Do.[a] evg.	–	–	–	–	–	–	–	–
234	12458	Do.	–	Annsborough[b], m. day,	–	Pres.	R.C.	Pres.	135	–	135	65
				Do. evg.	–	Pres.	R.C.	Pres.	70	–	70	30

[a] Including value of Free Residence.

[b] Including value of Free Residence and Garden.

Province of Ulster: County of Down—continued.

Amount paid for Books, Requisites, and Apparatus of School Prizes.	Aid granted by the Board during the Year 1874. In Free Stock of Books, Requisites, and Apparatus.	In Salaries, Premiums, and other Gratuities.	Results Fees, Financial Year.	Amount of Local Emoluments received in Aid of Teacher's Salary. School Fees.	Subscriptions, Endowments, &c.	Total Local Aid.	Vested or Non-Vested.	Number.
£ s. d.	£ s. d.	£ s. d.	£ s. d.	£ s. d.	£ s. d.	£ s. d.		
3 2 0	—	80 6 6	12 4 0	11 2 4	—	11 2 4		178
2 13 1	—	89 13 4	15 0 6	10 18 1	—	10 18 1		179
3 6 8	—	82 10 0	11 14 0	10 17 1	—	a 18 17 1		180
6 6 5	—	70 8 6	10 6 0	14 11 7	15 0 0	a 29 11 7		181
4 4 8	—	91 3 4	15 18 0	5 1 0	12 0 0	a 17 1 9		182
2 11 5	—	62 8 4	12 7 0	1 0 10	6 6 0	7 6 10		183
4 4 6	—	74 18 4	19 19 6	18 15 0	5 12 0	b 17 7 0		184
1 10 0	—	84 0 0	6 12 6	4 8 0	0 6 0	a 4 18 0		185
5 5 6	—	67 10 0	20 13 8	14 6 1	—	14 6 1		186
2 17 7	—	82 10 0	22 18 6	9 19 6	—	9 19 6		187
2 18 0	—	16 0 0	5 16 0	1 19 6	0 7 6	a 2 7 0		188
5 1 0	—	33 10 8	23 8 0	12 5 8	—	12 5 8		189
9 16 8	—	59 4 6	12 1 0	8 14 8	5 0 0	18 14 8		190
—	—	42 16 8	11 6 3	19 7 7	—	19 7 7		191
16 0 10	—	126 10 0	65 17 0	80 9 7	28 0 0	108 9 7		192
6 7 5	—	65 16 8	22 8 8	27 10 11	12 0 0	39 10 11		193
1 7 4	—	57 0 0	14 18 0	25 17 9	12 0 0	37 17 9		194
4 12 9	—	87 0 0	12 14 0	6 15 8	10 0 0	16 15 8		195
6 5 6	—	40 10 0	14 4 0	16 0 11	10 0 0	26 0 11		196
0 15 1	—	84 10 0	8 7 5	7 8 1	—	7 8 1		197
10 14 4	—	} 145 10 0	{ 37 6 0	61 18 1	—	61 18 1		198
—	—		4 7 0	4 12 10	—	4 12 10		
—	—	28 0 0	5 18 0	4 11 6	5 0 0	9 11 6		199
3 3 3	—	51 16 10	0 19 0	0 15 7	—	0 15 7		200
3 7 11	—	85 0 0	14 6 0	10 10 6	—	10 10 6		201
2 12 4	—	47 0 0	18 0 0	16 0 11	6 0 0	a 22 0 11		202
1 4 1	—	63 0 0	12 7 0	16 14 8	—	16 14 8		203
3 4 3	—	30 0 0	6 10 6	0 6 10	0 9 4	8 16 2		204
1 14 10	—	20 0 0	6 15 6	6 6 6	—	6 6 6		205
6 7 1	6 2 2	100 16 8	20 15 0	88 0 4	—	88 0 4	N.	206
6 17 5	4 10 0	3 0 0	—	3 14 7	—	3 14 7		207
6 15 3	5 0 0	0 8 4	—	4 13 9	—	4 13 9		208
—	—	24 0 0	6 8 0	6 15 0	—	6 15 0		209
7 3 9	—	70 16 8	24 0 0	24 14 8	31 2 0	55 16 8		210
1 7 7	—	81 0 0	19 11 8	12 12 2	3 10 0	b 16 2 2		211
8 0 6	—	45 0 0	19 0 0	9 15 0	—	9 15 0		212
1 7 8	—	20 0 0	11 10 0	6 0 0	—	6 0 0	V.T.	213
—	—	26 0 6	16 6 0	9 15 6	—	9 15 6	V.T.	214
} —	—	69 18 4	{ 27 10 0	12 6 0	—	12 6 0	V.T.	215
	—		8 6 8	3 8 0	—	3 8 0		
2 16 8	—	47 10 0	16 18 0	10 9 0	—	10 9 0	V.T.	216
1 18 0	—	35 0 0	17 6 0	9 12 9	—	9 12 9	V.T.	217
1 7 4	—	24 0 0	4 1 0	5 0 0	—	5 0 0		218
9 8 2	—	81 0 0	11 10 6	6 9 11	—	6 9 11		219
3 8 9	—	} 27 0 0	{ 8 10 6	5 15 9	—	5 15 0		220
—	—		3 10 0	1 17 0	—	1 17 0		
1 7 8	—	20 0 0	9 12 0	5 8 6	—	5 8 6		221
4 11 5	5 10 0	29 10 0	6 11 0	10 18 6	25 0 0	a 35 18 6		222
—	—	1 18 4	0 6 10	2 7 11	—	2 7 11		223
8 3 8	—	19 6 6	4 7 6	2 14 6	—	2 14 6		224
1 10 1	—	42 18 4	9 12 0	11 0 6	—	a 11 0 6		225
6 7 0	—	28 10 0	18 11 6	10 1 0	—	10 1 0		226
6 3 0	—	115 10 0	83 16 0	17 3 6	—	v 17 3 6		227
3 12 6	1 0 0	68 0 0	11 12 6	5 14 1	—	5 14 1		228
6 12 6	—	68 0 0	9 7 0	7 6 0	—	7 6 0		229
7 5 2	—	62 0 6	25 2 0	6 14 2	—	6 14 2		230
4 6 11	—	47 8 4	12 4 0	2 4 10	—	2 4 10		231
3 4 0	—	68 0 0	4 10 6	3 11 6	—	3 11 6		232
2 14 6	—	21 6 0	4 4 0	4 0 6	—	4 0 6	V.T.	233
—	—	—	—	—	—	—		
6 7 6	—	} 90 0 0	{ 23 6 6	14 18 0	50 0 0	a 64 18 0	V.T.	234
—	—		4 18 0	1 0 6	5 0 0	6 0 6		

a Including value of Free Garden.

b Chapel.

List of Schools in operation on the 31st December, 1874.—

Number.	Roll Number of School.	Parish.	District.	School.	Religious Denominations of Managers or Correspondents. Clerical.	Lay.	Religious Denominations of Teachers. Principals.	Assistants.	Total number of Pupils on Rolls within the Year 1874. Males.	Females.	Total.	Average daily attendance.
235	1488	Kilmegan,	17	Aghnamullen?, f. day,	–	Pres.	Dis.	E.C.	–	189	189	67
				Do. evg.	–	Pres.	Dis.	E.C.	–	123	123	65
236	8696	Do.	–	Clonvaraghan, day,	R.C.	–	R.C.	R.C.	122	97	220	87
				Do. evg.	R.C.	–	R.C.	–	63	10	73	32
237	[illegible]	Do.	–	Castlewellan, m.	R.C.	–	R.C.	R.C.	189	–	189	49
238	8187	Do.	–	Do. f.	R.C.	–	R.C.	R.C.	–	84	81	44
239	7496	Do.	–	Do. No. 2, day,	–	R.C.	Pres.	–	63	63	118	64
				Do. evg.	–	R.C.	Pres.	–	61	26	87	31
240	16551	Do.	–	Dundrum,	R.C.	–	R.C.	–	45	32	77	31
241	926	Kilcoo,	–	Ballymoney, m.	R.C.	–	R.C.	–	126	–	126	46
242	3155	Do.	–	Do. f.	R.C.	–	R.C.	–	–	128	128	46
243	1866	Do.	–	Ardaghy,	Pres.	–	Pres.	–	68	37	75	29
244	4237	Do.	–	Tullaree,	R.C.	–	R.C.	R.C.	96	64	160	52
245	7574	Do.	–	Slievanisnan,	–	E.C.	E.C.	–	28	16	46	21
246	7816	Do.	–	Burrenreagh,	–	R.C.	R.C.	R.C.	66	63	129	48
247	9686	Do.	–	Newcastle,	R.C.	–	R.C.	–	74	82	156	85
248	234	Killyleagh,	16	Derryboy,	–	Pres.	Pres.	Pres.	52	50	118	52
249	8226	Do.	–	Ballytrim,	–	Pres.	Pres.	–	46	28	74	34
250	2787	Do.	–	Killinchy Woods,	–	Pres.	Pres.	Pres.	74	47	121	62
251	8748	Do.	–	Shrigley, day,	–	E.C.	Pres.	Pres. E.C.	104	169	213	107
				Do. evg.	–	E.C.	Pres.	Pres. R.C. R.C.	148	123	261	109
252	9611	Do.	–	Do. i.	–	R.C.	E.C.	E.C.	60	61	121	67
253	4448	Do.	–	Killyleagh, Irish-st.	Pres.	–	Pres.	Pres.	133	90	223	104
254	6684	Do.	–	Do. m. day,	–	R.C.	Pres.	E.C. Pres.	65	109	174	78
				Do. evg.	–	R.C.	Pres.	E.C. Pres.	64	89	153	71
255	6094	Do.	–	Do.[a] i.	–	–	–	–	–	–	–	–
256	6516	Do.	–	Tullyveery,	Pres.	–	Pres.	–	25	18	43	19
257	11176	Do.	–	Tullymacnous,	Pres.	–	Pres.	–	59	60	99	39
258	825	Kilmore,	17	Crossgar,	–	Pres.	Pres.	Dis. Pres.	121	89	223	104
259	1622	Do.	–	Rademan,	Pres.	–	Dis.	–	16	33	48	22
260	6171	Do.	–	Drumaghlis,	–	Pres.	Pres.	Pres.	88	73	161	66
261	2612	Do.	–	Kilmore, No. 1,	R.C.	–	R.C.	–	61	26	81	29
262	2822	Do.	–	Drumgivan,	–	Pres.	Pres.	–	66	61	127	35
263	6120	Do.	–	Raleigh,	–	Pres.	Pres.	Pres.	52	66	118	43
264	1868	Kilbroney,	12	Rostrevor, m.	R.C.	–	R.C.	–	105	–	105	44
265	9788	Do.	–	Do. Conv., f.	R.C.	–	Nuns		32	212	244	102
266	10784	Do.	–	Killowenmy,	E.C.	–	Pres.	–	42	29	71	33
267	6462	Do.	–	Killowen,[c] m.	–	–	–	–	–	–	–	–
268	9011	Do.	–	Do. f.	R.C.	–	R.C.	–	–	97	97	68
269	6466	Do.	–	Drumreagh,	R.C.	–	R.C.	–	78	42	120	52
270	6637	Knockbreda,	16	Ballymacarrett,	–	Pres.	Pres.	2 Pres.	201	267	468	162
271	8466	Do.	–	Tullycarnet,	–	Pres.	Pres.	2 Pres.	124	77	201	69
272	6247	Do.	–	Mount Pottinger, m. day,	Pres.	–	Pres.	4 Pres.	617	–	617	143
				Do.[a] evg.	–	–	–	–	–	–	–	–
273	6649	Do.	–	Do. f.	Pres.	–	9 Pres.	2 Pres.	50	320	375	127
274	4387	Do.	–	Bridge-End, m. day,	R.C.	–	R.C.	–	188	–	188	44
				Do. evg.	R.C.	–	R.C.	–	67	–	67	27
275	6342	Do.	–	Do. f. day,	R.C.	–	R.C.	R.C.	–	244	244	62
				Do. evg.	R.C.	–	R.C.	R.C.	–	143	143	18
276	10486	Do.	–	Do. i.	R.C.	–	R.C.	R.C.	110	118	228	46
277	4032	Do.	–	Knock,[b]	–	–	–	–	–	–	–	–
278	7840	Do.	–	Logan Village,	Pres.	–	Pres.	3 Pres.	157	178	336	127
279	16641	Do.	–	Newtown Breda, m.	E.C.	–	E.C.	–	63	–	63	32
280	16616	Do.	–	Do. f.	E.C.	–	E.C.	E.C.	44	56	100	46
281	10114	Do.	–	Logan Village, No. 2,	R.C.	–	R.C.	4 R.C.	164	146	310	83
282	9266	Do.	–	New Road,	–	Pres.	Pres.	Pres.	102	74	144	61
283	10921	Do.	–	Do. i.	–	Pres.	R.C.	–	145	97	221	69

a Including value of Free Residence.

b Including value of Free Residence and Garden.

Province of Ulster: County of Down—*continued.*

Amount paid for Books, Requisites, and Apparatus of Second Year.	Aid granted by the Board during the Year 1874: In Free Stock of Books, Requisites, and Apparatus.	In Salaries, Premiums, and other Gratuities.	Results Fees, Financial Year.	Amount of Local Contributions received in Aid of Teacher's Salary: School Fees.	Subscriptions, Endowments, &c.	Total Local Aid.	Vested or Non-Vested.	Number.
£ s. d.	£ s. d.	£ s. d.	£ s. d.	£ s. d.	£ s. d.	£ s. d.		
18 1 1	—	81 0 0	20 9 5	8 19 0	10 0 0	18 18 9	V.T.	235
—	—		5 6 0	5 5 9	5 0 0	10 5 0		
3 5 5	—	62 0 0	20 0 0	10 19 9	—	10 19 9		236
—	—		6 18 0	3 1 4	—	3 1 4		
8 8 5	—	58 0 0	12 17 6	6 14 9	—	6 14 9	R.	237
1 6 7	—	46 0 0	12 3 8	4 9 10	—	4 9 10	R.	238
4 10 8	—	67 13 4	17 8 0	6 6 11	20 0 0	26 6 11		239
—	—		7 12 6	1 15 0	—	1 15 0		
—	—	27 0 0	7 13 0	6 0 0	—	6 0 0		240
2 11 4	—	37 10 0	13 16 6	4 0 0	1 0 0	5 0 0	R.	241
2 11 0	—	21 10 0	12 14 8	4 1 6	1 0 0	5 1 6		242
8 4 7	—	31 10 0	18 18 0	6 14 8	—	6 14 8		243
3 16 8	—	44 0 0	17 17 6	6 0 10	2 0 0	8 0 10		244
0 10 6	—	52 0 0	8 8 6	0 15 2	8 0 0	*8 15 2		245
1 8 0	—	48 0 0	11 16 6	2 19 11	8 10 0	*11 9 11		246
7 19 3	—	26 11 8	8 2 5	4 6 6	1 5 0	5 11 6		247
4 5 0	—	17 10 0	16 15 0	6 8 6	—	6 8 6		248
6 1 6	—	30 0 0	10 14 6	11 2 2	—	11 2 2		249
3 6 4	—	22 9 0	17 4 0	16 19 6	—	16 19 6		250
22 9 0	—	107 0 0	29 16 6	22 13 8	24 10 8	*[illegible] 6 11		251
—	—		18 18 0	26 10 0	37 10 0	64 0 0		
—	—	60 0 8	11 0 0	10 0 0	10 0 0	*20 0 0		252
7 12 11	—	55 13 4	23 2 6	30 16 7	—	30 16 7		253
6 10 3	—	86 10 0	14 0 0	20 0 0	6 0 0	*26 0 0		254
—	—		11 7 6	12 0 0	—	12 0 0		
—	—	—	—	—	—	—		255
1 17 9	—	24 0 0	2 11 4	2 15 0	—	2 15 0		256
1 10 8	4 0 0	6 18 4	—	6 3 7	—	6 3 7		257
8 8 2	—	118 0 0	36 15 8	38 3 7	10 0 0	48 3 7		258
0 10 9	—	20 0 0	4 18 6	1 11 0	—	1 11 0	V.T.	259
3 18 10	—	62 5 8	12 12 0	4 6 3	—	4 6 3		260
1 18 1	—	30 0 8	6 15 6	2 15 3	—	2 15 3		261
1 10 7	—	73 0 0	7 11 0	10 1 4	—	10 1 4		262
1 10 0	—	58 0 0	10 12 6	8 8 11	2 0 0	*10 8 11		263
1 16 1	—	24 10 0	6 14 6	0 8 4	—	0 8 4		264
10 14 0	—	70 16 4	16 8 0	3 3 10	—	3 3 10		265
—	—	80 10 0	7 1 6	1 16 2	23 0 0	*24 16 2		266
—	—	—	3 18 6	—	—	—		267
0 10 0	—	20 0 0	2 8 6	5 11 11	—	5 11 11		268
1 3 3	—	20 0 0	6 18 0	1 0 8	5 0 0	6 0 8		269
7 13 2	—	145 18 4	42 8 0	39 9 1	5 0 0	44 9 1		270
18 1 2	—	93 16 8	23 7 6	54 6 6	—	54 6 6		271
19 4 6	—	104 12 4	57 14 0	64 1 1	—	64 1 1		272
15 12 4	—	104 17 0	38 19 6	66 1 8	—	66 1 8		273
8 4 1	—	78 13 4	11 14 6	16 11 6	—	16 11 6		274
			4 9 0	8 7 0	—	8 7 0		
			12 0 0	10 5 2	—	10 5 2		275
—	—	64 18 4	0 10 0	1 8 9	—	1 8 9		276
—	—	44 0 0	7 8 0	6 19 6	—	6 19 6		277
5 5 2	—	55 13 4	22 6 0	22 12 6	—	22 12 6		278
3 6 6	—	36 0 0	5 16 0	6 4 1	61 0 0	67 4 1		279
7 0 1	0 1 0	50 6 8	10 0 6	7 12 11	25 0 0	*32 12 11		280
5 18 9	—	51 6 8	9 6 6	14 4 9	—	14 4 9		281
4 2 6	—	56 6 0	11 5 6	20 6 0	—	20 6 0		282
0 17 11	5 10 6	68 18 4	9 7 0	13 0 4	—	13 0 4		283

* Closed.

† Closed during latter part of year; no Teacher.

List of Schools in operation on the 31st December, 1874.—

Number.	Roll Number of School.	Parish.	District.	School.	Religious Denomination of Manager or Correspondent: Clerical.	Lay.	Number and Religious Denomination of Teachers: Principals.	Assistants.	Attendance for the Year: Total number of Pupils on Rolls within the Year: Males.	Fem.	Total.	Average Daily Attendance for the Year.
284	10[illegible]	Knockbreda,	10	Castlereagh,	Pres.	–	Pres.	–	65	32	97	34
285	4[illegible]	Kilmood,	–	Lisbarnet,	Pres.	–	Pres.	Pres.	66	36	102	43
286	[illegible]	Do.	–	Drumkirk, No. 1,	–	Pres.	Pres.	–	41	27	68	27
287	10[illegible]	Do.	–	Ballykeigle,	Pres.	–	Pres.	–	45	48	93	41
288	[illegible]	Killaney,	17	Carricknaveagh,	Pres.	–	Pres.	Pres.	71	52	123	44
289	1080[illegible]	Do.	–	First Boardmills,	Pres.	–	Pres.	–	39	40	79	35
290	782[illegible]	Kilclief,	–	Kilclief, m.	R.C.	–	R.C.	–	108	–	108	40
291	[illegible]	Do.	–	Do. f.	R.C.	–	R.C.	–	–	86	86	37
292	10[illegible]	Do.	–	Do. No. 2,	R.C.	–	R.C.	–	34	20	54	27
293	[illegible]	Loughinisland,	–	Loughinisland, m.	R.C.	–	R.C.	R.C.	128	–	128	61
294	781[illegible]	Do.	–	Do. f.	R.C.	–	R.C.	R.C.	–	117	117	63
295	7[illegible]	Do.	–	Drumaroad,	R.C.	–	R.C.	–	85	79	164	69
296	1[illegible]	Do.	–	Clough,	R.C.	–	Pres.	–	54	46	100	45
297	83[illegible]	Lambeg,	11	Lambeg, m.	–	E.C.	E.C.	E.C.	204	–	204	62
298	[illegible]	Do.	–	Do. f.	–	E.C.	Pres.	–	–	146	146	63
299	1580	Maghera,	17	Carnacaville,	R.C.	–	R.C.	–	55	44	99	41
300	[illegible]	Magheralin,	11	Magheralin,	R.C.	–	R.C.	–	64	44	108	46
301	[illegible]	Do.	–	Drumlin,	–	E.C.	E.C.	–	56	40	96	34
302	61[illegible]	Do.	–	Edenmore,	Pres.	–	Pres.	E.C.	65	52	117	50
303	[illegible]	Do.	–	Dollingstown,	–	E.C.	Pres.	–	92	76	168	68
304	[illegible]	Do.	–	Lisnashanker,	Pres.	–	Pres.	–	46	51	97	35
305	50[illegible]	Moira,	–	Lurganville, day,	R.C.	–	R.C.	R.C.	124	89	213	76
				Do. evg.	R.C.	–	R.C.	–	118	42	160	31
306	1100[illegible]	Do.	–	Moira, m.	–	E.C.	E.C.	–	104	–	104	50
307	110[illegible]	Do.	–	Do. f.	–	E.C.	E.C.	–	–	80	80	38
308	10615	Do.	–	[illegible]	–	E.C.	E.C.	–	66	27	93	44
309	4745	Magherally,	–	Mullafernaghan,	–	E.C.	Pres.	–	37	39	76	32
310	797[illegible]	Do.	–	Magherally,	Pres.	–	Pres.	Pres.	60	47	107	59
311	[illegible]	Do.	–	Do. No. 2, day,	R.C.	–	R.C.	–	35	57	92	41
				Do. evg.	E.C.	–	E.C.	–	40	52	92	32
312	[illegible]	Do.	–	Tonaghmore,	Pres.	–	Pres.	–	80	67	146	73
313	[illegible]	Magheradrool,	11	Ballymaglave,	Pres.	–	Pres.	Pres.	101	66	167	83
314	10[illegible]	Do.	–	Burren,	–	E.C.	Pres.	–	61	37	98	36
315	717[illegible]	Do.	–	Drumaness,	Pres.	–	Pres.	Pres.	82	85	167	76
316	10[illegible]	Do.	–	Ballynahinch, f.	Pres.	–	Pres.	–	36	36	72	38
317	[illegible]	Do.	–	Do. No. 2,	Dissen.	–	Dissen.	–	64	52	106	50
318	10[illegible]	Do.	–	Ballymacarn,	–	E.C.	Pres.	–	49	34	83	35
319	10[illegible]	Do.	–	Magheratimpany,	–	E.C.	Pres.	Pres.	78	64	142	48
320	922[illegible]	Do.	–	Ballynahinch (Church-st.), m.	R.C.	–	R.C.	–	110	–	110	47
321	[illegible]	Do.	–	Do. f.	R.C.	–	R.C.	R.C.	–	94	94	46
322	1030[illegible]	Do.	–	Glassdrummond,	–	E.C.	Pres.	–	63	48	111	40
323	101[illegible]	Do.	–	Ballinahinch,	Pres.	–	Pres.	Pres.	69	53	122	46
324	107[illegible]	Do.	–	Drumaness Mills,	–	Pres.	Pres.	2 Pres.	100	102	202	75
				Do. evg.	–	Pres.	Pres.	Pres.	57	55	112	45
325	27[illegible]	Newry,	19	Crobane,	Pres.	–	Pres.	–	43	27	70	22
326	2797	Do.	–	Loughorne,	–	Pres.	Pres.	–	51	31	82	30
327	275[illegible]	Do.	–	Sheepstown,	Pres.	–	E.C.	–	54	69	123	40
328	344[illegible]	Do.	–	Crownhill,	R.C.	–	R.C.	R.C.	83	77	160	60
329	4915	Do.	–	Shinn,	Pres.	–	R.C.	R.C.	76	60	133	45
330	064[illegible]	Do.	–	Windsor Hill, m.	R.C.	–	R.C.	–	166	–	166	74
331	604[illegible]	Do.	–	Do. f.	R.C.	–	R.C.	R.C.	81	100	181	62
332	72[illegible]	Do.	–	Boatstreet, Newry,	–	R.C.	R.C.	–	98	26	124	57
333	[illegible]	Do.	–	William-street, Newry,	Dissen.	–	Pres.	Pres.	66	60	126	39
334	07[illegible]	Do.	–	Grinan,	R.C.	–	R.C.	–	69	74	143	28
335	24[illegible]	Do.	–	High-street, Convent, f.	–	R.C.	Nuns	–	176	760	936	386
336	1008[illegible]	Do.	–	Rockvale,	Pres.	–	Pres.	–	50	45	95	35
337	24[illegible]	Newtownards,	10	Ballycullen,	Pres.	–	Pres.	Pres.	46	62	98	49
338	607[illegible]	Do.	–	Loughriscouse, No. 2,	Pres.	–	Pres.	Pres.	79	67	146	59
339	32[illegible]	Do.	–	Ballyblack,	Pres.	–	Pres.	Pres.	63	47	110	55
340	367[illegible]	Do.	–	Loughries, No. 1,	Pres.	–	Pres.	Pres.	73	68	141	49
341	347[illegible]	Do.	–	Mill-st., Newtownards,	Pres.	–	Pres.	E.C.	137	116	253	103
342	[illegible]	Do.	–	Newtownards, day,	Pres.	–	[a] Pres.	[b] Pres.	158	142	300	116
				Do. evg.	Pres.	–	Pres.	[a] Pres.	101	64	165	59

[a] Including value of Free Residence.

[b] Including value of Free Residence and Garden.

Province of Ulster: County of Down—*continued.*

Amount paid for Books, Requisites, and Apparatus at Reduced Prices.	Aid granted by the Board during the Year 1874. In Free Stock of Books, Requisites, and Apparatus.	In Salaries, Premiums, and other Gratuities.	Results Fees, Educational Year.	Amount of Local Contributions received in Aid of Teacher's Salary. School Fees.	Subscriptions, Endowments, &c.	Total Local Aid.	Vested or Non-Vested.	Number.
£ s. d.	£ s. d.	£ s. d.	£ s. d.	£ s. d.	£ s. d.	£ s. d.		
6 7 4	—	29 13 4	6 15 0	7 18 9	—	7 18 9		284
10 7 4	—	61 18 8	22 16 0	19 17 0	—	19 17 0		285
—	—	30 0 0	5 7 8	4 0 9	1 0 6	a 5 0 9		286
4 15 11	—	46 6 5	12 8 6	10 16 4	—	10 16 4		287
4 10 7	—	70 10 0	19 7 0	19 10 1	—	19 10 1		288
6 0 8	—	27 10 6	7 10 1	10 0 0	1 0 0	11 0 0		289
2 18 10	—	24 0 0	12 4 0	7 7 0	—	7 7 0		290
2 5 6	—	25 8 4	16 15 0	4 4 4	—	4 4 4		291
1 19 6	—	30 0 0	7 15 6	4 18 10	6 0 0	b 9 10 10		292
2 10 6	—	47 10 0	20 0 6	10 8 8	—	10 8 8	P.	293
9 16 8	—	36 0 0	21 0 0	9 1 0	—	9 1 0	B.	294
8 10 9	—	53 8 4	15 3 6	10 0 0	—	10 0 0		295
—	—	73 8 10	16 18 0	10 0 0	3 10 0	13 10 0		296
5 1 8	—	36 18 4	16 15 6	11 17 0½	19 6 0	a 31 3 0		297
4 5 0	—	39 10 6	15 0 6	9 15 8	6 0 0	16 15 3		298
1 12 11	—	45 19 2	18 18 0	8 18 10	1 0 0	8 18 10	V.E.	299
2 18 11	—	18 16 0	4 8 0	2 14 6	—	2 14 0		300
—	—	24 0 0	4 2 10	1 9 1	5 0 0	6 9 1		301
6 1 0	—	44 0 0	17 18 0	12 0 11	—	12 0 11		302
3 6 9	—	24 5 10	14 8 8	4 18 1	5 0 0	9 18 1		303
3 19 1	—	23 18 4	9 18 6	8 8 1	—	8 8 1	V.G.	304
6 18 6	—	71 8 8	24 1 0	18 7 1	—	18 7 1		305
—	—	—	0 15 0	3 13 3	—	3 13 3		
5 18 8	1 0 0	39 10 0	19 3 8	13 7 0	16 0 0	b 29 7 0		306
7 10 6	—	26 10 0	10 5 6	6 5 1	16 0 0	b 21 5 1		307
4 14 4	—	24 0 0	14 6 0	14 3 11	13 0 0	a 27 3 11		308
1 8 10	—	7 3 6	7 8 6	9 5 0	3 0 0	12 5 0	V.C.	309
4 8 8	—	45 10 0	21 5 6	15 0 0	1 6 0	a 16 6 0		310
6 19 11	—	37 0 0	18 2 0	8 7 8	—	8 7 8		311
—	—	—	10 15 0	4 16 6	—	4 16 6		
2 14 1	—	38 0 0	21 19 8	12 11 9	2 10 0	a 15 1 9		312
8 16 11	4 1 9	75 15 0	20 6 0	40 0 1	—	40 0 1		313
2 3 9	—	34 0 0	11 7 8	6 8 9	—	6 8 9		314
4 3 7	—	111 6 8	37 7 0	26 10 8	5 0 0	a 31 18 8		315
2 9 10	—	26 0 0	9 15 6	14 3 0	—	14 3 0		316
1 6 8	—	30 0 0	6 10 0	6 6 0	8 0 0	14 6 0		317
1 5 4	—	24 0 0	5 5 0	9 9 8	—	9 9 8		318
8 2 11	5 0 0	37 10 0	13 7 0	10 0 0	—	10 0 0		319
4 7 8	—	30 0 0	18 11 0	10 15 8	—	10 15 8		320
3 18 7	—	46 10 0	16 12 6	11 0 8	—	11 0 0		321
1 11 9	—	24 0 0	7 15 0	10 1 6	—	10 1 0		322
0 2 0	—	49 10 0	15 13 6	19 19 6	—	19 19 6		323
} 8 11 9	—	76 0 0	{ 25 15 6	30 10 7	21 0 0	a 57 10 7		324
			4 0 6	7 5 7	—	7 5 7		
4 6 1	—	30 0 0	—	5 1 6	4 0 0	a 9 1 6		325
4 4 8	—	24 0 0	8 8 6	9 9 8	7 0 0	16 9 8		326
0 10 6	—	23 0 0	9 8 0	5 13 4	—	5 13 4		327
1 6 6	—	38 16 8	5 18 0	7 1 6	—	7 1 6		328
2 19 7	—	51 10 0	9 18 6	7 0 0	9 0 0	a 16 0 0		329
6 18 0	—	100 8 4	19 6 8	17 13 6	9 0 0	b 26 13 6		330
10 18 8	—	63 10 0	20 4 0	18 8 10	—	18 8 10		331
1 4 8	—	25 0 0	4 3 0	7 1 1	—	7 1 1		332
6 0 0	—	31 0 0	9 0 6	15 3 8	8 0 0	23 3 8		333
—	—	30 0 0	4 9 6	5 6 9	6 0 0	10 6 0		334
37 15 1	—	160 1 6	74 1 0	—	—	—		335
1 9 4	—	30 0 0	5 0 8	4 10 8	—	4 10 8		336
3 4 0	—	34 0 0	10 17 0	7 17 8	—	7 17 8	4.	337
5 7 11	—	45 0 0	15 6 6	13 8 1	—	13 8 1		338
3 18 1	—	44 0 0	18 10 6	10 19 8	—	10 19 8		339
3 10 9	—	51 15 4	23 4 6	15 4 1	—	15 4 1		340
4 15 8	—	73 10 0	18 11 0	19 15 2	—	19 15 2		341
} 9 8 8	—	102 5 0	{ 29 7 8	20 4 8	4 10 0	a 24 1 8		342
			9 18 0	5 16 1	—	5 16 1		

a Including value of Free Copybooks.

List of Schools in operation on the 31st December, 1874.—

Number.	Roll Number of School.	Parish.	District.	School.	Religious Denomination of Managers or Correspondents: Clerical.	Lay.	Number and Religious Denomination of Teachers: Principals.	Assistants.	Attendance for the Year. Total number of Pupils on Rolls within the Year 1874: Males.	Fem.	Total.	Average [illegible]
343	6841	Newtownards,	16	Newtownards,	Pres.	–	Pres.	–	106	110	216	75
344	7774	Do.	–	Do. Dist. Mod. m.	Com.	N.E.	Pres.	Pres. R.C.	262	–	262	150
345	7775	Do.	–	Do. f.	Com.	N.E.	R.C.	R.C. Pres.	–	204	204	103
346	7776	Do.	–	Do. i.	Com.	N.E.	Pres.	R.C.	70	67	137	74
347	6850	Do.	–	Do. Workhouse,	P.L.	Gds.	2 Pres.	–	61	55	116	65
348	5185	Do.	–	Greengraves,	Pres.	–	Pres.	–	33	23	56	19
349	6912	Do.	–	Drumhirk, No. 2,	–	R.C.	Pres.	Pres.	79	57	136	73
350	7321	Do.	–	Movilla street.[a]	–	–	–	–	–	–	–	–
351	16296	Do.	–	Castlegarden st.,	–	E.C.	Pres.	Pres. Dis.	172	148	320	133
352	8194	Do.	–	Ballyregan,	Pres.	–	Pres.	–	50	45	95	27
353	8412	Do.	–	Zion-place,	Dis.	–	Pres.	Pres.	85	103	188	64
354	[illegible]	Do.	–	Anne-street, m.	R.C.	–	R.C.	–	68	–	68	24
355	[illegible]	Do.	–	Do. f.	R.C.	–	R.C.	–	–	120	120	45
356	9720	Newtownbreda,	–	Newtownbreda,	R.C.	–	Pres.	Pres. Dis.	116	108	224	109
357	2407	Rathmullan,	17	Killough, m.	R.C.	–	R.C.	–	96	–	96	46
358	2404	Do.	–	Do. f.	R.C.	–	R.C.	R.C.	–	118	118	64
359	2046	Do.	–	Rathmullan,[c]	–	–	–	–	–	–	–	–
360	[illegible]	Seapatrick,	11	Mulligans, day,	–	Pres.	R.C.	–	55	40	95	33
361	6860	Do.	–	Banbridge, m. day,	R.C.	–	R.C.	–	184	–	184	77
				Do. evg.	R.C.	–	R.C.	–	123	–	123	33
362	6053	Do.	–	Do. f. day,	R.C.	–	R.C.	2 R.C.	43	214	257	90
				Do.[d] evg.	–	–	–	–	–	–	–	–
363	4894	Do.	–	Do. No. 2, m.	Pres.	–	Pres.	–	118	–	118	44
364	4065	Do.	–	Do. f.	Pres.	–	R.C.	R.C.	63	120	183	75
365	3062	Do.	–	Do. Workhouse,	P.L.	Gds.	Pres. Dis.	–	34	40	74	41
366	6140	Do.	–	Scarva-street,	Pres.	–	Pres.	2 Pres.	121	79	200	107
367	9328	Do.	–	Ballydown, No. 2, day,	–	Pres.	Pres.	Pres.	70	61	127	61
				Do. evg.	–	–	Pres.	–	48	37	85	16
368	9541	Do.	–	Do. No. 1,	–	Pres.	R.C.	–	46	40	86	23
369	9544	Do.	–	Friar's place, day,	R.C.	–	Pres.	Dis.	163	122	274	101
				Do. evg.	–	–	Dis.	–	–	138	138	33
370	11094	Do.	–	Church street, f.	R.C.	–	R.C.	–	68	120	208	79
371	11167	Do.	–	Do. m.	R.C.	–	R.C.	–	106	–	106	61
372	11184	Do.	–	Do. i.	R.C.	–	R.C.	–	65	65	130	60
373	1092	Saint Andrew's,	10	Ballyhalbert,	–	Pres.	Pres.	Dis. Pres.	84	56	140	52
374	6518	Do.	–	Ballyeasborough,	Pres.	–	Pres.	Pres. E.C.	144	121	265	128
375	2276	Saul,	17	Ballintogher,	R.C.	–	R.C.	R.C.	125	116	241	75
376	2738	Saintfield,	–	Leggygowan,	Pres.	–	Pres.	–	20	53	73	24
377	6781	Do.	–	Lessans,	Pres.	–	Pres.	Pres.	49	43	92	14
378	5065	Do.	–	Tullywest,	Pres.	–	Pres.	Pres.	78	86	164	60
379	5912	Do.	–	Saintfield, m.	–	Pres.	Pres.	–	59	–	59	40
380	9811	Do.	–	Do. f.	–	Pres.	Pres.	–	–	73	76	34
381	10903	Do.	–	Do. No. 2,	R.C.	–	R.C.	–	40	39	79	35
382	6480	Do.	–	Ballyknockan,	–	E.C.	Pres.	Pres.	74	73	140	65
383	7347	Do.	–	Boardmills,	Pres.	–	Pres.	Pres.	52	45	97	43
384	6863	Do.	–	Tonaghmore,	Pres.	–	Pres.	–	47	26	73	38
385	10686	Do.	–	Ballymacarrennury,	–	E.C.	Pres.	–	35	29	64	22
386	10720	Do.	–	Killynure,	Pres.	–	Pres.	–	40	44	84	21
387	9167	Shankill,	11	Kilmore, No. 2,	–	E.C.	Pres.	–	30	37	67	24
388	[illegible]	Tullylish,	–	Bann, m. day,	R.C.	–	R.C.	R.C.	146	–	146	61
				Do. evg.	–	–	R.C.	–	96	–	96	24
389	6844	Do.	–	Do. f. day,	R.C.	–	R.C.	R.C.	19	117	136	58
				Do. evg.	–	–	R.C.	–	–	53	48	16
390	12564	Do.	–	Ballibagarrick, day,	–	E.C.	Pres.	Pres.	89	73	162	79
				Do.[f] evg.	–	–	Pres.	–	–	–	–	–
391	16238	Do.	–	Clare,	–	E.C.	E.C.	E.C.	74	86	160	68

a Closed. b Including value of Free Residence and Garden. c Closed; no returns.

Province of Ulster: County of Down—*continued.*

Amount paid for Books, Requisites, and Apparatus at Reduced Prices	Aid granted by the Board during the Year 1874: In Free Stock of Books, Requisites, and Apparatus	In Salaries, Premiums, and other Gratuities	Results Fees, Payment Year	Amount of Local Emoluments rendered in Aid of Teacher's Salary: School Fees	Subscriptions, Endowments, &c.	Total Local Aid	Vested or Non-Vested	Number
£ s. d.	£ s. d.	£ s. d.	£ s. d.	£ s. d.	£ s. d.	£ s. d.		
5 0 9	—	60 10 0	21 11 0	17 4 1	—	17 4 1		343
							V.C.	344
63 14 2	20 18 4	224 18 0	107 12 0	163 17 8	—	163 17 8	V.C.	345
							V.C.	346
3 15 1	—	—	—	—	—	—		347
0 12 0	—	15 3 4	8 11 6	2 10 6	—	2 10 6		348
4 17 0	—	72 8 6	21 10 6	24 13 9	—	24 18 0		349
—	—	—	—	—	—	—		350
6 0 8	—	60 17 8	22 5 0	20 18 6	8 0 0	28 18 9		351
9 8 4	—	24 0 0	7 18 8	5 13 6	6 5 0	ᵇ11 18 0		352
3 18 11	—	50 13 4	9 16 8	9 13 10	—	9 13 10		353
1 7 8	—	40 16 8	8 4 0	6 3 10	10 0 0	16 3 10	V.T.	354
2 10 7	—	64 0 8	15 15 6	7 18 6	10 6 0	17 18 6	V.T.	355
8 19 8	—	124 13 4	45 15 0	90 6 11	—	90 6 11		356
5 4 5	—	23 0 0	18 6 0	0 11 1	—	6 11 1		357
4 17 2	—	68 0 0	22 12 0	7 2 7	—	7 2 7		358
3 1 3	—	12 0 0	—	—	—	—		359
—	—	47 10 0	8 1 0	3 11 4	9 0 0	12 11 4		360
8 0 0	—	86 16 8	24 16 0	19 8 10	—	19 8 10		361
			5 4 6	4 8 0	—	4 8 0		
7 7 0	—	81 1 8	31 11 0	23 11 11	—	23 11 11		362
—	—	—	—	—	—	—		
8 0 2	—	28 6 8	18 10 0	15 13 2	6 17 6	22 10 8		363
1 7 8	—	49 6 8	21 6 0	16 10 6	6 0 0	22 16 6		364
5 5 6	—	—	—	—	—	—		365
4 13 11	—	143 10 0	15 4 6	50 5 0	—	50 5 0		366
8 14 9	—	47 0 0	19 2 0	10 8 0	—	16 8 0		367
—	—	—	8 19 0	1 14 0	—	1 14 0		
1 18 0	—	21 0 0	5 4 6	2 10 0	—	2 10 0	V.C.	368
6 1 2	—	69 16 8	16 10 0	12 14 10	2 2 0	15 6 10		369
—	—	—	6 8 6	8 0 0	—	8 0 0		
—	—	27 10 0	15 18 6	10 2 2	10 0 0	20 2 2		370
6 11 6	7 12 2	10 7 6	20 1 0	15 15 11	15 0 0	30 15 11		371
2 10 2	5 0 8	11 13 4	5 14 0	5 10 6	—	5 10 9		372
8 8 3	—	71 12 4	22 18 6	8 18 6	1 10 0	*11 8 9		373
6 11 5	—	116 10 0	44 6 6	41 12 6	8 10 0	*49 2 6		374
2 10 7	—	60 10 0	10 14 0	12 13 11	—	12 13 11	V.T.	375
1 14 11	—	28 0 8	4 19 6	6 14 8	—	6 14 8		376
6 0 1	—	54 10 0	7 10 0	13 11 6	—	13 11 6		377
8 18 10	—	74 10 0	19 9 0	10 4 9	—	10 4 9		378
4 15 7	—	46 13 9	10 16 6	17 8 8	3 0 0	*20 8 8		379
2 19 2	—	25 0 0	19 15 6	10 10 5	6 0 0	*16 10 5		380
1 7 11	—	23 0 0	11 7 0	9 12 11	3 0 0	11 12 11		381
8 19 11	—	65 15 0	23 14 6	19 16 8	14 0 0	*33 16 8		382
6 10 8	—	160 0 0	15 12 6	14 8 6	—	14 8 8		383
—	—	54 10 0	5 10 8	5 8 0	—	5 8 0		384
1 8 7	—	25 6 8	6 11 8	6 17 6	—	6 17 6		385
0 8 4	—	30 0 0	0 1 6	8 10 0	—	8 10 0		386
2 15 1	—	18 0 0	5 16 0	8 11 1	5 0 0	*8 11 1		387
			22 18 0	16 11 8	—	15 11 8		388
4 16 11	—	86 19 8	6 18 0	4 8 8	—	4 8 8		
			21 19 0	12 16 11	—	12 16 11		389
—	—	28 0 0	3 17 6	1 6 11	—	1 6 11		
5 1 4	—	68 0 0	23 14 8	12 0 0	4 0 0	16 0 0		390
—	—	—	4 1 0	—	—	—		
2 19 7	—	45 0 0	21 1 0	11 10 10	10 0 0	*21 10 10		391

ᵇ Only three months in operation. * Including value of Free Residence. † Closed December quarter.

List of Schools in operation on the 31st December, 1874.—

Number.	Roll Number of School.	Parish.	District.	School.	Religious Denomination of Manager or Correspondent: Clerical.	Lay.	Number and Religious Denominations of Teachers: Principals.	Assistants.	Attendance for the Year: Total number of Pupils on Rolls within the Year 1874: Males.	Fem.	Total.	Average Daily Attendance for the Year.
392	2580	Tullylish,	11	Ballydougan,	Pres.	–	Pres.	–	52	35	87	35
393	6238	Do.	–	Gilford, No. 1, day,	Pres.	–	Pres.	R.C. Pres.	177	80	258	88
				Do. evg.	–	–	Pres.	R.C.	187	34	221	81
394	4811	Do.	–	Gilford Mill, m. day,	–	R.C.	Pres.	R.C.	186	–	186	68
				Do. evg.	–	–	Pres.	R.C.	117	–	117	44
395	4812	Do.	–	Do. f. day,	–	R.C.	Pres.	2 Pres.	–	244	244	60
				Do. evg.	–	–	Pres.	Pres.	–	177	177	84
396	7111	Do.	–	Do. i.	–	R.C.	Pres.	2 R.C.	103	148	251	88
397	6748	Do.	–	Milltown, m. day,	–	Pres.	Pres.	–	111	23	134	64
				Do.[b] evg.	–	–	–	–	–	–	–	–
398	6958	Do.	–	Do. f.	–	Pres.	Pres.	–	82	99	181	60
399	8437	Do.	–	Mullabrack,	Pres.	–	Pres.	–	68	47	115	38
400	8118	Do.	–	Moyallen,	–	Dis.	Dis.	R.C.	127	103	230	108
401	9161	Do.	–	Ballydugan,	–	Pres.	Pres.	–	61	55	110	39
402	9728	Do.	–	Knocknagore,	–	R.C.	R.C.	R.C.	58	48	107	41
403	3030	Tullynakill,	10	Ballydrain,	–	Pres.	Pres.	–	63	51	110	50
404	7208	Tyrella,	17	Ballykinler, m.	R.C.	–	R.C.	–	108	–	108	58
405	7433	Do.	–	Do. f.	R.C.	–	R.C.	–	–	64	[illegible]	33
406	10818	Do.	–	Tyrella Parochial,	R.C.	–	R.C.	–	58	20	78	30
407	7044	Witter,	10	Ballygalget,	R.C.	–	R.C.	1 R.C.	170	100	270	91
408	10405	Whitechurch,	–	Ballywalter Park,	R.C.	–	Pres.	2 Pres.	88	48	136	60
409	10824	Warrenpoint,	19	Warrenpoint, i.	–	R.C.	R.C.	–	27	45	72	28
410	11019	Do.	–	Do.	–	R.C.	R.C.	R.C.	73	73	146	58
		Total for County of Down, 410,							30394	27349	57,743	21,6[illegible]

COUNTY OF

Number.	Roll Number of School.	Parish.	District.	School.	Religious Denomination of Manager or Correspondent: Clerical.	Lay.	Number and Religious Denominations of Teachers: Principals.	Assistants.	Attendance for the Year: Total number of Pupils on Rolls within the Year 1874: Males.	Fem.	Total.	Average Daily Attendance for the Year.
1	1847	Aghalurcher,	18	Mullaghfad,	R.C.	–	R.C.	R.C.	83	71	154	63
2	5044	Do.	–	Cavanaleck,	Pres.	–	R.C.	–	50	31	81	38
3	4123	Do.	–	Ballindarragh,	–	R.C.	Pres.	–	63	49	112	58
4	4717	Do.	–	Lisnaskea,	R.C.	–	R.C.	R.C.	95	61	156	54
5	8064	Do.	–	Maguire's Bridge,	R.C.	–	R.C.	R.C.	104	70	174	56
6	10206	Do.	–	Do. No. 2,	Pres.	–	Pres.	–	101	84	185	51
7	8780	Do.	–	Mullinabertin,	–	R.C.	R.C.	–	61	48	109	23
8	4287	Do.	–	Tyrahan,	R.C.	–	R.C.	–	80	50	108	40
9	10477	Do.	–	Tully,	–	R.C.	R.C.	–	51	63	114	58
10	11184	Do.	–	Aghavoory,	R.C.	–	Dis.	–	35	33	68	32
11	11148	Do.	–	Carrickapolin,	R.C.	–	Pres.	–	45	30	[illegible]	33
12	1745	Aghavea,	–	Ardmoney,	R.C.	–	R.C.	–	84	72	156	43
13	2261	Do.	–	Tattykeeran,	Pres.	–	R.C.	–	47	25	72	34
14	4538	Do.	–	Tamlaght,	Pres.	–	R.C.	–	60	47	108	43
15	4708	Do.	–	Edenagilhorn,	Pres.	–	Pres.	–	45	28	76	27
16	6604	Do.	–	Coonian,	R.C.	–	R.C.	–	57	37	94	34
17	7307	Do.	–	Brookeboro',	R.C.	–	R.C.	–	62	47	109	43
18	11109	Do.	–	Do. i.	R.C.	–	R.C.	–	38	40	78	49
19	8784	Do.	–	Crieve, Ord. Agr.	Pres.	–	R.C.	–	29	28	56	27
20	2457	Boho,	–	Carrickbeg,	R.C.	–	R.C.	–	34	35	69	30
21	8170	Do.	–	Treal,	R.C.	–	R.C.	–	66	44	110	43
22	10779	Do.	–	Aghaheirish,	R.C.	–	R.C.	–	50	36	86	38
23	6678	Belleek,	8	Townaghtown,	R.C.	–	R.C.	–	63	40	103	41
24	6407	Do.	–	Belleek,	R.C.	–	R.C.	–	40	48	88	33
25	7360	Do.	–	Mullek,	R.C.	–	R.C.	–	98	33	127	45
26	244	Clones,	16	Drumcrough,	R.C.	–	R.C.	R.C.	91	42	133	56
27	1250	Do.	–	Cornagague,	R.C.	–	R.C.	R.C.	89	64	153	58
28	8788	Do.	–	Lisreen,	Pres.	–	Pres.	–	35	20	56	23
29	8870	Do.	–	Mullanvaum,	R.C.	–	R.C.	R.C.	96	69	165	61
30	8878	Do.	–	Creaghawarren,	R.C.	–	R.C.	R.C.	103	73	176	58
31	10181	Do.	–	Gardoala,	R.C.	–	R.C.	2 R.C.	145	123	268	110

a Including value of Free Residence.

b Inoperative.

Province of ULSTER: County of DOWN—*continued.*

Amount paid for Books, Requisites, and Apparatus at Reduced Prices.	Aid granted by the Board during the Year 1874: In Free Stock of Books, Requisites, and Apparatus.	In Salaries, Premiums, and other Gratuities.	Results Fees, Financial Year.	Amount of Local Emoluments received in Aid of Teacher's Salary: School Fees.	Subscriptions, Endowments, &c.	Total Local Aid.	Vested or Non-Vested.	Number.
£ s. d.	£ s. d.	£ s. d.	£ s. d.	£ s. d.	£ s. d.	£ s. d.		
5 18 1	—	49 0 0	11 18 0	5 10 7	5 0 0	*8 10 7		392
6 8 0	—	102 6 4	23 12 6	17 15 4	—	17 15 4		393
—	—	—	5 6 6	8 6 1	—	8 6 1		
6 6 1	—	112 16 4	29 10 0	10 0 0	47 0 0	*57 0 0		394
			9 18 0	7 0 0	15 0 0	22 0 0		
11 6 6	—	99 0 0	33 14 0	19 15 7	21 0 0	40 15 7		395
			4 6 0	8 19 8	—	8 19 8		
9 3 6	—	70 0 0	20 1 8	—	21 0 0	21 0 0		396
3 8 8	—	44 10 0	14 11 6	15 1 10	20 0 0	*35 1 10		397
—	—	—	—	—	—	—		
2 17 8	—	41 15 0	18 8 0	9 18 9	10 0 0	19 18 9		398
8 15 6	—	21 0 0	7 1 8	4 1 4	—	4 1 4		399
6 18 1	—	64 16 0	67 18 6	20 8 8	61 0 0	*31 0 8		400
1 17 9	—	30 14 2	4 18 6	4 0 9	3 0 0	*0 6 9		401
2 17 11	—	33 0 0	6 1 11	4 8 2	7 0 0	*11 8 2		402
6 2 1	—	45 5 0	16 17 0	18 9 4	—	18 9 4		403
1 10 6	—	64 0 0	16 13 6	1 16 8	15 0 0	16 16 8		404
1 19 9	—	66 12 4	20 8 0	1 6 6	14 0 0	15 6 6		405
1 18 6	—	24 0 0	6 18 0	3 18 0	16 0 0	19 18 0		406
8 6 6	—	83 16 6	21 14 0	22 16 11	—	22 16 11		407
6 4 11	—	114 5 8	43 12 0	37 7 9	33 0 0	*70 7 9		408
0 16 4	—	91 16 4	3 0 0	1 4 4	5 0 0	*0 4 4		409
5 2 4	—	63 0 0	18 2 4	5 3 2	20 0 0	*25 3 2		410
1,851 14 7	106 17 5	20714 2 11	5,941 12 5	6,023 16 6	1579 1 10	6,819 16 4		

FERMANAGH—141 Schools.

1 16 5	—	84 0 0	16 4 6	5 13 8	—	5 13 8	V.C.	1
4 19 6	—	24 0 0	12 10 0	9 10 9	—	9 16 5		2
9 13 4	—	29 7 2	9 6 8	6 17 8	14 10 0	*20 7 8	V.A.	3
4 8 0	4 10 0	77 8 6	24 1 9	14 17 6	—	14 17 6		4
2 5 4	—	48 8 8	12 12 9	1 1 6	—	1 1 6		5
11 4 5	—	41 12 0	19 6 0	17 17 6	1 0 0	18 17 6		6
1 15 1	—	32 0 0	16 8 0	3 11 0	—	3 11 0	V.A.	7
8 14 6	—	30 6 8	14 11 0	6 0 0	8 0 0	10 0 0		8
2 8 7	—	24 0 0	7 1 0	4 18 6	6 0 0	10 18 6		9
—	—	8 15 0	—	6 0 6	4 9 0	6 9 0		10
—	—	18 0 0	0 19 6	6 1 6	10 0 0	16 1 6		11
1 4 1	—	21 0 0	11 18 0	2 16 6	—	2 16 6		12
9 1 0	—	24 0 0	7 13 0	1 14 0	—	1 14 6		13
8 0 11	—	27 10 0	16 17 0	5 0 0	—	5 0 0		14
1 16 8	—	24 0 0	8 13 0	1 8 6	—	1 8 6		15
0 14 5	—	24 0 0	12 3 6	2 17 0	—	2 17 0		16
6 7 9	—	27 10 8	7 8 0	1 10 2	—	1 10 2		17
1 16 6	4 10 0	8 0 8	—	8 0 0	20 0 0	*28 0 0		18
1 7 10	—	20 0 0	6 9 6	0 13 0	—	0 13 0		19
1 9 7	—	24 0 0	16 9 0	3 0 6	—	3 0 6	D.	20
1 11 5	—	27 0 0	18 12 6	4 0 0	—	4 0 0		21
1 12 0	—	24 0 0	5 12 0	3 15 6	—	3 15 6		22
1 11 6	—	24 0 0	16 1 0	0 16 6	0 5 0	†1 0 6		23
1 7 4	—	24 0 0	8 17 4	2 1 5	—	2 1 5		24
9 6 11	—	22 0 0	10 6 6	1 7 0	0 6 0	†1 13 0		25
3 16 9	—	61 16 8	19 16 0	9 17 6	—	9 17 6	A.	26
4 14 9	—	60 0 0	17 8 6	8 0 0	—	8 0 0	A.	27
0 10 2	—	30 0 0	9 11 0	2 1 3	—	2 1 3		28
8 9 4	—	57 0 0	21 5 4	8 10 0	—	8 10 0		29
5 18 1	—	78 1 8	23 16 0	6 14 0	1 0 0	*7 14 0		30
9 8 7	—	88 16 8	48 16 0	6 13 0	—	6 13 0	V.V.	31

* Including value of Free Residence and Garden.

† Including value of Free Garden.

List of Schools in operation on the 31st December, 1874.—

Number.	Roll Number of School.	Parish.	District.	School.	Religious Denomination of Manager or Correspondent: Clerical.	Lay.	Number and Religious Denomination of Teachers: Principals.	Assistants.	Attendance for the Year: Total number of Pupils on Rolls within the Year 1874: Males.	Females.	Total.	Average Daily Attendance for the Year.
32	8713	Clones,	16	Roslea,	–	R.C.	Pres.	–	88	13	[illegible]	[illegible]
33	11177	Do.	–	Do. f.	R.C.	–	R.C.	–	30	47	87	[illegible]
34	10187	Do.	–	Corranny,	R.C.	–	R.C.	R.C.	84	65	149	[illegible]
35	5182	Cleenish,	16	Carrygleas,	–	Diss.	Diss.	–	33	28	61	[illegible]
36	3703	Do.	–	Do., West,	R.C.	–	R.C.	–	61	36	97	[illegible]
37	8831	Do.	–	Carrick, 1st Cl. Agr.	–	R.C.	Pres.	–	43	49	92	[illegible]
38	4178	Do.	–	Lisbellaw, m.	–	R.C.	R.C.	–	112	–	112	49
39	4293	Do.	–	Do. f.	–	R.C.	R.C.	–	–	114	114	45
40	5433	Do.	–	Rossdoney,	R.C.	–	R.C.	–	112	64	176	[illegible]
41	5781	Do.	–	Belcoo,	R.C.	–	R.C.	–	80	37	117	[illegible]
42	7832	Do.	–	Lattone,	–	R.C.	R.C.	–	40	45	94	[illegible]
43	7037	Do.	–	Cornagrve,	–	R.C.	R.C.	–	83	65	148	[illegible]
44	8159	Do.	–	Rehoshock,	–	R.C.	R.C.	–	50	18	68	[illegible]
45	7687	Do.	–	Killyvanan,	–	R.C.	R.C.	–	39	35	73	[illegible]
46	0543	Do.	–	Mullymesker,	R.C.	–	R.C.	–	70	40	110	[illegible]
47	311	Derryvullan,	–	Slee,	–	Diss.	R.C.	–	49	37	79	[illegible]
48	2370	Do.	–	Coles,	R.C.	–	R.C.	–	46	53	99	[illegible]
49	[illegible]	Do.	–	Lisnarrivan,	–	Diss.	R.C.	–	49	22	71	[illegible]
50	4568	Do.	–	Drumgun,	R.C.	–	R.C.	–	54	40	94	[illegible]
51	9763	Do.	–	Coolaghey,	–	R.C.	R.C.	–	56	45	110	[illegible]
52	8712	Do.	–	Irvinestown,	R.C.	–	R.C.	R.C.	116	94	210	[illegible]
53	3677	Drumkeeran,	9	Aghakinne,	Pres.	–	R.C.	–	48	45	93	[illegible]
54	3915	Do.	–	Aghagruffin,	–	R.C.	R.C.	–	43	44	87	[illegible]
55	4531	Do.	–	Ednasleigh,	R.C.	–	R.C.	–	66	47	113	[illegible]
56	11121	Do.	–	Letterkeen,	R.C.	–	R.C.	–	52	38	90	[illegible]
57	8425	Do.	–	Drumskinny,	R.C.	–	R.C.	–	103	70	173	[illegible]
58	10926	Do.	–	Do. (1)	–	R.C.	Pres.	–	61	37	98	31
59	7619	Do.	–	Glenally,	Pres.	–	R.C.	–	52	70	[illegible]	[illegible]
60	8028	Do.	–	Drumnagleshan,	R.C.	–	R.C.	–	36	27	63	[illegible]
61	10103	Do.	–	Ranagh,	R.C.	–	R.C.	–	111	74	185	[illegible]
62	6909	Do.	–	Moneyvrieve,	R.C.	–	R.C.	R.C.	125	101	226	[illegible]
63	1742	Devenish,	16	Lisdoad,	R.C.	–	R.C.	–	47	56	103	[illegible]
64	10489	Do.	–	Moyglass, m.	–	R.C.	R.C.	–	97	–	97	44
65	10449	Do.	–	Do. f.	–	R.C.	R.C.	–	–	68	68	[illegible]
66	[illegible]	Do.	–	Monea,	R.C.	–	R.C.	–	80	76	156	53
67	8424	Do.	–	Gardeoa,	R.C.	–	R.C.	–	87	68	155	41
68	10453	Do.	–	Drumsawna,	–	R.C.	R.C.	–	48	30	78	[illegible]
69	5710	Do.	–	Drumbeggan,	R.C.	–	R.C.	–	55	49	104	[illegible]
70	5768	Do.	–	Rossinure more,	R.C.	–	R.C.	–	24	67	91	[illegible]
71	8591	Do.	–	Cashelnadrea, m.	R.C.	–	R.C.	–	106	–	106	[illegible]
72	5970	Do.	–	Do. f.	R.C.	–	R.C.	–	–	92	92	[illegible]
73	7469	Derrybrusk,	–	Derrybarney,	–	R.C.	R.C.	–	58	39	96	[illegible]
74	274	Enniskillen,	–	Killian,	–	R.C.	R.C.	–	93	56	149	[illegible]
75	9013	Do.	–	Tempo, m.	Pres.	–	R.C.	Pres.	86	96	182	51
76	4916	Do.	–	Do. f.	R.C.	–	R.C.	–	43	48	91	37
77	10304	Do.	–	Garvary,	R.C.	–	R.C.	–	47	60	107	47
78	8711	Do.	–	Enniskillen D. M. m.	Com.	N.B.	R.C.	Pres.	173	–	173	[illegible]
79	8079	Do.	–	Do. Do. f.	Com.	N.E.	R.C.	R.C.	–	129	129	[illegible]
80	9973	Do.	–	Do. Do. i.	Com.	N.E.	Pres.	R.C.	40	67	107	[illegible]
81	3934	Do.	–	Do. m.	R.C.	–	R.C.	–	117	–	117	49
82	2932	Do.	–	Do. f.	R.C.	–	R.C.	–	–	104	104	43
83	7497	Do.	–	Do. Convent, Nos. 1, 2, 3	–	R.C.	R.C.	4 R.C.	–	403	403	169
84	10735	Do.	–	Do. Workhouse,	P.T.	Gds.	R.C.	–	39	42	81	41
85	10167	Do.	–	Cleeby,	R.C.	–	R.C.	–	64	67	131	41
86	3143	Do.	–	Innismore,	–	Pres	R.C.	–	50	66	102	[illegible]
87	8777	Do.	–	Gleno,	R.C.	–	R.C.	–	76	38	114	[illegible]
88	4642	Do.	–	Carrowkeel,	–	R.C.	R.C.	–	66	47	113	40
89	8574	Do.	–	Mary-street,	Diss.	–	Diss.	–	29	78	107	[illegible]
90	9654	Do.	–	Carrickabraghan,	R.C.	–	R.C.	–	19	30	[illegible]	10
91	2711	Galloon,	19	Mullenagh,	R.C.	–	R.C.	–	35	41	76	[illegible]
92	2758	Do.	12	Newtownbutler, m.	R.C.	–	R.C.	–	84	–	84	[illegible]
93	4141	Do.	–	Do. f.	R.C.	–	R.C.	–	–	73	73	[illegible]
94	2759	Do.	–	Managhmore,	R.C.	–	R.C.	–	68	49	117	[illegible]

[a] Including value of Free Residence.

[b] Including value of Free Residence and Garden.

Province of Ulster: County of Fermanagh—*continued.*

Amount paid for Books, Stationery, and Apparatus at Reduced Prices.	Aid granted by the Board during the Year 1874. — In Free Stock of Books, Requisites, and Apparatus.	Aid granted by the Board during the Year 1874. — In Salaries, Premiums, and other Gratuities.	Aid granted by the Board during the Year 1874. — Results Fees, Financial Year.	Amount of Local Emoluments received in Aid of Teacher's Salary. — School Fees.	Amount of Local Emoluments received in Aid of Teacher's Salary. — Subscriptions, Endowments, &c.	Amount of Local Emoluments received in Aid of Teacher's Salary. — Total Local Aid.	Vested or Non-Vested.	Number.
£ s. d.	£ s. d.	£ s. d.	£ s. d.	£ s. d.	£ s. d.	£ s. d.		
2 1 4	—	22 11 1	5 5 6	0 17 0	14 0 0	14 17 0		32
1 10 1	4 0 0	6 0 0	—	0 14 0	—	0 14 0		33
0 13 0	—	43 10 0	10 7 0	8 7 0	—	8 7 0	V.T.	34
—	—	20 0 0	6 15 6	4 17 6	5 0 0	9 17 6		35
1 18 8	—	35 10 0	14 17 0	5 6 6	—	5 6 6		36
1 19 9	—	34 0 0	6 7 0	2 18 3	—	2 18 3	V.T.	37
6 9 5	4 0 0	24 0 0	8 8 6	5 11 9	21 10 0	a 40 1 9		38
—	—	23 1 8	9 10 6	8 9 9	10 0 0	18 9 9		39
2 13 9	—	47 4 8	20 14 5	9 6 8	—	9 6 8		40
4 2 4	—	61 8 6	0 11 6	6 9 7	1 10 0	a 0 19 7	V.C.	41
1 7 0	—	30 0 0	5 17 0	1 3 8	—	1 3 8		42
3 14 10	—	43 8 6	23 16 8	8 18 9	—	8 18 9		43
—	—	—	—	1 14 8	—	1 14 8		44
2 5 9	—	21 0 0	8 10 0	6 0 0	—	6 0 0		45
1 5 0	—	32 10 0	10 18 0	6 7 6	—	6 7 6	V.T.	46
2 7 8	—	24 0 0	7 10 6	5 7 4	—	5 7 4		47
1 7 6	—	20 0 0	8 18 0	4 0 0	—	4 0 0	A.	48
0 10 10	—	24 0 0	5 5 6	1 4 0	—	1 4 0	A.	49
2 11 11	—	24 0 0	9 11 0	1 0 9	—	1 0 9		50
4 7 2	—	24 0 0	12 5 8	4 1 0	—	4 1 0		51
6 3 0	—	21 0 0	10 5 0	7 3 7	—	7 3 7		52
1 10 9	—	24 0 0	8 8 6	2 18 8	6 0 0	a 8 18 8		53
1 5 2	—	20 0 0	9 15 8	1 7 6	—	1 7 6	A.	54
1 19 9	—	20 0 0	8 7 0	2 10 0	—	2 10 0		55
2 6 4	4 10 0	12 0 0	—	1 10 8	20 0 0	a 21 10 8		56
3 16 10	9 0 0	40 15 6	10 10 0	0 16 0	—	0 16 0		57
8 11 9	—	24 0 0	8 10 0	—	18 0 0	18 0 0		58
1 15 0	—	24 0 0	7 16 8	1 12 0	8 0 0	a 9 12 0		59
—	—	24 0 0	4 14 0	—	—	—		60
3 1 6	—	19 0 0	7 13 0	—	—	—		61
5 4 10	4 10 0	63 8 8	23 6 8	8 5 0	—	8 5 0		62
0 9 10	—	44 0 0	7 6 8	8 17 8	—	8 17 8	A.	63
4 9 7	—	61 0 0	20 14 0	11 0 0	23 0 0	a 34 0 0		64
8 11 10	—	20 0 0	14 18 6	9 0 0	15 0 0	24 0 0		65
2 15 3	—	20 10 0	13 17 0	1 0 0	—	1 0 0	A.	66
1 11 9	—	24 0 0	9 10 6	5 0 6	—	5 0 6		67
3 14 11	—	16 6 8	7 8 0	—	23 0 0	a 23 0 0		68
8 12 0	—	25 5 4	16 2 0	8 9 0	—	8 9 0		69
1 5 0	—	24 0 0	5 0 0	0 17 0	—	0 17 0	V.C.	70
1 10 0	—	23 10 0	18 17 0	4 7 8	—	4 7 8		71
1 12 3	—	20 0 0	10 18 0	1 2 0	—	1 2 0		72
1 6 5	—	20 13 4	9 17 5	2 15 8	5 0 0	7 15 8		73
1 11 8	—	24 0 0	9 8 0	1 10 0	0 10 0	a 1 0 0		74
2 8 0	—	23 0 0	11 14 6	4 16 8	—	4 16 8		75
8 17 2	—	20 0 0	8 0 0	—	—	—		76
4 10 1	—	28 0 0	17 8 0	4 18 0	—	4 18 0		77
30 1 8	11 13 4	}					V.C.	78
—	—	560 8 8	90 18 8	123 6 8	—	123 6 8	V.C.	79
—	—	}					V.C.	80
1 16 0	—	20 0 0	9 16 8	6 14 7	—	6 14 7	V.T.	81
0 14 5	—	26 6 8	9 0 0	6 2 0	—	6 2 0	V.T.	82
15 3 7	—	74 18 8	63 13 6	10 0 6	—	10 0 6		83
7 19 0	—	3 10 0	—	—	—	—		84
1 16 7	—	40 5 0	12 9 6	—	10 0 0	10 0 0		85
5 5 0	—	21 10 0	18 0 0	3 14 0	—	3 14 0	A.	86
1 5 10	—	27 10 0	18 5 6	4 1 0	—	4 1 0		87
4 8 2	—	47 10 0	21 5 6	4 0 0	—	4 0 0	V.T.	88
1 6 0	—	20 0 0	5 9 6	1 11 10	14 0 0	15 11 10		89
1 9 5	—	20 13 8	8 18 0	1 1 6	—	1 1 6		90
1 3 6	3 3 6	20 0 0	6 15 6	9 4 6	—	9 4 6		91
1 11 9	—	24 0 0	—	—	—	—		92
2 16 0	—	20 0 0	5 13 6	2 11 9	—	2 11 9		93
1 10 8	—	24 0 0	6 8 0	6 12 7	—	6 12 7	N.	94

a Including value of Free Garden.

List of Schools in operation on the 31st December, 1874.—

Number.	Roll Number of School.	Parish.	District.	School.		Religious Denomination of Manager or Correspondent: Clerical.	Lay.	Denomination of Teachers: Principals.	Assistants.	Total number of Pupils on Rolls within the Year 1874: Males.	Females.	Total.	Average Daily Attendance for the Year.
95	6251	Galloon,	19	Drumbarry,		R.C.	–	R.C.	–	30	18	48	18
96	11042	Do.	18	Drumskene,		R.C.	–	R.C.	–	91	59	150	59
97	17430	Do.	15	Kilmurk,		R.C.	–	R.C.	–	46	21	67	21
98	5458	Do.	13	Feragh,		–	R.C.	Pres.	R.C.	81	70	151	63
99	7257	Do.	–	Derrygonnelly,		R.C.	–	R.C.	–	50	43	93	33
100	7531	Do.	–	Cubb,		R.C.	–	R.C.	–	53	31	84	27
101	4348	Inishmacsaint,	–	Derrygonnelly,		R.C.	–	R.C.	–	70	57	127	44
102	5098	Do.	–	Carrickreagh,		R.C.	–	R.C.	–	49	64	113	51
103	5753	Do.	–	Rosscor,		–	R.C.	R.C.	–	77	57	134	50
104	6134	Do.	–	Glenn, East,		–	R.C.	R.C.	–	67	80	147	54
105	6354	Do.	–	Finnagh,		–	R.C.	R.C.	–	82	75	157	50
106	10910	Do.	–	Knockarevan,		–	R.C.	R.C.	–	47	30	77	33
107	10484	Do.	–	Churchhill,		–	R.C.	R.C.	–	33	38	71	33
108	10829	Do.	–	Drumbad,		–	R.C.	R.C.	–	42	33	75	31
109	2862	Killesher,	–	Gortmacnamee,		R.C.	–	R.C.	R.C.	98	69	167	66
110	8609	Do.	–	Arney,		R.C.	–	R.C.	–	115	50	165	43
111	9612	Do.	–	Drumbrochas,		R.C.	–	R.C.	–	80	63	143	60
112	0467	Do.	–	Lisblake,[b]		–	R.C.	–	–	–	–	–	–
113	10702	Do.	21	Derrylin,	m.	R.C.	–	R.C.	–	169	–	168	57
114	11031	Do.	13	Ballyreagh,		R.C.	–	R.C.	–	30	30	60	21
115	4445	Kinawley,	21	Derrylin,	f.	R.C.	–	R.C.	R.C.	–	153	153	61
116	241	Do.	–	Swanpark,		R.C.	–	R.C.	–	55	36	91	33
117	3864	Do.	–	Derrysteaghnamy,		R.C.	–	R.C.	–	50	50	100	38
118	[illegible]	Do.	–	Kilnacrannel,	m.	R.C.	–	R.C.	–	114	–	114	43
119	[illegible]	Do.	–	Do.	f.	R.C.	–	R.C.	–	–	75	75	38
120	4521	Do.	–	Corraleck,		R.C.	–	R.C.	–	33	31	64	23
121	4988	Do.	–	Swanlinbar, Drumderg,		R.C.	–	R.C.	R.C.	88	71	159	59
122	4247	Do.	–	Aughakillymaude,		R.C.	–	R.C.	R.C.	96	74	170	70
123	3462	Do.	18	Corrove,		R.C.	–	R.C.	–	57	27	84	29
124	6401	Do.	23	Drumshancyamore,		R.C.	–	R.C.	–	119	50	169	60
125	7414	Do.	18	Kinawley,	m.	R.C.	–	R.C.	–	63	–	63	19
126	8274	Do.	–	Do.	f.	R.C.	–	R.C.	–	–	55	55	20
127	0287	Do.	21	Aughnacloy,		Diss.	–	Diss.	–	34	55	80	29
128	6136	Killesher,	18	Teemore,		R.C.	–	R.C.	–	44	48	92	34
129	8945	Magheracloone,	–	Newtownbutler,		R.C.	–	R.C.	R.C.	101	71	172	77
130	8572	Do.	–	Clay,		–	R.C.	Diss.	–	51	40	91	39
131	3048	Do.	–	Aghagaffert,		–	R.C.	R.C.	–	78	49	127	57
132	6571	Do.	–	Crommeskea,[a]		R.C.	–	R.C.	–	–	–	–	–
133	9782	Do.	–	Leak, Ord. Agr.		–	R.C.	R.C.	–	67	64	131	39
134	3904	Magheraveely,	–	Cos,		R.C.	–	R.C.	–	78	58	136	34
135	8245	Do.	–	Grove,		–	R.C.	R.C.	–	78	60	138	45
136	8510	Do.	–	Sydare,		–	Diss.	R.C.	–	80	43	123	39
137	9732	Do.	–	Drumcullion,		–	Diss.	Diss.	–	08	69	104	35
138	9092	Rossory,	–	Ashwood,		R.C.	–	R.C.	–	40	45	85	20
139	8578	Templecarn,	6	Townavanny,		Pres.	–	R.C.	–	57	23	80	25
140	8091	Do. Drumkeeran	–	Boa Island,[b]		–	–	–	–	–	–	–	–
141	9788	Do.	–	Letter,		Pres.	–	Pres.	–	57	63	120	50
		Total for County Fermanagh, 1st,								9,446	7,136	16,580	6,594

COUNTY OF

Number.	Roll Number of School.	Parish.	District.	School.		Clerical.	Lay.	Principals.	Assistants.	Males.	Females.	Total.	Average Daily Attendance.
1	2972	Arditea,	16	Ballymaldery,		R.C.	–	R.C.	–	72	38	110	30
2	2982	Do.	–	Ballindrum,		Pres.	–	Pres.	–	68	43	111	37
3	11800	Do.	–	Annahavish,	day,	–	R.C.	R.C.	R.C.	125	73	198	75
				Do.	evg.	–	R.C.	R.C.	R.C.	70	38	108	65
4	2605	Do.	–	Ballymaguigh,		Pres.	–	Pres.	–	59	46	105	35
5	4316	Do.	–	Loup,		R.C.	–	R.C.	–	74	70	144	58
6	11185	Do.	–	Moneymore,	L.	–	R.C.	R.C.	–	48	49	95	36
7	5903	Do.	–	Warwick Lodge,		R.C.	–	R.C.	–	77	60	137	34

[a] Closed.

[b] Including value of Free Residence.

Province of Ulster: County of Fermanagh—*continued.*

Amount paid for Books, Requisites, and Apparatus at Reduced Prices.	Aid granted by the Board during the Year 1874. By Free Stock of Books, Requisites, and Apparatus.	In Salaries, Premiums, and other Gratuities.	Results Fees, Financial Year.	Amount of Local Emoluments received in Aid of Teacher's Salary. School Fees.	Subscriptions, Endowments, &c.	Total Local Aid.	Vested or Non-Vested.	Number.
£ s. d.	£ s. d.	£ s. d.	£ s. d.	£ s. d.	£ s. d.	£ s. d.		
0 14 0	—	12 0 0	0 10 5	1 16 6	—	1 16 6	V.T.	95
8 15 8	—	27 10 0	14 11 0	8 8 0	—	8 8 0	P.	96
1 17 6	—	44 0 0	7 11 0	3 14 9	—	3 14 9	P.	97
10 0 1	—	56 10 0	24 7 6	11 6 0	—	11 6 0		98
2 7 11	—	30 0 0	7 0 0	2 4 6	—	2 4 6		99
3 4 8	—	24 0 0	9 17 0	1 11 0	—	1 11 0		100
4 19 11	—	25 0 0	8 6 0	5 14 1	—	5 14 1		101
1 6 0	—	52 13 8	10 8 6	0 6 8	—	0 6 8		102
4 1 8	—	36 10 0	20 7 6	2 0 0	2 0 0	4 0 0		103
2 15 10	—	31 16 4	17 6 6	2 0 0	2 0 0	4 0 0		104
1 6 1	—	28 10 0	30 4 6	0 10 6	2 0 0	2 10 6		105
1 10 0	—	19 0 0	8 3 6	—	29 15 0	29 15 0		106
6 8 0	—	24 0 0	14 0 0	—	30 0 0	30 0 0		107
2 11 1	—	28 0 0	18 16 6	8 10 0	20 0 0	28 10 0		108
8 8 1	—	25 0 0	11 8 0	4 12 0	—	4 12 0		109
4 1 1	—	55 5 0	8 0 0	7 16 6	—	7 16 6		110
2 10 8	—	28 10 0	18 15 0	2 0 0	—	2 0 0		111
1 4 11	—	30 0 0	—	—	—	—	V.C.	112
2 15 4	—	40 10 0	28 19 8	8 8 6	—	8 8 6		113
8 6 0	4 10 0	16 6 8	—	—	17 10 0	a 17 10 0		114
6 16 10	—	53 8 8	26 11 0	6 16 10	—	6 16 10		115
1 8 1	—	44 0 0	2 19 0	0 7 0	—	0 7 0		116
0 12 2	—	20 0 0	6 1 6	4 0 0	—	4 0 0		117
4 6 2	—	24 0 0	14 3 6	8 14 0	—	8 14 0	V.T.	118
1 10 6	—	28 0 0	16 11 0	1 10 6	—	1 10 6	V.T.	119
1 5 8	—	24 0 0	3 16 0	2 0 0	—	2 0 0		120
1 10 11	—	28 0 0	16 12 0	2 2 6	—	2 2 6		121
8 13 6	—	48 0 0	26 10 6	7 10 2	—	7 10 2		122
0 19 0	—	24 0 0	6 2 6	6 0 6	—	6 0 6		123
6 8 5	—	28 0 0	10 16 6	8 0 0	—	8 0 0		124
0 11 0	—	24 0 0	2 17 6	1 16 6	—	1 16 6		125
1 16 6	—	43 8 4	17 9 6	4 6 8	—	4 6 8		126
2 17 8	—	17 0 0	7 8 0	5 1 8	10 0 0	15 1 8		127
8 2 4	—	44 0 0	10 19 0	1 2 6	—	1 2 6		128
4 8 7	—	79 10 0	31 13 6	8 18 6	—	8 18 6		129
6 14 9	—	35 0 0	14 15 0	8 18 6	—	8 18 6		130
8 6 8	—	42 16 8	24 0 8	4 5 0	—	4 5 0	V.T.	131
4 8 11	—	48 0 0	—	—	—	—		132
2 16 10	1 2 0	30 0 0	7 8 6	—	4 0 0	4 0 0	V.T.	133
1 12 0	—	24 0 0	6 1 0	4 11 6	—	4 11 6		134
4 8 1	—	35 0 0	16 10 0	6 10 0	—	6 10 0	A.	135
4 7 8	—	27 10 0	12 11 0	6 15 0	—	6 15 0	A.	136
6 2 11	—	60 0 0	9 15 0	6 12 6	—	6 12 6		137
0 13 4	—	20 0 0	8 8 0	1 19 4	—	1 19 4		138
1 9 7	—	24 0 0	10 4 6	6 4 6	—	6 4 6		139
—	—	—	—	—	—	—		140
6 12 11	—	24 0 0	10 19 0	—	—	—		141
435 6 2	80 9 10	3,018 10 9	1,769 18 11	628 19 8	296 4 0	1,023 3 6		

LONDONDERRY—262 Schools.

1 4 5	—	24 0 0	6 0 0	1 8 8	0 15 0	2 3 8		1
8 15 1	—	28 10 0	11 0 6	0 8 0	—	0 8 0		2
4 8 7	—	77 16 8	65 0 6	6 15 0	—	6 15 0		3
			26 11 0	3 0 0	—	* 3 0 0		
3 8 0	—	56 10 8	7 8 0	2 8 4	8 0 0	a 10 8 4		4
8 17 5	—	24 10 0	12 15 0	2 8 9	5 0 0	7 0 9		5
2 10 0	5 0 0	—	5 4 0	—	21 15 0	a 21 15 0		6
1 5 8	—	24 0 0	6 8 5	2 14 9	—	2 14 9	V.T.	7

* Returns not available. a Including value of Free Residence and Garden.

List of Schools in operation on the 31st December, 1874,—

Number.	Roll Number of School.	Parish.	District.	School.		Religious Denomination of Manager or Correspondent: Clerical.	Lay.	Number and Religious Denomination of Teachers: Principals.	Assistants.	Attendances for the Year: Total number of Pupils on Rolls within the Year 1874: Males.	Fem.	Total.	[illegible]
8	10916	Ardtrea,	16	Listinmorrow,		–	R.C.	R.C.	–	67	71	138	84
9	11118	Do.	–	Moneymore,	m.	–	R.C.	R.C.	–	107	–	107	65
10	11114	Do.	–	Do.	f.	–	R.C.	R.C.	–	–	80	80	56
11	9602	Aghadowey,	3	Rirgmad,		–	Pres.	Pres.	Pres.	93	58	151	57
12	2607	Do.	–	Aghadowey,	m.	–	Pres.	Pres.	–	100	–	100	51
13	6677	Do.	–	Do.	f.	–	Pres.	Pres.	–	–	105	105	53
14	3775	Do.	–	Cullycapple,	f.	–	Pres.	Pres.	Pres.	–	128	128	65
15	[illegible]	Do.	–	Moneycarrie,		–	Pres.	Pres.	–	64	45	109	44
16	8404	Do.	–	Miltown,	m.	–	R.C.	Pres.	–	65	–	65	41
17	7677	Do.	–	Do.	f.	–	R.C.	Pres.	–	–	60	66	[illegible]
18	6290	Do.	–	Ballinrees,		–	Pres.	Pres.	–	25	20	45	[illegible]
19	8278	Do.	–	Collins,		–	R.C.	Pres.	–	63	36	99	[illegible]
20	8976	Do.	–	Killeague,		–	R.C.	Pres.	–	56	55	111	[illegible]
21	8326	Do.	–	Drughed,		–	R.C.	Pres.	Pres.	108	49	157	76
22	9577	Do.	–	Mullaghinch,		–	R.C.	Pres.	Pres.	83	83	166	79
23	8917	Do.	–	Gorran,		Dis.	–	Pres.	Pres.	100	60	160	76
24	10496	Do.	–	Coolyrammer,		Dis.	–	Dis.	–	28	28	61	[illegible]
25	6578	Ardtrea,	16	Ballygurney,		Pres.	–	Pres.	–	41	31	75	[illegible]
26	9737	Do.	–	Drumullan,		R.C.	–	R.C.	R.C.	79	81	160	43
27	8008	Ardwen,	–	Ballyronan,		–	R.C.	Pres.	–	132	91	223	[illegible]
				Do.	evg.	–	–	Pres.	–	40	40	80	[illegible]
28	9352	Aghanloo,	3	Shanvey,		R.C.	–	R.C.	–	22	22	44	[illegible]
29	10580	Do.	–	Aghanloo,		–	Pres.	Pres.	–	44	41	85	37
30	296	Ballynascreen,	7	Straw,		R.C.	–	R.C.	R.C.	150	101	210	80
31	4719	Do.	–	Draperstown,	m.	R.C.	–	R.C.	–	83	–	83	54
32	296	Do.	–	Do.	f.	R.C.	–	R.C.	R.C.	–	143	143	48
33	1774	Do.	–	Altayeskey,	m.	–	R.C.	R.C.	–	142	–	142	64
34	8478	Do.	–	Do.	f.	–	R.C.	R.C.	–	–	118	128	50
35	4145	Do.	–	Bracka, Dysert,		R.C.	–	R.C.	–	80	69	151	45
36	4630	Do.	–	Moneyneena,		–	R.C.	R.C.	R.C.	96	91	187	41
37	8464	Do.	–	Drummard,		R.C.	–	R.C.	R.C.	71	55	126	63
38	10172	Do.	–	Strawmore,		R.C.	–	R.C.	–	81	40	117	[illegible]
39	11106	Do.	–	Cavanamoney,		–	R.C.	R.C.	–	30	29	65	37
40	11216	Do.	–	Bleachhill,[a]		–	R.C.	–	–	–	–	–	–
41	1608	Ballyscullion,	–	Ballyneese,	m.	R.C.	–	R.C.	–	108	–	109	80
42	4384	Do.	–	Do.	f.	R.C.	–	R.C.	–	–	117	117	31
43	[illegible]	Do.	–	Bellaghy,		R.C.	–	R.C.	–	103	69	172	61
44	[illegible]	Do.	–	Moyola,	day.	–	R.C.	R.C.	–	57	78	135	52
				Do.[a]	evg.	–	–	–	–	–	–	–	–
45	8246	Do.	–	Glenvale,		Pres.	–	Dis.	–	77	61	138	40
46	10478	Balteagh,	–	Balteagh,		R.C.	–	R.C.	–	65	97	162	47
47	10808	Do.	–	Lisane,		Pres.	–	Pres.	–	76	69	145	36
48	10941	Do.	–	Drumsurn,		R.C.	–	R.C.	–	64	70	134	39
49	1941	Bovevagh,	–	Burnfoot,		R.C.	–	R.C.	–	71	53	124	34
50	2006	Do.	–	Muldonagh,		R.C.	–	R.C.	–	84	65	149	40
51	4145	Do.	–	Ballyharrigan,		–	R.C.	R.C.	–	76	65	141	39
52	[illegible]	Do.	–	Derrinflaw,		R.C.	–	R.C.	–	62	57	[illegible]	[illegible]
53	[illegible]	Do.	7	Glenacutway,		–	R.C.	Pres.	–	–	–	–	–
54	[illegible]	Do.	6	Finvoy,	m.	–	R.C.	R.C.	–	97	–	97	33
55	[illegible]	Do.	–	Do.	f.	–	R.C.	R.C.	–	–	78	[illegible]	[illegible]
56	11108	Do.	7	Drumcovey,		–	R.C.	R.C.	–	57	33	90	37
57	[illegible]	Do.	–	Templemoyle,		R.C.	–	R.C.	–	74	50	124	51
58	[illegible]	Ballyrashane,	3	Ballyrashane,		Pres.	–	Pres.	–	74	58	132	61
59	7183	Ballyaghran,	–	Portstewart,		Pres.	–	Pres.	Pres.	60	33	93	39
60	[illegible]	Ballywillin,	–	Cloyfin,		–	Pres.	Pres.	–	40	31	70	[illegible]
61	8600	Do.	–	Carnalridge,		Pres.	–	Pres.	Pres.	47	80	127	43
62	8248	Ballinderry,	13	Ballylifford,		–	R.C.	R.C.	R.C.	126	96	220	[illegible]
				Do.	evg.	–	–	R.C.	–	87	21	108	61
63	10376	Do.	–	Church-hill,		Dis.	–	Dis.	–	49	21	70	[illegible]
				Do.	evg.	–	–	Dis.	–	48	–	48	[illegible]
64	10580	Banagher,	5	Tirglasson,		–	R.C.	Pres.	Pres.	83	82	165	[illegible]
65	803	Cumber, Lower,	2	Lower Cumber,		–	R.C.	Pres.	–	54	36	90	41
66	[illegible]	Do.	–	Ogill,		Pres.	–	Pres.	–	35	38	[illegible]	27

a Including value of Free Residence.

b Including value of Free Garden.

Province of Ulster: County of Londonderry—*continued.*

Amount paid for Books, Requisites, and Apparatus at Reduced Prices.	Aid granted by the Board during the Year 1874. In Free Stock of Books, Requisites, and Apparatus.	Aid granted by the Board during the Year 1874. In Salaries, Premiums, and other Gratuities.	Aid granted by the Board during the Year 1874. Results Fees, Payment Year.	Amount of Local Emoluments received in Aid of Teacher's Salary. School Fees.	Amount of Local Emoluments received in Aid of Teacher's Salary. Subscriptions, Endowments, &c.	Amount of Local Emoluments received in Aid of Teacher's Salary. Total Local Aid.	Vested or Non-Vested.	Number.
£ s. d.	£ s. d.	£ s. d.	£ s. d.	£ s. d.	£ s. d.	£ s. d.		
2 18 10	—	60 0 0	16 17 6	8 4 8	20 0 0	*28 4 8		8
1 7 8	4 10 0	14 0 0	5 4 0	—	28 0 0	*28 0 0		9
1 16 8	4 10 0	11 12 4	14 15 0	—	28 15 0	*28 15 0		10
0 5 6	—	44 0 0	4 18 0	9 6 8	—	9 6 8		11
6 8 8	—	52 18 4	20 0 6	10 12 9	—	10 12 9		12
8 18 7	—	54 10 0	28 11 6	8 1 10	6 0 0	14 1 10		13
4 5 8	—	81 18 8	28 8 6	8 0 0	17 0 0	*25 0 0		14
1 12 9	—	24 0 0	14 0 0	7 17 0	—	7 17 0		15
2 18 4	—	49 8 8	10 1 8	8 14 6	12 0 0	20 14 6		16
—	—	20 0 0	8 14 0	8 15 8	18 0 0	26 15 6		17
1 5 0	—	24 0 0	6 6 0	4 18 0	—	4 18 0		18
—	—	50 0 0	18 11 6	8 17 0	0 0 0	18 17 0		19
9 15 10	—	47 10 0	17 10 6	5 7 9	17 0 0	22 7 9		20
7 7 6	—	78 16 8	33 15 0	16 5 7	18 0 0	34 5 7		21
5 18 4	—	69 10 0	27 10 6	11 8 8	11 0 0	*24 8 8		22
6 10 8	—	38 5 8	38 0 0	14 0 0	5 0 0	18 0 0		23
—	—	30 0 0	6 12 5	9 12 8	10 0 0	19 12 8		24
2 8 6	—	22 0 0	7 8 0	1 11 0	—	1 11 0		25
1 11 6	—	45 18 4	9 12 0	2 17 6	—	2 17 6		26
20 1 3	—	57 8 0	16 19 5	6 10 0	23 0 0	*29 10 0		27
			10 8 0	4 5 0	—	4 5 0		
1 11 0	—	30 0 0	0 19 0	—	—	—		28
4 7 0	—	48 0 0	8 5 0	8 5 4	21 0 0	*30 5 4		29
6 13 8	—	67 0 0	20 12 0	8 8 11	—	8 8 11		30
6 18 4	—	21 0 0	10 10 9	0 18 0	—	0 18 0		31
4 8 6	—	46 0 0	24 5 8	3 9 8	—	3 9 8		32
1 18 11	—	68 0 0	9 2 0	4 16 1	—	4 16 1	V.T.	33
1 9 2	—	18 8 8	13 10 0	1 17 8	5 0 0	*6 17 8	V.C.	34
2 14 8	—	33 16 8	19 18 0	5 9 0	5 0 0	10 9 0		35
8 0 6	—	51 0 0	37 8 6	7 8 6	2 10 0	*9 18 6		36
0 17 8	—	85 0 0	22 18 0	4 10 0	18 0 0	18 10 0		37
1 11 0	—	32 0 0	5 15 0	3 6 9	—	8 6 0		38
1 7 9	4 10 0	11 18 4	10 14 0	8 0 0	8 0 0	*17 0 0		39
—	—	—	—	—	—	—		40
1 5 0	—	24 0 0	7 0 5	6 8 4	—	6 8 4	V.T.	41
1 7 4	—	20 0 0	10 18 6	8 5 8	—	8 5 8	V.T.	42
3 12 6	—	32 18 4	15 6 8	5 12 9	—	6 12 9		43
4 10 4	—	20 0 0	14 9 0	1 4 0	14 0 0	15 4 0		44
—	—	—	—	8 8 1	—	8 8 1		45
—	—	20 0 0	11 0 6	14 7 6	9 10 0	*23 17 6		46
5 4 7	—	34 10 0	24 15 0	12 12 8	—	10 19 8		47
6 8 6	—	24 0 0	18 4 6	1 8 6	5 5 0	1 3 6		48
—	—	21 0 0	6 12 8	4 11 3	1 0 0	5 11 8		49
1 14 10	—	24 0 0	9 18 8	5 11 8	1 0 0	*8 11 9	V.T.	50
4 11 8	—	30 0 0	17 8 8	5 5 0	—	6 8 0		51
8 7 6	—	28 10 0	8 15 6	3 10 8	—	8 10 8	V.C.	52
4 4 0	—	49 0 0	10 6 6	—	—	—		53
0 10 2	—	32 0 0	0 13 0	8 17 10	9 0 0	22 17 10		54
8 1 8	—	65 0 0	8 8 0	1 17 8	0 0 0	7 17 6		55
1 17 8	—	20 0 0	6 8 8	2 10 0	10 0 0	12 10 0		56
8 1 1	4 10 0	19 10 0	—	5 0 6	—	5 6 6	V.O.	57
2 11 0	—	30 0 0	8 17 8	10 14 0	5 0 0	15 14 0		58
8 8 2	—	30 0 0	6 8 0	5 0 0	—	6 0 0		59
1 11 5	—	44 0 0	8 1 0	6 3 7	4 0 0	*10 8 7		60
1 4 11	—	30 0 0	5 0 0	6 9 7	5 0 0	18 8 7	V.C.	61
3 15 11	—	41 10 0	11 8 0	4 10 0	5 0 0	9 10 0		62
8 6 10	—	56 19 9	37 0 6	8 0 0	—	5 0 0		
			17 14 0	1 6 0	8 0 0	8 0 0		63
1 6 11	—	27 8 0	10 0 6	1 10 0	—	1 10 8		
			10 11 8					
6 4 8	—	—	18 14 8	3 9 8	20 3 4	22 18 6		64
11 5 7	—	43 8 4	22 10 8	23 4 11	0 0 0	*20 4 11		65
1 15 9	—	24 0 0	10 8 6	8 11 4	—	8 11 4		66

* Including value of Free Residence and Garden. † Only two months in operation. ‡ Inoperative.

List of Schools in operation on the 31st December, 1874—

Number.	Roll Number of School.	Parish.	District.	School.	Religious Denomination of Managers or Correspondents: Clerical.	Lay.	Religious Denomination of Teachers: Principals.	Assistants.	Attendance for the Year: Total number of Pupils on Rolls within the Year 1874: Males.	Fem.	Total.	Average daily attendance.
67	9291	Cumber, Lower,	3	Ervey,	–	Pres.	Diss.	Pres.	73	46	123	40
68	11164	Do.	–	Bond's Glen,	R.C.	–	R.C.	–	35	20	55	21
69	6408	Cumber, Upper,	6	Glenmadle, m.	R.C.	–	R.C.	–	60	–	60	23
70	6497	Do.	–	Do. f.	R.C.	–	R.C.	–	–	101	102	32
71	8700	Coleraine,	8	Boghill,	–	Pres.	Pres.	–	64	43	107	35
72	4289	Do.	–	Coleraine, m.	R.C.	–	R.C.	–	97	–	97	41
73	4386	Do.	–	Do. f.	R.C.	–	R.C.	–	–	84	84	38
74	[illegible]	Do.		Do. No. 2, m.	–	R.C.	Pres.	Pres. R.C.	287	–	287	142
75	6591	Do.	–	Do. f.	–	R.C.	Pres.	R.C.	–	303	303	144
76	8392	Do.	–	Do. i.	–	R.C.	R.C.	Pres. Diss.	160	180	343	169
77	8881	Do.	–	Do. Workhouse,	P.L.	Gds.	R.C. Pres.	–	30	34	58	40
78	7807	Do.	–	Knocknamara,	–	Pres.	Pres.	–	35	41	76	25
79	11208	Clondermott,	9	Waterside, m.	R.C.	–	R.C.	R.C.	162	–	162	59
80	11209	Do.	–	Do. f.	R.C.	–	R.C.	R.C.	–	186	186	65
81	6101	Do.	–	Do. No. 2,	Pres.	–	Pres.	Pres.	104	101	205	83
82	1416	Do.	–	Rossnagalliagh,	–	R.C.	R.C.	–	41	56	97	35
83	8780	Do.	–	Lisdillon,	–	R.C.	Pres.	–	45	39	84	29
84	8042	Do.	–	Lismacarroll,	–	R.C.	R.C.	–	51	32	83	30
85	7872	Do.	–	Glendermott,	R.C.	–	R.C.	–	63	40	103	41
86	8105	Do.	–	Greysteown,	Pres.	–	Pres.	–	30	43	73	28
87	8840	Do.	–	Killymallaght,	–	Diss.	Pres.	–	64	25	89	10
88	81096	Do.	–	Gortinure,	–	R.C.	Pres.	Pres.	80	78	158	69
89	8441	Do.	–	Clooney Terrace,	Pres.	–	Pres.	Pres.	94	95	189	80
90	8510	Do.	–	Faughanbridge,	Pres.	–	Pres.	–	40	41	81	28
91	8891	Do.	–	Derry Workhouse,	P.L.	Gds.	R.C. Pres.	–	44	66	110	73
92	10788	Cumber,	–	Coolkeeragh,	R.C.	–	R.C.	–	35	32	66	34
93	800	Desertoghill,	7	Magheramore,	–	R.C.	R.C.	–	47	56	103	42
94	[illegible]	Do.	–	Ballyagan, m.	–	R.C.	Diss.	–	84	–	84	35
95	7770	Do.	–	Do. f.	–	R.C.	Pres.	–	–	52	63	31
96	2882	Do.	–	Moneydig,	–	Pres.	Pres.	–	59	43	102	37
97	8105	Do.	–	Tirnakilnagh,	–	R.C.	Pres.	–	41	27	68	30
98	[illegible]	Do.	–	Carhill,	–	R.C.	Pres.	–	–	–	–	–
99	10817	Do.	–	Moyletragh,	–	R.C.	R.C.	–	43	44	92	61
100	[illegible]	Desertmartin,	–	Knocknagin,	R.C.	–	R.C.	–	44	50	125	33
101	10432	Do.	–	Desertmartin, m.	R.C.	–	R.C.	–	89	–	69	29
102	10403	Do.	–	Do. f.	R.C.	–	R.C.	–	–	72	74	30
103	9783	Do.	–	Rosegarland, day.	R.C.	–	R.C.	–	60	48	108	46
				Do. evg.	–	–	R.C.	–	40	19	59	30
104	11168	Do.	–	Cranny,	–	R.C.	Pres.	Pres.	140	60	160	61
105	11128	Do.	–	Lisnamorn,	–	R.C.	R.C.	–	23	94	117	55
106	4146	Desertlynn,	14	Gorteagillie,	–	R.C.	Pres.	R.C.	79	55	134	41
107	[illegible]	Do.	–	Desertlynn,	–	R.C.	R.C.	–	44	47	91	28
108	2596	Dunboe,	3	Ballywildrick,	R.C.	–	Pres.	–	34	44	78	30
109	2650	Do.	–	Ballinrees, No. 1,	Pres.	–	Pres.	–	54	47	101	37
110	8416	Do.	–	Altibrunagh,	R.C.	–	R.C.	–	69	93	152	63
111	10[illegible]	Do.	–	Ballymaclan,	R.C.	–	R.C.	–	57	30	87	34
112	9448	Do.	–	Downhill,	R.C.	–	R.C.	–	45	24	69	31
113	0002	Do.	–	Formoyle,	R.C.	–	R.C.	–	37	29	66	31
114	6331	Do.	–	Articlave,	R.C.	–	R.C.	R.C.	67	66	133	79
115	2950	Drumachose,	2	Market-street,	Pres.	–	Pres.	Pres.	57	53	110	34
116	1107	Do.	–	Roe Mill,	R.C.	–	R.C.	–	32	45	77	34
117	4073	Do.	–	Newtownlimavady,	Pres.	–	Pres.	Pres.	67	40	108	53
118	9487	Do.	–	Do. Workhouse,	P.L.	Gds.	Pres.	–	29	24	53	31
119	1465	Do.	–	Isle of Man-street, m.	R.C.	–	R.C.	–	143	–	143	38
120	1611	Do.	–	Do. f.	R.C.	–	R.C.	–	–	66	66	30
121	[illegible]	Do.	8	Derrymore,	Pres.	–	Pres.	–	73	68	141	46
122	[illegible]	Do.	2	Drumrammer, tem.	R.C.	–	R.C.	–	36	23	60	19
123	9505	Do.	–	Drumachose,	Pres.	–	R.C.	–	24	24	48	23
124	11082	Do.	–	Do. i.	R.C.	–	Pres.	–	38	30	68	30

a Including value of Free Residence and Garden.

b Including value of Free Residence.

Province of Ulster: County of Londonderry—*continued.*

Amount paid for Books, Requisites, and Apparatus, at Reduced Prices.	Aid granted by the Board during the Year 1874. In Free Stock of Books, Requisites, and Apparatus.	In Salaries, Premiums, and other Gratuities.	Results Fees, Financial Year.	Amount of Local Emoluments received in Aid of Teacher's Salary. School Fees.	Subscriptions, Endowments, &c.	Total Local Aid.	Vested or Non-Vested.	Number.
£ s. d.	£ s. d.	£ s. d.	£ s. d.	£ s. d.	£ s. d.	£ s. d.		
—	—	48 0 0	11 18 6	6 19 9	20 0 0	[a] 25 19 9		67
1 5 1	—	6 0 0	—	1 7 4	11 0 0	12 7 4		68
0 18 9	—	24 0 0	6 18 0	2 0 3	—	2 0 3	V.C.	69
2 15 8	—	30 0 0	6 3 0	1 0 0	—	1 0 0	V.C.	70
1 6 8	—	30 0 0	0 8 6	—	28 0 0	[b] 28 0 0		71
3 19 5	—	92 5 4	12 16 6	0 5 7	11 16 5	21 0 0		72
2 17 8	—	73 16 8	9 19 0	4 15 6	5 5 6	10 0 0		73
16 18 3	—	134 13 4	52 15 0	—	100 0 0	[b] 109 0 0		74
15 19 0	—	137 6 8	57 15 6	—	118 0 0	[b] 118 0 0		75
1 7 11	—	84 16 8	80 15 0	—	100 0 0	[b] 108 0 0		76
4 10 0	—	—	—	—	—	—		77
—	—	97 0 0	4 10 4	1 7 4	3 0 0	6 7 6		78
5 0 4	—	36 10 0	11 14 6	17 13 10	10 0 0	37 18 10		79
3 5 6	—	80 0 0	18 19 0	15 17 10	5 0 0	80 11 10		80
1 15 10	—	67 8 8	20 8 6	11 7 8	18 0 0	[b] 29 7 8		81
2 5 0	—	27 0 4	10 0 6	8 3 8	15 0 0	15 8 8	[illegible]	82
1 10 3	—	80 0 0	—	2 0 0	5 0 0	7 0 0		83
—	—	24 0 0	9 10 0	6 19 7	13 5 0	[a] 19 4 7		84
—	—	15 0 0	9 18 0	11 1 8	—	11 1 8		85
8 3 10	—	24 0 0	8 2 0	3 18 6	8 0 0	[b] 11 18 6		86
1 5 7	—	13 10 0	2 15 0	4 10 8	—	4 10 8		87
6 13 8	—	37 1 8	28 6 0	51 15 8	86 0 0	[b] 67 15 8		88
4 13 4	—	55 0 0	15 16 6	20 17 7	10 0 0	30 17 7		89
5 10 0	—	80 0 0	9 4 6	6 10 7	1 0 0	7 10 7		90
—	—	10 10 0	—	—	—	—		91
1 14 7	—	20 0 0	6 19 6	3 18 0	5 0 0	8 15 0		92
6 17 4	—	40 10 0	11 17 6	2 18 6	12 0 0	14 15 6		93
2 2 1	—	40 0 0	11 6 0	4 11 8	12 0 0	16 11 8		94
3 0 8	—	23 0 6	17 19 0	1 1 6	12 0 0	13 1 6		95
1 15 0	—	24 0 0	13 1 6	4 15 10	—	4 15 10		96
1 18 11	—	24 0 0	0 11 0	1 15 8	6 0 0	7 15 8		97
2 1 8	—	27 0 0	12 15 6	—	—	—		98
—	—	24 0 0	10 4 0	0 1 6	6 0 0	11 1 6		99
0 1 2	—	24 0 0	20 6 0	5 9 1	—	5 9 1	V.C.	100
1 6 3	—	32 0 0	8 10 0	9 5 11	18 0 0	17 3 11		101
1 6 7	—	27 0 0	14 4 6	2 0 10	—	2 0 10		102
1 12 5	—	30 0 0	12 19 6	5 11 0	—	8 11 0		103
—	—	—	11 16 6	3 12 0	—	2 12 0		
4 16 4	5 0 0	16 0 0	11 9 6	—	45 0 0	[b] 45 0 0		104
1 10 6	5 0 0	14 0 0	13 2 6	—	30 15 0	[b] 35 15 0		105
4 1 11	—	27 0 0	21 4 0	7 13 11	16 0 0	[a] 23 13 11		106
2 10 5	—	30 0 0	7 0 0	0 10 0	5 0 0	[b] 5 10 0		107
2 4 0	—	24 0 0	11 14 0	4 15 0	10 15 0	[a] 15 10 0		108
2 5 7	—	27 10 0	11 1 6	4 10 6	—	4 10 0		109
4 0 7	—	30 5 8	27 8 6	3 7 0	0 14 0	[a] 4 1 0		110
—	—	24 0 0	2 8 0	1 17 6	10 0 0	11 17 6	V.C.	111
2 10 3	—	34 10 0	2 15 0	3 18 10	21 4 8	25 3 6		112
2 0 8	—	29 0 0	5 15 8	3 6 9	13 10 0	[a] 18 14 0		113
5 3 6	—	61 0 0	57 7 0	3 4 0	33 10 0	[a] 29 14 0		114
6 7 1	—	61 16 8	54 19 6	50 2 2	—	56 5 8		115
1 13 0	—	24 0 0	8 14 6	4 3 8	—	4 3 8		116
—	—	65 19 4	23 15 6	6 16 6	6 10 6	13 6 0		117
—	—	—	—	—	—	—		118
4 18 6	—	77 18 4	84 19 0	29 5 4	—	29 9 4		119
2 8 1	—	25 0 0	12 5 6	0 8 7	—	5 8 7		120
2 10 6	—	31 5 4	14 5 6	8 1 11	—	8 1 11		121
1 0 8	—	30 0 0	7 10 0	5 6 9	—	3 8 9		122
2 6 11	—	19 0 0	5 16 0	10 15 0	—	10 15 0		123
2 7 11	4 0 0	30 0 0	7 1 6	—	—	—		124

[a] Returns not available.

[b] Including value of Free Grants.

List of Schools in operation on the 31st December, 1874,—

Number.	Roll Number of School.	Parish.	District.	School.	Religious Denomination of Managers or Correspondents: Comm.	Lay.	Religious Denomination of Teachers: Principals.	Assistants.	Attendance for the Year. Total number of Pupils on Rolls within the Year 1874: Males.	Fem.	Total.	Average Daily Attendance.
125	4147	Dungiven,	7	Cashel, m.	–	R.C.	R.C.	–	108	–	108	60
126	[illegible]	Do.	–	Do. f.	–	R.C.	R.C.	–	–	103	103	[illegible]
127	4708	Do.	–	Tirgoland,	Pres.	–	R.C.	–	67	[illegible]	96	[illegible]
128	6431	Do.	–	Dungiven, m.	R.C.	–	R.C.	–	73	–	73	37
129	[illegible]	Do.	–	Do. f.	R.C.	–	R.C.	–	–	60	60	[illegible]
130	6918	Do.	–	Do.	–	R.C.	Pres.	–	18	46	64	[illegible]
131	11188	Do.	–	Ballymonaghan,	–	R.C.	R.C.	–	81	[illegible]	54	[illegible]
132	912	Errigal,	–	Lisnamurragh,	–	R.C.	R.C.	–	113	99	212	84
133	2564	Do.	–	Ballinaugh,	Pres.	–	Pres.	–	60	84	70	41
134	4574	Do.	–	Glenullin,	–	R.C.	R.C.	Pres.	76	80	158	47
135	5497	Do.	–	Garvagh,	Pres.	–	Pres.	Pres.	93	35	128	50
136	6897	Do.	–	Do. f.	–	R.C.	Pres.	–	–	108	108	53
137	[illegible]	Do.	–	Cah,	Pres.	–	Pres.	–	47	37	84	33
138	[illegible]	Do.	–	Ballerin,	R.C.	–	R.C.	R.C.	74	68	142	52
139	8762	Faughanvale,	2	Faughanvale,	–	Pres.	R.C.	–	45	61	90	[illegible]
140	9712	Do.	–	Greysteel,	–	R.C.	Pres.	–	60	68	128	61
141	9807	Do.	–	Craigbrack,	R.C.	–	R.C.	–	103	61	164	66
142	[illegible]	Do.	–	Carmoney, m.	–	R.C.	Pres.	–	80	–	80	[illegible]
143	10801	Do.	–	Do. f.	–	R.C.	Pres.	–	–	67	67	31
144	11077	Glendermot,	–	Ardmore,	–	R.C.	R.C.	–	53	33	86	32
145	10844	Killowen,	9	Cranagh Hill,	R.C.	–	R.C.	–	[illegible]	[illegible]	101	37
146	[illegible]	Do.	–	Killowen-street, Coleraine, m.	R.C.	–	R.C.	–	50	–	50	35
147	4874	Do.	–	Do. f.	R.C.	–	R.C.	–	–	77	77	31
148	11028	Do.	–	Killowen-street,	R.C.	–	R.C.	–	60	60	120	56
		Do.	–	Do. evg.	R.C.	–	R.C.	–	41	7	48	[illegible]
149	8618	Do.	–	Coleraine District Model, m.	Com.	N.R.	Pres.	R.C.	173	–	173	61
150	8619	Do.	–	Do. f.			Pres.	R.C. / Pres.	–	111	111	60
151	8620	Do.	–	Do. i.			R.C.	–	43	43	86	48
152	8080	Kilcronaghan,	7	Killyrammer,	–	Pres.	Pres.	–	23	30	53	20
153	6152	Do.	–	Tobermore,	Pres.	–	Pres.	–	88	87	175	44
154	7747	Do.	–	Kilcronaghan,	R.C.	–	R.C.	R.C.	76	84	160	56
155	9008	Do.	–	Keenaght, day.	R.C.	–	R.C.	–	77	[illegible]	[illegible]	[illegible]
				Do. evg.	–	–	R.C.	–	73	1	74	[illegible]
156	[illegible]	Do.	–	Brackaghlislea,	R.C.	–	R.C.	–	59	[illegible]	80	[illegible]
157	9168	Killelagh,	–	Tirkane,	R.C.	–	R.C.	–	88	80	168	65
158	[illegible]	Do.	–	Corlacky,	R.C.	–	R.C.	R.C.	105	100	205	89
159	[illegible]	Do.	8	Fallagloon, No. 1, m.	Pres.	–	Pres.	–	60	–	[illegible]	37
160	7677	Do.	–	Do. No. 2, f.	Pres.	–	Pres.	–	–	50	[illegible]	[illegible]
161	[illegible]	Do.	7	Swatragh, m.	–	R.C.	R.C.	–	78	–	78	55
162	[illegible]	Do.	–	Do. f.	–	R.C.	R.C.	–	–	74	74	37
163	10381	Do.	–	Killelagh,	R.C.	–	R.C.	–	84	80	164	53
164	[illegible]	Kildollagh,	8	Dunalis,	Pres.	–	Pres.	Pres.	80	[illegible]	168	61
165	[illegible]	Do.	–	Coolderragh,	–	R.C.	Pres.	–	24	23	47	33
166	[illegible]	Kilrea,	7	Movanagher, m.	–	R.C.	R.C.	–	108	–	108	41
167	[illegible]	Do.	–	Do. f.	–	R.C.	Pres.	–	–	61	64	34
168	[illegible]	Do.	–	Lislea, m.	–	R.C.	R.C.	–	88	–	88	48
169	[illegible]	Do.	–	Do. f.	–	R.C.	R.C.	–	–	83	83	47
170	[illegible]	Do.	–	Kilrea, m.	–	R.C.	R.C.	–	100	–	100	43
171	[illegible]	Do.	–	Do. f.	–	R.C.	R.C.	Pres.	–	180	180	55
172	4101	Lissan,	–	Drumsaan,	Pres.	–	Pres.	–	43	40	83	34
173	[illegible]	Do.	16	Derran,	R.C.	–	R.C.	–	61	57	118	36
174	[illegible]	Do.	–	Claggan,	Pres.	–	Pres.	Pres.	88	70	158	63
175	[illegible]	Learmount,	8	Park,	R.C.	–	R.C.	–	90	62	152	41
176	[illegible]	Do.	–	Moneyboghan, m.	R.C.	–	R.C.	–	144	–	144	44
177	[illegible]	Do.	–	Do. f.	R.C.	–	R.C.	–	–	87	87	31
178	[illegible]	Magherafelt,	7	Aghagaskin,	–	R.C.	R.C.	–	51	20	70	34
179	4182	Do.	–	Magherafelt, No. 2, m.	Pres.	–	Pres.	–	178	–	102	44
180	[illegible]	Do.	–	[illegible], m.	R.C.	–	R.C.	–	68	–	68	[illegible]
				Do. evg.	R.C.	–	R.C.	–	63	–	63	[illegible]
181	8302	Do.	–	Do. f.	R.C.	–	R.C.	–	–	66	65	[illegible]

a Including value of Free Residence.

b Including value of Free Residence and Garden.

Province of Ulster : County of Londonderry—continued.

Amount paid for Books, Requisites, and Apparatus, at Reduced Prices.	Aid granted by the Board during the Year 1874. In Free Stock of Books, Requisites, and Apparatus.	In Salaries, Premiums, and other Gratuities.	Results Fees, Financial Year.	Amount of Local Endowments received in Aid of Teacher's Salary. School Fees.	Subscriptions, Endowments, &c.	Total Local Aid.	Vested or Non-Vested.	Number.
£ s. d.	£ s. d.	£ s. d.	£ s. d.	£ s. d.	£ s. d.	£ s. d.		
0 8 11	—	31 0 0	14 4 6	1 1 0	12 10 0	[a] 13 11 0		125
1 14 4	—	37 6 8	10 6 0	0 0 0	11 0 0	11 6 0		126
9 12 5	—	30 0 0	4 7 6	4 16 8	6 0 0	10 16 0		127
2 19 7	—	34 0 0	9 18 6	7 17 4	1 0 0	8 17 4		128
1 7 10	—	20 0 0	9 0 0	1 14 10	1 0 0	2 14 10		129
1 12 3	—	30 0 0	7 8 6	2 19 0	10 0 0	12 19 0		130
1 15 6	4 10 0	10 0 0	—	1 0 0	14 0 0	[b] 15 0 0		131
1 10 0	—	30 0 0	6 4 8	—	9 0 0	9 0 0		132
1 6 9	—	55 0 0	17 8 0	2 2 0	—	2 2 0		133
4 9 3	—	70 0 0	24 6 8	3 1 0	7 10 0	10 11 0		134
5 15 0	—	91 8 4	17 8 8	14 0 8	—	14 0 8		135
—	—	14 16 8	21 5 0	9 1 8	5 0 0	14 1 8		136
—	—	20 0 0	10 9 0	2 0 0	—	2 6 8		137
6 6 8	—	55 0 0	21 4 0	8 18 9	—	8 18 9		138
1 15 1	—	24 0 0	4 15 6	1 10 6	—	1 10 6		139
15 0 8	—	6 0 0	26 16 6	8 1 0	55 0 0	[b] 63 1 0		140
8 15 0	—	40 10 0	22 9 6	8 14 10	10 0 0	18 14 10		141
3 15 1	—	80 0 0	28 0 6	12 2 1	20 0 0	[a] 32 2 1		142
6 19 0	—	21 0 0	20 6 5	6 10 9	16 0 0	22 10 9		143
1 15 8	4 10 0	30 0 0	2 8 0	3 17 8	15 0 0	[a] 18 17 8		144
6 8 8	—	15 10 0	—	2 17 4	11 6 0	14 3 4	V.C.	145
0 12 6	—	24 0 0	4 19 0	—	10 0 0	10 0 0	V.N.S.	146
1 14 11	—	26 0 0	9 10 0	2 8 0	5 0 0	7 6 0	V.N.S.	147
7 6 3	—	—	17 18 0	—	22 0 0	22 6 0		148
—	—	87 6 8	—	1 12 0	—	1 12 0		
57 8 6	—						V.C.	149
—	—	573 2 1	88 19 6	140 10 9	—	140 10 9	V.C.	150
—	—						V.C.	151
0 14 8	—	20 0 0	8 17 0	1 8 0	—	1 8 0		152
8 15 8	—	25 8 4	14 18 8	5 5 0	—	5 5 0		153
2 7 2	—	55 6 8	15 9 6	6 11 6	5 0 0	8 11 6		154
4 6 8	—	30 18 4	15 18 0	7 10 0	—	7 10 0		155
—	—	—	8 16 0	3 0 0	—	3 0 0		
1 18 8	—	24 0 0	15 4 0	1 0 0	—	1 0 0		156
6 7 8	—	25 0 0	24 3 0	2 16 6	—	2 16 6	V.T.	157
6 7 4	—	44 0 0	37 8 8	6 12 4	2 0 0	8 12 4	V.T.	158
2 19 7	—	41 10 0	16 4 0	13 10 2	10 0 0	23 10 2		159
4 15 8	—	40 0 0	24 5 0	12 8 8	10 0 0	22 8 8		160
—	—	21 0 0	8 18 6	0 8 9	17 10 8	[b] 27 17 6		161
1 16 0	—	61 0 0	5 11 0	0 0 0	20 0 0	[a] 20 0 0		162
8 4 9	—	18 0 0	10 9 8	8 3 0	4 0 0	7 3 0		163
1 10 2	—	44 0 0	18 6 0	3 13 4	5 0 0	8 16 4		164
0 11 10	—	—	4 14 0	—	—	—		165
4 11 5	—	22 0 0	14 15 6	0 19 0	25 10 0	[a] 33 3 0		166
6 17 10	—	26 0 0	19 8 0	8 10 8	21 10 0	[b] 29 0 8		167
8 14 7	—	35 0 0	19 18 2	9 11 9	26 10 0	[b] 36 4 2		168
6 8 10	—	30 0 0	23 10 8	9 14 11	21 10 0	[a] 31 4 11		169
8 16 6	—	72 15 0	18 8 0	13 11 0	30 0 0	[a] 48 16 0		170
3 10 10	—	47 0 0	18 12 0	6 0 7	25 0 0	[b] 30 0 7		171
8 2 0	—	20 0 0	6 15 0	4 3 0	—	4 3 0	R.	172
3 1 10	—	24 0 0	10 18 0	5 7 0	—	5 7 0		173
11 8 10	—	53 0 0	14 10 0	16 0 0	5 8 8	10 0 0	V.C.	174
2 14 2	—	69 10 0	20 7 0	1 17 9	11 10 0	[a] 19 7 8		175
8 7 8	—	72 13 4	13 11 0	5 14 7	—	3 16 7	V.T.	176
1 10 7	—	20 0 0	11 1 0	0 16 0	—	0 16 9	V.T.	177
1 11 0	—	22 0 0	18 6 5	3 7 0	5 0 0	8 7 0		178
15 1 8	—	37 0 0	19 19 0	10 17 8	6 0 8	16 17 6		179
9 6 7	—	40 10 0	16 4 0	6 17 0	17 10 0	[a] 23 7 0		180
—	—	—	—	1 19 1	—	[a] 1 19 1		
9 19 11	—	26 0 0	6 14 6	6 10 10	5 0 0	11 10 10		181

[a] Including value of Free Grants.

[b] No Results Examination.

List of Schools in operation on the 31st December, 1874.—

Number.	Roll Number of School.	Parish.	District.	School.	Religious Denomination of Manager or Correspondent. Clerical.	Lay.	Number and Religious Denominations of Teachers. Principals.	Assistants.	Attendance for the Year. Total number of Pupils on Rolls within the Year 1874. Males.	Fem.	Total.	Average Daily Attendance for Year 1874.
182	8519	Magherafelt,	7	Castledawson, No. 2,	Pres.	–	Pres.	–	58	61	119	43
183	9110	Do.	–	Coolshinny,	–	R.C.	Pres.	–	82	72	154	47
184	10087	Do.	–	New Row,	R.C.	–	R.C.	R.C.	130	100	230	79
				Do. evg.	R.C.	–	R.C.	–	102	87	189	34
185	[illegible]	Do.	–	Drumrainey, day,	–	R.C.	R.C.	–	30	31	60	25
				Do. evg.	–	R.C.	R.C.	–	63	47	110	26
186	10478	Do.	–	Magherafelt, f.	Pres.	–	Pres.	–	–	79	79	30
187	[illegible]	Do.	–	Do. Parochial, f.	R.C.	–	R.C.	Dep.	28	10	38	14
188	[illegible]	Do.	–	Do. Workhouse,	P.L. Gdns.		Pres.	–	41	40	[illegible]	[illegible]
189	827	Magilligan,	8	Ballymaclary,	R.C.	–	R.C.	–	71	46	117	34
190	7139	Do.	–	Margymonaghan,	Pres.	–	R.C.	–	17	46	63	24
191	[illegible]	Do.	–	Duncrun,	–	R.C.	R.C.	–	48	44	92	37
192	[illegible]	Do.	–	Bellarena,	–	R.C.	R.C.	–	50	60	108	46
193	11117	Do.	–	Gortmore,	Pres.	–	Pres.	–	31	25	56	23
194	1871	Maghera,	9	Maghera,	R.C.	–	R.C.	–	112	66	177	78
195	[illegible]	Do.	–	Do. f.	Pres.	–	Pres.	–	–	112	112	49
196	6878	Do.	–	Do. Parochial,	R.C.	–	R.C.	–	47	43	90	35
197	3039	Do.	–	Drum[illegible], m.	R.C.	–	R.C.	R.C.	82	68	148	60
198	[illegible]	Do.	–	Do. f.	R.C.	–	R.C.	–	157	–	157	60
199	[illegible]	Do.	–	Lisnamuck, m.	R.C.	–	R.C.	–	157	–	157	60
200	2891	Do.	–	Do. f.	R.C.	–	R.C.	–	–	130	130	35
201	[illegible]	Do.	–	Culnady,	R.C.	–	R.C.	R.C.	101	90	198	80
202	[illegible]	Do.	–	Lemnaroy, m.	–	Pres.	R.C.	–	80	–	80	37
203	[illegible]	Do.	–	Do. f.	–	Pres.	R.C.	–	–	92	92	39
204	4877	Do.	–	Toberhead,	Pres.	–	Pres.	–	40	36	76	19
205	4352	Do.	–	Ballynahone,	Pres.	–	Pres.	–	74	41	115	41
206	7432	Do.	–	Crew,	Pres.	–	Pres.	–	65	46	111	30
207	7419	Do.	–	Hall-st., Maghera, m.	Pres.	–	Pres.	–	88	–	88	36
208	8077	Do.	–	Beagh,	Pres.	–	Pres.	–	45	31	76	34
209	8457	Do.	–	Derganagh,	Pres.	–	Pres.	–	37	36	73	36
210	[illegible]	Do.	–	Tamnymarny,	R.C.	–	R.C.	–	52	65	97	34
211	9184	Do.	–	Curran,	R.C.	–	R.C.	–	48	44	92	38
212	[illegible]	Do.	–	Ampertain, m.	–	R.C.	R.C.	–	85	–	85	38
213	[illegible]	Do.	–	Do. f.	–	R.C.	R.C.	–	–	102	102	30
214	10098	Do.	–	Fallagloon, day,	R.C.	–	R.C.	–	129	79	208	61
				Do. evg.	R.C.	–	R.C.	–	42	7	49	22
215	8819	Do.	–	Brocktown,	R.C.	–	R.C.	–	77	39	110	41
216	[illegible]	Do.	–	Ballymacpeake,	R.C.	–	R.C.	–	38	42	80	41
217	[illegible]	Macosquin,	3	Castleroe,	Pres.	–	Pres.	Pres.	47	67	114	48
218	2801	Do.	–	Killure,	–	R.C.	Pres.	–	65	63	128	27
219	1947	Do.	–	Coolyvenny,	Pres.	–	Pres.	–	57	59	116	19
220	[illegible]	Do.	–	Killeague,	Pres.	–	Pres.	–	35	67	92	23
221	[illegible]	Do.	–	Ballinteer,	R.C.	–	Pres.	–	61	53	114	13
222	8416	Do.	–	Macosquin,	R.C.	–	R.C.	Pres.	83	73	156	73
223	[illegible]	Do.	–	Camus,	Pres.	–	Pres.	–	37	23	60	15
224	321	Templemore,	2	St. Columb's, m.	R.C.	–	R.C.	–	228	–	228	99
225	825	Do.	–	Do. f.	R.C.	–	R.C.	R.C.	–	139	139	61
226	6181	Do.	–	Do. Convent, No. 2, f.	R.C.	–	Nuns.		139	110	249	153
227	[illegible]	Do.	–	Derry, m.	Pres.	–	Pres.	–	116	–	116	45
				Do. evg.	–	–	Pres.	–	119	–	149	50
228	8049	Do.	–	Do. f.	Pres.	–	Pres.	2 Pres.	–	200	200	96
229	1580	Do.	–	Shantallow,	R.C.	–	R.C.	–	45	30	75	31
230	[illegible]	Do.	–	Race Course,	Pres.	–	Pres.	–	43	21	69	33
231	[illegible]	Do.	–	Bennett-street,	Pres.	–	Pres.	2 Pres.	110	123	233	83
232	7660	Do.	–	Londonderry District Model, m.	Com.	N.E.	–	–	314	–	314	159
233	7661	Do.	–	Do. f.	Com.	N.E.	n.e.	2 R.C. Pres.	–	219	219	95
234	7662	Do.	–	Do. i.	Com.	N.E.	n.e.	R.C. Pres.	96	73	169	79
235	8100	Do.	–	Creevagh,	Pres.	–	Pres.	–	75	60	134	46
236	[illegible]	Do.	–	Culmore, m.	–	R.C.	Pres.	–	54	–	54	25
237	[illegible]	Do.	–	Do. f.	–	R.C.	R.C.	–	–	71	71	30

a Including value of Free Residence and Garden. b Including value of Free Residence.

Province of ULSTER: County of LONDONDERRY—*continued.*

Amount paid for Books, Requisites, and Apparatus at Reduced Prices.	Aid granted by the Board during the Year 1874. In Purchase of Books, Requisites, and Apparatus.	In Salaries, Premiums, and other Gratuities.	Results Fees, Financial Year.	Amount of Local Endowments received in Aid of Teacher's Salary. School Fees.	Subscriptions, Endowments, &c.	Total Local Aid.	Vested or Non-Vested.	Number.
£ s. d.	£ s. d.	£ s. d.	£ s. d.	£ s. d.	£ s. d.	£ s. d.		
2 10 10	—	26 0 0	8 18 6	4 8 6	—	4 8 6		182
3 10 2	—	22 18 10	8 15 8	6 0 0	14 0 0	b 20 0 0		183
6 14 4	—	23 0 0	21 17 0	8 10 0	—	8 10 0	V.T.	184
—	—	—	10 16 0	8 3 7	—	8 3 7		
3 2 8	—	20 0 0	8 2 6	6 15 6	—	6 15 6		185
—	—	—	8 11 8	9 9 0	15 0 0	24 9 0		
4 18 8	—	21 0 0	11 6 8	17 6 4	6 0 0	23 6 4		186
2 7 0	—	44 0 0	10 0 0	7 2 2	28 0 0	b 35 2 2		187
8 18 8	—	6 10 0	—	—	—	—		188
1 10 8	—	44 18 7	6 10 0	8 18 8	—	8 18 8		189
0 12 8	—	24 0 0	4 7 6	3 16 6	—	3 16 6		190
—	—	20 0 0	7 3 6	0 4 0	—	0 4 0		191
4 17 4	—	55 10 0	17 16 0	0 10 0	22 10 0	b 23 0 0		192
1 6 0	4 0 0	13 10 8	—	1 10 0	1 0 0	a 2 10 0		193
2 10 4	—	25 0 0	10 17 0	4 18 2	—	4 18 2	V.T.	194
2 12 10	—	20 10 8	22 16 6	10 11 6	—	10 11 6		195
2 13 6	—	20 0 0	3 9 0	6 0 0	15 10 0	a 21 10 0		196
1 8 10	—	28 0 0	7 0 0	1 0 0	6 0 0	7 0 0		197
—	—	—	—	3 3 0	—	a 3 3 0		198
1 14 4	—	20 8 4	21 19 0	3 3 0	—	3 3 0	V.T.	199
8 12 10	—	26 0 6	15 17 8	6 8 4	—	6 8 4	V.N.	200
6 14 4	—	27 0 0	19 8 8	5 18 8	—	5 18 8		201
0 10 9	—	24 0 0	4 13 0	1 6 0	3 0 0	4 6 0	A.	202
1 11 0	—	20 0 0	4 4 0	2 8 8	—	2 8 8	A.	203
1 8 9	—	28 0 0	4 16 0	1 8 0	8 8 0	9 16 0		204
3 10 3	—	25 0 0	10 8 6	7 6 0	—	7 6 0		205
8 17 1	—	24 0 0	14 13 0	10 14 0	—	10 14 0		206
7 10 7	—	35 15 4	21 11 6	12 12 7	3 0 0	b 15 12 7		207
—	—	20 0 0	10 0 6	7 8 0	—	7 8 0		208
0 18 8	—	20 0 0	7 7 0	9 4 11	—	9 4 11		209
1 19 9	—	24 0 0	7 8 6	1 7 4	1 6 0	2 13 4		210
2 15 6	—	24 0 0	5 5 0	0 16 6	5 10 0	a 6 6 6		211
8 13 0	—	32 0 0	13 6 0	6 10 0	20 0 0	b 26 10 0		212
2 9 11	—	20 0 0	10 12 0	4 4 0	23 0 0	b 27 4 0		213
1 8 8	—	38 10 0	24 17 0	5 10 0	—	5 10 0		214
—	—	—	4 8 0	1 18 0	—	1 18 0		
3 10 0	—	27 0 0	10 2 0	4 17 8	3 3 0	8 0 8		215
1 0 4	—	30 0 0	3 13 6	2 4 11	—	2 4 11		216
7 14 8	1 0 0	84 0 0	15 2 6	6 0 6	16 10 0	22 10 6		217
1 12 9	—	24 0 0	5 0 0	5 0 0	6 0 0	11 0 0		218
3 11 6	4 0 0	24 10 0	16 3 8	0 12 6	—	0 12 6		219
3 4 9	—	20 0 0	9 8 6	5 0 0	—	5 0 0		220
1 6 11	—	84 18 4	18 8 0	4 11 6	19 0 0	a 23 11 6		221
2 14 5	—	87 10 8	22 14 6	8 11 2	21 0 0	a 29 11 2		222
3 8 1	—	20 0 0	6 16 0	3 14 0	4 0 0	7 14 0		223
6 4 8	—	29 18 4	21 15 0	30 7 0	10 0 0	40 7 0		224
1 10 8	—	40 16 8	17 11 6	17 1 6	13 10 0	b 30 11 6		225
22 10 0	—	116 6 8	62 0 9	58 2 0	10 0 0	68 2 0		226
8 14 9	—	20 5 0	10 9 6	15 7 4	20 0 0	35 7 4		227
—	—	—	17 10 8	21 6 0	—	21 6 0		
6 7 3	—	61 6 8	44 6 0	27 7 2	20 0 0	47 7 2		228
1 18 6	—	50 0 0	3 14 0	8 8 5	10 0 0	18 8 5	V.T.	229
4 0 7	—	81 0 0	12 8 6	9 0 0	20 0 0	a 29 0 0		230
7 2 5	—	87 10 0	22 18 5	10 7 9	10 0 0	20 7 9		231
57 18 1	2 0 0	—					V.C.	232
15 8 9	1 10 0	849 7 8	162 14 6	230 19 4	—	230 19 4	V.C.	233
—	—	—					V.C.	234
8 6 8	—	26 0 0	17 1 8	18 18 0	10 0 0	28 18 0		235
4 8 5	—	24 0 0	4 19 6	4 11 11	17 0 0	b 21 11 11		236
2 19 4	—	23 13 4	15 11 0	7 1 11	12 0 0	19 1 11		237

a Including value of Free Garden.

b No Results Examination.

List of Schools in operation on the 31st December, 1874.—

Number.	Roll Number of School.	Parish.	District.	School.		Religious Denomination of Manager or Correspondent: Clerical.	Lay.	Number and Religious Denominations of Teachers: Principals.	Assistants.	Attendance for the Year. Total number of Pupils on Rolls within the Year 1874: Males.	Fem.	Total.	Average Daily Attendance for Year 1874.
238	6607	Templemore,	8	Strand-road,	day.	Pres.	–	Pres.	Pres.	128	60	188	88
				Do.	evg.	–	–	Pres.	–	61	–	61	39
239	11077	Do.	–	Rasnagonnell,		Pres.	–	Pres.	–	64	66	130	46
240	6711	Do.	–	Ballinagarry,		–	R.C.	Pres.	–	54	46	100	28
241	10838	Tamlaght,	18	Tamlaght,		R.C.	–	R.C.	Pres.	91	84	175	84
				Do.	evg.	–	–	–	–	72	44	116	83
242	1146	Tamlaght Finlagan,	8	Ballymarig,		Pres.	–	Pres.	–	62	56	118	58
243	1166	Do.	–	Carrymena,		R.C.	–	R.C.	–	47	48	95	31
244	8826	Do.	–	Drumore,		Pres.	–	R.C.	–	66	52	118	43
245	7909	Do.	–	Myroe,	m.	Pres.	–	Pres.	–	68	–	68	34
246	7908	Do.	–	Do.	f.	Pres.	–	Pres.	–	–	84	84	30
247	6790	Do.	–	Largy,		–	R.C.	Pres.	Pres.	85	67	152	54
248	6031	Do.	–	Tartnakelly,		R.C.	–	R.C.	–	47	45	92	34
249	10915	Do.	–	Ballykelly,	m.	–	R.C.	R.C.	–	64	–	64	44
250	10916	Do.	–	Do.	f.	–	R.C.	R.C.	–	–	88	88	37
251	1572	Tamlaght O'Crilly,	7	Glenone,	m.	R.C.	–	R.C.	–	86	–	86	34
252	1457	Do.	–	Do.	f.	R.C.	–	R.C.	–	–	86	86	35
253	1801	Do.	–	Greenlough,	day.	R.C.	–	R.C.	–	90	66	156	39
				Do.	evg.	R.C.	–	R.C.	–	37	30	67	15
254	2762	Do.	–	Drumagarner,		R.C.	–	R.C.	R.C.	119	95	214	61
255	2686	Do.	–	Ranaghan,		Pres.	–	Pres.	–	65	52	97	37
256	4326	Do.	–	Tyanee, West,		Pres.	–	Pres.	–	65	34	99	39
257	5715	Do.	–	Tamlaght O'Crilly,		–	R.C.	R.C.	R.C.	120	115	235	73
258	7877	Do.	–	Bovedy,		Pres.	–	Pres.	–	30	48	64	30
259	8654	Do.	–	Lisnacoyle,	m.	–	R.C.	Pres.	–	70	–	70	31
260	9158	Do.	–	Do.	f.	–	R.C.	Pres.	–	–	73	73	29
261	8806	Do.	–	Eden,		R.C.	–	R.C.	–	56	71	127	51
262	8611	Do.	–	Harvy Hill,		R.C.	–	R.C.	–	56	57	113	51
		Total for County Londonderry, 262,								10281	1804[illegible]	28,017	1[illegible]

COUNTY OF

Number.	Roll Number of School.	Parish.	District.	School.		Clerical.	Lay.	Principals.	Assistants.	Males.	Fem.	Total.	Average Daily Attendance.
1	326	Aghnamullen,	24	Raw,	m.	–	R.C.	R.C.	–	71	–	71	29
2	6057	Do.	–	Do.	f.	–	R.C.	R.C.	–	–	63	63	24
3	1752	Do.	–	Lisinisky,		R.C.	–	R.C.	–	70	25	95	31
4	3474	Do.	–	Aghnakerry,		R.C.	–	R.C.	R.C.	164	108	272	84
5	6578	Do.	–	Crieve,		–	R.C.	R.C.	–	78	69	147	65
6	8877	Do.	–	Lisdrumcleve,		R.C.	–	R.C.	R.C.	111	133	244	77
7	6317	Do.	–	Lavagh,		R.C.	–	R.C.	R.C.	105	82	187	62
8	6541	Do.	–	Carrickmaclim,	m.	–	R.C.	R.C.	–	74	–	74	25
9	6545	Do.	–	Do.	f.	–	R.C.	R.C.	–	–	90	65	24
10	6251	Do.	–	Aughnamullen,		R.C.	–	R.C.	–	43	67	110	50
11	8594	Do.	–	Ullinagh, *		–	–	–	–	–	–	–	–
12	9468	Do.	–	Shanntonagh,		–	R.C.	R.C.	–	13	21	34	18
13	6732	Do.	17	Mullanagore,		R.C.	–	R.C.	–	35	31	66	29
14	10676	Do.	24	Drumafreeha,		R.C.	–	R.C.	R.C.	91	73	164	56
15	1911	Do.	–	Derrygorthey,		–	R.C.	R.C.	–	101	73	174	54
16	9074	Do.	–	Annahale,		R.C.	–	R.C.	R.C.	165	109	274	70
17	10116	Do.	–	Corlatt,		R.C.	–	R.C.	R.C.	140	111	251	63
18	331	Aghabog,	16	Latnamard,		R.C.	–	R.C.	R.C.	71	68	139	50
19	1315	Do.	–	Drumgarley,		R.C.	–	R.C.	–	71	53	124	37
20	1192	Do.	–	Drumcon,		R.C.	–	R.C.	R.C.	114	83	197	77
21	6629	Do.	–	Tattenaheive,		R.C.	–	R.C.	–	61	50	117	46
22	10849	Do.	–	Claraclough,		Pres.	–	R.C.	–	54	55	109	44
23	7526	Do.	–	Creenagh,		R.C.	–	R.C.	R.C.	75	68	143	56
24	11041	Do.	–	Mullagreenan,		Pres.	–	Pres.	–	41	44	85	32
25	8186	Ballybay,	–	Ballydian,		Pres.	–	Pres.	–	63	41	91	30
26	6378	Do.	–	Derryvalley,		Pres.	–	Pres.	Pres.	75	78	153	6[illegible]

a Including value of Free Residence.

b Including value of Free Residence and Garden.

Province of ULSTER: County of LONDONDERRY—*continued.*

Amount paid for Books, Requisites, and Apparatus at Reduced Prices.	Aid granted by the Board during the Year 1874. In Free Stock of Books, Requisites, and Apparatus.	In Salaries, Premiums, and other Gratuities.	Results Fees, Financial Year.	Amount of Local Emoluments received in Aid of Teacher's Salary. School Fees.	Subscriptions, Endowments, &c.	Total Local Aid.	Vested or Non-Vested.	Number.
£ s. d.	£ s. d.	£ s. d.	£ s. d.	£ s. d.	£ s. d.	£ s. d.		
5 1 6	—	61 13 4	37 10 6	24 19 7	10 0 0	34 19 7		233
—	—	—	9 16 0	12 7 6	—	12 7 0		
0 8 4	4 0 0	17 13 0	8 6 0	6 4 9	15 0 0	21 4 9		239
1 11 8	—	30 0 0	8 4 6	—	15 0 0	15 0 0		240
11 11 6	—	58 17 8	{ 28 14 8	3 4 8	—	3 4 8		241
			20 17 6	1 16 6	—	1 16 6		
2 9 8	—	24 5 8	—	4 2 4	—	4 2 4	V.T.	242
1 19 8	—	24 0 0	6 10 6	2 16 0	7 10 0	a10 6 0		243
3 5 6	—	24 6 8	6 19 6	5 15 11	—	5 15 11		244
—	—	22 0 0	14 15 0	5 19 6	6 0 0	11 19 6		245
2 7 8	—	24 0 0	11 9 0	8 6 6	6 0 0	11 6 6		246
6 15 6	—	34 19 8	28 7 0	16 17 9	9 2 8	b20 0 0		247
2 0 11	—	29 18 0	11 16 0	1 6 6	—	1 6 0		248
16 8 0	—	—	21 9 6	1 0 0	61 0 0	b62 0 0		249
—	—	—	16 14 6	5 5 0	53 0 0	b58 5 9		250
1 15 10	—	25 2 6	2 18 6	1 1 0	—	1 1 0	F.T.	251
2 4 10	—	31 10 0	6 17 0	1 16 8	—	1 16 8		252
1 8 0	—	30 0 0	4 19 6	1 5 0	—	1 5 8		253
—	—	—	0 12 6	0 2 0	—	0 2 0		
8 2 11	—	60 10 0	13 10 6	8 8 6	—	8 8 6	V.T.	254
1 13 7	—	21 0 0	10 11 0	5 11 6	—	5 11 6		255
1 18 8	—	18 0 0	10 13 0	6 10 0	0 10 0	7 0 0		256
10 6 0	—	68 5 8	27 16 8	12 0 6	10 0 0	a22 0 6		257
1 11 4	—	20 0 0	6 6 0	0 14 0	1 0 0	1 14 0		258
1 6 0	—	32 0 0	10 7 6	3 0 0	26 0 0	b29 0 0		259
2 1 11	—	28 0 0	8 16 0	1 5 0	15 0 0	16 5 0		260
1 5 6	—	24 0 0	16 11 6	4 10 0	3 0 0	7 10 0		261
1 16 1	—	30 0 0	12 13 0	3 4 6	4 0 0	7 4 6		262
253 8 5	68 10 0	9,262 4 11	3,083 1 5	1,230 17 5	2,109 8 5	3,339 5 8		

MONAGHAN—174 Schools.

2 0 6	—	24 0 0	9 3 0	2 7 0	6 0 0	8 7 0		1
4 10 5	—	22 6 0	10 5 0	1 6 0	—	1 6 0		2
—	—	24 0 0	4 3 8	0 8 0	—	0 8 0		3
8 15 5	—	40 16 8	28 6 0	12 4 11	—	12 4 11		4
5 9 6	—	42 10 0	31 2 6	8 0 0	10 0 0	18 0 0		5
4 14 6	—	54 10 0	23 16 0	2 7 0	—	2 7 0		6
5 12 6	—	50 8 4	19 0 6	10 0 0	—	10 0 0		7
1 8 9	—	24 0 0	4 8 0	—	—	—		8
1 9 6	—	30 0 0	6 7 8	—	—	—		9
1 13 4	—	65 2 4	9 15 6	2 16 7	3 18 5	b6 10 0		10
—	—	—	—	—	—	—		11
—	—	14 0 0	5 18 6	2 8 0	25 0 0	b27 8 0		12
1 0 5	—	24 0 0	7 16 6	2 9 0	16 0 0	a18 9 0		13
6 18 9	—	37 18 4	17 18 0	7 5 0	—	7 5 0		14
3 5 6	—	51 10 0	22 6 8	5 11 0	—	5 11 0		15
6 0 2	—	48 3 4	13 9 0	6 15 4	—	6 15 4		16
2 10 6	—	41 0 0	15 5 6	0 19 0	—	0 19 0	V.T.	17
5 11 1	—	51 10 0	30 17 0	1 5 0	—	1 5 0		18
—	—	24 0 0	9 10 6	8 3 10	—	8 3 10		19
7 10 6	—	53 8 4	31 17 6	7 17 10	—	7 17 10	V.T.	20
1 6 0	—	30 3 0	6 3 10	0 18 1	—	0 18 1		21
1 7 8	—	30 0 0	6 16 4	2 16 0	2 0 0	4 16 0		22
2 18 6	—	61 0 0	22 6 0	4 18 6	—	4 18 6		23
2 8 4	4 10 0	38 16 4	14 13 0	5 10 0	—	5 10 0		24
1 6 8	—	27 10 0	5 14 8	0 10 0	0 10 0	a1 0 0		25
8 0 10	—	68 0 0	11 19 0	4 13 0	—	4 13 0		26

a Inoperative.

b Including value of Free Garden.

List of Schools in operation on the 31st December, 1874.—

Number.	Roll Number of School.	Parish.	District.	School.	Religious Denomination of Manager or Correspondent.		Number and Religious Denomination of Teachers.		Attendance for the Year.			
									Total number of Pupils on the Rolls within the Year 1874.			Average Daily Attendance.
					Clerical.	Lay.	Principals.	Assistants.	Males.	Fem.	Total.	
27	4467	Ballybay,	15	Clogher,	Pres.	–	Pres.	–	63	48	111	45
28	5004	Do.	–	Ballybay, m.	R.C.	–	R.C.	R.C.	188	–	188	97
29	7001	Do.	–	Do. f.	R.C.	–	R.C.	R.C.	–	184	184	47
30	9931	Do.	–	Do. No. 2,	R.C.	–	Pres.	2R.C.	146	69	215	115
31	8501	Do.	–	Shane,	R.C.	–	R.C.	R.C.	124	121	245	81
32	331	Clones,	–	Aghnashalvy,	R.C.	–	R.C.	R.C.	101	77	178	71
33	1499	Do.	–	Lemgy, m.	R.C.	–	R.C.	R.C.	244	–	244	86
34	[illegible]	Do.	–	Do. f.	R.C.	–	R.C.	R.C.	–	158	158	84
35	[illegible]	Do.	–	Stonebridge,	Pres.	–	R.C.	–	37	29	66	33
36	8687	Do.	–	Killeevan,	–	Pres.	R.C.	–	75	65	140	42
37	3791	Do.	–	Glear,	R.C.	R.C.	R.C.	–	68	66	134	80
38	[illegible]	Do.	–	Clones, f.	R.C.	–	R.C.	–	34	82	116	49
39	[illegible]	Do.	–	Do. Parish,	R.C.	–	R.C.	2R.C.	168	51	219	73
40	[illegible]	Do.	–	Do. Workhouse,[a]	–	–	–	–	–	–	–	–
41	8447	Do.	–	Garrasmuinny,	R.C.	–	R.C.	–	47	23	70	30
42	9817	Do.	–	Granshaw,	R.C.	–	R.C.	–	53	36	89	38
43	9164	Do.	–	Magheraveney,	R.C.	–	R.C.	R.C.	88	79	167	77
44	10101	Do.	–	Scotshouse,	Pres.	–	R.C.	–	55	24	79	31
45	27	Currin,	22	Killyfargy,	R.C.	–	R.C.	R.C.	103	113	216	89
46	1362	Do.	–	Laurel-hill, m.	R.C.	–	R.C.	–	68	–	68	27
47	1821	Do.	–	Do. f.	R.C.	–	R.C.	–	–	70	70	32
48	2100	Do.	–	Clonrich,	R.C.	–	R.C.	–	86	92	178	68
49	6155	Do.	–	Kevenaghoge,	Pres.	–	Pres.	–	44	32	76	34
50	7149	Do.	–	Drum,	Pres.	–	Pres.	–	113	71	184	60
51	[illegible]	Do.	–	Do. f.	R.C.	–	R.C.	–	36	41	77	32
52	11614	Do.	–	Largysaboy,	R.C.	–	R.C.	–	37	41	78	36
53	336	Clontibret,	16	Mullanacross,	Pres.	–	Pres.	Pres.	93	123	216	68
54	[illegible]	Do.	–	Annyalla, m.	R.C.	–	R.C.	R.C.	168	–	168	97
55	3297	Do.	–	Do. f.	R.C.	–	R.C.	R.C.	–	138	138	59
56	[illegible]	Do.	–	Creeve,	–	R.C.	Pres.	–	93	67	160	79
57	4811	Do.	–	Lisnagrieve,	–	Pres.	R.C.	R.C.	63	80	[illegible]	55
58	8117	Do.	–	Dunlamalet, m.	R.C.	–	R.C.	R.C.	137	177	246	74
59	[illegible]	Do.	–	Mayo,	R.C.	–	R.C.	–	137	111	248	76
60	[illegible]	Do.	–	Killeenly,	R.C.	–	R.C.	R.C.	116	85	201	67
61	8162	Do.	–	Lattinagh, m.	R.C.	–	R.C.	–	110	–	110	45
62	[illegible]	Do.	–	Do. f.	R.C.	–	R.C.	–	–	128	128	50
63	8764	Do.	–	Lemgare,	R.C.	–	R.C.	R.C.	76	81	157	66
64	[illegible]	Do.	–	Drumsnick,	R.C.	–	R.C.	R.C.	114	78	192	75
65	10731	Do.	–	Clontibret,	R.C.	–	R.C.	Pres.	68	61	129	67
66	315	Donagh,	–	Ballanagay,	R.C.	–	R.C.	–	63	24	87	30
67	2119	Do.	–	Corraerin,	R.C.	–	R.C.	2R.C.	125	163	288	79
68	2213	Do.	–	Clonraw,	R.C.	–	R.C.	R.C.	66	65	131	59
69	[illegible]	Do.	–	Knockmagraws,	R.C.	–	R.C.	–	65	46	119	38
70	[illegible]	Do.	–	Tyrnamull,	Pres.	–	Pres.	–	40	22	61	25
71	[illegible]	Do.	–	Killyvane,	R.C.	–	R.C.	R.C.	59	78	137	45
72	4807	Do.	–	Edenmore,	R.C.	–	R.C.	R.C.	60	59	124	66
73	[illegible]	Do.	–	Glaslough, No. 2,	Pres.	–	Pres.	–	51	33	84	31
74	[illegible]	Do.	–	Stille,	R.C.	–	R.C.	–	40	64	104	34
75	6073	Donaghmoyne,	24	Donaghmoyne,	R.C.	–	R.C.	R.C.	146	102	248	68
76	[illegible]	Do.	–	Lisdoonan,	R.C.	–	R.C.	–	152	97	246	85
77	8113	Do.	–	Drumkeeny,	–	R.C.	R.C.	R.C.	173	132	304	89
78	[illegible]	Do.	–	Aghadreenan,	–	R.C.	R.C.	–	91	110	201	70
79	[illegible]	Do.	–	Bath Ins Class Ag.[a]	–	–	–	–	–	–	–	–
80	4116	Do.	–	Broomfield Gr. Ag.	–	R.C.	R.C.	R.C.	90	73	163	62
81	5180	Do.	–	Ashburton Gr. Ag.	–	R.C.	R.C.	–	132	99	231	78
82	[illegible]	Drummully,	22	Rocks,	–	R.C.	Pres.	–	64	57	121	35
83	10160	Drumsnat,	17	Drumsnat, m.	R.C.	–	R.C.	–	61	–	61	30
84	[illegible]	Do.	–	Do. f.	R.C.	–	R.C.	–	–	69	64	26
85	[illegible]	Do.	–	Corlanore,	R.C.	–	R.C.	–	68	63	131	35
86	373	Errigal,	–	Derrywoy,	R.C.	–	R.C.	2R.C.	137	118	256	83
87	1182	Do.	–	Killybrone,	R.C.	–	R.C.	–	71	80	151	47
88	3319	Do.	–	Knockconan,	R.C.	–	R.C.	2R.C.	103	119	222	74
89	10748	Do.	–	Aghamacklin,	R.C.	–	R.C.	R.C.	78	67	145	61

a No Return. b Including value of Free Garden. c Including value of Free Residence.

Province of Ulster: County of Monaghan—*continued.*

Amount paid for Books, Requisites, and Apparatus at Reduced Prices.	Aid granted by the Board during the Year 1873. In Free Stock of Books, Requisites, and Apparatus.	In Salaries, Premiums, and other Gratuities.	Results Fees, Financial Year.	Amount of Local Emoluments received in Aid of Teacher's Salary. School Fees.	Subscriptions, Endowments, &c.	Total Local Aid.	Vested or Non-Vested.	Number.
£ s. d.	£ s. d.	£ s. d.	£ s. d.	£ s. d.	£ s. d.	£ s. d.		
9 0 0	—	21 0 0	10 18 6	4 18 0	—	4 18 0		27
1 17 9	—	70 11 6	7 3 6	6 5 7	—	6 5 7		28
8 15 8	—	54 7 9	13 10 0	9 0 10	—	9 0 10		29
16 9 10	—	67 8 4	44 3 6	24 17 0	20 0 0	44 17 0		30
8 18 0	—	62 0 0	27 14 0	11 6 9	—	11 6 9		31
7 10 8	—	66 3 4	36 0 6	5 4 0	—	5 4 0		32
6 10 10	—	50 8 4	20 0 0	0 13 4	—	0 13 4		33
1 18 7	—	33 0 6	16 11 6	4 15 4	—	4 15 4		34
0 15 8	—	17 0 0	4 11 6	3 1 6	—	3 1 6		35
3 10 0	—	78 0 0	18 12 0	6 7 6	—	6 7 6		36
3 15 5	—	19 8 11	6 3 6	1 0 0	—	1 0 0		37
3 11 0	—	20 0 0	12 5 6	10 4 1	—	10 4 1		38
7 1 6	—	80 0 0	25 0 0	30 0 0	—	30 0 0		39
—	—	—	—	—	—	—		40
2 18 1	3 18 0	16 0 0	6 7 0	—	—	—		41
1 16 10	—	20 0 0	6 18 0	0 4 0	—	0 4 0	V.T.	42
7 1 6	—	51 3 4	28 18 0	8 17 6	2 0 0	b 10 17 6	V.T.	43
1 18 11	—	24 0 0	7 2 0	1 10 0	—	1 10 0		44
0 11 7	—	78 8 4	30 7 0	14 14 9	3 10 0	17 4 9	V.T.	45
2 10 0	—	27 0 0	0 12 0	3 10 11	—	3 15 11	V.T.	46
1 10 6	—	30 0 0	7 10 3	4 11 10	—	4 11 10	V.T.	47
—	—	63 15 0	23 11 6	4 3 6	—	4 3 6		48
1 5 3	—	31 0 0	6 1 4	2 0 0	2 10 0	4 10 0		49
10 16 9	—	43 6 8	23 9 8	10 10 6	1 13 0	11 11 6		50
2 8 0	4 10 0	15 0 0	6 5 6	2 4 0	2 5 0	4 9 0		51
4 8 1	—	20 0 0	10 8 6	3 0 0	2 0 0	5 0 0		52
4 16 7	—	42 0 6	23 18 0	0 3 7	—	0 3 7		53
4 14 0	—	65 0 0	70 4 11	10 2 6	1 0 0	a 11 2 6		54
1 14 8	—	40 0 0	15 9 0	3 8 0	3 10 0	6 18 0		55
0 17 6	—	31 0 0	31 13 0	13 1 6	12 0 0	a 25 1 6		56
1 13 4	—	41 0 0	11 15 6	3 10 0	—	3 10 0	V.A.	57
4 17 4	—	56 0 0	25 11 0	0 10 10	—	0 10 10		58
12 9 0	—	23 0 0	30 1 0	6 13 6	—	6 13 0		59
0 8 2	—	40 18 4	17 19 5	10 17 5	—	10 17 5	V.T.	60
1 17 4	—	24 0 0	0 14 0	3 11 0	—	3 11 0		61
3 11 9	—	30 16 6	16 6 6	5 14 6	—	5 11 0		62
3 11 3	—	67 16 6	15 18 8	3 0 0	—	3 0 0		63
4 5 10	—	59 0 0	29 8 0	4 3 0	—	4 3 0		64
—	—	44 0 0	24 0 0	16 7 10	14 18 0	a 31 17 10		65
2 5 8	—	30 0 0	11 16 0	4 9 1	—	4 9 1		66
10 0 11	—	111 10 0	30 11 1	6 7 10	—	6 7 10		67
7 5 3	—	38 2 0	19 10 6	7 0 0	—	7 0 0		68
1 15 6	—	24 0 0	18 18 0	1 7 0	—	1 7 0	V.T.	69
1 8 9	—	24 0 0	6 5 0	2 5 6	1 10 0	b 3 15 6		70
2 8 6	—	34 0 0	12 6 9	0 16 6	—	0 16 6	V.T.	71
4 4 0	—	47 10 0	21 10 6	3 7 6	—	3 7 6		72
1 5 0	—	24 13 6	7 10 0	3 18 6	0 5 0	b 4 3 6		73
6 3 1	—	30 0 0	8 7 6	3 19 4	20 0 0	a 23 19 4		74
5 3 8	—	44 0 0	20 8 6	6 1 6	—	6 1 6		75
4 0 5	—	44 10 0	22 18 10	6 19 0	—	6 19 0		76
10 3 11	—	110 8 4	37 0 0	10 0 0	14 0 0	b 24 0 0	V.C.	77
5 1 6	—	61 10 0	30 15 0	18 6 0	4 0 0	22 6 0	V.A.	78
—	0 1 0	41 17 9	—	—	—	—	V.A.	79
5 17 5	—	30 0 0	17 1 6	6 13 9	4 0 0	b 10 13 9	V.A.	80
8 9 10	—	67 0 0	29 9 0	7 8 6	12 0 0	b 19 8 6	V.A.	81
10 3 4	—	20 0 0	8 18 6	6 0 0	13 0 0	a 19 0 0		82
2 19 7	—	86 18 4	6 17 0	0 15 2	1 7 6	b 2 2 8	V.T.	83
—	—	20 0 0	0 8 1	1 5 0	—	1 5 0	V.T.	84
9 14 6	—	35 10 0	21 10 6	3 15 6	—	3 15 6		85
5 8 1	—	78 10 0	44 18 0	2 12 6	—	2 12 6	V.T.	86
8 7 4	3 2 2	48 0 0	21 0 6	1 5 0	—	1 5 0	V.T.	87
10 7 0	—	71 0 0	40 0 0	0 10 0	—	0 10 0		88
8 8 1	—	80 18 4	20 7 6	0 9 1	—	0 9 1		89

b Including value of Free Residence and Garden.

a Inoperative.

List of Schools in operation on the 31st December, 1874.—

Number.	Roll Number of School.	Parish.	District.	School.	Religious Denomination of Manager or Correspondent. Clerical.	Lay.	Teacher and Religious Denomination of Teachers. Principals.	Assistants.	Attendance for the Year. Total number of Pupils on Rolls within the Year 1874. Males.	Females.	Total.	Average Daily Attendance for the Year 1874.
90	2827	Ematris,	18	Dartrey,	R.C.	R.C.	Pres.	Pres.	54	54	108	31
91	10482	Do.	–	Corravacan, m.	R.C.	–	R.C.	–	103	–	103	31
92	10483	Do.	–	Do. f.	R.C.	–	R.C.	–	–	101	101	34
93	4290	Do.	–	Tattygare,	R.C.	–	R.C.	–	43	33	76	30
94	7703	Do.	–	Unshinagh,	–	R.C.	Pres.	–	49	31	80	27
95	10[illegible]	Do.	–	Rockcorry,	R.C.	R.C.	R.C.	R.C.	90	78	168	81
96	10173	Do.	–	Drumgole,	Pres.	–	R.C.	–	17	33	50	23
97	11103	Do.	–	Kilmore,	R.C.	–	R.C.	–	37	33	70	30
98	6181	Inishkeen,	24	Inishkeen,	R.C.	–	R.C.	–	118	151	269	98
99	3108	Do.	–	[illegible],	–	R.C.	R.C.	–	61	48	113	25
100	11107	Do.	–	Magrany,	R.C.	–	R.C.	–	112	90	201	57
101	6302	Do.	–	Blackstaff,[a]	–	–	–	–	–	–	–	–
102	346	Kilmore,	18	Threemilehouse,	R.C.	–	R.C.	R.C.	98	71	169	68
103	10451	Do.	–	Tappa,	R.C.	–	R.C.	R.C.	88	82	170	68
104	330	Do.	–	Corraghan, m.	R.C.	–	R.C.	–	123	–	123	68
105	3975	Do.	–	Do. f.	R.C.	–	R.C.	–	–	111	111	67
106	5736	Do.	–	Graham,	Pres.	–	Pres.	–	55	51	106	37
107	6601	Killany,	24	Ballymackney,	–	R.C.	R.C.	–	75	62	137	60
108	331	Killeevan,	16	Killeevan,	R.C.	–	R.C.	–	73	65	137	52
109	6326	Do.	–	Tom,	R.C.	–	R.C.	–	89	64	153	60
110	6832	Do.	–	Drumhillagh,	Pres.	–	Pres.	–	48	35	83	34
111	1611	Do.	–	Killycrummy,	–	Pres.	Pres.	Pres.	66	53	119	41
112	6274	Do.	–	Newbliss,	–	R.C.	Pres.	R.C.	64	65	129	67
113	10[illegible]	Do.	–	[illegible]park,	R.C.	–	R.C.	R.C.	104	78	182	61
114	2273	Lisletrim,	–	Lisletrim,	R.C.	–	R.C.	–	62	38	100	39
115	5708	Monaghan,	–	Coolshannagh,	–	R.C.	Pres.	Pres.	80	62	142	61
116	6931	Do.	–	Cornaveagh,	–	R.C.	Pres.	–	48	30	78	34
117	7458	Do.	–	Agnaclogh,	R.C.	–	R.C.	R.C.	67	77	144	65
118	7363	Do.	–	Rakeeragh,	R.C.	–	R.C.	R.C.	81	61	142	61
119	6308	Do.	–	Legnacrase,	Pres.	–	Pres.	–	33	30	63	25
120	3731	Do.	–	Monaghan Minor Model, m.	Com.	N.M.	R.C.	R.C.	140	–	140	78
121	7752	Do.	–	Do. f.	Com.	N.M.	Pres.	R.C.	–	104	104	78
122	2533	Do.	–	Do. i.	Com.	N.M.	R.C.	–	57	60	117	65
123	330	Do.	–	Do. Conv. f.	R.C.	–	Nuns	–	88	341	[illegible]	153
124	2949	Do.	–	Do. Workhse.	P.L.	Gds.	[b] Pres.	–	33	30	63	30
125	[illegible]	Do.	–	Drumsnatton,	–	R.C.	Pres.	–	25	22	47	33
126	11011	Do.	–	[illegible],	–	R.C.	Pres.	–	38	24	62	19
127	352	Muckno,	–	Tullyvahattina,	–	Pres.	Pres.	–	43	38	81	33
128	3422	Do.	–	Carrickaslane,	–	Pres.	Pres.	–	47	37	84	30
129	1816	Do.	–	Tullyvaleen,	R.C.	–	R.C.	R.C.	68	64	132	42
130	4242	Do.	–	Castleblayney, m.	R.C.	–	R.C.	R.C.	143	–	143	80
131	6216	Do.	–	Do. f.	R.C.	–	R.C.	R.C.	–	148	148	68
132	10237	Do.	–	Do. inf.	R.C.	–	R.C.	R.C.	56	60	116	58
133	10513	Do.	–	Do. No. 2,	–	R.C.	R.C.	R.C.	74	80	154	60
134	[illegible]	Do.	–	Do. Workhouse,	P.L.	Gds.	R.C.	–	43	27	70	37
135	[illegible]	Do.	–	Drumcoose,	R.C.	–	R.C.	R.C.	60	73	134	50
136	[illegible]	Do.	–	Drumskill,	Pres.	–	Pres.	–	35	50	85	33
137	6416	Do.	–	Oram,	R.C.	–	R.C.	R.C.	159	140	299	94
138	9120	Do.	–	M'Kelvey's Grove,	Pres.	–	Pres.	Pres.	95	106	201	57
139	10073	Do.	–	Annaghbane,	R.C.	–	R.C.	R.C.	87	102	189	53
140	346	Magheross,	24	Carrickmacross, m.	R.C.	–	R.C.	R.C.	175	–	175	75
141	347	Do.	–	Do. f.	R.C.	–	R.C.	–	–	140	140	68
142	10[illegible]	Do.	–	Magheross,	R.C.	–	R.C.	R.C.	84	74	158	49
143	5617	Do.	–	Do. Industrial,	–	R.C.	[b] R.C.	–	–	101	101	44
144	8046	Do.	–	Do. Workhse.	P.L.	Gds.	R.C.	–	20	27	47	31
145	[illegible]	Do.	–	Coolfore,	–	R.C.	R.C.	R.C.	181	107	288	109
146	9167	Do.	–	Corlaff, m.	R.C.	–	R.C.	–	134	–	134	44
147	9168	Do.	–	Do. f.	R.C.	–	R.C.	R.C.	–	161	161	50
148	10706	Do.	–	Carnally,	R.C.	–	R.C.	–	41	31	72	30
149	9015	Do.	–	Greaty,	–	R.C.	R.C.	R.C.	113	91	204	56
150	10720	Do.	–	Carrickamaddle,	R.C.	–	R.C.	R.C.	72	75	147	61
151	9659	Do.	–	Corcreaghagh,	R.C.	–	R.C.	–	77	68	145	50

[a] Including value of Free Residence. [b] Including value of Free Residence and Garden.

Province of Ulster: County of Monaghan—*continued.*

Amount paid for Books, Requisites, and Apparatus at Reduced Prices.	Aid granted by the Board during the Year 1874. For Purchase of Books, Requisites, and Apparatus.	In Salaries, Premiums, and other Gratuities.	Results Fees, Remunerative Fees.	Amount of Local Endowments received in Aid of Teacher's Salary. School Fees.	Subscriptions, Endowments, &c.	Total Local Aid.	Vested or Non-Vested.	Number.
£ s. d.	£ s. d.	£ s. d.	£ s. d.	£ s. d.	£ s. d.	£ s. d.		
5 5 0	—	69 0 0	25 14 8	7 10 5	20 0 0	a 29 10 5		90
—	—	80 0 0	6 9 0	1 8 0	—	1 8 0	V.T.	91
3 18 4	—	89 8 4	13 11 8	1 5 0	—	1 5 0	V.T.	92
0 9 9	—	24 0 6	4 0 7	8 10 0	—	8 10 0		93
0 1 4	—	82 0 0	8 4 6	1 17 4	12 10 0	b 14 7 4		94
9 8 10	—	70 16 8	43 14 6	16 11 6	20 0 0	a 36 14 6		95
1 8 0	—	24 0 0	6 18 11	—	9 0 0	9 0 0		96
2 8 9	4 10 0	16 0 0	7 10 4	0 19 0	10 0 0	10 19 0		97
1 19 3	—	39 0 0	5 10 5	8 5 0	—	8 5 0		98
1 10 0	—	31 0 0	9 10 4	1 6 0	—	1 6 0	V.C.	99
8 6 11	6 10 0	20 0 0	14 17 6	6 8 1	—	6 8 1		100
—	—	—	—	—	—	—	V.N.	101
4 4 8	—	54 10 8	28 8 0	1 16 0	—	1 16 0		102
6 18 7	—	60 0 0	17 13 4	3 9 8	—	3 9 0	V.T.	103
4 11 8	—	24 8 0	8 8 6	1 8 8	—	1 8 8		104
8 11 9	—	30 13 7	—	8 0 0	8 0 0	4 0 0		105
2 5 2	—	30 0 0	0 17 0	3 0 6	10 0 0	b 13 6 6		106
9 1 9	—	67 0 0	18 4 6	6 15 10	10 4 0	a 16 19 10	V.C.	107
1 18 8	—	19 0 0	81 6 0	2 17 0	—	2 17 0		108
2 9 0	—	86 11 8	20 6 0	7 4 4	—	7 4 4		109
6 19 1	—	99 9 0	19 8 0	3 10 0	20 0 0	a 23 10 0		110
0 12 10	—	44 0 0	11 12 0	8 18 0	—	8 18 0		111
7 8 10	—	85 0 0	62 5 0	17 12 4	10 0 0	27 12 4		112
9 18 9	—	36 0 0	20 4 8	3 7 0	—	3 7 0	V.T.	113
1 5 8	—	95 16 0	15 6 0	4 9 8	—	4 9 8		114
6 16 8	—	65 0 0	23 18 0	10 11 4	24 4 0	a 34 15 4		115
—	—	37 0 0	8 7 6	1 9 0	19 0 0	a 14 9 6		116
3 11 1	—	51 10 0	25 7 0	4 0 0	—	4 0 0		117
8 19 2	—	80 0 0	13 19 0	8 0 0	—	8 0 0		118
1 5 8	—	24 8 0	7 8 0	1 13 0	—	1 13 0		119
—	—	480 6 4	114 10 8	100 5 4	—	100 5 4	V.C.	120
—	—						V.C.	121
—	—						V.C.	122
20 4 8	—	91 1 0	68 11 7	—	—	—		123
1 14 8	—	—	—	—	—	—		124
1 8 2	—	81 10 0	11 18 0	9 8 2	4 0 0	a 6 9 8		125
0 18 8	—	33 10 0	8 4 0	8 12 10	5 12 0	a 9 6 10		126
3 0 0	—	24 0 0	6 12 0	1 18 0	1 0 0	a 8 18 0		127
6 0 0	—	34 0 0	18 9 0	6 18 8	8 0 0	10 18 8		128
3 3 4	—	70 10 8	14 0 0	6 18 0	—	6 18 0		129
7 8 3	—	75 12 4	15 18 8	11 6 4	—	11 6 4		130
2 14 2	—	39 8 8	25 18 0	7 8 0	—	7 8 0		131
1 10 10	—	40 0 0	10 17 0	0 18 0	—	0 18 0		132
6 18 10	—	80 0 0	20 8 0	13 10 4	60 0 0	a 73 10 4		133
—	—	1 10 0	—	—	—	—		134
4 18 0	—	41 0 0	16 8 8	4 8 10	—	4 8 10		135
1 11 6	—	82 0 0	11 15 0	2 3 8	—	2 3 8		136
9 10 4	—	61 10 8	29 8 8	18 1 0	—	18 1 0		137
3 10 11	—	80 0 3	14 19 6	3 15 8	—	3 15 8		138
3 9 4	5 0 0	13 0 0	25 9 4	0 10 6	—	0 10 6	V.T.	139
7 8 1	—	73 16 4	24 0 8	7 10 11	—	7 10 11	V.T.	140
7 13 8	—	36 10 0	22 17 0	7 18 8	—	7 18 8	V.T.	141
11 13 8	—	65 10 0	15 4 8	7 4 8	60 0 0	b 67 4 8		142
—	—	80 0 0	8 15 8	—	—	—		143
—	—	—	—	—	—	—		144
8 1 7	—	65 0 0	68 15 6	8 9 10	14 0 0	b 22 9 10		145
1 8 10	—	20 0 0	9 6 0	4 8 0	—	4 8 0	V.T.B.	146
8 18 8	—	57 18 8	14 1 0	8 7 0	—	8 7 0	V.T.C.	147
0 8 1	—	84 13 0	8 8 6	8 6 0	32 10 0	b 41 16 0		148
3 12 4	—	36 10 0	18 8 0	0 15 0	16 10 0	b 16 5 0		149
3 5 6	—	41 13 0	17 2 0	8 0 0	12 19 0	b 20 19 0		150
0 12 5	—	24 0 0	3 7 0	—	—	—		151

a Inoperative.

b Including value of Farm Garden.

List of Schools in operation on the 31st December, 1874,—

Number.	Roll Number of School.	Parish.	District.	School.	Religious Denomination of Manager or Correspondent: Clerical.	Lay.	Number and Religious Denomination of Teachers: Principals.	Assistants.	Attendance for the Year. Total number of Pupils on Rolls within the Year 1874: Males.	Fem.	Total.	Average Daily Attendance.
152	4087	Magheracloone,	24	Corlderry,	–	R.C.	R.C.	–	104	80	184	55
153	9911	Do.	–	Mayhevna, m.	R.C.	–	R.C.	–	127	–	127	65
154	7019	Do.	–	Do. f.	R.C.	–	R.C.	–	–	130	130	80
155	8971	Do.	–	Ballymagrera,	–	R.C.	R.C.	R.C.	118	116	234	88
156	7412	Do.	–	Drumcanal,	R.C.	–	R.C.	–	73	98	171	50
157	10720	Do.	–	Lisnalta,	R.C.	–	R.C.	R.C.	84	99	184	73
158	272	Tedavnet,	18	Tedavnet,	R.C.	–	R.C.	R.C.	129	109	238	61
159	1220	Do.	–	Tullycorcan,	R.C.	–	R.C.	–	42	32	75	18
160	1716	Do.	–	Rackwallace,	R.C.	–	R.C.	R.C.	107	78	179	61
161	1877	Do.	–	Killycarran, [b]	–	–	–	–	–	–	–	–
162	8142	Do.	–	Ballyalbany,	Pres.	–	Pres.	–	41	33	74	26
163	12910	Do.	–	Urbleshanny,	R.C.	–	R.C.	R.C.	109	98	207	57
164	7599	Do.	–	Derrynashallog,	–	R.C.	R.C.	R.C.	104	110	214	81
165	870	Do.	–	Corwillis, 1st Class Agricultural,	–	R.C.	R.C.	–	80	98	178	45
166	10411	Do.	–	Tirnaneill, [a]	–	R.C.	–	–	–	–	–	–
167	10463	Do.	–	Bellanode,	R.C.	–	R.C.	–	53	40	93	28
168	1742	Tehallan,	–	Fedoo,	R.C.	–	R.C.	–	65	51	116	30
169	9168	Do.	–	Lappan, m.	R.C.	–	R.C.	–	118	–	118	43
170	2937	Do.	–	Do. f.	R.C.	–	R.C.	–	–	113	113	60
171	8458	Leitrim,	–	Leitrim,	R.C.	–	R.C.	–	87	65	152	44
172	2841	Tullycorbet,	–	Carrowy,	R.C.	–	R.C.	R.C.	121	106	227	67
173	8271	Do.	–	Braddocks,	Pres.	–	Pres.	R.C.	51	51	102	46
174	9915	Do.	–	Cornanure,	–	R.C.	R.C.	–	77	57	134	43
		Total for County Monaghan, 174,							12725	11606	24,331	8,449

COUNTY OF

Number.	Roll Number of School.	Parish.	District.	School.	Clerical.	Lay.	Principals.	Assistants.	Males.	Fem.	Total.	Average Daily Attendance.
1	10522	Altedesert,	15	Pomeroy, [b]	–	R.C.	–	–	–	–	–	–
2	7708	Ardstraw,	6	Newtown-Stewart Minor Model, m.	[illegible]	[illegible]	Pres.	R.C.	81	–	81	40
3	7706	Do.	–	Do. f.	[illegible]	[illegible]	R.C.	–	–	84	84	44
4	4734	Do.	–	Do. i.	[illegible]	[illegible]	R.C.	–	38	39	77	42
5	1567	Do.	14	N. T. Stewart, m.	R.C.	–	R.C.	–	105	–	105	41
6	8601	Do.	–	Do. f.	R.C.	–	R.C.	–	–	106	106	36
7	1317	Do.	–	Tullymuck,	–	R.C.	R.C.	–	69	62	131	41
8	8777	Do.	6	Tirenny, [c]	Pres.	–	–	–	–	–	–	–
9	3407	Do.	–	Killymore, [b]	Pres.	–	Pres.	–	–	–	–	15
10	6539	Do.	–	Douglas,	Pres.	–	Pres.	–	59	40	108	36
11	5810	Do.	–	Garvetagh,	Pres.	–	Pres.	–	58	48	106	34
12	5485	Do.	–	Lisnatunny,	R.C.	–	R.C.	–	34	58	92	37
13	5884	Do.	–	Crosh,	R.C.	–	R.C.	–	37	56	93	30
14	6886	Do.	–	Magheracolton,	R.C.	–	R.C.	–	70	48	157	32
15	6805	Do.	–	Ervey,	R.C.	–	R.C.	–	45	67	91	20
16	7161	Do.	–	Drumnabey,	–	Pres.	R.C.	R.C.	80	98	177	65
17	7408	Do.	–	Gallan,	R.C.	–	R.C.	–	53	73	126	31
18	7811	Do.	–	Drumlegagh,	Pres.	–	Pres.	–	41	48	89	46
19	7878	Do.	–	Magherakeerogue,	–	R.C.	Pres.	–	44	33	77	33
20	7834	Do.	–	Carnkenny,	–	Pres.	Pres.	Pres.	66	94	160	36
21	7902	Do.	–	Letterbin,	R.C.	–	R.C.	–	80	68	148	50
22	4447	Do.	–	Clare,	R.C.	–	Pres.	–	76	80	182	41
23	8379	Do.	–	Legfordrum,	R.C.	–	R.C.	–	54	23	77	21
24	9795	Do.	–	Scarvagh, [b]	–	R.C.	R.C.	R.C.	–	–	–	41
25	10168	Do.	–	Altdoghal,	Pres.	Pres.	R.C.	–	34	19	53	18
26	878	Aghaloo,	15	Sheskinshule,	Pres.	–	Pres.	–	49	86	84	20
				Do. [b] avg.	–	–	Pres.	–	–	–	–	–
27	8860	Do.	–	Rehaghy,	–	R.C.	Pres.	–	67	60	123	37
28	11192	Do.	–	Mullaghmore, [c]	–	–	–	–	–	–	–	–
29	7822	Do.	–	Minterburn,	–	Pres.	Pres.	Pres.	118	85	198	69

[a] Including value of Free Residence and Garden. [b] No Returns. [c] No Teacher.

Province of Ulster: County of Monaghan—*continued.*

Amount paid for Books, Requisites, and Apparatus of National Grants. £ s. d.	Aid granted by the Board during the Year 1874. To Free Stock of Books, Requisites, and Apparatus. £ s. d.	In Salaries, Premiums, and other Gratuities. £ s. d.	Results Fees, Financial Year. £ s. d.	Amounts of Local Emoluments received in Aid of Teacher's Salary. School Fees. £ s. d.	Subscriptions, Endowments, &c. £ s. d.	Total Local Aid. £ s. d.	Vested or Non-Vested.	Number.
—	—	50 10 0	17 8 0	8 17 0	2 0 0	4 17 0		152
8 4 4	—	53 0 0	7 18 0	6 6 0	1 0 0	6 6 8		153
1 10 8	—	20 0 0	8 8 0	1 10 3	1 0 0	2 10 3		154
4 1 10	—	28 0 0	16 10 0	1 13 6	13 0 0	* 14 13 0		155
2 12 3	—	17 1 1	—	5 16 3	—	5 16 3		156
5 14 7	—	8 0 0	10 14 0	3 6 3	10 0 0	* 18 6 3		157
3 10 1	—	68 0 0	17 17 0	0 15 0	—	0 15 0		158
—	—	24 16 0	2 8 6	—	—	—	V.T.	159
9 15 5	—	54 0 0	24 16 6	3 0 0	—	3 0 0	V.T.	160
1 14 6	—	48 16 7	—	—	—	—		161
1 8 0	—	47 10 0	5 8 0	8 18 6	—	8 13 6		162
11 5 2	—	50 4 5	29 8 6	3 5 0	—	3 5 0		163
5 7 0	—	44 10 0	23 5 8	4 8 0	8 0 0	* 15 8 0		164
1 18 7	—	87 18 8	8 18 0	—	20 0 0	20 0 0		165
0 16 8	—	23 0 0	—	—	—	—		166
8 8 8	—	35 18 0	8 14 0	1 1 6	—	1 1 3		167
0 14 6	—	81 0 0	0 12 6	1 11 8	—	1 11 8	V.T.	168
0 18 4	—	84 0 0	17 10 0	6 4 6	—	6 4 6	N.	169
8 18 9	—	45 0 0	18 2 6	5 9 0	—	5 9 0		170
1 16 10	—	84 0 0	15 14 8	3 10 0	—	0 10 0	V.T.	171
0 14 0	—	60 10 0	18 19 6	4 19 6	—	4 19 6		172
3 5 10	—	58 10 0	14 17 0	5 18 9	0 0 0	11 18 9		173
6 1 8	—	24 16 8	7 18 0	4 17 6	—	4 17 6		174
120 11 8	80 16 2	7,388 18 7	2,816 11 2	820 11 4	465 2 0	1,467 15 1		

TYRONE—301 Schools.

1 5 0	—	40 10 0	—	—	—	—		1
—	—	} 376 10 11	61 17 0	61 2 5	—	61 2 9	V.A. {	2
—	—							3
—	—							4
1 13 9	—	40 0 0	7 8 0	5 18 0	—	5 10 0	V.T.	5
1 8 1	—	20 0 0	10 6 0	4 14 9	—	4 14 9	V.L.	6
3 16 9	—	24 8 0	14 10 6	4 8 0	—	4 0 6	A.	7
—	—	18 0 0	—	—	—	—		8
0 10 4	—	24 0 0	0 18 5	—	—	—		9
2 10 1	—	24 0 0	10 2 6	—	9 0 0	3 0 0		10
0 3 1	—	21 0 0	7 0 6	4 18 0	—	4 18 0		11
—	—	30 10 0	8 18 6	4 18 8	—	4 13 8		12
1 8 3	—	18 0 0	2 7 0	1 16 3	—	1 16 3		13
2 7 7	—	23 13 4	2 1 0	2 13 4	—	2 13 4		14
1 16 11	—	24 0 0	2 3 0	1 1 9	—	1 1 9		15
2 9 10	—	14 0 0	9 17 0	16 1 6	1 0 0	16 1 6		16
1 8 2	—	24 8 0	5 14 6	0 14 0	—	0 14 0		17
3 5 4	—	30 0 0	15 16 0	0 17 3	—	0 17 3		18
2 10 7	—	24 0 0	10 14 0	0 11 0	—	0 11 0		19
8 1 6	—	44 0 0	15 15 0	11 18 10	—	11 18 10		20
4 6 6	—	40 0 0	30 5 0	12 6 8	35 0 0	* 47 8 8		21
3 2 5	—	40 3 4	12 11 0	15 1 0	10 4 8	* 25 5 8		22
1 8 2	—	34 0 0	2 17 0	1 4 10	—	1 4 10		23
2 7 0	—	44 0 0	11 18 6	—	—	—		24
1 6 10	—	24 0 0	4 10 0	2 15 0	—	2 15 0	V.G.	25
—	—	} 35 0 0	{ 11 18 8	9 8 0	6 0 0	16 8 0		26
—	—		16 18 8	6 1 7	—	6 1 7		27
—	—	29 0 0	14 16 6	—	—	—	V.T.	28
3 14 0	—	73 0 0	34 10 0	12 9 10	3 0 0	* 15 9 10		29

* Closed.

* Including value of Free Residence.

List of Schools in operation on the 31st December, 1874.—

Number.	Roll Number of School.	Parish.	District.	School.		Religious Denomination of Manager or Correspondent. Clerical.	Lay.	Religious Denomination of Teachers. Principal.	Assistant.	Attendance for the Year. Total number of Pupils on Rolls within the Year 1874. Males.	Fem.	Total.	Average Number in daily attendance for the Year.
30	11098	Aughaloo,	15	Caledon,		R.C.	–	R.C.	–	41	50	90	32
31	8239	Do.	–	Knockmoyle,		–	Pres.	R.C.	–	43	35	78	32
32	10636	Do.	15	Killey,		–	Diss.	R.C.	–	46	40	86	38
33	6390	Do.	15	Church-lane,		Pres.	–	Pres.	–	73	27	100	46
34	1969	Aughalisnaker,	15	Aldermoond,		–	R.C.	R.C.	–	41	26	67	36
35	6946	Arboe,	15	Albany,		Pres.	–	Pres.	–	77	73	150	65
36	4160	Do.	–	Maghine,	m.	R.C.	–	R.C.	–	150	–	150	69
37	7624	Do.	–	Do.	f.	R.C.	–	R.C.	–	–	167	167	69
38	5952	Do.	–	Drumnamoney,		–	Pres.	Pres.	–	44	50	94	36
39	9401	Do.	–	Armaloughey,		–	R.C.	Pres.	–	70	52	122	45
40	6134	Do.	–	Ballymaguire,		R.C.	–	Pres.	Pres.	89	80	171	77
				Do. ᵃ	evg.	–	–	–	–	–	–	–	–
41	6261	Do.	–	Arboe,		R.C.	–	R.C.	–	97	74	171	49
				Do. ᵃ	evg.	–	–	–	–	–	–	–	–
42	6962	Do.	–	Do. (Old),		R.C.	–	R.C.	–	64	50	104	36
43	8191	Do.	–	Moortown,		R.C.	–	R.C.	R.C.	121	104	225	89
44	9778	Do.	–	Gortnagwig,		R.C.	–	R.C.	–	46	43	89	39
45	10676	Ardtrea,	–	Ardtrea,		R.C.	–	R.C.	R.C.	83	77	160	67
46	3939	Barr,	14	Minagar,		R.C.	–	R.C.	–	66	41	107	42
47	10629	Ballygawley,	15	Ballygawley (2),		R.C.	–	R.C.	–	48	55	103	38
48	3339	Ballyclog,	–	Brigh,		Pres.	–	Pres.	–	50	44	94	38
49	4641	Badoney, Lower,	6	Aghnamoyle,		–	R.C.	R.C.	–	63	66	129	56
50	3028	Do.	–	Disewnaile,	m.	R.C.	–	R.C.	–	163	–	163	81
51	5737	Do.	–	Do.	f.	R.C.	–	R.C.	–	–	180	180	67
52	6734	Do.	–	Greenan,		–	R.C.	Pres.	–	64	66	130	34
53	6741	Do.	–	Glenmacaffer,		R.C.	–	R.C.	–	60	55	115	61
54	6831	Do.	6	Lisnacreaght,		–	R.C.	R.C.	–	63	42	105	31
55	7161	Do.	–	Gortin,	m.	–	R.C.	R.C.	–	113	67	180	46
56	9439	Do.	–	Do.	f.	–	R.C.	R.C.	–	40	103	143	57
57	8522	Do.	–	Loughgreagh,		–	Diss.	R.C.	–	58	53	111	30
58	9678	Do.	–	Cashel,		–	R.C.	R.C.	–	67	63	130	37
59	8916	Badoney, Upper,	–	Leaghcloghin,	m.	R.C.	–	R.C.	–	164	–	164	43
60	8937	Do.	–	Do.	f.	R.C.	–	R.C.	–	–	128	128	45
61	10698	Do.	–	Carrickbridge, ᶜ		–	Pres.	Pres.	–	–	–	–	50
62	10166	Do.	–	Grais,		R.C.	–	R.C.	–	69	47	116	33
63	10168	Do.	–	Barnes,	m.	R.C.	–	R.C.	–	108	–	108	33
64	10170	Do.	–	Do.	f.	R.C.	–	R.C.	–	–	126	126	31
65	6189	Do.	–	Carrick, ᶜ		R.C.	–	–	–	–	–	–	–
66	3631	Do.	–	Crosh,		R.C.	–	Pres.	–	38	52	90	33
67	8846	Do.	–	Letterbrat,	m.	R.C.	–	Pres.	–	50	23	73	23
68	11342	Do.	–	Plumbridge,	m.	R.C.	–	R.C.	–	118	–	118	30
69	11348	Do.	–	Do.	f.	R.C.	–	R.C.	–	–	103	103	39
70	9064	Do.	–	Eden,		Pres.	–	Pres.	–	71	45	116	38
71	9816	Do.	15	Derrygleen,		–	R.C.	R.C.	–	74	53	122	29
72	391	Clogher,	15	Fivemiletown,	m.	–	R.C.	Pres.	–	115	–	115	56
73	392	Do.	–	Do.	f.	–	R.C.	Pres.	Pres.	–	126	126	59
74	8046	Do.	14	Scarnaghan,		R.C.	–	R.C.	–	68	72	140	51
75	8734	Do.	–	Cavanall, ᶜ		–	–	–	–	–	–	–	–
76	4634	Do.	–	Killyfaddy,		–	Pres.	R.C.	–	88	73	161	51
77	4713	Do.	–	Aughnaclroy,		–	R.C.	R.C.	R.C.	112	97	209	51
78	4734	Do.	–	Ballymacally, ᶜ		–	R.C.	–	–	–	–	–	–
79	5317	Do.	–	Killclay,		R.C.	–	R.C.	–	44	34	78	37
80	7404	Do.	–	Eskra,		–	R.C.	R.C.	R.C.	87	85	172	67
81	7846	Do.	–	Corleghan, ᶜ		–	R.C.	–	–	–	–	–	–
82	8257	Do.	–	Ballynagurragh,		R.C.	–	R.C.	R.C.	84	73	157	40
83	8912	Do.	–	Aughintaine,		Pres.	–	Pres.	–	47	29	76	16
84	8973	Do.	–	Clogher Parochial,	m.	R.C.	–	R.C.	R.C.	106	64	170	57
85	9184	Do.	–	Do.	f.	R.C.	–	R.C.	–	22	55	77	35
86	9697	Do.	–	Murley,		–	Pres.	R.C.	–	53	35	88	25
87	10719	Do.	–	Augher,		R.C.	–	R.C.	–	66	53	119	42
88	391	Clonoe,	15	Aughamullan,		R.C.	–	R.C.	R.C.	96	67	163	56
89	2415	Do.	–	Mountjoy,		R.C.	–	R.C.	R.C.	97	70	167	40
90	11171	Do.	–	Aughagheare,		R.C.	–	R.C.	–	90	70	160	70

ᵃ Including value of Free Residence. ᵇ Including value of Free Garden. ᶜ Inoperative during latter part of year.

Province of Ulster: County of Tyrone—*continued.*

Amount paid for Books, Requisites, and Apparatus at Reduced Prices.	Aid granted by the Board during the Year 1874: In Free Stock of Books, Requisites, and Apparatus.	In Salaries, Premiums, and other Remuneration.	Results Fees, Financial Year.	Amount of Local Emoluments received in Aid of Teacher's Salary: School Fees.	Subscriptions, Endowments, &c.	Total Local Aid.	Vested or Non-Vested.	Number.
£ s. d.	£ s. d.	£ s. d.	£ s. d.	£ s. d.	£ s. d.	£ s. d.		
—	4 0 0	21 0 0	19 4 6	5 18 4	—	5 18 4		30
2 17 8	—	80 0 0	8 2 6	7 7 6	0 0 0	7 7 6		31
2 16 10	—	24 0 0	6 19 6	4 8 6	—	4 8 6		32
9 18 8	—	42 8 4	8 18 0	14 18 4	7 0 0	21 18 4		33
5 0 4	—	24 0 8	12 8 0	8 18 6	6 6 8	18 5 8		34
6 4 10	—	41 10 0	19 10 6	—	8 0 0	[a] 8 0 0		35
2 12 1	—	24 0 0	8 9 6	0 5 7	—	0 5 7		36
1 9 8	—	23 10 0	8 1 6	0 6 6	—	0 6 6		37
6 7 4	—	31 11 1	7 0 0	11 0 0	4 10 0	[b] 36 10 0		38
5 1 4	—	65 0 0	15 16 6	1 10 6	—	1 10 6		39
4 12 10	—	00 0 0 }	{ 48 7 6 8 16 0	8 14 0	8 0 0	10 14 0		40
4 14 11	—	16 0 0 }	{ 20 15 8 0 8 0	0 8 4	8 0 0	49 8 4		41
1 7 4	—	65 0 0	9 16 0	0 16 0	1 10 0	2 6 0		42
2 10 8	—	80 0 0	23 14 0	1 3 0	—	1 3 0		43
7 12 4	—	24 0 0	11 16 6	2 0 0	7 0 0	[a] 0 0 0		44
7 10 6	—	47 0 0	33 0 0	2 10 7	20 10 0	[d] 23 0 7		45
1 15 8	—	24 0 0	16 1 0	1 10 0	—	1 10 0		46
4 0 0	—	34 6 0	10 6 6	2 17 4	20 0 0	22 17 4		47
1 6 0	—	27 0 0	7 16 6	3 8 7	—	3 8 7		48
2 11 10	—	35 6 8	20 6 6	2 18 0	—	2 18 0		49
2 5 6	—	23 0 0	14 19 6	0 16 7	—	0 16 7		50
5 1 9	—	24 6 9	27 18 0	—	—	—		51
0 10 9	—	25 0 0	1 8 0	1 1 11	5 16 0	[e] 6 16 11		52
6 16 6	—	71 0 0	22 18 0	1 15 6	3 0 0	[a] 4 15 6		53
8 0 4	—	23 3 4	5 0 6	5 17 4	6 0 0	[a] 11 17 4		54
9 9 8	—	41 12 4	17 1 0	7 6 4	8 18 10	15 19 2		55
6 11 8	—	30 3 4	9 10 0	0 8 7	0 0 0	[b] 0 8 7	E	56
1 7 8	—	24 0 0	0 7 6	2 10 0	—	2 10 0		57
1 6 10	—	21 0 0	7 11 0	1 10 0	—	1 10 0		58
4 15 11	—	67 10 0	30 10 6	6 17 0	—	6 17 0	V.V.	59
5 19 4	—	21 10 0	20 18 0	9 17 6	—	9 17 6	V.V.	60
8 4 10	—	6 0 0	—	—	—	—		61
1 6 6	—	27 0 0	7 16 0	3 1 6	—	3 1 6		62
2 11 8	—	34 0 0	11 3 6	8 4 6	—	8 4 6		63
2 17 10	—	23 18 4	11 17 6	0 18 6	—	0 18 6		64
—	—	18 0 0	—	—	—	—		65
6 6 0	—	24 0 0	9 5 0	0 16 8	—	0 16 8	V.d.	66
1 3 1	—	17 15 10	1 14 0	1 7 1	—	1 7 1	V.d.	67
1 5 8	—	32 0 0	11 13 0	5 11 4	2 10 0	[a] 8 1 4		68
2 14 0	—	26 0 0	12 8 0	2 19 1	2 10 0	[a] 5 9 1		69
4 2 8	—	65 15 4	16 1 0	4 1 11	3 0 0	[e] 7 1 11		70
9 19 6	—	80 0 0	0 15 6	0 14 0	—	0 14 0		71
4 14 7	—	59 6 4	12 5 0	13 9 10	14 0 0	[e] 27 9 10		72
4 15 7	—	72 0 0	23 2 6	8 11 2	6 0 0	14 11 2		73
1 6 8	—	68 0 0	5 8 0	6 16 4	—	6 16 4		74
—	—	—	—	—	—	—		75
8 7 8	—	23 16 8	19 8 0	6 14 0	—	6 14 0		76
6 0 11	—	63 0 0	25 16 0	4 8 6	7 0 0	11 8 6		77
0 10 2	—	25 18 4	—	—	—	—	V.d.	78
1 8 8	—	24 0 0	3 1 0	0 14 0	—	0 14 0		79
1 9 5	—	62 0 0	10 4 6	5 10 0	1 6 0	[a] 6 16 0	V.d.	80
—	—	14 16 0	—	—	—	—	V.d.	81
5 6 9	—	21 0 0	16 18 0	8 4 6	—	8 4 6		82
—	—	24 0 0	4 6 0	2 5 0	—	2 5 0		83
6 7 7	6 0 0	48 0 0	24 11 6	4 10 0	19 15 10	[a] 24 5 10		84
—	—	20 0 0	4 16 6	1 15 11	10 0 0	11 15 11		85
1 6 8	—	24 0 0	5 13 6	4 0 0	2 10 0	[a] 6 10 0		86
1 11 9	—	18 5 8	6 0 0	6 16 6	—	6 16 6		87
2 10 6	—	44 0 0	17 16 6	2 15 0	—	2 15 0		88
4 0 5	—	24 0 0	10 7 0	4 0 0	—	4 0 0	n.	89
1 15 5	6 0 0	6 0 0	10 8 0	5 0 0	—	5 0 0		90

d Including value of Free Residence and Garden. a No returns. f Closed. e Inoperative.

List of Schools in operation on the 31st December, 1874.—

Number.	Roll Number of School.	Parish.	District.	School.	Religious Denomination of Manager or Correspondent.		Religious Denomination of Teachers.		Attendance for the Year. Total number of Pupils on Rolls within the Year.			Average Daily Attendance for the Year.
					Clerical.	Lay.	Principals.	Assistants.	Males.	Fem.	Total.	
91	10198	Clones,	15	King's Island,	–	Pres.	R.C.	R.C.	86	93	179	50
92	10383	Do.	–	Clones Parochial,	R.C.	–	R.C.	–	48	27	75	17
93	397	Comber, Upper,	6	Stranagalwilly,	R.C.	–	R.C.	–	93	48	140	26
94	8257	Clogherny,	12	Beragh, m.	R.C.	–	R.C.	–	107	–	107	36
95	4891	Do.	–	Do. f.	R.C.	–	R.C.	–	–	101	101	34
96	8604	Do.	–	Seskinore,	R.C.	–	R.C.	–	50	40	98	23
97	10918	Do.	–	Do.* f.	–	R.C.	R.C.	–	–	–	–	22
98	4917	Do.	–	Derraghbrey,	Pres.	–	Pres.	–	54	44	98	34
99	8859	Do.	–	Mullaghslin,	R.C.	–	R.C.	–	58	24	82	34
100	8640	Do.	–	Roscavey,	R.C.	–	R.C.	–	56	37	93	23
101	8608	Do.	–	Radergan,	R.C.	–	R.C.	–	53	44	97	30
102	8609	Do.	–	Clogherny,	R.C.	–	R.C.	–	50	60	110	33
103	10690	Do.	–	Tullyvreah,	Pres.	–	Pres.	–	67	41	108	32
104	7048	Do.	–	Hilladroy,	Pres.	–	Pres.	–	50	51	101	30
105	7065	Do.	–	Tattykeeran,	–	Pres.	R.C.	–	40	65	101	30
106	6008	Carnteel,	16	Aughnacloy, m.	R.C.	–	R.C.	–	101	–	101	42
107	6408	Do.	–	Do. f.	R.C.	–	R.C.	–	–	63	63	30
108	8836	Do.	–	Do. No. 2,	Diss.	–	Diss.	–	40	53	93	31
109	6880	Do.	–	Innisnagh,	–	R.C.	R.C.	R.C.	81	66	147	67
110	8478	Do.	–	Carnteel,	–	–	Pres.	Pres.	86	73	159	43
				Do. evg.	–	Diss.	Pres.	Pres.	78	19	97	46
111	398	Camus,	9	Strabane,	R.C.	–	R.C.	–	75	30	105	37
112	7024	Do.	–	Do. No. 2,	Pres.	–	Pres.	–	71	–	71	31
113	7890	Do.	–	Do. f.	Pres.	–	Pres.	–	–	105	105	38
114	8348	Do.	–	Do. Parochial, m.	R.C.	–	R.C.	–	97	–	97	30
115	10110	Do.	–	Do. Convent,* f.	R.C.	–	None.		–	–	–	160
116	5785	Do.	–	Camus,	R.C.	–	R.C.	–	61	40	101	43
117	5788	Do.	–	Derrygalt,	R.C.	–	R.C.	–	45	39	84	37
118	2488	Clonfeacle,	16	Roxo, m.	R.C.	–	R.C.	–	108	–	108	34
				Do. evg.	R.C.	–	R.C.	–	74	–	74	29
119	8420	Do.	–	Do. f.	R.C.	–	R.C.	–	–	108	104	30
120	7488	Do.	–	Derrylatinee,	R.C.	–	R.C.	–	70	108	178	49
				Do. evg.	R.C.	–	R.C.	–	73	–	73	21
121	8017	Do.	–	Moy, m.	R.C.	–	R.C.	–	131	–	131	52
122	8018	Do.	–	Do. f.	R.C.	–	R.C.	–	–	129	129	56
123	8231	Do.	–	Do. No. 2,	R.C.	–	R.C.	R.C.	53	87	140	74
124	9019	Do.	–	Mullycar,	–	Diss.	Diss.	–	34	30	70	16
125	9118	Do.	–	Eglish,	Pres.	–	Pres.	–	50	67	129	21
126	9792	Do.	–	Drumnamoe,	R.C.	–	R.C.	–	53	40	81	27
127	10178	Do.	–	Benburb, m.	R.C.	–	R.C.	–	98	–	98	44
128	10179	Do.	–	Do. f.	R.C.	–	R.C.	–	–	107	107	45
129	10280	Do.	–	Stangmore,	–	Diss.	R.C.	–	40	36	77	31
				Do. evg.	–	–	R.C.	–	31	35	66	18
130	9990	Do.	–	Derryfubble,	R.C.	–	R.C.	–	24	37	61	10
131	10585	Do.	–	Moygashel,	Pres.	–	Pres.	–	36	44	80	16
132	382	Cappagh,	14	Killyclogher, m.	R.C.	–	R.C.	–	101	–	101	36
133	4502	Do.	–	Do. f.	R.C.	–	R.C.	–	–	91	94	38
134	690	Do.	–	Tattinkenought,	R.C.	–	R.C.	–	78	61	139	61
135	390	Do.	–	Carrigans, Lower,	R.C.	–	R.C.	–	37	29	63	27
136	391	Do.	–	Beltany,	R.C.	–	R.C.	–	53	30	81	34
137	9735	Do.	–	Calkill,	Pres.	–	Pres.	–	54	44	98	26
138	8468	Do.	–	Ballinamullard,	R.C.	–	R.C.	–	65	45	100	33
139	4361	Do.	–	Castletown,	Pres.	–	R.C.	–	81	36	119	33
140	5531	Do.	–	Edenderry,	R.C.	–	Pres.	–	97	55	152	51
141	6104	Do.	–	Tattysure,	–	Pres.	R.C.	–	47	23	70	23
142	6135	Do.	–	Dunmullan, f.	R.C.	–	R.C.	–	–	97	97	30
143	6811	Do.	–	Do. m.	R.C.	–	R.C.	–	63	–	63	22
144	8404	Do.	–	Recarson,	–	Pres.	R.C.	R.C.	100	77	177	54
145	7630	Do.	–	Garvaghy,	–	Diss.	R.C.	–	86	42	128	33
146	8101	Do.	–	Mountfield,	R.C.	–	R.C.	R.C.	83	70	152	58
147	10247	Do.	–	Tyrcur,	–	R.C.	R.C.	–	42	38	80	41
148	9011	Do.	–	Castlereddy,	R.C.	–	R.C.	–	25	25	50	23
149	10294	Do.	–	Knockmoyle,	R.C.	–	R.C.	–	30	31	61	24

a Including value of Free Residence and Garden.

b Including value of Free Garden.

Province of Ulster: County of Tyrone—*continued.*

Amount paid for Books, Requisites, and Apparatus, at Reduced Prices.	Aid granted by the Board during the Year 1874. In Free Stock of Books, Requisites, and Apparatus.	In Salaries, Premiums, and other Gratuities.	Results Fees, Financial Year.	Amount of Local Emoluments received in Aid of Teacher's Salary. School Fees.	Subscriptions, Endowments, &c.	Total Local Aid.	Vested or Non-Vested.	Number.
£ s. d.	£ s. d.	£ s. d.	£ s. d.	£ s. d.	£ s. d.	£ s. d.		
1 10 1	—	30 0 0	10 18 6	5 5 11	67 0 0	a 43 5 11		91
1 5 10	—	17 11 6	1 19 0	—	10 0 0	10 0 0		92
1 13 5	—	24 0 0	5 0 6	1 2 0	2 10 0	b 9 12 6		93
1 5 6	—	25 18 4	10 14 8	0 8 6	—	8 2 8		94
1 5 5	—	41 14 0	14 8 0	1 10 0	—	1 10 0		95
2 3 6	—	24 0 0	—	6 14 8	—	6 14 3		96
—	—	24 0 0	6 18 0	—	—	—		97
6 8 11	—	24 0 0	9 18 6	8 2 0	—	8 2 0		98
5 0 6	—	24 0 0	15 0 4	5 18 9	—	5 18 9		99
—	—	24 0 0	8 13 6	1 7 6	—	1 7 6		100
—	—	24 0 0	5 10 6	8 10 0	—	8 10 0		101
4 18 1	—	23 18 8	8 8 6	5 9 7	15 0 0	20 9 7		102
1 8 4	—	24 0 0	5 17 0	8 10 0	—	8 10 0		103
1 2 0	—	20 0 0	6 17 6	1 8 0	—	1 8 0		104
1 9 1	—	30 0 0	7 1 6	1 16 0	—	1 16 0		105
8 0 7	—	34 18 8	12 11 0	6 13 8	—	6 13 6		106
1 10 7	—	20 0 0	9 18 6	2 2 7	—	2 2 7		107
—	—	27 10 0	11 0 0	8 8 6	10 0 0	18 8 6		108
6 1 9	—	30 0 0	10 17 0	8 15 8	46 8 0	a 44 0 3		109
2 15 11	—	44 0 0	19 18 6	5 8 6	0 0 0	a 11 3 6		110
—			15 3 6	8 19 0	—	3 19 0		
1 16 0	—	24 0 0	8 14 0	4 1 8	1 10 8	a 5 11 8		111
3 18 10	—	48 0 0	12 18 6	8 5 4	12 0 0	20 5 4		112
4 6 10	—	68 0 0	17 0 6	23 13 10	8 0 0	25 13 10		113
9 19 0	—	38 10 0	11 18 6	11 5 0	28 0 0	39 5 0		114
15 6 0	—	72 11 4	48 4 6	—	—	—		115
2 12 3	—	36 0 0	6 10 6	6 4 8	—	6 4 8	V.T.	116
1 14 11	—	21 0 0	6 6 6	2 0 6	1 8 0	b 3 8 0	V.T.	117
3 5 10	—	48 0 0	21 6 6	1 0 6	—	1 6 6	P.	118
—			16 14 0	1 18 0	—	1 18 0		
1 19 5	—	20 0 0	8 15 0	1 15 4	1 0 0	2 15 4	P.	119
3 0 10	—	41 18 8	20 8 0	2 18 6	—	2 13 6		120
—			12 11 0	1 16 0	—	1 16 0		
8 4 10	—	30 6 8	21 8 0	16 18 0	—	16 18 0		121
4 2 0	—	66 8 8	22 17 0	18 0 0	—	18 0 0		122
11 14 9	—	60 6 2	62 2 0	80 1 8	61 7 4	b 61 6 7		123
—	—	24 0 0	4 8 0	0 6 0	0 0 0	6 6 0		124
1 8 3	—	65 4 5	11 18 0	5 6 0	10 0 0	15 6 0		125
5 1 10	—	28 0 0	8 11 0	8 11 6	15 0 0	a 23 11 6		126
5 8 6	—	30 8 4	16 4 6	15 18 1	60 0 0	a 43 18 1		127
4 15 1	—	55 8 4	20 1 0	12 18 2	15 0 0	a 27 18 8		128
4 12 6	—	27 10 0	19 15 6	5 11 6	10 0 0	15 11 6		129
—			9 9 0	8 10 0	—	8 10 0		
1 8 4	—	24 0 0	8 10 6	3 10 6	17 18 0	21 6 8	V.C.	130
0 8 10	—	34 0 0	4 4 0	2 14 6	—	2 14 6		131
0 7 4	—	24 0 0	8 11 6	0 8 7	—	0 8 7	V.T.	132
0 4 11	—	30 0 0	8 14 0	0 11 0	—	0 11 0		133
3 18 9	—	75 10 0	14 19 6	6 19 0	0 5 0	b 1 4 6	V.T.	134
—	—	24 0 0	21 6 0	0 14 0	—	0 14 0	V.T.	135
—	—	24 0 0	8 6 0	6 0 0	—	6 0 0	V.T.	136
2 1 2	—	24 0 0	4 11 6	—	—	—		137
1 6 0	—	36 0 0	15 7 0	1 0 0	—	1 0 0	V.T.	138
—	—	29 16 4	13 0 6	2 2 4	—	6 2 4		139
6 6 1	—	39 16 6	23 4 6	5 5 5	5 0 0	a 10 5 5		140
—	—	22 0 0	4 4 6	1 12 6	—	1 12 6	V.C.	141
1 10 9	—	36 0 0	18 16 6	—	8 8 10	8 8 10		142
2 2 11	—	24 18 4	12 11 0	1 5 0	5 3 10	6 8 10		143
4 13 9	—	42 16 6	17 2 6	6 16 0	—	6 16 0		144
1 4 11	—	33 1 8	6 18 0	1 18 5	4 0 0	5 18 5		145
6 1 4	—	36 0 0	15 2 0	6 7 5	25 0 0	28 7 5		146
1 6 7	—	24 0 0	18 7 6	0 13 6	5 0 0	5 13 6		147
1 17 1	—	26 10 0	9 10 0	—	—	—		148
1 6 8	—	22 0 0	4 16 0	6 9 8	—	0 9 8		149

b No returns.

a Including value of Free Residence.

List of Schools in operation on the 31st December, 1874.—

Number.	Roll Number of School.	Parish.	District.	School.	Religious Denomination of Managers or Correspondents. Clerical.	Lay.	Principal and Religious Denomination of Teachers. Principals.	Assistants.	Attendance for the Year. Total number of Pupils on Rolls within the Year 1874. Males.	Fem.	Total.	Average Daily Attendance for the Year.
150	6316	Cappagh,	14	Omagh Workhouse,	P.L.	Gds.	2 Pres.	–	39	19	58	24
151	9526	Do.	–	Mayne,	Diss.	–	Diss.	–	62	40	102	35
152	401	Donaghedy,	–	Tattymoyle,	R.C.	–	R.C.	–	54	46	100	43
153	1669	Do.	6	Donaghedy,	–	Pres.	Diss.	–	27	47	74	29
154	2411	Do.	–	Doorat,	R.C.	–	R.C.	–	51	49	100	31
155	6972	Do.	–	Upper Bells,	–	R.C.	R.C.	–	40	53	93	34
156	5515	Do.	–	Elliggs,	R.C.	–	R.C.	R.C.	102	60	162	40
157	7047	Do.	–	Sandville,	–	Pres.	Pres.	Pres.	73	70	143	55
158	8708	Do.	–	Carnkenallen,	Pres.	–	Pres.	–	81	43	124	44
159	9786	Do.	–	Bready,	–	R.C.	Pres.	–	70	56	126	63
160	402	Do.	–	Loughash 1st class Agricultural, [a]	–	–	–	–	–	–	–	–
161	9258	Do.	–	Do.	R.C.	–	R.C.	–	50	68	118	34
162	1037	Do.	–	Ballyneaner Ord. Ag.	–	Pres.	Pres.	–	59	33	92	39
163	11073	Do.	–	Earl's G(i)ft,	R.C.	–	R.C.	–	–	77	77	39
164	8225	Do.	15	Drumnaslera Ord. Ag.	Pres.	–	Pres.	Pres.	92	78	170	46
				Do. evg.	–	–	Pres.	–	66	–	66	30
165	10671	Do.	6	Glenagoorland,	R.C.	–	R.C.	–	69	44	113	40
166	404	Donagheady,	16	Shankey,	Pres.	–	Pres.	–	46	46	92	29
167	11116	Do.	–	Donagby, (2),	R.C.	–	Pres.	–	56	49	116	40
168	11020	Do.	–	Do. (1),	Diss.	–	R.C.	–	50	39	89	27
169	2231	Do.	–	Brickfield, m.	R.C.	–	2 R.C.	R.C.	221	–	221	95
170	2253	Do.	–	Do. f.	R.C.	–	R.C.	R.C.	–	158	158	55
171	10683	Do.	–	Donagheady,	–	R.C.	R.C.	–	24	38	62	24
172	10718	Do.	–	Do. i.	–	R.C.	R.C.	–	30	40	70	31
173	8430	Do.	–	Stewartstown,	R.C.	–	R.C.	R.C.	79	91	170	65
174	7150	Do.	–	Do. No. 2, day,	Pres.	–	Pres.	–	71	56	120	65
				Do. evg.	–	–	Pres.	–	66	11	77	58
175	10500	Do.	–	Do. i.	Pres.	–	Pres.	–	42	34	76	33
176	407	Derryloran,	–	Gortalowry,	R.C.	–	R.C.	–	103	104	207	82
				Do. evg.	–	–	R.C.	–	102	–	102	33
177	4020	Do.	–	Drumcraw,	Pres.	–	Pres.	–	36	37	73	21
178	5184	Do.	–	Loy,	Diss.	–	Pres.	–	54	58	112	39
179	9891	Do.	–	Do. m.	R.C.	–	R.C.	–	101	–	101	51
180	9892	Do.	–	Do. f.	R.C.	–	R.C.	–	–	114	114	48
181	7548	Do.	–	Cookstown,	Pres.	–	Pres.	Pres.	122	105	227	18
182	8074	Do.	–	Do. Workhouse,	P.L.	Gds.	Pres.	–	22	24	46	30
183	10063	Do.	–	Tobermore,	Pres.	–	Pres.	Pres.	87	76	163	60
184	410	Drumglass,	–	Dungannon, m.	R.C.	–	R.C.	R.C.	222	–	222	63
185	411	Do.	–	Do. f.	R.C.	–	R.C.	R.C.	–	193	193	73
186	10337	Do.	–	Do. Factory, [b] evg.	–	–	–	–	–	–	–	–
187	9522	Do.	–	Do. Workhouse,	P.L.	Gds.	R.C.	–	40	33	73	21
188	8768	Do.	–	Anne-st., Dungannon,	Pres.	–	Pres.	–	93	–	93	47
				Do. evg.	–	–	Pres.	–	49	–	49	26
189	418	Dromore,	14	Tummery,	R.C.	–	R.C.	–	69	63	131	46
190	1261	Do.	–	Gortaclay,	R.C.	–	R.C.	–	47	37	84	33
191	2816	Do.	–	Dromore, m.	R.C.	–	R.C.	–	73	–	73	30
192	4284	Do.	–	Do. f.	R.C.	–	R.C.	–	–	55	55	30
193	3125	Do.	–	Curley,	–	Pres.	R.C.	–	53	49	102	38
194	3511	Do.	–	Aghindarragh,	R.C.	–	R.C.	R.C.	95	81	176	55
195	5046	Do.	–	Mullaghshane,	Pres.	–	R.C.	–	75	42	117	41
196	5020	Do.	–	Edernay Hill,	Pres.	–	R.C.	–	66	51	117	39
197	6368	Do.	–	Eskar,	R.C.	–	R.C.	–	80	80	169	47
198	7620	Do.	–	Bellisle,	R.C.	–	R.C.	–	64	40	116	43
199	31728	Do.	–	Drumliske,	R.C.	–	R.C.	–	61	82	143	48
200	10231	Donacavey,	–	Garvaghey,	–	R.C.	R.C.	–	111	99	210	83
201	1279	Do.	–	Legamaghery,	R.C.	–	R.C.	R.C.	55	66	121	36
202	11680	Do.	–	Fintona, f.	R.C.	–	R.C.	–	–	124	124	45
203	1930	Do.	–	Do. m.	R.C.	–	R.C.	–	124	–	124	46
204	1634	Do.	–	Blacktort, m.	–	Pres.	R.C.	–	58	–	58	37
205	2156	Do.	–	Do. f.	–	Pres.	R.C.	–	–	40	40	14
206	2171	Do.	–	Shanogue,	–	Pres.	R.C.	–	79	48	127	40
207	8632	Do.	–	Lisnacreive,	R.C.	–	R.C.	–	59	54	113	37

[a] Including value of Free Residence and Garden.

[b] Inoperative.

Province of Ulster: County of Tyrone—*continued.*

Amount paid for Books, Requisites, and Apparatus, at Reduced Prices.	Aid granted by the Board during the Year 1874. In Free Stock of Books, Requisites, and Apparatus.	In Salaries, Premiums, and other Gratuities.	Results Fees, Financial Year.	Amount of Local Emoluments received in Aid of Teacher's Salary. School Fees.	Subscriptions, Endowments, &c.	Total Local Aid.	Vested or Non-Vested.	Number.
£ s. d.	£ s. d.	£ s. d.	£ s. d.	£ s. d.	£ s. d.	£ s. d.		
6 8 11	—	—	—	—	—	—		150
—	—	20 0 0	12 2 0	3 12 7	18 0 0	21 12 7		151
4 4 2	—	22 8 9	10 2 0	—	—	—		152
1 8 8	—	26 0 0	11 18 8	8 17 0	6 0 0	*9 17 0	A.	153
2 18 1	—	21 0 0	6 7 8	8 5 8	—	3 6 8	V.T.	154
2 14 2	—	24 0 0	6 3 8	0 7 1	—	0 7 1	V.A.	155
1 6 7	—	40 0 0	9 8 8	9 7 2	—	0 7 0	V.C.	156
8 8 0	—	52 0 0	20 16 0	11 17 8	5 15 0	16 12 8		157
3 17 9	—	66 10 0	17 11 0	12 14 8	—	12 14 8		158
6 6 0	—	20 0 0	27 6 0	15 12 1	9 0 0	*24 12 1		159
—	—	—	—	—	—	—	V.T.	160
1 13 8	—	29 10 0	11 12 8	2 17 11	—	2 17 11	V.A.	161
1 15 11	—	62 0 0	6 0 0	4 0 0	6 0 0	*10 0 9		162
—	—	18 0 0	5 18 0	4 0 0	5 0 0	9 0 0		163
2 14 11	—	33 0 8	17 12 6	9 8 0	2 10 0	5 10 0		164
	—	—	7 17 0	1 11 0	—	1 11 0		
9 9 6	—	19 0 0	9 16 6	11 6 4	4 0 0	*15 6 4		165
—	—	24 0 0	7 0 0	3 1 0	—	3 1 0		166
1 18 10	4 0 0	8 0 0	6 0 8	5 10 4	6 0 0	11 16 4		167
0 6 6	—	21 0 0	7 15 0	5 19 7	7 10 0	11 8 7		168
1 8 10	—	45 0 0	16 6 0	8 16 11	—	8 15 11	V.T.	169
2 18 5	—	37 0 0	13 0 6	4 10 11	—	4 10 11	V.T.	170
4 3 6	—	24 0 0	13 0 0	0 10 0	11 0 0	*11 10 0		171
—	—	20 0 0	6 8 0	1 10 6	10 0 0	11 10 6		172
4 14 2	—	45 0 0	18 0 0	8 18 10	—	8 18 10	[illegible]	173
10 7 11	—	69 18 4	52 16 0	13 12 9	1 6 0	*24 17 9		174
	—	—	6 10 0	0 14 0	—	0 14 0		
—	—	27 10 0	6 13 0	1 2 6	—	1 2 6	V.A.	175
—	—	29 0 0	11 17 0	5 1 1	5 0 0	*5 1 1		176
—	—	—	6 17 0	0 10 0	—	0 10 0		
1 13 11	—	20 0 0	5 7 8	8 5 0	—	2 5 0	V.P.	177
2 18 6	—	35 0 0	5 15 8	7 0 0	18 0 0	*25 0 0		178
3 16 4	—	44 0 0	24 18 6	6 12 0	—	6 12 0		179
4 4 9	—	27 10 0	20 4 0	6 2 9	—	6 2 9		180
5 10 6	—	34 0 0	36 0 0	22 0 0	—	22 0 0		181
2 18 6	—	2 10 0	—	—	—	—		182
11 7 9	—	45 0 0	10 9 6	12 0 0	—	12 0 0		183
6 12 6	—	36 6 10	21 8 8	14 16 8	—	14 16 8		184
1 18 3	—	22 13 4	26 8 0	12 4 1	—	12 4 1		185
—	—	—	—	—	—	—		186
2 17 6	—	1 10 0	—	—	—	—		187
11 18 10	—	[illegible] 0 0	40 6 0	30 0 0	—	30 0 0		188
—	—	—	—	8 0 0	—	3 0 0		
1 5 0	—	16 6 8	16 5 0	1 0 0	—	1 0 0		189
1 6 8	—	24 0 0	6 5 0	1 15 0	—	1 15 0		190
—	—	32 0 0	0 15 4	18 0 0	—	48 0 0		191
1 6 10	—	20 0 0	6 16 6	2 4 0	—	2 4 0		192
6 6 1	—	20 16 4	16 13 6	1 7 6	—	1 7 6	V.T.	193
6 12 6	—	76 13 4	27 19 0	10 0 0	1 0 0	*11 0 0	V.T.	194
6 11 4	—	25 12 4	12 10 6	4 3 0	—	4 8 0	V.A.	195
6 4 6	—	26 6 8	14 11 6	8 0 6	—	2 9 8		196
1 6 11	—	27 16 0	12 8 0	0 14 6	—	8 14 6		197
0 16 2	—	27 0 8	20 4 8	7 2 6	—	7 8 6		198
8 6 11	—	20 6 8	12 4 6	6 14 6	—	4 14 6		199
8 19 1	—	30 10 0	25 10 6	1 4 0	5 0 0	6 5 0	V.A.	200
3 1 4	—	44 16 0	14 11 0	3 16 6	—	8 16 6	V.T.	201
4 14 4	5 0 0	22 0 0	27 10 6	0 4 0	—	6 4 0		202
6 11 6	—	37 12 4	18 16 6	6 12 6	—	8 12 6		203
8 16 10	—	21 0 0	6 8 6	3 14 6	—	3 14 6	A.	204
—	—	20 0 0	6 12 0	9 18 6	—	9 18 6	A.	205
4 8 4	—	60 0 0	17 12 6	10 0 6	—	10 0 6	A.	206
8 10 10	—	59 10 0	18 16 0	1 15 0	1 0 0	*3 0 0		207

* Including value of Free Residence.

* Including value of Free Garden.

List of Schools in operation on the 31st December, 1874.—

Number.	Roll Number of School.	Parish.	District.	School.	Religious Denomination of Manager or Correspondent. Clerical.	Lay.	Number and Religious Denomination of Teachers. Principals.	Assistants.	Attendance for the Year. Total number of Pupils on Rolls within the Year 1874. Males.	Fem.	Total.	Average Daily Attendance for Year 1874.
208	6300	Donacavey,	14	Tyrenan,	R.C.	–	R.C.	–	46	38	84	34
209	7001	Do.	–	Aughafad,	R.C.	–	R.C.	–	70	69	139	37
210	7985	Do.	–	Dergraberd,	–	R.C.	Pres.	–	76	80	156	46
211	10572	Do.	–	Cranny,	–	R.C.	R.C.	–	83	59	142	62
212	1376	Donaghmore,	15	Aughnagar,	R.C.	–	R.C.	–	123	93	216	69
213	9812	Do.	–	Donaghmore (old),	–	R.C.	R.C.	R.C.	57	43	100	43
214	8080	Do.	–	Do. m.	R.C.	–	R.C.	–	113	–	113	27
				Do. evg.	R.C.	–	R.C.	–	39	–	39	20
215	11071	Do.	–	Do.[b] evg.	–	Pres.	–	–	–	–	–	–
216	6612	Do.	–	Do. f.	R.C.	–	R.C.	–	–	100	100	36
217	2302	Do.	–	Tullyallen,	R.C.	–	R.C.	R.C.	49	46	95	52
				Do. evg.	–	–	R.C.	–	73	–	73	20
218	5279	Do.	–	Tullyaran,	Pres.	–	Pres.	–	67	57	114	64
219	6785	Do.	–	Dernaseer,	R.C.	–	R.C.	–	61	66	127	56
220	5272	Do.	–	Gortnagrush,	Pres.	–	Pres.	–	66	63	129	41
221	9266	Do.	–	Parkanaure, day,	–	R.C.	R.C.	–	47	67	114	45
				Do. evg.	–	R.C.	R.C.	–	63	–	63	22
222	9420	Do.	–	Killeeslea,	–	Diss.	Diss.	–	33	47	80	28
223	10284	Do.	–	Castlecaulfield,	R.C.	–	R.C.	R.C.	95	161	196	67
224	8029	Drumragh,	16	Ballynahatty,	Pres.	–	Pres.	–	42	27	69	20
225	7383	Do.	–	Omagh Mis. Mod. m.		–	Diss.	Pres., R.C.	206	–	200	90
226	6178	Do.	–	Do. f.		–	R.C.	Pres., R.C.	–	141	141	66
227	6179	Do.	–	Do. i.		–	Pres.	–	77	75	152	76
228	6326	Do.	–	Do. Convent, f.	R.C.	–	None.		–	311	311	111
229	7068	Do.	–	Cavanacaw,[c]	–	Pres.	–	–	–	–	–	–
230	4300	Do.	–	Tattyreagh,	R.C.	–	R.C.	–	53	58	111	30
231	4870	Do.	–	Cornabracken,	R.C.	–	R.C.	–	60	48	108	33
232	4742	Do.	–	Aughare,	R.C.	–	R.C.	–	48	37	85	29
233	5330	Do.	–	Drumragh,	R.C.	–	R.C.	–	30	33	63	31
234	8210	Do.	–	Gorten,	R.C.	–	Pres.	–	31	46	77	24
235	9484	Do.	–	Gillygooly,	R.C.	–	Pres.	–	45	30	75	22
236	4106	[illegible]	16	Rock,	R.C.	–	R.C.	R.C.	116	101	214	56
237	7490	Do.	–	Moneyquinny,	R.C.	–	R.C.	–	53	62	116	33
238	8417	Do.	–	Cady,[b]	–	Diss.	–	–	–	–	–	–
239	8214	Do.	–	Grange,	Pres.	–	Pres.	Pres.	64	52	116	48
240	10410	Do.	–	Moore,	–	Diss.	Pres.	–	65	55	120	38
241	10743	Do.	–	Sandholes,	Pres.	–	Pres.	–	64	59	123	34
242	414	Errigal Keerogue	–	Gort,	R.C.	–	R.C.	R.C.	88	51	139	66
243	416	Do.	–	Glencull,	R.C.	–	R.C.	–	48	54	102	27
244	1382	Do.	–	Barrogue,	–	R.C.	R.C.	–	58	46	90	30
245	2934	Do.	–	Ballygawley,	R.C.	–	R.C.	R.C.	62	53	115	42
246	5277	Do.	–	Altamuskin,	R.C.	–	R.C.	–	72	63	135	48
247	5838	Do.	–	Altcloghfin,	R.C.	–	R.C.	–	68	54	122	37
248	6855	Do.	–	Tursallan,	R.C.	–	R.C.	–	47	19	66	28
249	7324	Do.	–	Fallaghearn,	R.C.	–	R.C.	–	53	89	140	30
250	8357	Do.	–	Dunmoyle,	–	R.C.	R.C.	–	61	25	86	31
251	414	[illegible]	–	Dunamore,	R.C.	–	R.C.	R.C.	116	104	216	60
252	420	Do.	–	Killeenan,	R.C.	–	R.C.	–	119	94	213	61
253	421	Do.	–	Glenarney,	–	Diss.	R.C.	–	83	63	146	40
254	423	Do.	–	Corrachrummen,[b]	Pres.	–	–	–	–	–	–	–
255	1378	Do.	–	Stramackilmartin,	R.C.	–	R.C.	–	63	71	134	41
256	9757	Do.	–	Gortnaglaidy,	–	Diss.	R.C.	–	100	92	192	56
257	7206	Do.	–	Drumshambo, f.	R.C.	–	R.C.	–	61	183	139	37
258	8971	Do.	–	Drumamalia,	Diss.	–	Pres.	–	56	33	89	29
259	10256	Do.	–	Ballynasollus,[b]	Pres.	–	–	–	–	–	–	–
260	2780	Kilskeery,	16	Crossan,	–	Diss.	R.C.	–	39	37	76	20
261	3118	Do.	–	Feglish,	–	R.C.	R.C.	–	64	60	123	40
262	3477	Do.	–	Tullick,	R.C.	–	R.C.	–	40	44	83	33
263	6675	Do.	–	Drumharvey,	R.C.	–	R.C.	–	51	41	92	33
264	6713	Do.	–	Stramaguerty,	R.C.	–	R.C.	–	53	58	93	34
265	8061	Do.	–	Knockmoyle,	R.C.	–	R.C.	–	48	39	87	28

[a] Including value of Free Residence and Garden. [b] Closed. [c] Including value of Free Garden.

Province of Ulster: County of Tyrone—*continued.*

Amount paid for Books, Requisites, and Apparatus, and Sale of Prizes.	Aid granted by the Board during the Year 1874: In Free Stock of Books, Requisites, and Apparatus.	Aid granted by the Board during the Year 1874: In Salaries, Premiums, and other Emoluments.	Aid granted by the Board during the Year 1874: Results Fees, Financial Year.	Amount of Local Emoluments received in Aid of Teacher's Salary: School Fees.	Amount of Local Emoluments received in Aid of Teacher's Salary: Subscriptions, Endowments, &c.	Amount of Local Emoluments received in Aid of Teacher's Salary: Total Local Aid.	Vested or Non-Vested.	Number.
£ s. d.	£ s. d.	£ s. d.	£ s. d.	£ s. d.	£ s. d.	£ s. d.		
1 10 4	—	44 0 0	10 16 0	1 0 0	—	1 0 0		208
1 16 8	—	85 0 0	11 16 8	2 0 0	—	2 8 0		209
1 9 4	—	59 8 6	14 17 0	7 10 1	7 0 0	* 14 18 1	V.C.	210
1 7 6	—	44 16 8	19 8 0	4 7 0	—	4 7 0	V.C.	211
1 4 8	—	48 0 0	7 11 6	4 8 6	—	4 8 6		212
1 16 8	—	44 0 0	11 15 8	5 0 0	16 0 0	21 0 0		213
9 12 0	—	60 0 0	7 11 0	4 14 6	—	4 14 6	V.T.	214
			7 18 0	8 17 6	—	8 17 0		
—	—	1 5 0	—	—	—	—		215
0 15 0	—	96 0 0	9 6 6	2 8 0	—	2 0 0		216
6 0 7	—	41 0 0	11 5 0	1 10 6	—	1 10 6	V.T.	217
			6 18 6	1 0 0	—	1 0 0		
1 9 9	—	85 17 8	9 9 6	4 0 0	0 10 0	* 4 10 0		218
1 6 4	0 15 0	84 0 0	19 6 6	2 0 0	—	2 0 0		219
1 7 6	—	66 0 0	14 8 6	7 8 5	—	7 8 5		220
4 14 8	—	—	16 4 0	1 10 0	27 8 5	29 18 5		221
			10 15 6	6 0 0	—	6 0 0		
2 10 1	—	24 0 0	8 14 0	2 9 0	0 0 0	7 9 0		222
3 8 10	—	41 15 0	16 1 0	4 4 0	15 0 0	* 19 4 0		223
1 11 2	—	24 0 0	18 7 0	1 10 3	—	1 10 3		224
—	—	487 6 4	100 8 6	198 4 0	—	198 4 0	V.C.	225
	—						V.C.	226
—	—						V.C.	227
10 10 0	—	67 1 0	55 18 6	8 8 9	—	8 8 9		228
—	—	32 0 0	—	—	—	—	V.C.	229
1 18 11	—	24 0 0	—	2 10 0	—	2 10 0		230
1 0 8	—	49 16 8	6 14 0	6 0 2	—	6 0 2		231
1 8 10	—	24 0 0	8 1 0	2 8 0	—	2 8 0	V.C.	232
—	—	60 0 0	9 0 6	1 0 8	1 15 0	* 2 18 8		233
2 0 6	—	24 0 0	11 14 8	—	6 0 0	6 0 0		234
1 11 11	—	36 0 8	16 8 8	2 10 0	5 0 0	7 10 0		235
8 10 6	—	68 0 0	18 11 9	7 4 0	—	7 4 0		236
3 10 11	—	43 6 0	10 14 0	3 6 0	—	3 6 0		237
—	—	—	—	—	—	—		238
5 8 0	—	47 0 0	18 7 6	7 4 8	—	7 4 8		239
2 10 0	—	41 0 0	14 3 6	2 4 0	10 0 0	12 4 0		240
6 0 10	—	40 0 0	25 9 0	—	—	—		241
5 6 2	—	58 0 0	22 18 6	5 6 2	—	5 6 2		242
—	—	20 0 0	7 8 6	1 10 6	—	1 10 6	V.T.	243
1 16 7	—	24 0 0	9 4 6	4 11 10	—	4 11 10	V.T.	244
1 0 6	—	51 0 0	6 16 6	0 11 0	—	0 11 0		245
8 10 2	—	35 10 0	6 5 6	3 17 6	—	3 17 6		246
5 6 3	—	60 0 0	11 6 0	6 0 0	—	6 0 0		247
8 1 4	—	24 0 0	5 19 0	4 8 0	—	4 8 0		248
1 15 6	—	24 0 0	9 14 6	2 0 0	—	2 0 0		249
1 6 3	—	1 1 1	—	—	—	—	V.C.	250
4 19 7	—	47 10 0	13 11 0	8 14 9	—	8 14 9	V.T.	251
4 6 4	—	34 0 6	18 1 0	4 0 0	—	4 0 0		252
5 1 7	—	24 0 0	10 17 5	6 10 1	9 18 1	* 15 8 2		253
—	—	20 0 0	—	—	—	—		254
1 8 4	—	24 0 0	5 3 6	2 4 6	2 2 0	4 6 6	V.T.	255
2 10 3	—	21 0 0	11 4 0	4 8 8	2 0 0	* 6 8 8	V.T.	256
1 6 6	—	24 0 0	8 17 6	3 5 6	2 15 0	* 6 8 0		257
1 19 2	—	60 0 0	12 1 0	4 18 7	—	4 18 7		258
—	—	—	—	—	—	—		259
1 18 5	—	24 0 0	6 7 0	1 5 6	—	1 5 6	A.	260
4 18 8	—	23 8 4	11 1 5	2 9 5	—	2 9 5	A.	261
2 15 9	—	21 0 0	9 6 5	2 0 0	—	2 0 0		262
1 16 6	—	54 0 0	19 8 4	2 11 0	—	2 11 0		263
1 10 6	—	30 0 0	12 18 0	6 5 6	—	3 5 6		264
1 8 4	—	24 0 0	—	—	—	—		265

d No Teacher.

* Including value of Free Residence.

List of Schools in operation on the 31st December, 1874.—

Number.	Roll Number of School.	Parish.	District.	School.	Religious Denomination of Manager or Correspondent: Clerical	Lay.	Number and Religious Denomination of Teachers: Principals.	Assistants.	Attendance for the Year: Total Number of Pupils on Rolls within the Year ago: Males.	Fem.	Total.	Average Number in daily attendance.
266	7204	Kilskerry,	16	Cranagh,	R.C.	–	R.C.	–	50	56	106	37
267	7412	Do.	–	Relaghguanais,	R.C.	–	R.C.	R.C.	61	59	120	55
268	9487	Do.	–	Drumlea,[a]	–	–	–	–	–	–	–	–
269	9620	Do.	–	Greenan,	R.C.	–	R.C.	R.C.	60	64	124	42
270	9794	Killyman,	16	Cavan, or Killyman,	R.C.	–	R.C.	–	71	40	111	61
271	8830	Do.	–	Gortaclogan,	R.C.	–	R.C.	–	58	51	89	37
272	8295	Do.	–	Tamnamore,	R.C.	–	R.C.	–	60	53	116	45
273	10036	Do.	–	Killyman, m.	R.C.	–	R.C.	–	101	–	101	59
274	10036	Do.	–	Do. f.	R.C.	–	Pres.	–	–	108	108	48
275	10457	Do.	–	Trew,	–	Diss.	R.C.	–	64	66	130	46
276	9152	Kilkeenill,	–	Clonmackate,	Pres.	–	Pres.	–	54	52	106	53
				Do. evg.	–	–	Pres.	–	54	–	41	33
277	434	Leckpatrick,	6	Cloughcorr, m.	R.C.	–	R.C.	–	98	–	98	30
278	1891	Do.	–	Do. f.	R.C.	–	R.C.	–	–	108	108	50
279	9106	Do.	–	Glenagoorland,	R.C.	–	R.C.	R.C.	106	80	189	45
280	4515	Do.	–	Strabane Workhouse,	P.L.	Gds.	R.C. / Diss.	–	34	32	66	37
281	1194	Lisson,	16	Grievagh,	R.C.	–	R.C.	–	56	61	126	61
282	2416	Do.	–	Broughderg,	–	Pres.	R.C.	–	59	27	86	54
283	11144	Do.	–	Lisnaharney,	R.C.	–	R.C.	–	73	49	122	45
284	2071	Longfield, East,	14	Drumnafusha,	R.C.	–	R.C.	R.C.	71	60	140	50
285	8148	Do.	–	Gorteyshallon,	R.C.	–	R.C.	–	62	66	128	59
286	6677	Do.	–	Dreenan,	R.C.	–	R.C.	–	51	48	100	31
287	9467	Do.	–	Cornavarrow,	R.C.	–	R.C.	–	47	48	90	23
288	4916	Longfield, West,	–	Donish, m.	R.C.	–	R.C.	–	73	–	73	28
289	8968	Do.	–	Do. f.	Pres.	–	Pres.	–	–	63	63	26
290	5756	Do.	–	Carrick,[a]	R.C.	–	–	–	–	–	–	–
291	5707	Do.	–	Lisnacreaght,	R.C.	–	R.C.	–	47	33	80	35
292	8764	Do.	–	Drumgallon,	Pres.	–	Pres.	–	30	23	51	23
293	10150	Longfield, Lower,	–	Mulnavar,	R.C.	–	R.C.	R.C.	44	30	80	45
294	7708	Do.	–	Williamstown,	R.C.	–	R.C.	–	60	54	106	50
295	10815	Do.	–	Lough Mulhern,	R.C.	–	R.C.	–	56	42	99	37
296	8016	Do.	–	Lower Longfield,	R.C.	–	R.C.	–	57	41	98	37
297	7648	Lettera,	–	Lettera,	R.C.	–	R.C.	–	70	57	127	41
298	428	Pomeroy,	13	Pomeroy, m.	R.C.	–	R.C.	–	120	–	120	56
299	8536	Do.	–	Do. f.	R.C.	–	R.C.	–	–	111	111	57
300	1168	Do.	–	Altmore, m.	–	R.C.	R.C.	–	105	–	105	29
				Do.[f] evg.	–	–	–	–	–	–	–	–
301	1488	Do.	–	Do. f.	–	R.C.	R.C.	–	–	118	118	33
302	5028	Do.	–	Coolnasoghery,	R.C.	–	R.C.	–	67	45	112	37
303	2280	Do.	–	Limnagore,	–	R.C.	Diss.	–	58	64	112	43
304	2714	Do.	–	Claggan,	Pres.	–	R.C.	–	40	35	75	23
305	5014	Do.	–	Gallaly,	R.C.	–	R.C.	–	129	88	220	64
306	435	Termonamongan,	6	Altanaffan,	Pres.	–	Pres.	–	37	29	60	25
307	436	Do.	–	Magherakeel,	R.C.	–	R.C.	–	57	49	100	32
308	438	Do.	–	Aghnahoe,	R.C.	–	Pres.	Pres.	89	51	140	50
309	1193	Do.	–	Carrowaglass,	R.C.	–	R.C.	–	64	41	105	40
310	1850	Do.	–	Laght,	R.C.	–	R.C.	–	56	45	101	44
311	2761	Do.	–	Magheranageeragh,	Pres.	–	Pres.	Pres.	89	60	149	59
312	4679	Do.	–	Lisnacloon,	R.C.	–	R.C.	–	40	55	101	36
313	4539	Do.	–	Scraghy,	R.C.	–	R.C.	–	50	31	81	23
314	5146	Do.	–	Third Corgary,	R.C.	–	R.C.	–	41	54	95	30
315	7329	Do.	–	Tullywhisker,	R.C.	–	R.C.	–	49	39	89	35
316	8163	Do.	–	Oraigh,	R.C.	–	R.C.	–	44	48	92	30
317	437	Termonmaguirk,	16	Aughnagar,	R.C.	–	R.C.	–	116	94	209	49
318	438	Do.	–	Creggan,	R.C.	–	R.C.	–	80	90	170	42
319	1202	Do.	14	Tandaragee,	R.C.	–	R.C.	–	80	71	151	51
320	2846	Do.	15	Tyrcoomeague,	R.C.	–	R.C.	R.C.	86	84	170	55
321	4677	Do.	14	Sheskinshule,	–	R.C.	Pres.	Pres.	97	79	170	30
322	5162	Do.	–	Drumlester,	R.C.	–	R.C.	–	59	33	90	35
323	8247	Do.	13	Carrickmore,[a]	–	–	–	–	–	–	–	–
324	10922	Do.	–	Termon,	R.C.	–	R.C.	–	25	24	49	17
325	5528	Do.	14	Rathmaskle, m.	Pres.	–	R.C.	–	46	42	88	29

[a] Inoperative. [e] Including value of Free Garden. [f] Closed last part of year. [g] Including value of Free Residence.

Province of Ulster: County of Tyrone—*continued.*

Amount paid for Books, Requisites, and Apparatus, at Reduced Prices.	Aid granted by the Board during the Year 1874. In Free Grants of Books, Requisites, and Apparatus.	In Salaries, Premiums, and other Gratuities.	Results Fees, Financial Year.	Amount of Local Emoluments received in Aid of Teacher's Salary. School Fees.	Subscriptions, Endowments, &c.	Total Local Aid.	Vested or Non-Vested.	Number.
£ s. d.	£ s. d.	£ s. d.	£ s. d.	£ s. d.	£ s. d.	£ s. d.		
4 13 1	—	50 0 0	10 7 0	2 3 6	—	2 3 6		266
1 9 4	—	44 0 0	24 2 0	5 13 6	—	5 13 6		267
—	—	—	—	—	—	—		268
8 2 10	—	44 3 4	16 10 0	9 11 0	—	9 11 0	V.T.	269
1 6 5	—	33 16 0	6 16 0	6 13 3	—	6 13 3	R.	270
3 6 0	—	20 0 0	3 6 0	2 7 6	4 0 0	6 7 6		271
9 0 3	—	24 10 0	7 16 0	4 1 5	3 0 0	7 1 5		272
1 6 5	—	42 8 4	8 15 0	4 1 11	6 3 9	b 10 5 8		273
3 0 10	—	10 15 0	16 1 6	5 1 2	10 0 0	15 1 2		274
1 10 10	—	25 0 0	15 6 0	4 16 0	4 0 0	8 16 0		275
8 1 0	—	30 16 0	18 1 0	10 6 8	6 0 0	16 6 8		276
			8 10 6	6 19 8	5 0 0	11 19 8		
1 13 0	—	24 0 0	9 0 0	3 6 1	—	3 6 1		277
6 10 10	—	20 0 0	8 6 8	4 0 8	1 0 0	* 5 0 8		278
8 0 10	—	65 8 4	12 14 0	7 10 3	—	7 10 3		279
—	—	—	—	—	—	—		280
1 6 3	—	20 0 0	3 15 0	2 19 6	3 10 0	* 6 9 6		281
8 9 0	—	24 0 0	6 14 2	—	5 0 0	5 0 0	T.T.	282
—	—	5 0 0	* —	12 0 0	4 0 0	16 0 0		283
3 4 9	—	67 0 0	30 15 6	8 16 8	—	8 16 8		284
4 10 1	—	50 0 0	19 11 6	6 10 6	—	6 10 6	V.T.	285
1 18 9	—	24 0 0	6 4 6	1 1 0	3 15 0	4 16 0	V.A.	286
0 16 5	—	30 0 0	7 5 4	—	—	—		287
0 13 6	—	24 0 0	4 15 0	0 10 0	—	0 10 0	V.C.	288
9 11 6	—	30 0 0	6 15 0	2 6 0	—	2 6 0	V.C.	289
—	—	—	—	—	—	—		290
—	—	24 0 0	10 4 6	0 4 0	—	0 4 0		291
1 6 8	—	21 0 0	6 12 0	6 19 6	—	5 15 0		292
0 10 8	—	66 0 0	16 6 0	—	14 0 0	* 14 0 0	V.C.	293
2 0 4	—	56 0 0	10 6 6	2 10 6	—	2 10 6		294
4 0 10	4 0 0	24 0 0	11 18 6	—	—	—		295
2 6 5	—	40 2 2	11 2 0	—	10 0 0	* 10 0 0		296
—	—	57 0 0	16 16 0	9 4 6	—	9 4 6		297
8 0 4	—	24 0 0	7 10 6	1 11 8	—	1 11 8		298
—	—	30 0 0	11 1 0	3 0 8	—	3 0 2		299
1 16 6	—	23 8 0	4 16 0	1 17 2	—	b 1 17 2	A.	300
			7 13 0	—	—	—		
1 9 3	—	24 0 0	7 7 6	2 16 7	—	2 16 7	A.	301
2 10 10	—	23 0 0	6 1 6	2 10 1	4 10 0	7 0 1	V.T.	302
1 8 5	—	31 10 8	18 16 6	3 14 5	—	3 14 5		303
1 12 10	—	24 0 0	7 17 8	0 17 0	—	0 17 0	V.T.	304
5 9 10	—	44 13 4	12 19 8	3 19 0	—	3 19 0		305
1 3 6	—	24 0 0	0 17 0	4 17 0	—	4 17 0		306
1 16 3	—	17 16 0	0 16 6	—	0 15 0	0 15 0		307
8 18 4	—	44 16 8	16 19 6	11 7 6	4 0 0	15 7 6	R.	308
1 16 0	—	25 8 6	13 10 6	4 2 6	—	4 2 6	A.	309
1 14 8	—	47 8 4	10 18 6	1 6 0	—	1 6 0	A.	310
4 0 0	—	74 3 4	26 18 6	6 4 6	—	6 4 6	A.	311
1 9 5	—	26 15 6	9 9 0	6 0 0	—	6 0 0		312
8 6 1	—	24 0 0	10 14 0	—	—	—	R.C.	313
0 9 1	—	26 10 0	9 1 0	0 12 6	3 0 0	b 3 12 6		314
1 8 0	—	24 0 0	11 6 6	5 17 6	4 0 0	* 9 17 6		315
1 7 10	—	25 10 0	6 10 0	—	1 1 0	1 1 0		316
9 19 7	—	30 0 0	12 3 0	4 1 6	—	4 1 6	V.T.	317
8 10 11	—	24 0 0	16 1 0	6 12 6	—	6 12 6		318
1 5 0	—	24 0 0	4 15 0	5 8 6	—	5 8 6		319
1 15 7	—	45 10 0	12 15 8	—	—	—		320
4 0 4	—	53 16 6	17 3 6	5 2 6	18 0 0	* 23 2 6		321
2 9 9	—	24 0 0	5 13 6	2 4 6	—	2 4 6		322
—	—	—	—	—	—	—		323
0 17 0	—	29 0 0	4 5 0	1 15 6	67 1 8	* 68 17 2		324
1 4 11	—	24 0 0	12 4 6	3 1 6	—	3 1 6		325

b Including value of Free Residence and Garden.

c Chapel.

* Results Examination cancelled.

List of Schools in operation on the 31st December, 1874.—

Number.	Roll Number of School.	Parish.	District.	School.	Religious Denomination of Manager or Correspondent: Clerical.	Lay.	Number and Religious Denomination of Teachers: Principals.	Assistants.	Attendance for the Year: Total number of Pupils on Rolls within the Year 1874: Males.	Females.	Total.	Average Attendance for the Year 1874.
326	8004	Termonmaguirk,	16	Rathmackin, . c.	R.C.	–	R.C.	–	45	55	101	56
327	10298	Do.	–	Altinagh, . .	R.C.	–	R.C.	–	146	109	255	46
328	3951	Do.	16	Cary, . .	R.C.	–	R.C.	–	32	48	79	34
329	7590	Do.	16	Bracky, . m.	R.C.	–	R.C.	–	108	–	108	58
330	8566	Do.	–	Do. . f.	R.C.	–	R.C.	–	–	121	124	34
331	6118	Do.	16	Inishatrack, . .	R.C.	–	R.C.	–	72	74	140	67
332	9215	Do.	–	Mullans, . .	R.C.	–	R.C.	–	70	107	177	54
			–	Do. . evg.	R.C.	–	R.C.	–	54	16	73	51
333	8829	Do.	16	Drumnakilly, . .	R.C.	–	R.C.	–	44	34	78	39
334	10531	Do.	–	Inishative,[b] . .	–	–	–	–	–	–	–	–
335	4290	Tamlaght,	16	Aughavey, . .	Pres.	–	Pres.	–	56	35	91	41
336	7479	Do.	–	Cough, . .	Pres.	–	Pres.	Pres.	80	74	154	58
337	10217	Do.	–	Do. . No. 2,	R.C.	–	R.C.	R.C.	50	30	85	50
338	1165	Tullyniskan,	–	Edendork, . .	R.C.	–	[a] R.C.	R.C.	120	98	218	73
339	9154	Do.	–	Coal Island, . L.	Pres.	–	Pres.	–	39	71	110	38
340	10280	Do.	–	Newmills, . .	R.C.	–	R.C.	R.C.	101	95	196	72
341	430	Urney,	8	Kilclean, . .	R.C.	–	Pres.	–	71	61	132	38
342	1391	Do.	–	Rabstown, . .	R.C.	–	R.C.	–	80	60	140	48
343	9407	Do.	–	Bridge End, . .	R.C.	–	R.C.	–	96	60	156	77
344	7430	Do.	–	Urney, . .	Pres.	–	Pres.	–	35	18	53	18
345	10296	Do.	–	Do. . .	R.C.	–	R.C.	–	34	29	63	27
346	8271	Do.	–	Sion Mills, . .	–	R.C.	R.C.	Pres. R.C.	150	78	228	119
347	8438	Do.	–	Castlederg, No. 1 (Edward's), . .	R.C.	–	Pres.	–	101	39	100	61
348	8707	Do.	–	Tullywhisker, . .	–	R.C.	R.C.	R.C.	85	75	160	64
349	2036	Skirts of Urney,	–	Castlederg Workhouse,	P.L.	Gds.	R.C.	–	9	10	19	10
350	10188	Do.	–	Castlederg, . .	R.C.	–	R.C.	R.R.C.	130	129	259	84
351	8842	Urney and Ardstraw,	–	Gortaghan, . .	R.C.	–	Pres.	–	40	68	114	41
		Total for County Tyrone, 351, .							21606	18344	20,046	18503

MUNSTER—

COUNTY OF

1	7703	Abbey, . .	42	Ballyvelahan, . m.	R.C.	–	R.C.	–	80	–	80	58
2	7729	Do. . .	–	Do. . f.	R.C.	–	R.C.	–	–	78	78	51
3	2258	Drumcreehy, .	45	Glenmoney, . m.	R.C.	–	R.C.	–	69	–	69	38
4	2757	Do. . .	–	Do. . f.	R.C.	–	R.C.	R.C.	–	103	103	43
5	1223	Clonlea, . .	61	Belvoir, . m.	R.C.	–	R.C.	–	93	–	91	45
6	1926	Do. . .	–	Do. . f.	R.C.	–	R.C.	–	–	86	86	40
7	4475	Do. . .	46	Kilkishen, . m.	R.C.	–	R.C.	–	84	–	85	31
8	4459	Do. . .	–	Do. . f.	R.C.	–	R.C.	–	–	115	115	53
9	6317	Do. . .	61	Derrynaveagh, .	R.C.	–	R.C.	R.C.	93	84	179	62
10	3186	Do. . .	42	Oatfield Jail C. Agr.	–	R.C.	R.C.	–	154	–	154	58
11	8240	Do. . .	–	Do. . f.	–	R.C.	R.C.	–	–	131	131	47
12	10241	Clenagh, . .	45	Shannon View, .	R.C.	–	R.C.	R.C.	143	133	273	117
13	8000	Clare Abbey, .	–	Clare Castle, . m.	R.C.	–	R.C.	–	140	–	140	39
14	8087	Do. . .	–	Do. . f.	R.C.	–	R.C.	R.C.	–	133	133	64
15	1842	Carran, . .	42	Glencolumbkill, .	–	R.C.	R.C.	–	29	28	57	27
16	7573	Do. . .	–	Carran, . .	R.C.	–	R.C.	–	52	45	97	43
17	9773	Clooney, . .	45	Carrahan, . m.	R.C.	–	R.C.	–	119	–	119	45
18	10161	Do. . .	–	Do. . f.	R.C.	–	R.C.	–	–	93	93	57
19	8770	Do. . .	–	Spancel Hill, .	R.C.	–	R.C.	–	31	24	55	27
20	10309	Do. . .	–	Maghera, . .	R.C.	–	R.C.	–	31	32	63	23
21	8691	Clondagad, .	–	Phifield, . .	R.C.	–	R.C.	R.C.	96	94	190	61
22	7003	Do. . .	–	Killerk, . .	R.C.	–	R.C.	R.C.	46	89	135	41
23	10671	Do. . .	–	Lissycasey, . .	R.C.	–	R.C.	R.R.C.	133	126	259	88

a Including value of Free Residences. b Inoperative.

Province of Ulster: County of Tyrone—*continued.*

Amount paid for Books, Requisites, and Apparatus, at Reduced Prices.	Aid granted by the Board during the Year 1874.			Amount of Local Emoluments received in Aid of Teacher's Salary.			Vested or Non-Vested.	Number.
	In Free Stock of Books, Requisites, and Apparatus.	In Salaries, Premiums, and other Gratuities.	Results Fees, Financial Year.	School Fees.	Subscriptions, Endowments, &c.	Total Local Aid.		
£ s. d.	£ s. d.	£ s. d.	£ s. d.	£ s. d.	£ s. d.	£ s. d.		
1 6 6	—	77 10 0	18 3 8	9 2 6	—	9 2 6		326
3 10 6	—	24 0 0	8 16 6	0 12 0	—	0 12 0		327
0 16 9	—	20 0 0	10 11 0	—	—	—		328
1 4 11	—	24 0 0	10 0 0	8 18 0	—	8 18 0		329
2 18 0	—	20 0 0	8 14 8	3 9 5	—	3 9 5		330
1 14 8	—	24 0 0	10 4 6	0 19 7	—	0 19 7		331
3 13 10	—	} 30 0 0	{ 16 11 0	0 14 0	—	0 14 0		332
—	—		13 16 0	0 10 0	—	0 16 0		
—	—	17 0 0	10 12 0	0 11 9	14 8 0	* 14 19 9		333
0 7 0	—	—	—	—	—	—		334
0 11 0	—	84 0 0	20 14 0	5 10 0	—	5 10 0		335
7 17 0	—	44 0 0	20 0 0	8 8 0	8 15 0	10 8 0		336
3 2 1	—	30 0 0	7 10 6	1 8 0	—	1 8 0		337
8 4 8	—	54 0 0	28 18 0	18 16 11	—	18 16 11		338
—	—	20 0 0	7 0 0	3 18 4	—	3 18 4		339
—	—	78 0 0	32 13 6	14 7 1	28 0 0	* 40 7 1		340
5 9 1	—	31 0 0	7 16 6	7 4 0	4 0 0	* 11 4 0		341
7 1 10	—	35 18 6	17 18 8	9 0 6	—	9 0 6		342
6 18 3	—	70 0 0	14 19 0	14 10 4	—	14 10 4		343
1 13 10	—	24 0 0	1 7 5	2 11 0	—	2 11 0		344
1 19 4	—	27 8 6	10 16 6	6 8 10	10 10 0	* 17 18 10		345
4 6 8	—	85 16 8	30 10 4	16 6 8	20 0 0	36 6 9		346
5 14 1	—	48 10 0	81 1 6	23 12 0	41 8 2	* 65 0 8		347
3 17 6	—	64 0 0	80 8 5	9 6 0	—	9 6 0		348
—	—	—	—	—	—	—		349
5 18 0	—	64 6 10	23 15 0	8 1 9	—	8 1 0		350
5 10 0	—	69 0 0	9 13 0	13 10 6	—	13 16 6	A.	351
576 16 2	27 16 0	11,802 6 1	4,180 10 7	1,881 13 6	1,160 7 2	2,816 0 7		

1,791 Schools.

CLARE—221 Schools.

2 14 10	—	24 0 0	7 7 8	4 19 1	—	4 11 1	V.C.	1
1 16 5	—	20 6 8	8 18 0	4 19 9	—	4 19 9	V.C.	2
2 8 7	—	21 0 0	10 3 0	4 11 5	—	4 11 8	V.T.	3
3 8 7	—	40 0 0	10 5 0	3 4 10	—	* 8 4 10	V.T.	4
1 11 1	—	27 6 8	21 6 0	2 15 10	4 5 0	* 7 0 10	V.T.	5
1 7 0	—	29 10 0	14 15 0	3 3 10	8 0 0	8 3 10	V.T.	6
2 10 6	—	33 8 4	6 0 6	4 19 10	—	4 19 10	V.T.	7
—	—	60 0 0	18 4 0	10 9 4	—	10 9 4	V.T.	8
4 15 1	—	60 19 8	41 16 0	17 13 6	0 15 0	* 18 8 6	V.C.	9
1 5 10	—	43 0 0	19 3 0	1 8 6	10 0 0	12 5 6		10
4 5 4	—	24 0 0	16 9 6	1 3 0	6 0 0	7 3 0		11
13 8 0	—	60 18 4	40 9 6	18 1 6	—	18 1 6	V.T.	12
5 9 7	—	39 0 0	27 9 0	4 10 0	—	4 10 0	V.T.	13
8 12 0	—	62 15 0	17 7 6	5 15 10	—	5 15 10	V.T.	14
6 17 1	—	33 0 0	8 14 6	5 1 0	—	5 1 0	A.	15
1 12 4	—	38 16 8	15 19 0	6 8 8	3 0 0	* 18 8 8	V.C.	16
1 6 8	—	40 0 0	18 18 9	5 11 0	—	5 11 0		17
1 10 10	—	61 0 0	16 6 0	6 10 8	—	6 10 8		18
1 17 0	—	18 6 8	6 10 0	5 10 0	—	5 10 0		19
2 17 8	—	24 0 0	13 12 0	9 19 6	—	9 10 0		20
6 5 0	—	48 0 0	23 7 8	10 18 2	—	10 18 2		21
—	—	44 0 0	3 4 6	6 2 8	—	6 2 8		22
18 6 0	—	59 16 4	67 16 8	10 8 4	—	10 8 4	V.T.	23

* Including value of Free Residence and Garden.

* Including value of Free Garden.

List of Schools in operation on the 31st December, 1874.—

Number.	Roll Number of School.	Parish.	District.	School.	Religious Denomination of Manager or Correspondent. Clerical.	Lay.	Number and Religious Denomination of Teachers. Principals.	Assistants.	Attendance for the Year. Total number of Pupils on Rolls within the Year 1874. Males.	Fem.	Total.	Average Daily Attendance for Year 1874.
24	[illegible]	Clondegad,	42	Fergus View,	R.C.	–	R.C.	3R.C.	139	137	276	119
25	8918	Dysert,	–	Toonagh, m.	–	R.C.	R.C.	–	98	–	98	55
26	4393	Do.	–	Do. f.	–	R.C.	R.C.	–	–	80	80	39
27	7881	Do.	–	Dysert,	R.C.	–	R.C.	R.C.	85	80	165	74
28	10727	Doora,	–	Doora,	R.C.	–	R.C.	–	54	38	92	35
29	8589	Do.	–	Knockanean, m.	R.C.	–	R.C.	–	90	–	90	27
30	8604	Do.	–	Do. f.	R.C.	–	R.C.	–	–	88	88	37
31	7315	Drumcliff,	–	Ennis Convent, f.	R.C.	–	Nuns.		–	923	923	571
32	3225	Do.	–	Do. Workhouse,	P.L.	Gds.	2R.C.	R.C.	66	74	140	84
33	22064	Do.	–	Do. Gaol,[b]	R.C.	–	–	–	–	–	–	–
34	6436	Drumcreehy,	42	Ballyvaughan, m.	R.C.	–	R.C.	–	152	–	152	66
35	6287	Do.	–	Do. f.	R.C.	–	R.C.	R.C.	–	131	131	62
36	6859	Do.	–	Do. Workhouse,	P.L.	Gds.	R.C.	–	24	11	35	15
37	2129	Feakle,	–	Feakle, 1st Cl. Agr., m.	R.C.	–	R.C.	R.C.	153	–	153	64
38	2440	Do.	–	Do. f.	R.C.	–	R.C.	R.C.	–	231	231	69
39	3279	Do.	–	[illegible]	R.C.	–	R.C.	–	67	52	118	45
40	4187	Do.	–	Carrakyle,	R.C.	–	R.C.	–	49	35	84	29
41	4141	Do.	–	Mountainview,	R.C.	–	R.C.	–	70	72	151	53
42	8804	Do.	–	[illegible]	R.C.	–	R.C.	R.C.	90	108	202	76
43	8400	Do.	–	Drumandoora, Ord. Agr.	R.C.	–	R.C.	–	75	82	157	47
44	4452	Do.	–	Gurtavaha,[a]	–	–	–	–	–	–	–	–
45	9719	Inagh,	43	Letterkelly, m.	R.C.	–	R.C.	–	63	–	63	44
46	9224	Do.	–	Do. f.	R.C.	–	R.C.	–	–	77	77	31
47	9543	Do.	–	Inagh, f.	R.C.	–	R.C.	R.C.	–	177	177	60
48	9571	Do.	–	Do. m.	R.C.	–	R.C.	–	245	–	245	71
49	8101	Inch,	–	Inch,	R.C.	–	R.C.	1R.C.	89	83	172	59
50	4019	Inchicronan,	43	Crusheen, m.	R.C.	–	R.C.	–	91	–	91	33
51	6340	Do.	–	Do. f.	R.C.	–	R.C.	–	–	99	99	33
52	7980	Do.	–	Drumbaniff,	R.C.	–	R.C.	–	55	42	97	42
53	2292	Do.	–	Ballinruan, Ord. Agr.,	R.C.	–	R.C.	2R.C.	100	79	179	66
54	1130	Killinaboy,	–	Richmond,	R.C.	–	R.C.	R.C.	159	–	159	81
55	8851	Do.	–	Corofin, f.	R.C.	–	R.C.	R.C.	–	134	134	49
56	6585	Do.	–	Do. Workhouse,	P.L.	Gds.	R.C.	–	33	11	44	22
57	7182	Do.	–	Kilnaboy,	R.C.	–	R.C.	–	71	76	147	60
58	1302	Killadysert,	43	Killadysert, m.	R.C.	–	R.C.	4R.C.	220	–	220	94
59	1379	Do.	–	Do. f.	R.C.	–	R.C.	R.C.	–	168	168	73
60	6234	Do.	–	Do. Workhouse,	P.L.	Gds.	R.C.	–	30	14	44	19
61	6011	Do.	–	Canon Island,	R.C.	–	R.C.	–	19	10	29	17
62	1679	Kilfinaghta,	51	Sixmilebridge, m.	R.C.	–	R.C.	R.C.	109	–	109	61
63	2409	Do.	–	Do. f.	R.C.	–	R.C.	R.C.	–	219	219	71
64	1831	Killilagh,	42	Ballynalackan, m.	R.C.	–	R.C.	–	104	–	104	38
65	8041	Do.	–	Do. f.	R.C.	–	R.C.	–	–	101	101	30
66	8671	Do.	–	Doolin, m.	R.C.	–	R.C.	–	159	–	159	63
67	4871	Do.	–	Do. f.	R.C.	–	R.C.	–	–	114	114	46
68	2155	Kilfenora,	–	Kilfenora, m.	R.C.	–	R.C.	–	107	–	107	50
69	2156	Do.	–	Do. f.	R.C.	–	R.C.	R.C.	–	178	178	69
70	2150	Kilchreest,	43	Ballinacally, m.	–	R.C.	R.C.	–	74	–	74	33
71	2184	Do.	–	Do. f.	–	R.C.	R.C.	–	–	61	61	31
72	7484	Do.	–	Lack,	R.C.	–	R.C.	R.C.	63	100	163	70
73	8241	Kilfearagh,	–	Kilkee, m.	R.C.	–	R.C.	2R.C.	236	–	236	159
74	2522	Do.	–	Do. f.	R.C.	–	R.C.	4R.C.	–	272	272	103
75	10816	Do.	–	Do. No. 2,	R.C.	–	R.C.	–	19	21	40	20
76	7781	Do.	–	Termon,	R.C.	–	R.C.	–	73	80	153	30
77	8806	Do.	–	[illegible]	R.C.	–	R.C.	–	87	80	167	61
78	6418	Do.	–	Moyasta, m.	–	R.C.	R.C.	–	142	–	142	47
79	6811	Do.	–	Do. f.	–	–	R.C.	–	–	183	183	45
80	6430	Do.	–	[illegible]	R.C.	–	R.C.	–	64	45	109	30
81	8004	Kilmurry,	–	Shanahill, m.	R.C.	–	R.C.	–	98	–	98	34
82	3005	Do.	–	Do. f.	R.C.	–	R.C.	–	–	121	121	43
83	8201	Killaloe,	42	Killaloe, m.	R.C.	–	R.C.	2R.C.	231	–	231	98
84	8582	Do.	–	Do. f.	R.C.	–	R.C.	R.C.	–	196	196	71
85	10153	Do.	–	Do. (3).	R.C.	–	R.C.	–	6	8	14	7
86	6529	Do.	–	Carrowbane,	R.C.	–	R.C.	–	61	30	87	33

[a] No returns. [b] Including value of Free Garden. [c] No Teacher.

Province of Munster: County of Clare—continued.

Amount paid for Books, Requisites, and Apparatus, at Reduced Prices.	Aid granted by the Board during the Year 1873: In Free Stock of Books, Requisites, and Apparatus.	In Salaries, Premiums, and other Gratuities.	Results Fees, Financial Year.	Amount of Local Emoluments received in Aid of Teacher's Salary: School Fees.	Subscriptions, Endowments, &c.	Total Local Aid.	Vested or Non-vested.	Number.
£ s. d.	£ s. d.	£ s. d.	£ s. d.	£ s. d.	£ s. d.	£ s. d.		
6 1 4	—	104 16 4	67 13 8	20 16 0	—	20 16 0	V.T.	24
—	—	24 0 0	7 3 0	—	10 0 0	10 0 0	N.	25
—	—	20 0 0	10 10 8	6 0 0	10 0 0	16 0 0	N.	26
1 17 8	—	60 13 4	20 15 0	14 1 11	—	14 1 11		27
—	—	49 10 0	10 3 8	0 11 0	—	0 11 0	V.C.	28
1 7 1	—	24 0 0	5 1 0	3 10 0	—	3 10 0		29
2 10 0	—	22 1 8	8 18 0	4 14 0	—	4 14 6		30
11 16 11	—	163 11 4	119 6 8	18 14 7	—	18 14 7		31
8 11 3	—	7 10 0	—	—	—	—		32
—	—	—	—	—	—	—		33
1 15 1	—	81 18 4	11 7 8	6 16 2	—	6 16 2	V.C.	34
4 9 0	—	67 13 4	19 14 0	6 3 4	—	6 3 4	V.C.	35
4 2 11	—	—	—	—	—	—		36
4 1 8	—	64 0 0	8 5 0	7 4 6	27 12 6	b 34 17 0	N.	37
3 16 1	—	56 18 0	17 11 8	3 15 5	—	3 15 5	N.	38
2 16 1	—	80 0 0	18 8 6	1 9 6	—	1 9 6		39
0 4 7	—	28 0 0	8 18 0	1 10 0	—	1 10 0	V.C.	40
1 10 8	—	24 0 0	7 9 6	3 3 8	—	3 3 8	V.C.	41
2 13 6	—	11 0 0	23 4 0	0 10 8	9 9 6	b 11 12 9		42
1 0 10	—	20 0 0	14 1 0	4 7 0	14 15 1	b 10 2 1		43
1 12 4	—	—	—	—	—	—		44
3 7 2	—	83 8 4	16 4 0	0 16 4	—	8 16 4	V.T.	45
—	—	20 0 0	7 15 0	4 13 4	—	4 13 4	V.T.	46
4 17 8	—	40 0 0	22 1 8	11 9 2	—	11 9 2		47
1 12 4	—	45 0 0	21 14 0	12 8 0	—	12 8 0		48
6 9 7	—	51 10 0	23 3 0	22 0 0	—	22 0 0		49
1 16 11	—	24 0 0	7 4 6	2 15 10	—	2 15 10		50
2 6 7	—	25 0 0	18 15 0	3 15 6	—	3 15 6		51
2 15 8	—	26 0 8	12 14 0	3 10 0	2 0 0	5 10 0		52
4 8 4	—	63 0 0	60 3 6	6 3 6	15 7 0	b 21 10 0	V.T.	53
18 11 7	—	39 0 0	27 12 8	33 0 0	—	33 0 0		54
6 18 11	—	44 0 0	21 12 6	10 0 0	—	10 0 0		55
3 10 2	—	—	—	—	—	—		56
0 3 11	—	80 0 0	18 11 6	8 5 8	—	8 5 8		57
4 18 0	—	118 0 0	45 6 0	26 17 8	—	26 17 8		58
5 1 7	—	87 18 8	20 17 0	20 14 0	—	20 14 6		59
2 5 8	—	1 10 0	—	—	—	—		60
—	—	24 0 0	2 19 6	4 0 0	—	4 0 0		61
2 11 11	—	59 0 0	20 7 6	10 8 0	—	10 8 0		62
7 9 8	—	64 0 0	14 8 0	11 19 2	—	11 19 2		63
3 4 11	—	24 0 0	4 3 0	6 9 0	—	6 9 0	N.	64
—	—	20 0 0	6 10 0	4 7 0	—	4 7 0	N.	65
7 8 10	—	24 0 0	13 18 0	7 8 7	—	7 8 7	V.C.	66
1 10 0	—	20 0 0	9 12 0	3 10 6	—	3 10 6	V.C.	67
2 4 4	—	24 0 0	8 0 6	6 2 0	—	6 2 0	N.	68
0 9 9	—	71 6 6	25 12 0	8 0 6	—	8 0 6	N.	69
1 13 6	—	60 0 0	10 19 0	7 2 2	4 0 0	a 11 2 2	V.T.	70
2 2 1	—	20 0 0	13 7 0	4 3 0	—	4 3 0	V.T.	71
2 18 4	—	44 0 0	13 19 0	11 9 0	—	11 9 0		72
9 8 1	—	126 0 0	60 9 8	10 9 11	2 0 0	12 9 11	V.T.	73
4 18 0	—	114 16 8	47 14 8	5 14 6	2 0 0	7 14 6	V.T.	74
1 8 4	—	21 0 0	9 18 8	12 10 0	30 0 0	a 42 10 0		75
1 11 11	—	20 0 0	8 0 0	0 7 11	—	0 7 11		76
1 15 11	—	30 16 8	8 9 0	3 0 0	—	3 0 0		77
4 19 9	—	65 0 0	18 11 0	5 10 8	10 0 0	15 10 8		78
2 16 2	—	62 0 0	12 9 0	4 18 4	8 0 0	a 12 18 4		79
4 5 8	—	24 0 0	10 1 0	4 10 0	—	4 10 0		80
2 17 11	—	20 0 0	14 0 0	5 10 0	1 10 0	b 7 0 0		81
8 11 9	—	81 10 8	18 14 0	4 19 6	1 10 0	b 6 9 6		82
6 12 0	—	129 6 8	28 15 0	37 11 4	—	37 11 4		83
4 17 3	—	79 10 6	19 18 0	15 1 8	—	15 1 8		84
—	—	—	0 19 0	1 7 6	—	1 7 6		85
1 18 10	—	45 3 4	12 9 6	7 8 0	—	7 8 0		86

a Including value of Free Residence.

b Including value of Free Residence and Garden.

List of Schools in operation on the 31st December, 1874.—

Number.	Roll Number of School.	Parish.	District.	School.	Religious Denomination of Manager or Correspondent: Clerical.	Lay.	Teacher and Religious Denomination of Teachers: Principals.	Assistants.	Attendance for the Year: Total number of Pupils on Rolls within the Year 1874: Males.	Fem.	Total.	Average Daily Attendance for the Year.
87	7154	Killaloe,	42	Ballycorney, f.	R.C.	–	R.C.	–	–	79	79	41
88	7256	Do.	–	Do. m.	R.C.	–	R.C.	–	80	–	80	39
89	8970	Do.	–	Glee,	R.C.	–	R.C.	–	48	35	73	38
90	4696	Kilrush,	45	Knockerra,	R.C.	–	R.C.	3 R.C.	140	114	253	125
91	8821	Do.	–	Kilrush, m.	R.C.	–	R.C.	4 R.C.	339	–	339	177
92	7025	Do.	–	Do. No. 2,	R.C.	–	R.C.	–	197	–	197	80
93	7892	Do.	–	Do. Convent, f.	R.C.	–	Nuns.		–	490	498	219
94	[illegible]	Do.	–	Do. Workhouse,	P.L.	Gds.	R.C.	–	40	–	40	39
95	10316	Do.	–	Scattery,	R.C.	–	R.C.	–	19	15	34	35
96	8484	Kilseily,	51	Broadford, m.	R.C.	–	R.C.	–	89	–	89	40
97	4168	Do.	–	Do. f.	R.C.	–	R.C.	R.C.	35	110	145	66
98	11172	Do.	–	Meelick, m.	R.C.	–	R.C.	–	89	–	89	37
99	11173	Do.	–	Do. f.	R.C.	–	R.C.	–	2	67	69	–
100	8871	Kilmacreehy,	42	St. Bridget's, m.	R.C.	–	R.C.	–	116	–	116	65
101	4857	Do.	–	Do. f.	R.C.	–	R.C.	–	–	130	130	60
102	4456	Do.	–	Liscannor, m.	R.C.	–	R.C.	–	153	–	153	69
103	4156	Do.	–	Do. f.	R.C.	–	R.C.	R.C.	–	139	139	56
104	3626	Kilmurry,	42	Mullagh,	R.C.	–	R.C.	3 R.C.	121	163	284	132
105	4431	Do.	–	Kilmurry, m.	–	R.C.	R.C.	–	118	–	118	46
106	4452	Do.	–	Do. f.	–	R.C.	R.C.	–	–	100	100	41
107	5201	Do.	–	Clonadrum,	–	R.C.	R.C.	R.C.	101	110	212	62
108	7113	Do.	–	Kilmurry McMahon,	R.C.	–	R.C.	2 R.C.	164	129	293	110
109	7704	Do.	–	Tullycrine, m.	–	R.C.	R.C.	–	92	–	92	37
110	7700	Do.	–	Do. f.	–	R.C.	R.C.	–	–	100	100	40
111	9411	Do.	–	Scropul,	–	R.C.	R.C.	R.C.	81	60	141	63
112	[illegible]	Do.	–	Annagh,	R.C.	–	R.C.	2 R.C.	107	130	237	[illegible]
113	[illegible]	Do.	–	Cahir-a-curra,	R.C.	–	R.C.	–	96	80	176	69
114	[illegible]	Kilmacduane,	–	Cranny,	R.C.	–	R.C.	2 R.C.	140	180	[illegible]	183
115	[illegible]	Do.	–	Cooraclare,	R.C.	–	R.C.	5 R.C.	[illegible]	[illegible]	[illegible]	[illegible]
116	[illegible]	Do.	–	Tullabrack, f.	R.C.	–	R.C.	–	–	115	115	47
117	[illegible]	Do.	–	Do. m.	R.C.	–	R.C.	–	66	–	66	28
118	7500	Do.	–	Clogher Day,[a]	–	–	–	–	–	–	–	–
119	[illegible]	[illegible]	42	Rathbane, m.	R.C.	–	R.C.	–	145	–	145	47
120	[illegible]	Do.	–	Do. f.	R.C.	–	R.C.	–	–	84	84	30
121	4453	Kilmihil,	42	Leitrim, m.	R.C.	–	R.C.	–	130	–	126	48
122	4431	Do.	–	Do. f.	R.C.	–	R.C.	–	–	91	91	34
123	4731	Do.	–	Lacken, m.	R.C.	–	R.C.	R.C.	119	–	119	57
124	4732	Do.	–	Do. f.	R.C.	–	R.C.	R.C.	–	141	141	65
125	4870	Do.	–	Cahermurphy,	R.C.	–	R.C.	2 R.C.	77	100	[illegible]	[illegible]
126	[illegible]	[illegible]	51	[illegible], m.	R.C.	–	R.C.	–	90	–	90	35
127	8527	Do.	–	Do. f.	R.C.	–	R.C.	R.C.	–	157	157	62
128	6978	Do.	–	Sallybank 1st Class Agricultural,	Com.	N.B.	R.C.	R.C.	110	83	203	84
129	4816	Kilnoe,	45	Aughnaneal,	R.C.	–	R.C.	–	50	41	91	29
130	8821	Do.	–	Bodyke, m.	R.C.	–	R.C.	R.C.	184	–	184	63
131	4822	Do.	–	Do. f.	R.C.	–	R.C.	R.C.	–	179	179	63
132	4919	Kilfintinan,	51	Cratloe, m.	R.C.	–	R.C.	–	114	–	114	41
133	[illegible]	Do.	–	Do. f.	R.C.	–	R.C.	–	–	97	97	35
134	4691	Kilfarboy,	45	Moy, m.	R.C.	–	R.C.	R.C.	160	–	160	54
135	[illegible]	Do.	–	Do. f.	R.C.	–	R.C.	–	–	180	180	79
136	[illegible]	Do.	–	Miltown Malbay, m.	R.C.	–	R.C.	2 R.C.	211	–	211	60
137	9201	Do.	–	Do. f.	R.C.	–	R.C.	2 R.C.	–	208	208	68
138	[illegible]	Do.	–	Do. i.	R.C.	–	R.C.	2 R.C.	142	141	283	180
139	9390	Do.	–	Rockmount, m.	R.C.	–	R.C.	–	129	–	129	46
140	9391	Do.	–	Do. f.	R.C.	–	R.C.	–	–	109	109	47
141	[illegible]	Do.	–	Spanish Point,	R.C.	–	R.C.	–	41	46	87	45
142	[illegible]	Killuran,	45	O'Callaghan's Mills, m.	R.C.	–	R.C.	R.C.	103	–	103	71
143	9678	Do.	–	Do. f.	R.C.	–	R.C.	R.C.	–	157	157	60
144	6728	Killard,	45	Baunta,	–	R.C.	R.C.	R.C.	93	60	151	69
145	6763	Do.	–	Doonbeg,	R.C.	–	R.C.	3 R.C.	109	108	211	105
146	9045	Do.		Ballard,	–	R.C.	R.C.	2 R.C.	93	66	159	79
147	10756	Do.	–	Shragh,	R.C.	–	R.C.	R.C.	69	73	142	61
148	9124	Kilmanaheen,	45	Rannane, m.	–	R.C.	R.C.	–	86	–	86	42

a Including value of Free Residence. b Including value of Free Residence and Garden.

Province of MUNSTER: County of CLARE—continued.

Amount paid for Books, Requisites, and Apparatus, at Reduced Prices.	Aid granted by the Board during the Year 1874. In Free Stock of Books, Requisites, and Apparatus.	In Salaries, Premiums, and other Gratuities.	Results Fees, Financial Year.	Amount of Local Emoluments received in Aid of Teacher's Salary. School Fees.	Subscriptions, Endowments, &c.	Total Local Aid.	Vested or Non-Vested.	Number.
£ s. d.	£ s. d.	£ s. d.	£ s. d.	£ s. d.	£ s. d.	£ s. d.		
3 1 8	—	20 0 0	13 16 6	9 16 6	—	9 16 6		87
1 11 0	—	24 0 0	9 3 0	9 18 6	—	9 18 6		88
9 1 10	—	24 0 0	4 14 0	5 16 9	—	5 18 0		89
7 13 8	—	122 8 8	53 0 6	30 8 2	—	30 8 4		90
11 15 10	—	165 6 5	67 17 6	24 8 4	—	23 8 4		91
—	—	52 13 4	95 0 6	17 6 7	—	17 6 7		92
12 4 3	—	98 6 6	77 8 6	15 5 6	—	15 5 0		93
4 1 4	—	1 10 0	—	—	—	—		94
2 5 4	—	24 0 0	8 18 6	4 8 6	—	4 8 6		95
4 3 9	—	28 6 9	16 8 11	5 0 0	—	5 0 0		96
2 13 7	—	40 3 4	14 9 1	5 0 0	—	5 0 0		97
1 14 6	4 10 0	9 6 5	—	5 0 6	—	5 0 6		98
1 13 5	4 10 0	13 3 8	—	5 18 1	—	5 18 1		99
0 10 5	—	23 0 0	8 9 0	3 14 6	—	3 14 6	A.	100
2 8 2	—	27 0 0	19 12 6	4 16 9	1 0 0	*5 16 9	A.	101
6 18 6	—	23 0 0	25 8 0	8 10 0	—	8 10 0	V.C.	102
4 0 7	—	43 0 0	23 8 0	3 5 3	—	3 5 3	V.C.	103
14 10 5	—	177 16 8	41 10 0	8 1 0	—	8 1 4	V.T.	104
9 18 6	—	24 0 0	12 1 0	2 8 10	—	2 3 10	V.T.	105
1 5 3	—	24 0 0	18 18 6	4 18 0	—	4 18 0	V.T.	106
1 16 4	—	44 0 0	15 7 8	3 15 6	—	3 15 6	V.C.	107
5 0 0	—	74 0 0	37 0 6	25 1 0	—	25 1 0		108
4 17 10	—	62 10 0	10 18 6	5 14 9	19 6 10	*25 1 7		109
5 10 10	—	63 6 0	18 12 0	4 11 10	—	4 12 10		110
4 5 0	—	41 10 6	10 0 6	7 10 3	14 13 1	*23 3 4	V.C.	111
1 11 1	—	71 10 6	23 16 0	7 5 10	—	7 5 10		112
3 13 11	—	33 18 4	24 0 0	7 0 0	—	7 0 0		113
4 17 8	—	71 11 6	48 9 0	11 13 0	—	11 13 0	V.T.	114
31 3 10	—	212 10 0	142 7 0	43 16 6	—	43 16 6	V.T.	115
1 18 0	—	20 0 0	16 16 6	4 15 0	—	4 15 0	V.T.	116
6 8 9	—	24 0 0	7 18 6	5 8 0	—	5 8 0	V.T.	117
—	—	—	—	—	—	—		118
6 6 8	—	37 0 0	21 19 6	9 11 6	—	9 11 0	A.	119
3 9 8	—	29 10 0	12 7 0	8 11 4	—	8 11 4	A.	120
6 13 7	—	33 0 0	30 9 6	4 18 7	—	4 18 7	V.C.	121
5 8 1	—	24 0 0	9 16 0	5 17 6	—	5 17 6	V.C.	122
7 4 0	—	36 6 8	21 9 6	5 10 0	—	5 10 0	V.C.	123
3 5 8	—	48 10 0	25 17 0	7 5 0	—	7 5 0	V.C.	124
10 3 3	—	100 18 6	27 0 6	10 12 0	—	10 12 4		125
3 1 0	—	30 0 0	11 6 0	18 0 0	—	18 0 0		126
0 18 4	—	56 10 0	27 18 0	7 1 6	—	7 1 6		127
8 17 9	—	80 10 0	30 10 6	20 6 6	9 10 11	*29 17 5	A.	128
8 11 0	—	24 0 0	4 9 6	4 3 6	8 0 0	7 3 6		129
4 6 11	—	33 5 6	73 8 6	6 9 0	—	6 9 0		130
4 18 4	—	36 0 0	38 9 6	8 13 0	—	8 13 0		131
—	—	47 10 6	30 4 7	11 0 9	—	11 0 0	V.C.	132
1 10 10	—	29 6 0	13 16 6	5 18 8	—	5 18 8	V.C.	133
4 17 10	—	49 0 0	27 6 0	6 15 8	—	6 15 8	V.C.	134
8 10 2	—	33 3 4	25 19 6	4 18 6	—	4 18 6	V.C.	135
20 11 9	—	33 6 8	55 10 0	15 15 3	—	15 16 3	V.T.	136
23 8 0	—	71 10 0	47 19 6	7 15 0	—	7 15 0	V.T.	137
10 0 11	—	73 0 0	53 19 0	7 10 6	—	7 10 6	V.T.	138
8 13 5	—	40 0 0	13 0 0	8 11 0	—	6 11 0	V.T.	139
1 17 0	—	51 0 0	19 5 6	8 12 6	—	8 12 6	V.T.	140
1 5 8	—	31 3 4	17 4 0	4 8 0	—	4 8 0		141
7 19 6	—	61 18 4	53 15 0	18 6 5	—	18 6 5	V.C.	142
8 5 8	—	64 10 0	94 2 0	12 10 3	—	12 10 3	V.C.	143
6 11 1	—	63 0 0	16 6 0	9 11 6	—	9 11 6		144
4 15 9	—	35 10 0	49 17 0	16 7 0	—	16 7 0		145
2 10 5	2 10 0	44 0 0	27 15 6	15 7 0	4 10 0	*19 17 0		146
—	—	44 0 0	18 0 6	5 6 1	—	5 6 1		147
5 8 5	—	43 6 4	16 16 0	7 10 6	—	7 10 0	V.T.	148

* Including value of Free Grants.

d Inoperative.

List of Schools in operation on the 31st December, 1874.—

Number.	Roll Number of School.	Parish.	District.	School.	Religious Denominations of Patrons or Correspondents: Clerical.	Lay.	Religious Denominations of Teachers: Principals.	Assistants.	Attendance for the Year: Total number of Pupils on Rolls within the Year: Males.	Fem.	Total.	Average daily attendance.
149	9459	Kilbranahan,	48	Burgess, . . f.	–	R.C.	R.C.	–	–	98	98	63
150	1804	Do.	–	Ennistymon, ᵃ . f.	–	–	–	–	–	–	–	–
151	8534	Do.	–	Do. Workhse.	P.L.	Gds.	R.C.	–	40	37	77	40
152	10514	Do.	–	Do. Convent,	R.C.	–	Nuns.		–	813	813	178
153	8408	Kilshanny,	41	Kilfenora, . . m.	R.C.	–	R.C.	–	100	–	109	49
154	9203	Do.	–	Do. . . f.	R.C.	–	R.C.	–	–	100	100	43
155	0149	Killanena,	49	Killanena, . . m.	R.C.	–	R.C.	–	229	–	229	61
156	8810	Do.	–	Do. . . f.	R.C.	–	R.C.	–	–	129	129	66
157	10316	Kilballyowen,	–	Kilbaha, . . m.	R.C.	–	R.C.	R.C.	141	–	141	68
158	10316	Do.	–	Do. . . f.	R.C.	–	R.C.	R.C.	–	129	129	65
159	6270	Do.	–	Cross, . . .	R.C.	–	R.C.	R.C.	113	87	200	70
160	7456	Kilfiddane,	–	Coolmeen, . . .	R.C.	–	R.C.	R.C.	187	107	294	79
161	7562	Do.	–	Cranny, ᵃ . . .	R.C.	–	R.C.	2R.C.	–	–	–	–
162	10334	Do.	–	Kilrush, . . .	–	R.C.	R.C.	R.C.	98	108	206	68
163	6406	Kilfinane,	–	Burrane, . . .	R.C.	–	R.C.	R.C.	104	97	201	77
164	7506	Do.	–	Carrowdotia, . .	R.C.	–	R.C.	–	63	44	107	46
165	10763	Kilchreest,	48	Boston, . . .	R.C.	–	R.C.	–	74	81	155	57
166	10912	Do.	–	Kells, . . .	R.C.	–	R.C.	–	60	64	124	46
167	6765	Do.	–	Tubber, . . .	R.C.	–	R.C.	R.C.	101	105	206	79
168	10185	Kilkeedy,	–	Kilkeedy, . . m.	R.C.	–	R.C.	R.C.	185	–	185	68
169	10495	Do.	–	Do. . . f.	R.C.	–	R.C.	2R.C.	–	179	179	74
170	9911	Killofin,	48	Labasheeda, . . m.	R.C.	–	R.C.	–	118	–	118	41
171	6904	Do.	–	Do. . . f.	R.C.	–	R.C.	–	–	189	189	65
172	7166	Killonaghan,	49	Inchovea, . . m.	R.C.	–	R.C.	–	61	–	61	38
173	7153	Do.	–	Do. . . f.	R.C.	–	R.C.	–	–	80	80	37
174	10530	Kilmaleery,	–	Fanore, . . .	R.C.	–	R.C.	–	70	66	136	48
175	7769	Kilmaley,	45	Connolly, . . m.	R.C.	–	R.C.	–	104	–	104	47
176	8740	Do.	–	Do. . . f.	R.C.	–	R.C.	R.C.	–	129	129	56
177	7684	Do.	–	Kilmaley, . . m.	R.C.	–	R.C.	–	140	–	148	56
178	7076	Do.	–	Do. . . f.	R.C.	–	R.C.	R.C.	–	183	183	58
179	8837	Do.	–	Kanturk, . . .	R.C.	–	R.C.	R.C.	76	71	147	65
180	0639	Do.	–	Lisroe, . . .	R.C.	–	R.C.	–	70	53	123	41
181	8871	Kilmurry,	–	Darrfield, . . m.	R.C.	–	R.C.	–	136	–	136	45
182	8672	Do.	–	Do. . . f.	R.C.	–	R.C.	–	–	121	121	46
183	6272	Killone,	–	Tiermaclane, . .	R.C.	–	R.C.	R.C.	68	89	157	64
184	10246	Moyarta,	–	Carrigaholt, . . m.	R.C.	–	R.C.	R.C.	158	–	158	71
185	10240	Do.	–	Do. . . f.	R.C.	–	R.C.	R.C.	–	171	171	67
186	6573	Do.	–	Moveen, . . .	R.C.	–	R.C.	R.C.	94	97	191	67
187	6574	Do.	–	Querrin, . . .	R.C.	–	R.C.	R.C.	86	97	183	68
188	9707	Do.	–	Doonaha, . . .	R.C.	–	R.C.	R.C.	62	60	122	61
189	4516	O'Gonnelloe,	42	Ballybran, . . .	R.C.	–	R.C.	R.C.	76	65	141	65
190	7874	Do.	–	Ballylongbannan, .	R.C.	–	R.C.	R.C.	78	65	143	60
191	6997	O'Brien's Bridge,	31	Bridgetown, . . m.	R.C.	–	R.C.	–	200	–	200	60
192	9079	Do.	–	Do. . . f.	R.C.	–	R.C.	R.C.	–	268	268	64
193	7831	Ogonnelloe,	42	Garra Clare, . . .	R.C.	–	R.C.	–	88	61	79	38
194	4716	Quin,	45	Quin, . . m.	R.C.	–	R.C.	–	108	–	108	49
195	6823	Do.	–	Do. . . f.	R.C.	–	R.C.	R.C.	–	115	115	59
196	11004	Do.	–	Dangan, . . .	R.C.	–	R.C.	–	99	74	167	62
197	441	Ruan,	42	Ruan, . . .	R.C.	–	R.C.	R.C.	116	81	167	69
198	1984	Do.	–	Moyrhee, ᵃ . . m.	–	–	–	–	–	–	–	–
199	4683	Do.	–	Do. . . f.	R.C.	–	R.C.	R.C.	79	93	173	60
200	648	St. Patrick's,	31	Parteen, Cml. Agr.	–	R.C.	R.C.	–	104	–	104	40
201	819	Do.	–	Do. . . f.	–	R.C.	R.C.	–	–	78	78	39
202	7094	Sixmilebridge,	45	Kilmurry, . . .	R.C.	–	R.C.	R.C.	96	65	161	63
203	1912	Tulla,	42	Tulla, . . m.	R.C.	–	R.C.	R.C.	169	–	169	64
204	3708	Do.	–	Do. . . f.	R.C.	–	R.C.	R.C.	–	169	169	57
205	8444	Do.	–	Do. . . i.	R.C.	–	R.C.	R.C.	89	128	217	69
206	6150	Do.	–	Do. Workhouse,	P.L.	Gds.	R.C.	–	30	28	58	39
207	6860	Do.	–	Glandree, . . m.	R.C.	–	R.C.	–	94	39	133	59
208	6142	Do.	–	Do. . . f.	R.C.	–	R.C.	–	–	73	73	38
209	7669	Do.	–	Knockjames, . . .	R.C.	–	R.C.	–	77	67	144	58
210	7678	Do.	42	Drumcharley, . . .	R.C.	–	R.C.	–	68	80	148	58
211	2460	Tomfinlough,	45	Newmarket-on-Fergus, . . m.	R.C.	–	R.C.	–	169	–	169	73

ᵃ Suspended. ¹ Including value of Free Residence. ᵃ No returns.

Province of Munster: County of Clare—*continued.*

Amount paid for Books, Requisites, and Apparatus, at Reduced Prices.			Aid granted by the Board during the Year 1874. In Free Stock of Books, Requisites, and Apparatus.			In Salaries, Premiums, and other Gratuities.			Results Fees, Financial Year.			Amount of Local Emoluments received in Aid of Teacher's Salary. School Fees.			Subscriptions, Endowments, &c.			Total Local Aid.			Vested or Non-Vested.	Number.
£	s.	d.	£	s.	d.	£	s.	d.	£	s.	d.	£	s.	d.	£	s.	d.	£	s.	d.		
	—			—		24	0	0	16	8	0	5	10	0		—		5	10	0	V.N.	149
	—			—			—			—			—			—			—			150
	—			—			—			—			—			—			—			151
10	4	8		—		59	5	4	33	6	8	41	0	0		—		41	0	0		152
6	7	7		—		49	8	4	26	13	0	20	17	8		—		20	17	8		153
1	19	9		—		20	0	0	11	10	6	6	19	0	6	0	0	b 12	19	0		154
3	18	11		—		85	16	4	26	8	0	11	7	0		—		11	7	0		155
0	4	6		—		36	15	6	14	18	0	6	9	0		—		6	9	0		156
4	16	8	4	10	0	29	13	0	17	16	6	11	18	5		—		11	18	5	V.T.	157
8	19	6	4	10	0	15	10	0	16	6	0	5	18	4		—		5	18	4	V.T.	158
8	6	10		—		71	0	0	20	0	0	15	2	10		—		15	2	10		159
5	10	6		—		58	4	4	20	10	6	7	14	5		—		7	14	5		160
4	0	11		—		78	10	9	30	6	5		—			—			—			161
2	18	0	5	0	0	104	13	4	20	18	6	15	16	2		—		15	16	2	V.C.	162
4	18	1		—		64	0	0	24	12	0	12	2	10		—		12	2	10		163
0	10	2		—		24	0	0	13	17	0	3	19	10		—		3	19	10		164
1	13	6	4	10	0	18	0	0	14	11	6	5	6	4		—		5	6	4	V.T.	165
2	16	0	4	10	0	21	0	0	19	7	6	6	0	6		—		6	0	6		166
4	13	4		—		68	0	0	26	16	8	18	0	0		—		18	0	0		167
0	8	6		—		42	0	0	20	19	6	17	8	6		—		17	8	6		168
4	13	2		—		40	0	0	28	11	0	18	9	1		—		18	9	1		169
3	11	9		—			—		11	6	0	9	13	0		—		9	18	6		170
1	16	0		—		39	18	8	16	15	0	4	8	8		—		4	3	8		171
2	0	9		—		24	0	0	11	14	6	4	11	4		—		4	11	4		172
1	6	0		—		20	0	0	18	15	0	5	18	0		—		5	18	0		173
0	6	0		—		27	0	6	8	0	0	8	10	1		—		8	16	1		174
1	17	10		—		25	0	0	18	9	0	10	2	0		—		10	2	0		175
1	19	9		—		64	0	0	20	15	6	9	17	0		—		9	17	0		176
4	8	4		—		31	10	0	18	2	0	17	0	0		—		17	0	0		177
2	16	1		—		44	0	0	20	8	6	11	13	4		—		11	13	4		178
6	9	6		—		46	0	0	25	0	0	12	12	11		—		19	12	11		179
2	5	8		—		24	0	0	24	8	8	6	8	10		—		6	8	10		180
	—			—		22	0	0	14	11	0	4	18	8		—		4	18	8		181
6	2	0		—		85	15	8	11	2	8	12	6	8	1	0	0	b 13	6	8		182
4	14	10		—		50	15	8	31	6	6	19	17	4	1	6	0	b 21	3	4		183
5	1	6		—		65	0	0	23	0	8	12	14	4		—		12	14	4	V.T.	184
4	0	1		—		75	10	0	26	13	0	9	5	0		—		9	5	0	V.T.	185
4	4	8		—		59	0	0	25	10	0	13	9	0	7	4	0	b 16	13	0		186
5	3	10		—		52	5	4	21	10	6	13	6	0		—		13	6	0		187
2	14	7		—		48	0	0	21	19	0	12	9	0		—		12	9	6		188
2	11	8		—		65	12	4	13	0	0	17	2	10		—		17	2	10		189
0	7	4		—		60	6	8	15	15	0	13	4	8		—		13	4	8		190
8	18	9		—		48	7	4	45	19	8	25	10	1		—		25	10	1		191
2	1	9		—		52	16	8	43	14	6	10	18	8		—		10	18	8		192
3	0	11		—		24	0	0	6	10	5	1	10	0		—		1	16	0		193
8	1	11		—		10	5	8	21	7	0	15	4	6		—		15	4	6		194
2	15	6		—		50	5	6	10	0	5	7	0	0		—		7	0	0		195
4	7	4		—		23	6	8		—		4	3	8		—		4	3	5		196
	—			—		32	0	0	67	7	0	20	8	10		—		28	8	10	V.C.	197
	—			—			—			—			—			—			—		A.	198
1	10	5		—		53	10	0	23	9	5	3	19	2		—		3	19	8	A.	199
4	10	5		—		19	10	0	18	12	0	12	0	0	12	12	6	a 24	12	6		200
1	15	10		—		20	0	0	11	10	6	5	10	0	5	0	0	b 10	10	0		201
4	14	8		—		44	2	4	18	15	0	5	1	6		—		5	1	6		202
6	8	9		—		180	8	4	27	7	0	11	18	6		—		11	18	6	A.	203
3	3	2		—		60	16	8	23	14	6	9	0	3		—		9	0	3	A.	204
0	10	2		—		65	8	4	10	19	0	5	15	10		—		5	15	10		205
5	14	9		—			—			—			—			—			—			206
2	8	7		—		21	0	0	10	15	0	4	7	6		—		4	7	6	V.C.	207
1	18	6		—		28	0	0	5	19	0	2	16	5		—		2	16	5	V.C.	208
6	13	9		—		56	16	8	24	5	6	8	8	6		—		8	8	6		209
2	14	6		—		21	0	0	12	0	0	7	19	1		—		7	19	1		210
7	0	8		—		56	10	0	26	17	6	13	15	4		—		13	15	4		211

a Including value of Free Residence and Garden.

b Including value of Free Garden.

List of Schools in operation on the 31st December, 1874—

212	2481	Tomfinlough,	43	Newmarket-on-Fergus, f.	R.C.	–	R.C.	R.C.	–	155	155	75
213	4819	Do.	–	Ballycar,	R.C.	–	R.C.	–	96	61	158	48
214	4720	Do.	–	Moughane,	R.C.	–	R.C.	–	40	61	100	26
215	4874	Tomgraney,	49	Scarriff, m.	R.C.	–	R.C.	R.C.	270	–	270	100
216	4975	Do.	–	Do. f.	R.C.	–	R.C.	R.C.	–	217	217	81
217	5407	Do.	–	Do. Workhouse,	P.L.	Gds.	R.C.	–	59	36	95	53
218	7692	Do.	–	Cooleagorry,	R.C.	–	R.C.	–	70	65	135	52
219	7236	Do.	–	Tomgraney, m.	R.C.	–	R.C.	–	96	–	96	56
220	8094*	Do.	–	Do. f.	R.C.	–	R.C.	–	–	86	86	41
221	7075	Do.	–	Clonusker,	R.C.	–	R.C.	R.C.	67	63	130	67
		Total for County Clare, 221,							19,025	18,0[illegible]	[illegible]	[illegible]

COUNTY OF

1	486	Ardnageehy,	56	Glenville, m.	–	Diss.	R.C.	–	124	–	124	56
2	3248	Do.	–	Do. f.	–	Diss.	R.C.	–	–	119	119	47
3	8011	Do.	–	Nunstown, m.	R.C.	–	R.C.	–	150	–	150	51
4	3135	Do.	–	Do. f.	R.C.	–	R.C.	–	–	115	115	65
5	8024	Do.	–	Killgullane, f.	–	R.C.	R.C.	–	21	39	60	[illegible]
6	7401	Do.	–	Chimneyfield,	R.C.	–	R.C.	R.C.	73	93	165	71
7	455	Aghada,	45	Aghada, m.	R.C.	–	R.C.	R.C.	152	52	154	75
8	2290	Do.	–	Farsid, f.	R.C.	–	R.C.	R.C.	38	129	168	62
9	1068	Do.	–	Ballymacandrick,	R.C.	–	R.C.	–	43	46	89	44
10	464	Athnowen,	57	Ovens, m.	R.C.	–	R.C.	R.C.	173	–	173	85
11	5686	Do.	–	Do. f.	R.C.	–	R.C.	R.C.	–	173	173	76
12	2016	Aghabulloge,	–	Knockanagoum, m.	R.C.	–	R.C.	–	73	–	73	33
13	2017	Do.	–	Do. f.	R.C.	–	R.C.	–	–	118	118	45
14	3366	Do.	–	Aghabulloge, m.	R.C.	–	R.C.	–	154	–	154	61
15	8566	Do.	–	Do. f.	R.C.	–	R.C.	–	–	122	122	56
16	1257	Ardfield,	58	Ardfield, f.	R.C.	–	R.C.	R.C.	–	167	167	81
17	10287	Do.	–	Do. m.	R.C.	–	R.C.	R.C.	228	–	228	122
18	3461	Abbeymahon,	–	Lislevane, m.	R.C.	–	R.C.	R.C.	160	–	160	80
19	7973	Do.	–	Do. f.	R.C.	–	R.C.	R.C.	–	135	135	79
20	2280	Aghadown,	58	Lisheen,	R.C.	–	R.C.	R.C.	147	107	254	91
21	7833	Do.	–	Hare Island,	R.C.	–	R.C.	–	30	50	74	36
22	2836	Abbey,	–	Abbey,	R.C.	–	R.C.	R.C.	87	75	162	68
23	3464	Ardagh,	43	Inch, m.	R.C.	–	R.C.	–	131	–	131	63
24	3466	Do.	–	Do. f.	R.C.	–	R.C.	R.C.	–	107	107	64
25	6201	Do.	–	Park,	R.C.	–	R.C.	–	61	38	99	41
26	2312	Aghinagh,	57	Aghinagh,	R.C.	–	R.C.	–	80	60	140	45
27	4519	Do.	–	Ballyvongane, m.	R.C.	–	R.C.	–	137	–	137	65
28	4576	Do.	–	Do. f.	R.C.	–	R.C.	R.C.	–	140	140	75
29	8677	Abbeystrowry,	66	Lissaclarig,	R.C.	–	R.C.	R.C.	54	44	98	44
30	3417	Do.	–	Skibbereen Workhouse,	P.L.	Gds.	R.C.	R.C.	44	53	97	52
31	7413	Aglish,	56	Farran, m.	R.C.	–	R.C.	–	118	–	118	56
32	7414	Do.	–	Do. f.	R.C.	–	R.C.	–	–	129	129	58
33	1188	Ballintemple,	46	Churchtown, m.	R.C.	–	R.C.	–	114	–	114	49
34	6778	Do.	–	Do. f.	R.C.	–	R.C.	R.C.	–	110	115	49
35	1017	Buttevant,	56	Buttevant, m.	R.C.	–	R.C.	R.C.	210	–	210	88
36	4139	Do.	–	Do. f.	R.C.	–	R.C.	R.C.	–	224	224	95
37	7898	Do.	–	Grange, m.	R.C.	–	R.C.	–	63	–	63	36
38	10032	Do.	–	Do. f.	R.C.	–	R.C.	–	–	107	107	47
39	1079	Ballinaboy,	56	Goggin's-hill,	R.C.	–	R.C.	–	94	63	157	75
40	2114	Brigown,	46	Ballygiblin, m.	R.C.	–	R.C.	–	121	–	121	46
41	10229	Do.	–	Do. f.	R.C.	–	R.C.	–	–	94	94	35
42	8216	Do.	–	Mitchelstown Workh.	P.L.	Gds.	R.C.	–	69	66	135	86
43	11153	Ballyvourney,	56	Ballyvourney, m.	R.C.	–	R.C.	R.C.	144	–	144	69
44	11154	Do.	–	Do. f.	R.C.	–	R.C.	R.C.	–	143	143	58
45	6814	Do.	–	Coolea,	R.C.	–	R.C.	R.C.	118	119	237	105

* Including value of Free Residence.

Province of Munster: County of Clare—continued.

Amount paid for Books, Requisites, and Apparatus, at reduced Prices.	Aid granted by the Board during the Year 1874. In Free Stock of Books, Requisites, and Apparatus.	In Salaries, Premiums, and other Gratuities.	Results Fees, Financial Year.	Amount of Local Emoluments received in Aid of Teacher's Salary. School Fees.	Subscriptions, Endowments, &c.	Total Local Aid.	Vested or Non-Vested.	Number.
£ s. d.	£ s. d.	£ s. d.	£ s. d.	£ s. d.	£ s. d.	£ s. d.		
4 8 7	—	33 13 4	24 1 0	8 8 0	—	8 8 0		212
1 17 1	—	15 6 8	18 8 0	4 8 6	—	4 3 6		213
1 16 0	—	16 0 0	6 19 0	1 18 0	—	1 18 0		214
6 2 11	—	162 0 0	85 1 8	16 15 9	—	16 15 9		215
12 6 8	—	61 4 11	82 14 0	7 17 8	—	7 17 8		216
8 19 10	—	3 0 0	—	—	—	—		217
0 9 8	—	25 8 6	5 4 8	4 4 0	—	4 4 8		218
2 11 4	—	24 0 0	8 8 4	8 17 6	—	8 17 6		219
8 12 7	—	27 0 0	16 1 0	2 18 0	—	2 18 0		220
4 8 8	—	37 10 0	86 1 0	2 5 0	—	2 5 0		221
802 14 4	84 10 0	8,804 14 0	4,421 12 1	1,033 4 0	219 19 11	2,167 3 11		

CORK—318 Schools.

Amount paid for Books, Requisites, and Apparatus, at reduced Prices.	In Free Stock of Books, Requisites, and Apparatus.	In Salaries, Premiums, and other Gratuities.	Results Fees, Financial Year.	School Fees.	Subscriptions, Endowments, &c.	Total Local Aid.	Vested or Non-Vested.	Number.
4 1 10	—	40 13 4	18 8 0	6 13 0	21 0 6	28 13 6		1
1 10 5	—	37 0 0	10 2 0	4 5 9	20 0 11	b24 5 8		2
0 5 8	—	53 10 0	11 11 0	11 14 2	—	11 14 2	V.T.	3
8 1 6	—	68 3 4	16 8 8	6 7 8	—	6 7 8	V.T.	4
—	—	20 18 4	5 10 2	8 18 4	—	8 18 4	V.T.	5
4 5 9	—	56 0 0	21 4 8	12 17 4	—	12 17 4		6
5 0 3	—	50 0 0	41 0 0	3 2 10	18 0 3	21 12 1		7
2 11 9	—	48 0 0	18 7 8	6 7 10	—	6 7 10		8
4 18 8	4 10 0	72 0 0	11 8 6	2 7 11	—	2 7 11		9
1 18 5	—	75 0 0	15 3 0	6 18 6	0 15 0	7 13 6		10
2 8 8	—	80 8 4	18 11 6	6 8 8	—	6 8 8		11
2 10 0	—	24 0 0	18 18 0	8 16 9	—	8 16 9	V.T.	12
1 7 11	—	24 0 0	13 11 0	4 8 0	—	4 8 0	V.T.	13
—	—	34 15 8	21 2 6	11 1 0	—	11 1 0		14
—	—	14 0 0	17 8 0	7 4 0	—	7 4 0		15
6 2 8	—	67 13 4	29 6 0	11 17 10	—	11 17 10	V.T.	16
6 8 0	—	67 8 4	48 12 0	22 14 11	—	22 14 11		17
2 18 9	—	48 0 0	28 18 6	8 0 0	—	8 0 0	V.T.	18
4 8 0	—	71 10 0	64 4 8	10 10 0	—	10 10 0	V.T.	19
8 0 6	—	63 0 0	18 7 0	9 0 0	—	9 0 0		20
1 0 6	—	20 0 0	10 9 0	3 0 0	1 10 0	b4 10 0		21
8 12 0	—	59 10 0	14 3 0	4 18 6	—	4 18 6	V.T.	22
2 18 6	—	24 0 0	18 15 6	4 12 4	2 10 0	7 2 4	V.T.	23
2 10 6	—	43 0 0	20 9 0	4 0 0	2 10 0	7 10 0	V.T.	24
8 10 0	—	31 0 0	16 8 6	8 15 2	5 0 0	8 16 2		25
1 5 7	—	34 0 0	6 3 0	4 8 0	—	4 8 0		26
4 10 9	—	23 0 0	29 13 6	0 13 6	—	0 13 6		27
6 4 10	—	59 8 4	28 9 0	14 5 0	—	14 5 0		28
0 15 8	—	41 1 8	14 6 1	4 10 6	—	4 10 6		29
—	—	3 10 0	—	—	—	—		30
4 0 7	—	65 0 0	10 14 0	6 15 0	—	6 15 0		31
1 18 2	—	55 15 0	11 16 6	4 7 0	—	4 7 0		32
1 4 0	—	52 0 0	18 11 6	2 5 0	2 0 0	b4 5 0		33
2 10 1	—	40 0 0	19 8 6	8 16 6	—	8 16 6		34
4 5 7	—	68 8 8	27 17 0	9 17 5	—	9 17 5		35
4 14 8	—	67 8 8	17 4 8	5 12 11	—	5 12 10		36
2 9 11	—	24 0 0	4 18 0	2 2 8	4 0 0	b6 2 8		37
8 12 1	—	52 0 0	12 16 6	8 10 0	2 0 0	b10 10 0		38
1 0 11	—	64 18 4	32 8 6	22 7 8	—	22 7 8		39
0 15 8	—	24 0 0	8 16 5	12 8 0	—	12 8 0	V.T.	40
—	—	53 8 0	6 12 8	8 4 8	—	8 4 8	V.T.	41
2 0 7	—	—	—	—	—	—		42
2 3 9	5 0 0	20 18 4	—	10 7 4	—	10 7 4		43
4 4 9	5 0 0	8 8 8	—	8 1 8	—	8 1 8		44
8 18 10	—	61 0 8	20 0 6	18 0 8	—	18 0 8		45

b Including value of Free Residence and Garden.

List of Schools in operation on the 31st December, 1874.—

Number.	Roll Number of School.	Parish.	District.	School.	Religious Denomination of Manager or Correspondent: Clerical.	Lay.	Religious Denominations of Teachers: Principals.	Assistants.	Attendance for the Year: Total number of Pupils on Rolls within the Year 1874: Males.	Fem.	Total.	Average Daily Attendance.
46	7491	Ballyvourney,	45	Slievereagh,	R.C.	–	R.C.	R.C.	115	106	221	88
47	8993	Driway,	66	Briway,	R.C.	–	R.C.	–	80	33	113	50
48	3997	Ballyhooly,	–	Ballyhooly, m.	R.C.	–	R.C.	4R.C.	253	–	256	108
49	3998	Do.	–	Do. f.	R.C.	–	R.C.	1R.C.	–	229	229	112
50	4834	Ballydeloughy,	–	Ballindangan, m.	R.C.	–	R.C.	R.C.	156	–	156	88
51	[illegible]	Do.	–	Do. f.	R.C.	–	R.C.	R.C.	–	145	145	69
52	4690	[illegible]	66	[illegible] m.	R.C.	–	R.C.	–	120	–	120	55
53	7241	Do.	–	Do. f.	R.C.	–	R.C.	–	–	108	108	[illegible]
54	5029	Ballymodan,	32	Bandon, m.	R.C.	–	R.C.	R.C.	240	–	245	77
55	9152	Do.	–	Do. Workhouse,	P.L.	Gds.	R.C.	R.C.	48	38	86	65
56	9065	Do.	–	Cronamahon,	R.C.	–	R.C.	–	63	56	119	41
57	10375	Do.	–	Gurteen O'Mahon,*	R.C.	–	–	–	–	–	–	–
58	5345	Ballymoe,	15	Ballymoe, m.	R.C.	–	R.C.	R.C.	160	–	160	72
59	5346	Do.	–	Do. f.	R.C.	–	R.C.	R.C.	–	119	119	66
60	6590	Bandon,	56	Shannon-st. (Bandon),	R.C.	–	R.C.	R.C.	169	–	169	80
61	10739	Ballymoney,	–	Ballinacarriga, m.	R.C.	–	R.C.	R.C.	170	–	175	73
62	10740	Do.	–	Do. f.	R.C.	–	R.C.	R.C.	–	158	158	70
63	8150	Do.	–	Ballyneen, m.	R.C.	–	R.C.	R.C.	181	–	181	64
64	8318	Do.	–	Do. f.	R.C.	–	R.C.	R.C.	–	141	141	66
65	4605	Blarney,	60	Blarney Village, m.	R.C.	–	R.C.	–	130	–	130	65
66	6804	Ballydeloher,	–	Brookledge,	R.C.	–	R.C.	R.C.	103	73	176	68
67	5093	Ballyfeard,	–	Ballinagarry,	R.C.	–	R.C.	–	66	31	97	45
68	7361	Ballymartle,	–	Ballymartle, m.	R.C.	–	R.C.	–	56	–	56	58
69	8446	Do.	–	Do. f.	R.C.	–	R.C.	R.C.	–	104	104	43
70	7086	Ballyclogh,	35	Ballyclogh, m.	R.C.	–	R.C.	R.C.	160	–	160	71
71	7707	Do.	–	Do f.	R.C.	–	R.C.	R.C.	–	158	158	70
72	7237	Ballyhedy,	–	Newtown, f.	R.C.	–	R.C.	R.C.	16	248	264	78
73	6582	Ballygarvan,	66	Ballygarvan, m.	R.C.	–	R.C.	–	152	–	152	48
74	6426	Do.	–	Do. f.	R.C.	–	R.C.	R.C.	–	130	130	56
75	9587	Ballinadee,	56	Ballinadee, m.	R.C.	–	R.C.	R.C.	122	–	122	60
76	8327	Do.	–	Do. f.	R.C.	–	R.C.	–	–	83	83	58
77	6973	Brinny,	–	Coolaleast,	R.C.	–	R.C.	R.C.	73	63	136	57
78	460	Clondrohid,	36	Gurrane, m.	R.C.	–	R.C.	R.C.	179	–	179	85
79	461	Do.	–	Do. f.	R.C.	–	R.C.	R.C.	–	166	169	85
80	4157	Do.	–	Carrigcashel,	R.C.	–	R.C.	R.C.	190	155	345	105
81	10279	Do.	–	Marlfield,	R.C.	–	R.C.	2R.C.	78	84	156	73
82	462	Caherlag,	66	New Glanmire, m.	R.C.	–	R.C.	–	103	–	103	48
83	6186	Do.	–	Do. f.	R.C.	–	R.C.	–	–	109	107	61
84	482	Clonpriest,	45	Clonpriest, m.	R.C.	–	R.C.	–	123	–	123	49
85	4654	Do.	–	Do. f.	R.C.	–	R.C.	R.C.	–	187	157	56
86	4413	Do.	–	Kyle,	R.C.	–	R.C.	–	45	63	108	47
87	483	Corkbeg,	–	Whitegate, m.	R.C.	–	R.C.	R.C.	140	–	146	73
88	7946	Do.	–	Do. f.	R.C.	–	R.C.	R.C.	–	170	170	73
89	11108	Do.	–	Corkbeg,	–	R.C.	R.C.	–	23	20	43	34
90	470	Caheragh,	66	Killeenleagh, m.	R.C.	–	R.C.	R.C.	183	–	183	69
91	7361	Do.	–	Killeenleagh, f.	R.C.	–	R.C.	R.C.	–	165	165	60
92	3047	Do.	–	Dromore,	R.C.	–	R.C.	1R.C.	185	140	325	135
93	4736	Do.	–	[illegible]	R.C.	–	R.C.	2R.C.	90	119	212	81
94	9847	Do.	66	Baurnville, m.	R.C.	–	R.C.	–	131	–	131	63
95	6848	Do.	–	Do. f.	R.C.	–	R.C.	R.C.	–	145	145	77
96	10543	Do.	66	Caheragh,	–	R.C.	R.C.	–	20	15	35	23
97	11216	Do.	–	Dromore, f.	R.C.	–	R.C.	R.C.	–	127	127	68
98	480	Clear Island,	–	Cape Clear Island, m.	R.C.	–	R.C.	–	65	–	65	40
99	8557	Do.	–	Do. f.	R.C.	–	R.C.	–	–	60	60	31
100	1026	Clondulane,	54	Clondulane,	R.C.	–	R.C.	R.C.	103	94	197	61
101	1637	Clonmel,	60	Cove, m.	R.C.	–	R.C.	3R.C.	240	–	240	155
102	1407	Do.	–	Do. prep. m.	R.C.	–	R.C.	3R.C.	431	–	431	184
103	10777	Do.	–	Queenstown, m.	–	R.C.	R.C.	–	89	–	89	55
104	10772	Do.	–	Do. f.	–	R.C.	Prm.	–	–	87	87	38
105	6376	Do.	–	Do. Conv. f.	R.C.	–	None		60	820	880	672
106	10981	Do.	–	Do. i.	–	R.C.	Prm.	–	43	37	80	45
107	1789	Clonfert,	53	Kanturk, m.	R.C.	–	R.C.	1R.C.	241	–	217	128
108	1283	Do.	–	Do. prep. m.	R.C.	–	R.C.	R.C.	186	–	[illegible]	98

* Inoperative.

b Including value of Free Residence and Garden.

Province of MUNSTER: County of CORK—*continued.*

Amount paid for Books, Requisites, and Apparatus, at Reduced Prices.	Aid granted by the Board during the Year 1874: In Free Stock of Books, Requisites, and Apparatus.	Aid granted by the Board during the Year 1874: In Salaries, Premiums, and other Gratuities.	Aid granted by the Board during the Year 1874: Results Fees, Financial Year.	Amount of Local Endowments provided in Aid of Teacher's Salary: School Fees.	Amount of Local Endowments provided in Aid of Teacher's Salary: Subscriptions, Endowments, &c.	Amount of Local Endowments provided in Aid of Teacher's Salary: Total Local Aid.	Vested or Non-Vested.	Number.
£ s. d.	£ s. d.	£ s. d.	£ s. d.	£ s. d.	£ s. d.	£ s. d.		
8 17 3	—	42 17 8	26 17 8	8 0 0	—	8 0 0		46
1 4 11	—	24 0 0	7 0 0	6 10 5	—	6 10 5	V.T.	47
8 1 8	—	131 8 4	83 14 0	17 7 0	12 0 0	29 7 0	V.T.	48
0 12 3	—	94 13 4	53 8 0	10 8 4	8 0 0	27 8 4	V.T.	49
8 11 3	—	54 13 0	24 7 0	20 17 0	—	20 17 0		50
4 8 8	—	41 0 0	19 9 0	13 7 9	—	13 7 9		51
2 19 9	—	41 0 0	14 3 0	18 8 4	—	18 8 4		52
0 0 6	—	68 10 0	11 14 0	8 1 0	—	8 1 0		53
1 6 1	—	69 2 0	13 6 0	10 12 1	11 0 0	21 12 1		54
6 10 4	—	1 10 0	—	—	—	—		55
1 7 0	—	24 0 0	20 12 0	10 10 0	—	10 19 0		56
—	—	—	—	—	—	—		57
8 19 9	—	80 10 0	30 4 0	8 12 8	3 15 0	12 7 8	V.C.	58
0 17 6	—	60 0 0	28 5 0	10 6 7	3 15 0	14 1 7	V.C.	59
8 19 5	—	90 0 0	52 18 0	27 16 0	8 0 0	35 16 0		60
1 17 9	5 0 0	50 10 0	70 14 11	22 17 0	—	22 17 0		61
6 14 7	5 0 0	30 10 0	30 14 5	7 9 8	—	7 9 8		62
4 0 6	—	65 10 0	21 11 6	16 8 8	—	16 8 8		63
2 8 7	—	36 0 0	27 17 6	8 0 4	—	8 0 4		64
4 12 11	—	60 18 4	18 0 8	20 17 2	—	20 17 2		65
1 18 4	—	63 10 0	20 17 1	11 0 5	—	11 0 0		66
3 16 9	—	20 0 0	15 1 0	9 16 0	—	9 15 8		67
1 10 0	—	37 18 4	13 6 0	16 2 5	—	16 2 5		68
1 17 7	—	39 14 5	14 5 0	8 14 1	—	8 14 1		69
7 19 0	—	99 0 0	25 6 0	18 19 0	—	18 19 0		70
4 0 0	—	69 8 4	33 12 6	33 11 6	2 10 0	35 1 6		71
0 0 8	6 6 6	74 8 4	26 17 0	18 0 0	8 0 0	*18 0 0		72
1 17 11	—	80 16 6	15 8 0	11 15 11	—	11 15 11		73
4 10 4	—	65 15 4	24 18 0	18 3 6	—	18 3 6		74
6 1 0	—	50 10 0	20 3 4	18 8 4	—	18 4 0	V.T.	75
2 8 11	—	10 8 11	9 4 0	6 9 11	—	8 8 11		76
1 18 9	—	53 10 0	17 10 0	7 0 0	—	7 0 0	V.T.	77
6 17 2	—	74 0 0	60 8 0	15 8 0	—	15 2 0		78
2 7 0	—	42 6 8	26 15 0	13 0 0	—	12 0 0		79
0 19 0	—	82 0 0	40 19 0	12 8 0	—	12 3 0	V.T.	80
6 10 4	—	61 0 0	28 2 0	12 15 6	2 10 0	*15 5 6		81
2 10 10	—	64 13 4	10 15 0	14 6 0	—	14 6 9		82
1 14 8	—	25 6 0	30 4 0	17 0 0	—	17 0 0		83
5 7 8	2 11 6	58 0 0	12 16 6	5 10 1	1 0 0	6 10 1		84
8 7 11	2 1 6	40 0 0	21 8 0	4 0 7	2 0 0	6 0 7		85
2 1 0	—	24 0 0	12 1 0	9 10 0	—	9 10 0	V.C.	86
2 19 5	—	40 0 0	14 14 6	3 18 0	—	3 18 0		87
8 11 11	—	55 2 6	18 17 0	5 9 2	—	5 9 2		88
8 14 11	4 0 0	10 0 0	6 19 6	12 0 0	44 0 0	*56 0 0		89
8 18 0	—	62 5 0	21 0 0	11 15 2	—	11 14 2		90
3 6 8	—	47 0 0	26 17 2	11 6 0	—	11 6 0		91
8 11 10	—	85 6 0	49 0 8	9 13 1	—	9 13 1		92
4 16 11	—	60 10 0	25 9 10	18 1 7	—	15 1 7		93
3 4 8	—	63 0 0	34 8 8	0 9 8	—	0 9 8	V.C.	94
2 0 10	—	64 1 1	57 3 6	12 14 8	—	12 14 6	V.T.	95
1 5 8	—	20 0 0	8 4 10	5 5 0	20 0 0	25 5 0		96
—	—	—	—	—	—	—		97
2 2 6	—	24 0 0	5 11 6	2 0 0	—	2 0 0		98
—	—	20 0 0	0 11 6	2 12 0	—	2 12 0		99
—	—	59 0 0	18 6 2	18 18 9	1 10 0	*20 8 6		100
15 15 1	—	149 10 0	80 10 6	41 18 11	—	41 10 11	V.T.	101
2 14 10	—	108 0 0	98 15 0	27 0 1	4 0 0	31 0 1	V.T.	102
9 8 2	—	71 10 0	40 0 6	57 1 6	63 0 0	*90 1 0		103
8 17 8	—	29 0 0	23 8 6	62 3 5	25 0 0	*87 3 5		104
58 4 3	—	277 15 0	114 0 6	80 14 6	—	80 14 6		105
0 17 8	—	98 10 0	7 15 0	11 17 1	95 0 0	*85 17 1		106
14 11 11	—	108 0 0	41 15 0	58 10 1	—	58 10 1	N.	107
6 14 10	—	81 18 0	20 15 0	14 9 5	—	14 9 5	N.	108

* Including value of Free Residence.

List of Schools in operation on the 31st December, 1874.—

Number.	Roll Number of School.	Parish.	District.	School.	Religious Denomination of Manager or Correspondent. Clerical.	Lay.	Number and Religious Denomination of Teachers. Principals.	Assistants.	Attendance for the Year. Total Number of Pupils on Rolls within the Year 1874. Males.	Females.	Total.	Average Daily Attendance for the Year 1874.
109	16[illegible]	Clonfert,	58	Kanturk, Convent, f.	R.C.	–	Nuns	–	–	896	[illegible]	178
110	8[illegible]	Do.	–	Do. Workhouse,	P.L.	Gds.	2R.C.	R.C.	9[illegible]	134	[illegible]	1[illegible]5
111	216[illegible]	Do.	–	Lismire, m.	R.C.	–	R.C.	–	60	–	60	36
112	216[illegible]	Do.	–	Do. f.	R.C.	–	R.C.	R.C.	–	137	137	57
113	6476	Do.	58	Rockchapel, m.	R.C.	–	R.C.	R.C.	165	–	165	71
114	6476	Do.	–	Do. f.	R.C.	–	R.C.	R.C.	–	178	178	75
115	[illegible]	Do.	–	Tooreard, m.	R.C.	–	R.C.	–	129	–	129	54
116	[illegible]	Do.	–	Do. f.	R.C.	–	R.C.	R.C.	–	108	108	54
117	718[illegible]	Do.	–	Meelin, m.	R.C.	–	R.C.	R.C.	180	–	180	71
118	7376	Do.	–	Do. f.	R.C.	–	R.C.	R.C.	–	169	169	74
119	[illegible]	Do.	–	Tour,	R.C.	–	R.C.	R.C.	118	186	248	91
120	10764	Do.	–	Knocknacolan,	R.C.	–	R.C.	–	69	68	130	44
121	1667	Castlelyons,	56	Castlelyons, m.	–	R.C.	R.C.	R.C.	161	–	161	76
122	6548	Do.	–	Do. f.	–	R.C.	R.C.	R.C.	–	188	188	78
123	2048	Castletownroche,	–	Castletownroche, m.	R.C.	–	R.C.	R.C.	196	–	196	88
124	2410	Do.	–	Do. f.	R.C.	–	R.C.	2R.C.	–	208	208	80
125	[illegible]	Carrigtohill,	60	Carrigtohill, m.	R.C.	–	R.C.	R.C.	167	–	167	81
126	7416	Do.	–	Do. f.	R.C.	–	R.C.	2R.C.	–	163	163	69
127	8159	Creagh,	56	Creagh,	R.C.	–	R.C.	R.C.	84	79	163	80
128	[illegible]	Do.	–	Rossnagrogue,	R.C.	–	R.C.	–	90	63	153	44
129	8440	Do.	–	Skibbereen, (1), m.	R.C.	–	R.C.	R.C.	181	–	181	68
130	8441	Do.	–	Do.	R.C.	–	R.C.	R.C.	164	–	169	75
131	[illegible]	Do.	–	Do. No. 2, Conv. f.	–	R.C.	R.C.	–	–	696	696	329
132	5146	Do.	–	Do. (2), m.	R.C.	–	R.C.	R.C.	163	–	162	64
133	5141	Do.	–	Do.[a] (3), m.	R.C.	–	–	–	–	–	–	–
134	[illegible]	Do.	–	Tragumna, m.	R.C.	–	R.C.	–	101	–	101	48
135	[illegible]	Do.	–	Do. f.	R.C.	–	R.C.	–	–	88	88	41
136	[illegible]	Cloyne,	58	Cloyne, m.	R.C.	–	R.C.	2R.C.	209	–	209	166
137	[illegible]	Do.	–	Do. f.	R.C.	–	R.C.	R.C.	–	150	150	66
138	8449	Do.	–	Do. i.	R.C.	–	R.C.	R.C.	46	81	12[illegible]	46
139	9601	Do.	–	Ballycotton, m.	R.C.	–	R.C.	R.C.	121	–	121	57
140	6002	Do.	–	Do. f.	R.C.	–	R.C.	R.C.	–	108	108	58
141	[illegible]	Do.	–	Ballymacoda, m.	R.C.	–	R.C.	R.C.	129	–	129	68
142	10394	Do.	–	Do. f.	R.C.	–	R.C.	–	–	88	88	64
143	[illegible]	Clontead,	56	Belgooly, m.	R.C.	–	R.C.	R.C.	104	–	104	57
144	[illegible]	Do.	–	Do. f.	R.C.	–	R.C.	R.C.	–	146	146	61
145	[illegible]	Do.	–	Lyre, m.	R.C.	–	R.C.	–	97	–	97	59
146	[illegible]	Do.	–	Do. f.	R.C.	–	R.C.	R.C.	–	176	176	61
147	4148	Do.	–	Clonmeen, m.	R.C.	–	R.C.	R.C.	175	–	175	90
148	4146	Do.	–	Do. f.	R.C.	–	R.C.	R.C.	–	163	163	61
149	8150	Canovee,	56	Canovee, m.	R.C.	–	R.C.	–	148	–	148	60
150	[illegible]	Do.	–	Do. f.	R.C.	–	R.C.	R.C.	–	139	139	68
151	[illegible]	Carrigrohane,	60	Ballincollig, m.	R.C.	–	R.C.	2R.C.	283	–	283	114
152	[illegible]	Do.	–	Do. f.	R.C.	–	R.C.	2R.C.	–	199	199	82
153	[illegible]	Do.	–	Do. i.	R.C.	–	R.C.	R.C.	94	97	191	118
154	[illegible]	Do.	–	Carrigrohane, pay.	–	R.C.	R.C.	–	31	6	38	19
155	[illegible]	Cullen,	56	Cullen, m.	R.C.	–	R.C.	R.C.	191	–	191	76
156	[illegible]	Do.	–	Do. f.	R.C.	–	R.C.	3R.C.	–	314	314	148
157	4441	Castlehaven,	56	Drombeg, m.	R.C.	–	R.C.	–	99	–	99	41
158	4443	Castlehaven,	56	Drombeg, f.	R.C.	–	R.C.	–	–	126	129	43
159	5716	Do.	–	Castletownshend, m.	R.C.	–	R.C.	2R.C.	146	–	146	64
160	5717	Do.	–	Do. f.	R.C.	–	R.C.	2R.C.	–	181	181	85
161	[illegible]	Do.	–	Do.	R.C.	–	R.C.	–	17	17	34	12
162	[illegible]	Carrigaline,	60	Shanbally,	R.C.	–	R.C.	R.C.	161	47	148	58
163	5375	Do.	–	Douglas, m.	R.C.	–	R.C.	R.C.	188	–	188	79
164	[illegible]	Do.	–	Do. f.	R.C.	–	R.C.	R.C.	–	287	287	101
165	[illegible]	Castlemagner,	56	Ballyhass, m.	–	R.C.	R.C.	–	146	–	146	65
166	[illegible]	Do.	–	Do. f.	–	R.C.	R.C.	R.C.	–	138	136	64
167	[illegible]	Carrigleamleary,	–	Clogher & Carrig, m.	R.C.	–	R.C.	–	91	–	91	63
168	[illegible]	Do.	–	Do. f.	R.C.	–	R.C.	–	–	69	69	37
169	[illegible]	Churchtown,	–	Churchtown, m.	R.C.	–	R.C.	R.C.	147	–	147	69
170	[illegible]	Do.	–	Do. f.	R.C.	–	R.C.	R.C.	–	138	168	54
171	[illegible]	Clondrohid,	48	Clondrohid, m.	R.C.	–	R.C.	–	78	–	78	41

[a] Inoperative.

[b] Including value of Free Residence.

Province of Munster: County of Cork—*continued.*

Amount paid for Books, Requisites, and Apparatus, at Reduced Prices.	Aid granted by the Board during the Year 1874. In Free Stock of Books, Requisites, and Apparatus.	In Salaries, Premiums, and other Gratuities.	Results Fees, Financial Year.	Amount of Local Emoluments received in Aid of Teacher's Salary. School Fees.	Subscriptions, Endowments, &c.	Total Local Aid.	Vested or Non-Vested.	Number.
£ s. d.	£ s. d.	£ s. d.	£ s. d.	£ s. d.	£ s. d.	£ s. d.		
14 15 0	—	104 14 4	45 16 0	—	—	—		109
11 16 1	—	—	—	—	—	—		110
1 18 11	—	24 0 0	11 15 0	11 3 8	—	11 3 8	v.r.	111
3 8 0	—	51 8 8	20 4 0	8 0 0	—	8 0 0	v.r.	112
3 5 1	—	68 0 0	25 8 0	18 0 2	—	13 0 2	v.c.	113
6 8 2	—	48 7 4	24 19 0	16 10 6	—	16 10 6	v.c.	114
1 12 0	—	21 0 0	31 9 0	11 8 5	—	11 8 5	v.r.	115
6 17 1	—	40 0 0	16 6 8	11 1 11	—	11 1 11	v.r.	116
4 12 11	—	65 0 0	28 5 0	15 8 8	—	15 8 8	v.c.	117
4 3 0	—	65 10 0	27 8 0	12 0 0	—	12 0 0	v.c.	118
5 2 1	—	48 0 0	27 15 0	12 6 8	—	12 6 8		119
2 14 0	—	24 0 0	12 4 0	8 0 0	—	8 0 0		120
6 6 0	—	68 10 0	20 18 0	11 8 9	2 10 0	13 18 9	v.c.	121
2 10 6	—	50 0 0	17 18 0	9 8 4	2 10 0	11 18 4	v.c.	122
2 1 4	—	72 8 4	28 15 8	17 8 1	—	17 8 1		123
6 9 0	—	73 0 0	26 7 8	18 7 2	—	18 7 2		124
5 18 9	—	71 0 8	22 18 0	17 0 0	—	17 0 0		125
7 9 6	—	74 18 4	24 19 6	15 12 10	—	15 12 10		126
4 16 11	—	68 10 0	34 7 0	9 15 0	—	9 15 0	v.r.	127
3 14 11	—	24 0 0	10 6 7	3 19 4	—	3 19 4		128
2 6 9	—	81 0 8	29 4 0	11 15 8	—	11 15 8	v.r.	129
1 17 6	—	67 13 4	14 17 0	5 6 6	—	5 6 6	v.r.	130
27 9 4	—	101 2 10	62 9 6	18 7 9	—	18 7 9		131
6 10 6	—	62 18 4	28 16 0	9 10 11	—	9 10 11	v.r.	132
—	—	—	—	—	—	—	v.r.	133
4 0 9	—	21 0 0	18 4 2	16 3 6	—	16 3 6		134
—	—	88 10 0	12 0 6	9 8 10	—	9 8 10		135
1 8 9	—	121 0 0	47 2 0	19 15 6	—	19 15 6		136
4 6 11	—	82 0 0	63 17 0	10 3 2	—	10 3 2		137
—	—	41 0 0	5 0 0	2 3 4	—	2 3 4		138
5 6 8	—	55 8 0	21 14 0	7 12 8	—	7 12 8		139
2 13 4	—	52 0 0	31 2 6	5 1 6	—	5 1 6		140
—	—	57 0 0	30 5 6	4 1 8	—	4 1 8		141
—	—	26 0 0	12 0 0	1 12 8	—	1 12 0		142
2 17 8	—	83 3 4	14 17 6	11 11 6	—	11 11 6	v.r.	143
4 17 0	—	46 10 6	15 10 0	10 4 6	—	10 4 6	v.r.	144
4 11 0	—	57 0 0	11 8 0	4 16 6	—	4 16 6	v.r.	145
3 0 3	—	50 0 0	18 18 1	7 17 0	—	7 17 0		146
1 15 11	—	69 10 0	30 10 5	6 15 0	—	6 15 0	v.c.	147
6 6 7	—	63 6 6	34 2 5	4 19 6	—	4 19 6	v.c.	148
6 3 5	—	44 13 4	14 7 2	10 6 3	—	10 6 3	v.r.	149
3 3 0	—	40 0 0	29 10 3	8 0 0	—	8 0 0	v.r.	150
9 0 5	—	69 0 0	28 10 0	21 1 7	—	21 1 7		151
6 2 6	—	56 0 6	25 0 5	15 8 5	—	13 8 5		152
1 10 0	5 0 0	51 0 6	20 5 0	8 10 5	—	8 10 5		153
—	—	29 5 0	7 1 6	0 17 8	20 0 0	*35 18 8		154
2 15 2	2 5 0	56 0 0	17 1 0	—	—	—	v.r.	155
10 1 1	3 2 8	112 10 0	30 10 0	6 4 6	—	6 4 6	v.r.	156
3 10 8	—	59 5 9	18 3 0	5 5 1	—	5 5 1	v.c.	157
5 12 9	—	82 13 4	16 10 0	4 0 6	—	4 0 6	v.c.	158
0 0 10	—	48 0 0	15 19 6	0 8 2	—	5 8 2	v.c.	159
5 17 6	—	68 0 0	21 19 0	5 6 10	—	5 6 10	v.c.	160
3 5 6	4 0 0	17 13 4	4 8 0	4 10 0	16 0 0	*30 10 0		161
5 4 2	—	46 10 8	19 2 0	12 1 6	—	12 1 6		162
5 3 9	—	56 8 4	10 18 8	13 6 1	—	15 6 1		163
4 12 7	—	88 0 0	21 5 8	15 7 7	—	15 7 7		164
5 6 5	—	78 10 6	18 17 0	18 0 0	15 0 0	*33 0 0	v.c.	165
5 1 3	—	35 5 0	17 11 6	10 2 0	3 0 0	13 2 0	v.c.	166
2 6 10	—	24 0 0	10 7 6	4 11 6	—	4 11 6		167
1 12 4	—	80 0 0	8 4 6	7 8 1	—	7 8 1		168
4 0 7	—	71 10 0	22 12 8	5 0 11	6 0 0	13 0 11		169
7 15 4	—	45 0 0	18 13 0	6 15 0	3 0 0	12 15 0		170
3 13 6	—	27 10 0	12 15 0	6 3 9	—	6 3 9		171

* Including value of Free Residence and Garden.

† Including value of Free Garden.

List of Schools in operation on the 31st December, 1874.—

Number.	Roll Number of School.	Parish.	District.	School.	Religious Denomination of Manager or Correspondent. Clerical.	Lay.	Number and Religious Denominations of Teachers. Principals.	Assistants.	Attendance for the Year. Total number of Pupils on Rolls within the Year 1874. Males.	Females.	Total.	[illegible]
172	9538	Clonmult,	46	Clonmult, f.	R.C.	–	R.C.	–	–	78	78	39
173	7637	Cloghean,	60	Cloghean,	R.C.	–	R.C.	–	71	44	115	43
174	473	Durrus,	56	Fourmilewater, m.	R.C.	–	R.C.	R.C.	146	–	146	71
175	845	Do.	–	Do. f.	R.C.	–	R.C.	R.C.	–	179	179	77
176	1684	Drishane,	55	Millstreet, day, m.	R.C.	–	R.C.	R.C.	204	–	204	62
177	103	Do.	–	Do. preparatory, m.	R.C.	–	R.C.	R.C.	279	–	279	102
178	227	Do.	–	Do. convent, f.	–	R.C.	Nuns	–	–	462	462	229
179	6012	Do.	–	Do. workhouse,	P.L.	Gds.	2 R.C.	–	67	78	145	83
180	[illegible]	Do.	–	Rathduane, m.	R.C.	–	R.C.	R.C.	130	–	130	57
181	8408	Do.	–	Do. f.	R.C.	–	R.C.	R.C.	–	107	107	50
182	897	Do.	–	Hollymount, m.	R.C.	–	R.C.	R.C.	170	–	170	65
183	8871	Do.	–	Do. f.	R.C.	–	R.C.	R.C.	–	109	109	54
184	6879	Do.	–	Cloghboola, m.	R.C.	–	R.C.	R.C.	181	–	181	66
185	9779	Do.	–	Do. f.	R.C.	–	R.C.	R.C.	–	164	164	80
186	1001	Donaghmore,	–	Ballykurwick, m.	R.C.	–	R.C.	R.C.	103	–	103	58
187	2294	Do.	–	Do. f.	R.C.	–	R.C.	R.C.	–	137	137	60
188	1682	Do.	60	Firmount, m.	R.C.	–	R.C.	–	126	–	126	67
189	12296	Do.	–	Do. f.	R.C.	–	R.C.	R.C.	–	134	134	70
190	2500	Do.	55	Kilcullen, m.	R.C.	–	R.C.	–	118	–	118	63
191	3146	Do.	–	Do. f.	R.C.	–	R.C.	–	–	96	96	43
192	2707	Do.	–	Rathcoole, m.	R.C.	–	R.C.	–	78	–	78	37
193	3343	Do.	–	Do. f.	R.C.	–	R.C.	–	–	89	89	40
194	5374	Drinagh,	50	Letterguesane,	R.C.	–	R.C.	–	78	63	141	54
195	9101	Do.	–	Drominidy,	R.C.	–	R.C.	R.C.	69	74	143	78
196	8554	Do.	–	Lisheenleigh,	R.C.	–	R.C.	R.C.	69	73	[illegible]	73
197	8706	Do.	–	Shandrum,	R.C.	–	R.C.	–	34	34	68	45
198	8477	Do.	–	Drinagh, m.	R.C.	–	R.C.	–	138	–	138	63
199	8575	Do.	–	Do. f.	R.C.	–	R.C.	R.C.	–	177	177	65
200	1874	Dundarrow,	60	Ballyheedy, m.	R.C.	–	R.C.	–	130	–	130	59
201	1086	Do.	–	Do. f.	R.C.	–	R.C.	–	–	100	100	48
202	2267	Do.	–	Dundarrow,	R.C.	–	R.C.	–	60	90	150	55
203	2151	Dromtarriff,	55	Dromagh, m.	R.C.	–	R.C.	R.C.	171	–	171	71
204	2156	Do.	–	Do. f.	R.C.	–	R.C.	R.C.	–	201	201	70
205	8717	Do.	–	[illegible], m.	R.C.	–	R.C.	R.C.	187	–	187	69
206	8718	Do.	–	Do. f.	R.C.	–	R.C.	R.C.	–	180	180	63
207	7450	Do.	–	Derrinagree, m.	R.C.	–	R.C.	2 R.C.	242	–	242	90
208	7401	Do.	–	Do. f.	R.C.	–	R.C.	2 R.C.	–	217	217	68
209	9767	Do.	–	Derrygallon, m.	R.C.	–	R.C.	–	82	–	82	53
210	9768	Do.	56	Do. f.	R.C.	–	R.C.	–	–	83	83	39
211	2271	Dungandonovan,	45	Kilcanaty,	R.C.	–	R.C.	R.C.	84	76	160	48
212	10246	Desertserges,	59	Ahiohill, m.	R.C.	–	R.C.	–	80	–	80	35
213	10244	Do.	–	Do. f.	R.C.	–	R.C.	R.C.	–	113	113	46
214	8794	Do.	59	Knocks,	R.C.	–	R.C.	R.C.	85	64	149	75
215	8134	Do.	–	Kilcolman,	R.C.	–	R.C.	R.C.	71	73	144	63
216	8501	Dungourney,	45	Dungourney, m.	R.C.	–	R.C.	R.C.	161	–	161	71
217	8737	Do.	–	Do. f.	R.C.	–	R.C.	R.C.	–	127	127	60
218	4128	Doneraile,	56	Skahanagh,	R.C.	–	R.C.	R.C.	102	90	192	61
219	4254	Do.	–	Ballinvonear,	R.C.	–	R.C.	R.C.	96	87	183	70
220	4293	Do.	–	Doneraile Convent, f.	R.C.	–	Nuns		–	425	425	239
221	3185	Dromdaleague,	59	Dromdaleague, m.	R.C.	–	R.C.	R.C.	194	–	194	95
222	8324	Do.	–	Do. f.	R.C.	–	R.C.	2 R.C.	–	180	180	102
223	8718	Do.	–	Dunfeh,	R.C.	–	R.C.	R.C.	93	83	176	57
224	10563	Do.	–	Meenies,	R.C.	–	R.C.	–	47	20	62	29
225	9059	Do.	–	Knockeenbwee,	R.C.	–	R.C.	R.C.	90	90	180	65
226	10585	Do.	–	Claidagh,	R.C.	–	R.C.	–	37	34	71	40
227	2824	Dunbulloge,	60	Carrignavar, m.	R.C.	–	R.C.	R.C.	173	–	173	74
228	10596	Do.	–	Do. f.	R.C.	–	R.C.	R.C.	–	169	169	69
229	10409	Do.	–	Glashaboy, m.	R.C.	–	R.C.	–	114	–	114	41
230	10570	Do.	–	Do. f.	R.C.	–	R.C.	–	–	114	114	37
231	476	Fanlobbus,	60	Dunmanway,	R.C.	–	R.C.	2 R.C.	177	205	382	113
232	10485	Do.	–	Do., No. 2,	–	R.C.	R.C.	–	38	37	75	34
233	5626	Do.	–	Do. Dist. Mod., m.	Com.	N.E.	R.C.	R.C.	209	–	209	153
234	5637	Do.	–	Do. f.	Com.	N.E.	R.C.	R.C. [illegible]	–	516	516	189

a Including value of Free Residence and Garden.

b Including value of Free Residence.

Province of MUNSTER: County of CORK—*continued.*

Amount paid for Books, Requisites, and Apparatus at reduced Prices.	Aid granted by the Board during the Year 1874. In Free Stock of Books, Requisites, and Apparatus.	In Salaries, Premiums, and other Gratuities.	Results Fees, Payments Fees.	Amount of Local Emoluments received in Aid of Teacher's Salary. School Fees.	Subscriptions, Endowments, &c.	Total Local Aid.	Vested or Non-Vested.	Number.
£ s. d.	£ s. d.	£ s. d.	£ s. d.	£ s. d.	£ s. d.	£ s. d.		
—	—	63 10 0	10 10 0	7 16 4	—	7 16 4		172
4 7 8	—	21 0 0	13 11 0	6 12 0	—	6 12 0		173
1 0 10	—	42 0 0	17 8 0	12 12 4	—	12 12 4		174
6 10 11	—	56 1 8	20 8 2	13 10 0	—	13 10 0		175
17 18 0	—	74 18 8	81 14 0	9 19 6	8 3 4	19 8 0	V.T.	176
1 10 6	—	51 0 0	27 1 0	9 9 0	—	9 9 0		177
21 18 6	—	62 11 8	71 18 0	—	—	—	N.	178
0 14 9	—	6 10 0	—	—	—	—		179
6 8 3	—	47 3 0	10 14 6	0 10 0	—	0 10 0	V.C.	180
6 8 0	—	44 0 0	10 2 6	4 18 5	—	4 18 5	V.C.	181
4 10 4	—	44 0 0	15 12 8	8 14 6	—	8 14 6	V.T.	182
8 13 9	—	47 10 0	31 8 6	4 13 0	—	4 13 0	V.T.	183
8 16 8	—	57 0 0	10 6 0	9 18 4	—	9 18 4	V.C.	184
8 14 8	—	90 10 0	28 17 0	7 18 6	—	7 18 6	V.T.	185
10 8 3	—	60 4 8	18 8 0	6 5 0	—	6 5 0	N.	186
6 17 7	—	63 10 0	22 8 0	6 8 0	—	6 8 0	N.	187
9 1 8	—	62 10 0	12 8 0	3 6 8	—	3 6 8	N.	188
8 17 11	—	45 10 0	21 15 0	6 0 9	—	6 0 9	N.	189
—	—	60 0 0	14 14 6	7 3 0	—	7 3 0	V.T.	190
6 17 1	—	65 0 0	17 11 6	7 0 8	—	7 0 8	V.T.	191
1 0 8	—	51 0 0	10 1 6	8 4 0	—	8 4 0	V.T.	192
4 1 3	—	30 0 0	17 11 0	7 18 0	—	7 18 0	V.T.	193
0 14 11	—	58 0 0	37 18 6	7 15 0	—	7 15 0		194
3 0 0	—	57 6 8	33 16 6	12 19 0	—	12 19 0		195
4 18 0	—	60 10 0	38 11 0	15 0 1	—	15 0 1		196
8 18 0	—	47 0 0	21 4 6	10 16 6	21 0 0	*31 16 6		197
3 18 9	—	51 10 0	23 18 6	12 17 0	—	12 17 0	V.T.	198
3 8 8	—	64 10 0	20 12 0	6 6 2	—	6 6 2	V.T.	199
8 16 8	—	33 0 0	16 16 6	14 10 0	—	14 10 0		200
1 8 8	—	34 0 0	12 6 0	11 8 1	—	11 8 1		201
1 7 0	—	78 0 0	10 6 6	18 7 4	5 0 0	*23 7 4	V.T.	202
8 16 6	—	78 8 4	25 8 6	10 8 8	—	10 8 8	V.T.	203
4 6 7	—	70 10 0	31 8 6	10 0 0	—	10 0 0	V.T.	204
1 7 0	—	74 0 0	21 11 0	6 18 0	1 0 0	*7 18 0	V.C.	205
6 4 6	—	70 0 8	20 8 0	6 1 1	—	6 1 1	V.C.	206
6 17 11	—	167 0 0	48 19 0	0 12 0	—	0 12 0	V.C.	207
0 8 7	—	150 10 0	40 8 0	10 1 8	—	10 1 8	V.C.	208
3 18 6	—	82 0 0	10 7 0	8 18 0	—	8 18 0	V.C.	209
3 0 2	—	42 8 8	12 4 0	8 17 0	—	8 17 0	V.C.	210
3 7 1	—	44 0 0	20 2 6	8 1 7	—	8 1 7	V.T.	211
1 8 1	—	65 0 0	9 18 6	5 8 8	—	5 8 8	V.T.	212
7 18 9	—	46 0 0	20 11 6	10 6 0	—	10 6 0	V.T.	213
4 14 9	—	68 0 0	21 15 6	13 7 1	—	13 7 1	V.T.	214
3 11 6	—	50 0 0	24 13 0	14 10 6	3 10 0	*17 0 6		215
3 0 0	—	64 18 4	23 7 6	14 10 8	—	14 10 8		216
8 1 8	—	62 8 4	22 10 0	7 10 0	—	7 10 0		217
4 14 10	2 18 0	44 0 0	26 7 6	2 8 0	—	2 8 0	V.T.	218
6 6 2	—	60 0 0	15 11 0	8 4 7	2 0 0	*10 4 7		219
20 0 5	—	118 12 8	62 6 0	—	—	—		220
4 10 0	—	98 16 4	50 13 0	16 19 0	—	16 19 0		221
7 18 9	—	80 0 0	46 14 6	15 19 0	—	15 18 0		222
8 17 9	—	49 10 0	60 6 6	17 10 0	—	17 10 0	V.C.	223
2 10 8	—	29 10 0	7 11 0	8 18 1	28 0 0	*36 18 1		224
0 8 7	—	45 6 4	26 0 0	12 10 9	—	12 10 9	V.T.	225
4 7 4	—	58 0 8	16 11 0	9 4 0	25 6 0	*34 4 0		226
6 18 6	—	62 10 8	15 18 6	21 18 10	—	21 18 10		227
—	—	44 7 9	15 18 0	14 17 6	—	14 17 6		228
6 0 0	—	78 0 0	14 4 6	5 15 0	—	5 15 0	V.T.	229
2 16 7	—	84 0 0	11 8 6	6 6 6	—	6 6 6	V.T.	230
8 8 0	—	117 8 8	60 8 0	—	—	—		231
1 11 0	—	24 0 0	11 18 0	9 14 2	10 0 0	*19 14 2		232
16 10 2	9 18 0	626 0 7	182 16 2	68 7 6	—	68 7 6	V.C.	233
19 2 2	9 0 0						V.C.	234

* Including value of Free Garden.

List of Schools in operation on the 31st December 1874.—

Number.	Roll Number of School.	Parish.	District.	School.	Religious Denomination of Patrons or Correspondents: Clerical.	Lay.	Number and Religious Denomination of Teachers: Principals.	Assistants.	Attendance for the Year. Total number of Pupils on Rolls within the Year 1874: Male.	Fem.	Total.	Average Daily Attendance for Year 1874.
235	3568	Fanlobbus,	52	Dunmanway Workhs.	P.L.	Gds.	R.C.	-	80	55	135	61
236	478	Do.	-	Derrynacaheragh,	R.C.	-	R.C.	2R.C.	133	118	251	119
237	6457	Do.	-	Inch,	R.C.	-	R.C.	-	66	60	126	63
238	6708	Do.	-	Behagh,	R.C.	-	R.C.	-	76	86	159	79
239	10562	Do.	-	Kilronane,	-	E.C.	E.C.	-	36	47	83	39
240	7870	Do.	-	Togher,	R.C.	-	R.C.	R.C.	53	61	114	67
241	10542	Do.	-	Ahakeera,	R.C.	-	R.C.	R.C.	64	65	129	68
242	8181	Fermoy,	56	Grange,	R.C.	-	R.C.	R.C.	140	66	206	87
243	9708	Do.	-	Fermoy, Convent, f.	R.C.	-	R.C.	-	224	645	844	329
244	11110	Do.	-	Adair, m.	R.C.	-	R.C.	-	29	-	29	13
245	3245	Do.	-	Fermoy, Workhs.	P.L.	Gds.	2R.C.	-	86	52	138	66
246	10322	Do.	-	Do. Infant,	R.C.	-	R.C.	-	40	62	103	40
247	6287	Farahy,	-	Farahy 1st Class Agr.,	R.C.	-	R.C.	R.C.	169	-	169	77
248	6834	Do.	-	Do. f.	R.C.	-	R.C.	R.C.	-	124	124	84
249	1258	Garrycloyne,	60	Blarney, m.	R.C.	-	R.C.	R.C.	105	56	161	65
250	7036	Do.	-	Do. Village, f.	R.C.	-	R.C.	R.C.	-	158	158	67
251	9057	Do.	-	Do. No. 3,	R.C.	-	R.C.	-	6	11	17	10
252	9622	Garrane Kinlaske,	61	Scarteigh, m.	R.C.	-	R.C.	-	88	-	88	55
253	6302	Do.	-	Do. f.	R.C.	-	R.C.	-	-	67	67	35
254	1452	Gortroe,	56	Gortroe, m.	R.C.	-	R.C.	-	61	-	61	27
255	1534	Do.	-	Do. f.	R.C.	-	R.C.	-	-	83	83	40
256	4627	Glanworth,	-	Glanworth, m.	R.C.	-	R.C.	R.C.	163	-	163	46
257	1525	Do.	-	Do. f.	R.C.	-	R.C.	2R.C.	-	218	212	94
258	8305	Granagh,	-	Rathduff, m.	R.C.	-	R.C.	R.C.	109	96	205	99
259	10516	Do.	-	Ballyglass,	R.C.	-	R.C.	R.C.	107	100	207	78
260	10773	Holy Trinity,	66	Queen-street,	Pres.	-	Pres.	Pres.	48	66	114	43
261	10044	Do.	-	Christ Church,	R.C.	R.C.	R.C.	-	60	-	60	26
262	10547	Do.	-	Do. i.	E.C.	E.C.	E.C.	-	16	71	87	60
263	451	Inchigeelagh,	66	Kilberry,	R.C.	-	R.C.	2R.C.	91	74	165	73
264	[illegible]	Do.	-	[illegible] m.	R.C.	-	R.C.	R.C.	186	-	186	69
265	486	Do.	-	Do. f.	R.C.	-	R.C.	R.C.	-	147	147	71
266	1394	Do.	56	Coolmountain,	R.C.	-	R.C.	R.C.	80	78	158	72
267	1782	Do.	66	Inchigeelagh, m.	R.C.	-	R.C.	R.C.	183	-	183	65
268	4162	Do.	-	Do. f.	R.C.	-	R.C.	R.C.	-	141	141	56
269	8408	Do.	-	Tooreenalour,	R.C.	-	R.C.	-	37	37	74	36
270	10551	Do.	-	Keimaneigh, m.	R.C.	-	R.C.	-	34	61	95	34
271	456	Ightermurragh,	45	Ladysbridge, m.	R.C.	-	R.C.	R.C.	165	-	165	69
272	1576	Do.	-	Do. f.	R.C.	-	R.C.	R.C.	-	153	153	69
273	1948	Inishannon,	66	Inishannon, m.	R.C.	-	R.C.	R.C.	133	-	133	64
274	7366	Do.	-	Do. f.	R.C.	-	R.C.	R.C.	-	180	180	71
275	4186	Inishcarra,	56	Berrings, m.	R.C.	-	R.C.	-	147	-	147	63
276	4187	Do.	-	Do. f.	R.C.	-	R.C.	R.C.	-	141	141	63
277	7242	Do.	-	Cloghroe, m.	R.C.	-	R.C.	R.C.	170	-	170	78
278	7243	Do.	-	Do. f.	R.C.	-	R.C.	R.C.	-	168	168	74
279	8014	Do.	-	Dripsey, m.	R.C.	-	R.C.	-	114	-	114	57
280	10053	Do.	-	Do. f.	R.C.	-	R.C.	R.C.	-	125	125	54
281	6782	Inishkenny,	56	Newtown Ballyhea, m.	R.C.	-	R.C.	R.C.	261	-	261	97
282	9712	Inch,	45	Gallane,	R.C.	-	R.C.	R.C.	117	101	218	91
283	10268	Do.	-	Inch, No. 2,	R.C.	-	R.C.	-	12	22	34	16
284	11107	Do.	-	Ballytibbot,	R.C.	-	R.C.	-	76	63	139	63
285	11130	Kanturk,	55	Kanturk,	E.C.	-	-	-	-	-	-	-
286	434	Kilmocomogue,	55	Bantry, m.	R.C.	-	R.C.	R.C.	161	-	161	65
287	437	Do.	-	Do. prep.	R.C.	-	R.C.	R.C.	135	-	135	48
288	6594	Do.	-	Do. No. 2,	R.C.	-	R.C.	-	98	-	98	34
289	9146	Do.	-	Do. Convent, f.	R.C.	Nuns		-	-	443	443	213
290	4411	Do.	-	Do. Workhouse,	P.L.	Gds.	R.C.	-	36	24	59	13
291	10548	Do.	-	Do. Parochial,	E.C.	-	E.C.	E.C.	38	29	67	38
292	5497	Do.	-	Droumgarriff,	R.C.	-	R.C.	-	76	62	138	41
293	6469	Do.	-	Whiddy Island,	R.C.	-	R.C.	-	44	55	99	44
294	9628	Do.	-	Kealkil,	R.C.	-	R.C.	2R.C.	117	111	228	105
295	7101	Do.	-	Inchiclogh,	R.C.	-	R.C.	2R.C.	118	110	228	94
296	7597	Do.	-	Dromacloough,	R.C.	-	R.C.	R.C.	75	56	131	48
297	7598	Do.	-	Maughanaclea,	R.C.	-	R.C.	R.C.	49	66	105	45

a Including value of Free Residence.

Province of MUNSTER: County of CORK—*continued.*

Amount paid for Books, Requisites, and Apparatus, at Reduced Prices.	Aid granted by the Board during the Year 1874: In Free Stock of Books, Requisites, and Apparatus.	In Salaries, Premiums, and other Gratuities.	Results Fees, Financial Year.	Amount of Local Emoluments received in Aid of Teacher's Salary: School Fees.	Subscriptions, Endowments, &c.	Total Local Aid.	Vested or Non-Vested.	Number.
£ s. d.	£ s. d.	£ s. d.	£ s. d.	£ s. d.	£ s. d.	£ s. d.		
4 4 0	—	1 10 0	—	—	—	—		835
7 6 11	—	117 18 4	56 6 0	29 1 0	—	29 1 0		836
2 0 7	—	24 0 0	6 18 6	0 18 0	—	0 18 0		837
3 8 3	—	61 10 0	61 18 0	19 14 0	—	19 14 0		838
1 7 6	—	26 6 6	15 8 0	6 0 0	20 10 0	[a] 26 10 0		839
1 11 5	—	41 0 0	17 16 11	16 12 6	—	16 12 6		840
8 18 4	—	55 10 0	25 18 6	12 1 0	—	12 1 0		841
2 4 8	—	23 0 0	17 0 0	8 18 2	—	8 18 2	V.T.	842
15 14 0	—	129 18 10	60 8 8	—	—	—		843
1 5 8	4 10 0	—	1 4 0	8 0 0	47 0 0	[a] 40 0 0		844
4 16 0	—	10 10 0	—	—	—	—		845
4 17 4	—	67 6 4	11 7 6	7 13 10	0 0 0	[a] 15 15 10		846
4 14 1	—	113 17 4	24 6 6	18 18 0	—	18 18 0	V.C.	847
4 7 8	—	31 0 0	81 8 0	8 18 0	—	8 18 0	V.C.	848
1 13 8	—	48 18 8	84 11 0	12 11 0	5 0 0	17 11 0	V.T.	849
6 6 8	—	61 10 8	10 10 0	10 3 0	—	16 5 0		850
0 18 0	—	—	4 4 0	1 4 8	65 0 0	[a] 66 4 8		851
0 18 8	—	20 10 0	8 16 0	8 16 4	—	8 16 4	V.T.	852
11 18 0	—	20 0 0	10 1 0	4 1 7	—	4 1 7		853
1 8 7	—	24 0 0	4 16 0	5 1 6	—	5 1 6	V.T.	854
2 1 6	—	30 0 0	12 3 6	5 9 6	—	5 9 6	V.T.	855
1 13 5	—	63 7 4	17 18 6	15 15 4	—	15 15 4	V.C.	856
9 9 8	—	60 10 8	30 14 6	18 18 8	—	18 18 8	V.C.	857
4 8 8	—	63 8 4	22 19 6	15 0 0	—	15 0 0	V.C.	858
8 11 11	—	44 0 0	13 3 9	4 19 5	—	4 19 5		859
6 18 11	—	63 16 0	17 7 6	18 8 8	—	18 8 8		860
8 1 0	—	35 0 0	31 7 0	1 4 5	81 0 0	[a] 82 4 5		861
1 15 7	—	35 0 0	5 8 6	16 0 4	—	16 0 4		862
4 18 11	—	77 0 0	20 0 6	8 15 6	—	8 15 0		863
8 6 8	—	53 0 0	14 10 0	3 0 0	—	3 0 0	V.T.	864
5 3 9	—	31 18 4	21 5 6	3 0 0	—	3 0 0		865
4 18 0	—	53 0 0	23 12 0	12 8 4	—	14 8 4	V.T.	866
6 8 4	—	75 0 0	38 14 0	13 8 0	—	13 8 0		867
4 12 8	—	60 8 0	26 8 6	7 15 0	—	7 15 0		868
2 0 10	—	24 0 0	10 17 0	6 0 0	—	6 0 0		869
2 0 2	—	36 0 0	8 17 0	4 0 0	—	4 0 0		870
3 0 10	—	81 18 4	17 2 6	7 14 3	1 10 0	[a] 9 4 3	V.T.	871
2 11 6	—	45 18 4	18 7 6	7 0 10	—	7 0 10	V.T.	872
3 6 3	—	49 0 0	11 7 9	8 18 7	—	8 18 7		873
8 0 8	—	64 0 0	23 18 0	6 7 6	—	6 7 6		874
5 19 9	—	23 0 0	23 5 6	10 8 0	—	10 8 0	V.T.	875
4 7 3	—	27 16 8	17 0 0	14 17 3	—	14 17 8	V.T.	876
0 18 4	—	88 18 4	25 19 0	20 8 9	—	20 8 9		877
0 0 9	—	50 8 10	34 0 6	16 7 0	—	16 7 0		878
3 18 1	—	34 0 0	16 11 0	6 8 5	—	6 8 5		879
3 8 7	—	54 10 0	22 0 0	5 18 5	—	5 18 5		880
8 8 9	8 12 0	41 16 6	21 10 0	12 2 6	—	12 2 0		881
4 10 9	—	46 18 4	19 11 0	4 14 4	—	4 14 4		882
1 10 4	—	13 8 8	5 15 6	6 13 0	13 0 4	[a] 19 13 4		883
3 3 3	—	13 8 11	13 15 6	4 14 6	1 0 0	[a] 5 14 6	V.T.	884
3 6 1	4 0 0	—	—	—	—	—		885
5 11 9	—	[b] 55 6 8	81 10 8	8 6 0	—	8 6 0		886
1 1 1	—	87 10 0	7 18 0	1 4 10	—	1 4 10		887
5 15 5	—	47 16 8	33 11 0	15 7 6	—	15 7 6		888
18 2 11	—	110 0 6	44 0 0	—	—	—		889
2 17 0	—	2 10 0	—	—	—	—		890
6 8 10	4 3 8	86 0 0	59 18 6	28 17 0	69 10 0	[a] 98 7 0		891
4 8 9	—	88 0 0	15 18 0	8 9 0	—	8 9 0		892
2 5 11	—	30 10 0	17 0 5	5 8 8	—	5 8 8		893
7 14 1	—	34 5 4	45 19 0	11 0 6	1 0 0	[a] 12 0 6		894
4 17 6	—	80 15 8	67 8 0	19 17 0	—	19 17 0		895
4 4 7	—	63 15 0	8 8 8	8 7 6	—	8 7 6		896
1 10 11	—	20 0 0	18 5 6	7 0 0	—	7 0 0		897

[b] No Returns.

List of Schools in operation on the 31st December, 1874.—

No.	Roll Number of School	Parish.	District.	School.		Religious Denomination of Manager or Correspondent: Clerical	Lay.	Teaching and Religious Denomination of Teachers: Principals.	Assistants.	Attendance for the Year. Total number of Pupils on Rolls within the Year 1874: Males.	Fem.	Total.	Average Daily Attendance for the Year 1874.
298	7967	Kilmocomogue,	53	Bocktra,		R.C.	–	R.C.	–	29	38	67	35
299	8147	Do.	–	Coomhola,		R.C.	–	R.C.	R.C.	113	112	225	74
300	5514	Do.	–	Cappabue,		R.C.	–	R.C.	R.C.	79	80	159	69
301	8592	Do.	–	Coomleigh,		R.C.	–	R.C.	–	43	91	134	29
302	480	Kilgarriff,	50	Clonakilty,	m.	R.C.	–	R.C.	2 R.C.	218	–	218	137
303	481	Do.	–	Do.	f.	–	R.C.	R.C.	3 R.C.	160	235	341	159
304	7545	Do.	–	Do. M., No. 2,		R.C.	–	R.C.	–	33	23	56	38
305	7641	Do.	–	Do. Convent,	f.	R.C.	–	Nuns.		179	550	729	[illegible]
306	7919	Do.	–	Do. Workhouse,		P.L. Gds.		R.C.	–	52	40	92	44
307	8131	Do.	–	Shannon-square,		–	Pres.	Pres.	–	53	33	86	55
308	9829	Do.	–	Knockeenagh,		R.C.	–	R.C.	R.C.	83	53	136	65
309	10480	Do.	–	Kilgarriff,		–	R.C.	R.C.	R.C.	84	33	117	49
310	487	Kilnamartery,	55	Ballyvoge,	m.	R.C.	–	R.C.	R.C.	182	–	182	95
311	184	Do.	–	Do.	f.	R.C.	–	R.C.	R.C.	–	210	210	98
312	9160	Do.	–	Renaniree,		R.C.	–	R.C.	R.C.	65	102	167	67
313	10451	Do.	–	Coolavokig,		R.C.	–	R.C.	R.C.	119	105	224	87
314	10678	Kilmeen,	56	Rossmore,	m.	R.C.	–	R.C.	–	146	–	146	89
315	10670	Do.	–	Do.	f.	R.C.	–	R.C.	R.C.	–	108	108	53
316	6660	Do.	–	Ballygurteen,		R.C.	–	R.C.	–	71	64	135	69
317	6868	Do.	56	Kilshinahan,	m.	R.C.	–	R.C.	R.C.	221	–	221	85
318	10079	Do.	–	Do.	f.	R.C.	–	R.C.	2 R.C.	–	258	258	111
319	4449	Do.	–	Boherbue,	m.	R.C.	–	R.C.	2 R.C.	207	–	207	101
320	4447	Do.	–	Do.	f.	R.C.	–	R.C.	3 R.C.	–	241	241	109
321	7457	Do.	–	Cloghdubhlea,		R.C.	–	R.C.	2 R.C.	133	127	260	93
322	9410	Do.	–	Cranroe,	m.	R.C.	–	R.C.	R.C.	154	–	154	91
323	9082	Do.	–	Do.	f.	R.C.	–	R.C.	R.C.	–	168	157	79
324	9817	Do.	–	Umeraboy,	m.	R.C.	–	R.C.	–	195	–	165	84
325	9418	Do.	–	Do.	f.	R.C.	–	R.C.	R.C.	–	169	159	89
326	10841	Do.	–	Drumscarrigle,	m.	R.C.	–	R.C.	–	101	–	101	67
327	10867	Do.	–	Do.	f.	R.C.	–	R.C.	–	–	75	75	61
328	8714	Do.	57	Knockskeagh,		R.C.	–	R.C.	3 R.C.	162	105	258	98
329	501	Kilmoney,	57	Kilmoney,	m.	R.C.	–	R.C.	R.C.	155	–	155	89
330	9478	Do.	–	Do.	f.	R.C.	–	R.C.	R.C.	–	134	131	62
331	1271	Kilmalane,	56	Kilmalane,	m.	R.C.	–	R.C.	R.C.	101	–	101	79
332	1801	Do.	–	Do.	f.	R.C.	–	R.C.	R.C.	–	185	185	96
333	7745	Do.	55	Kilbeacane,		R.C.	–	R.C.	2 R.C.	93	80	173	78
334	1330	Kilnamanagh,	56	Rossmanagh,	m.	–	R.C.	R.C.	–	118	–	118	59
335	7835	Do.	–	Do.	f.	–	R.C.	R.C.	–	–	119	119	67
336	4330	Do.	–	Ballyhealy,		–	R.C.	R.C.	–	62	55	117	55
337	4848	Do.	–	Castletown,	m.	R.C.	–	R.C.	R.C.	145	–	145	87
338	4844	Do.	–	Do.	prep.	R.C.	–	R.C.	–	93	1	94	69
339	9928	Do.	–	Do. Convent,	f.	–	R.C.	Nuns.		–	248	249	153
340	5932	Do.	–	Do. Workhouse,		P.L. Gds.		R.C.	–	27	30	57	30
341	7155	Do.	–	Laragh Cove,	m.	R.C.	–	R.C.	–	58	–	58	40
342	7463	Do.	–	Do.	f.	R.C.	–	R.C.	R.C.	–	114	114	54
343	7454	Do.	–	Ballinakilla,		R.C.	–	R.C.	R.C.	88	77	165	79
344	7830	Do.	–	Caherguriffe,		R.C.	–	R.C.	–	55	45	100	45
345	1012	Kinsale,	56	Kinsale, No. 1,	m.	R.C.	–	R.C.	R.C.	185	–	185	99
346	8230	Do.	–	Do. No. 2,	m.	R.C.	–	R.C.	–	206	–	206	78
347	4572	Do.	–	Do. (St. Joseph's) Convent,	f.	R.C.	–	Nuns.		–	710	710	378
348	4935	Do.	–	Do. Workhouse,		P.L. Gds.		R.C.	–	43	22	65	21
349	10754	Do.	–	Do. (5).		–	R.C.	R.C.	R.C.	70	28	98	60
350	1897	Kilmichael,	55	Dromleigh,		R.C.	–	R.C.	R.C.	93	91	184	78
351	5376	Do.	–	Gurranes,		R.C.	–	R.C.	R.C.	76	60	136	61
352	7650	Do.	55	Kilnadur,		R.C.	–	R.C.	R.C.	78	81	157	67
353	9118	Do.	55	Lackareigh,		R.C.	–	R.C.	R.C.	68	47	115	45
354	1878	Kilkerranmore,	56	Brahid,		R.C.	–	R.C.	R.C.	109	75	184	73
355	8705	Do.	–	Rathbarry,	f.	R.C.	–	R.C.	–	–	140	140	98
356	1674	Kilworth,	56	Kilworth,	m.	R.C.	–	*R.C.	2 R.C.	217	–	217	85
357	1761	Do.	–	Do.	f.	R.C.	–	R.C.	R.C.	–	173	173	74
358	1957	Kilmahon,	48	Kilmahon,	m.	R.C.	–	R.C.	–	89	–	89	47
359	5891	Do.	–	Do.	f.	R.C.	–	R.C.	R.C.	–	125	125	68

* Including value of Free Residence.

Province of Munster: County of Cork—*continued.*

Amount paid for Books, Requisites, and Apparatus at Reduced Prices.	Aid granted by the Board during the Year 1874. In Free Stock of Books, Requisites, and Apparatus.	In Salaries, Premiums, and other Gratuities.	Results Fees, Financial Year.	Amount of Local Fund received in Aid of Teacher's Salary. School Fees.	Subscriptions, Endowments, &c.	Total Local Aid.	Vested or Non-Vested.	Number.
£ s. d.	£ s. d.	£ s. d.	£ s. d.	£ s. d.	£ s. d.	£ s. d.		
1 5 3	—	21 0 0	8 1 0	8 11 0	—	8 11 0		298
5 11 8	—	44 0 0	25 16 5	9 18 8	—	9 18 8		299
4 12 3	—	46 18 4	21 19 6	4 8 0	—	4 8 0		300
4 1 6	—	24 0 0	5 18 9	4 18 5	—	4 18 5		301
11 6 5	—	108 18 8	45 9 6	30 0 6	—	30 0 6		302
14 10 7	—	124 10 0	48 1 0	—	5 0 0	5 0 0	V.T.	303
6 5 6	—	36 0 0	14 1 0	40 0 0	30 0 0	70 0 0		304
30 11 3	—	191 9 4	114 5 0	—	—	—		305
0 12 3	—	—	—	—	—	—		306
—	—	80 1 6	18 5 6	21 5 0	16 15 0	43 0 0		307
5 1 8	—	51 10 0	26 16 5	4 18 1	—	4 18 1		308
18 7 7	—	68 13 4	24 16 0	26 9 10	23 10 2	50 0 0		309
—	—	80 0 0	80 13 6	5 10 0	—	5 10 0		310
8 6 0	—	50 3 4	29 3 0	5 1 0	—	5 1 0		311
4 8 8	—	14 0 0	27 2 0	8 18 0	—	8 18 0	V.T.	312
8 1 11	—	64 6 8	10 7 4	8 6 0	—	8 0 0		313
5 15 7	—	42 10 0	20 5 5	7 16 0	—	7 18 0	V.T.	314
9 10 8	—	63 0 0	34 8 0	6 1 6	—	6 1 0	V.T.	315
1 11 0	—	81 10 6	13 9 1	7 18 0	—	7 18 0		316
9 15 6	—	80 10 0	47 3 6	14 10 3	—	14 10 3	V.T.	317
4 17 8	—	73 7 0	48 10 0	8 9 10	—	8 9 10	V.T.	318
1 6 5	—	69 6 8	40 10 6	19 16 0	—	19 16 0	V.T.	319
7 13 7	—	86 15 8	46 11 10	14 10 6	—	14 10 6	V.T.	320
0 7 7	—	76 0 0	20 1 6	12 1 0	—	12 1 6		321
9 10 0	—	38 0 0	10 19 6	18 0 0	—	18 0 0	V.T.	322
4 8 8	—	53 18 6	29 7 0	6 11 0	—	6 11 0	V.T.	323
8 14 4	—	85 10 0	25 18 0	15 0 0	—	15 0 0	V.T.	324
8 9 0	—	42 10 0	21 8 5	8 1 6	—	8 1 6	V.T.	325
1 11 3	—	30 0 0	12 18 6	8 18 0	—	8 18 0	V.T.	326
8 3 4	—	20 0 0	19 5 5	5 10 0	—	5 10 0	V.T.	327
6 19 6	—	40 0 0	30 18 0	25 0 0	—	25 0 0		328
11 6 5	—	44 0 0	29 8 0	28 7 1	—	28 7 1		329
8 8 1	—	60 18 4	18 4 6	11 9 5	—	11 9 5		330
4 12 9	—	67 16 4	19 10 0	12 0 0	—	12 0 0	V.T.	331
1 16 2	—	44 0 0	18 16 6	8 19 1	—	8 19 1	V.T.	332
6 18 6	—	88 0 0	22 1 6	12 0 0	—	15 0 0		333
1 10 7	—	41 10 0	18 16 0	8 8 0	—	8 8 0	A.	334
8 17 8	—	61 0 0	28 7 0	9 11 6	—	9 11 6	A.	335
1 19 8	—	67 2 8	10 11 8	4 8 0	—	4 8 0	V.C.	336
2 12 11	—	104 10 0	23 6 8	50 8 6	—	50 8 0	V.C.	337
1 11 9	—	18 18 5	—	1 17 0	—	1 17 0	V.C.	338
8 9 6	—	118 18 6	44 10 6	—	—	—		339
2 18 0	—	2 10 0	Nil.	—	—	—		340
2 16 0	—	62 8 0	15 14 6	2 14 10	—	2 14 10	V.C.	341
—	—	74 10 0	18 14 10	2 12 0	—	2 12 0	V.A.	342
6 8 6	—	66 10 0	19 12 4	5 10 0	—	5 10 0	V.C.	343
1 10 4	—	30 0 0	8 19 0	2 16 6	—	2 16 6		344
9 2 8	—	67 0 0	24 0 0	61 17 9	—	61 17 9	V.T.	345
4 6 9	—	61 0 0	16 16 0	6 6 5	—	6 6 5	V.T.	346
53 17 6	—	130 0 4	65 6 8	—	—	—		347
5 3 4	—	Nil.	Nil.	—	—	—		348
9 7 8	—	37 6 4	19 11 6	53 10 0	5 0 0	58 10 0		349
2 15 0	—	56 18 4	60 0 0	6 9 4	—	6 6 4	V.T.	350
2 1 10	—	44 0 0	16 11 6	7 10 8	—	7 10 8		351
4 12 9	—	60 16 4	26 6 0	30 12 8	—	30 12 8		352
1 7 7	—	44 0 0	16 10 0	4 8 0	—	4 8 0	V.T.	353
6 0 4	—	51 10 0	25 6 8	8 11 7	—	5 11 7		354
2 10 7	8 6 9	40 16 8	37 15 0	15 11 6	—	18 11 6		355
9 18 6	—	97 6 6	29 9 6	29 11 4	—	30 11 4		356
7 4 9	—	101 6 0	41 17 5	14 13 0	—	15 13 0		357
2 2 1	—	30 6 10	18 6 6	7 10 5	—	7 16 5		358
2 5 0	—	46 0 0	20 5 6	9 6 2	—	9 6 2		359

List of Schools in operation on the 31st December, 1874.—

Number.	Roll Number of School.	Parish.	District.	School.	Religious Denomination of Manager or Correspondent: Clerical.	Lay.	Teachers' Religious Denomination: Principals.	Assistants.	Total number of Pupils on Rolls within the Year 1874: Males.	Fem.	Total.	Average Daily Attendance for Year 1874.
360	3048	Kilquane,	57	Knockraha, m.	R.C.	–	R.C.	–	88	–	88	35
361	6332	Do.	–	Do. f.	R.C.	–	R.C.	–	–	104	104	51
362	3117	Kilmacabea,	58	Meenlagrahan, m.	R.C.	–	R.C.	R.C.	128	–	128	61
363	3018	Do.	–	Do. f.	R.C.	–	R.C.	R.C.	–	115	115	55
364	9582	Do.	–	Knockskeagh, f.	R.C.	–	R.C.	R.C.	4	155	159	56
365	10603	Do.	–	Do. m.	R.C.	–	R.C.	–	181	–	181	41
366	3816	Do.	–	Kilmacabea,	R.C.	–	R.C.	–	61	53	114	44
367	3718	Do.	–	Glenkeen Ord. Ag.	R.C.	–	R.C.	–	160	–	160	54
368	3701	Do.	–	Do. f.	R.C.	–	R.C.	–	–	123	123	66
369	10566	Do.	–	Corran,	R.C.	–	R.C.	–	28	19	50	31
370	3174	Kilfaughnabeg,	–	Glandore 1st al. ag.	Conv.	N.B.	R.C.	–	117	–	117	45
371	3238	Do.	–	Do. f.	Conv.	N.E.	R.C.	R.C.	–	[illegible]	[illegible]	41
372	9320	Do.	–	Benagroum, m.	R.C.	–	R.C.	–	116	–	116	46
373	9014	Do.	–	Do. f.	R.C.	–	R.C.	–	–	106	106	46
374	3379	Kilcaskin,	65	Cloghfin,	R.C.	–	R.C.	–	79	77	156	53
375	4948	Do.	–	Derryconnery,	R.C.	–	R.C.	–	80	30	108	50
376	5562	Do.	–	Tralum, m.	R.C.	–	R.C.	–	128	–	128	58
377	5564	Do.	–	Do. f.	R.C.	–	R.C.	R.C.	–	160	160	68
378	5367	Do.	–	Adrigole, m.	R.C.	–	R.C.	–	105	–	105	41
379	5568	Do.	–	Do. f.	R.C.	–	R.C.	–	–	118	118	44
380	3597	Kilmacdonogh,	46	Kilmacdonogh,	R.C.	–	R.C.	2R.C.	130	93	223	110
381	3541	Kilcredan,	–	Kilcredan,	R.C.	–	R.C.	2R.C.	111	103	214	60
382	3722	Kilmaloda,	58	Clogagh, m.	R.C.	–	R.C.	–	130	–	130	62
383	3223	Do.	–	Do. f.	R.C.	–	R.C.	–	–	103	103	48
384	9987	Do.	–	Kilmalooda,	R.C.	–	R.C.	–	26	41	67	23
385	8481	Kilbrin,	60	Ballygraddy, m.	R.C.	–	R.C.	R.C.	203	–	203	91
386	3433	Do.	–	Do. f.	R.C.	–	R.C.	R.C.	–	171	171	77
387	3247	Kilshannig,	–	Lahana,	R.C.	–	R.C.	–	90	93	183	61
388	8881	Do.	–	Kilpadder,	R.C.	–	R.C.	R.C.	99	81	100	71
389	4738	Do.	–	Glantane, m.	R.C.	–	R.C.	–	131	–	131	46
390	4739	Do.	–	Do. f.	R.C.	–	R.C.	–	–	116	116	49
391	5117	Do.	–	Glashaboy,	R.C.	–	R.C.	R.C.	61	80	140	53
392	7710	Do.	–	Dana,	R.C.	–	R.C.	–	–	94	89	35
393	8412	Do.	–	Glanagarry,	R.C.	–	R.C.	R.C.	100	93	193	66
394	8728	Kilnaglory,	60	Ballynora, m.	R.C.	–	R.C.	R.C.	174	–	174	59
395	8732	Do.	–	Do. f.	R.C.	–	R.C.	R.C.	–	149	149	72
396	4956	Kinneigh,	58	Enniskean, m.	R.C.	–	R.C.	–	116	–	116	48
397	9638	Do.	–	Do. f.	R.C.	–	R.C.	R.C.	–	158	158	66
398	8488	Do.	–	Castletown (3), m.	R.C.	–	R.C.	R.C.	148	–	149	66
399	0992	Do.	–	Do. (3), f.	R.C.	–	R.C.	R.C.	–	119	119	60
400	3479	Do.	–	Coppeen, m.	R.C.	–	R.C.	–	119	–	119	56
401	10481	Do.	–	Do. f.	R.C.	–	R.C.	R.C.	–	144	144	60
402	10851	Do.	–	Connagh,	R.C.	–	R.C.	R.C.	70	88	158	64
403	11074	Do.	–	Moneygaskerry,	R.C.	–	R.C.	–	30	17	48	17
404	4186	Kildorrery,	56	Scart, m.	R.C.	–	R.C.	–	145	–	145	56
405	4187	Do.	–	Do. f.	R.C.	–	R.C.	R.C.	–	155	155	71
406	4132	Knockavilly,	56	Knockavilly, m.	R.C.	–	R.C.	R.C.	161	–	161	74
407	7164	Do.	–	Do. f.	R.C.	–	R.C.	R.C.	–	118	118	58
408	8898	Killeagh,	48	Killeagh, m.	R.C.	–	R.C.	–	110	–	110	41
409	3384	Do.	–	Do. f.	R.C.	–	R.C.	R.C.	–	129	129	42
410	3348	Knockmourne,	–	Conna, m.	R.C.	–	R.C.	R.C.	169	–	169	52
411	3349	Do.	–	Do. f.	R.C.	–	R.C.	2R.C.	–	153	153	55
412	5477	Kilnamanagh,	56	Glen, m.	R.C.	–	R.C.	R.C.	100	107	218	56
413	8881	Do.	–	Cahermore,	R.C.	–	R.C.	R.C.	117	102	219	60
414	7808	Do.	–	Dursey Island,	R.C.	–	R.C.	–	66	34	80	26
415	3914	Do.	–	Bawnaskehy,	R.C.	–	R.C.	–	61	35	87	37
416	5177	Kilbrogan,	58	Laragh,	R.C.	–	R.C.	R.C.	70	94	170	58
417	8806	Do.	–	Watergate,	Pres.	–	Pres.	Pres.	72	58	130	55
418	8728	Do.	–	Watergate-place,	Diss.	–	Diss.	Diss.	68	44	112	41
419	9857	Do.	–	Bandon Convent, f.	–	R.C.	Nuns		110	646	756	393
420	10413	Kilnagross,	–	Kilnagross,	–	R.C.	R.C.	–	31	26	56	24
421	9846	Kilmore,	58	Galeen, m.	R.C.	–	R.C.	–	116	–	116	42
422	9847	Do.	–	Do. f.	R.C.	–	R.C.	–	–	90	90	43

* Including value of Free Garden.

Province of Munster: County of Cork—*continued.*

Amount paid for Books, Requisites, and Apparatus at Reduced Prices.	Aid granted by the Board during the Year 1874.			Amount of Local Endowments received in Aid of Teacher's Salary.			Vested or Non-Vested.	Number.
	In Free Stock of Books, Requisites, and Apparatus.	In Salaries, Premiums, and other Gratuities.	Results Fees, Financial Year.	School Fees.	Subscriptions, Local Funds, &c.	Total Local Aid.		
£ s. d.	£ s. d.	£ s. d.	£ s. d.	£ s. d.	£ s. d.	£ s. d.		
4 18 6	—	21 0 0	0 12 6	3 13 0	—	3 15 0		360
6 5 9	—	20 0 0	12 18 6	14 7 4	—	14 7 4		361
6 10 3	—	57 0 0	23 16 6	5 3 0	—	5 3 0	A.	362
3 4 3	—	42 0 0	15 3 6	6 7 6	—	3 7 6	A.	363
3 5 4	—	44 13 1	18 10 0	1 4 6	—	1 4 6	A.	364
2 14 11	—	40 10 0	24 8 0	2 7 6	—	2 7 6		365
1 7 1	—	20 18 8	0 8 2	2 5 8	—	2 6 8		366
6 7 11	—	97 11 8	16 5 0	1 8 0	7 13 0	b 9 1 0	V.C.	367
1 19 0	—	81 8 8	23 8 6	1 16 6	—	1 16 6	V.C.	368
1 0 1	—	28 0 0	8 0 0	4 15 4	32 19 0	b 34 15 1		369
—	1 1 0	77 10 0	9 8 0	6 0 8	—	0 11 0	A.	370
6 3 0	—	32 10 0	36 10 6	7 18 10	—	7 13 10	A.	371
2 16 11	—	68 0 0	19 5 0	6 11 6	—	6 11 6	V.C.	372
1 6 1	—	29 10 0	16 6 0	8 11 4	—	8 12 1	V.C.	373
1 10 3	—	81 14 5	19 8 10	18 0 0	—	18 5 8	A.	374
2 18 0	—	30 18 4	10 18 6	4 0 0	—	4 0 0	V.C.	375
1 18 1	—	81 13 4	18 5 6	6 10 0	—	6 10 0	V.C.	376
1 17 3	—	56 5 0	24 12 0	2 18 0	—	2 18 0	V.C.	377
—	—	24 13 4	17 14 0	6 0 0	—	6 0 0	V.C.	378
4 18 0	—	26 0 0	15 16 1	5 7 10	—	5 7 10	V.C.	379
3 15 0	—	71 0 0	35 17 6	13 19 4	—	18 19 4	V.T.	380
2 8 6	—	72 18 0	20 12 0	9 10 11	2 5 0	b 11 15 11	V.T.	381
4 18 8	—	64 10 0	25 17 0	15 1 5	—	16 1 5	V.T.	382
6 15 6	—	58 6 8	13 17 0	6 18 7	—	6 18 7	V.T.	383
2 0 2	—	20 12 4	9 19 0	4 10 0	15 0 0	b 22 10 0		384
7 15 11	—	101 16 8	19 15 0	18 4 8	—	19 4 8	V.T.	385
9 16 7	—	66 0 9	23 1 6	6 10 6	—	6 10 6	V.T.	386
4 19 2	—	38 18 4	12 0 5	9 8 7	—	9 8 7	V.T.	387
1 7 9	—	30 0 0	16 10 6	7 5 2	—	7 5 3	V.T.	388
5 2 8	—	42 0 0	12 1 6	6 18 6	—	6 13 8	V.C.	389
3 18 4	—	67 10 0	15 8 0	8 18 0	—	8 15 0	V.C.	390
1 4 11	—	81 10 0	9 0 0	8 18 6	—	0 16 6	V.C.	391
0 12 5	—	29 0 0	4 16 0	3 10 0	—	1 10 0		392
5 5 6	—	60 8 8	22 14 6	10 4 4	0 10 0	10 14 4	V.C.	393
6 1 11	—	113 18 4	25 16 0	18 14 6	—	18 14 0		394
5 4 6	—	50 10 0	21 0 0	16 6 7	—	16 3 7		395
2 16 0	—	49 10 0	23 4 0	7 8 0	1 7 8	b 8 10 0		396
2 16 0	—	48 13 4	23 15 6	6 7 0	0 10 0	b 0 17 0		397
3 14 4	—	84 16 8	27 7 6	6 8 6	—	8 8 3		398
6 4 6	—	84 8 4	19 7 0	7 0 0	—	7 0 0		399
7 8 0	—	68 10 8	24 12 0	8 19 8	—	8 19 2		400
4 0 8	—	55 19 0	20 4 6	20 14 8	—	14 15 6		401
3 4 1	—	52 6 0	21 9 0	13 8 7	—	13 8 7		402
5 5 8	4 0 0	31 0 8	9 1 6	—	40 0 0	40 0 0		403
4 14 7	—	41 10 0	15 0 6	23 19 6	—	13 18 6	V.T.	404
6 5 4	—	52 10 0	25 7 6	13 15 8	—	15 16 2	V.T.	405
5 18 2	—	60 10 0	19 15 0	10 8 4	—	16 8 6		406
5 1 9	—	46 10 0	20 13 0	8 4 0	—	8 4 0		407
8 4 11	—	35 10 0	19 18 6	4 8 0	—	4 8 0		408
2 18 10	—	32 16 8	13 15 6	6 0 5	—	6 0 5		409
5 18 8	—	48 6 0	22 3 0	10 17 8	3 15 0	14 18 8	V.C.	410
—	—	59 10 0	33 1 0	6 4 1	8 15 0	11 19 1	V.C.	411
6 18 11	—	21 8 0	—	6 13 0	—	6 18 0		412
3 10 6	—	58 0 0	20 9 0	24 9 0	—	24 9 0		413
6 15 11	—	24 0 0	6 0 0	1 10 0	0 10 0	2 0 0		414
—	—	20 0 0	7 17 0	5 16 4	—	5 16 4		415
5 18 8	—	74 10 0	23 2 6	12 10 10	5 0 0	17 10 10	V.C.	416
10 17 8	—	69 0 8	21 7 0	48 9 9	5 0 0	53 9 9		417
2 15 8	—	52 0 0	20 13 6	18 0 0	30 10 0	b 47 10 0		418
21 14 2	—	216 14 4	23 9 0	—	—	—		419
1 6 3	—	24 0 0	6 16 0	8 4 0	37 0 0	b 29 4 0		420
1 14 5	—	57 16 8	12 2 2	8 19 0	—	6 19 6		421
1 10 3	—	51 0 0	19 3 0	1 10 0	—	1 10 0		422

b Including value of Free Residence and Garden.

List of Schools in operation on the 31st December, 1874—

Number.	Roll Number of School.	Parish.	District.	School.	Religious Denomination of Managers or Correspondents: Clerical.	Lay.	Number and Religious Denomination of Teachers: Principals.	Assistants.	Total number of Pupils on Rolls within the Year 1874: Males.	Fem.	Total.	Average daily attendance.
423	6748	Kilcatherine,	58	Inner Ardgroom, m.	R.C.	–	R.C.	–	118	–	118	48
424	6846	Do.	–	Do. f.	R.C.	–	R.C.	–	–	81	81	32
425	7153	Do.	–	Urhin,	R.C.	–	R.C.	R.C.	104	110	214	76
426	8071	Do.	–	Eyeries,	R.C.	–	R.C.	R.C.	74	71	145	72
427	9389	Do.	–	Ballycrovane,	R.C.	–	R.C.	–	55	56	111	44
428	9847	Do.	–	Kilmacowen, m.	R.C.	–	R.C.	–	90	–	90	47
429	9847	Do.	–	Do. f.	R.C.	–	R.C.	R.C.	–	63	63	36
430	6858	Kilmurry,	58	Kilmurry, m.	R.C.	–	R.C.	2R.C.	216	–	216	83
431	6859	Do.	–	Do. f.	R.C.	–	R.C.	2R.C.	–	221	221	89
432	8868	Kilcrohane,	58	Rossnacaheragh,	R.C.	–	R.C.	R.C.	79	78	155	58
433	8760	Do.	–	Cahir,	R.C.	–	R.C.	2R.C.	103	98	201	91
434	9186	Do.	–	Gortalassa,	R.C.	–	R.C.	R.C.	70	55	125	51
435	9484	Do.	–	Hopsladen,	R.C.	–	R.C.	–	40	45	85	37
436	1782	Do.	–	Kilcrohane,	R.C.	–	2R.C.	R.C.	92	87	179	88
437	9142	Kilmacomoge,	57	Balgrady,	R.C.	–	R.C.	R.C.	110	78	188	75
438	10784	Do.	–	Ballinacalaba,*	R.C.	–	–	–	–	–	–	–
439	5246	Kilmona,	57	Kilmona, m.	R.C.	–	R.C.	–	113	–	113	48
440	5941	Do.	–	Do. f.	R.C.	–	R.C.	–	–	118	118	46
441	9900	Kilbrittain,	60	Rosleigh,	R.C.	–	R.C.	–	97	56	153	58
442	10800	Do.	–	Ballyjames, f.	R.C.	–	R.C.	–	–	80	80	33
443	10880	Do.	–	Barren,	R.C.	–	R.C.	–	48	53	101	32
444	6294	Knocktemple,	56	Promontory Ord. Ag.	R.C.	–	R.C.	R.C.	164	–	164	61
445	6295	Do.	–	Do. f.	R.C.	–	R.C.	R.C.	–	148	148	59
446	6368	Kinure,	60	Oysterhaven,	R.C.	–	R.C.	–	103	86	189	58
447	7630	Kilmoe,	58	Crookhaven,	R.C.	–	R.C.	–	53	41	94	39
448	8284	Do.	–	Ballygriffin,	R.C.	–	R.C.	2R.C.	118	103	221	114
449	8898	Kilcorney,	56	Kilcorney, m.	R.C.	–	R.C.	R.C.	164	–	164	63
450	8899	Do.	–	Do. f.	R.C.	–	R.C.	R.C.	–	144	144	69
451	607	Liscarroll,	56	Liscarroll, m.	–	R.C.	R.C.	R.C.	184	–	184	96
452	7115	Do.	–	Do. f.	R.C.	–	R.C.	R.C.	–	177	177	89
453	1671	Lislee,	59	Butlerstown, m.	R.C.	–	R.C.	R.C.	178	–	178	85
454	6830	Do.	–	Do. f.	R.C.	–	R.C.	R.C.	–	184	184	82
455	2824	Do.	–	Callinagh,	R.C.	–	R.C.	2R.C.	116	95	211	143
456	6891	Little Island,	60	Little Island, m.	R.C.	–	R.C.	R.C.	141	–	141	79
457	7844	Do.	–	Do. f.	R.C.	–	R.C.	–	–	111	111	65
458	4174	Lisgoold,	46	Leamlara, m.	R.C.	–	R.C.	–	95	–	95	39
459	6914	Do.	–	Do. f.	R.C.	–	R.C.	–	–	86	86	32
460	4230	Do.	–	Lisgoold, m.	R.C.	–	R.C.	R.C.	186	–	186	85
461	4231	Do.	–	Do. f.	R.C.	–	R.C.	–	–	181	181	67
462	9647	Leitrim,	56	Kilmurray, m.	–	R.C.	R.C.	–	61	–	61	34
463	9654	Do.	–	Do. f.	–	R.C.	R.C.	–	12	48	60	24
464	530	Macloneigh,	58	Toames, m.	R.C.	–	R.C.	R.C.	165	–	165	67
465	2708	Do.	–	Do. f.	R.C.	–	R.C.	R.C.	–	159	159	72
466	9846	Do.	–	Castleview, m.	R.C.	–	R.C.	–	40	–	40	30
467	9796	Do.	–	Do. f.	R.C.	–	R.C.	–	–	58	58	29
468	606	Macroom,	–	Macroom, m.	R.C.	–	R.C.	3R.C.	–	275	275	177
469	6468	Do.	–	Do. prep. m.	R.C.	–	R.C.	2R.C.	325	–	325	117
470	10347	Do.	–	Do. Conv., f.	R.C.	–	Nuns		–	514	514	325
471	4606	Do.	–	Do. Workhouse,	P.L.	Gds.	R.C.	–	36	25	61	50
472	6784	Do.	–	Ballymagree, m.	R.C.	–	R.C.	–	145	–	145	60
473	9785	Do.	–	Do. f.	R.C.	–	R.C.	–	–	111	111	50
474	9241	Magourney,	56	Aregith, m.	R.C.	–	R.C.	–	140	–	140	58
475	9245	Do.	–	Do. f.	R.C.	–	R.C.	R.C.	–	126	126	56
476	413	Middleton,	46	Ballinacollig,	R.C.	–	R.C.	R.C.	169	49	218	88
477	413	Do.	–	Middleton Conv. f.	R.C.	–	Nuns		181	738	919	446
478	8161	Do.	–	Do. Workhouse,	P.L.	Gds.	2R.C.	–	87	59	146	94
479	511	Movidy,	58	Aharler, m.	R.C.	–	R.C.	R.C.	168	–	168	74
480	6681	Do.	–	Do. f.	R.C.	–	R.C.	2R.C.	–	169	169	80
481	10142	Mallow,	56	Mallow, m.	R.C.	–	R.C.	R.C.	313	–	313	71
482	4620	Do.	–	Do. Convent, f.	R.C.	–	Nuns		–	647	647	360
483	3631	Do.	–	Do. Workhouse,	P.L.	Gds.	2R.C.	–	106	81	187	63
484	11183	Do.	–	Mallow,	R.C.	–	R.C.	–	46	25	71	38
485	2112	Myross,	59	Caheragh, m.	R.C.	–	R.C.	R.C.	176	–	176	65

* Closed.

Province of Munster: County of Cork—*continued.*

Amount paid for Books, Requisites, and Apparatus, at Reduced Prices.	Aid granted by the Board during the Year 1874: In Free Stock of Books, Requisites, and Apparatus.	In Salaries, Premiums, and other Gratuities.	Results Fees, Financial Year.	Amount of Local Emoluments received in Aid of Teacher's Salary: School Fees.	Subscriptions, Endowments, &c.	Total Local Aid.	Vested or Non-Vested.	Number.
£ s. d.	£ s. d.	£ s. d.	£ s. d.	£ s. d.	£ s. d.	£ s. d.		
5 16 8	—	63 4 8	70 17 10	2 4 8	—	2 4 8		423
—	—	30 0 0	8 4 6	1 0 0	—	1 0 0		424
—	—	69 0 0	15 6 8	4 10 6	—	4 10 6		425
1 17 2	—	70 6 8	20 18 7	5 3 0	—	5 3 0		426
1 6 11	—	40 10 0	20 10 0	4 0 0	—	4 0 0		427
5 5 5	—	30 16 8	16 5 0	4 16 6	—	4 16 6	V.C.	428
1 15 5	—	43 13 4	17 0 0	4 15 10	—	4 15 10	V.C.	429
4 10 2	—	21 6 8	29 3 0	18 10 5	—	18 10 5		430
6 12 2	—	75 3 4	30 14 7	11 14 5	—	18 14 0		431
6 16 0	—	64 0 0	6 8 10	5 6 11	—	5 6 11		432
7 11 6	—	73 14 0	46 17 0	12 7 6	—	12 7 6		433
5 4 11	—	44 0 0	22 8 6	8 11 0	—	8 11 0		434
2 11 0	—	20 0 0	12 8 0	4 0 0	—	4 0 0		435
1 10 10	—	40 0 0	15 15 0	3 4 0	—	3 4 0		436
2 16 1	—	40 14 6	19 16 0	16 13 6	—	16 13 5	V.T.	437
—	—	—	—	—	—	—		438
1 8 1	—	57 0 0	12 7 0	4 14 1	—	4 14 1		439
1 10 8	—	50 0 0	10 1 0	5 7 3	—	5 7 3		440
2 5 11	—	27 0 0	19 5 6	10 15 6	—	10 15 6		441
2 13 8	—	19 16 0	12 15 6	6 10 10	—	6 10 10		442
3 7 5	—	21 0 0	9 15 0	3 1 8	—	3 1 8	V.T.	443
10 1 11	—	77 18 3	27 10 0	20 0 10	—	20 0 10	V.C.	444
2 10 10	—	57 0 0	15 15 6	6 19 1	—	6 19 1	V.C.	445
3 14 8	—	52 0 5	22 12 6	17 0 3	—	17 0 3		446
—	—	50 0 0	7 7 2	—	—	—		447
10 9 3	—	65 10 0	48 18 0	8 14 0	—	8 14 0		448
1 5 8	—	22 10 0	18 15 6	7 12 6	—	7 12 6	V.T.	449
6 4 9	—	22 0 0	24 7 5	5 15 0	—	5 15 0	V.T.	450
2 9 11	—	60 0 0	21 10 0	22 18 2	—	22 18 2		451
3 0 5	—	52 6 4	36 0 5	21 0 0	—	21 0 0		452
6 12 11	—	51 12 5	37 10 0	12 6 0	—	12 6 0		453
7 8 8	—	65 10 0	28 11 0	18 8 1	—	18 8 1		454
2 10 0	—	63 0 0	28 11 0	10 0 0	—	19 0 0	V.T.	455
4 5 11	—	41 10 0	25 4 0	20 5 7	—	20 5 7		456
1 7 1	—	27 0 5	11 17 0	18 1 9	—	18 1 9		457
—	—	24 0 0	11 17 6	8 18 6	—	8 18 6	V.T.	458
1 8 4	—	20 0 6	8 9 0	8 11 6	—	8 11 6	V.T.	459
5 17 11	—	48 10 8	21 12 4	10 15 0	—	10 16 6	V.T.	460
4 2 8	—	88 15 4	30 10 5	9 3 8	—	9 3 8	V.T.	461
5 13 9	—	24 0 0	18 8 6	14 13 0	—	14 13 0		462
3 1 2	—	50 0 0	13 7 0	11 15 6	8 10 0	b20 6 0		463
—	—	71 18 4	30 11 6	8 17 0	—	8 17 0		464
6 19 6	—	48 0 0	35 7 8	6 1 0	—	6 1 0		465
1 9 2	—	24 0 0	7 14 0	6 12 0	—	6 12 0	V.T.	466
1 10 8	—	24 0 0	9 1 0	5 10 10	—	5 10 10	V.T.	467
12 19 1	—	154 8 4	71 10 5	21 7 5	—	21 7 5		468
7 16 0	—	100 10 0	65 7 0	11 8 4	—	11 8 4		469
19 6 4	—	142 7 9	97 10 8	23 7 9	—	23 7 9		470
—	—	1 10 0	—	—	—	—		471
4 0 10	—	24 0 0	18 10 9	10 11 11	—	10 11 11		472
1 11 1	—	50 0 0	13 16 6	6 18 0	—	6 18 0		473
3 10 7	—	63 8 8	12 6 6	18 0 0	—	18 0 0		474
1 15 6	—	55 0 0	25 8 6	11 17 4	—	11 17 4		475
—	—	47 6 0	12 14 0	8 0 0	6 0 0	b14 0 0		476
58 2 4	14 7 0	212 2 0	154 1 0	—	—	—		477
2 10 5	—	2 10 0	—	—	—	—		478
4 8 9	—	62 10 0	21 7 8	11 12 2	—	11 12 2		479
8 10 0	—	60 0 0	20 2 6	16 18 6	—	15 18 6		480
4 5 5	—	68 10 0	15 8 0	9 15 2	—	9 15 2		481
19 18 2	—	126 0 4	74 12 0	—	—	—		482
7 5 8	—	11 0 0	—	—	—	—		483
1 14 9	4 10 0	16 0 0	8 5 6	5 7 4	38 0 0	b44 7 4		484
11 9 2	—	63 8 4	44 18 0	14 18 6	—	24 12 0	A.	485

b Including value of Free Residence.

List of Schools in operation on the 31st December, 1874—

Number.	Roll Number of School.	Parish.	District.	School.	Religious Denominations of Managers or Correspondents. Clerical.	Lay.	Number and Religious Denominations of Teachers. Principals.	Assistants.	Attendance for the Year. Total Number of Pupils on Rolls within the Year 1874. Males.	Females.	Total.	Average Daily Attendance for the Year.
494	8118	Myross,	69	Coonvoran, . f.	R.C.	–	R.C.	R.C.	4	186	190	119
497	9118	Marshalstown,	66	Gortroe,	R.C.	–	R.C.	R.C.	66	64	130	59
498	6456	Do.	–	Glenahulla, . m.	R.C.	–	R.C.	–	63	–	63	41
498	9080	Do.	–	Do. . f.	R.C.	–	R.C.	–	7	81	88	65
499	2292	Mitchelstown?	–	Kilbeheny? . m.	R.C.	–	R.C.	R.C.	180	–	161	99
501	2296	Do.	–	Do. . f.	R.C.	–	R.C.	R.C.	–	164	164	90
502	9367	Do.	–	Knocknacallery? . m.	R.C.	–	R.C.	–	53	–	53	36
503	9367	Do.	–	Do. . f.	R.C.	–	R.C.	–	–	67	67	44
494	2825	Murragh.	68	Newcestown, . m.	R.C.	–	R.C.	–	111	–	111	49
503	6391	Do.	–	Do. . f.	R.C.	–	R.C.	R.C.	–	107	107	61
504	11976	Do.	–	Farnthomas?,	R.C.	–	R.C.	–	17	25	37	22
497	2374	Magourney,	63	Clonlead?, . m.	R.C.	–	R.C.	–	182	–	183	84
498	2870	Do.	–	Do. . f.	R.C.	–	R.C.	R.C.	–	131	131	45
506	6461	Do.	–	Tullig, . m.	R.C.	–	R.C.	–	61	–	61	28
506	4465	Do.	–	Do. . f.	R.C.	–	R.C.	–	–	103	103	52
501	6824	Marmullane,	66	Passage West, . m.	R.C.	–	R.C.	R.C.	216	–	219	97
502	8414	Do.	–	Do. . Conv. f.	R.C.	–	Nuns		65	280	345	164
503	10643	Monkstown,	–	Monkstown, . f.	R.C.	–	R.C.	–	105	100	205	74
504	6976	Mourne Abbey,	66	Burnfort,	R.C.	–	R.C.	R.C.	142	129	271	89
505	6576	Do.	–	Kilquane,	R.C.	–	R.C.	–	67	76	143	68
506	6327	Mogeely,	16	Curraglass,	R.C.	–	R.C.	R.C.	73	74	147	60
507	9788	Do.	–	Castlemartyr, . m.	R.C.	–	R.C.	R.C.	172	–	172	60
508	7871	Do.	–	Do. . f.	R.C.	–	R.C.	R.C.	–	164	164	97
509	10285	Do.	–	Glengoura, . m.	R.C.	–	R.C.	–	60	–	60	37
510	10286	Do.	–	Do. . f.	R.C.	–	R.C.	–	–	43	43	31
511	6345	Matehy,	66	Vicarstown, . m.	R.C.	–	R.C.	R.C.	186	–	186	73
512	7896	Do.	–	Do. . f.	R.C.	–	R.C.	R.C.	–	190	190	98
513	1966	Nohavaldaly,	–	Knocknagree, . m.	R.C.	–	R.C.	R.C.	237	–	237	95
514	8616	Do.	–	Do. . f.	R.C.	–	R.C.	R.C.	–	216	217	85
515	6214	Do.	–	King Williamstown, m.	R.C.	–	R.C.	–	156	–	156	29
516	6216	Do.	–	Do. . f.	R.C.	–	R.C.	R.C.	–	130	130	66
517	4443	Nohaval,	60	Reanies,	R.C.	–	R.C.	R.C.	63	86	149	36
518	4442	Newmarket,	66	Newmarket Ord. Agl.	R.C.	–	R.C.	R.C.	273	–	273	167
519	4436	Do.	–	Do. . f.	R.C.	–	R.C.	R.C.	–	256	256	169
520	316	Ross?,	56	Old Chapel,	R.C.	–	R.C.	R.C.	313	–	316	111
521	1376	Do.	–	Ardagh, . f.	R.C.	–	R.C.	R.C.	–	143	143	89
522	2166	Do.	–	Do. . prep. f.	R.C.	–	R.C.	R.C.	–	170	190	70
523	6197	Do.	–	Rossmacowen?, . m.	–	R.C.	R.C.	–	168	–	169	89
524	6796	Do.	–	Do. . f.	–	R.C.	R.C.	R.C.	–	116	116	69
525	6697	Do.	–	Lisavaird, . m.	R.C.	–	R.C.	–	123	–	121	57
526	6011	Do.	–	Do. . f.	R.C.	–	R.C.	R.C.	–	176	176	68
527	10547	Little Island?,	66	Glanmire,	–	R.C.	–	–	14	26	30	29
528	10666	Do.	–	Lower Glanmire, . m.	R.C.	–	R.C.	R.C.	157	–	157	61
529	10661	Do.	–	Do. . f.	R.C.	–	R.C.	–	–	115	115	55
530	1776	Rathgoggan,	56	Charleville, . m.	R.C.	–	R.C.	–	163	–	152	39
531	1045	Do.	–	Do. . Conv. f.	R.C.	–	Nuns.		81	375	456	221
532	1565	Rathcormack,	–	Rathcormack, . m.	R.C.	–	R.C.	R.C.	182	–	182	76
533	1579	Do.	–	Do. . f.	R.C.	–	R.C.	R.C.	–	212	212	83
534	6433	Do.	–	Kildinan Ord. Agri.,	R.C.	–	R.C.	–	78	68	161	58
535	2784	Ringcurran,	66	Cove of Kinsale,	R.C.	–	R.C.	R.C.	120	86	106	84
536	4825	Ringrone,	55	Ringrone,	R.C.	–	R.C.	R.C.	62	71	133	66
537	9659	Do.	–	Old Head of Kinsale, m.	R.C.	–	R.C.	–	113	–	113	59
538	10315	Do.	–	Do. . f.	R.C.	–	R.C.	R.C.	–	117	117	55
539	7662	Do.	–	Ballyduane?, . m.	R.C.	–	R.C.	–	67	2	69	35
540	9086	Rahan,	66	Rahan,	R.C.	–	R.C.	R.C.	110	63	169	62
541	10470	Do.	–	Kanturk?, . m.	R.C.	–	R.C.	–	97	–	97	48
542	10634	Do.	–	Do. . f.	R.C.	–	R.C.	–	–	86	80	37
543	6851	Rathclarin,	59	Kilbrittain, . m.	R.C.	–	R.C.	R.C.	186	–	168	59
544	11104	Do.	–	Do. . f.	R.C.	–	R.C.	R.C.	–	179	178	91
545	9246	Do.	–	Barryroe, ᵈ	R.C.	–	–	–	–	–	–	–
546	8007	Rathberry,	–	Rathberry,	R.C.	–	R.C.	–	103	–	103	48
547	10180	Rostellan,	48	Rostellan, ᵉ	–	E.C.	–	–	–	–	–	–
548	1107	St. Mary's, Shandon,	60	Sundaywell, . m.	R.C.	–	R.C.	R.C.	200	–	208	70

ᵃ Including value of Free Residence.

ᵇ Including value of Free Residence and Garden.

Province of MUNSTER: County of CORK—*continued.*

Amount paid for Books, Requisites, and Apparatus, at Reduced Prices.	Aid granted by the Board during the Year 1874: In Free Stock of Books, Requisites, and Apparatus.	In Salaries, Premiums, and other Gratuities.	Results Fees, Financial Year.	Amount of Local Emoluments received in Aid of Teacher's Salary: School Fees.	Subscriptions, Endowments, &c.	Total Local Aid.	Vested or Non-Vested.	Number.
£ s. d.	£ s. d.	£ s. d.	£ s. d.	£ s. d.	£ s. d.	£ s. d.		
5 2 4	—	65 0 0	40 9 3	15 1 11	—	15 1 11	d.	486
7 3 5	—	51 6 8	15 5 0	8 0 0	—	8 0 0	V.T.	487
5 4 10	—	37 0 0	17 15 0	7 13 0	—	7 13 0		488
3 18 5	—	29 0 0	19 2 6	8 6 0	—	8 6 0		489
4 7 6	—	96 1 8	27 18 0	18 7 2	—	18 7 2		490
8 14 1	—	56 0 0	28 9 6	14 4 9	—	14 4 9		491
—	—	8 0 0	8 0 0	0 11 0	2 0 0	*2 11 0	V.T.	492
8 4 10	—	63 6 8	15 11 0	6 8 6	—	6 8 6	V.T.	493
0 6 8	—	48 0 0	12 15 6	13 11 0	—	13 14 0		494
2 14 1	—	15 16 8	8 15 6	8 0 0	—	8 0 0		495
4 6 4	4 0 0	24 0 0	10 2 6	8 0 0	10 0 0	b18 0 0		496
2 18 7	—	40 6 8	22 15 6	8 7 6	—	8 7 6	V.T.	497
4 13 10	—	62 16 0	27 11 0	7 5 0	—	7 5 0	V.T.	498
1 6 6	—	24 0 0	4 13 0	4 1 6	—	4 1 6	V.T.	499
—	—	32 16 8	18 6 8	6 9 2	—	6 9 2	V.T.	500
0 18 11	—	93 0 0	98 8 0	84 13 8	—	84 13 8		501
13 0 4	—	70 14 0	71 0 0	4 10 6	—	4 10 6		502
8 1 4	—	45 0 0	14 16 0	13 8 11	—	13 8 11		503
11 7 6	—	61 0 0	70 1 8	15 6 0	—	15 6 0		504
3 6 8	—	41 0 0	18 14 0	4 15 3	—	4 10 3		505
4 8 1	—	40 13 4	21 18 6	5 0 5	—	5 0 5		506
4 18 0	—	61 1 8	31 8 6	10 15 0	4 0 0	*14 15 0		507
1 9 6	—	61 6 8	25 7 6	10 18 7	—	10 18 7		508
1 13 4	—	24 0 0	13 16 6	4 1 6	—	4 1 6		509
2 10 10	—	34 0 0	13 5 0	5 15 6	4 0 0	b9 15 6		510
6 4 1	—	62 0 0	82 6 0	17 15 0	—	17 15 0		511
...	—	40 0 0	21 0 11	6 5 0	—	6 5 0		512
5 6 11	—	30 10 8	36 16 0	7 10 0	—	7 10 0	V.T.	513
4 1 0	—	54 0 0	31 2 0	3 10 0	—	3 10 0	V.T.	514
6 5 10	—	91 0 0	10 14 6	4 4 6	—	4 4 6	V.T.	515
6 15 6	—	51 8 4	23 13 6	1 19 10	—	1 19 10	V.T.	516
2 17 6	—	30 0 8	10 0 0	7 0 0	—	7 0 0	V.T.	517
6 13 3	—	116 8 4	26 13 6	26 15 0	—	26 15 0	V.T.	518
6 14 11	—	130 0 0	45 16 6	13 13 0	—	13 13 0	V.T.	519
5 0 1	—	86 0 6	30 11 6	15 6 1	—	15 6 1		520
7 5 6	—	64 10 6	41 7 6	7 4 11	—	7 4 11		521
3 0 4	—	47 6 8	13 4 6	3 1 1	—	3 1 1		522
4 2 0	—	49 10 0	28 12 6	16 6 0	—	16 6 0	V.T.	523
9 13 9	—	22 5 0	25 17 0	10 7 6	—	10 7 6	V.T.	524
8 1 1	—	37 10 0	22 1 0	6 6 9	—	6 6 9		525
7 11 11	—	32 4 8	30 4 0	9 16 0	—	9 16 0		526
—	—	8 0 0	0 14 7	—	20 0 0	*20 0 0		527
0 17 9	—	65 16 4	12 17 5	18 7 1	—	18 7 1		528
1 6 0	—	30 0 0	6 13 0	6 18 4	—	6 18 4		529
9 13 9	—	50 0 0	6 19 0	15 16 0	1 0 0	16 16 0	V.T.	530
11 13 6	—	78 19 4	63 4 0	—	—	—	V.T.	531
4 14 11	—	54 0 0	15 10 2	7 6 8	—	7 6 8	V.T.	532
8 3 1	—	115 5 0	26 18 6	6 7 5	—	6 7 5	V.T.	533
8 12 8	—	48 0 0	8 8 0	7 0 0	12 0 0	*10 0 0	V.T.	534
9 7 5	—	44 0 0	11 0 0	14 10 6	—	14 10 6		535
—	—	19 11 8	19 12 8	8 15 8	—	8 15 8		536
8 8 5	—	25 0 0	18 0 0	11 8 8	—	11 8 8	V.T.	537
4 17 6	—	40 0 0	16 6 6	6 18 6	—	6 18 6	V.T.	538
1 18 7	—	24 0 0	8 17 0	2 1 0	—	2 1 0		539
4 5 11	—	81 10 0	17 17 0	10 8 5	14 0 0	*24 8 5		540
8 6 6	—	24 0 0	7 18 0	—	20 0 0	*20 0 0		541
3 18 0	—	20 0 0	4 18 2	—	8 0 0	8 0 0		542
7 4 4	—	60 0 8	27 5 0	20 17 6	—	20 17 6		543
9 0 1	5 0 0	40 10 0	21 18 7	13 2 6	—	13 2 6		544
—	—	—	—	—	—	—		545
2 10 0	1 6 1	24 0 0	13 18 7	6 1 6	—	6 1 6		546
—	—	—	1 10 0	—	—	—		547
4 7 11	—	45 0 0	20 10 0	17 18 8	—	17 15 3	V.T.	548

* Including value of Free Garden. d Inoperative. c Returns not available.

List of Schools in operation on the 31st December, 1874.—

No.	Roll Number of School	Parish	District	School	Religious Denomination of Trustees or Correspondents: Clerical	Religious Denomination of Trustees or Correspondents: Lay	Teachers and Religious Denominations of Teachers: Principals	Teachers and Religious Denominations of Teachers: Assistants	Total number of Pupils on Rolls within the Year 1874: Males	Females	Total	Average daily attendance
549	2707	St. Mary's, Shandon,	60	Sundayswell, f.	R.C.	–	R.C.	2R.C.	81	207	[illegible]	115
550	[illegible]	Do.	–	Blackpool,	R.C.	–	R.C.	3R.C.	347	–	387	141
551	[illegible]	Do.	–	St. Mary's (Shandon), evg.	R.C.	–	R.C.	–	65	49	119	87
552	10778	St. Edmund's,	60	St. Edmund's,	R.C.	–	R.C.	R.C.	42	31	73	45
553	1848	St. Peter's,	60	SS. Peter & Paul's, No. 1,	R.C.	–	R.C.	2R.C.	–	239	[illegible]	103
554	8767	Do.	–	Do. No. 2, f.	R.C.	–	R.C.	2R.C.	101	278	374	120
555	11187	Do.	–	St. Peter's,	R.C.	–	R.C.	–	33	54	87	44
556	11184	Do.	–	Do. infant,	R.C.	–	R.C.	–	[illegible]	[illegible]	[illegible]	50
557	1654	Skull,	58	Ballydehob, m.	R.C.	–	R.C.	R.C.	173	–	173	61
558	1774	Do.	–	Do. f.	R.C.	–	R.C.	R.C.	–	129	129	56
559	1697	Do.	–	Skull, m.	R.C.	–	R.C.	R.C.	118	–	179	78
560	2276	Do.	–	Do. f.	R.C.	–	R.C.	3R.C.	–	161	161	80
561	8140	Do.	–	Do. Workhouse,	P.L.	Gds.	R.C.	–	30	34	64	[illegible]
562	[illegible]	Do.	–	Dunbeacon,	R.C.	–	R.C.	R.C.	78	95	173	75
563	4178	Do.	–	Lowertown,	R.C.	–	R.C.	R.C.	64	100	160	75
564	8718	Do.	–	Dunmanus,	R.C.	–	R.C.	3R.C.	93	86	179	72
565	8788	Do.	–	Kilthomane,	R.C.	–	R.C.	–	48	66	114	46
566	[illegible]	Do.	–	Long Island,	R.C.	–	R.C.	–	16	27	43	15
567	8173	Do.	–	Dereenlamane,	R.C.	–	R.C.	R.C.	60	48	108	45
568	[illegible]	Do.	–	Rossbrin, m.	R.C.	–	R.C.	–	61	–	61	30
569	9072	Do.	–	Do. f.	R.C.	–	R.C.	R.C.	–	125	125	60
570	[illegible]	Do.	–	Bawnakeana,	Diss.	–	Diss.	–	[illegible]	[illegible]	43	23
571	[illegible]	Do.	–	Dunmanas,	R.C.	–	R.C.	R.C.	91	73	164	61
572	8813	Do.	–	Glaun,	R.C.	–	R.C.	–	[illegible]	38	74	29
573	9059	Do.	–	Rockwood,	R.C.	–	R.C.	R.C.	67	61	[illegible]	59
574	1858	St. Finbar's,	60	Blackrock, m.	R.C.	–	R.C.	R.C.	164	–	164	160
575	5040	Do.	–	Do. Convent, f.	R.C.	–	Nuns		–	167	167	95
576	4230	Do.	–	Ballintemple,	R.C.	–	R.C.	R.C.	96	61	157	65
577	[illegible]	Do.	–	Tugher,	R.C.	–	R.C.	R.C.	123	83	210	67
578	8062	Do.	–	St. Michael's,	R.C.	–	R.C.	–	21	16	40	15
579	5069	Do.	–	Great George's-street, Monastic, m.	–	R.C.	Monks		780	–	770	[illegible]
580	[illegible]	Do.	–	Douglas-st. Monastic, m.	–	R.C.	Monks		1,115	–	1,118	490
581	6626	Do.	–	St. Joseph's Convent, f.	–	R.C.	Nuns		–	1,089	1,089	384
582	10099	Do.	–	Ballinlough,	R.C.	–	R.C.	R.C.	81	96	177	95
583	8345	Do.	–	Cork Workhouse,	P.L.	Gds.	3R.C.	5R.C.	364	[illegible]	700	[illegible]
584	[illegible]	Do.	–	County Gaol, No. 1, c	Governor		R.C.	–	–	–	–	–
585	[illegible]	Do.	–	Do. No. 2, c	Governor		–	–	–	–	–	–
586	6799	Do.	–	Munster Model Agr.	–	E.C.	R.C.	{R.C. / [illegible]}	17	–	17	8
587	10284	Do.	–	St. Finbar's, m.	R.C.	–	R.C.	–	67	–	67	35
588	[illegible]	Do.	–	Do. f.	R.C.	–	R.C.	R.C.	34	83	117	43
589	5884	St. Anne's (Shandon),	–	St. Patrick's, m.	R.C.	–	R.C.	2R.C.	280	–	280	123
590	8155	Do.	–	Do. f.	R.C.	–	R.C.	3R.C.	–	274	274	118
591	9170	Do.	–	Do. i.	R.C.	–	R.C.	2R.C.	231	264	495	151
592	[illegible]	Do.	–	Carmichael, m.	Pres.	–	Pres.	R.C.	164	–	164	81
593	7320	Do.	–	Do. f.	Pres.	–	Pres.	Pres.	45	105	150	79
594	10340	Do.	–	Blackpool, f.	R.C.	–	R.C.	R.C.	–	280	280	15
595	9920	Do.	–	Angel Guardians,	R.C.	–	R.C.	2R.C.	62	145	[illegible]	60
596	10571	Do.	–	St. Mary's of the Rock,	–	R.C.	R.C.	R.C.	–	544	544	239
597	6109	St. Michael's,	–	Upper Glanmire,	R.C.	–	R.C.	R.C.	107	67	174	77
598	8508	Shandrum,	58	Newtown, Shandrum, m.	R.C.	–	R.C.	–	178	–	178	64
599	7488	Do.	–	Do. f.	R.C.	–	R.C.	R.C.	13	168	181	86
600	10500	Do.	–	Dromina,	R.C.	–	R.C.	–	176	157	[illegible]	135
601	10784	St. Mary's,	48	Friar-street,	R.C.	–	R.C.	R.C.	69	40	[illegible]	30
602	6201	St. Nicholas,	60	Cork Dis. Mod. m.	Com.	N.B.	R.C.	{3R.C. / [illegible]}	300	–	[illegible]	161
603	[illegible]	Do.	–	Do. f.	Com.	N.B.	R.C.	{Paid / R.C. / R.C.}	–	348	378	144
604	[illegible]	Do.	–	Do. i.	Com.	N.B.	R.C.	R.C.	111	96	208	85

a Including value of Free Residence. b Including value of Free Residence and Garden.
c This includes Male and Female School as well as Residence.

Province of MUNSTER: County of CORK—*continued.*

Amount paid for Books, Requisites, and Apparatus, at Reduced Prices.	Aid granted by the Board during the Year 1874: In Free Stock of Books, Requisites, and Apparatus.	In Salaries, Premiums, and other Gratuities.	Results Fees, Financial Year.	Amount of Local Emoluments received in Aid of Teacher's Salary: School Fees.	Subscriptions, Endowments, &c.	Total Local Aid.	Vested or Non-Vested.	Number.
£ s. d.	£ s. d.	£ s. d.	£ s. d.	£ s. d.	£ s. d.	£ s. d.		
6 5 9	—	110 6 4	29 2 6	16 3 6	10 0 0	26 3 6	V.T.	549
—	—	112 0 0	30 2 0	46 19 11	—	46 19 11		550
6 1 10	—	41 7 10	12 16 0	6 13 4	28 0 0	* 34 13 4		551
8 3 2	—	28 0 0	17 10 5	6 0 0	35 0 0	* 41 0 0		552
12 14 2	—	103 3 4	18 10 6	10 18 5	—	10 18 5		553
4 8 0	—	40 16 8	25 17 0	27 16 11	—	27 16 11		554
9 11 1	4 10 0	16 0 0	17 1 6	—	50 0 0	50 0 0		555
1 7 2	4 0 0	10 0 0	3 13 6	—	21 0 0	21 0 0		556
4 0 8	—	73 10 0	28 1 0	7 19 11	—	7 19 11		557
2 15 4	—	64 15 0	20 12 6	6 12 0	—	6 12 0		558
6 9 2	—	64 10 0	30 17 6	15 0 1	—	15 0 1		559
7 7 7	—	66 10 0	19 0 6	5 10 9	—	5 10 9	N.	560
1 14 11	—	—	—	—	—	—		561
3 6 1	—	77 10 0	24 6 6	7 10 0	—	7 10 0	V.T.	562
1 17 9	—	66 18 4	23 18 0	2 10 0	—	2 10 0	V.T.	563
1 18 2	—	52 0 0	25 18 6	4 14 0	—	4 14 0		564
5 7 1	—	24 0 0	17 0 6	4 8 2	—	4 8 2		565
—	—	14 0 8	1 16 0	0 10 0	—	0 10 0		566
1 13 7	—	30 10 0	14 8 11	6 9 2	—	6 9 2		567
1 4 11	—	31 0 0	1 16 7	3 2 6	2 0 0	* 5 8 0		568
9 6 4	6 0 0	50 10 0	17 7 0	4 2 6	—	4 2 0		569
3 3 0	—	30 0 0	7 19 8	2 0 0	22 0 0	* 24 0 0		570
4 9 8	—	47 6 8	23 11 0	0 17 0	—	0 17 0		571
2 4 0	—	24 0 0	8 1 6	4 10 7	—	4 10 7		572
0 8 10	—	41 0 0	20 17 6	4 8 0	—	4 8 0		573
9 12 6	—	69 16 5	22 6 0	29 15 2	4 0 0	33 15 2	V.T.	574
4 10 9	—	60 11 0	10 3 6	—	—	—		575
4 9 7	—	58 10 0	10 12 6	10 15 6	—	10 15 6		576
3 19 4	—	61 0 0	11 10 6	11 8 9	10 0 0	21 8 9		577
0 14 7	—	21 8 10	2 14 6	1 11 1	27 10 0	28 1 1		578
29 7 6	—	119 10 2	60 9 0	—	84 0 0	61 0 0		579
16 7 1	—	150 17 8	69 8 6	—	124 0 0	124 0 0		580
19 6 1	—	180 4 1	71 14 0	25 0 0	—	25 0 0		581
4 9 8	—	63 0 0	21 13 0	15 10 1	—	15 10 1		582
15 19 9	—	23 0 0	—	—	—	—		583
—	—	—	—	—	—	—		584
—	—	—	—	—	—	—		585
—	4 10 6	211 16 0	—	—	—	—	V.C.	586
8 18 9	—	27 15 0	8 11 6	4 11 0	* 45 15 0	* 50 6 0		587
1 7 6	—	40 15 2	14 17 6	4 10 4	13 15 0	* 18 10 4		588
0 19 11	—	101 19 4	54 8 6	31 6 4	10 0 0	41 6 4		589
—	—	90 18 1	54 16 6	25 3 11	—	25 3 11		590
—	—	111 3 4	25 18 6	30 9 10	—	30 9 10		591
11 5 0	—	92 1 0	66 19 0	38 15 1	—	38 15 1		592
4 8 2	—	58 10 0	41 6 0	58 17 10	—	58 17 10		593
0 6 7	—	65 6 6	20 7 6	34 14 4	—	34 14 4		594
8 18 0	—	68 10 0	10 10 0	21 16 10	—	21 16 10		595
9 18 7	14 6 0	215 8 4	41 11 0	20 0 0	—	20 0 0		596
4 1 6	—	44 0 0	26 0 0	19 19 0	—	19 19 0		597
8 16 4	—	24 0 0	20 10 0	16 8 4	—	16 8 4		598
6 11 7	—	40 0 0	23 0 0	12 1 4	—	12 1 4		599
5 13 8	—	68 0 0	60 3 8	18 12 0	—	18 12 0		600
4 7 5	—	56 6 0	17 5 0	20 18 5	16 0 0	* 36 18 5		601
29 4 1	11 4 0	1,083 16 11	166 0 0	323 10 5	—	323 10 5	V.C.	602
24 1 5	30 10 0							603
19 1 11	—							604

* Including value of Free Garden. † Not in operation during last quarter. ‡ Inoperative.

List of Schools in operation on the 31st December, 1874.—

Number.	Roll Number of School.	Parish.	District.	School.		Religious Denomination of Patrons or Correspondents: Clerical.	Lay.	Religious Denomination of Teachers: Principals.	Assistants.	Attendance for the Year: Total number of Pupils on Rolls within the Year 1874: Males.	Females.	Total.	Average Daily Attendance.
605	6720	St. Nicholas,	60	St. Nicholas,	m.	R.C.	–	R.C.	–	72	–	72	24
606	3831	Do.	–	Do.	f.	R.C.	–	R.C.	–	–	73	73	60
607	6556	Do.	–	Do.	m. i.	R.C.	–	R.C.	–	97	–	97	30
608	6504	Do.	–	Do.	f. i.	R.C.	–	R.C.	–	–	87	87	35
609	6152	Do.	–	St. Finbar's Conv.	f.	R.C.	–	Nuns		–	1,765	1,765	641
610	457	Templetrine,	59	Ballinspittle,	m.	R.C.	–	R.C.	R.C.	138	–	138	66
611	465	Do.	–	Do.	f.	R.C.	–	R.C.	R.C.	–	119	119	54
612	6220	Templebreedy,	60	Myrtleville,		R.C.	–	R.C.	R.C.	113	56	169	68
613	8474	Do.	–	Crosshaven,		R.C.	–	R.C.	R.C.	66	103	169	77
614	1275	Tullagh,	58	Sherkin Island,	m.	R.C.	–	R.C.	–	68	–	68	36
615	4929	Do.	–	Do.	f.	R.C.	–	R.C.	–	–	66	66	31
616	2292	Do.	–	Baltimore,	m.	R.C.	–	R.C.	aR.C.	68	98	166	73
617	6126	Do.	–	Lough Ine,		R.C.	–	R.C.	R.C.	79	69	148	72
618	1891	Tracton,	60	Knocknamanagh,	m.	R.C.	–	R.C.	–	138	–	138	51
619	1677	Do.	–	Do.	f.	R.C.	–	R.C.	–	–	108	108	35
620	3814	Do.	–	Robert's Cove,		–	R.C.	R.C.	–	101	68	169	53
621	2354	Timoleague,	59	Timoleague,	m.	R.C.	–	R.C.	aR.C.	201	–	201	97
622	8672	Do.	–	Do.	f.	R.C.	–	R.C.	aR.C.	–	185	185	102
623	1083	Do.	–	Do.		–	R.C.	R.C.	–	9	22	31	11
624	6195	Templerobin,	60	Haulbowline Island,		–	R.C.	R.C.	–	35	28	63	34
625	4701	Do.	–	Spike Island,	m.	–	R.C.	R.C.	–	74	–	74	33
626	8816	Do.	–	Do.	f.	–	R.C.	R.C.	–	–	43	43	16
627	7600	Do.	–	Walterstown,		R.C.	–	R.C.	aR.C.	74	72	146	46
628	3704	Templeroan,	58	Shanballymore,	m.	R.C.	–	R.C.	R.C.	123	–	123	67
629	8708	Do.	–	Do.	f.	R.C.	–	R.C.	–	–	116	116	48
630	4128	Templemolaga,	–	Knockanevin,	m.	R.C.	–	R.C.	R.C.	168	–	168	64
631	4129	Do.	–	Do.	f.	R.C.	–	R.C.	R.C.	–	135	135	58
632	4144	Do.	–	Graigue,	m.	R.C.	–	R.C.	–	100	–	100	48
633	4125	Do.	–	Do.	f.	R.C.	–	R.C.	–	–	78	78	33
634	6187	Templeusque,	60	Riverstown,	m.	R.C.	–	R.C.	–	111	–	111	50
635	6708	Do.	–	Do.	f.	R.C.	–	R.C.	–	–	109	109	30
636	3844	Templecurraheen,	57	Derrivry,		R.C.	–	R.C.	R.C.	105	102	207	93
637	6156	Templemartin,	–	Mossgrove,		R.C.	–	R.C.	R.C.	64	75	139	73
638	6463	Do.	–	Garranes,		R.C.	–	R.C.	R.C.	72	77	149	62
639	6465	Do.	–	Templemartin,		R.C.	–	R.C.	–	21	7	28	17
640	6816	Tullylease,	56	Tullylease,	m.	R.C.	–	R.C.	R.C.	126	–	126	58
641	9818	Do.	–	Do.	f.	R.C.	–	R.C.	R.C.	–	129	129	66
642	10770	Whitechurch,	62	Kilcard,		R.C.	–	R.C.	R.C.	76	57	133	54
643	631	Do.	–	Whitechurch,	m.	R.C.	–	R.C.	R.C.	168	–	168	72
644	632	Do.	–	Do.	f.	R.C.	–	R.C.	aR.C.	–	161	161	75
645	6190	Wallstown,	56	Wallstown,	m.	R.C.	–	R.C.	–	67	–	67	41
646	7067	Do.	–	Do.	f.	R.C.	–	R.C.	–	–	80	80	53
647	6526	Youghal,	48	Youghal Convent,	f.	R.C.	–	Nuns		–	672	672	356
648	6121	Do.	–	Do. Workhouse,		P.L.	Gds.	aR.C.	–	65	41	106	56
		Total for County Cork, 648,								51099	53311	104410	43347

COUNTY OF

1	1159	Annagh,	54	Blennerville,	m.	R.C.	–	R.C.	R.C.	140	–	140	49
2	1140	Do.	–	Do.	f.	R.C.	–	R.C.	–	–	98	98	44
3	6637	Do.	–	Derryquay,		R.C.	–	R.C.	–	88	82	170	68
4	11180	Annascaul,	–	Glenmore,		R.C.	–	R.C.	–	78	68	146	60
5	1270	Aghavallen,	56	Ballylongford,	m.	R.C.	–	R.C.	R.C.	205	–	205	117
6	1506	Do.	–	Do.	f.	R.C.	–	R.C.	aR.C.	–	243	243	95
7	10301	Do.	–	Asdee,	m.	R.C.	–	R.C.	R.C.	174	–	174	66
8	10302	Do.	–	Do.	f.	R.C.	–	R.C.	R.C.	–	186	186	80
9	11308	Do.	–	Lenamore,		R.C.	–	R.C.	R.C.	74	57	131	61
10	3876	Ardfert,	54	Ardfert,	m.	R.C.	–	R.C.	R.C.	173	–	173	70
11	10961	Do.	–	Do.	m.	–	Christian	Bros.	–	50	12	62	17

a Including value of Free Residence. b Including value of Free Garden.

Province of MUNSTER: County of CORK—*continued.*

Amount paid for Books, Requisites, and Apparatus, at Reduced Prices.	Aid granted by the Board during the Year 1874. In Free Stock of Books, Requisites, and Apparatus.	To Salaries, Premiums, and other Gratuities.	Results Fees, Financial Year.	Amount of Local Emoluments received in Aid of Teacher's Salary. School Fees.	Subscriptions, Endowments, &c.	Total Local Aid.	Vested or Non-Vested.	Number.
£ s. d.	£ s. d.	£ s. d.	£ s. d.	£ s. d.	£ s. d.	£ s. d.		
14 9 8	—	24 0 0	5 18 0	2 7 3	25 0 0	27 7 3		605
3 8 11	—	23 8 8	9 17 0	0 17 3	24 0 0	25 17 3		606
—	—	26 0 0	5 5 0	4 14 8	13 15 0	17 8 0		607
—	—	25 10 0	2 5 0	2 2 8	12 0 0	14 2 8		608
20 17 10	—	220 1 8	61 1 0	—	—	—		609
3 18 6	—	61 8 4	18 13 0	15 10 6	—	15 10 6	N.	610
2 14 1	—	40 0 0	9 9 0	6 4 3	—	6 4 3	N.	611
6 4 5	—	59 0 0	15 8 6	18 8 0	—	18 8 0		612
4 10 6	—	80 6 8	19 1 6	24 17 11	—	24 17 11		613
1 17 5	—	21 0 0	4 8 5	2 10 0	—	2 10 0	V.V.	614
1 6 8	—	44 0 0	10 17 6	8 10 0	—	8 10 0	V.C.	615
5 10 4	—	64 0 0	16 17 0	7 17 11	—	7 17 11		616
7 0 3	—	74 0 0	24 18 6	12 10 8	—	12 16 8		617
2 8 3	—	27 6 8	16 8 0	12 13 11	—	12 18 11	V.V.	618
1 15 8	—	29 8 8	11 13 8	8 18 3	—	8 18 3	V.V.	619
2 18 1	—	31 15 0	8 16 0	3 18 10	—	5 18 10		620
5 0 6	—	25 0 8	55 4 6	20 0 0	—	20 0 0		621
6 8 2	—	28 0 0	36 14 0	16 6 4	—	16 6 4		622
1 12 7	—	—	4 2 0	1 0 0	84 0 0	*85 0 0		623
—	—	30 10 0	3 7 6	23 8 10	3 0 0	*26 0 10		624
6 8 1	—	47 10 0	18 10 0	21 8 4	6 10 0	*27 15 8		625
—	—	20 0 0	10 5 0	8 1 4	6 10 0	*15 11 4		626
9 15 6	—	67 14 4	29 4 6	11 3 6	—	11 3 6		627
3 18 10	3 7 8	48 0 0	17 18 0	3 8 8	3 0 0	6 8 8		628
6 14 3	2 19 3	40 0 0	18 7 6	2 18 10	—	2 18 10		629
7 1 11	—	49 10 0	23 14 6	26 0 0	—	26 0 0	V.V.	630
6 6 3	—	52 0 0	34 18 6	18 0 0	—	18 0 0	V.V.	631
1 6 9	—	67 6 1	11 9 1	18 4 8	—	13 4 8	V.V.	632
—	—	30 0 0	9 5 6	5 16 6	—	5 16 6	V.V.	633
1 15 9	—	34 0 0	8 15 8	8 0 7	—	8 0 7		634
1 11 8	—	24 0 0	6 17 11	5 8 5	—	5 0 5		635
4 17 0	—	51 15 5	52 12 0	9 3 0	15 2 0	*24 4 0		636
3 16 4	—	80 10 0	23 11 6	12 19 10	—	12 19 10		637
2 3 4	—	68 10 6	34 10 6	27 15 6	—	29 15 6		638
1 18 8	—	24 0 0	4 6 6	3 10 0	8 0 0	*18 10 0		639
6 8 2	—	53 6 8	19 8 5	14 17 6	—	14 17 6	V.V.	640
8 1 7	—	58 0 0	19 11 0	10 10 6	—	10 10 6	V.V.	641
3 11 2	—	40 18 4	20 6 6	14 15 5	—	16 13 5		642
7 0 8	—	57 10 0	27 8 0	13 0 4	—	13 6 4		643
5 14 5	—	72 16 6	27 18 0	13 0 8	—	13 0 8		644
0 10 2	—	83 13 4	9 7 6	5 7 3	2 0 0	*7 7 3		645
1 6 5	—	24 0 0	9 7 6	4 7 4	—	4 7 4		646
15 19 0	10 0 0	117 9 0	64 5 6	—	—	—		647
6 9 6	—	2 10 0	—	—	—	—		649
3,107 4 5	218 11 6	33,018 8 2	14,214 4 2	6,502 15 1	1,720 4 4	8,331 17 5		

KERRY—296 Schools.

1 18 4	—	78 0 0	18 12 6	—	—	—		1
1 7 3	—	30 0 0	12 16 0	—	—	—		2
1 5 0	—	41 0 0	19 1 6	6 10 8	—	0 10 8		3
1 14 1	—	18 10 0	14 3 0	5 5 0	—	5 5 0		4
6 4 4	—	62 0 0	63 18 6	17 19 0	—	17 19 0	V.V.	5
6 18 5	—	80 10 0	39 9 0	12 13 9	—	12 13 9	V.V.	6
4 13 4	—	51 16 0	33 1 0	20 6 3	—	20 6 3	V.V.	7
7 0 3	—	63 10 0	60 15 0	24 10 6	—	34 10 6	V.V.	8
6 13 7	—	49 10 0	18 2 6	14 3 4	—	14 3 4	V.V.	9
5 9 6	—	54 5 8	30 6 0	8 10 9	—	8 10 9	V.V.	10
—	—	18 0 0	5 19 6	4 0 0	84 0 0	37 0 0		11

* Including value of Free Residence and Garden.

List of Schools in operation on the 31st December, 1874.—

Number.	Roll Number of School.	Parish.	District.	School.	Religious Denomination of Manager or Correspondent: Clerical.	Lay.	Number and Religious Denomination of Teachers: Principals.	Assistants.	Attendance for the Year: Total number of Pupils on Rolls within the Year 1874: Males.	Females.	Total.	Average daily attendance.
12	9976	Ardfert,	64	Ardfert, f.	R.C.	–	R.C.	aR.C.	–	212	212	62
13	[illegible]	Do.	–	Barrow,	R.C.	–	R.C.	R.C.	58	52	110	41
14	6250	Do.	–	Tubrid, m.	R.C.	–	R.C.	–	110	–	110	46
15	[illegible]	Do.	–	Do. f.	R.C.	–	R.C.	–	–	103	103	48
16	1800	Aghadoe,	57	Fossa, m.	R.C.	–	R.C.	–	92	–	92	42
17	[illegible]	Do.	–	Do. f.	R.C.	–	R.C.	R.C.	–	63	63	33
18	8474	Do.	–	[illegible]	R.C.	–	R.C.	R.C.	140	80	220	78
19	5376	Do.	–	[illegible]bridge,	R.C.	–	R.C.	aR.C.	148	100	[illegible]	160
20	6304	Do.	–	[illegible], m.	R.C.	–	R.C.	–	95	–	95	31
21	[illegible]	Do.	–	Do. f.	R.C.	–	R.C.	–	–	103	103	47
22	2406	Aglish,	–	[illegible], m.	R.C.	–	R.C.	–	109	–	109	43
23	8406	Do.	–	Do. f.	R.C.	–	R.C.	R.C.	–	93	93	31
24	1148	Ballincuslane,	64	Knockaclare,	–	R.C.	R.C.	R.C.	88	87	175	60
25	7448	Do.	–	Glountane,	R.C.	–	R.C.	R.C.	56	69	125	59
26	6450	Do.	–	Loughfouder,	R.C.	–	R.C.	–	63	76	140	60
27	10020	Do.	–	[illegible], m.	R.C.	–	R.C.	–	115	–	115	47
28	10721	Do.	–	Do. f.	R.C.	–	R.C.	–	–	96	96	40
29	10904	Do.	–	Kilmurry, m.	R.C.	–	R.C.	R.C.	205	–	205	92
30	[illegible]	Do.	–	Do. f.	R.C.	–	R.C.	R.C.	–	191	191	70
31	1977	Ballyheigue,	–	[illegible], m.	R.C.	–	R.C.	R.C.	135	–	135	60
32	1510	Do.	–	Do. f.	R.C.	–	R.C.	R.C.	–	100	100	41
33	10402	Do.	–	Glenderry, m.	R.C.	–	R.C.	–	116	–	116	64
34	10404	Do.	–	Do. f.	R.C.	–	R.C.	R.C.	–	96	96	55
35	10054	Do.	–	[illegible],	R.C.	–	R.C.	R.C.	86	98	184	81
36	8118	[illegible],	–	[illegible], m.	R.C.	–	R.C.	R.C.	231	–	231	98
37	8117	Do.	–	Do. f.	R.C.	–	R.C.	R.C.	–	256	256	95
38	9761	Ballymacelligott,	–	Clogher, m.	R.C.	–	R.C.	aR.C.	175	–	175	65
39	8705	Do.	–	Do. f.	R.C.	–	R.C.	R.C.	–	175	175	66
40	9798	Do.	–	Ballymacelligott, m.	R.C.	–	R.C.	R.C.	169	–	169	76
41	9766	Do.	–	Do. f.	R.C.	–	R.C.	R.C.	–	139	139	67
42	9966	Do.	–	The O'Brennan, m.	R.C.	–	R.C.	–	68	–	68	40
43	9951	Do.	–	Do. f.	R.C.	–	R.C.	R.C.	–	114	114	47
44	5991	Ballynahaglish,	–	Chapeltown,	R.C.	–	R.C.	R.C.	119	110	229	67
45	0482	Do.	–	Spa, m.	R.C.	–	R.C.	–	70	–	70	34
46	8425	Do.	–	Do. f.	R.C.	–	R.C.	–	–	68	68	16
47	6653	Brosna,	–	Brosna, m.	R.C.	–	R.C.	aR.C.	108	182	[illegible]	117
48	8018	Ballyseedy,	–	Ballyseedy, m.	R.C.	–	R.C.	–	91	–	91	34
49	9053	Do.	–	Do. f.	R.C.	–	R.C.	–	–	93	93	37
50	450	Caher,	67	Cahersiveen, m.	R.C.	–	R.C.	R.C.	214	–	214	99
51	[illegible]	Do.	–	Do. Convent, f.	R.C.	Nuns	R.C.	aR.C.	–	484	484	189
52	4990	Do.	–	Do. Workhouse,	P.L.	Gdns.	R.C.	–	20	24	50	19
53	11042	Do.	–	Do. [illegible],	R.C.	–	R.C.	–	21	17	38	24
54	9716	Do.	–	Aghatubrid, m.	R.C.	–	R.C.	–	108	–	108	47
55	[illegible]	Do.	–	Do. f.	R.C.	–	R.C.	R.C.	–	83	83	43
56	9676	Do.	–	Kimego,	R.C.	–	R.C.	R.C.	95	89	184	55
57	[illegible]	Castle Island,	64	Castle Island, m.	R.C.	–	R.C.	–	128	–	128	55
58	8216	Do.	–	Do. Convent, f.	–	R.C.	Nuns.		130	[illegible]	703	257
59	[illegible]	Do.	–	Do. i.	R.C.	–	R.C.	–	214	–	214	81
60	[illegible]	Do.	–	Currow, m.	R.C.	–	R.C.	–	95	–	95	41
61	[illegible]	Do.	–	Do. f.	R.C.	–	R.C.	–	–	88	88	40
62	[illegible]	Do.	–	[illegible],	R.C.	–	R.C.	R.C.	83	98	181	65
63	6181	Do.	–	Scartaglin,	R.C.	–	R.C.	R.C.	126	90	[illegible]	63
64	[illegible]	Do.	–	Knocknagoshel, m.	R.C.	–	R.C.	R.C.	[illegible]	–	[illegible]	108
65	[illegible]	Do.	–	Do. f.	R.C.	–	R.C.	R.C.	–	267	267	110
66	[illegible]	Currans,	–	Currans, m.	R.C.	–	R.C.	R.C.	198	–	198	85
67	4500	Do.	–	Do. f.	R.C.	–	R.C.	–	–	104	104	51
68	8403	Cloghane,	–	Ballyquin,	R.C.	–	R.C.	–	84	98	182	47
69	7879	Do.	–	Clahane,	R.C.	–	R.C.	R.C.	79	72	151	60
70	6904	Clogherbrien,	–	Ballyroe,	R.C.	–	R.C.	R.C.	74	66	140	67
71	1819	Dunurlin,	–	Ferriter,	R.C.	–	R.C.	aR.C.	167	119	286	122
72	1697	Dunquin,	–	Vicarstown,	R.C.	–	R.C.	–	68	37	105	67
73	[illegible]	Do.	–	Blasket Island,	R.C.	–	R.C.	–	26	14	40	15
74	2171	Dromod,	67	Spunkane, m.	R.C.	–	R.C.	R.C.	162	–	162	63 b

a Including value of Free Residence and Garden.

b Including value of Free garden.

MUNSTER: County of KERRY—*continued.*

Aid granted by the Board during the Year 1873.			Amount of Local Endowments received in Aid of Teacher's Salary.				
In Free Stock of Books, Requisites, and Apparatus.	In Salaries, Premiums, and other Emoluments.	Results Fees, Pupil-Teachers, &c.	School Fees.	Subscriptions, Endowments, &c.	Total Local Aid.	Vested or Non-Vested.	Number.
£ s. d.	£ s. d.	£ s. d.	£ s. d.	£ s. d.	£ s. d.		
—	71 0 0	22 11 6	6 0 0	—	6 0 0	V.T.	12
—	44 0 0	18 16 6	6 4 2	—	6 4 2		13
—	43 10 0	10 8 8	4 14 8	—	4 14 0	V.T.	14
—	31 18 6	16 15 8	3 18 6	—	5 13 6	V.T.	15
—	30 0 0	21 15 0	9 0 4	1 3 0	10 3 1	V.T.	16
—	41 8 4	11 18 6	4 10 6	1 3 0	5 13 0	V.T.	17
—	60 8 4	21 1 0	9 0 6	—	6 0 0	V.T.	18
—	61 0 0	45 14 6	20 17 4	—	20 17 4	V.C.	19
—	38 0 0	21 0 0	0 14 11	—	6 14 11	V.C.	20
—	30 0 0	14 8 0	6 4 4	—	6 4 4	V.C.	21
—	33 9 8	14 16 8	9 13 6	—	9 18 6	V.T.	22
—	44 0 0	18 4 0	5 6 0	—	5 6 0	V.T.	23
—	44 0 0	13 8 0	10 5 1	0 0 0	*13 5 1	V.T.	24
—	44 0 0	7 14 0	4 5 0	0 10 0	*4 15 0	V.C.	25
—	38 10 0	15 7 0	6 11 6	—	6 11 6		26
—	32 8 4	6 7 8	6 0 0	—	6 0 0	V.T.	27
—	30 0 0	14 3 6	6 6 6	—	6 6 6	V.T.	28
—	60 0 0	21 5 6	11 11 6	3 0 0	14 11 6	V.T.	29
—	40 0 0	29 4 0	6 18 0	—	6 18 0	V.T.	30
—	72 0 0	25 18 0	12 8 0	—	12 8 8	V.C.	31
—	40 0 0	29 9 6	6 0 0	—	6 0 0	V.T.	32
4 10 0	7 13 4	—	3 11 0	—	3 11 0	V.T.	33
4 10 0	10 0 0	—	2 8 0	—	2 3 0	V.T.	34
—	29 0 0	19 14 0	6 8 6	—	6 5 6	V.T.	35
—	43 10 0	29 15 0	7 10 0	5 0 0	12 10 0	V.T.	36
—	45 0 0	30 6 10	7 8 0	5 0 0	12 8 0	V.T.	37
—	45 0 0	14 16 6	2 10 0	—	2 10 0		38
—	78 16 0	31 17 8	8 0 0	1 0 0	*4 0 0		39
—	63 13 0	24 9 0	7 6 4	—	7 6 4	V.T.	40
—	41 0 0	20 8 5	3 0 0	—	3 0 0	V.T.	41
—	44 0 0	15 10 0	4 8 0	—	4 8 6	V.T.	42
—	37 18 4	20 13 6	6 0 0	—	6 0 0	V.T.	43
—	61 16 5	53 0 6	14 6 0	—	14 0 0		44
—	44 0 0	8 8 6	7 4 4	—	7 4 4	V.T.	45
—	30 0 0	6 12 9	6 11 4	—	6 11 4	V.T.	46
—	107 8 4	67 10 0	29 8 0	—	29 8 0		47
—	23 18 4	5 7 6	1 10 0	—	1 10 0		48
—	27 18 4	10 6 0	1 0 0	—	1 0 0		49
—	81 0 0	48 0 6	0 8 7	—	0 8 7	V.T.	50
—	148 0 0	54 8 6	—	—	—		51
—	1 10 0	Nil.	—	—	—		52
4 0 0	29 0 0	7 14 8	8 5 8	47 0 0	*63 5 8		53
—	52 10 0	11 2 6	9 0 0	—	0 0 0	V.C.	54
—	46 0 0	18 11 0	6 0 0	—	6 0 0	V.C.	55
—	48 10 6	38 18 0	10 15 0	—	10 14 0	V.C.	56
—	64 0 0	45 18 6	14 18 7	—	14 18 7	V.T.	57
—	150 11 2	18 1 6	112 0 0	—	112 0 0		58
—	41 0 0	19 8 6	6 18 0	—	6 18 0	V.T.	59
—	21 0 0	10 11 6	9 12 10	—	9 12 10	V.T.	60
—	30 0 0	16 18 6	6 8 0	—	6 8 0	V.T.	61
—	45 0 0	10 14 6	7 10 0	—	7 10 0		62
—	50 15 4	20 16 6	11 19 6	1 0 0	*12 19 6	V.C.	63
—	61 10 0	7 8 10	15 10 0	1 0 0	*16 10 0	V.T.	64
—	80 0 0	53 4 0	8 10 8	2 0 0	10 10 8	V.T.	65
—	49 0 0	27 9 0	19 3 6	—	19 3 6	V.C.	66
—	20 0 0	19 0 6	6 0 0	—	6 0 0	V.C.	67
—	84 0 0	34 0 0	10 0 0	—	10 0 0		68
—	34 0 0	17 14 5	8 13 8	—	8 13 8		69
—	37 0 0	14 14 8	6 8 6	—	5 8 5		70
—	31 0 0	60 1 6	7 10 6	3 0 0	10 10 6	N.	71
—	27 10 0	18 15 0	4 0 6	4 0 0	8 0 0	V.T.	72
—	31 0 0	1 0 6	—	—	—		73
—	49 8 0	18 11 6	1 10 0	3 10 0	4 0 0	N.	74

* Including value of Free Residence.

List of Schools in operation on the 31st December, 1874—

Number.	Roll Number of School.	Parish.	District.	School.		Religious Denomination of Manager or Correspondent: Clerical.	Lay.	Number and Religious Denomination of Teachers: Principals.	Assistants.	Attendance for the Year. Total number of Pupils on Rolls within the Year ended: Males.	Fem.	Total.	Average daily Attendance.
75	2106	Dromod,	67	Spunkane,	f.	R.C.	–	R.C.	R.C.	–	167	157	97
76	4484	Do.	–	Ballinakilla,		R.C.	–	R.C.	R.C.	80	73	153	66
77	4563	Do.	–	Mastergeehy,		R.C.	–	R.C.	R.C.	131	108	240	109
78	9648	Do.	–	Caherulvane,		R.C.	–	R.C.	R.C.	97	86	183	88
79	10603	Do.	–	Kilmakerrin,		R.C.	–	R.C.	R.C.	80	105	184	101
80	7255	Dysert,	64	Kilcarran,		R.C.	–	R.C.	R.C.	121	88	210	73
81	2348	Duagh,	–	Duagh,	m.	R.C.	–	R.C.	R.C.	158	–	158	98
82	4614	Do.	–	Do.	f.	R.C.	–	R.C.	R.C.	–	143	143	69
83	10567	Do.	–	Islandanny,	m.	R.C.	–	R.C.	R.C.	116	–	116	61
84	10569	Do.	–	Do.	f.	R.C.	–	R.C.	–	–	97	97	44
85	8394	Do.	–	Trienearagh,		R.C.	–	R.C.	2 R.C.	170	113	283	127
86	10879	Do.	–	Lyre a crompane,		R.C.	–	R.C.	R.C.	84	46	130	65
87	6496	Do.	–	Knockalongan,		R.C.	–	R.C.	–	64	42	106	43
88	9914	Do.	–	Drumakeenagh,		R.C.	–	R.C.	–	76	31	107	52
89	535	Dingle,	–	Dingle Convent,	f.	R.C.	–	Nuns.		–	434	431	253
90	5911	Do.	–	Do. Workhouse,		P.L.	Gds.	R.C.	–	29	26	55	35
91	2495	Do.	–	Ballyrannaun,[b]		R.C.	–	–	–	–	–	–	–
92	6479	Fieries,	–	Fieries,		R.C.	–	R.C.	R.C.	80	87	167	66
93	4261	Galey,	–	Coolard,		R.C.	–	R.C.	2 R.C.	230	138	368	141
94	4762	Glenbeigh,	67	Glenbeigh,	m.	R.C.	–	R.C.	R.C.	109	–	109	68
95	4763	Do.	–	Do.	f.	R.C.	–	R.C.	R.C.	–	144	141	73
96	5770	Do.	–	Keelnabrack,	m.	R.C.	–	R.C.	R.C.	130	–	130	68
97	5786	Do.	–	Do.	f.	R.C.	–	R.C.	R.C.	–	166	166	72
98	10401	Do.	–	Rangleah,		R.C.	–	R.C.	–	41	47	88	49
99	10864	Glanarought,	–	Drimagh,		R.C.	–	R.C.	R.C.	71	83	153	73
100	6108	Killallagh,	56	Castlemaine,	m.	R.C.	–	R.C.	–	101	–	101	55
101	6170	Do.	–	Do.	f.	R.C.	–	R.C.	–	–	130	135	64
102	5347	Kilcrohane,	67	Derrynane,	m.	R.C.	–	R.C.	–	101	–	101	45
103	6315	Do.	–	Do.	f.	R.C.	–	R.C.	–	–	109	109	49
104	10588	Do.	–	Letterfinish,	m.	R.C.	–	R.C.	–	63	–	63	32
105	10599	Do.	–	Do.	f.	R.C.	–	R.C.	–	–	60	60	37
106	10336	Do.	–	Caherdaniel,	m.	R.C.	–	R.C.	–	130	–	130	52
107	10440	Do.	–	Do.	f.	R.C.	–	R.C.	–	–	104	104	48
108	9291	Do.	–	Sneem Ordinary Agr.	m.	R.C.	–	R.C.	2 R.C.	201	–	201	86
109	9284	Do.	–	Do.	f.	R.C.	–	R.C.	R.C.	–	181	181	77
110	8457	Do.	–	Glenlough,	temp.	R.C.	–	R.C.	R.C.	84	71	155	60
111	10846	Do.	–	Lohar,	m.	R.C.	–	R.C.	–	148	–	148	54
112	11046	Do.	–	Do.	f.	R.C.	–	R.C.	–	–	80	80	68
113	8411	Do.	–	Baunreagh,	m.	R.C.	–	R.C.	R.C.	107	–	107	44
114	10842	Do.	–	Do.	f.	R.C.	–	R.C.	R.C.	–	107	107	67
115	10087	Do.	–	Blackwater,		R.C.	–	R.C.	R.C.	80	75	161	46
116	5392	Kilflynn,	54	Kilflynn,		R.C.	–	R.C.	2 R.C.	154	141	295	116
117	5869	Killeentierna,	57	Farranfore,		R.C.	–	R.C.	–	71	68	139	63
118	8187	Do.	–	The Glen,		R.C.	–	R.C.	R.C.	64	52	116	61
119	6316	Kilconly,	56	Lisnaw,	m.	R.C.	–	R.C.	R.C.	201	–	201	84
120	6071	Do.	–	Do.	f.	R.C.	–	R.C.	R.C.	–	194	194	74
121	6118	Kilquane,	–	Kilquane,		R.C.	–	R.C.	R.C.	87	87	174	80
122	9891	Do.	–	St. Brendan's,		R.C.	–	R.C.	R.C.	43	68	111	58
123	6357	Kilmalkedar,	–	Smerwick,	m.	R.C.	–	R.C.	–	160	–	160	59
124	6358	Do.	–	Do.	f.	R.C.	–	R.C.	R.C.	–	118	118	58
125	9726	Kilgobbin,	56	Camp,		R.C.	–	R.C.	R.C.	84	97	181	88
126	2167	Killehenny,	–	Gortnaskehy,	m.	R.C.	–	R.C.	R.C.	171	–	171	73
127	2181	Do.	–	Do.	f.	R.C.	–	R.C.	R.C.	–	162	162	63
128	9766	Do.	–	Rahea,	temp.	R.C.	–	R.C.	R.C.	108	63	171	70
129	8191	Killiney,	–	Castlegregory,	m.	R.C.	–	R.C.	2 R.C.	271	–	271	118
130	8182	Do.	–	Do.	f.	R.C.	–	R.C.	R.C.	–	240	240	109
131	2462	Kilnaughtin,	67	Fahs,		R.C.	–	R.C.	2 R.C.	280	201	480	171
132	8481	Do.	–	Kilbonane,	m.	R.C.	–	R.C.	–	111	–	111	57
133	6468	Do.	–	Do.	f.	R.C.	–	R.C.	R.C.	–	106	106	67
134	8610	Kilmoyley,	64	Kilmoyley,	m.	R.C.	–	R.C.	R.C.	151	–	151	61
135	8511	Do.	–	Do.	f.	R.C.	–	R.C.	R.C.	–	146	146	63
136	9684	Do.	–	Banna,	m.	R.C.	–	R.C.	R.C.	157	–	157	71
137	6626	Do.	–	Do.	f.	R.C.	–	R.C.	R.C.	–	150	150	66

[a] Including value of Free Residence.

[b] Inoperative.

Province of MUNSTER: County of KERRY—*continued.*

Amount paid for Books, Requisites, and Apparatus at Reduced Prices.			Aid granted by the Board during the Year 1874. In Free Stock of Books, Requisites, and Apparatus.			In Salaries, Premiums, and other Gratuities.			Results Fees, Financial Year.			Amount of Local Contributions in Aid of Teacher's Salary. School Fees.			Subscriptions, Endowments, &c.		
£	s.	d.	£	s.	d.	£	s.	d.	£	s.	d.	£	s.	d.	£	s.	d.
4	8	7		—		69	18	8	44	11	6	4	10	0	9	10	0
1	9	9		—		62	10	0	45	18	0	5	10	0		—	
7	17	11		—		68	10	0	40	5	0	13	18	8		—	
5	8	1		—		64	5	4	80	4	0	9	4	0	6	0	0
1	10	9	5	10	0	12	10	0	34	11	6	5	17	0		—	
2	17	0		—		44	0	0	30	19	0	10	18	0		—	
5	9	8		—		60	18	4	84	6	6	20	19	10		—	
1	6	5		—		57	18	4	22	4	8	8	7	0		—	
0	11	4		—		41	16	8	23	8	0	16	17	0		—	
5	6	1	5	0	0	25	0	0	18	6	6	6	10	0		—	
8	9	1		—		100	8	0	47	10	6	34	4	11		—	
8	2	1		—		24	0	0	13	12	6	18	8	0		—	
1	17	6		—		31	10	0	18	8	0	5	11	0		—	
1	8	1		—		89	3	4	8	10	0	10	8	0		—	
22	19	0	11	12	3	140	14	0	87	14	8		—			—	
2	10	8		—		1	10	0		—			—			—	
	—			—			—			—			—			—	
5	11	6		—		60	0	0	81	1	0	16	4	6		—	
9	8	0		—		69	0	0	56	0	0	15	7	6		—	
	—			—		61	0	0	32	0	0	11	5	8	1	18	0
6	4	6		—		44	0	0	26	7	0	7	4	10		—	
3	0	5		—		33	0	0	14	16	0	7	2	10		—	
1	10	10		—		40	0	0	19	7	0	2	5	0		—	
1	0	0		—		24	0	0	13	12	5	0	18	6		—	
2	12	1		—		63	0	0	24	18	0		—			—	
1	12	6		—		42	16	4	15	8	0	6	7	0	0	10	0
1	10	5		—		35	10	0	29	8	6	1	7	0		—	
	—			—		21	0	0	18	5	0	8	10	0		—	
4	9	10		—		25	16	4	19	8	6	7	0	0		—	
1	10	0		—		60	16	0	11	7	6	7	11	2		—	
7	10	10		—		84	0	0	22	10	0	7	10	0		—	
1	9	1		—		30	10	0	12	19	6	3	8	6	9	0	0
1	8	2		—		41	0	8	36	0	0	4	0	0	8	0	0
8	15	10		—		117	0	0	40	4	6	12	8	5		—	
8	0	9		—		67	8	4	58	18	6	8	10	8		—	
3	12	1		—		72	6	4	28	18	6	7	4	8		—	
1	6	4		—		21	0	0	7	10	6	4	8	6		—	
3	0	6		—		23	6	0	0	8	6	4	0	6		—	
4	15	1		—		65	8	8	25	10	6	8	18	6		—	
4	18	11		—		62	18	4	24	7	0	12	0	0		—	
1	10	11		—		66	10	0	43	9	0	8	0	0	5	0	0
4	10	0		—		61	0	0	26	2	6	15	7	6		—	
5	9	1		—		30	0	0	15	6	0	7	16	2		—	
8	1	8		—		63	0	0	38	14	6	6	8	0		—	
3	10	1		—		18	0	0	21	8	6	12	19	0		—	
2	16	8		—		34	0	0	29	17	6	10	2	6		—	
2	18	9		—		44	0	0	25	0	0	11	0	0	1	0	0
1	18	0		—		51	0	0	25	8	0	18	4	0		—	
1	5	4		—		69	15	0	32	8	6	9	0	0	1	10	8
1	8	6		—		51	0	0	17	10	0	2	0	0	1	6	6
1	19	11		—		44	0	0	11	16	0	8	4	0		—	
6	0	10		—		65	0	0	17	7	0	10	17	4	5	0	0
1	8	8		—		26	18	4	17	6	0	10	17	2		—	
6	15	1		—		60	0	0	41	18	0	28	0	0		—	
12	3	6		—		60	16	8	32	11	6	22	15	0	7	0	0
4	18	2		—		56	10	0	33	5	6	17	8	6	2	0	0
10	8	9		—		102	18	4	40	8	8	16	0	0	4	0	0
3	18	6		—		40	0	8	31	16	0	4	0	8	8	0	0
	—			—		44	0	0	18	9	0	6	15	8	6	0	0
8	1	8		—		65	15	0	31	1	0	8	6	0	0	12	0
5	11	1		—		52	0	0	29	18	6	4	6	0	0	10	0
8	18	11		—		48	0	0	24	11	8	6	19	8		—	
4	18	0		—		40	0	0	26	17	0	11	8	5		—	

* Including value of Free Garden.

List of Schools in operation on the 31st December, 1874.—

No.	Roll Number of School.	Parish.	District.	School.	Religious Denomination of Patrons or Correspondents: Clerical.	Lay.	Number and Religious Denomination of Teachers: Principals.	Assistants.	Attendance for the Year: Total number of Pupils on Rolls within the Year 1874: Males.	Fem.	Total.	Average daily attendance.
138	9748	Kenmare,	57	Kenmare, m.	Others.		R.C.	R.R.C.	108	–	128	114
139	6911	Do.	–	Do. Parochial,	R.C.	–	R.C.	–	8	19	35	16
140	10230	Do.	–	Do. Convent, f.	R.C.	–	R.C.	9R.C.	78	479	557	325
141	4578	Do.	–	Do. Workhouse,	P.L.	Gds.	R.C.	–	41	22	63	39
142	4119	Do.	–	Cahir,	R.C.	–	R.C.	2R.C.	130	107	237	137
143	5622	Do.	–	Sheilmore, No. 1,	R.C.	–	R.C.	–	52	62	114	63
144	5422	Do.	–	Gortalea,	R.C.	–	R.C.	–	57	45	102	41
145	5874	Do.	–	Lauragh,	R.C.	–	R.C.	–	57	26	83	30
146	4707	Kilcrohane,	58	Cloonaghlogh, m.	R.C.	–	R.C.	–	120	–	120	57
147	4708	Do.	–	Do. f.	R.C.	–	R.C.	–	–	124	124	59
148	515	Killury,	–	Killury, m.	R.C.	–	R.C.	R.C.	287	–	287	80
149	525	Do.	–	Do. f.	R.C.	–	R.C.	R.C.	–	148	148	56
150	8162	Do.	–	Drumnacurra, m.	R.C.	–	R.C.	–	65	–	65	44
151	8163	Do.	–	Do. f.	R.C.	–	R.C.	–	–	65	65	30
152	3498	Do.	–	Ballynace,	R.C.	–	–	–	–	–	–	–
153	10648	Do.	–	Ballincarrell, m.	R.C.	–	R.C.	–	73	–	73	33
154	10649	Do.	–	Do. f.	R.C.	–	R.C.	–	–	84	84	48
155	544	Kilcummin,	57	Inch, m.	R.C.	–	R.C.	–	183	–	183	42
156	9687	Do.	–	Do. f.	R.C.	–	R.C.	–	–	111	111	51
157	1748	Do.	–	Gneeveguilla, m.	R.C.	–	R.C.	R.C.	204	–	204	60
158	8898	Do.	–	Do. f.	R.C.	–	R.C.	R.C.	–	152	152	69
159	9652	Do.	–	Meentogues, m.	R.C.	–	R.C.	R.C.	229	–	229	82
160	9801	Do.	–	Do. f.	R.C.	–	R.C.	2R.C.	–	230	230	110
161	10116	Do.	–	Coolick, m.	R.C.	–	R.C.	–	85	–	85	45
162	10046	Do.	–	Do. f.	R.C.	–	R.C.	–	–	81	81	43
163	8704	Do.	–	Rathmore, m.	R.C.	–	R.C.	2R.C.	194	–	194	56
164	8980	Do.	–	Do. f.	R.C.	–	R.C.	2R.C.	–	276	276	118
165	2978	Do.	–	Clonkeen, m.	R.C.	–	R.C.	–	96	–	96	48
166	2083	Do.	–	Do. f.	R.C.	–	R.C.	R.C.	–	191	191	64
167	9780	Do.	–	Shrone, m.	R.C.	–	R.C.	R.C.	189	–	189	84
168	8091	Do.	–	Do. f.	R.C.	–	R.C.	R.C.	–	184	184	83
169	11181	Kilcummin, East,	–	Tureencahill, f.	R.C.	–	R.C.	R.C.	–	185	185	69
170	10802	Do.	–	Do. m.	R.C.	–	R.C.	R.C.	129	–	129	67
171	11088	Kilnanare,	–	Callinagh, m.	–	R.C.	R.C.	R.C.	109	–	109	77
172	9706	Do.	–	Do. f.	–	R.C.	R.C.	2R.C.	–	237	237	66
173	6169	Do.	–	Carraghbeg, m.	R.C.	–	R.C.	–	159	–	159	52
174	6726	Do.	–	Do. f.	R.C.	–	R.C.	–	–	67	67	41
175	7841	Do.	–	Kilgobnet, m.	R.C.	–	R.C.	R.C.	177	–	177	70
176	7842	Do.	–	Do. f.	R.C.	–	R.C.	R.C.	–	161	161	55
177	9672	Do.	–	Gap of Dunloe,	R.C.	–	R.C.	–	53	40	93	32
178	10778	Knockanure,	58	Knockanure, m.	R.C.	–	R.C.	R.C.	120	69	189	86
179	10779	Do.	–	Do. f.	R.C.	–	R.C.	–	–	189	189	91
180	10000	Kilnaughtin,	–	Tarbert, m.	R.C.	–	R.C.	R.C.	–	163	163	62
181	10001	Do.	–	Do. f.	R.C.	–	R.C.	2R.C.	–	176	176	77
182	4831	Do.	–	Tarmon's, m.	R.C.	–	R.C.	–	141	–	141	59
183	4832	Do.	–	Do. f.	R.C.	–	R.C.	–	–	185	185	56
184	9632	Do.	–	Reenturk, m.	R.C.	–	R.C.	–	64	–	64	36
185	9633	Do.	–	Do. f.	R.C.	–	R.C.	–	–	60	64	18
186	1906	[illegible],	36	Tullaha, m.	–	Chris.	R.C.	–	69	–	69	26
187	7657	Do.	–	Do. f.	–	Chris.	R.C.	–	–	56	56	29
188	6746	Do.	–	Gurranebane,	R.C.	–	R.C.	R.C.	75	65	140	63
189	1658	Killorglin,	57	Glounaguillagh, m.	R.C.	–	R.C.	–	136	–	118	42
190	6192	Do.	–	Do. f.	R.C.	–	R.C.	–	–	63	63	27
191	1622	Do.	–	Killorglin, m.	R.C.	–	R.C.	2R.C.	259	–	248	143
192	9749	Do.	–	Do. f.	R.C.	–	R.C.	R.C.	–	570	578	162
193	9862	Do.	–	Cromane,	R.C.	–	R.C.	R.C.	134	78	212	67
194	1607	Killarney,	–	Tiernaboul, m.	R.C.	–	R.C.	–	147	–	147	65
195	1622	Do.	–	Do. f.	R.C.	–	R.C.	R.C.	–	161	161	51
196	8134	Do.	–	Killarney, adult evg.	–	R.C.	R.C.	–	60	–	60	12
197	1792	Do.	–	Do. Monastic, m.	R.C.	–	Monks		638	–	638	230
198	524	Do.	–	Do. Convent, f.	–	R.C.	Nuns		–	701	701	312
199	6890	Do.	–	Do. do. No. 2,	–	R.C.	Nuns		70	284	354	148
200	4348	Do.	–	Do. Workhs.	P.L.	Gds.	2R.C.	R.C.	63	29	103	85

* Including value of Free Residence.

Province of Munster: County of Kerry—*continued.*

Amount paid for Books, Requisites, and Apparatus, at Reduced Prices.			Aid granted by the Board during the Year 1874. In Free Stock of Books, Requisites, and Apparatus.			In Salaries, Premiums, and other Gratuities.			Results Fees, Financial Year.			Amount of Local Emoluments received in Aid of Teacher's Salary. School Fees.			Subscriptions, Endowments, &c.			Total Local Aid.			Vested or Non-Vested.	Number.
£	s.	d.	£	s.	d.	£	s.	d.	£	s.	d.	£	s.	d.	£	s.	d.	£	s.	d.		
5	2	8	—			107	12	10	56	3	0	31	16	2	—			81	18	2	A.	138
4	8	10	—			11	3	8	5	15	0	9	18	0	29	14	8	a 39	14	3		139
—			—			219	12	8	109	0	0	—			10	0	0	10	0	0		140
3	4	4	—			Nil.			Nil.			—			—			—				141
3	17	8	—			160	0	0	60	8	0	10	15	6	—			10	15	0	V.C.	142
—			—			35	10	0	20	18	0	6	10	6	—			6	10	6	V.C.	143
8	8	5	—			69	8	8	23	0	0	3	18	9	2	11	0	b 6	0	9	V.C.	144
—			—			24	0	0	6	11	6	2	0	0	—			2	0	0	V.C.	145
1	10	1	—			24	0	0	32	7	0	8	0	0	—			8	0	0	V.C.	146
5	15	3	—			25	0	0	25	14	0	6	13	10	—			6	13	10	V.C.	147
8	0	11	—			60	8	4	45	8	0	10	8	0	5	0	0	15	8	0		148
3	3	8	—			31	0	0	21	16	0	1	10	9	5	0	0	6	10	9		149
2	10	6	—			28	10	0	14	8	6	4	14	0	—			4	14	0	V.V.	150
1	12	5	—			28	10	0	15	6	6	4	19	0	—			6	19	0	V.V.	151
—			—			23	18	4	—			—			—			—				152
1	8	1	4	10	0	9	0	0	10	18	0	0	10	6	—			0	10	6	V.V.	153
1	9	6	4	10	0	8	9	8	18	0	0	0	11	6	—			0	11	6	V.V.	154
1	2	0	—			24	0	0	8	14	6	6	5	8	2	6	1	8	11	0	V.V.	155
—			—			20	0	0	18	8	0	3	14	6	2	6	1	6	0	7		156
3	8	7	—			30	10	0	25	10	6	2	4	0	—			a 2	4	0	V.V.	157
2	16	2	—			53	0	0	24	8	0	0	4	0	8	0	0	8	4	0	V.V.	158
10	10	3	—			61	18	4	81	0	0	2	10	0	—			2	10	0	V.V.	159
8	5	7	—			81	10	0	48	0	6	10	0	7	8	0	0	a 18	8	7	V.V.	160
—			—			30	0	0	10	18	6	10	10	6	—			10	10	6	V.C.	161
—			—			28	15	4	16	7	6	5	10	0	—			5	10	0	V.C.	162
7	0	8	—			112	10	0	32	8	0	4	19	8	—			4	19	8	V.V.	163
3	0	8	—			108	5	4	60	10	0	16	0	0	—			16	0	0	V.V.	164
5	7	3	—			44	8	4	12	0	6	8	17	6	5	8	1	a 14	8	7	V.V.	165
3	18	10	—			65	8	4	29	6	6	6	18	6	2	0	8	8	6	8	V.V.	166
—			—			67	0	0	18	14	0	1	6	8	—			1	6	8		167
—			—			40	0	0	39	16	0	5	8	6	—			5	8	0		168
8	7	7	0	0	0	14	13	4	—			—			—			—			V.V.	169
2	17	11	5	10	0	18	0	0	—			—			—			—			V.V.	170
4	9	10	—			66	0	0	16	14	0	4	16	0	2	0	0	a 6	12	0	V.V.	171
6	14	8	—			107	1	8	28	19	6	8	18	6	—			3	18	0	V.V.	172
—			—			20	0	0	9	8	0	8	4	0	6	0	0	a 18	4	0	V.C.	173
1	18	4	—			21	10	0	7	2	0	6	14	0	6	0	0	6	14	0	V.C.	174
1	6	8	—			54	0	0	18	7	0	7	3	6	—			7	3	6	V.V.	175
8	15	0	—			40	0	0	6	15	0	6	11	9	—			6	11	9	V.V.	176
3	16	1	—			88	0	0	6	15	0	3	18	8	—			3	18	8	V.C.	177
1	8	9	4	10	0	—			21	1	0	10	1	0	—			10	1	0	V.V.	178
3	15	4	4	10	0	—			19	8	6	9	15	2	—			9	15	2	V.V.	179
9	8	6	—			90	18	4	23	12	0	19	8	7	—			19	9	7		180
—			—			73	15	0	30	13	0	15	4	6	—			15	4	6		181
—			—			81	10	0	15	6	8	10	15	8	—			10	15	0	V.V.	182
—			—			33	6	7	10	14	0	8	8	1	—			9	8	1	V.V.	183
1	6	4	—			31	0	0	} 18	8	6	{ 10	11	1	—			10	11	1	V.V.	184
—			—			11	18	4				8	8	0	—			8	8	0	V.V.	185
1	16	0	—			24	0	0	8	8	6	8	16	6	10	0	0	18	16	6	A.	186
1	6	0	—			24	0	0	16	16	0	6	16	0	8	0	0	15	16	0	A.	187
5	9	8	—			54	16	8	26	15	8	8	10	6	—			8	18	6	V.C.	188
—			—			85	0	0	18	17	0	7	7	7	—			7	7	7	A.	189
8	9	6	—			80	0	0	9	16	0	3	18	4	—			3	18	4	A.	190
6	12	6	—			100	8	8	29	6	8	16	18	8	—			16	18	8	V.C.	191
4	0	7	—			108	0	8	32	14	6	15	15	0	—			15	15	0	V.V.	192
—			—			68	10	0	26	8	6	6	11	9	—			6	14	9		193
1	11	4	—			48	10	0	22	3	6	6	0	0	—			6	0	0	V.V.	194
8	18	8	—			41	10	0	30	17	0	4	7	6	—			4	7	0	V.V.	195
1	8	0	—			7	4	6	6	4	6	—			—			—				196
14	14	1	—			110	10	8	49	10	0	—			—			—				197
11	1	11	—			140	6	4	61	4	6	—			—			—			B.	198
10	18	8	—			81	18	8	20	6	6	—			—			—				199
6	18	8	—			15	0	0	Nil.			—			—			—				200

b Including value of Free Garden.

List of Schools in operation on the 31st December, 1874.—

Number.	Roll Number of School.	Parish.	District.	School.		Religious Denomination of Manager or Correspondent: Clerical.	Lay.	Teachers and Religious Denomination of Teachers: Principals.	Assistants.	Attendance for the Year. Total number of Pupils on Rolls within the Year: Males.	Females.	Total.	Average Daily Attendance.
201	1670	Killarney,	57	Gortnagullane, a		R.C.	–	–	–	–	–	–	–
202	6791	Do.	–	Lissivigeen,	m.	R.C.	–	R.C.	R.C.	210	–	210	69
203	6792	Do.	–	Do.	f.	R.C.	–	R.C.	–	–	117	117	62
204	9237	Do.	–	Scarna,		R.C.	–	R.C.	–	21	20	41	30
205	10019	Do.	–	Loughguittane,	m.	R.C.	–	R.C.	R.C.	141	40	181	93
206	10850	Do.	–	St. Gertrude's,		R.C.	–	R.C.	R.C.	84	85	169	93
207	9086	Kilcolman,	–	Milltown Monastic,	m.	R.C.	–	Monks.		202	–	202	145
208	1619	Do.	–	Do. Convent,	f.	–	R.C.	Nuns.		–	488	488	216
209	1034	Kinnard,	54	Ardamore,		R.C.	–	R.C.	R.C.	142	158	300	107
210	2123	Killinane,	57	Aghamore,	m.	R.C.	–	R.C.	–	110	–	110	61
211	9198	Do.	–	Do.	f.	R.C.	–	R.C.	R.C.	–	128	128	66
212	9149	Do.	–	Kells,		–	R.C.	R.C.	R.C.	59	58	117	71
213	9257	Do.	–	Coars,		R.C.	–	R.C.	R.C.	67	62	129	64
214	2084	Do.	–	Killurly,		R.C.	–	R.C.	R.C.	78	65	143	69
215	2417	Kilnanare,	–	Firies,	m.	R.C.	–	R.C.	2R.C.	215	–	215	108
216	6290	Do.	–	Do.	f.	R.C.	–	R.C.	2R.C.	–	206	206	104
217	10084	Kilfeighny,	54	Kilfeighny,		R.C.	–	R.C.	–	116	107	223	109
218	7418	Kilgarvan,	57	Morleysbridge,		R.C.	–	R.C.	R.C.	80	82	162	68
219	7336	Do.	–	Kilgarvan,	m.	R.C.	–	R.C.	2R.C.	217	–	217	100
220	7337	Do.	–	Do.	f.	R.C.	–	R.C.	2R.C.	–	211	211	94
221	10281	Kilmeany,	54	Beale,		R.C.	–	R.C.	R.C.	48	69	116	60
222	7640	Do.	–	Do.	m.	R.C.	–	R.C.	–	50	81	131	44
223	10190	Do.	–	Kahervanig,	m.	R.C.	–	R.C.	–	98	–	98	40
224	11421	Do.	–	Do.	f.	R.C.	–	R.C.	–	–	115	115	45
225	7735	Killahan,	54	Killahan,	m.	R.C.	–	R.C.	–	92	–	92	60
226	7830	Do.	–	Do.	f.	R.C.	–	R.C.	–	–	100	100	48
227	8703	Do.	57	Clounabreen,		R.C.	–	R.C.	R.C.	124	100	224	103
228	9372	Do.	–	Glanfesk,		R.C.	–	R.C.	R.C.	85	68	143	67
229	9896	Kilgarrylander,	54	Castledrum,	m.	R.C.	–	R.C.	–	177	–	177	83
230	9280	Do.	–	Do.	f.	R.C.	–	R.C.	R.C.	–	170	170	78
231	10115	Do.	–	Vilrough,	m.	R.C.	–	R.C.	–	123	–	123	48
232	10112	Do.	–	Do.	f.	R.C.	–	R.C.	–	–	159	159	61
233	5497	Kilmacalogue,	56	Lohart,		R.C.	–	R.C.	R.C.	60	12	172	61
234	6701	Do.	–	Lansdowne Ord. Ag.		R.C.	–	R.C.	R.C.	83	78	161	84
235	1787	Listowel,	54	Listowel,	m.	R.C.	–	R.C.	R.C.	230	–	236	91
236	4707	Do.	–	Do. Convent	f.	–	R.C.	Nuns.		–	841	841	352
237	4416	Do.	–	Do. Workhouse,		P.L.	Gds.	R.C.	–	23	22	45	30
238	10299	Do.	–	Do. No. 2,	m.	R.C.	–	R.C.	2R.C.	318	–	318	112
239	10101	Lisselton,	–	Mirard Castle,		R.C.	–	R.C.	R.C.	101	105	206	82
240	4004	Lissauham,	–	Ballyorney,		R.C.	–	R.C.	2R.C.	118	101	219	111
241	10381	Do.	–	Lixnaw,	m.	R.C.	–	R.C.	–	102	–	102	48
242	10382	Do.	–	Do.	f.	R.C.	–	R.C.	–	–	100	100	45
243	6416	Molahiffe,	57	Knockaderry,	m.	R.C.	–	R.C.	R.C.	209	–	209	68
244	6410	Do.	–	Do.	f.	R.C.	–	R.C.	2R.C.	–	170	170	70
245	7080	Do.	–	Ballyfinnane,	m.	R.C.	–	R.C.	R.C.	144	–	144	64
246	7081	Do.	–	Do.	f.	R.C.	–	R.C.	R.C.	–	194	194	64
247	7816	Marhin,	56	Marhin,	m.	R.C.	–	R.C.	3R.C.	278	–	278	141
248	7816	Do.	–	Do.	f.	R.C.	–	R.C.	2R.C.	–	318	318	150
249	10187	Nohoval,	56	Nohoval,	m.	R.C.	–	R.C.	–	96	–	96	58
250	10726	Do.	–	Do.	f.	R.C.	–	R.C.	–	–	107	107	40
251	10200	O'Brennan,	–	Meens,		R.C.	–	R.C.	–	34	23	57	30
252	4161	O'Dorney,	–	O'Dorney,	m.	R.C.	–	R.C.	R.C.	107	–	167	91
253	4462	Do.	–	Do.	f.	R.C.	–	R.C.	R.C.	–	194	194	77
254	2781	Prior,	57	Innalaghmore,	m.	R.C.	–	R.C.	–	90	–	90	47
255	4809	Do.	–	Do.	f.	R.C.	–	R.C.	–	–	118	118	44
256	4816	Do.	–	Ballinskelligs,	m.	–	R.C.	R.C.	R.C.	180	–	180	68
257	8850	Do.	–	Do.	f.	–	R.C.	R.C.	R.C.	–	145	145	83
258	1696	Rattoo,	54	Ballyduff,	m.	R.C.	–	R.C.	R.C.	170	–	170	78
259	8123	Do.	–	Do.	f.	R.C.	–	R.C.	2R.C.	–	191	191	84
260	1182	Do.	–	Glenvanadder,	m.	R.C.	–	R.C.	R.C.	187	–	187	78
261	8128	Do.	–	Do.	f.	R.C.	–	R.C.	R.C.	–	147	147	61
262	9641	Do.	–	Ballincrossig,	m.	R.C.	–	R.C.	R.C.	187	–	187	48
263	8512	Do.	–	Do.	f.	R.C.	–	R.C.	R.C.	–	183	183	59

a Closed; no Report up.

b Including value of Free Residence.

Province of Munster: County of Kerry—*continued.*

Amount paid for Books, Requisites, and Apparatus at Reduced Prices.			Aid granted by the Board during the Year 1874: By Free Stock of Books, Requisites, and Apparatus.			In Salaries, Premiums, and other Gratuities.			Results Fees, Financial Year.			Amount of Local Emoluments received in Aid of Teacher's Salary: School Fees.			Subscriptions, Endowments, &c.			Total Local Aid.			Vested or Non-Vested.	Number.
£	s.	d.	£	s.	d.	£	s.	d.	£	s.	d.	£	s.	d.	£	s.	d.	£	s.	d.		
	—			—			—			—			—			—			—		V.E.	201
2	8	10		—		80	8	4	10	1	0	10	11	8		—		10	11	8		202
5	8	6		—		84	0	0	8	5	0	5	5	0		—		5	5	0		203
1	10	3		—		31	0	0	8	11	6		—		28	15	0	*28	15	0		204
	—			—		48	10	0	28	8	0	8	4	0	2	6	0	10	10	0	V.E.	205
3	18	6		—		46	0	0	13	12	0	4	18	0	2	6	3	7	4	3	V.E.	206
0	14	4		—		73	7	8	51	4	6		—			—			—			207
15	5	0		—		60	8	0	54	13	6		—			—			—		N.	208
2	1	9		—		44	0	0	28	18	0	5	0	0	5	0	0	10	0	0	V.E.	209
1	11	7		—		65	10	0	30	18	6	4	18	0	1	15	0	*10	13	0	V.E.	210
0	17	1		—		36	0	0	23	4	6	8	10	0	1	0	0	9	10	0	N.V.	211
3	13	6		—		41	0	0	29	3	6	8	0	0		—		8	0	0	V.E.	212
3	14	9		—		56	0	0	24	14	0	9	13	4		—		9	13	4	V.E.	213
4	2	6		—		56	8	4	28	18	0	9	5	6		—		9	5	6		214
6	6	4		—		91	10	0	31	12	0	18	1	8		—		18	1	8	V.V.	215
6	2	8		—		65	0	0	44	8	6	20	0	5		—		20	0	5	V.V.	216
6	3	9		—		47	0	0	65	13	0	24	17	0		—		24	17	0		217
3	6	7		—		94	10	0	45	6	0	4	10	8		—		4	10	8	V.E.	218
6	18	8		—		64	6	0	60	8	6	9	13	0	1	5	0	10	18	0	V.E.	219
2	15	6		—		111	0	0	55	17	6	10	0	0		—		10	0	0	V.E.	220
3	19	11		—		30	18	4	13	5	0	8	10	0		—		8	10	0	V.E.	221
1	5	0		—		17	0	0	15	5	6	7	14	6		—		7	14	6		222
	—			—		29	0	0	17	15	0	12	5	6		—		12	5	6	V.V.	223
	—			—		30	0	0	11	1	6	10	10	0		—		10	10	0	V.E.	224
1	19	4		—		34	0	0	0	4	6	6	5	0		—		6	5	0		225
1	0	4		—		30	0	0	18	5	6	6	9	0		—		6	9	0		226
0	19	11		—		44	0	0	28	7	0	4	11	8		—		4	11	8	V.E.	227
2	1	8		—		35	6	8	11	16	0	3	12	9		—		3	14	0	V.E.	228
3	7	7		—		48	3	4	25	6	0	5	13	0		—		5	17	0	V.E.	229
	—			—		43	8	0	30	3	0	8	15	0		—		2	15	0	V.E.	230
5	11	10		—		34	0	0	18	10	0	9	16	0		—		0	16	0	V.V.	231
3	12	0		—		23	0	0	15	15	0		—			—			—		V.V.	232
4	19	9		—		42	9	6	8	13	2	6	0	0		—		6	6	0	V.E.	233
4	4	10		—		56	10	0	67	11	6	16	0	0	27	10	0	*43	16	0	V.E.	234
12	17	7		—		102	10	6	97	0	6	28	16	0	13	0	0	41	16	0	V.V.	235
14	16	3		—		104	8	0	109	8	6		—		9	0	0	9	0	0		236
0	16	6		—			—			—			—			—			—			237
4	3	11		—		81	0	8	21	16	8	24	19	6		—		24	19	6		238
1	14	10	5	10	0	10	0	0	33	4	6	5	6	6		—		5	6	6	V.E.	239
0	6	10		—		80	0	0	43	6	6	5	14	0		—		5	14	0		240
1	10	8	6	0	0	18	0	0	10	16	0	5	1	9		—		5	1	9	V.E.	241
1	10	8	6	0	0	15	0	0	15	10	6	5	16	6		—		5	16	6	V.E.	242
3	16	4		—		64	17	7	17	8	0	10	4	3		—		10	4	3	V.E.	243
5	1	6		—		74	0	0	16	17	6	11	18	2		—		11	18	2	V.V.	244
3	8	4		—		53	18	4	36	4	0	8	7	6		—		8	7	6	V.E.	245
1	12	3		—		61	0	0	35	1	6	6	3	0		—		6	3	0	V.E.	246
13	15	11		—		109	0	0	40	0	0	35	17	6		—		35	17	6		247
8	1	4		—		65	0	0	44	5	6	37	7	8		—		37	7	6		248
	—			—		80	0	0	10	12	6	6	4	8		—		6	4	8	V.V.	249
	—			—		84	0	0	19	14	6	3	1	0		—		3	1	0	V.E.	250
1	18	2		—		21	0	0	8	17	6		—			—			—		V.V.	251
6	4	3		—		17	13	0	21	18	6	21	15	6		—		21	15	6	V.E.	252
7	15	10		—		19	0	0	29	6	6	11	15	0		—		11	15	0	V.E.	253
4	12	7		—		44	0	0	16	18	6	5	14	6	3	0	0	8	18	6	V.V.	254
4	4	9		—		80	0	0	18	18	0	8	2	0	4	0	0	*8	2	0	V.V.	255
8	16	11		—		65	0	0	69	8	6	12	0	0		—		12	0	0	V.E.	256
3	16	4		—		97	16	8	24	17	6	7	0	0		—		7	0	0	V.E.	257
4	14	0		—		64	0	0	22	19	6	12	0	6		—		12	0	6	V.V.	258
7	4	0		—		60	0	0	27	16	11	10	2	6		—		10	2	6	V.V.	259
8	2	10		—		36	14	6	11	12	0	4	18	6		—		4	18	6	V.V.	260
	—			—		40	0	6	25	10	0	3	17	6		—		3	17	6	V.E.	261
1	5	0		—		52	14	8	10	4	6	5	5	6		—		5	5	6	V.E.	262
	—			—		44	0	0	26	2	6	5	0	6		—		5	0	6	V.V.	263

* Including value of Free Garden.

List of Schools in operation on the 31st December, 1874.—

Number.	Roll Number of School.	Parish.	District.	School.	In Nature Denomination of Managers or Correspondents. Clerical.	Lay.	Religious Denomination of Teachers. Principals.	Assistants.	Total number of Pupils on Rolls within the Year 1874. Males.	Females.	Total.	Average No. in Attendance.
264	9410	Rattoo,	54	Drumclanihan, m.	R.C.	–	R.C.	–	79	–	79	37
265	9411	Do.	–	Do. f.	R.C.		R.C.	–	–	62	62	31
266	9460	Do.	–	Tralee Workhouse,	P.L.	Gdn.	2R.C.	R.C.	161	124	285	173
267	6082	Do.	–	Do. Gaol,	Gove	rnor	2R.C.	–	37	15	52	11
268	4317	Stradbally,	–	Magharees,	R.C.	–	R.C.	R.C.	89	66	155	78
269	1702	Do.	–	Farranakilla,	R.C.	–	R.C.	R.C.	118	46	164	68
270	1790	Tonakel,	51	Dromes, m.	–	Chris.	R.C.	–	101	–	101	45
271	7192	Do.	–	Do. f.	–	Chris.	R.C.	–	78	–	78	53
272	5184	Do.	–	Shelbourne, No. 2,	R.C.	–	R.C.	R.C.	63	69	132	68
273	5390	Do.	–	Lerrigh, m.	–	Chris.	R.C.	–	181	–	181	82
274	7610	Do.	–	Do. f.	–	Chris.	R.C.	R.C.	–	189	189	86
275	4759	Templemore,	67	Rostermore, m.	R.C.	–	R.C.	–	104	–	104	38
276	6349	Do.	–	Do. f.	R.C.	–	R.C.	–	–	116	116	49
277	8149	Do.	–	Gurrangharnlagh,	R.C.	–	R.C.	–	26	22	48	28
278	3492	Do.	–	Direen,	R.C.	–	R.C.	–	88	69	57	32
279	7815	Do.	–	Dirreendarragh Ord. Agricultural), m.	R.C.	–	R.C.	–	186	–	186	70
280	7816	Do.	–	Do. f.	R.C.	–	R.C.	–	–	123	123	60
281	11059	Do.	–	Capparcoe,	–	–	–	–	–	–	–	–
282	9280	Tralee,	51	Lisardlick, m.	R.C.	–	R.C.	–	117	–	117	40
283	9281	Do.	–	Do. f.	R.C.	–	R.C.	–	–	120	120	47
284	11184	Do.	–	Tralee, f.	R.C.	–	R.C.	–	–	65	65	22
285	346	Do.	–	Do. Convent, f.	–	R.C.	R.C.	15R.C.	–	928	928	462
286	9286	Do.	–	Do. f. No. 2.	–	R.C.	Nuns		–	594	594	219
287	11062	Do.	–	Do. m.	R.C.	–	R.C.	–	56	17	73	48
288	11037	Do.	–	Do. f.	R.C.	–	R.C.	–	57	48	105	49
289	2415	Valentia,	51	Valentia, m.	R.C.	–	R.C.	R.C.	146	–	146	60
290	2416	Do.	–	Do. f.	R.C.	–	R.C.	R.C.	–	115	115	47
291	7897	Do.	–	Knightstown, m.	R.C.	–	R.C.	–	90	–	90	40
292	7898	Do.	–	Do. f.	R.C.	–	R.C.	–	16	93	109	45
293	10596	Do.	–	Coroberg,	R.C.	–	R.C.	–	49	48	97	53
294	5593	Ventry,	54	Ventry, m.	R.C.	–	R.C.	–	119	–	119	45
295	7444	Do.	–	Do. f.	R.C.	–	R.C.	R.C.	–	189	189	85
296	11146	Do.	–	Kealvienhenig,	R.C.	–	R.C.	–	66	81	147	75
		Total for County of Kerry, 296.							23477	24834	48,311	21800

COUNTY OF

1	402	Athington,	61	Kilabyquirk, m.	–	R.C.	R.C.	–	118	–	118	46
2	403	Do.	–	Do. f.	–	R.C.	R.C.	R.C.	–	112	112	54
3	4960	Do.	–	Mucron, m.	–	R.C.	R.C.	R.C.	268	–	268	81
4	4961	Do.	–	Do. f.	–	R.C.	R.C.	R.C.	–	260	260	77
5	1291	Ardagh,	58	Ardagh, m.	R.C.	–	R.C.	R.C.	175	–	170	76
6	1292	Do.	–	Do. f.	R.C.	–	R.C.	R.C.	–	182	182	79
7	4877	Do.	–	Killeighteen,	–	R.C.	R.C.	R.C.	126	100	226	100
8	8783	Do.	–	Ballyloghane, m.	R.C.	–	R.C.	–	120	–	120	60
9	8784	Do.	–	Do. f.	R.C.	–	R.C.	R.C.	–	160	150	63
10	1720	Aglish Cormick,	58	Cloverfield, m.	R.C.	–	R.C.	–	71	–	71	35
11	1773	Do.	–	Do. f.	R.C.	–	R.C.	–	–	73	73	34
12	2039	Askeaton,	58	Askeaton, m.	R.C.	–	R.C.	R.C.	101	–	161	65
13	2040	Do.	–	Do. f.	R.C.	–	R.C.	R.C.	–	163	163	68
14	8020	Do.	–	Do. f.	R.C.	–	R.C.	R.C.	63	80	143	64
15	2839	Abbeyfeale,	–	Abbeyfeale, m.	R.C.	–	R.C.	R.C.	247	–	247	131
16	7182	Do.	–	Do. f.	R.C.	–	Nuns		–	498	498	232
17	7287	Do.	–	Mountkilly,	R.C.	–	R.C.	R.C.	108	81	189	84
18	10379	Do.	–	Springmount, m.	R.C.	–	R.C.	R.C.	180	–	180	70
19	10403	Do.	–	Do. f.	R.C.	–	R.C.	–	–	77	77	37
20	8411	Do.	–	Dromtrasna,	R.C.	–	R.C.	R.C.	136	105	241	91
21	8607	Adare,	–	Shanagolden,	R.C.	–	R.C.	–	54	47	101	31

a Including value of Free Garden. b Including value of Free Residence.

Province of Munster: County of Kerry—*continued.*

Amount paid for Books, Requisites, and Apparatus at Reduced Prices.	Aid granted by the Board during the Year 1874. In Free Stock of Books, Requisites, and Apparatus.	In Salaries, Premiums, and other Gratuities.	Results Fees, Financial Year.	Amount of Local Emoluments received in Aid of Teacher's Salary. School Fees.	Subscriptions, Endowments, &c.	Total Local Aid.	Vested or Non-Vested.	Number.
£ s. d.	£ s. d.	£ s. d.	£ s. d.	£ s. d.	£ s. d.	£ s. d.		
1 19 5	—	24 0 0	9 19 8	2 11 9	—	2 11 9	V.T.	[illegible]
1 11 9	—	26 5 0	9 10 6	4 10 6	—	4 10 0	V.T.	[illegible]
11 1 5	—	8 0 0	—	—	—	—		[illegible]
—	—	—	—	—	—	—		[illegible]
4 19 1	—	77 0 0	60 13 0	10 0 0	—	10 0 0	V.C.	[illegible]
5 0 4	—	50 10 9	1 18 11	6 1 9	—	6 1 0	V.T.	[illegible]
4 9 0	—	84 0 0	18 9 6	11 0 7	10 0 0	21 0 7	A.	[illegible]
2 18 11	—	28 0 0	46 9 0	4 15 8	5 0 0	9 15 8	A.	[illegible]
—	—	41 0 0	20 10 6	5 11 0	—	5 11 0	V.C.	[illegible]
8 15 0	—	24 0 0	12 19 0	2 8 0	10 0 0	12 8 0	V.C.	[illegible]
4 4 8	—	44 0 0	25 0 6	6 8 0	6 0 0	12 8 0	V.C.	[illegible]
2 16 9	—	80 0 0	9 7 8	5 1 8	—	5 1 8	V.C.	[illegible]
8 11 5	—	26 0 0	18 14 6	5 11 0	—	5 11 0	V.C.	[illegible]
9 12 11	—	20 0 0	6 8 0	8 0 0	—	8 0 0	V.C.	[illegible]
1 17 8	—	21 0 0	10 14 6	5 9 0	—	5 9 0	V.C.	[illegible]
—	—	62 16 8	32 13 6	14 1 4	8 0 0	* 17 1 4	V.C.	[illegible]
6 1 0	—	62 10 0	26 9 8	7 13 0	—	7 19 0	V.C.	[illegible]
1 6 8	4 0 0	—	—	—	—	—		[illegible]
1 19 8	—	29 18 4	11 8 0	2 5 10	—	2 5 10	V.T.	[illegible]
8 0 2	—	22 0 0	10 13 6	3 5 0	—	3 5 0	V.T.	[illegible]
4 14 9	6 0 0	62 0 0	9 16 4	14 10 0	17 0 0	31 10 0		[illegible]
55 1 9	—	637 11 4	160 9 6	—	—	—		[illegible]
16 0 5	—	72 8 0	88 15 0	—	—	—		[illegible]
5 14 9	—	58 18 4	9 7 8	8 8 10	5 0 0	18 8 10		[illegible]
—	—	26 16 4	8 8 0	4 10 0	5 0 0	9 10 0		[illegible]
—	—	48 0 0	18 1 0	4 0 8	—	4 0 8	V.T.	[illegible]
—	—	49 18 4	20 5 0	8 0 0	—	8 0 0	V.T.	[illegible]
1 5 11	—	47 8 4	15 18 0	10 19 8	6 0 0	* 10 10 8	V.C.	[illegible]
8 11 7	—	62 8 4	22 0 0	8 18 10	—	8 18 10	V.C.	[illegible]
4 19 8	—	20 0 0	12 18 0	4 0 0	—	4 0 0		[illegible]
8 14 10	—	27 0 0	13 1 0	8 14 0	—	8 14 0		[illegible]
9 18 9	—	25 0 0	13 1 0	8 12 4	—	8 12 4		[illegible]
8 9 8	—	19 0 0	16 17 8	9 8 0	—	9 8 0		[illegible]
1,286 10 5	87 2 0	14,693 18 10	6,050 10 10	2,505 7 8	436 8 4	2,940 7 0		

LIMERICK—[illegible] Schools.

Amount paid for Books, Requisites, and Apparatus at Reduced Prices.	In Free Stock of Books, Requisites, and Apparatus.	In Salaries, Premiums, and other Gratuities.	Results Fees, Financial Year.	School Fees.	Subscriptions, Endowments, &c.	Total Local Aid.	Vested or Non-Vested.	Number.
5 8 9	—	65 13 4	80 6 8	15 2 0	7 0 0	22 8 0		1
3 10 7	—	50 0 0	26 14 0	11 0 0	16 15 9	* 24 15 9		2
6 16 0	—	63 8 4	40 0 0	14 8 0	4 0 0	* 18 8 6	V.C.	3
8 8 6	—	74 18 8	65 18 6	18 16 5	4 10 0	* 23 0 5	V.C.	4
4 4 7	—	62 0 0	28 18 8	13 0 0	3 0 0	16 0 0		5
0 11 8	—	46 0 0	19 11 0	5 7 6	2 0 0	7 7 6		6
10 0 9	—	84 13 4	28 0 0	11 10 5	18 0 0	* 29 10 5		7
2 18 9	—	89 8 4	19 9 0	9 10 0	4 0 0	13 10 0	V.C.	8
2 14 7	—	29 8 2	15 16 8	8 8 0	4 0 0	12 0 0	V.C.	9
1 5 2	—	24 16 5	0 10 0	6 9 6	—	6 9 6	[illegible]	10
1 17 0	—	20 0 0	8 11 8	5 3 0	—	5 8 0	[illegible]	11
—	—	24 1 1	80 9 0	13 8 4	—	15 8 4	V.T.	12
—	—	24 1 5	14 4 5	8 1 0	—	8 1 0	V.T.	13
0 11 2	—	42 0 0	11 19 0	6 0 0	—	0 0 0		14
7 0 10	—	56 8 8	47 12 0	20 0 0	—	20 0 0		15
7 7 8	—	109 18 6	93 10 6	—	—	—		16
5 14 1	—	92 8 4	81 18 0	13 11 8	—	13 11 8		17
4 18 4	—	65 8 8	33 6 0	13 1 4	1 0 0	* 19 1 4		18
3 0 10	—	20 0 0	18 2 0	0 10 0	—	0 10 0		19
6 16 4	—	67 8 4	33 6 8	16 0 0	—	16 0 0		20
2 11 10	—	24 0 0	0 14 6	5 18 6	10 0 0	15 18 6		21

* Including value of Free Residence and Garden.

List of Schools in operation on the 31st December, 1874.—

Number.	Roll Number of School.	Parish.	District.	School.	Religious Denomination of Managers or Correspondents: Clerical.	Lay.	Number and Religious Denomination of Teachers: Principals.	Assistants.	Attendance for the Year: Total number of Pupils on Rolls within the Year Ended: Males.	Fem.	Total.	Average [illegible]
22	[illegible]	Adare,	61	Adare,	R.C.	–	R.C.	–	41	41	82	64
23	[illegible]	Do.	–	Do. Convent, f.	–	–	R.C.	–	–	241	241	122
24	6911	Athlacca,	46	Athlacca,	R.C.	–	R.C.	aR.C.	71	66	137	63
25	6419	Ardpatrick,	–	Ardpatrick, m.	R.C.	–	R.C.	R.C.	164	–	164	80
26	6120	Do.	–	Do. f.	R.C.	–	R.C.	R.C.	–	167	167	77
27	[illegible]	Athneasy,	–	Martinstown, m.	R.C.	–	R.C.	R.C.	151	–	151	74
28	[illegible]	Do.	–	Do. f.	R.C.	–	R.C.	R.C.	–	126	126	64
29	[illegible]	Ballybrood,	–	Caherline,	R.C.	–	R.C.	2R.C.	137	103	240	119
30	[illegible]	Ballingarry,	52	Ballingarry, m.	R.C.	–	R.C.	2R.C.	216	–	216	90
31	2916	Do.	–	Do. f.	R.C.	–	R.C.	aR.C.	–	173	173	75
32	7020	Do.	47	Glenbrohane, m.	R.C.	–	R.C.	R.C.	169	–	165	63
33	[illegible]	Do.	–	Do. f.	R.C.	–	R.C.	R.C.	2	128	130	69
34	[illegible]	Do.	52	Granagh, m.	R.C.	–	R.C.	R.C.	137	–	137	68
35	[illegible]	Do.	–	Do. f.	R.C.	–	R.C.	–	–	180	180	60
36	[illegible]	Ballylanders,	48	Ballylanders, m.	R.C.	–	R.C.	R.C.	177	–	177	63
37	[illegible]	Do.	–	Do. f.	R.C.	–	R.C.	R.C.	–	190	190	84
38	[illegible]	Banogue,	51	Banogue, m.	R.C.	–	R.C.	–	169	–	165	51
39	[illegible]	Do.	–	Do. f.	R.C.	–	R.C.	–	–	130	130	60
40	7857	Bohar,	46	Kyne, m.	R.C.	–	R.C.	–	74	–	74	35
41	[illegible]	Do.	–	Do. f.	R.C.	–	R.C.	–	–	71	71	34
42	11107	Bruff,	–	Bruff, f.	R.C.		Nuns	–	–	177	177	–
43	[illegible]	Bruree,	–	Bruree, m.	R.C.	–	R.C.	R.C.	157	–	157	63
44	[illegible]	Do.	–	Do. f.	R.C.	–	R.C.	R.C.	–	180	150	63
45	8707	Do.	–	Rockhill, m.	R.C.	–	R.C.	–	78	–	78	34
46	[illegible]	Do.	–	Do. f.	R.C.	–	R.C.	R.C.	–	94	94	45
47	[illegible]	Caherconlish,	51	Inch St. Lawrence,	R.C.	–	R.C.	R.C.	87	69	156	65
48	[illegible]	Do.	–	Kilmurry,	R.C.	–	R.C.	–	45	62	107	44
49	[illegible]	Do.	–	Caherconlish,	R.C.	–	R.C.	–	69	78	147	70
50	[illegible]	Do.	–	Bohermore,	R.C.	–	R.C.	–	45	42	87	39
51	[illegible]	Clonkeen,	–	Clonkeen,	–	R.C.	R.C.	R.C.	61	86	147	67
52	[illegible]	Croagh,	52	Croagh, m.	R.C.	–	R.C.	–	91	–	91	30
53	[illegible]	Do.	–	Do. f.	R.C.	–	R.C.	–	–	63	63	30
54	[illegible]	Caherelly,	46	Caherelly,	R.C.	–	R.C.	R.C.	78	44	122	57
55	[illegible]	Croom,	51	Croom, m.	R.C.	–	R.C.	R.C.	235	–	235	68
56	[illegible]	Do.	–	Do. f.	R.C.	–	R.C.	R.C.	–	198	198	80
57	8015	Do.	–	Do. Workhouse,	Official		R.C.	R.C.	42	37	79	44
58	[illegible]	Chapel Russell,	52	Pallaskenry, m.	R.C.	–	R.C.	R.C.	163	–	163	73
59	[illegible]	Do.	–	Do. f.	R.C.	–	R.C.	R.C.	–	121	121	60
60	[illegible]	Clonelty,	–	Athea, m.	R.C.	–	R.C.	R.C.	154	–	154	79
61	[illegible]	Do.	–	Do. f.	R.C.	–	R.C.	R.C.	–	161	161	70
62	[illegible]	Corcomohide,	–	Kilfinny, m.	R.C.	–	R.C.	–	161	–	161	61
63	[illegible]	Do.	–	Do. f.	R.C.	–	R.C.	–	–	118	118	47
64	[illegible]	Do.	–	Castletown, day.	R.C.	–	R.C.	R.C.	79	81	152	66
65	[illegible]	Do.	–	Ballygran, m. day.	R.C.	–	R.C.	–	116	–	116	52
66	[illegible]	Do.	–	Do. f.	R.C.	–	R.C.	–	–	112	[illegible]	47
67	[illegible]	Cahercorney,	51	Kennakam, m.	R.C.	–	R.C.	–	108	–	108	56
68	7104	Cloncagh,	52	Coolcappagh,	R.C.	–	R.C.	–	73	57	130	60
69	[illegible]	Colmanswell,	46	Colmanswell,	R.C.	–	R.C.	–	64	46	110	41
70	[illegible]	Crecora,	51	Crecora, m.	R.C.	–	R.C.	–	130	–	130	64
71	[illegible]	Do.	–	Do. f.	R.C.	–	R.C.	R.C.	–	111	111	60
72	[illegible]	Darragh,	40	Glenroe, m.	R.C.	–	R.C.	R.C.	184	–	184	82
73	[illegible]	Do.	–	Do. f.	R.C.	–	R.C.	R.C.	–	140	140	68
74	10314	Do.	–	Ballintubber,	R.C.	–	R.C.	R.C.	106	79	184	73
75	[illegible]	Dromcolliher,	42	Dromcolliher, m.	R.C.	–	R.C.	R.C.	182	–	182	80
76	[illegible]	Do.	–	Do. f.	R.C.	–	R.C.	R.C.	–	183	183	78
77	[illegible]	Drehidtarsna,	61	Drehidtarsna,	R.C.	–	R.C.	–	42	27	69	34
78	[illegible]	Doon,	46	Bilboa,	R.C.	–	R.C.	2R.C.	163	134	297	133
79	[illegible]	Do.	–	Gortavalla,	R.C.	–	R.C.	R.C.	106	90	196	84
80	[illegible]	Do.	–	Doon, Convent, f.	–	R.C.	Nuns		–	[illegible]	[illegible]	[illegible]
81	[illegible]	Donaghmore,	61	Donaghmore,	R.C.	–	R.C.	–	59	51	110	39
82	[illegible]	Dromin,	46	Dromin,	R.C.	–	R.C.	R.C.	60	62	122	58
83	[illegible]	Dunmoylan,	52	Mountmahill, m.	–	R.C.	R.C.	–	168	–	168	68
84	[illegible]	Do.	–	Do. f.	–	R.C.	R.C.	–	–	140	140	48

a Including value of Free Residence.

b Including value of Free Garden.

Province of Munster: County of Limerick—*continued.*

Amount paid for Books, Requisites, and Apparatus, at Reduced Prices.			Aid granted by the Board during the Year 1874. In Free Stock of Books, Requisites, and Apparatus.			In Salaries, Gratuities, and other Emoluments.			Results Fees, Financial Year.			Amount of Local Contributions in Aid of Teacher's Sa[laries]. School Fees.			Subscriptions, Endowments, &c.		
£	s.	d.	£	s.	d.	£	s.	d.	£	s.	d.	£	s.	d.	£	s.	d.
8	17	4		—		21	0	0	9	0	8	6	0	0	22	0	0
11	14	1		—		103	1	8	48	18	0		—			—	
9	14	2	1	0	0	59	16	4	42	10	8	30	0	0		—	
7	8	9		—		56	3	4	38	8	6	26	17	8	2	0	0
7	1	0		—		66	0	0	38	16	4	30	10	8	2	0	0
8	1	8		—		58	16	4	30	18	6	13	15	0		—	
4	17	4		—		73	18	0	30	17	0	18	0	0		—	
10	12	4		—		124	8	10	61	16	4	30	12	8		—	
5	8	8		—		107	8	8	57	8	0	21	12	0		—	
1	17	4		—		84	18	4	23	8	0	16	9	8		—	
4	8	5		—		43	0	0	21	17	0	18	0	0		—	
10	18	9		—		62	10	0	45	1	0	36	18	8		—	
4	17	8		—		97	0	8	28	0	0	28	0	0		—	
8	19	8		—		87	0	0	18	8	0	17	10	0		—	
6	9	0		—		05	0	0	20	8	0	10	15	8		—	
8	8	8		—		82	16	4	30	14	6	12	10	0		—	
5	8	6		—		55	0	8	45	17	0	7	17	8	12	0	0
1	17	6		—		39	15	0	18	4	8	6	17	4	3	0	0
1	18	7		—		24	0	0	18	11	0	7	0	0	1	10	0
1	8	4		—		25	0	0	12	10	6	6	2	8	1	10	0
12	8	6	7	0	0		—			—		4	0	0		—	
10	11	2		—		32	10	0	31	8	6	20	15	8	8	0	0
2	9	5		—		40	0	0	26	8	0	21	8	6		—	
2	10	4		—		30	0	0	13	10	0	8	16	8		—	
6	1	9		—		30	0	0	18	10	4	18	10	0		—	
8	2	6		—		56	8	8	28	17	0	17	12	6		—	
1	10	10		—		42	18	8	18	17	0	8	0	0		—	
3	10	11		—		47	0	0	30	6	0	8	12	8		—	
1	18	2		—		61	0	0	7	0	0	7	18	0	1	10	0
3	1	1		—		52	0	0	20	18	0	0	0	0	4	0	0
	—			—		24	0	0	7	17	0	6	8	4		—	
	—			—		20	0	0	7	16	0	7	15	4		—	
3	8	8		—		39	10	0	21	0	8	16	17	0		—	
6	2	9		—		62	8	4	61	18	0	30	4	9	18	0	0
4	0	7		—		52	10	0	16	2	8	2	18	2	10	0	0
	—			—			—			—			—			—	
4	18	8		—		78	10	8	24	9	8	18	6	0	9	0	0
5	19	4		—		82	10	0	20	2	8	10	2	9		—	
1	8	0		—		78	8	4	27	0	0	39	10	0	7	0	0
8	8	4		—		81	0	8	30	4	0	14	17	0		—	
8	8	0		—		30	8	4	18	8	8	16	14	8		—	
5	17	8		—		34	18	4	17	14	0	16	7	0		—	
5	11	0		—		11	0	0	10	12	0	30	0	0		—	
6	18	9		—		58	6	8	17	8	6	9	0	0		—	
1	17	8		—		85	3	4	38	18	6	8	14	0		—	
4	0	8		—		36	0	0	31	17	6	22	0	0	1	0	0
6	0	7		—		85	10	0	16	8	6	8	0	0		—	
8	8	2		—		38	8	4	13	0	6	8	0	0		—	
7	14	4		—		53	18	4	24	19	8	24	10	6		—	
2	8	8		—		50	0	0	30	0	0	30	11	1		—	
4	16	7		—		60	0	0	28	13	9	14	10	0		—	
3	19	8		—		62	8	4	25	10	6	10	11	10		—	
8	8	10		—		69	0	0	20	1	8	18	0	0		—	
8	11	9		—		60	6	8	17	8	0	21	6	0		—	
7	15	0		—		78	16	6	19	1	6	23	19	11		—	
2	12	7		—		30	0	0	11	5	0	8	12	7	10	0	0
8	7	4		—		76	0	0	23	15	0	20	18	6		—	
7	10	8		—		58	8	4	24	2	0	24	17	0		—	
11	18	8		—		57	6	8	23	17	0	18	17	1		—	
9	16	9		—		44	0	0	10	4	6	11	14	5		—	
8	16	4		—		44	0	0	22	0	0	18	14	0		—	
1	14	4		—		39	10	0	19	2	0	10	0	0	8	0	0
8	17	8		—		29	8	8	14	15	8	7	0	0	6	0	0

* Including value of Free Residence and Garden.

List of Schools in operation on the 31st December, 1874.—

Number.	Roll Number of School.	Parish.	District.	School.		Religious Denomination of Manager or Correspondent.		Number and Religious Denomination of Teachers.		Attendances for the Year. Total Number of Pupils on Rolls within the Year 1874.			[illegible]
						Clerical.	Lay.	Principals.	Assistants.	Males.	Fem.	Total.	
85	5782	Effin,	36	Effin,	m.	R.C.	–	R.C.	–	137	–	137	48
86	8231	Do.	–	Do.	f.	R.C.	–	R.C.	R.C.	29	143	172	73
87	9132	Fedamore,	51	Caramee,	m.	–	R.C.	R.C.	–	126	–	126	62
88	9541	Do.	–	Do.	f.	–	R.C.	R.C.	–	–	108	108	44
89	10304	Do.	–	Fedamore,		R.C.	–	R.C.	R.C.	91	64	164	66
90	10731	Galbally,	46	Knockcarron,	m.	–	R.C.	R.C.	R.C.	139	–	139	60
91	10732	Do.	–	Do.	f.	–	R.C.	R.C.	R.C.	–	128	128	56
92	1143	Do.	–	Lowtown,	m.	R.C.	–	R.C.	aR.C.	166	–	189	71
93	1141	Do.	–	Do.	f.	R.C.	–	R.C.	R.C.	–	180	185	92
94	10[illegible]	Glenogra,	51	Mountain,	f.	R.C.	–	R.C.	–	–	59	59	33
95	6342	Grean,	46	Derk,	m.	–	R.C.	R.C.	–	96	–	96	44
96	6343	Do.	–	Do.	f.	–	R.C.	R.C.	–	–	88	88	41
97	6[illegible]	Do.	–	Nicker,	m.	R.C.	–	R.C.	R.C.	187	–	187	77
98	7925	Do.	–	Do.	f.	R.C.	–	R.C.	R.C.	–	132	132	51
99	10216	Do.	–	Brookhill,		R.C.	–	R.C.	R.C.	82	74	156	62
100	9970	Grange,	51	Grange,	m.	R.C.	–	R.C.	–	59	–	59	13
101	9971	Do.	–	Do.	f.	R.C.	–	R.C.	–	–	89	89	42
102	6848	Hospital,	46	Hospital,	m.	R.C.	–	R.C.	R.C.	218	–	218	109
103	6841	Do.	–	Do.	f.	R.C.	–	R.C.	aR.C.	–	183	185	83
104	7900	Iverus,	52	Ballysteen,		R.C.	–	R.C.	bR.C.	116	106	222	107
105	10[illegible]	Kilbehenny,	46	Anglesborough,	m.	R.C.	–	R.C.	R.C.	189	–	189	74
106	10[illegible]	Do.	–	Do.	f.	R.C.	–	R.C.	aR.C.	–	181	182	97
107	581	Killeedy,	52	Raheenagh,	m.	R.C.	–	R.C.	–	114	–	114	46
108	1[illegible]	Do.	–	Do.	f.	R.C.	–	R.C.	R.C.	–	153	153	67
109	7817	Do.	–	Glenagurt,	m.	R.C.	–	R.C.	R.C.	270	–	205	100
110	7820	Do.	–	Do.	f.	R.C.	–	R.C.	R.C.	–	178	178	19
111	7357	Do.	–	Ashford,	m.	R.C.	–	R.C.	R.C.	123	–	123	66
112	8470	Do.	–	Do.	f.	R.C.	–	R.C.	–	–	90	90	36
113	10107	Do.	–	Mount Collins,	m.	R.C.	–	R.C.	R.C.	108	–	108	37
114	10109	Do.	–	Do.	f.	R.C.	–	R.C.	R.C.	–	130	164	44
115	585	Killeenagarriff,	51	Ahane,	m.	–	R.C.	R.C.	–	148	–	148	65
116	[illegible]	Do.	–	Do.	f.	–	R.C.	R.C.	–	–	100	100	43
117	[illegible]	Kilfinane,	46	Kilfinane,	m.	R.C.	–	R.C.	R.C.	220	–	220	82
118	8409	Do.	–	Do.	f.	R.C.	–	R.C.	aR.C.	16	230	246	146
119	[illegible]	Killagholehane,	53	Broadford,	m.	R.C.	–	R.C.	R.C.	146	–	146	6[illegible]
120	[illegible]	Do.	–	Do.	f.	R.C.	–	R.C.	R.C.	–	152	152	60
121	1007	Do.	–	[illegible],		R.C.	–	R.C.	R.C.	110	126	235	93
122	1690	Killeely,	46	Killeely,	m.	R.C.	–	R.C.	R.C.	174	–	174	61
123	1967	Do.	–	Do.	f.	R.C.	–	R.C.	–	–	174	174	64
124	8011	Kilcornan,	52	Kilcornan,	m.	R.C.	–	R.C.	–	109	–	109	46
125	10114	Do.	–	Do.	f.	R.C.	–	R.C.	–	–	77	77	37
126	[illegible]	Kilfergus,	–	Glin,	f.	R.C.	–	R.C.	aR.C.	–	188	188	64
127	2291	Do.	–	Do.	m.	R.C.	–	R.C.	R.C.	200	–	200	64
128	10[illegible]	Do.	–	Do.	I.	R.C.	–	R.C.	–	54	54	108	48
129	[illegible]	Do.	–	Do. Workhouse,		P.L.	Gds.	iR.C.	–	20	23	43	33
130	[illegible]	Kil[illegible],	–	[illegible],	m.	R.C.	–	R.C.	–	130	–	130	54
131	4016	Do.	–	Do.	f.	R.C.	–	R.C.	–	–	109	109	48
132	44[illegible]	Kilmeedy,	–	Feenagh,	m.	R.C.	–	R.C.	–	109	–	109	45
133	4474	Do.	–	Do.	f.	R.C.	–	R.C.	–	–	71	71	30
134	7181	Do.	–	Kilmeedy,	m.	R.C.	–	R.C.	R.C.	147	–	147	69
135	7909	Do.	–	Do.	f.	R.C.	–	R.C.	R.C.	–	142	142	76
136	8130	Knockainey,	46	Knockainey,	m.	R.C.	–	R.C.	–	101	–	101	40
137	8127	Do.	–	Do.	f.	R.C.	–	R.C.	R.C.	–	148	148	64
138	7117	Do.	–	Loughgur,		R.C.	–	R.C.	aR.C.	121	100	221	79
139	[illegible]	Do.	–	[illegible],		R.C.	–	R.C.	aR.C.	104	66	170	69
140	8464	Kilkeedy,	51	Tervoe, 1st Cl. Agl.	m.	R.C.	–	R.C.	–	120	–	120	60
141	[illegible]	Do.	–	Do.	f.	R.C.	–	R.C.	–	–	122	122	64
142	10818	Do.	–	Lurriga,	m.	R.C.	–	R.C.	–	123	–	123	42
143	10817	Do.	–	Do.	f.	R.C.	–	R.C.	–	–	81	81	35
144	6129	Killeely,	–	Thomondgate,	f.	R.C.	–	R.C.	R.C.	–	187	187	71
145	6316	Kildimo,	–	Kildimo,	m.	R.C.	–	R.C.	R.C.	137	–	137	62
146	6317	Do.	–	Do.	f.	R.C.	–	R.C.	R.C.	–	114	114	40
147	7660	Knocklong,	46	Knocklong,	m.	R.C.	–	R.C.	R.C.	157	–	157	57

a Including value of Free Residence. b Including value of Free Residence and Garden.

Province of Munster: County of Limerick—*continued.*

Amount paid for Books, Requisites, and Apparatus, at Reduced Prices.	Aid granted by the Board during the Year 1874: In Free Stock of Books, Requisites, and Apparatus.	In Salaries, Premiums, and other Gratuities.	Results Fees, Financial Year.	Amount of Local Funds received in Aid of Teacher's Salary: School Fees.	Subscriptions, Endowments, &c.	Total Local Aid.	Vested or Non-Vested.	Number.
£ s. d.	£ s. d.	£ s. d.	£ s. d.	£ s. d.	£ s. d.	£ s. d.		
8 1 0	—	24 0 0	13 6 6	18 0 0	—	18 0 0		85
4 7 7	—	30 0 0	29 9 0	20 0 0	—	21 0 0		86
1 12 7	—	31 6 8	19 10 6	15 3 6	2 10 0	17 13 6		87
8 3 11	—	20 10 0	13 12 0	10 15 0	—	10 15 0		88
4 10 5	—	43 6 8	25 17 6	15 1 0	—	15 1 0		89
4 10 11	5 0 0	37 6 8	17 12 0	18 10 8	—	18 10 8	V.C.	90
4 18 8	5 0 0	29 13 4	21 8 6	15 16 6	—	15 16 6	V.C.	91
0 14 7	—	121 10 0	55 3 0	62 14 4	—	62 14 1	V.C.	92
7 13 7	—	70 0 0	33 6 6	20 4 6	—	20 4 6	V.V.	93
5 16 9	—	29 0 0	14 10 0	13 18 7	—	13 18 7		94
2 10 5	—	24 0 0	16 10 6	0 7 0	2 0 0	*11 7 6		95
3 14 10	—	24 0 0	16 11 6	6 0 0	—	6 0 0		96
4 14 1	—	78 0 8	23 19 0	12 16 8	—	12 16 8		97
8 4 8	—	60 0 8	16 1 0	14 0 0	—	14 0 0		98
4 10 8	—	60 0 0	20 10 0	9 7 6	—	9 7 0		99
8 11 0	—	31 6 8	29 18 0	10 10 0	—	10 10 0		100
—	—	38 0 8	28 6 0	18 3 2	—	18 3 2		101
9 1 3	—	80 0 0	40 0 0	17 10 0	14 10 0	*32 0 0		102
12 3 9	—	104 10 0	64 1 0	20 17 0	16 0 0	*36 17 0		103
10 0 0	—	102 0 0	37 11 0	30 0 0	16 0 0	*45 0 0		104
7 11 1	—	10 0 0	31 11 0	18 10 8	—	18 10 8		105
8 7 8	—	73 10 4	30 18 0	18 6 10	—	18 6 10		106
1 4 11	—	31 10 8	10 16 0	18 16 0	—	18 16 0		107
6 4 3	—	68 0 8	28 8 6	28 4 0	3 0 0	31 4 0		108
7 13 5	—	78 10 0	31 2 6	18 0 0	8 0 0	26 0 0	V.C.	109
5 18 0	—	65 0 8	18 6 0	10 13 6	5 0 0	15 13 6	V.C.	110
4 1 2	—	60 0 0	21 1 0	27 17 3	2 0 0	29 17 3	V.C.	111
3 8 3	—	50 0 0	9 16 0	8 14 0	2 0 0	10 14 0	V.V.	112
—	—	56 0 0	30 3 8	21 15 0	—	21 15 0	V.V.	113
—	—	49 0 0	10 6 6	13 10 0	—	13 10 0	V.V.	114
7 18 6	—	128 16 8	84 16 8	16 3 3	20 0 0	*34 3 3		115
0 9 9	—	42 15 0	18 4 0	12 5 0	9 10 0	*12 16 6		116
12 8 7	—	58 0 0	27 8 0	60 0 0	—	60 0 0		117
5 8 10	—	88 8 8	47 6 0	40 0 0	—	40 0 0		118
4 10 8	—	86 0 0	17 11 8	13 15 8	1 0 0	14 13 0		119
3 2 0	—	56 3 4	14 11 6	7 0 4	—	7 0 4		120
0 14 8	—	85 10 0	24 18 6	18 0 0	—	18 0 0		121
5 6 8	—	52 0 0	29 4 6	10 15 0	—	20 12 8	V.V.	122
—	—	41 0 0	27 18 0	12 19 0	—	12 19 0	V.V.	123
3 9 8	—	30 0 0	18 10 0	10 15 0	—	10 15 0	V.V.	124
5 2 6	—	31 0 0	10 6 0	10 10 10	—	10 10 10	V.V.	125
7 8 3	—	64 10 0	22 8 5	23 0 0	—	23 0 0	A.	126
11 0 5	—	18 0 0	26 17 0	20 10 6	—	20 19 6	A.	127
0 11 8	4 0 0	23 0 0	8 10 5	3 10 0	—	8 10 0		128
3 8 4	—	—	—	—	—	—		129
4 17 3	—	61 18 4	17 13 0	19 12 8	11 0 0	*30 12 8	V.V.	130
1 10 8	—	27 6 8	8 4 6	6 18 0	5 0 0	11 13 0	V.V.	131
5 11 9	—	83 0 0	12 4 0	9 6 0	2 0 0	11 6 0	V.C.	132
8 1 4	—	24 0 0	0 16 6	6 18 0	3 0 0	8 15 0	V.C.	133
8 18 4	—	60 8 4	15 14 0	9 10 0	—	9 10 0		134
4 0 0	—	72 16 8	17 18 0	7 0 0	—	7 0 0		135
1 0 8	—	97 8 8	6 18 0	8 16 0	8 0 0	*11 15 8		136
4 0 2	—	38 3 4	22 16 0	10 10 0	1 10 0	*18 0 0		137
4 10 8	—	60 10 0	28 8 0	21 0 0	2 0 0	*28 8 0		138
6 12 4	—	98 0 8	30 12 0	20 10 0	2 0 0	*32 10 0		139
3 10 0	—	40 3 4	21 16 0	14 0 0	5 0 0	*19 0 0	V.C.	140
4 1 4	—	57 0 0	21 19 6	10 0 0	0 0 0	25 6 0		141
4 9 11	—	84 0 0	11 1 0	8 12 6	—	8 12 6	V.V.	142
1 17 4	—	24 0 0	7 7 6	6 0 10	—	6 0 10	V.V.	143
2 10 1	—	75 0 0	24 18 0	9 1 4	—	9 1 4		144
1 15 8	—	57 0 0	25 2 0	16 8 0	3 0 0	*19 8 0	V.C.	145
1 0 4	—	60 0 0	31 14 0	14 11 0	4 0 0	*18 11 0	V.C.	146
8 14 5	—	79 10 0	26 15 0	16 13 6	—	16 13 6		147

* Including value of Free Garden.

List of Schools in operation on the 31st December, 1874.—

Number.	Roll Number of School.	Parish.	District.	School.		Religious Denomination of Manager or Correspondent: Clerical.	Lay.	Number and Religious Denomination of Teachers: Principals.	Assistants.	Total number of Pupils on Rolls within the Year: Males.	Fem.	Total.	Average Daily Attendance for the Year.
148	7805	Knocklong,	44	Knocklong,	f.	R.C.	–	R.C.	R.C.	–	181	181	46
149	7287	Kilflyn,	–	Ballyorgan,	m.	R.C.	–	R.C.	–	78	–	78	30
150	9248	Do.	–	Do.	f.	R.C.	–	R.C.	–	–	67	67	40
151	7376	Kilcullane,	–	Herbertstown,	m.	R.C.	–	R.C.	R.C.	145	–	145	65
152	7811	Do.	–	Do.	f.	R.C.	–	R.C.	R.C.	–	145	145	56
153	7145	Kilmurry,	64	Monaleen,	m.	R.C.	–	R.C.	–	108	–	108	46
154	7816	Do.	–	Do.	f.	R.C.	–	R.C.	–	–	71	71	34
155	8148	Knocken,	–	Knocken,	f.	R.C.	–	R.C.	R.C.	–	181	181	58
156	6760	Kilbehenny,	54	Cloonadaharde,[b]	m.	–	–	–	–	–	–	–	–
157	6761	Do.	–	Do.	f.	R.C.	–	R.C.	–	–	160	160	48
158	10262	Do.	–	Nusgrove,	m.	R.C.	–	R.C.	–	124	–	124	58
159	10827	Do.	–	Do.	f.	R.C.	–	R.C.	–	–	110	110	43
160	7818	Kilfinny,	–	Kilfinny,	m.	R.C.	–	R.C.	–	67	–	67	46
161	9318	Do.	–	Do.	f.	R.C.	–	R.C.	–	–	65	65	30
162	6481	Kilbreedymajor,	46	Bulgaden,	m.	R.C.	–	R.C.	R.C.	114	–	114	48
163	6482	Do.	–	Do.	f.	R.C.	–	R.C.	R.C.	–	169	169	64
164	9254	Monagay,	58	Templeglantane,	m.	R.C.	–	R.C.	aR.C.	227	–	227	123
165	9256	Do.	–	Do.	f.	R.C.	–	R.C.	aR.C.	149	–	243	97
166	9401	Do.	–	Monagea,	m.	R.C.	–	R.C.	R.C.	189	–	189	80
167	9197	Do.	–	Do.	f.	R.C.	–	R.C.	aR.C.	–	197	197	89
168	1984	Mahoonagh,	–	Feohanagh,	.	R.C.	–	R.C.	aR.C.	118	124	242	123
169	8772	Do.	–	Mahoonagh,	.	R.C.	–	R.C.	aR.C.	181	114	295	151
170	4402	Monasteranenagh	61	Ballyneety,	.	R.C.	–	R.C.	aR.C.	109	59	168	78
171	9687	Morgans,	55	Mountpleasant,	.	R.C.	–	R.C.	R.C.	85	62	147	65
172	4756	Mungret,	52	Patrickswell,	m.	R.C.	–	R.C.	–	110	–	110	43
173	4702	Do.	–	Do.	f.	R.C.	–	R.C.	–	–	107	107	40
174	8068	Do.	–	Limerick 1st class Agl. (at Mungret),	.	Com.	N.B.	R.C.	–	94	–	94	17
175	8149	Do.	–	Do.	f.	Com.	N.B.	R.C.	–	–	113	113	52
176	9752	Meanus,	–	Meanus,	.	R.C.	–	R.C.	–	68	–	68	38
177	9705	Nantinan,	62	St. James,	m.	R.C.	–	R.C.	R.C.	159	–	159	63
178	6703	Do.	–	Do.	f.	R.C.	–	R.C.	R.C.	–	127	127	44
179	9116	Newcastle,	–	Newcastle Workhouse,	.	P.L.	Gds.	aR.C.	–	49	80	129	64
180	10224	Do.	–	St. Catherine's Con.	f.	R.C.	–	None		–	641	641	281
181	7373	Oola,	49	Oola,	m.	R.C.	–	R.C.	R.C.	212	–	212	73
182	7374	Do.	–	Do.	f.	R.C.	–	R.C.	R.C.	–	161	161	75
183	10692	Pallasgreen,	–	Cappamore,	m.	R.C.	–	R.C.	–	149	–	149	60
184	10693	Do.	–	Do.	f.	R.C.	–	R.C.	R.C.	–	128	128	51
185	1276	Rathkeale,	57	Rathkeale,	m.	R.C.	–	R.C.	–	188	–	188	80
186	1311	Do.	–	Do.[b]	f.	–	–	–	–	–	–	–	–
187	10928	Do.	–	Do.	(9)	R.C.	–	R.C.	R.C.	37	39	76	40
188	8416	Do.	–	Do. Workhse.	.	P.L.	Gds.	aR.C.	–	49	66	115	32
189	6306	Do.	–	St. Anne's Convent,	f.	R.C.	–	None.		–	484	484	229
190	8546	Do.	–	Dunterm,	.	R.C.	–	R.C.	–	78	34	112	41
191	8046	Robertstown,	–	Mt. Trenchard,	m.	–	R.C.	R.C.	–	92	–	92	35
192	9131	Do.	–	Do.	f.	–	R.C.	R.C.	–	–	65	65	30
193	9816	Do.	–	Foynes,	m.	–	R.C.	R.C.	–	154	–	154	49
194	9714	Do.	–	Do.	f.	–	R.C.	R.C.	R.C.	–	140	140	63
195	5618	Do.	–	Mount Trenchard Central Ag.[d]	.	–	–	–	–	–	–	–	–
196	7891	Rathronan,	–	Athea,	m.	R.C.	–	R.C.	aR.C.	249	–	249	108
197	7807	Do.	–	Do.	f.	R.C.	–	R.C.	aR.C.	–	282	282	102
198	10408	Rathnaseare,	51	Sheehan's Cross,	.	R.C.	–	R.C.	–	59	45	104	42
199	6646	Stradbally,	–	Richhill,	f.	–	R.C.	R.C.	–	55	128	183	67
200	9930	Do.	–	Castlematrell,	m.	R.C.	–	R.C.	R.C.	173	–	173	68
201	9948	Do.	–	Do.	f.	R.C.	–	R.C.	–	–	170	170	69
202	7811	Do.	–	Mount Pallas,	.	–	R.C.	R.C.	–	49	67	116	38
203	8786	Shanagolden,	52	Shanagolden,	m.	–	R.C.	R.C.	aR.C.	169	–	169	60
204	1181	Do.	–	Do.	f.	–	R.C.	R.C.	R.C.	–	97	97	47
205	4087	Do.	–	Do.	i.	–	R.C.	R.C.	R.C.	87	61	148	54
206	3696	St. Mary's,	51	Limerick model,	org.	R.C.	–	R.C.	–	77	–	77	34
207	10851	Do.	–	St. Mary's,	.	R.C.	–	R.C.	–	108	–	108	48
208	10852	Do.	–	Do.	f.	R.C.	–	R.C.	–	50	45	95	37

a Including value of Free Residence.

b Closed.

Province of MUNSTER: County of LIMERICK—*continued.*

Amount paid for Books, Requisites, and Apparatus at Reduced Prices.	Aid granted by the Board during the Year 1874.			Amount of Local Emoluments received in Aid of Teacher's Salary.			Vested or Non-Vested.	Number.
	In Free Stock of Books, Requisites, and Apparatus.	In Salaries, Premiums, and other Gratuities.	Results Fees, Financial Year.	School Fees.	Subscriptions, Endowments, &c.	Total Local Aid.		
£ s. d.	£ s. d.	£ s. d.	£ s. d.	£ s. d.	£ s. d.	£ s. d.		
8 8 0	—	40 0 0	20 6 0	17 12 8	—	17 12 8		148
1 10 0	—	21 0 0	10 14 8	8 4 0	—	8 4 0		149
1 14 9	—	24 0 0	18 4 0	11 14 0	—	11 14 0		150
6 14 8	—	51 0 0	20 7 0	11 2 6	6 6 0	*14 2 6		151
3 0 8	—	54 16 8	23 3 8	21 14 10	5 6 0	*24 14 10		152
4 6 9	—	34 18 4	10 15 8	6 8 0	—	6 8 0		153
8 9 8	—	20 0 0	14 1 0	8 8 6	—	6 8 6		154
2 16 1	—	58 12 4	20 1 8	12 6 8	1 0 0	20 6 6		155
—	—	24 0 0	—	—	—	—		156
4 9 1	—	23 16 8	15 19 0	4 16 8	2 10 0	*7 6 6		157
6 5 0	—	30 8 8	18 15 0	15 18 8	6 0 0	20 18 8	V.T.	158
8 18 5	—	31 16 8	14 1 0	9 6 9	6 0 0	14 6 9	V.T.	159
1 7 4	—	37 0 0	16 8 6	10 0 0	8 10 0	18 10 0		160
2 12 8	—	34 0 0	11 0 8	9 12 8	2 10 0	12 4 8		161
8 16 8	—	30 0 0	14 17 8	14 0 0	—	14 0 0		162
1 7 5	—	53 0 0	20 6 0	20 0 0	—	20 0 0		163
11 8 10	—	122 16 0	43 6 6	45 8 10	20 0 0	*65 8 10	V.T.	164
7 6 9	—	37 18 8	26 0 0	32 4 0	5 0 0	37 4 0	V.T.	165
7 14 4	—	53 8 6	27 12 8	14 16 6	5 0 0	19 16 6	V.T.	166
5 5 9	—	76 18 4	63 18 8	13 13 6	5 0 0	18 13 6	V.T.	167
10 16 0	—	90 18 4	46 16 0	25 14 3	0 10 0	*26 4 5		168
9 8 6	—	153 10 0	57 4 8	25 2 0	1 10 0	26 12 0		169
6 11 11	—	53 6 0	57 16 0	23 3 6	—	23 3 6	V.C.	170
6 11 10	—	55 0 0	18 8 8	6 15 1	—	6 15 1		171
8 0 8	—	61 6 8	17 4 0	8 0 2	2 10 0	*10 10 2	V.C.	172
8 8 8	—	30 10 0	15 8 0	7 9 0	2 10 0	*6 19 0	V.C.	173
5 8 4	—	}776 12 4	{30 18 6	—	—	—	V.C.	174
—	—		28 1 6	—	—	—	V.C.	175
5 8 8	—	31 0 0	19 17 6	6 11 7	—	6 11 7		176
4 0 1	—	51 8 4	16 3 6	11 2 6	2 10 0	*13 14 8		177
1 17 6	—	48 0 0	16 4 0	6 10 0	—	6 10 0		178
3 18 8	—	5 10 8	—	—	—	—		179
15 8 10	—	162 11 4	74 11 6	—	—	—		180
8 17 0	—	71 8 11	29 8 8	15 19 6	5 0 0	20 19 0		181
8 2 9	—	63 1 8	24 12 0	25 16 0	5 0 0	30 16 0		182
4 16 11	—	86 0 0	20 18 0	18 0 0	—	18 0 0		183
8 8 7	—	46 0 0	26 19 0	23 16 0	—	23 16 0		184
2 10 6	—	61 0 0	11 0 8	8 18 8	—	8 18 8	V.T.	185
—	—	—	—	—	—	—	V.T.	186
8 10 8	—	42 0 0	11 11 6	7 8 6	16 6 0	*23 18 6		187
—	—	8 0 0	—	—	—	—		188
19 0 1	—	127 8 8	20 4 0	—	1 0 0	1 0 0		189
4 11 0	—	27 0 0	20 8 0	7 15 0	—	7 15 0		190
3 8 11	—	48 8 4	19 1 0	6 8 6	6 0 0	*15 8 6		191
1 15 10	—	20 0 0	10 16 6	3 16 9	5 0 0	8 16 9		192
3 18 11	—	49 1 8	17 18 8	12 0 0	5 0 0	17 0 0	L.	193
7 8 4	—	65 18 8	35 12 0	10 6 0	5 0 0	15 6 0	L.	194
—	—	62 0 0	—	—	—	—	V.C.	195
9 17 2	—	24 18 4	67 7 0	23 0 0	—	23 0 0		196
5 3 6	—	60 0 0	30 8 6	14 0 0	—	14 0 0		197
1 15 6	—	36 0 0	16 14 0	16 0 0	—	16 4 0		198
6 5 8	—	24 0 0	17 18 0	8 13 7	7 0 0	*16 18 7		199
4 8 8	—	63 18 4	47 17 8	24 1 6	—	24 1 6	V.C.	200
7 10 8	—	50 0 0	25 9 0	10 6 8	—	10 6 8	V.C.	201
9 18 6	—	23 0 0	6 16 0	4 11 6	—	4 11 6		202
7 8 4	—	51 8 8	17 19 0	10 0 10	6 0 0	16 0 10	L.	203
8 18 1	—	44 16 4	17 8 6	6 18 0	18 12 0	*24 6 0		204
1 10 8	—	51 10 0	7 0 0	2 10 0	8 0 0	*10 10 0		205
1 8 8	—	20 0 0	6 16 0	9 10 9	—	9 10 9		206
6 11 8	—	43 0 0	10 18 6	25 6 7	—	25 6 7		207
8 7 8	—	24 10 0	11 19 6	10 1 6	—	10 1 6		208

* Including value of Free Residence and Garden.

† No Returns.

List of Schools in operation on the 31st December, 1874.—

Number.	Roll Number of School.	Parish.	District.	School.	Religious Denomination of Managers or Correspondents: Clerical.	Lay.	Number and Religious Denomination of Teachers: Principals.	Assistants.	Attendance for the Year. Total number of Pupils on Rolls within the Year: Males.	Fem.	Total.	[illegible]
209	6021	St. Munchin's,	61	Villiers, f.	R.C.	–	R.C.	–	19	33	52	24
210	6141	Do.	–	Do. m.	Pres.	–	R.C.	–	52	–	52	21
211	576	Do.	–	SS. Mary's and Munchin's Convent,	R.C.	–	Nuns		–	1070	1,070	361
212	9224	St. John's,	–	St. John's-square, m.	R.C.	–	R.C.	–	176	–	176	49
213	[illegible]	Do.	–	Do. Convent f.	R.C.	–	Nuns		–	856	856	445
214	9637	St. Michael's,	–	Perry-square, m. i.	R.C.	–	2R.C.	–	201	–	201	81
215	3142	Do.	–	Do. Conv. f.	R.C.	–	Nuns		–	699	699	[illegible]
216	6776	Do.	–	Limerick [illegible] m.	Com.	N.R.	R.C.	–	191	–	191	93
217	6971	Do.	–	Do. f.	Com.	N.R.	R.C.	Pres.	–	148	148	78
218	6972	Do.	–	Do. i.	Com.	N.R.	–	R.C.	75	64	139	58
219	10034	Do.	–	Mount St. Vincent,	R.C.	–	Nuns		–	110	110	77
220	6511	Do.	–	Sexton-st. Conv. f.	R.C.	–	Nuns		–	1128	1,128	484
221	9098	St. Patrick's,	–	St. Patrick's, m.	R.C.	–	R.C.	R.C.	205	–	205	57
222	8378	Do.	–	Do. f.	R.C.	–	R.C.	R.C.	–	198	198	85
223	1634	SS. Peter & Paul's	48	SS. Peter & Paul's m.	R.C.	–	R.C.	R.C.	259	–	259	188
224	8157	Do.	–	Do. f.	R.C.	–	R.C.	2R.C.	35	273	308	160
225	3046	Do.	–	Kilmallock Workh.	P.L.	Gds.	2R.C.	R.C.	107	107	214	109
226	3656	St. Nicholas,	–	Limerick Workh.	P.L.	Gds.	2R.C.	–	401	331	[illegible]	300
227	7479	Tuogh,	–	Cappamore, m.	R.C.	–	R.C.	R.C.	240	–	240	91
228	7318	Do.	–	Do. f.	R.C.	–	R.C.	R.C.	–	224	224	92
229	7360	Do.	–	Tinnakilla,	R.C.	–	R.C.	R.C.	118	59	176	75
		Total for County Limerick, 229 Schools,							17412	20046	[illegible]	[illegible]

COUNTY OF

1	571	Ardmoyle,	43	Ardmoyle,	R.C.	–	R.C.	R.C.	75	66	142	81
[illegible]	2570	Do.	–	Nodstown, m.	R.C.	–	R.C.	–	108	–	108	44
[illegible]	2577	Do.	–	Do. f.	R.C.	–	R.C.	–	–	107	107	41
[illegible]	416	Ardmayle	–	Toomyvara, m.	R.C.	–	R.C.	R.C.	162	–	162	77
[illegible]	6724	Do.	–	Do. f.	R.C.	–	R.C.	R.C.	–	126	126	63
[illegible]	6408	Do.	–	Borrisnafarney,	R.C.	–	R.C.	–	40	42	82	41
[illegible]	4932	Do.	–	Ballinlough,	R.C.	–	R.C.	R.C.	68	73	141	63
[illegible]	[illegible]	Ardfinnan,	53	Ardfinnan, m.	R.C.	–	R.C.	–	99	–	99	39
[illegible]	7715	Do.	–	Do. f.	R.C.	–	R.C.	–	–	115	113	44
10	10400	Ardcroney,	36	Ardcroney,	R.C.	–	R.C.	R.C.	94	83	177	58
11	6410	Athnid	–	Eglish, m.	R.C.	–	R.C.	–	94	–	94	50
[illegible]	6041	Do.	–	Do. f.	R.C.	–	R.C.	–	–	76	76	31
13	578	Burdick,	49	Ballyduag,	R.C.	–	R.C.	R.C.	62	61	113	47
14	574	Do.	–	Clonmichael,	R.C.	–	R.C.	R.C.	91	67	158	63
[illegible]	575	Do.	–	Garranahon, m.	R.C.	–	R.C.	–	60	–	60	30
[illegible]	6305	Do.	–	Do. f.	R.C.	–	R.C.	–	–	63	63	37
[illegible]	[illegible]	Ballycahill,	–	Ballycahill, m.	R.C.	–	R.C.	–	101	–	101	48
[illegible]	1640	Do.	–	Do.[a] f.	R.C.	–	R.C.	–	–	68	68	37
[illegible]	2803	Ballynaclogh	53	Clerahan, m.	R.C.	–	R.C.	–	181	–	181	67
[illegible]	[illegible]	Do.	–	Do. f.	R.C.	–	R.C.	–	–	108	108	41
21	3227	Ballingarry,	47	Killavenoge, m.	–	R.C.	R.C.	–	142	–	142	61
[illegible]	6941	Do.	–	Do. f.	–	R.C.	R.C.	–	–	100	100	38
[illegible]	6084	Do.	56	Pike,	R.C.	–	R.C.	–	60	89	149	41
[illegible]	7048	Do.	47	Mohober,	R.C.	–	R.C.	R.C.	72	86	158	58
[illegible]	7049	Do.	–	Copper,	R.C.	–	R.C.	R.C.	120	41	161	60
[illegible]	7281	Do.	–	Ballybeg	R.C.	–	R.C.	–	67	23	90	39
27	7431	Do.	–	Ballingarry, f.	R.C.	–	R.C.	R.C.	60	99	159	78
[illegible]	4032	Ballytarsna,	53	Crumpa, m.	R.C.	–	R.C.	–	92	–	92	32
[illegible]	7811	Do.	–	Do. f.	R.C.	–	R.C.	–	–	74	73	34
30	6515	Do.	–	Garrinnamore Class Agr. [illegible] m.	Com.	N.R.	R.C.	–	162	–	166	68
31	6941	Do.	–	Do. f.	Com.	N.R.	R.C.	–	–	90	95	19
32	4120	Borrisoleigh,	56	Borrisoleigh, m.	R.C.	–	R.C.	–	149	–	149	64

[a] Including value of Free Residence.

[b] Including value of Free Residence and Garden.

Province of Munster: County of Limerick—*continued.*

Amount paid for Books, Requisites, and Apparatus, at Reduced Prices.	Aid granted by the Board during the Year 1874: In Free Stock of Books, Requisites, and Apparatus.	In Salaries, Premiums, and other Gratuities.	Results Fees, Financial Year.	Amount of Local Payments received in Aid of Teacher's Salary: School Fees.	Subscriptions, Endowments, &c.	Total Local Aid.	Vested or Non-Vested.	Number.
£ s. d.	£ s. d.	£ s. d.	£ s. d.	£ s. d.	£ s. d.	£ s. d.		
1 0 1	—	38 0 0	7 8 8	4 3 0	53 0 0	*57 3 0		209
—	—	81 0 0	10 5 0	6 0 11	35 0 0	*40 0 11		210
21 18 8	—	316 10 8	133 5 2	—	—	—		211
11 17 11	—	43 0 0	17 3 0	100 11 6	—	100 11 6		212
9 18 5	—	220 6 8	40 0 0	—	—	—		213
—	—	77 18 4	21 0 0	6 9 7	—	6 9 7		214
21 3 4	—	220 18 8	118 19 8	—	—	—		215
38 4 2	8 3 6	}					V.C.	216
13 17 0	9 14 9	353 2 0	96 17 0	123 10 0	—	123 10 0	V.C.	217
—	—	}					V.C.	218
14 16 7	8 3 0	29 9 8	61 17 0	—	—	—		219
23 17 0	—	234 0 0	127 17 6	—	100 0 0	100 0 0		220
1 17 9	—	65 8 4	7 17 0	14 6 6	—	14 0 6		221
5 1 1	—	83 5 4	16 17 0	16 18 4	—	16 18 4		222
6 7 5	—	98 0 0	43 18 6	35 10 0	—	35 10 0		223
6 17 11	—	130 10 6	64 17 0	24 0 0	—	24 0 0		224
0 13 0	—	8 10 0	—	—	—	—		225
—	—	—	—	—	—	—		226
7 10 6	—	77 0 0	31 16 0	25 12 0	—	25 12 0		227
3 5 1	—	65 14 4	18 0 0	15 8 10	—	15 8 10		228
6 5 8	—	58 13 4	21 3 0	10 13 6	—	10 13 6		229
1,140 17 6	37 19 9	14073 6 7	3,024 16 8	8,874 11 8	638 18 9	3,994 10 5		

TIPPERARY—[illegible] Schools.

Amount paid for Books, Requisites, and Apparatus, at Reduced Prices.	In Free Stock of Books, Requisites, and Apparatus.	In Salaries, Premiums, and other Gratuities.	Results Fees, Financial Year.	School Fees.	Subscriptions, Endowments, &c.	Total Local Aid.	Vested or Non-Vested.	Number.
6 1 4	—	80 0 0	28 7 0	19 6 0	—	19 3 0		1
5 7 1	—	60 0 0	16 7 0	18 14 0	—	18 14 0		2
3 1 0	—	31 0 0	10 17 6	11 3 8	—	11 3 8		3
0 17 0	8 0 3	58 0 8	57 9 8	35 16 9	—	35 16 8		4
3 6 4	—	46 16 8	24 5 5	7 11 5	—	7 11 5		5
1 5 8	—	31 0 0	18 0 0	8 18 0	—	8 18 0		6
2 16 2	6 3 0	50 0 0	30 11 6	18 10 0	—	18 10 0		7
2 16 7	—	34 4 8	7 6 9	12 6 7	—	12 6 7		8
3 11 2	—	25 10 0	16 0 0	10 10 8	10 0 0	20 10 8		9
4 8 6	—	41 0 0	17 7 0	15 12 0	—	15 12 0		10
6 12 4	—	20 0 0	11 8 0	7 13 4	—	7 13 4	V.C.	11
1 6 6	—	20 0 0	11 18 0	6 14 9	—	6 14 9	V.C.	12
2 10 8	—	44 0 0	19 8 8	6 16 0	5 0 0	*11 16 0		13
5 14 10	—	10 10 0	27 18 0	15 1 6	—	15 1 6		14
1 10 8	—	23 0 0	11 18 0	5 0 0	2 0 0	7 6 0		15
4 16 2	—	20 0 0	19 1 0	6 7 6	5 4 0	*16 11 0		16
1 5 8	—	24 0 0	16 11 0	8 0 0	—	8 0 0	V.T.	17
1 5 6	—	24 0 0	7 12 0	0 0 0	—	0 0 0	V.T.	18
6 12 6	—	64 6 8	18 17 6	20 11 8	—	20 11 8		19
1 12 9	—	26 6 8	10 11 0	7 18 6	—	7 18 0		20
4 0 9	—	58 14 8	24 1 0	13 18 6	5 0 0	*21 12 6		21
1 0 8	—	80 18 4	31 8 0	14 6 0	4 0 0	*18 8 6		22
2 1 8	—	28 10 2	8 7 6	3 19 4	—	3 19 4		23
2 10 6	—	41 0 0	26 10 6	17 16 6	—	17 15 6		24
5 17 4	—	53 6 8	26 18 0	26 9 0	—	26 9 0		25
8 15 7	—	30 0 0	19 10 0	20 17 6	—	20 17 6		26
8 8 6	—	50 18 4	35 16 0	7 7 0	1 10 0	*8 17 0		27
—	—	21 0 0	4 8 6	7 1 5	—	7 1 5	N.V.	28
—	—	20 0 0	6 18 10	7 10 10	0 10 0	*8 0 10	V.T.	29
8 16 7	8 0 0	} 158 6 8	41 0 6	{ 24 10 10	—	24 10 10	V.C.	30
—	—			16 10 0	—	16 10 0	V.C.	31
4 10 1	—	63 10 8	18 10 6	13 1 5	—	13 1 6	V.T.	32

* Including value of Free Garden.

List of Schools in operation on the 31st December, 1871.—

Number.	Roll Number of School.	Parish.	District.	School.	Religious Denomination of Patrons or Correspondents: Clerical.	Lay.	Number and Religious Denomination of Teachers: Principals.	Assistants.	Attendance for the Year: Total number of Pupils on Rolls within the Year 1871: Males.	Fem.	Total.	Average daily attendance
33	4151	Barrinahane,	36	Barrinahane, f.	R.C.	–	R.C.	R.C.	–	196	196	80
34	3694	Do.	–	Kyle Park 1st Cl. Agr.	–	R.C.	R.C.	–	124	–	124	38
35	4251	Do.	–	Do. f.	–	R.C.	R.C.	–	–	109	109	59
36	9081	Do.	–	Barrinahane Workh.	P.L.	Gds.	R.C.	–	16	13	30	22
37	4915	Bruis,	45	Mount Bruis,	R.C.	–	R.C.	R.C.	106	80	186	78
38	8646	Barrane Kly,	45	Barrane,	–	R.C.	R.C.	–	44	25	69	35
39	8547	Bourney,	–	St. Cronan's, m.	R.C.	–	R.C.	–	66	–	66	29
40	6402	Do.	–	Do. f.	R.C.	–	R.C.	–	–	100	100	41
41	8763	Do.	–	Corrigeenmore,	–	R.C.	R.C.	–	20	18	38	27
42	9587	Do.	–	Rouskahane,	R.C.	–	R.C.	–	96	58	153	56
43	7447	Ballygriffin,	46	Ballinahinch,	–	R.C.	R.C.	–	63	51	110	47
44	6806	Burgess Beg,	36	Burgess, m.	R.C.	–	R.C.	–	118	–	118	51
45	6501	Do.	–	Do. f.	R.C.	–	R.C.	–	–	125	125	55
46	6602	Ballymackey,	–	Clash,	R.C.	–	R.C.	–	70	55	125	48
47	2837	Ballysheehan,	45	Dually,	R.C.	–	R.C.	R.C.	84	77	161	65
48	6082	Ballynaclogh,	–	Ballynaclogh,	R.C.	–	R.C.	–	58	36	69	32
49	10636	Ballygibbon,	36	Glenahilty,	R.C.	–	R.C.	–	72	76	148	66
50	7047	Ballymackey,	–	Ballinree,	R.C.	–	R.C.	–	50	58	108	39
51	10626	Boherlahan,	45	Ballytarsna,	R.C.	–	R.C.	R.C.	108	108	217	78
52	10190	Cahir,	53	Cahir Convent, f.	R.C.	–	Nuns		274	410	684	288
53	10187	Do.	–	Do. m.	–	R.C.	R.C.	–	107	–	107	44
54	10884	Do.	–	Do. f.	–	R.C.	R.C.	–	31	40	71	30
55	10800	Do.	–	Garryduagher,	–	R.C.	R.C.	R.C.	76	58	134	64
56	518	Clonoulty,	45	Clonoulty, m.	R.C.	–	R.C.	–	124	–	124	44
57	8456	Do.	–	Do. f.	R.C.	–	R.C.	R.C.	–	130	130	61
58	582	Do.	–	Rossmore,	R.C.	–	R.C.	R.C.	70	70	140	71
59	1131	Do.	–	Ballagh,	R.C.	–	R.C.	–	42	62	104	47
60	8824	Do.	–	Glenough,	R.C.	–	R.C.	–	44	47	91	46
61	10678	Callan,	47	Ballingarry Convt., f.	–	R.C.	Nuns		23	208	230	81
62	861	Clonoura,	53	Clonmore,	R.C.	–	R.C.	–	78	47	125	43
63	1766	Clogher,	45	Cloneyharp,	R.C.	–	R.C.	–	66	31	97	39
64	9210	Do.	–	Tarynheen,	R.C.	–	R.C.	R.C.	110	95	205	88
65	2077	Cloghprior,	36	Carney, f.	R.C.	–	R.C.	–	71	41	112	54
66	2829	Crohane,	45	Marlfield, m.	–	R.C.	R.C.	R.C.	163	–	163	65
67	7489	Do.	–	Do. f.	–	R.C.	R.C.	R.C.	–	151	151	56
68	8040	Do.	–	Croinane,	R.C.	–	R.C.	R.C.	67	48	115	60
69	4648	Colman,	53	Colman,	R.C.	–	R.C.	–	29	35	64	28
70	9610	Cordangan,	46	Cordangan,	–	R.C.	R.C.	–	31	48	79	35
71	6802	Clonbeg,	–	Newtown,	R.C.	–	R.C.	R.C.	102	88	190	71
72	7721	Do.	–	Garranroher,	R.C.	–	R.C.	–	39	39	78	37
73	8072	Do.	–	Lisvernane,	R.C.	–	R.C.	R.C.	86	80	166	61
74	10381	Do.	–	Kilross, m.	R.C.	–	R.C.	–	112	–	112	40
75	10382	Do.	–	Do. f.	R.C.	–	R.C.	R.C.	9	94	103	41
76	6845	Corbally,	36	Corville,	R.C.	–	R.C.	–	45	66	118	45
77	6544	Do.	–	Knock,	R.C.	–	R.C.	–	32	35	67	33
78	3414	Do.	–	Roscrea Workhouse,	P.L.	Gds.	2R.C.	–	35	15	50	30
79	10366	Do.	–	Ballinakill,	–	R.C.	R.C.	–	37	35	72	27
80	3316	Carrick-on-Suir,	52	Carrick-on-Suir Wkh.	P.L.	Gds.	2R.C.	–	48	90	88	38
81	7125	Castletown Arra,	38	Castletown Arra, m.	R.C.	–	R.C.	–	115	–	115	45
82	7119	Do.	–	Do. f.	R.C.	–	R.C.	–	–	119	119	45
83	7756	Do.	–	Carbally, m.	R.C.	–	R.C.	–	118	–	118	40
84	7854	Do.	–	Do. f.	R.C.	–	R.C.	–	–	123	123	49
85	7815	Cullen,	46	Cullen, m.	R.C.	–	R.C.	R.C.	129	–	129	71
86	7276	Do.	–	Do. f.	R.C.	–	R.C.	2R.C.	–	106	155	64
87	9037	Clonbullogue,	–	Tankerstown,	R.C.	–	R.C.	2R.C.	187	99	286	85
88	10232	Derrygrath,	53	Garnavilla,	–	R.C.	R.C.	–	57	52	109	40
89	572	Donohill,	45	Annacarty, m.	R.C.	–	R.C.	R.C.	129	–	129	56
90	8637	Do.	–	Do. f.	R.C.	–	R.C.	R.C.	–	140	140	68
91	1695	Do.	–	Garryshane, m.	R.C.	–	R.C.	R.C.	181	–	181	63
92	1697	Do.	–	Do. f.	R.C.	–	R.C.	R.C.	–	144	144	68
93	8084	Do.	–	Mobarnagh,	R.C.	–	R.C.	R.C.	78	69	141	60
94	8588	Do.	–	Carbane,	R.C.	–	R.C.	R.C.	72	64	136	56
95	580	Drum,	45	Drum, m.	R.C.	–	R.C.	–	74	–	74	29

a Including value of Free Residence. b Including value of Free Residence and Garden.

Province of Munster: County of Tipperary—*continued.*

Amount paid for Books, Requisites, and Apparatus, of Reduced Prices.			Aid granted by the Board during the Year 1874. In Free Stock of Books, Requisites, and Apparatus.	In Salaries, Premiums, and other Gratuities.			Results Fees, Personal Total.			Amount of Local Emoluments received in Aid of Teacher's Salary. School Fees.			Subscriptions, Endowments, &c.			Total Local Aid.	
£	s.	d.	£ s. d.	£	s.	d.	£	s.	d.	£	s.	d.	£	s.	d.	£	s.
6	4	2	—	78	9	5	23	17	6	15	9	1	—			15	6
2	3	6	—	127	13	6	11	0	6	3	4	11	10	0	0	a 18	4
—			—	24	10	0	7	0	6	6	2	7	—			3	6
2	0	0	—	2	10	0	—			—			—			—	
4	2	0	—	43	0	0	26	18	0	19	5	2	—			19	5
—			—	45	0	0	18	2	0	4	4	0	14	0	0	a 18	4
1	7	2	—	30	0	0	7	10	0	6	8	2	—			0	8
2	17	5	—	56	8	4	10	2	6	4	12	0	—			4	12
—			—	24	0	0	Cancelled.			1	0	0	23	10	0	b 24	10
8	2	5	—	44	3	4	16	12	8	8	19	0	—			8	19
8	17	4	—	62	13	4	11	6	8	9	15	0	21	0	0	b 30	15
1	10	4	—	28	10	0	17	2	8	5	19	6	1	10	0	a 7	9
4	7	0	—	43	6	8	19	10	0	14	14	9	—			14	14
2	15	1	—	34	0	6	8	18	0	12	1	6	—			12	1
1	14	9	—	45	10	0	19	14	6	14	16	10	—			14	16
1	5	6	—	34	0	0	9	11	6	6	7	0	—			6	7
1	5	8	—	51	0	0	11	3	0	5	11	1	—			5	11
2	12	10	—	24	0	0	18	0	6	8	0	0	—			8	0
4	0	6	—	44	0	0	21	4	0	14	19	1	—			14	19
14	11	8	—	114	6	4	60	1	0	28	2	7	100	0	0	143	2
8	17	8	—	60	9	8	16	10	6	17	18	6	22	0	0	b 39	13
1	0	8	—	26	9	8	10	19	5	2	18	0	25	0	0	a 27	18
6	1	11	—	64	10	0	31	2	6	22	0	6	10	0	0	a 32	0
—			—	48	10	0	19	3	0	16	10	0	—			16	10
2	1	4	—	40	0	0	24	18	8	12	8	0	—			12	8
—			—	61	10	0	21	0	0	15	6	6	—			15	6
4	3	0	—	32	0	8	11	6	0	5	8	6	—			5	8
8	4	0	—	24	0	8	15	10	9	10	18	8	—			10	18
13	18	0	—	47	0	0	44	14	6	—			—			—	
0	10	3	—	24	0	0	8	0	9	6	5	10	—			6	5
—			—	24	0	0	0	0	8	6	0	0	—			0	0
0	1	6	—	14	0	0	22	8	0	16	0	0	1	0	0	17	0
2	10	0	—	24	0	0	7	7	0	4	18	0	—			4	10
9	0	1	—	60	10	0	62	1	0	15	12	4	20	0	0	b 35	12
8	17	5	—	61	8	4	51	1	6	11	15	0	20	0	0	b 31	15
2	14	7	—	24	5	4	20	9	0	25	16	8	—			25	15
—			—	24	0	0	4	10	10	4	14	0	—			4	14
2	10	6	—	30	0	0	8	10	0	6	15	2	13	0	0	b 18	18
2	10	3	—	44	8	0	20	0	0	17	17	6	3	10	0	b 21	7
1	4	10	—	24	0	0	10	11	0	10	17	6	—			10	17
1	0	10	—	48	18	4	17	1	0	20	12	0	—			20	12
5	0	0	—	34	10	6	29	0	6	19	15	6	—			19	15
3	12	6	—	44	0	0	30	0	0	20	2	6	—			20	2
1	4	11	—	97	1	8	6	13	6	8	10	0	0	10	0	a 5	0
1	6	0	—	35	6	8	4	14	0	8	4	0	—			8	4
4	13	4	—	4	0	0	—			—			—			—	
3	2	4	—	24	0	0	4	15	6	5	8	0	10	0	0	15	8
1	15	0	—	—			—			—			—			—	
0	3	11	—	30	0	0	17	7	8	12	4	0	—			12	4
1	10	1	—	30	15	0	17	7	6	7	17	6	—			7	17
2	15	11	—	36	10	0	12	0	9	8	4	7	—			8	4
2	18	6	—	33	6	8	24	8	6	12	7	9	—			12	7
0	2	10	—	37	10	0	21	18	8	12	5	0	5	0	0	17	5
8	4	9	—	36	5	4	38	12	6	16	7	0	5	0	0	21	7
7	1	0	—	61	13	4	37	11	6	24	14	6	—			24	14
2	0	5	—	32	10	0	17	4	6	9	0	3	11	0	0	c 20	0
1	10	3	—	56	0	0	10	2	6	13	14	0	—			13	14
7	12	6	—	61	0	5	24	10	0	25	3	0	—			25	3
4	3	11	—	51	18	8	20	3	6	17	8	0	—			17	8
4	18	3	—	48	0	0	30	0	0	18	0	8	—			18	0
2	0	11	—	40	0	0	27	12	0	11	6	0	—			11	6
8	12	10	—	44	0	0	18	10	0	10	7	6	—			10	7
0	0	6	—	24	0	0	11	7	0	0	8	0	—			0	8

c Including value of Free Garden.

List of Schools in operation on the 31st December, 1874—

Number.	Roll Number of School.	Parish.	District.	School.		Religious Denomination of Managers or Correspondents.		Religious Denomination of Teachers.		Attendance for the Year.			
										Total number of Pupils on Rolls within the Year 1874.			Average Daily Attendance for the Year 1874.
						Clerical.	Lay.	Principals.	Assistants.	Males.	Fem.	Total.	
96	10177	Drum,	48	Drum,	f.	R.C.	–	R.C.	–	–	66	66	30
97	[illegible]	Dolla,	–	Bollingbrooke,		R.C.	–	R.C.	–	69	–	69	39
98	11109	Do.	–	Do.	f.	R.C.	–	R.C.	–	–	74	74	31
99	545	Dorrha,	50	Carrigeen,	m.	R.C.	–	R.C.	–	109	–	105	44
100	5435	Do.	–	Do.	f.	R.C.	–	R.C.	–	–	58	58	24
101	5377	Do.	–	Aumagh,		R.C.	–	R.C.	–	51	60	111	32
102	7251	Drangan,	53	Drangan,	m.	R.C.	–	R.C.	–	134	–	131	47
103	7252	Do.	–	Do.	f.	R.C.	–	None		–	115	175	58
104	10577	Dangan,	45	Dangan,		R.C.	–	R.C.	–	42	31	74	35
105	4331	Emly,	–	Emly,	m.	R.C.	–	R.C.	–	119	–	119	35
106	1125	Do.	–	Do.	f.	R.C.	–	R.C.	R.C.	–	151	151	77
107	647	Fennor,	45	Graigue,		R.C.	–	R.C.	R.C.	70	51	121	67
108	649	Do.	–	Drand,		R.C.	–	R.C.	–	47	41	88	37
109	9920	Fethard,	56	Fethard Convent,	f.	R.C.	–	None		56	540	596	245*
110	10118	Finnoe,	35	Finnoe,		–	E.C.	E.C.	–	40	30	70	19
111	5411	Glenkeen,	45	Borrisoleigh,	m.	R.C.	–	R.C.	–	163	–	163	47
112	3165	Do.	–	Do.	f.	R.C.	–	R.C.	R.C.	–	155	155	53
113	401	Do.	–	Ileigh,		R.C.	–	R.C.	R.C.	87	75	162	72
114	2742	Do.	–	Curraghgraigue,		R.C.	–	R.C.	R.C.	66	98	164	55
115	4919	Do.	–	Coolderry,		R.C.	–	R.C.	–	78	45	123	50
116	4931	Graystown,	–	Nora,		R.C.	–	R.C.	R.C.	80	63	173	57
117	5111	Glenbane,	46	Glenbane,		R.C.	–	R.C.	R.C.	105	63	168	72
118	7505	Grangemockler,	55	Grangemockler,	m.	R.C.	–	R.C.	–	169	–	169	68
119	7506	Do.	–	Do.	f.	R.C.	–	R.C.	R.C.	–	130	136	73
120	1311	Holycross,	47	Holycross,	m.	R.C.	–	R.C.	–	118	–	114	46
121	1312	Do.	–	Do.	f.	R.C.	–	R.C.	–	–	120	120	41
122	10912	Inishlounaght,	56	Marlfield,		–	R.C.	R.C.	–	48	74	121	56
123	2635	Inch,	–	Inch,	m.	R.C.	–	R.C.	–	99	–	99	41
124	2636	Do.	–	Do.	f.	R.C.	–	R.C.	R.C.	–	104	104	45
125	3605	Kilcooley,	–	New Birmingham,		R.C.	–	R.C.	R.C.	81	79	160	57
126	5107	Kilcash,	55	Kilcash,	m.	R.C.	–	R.C.	–	108	–	108	45
127	5614	Do.	–	Do.	f.	R.C.	–	R.C.	–	–	93	93	41
128	5098	Kilkeary,	–	Killeany,		R.C.	–	R.C.	–	83	53	136	51
129	1324	Kilcommonty,	51	Birdhill,	m.	R.C.	–	R.C.	–	89	–	96	31
130	2071	Do.	–	Do.	f.	R.C.	–	R.C.	–	–	92	92	35
131	1402	Killea,	45	Killea,	m.	R.C.	–	R.C.	–	94	–	91	34
132	1116	Do.	–	Do.	f.	R.C.	–	R.C.	–	–	80	80	34
133	1536	Killaloan,	56	Newtown Anner,		–	E.C.	R.C.	R.C.	117	57	214	63
134	1570	Kilfithmone,	45	Ballinlonty,		R.C.	–	R.C.	R.C.	71	36	107	61
135	1776	Kilnarath,	51	Ballinahinch,	f.	R.C.	–	R.C.	–	40	80	113	49
136	11101	Do.	–	Ballinahinch,		R.C.	–	R.C.	–	61	–	61	12
137	4476	Do.	–	Toor,		R.C.	–	R.C.	–	71	41	110	17
138	10620	Killardry,	48	Ballydrehid,		–	R.C.	R.C.	R.C.	46	67	124	35
139	2525	Kilvellane,	51	Lackamore,		R.C.	–	R.C.	R.C.	70	80	150	51
140	4006	Do.	–	Newport,	m.	R.C.	–	R.C.	R.C.	282	–	281	82
141	4077	Do.	–	Do.	f.	R.C.	–	R.C.	2R.C.	–	277	277	91
142	8546	Kilmore,	45	Silvermines,	m.	R.C.	–	R.C.	–	80	–	80	37
143	8544	Do.	–	Do.	f.	R.C.	–	R.C.	–	–	108	108	39
144	8456	Do.	–	Lissenhall,	m.	R.C.	–	R.C.	–	129	–	129	39
145	8124	Do.	–	Do.	f.	R.C.	–	R.C.	–	–	78	78	35
146	8526	Do.	–	Bishopswood,		R.C.	–	R.C.	R.C.	52	49	101	43
147	2720	Killenaule,	–	Killenaule,	m.	R.C.	–	R.C.	R.C.	173	–	173	63
148	5899	Do.	–	Do.	f.	R.C.	–	R.C.	R.C.	–	183	183	63
149	4772	Do.	–	Graystown,		R.C.	–	R.C.	–	50	30	80	35
150	4074	Do.	–	Lanespark,		R.C.	–	R.C.	–	63	33	96	19
151	4075	Do.	–	Moyglass,		R.C.	–	R.C.	–	40	68	114	45
152	5627	Kilbarron,	38	Kilbarron,	m.	R.C.	–	R.C.	–	63	–	63	31
153	8034	Do.	–	Do.	f.	R.C.	–	R.C.	–	–	77	77	33
154	3099	Kilnaneave,	45	Kilnaneave,		R.C.	–	R.C.	R.C.	84	77	171	73
155	3144	Knockgraffon,	56	New Inn,	m.	R.C.	–	R.C.	–	115	–	115	49
156	3179	Do.	–	Do.	f.	R.C.	–	R.C.	–	–	114	114	53
157	10580	Do.	–	Knockgraffon,		R.C.	–	R.C.	R.C.	101	79	180	51
158	6743	Killavinoge,	45	Clonmore,	m.	R.C.	–	R.C.	–	65	–	65	33

* Including value of Free Residence.

Province of MUNSTER: County of TIPPERARY—*continued.*

Amount paid for Books, Requisites, and Apparatus, at Reduced Prices.	Aid granted by the Board during the Year 1874: In Free stock of Books, Requisites, and Apparatus.	Aid granted by the Board during the Year 1874: In Salaries, Premiums, and other Gratuities.	Aid granted by the Board during the Year 1874: Results Fees, Financial Year.	Amount of Local Emoluments received in Aid of Teacher's Salary: School Fees.	Amount of Local Emoluments received in Aid of Teacher's Salary: Subscriptions, Endowments, &c.	Amount of Local Emoluments received in Aid of Teacher's Salary: Total Local Aid.	Vested or Non-Vested.	Number.
£ s. d.	£ s. d.	£ s. d.	£ s. d.	£ s. d.	£ s. d.	£ s. d.		
1 4 11	—	30 0 0	15 17 0	3 17 6	—	3 17 6		96
4 19 8	—	24 0 0	6 8 6	6 17 6	—	6 17 6		97
2 18 6	4 10 0	15 0 0	13 5 6	8 0 0	—	8 0 0		98
8 7 8	—	54 16 8	14 7 0	17 12 4	—	17 12 4	V.T.	99
3 3 3	—	30 0 0	8 8 0	6 13 6	—	6 13 6	V.T.	100
0 10 9	—	24 0 0	3 10 0	1 11 0	—	1 11 0	A.	101
3 9 10	—	24 0 0	11 18 6	4 10 7	—	4 10 7		102
10 10 5	—	40 1 0	33 10 6	18 5 10	—	18 5 10		103
1 0 8	—	24 0 0	11 0 6	13 4 6	—	13 4 6		104
3 12 6	—	30 0 0	7 7 8	8 0 0	—	8 0 0		105
1 6 7	—	44 0 0	18 18 0	10 0 0	3 0 0	b 18 0 0		106
3 8 8	—	40 6 8	24 10 0	12 18 8	5 0 0	b 17 15 6		107
3 13 10	—	24 0 0	7 7 0	3 9 0	—	3 9 0		108
20 5 9	—	101 8 0	57 5 0	—	—	—		109
1 10 3	—	20 0 0	8 11 6	5 0 0	12 0 0	17 0 0		110
0 19 10	—	30 10 0	17 13 6	11 6 6	—	11 6 6		111
4 2 3	—	54 8 4	14 13 0	13 8 3	—	13 8 3		112
4 10 6	—	51 8 6	29 11 0	14 15 0	—	14 15 0		113
2 7 8	—	50 0 0	15 17 6	10 0 0	—	10 0 0	V.T.	114
2 10 0	—	31 0 0	21 11 0	11 15 6	—	11 15 6		115
—	—	34 0 0	0 10 0	11 3 5	—	11 3 5		116
5 0 0	—	56 0 0	29 11 6	20 0 0	—	20 0 0		117
8 5 0	—	29 0 0	15 18 8	14 10 9	—	14 10 9		118
6 19 11	—	30 8 8	31 4 0	17 10 0	—	17 10 0		119
2 11 7	—	28 10 0	13 15 6	8 17 0	—	8 17 0	V.T.	120
5 1 2	—	27 10 0	12 5 6	8 5 0	—	8 5 0	V.T.	121
3 19 8	—	56 6 8	14 11 0	7 11 1	16 0 0	b 23 11 1		122
3 9 9	—	24 0 0	18 10 6	6 10 0	—	6 10 0	V.T.	123
9 18 0	—	42 3 4	21 17 6	9 8 6	—	9 8 6	V.T.	124
—	—	52 0 0	19 5 0	13 0 6	5 0 0	b 19 0 0		125
1 11 9	—	25 6 8	11 14 6	6 16 0	6 10 0	b 13 6 0	V.C.	126
1 5 8	—	24 0 0	14 10 0	7 11 3	—	7 11 3	V.C.	127
6 18 1	—	32 0 0	18 10 6	15 5 0	—	15 5 0		128
0 10 0	—	24 0 0	8 18 0	9 5 4	—	9 5 4	V.T.	129
1 6 0	—	20 0 0	9 11 0	5 10 6	—	5 10 6	V.T.	130
3 7 10	—	41 6 8	10 18 8	7 7 6	—	7 7 6	V.T.	131
3 15 5	—	30 15 4	18 1 0	6 16 0	—	6 16 0	V.T.	132
7 11 8	—	36 3 4	34 8 0	9 17 0	34 0 0	b 43 17 0		133
5 7 4	—	34 6 8	22 8 6	6 1 0	—	6 1 0	V.T.	134
—	—	31 1 8	—	8 10 0	—	8 10 0		135
1 16 8	4 10 0	11 6 8	—	3 10 0	—	3 10 0		136
9 16 10	—	31 0 0	18 0 6	5 3 6	—	5 3 6	V.T.	137
1 15 4	—	60 0 0	11 7 8	5 5 6	5 0 0	b 10 5 6	V.T.	138
1 5 3	—	44 0 0	25 9 0	3 7 6	—	3 7 6	V.T.	139
4 5 0	—	74 0 0	21 5 6	5 15 8	—	5 15 8	V.T.	140
4 8 11	—	80 0 0	38 15 6	12 14 6	4 0 0	b 16 14 6	V.T.	141
9 17 11	—	40 0 0	9 13 6	6 16 0	—	6 16 0		142
1 12 0	—	32 0 0	14 10 6	7 18 10	—	7 18 10		143
1 5 7	—	21 0 0	13 9 0	6 0 6	—	6 0 6		144
—	—	30 0 0	9 9 6	5 5 6	—	5 5 6		145
8 0 6	—	44 0 0	18 8 0	5 10 0	—	5 10 0		146
5 17 4	—	68 16 8	37 5 6	14 8 6	—	14 8 6		147
3 0 4	—	83 18 4	46 5 6	17 5 0	—	17 5 0		148
6 6 7	—	32 0 0	42 8 6	11 19 6	—	11 19 6		149
—	—	24 0 0	8 13 4	8 11 6	—	8 11 6		150
9 1 7	—	24 0 0	18 9 6	10 19 11	—	10 19 11		151
1 5 8	—	34 0 0	5 16 0	5 0 4	—	5 0 4		152
2 6 5	—	20 0 0	6 8 6	2 11 6	—	2 11 6		153
6 17 2	—	48 10 0	37 4 6	16 10 1	—	16 10 1	V.T.	154
6 19 6	—	64 8 8	16 5 0	19 19 0	5 0 0	b 24 19 0		155
1 10 7	—	35 15 4	15 5 0	19 0 8	—	19 0 8		156
2 8 11	—	47 10 0	15 12 0	14 10 0	4 10 0	b 19 0 0		157
3 15 5	—	24 0 0	9 5 6	4 6 8	1 10 0	b 5 16 8		158

b Including value of Free Residence and Garden.

List of Schools in operation on the 31st December, 1874.—

Number.	Roll Number of School.	Parish.	Barony.	School.	Religious Denomination of Patrons or Correspondents: Clerical.	Lay.	Teachers and Religious Denomination: Principals.	Assistants.	Attendance for the Year: Total number of Pupils on the Rolls within the Year 1874: Males.	Fem.	Total.	Average Daily Attendance.
159	7196	Killavinoge,	43	Clonmore, f.	R.C.	–	R.C.	R.C.	29	137	166	60
160	7139	Do.	–	Shanaskill,	R.C.	–	R.C.	R.C.	69	70	139	63
161	6186	Killoscully,	61	Killoscully,	R.C.	–	R.C.	R.C.	82	61	143	76
162	6213	Do.	–	Shallee,	R.C.	–	R.C.	–	73	94	167	60
163	9741	Do.	–	Drumbane, m.	R.C.	–	R.C.	–	66	–	66	35
164	9790	Do.	–	Do. f.	R.C.	–	R.C.	–	–	89	95	35
165	11053	Do.	–	Glenculloo,	–	R.C.	R.C.	–	24	49	74	35
166	[illegible]	Killodiernan,	56	Kildangan, m.	R.C.	–	R.C.	–	93	–	93	34
167	[illegible]	Do.	–	Do. f.	R.C.	–	R.C.	–	–	83	83	41
168	6918	Kilgrant,	63	Powerstown,	R.C.	–	R.C.	–	64	34	98	45
169	7980	Kilruane,	26	Kilruane, m.	R.C.	–	R.C.	–	108	–	108	35
170	10014	Do.	–	Do. f.	R.C.	–	R.C.	–	–	81	81	34
171	7697	Kilvemnon,	62	Clonagoose, m.	R.C.	–	R.C.	–	156	–	156	67
172	7622	Do.	–	Do. f.	R.C.	–	R.C.	–	–	118	118	63
173	7807	Kilshelan,	–	Kilshelan, m.	R.C.	–	R.C.	–	80	–	80	38
174	6199	Do.	–	Do. f.	R.C.	–	R.C.	–	–	84	84	36
175	9861	Kilmurry,	–	Ballyneal, m.	R.C.	–	R.C.	–	119	–	119	41
176	8332	Do.	–	Do. f.	R.C.	–	R.C.	–	–	119	119	59
177	6499	Kilbarry,	36	Kilbarry, m.	–	E.C.	R.C.	–	80	49	129	54
178	9428	Do.	–	Do.[a] f.	–	E.C.	–	–	–	–	–	–
179	[illegible]	Lorrha,	–	Lorrha,[a] m.	R.C.	–	–	–	–	–	–	–
180	6011	Do.	–	Do. f.	R.C.	–	R.C.	–	–	91	91	53
181	6919	Do.	–	Lehinch,	R.C.	–	R.C.	–	51	16	67	30
182	4320	Loughkeen,	–	Carrig, temp.	R.C.	–	R.C.	–	65	36	101	34
183	4605	Do.	–	Riverstown,	R.C.	–	R.C.	–	50	39	89	37
184	9771	Lisronagh,	63	Lisronagh, m.	R.C.	–	R.C.	–	83	–	83	33
185	9917	Do.	–	Do. f.	R.C.	–	R.C.	–	–	60	60	33
186	7344	Loughmoe,	43	Loughmoe, f.	R.C.	–	R.C.	–	–	199	199	59
187	7894	Do., West,	–	Do. m.	R.C.	–	R.C.	–	129	–	129	47
188	7799	Lismalin,	47	Ballydonnell,[a]	R.C.	–	–	–	–	–	–	–
189	[illegible]	Moyne,	47	Moyne, m.	R.C.	–	R.C.	–	85	–	85	35
190	6732	Do.	–	Do. f.	R.C.	–	R.C.	–	–	89	89	36
191	[illegible]	Do.	–	Kilcomahill,	R.C.	–	R.C.	–	27	30	57	23
192	[illegible]	Moyaliff,	–	Clareen,	R.C.	–	R.C.	–	61	48	109	44
193	8427	Do.	–	Reakeen, m.	R.C.	–	R.C.	–	85	–	85	35
194	8438	Do.	–	Do. f.	R.C.	–	R.C.	–	–	86	86	35
195	[illegible]	Moycarky,	–	Moycarky,	R.C.	–	R.C.	R.C.	91	61	152	59
196	[illegible]	Mortlestown,	55	Ballingarry,	R.C.	–	R.C.	–	40	67	107	44
197	[illegible]	Mowney,	64	Carrig, m.	R.C.	–	R.C.	–	83	–	83	11
198	6847	Do.	–	Do. f.	R.C.	–	R.C.	–	–	70	70	27
199	9344	Modreeny,	–	Newtown,[f]	–	–	Disc.	–	–	–	–	–
200	[illegible]	Do.	–	Cloghjordan,[f]	R.C.	–	–	–	–	–	–	–
201	7880	Newcastle,	59	Croughshancony,	R.C.	–	R.C.	–	82	98	180	49
202	9249	Do.	–	Newcastle, m.	R.C.	–	R.C.	–	144	–	144	55
203	[illegible]	Do.	–	Do. f.	R.C.	–	R.C.	R.C.	–	114	114	60
204	7592	Nenagh,	26	Nenagh Convent, f.	–	R.C.	Nuns		–	569	569	299
205	8516	Do.	–	Do. Workhouse,	P.L.	Gds.	R.C.	–	45	69	114	73
206	8520	Do.	–	Do. Gaol, m.	–	–	R.C.	–	77	–	77	23
207	8521	Do.	–	Do.[a] Do. f.	–	–	R.C.	–	–	–	–	–
208	[illegible]	Newtown Lennan,	52	Upper Newtown, m.	R.C.	–	R.C.	–	114	–	114	44
209	[illegible]	Do.	–	Do. f.	R.C.	–	R.C.	–	–	125	125	60
210	[illegible]	Oughterleague,	48	Kennedyville,	R.C.	–	R.C.	R.C.	104	113	217	73
211	10184	Rathronan,	65	Rathkeevin,	R.C.	–	R.C.	R.C.	90	71	161	61
212	1704	Roscrea,	86	Roscrea, m.	R.C.	–	R.C.	R.C.	269	–	269	118
213	9153	Do.	–	Airhill Convent, f.	–	R.C.	Nuns		–	685	685	275
214	8061	Rathsaveage,	–	Lisdaff,	R.C.	–	R.C.	R.C.	84	69	143	34
215	[illegible]	Rathcool,	65	Coolmoyne,	R.C.	–	R.C.	–	69	49	131	57
216	4515	Rahelty,	45	Rahelty,	R.C.	–	R.C.	R.C.	87	69	146	35
217	[illegible]	Relickmurry and Athassel,	46	Thomastown,	R.C.	–	R.C.	R.C.	82	96	179	76
218	7894	Do.	–	Laganstown,	R.C.	–	R.C.	–	29	44	73	33
219	7920	Do.	–	Golden, m.	R.C.	–	R.C.	–	86	–	85	29
220	7921	Do.	–	Do. f.	R.C.	–	R.C.	–	–	69	81	30

[a] Including value of Free Garden.

[b] Including value of Free Residence and Garden.

Province of Munster: County of Tipperary—*continued.*

Amount paid for Books, Requisites, and Apparatus, at Reduced Prices.	Aid granted by the Board during the Year 1874. In Free Stock of Books, Requisites, and Apparatus.	In Salaries, Premiums, and other Gratuities.	Results Fees, Financial Year.	Amount of Local Contributions received in Aid of Teacher's Salary. School Fees.	Subscriptions, Endowments, &c.	Total Local Aid.	Vested or Non-Vested.	Roll Number.
£ s. d.	£ s. d.	£ s. d.	£ s. d.	£ s. d.	£ s. d.	£ s. d.		
1 9 6	—	46 13 4	23 15 0	6 8 0	—	0 9 6		159
8 8 2	—	30 13 4	15 0 6	8 10 0	1 0 0	*3 10 0		160
5 19 0	—	37 8 8	24 0 0	8 10 0	—	0 10 0		161
8 6 7	—	23 8 4	9 6 0	5 1 0	—	5 1 0		162
5 3 8	—	20 1 8	13 18 8	—	27 0 0	*27 0 0		163
—	—	30 0 0	13 3 8	—	6 0 0	6 0 0		164
1 18 5	4 10 0	15 11 1	9 3 6	7 18 0	—	7 18 0		165
—	—	23 0 0	5 10 8	4 9 3	—	4 9 8		166
1 16 0	—	20 0 0	5 15 0	8 4 8	—	8 4 8		167
8 4 8	—	30 0 0	19 13 6	13 4 5	—	13 4 5		168
3 13 4	—	21 10 0	18 1 8	9 16 9	—	9 16 9		169
1 11 10	—	24 0 0	21 10 0	9 16 5	—	9 16 5		170
4 11 9	1 0 0	21 0 0	28 8 0	11 8 0	—	11 8 0		171
8 8 0	1 0 0	28 0 0	10 18 0	14 8 9	—	14 8 0		172
—	—	24 0 0	0 8 6	9 9 2	4 10 0	*13 10 2		173
8 0 0	—	21 0 0	10 17 0	5 8 5	4 10 0	*9 18 5		174
2 11 8	—	24 0 0	12 7 8	18 7 0	—	18 7 0		175
8 1 6	—	28 10 0	14 4 8	10 18 5	—	10 18 5		176
1 17 0	—	18 0 0	0 14 6	6 8 8	13 0 0	*19 8 8		177
—	—	—	—	—	—	—		178
1 9 8	—	18 18 4	—	—	—	—	V.T.	179
1 11 5	—	32 2 4	0 0 0	5 18 4	—	5 18 4	V.T.	180
—	—	21 0 0	8 8 0	1 11 9	1 10 0	*8 1 9		181
3 14 8	—	41 18 4	8 11 6	0 15 1	—	0 15 1		182
2 10 8	—	24 0 0	9 17 6	13 8 5	—	13 8 5		183
1 12 7	—	20 0 0	7 15 6	10 7 1	—	10 7 1		184
8 0 11	—	21 0 0	7 19 4	0 10 10	—	0 10 10		185
9 14 7	—	20 0 0	0 17 0	5 17 8	—	5 17 8		186
4 8 0	—	37 8 4	15 15 6	18 1 6	—	18 1 6		187
—	—	—	—	—	—	—		188
—	—	24 0 0	4 7 6	8 18 10	—	8 18 10	V.T.	189
0 10 2	—	24 0 0	7 1 0	1 7 0	—	1 7 0		190
0 10 0	—	24 0 0	8 9 6	1 16 0	—	1 16 0		191
1 4 10	—	24 0 0	14 17 6	14 7 6	—	14 7 6		192
1 8 8	—	24 0 0	6 18 6	8 0 0	—	8 0 0		193
0 10 8	—	20 0 0	1 9 4	8 8 2	—	8 8 2		194
4 9 3	—	49 10 0	19 10 6	8 10 0	—	8 10 0	V.T.	195
2 0 4	—	30 0 0	18 8 7	13 18 6	—	13 18 0		196
5 10 6	—	32 0 0	10 19 6	18 18 6	—	13 18 0		197
1 18 10	—	20 0 0	31 8 6	8 2 8	1 0 0	*9 2 8		198
—	—	—	—	—	—	—		199
—	—	—	—	—	—	—		200
1 9 8	—	24 0 0	31 12 0	12 1 0	—	12 1 0		201
5 14 8	—	33 0 0	10 8 8	12 4 8	—	12 4 8		202
8 2 10	—	43 0 0	22 4 6	15 6 0	—	15 6 0		203
14 8 0	—	110 10 2	61 8 6	21 8 8	—	21 8 8		204
—	—	11 10 0	—	—	—	—		205
—	—	—	—	—	—	—		206
—	—	—	—	—	—	—		207
1 8 9	—	24 0 0	10 18 0	8 8 8	—	8 8 0		208
3 10 8	—	35 0 0	18 3 1	8 14 10	—	8 14 10		209
5 0 11	—	50 0 0	11 10 0	16 10 0	—	16 10 0		210
4 3 1	—	58 8 4	15 4 6	16 10 9	—	16 10 9		211
29 17 0	—	144 11 8	45 10 0	65 4 4	15 0 0	81 4 4	V.T.	212
20 0 4	—	27 15 4	58 17 6	18 8 4	15 0 0	33 8 4	N.	213
4 12 8	—	41 0 0	13 8 8	18 8 11	—	18 8 11		214
—	—	24 0 0	8 4 6	5 0 0	—	5 0 0		215
8 0 1	—	65 0 0	12 18 0	6 12 0	—	6 12 6		216
6 6 7	—	58 10 8	17 14 0	14 10 0	—	14 10 0	V.T.	217
1 8 11	—	20 0 0	18 8 0	5 0 0	5 0 0	*10 0 0		218
8 11 7	—	22 0 0	6 4 6	—	—	—		219
1 14 8	—	20 0 0	7 18 6	6 7 8	—	6 7 8		220

* Including value of Free Residences. † Suspended. ‡ No returns; Teacher not recognised. § No Returns.

List of Schools in operation on the 31st December, 1874.—

Number.	Roll Number of School.	Parish.	District.	School.	Religious Denomination of Manager or Correspondent: Clerical.	Lay.	Popular and Religious Denomination of Teachers: Principals.	Assistants.	Attendance for the Year: Total number of Pupils on Rolls within the Year 1874: Males.	Fem.	Total.	Average daily attendance.
221	9203	[illegible]	46	Cloughleigh, * . .	–	–	–	–	–	–	–	–
222	8450	Do. . .	–	Ballyvarren, . m.	–	R.C.	R.C.	–	67	–	67	33
223	8460	Do. . .	–	Do. . . f.	–	R.C.	R.C.	–	–	86	86	31
224	7478	Rathlynin,	–	Curraghpoor, . .	R.C.	–	R.C.	R.C.	86	73	164	67
225	5??	St. John Baptist,	53	Cashel, . . m.	R.C.	–	R.C.	R.C.	319	–	243	84
226	4911	Do. . .	–	Do. Convent, f.	–	R.C.	Nuns		67	650	718	464
227	3768	Do. . .	–	Do. Workhouse,	P.L.	Gds.	2R.C.	R.C.	92	71	163	96
228	3070	Do. . .	–	[illegible], . .	R.C.	–	R.C.	–	65	64	129	46
229	5??	Solloghodmore,	46	Monard, . . m.	R.C.	–	R.C.	R.C.	109	2	171	50
230	2012	Do. . .	–	Do. . . f.	R.C.	–	R.C.	R.C.	–	127	127	64
231	6318	Solloghodbeg, .	–	Newtown, . m.	R.C.	–	R.C.	–	133	–	133	44
232	6317	Do. . .	–	Do. . . f.	R.C.	–	R.C.	R.C.	–	98	98	41
233	7010	Shanrahan, .	53	Burncourt, . m.	R.C.	–	R.C.	–	118	–	118	65
234	3073	Do. . .	–	Do. . . f.	R.C.	–	R.C.	R.C.	–	127	127	62
235	4132	Do. . .	–	Clogheen, . m.	R.C.	–	R.C.	R.C.	202	–	202	96
236	4133	Do. . .	–	Do. . . f.	R.C.	–	R.C.	R.C.	–	219	213	84
237	8450	Do. . .	–	Do. Workhouse,	–	R.C.	R.C.	–	40	–	46	36
238	4060	St. Patrick's Rock, . .	–	Mocklershill, . .	R.C.	–	R.C.	–	40	27	67	36
239	4071	Shronell, . .	46	Shronell, . .	R.C.	–	R.C.	R.C.	82	65	149	84
240	6633	St. Mary's, .	53	Clonmel Dis. Mod. m.	Com.	N.E.	R.C.	R.C.	165	–	165	77
241	6634	Do. . .	–	Do. do. f.	Com.	N.E.	R.C.	Pres.	–	93	93	40
242	6635	Do. . .	–	Do. do. i.	Com.	N.E.	R.C.	–	39	32	70	35
243	3224	Do. . .	–	Do. Workhouse,	P.L.	Gds.	2R.C.	2R.C.	82	90	172	96
244	692	Toem, . .	46	Hollyford, . .	R.C.	–	R.C.	2R.C.	104	137	241	115
245	1706	Do. . .	–	Cappawhite, . m.	R.C.	–	R.C.	R.C.	224	–	224	90
246	1707	Do. . .	–	Do. . . f.	R.C.	–	R.C.	2R.C.	84	163	240	164
247	614	Tullamain, .	53	Rosegreen, . .	R.C.	–	R.C.	–	69	69	118	54
248	513	Templetouhy, .	42	Toher, . . .	R.C.	–	R.C.	–	65	65	101	38
249	2443	Do. . .	–	Templetouhy, . m.	–	R.C.	R.C.	–	94	–	94	63
250	2444	Do. . .	–	Do. . . f.	–	R.C.	R.C.	–	–	123	123	61
251	1361	Templebeg, .	–	Kilbrannish, . m.	R.C.	–	R.C.	–	182	–	182	54
252	8491	Do. . .	–	Do. . . f.	R.C.	–	R.C.	R.C.	–	179	179	80
253	8640	Do. . .	–	Newtown, . . f.	R.C.	–	R.C.	R.C.	80	97	180	69
254	7656	Tipperary, .	46	Tipperary, . m.	R.C.	–	R.C.	3R.C.	264	–	264	113
255	1492	Do. . .	–	Do. . . f.	R.C.	–	R.C.	3R.C.	67	108	273	117
256	9452	Do. . .	–	Do. Convent, f.	R.C.	–	Nuns.		–	778	778	317
257	9903	Do. . .	–	Do. . . m. i.	R.C.	–	R.C.	3R.C.	282	–	282	80
258	8140	Do. . .	–	Do. Workhouse,	P.L.	Gds.	R.C.	R.C.	124	50	174	66
259	2457	Templemore, .	46	Templemore, . m.	R.C.	–	R.C.	R.C.	160	–	160	90
260	8417	Do. . .	–	Do. . Conv. f.	–	R.C.	Nuns.		–	289	289	154
261	2458	Do. . .	–	Do. . . prep.	R.C.	–	R.C.	R.C.	146	–	146	77
262	3699	Templeree, .	46	Grenane, . .	–	R.C.	R.C.	–	57	13	73	91
263	4564	Do. . .	–	Ballyhuss, . .	R.C.	–	R.C.	–	40	31	71	62
264	7762	Do. . .	42	Castle Iney, . m.	R.C.	–	R.C.	–	73	–	73	80
265	7763	Do. . .	–	Do. . . f.	R.C.	–	R.C.	–	–	93	93	61
266	4600	Templederry, .	–	Templederry, . .	R.C.	–	R.C.	–	66	47	112	42
267	8680	Do. . .	–	Clohinch, . . m.	R.C.	–	R.C.	–	114	–	114	46
268	9001	Do. . .	–	Do. . . f.	R.C.	–	R.C.	R.C.	–	113	113	49
269	9304	Do. . .	–	Curreeny, . .	R.C.	–	R.C.	R.C.	86	78	164	56
270	4003	Twomileborris, .	–	Twomileborris, .	R.C.	–	R.C.	R.C.	91	78	168	60
271	4004	Do. . .	–	Littleton, . .	R.C.	–	R.C.	R.C.	97	111	208	72
272	7416	Toem, . .	46	Cahirvahalla, . .	R.C.	–	R.C.	R.C.	145	46	161	67
273	7258	Templetenny, .	56	Skeheenarinky, m.	–	R.C.	R.C.	R.C.	219	–	219	79
274	7259	Do. . .	–	Do. . . f.	–	R.C.	R.C.	R.C.	–	169	169	79
275	10436	Do. . .	–	Ballyporeen, . m.	R.C.	–	R.C.	R.C.	240	–	240	121
276	10437	Do. . .	–	Do. . . f.	R.C.	–	R.C.	R.C.	–	220	220	60
277	10423	Templeneiry, .	46	Ardane, . . m.	Com.	N.E.	R.C.	–	61	–	61	32
278	10424	Do. . .	–	Do. . . f.	Com.	N.E.	R.C.	–	–	56	53	35
279	10425	Do. . .	–	Ballagh, . . m.	–	–	–	–	–	–	–	–
280	10422	Do. . .	–	Do. . . f.	Com.	N.E.	R.C.	R.C.	18	164	182	60
281	9306	Tubbrid, . .	53	Ballylooby, . m.	R.C.	–	R.C.	R.C.	134	–	131	79
282	9307	Do. . .	–	Do. . . f.	R.C.	–	R.C.	R.C.	–	172	182	57

* Temporarily closed.

† Including value of Free Residence.

Province of Munster: County of Tipperary—*continued.*

Amount paid for Books, Requisites, and Apparatus, of Reduced Prices	Aid granted by the Board during the Year 1874: In Free Stock of Books, Requisites, and Apparatus	In Salaries, Premiums, and other Gratuities	Results Fees, Financial Year	Amount of Local Endowments received in Aid of Teacher's Salary: School Fees	Subscriptions, Endowments, &c.	Total Local Aid	Vested or Non-vested	Number
£ s. d.	£ s. d.	£ s. d.	£ s. d.	£ s. d.	£ s. d.	£ s. d.		
—	—	—	—	—	—	—		220
8 10 6	—	22 0 0	11 0 0	6 7 6	5 0 0	*11 7 6	V.C.	221
9 17 4	—	49 15 0	16 8 0	7 0 0	—	7 0 0	V.C.	222
3 18 0	—	48 10 0	20 18 4	16 10 0	—	16 10 0		223
8 2 8	—	61 0 0	23 7 0	6 12 3	80 0 0	86 12 3		224
21 7 5	—	118 8 1	58 2 0	—	60 0 0	60 0 0		225
5 18 1	—	2 0 0	—	—	—	—		226
1 13 8	—	24 0 0	0 15 8	0 10 0	—	0 10 0		227
7 11 1	—	70 15 6	46 8 8	16 14 0	17 15 0	*34 9 0		228
6 19 10	—	179 0 0	24 18 6	21 6 7	15 0 0	*36 6 7		229
5 18 4	—	35 1 8	16 19 0	9 15 0	—	9 15 0		230
1 11 6	—	46 0 0	15 12 8	—	—	—		231
2 9 0	—	87 18 4	16 16 4	9 9 0	10 4 0	19 13 0	V.T.	232
2 16 3	—	48 10 8	20 15 6	19 15 4	7 4 6	27 19 4	V.T.	233
2 15 8	—	51 6 8	28 7 4	20 18 1	—	20 18 1	V.T.	234
7 10 4	—	85 0 0	23 14 6	27 13 3	—	27 13 3	V.T.	235
6 9 5	—	1 10 0	—	—	—	—		236
1 6 10	—	24 0 0	3 6 0	4 14 6	—	4 14 6		238
5 10 3	—	33 8 4	19 19 0	13 7 0	—	13 7 0		239
15 12 5	7 15 5	601 0 8	87 16 0	70 11 7	—	70 11 7	V.C.	240
6 5 9	17 7 8						V.C.	241
—	—						V.C.	242
6 18 7	—	3 0 0	—	—	—	—		243
5 15 0	—	104 0 0	40 0 6	19 4 6	—	19 4 6		244
6 4 2	—	67 18 4	28 0 4	18 19 0	—	18 19 0		245
8 19 9	—	80 10 0	33 1 8	22 15 8	—	22 15 8		246
6 1 11	—	65 10 0	11 0 6	12 18 0	—	12 18 0		247
1 7 3	—	20 0 0	13 15 8	5 17 6	—	5 17 6		248
4 9 7	—	20 0 0	10 5 8	4 18 0	6 10 0	*11 8 0	V.T.	249
6 12 0	—	36 18 7	14 12 0	3 4 0	1 10 0	4 14 0	V.C.	250
2 2 9	—	24 0 0	18 10 6	10 0 0	—	10 0 0		251
2 12 0	—	44 0 0	15 17 0	10 5 0	—	10 5 0		252
4 0 6	—	62 16 8	17 19 0	10 2 6	—	10 2 6		253
5 6 2	—	118 16 8	18 1 6	24 10 6	5 0 0	29 10 6	V.T.	254
9 1 6	—	81 10 8	28 5 0	25 6 8	6 0 0	*61 6 8	V.T.	255
40 9 11	—	188 12 0	66 18 0	—	—	—		256
2 11 0	—	108 8 4	19 0 6	0 6 6	—	0 6 6		257
4 3 0	—	1 10 0	—	—	—	—		258
1 5 0	—	61 3 4	20 4 0	15 5 4	—	18 8 4	B.	259
24 9 9	—	81 0 8	41 7 6	9 5 0	—	9 5 0		260
1 19 5	—	56 0 0	10 4 0	15 11 8	—	15 11 8	B.	261
2 7 10	—	30 0 0	6 12 0	9 15 6	—	9 15 6	V.T.	262
2 0 7	—	24 0 0	4 6 6	6 16 0	—	6 16 0	V.C.	263
1 0 0	—	18 0 0	5 11 6	2 17 8	—	2 17 8		264
8 8 8	—	20 0 0	14 6 6	6 19 0	—	6 19 0		265
9 5 9	—	22 0 0	18 6 0	23 18 6	—	23 18 6	V.T.	266
1 8 9	—	28 10 0	18 1 6	9 8 4	—	9 8 4		267
0 4 6	—	46 0 0	23 9 0	8 11 4	—	8 11 4		268
3 6 0	—	44 0 0	10 17 6	8 0 6	—	8 0 6		269
8 0 0	—	65 10 0	12 18 0	6 5 0	—	6 5 0	V.T.	270
2 10 0	—	56 10 0	14 8 0	7 17 11	—	7 17 11	V.T.	271
—	—	56 0 0	17 18 0	16 15 0	5 0 9	*21 15 0		272
6 7 8	—	54 0 0	6 12 0	—	30 10 0	*34 10 0	V.C.	273
4 12 11	—	83 8 4	20 15 4	—	23 10 0	*21 10 0	V.C.	274
4 8 5	—	75 9 0	29 14 10	29 14 5	—	27 14 5		275
—	—	63 9 0	25 17 4	27 5 10	—	27 5 10		276
1 14 9	—	24 9 0	11 18 4	8 8 6	—	8 0 6	V.T.	277
—	—	30 0 0	13 4 6	6 19 0	—	6 19 0	V.T.	278
2 19 1	—	85 10 0	9 10 0	—	—	—	V.T.	279
6 13 8	—	48 0 0	23 15 6	14 6 7	—	14 6 7	V.T.	280
3 1 0	—	46 0 0	24 8 0	35 7 8	—	35 7 8		281
5 0 0	—	57 5 6	34 3 6	24 10 7	—	24 10 7		282

* Including value of Free Residence and Garden.

List of Schools in operation on the 31st December, 1874.—

Number.	Roll Number of School.	Parish.	District.	School.	Religious Denomination of Managers or Correspondents: Clerical.	Lay.	Religious Denomination of Teachers: Principals.	Assistants.	Attendance for the Year: Total number of Pupils on Rolls within the Year 1874: Males.	Fem.	Total.	Average Daily Attendance for the Year.
283	7092	Thurles,	43	Lough,	R.C.	–	R.C.	–	49	62	101	62
284	8168	Do.	–	Thurles Convent, f.	–	R.C.	Nuns		46	576	622	234
285	3617	Do.	–	Do. Workhouse,*	P.L. Gds.		–	–	–	–	–	–
286	10249	Templeachally,	51	Ballina, m.	R.C.	–	R.C.	–	146	–	146	56
287	7839	Do.	–	Do. f.	R.C.	–	R.C.	R.C.	–	197	197	55
288	6196	Do.	–	Boher, m.	R.C.	–	R.C.	–	105	–	105	30
289	6923	Do.	–	Do. f.	R.C.	–	R.C.	–	–	79	79	31
290	5424	Do.	–	Derrycastle 1st Cl. Agr.	Com.	N.B.	R.C.	R.C.	85	47	132	45
291	7968	Tullaghmelan,	53	Grange, m.	R.C.	–	R.C.	–	113	–	113	37
292	7065	Do.	–	Do. f.	R.C.	–	R.C.	–	–	79	79	41
293	615	Uskane,	50	Sopwell,	–	E.C.	E.C.	–	44	55	98	17
294	4876	Upper Church,	43	Garranakilla,	R.C.	–	R.C.	R.C.	74	75	149	65
295	6741	Do.	–	Upper Church,* m.	R.C.	–	–	–	–	–	–	–
296	8448	Do.	–	Do.* f.	R.C.	–	–	–	–	–	–	–
297	8748	Do.	–	Inchavallane,	R.C.	–	R.C.	R.C.	93	80	173	61
298	6649	Youghalarra,	56	Youghalarra, m.	R.C.	–	–	–	85	–	85	31
299	6874	Do.	–	Do. f.	R.C.	–	R.C.	–	–	78	78	31
		Total for County Tipperary, 299,							16183	20485	36,668	10602

COUNTY OF

1	1620	Aglish,	48	Aglish, m.	R.C.	–	R.C.	R.C.	180	–	180	65
2	6785	Do.	–	Do. f.	R.C.	–	R.C.	R.C.	–	165	165	71
3	6770	Do.	–	Mount Stuart,	R.C.	–	R.C.	–	64	56	120	60
4	1737	Affane,	–	Villierstown, m.	E.C.	–	R.C.	–	88	–	88	44
5	8820	Do.	–	Do. f.	E.C.	–	R.C.	–	–	116	116	–
6	9820	Do.	–	Affane,	R.C.	–	R.C.	R.C.	83	87	170	64
7	8834	Ardmore,	–	Ardmore, m.	R.C.	–	R.C.	R.C.	160	–	161	75
8	5086	Do.	–	Do. f.	R.C.	–	R.C.	R.C.	–	168	169	61
9	5541	Ardmore East,	–	Ballymacart, m.	R.C.	–	R.C.	R.C.	133	–	133	75
10	6988	Do.	–	Do. f.	R.C.	–	R.C.	R.C.	–	115	115	55
11	619	Ballygunner,	49	Ballygunner, m.	R.C.	–	R.C.	–	66	–	66	46
12	5187	Do.	–	Do. f.	R.C.	–	R.C.	R.C.	–	105	105	65
13	1207	Ballyduff,	46	Ballyduff, No. 1,	R.C.	–	R.C.	–	65	73	138	43
14	10694	Do.	–	Do. No. 2,	R.C.	–	R.C.	R.C.	69	81	150	53
15	10357	Do.	–	Ballyheafy, m.	R.C.	–	R.C.	–	111	–	111	45
16	10807	Do.	–	Do. f.	R.C.	–	R.C.	R.C.	–	112	112	55
17	1037	Ballylaneen,	49	Bunmahon, m.	R.C.	–	R.C.	–	146	–	146	55
18	8927	Do.	–	Do. f.	R.C.	–	R.C.	R.C.	–	164	164	70
19	2761	Do.	–	Ballylaneen, m.	R.C.	–	R.C.	–	93	–	93	46
20	11207	Do.	–	Do. f.	R.C.	–	R.C.	–	–	104	104	47
21	2314	Do.	–	Carrahaha, m.	R.C.	–	R.C.	–	116	–	116	46
22	11846	Do.	–	Do. f.	R.C.	–	R.C.	–	–	90	90	37
23	1784	Corbally,	–	Summerville, m.	–	E.C.	R.C.	–	100	–	100	45
24	497	Do.	–	Do. f.	–	E.C.	R.C.	R.C.	–	95	95	40
25	2590	Clashmore,	46	Clashmore, m.	R.C.	–	R.C.	R.C.	164	–	164	74
26	8197	Do.	–	Do. f.	R.C.	–	R.C.	R.C.	–	146	141	61
27	3491	Do.	–	Kilcolf,	R.C.	–	R.C.	–	34	44	78	33
28	3411	Do.	–	Ballycurrane,	R.C.	–	R.C.	–	48	49	97	39
29	7224	Clonegam,	49	Mayfield, m.	–	Dim.	R.C.	R.C.	254	–	254	122
30	7874	Do.	–	Do. f.	–	Dim.	R.C.	R.C.	–	246	246	81
31	8251	Do.	–	Do. i.	–	Dim.	R.C.	R.C.	139	98	237	73
32	8491	Drumcannon,	–	Castletown,	R.C.	–	R.C.	–	45	30	75	22
33	2099	Dungarvan,	48	Garrynageragh,	R.C.	–	R.C.	–	83	14	97	37
34	6784	Do.	–	Carriglea,	–	E.C.	R.C.	–	50	59	109	55
35	10164	Do.	–	Ballinacourty,	R.C.	–	R.C.	–	19	63	81	41
36	4620	Dunhill,	49	Dunhill, m.	R.C.	–	R.C.	–	111	–	111	49
37	4680	Do.	–	Do. f.	R.C.	–	R.C.	–	–	114	114	55
38	6038	Dysert,	58	Windgap,	R.C.	–	R.C.	–	59	37	96	41

* Returns not available.

b Including value of Free Residence and Garden.

Province of MUNSTER: County of TIPPERARY—*continued.*

Amount paid for Books, Requisites, and Apparatus, at Reduced Prices.	Aid granted by the Board during the Year 1874: In Free Stock of Books, Requisites, and Apparatus.	In Salaries, Premiums, and other Gratuities.	Results Fees, Financial Year.	Amount of Local Emoluments received in Aid of Teacher's Salary: School Fees.	Subscriptions, Endowments, &c.	Total Local Aid.	Vested or Non-Vested.	Number.
£ s. d.	£ s. d.	£ s. d.	£ s. d.	£ s. d.	£ s. d.	£ s. d.		
—	—	35 3 4	—	1 11 9	—	1 11 9		[illegible]
86 1 7	5 0 0	142 1 8	100 16 0	—	—	—		[illegible]
—	—	8 10 0	—	—	—	—		[illegible]
1 8 8	—	43 0 0	18 16 0	9 10 4	—	9 10 4		[illegible]
1 11 6	—	60 8 4	16 15 6	5 17 1	—	5 17 4		[illegible]
8 16 6	—	30 0 0	15 16 0	8 16 4	—	0 15 0		[illegible]
4 2 2	—	20 0 0	16 5 0	5 5 0	—	5 5 0		[illegible]
3 0 0	—	114 3 4	24 3 11	9 8 3	—	9 8 3	V.C.	[illegible]
8 17 3	—	60 18 4	21 8 0	25 4 1	—	25 4 1		[illegible]
2 16 8	—	46 6 8	19 10 0	21 13 11	—	21 18 11		[illegible]
0 4 6	—	10 0 0	8 9 0	—	21 8 4	*21 8 4		[illegible]
4 8 9	—	41 0 0	24 18 0	18 18 6	—	18 18 0		[illegible]
—	—	17 0 6	—	—	—	—		[illegible]
—	—	37 8 4	—	—	—	—		[illegible]
2 18 0	—	44 0 0	13 11 0	12 0 0	—	12 0 0		[illegible]
2 18 10	—	—	3 6 6	6 2 0	—	6 8 0		[illegible]
—	—	—	21 1 0	0 17 6	—	6 17 6		[illegible]
1,060 19 6	64 17 1	12,257 9 11	6,138 0 6	3,043 10 1	625 17 4	3,669 16 8		

WATERFORD—139 Schools.

Amount paid for Books, Requisites, and Apparatus, at Reduced Prices.	In Free Stock of Books, Requisites, and Apparatus.	In Salaries, Premiums, and other Gratuities.	Results Fees, Financial Year.	School Fees.	Subscriptions, Endowments, &c.	Total Local Aid.	Vested or Non-Vested.	Number.
3 18 6	—	60 10 0	20 6 0	18 0 8	0 0 0	23 8 8	A.	1
5 15 3	—	44 0 0	24 2 0	11 18 10	—	11 18 10	A.	2
1 6 6	—	24 0 0	14 7 6	3 4 6	8 12 0	*11 16 6	V.C.	3
2 19 0	—	20 0 0	11 0 0	6 0 0	0 0 0	11 0 0		4
3 12 0	—	25 0 0	13 5 0	3 5 5	—	3 5 5		5
3 4 0	—	47 13 4	18 14 0	12 0 0	5 0 0	17 0 0		6
3 5 8	—	60 13 4	21 15 0	16 8 0	5 0 0	19 8 0		7
3 0 7	—	50 8 4	29 4 8	10 0 0	5 0 0	15 0 0		8
8 10 5	—	48 0 0	23 7 0	20 8 4	4 10 0	*30 18 4		9
4 17 10	—	40 0 0	40 18 6	18 17 2	2 10 0	21 7 2		10
2 1 1	—	23 10 0	10 6 0	8 4 0	8 0 0	*18 4 0		11
11 6 7	—	30 8 4	24 12 6	8 8 11	8 0 0	17 8 11		12
1 8 2	—	22 16 4	11 4 0	8 18 5	1 10 0	*10 8 5	V.T.	13
4 6 0	—	57 10 0	10 6 0	10 0 0	—	10 0 0		14
—	—	24 0 0	8 7 0	9 10 6	—	9 10 6		15
—	—	60 0 0	12 11 9	9 11 6	—	9 11 6		16
1 6 8	—	30 10 0	16 15 6	1 4 7	—	4 4 5		17
2 5 0	—	46 18 4	61 16 6	7 7 2	—	7 7 2		18
2 16 0	—	44 0 0	14 4 0	9 10 3	—	9 10 3		19
1 18 7	4 10 0	—	17 11 6	7 18 2	—	7 13 2		20
1 6 0	—	38 10 0	15 18 0	10 7 0	—	10 7 11		21
3 17 0	5 0 0	15 0 0	9 11 0	4 11 11	—	4 11 11		22
2 8 0	—	50 0 0	20 0 0	5 19 0	10 0 0	15 15 0	V.I.	23
1 15 8	—	61 16 4	24 4 0	5 6 1	7 0 0	12 6 1		24
0 13 10	—	48 0 0	21 7 8	8 8 6	11 10 0	*19 18 6		25
9 6 6	—	50 0 0	17 12 0	4 10 6	—	4 10 6		26
—	—	55 0 0	2 17 0	4 18 8	5 0 0	9 18 8	A.	27
1 11 6	—	40 16 8	18 16 6	5 6 1	2 0 0	*7 6 1		28
6 16 0	—	67 10 0	49 8 6	51 10 1	20 10 0	72 0 1		29
7 17 7	—	75 18 4	43 1 6	54 8 9	8 0 0	62 8 9		30
—	—	40 0 0	30 4 0	12 0 11	16 0 0	28 0 11		31
2 0 11	—	24 0 0	10 6 0	9 15 6	6 0 0	15 15 6		32
2 6 0	—	41 8 4	15 13 8	4 10 0	—	4 10 0		33
1 14 2	—	51 8 4	23 8 0	10 2 6	20 2 0	*30 4 6	V.C.	34
2 10 7	—	20 0 0	10 10 0	8 10 6	3 0 0	*8 10 6		35
0 4 7	—	24 0 0	16 11 6	16 16 7	—	16 16 7		36
4 17 0	—	30 18 4	26 14 0	17 0 2	3 0 0	*19 0 2		37
3 3 8	—	20 0 0	6 7 6	9 11 4	5 0 0	*14 11 4		38

* No Returns; dismissed Teachers in charge.

b Including value of Free Residence.

List of Schools in operation on the 31st December, 1874.—

Number.	Roll Number of School.	Parish.	Barony.	School.		Religious Denomination of Manager or Correspondent: Clerical.	Lay.	Number and Religious Denomination of Teachers: Principals.	Assistants.	Attendance for the Year: Total number of Pupils on Rolls within the Year 1874: Males.	Fem.	Total.	Average daily attendance.
39	7689	Faithlegg,	49	Faithlegg,	m.	–	R.C.	R.C.	–	86	–	86	35
40	8107	Do.	–	Do.	f.	–	R.C.	R.C.	–	–	63	63	30
41	6233	Grange,	48	Grange Ord. Agricul.		R.C.	–	R.C.	–	97	–	97	39
42	10158	Do.	–	Do.	f.	R.C.	–	R.C.	–	–	121	121	64
43	4866	Islandikane,	49	Fenor,	m.	R.C.	–	R.C.	–	78	–	78	43
44	4890	Do.	–	Do.	f.	R.C.	–	R.C.	R.C.	–	116	116	49
45	620	Kilbarrymeaden,	–	Kill,	m.	R.C.	–	R.C.	–	160	–	160	62
46	6799	Do.	–	Do.	f.	R.C.	–	R.C.	R.C.	–	140	140	55
47	634	Kilburne,	–	Butlerstown,	m.	R.C.	–	R.C.	–	84	–	84	36
48	6727	Do.	–	Do.	f.	R.C.	–	R.C.	–	–	83	83	41
49	1287	Kilculliheen,	–	Kilculliheen,	m.	R.C.	–	R.C.	–	120	–	120	52
50	1516	Do.	–	Do.	f.	R.C.	–	R.C.	R.C.	31	165	190	94
51	1677	Kilronan,	48	Bennettstown,		–	R.C.	R.C.	–	74	88	164	69
52	4036	Do.	–	Bennet's Church,		R.C.	–	R.C.	–	96	77	173	67
53	6479	Do.	–	Newtown,		R.C.	–	R.C.	R.C.	85	73	163	91
54	1703	Kilmeadan,	49	Ballyduff, No. 2,	m.	R.C.	–	R.C.	–	156	–	156	82
55	1777	Do.	–	Do.	f.	R.C.	–	R.C.	–	–	138	138	43
56	5711	Kilrossanty,	48	Kilrossanty,	m.	R.C.	–	R.C.	–	173	–	173	75
57	1778	Do.	–	Do.	f.	R.C.	–	R.C.	–	–	181	181	67
58	5764	Kilsheelan,	–	Knockanore,	m.	R.C.	–	R.C.	–	129	–	129	66
59	10290	Do.	–	Do.	f.	R.C.	–	R.C.	R.C.	–	130	130	56
60	4134	Kilgobnet,	–	Coolnasmear,	m.	–	R.C.	R.C.	–	120	–	120	48
61	4183	Do.	–	Do.	f.	–	R.C.	R.C.	R.C.	18	108	126	54
62	4613	Do.	–	Garranbane,	m.	R.C.	–	R.C.	–	65	–	65	35
63	9774	Do.	–	Do.	f.	R.C.	–	R.C.	–	–	48	48	27
64	4901	Kill, St. Nicholas,	49	Passage, East,	m.	R.C.	–	R.C.	R.C.	164	–	164	83
65	8284	Do.	–	Do.	f.	R.C.	–	R.C.	R.C.	–	152	149	74
66	3395	Kilwatermoy,	48	Kilwatermoy,	m.	R.C.	–	R.C.	–	80	–	69	38
67	4611	Do.	–	Do.	f.	R.C.	–	R.C.	–	–	107	107	53
68	6905	Kilmolerane,	52	Carrickbeg,	m.	R.C.	–	R.C.	–	77	–	77	38
69	7810	Do.	–	Do.	f.	R.C.	–	R.C.	–	–	70	70	37
70	7460	Killea,	49	Dunmore, East,	f.	R.C.	–	R.C.	–	–	88	88	39
71	10068	Do.	–	Ballyglan,		R.C.	–	R.C.	–	41	45	86	31
72	10248	Do.	–	Killea,	m.	R.C.	–	R.C.	–	83	–	83	38
73	8181	Kinsalebeg,	48	Piltown,	m.	R.C.	–	R.C.	–	118	–	118	54
74	8538	Do.	–	Do.	f.	R.C.	–	R.C.	R.C.	–	139	139	57
75	9069	Do.	–	D'Loughtane,		R.C.	–	R.C.	R.C.	77	81	158	82
76	8418	Lismore and Mocollop,	–	Lismore Workhouse,		P.L.	Gds.	R.C.	–	37	43	78	33
77	1710	Do.	–	Glencairn 1st Class Agricultural,		–	R.C.	R.C.	–	101	–	101	50
78	6842	Do.	–	Do.	f.	–	R.C.	R.C.	–	–	68	68	37
79	7880	Do.	–	Ballinvella,		–	R.C.	R.C.	–	46	46	91	33
80	1036	Do.	–	Cappoquin,	m.	R.C.	–	R.C.	R.C.	156	–	156	62
81	6226	Do.	–	Do. Convent,	f.	R.C.	–	Nuns		113	297	410	221
82	1404	Do.	–	Tourin,		–	R.C.	R.C.	–	51	21	73	31
83	7811	Do.	–	Mount Melleray,	f.	R.C.	–	R.C.	–	–	135	135	69
84	9148	Do.	–	Ballysaggart,		R.C.	–	R.C.	R.C.	88	77	165	60
85	10075	Do.	–	Lismore,		–	R.C.	R.C.	–	18	28	46	25
86	1578	Monksland,	49	Knockmahon,	m.	–	R.C.	R.C.	R.C.	271	–	271	79
87	5536	Do.	–	Do.	f.	–	R.C.	R.C.	R.C.	–	177	177	75
88	9068	Modeligo,	48	Modeligo,	m.	R.C.	–	R.C.	R.C.	172	–	172	81
89	9890	Do.	–	Do.	f.	R.C.	–	R.C.	R.C.	–	153	153	73
90	1807	Mothel,	53	Clonea,	m.	R.C.	–	R.C.	R.C.	124	–	124	60
91	7772	Do.	–	Do.	f.	R.C.	–	R.C.	–	–	100	100	44
92	4186	Do.	–	Coolnahorna,		R.C.	–	R.C.	–	27	41	68	37
93	628	Rossmire,	49	Newtown,	m.	R.C.	–	R.C.	–	116	–	116	48
94	1188	Do.	–	Do.	f.	R.C.	–	R.C.	–	–	107	107	58
95	1830	Ringagonagh,	48	Mullinasharna,	m.	R.C.	–	R.C.	–	110	–	110	60
96	6537	Do.	–	Do.	f.	R.C.	–	R.C.	R.C.	–	119	119	67
97	4640	Rathgormack,	53	Rathgormack,	m.	R.C.	–	R.C.	–	107	–	107	55
98	6371	Do.	–	Do.	f.	R.C.	–	R.C.	–	–	112	112	66
99	9710	Do.	–	Glenaphore,	m.	R.C.	–	R.C.	–	80	–	80	38

a Including value of Free Residence. b Including value of Free Residence and Garden.

Province of Munster: County of Waterford—*continued.*

Amount paid for Books, Requisites, and Apparatus, at Reduced Prices.	Aid granted by the Board during the Year 1874. In Free Stock of Books, Requisites, and Apparatus.	In Salaries, Premiums, and other Gratuities.	Results Fees, Financial Year.	Amount of Local Emoluments received in Aid of Teacher's Salary. School Fees.	Subscriptions, Endowments, &c.	Total Local Aid.	Vested or Non-Vested.	Number.
£ s. d.	£ s. d.	£ s. d.	£ s. d.	£ s. d.	£ s. d.	£ s. d.		
1 6 1	—	81 2 3	0 9 9	3 11 9	7 6 0	* 10 11 9		39
1 10 2	—	19 8 10	—	3 0 3	6 0 0	9 8 3		40
1 5 3	—	47 10 0	11 7 6	6 14 4	18 0 0	* 19 10 4		41
3 8 8	—	40 14 6	21 1 6	8 5 7	4 0 0	12 5 7		42
2 11 0	—	31 0 0	13 12 6	9 0 9	—	9 0 9		43
1 15 7	—	50 0 0	20 10 0	21 14 1	3 0 0	* 24 11 4		44
1 17 11	—	44 0 0	18 8 0	11 13 4	—	11 13 4		45
1 5 8	—	46 6 8	18 19 0	8 11 2	—	8 11 2		46
8 5 0	—	47 10 0	9 18 6	8 16 9	12 13 9	* 21 7 6		47
2 1 9	—	27 10 2	12 9 4	7 0 9	1 0 0	* 9 9 9		48
0 18 0	—	19 10 6	4 0 3	4 11 8	—	4 14 4	V.N.	49
1 3 3	—	30 0 0	14 5 4	20 0 10	—	20 0 10	V.N.	50
6 10 2	—	51 18 4	21 12 6	17 15 0	15 0 0	* 33 15 0		51
5 12 0	—	30 0 8	27 6 0	27 7 10	—	27 7 10		52
—	—	46 0 0	31 10 6	21 18 0	—	21 19 6		53
0 18 8	—	30 8 4	21 10 6	17 8 11	—	17 8 11	N.	54
3 12 8	—	28 10 0	17 14 6	8 13 0	3 10 0	* 14 8 0	N.	55
2 12 1	—	38 8 10	21 3 0	9 0 0	—	9 0 0	V.N.	56
0 9 4	—	30 0 0	17 11 0	8 6 6	—	8 6 6	V.N.	57
2 19 8	—	21 0 0	18 1 0	10 4 5	1 10 0	* 11 14 5		58
1 17 4	—	40 0 0	16 0 6	5 14 3	—	5 14 3		59
3 12 1	—	34 0 0	6 13 0	7 17 0	6 15 0	* 18 12 6	V.N.	60
1 14 1	—	30 0 0	13 6 0	3 17 0	8 10 0	* 12 7 6	V.N.	61
1 15 0	—	24 0 0	7 16 0	7 0 0	0 10 0	* 7 10 6		62
2 8 4	—	20 0 0	0 1 6	4 4 0	—	4 4 0		63
8 17 0	—	67 18 6	83 8 0	28 9 4	7 10 0	35 19 4		64
4 9 3	—	78 11 8	39 0 0	15 7 6	5 0 0	* 20 7 6		65
—	—	41 0 0	14 9 0	5 10 0	1 6 0	* 7 1 0		66
3 13 8	—	25 0 0	11 14 6	8 1 10	1 10 0	* 10 11 10		67
4 7 4	—	34 0 0	9 6 0	7 10 9	3 10 0	* 11 0 8		68
1 10 0	—	20 0 0	6 0 0	2 13 7	—	2 13 7		69
4 0 1	—	36 16 8	20 4 6	8 1 0	—	8 1 0		70
1 11 0	—	24 0 0	10 11 0	6 9 6	—	6 9 6		71
1 5 3	—	38 17 8	7 8 0	4 6 0	—	4 6 0		72
2 9 3	—	29 0 0	11 10 0	12 16 9	2 0 0	* 14 16 9		73
4 0 10	—	53 18 4	23 18 8	11 16 8	—	11 16 8		74
2 11 0	—	44 9 0	30 19 0	8 18 4	1 0 0	* 9 18 4		75
1 0 8	—	8 10 0	—	—	—	—		76
2 11 7	—	60 19 4	10 6 0	—	16 0 0	* 16 0 0	V.N.	77
2 13 3	—	40 0 0	18 13 0	—	13 10 0	* 13 10 0	V.N.	78
1 16 3	—	81 0 0	7 10 0	1 15 6	10 0 0	11 15 6	V.N.	79
0 0 1	—	57 0 0	30 10 0	10 9 8	12 0 0	22 9 8		80
22 0 11	—	117 5 1	77 17 0	11 13 11	—	11 13 11		81
3 10 6	—	31 0 5	11 10 0	5 0 0	6 0 0	* 11 0 0		82
4 7 2	4 5 0	31 0 8	16 3 4	—	—	—		83
3 8 4	2 16 0	63 0 0	23 18 6	3 4 6	2 0 0	* 5 4 6		84
5 5 5	—	31 0 0	13 12 4	8 6 0	32 0 6	* 40 6 6		85
5 6 3	—	76 15 0	21 13 0	5 4 6	12 0 0	17 4 2		86
4 2 8	—	48 0 0	15 14 6	7 15 9	8 0 0	15 15 9		87
4 0 9	—	62 6 8	23 8 0	16 8 0	5 0 0	21 8 0		88
4 3 11	—	57 10 6	23 11 0	9 11 7	5 0 0	14 11 7		89
1 9 3	—	60 16 8	24 3 6	12 12 6	—	12 12 6		90
4 14 4	—	15 8 8	17 17 0	7 19 6	—	7 19 6		91
1 8 8	—	20 0 0	10 7 0	5 6 0	—	5 6 0	V.N.	92
5 6 7	—	34 0 0	11 4 0	9 0 0	1 0 0	* 10 0 0		93
10 12 0	—	21 0 0	23 5 8	14 0 0	3 0 0	* 17 0 0		94
8 1 9	—	40 10 0	30 1 6	18 10 5	2 10 0	21 0 8	N.	95
3 8 1	—	40 0 0	18 6 6	16 18 5	2 10 0	18 8 5	N.	96
4 15 7	—	34 8 5	17 8 0	13 0 0	—	13 0 0		97
4 10 2	—	51 16 8	16 17 0	9 4 10	—	9 4 10		98
0 10 2	—	24 0 0	8 8 6	15 2 0	—	15 2 0		99

* Including value of Free Garden.

List of Schools in operation on the 31st December, 1874.—

Number.	Roll Number of School.	Parish.	District.	School.	Religious Denomination of Managers or Correspondent. Clerical.	Lay.	Number and Religious Denomination of Teachers. Principals.	Assistants.	Attendance for the Year. Total number of Pupils on Rolls within the Year 1874. Males.	Females.	Total.	Average daily Attendance for the Year 1874.
100	6740	Rathgormuck,	53	Glenstown, f.	R.C.	–	R.C.	–	–	73	73	33
101	6743	Rossmore,	41	Kilmacthomas Work. a	P.L.	Gds.	–	–	–	–	–	–
102	1787	Stradbally,	45	Stradbally, m.	R.C.	–	R.C.	R.C.	207	–	207	74
103	1788	Do.	–	Do. f.	R.C.	–	R.C.	R.C.	–	157	157	73
104	8182	Seskinan,	33	Touraneena, m.	R.C.	–	R.C.	R.C.	163	–	163	78
105	8183	Do.	–	Do. f.	R.C.	–	R.C.	R.C.	–	178	178	73
106	6971	St. John's,	40	Waterford District Model, m.	Com.	N.E.	R.C.	Prot.	153	–	153	78
107	6975	Do.	–	Do. f.	Com.	N.E.	R.C.	R.C.	–	165	165	69
108	6976	Do.	–	Do. i.	Com.	N.E.	R.C.	–	47	49	96	38
109	6977	Do.	–	Do. Maritime, a	Com.	N.E.	–	–	–	–	–	–
110	6529	Do.	–	Do. Workhouse,	P.L.	Gds.	3R.C.	–	214	153	367	151
111	546	St. Patrick's,	–	St. Patrick's,	R.C.	–	R.C.	R.C.	–	199	199	62
112	9159	Trinity Within,	–	Waterford Gaol,	Gov.	Gaol	2R.C.	–	36	34	70	12
113	1179	Tallow,	48	Glenmore,	R.C.	–	R.C.	–	35	49	84	30
114	1888	Do.	–	Tallow, m.	R.C.	–	R.C.	2R.C.	237	–	237	104
115	1889	Do.	–	Do. Convent, f.	R.C.	–	R.C.	2R.C.	–	344	344	16[illegible]
116	7115	Templemichael,	–	Glentine,	R.C.	–	R.C.	–	64	46	110	46
117	8549	Whitechurch,	–	Whitechurch, m.	R.C.	–	R.C.	–	101	–	101	46
118	8550	Do.	–	Do. f.	R.C.	–	R.C.	–	–	85	85	41
119	8736	Do.	–	Ballinaparka,	–	R.C.	R.C.	R.C.	60	51	111	56
120	8180	Do.	–	Killahala,	R.C.	–	R.C.	–	64	63	127	46
		Total for County Waterford, 120,							7,227	7,303	14,530	6,271

LEINSTER—

COUNTY OF

Number.	Roll Number of School.	Parish.	District.	School.	Clerical.	Lay.	Principals.	Assistants.	Males.	Females.	Total.	Average daily Attendance.
1	670	Agha,	20	Leighlinbridge, m.	R.C.	–	R.C.	R.C.	240	–	240	103
2	671	Do.	–	Do. f.	R.C.	–	R.C.	R.C.	–	224	224	93
3	647	Ballon,	–	Ballon, m.	R.C.	–	R.C.	–	118	–	118	69
4	6852	Do.	–	Do. f.	R.C.	–	R.C.	R.C.	–	180	180	11
5	649	Barragh,	–	Kildavin, m.	R.C.	–	R.C.	–	110	–	110	53
6	650	Do.	–	Do. f.	R.C.	–	R.C.	–	–	101	101	35
7	666	Carlow,	–	Carlow Convent, f.	–	R.C.	Nuns		–	644	644	233
8	10010	Do.	–	Do. do. m. i.	–	R.C.	Nuns		163	–	163	67
9	11164	Do.	–	Do. Workhouse,	P.L.	Gds.	R.C. / R.C.	R.C.	87	97	184	39
10	651	Clonmore,	–	Clonmore,	R.C.	–	R.C.	–	–	90	90	67
11	10041	Do.	–	Do. m.	R.C.	–	R.C.	–	86	–	86	61
12	651	Clonygoose,	–	Borris, a m.	–	–	–	–	–	–	–	–
13	652	Do.	–	Do. f.	R.C.	–	R.C.	3R.C.	61	224	285	117
14	653	Do.	–	Ballymurrin,	R.C.	–	R.C.	–	57	47	94	34
15	6522	Cloydagh,	–	Ballinabranagh, m.	R.C.	–	R.C.	–	135	–	135	55
16	10397	Do.	–	Do. f.	R.C.	–	R.C.	–	–	108	108	52
17	1216	Dunleckney,	–	Newtown Dunleckney, m.	R.C.	–	R.C.	–	94	–	94	36
18	1435	Do.	–	Do. f.	R.C.	–	R.C.	–	–	105	105	47
19	1926	Do.	–	Bagenalstown, Conv. f.	–	R.C.	Nuns		68	390	458	142
20	[illegible]	Do.	–	Garryhill, [illegible]	–	R.C.	R.C.	–	115	–	115	38
21	[illegible]	Do.	–	Do. f.	–	R.C.	R.C.	–	–	75	75	45
22	11180	Do.	–	Bagenalstown,	R.C.	–	R.C.	–	31	40	71	43
23	[illegible]	Fenagh,	–	Rathnageera,	R.C.	–	R.C.	R.C.	75	59	134	52
24	11043	Do.	–	Fenagh,	R.C.	–	R.C.	–	31	30	61	31
25	1412	Gilbertstown,	–	Rathoe, m.	R.C.	–	R.C.	–	63	–	63	32
26	[illegible]	Do.	–	Do. f.	R.C.	–	R.C.	–	–	65	65	39
27	4077	Grangeford,	–	Grange, m.	R.C.	–	R.C.	–	60	–	60	31
28	6778	Do.	–	Do. f.	R.C.	–	R.C.	–	–	67	67	39
29	[illegible]	Do.	–	Grangeford,	–	R.C.	R.C.	–	29	29	58	27
30	1291	Hacketstown,	–	Hacketstown, m.	R.C.	–	R.C.	–	150	–	150	60

a No Return.

b Including value of Free Residence.

Province of MUNSTER: County of WATERFORD—*continued.*

Amount paid for Books, Requisites, and Apparatus, at Reduced Prices.	Aid granted by the Board during the Year 1874: In Free Stock of Books, Requisites, and Apparatus.	In Salaries, Premiums, and other Gratuities.	Results Fees, Financial Year.	Amount of Local Emoluments received in Aid of Teacher's Salary: School Fees.	Subscriptions, Endowments, &c.	Total Local Aid.	Vested or Non-Vested.	Number.
£ s. d.	£ s. d.	£ s. d.	£ s. d.	£ s. d.	£ s. d.	£ s. d.		
1 8 3	—	20 0 0	8 0 0	18 0 0	—	18 0 0		100
1 17 1	—	1 10 0	—	—	—	—		101
4 18 7	—	48 0 0	17 17 8	7 19 0	8 0 0	15 19 0		102
4 8 9	—	47 10 0	20 3 8	6 17 4	10 0 0	16 17 4		103
6 8 6	—	68 1 8	18 0 8	28 18 0	—	28 18 0		104
1 8 8	—	64 0 0	19 11 8	18 11 10	4 0 0	b 22 14 10		105
24 6 0	4 1 10	617 14 6	43 2 0	80 5 7	—	86 5 7	V.C.	106
14 4 7	23 14 5						V.C.	107
—	—						V.C.	108
—	—	—	—	—	—	—	V.C.	109
14 1 8	—	10 0 0	—	—	—	—		110
0 10 2	—	36 0 0	4 18 0	2 8 0	—	2 8 6		111
—	—	—	—	—	—	—		112
2 16 0	—	34 0 0	8 0 0	7 10 8	3 0 0	b 10 10 9		113
8 11 0	—	106 10 0	37 16 0	27 10 0	—	27 10 0	A.	114
7 18 11	8 0 0	68 2 11	24 17 0	2 0 2	7 10 0	10 10 2	A.	115
1 18 8	—	30 0 0	13 12 0	7 8 2	—	7 8 2		116
3 4 5	—	53 18 4	13 13 0	16 17 1	—	16 17 1	V.T.	117
3 14 7	—	31 0 0	16 19 0	12 14 0	—	12 14 0	V.T.	118
—	—	53 0 0	8 4 0	6 1 0	10 10 0	a 16 11 0		119
1 0 0	—	20 0 0	9 13 6	4 0 2	—	4 0 2		120
148 10 0	41 18 3	3,232 8 2	1,028 8 7	1,375 8 1	432 17 9	1,347 8 10		

1,346 Schools.

CARLOW—64 Schools.

10 8 7	—	118 0 0	41 11 0	16 2 8	—	16 2 8	R.	1
7 10 6	—	97 10 8	40 11 6	41 17 4	5 0 0	46 17 4	V.	2
2 0 0	—	24 0 0	7 19 8	8 12 10	—	8 12 10		3
3 10 0	—	44 0 0	15 2 0	4 1 1	—	4 1 1		4
—	—	24 0 0	—	1 2 7	—	1 2 7	V.T.	5
3 1 0	—	30 0 0	8 0 6	1 16 0	—	1 16 0	V.T.	6
12 13 10	—	180 7 6	72 2 0	—	—	—	R.	7
5 7 8	—	30 14 0	18 13 0	4 8 0	—	4 8 0		8
6 1 1	5 0 0	—	—	—	—	—		9
4 1 9	—	38 2 4	12 9 0	3 17 0	—	3 17 0		10
3 5 6	—	24 0 0	9 4 0	5 5 6	—	5 5 6		11
—	—	—	—	—	—	—	V.T.	12
7 10 1	—	128 0 0	40 11 6	8 18 0	—	8 18 0	V.T.	13
1 18 4	—	20 0 0	11 4 6	2 18 9	1 0 0	b 8 18 9		14
6 0 6	—	21 8 4	14 16 0	6 2 4	—	6 2 4	V.T.	15
2 0 6	—	20 0 6	15 1 6	3 16 0	—	3 16 0	V.T.	16
2 10 11	—	24 0 0	8 16 0	6 10 3	—	6 10 3	V.T.	17
—	—	20 0 0	19 18 8	4 6 2	—	4 6 2	V.T.	18
10 8 8	—	71 0 4	47 18 6	18 18 11	—	18 13 11		19
6 7 11	—	47 0 0	24 8 8	6 8 0	41 11 9	a 49 19 9		20
9 8 6	—	30 10 0	16 16 0	9 0 0	3 10 0	b 18 10 0		21
6 15 6	5 0 0	14 0 0	—	—	68 18 5	a 68 18 5		22
5 0 10	—	44 0 0	62 0 0	7 3 0	—	7 3 0		23
4 6 11	4 0 0	24 0 0	9 10 6	10 8 0	18 0 0	b 28 8 0		24
0 16 6	—	24 0 0	7 14 0	5 10 6	—	5 10 6	V.T.	25
—	—	20 0 0	6 14 0	3 5 2	—	3 5 2	V.T.	26
3 7 7	—	20 0 0	9 19 6	8 14 6	—	8 14 6		27
3 4 11	—	20 0 0	6 0 6	6 11 0	—	6 11 0		28
0 10 2	—	20 0 0	9 7 0	1 18 0	7 1 0	a 8 18 8		29
0 3 8	—	58 0 0	17 18 6	18 11 8	—	18 11 8	V.T.	30

a Inoperative.

b Including value of Free Residence and Garden.

List of Schools in operation on the 31st December, 1874.—

Number.	Roll Number of School.	Parish.	District.	School.	Religious Denomination of Manager or Correspondent: Clerical.	Lay.	Number and Religious Denominations of Teachers: Principals.	Assistants.	Attendance for the Year: Total Number of Pupils on Rolls within the Year: Male.	Fem.	Total.	[illegible]
31	1198	Hacketstown,	89	Hacketstown, f.	R.C.	–	R.C.	R.C.	–	173	173	[illegible]
32	[illegible]	Kiltennel,	–	Raheene, m.	R.C.	–	R.C.	–	153	–	153	[illegible]
33	[illegible]	Do.	–	Do. f.	R.C.	–	R.C.	–	–	137	137	[illegible]
34	[illegible]	Do.	–	Tynaclash,	R.C.	–	R.C.	R.C.	94	91	185	[illegible]
		Do.	–	Do.[b] evg.	–	–	–	–	–	–	–	–
35	11[illegible]	Do.	–	Killedmond,	R.C.	–	R.C.	–	[illegible]	22	[illegible]	[illegible]
36	1116	Lorum,	–	Ballinkillen, m.	R.C.	–	R.C.	–	77	–	77	[illegible]
37	1117	Do.	–	Do. f.	R.C.	–	R.C.	–	–	90	90	[illegible]
38	627	Moyacomb,	–	Clonegal, m.	R.C.	–	R.C.	–	108	–	108	[illegible]
39	628	Do.	–	Do. f.	R.C.	–	R.C.	–	–	90	[illegible]	[illegible]
40	673	Myshall,	–	Myshall, m.	R.C.	–	R.C.	–	99	–	[illegible]	[illegible]
41	1[illegible]	Do.	–	Do. f.	R.C.	–	R.C.	R.C.	–	110	110	[illegible]
42	1418	Old Leighlin,	–	Ridge,	R.C.	–	R.C.	R.C.	60	69	129	[illegible]
43	2124	Do.	–	Old Leighlin, m.	R.C.	–	R.C.	–	75	–	75	[illegible]
44	[illegible]	Do.	–	Do. f.	R.C.	–	R.C.	–	–	86	86	[illegible]
45	[illegible]	Do.	–	Ballinree,	R.C.	–	R.C.	–	40	36	76	[illegible]
46	3139	Rathvilly,	–	Hacketstown	R.C.	–	R.C.	R.C.	60	63	123	[illegible]
47	674	Do.	–	Rathvilly, m.	R.C.	–	R.C.	–	177	–	177	[illegible]
48	675	Do.	–	Do. f.	R.C.	–	R.C.	–	–	104	104	[illegible]
49	[illegible]	Do.	–	Rathmore,	R.C.	–	R.C.	–	80	[illegible]	[illegible]	[illegible]
50	635	St. Mullins,	–	Ballymurphy, m.	R.C.	–	R.C.	–	80	–	[illegible]	[illegible]
51	636	Do.	–	Do. f.	R.C.	–	R.C.	–	–	73	73	[illegible]
52	677	Do.	–	Glynn, m.	R.C.	–	R.C.	–	91	–	91	[illegible]
53	678	Do.	–	Do. f.	R.C.	–	R.C.	–	–	[illegible]	[illegible]	[illegible]
54	679	Do.	–	Newtown St. Mullins,	R.C.	–	R.C.	R.C.	74	55	129	[illegible]
55	11[illegible]	Do.	–	Drummond,	R.C.	–	R.C.	–	69	62	131	[illegible]
56	[illegible]	Do.	–	Inch, m.	R.C.	–	R.C.	–	107	–	107	[illegible]
57	[illegible]	Do.	–	Do. f.	R.C.	–	R.C.	–	–	110	110	[illegible]
58	7[illegible]	Slyguff,	–	Killoughternane,	R.C.	–	R.C.	–	[illegible]	[illegible]	110	[illegible]
59	[illegible]	Tullowmagimma,	–	Tinryland, m.	R.C.	–	R.C.	–	97	–	97	[illegible]
60	[illegible]	Do.	–	Do. f.	R.C.	–	R.C.	–	–	91	91	[illegible]
61	[illegible]	Tullow,	–	Ardattin,	R.C.	–	R.C.	R.C.	114	70	184	[illegible]
62	681	Do.	–	Tullow Monastery, m.	R.C.	–	Monks		212	–	212	[illegible]
63	682	Do.	–	Do. Convent, f.	R.C.	–	Nuns		184	310	494	[illegible]
64	10270	Urglin,	–	Bennekerry,	R.C.	–	R.C.	–	65	51	116	[illegible]
		Total for County of Carlow, 64 Schools,							[illegible]	1510	[illegible]	[illegible]

COUNTY OF

Number.	Roll Number of School.	Parish.	District.	School.	Clerical.	Lay.	Principals.	Assistants.	Male.	Fem.	Total.	[illegible]
1	[illegible]	Artane,	30	Artane, m.	R.C.	–	R.C.	–	117	–	117	[illegible]
2	[illegible]	Do.	–	Do. f.	R.C.	–	R.C.	–	–	84	84	[illegible]
3	[illegible]	Baldoyle,	–	Baldoyle, m.	R.C.	–	R.C.	–	110	–	110	[illegible]
4	[illegible]	Do.	–	Portmarnock,	R.C.	–	R.C.	R.C.	48	[illegible]	[illegible]	[illegible]
5	[illegible]	Balrothery,	[illegible]	St. Mary's (Balbriggan), f.	R.C.	–	R.C.	R.C.	–	121	121	[illegible]
6	[illegible]	Do.	–	Do. f.	R.C.	–	R.C.	R.C.	[illegible]	[illegible]	177	[illegible]
7	[illegible]	Do.	–	St. Peter's (Balbriggan), m.	R.C.	–	R.C.	R.C.	163	–	163	[illegible]
8	[illegible]	Do.	–	Balrothery,	R.C.	–	R.C.	R.C.	60	[illegible]	[illegible]	[illegible]
9	[illegible]	Blanchardstown,	[illegible]	Blanchardstown, m.	R.C.	–	R.C.	–	119	–	119	[illegible]
10	[illegible]	Do.	–	Do. Conv. f.	R.C.	–	Nuns		[illegible]	164	[illegible]	[illegible]
11	[illegible]	Balscadden,	25	Ring,	R.C.	–	R.C.	R.C.	64	68	137	[illegible]
12	[illegible]	Do.	–	Balscadden,	R.C.	–	R.C.	–	48	40	[illegible]	[illegible]
13	[illegible]	Clondalkin,	37	Clondalkin, m.	–	R.C.	R.C.	R.C.	108	–	[illegible]	[illegible]
				Do. evg.	–	R.C.	R.C.	–	[illegible]	–	[illegible]	[illegible]
14	[illegible]	Do.	–	Do. Convent, f.	R.C.	–	Nuns		[illegible]	[illegible]	[illegible]	[illegible]
15	[illegible]	Do.	–	Do. village,	R.C.	–	R.C.	–	17	19	[illegible]	14
16	[illegible]	Castleknock,	–	St. Bridget's, m.	R.C.	–	R.C.	–	[illegible]	–	[illegible]	[illegible]
17	[illegible]	Do.	–	Do. f.	R.C.	–	R.C.	–	[illegible]	73	[illegible]	[illegible]
18	[illegible]	Do.	–	Lower Road,	R.C.	–	R.C.	–	[illegible]	[illegible]	[illegible]	[illegible]

a Including value of Free Residence.] b No Return.

Province of Leinster: County of Carlow—*continued.*

Amount paid for Books, Requisites, and Apparatus at reduced Prices.	Aid granted by the Board during the Year 1874: In Free Stock of Books, Requisites, and Apparatus.	In Salaries, Premiums, and other Gratuities.	Results Fees, Financial Year.	Amount of Local Emoluments received in Aid of Teacher's Salary: School Fees.	Subscriptions, Endowments, &c.	Total Local Aid.	Vested or Non-vested.	Number.
£ s. d.	£ s. d.	£ s. d.	£ s. d.	£ s. d.	£ s. d.	£ s. d.		
1 8 4	—	109 8 4	34 15 8	17 19 2	—	17 19 2	V.T.	31
3 8 0	—	47 13 10	28 11 8	14 6 7	1 0 0	*15 6 7		32
2 13 3	—	30 4 0	16 10 6	6 7 6	1 0 0	*7 7 6		33
4 0 10	—	50 10 0	10 6 8 / —	6 11 11	—	6 11 11	V.T.	34
3 1 6	4 0 0	18 4 8	7 9 0	9 16 6	10 0 0	19 16 6		35
4 5 6	—	31 0 0	13 8 0	4 2 6	—	4 2 6		36
1 12 4	—	24 0 0	6 10 0	1 0 4	—	1 0 4		37
1 3 0	—	24 0 0	—	6 1 6	—	6 1 6	V.T.	38
2 6 8	—	20 0 0	7 18 0	5 0 0	—	5 0 0	V.T.	39
1 17 9	—	38 0 0	7 10 9	4 14 4	1 10 0	*6 4 4		40
1 17 5	—	48 10 0	11 13 6	6 5 0	3 0 0	*9 5 0	V.T.	41
3 1 4	—	40 0 0	23 3 4	4 4 8	—	4 4 8		42
1 5 9	—	24 0 0	6 4 0	3 16 8	—	3 16 8	V.T.	43
1 13 11	—	64 0 0	9 6 8	8 4 0	—	8 4 0	V.T.	44
—	—	24 0 0	6 0 0	1 9 0	—	1 9 0		45
6 4 9	—	34 10 0	21 8 6	17 6 6	—	17 6 6		46
3 18 0	—	38 2 0	17 13 0	8 6 1	—	8 6 1	V.T.	47
3 7 2	—	35 0 0	11 6 6	14 8 6	—	14 8 6	V.T.	48
0 10 4	—	30 0 0	5 5 0	3 17 0	—	3 17 0		49
1 5 3	—	24 0 0	10 13 0	5 16 6	—	5 16 6	N.	50
1 0 11	—	30 0 0	7 14 9	3 8 8	4 10 0	*8 18 8	N.	51
0 1 3	—	24 0 0	7 13 6	1 5 11	0 10 0	*1 15 11	N.	52
0 18 5	—	30 0 0	6 17 0	0 14 6	1 0 0	*1 14 6	N.	53
1 7 1	—	40 0 0	10 14 6	0 13 2	—	0 13 2	V.T.	54
3 0 8	—	44 0 0	20 18 0	6 3 8	—	6 3 8	V.T.	55
2 4 10	—	21 0 0	14 0 0	4 16 1	—	4 16 1		56
1 0 7	—	27 18 0	17 3 0	4 10 0	—	4 10 0		57
2 14 10	—	24 10 0	12 4 0	2 17 2	—	2 17 2		58
2 2 6	—	21 0 0	12 8 0	10 3 0	6 0 0	16 3 0	N.	59
2 10 6	—	24 10 0	18 18 6	4 15 6	2 0 0	*6 15 6	N.	60
4 11 3	—	41 0 0	10 6 5	15 9 2	—	15 9 2		61
8 8 4	—	24 15 0	23 18 6	—	—	—		62
7 18 1	—	30 10 4	24 3 0	—	—	—		63
2 16 5	—	24 18 4	18 9 0	10 14 6	3 0 0	*13 14 6		64
370 11 9	16 0 0	2,817 10 10	1,010 16 9	384 8 8	171 6 4	555 9 7		

DUBLIN—[illegible] Schools.

Amount paid for Books, Requisites, and Apparatus at reduced Prices.	In Free Stock of Books, Requisites, and Apparatus.	In Salaries, Premiums, and other Gratuities.	Results Fees, Financial Year.	School Fees.	Subscriptions, Endowments, &c.	Total Local Aid.	Vested or Non-vested.	Number.
3 17 0	—	69 18 4	5 14 0	5 18 0	0 10 0	*14 8 8	V.T.	1
4 10 9	—	58 10 8	7 15 0	4 3 8	6 10 0	*10 12 8	V.T.	2
2 8 10	—	58 0 0	7 8 5	9 7 5	6 0 0	15 7 5		3
5 8 8	—	60 0 0	13 14 0	8 18 1	10 0 0	*22 18 1		4
9 19 6	—	44 0 0	15 6 6	7 16 7	—	7 16 7		5
1 8 3	—	48 0 0	11 17 0	8 16 8	—	8 16 3		6
5 10 6	—	55 12 4	12 3 6	18 0 4	—	13 0 4		7
3 8 4	—	44 10 0	17 0 6	6 13 10	—	6 13 10		8
5 13 10	—	58 10 0	14 9 6	4 3 9	13 0 0	17 3 9	V.C.	9
6 11 3	—	60 12 0	11 10 6	10 15 0	—	10 15 0		10
1 6 8	—	50 0 0	13 17 0	7 16 9	—	7 16 9		11
8 8 5	—	61 6 8	6 8 8	5 3 6	—	5 3 6		12
16 12 7	—	80 5 0	23 5 5 / 4 10 0	— / 4 7 0	—	— / 4 7 0		13
16 14 0	—	58 11 0	81 11 0	6 8 4	—	8 3 4		14
2 8 7	—	30 10 0	8 13 0	—	40 0 0	*50 0 0	V.N.	15
1 8 0	—	34 18 4	4 7 0	5 0 10	10 0 8	*16 0 10		16
1 13 10	—	35 10 0	5 11 0	3 14 8	11 0 0	*16 14 8		17
2 1 0	—	30 0 0	5 0 0	2 0 0	—	2 0 0		18

* Including value of Free Garden.

* Including value of Free Residence and Garden.

List of Schools in operation on the 31st December, 1874.—

No. of ref.	Roll Number of School.	Parish.	District.	School.	Religious Denomination of Managers or Correspondents: Clerical.	Lay.	Religious Denomination of Teachers: Principals.	Assistants.	Attendance for the Year: Total number of Pupils on Rolls within the Year: Males.	Females.	Total.	Average Daily Attendance for the Year.
19	5473	Castleknock,	80	Phoenix Park,	R.C.	—	R.C.	R.C.	[illegible]	70	[illegible]	[illegible]
20	[illegible]	Do.	67	Blanchardstown,	R.C.	—	R.C.	R.C.	[illegible]	[illegible]	146	57
21	7097	Do.	—	Clonsilla, m.	R.C.	—	R.C.	—	61	—	[illegible]	[illegible]
22	7026	Do.	—	Do. f.	R.C.	—	R.C.	—	—	76	76	[illegible]
23	[illegible]	Do.	—	Mulhuddart,	R.C.	—	R.C.	R.C.	63	56	119	44
24	700	Chapelizod,	81	Chapelizod, m.	R.C.	—	R.C.	R.C.	166	—	[illegible]	65
25	701	Do.	—	Do. f.	R.C.	—	R.C.	R.C.	—	166	[illegible]	[illegible]
26	10643	Do.	—	Do. No. 2,	R.C.	—	R.C.	—	16	[illegible]	[illegible]	[illegible]
27	[illegible]	Clontarf,	—	Ballybough,	R.C.	—	R.C.	R.C.	77	[illegible]	[illegible]	[illegible]
28	1292	Clonmethan,	—	Ballyboghill, m.	R.C.	—	R.C.	—	56	—	[illegible]	[illegible]
29	[illegible]	Do.	—	Do. f.	R.C.	—	R.C.	—	—	46	46	[illegible]
30	7470	Do.	—	Oldtown,	R.C.	—	R.C.	—	41	30	71	[illegible]
31	4817	Crumlin,	38	Crumlin, m.	R.C.	—	R.C.	—	[illegible]	—	[illegible]	21
32	9018	Do.	—	Do. f.	R.C.	—	R.C.	—	18	[illegible]	77	[illegible]
33	[illegible]	Clontarf,	80	Clontarf, m.	R.C.	—	R.C.	—	119	—	119	49
34	4831	Do.	—	Do. f.	R.C.	—	R.C.	—	—	101	101	[illegible]
35	8475	Coolock,	—	Clonshaugh,	R.C.	—	R.C.	—	40	[illegible]	71	39
36	8216	Cloghran,	—	Cloghran, m.	R.C.	—	R.C.	—	60	60	108	[illegible]
37	704	Dalkey,	40	Dalkey, m.	R.C.	—	R.C.	—	227	—	227	[illegible]
38	7191	Do.	—	Do. Convent, f.	—	R.C.	R.C.	R.C.	74	196	[illegible]	[illegible]
39	[illegible]	Donabate,	67	Portrane, m.	—	R.C.	R.C.	—	65	—	[illegible]	[illegible]
				Do. [illegible]	—	R.C.	R.C.	—	65	—	[illegible]	[illegible]
40	4601	Do.	—	Do. f.	—	R.C.	R.C.	—	—	100	100	[illegible]
41	705	Finglas,	—	Finglas, m.	R.C.	—	R.C.	—	[illegible]	—	[illegible]	[illegible]
42	8106	Do.	—	Do. f.	R.C.	—	R.C.	—	—	66	66	37
43	706	Garristown,	—	Garristown, m.	R.C.	—	R.C.	—	[illegible]	—	[illegible]	[illegible]
44	7912	Do.	—	Do. f.	R.C.	—	R.C.	—	—	[illegible]	[illegible]	[illegible]
45	8081	Grangegorman,	—	St. Peter's (No. 1, Phibsboro'), m.	R.C.	—	R.C.	R.C.	620	—	[illegible]	[illegible]
46	[illegible]	Do.	—	Do. f.	R.C.	—	R.C.	²R.C.	—	240	240	[illegible]
47	[illegible]	Do.	—	Do. i.	R.C.	—	R.C.	²R.C.	219	224	443	[illegible]
48	7716	Do.	—	Do. (No. 2), m.	R.C.	—	R.C.	—	[illegible]	—	[illegible]	[illegible]
49	10010	Do.	—	Grangegorman,	R.C.	—	R.C.	—	[illegible]	[illegible]	84	[illegible]
50	7494	Do.	—	Richmond Penitentiary, f.	Governor		R.C.	—	—	674	674	[illegible]
51	[illegible]	Do.	—	Richmond Lunatic Asylum, m.	Governor		R.C.	—	290	—	[illegible]	[illegible]
52	[illegible]	Do.	—	Do. f.	Governor		R.C.	1R.C. 1R.C.	—	206	206	[illegible]
53	[illegible]	Glasnevin,	—	Glasnevin, m.	Com.	N.E.	R.C.	—	117	—	117	[illegible]
54	[illegible]	Do.	—	Do. f.	Com.	N.E.	R.C.	R.C.	32	[illegible]	[illegible]	[illegible]
55	1147	Holmpatrick,	—	Skerries, m.	R.C.	—	R.C.	R.C.	270	—	270	141
56	1148	Do.	—	Do. f.	R.C.	—	R.C.	²R.C.	—	219	[illegible]	115
57	7278	Do.	—	Grange,	R.C.	—	²R.C.	—	41	[illegible]	[illegible]	37
58	7847	Howth,	—	Howth, m.	R.C.	—	R.C.	—	129	—	[illegible]	[illegible]
59	[illegible]	Do.	—	Do. f.	R.C.	—	R.C.	R.C.	—	163	[illegible]	[illegible]
60	[illegible]	Do.	—	Barrow,*	—	—	—	—	—	—	—	—
61	710	Kilsaleghan,	—	Killsamery,	R.C.	—	R.C.	—	[illegible]	[illegible]	[illegible]	[illegible]
62	711	Kiltiernan,	4	Glencullen, m.	—	R.C.	R.C.	—	40	—	[illegible]	[illegible]
63	[illegible]	Do.	—	Do. f.	—	R.C.	R.C.	—	—	103	[illegible]	[illegible]
64	4970	Kill of the Grange	—	Cabinteely, m.	R.C.	—	R.C.	—	120	—	[illegible]	[illegible]
65	[illegible]	Do.	—	Do. f.	R.C.	—	R.C.	—	—	110	110	[illegible]
66	[illegible]	Killiney,	—	Ballybrack,	R.C.	—	R.C.	R.C.	41	91	[illegible]	[illegible]
67	714	Lucan,	67	Lucan, m.	R.C.	—	R.C.	—	107	—	[illegible]	[illegible]
68	[illegible]	Do.	—	Do. Convent, f.	R.C.	—	Nuns		48	190	[illegible]	[illegible]
69	716	Lusk,	80	Lusk, m.	R.C.	—	R.C.	—	183	—	[illegible]	[illegible]
70	[illegible]	Do.	—	Do. f.	R.C.	—	R.C.	—	—	[illegible]	[illegible]	[illegible]
71	[illegible]	Do.	—	Corduff,	—	R.C.	R.C.	—	44	29	73	[illegible]
72	[illegible]	Do.	—	Lambay Island,	R.C.	—	R.C.	—	18	9	27	18
73	[illegible]	Do.	—	Rush, m.	R.C.	—	R.C.	R.C.	194	—	[illegible]	[illegible]
74	[illegible]	Do.	—	Do. f.	R.C.	—	²R.C.	²R.C.	—	[illegible]	[illegible]	[illegible]
75	8434	Do.	—	Loughshinny,	R.C.	—	R.C.	—	70	[illegible]	[illegible]	[illegible]
76	8144	Do.	—	Balrothery Workhouse,	P.L. Gds.		R.C.	—	24	20	41	[illegible]
77	[illegible]	Do.	—	Hedgestown,	R.C.	—	R.C.	—	63	[illegible]	[illegible]	[illegible]
78	1036	Monkstown,	40	Blackrock, m.	R.C.	—	R.C.	—	—	160	[illegible]	77

* Including value of Free Residence. ¹ Including value of Free Residence and Garden.

Province of Leinster: County of Dublin—*continued.*

Amount paid for Books, Requisites, and Apparatus at Reduced Prices.	Aid granted by the Board during the Year 1874. In Free Stock of Books, Requisites, and Apparatus.	In Salaries, Premiums, and other Gratuities.	Results Fees, Financial Year.	Amount of Local Emoluments received in Aid of Teacher's Salary. School Fees.	Subscriptions, Endowments, &c.	Total Local Aid.	Vested or Non-Vested.	Number.
£ s. d.	£ s. d.	£ s. d.	£ s. d.	£ s. d.	£ s. d.	£ s. d.		
1 17 10	—	54 18 4	9 6 0	8 8 7	28 0 0	* 30 8 7		19
3 7 4	—	69 10 0	13 17 6	7 18 2	—	7 18 2		20
4 8 3	—	58 3 4	13 0 6	8 14 8	10 0 0	* 18 14 8		21
1 15 6	—	83 10 0	11 6 6	8 0 11	0 0 0	8 0 11		22
1 5 0	—	55 13 4	19 13 0	28 7 0	5 0 0	33 7 0		23
5 18 0	1 0 0	59 3 4	16 17 0	10 8 7	5 8 0	* 16 3 7	N.V.	24
9 0 11	—	60 0 0	10 16 0	4 0 1	6 0 0	* 10 6 1	V.S.	25
1 4 0	—	12 6 8	8 11 6	8 17 8	16 13 4	25 11 0		26
4 8 2	—	76 3 4	34 5 6	11 14 11	10 0 0	21 14 11		27
1 10 3	—	30 0 0	19 8 0	18 14 0	—	18 14 0	V.T.	28
3 1 9	—	26 0 0	10 8 0	9 10 1	—	9 10 1	V.T.	29
1 15 7	—	37 6 8	14 1 0	6 4 7	—	6 4 7		30
—	—	81 10 0	1 17 0	2 11 10	0 0 0	6 11 10		31
1 4 8	—	20 0 0	6 7 8	8 15 0	4 0 0	7 15 9		32
8 14 2	—	44 10 0	9 17 0	14 3 0	10 0 0	24 3 0	V.T.	33
4 18 6	—	84 10 0	18 11 0	10 4 5	8 0 0	18 4 5	V.T.	34
0 12 1	—	20 0 0	5 3 6	3 8 5	8 0 0	11 8 5		35
—	—	20 10 0	5 10 0	6 1 6	5 0 0	* 11 1 6		36
6 3 9	—	68 10 0	22 15 0	11 8 0	10 0 0	* 21 8 0		37
7 8 3	—	65 19 8	30 0 0	3 10 4	—	3 10 4		38
3 6 6	—	83 10 0	14 0 0	7 17 2	17 0 0	* 24 17 2		39
			—	12 18 1	—	12 18 1		
3 6 9	—	47 1 8	16 1 0	7 17 10	18 0 0	* 25 17 10		40
9 17 1	—	28 10 0	5 10 0	1 4 0	10 0 0	* 11 4 0		41
1 4 4	—	30 0 0	6 6 0	0 17 4	5 2 8	6 0 0		42
1 17 1	—	24 0 0	4 17 0	4 17 0	20 0 0	24 17 0		43
1 6 11	—	20 0 0	12 4 0	7 0 4	—	7 0 4		44
16 6 11	—	66 0 7	30 3 6	23 10 8	18 1 10	41 18 1	V.S.	45
4 19 0	—	73 8 4	24 3 0	7 19 0	8 14 9	11 13 9	V.T.	46
8 6 8	—	94 8 4	15 10 0	11 17 5	—	11 17 5	V.T.	47
3 6 11	—	41 0 0	19 6 0	9 8 0	8 19 0	18 0 0	V.T.	48
2 19 2	—	24 10 0	8 3 6	6 15 7	20 0 0	26 15 7		49
—	—	—	—	—	—	—		50
8 2 3	—	—	—	—	—	—		51
11 13 7	—	—	—	—	—	—		52
—	—	221 6 8	23 3 0	4 17 10	—	4 17 10	V.S.	53
—	—			15 1 2	—	15 1 2	V.S.	54
10 12 4	—	71 10 8	38 16 0	24 0 4	—	24 0 4	V.S.	55
10 2 6	—	30 1 8	31 8 0	14 9 2	—	14 9 2	V.T.	56
1 8 3	—	31 6 4	6 11 0	4 17 10	—	4 17 10		57
6 11 8	—	48 10 0	8 15 6	14 18 3	17 4 0	31 10 3		58
2 14 1	—	54 6 8	17 11 0	13 9 2	—	13 9 2		59
0 17 8	—	—	—	—	—	—		60
0 17 10	—	21 0 0	2 9 0	5 18 10	4 0 0	* 9 18 10	V.T.	61
1 6 8	—	23 0 0	9 13 0	8 1 10	10 10 0	* 18 11 10		62
1 14 9	—	20 0 0	7 13 0	1 19 8	7 10 0	* 9 9 8	V.T.	63
1 4 8	—	25 13 0	4 19 0	5 0 4	10 0 0	* 15 0 4		64
8 13 1	—	67 6 8	13 18 0	4 17 2	6 0 0	* 10 17 2		65
2 16 0	—	24 1 8	11 9 0	4 19 8	—	4 19 8		66
0 15 8	—	85 15 0	6 7 0	17 11 7	10 0 0	27 11 7		67
7 2 9	—	54 16 4	25 6 0	4 17 0	4 0 0	8 17 0		68
4 16 0	—	33 13 4	9 5 0	10 19 5	—	10 19 5		69
1 11 0	8 0 6	80 10 0	21 10 6	13 10 10	1 14 0	* 15 4 10		70
3 19 3	—	20 10 0	11 16 0	8 1 9	2 10 0	* 10 11 9		71
—	—	24 0 0	4 11 0	11 11 3	—	11 11 3		72
9 3 9	—	34 16 8	21 10 6	23 7 8	—	23 7 8		73
12 12 1	—	78 10 0	45 14 0	35 2 6	—	35 2 6		74
5 4 4	—	30 6 8	10 16 0	15 5 4	—	15 5 4		75
5 6 1	—	1 10 0	—	—	—	—		76
6 18 6	—	24 0 0	16 2 0	10 1 0	1 10 0	11 11 0		77
4 18 3	—	68 10 0	13 6 0	8 8 8	18 0 0	26 8 8		78

* [illegible]

List of Schools in operation on the 31st December, 1874.—

Number.	Roll Number of School.	Parish.	District.	School.	Religious Denomination of Manager or Correspondent.		Religious Denomination of Teachers.		Attendance for the Year.			
									Total number of Pupils on Rolls within the Year 1874.			[illegible]
					Clerical.	Lay.	Principals.	Assistants.	Males.	Females.	Total.	
79	731	Monkstown, .	40	Blackrock Convent,	R.C.	–	Nuns		264	300	564	277
81	[illegible]	Do. .	–	Glasthule, . m.	R.C.	–	R.C.	–	174	–	174	[illegible]
81	[illegible]	Do. .	–	Do. Convent, f.	R.C.	–	Nuns		102	311	413	[illegible]
87	[illegible]	Do. .	–	Kingstown Convt. f.	–	R.C.	Nuns		233	904	1,137	[illegible]
88	[illegible]	Malahide, .	34	Malahide, . m.	R.C.	–	R.C.	–	94	–	94	[illegible]
84	5719	Do. .	–	Do. . f.	R.C.	–	R.C.	–	–	107	107	[illegible]
[illegible]	[illegible]	Milltown, .	36	Milltown, . m.	R.C.	–	R.C.	–	104	–	103	[illegible]
[illegible]	[illegible]	Do. .	–	Do. . f.	R.C.	–	R.C.	–	40	123	163	51
87	[illegible]	Newcastle, .	37	Newcastle, .	R.C.	–	R.C.	–	63	43	[illegible]	[illegible]
[illegible]	1178	Naul, .	35	Naul, . f.	R.C.	–	R.C.	–	39	33	72	[illegible]
[illegible]	1170	Do. .	–	Do.* . m.	–	–	–	–	–	–	–	–
[illegible]	[illegible]	Old Connaught,	40	St. Peter's, Little Bray, . m.	R.C.	–	R.C.	–	241	–	241	107
93	7748	Do. .	–	Do. . f.	R.C.	–	R.C.	R.C.	–	168	168	57
94	728	Palmerstown, .	39	Palmerstown, .	R.C.	–	R.C.	–	38	40	78	[illegible]
[illegible]	1294	Raheny, .	32	Raheny, . m.	R.C.	–	R.C.	–	77	–	77	[illegible]
[illegible]	1578	Do. .	–	Do. . f.	R.C.	–	R.C.	–	–	78	78	[illegible]
[illegible]	[illegible]	Rathfarnham, .	38	Rathfarnham, .	R.C.	–	R.C.	–	198	–	198	[illegible]
[illegible]	[illegible]	Do. .	–	Kilmashogue, m.	R.C.	–	R.C.	–	73	–	78	[illegible]
97	[illegible]	Do. .	–	Do. . f.	R.C.	–	R.C.	–	–	57	57	27
[illegible]	749	Do. .	–	Loretto Convent, f.	–	R.C.	Nuns		35	131	[illegible]	[illegible]
[illegible]	[illegible]	Do. .	–	Roundtown Convt. f.	–	R.C.	Nuns		118	310	[illegible]	[illegible]
[illegible]	0704	Do. .	–	Do. . m.	R.C.	–	R.C.	–	153	–	153	[illegible]
101	5746	Rathmichael, .	40	Loughlinstown, m.	R.C.	–	R.C.	–	174	–	174	81
102	5745	Do. .	–	Do. . f.	R.C.	–	R.C.	–	27	70	97	31
[illegible]	[illegible]	Do. .	–	Ballycorus, . m.	–	R.C.	R.C.	–	[illegible]	–	[illegible]	[illegible]
[illegible]	[illegible]	Do. .	–	Do. . f.	–	R.C.	R.C.	–	–	70	79	[illegible]
[illegible]	[illegible]	Do. .	–	Rathdown, Workhouse,	P.L. Gdns.		R.C.	–	71	50	121	[illegible]
[illegible]	[illegible]	Do. .	–	Tillystown, .	R.C.	–	R.C.	–	47	45	[illegible]	[illegible]
107	[illegible]	Rathcoole, .	37	Rathcoole, .	–	R.C.	R.C.	R.C.	74	[illegible]	137	[illegible]
108	[illegible]	Swords, .	33	Swords, . m.	R.C.	–	R.C.	R.C.	343	–	343	[illegible]
109	[illegible]	Do. .	–	Do. . f.	R.C.	–	R.C.	2R.C.	–	*301	301	[illegible]
110	[illegible]	St. Audoen's, .	36	St. Audoen's, . m.	R.C.	–	R.C.	R.C.	314	–	314	[illegible]
111	[illegible]	Do. .	–	Do. . f.	R.C.	–	R.C.	2R.C.	58	291	349	[illegible]
112	7032	St. Anne's, .	–	Lorcan-lane, . f.	–	R.C.	R.C.	2R.C.	–	218	279	81
113	[illegible]	Do. .	–	Do. . i.	–	R.C.	R.C.	3R.C.	150	170	[illegible]	[illegible]
114	[illegible]	St. Bride's, .	–	St. Bride's, . m.	R.C.	–	R.C.	–	63	–	63	[illegible]
115	[illegible]	Do. .	–	Do. . f.	R.C.	–	R.C.	–	–	24	24	[illegible]
116	[illegible]	Do. .	–	Do. . i.	R.C.	–	R.C.	R.C.	90	94	184	[illegible]
117	137	St. Catherine's,	–	St. Catherine's, m.	R.C.	–	R.C.	R.C.	[illegible]	–	[illegible]	[illegible]
				Do. . evg.	R.C.	–	R.C.	–	141	–	141	[illegible]
118	[illegible]	Do. .	–	Do. . f.	R.C.	–	R.C.	4R.C.	–	393	[illegible]	[illegible]
119	[illegible]	Do. .	–	Do. . i.	R.C.	–	R.C.	3R.C.	[illegible]	[illegible]	[illegible]	[illegible]
120	[illegible]	Do. .	–	Harold's-cross, m.	R.C.	–	R.C.	–	190	–	190	[illegible]
121	[illegible]	Do. .	–	St. Clare's, . f.	R.C.	–	R.C.	R.C.	[illegible]	250	317	[illegible]
122	[illegible]	Do. .	–	John-street, . f.	R.C.	–	R.C.	3R.C.	–	294	294	[illegible]
123	[illegible]	Do. .	–	Do. . i.	R.C.	–	R.C.	4R.C.	140	120	260	[illegible]
124	[illegible]	Do. .	–	Weavers'-square Convent, .	–	R.C.	Nuns		[illegible]	[illegible]	1,370	[illegible]
[illegible]	[illegible]	Do. .	37	West Dublin Mod. m.	Com.	N.E.	R.C.	[illegible]	303	–	[illegible]	[illegible]
126	[illegible]	Do. .	–	Do. . f.	Com.	N.E.	R.C.	[illegible]	–	273	273	111
127	[illegible]	Do. .	–	Do. . i.	Com.	N.E.	R.C.	R.C.	109	118	221	[illegible]
[illegible]	[illegible]	Do. .	37	Cork-street, .	Dis.	–	Dis.	–	28	30	[illegible]	[illegible]
[illegible]	[illegible]	Do. .	–	Richmond Bridewell,	Governor		R.C.	–	178	–	178	17
[illegible]	[illegible]	St. Doloughs's, .	37	Kinsealy, . m.	R.C.	–	R.C.	–	108	–	108	57
131	[illegible]	Do. .	–	Do. . f.	R.C.	–	R.C.	–	–	81	81	[illegible]
132	[illegible]	St. George's, .	–	St. Francis Xavier's, f.	R.C.	–	R.C.	R.C.	–	160	160	[illegible]
133	6196	Do. .	–	Do. . i.	R.C.	–	R.C.	3R.C.	170	114	284	[illegible]
134	6017	Do. .	–	Josephian, . f.	R.C.	–	R.C.	2R.C.	–	293	[illegible]	[illegible]
				Do. . evg.	R.C.	–	R.C.	R.C.	–	97	97	[illegible]
135	7013	St. James's, .	36	Dolphin's Barn, .	R.C.	–	R.C.	R.C.	60	68	128	[illegible]

a Including value of Free Residence. b Including value of Free Residence and Garden.

Province of Leinster: County of Dublin—*continued.*

Amount paid for Books, Requisites, and Apparatus at Reduced Prices.	Aid granted by the Board during the Year 1874: In Free Stock of Books, Requisites, and Apparatus.	In Salaries, Premiums, and other Gratuities.	Results Fees, Preceding Year.	Amount of Local Endowments received in Aid of Teacher's Salary: School Fees.	Subscriptions, Endowments, &c.	Total Local Aid.	Vested or Non-Vested.	Number.
£ s. d.	£ s. d.	£ s. d.	£ s. d.	£ s. d.	£ s. d.	£ s. d.		
78 13 10	—	170 6 6	20 4 0	19 3 1	—	19 3 1		79
4 11 3	—	33 16 0	24 7 6	7 4 2	40 0 0	* 47 1 2		80
13 14 4	—	152 1 8	37 0 8	81 19 6	—	81 19 6		81
20 1 11	—	234 7 8	105 1 0	18 7 4	50 0 0	68 7 4		82
6 7 1	—	37 10 0	4 14 6	6 4 6	4 0 0	10 4 6		83
1 18 1	—	36 16 8	13 3 6	8 4 2	12 0 0	20 4 2		84
6 0 1	—	28 10 0	8 18 0	5 4 1	6 0 0	11 4 1		85
2 10 1	—	31 8 4	10 1 0	10 15 0	—	10 15 0		86
4 2 11	—	24 0 0	11 15 0	5 1 8	5 0 0	* 10 1 8		87
4 11 11	—	28 0 0	5 10 0	5 1 8	9 10 0	b 14 11 8	V.T.	88
—	—	—	—	—	—	—	V.T.	89
—	—	64 6 8	35 15 0	24 0 3	—	24 0 3		90
10 8 7	—	40 18 8	12 8 0	10 16 10	—	10 16 10		91
1 7 0	—	21 0 8	0 16 0	6 10 0	2 0 0	* 5 10 0		92
1 9 7	—	37 10 8	8 0 0	6 3 11	8 0 0	14 3 11		93
2 3 5	—	24 0 0	10 2 0	6 6 8	6 0 0	12 6 8		94
5 17 0	—	81 0 0	31 11 0	25 8 8	4 0 0	29 8 8		95
1 18 10	—	21 0 0	8 0 8	6 1 7	4 0 0	10 1 7		96
0 18 7	—	30 0 0	0 16 0	3 11 2	6 3 0	9 14 2		97
8 4 8	—	87 11 4	12 17 6	7 13 1	—	7 13 1		98
12 12 1	—	102 9 8	88 19 6	13 8 0	—	13 8 0		99
2 0 2	—	79 18 4	10 12 6	0 1 4	4 0 0	18 1 8		100
6 3 8	—	45 3 4	10 4 6	7 5 3	—	7 5 3		101
1 17 0	—	20 0 0	5 10 6	2 18 10	—	2 18 10		102
4 1 10	—	64 3 4	13 18 0	14 11 2	17 11 4	* 32 2 6	V.C.	103
2 0 4	—	64 8 8	16 15 0	11 14 4	10 3 2	21 17 10	V.C.	104
11 8 5	—	1 18 8	—	—	—	—		105
1 5 8	—	20 0 0	0 8 6	3 15 6	—	3 15 6		106
2 11 0	—	40 0 0	0 1 6	2 16 0	—	2 16 0		107
13 8 6	—	64 10 0	97 5 0	5 5 0	10 0 0	15 5 0		108
11 14 3	—	107 13 4	47 8 0	12 7 0	10 0 0	* 22 7 0		109
8 8 0	—	64 0 0	17 0 0	3 18 7	8 0 0	11 18 7		110
2 14 8	—	109 19 8	19 8 0	5 3 11	4 17 1	10 0 0		111
11 0 7	—	12 0 0	25 0 0	—	—	—		112
—	—	73 0 8	17 10 6	11 15 6	—	11 15 6		113
—	—	21 0 0	4 11 0	—	58 0 0	* 58 0 0		114
2 1 10	—	20 0 0	8 4 6	—	30 0 0	30 0 0		115
1 5 0	—	47 8 8	14 7 6	—	35 0 0	* 35 0 0		116
} 9 18 10	—	94 6 4	{ 30 18 8	12 10 0	86 0 0	. 42 10 0		117
			1 10 0	11 7 8	—	11 7 8		
16 18 11	—	158 8 4	25 18 6	14 8 6	16 3 6	. 30 7 0		118
5 9 5	—	145 0 0	26 9 6	11 18 1	8 6 11	16 0 0		119
11 6 0	—	77 6 0	35 4 6	16 5 0	18 0 0	34 5 0	V.T.	120
10 8 1	—	59 5 5	20 0 6	—	—	—		121
3 10 0	—	84 10 0	10 10 0	8 0 9	10 0 0	18 0 9		122
—	—	73 10 8	2 5 0	1 16 7	5 0 0	6 16 7		123
—	—	101 10 8	197 9 0	47 3 8	—	67 3 8		124
10 11 0	18 1 4	1,017 7 11	97 8 6	120 5 11	—	220 5 11	V.C.	125
18 7 9	14 12 6						V.C.	126
2 7 4	—						V.C.	127
—	—	28 10 0	8 18 6	7 0 6	14 0 0	21 0 6		128
—	—	—	—	—	—	—		129
3 14 11	—	31 8 0	11 8 0	6 4 11	8 7 0	* 8 11 11	E.	130
1 18 6	—	24 0 0	9 13 0	4 19 6	8 7 0	* 8 6 4	E.	131
7 8 11	—	30 0 0	22 12 6	11 12 0	18 0 0	* 30 12 0		132
0 10 0	—	20 5 0	18 8 0	14 15 8	8 0 0	17 15 8		133
} 13 17 4	—	[145 11 8	60 4 6	10 4 11	—	10 4 11		134
		4 18 0	25 0 6	0 11 6	20 0 0	20 11 6		
1 17 1	—	44 0 0	0 2 6	6 14 9	—	. 6 14 9		135

* Inoperative.

b Including value of Free Garden.

List of Schools in operation on the 31st December, 1874—

Number.	Roll Number of School.	Parish.	District.	School.	Religious Denomination of Managers or Correspondent: Clerical.	Lay.	Principal and Religious Denomination of Teachers: Principals.	Assistants.	Attendance for the Year. Total number of Pupils on Rolls within the Year 1874: Males.	Fem.	Total.	Average Daily Attendance for the Year.
136	6975	St. James's,	38	Inchicore Rail. Model, day, m.	Com.	N.E.	Pres.	R.C.	310	–	140	[illegible]
				Do. evg.	Com.	N.E.	Pres.	R.C.	145	–	145	81
137	6976	Do.	–	Do. f.	Com.	N.E.	R.C.	R.C.	–	[illegible]	89	[illegible]
138	6966	Do.	–	Do. i.	Com.	N.E.	R.C.	–	60	[illegible]	108	[illegible]
139	[illegible]	Do.	–	St. James's, f.	R.C.	–	R.C.	–	–	[illegible]	[illegible]	[illegible]
140	8242	Do.	–	Do. i.	R.C.	–	R.C.	R.C.	187	171	[illegible]	[illegible]
141	7546	Do.	–	Golden Bridge Convt., f.	–	R.C.	Nuns		145	501	646	213
142	744	St. John's,	–	SS. Michael & John's day m.	R.C.	–	R.C.	3R.C.	647	–	647	141
				Do. evg.	R.C.	–	R.C.	R.C.	550	–	550	81
143	745	Do.	–	Do. f.	R.C.	–	R.C.	1R.C.	–	515	515	149
144	8171	Do.	–	Do. i.	R.C.	–	R.C.	5R.C.	391	402	793	206
145	[illegible]	St. Jude's,	–	Kilmainham Gaol,	Governor		R.C.	R.C.	46	17	63	11
146	[illegible]	Do.	–	Inchicore, South,	–	R.C.	R.C.	R.C.	212	–	212	177
147	4742	St. Luke's,	–	Warrenmount Convt. f.	R.C.	–	Nuns		–	731	731	221
148	747	St. Margaret's,	39	St. Margaret's,	R.C.	–	R.C.	–	67	60	127	87
149	6405	Do.	–	Kilcoskan,	R.C.	–	R.C.	–	25	[illegible]	84	34
150	6668	St. Mary's,	–	Denmark-street, m.	R.C.	–	R.C.	–	102	–	102	46
151	[illegible]	Do.	–	Do. (1), m.	R.C.	–	R.C.	R.C.	481	–	481	152
152	10346	Do.	–	Do. (1), f.	R.C.	–	R.C.	3R.C.	–	408	408	83
153	1149	Do.	–	King's Inns-street, Convent, f.	R.C.	–	Nuns		334	1,449	1,783	744
154	[illegible]	Do.	–	Dominick-street, m.	–	Pres.	Pres.	–	81	–	81	46
155	10019	Do.	–	Do. f.	–	Pres.	Pres.	–	–	81	81	41
156	[illegible]	Do.	–	Do. i.	–	Pres.	Pres.	–	19	43	60	[illegible]
157	8017	St. Mary's, Donnybrook,	39	Ringsend, day, m.	–	R.C.	R.C.	R.C.	301	–	301	[illegible]
				Do. evg.	–	R.C.	R.C.	–	163	–	163	87
158	2614	Do.	–	Do. f.	–	R.C.	R.C.	R.C.	–	158	158	[illegible]
159	8471	Do.	–	Do. i.	–	R.C.	R.C.	R.C.	80	80	164	76
160	10468	Do.	–	Donnybrook,	R.C.	–	R.C.	–	234	–	234	[illegible]
161	[illegible]	Do.	–	Irishtown, m.	–	R.C.	R.C.	–	116	–	116	31
162	[illegible]	Do.	–	Do. f.	–	R.C.	R.C.	–	25	86	111	[illegible]
163	747	St. Mark's,	–	St. Andrew's (1), f.	–	R.C.	R.C.	3R.C.	–	634	634	97
164	8162	Do.	–	Do. (2), f.	–	R.C.	R.C.	3R.C.	282	–	282	104
165	8162	Do.	–	Do. i.	–	R.C.	R.C.	4R.C.	858	–	858	114
166	9215	Do.	–	Townsend-street, f.	–	R.C.	R.C.	4R.C.	–	347	347	139
167	9212	Do.	–	Do. i.	–	R.C.	R.C.	4R.C.	–	539	539	[illegible]
168	10043	Do.	–	Lombard-street,	Diss.	–	Diss.	–	15	37	52	[illegible]
169	3607	St. Michan's,	30	St. Michan's, m.	R.C.	–	R.C.	R.C.	203	–	203	[illegible]
				Do. evg.	R.C.	–	R.C.	–	285	–	285	[illegible]
170	[illegible]	Do.	–	Do. f.	R.C.	–	R.C.	–	–	118	118	38
171	8615	Do.	–	Do. i.	R.C.	–	R.C.	3R.C.	124	94	218	81
172	7718	Do.	–	Do. (No. 2), m.	R.C.	–	R.C.	–	317	–	317	93
173	7482	Do.	–	North Anne-st. i.	R.C.	–	R.C.	3R.C.	153	108	261	167
174	[illegible]	Do.	–	George's-hill Convent, f.	R.C.	–	Nuns		–	1,231	1,231	[illegible]
175	8222	Do.	–	Josephian, i.	R.C.	–	R.C.	R.C.	182	111	293	87
176	[illegible]	St. Nicholas Without,	[illegible]	St. Nicholas Without, (No. 1), f.	R.C.	–	R.C.	3R.C.	–	808	808	91
177	[illegible]	Do.	–	Do. i.	R.C.	–	R.C.	4R.C.	206	433	639	83
178	7062	Do.	–	Do. (No. 2), f.	R.C.	–	R.C.	4R.C.	–	273	273	83
179	1784	St. Paul's,	30	St. Paul's, day, m.	R.C.	–	R.C.	–	190	–	190	83
				Do. evg.	R.C.	–	R.C.	–	186	–	186	19
180	178	Do.	–	Do. f.	R.C.	–	R.C.	2R.C.	–	263	263	87
181	8728	Do.	–	Do. i.	R.C.	–	R.C.	4R.C.	138	160	298	116
182	7917	Do.	–	Do. (No. 2), m.	R.C.	–	R.C.	R.C.	197	–	197	69
183	7918	Do.	–	Do. f.	R.C.	–	R.C.	–	–	180	180	38
184	9018	Do.	–	North Brunswick-st. f.	R.C.	–	R.C.	4R.C.	163	319	482	141
185	9156	Do.	–	Blackhall-place, f.	Diss.	–	Diss.	–	45	52	97	[illegible]
186	7157	Do.	–	North Dublin Workho.	P.L.	Gds.	1E.C. 1R.C.	1E.C. 3R.C.	193	174	367	185
187	9025	Do.	–	Manor-street, f.	–	R.C.	R.C.	3R.C.	–	341	341	[illegible]
188	[illegible]	Do.	–	Do. i.	–	R.C.	R.C.	3R.C.	140	313	453	[illegible]
189	[illegible]	St. Peter's,	[illegible]	St. Peter's, m.	R.C.	–	R.C.	R.C.	165	–	165	35
190	744	Do.	–	Do. f.	R.C.	–	R.C.	3R.C.	–	416	416	101

* Including value of Free Breakfasts.

Province of Leinster: County of Dublin—continued.

Amount paid for Books, Requisites, and Apparatus at Reduced Prices.	Aid granted by the Board during the Year 1874: In Free stock of Books, Requisites, and Apparatus.	In Salaries, Premiums, and other Gratuities.	Results Fees, Financial Year.	Amount of Local Emoluments received in Aid of Teacher's Salary: School Fees.	Subscriptions, Endowments, &c.	Total Local Aid.	Vested or Non-Vested.	Number.
£ s. d.	£ s. d.	£ s. d.	£ s. d.	£ s. d.	£ s. d.	£ s. d.		
13 9 8	4 11 7							136
14 5 7	—	208 16 8	77 17 0	90 6 11	—	90 6 11	N.V.	137
—	—							138
—	—	80 0 0	4 13 0	6 15 2	10 0 0	16 15 2		139
—	—	48 0 0	5 18 0	9 4 1	4 0 0	13 4 1		140
—	—	138 10 6	12 0 0	15 11 10	—	15 11 10		141
—	—	94 6 0	86 7 0	6 7 3	24 12 9	31 0 0		142
17 5 0	—	16 0 0	25 15 0	—	—	—		
7 5 4	—	116 6 4	34 19 6	10 0 5	—	10 0 5		143
7 18 2	—	147 4 5	81 16 0	14 18 4	—	14 18 4		144
—	—	—	—	—	—	—		145
4 9 1	8 10 0	—	—	10 10 6	—	16 19 6		146
11 14 2	—	118 2 0	46 9 6	87 10 11	—	87 10 11		147
9 5 10	—	12 0 0	6 10 0	6 19 1	2 10 0	9 0 1		148
2 4 6	—	26 0 0	5 5 6	4 10 2	6 0 0	* 10 10 2		149
2 11 6	—	87 11 8	8 10 0	—	12 0 0	12 0 0		150
0 10 9	—	68 18 4	10 13 6	20 14 7	—	20 14 7		151
6 4 2	—	85 16 10	17 11 0	13 12 0	—	13 12 0		152
77 0 0	—	565 16 6	248 5 6	109 6 2	20 0 0	129 6 2	N.V.	153
9 18 8	—	65 10 10	18 9 0	28 0 0	21 0 0	49 0 0		154
4 12 6	—	40 1 6	22 14 6	11 8 8	10 0 0	21 8 8		155
—	—	21 6 0	4 15 0	10 0 0	4 0 0	14 0 0		156
10 5 11	—	106 0 0	21 0 6	1 8 4	22 10 0	* 24 18 4	V.C.	157
—	—	—	2 0 0	2 0 4	40 4 6	* 42 9 10		
8 1 8	—	52 18 4	18 0 0	2 16 1	30 0 0	* 32 16 1	V.C.	158
0 12 4	—	61 0 0	11 5 0	4 17 4	37 0 0	* 41 17 4	V.C.	159
11 11 4	—	32 16 8	15 15 6	7 9 0	4 11 0	12 0 0		160
6 5 8	—	27 10 0	3 13 6	7 10 8	35 0 0	* 42 10 8		161
1 6 11	—	37 0 0	4 17 6	5 18 11	20 0 0	25 18 11		162
—	—	40 13 4	17 14 6	—	—	—		163
0 10 1	—	106 6 8	15 19 0	—	—	—		164
—	—	119 6 8	32 18 0	—	—	—		165
22 14 8	—	140 0 0	57 4 0	—	—	—		166
1 7 3	—	167 0 0	30 8 0	—	—	—		167
2 11 10	—	23 10 0	6 12 6	12 16 7	6 0 0	18 16 7		168
6 2 6	—	72 0 0	21 19 6	5 12 0	14 8 0	20 0 0		169
—	—		12 16 6	11 8 0	2 0 0	13 8 0		
1 5 0	—	20 18 4	8 6 0	2 7 1	—	2 7 1		170
1 7 11	—	60 0 0	12 3 0	3 2 5	11 17 7	14 0 0		171
1 6 10	—	34 6 8	12 3 0	6 10 9	6 9 3	13 0 0		172
2 18 3	—	70 0 8	21 19 0	2 10 6	11 9 6	14 0 0		173
24 16 11	—	256 19 8	71 14 6	14 6 6	72 0 0	86 6 6		174
—	—	60 18 4	6 16 0	6 11 10	—	6 11 10		175
2 10 1	—	37 0 0	27 6 6	16 0 0	4 0 0	11 0 0		176
0 12 10	—	103 3 4	15 4 6	18 0 0	—	18 0 0		177
2 4 1	—	73 10 0	27 14 0	8 0 0	4 0 0	12 0 0		178
5 5 10	—	48 13 4	20 11 6	7 0 10	18 0 0	25 0 10		179
—	—		2 18 0	4 1 1	—	4 1 1		
6 5 1	—	80 6 8	41 0 6	5 9 0	11 0 0	* 16 9 0		180
—	—	77 0 0	17 18 6	5 5 4	—	5 5 4		181
1 5 8	—	66 15 0	8 8 4	6 3 7	15 4 0	* 20 0 7		182
1 6 6	—	30 10 0	6 6 0	3 15 7	2 0 0	4 15 7		183
9 16 8	4 10 0	169 18 4	29 9 6	11 6 1	24 0 0	35 6 1		184
5 5 7	—	80 0 0	6 10 0	18 0 0	4 0 0	22 0 0		185
10 9 9	—	15 0 0	—	—	—	—		186
11 6 5	—	120 0 8	57 9 6	18 17 9	—	18 17 9		187
—	—	108 6 4	17 18 0	15 14 8	—	15 14 8		188
5 4 0	—	80 0 0	14 18 6	8 1 0	—	8 1 0		189
6 18 5	—	85 0 0	28 18 6	20 11 0	—	20 11 0		190

List of Schools in operation on the 31st December, 1874.—

Number.	Roll Number of School.	Parish.	District.	School.	Religious Denomination of Manager or Correspondent. Clerical.	Lay.	Number and Religious Denominations of Teachers. Principals.	Assistants.	Attendance for the Year. Total number of Pupils on Rolls within the Year were. Males.	Fem.	Total.	Average Daily Attendance for the Year.
191	6209	St. Peter's, . .	26	St. Peter's, junior department, m.	R.C.	–	R.C.	R.C.	297	–	297	67
192	6209	Do. . .	–	Do. Do. f.	R.C.	–	R.C.	4 R.C.	279	441	720	153
193	1659	Do. . .	–	Rathmines, m.	R.C.	–	R.C.	–	182	–	182	40
194	1351	Do. . .	–	Do. . . f.	R.C.	–	R.C.	R.C.	–	249	249	54
195	7767	Do. . .	–	Do. . . i.	R.C.	–	R.C.	R.C.	164	95	259	97
196	6255	Do. . .	–	Haddington-road, m.	R.C.	–	R.C.	–	170	–	170	56
197	7016	Do. . .	–	Ranelagh, . f.	–	R.C.	R.C.	–	–	143	143	44
198	[illegible]	Do. . .	–	Tranquilla Convent, f.	–	R.C.	Nuns		–	214	214	97
199	2018	Do. . .	–	Baggot-st. Convent, f.	–	R.C.	Nuns		730	1,004	2,[illegible]	[illegible]
200	10914	Do. . .	–	Whitefriar-street, .	Pres.	–	Pres.	–	71	62	133	31
201	792	St. Thomas's, . .	30	Central Mod. m. No. 1,	–	Commrs. of N. E.	R.C.	3 R.C. 1 R.C.	660	–	660	465
				Do. . . evg.	–		–	7 R.C. 2 R.C.	208	–	208	157
202	6652	Do. . .	–	Do. . No. 2,	–		R.C.	–	218	–	218	65
203	[illegible]	Do. . .	–	Do. . No. 3,	–		R.C.	–	124	–	124	58
204	[illegible]	Do. . .	–	Do. . No. 4,	–		R.C.	D.C.	146	–	146	65
205	[illegible]	Do. . .	–	Do. . No. 5,	–		R.C.	1 R.C. 1 R.C.	220	–	220	95
206	792	Do. . .	–	Do. . f. No. 1,	–		R.C.	4 R.C. 4 R.C. Fem.	–	637	637	374
207	[illegible]	Do. . .	–	Do. . No. 2,	–		R.C.	R.C.	–	208	208	64
208	[illegible]	Do. . .	–	Do. . f. No. 3,	–		R.C.	R.C.	–	115	115	44
209	[illegible]	Do. . .	–	Do. . No. 4,	–		R.C.	R.C.	–	140	140	84
210	1794	Do. . .	–	Do. . . i.	–		R.C.	2 R.C.	305	218	523	205
211	6468	Do. . .	–	Saint Laurence O'Toole's, No. 1, f.	R.C.	–	R.C.	R.C.	–	297	297	94
212	[illegible]	Do. . .	–	Do. . . i.	R.C.	–	R.C.	4 R.C.	218	601	819	275
213	[illegible]	Do. . .	–	Do. . No. 2, f.	R.C.	–	R.C.	R.C.	–	108	108	57
214	11091	Do. . .	–	Do. . . evg.	R.C.	–	R.C.	–	100	–	100	45
215	[illegible]	Do. . .	–	St. Patrick's, No. 1, m.	R.C.	–	R.C.	R.C.	231	–	231	87
216	[illegible]	Do. . .	–	Do. No. 1, f.	R.C.	–	R.C.	2 R.C.	–	246	246	77
217	6708	Do. . .	–	Do. No. 2, m. i.	R.C.	–	R.C.	R.C.	140	–	140	60
218	9707	Do. . .	–	Do. No. 2, f. i.	R.C.	–	R.C.	4 R.C.	160	140	290	82
219	1286	Stillorgan, .	33	Stillorgan, . m.	R.C.	–	R.C.	–	76	–	76	35
220	3477	Do. . .	–	Do. . . i.	R.C.	–	R.C.	R.C.	44	63	107	45
221	10484	Do. . .	–	Newtownpark, a .	R.C.	–	–	–	–	–	–	–
222	7700	Santry, . .	30	Ballymun, . .	R.C.	–	R.C.	–	73	42	115	60
223	730	Saggart, . .	37	Saggart, . . m.	R.C.	–	R.C.	–	123	–	123	51
224	6606	Do. . .	–	Do. . . f.	R.C.	–	R.C.	–	–	94	94	40
225	10457	Tallaght, . .	28	Tallaght, . m.	R.C.	–	R.C.	–	108	–	108	33
226	10458	Do. . .	–	Do. . . f.	R.C.	–	R.C.	–	15	96	111	34
227	6997	Do. . .	–	Glenasmole, m. day,	–	R.C.	R.C.	–	144	–	144	56
				Do. . . evg.	–	R.C.	R.C.	–	55	–	55	25
228	7616	Do. . .	–	Do. . . f.	–	R.C.	R.C.	R.C.	–	129	129	35
229	1167	Taney, . .	–	Dundrum, . m.	R.C.	–	R.C.	R.C.	130	–	130	54
230	1168	Do. . .	–	Do. . . f.	R.C.	–	R.C.	R.C.	67	149	216	67
231	2873	Do. . .	–	Sandyford, . m.	R.C.	–	R.C.	–	100	–	100	41
232	2878	Do. . .	–	Do. . . f.	R.C.	–	R.C.	R.C.	–	183	183	80
233	[illegible]	Whitechurch, .	–	Edmondstown, m.	R.C.	–	R.C.	–	79	–	79	34
234	3059	Do. . .	–	Do. . . f.	R.C.	–	R.C.	–	15	94	109	35
235	6379	Do. . .	–	Fir House, Convt., f.	–	R.C.	Nuns		72	110	182	74
		Total for County of Dublin, 223, .							23,610	30,049	53,[illegible]	20,179

a Returns not available.

b Including value of Free Residence.

Province of Leinster: County of Dublin—*continued.*

Amount paid for Books, Requisites, and Apparatus at Reduced Prices.	Aid granted by the Board during the Year 1874. In Free Stock of Books, Requisites, and Apparatus.	In Salaries, Premiums, and other Gratuities.	Results Fees, Financial Year.	Amount of Local Emoluments received in Aid of Teacher's Salary. School Fees.	Subscriptions, Endowments, &c.	Total Local Aid.	Vested or Non-Vested.	Number.
£ s. d.	£ s. d.	£ s. d.	£ s. d.	£ s. d.	£ s. d.	£ s. d.		
2 14 4	—	46 0 0	0 14 6	14 8 9	—	14 8 9		191
3 0 11	—	104 0 0	16 4 6	14 11 0	—	14 11 0		192
2 10 9	—	84 0 0	6 17 0	5 11 7	12 0 0	17 11 7		193
1 6 7	—	91 0 0	26 1 0	3 15 8	12 0 0	15 15 8		194
—	—	84 0 0	9 16 6	9 18 6	—	9 18 6		195
—	—	84 0 0	6 16 6	2 6 6	12 17 6	15 4 0		196
2 8 0	—	24 0 0	6 7 0	8 0 4	8 0 0	16 0 4		197
1 16 7	—	88 12 6	13 6 0	6 3 9	—	6 3 9		198
19 17 7	8 17 6	424 14 6	310 11 0	179 19 1	—	179 19 1		199
—	—	24 0 0	9 17 6	—	46 0 0	46 0 0		200
297 7 9	102 3 10	3,068 8 10	481 5 0	1,116 17 6	—	1,116 17 6	v.c.	201
							v.c.	202
							v.c.	203
							v.c.	204
							v.c.	205
							v.c.	206
							v.c.	207
							v.c.	208
							v.c.	209
							v.c.	210
8 10 1	—	65 18 4	24 18 6	9 0 0	—	9 0 0		211
5 17 9	—	146 18 4	41 4 4	11 16 7	—	11 16 7		212
—	—	65 8 4	18 9 0	7 6 9	—	7 6 9		213
1 5 0	—	9 9 6	7 1 0	10 0 6	—	10 0 0		214
2 18 5	—	56 17 9	18 4 0	4 18 6	10 0 0	14 18 6		215
6 1 11	—	76 14 5	18 8 0	6 11 8	5 0 0	11 11 8		216
2 14 11	—	48 10 0	9 14 0	5 5 6	5 0 0	10 5 6		217
1 7 8	—	81 6 8	19 15 0	7 14 6	2 0 0	9 14 2		218
6 18 1	—	24 0 0	14 1 0	1 16 9	12 0 0	13 16 9	A.	219
3 6 3	—	53 8 4	14 8 6	0 17 9	13 0 0	13 17 9	A.	220
—	—	—	4 15 0	—	—	—		221
1 18 7	—	38 0 0	6 1 0	4 8 6	10 0 0	b 14 8 6		222
4 1 0	—	18 8 0	4 11 4	13 18 7	2 10 0	b 16 8 7		223
8 6 1	—	20 0 0	6 5 6	3 9 11	—	3 9 11		224
1 9 1	—	23 0 0	5 0 11	3 2 4	6 0 0	9 2 4		225
1 0 8	—	20 0 0	6 6 0	5 4 6	5 10 0	10 14 6		226
4 8 9	—	29 13 6	12 7 0	8 0 0	10 0 0	b 18 0 0		227
—	—	—	—	—	5 0 0	b 5 0 0		228
6 0 10	—	84 0 0	20 19 0	10 0 0	10 0 0	b 20 0 0		229
8 15 0	—	71 0 0	22 14 8	4 10 8	18 0 0	22 10 8		230
2 2 5	—	72 5 4	29 14 0	4 19 11	12 0 0	16 19 11		231
8 1 6	—	56 0 0	16 9 6	10 0 6	14 10 0	a 25 10 6		232
1 10 1	—	40 0 0	18 8 6	5 10 1	13 10 0	b 19 0 1		233
6 2 9	—	54 0 0	6 16 6	8 0 7	6 15 0	14 15 7	v.v.	234
—	—	83 0 0	9 10 0	3 15 6	6 0 0	9 15 6	v.v.	235
8 2 6	4 3 7	83 4 0	14 10 6	8 3 0	—	8 3 0		236
1,028 19 6	1[illegible] 2 4	17782 9 0	1,673 6 11	8,[illegible] 10 5	1617 13 10	8,517 4 8		

a Including value of Free Residence and Garden.

List of Schools in operation on the 31st December, 1874.—

COUNTY OF

No.	Roll Number of School	Parish.	District.	School.	Religious Denomination of Manager or Correspondent: Clerical	Lay	Religious Denomination of Teachers: Principals	Assistants	Total number of Pupils on Rolls within the Year 1874: Males	Fem.	Total	[illegible]
1	8160	Ardkill,	37	Derinturn,	R.C.	–	R.C.	–	100	105	205	58
2	744	Ballybrackany,	–	Broadford, m.	R.C.	–	R.C.	–	76	–	76	37
3	1025	Do.	–	Do. f.	R.C.	–	R.C.	–	–	76	76	32
4	1417	Ballymore-Eustace,	–	Ballymore-Eustace, m.	R.C.	–	R.C.	–	190	–	190	49
5	1510	Do.	–	Do. f.	R.C.	–	R.C.	R.C.	–	122	122	44
6	8455	Do.	–	Do. i.	R.C.	–	R.C.	R.C.	90	51	141	54
7	2341	Ballymany,	44	Ballymany,	R.C.	–	R.C.	–	91	66	162	48
8	5022	Bodenstown,	37	Sallins, m.	R.C.	–	R.C.	–	93	–	93	39
9	6692	Do.	–	Do. f.	R.C.	–	R.C.	–	7	80	87	35
10	7316	Ballyshannon,	44	Ballyshannon,	R.C.	–	R.C.	–	93	81	174	50
11	706	Carragh,	37	Carragh, m.	R.C.	–	R.C.	–	118	–	118	44
12	707	Do.	–	Do. f.	R.C.	–	R.C.	–	–	60	60	29
13	708	Carn,	44	Bantroft,	R.C.	–	R.C.	–	62	60	121	43
14	1298	Clonecurry,	37	Newtown, m.	R.C.	–	R.C.	–	55	–	55	21
15	1497	Do.	–	Do. f.	R.C.	–	R.C.	–	–	73	73	35
16	772	Do.	–	Tiernaghten Ord. Agr.	R.C.	–	R.C.	–	33	43	76	37
17	2318	Cadamstown,	–	Balyna, m.	R.C.	–	R.C.	–	94	–	94	46
18	3427	Do.	–	Johnstown Bridge, m.	R.C.	–	R.C.	–	53	–	53	23
19	3428	Do.	–	Do. f.	R.C.	–	R.C.	–	9	47	56	23
20	6740	Do.	–	Cadamstown, f.	R.C.	–	R.C.	–	–	81	81	35
21	6127	Castledermot,	44	Castledermot, m.	R.C.	–	R.C.	R.C.	265	–	265	74
22	6171	Do.	–	Do. f.	R.C.	–	R.C.	–	–	204	204	76
23	5174	Clane,	37	Rathcoffey,	R.C.	–	R.C.	–	41	57	101	42
24	1713	Do.	–	Clane Ord. Agricul.	R.C.	–	R.C.	–	149	–	149	59
25	1161	Do.	–	Do. Convent, f.	R.C.	–	None		–	169	169	56
26	7132	Churchtown,	44	Churchtown,	R.C.	–	R.C.	–	56	66	118	46
27	2878	Do.	–	Athy Workhouse,	P.L.	Gds.	R.C.	–	58	60	118	13
28	1722	Dunmanoge,	–	Levitstown,	R.C.	–	R.C.	–	66	60	126	54
29	5308	Donaghcumper,	37	Abbey, m.	R.C.	–	R.C.	R.C.	202	–	202	83
30	5361	Do.	–	Do. f.	R.C.	–	R.C.	R.C.	–	181	181	85
31	11063	Downings,	–	Roseville,	R.C.	–	–	–	22	19	41	–
32	7020	Dunfierth,	–	Kilshanroe,	R.C.	–	R.C.	–	61	63	124	44
33	1734	Feighcullen,	–	Milltown,	R.C.	–	R.C.	–	57	34	91	38
34	8749	Do.	–	Clongowes, m.	–	R.C.	R.C.	–	69	–	69	30
35	8341	Do.	–	Do. f.	–	R.C.	R.C.	–	–	91	91	39
36	10216	Do.	–	Boston,	R.C.	–	R.C.	–	53	47	100	38
37	2105	Greatconnell,	14	Newbridge, m.	R.C.	–	R.C.	R.C.	201	–	201	86
38	2106	Do.	–	Do. f.	R.C.	–	–	–	–	257	257	86
39	6756	Do.	–	Athgarvan,	R.C.	–	R.C.	–	61	58	119	44
40	782	Kilmeague,	37	Allen,	R.C.	–	R.C.	–	80	64	144	44
41	1712	Do.	–	Allenwood,	R.C.	–	R.C.	–	82	57	139	59
42	1630	Do.	–	Robertstown, m.	R.C.	–	R.C.	–	90	24	114	44
43	2491	Do.	–	Do. f.	R.C.	–	R.C.	–	–	77	77	38
44	10280	Do.	–	Kilmeague,	R.C.	–	R.C.	–	52	51	103	45
45	7707	Kildare,	44	Kildare, m.	R.C.	–	R.C.	–	191	–	191	78
46	7711	Do.	–	Do. Convent, f.	–	R.C.	None		30	310	340	102
47	8227	Do.	–	Curragh,	–	–	Dissen.	–	68	47	115	54
48	776	Kilcock,	37	Kilcock, f.	R.C.	–	R.C.	R.C.	–	199	199	51
49	778	Kilcullen,	44	Halverstown,	–	R.C.	R.C.	–	62	51	113	57
50	4307	Do.	–	Kilcullenbridge, m.	R.C.	–	R.C.	–	215	–	215	80
51	6208	Do.	–	Do. f.	R.C.	–	R.C.	R.C.	–	185	185	75
52	1612	Kill,	37	Ardclough, m.	R.C.	–	R.C.	–	65	–	65	29
53	8236	Do.	–	Do. f.	R.C.	–	R.C.	–	–	73	73	33
54	1974	Do.	–	Kill, m. day,	R.C.	–	R.C.	–	57	–	57	38
				Do. evg.	R.C.	–	R.C.	–	66	–	66	36
55	1973	Do.	–	Do. f.	R.C.	–	R.C.	–	–	67	67	33
56	8813	Kilberry,	44	Kilberry,	R.C.	–	R.C.	–	43	49	92	35
57	10807	Do.	–	Do. paupl.	R.C.	–	R.C.	–	10	9	19	8
58	2201	Kildangan,	–	Kildangan, m.	R.C.	–	R.C.	–	121	–	121	44
59	2497	Do.	–	Do. f.	R.C.	–	R.C.	–	–	180	180	69
60	3022	Kilteel,	37	Kilteel,	R.C.	–	R.C.	–	89	75	164	44
61	5638	Killashee,	–	Twomilehouse, f.	R.C.	–	R.C.	–	–	101	101	49

a Including value of Free Residence and Garden.

b Including value of Free Residence.

Province of LEINSTER: County of KILDARE.

KILDARE—105 Schools.

Amount paid for Books, Requisites, and Apparatus, at Reduced Prices.	Aid granted by the Board during the Year 1874. In Free Stock of Books, Requisites, and Apparatus.	By Salaries, Gratuities, and other Emoluments.	Results Fees, Financial Year.	Amount of Local Emoluments received in Aid of Teacher's Salary. School Fees.	Subscriptions, Endowments, &c.	Total Local Aid.	Trained or Non-Trained.	Number.
£ s. d.	£ s. d.	£ s. d.	£ s. d.	£ s. d.	£ s. d.	£ s. d.		
12 8 3	—	50 17 6	21 0 8	17 2 3	8 10 0	*25 12 3	T.T.	1
8 15 11	—	24 0 0	7 7 0	4 14 1	4 0 0	*8 11 1		2
1 7 0	—	24 0 0	10 3 6	1 5 6	4 0 0	*5 5 6		3
6 8 0	—	28 10 0	13 7 0	6 18 0	—	6 18 0	n.	4
1 5 9	—	61 8 0	16 8 0	8 12 10	4 0 0	*12 12 10	n.	5
8 11 10	—	40 0 0	14 4 6	4 15 6	—	4 15 6	n.	6
1 5 7	—	30 0 0	12 13 0	7 11 6	2 0 0	*9 11 6		7
4 15 5	—	39 8 4	8 2 6	8 1 8	6 0 0	14 1 8		8
8 15 9	—	21 10 0	5 16 0	4 17 5	—	4 17 5		9
1 5 10	—	31 0 0	11 0 0	10 0 0	—	10 0 0		10
9 19 0	—	25 0 0	18 18 0	7 7 0	4 0 0	*11 7 0		11
—	—	24 0 0	11 8 6	8 11 11	4 0 0	*12 11 11		12
2 18 7	—	25 0 0	11 7 6	4 4 0	—	4 4 0		13
1 10 0	—	30 0 0	9 18 0	8 2 4	13 0 0	*15 2 4	T.T.	14
2 1 7	—	20 0 0	4 14 0	1 19 0	2 0 0	*3 19 6	T.T.	15
—	—	30 0 0	6 17 0	1 6 0	8 0 0	*10 6 0		16
7 0 1	—	71 10 0	15 19 0	11 7 6	10 0 0	*21 7 6	T.T.	17
—	—	24 0 0	8 3 0	5 10 5	—	5 10 5	T.T.	18
1 0 10	—	20 0 0	5 15 0	3 8 3	3 0 0	6 8 3	T.T.	19
1 15 8	—	19 13 4	10 16 0	4 1 7	3 0 0	*8 1 7		20
9 10 0	—	48 0 0	17 8 0	9 6 10	—	9 6 10		21
8 12 9	—	30 8 4	22 0 0	6 14 8	—	6 14 8		22
0 18 10	—	24 0 0	7 17 0	4 19 1	3 0 6	*8 19 1		23
7 6 2	—	63 10 0	14 18 6	20 10 2	10 0 0	*30 10 2	T.T.	24
—	—	26 6 8	25 8 0	6 9 0	—	6 9 0	T.T.	25
—	—	31 0 0	10 0 6	4 7 1	0 12 6	*4 19 7		26
5 15 10	—	6 0 0	—	—	—	—		27
8 2 8	—	20 0 0	5 11 0	9 9 11	—	8 0 11	T.T.	28
6 5 9	—	74 10 0	18 6 0	22 18 6	5 0 0	27 18 6	T.C.	29
8 18 11	—	30 0 8	16 10 0	7 0 6	5 0 0	12 0 6	T.C.	30
1 11 9	—	5 16 0	—	0 10 0	25 0 0	25 10 0		31
4 1 1	—	26 0 0	8 7 6	7 12 8	2 0 0	*9 12 8		32
4 0 1	—	15 8 8	8 15 0	5 6 0	4 0 0	*9 6 0		33
—	—	22 10 0	—	2 8 1	2 18 4	5 7 5		34
2 14 9	—	29 6 8	15 8 0	6 8 0	—	6 8 0		35
1 18 6	—	22 0 0	6 6 0	4 10 1	2 0 0	*6 10 1		36
5 6 5	—	69 16 8	22 17 6	25 18 6	—	25 18 6	T.T.	37
5 0 0	—	50 0 0	15 11 6	16 12 8	—	16 12 8	T.T.	38
6 1 0	—	25 0 0	8 18 0	7 4 5	5 0 0	*12 4 5		39
8 10 0	—	21 0 0	10 0 0	6 11 1	—	6 11 1		40
8 5 1	—	14 0 0	1 18 6	6 17 11	6 1 8	*11 19 7	T.T.	41
—	—	24 0 0	—	2 7 0	0 5 0	2 12 0	T.T.	42
—	—	24 0 0	5 12 6	8 8 1	—	8 8 1	T.T.	43
—	—	26 6 8	12 8 6	8 13 4	13 7 6	*45 0 10		44
12 8 7	—	50 10 0	24 8 0	5 15 0	—	5 15 0		45
5 0 5	—	41 0 4	14 8 8	—	—	—		46
8 14 4	—	44 0 0	10 9 0	42 11 8	4 0 0	*48 11 8		47
5 8 4	—	48 0 0	17 1 6	7 1 4	5 0 0	*13 1 4		48
1 15 6	—	63 0 0	7 18 6	8 10 6	3 0 0	6 10 6		49
—	—	56 0 0	16 4 0	6 7 11	—	6 7 11		50
—	—	107 18 4	17 6 6	4 2 11	—	4 2 11		51
1 9 0	—	24 0 0	5 15 6	6 13 6	—	6 13 6	T.T.	52
1 1 4	—	30 8 0	8 6 0	8 10 9	—	8 10 9	T.T.	53
			3 5 6	5 4 4	—	5 4 4	P.	54
2 8 1	—	55 0 0	2 1 6	1 10 0	3 0 0	4 10 0		
1 8 11	—	20 0 0	9 7 6	0 10 6	—	6 10 6	P.	55
—	—	18 6 8	11 18 6	8 10 0	—	8 10 0		56
1 7 7	4 0 0	—	2 8 0	—	—	—		57
1 8 6	—	24 10 0	12 8 0	5 8 7	2 0 0	5 8 7		58
8 12 7	—	56 0 0	30 2 0	4 1 5	8 10 0	*10 11 5		59
1 5 6	—	26 12 4	14 15 8	14 19 10	4 7 6	*19 0 4	T.T.	60
8 7 8	—	20 0 0	11 11 0	10 11 6	—	10 11 6		61

* Including value of Free Garden.

List of Schools in operation on the 31st December, 1874—

Number.	Roll Number of School.	Parish.	District.	School.	Religious Denomination of Manager or Correspondent: Clerical.	Lay.	Religious Denominations of Teachers: Principals.	Assistants.	Total number of Pupils on Rolls within the Year 1874: Males.	Fem.	Total.	[illegible]
62	8702	Killybegs,	37	Prosperous, m.	R.C.	–	R.C.	R.C.	149	–	149	–
63	8703	Do.	–	Do. f.	R.C.	–	R.C.	R.C.	–	100	100	62
64	8167	Kilkea,	44	Kilkea,	–	E.C.	R.C.	–	50	44	94	30
65	9272	Kildrought,	37	Celbridge, f.	R.C.	–	R.C.	R.C.	187	101	288	77
66	8296	Do.	–	Do. (adult) evg.	R.C.	–	R.C.	R.C.	–	103	103	40
67	8584	Do.	–	Do. Workho.	P.L.	Gds.	R.C.	–	24	20	44	26
68	8344	Leixlip,	–	Leixlip, m.	R.C.	–	R.C.	–	107	–	107	40
69	2545	Do.	–	Do. f.	R.C.	–	R.C.	R.C.	34	107	141	60
70	8636	Lackagh,	44	Lackagh,	R.C.	–	R.C.	R.C.	130	79	209	61
71	4192	Laraghbryan,	37	Maynooth, m.	R.C.	–	R.C.	–	151	–	151	58
72	7719	Do.	–	Do. Convent, f.	–	R.C.	Nuns		81	303	384	160
73	7378	Monasterevan,	18	Monasterevan, f.	R.C.	–	R.C.	2R.C.	–	256	256	110
74	10489	Moone,	–	Moone, m.	R.C.	–	R.C.	–	67	–	67	30
75	10490	Do.	–	Do. f.	R.C.	–	R.C.	–	–	112	112	43
76	7828	Nurney,	37	Cloghorinkan, m.	R.C.	–	R.C.	–	61	–	61	28
77	8126	Do.	–	Do. f.	R.C.	–	R.C.	–	–	53	53	25
78	8787	Do.	44	Nurney,	R.C.	–	R.C.	–	97	58	155	36
79	9284	Newbridge,	37	Twomilehouse Ord. Agricultural,	R.C.	–	R.C.	–	81	–	81	31
80	2083	Narraghmore,	44	Old Grange,	R.C.	–	R.C.	–	62	55	117	47
81	9414	Do.	–	Crookstown, m.	R.C.	–	R.C.	–	186	–	186	36
82	7207	Do.	–	Do. f.	R.C.	–	R.C.	R.C.	–	178	178	36
83	10875	Do.	–	Sharvins,	R.C.	–	R.C.	–	90	77	167	43
84	7240	Naas,	37	Naas, Convent, f.	–	R.C.	Nuns		23	351	374	160
85	8791	Do.	–	Do. Gaol,	Governors.		R.C.	–	61	–	61	10
86	7784	Rathangan,	44	Rathangan, m.	R.C.	–	R.C.	–	158	–	158	73
87	7785	Do.	–	Do. f.	R.C.	–	R.C.	R.C.	–	147	147	61
88	10481	Do.	37	Rathernan,	R.C.	–	R.C.	–	71	46	117	44
89	1821	Rathmore,	–	Rathmore, f.	R.C.	–	R.C.	–	8	50	58	28
90	6283	Do.	–	Eadestown,	R.C.	–	R.C.	–	46	–	46	24
91	1469	Staplestown,	–	Staplestown, m.	R.C.	–	R.C.	–	105	–	105	44
92	707	Do.	–	Do. f.	R.C.	–	R.C.	–	–	121	121	46
93	7623	Straffan,	–	Straffan, m.	R.C.	–	R.C.	–	54	–	54	25
94	7624	Do.	–	Do. f.	R.C.	–	R.C.	–	–	41	41	21
95	6209	St. Michael's,	41	Athy Dist. Model, m.	Com. N.E.		R.C.	–	85	–	85	18
96	6210	Do.	–	Do. f.	Com. N.E.		R.C.	Dis	–	71	71	41
97	6616	Do.	–	Do. i.	Com. N.E.		R.C.	–	34	24	58	28
98	4977	Do.	–	Do. Convent, f.	–	R.C.	Nuns		195	538	733	300
99	9758	St. John's,	–	Turnpike-road, m.i.	–	R.C.	R.C.	–	80	–	80	43
100	9763	Do.	–	Do. f.	–	R.C.	R.C.	R.C.	–	97	97	48
101	4318	Tipperkevin,	37	Tipperkevin,	R.C.	–	R.C.	–	29	55	84	24
102	8100	Tipper,	–	Naas Workhouse,	P.L.	Gds.	aR.C.	–	117	27	144	78
103	6318	Timahoe,	–	Timahoe,	–	R.C.	R.C.	–	60	30	90	36
104	7684	Tankardstown,	44	Ballyroe,	R.C.	–	R.C.	–	63	98	161	47
105	7500	Usk,	–	Ballymount,	R.C.	–	R.C.	–	118	100	218	82
		Total for County Kildare, 105 Schools,							6,808	7,1[illegible]1	13,[illegible]	3,400

COUNTY OF

1	7[illegible]	Aharney,	47	Lisdowney, m.	R.C.	–	R.C.	–	64	–	64	30
2	[illegible]	Do.	–	Do. f.	R.C.	–	R.C.	–	–	93	93	35
3	1714	Do.	–	Ballytamas,	–	R.C.	R.C.	–	20	35	55	31
4	2749	Do.	–	Ballyragget, m.	R.C.	–	R.C.	aR.C.	160	–	160	108
5	3632	Do.	–	Do. f.	R.C.	–	R.C.	aR.C.	–	103	103	58
6	5119	Attanagh,	44	Ballyouskill, m.	R.C.	–	R.C.	–	103	–	103	51
7	5113	Do.	–	Do. f.	R.C.	–	R.C.	R.C.	–	147	147	64
8	4881	Aghaviller,	57	Ballyhale Ord. Agric.	–	E.C.	R.C.	–	95	42	137	54
9	9906	Do.	47	Newmarket,	R.C.	–	R.C.	–	57	33	90	30

a Including value of Free Residence.

b Including value of Free Garden.

Province of Leinster: County of Kildare—*continued.*

Amount paid for Books, Requisites, and Apparatus, at Reduced Prices.	Aid granted by the Board during the Year 1874: In Free Stock of Books, Requisites, and Apparatus.	In Salaries, Premiums, and other Gratuities.	Results Fees, Teachers' Year.	Amount of Local Endowments received in Aid of Teacher's Salary: School Fees.	Subscriptions, Endowments, &c.	Total Local Aid.	Vested or Non-Vested.	Number.
£ s. d.	£ s. d.	£ s. d.	£ s. d.	£ s. d.	£ s. d.	£ s. d.		
8 1 6	—	69 0 0	13 10 6	19 0 1	—	19 9 1		62
6 19 0	—	52 6 8	21 15 0	12 14 11	—	12 14 11		63
2 13 4	—	40 10 0	8 0 6	1 10 0	22 0 0	* 23 10 0		64
8 7 6	—	62 13 4	11 8 0	7 13 1	—	7 13 1		65
1 5 8	—	3 10 0	4 17 6	—	—	—		66
1 8 6	—	3 0 0	—	—	—	—		67
2 16 3	—	23 0 9	9 1 6	5 18 9	—	5 18 9	N.	68
1 5 0	—	45 0 0	8 14 0	7 9 11	—	7 9 11	N.	69
8 5 11	—	48 13 4	10 0 6	7 8 8	1 10 0	8 18 8		70
8 6 11	—	64 10 0	23 9 4	4 10 2	25 0 0	* 29 10 2		71
11 11 8	—	61 10 0	21 14 4	—	20 0 0	20 0 0		72
7 17 8	—	64 0 0	30 5 6	14 4 0	4 0 0	* 18 4 0		73
—	—	21 0 0	13 4 0	12 0 0	—	12 0 0		74
6 15 1	—	28 0 0	18 6 6	5 1 6	—	5 1 6		75
1 13 8	—	24 0 0	6 3 5	0 4 10	3 0 0	* 12 1 10		76
1 16 3	—	20 0 0	6 0 0	4 11 0	3 0 0	* 7 11 6		77
1 19 5	—	38 0 0	14 13 6	13 0 7	1 10 0	* 13 10 7		78
2 5 3	—	28 0 0	8 10 0	8 15 1	—	8 15 1		79
4 7 6	—	27 10 0	11 18 6	11 7 11	—	11 7 11	V.N.	80
8 7 11	—	34 10 0	0 3 0	9 17 8	—	9 17 8		81
2 6 4	—	71 10 0	10 4 6	8 10 8	6 10 0	* 16 0 8		82
2 17 8	—	24 3 4	11 17 0	11 4 4	1 10 0	* 12 14 4		83
11 2 2	—	82 5 8	49 13 8	16 13 11	—	16 13 11		84
—	—	—	—	—	—	—		85
8 0 4	—	33 10 0	21 6 0	30 1 8	—	30 1 8		86
0 15 5	—	44 0 0	13 1 0	6 11 10	2 18 0	* 9 8 10		87
1 9 1	—	24 0 0	7 17 6	4 1 0	1 0 0	* 5 1 0		88
1 11 3	—	21 0 0	9 13 6	4 5 2	8 10 0	* 12 15 2		89
1 13 3	—	22 0 0	2 2 6	4 15 7	12 0 11	* 16 16 6		90
8 8 10	—	30 0 0	10 13 8	7 13 6	3 0 0	* 10 13 6	V.N.	91
2 9 0	—	43 0 8	13 13 0	6 16 8	3 0 0	* 9 16 8	V.N.	92
0 14 6	—	30 0 0	2 18 0	4 14 11	—	4 14 11		93
1 3 3	—	63 10 0	4 5 0	2 3 8	—	2 3 8		94
14 16 8	2 0 1						V.C.	95
10 16 6	—	696 18 4	42 0 0	92 14 1	—	92 14 1	V.C.	96
—	—						V.C.	97
24 15 0	—	163 7 8	65 10 0	16 18 10	—	16 18 10		98
1 5 8	—	20 0 0	7 0 0	—	—	—		99
2 14 3	—	44 0 0	10 15 6	—	—	—		100
2 8 10	—	24 0 0	1 19 6	3 6 0	—	3 6 6		101
16 10 11	—	—	—	—	—	—		102
1 14 3	—	48 3 4	5 2 6	8 4 6	22 0 0	* 25 4 6		103
2 18 0	—	31 0 0	12 8 0	5 11 0	3 10 0	* 9 1 0		104
2 11 3	—	64 0 0	18 0 6	9 3 0	2 0 0	11 3 0		105
321 4 6	7 0 1	4,401 7 2	1,277 9 0	775 6 11	560 8 5	1,335 16 4		

KILKENNY—176 Schools.

0 12 8	—	24 0 0	4 18 6	2 14 0	—	2 14 0		1
3 6 11	—	59 0 0	11 12 6	2 13 1	1 0 0	* 3 13 1		2
8 1 7	—	30 0 0	11 5 6	1 6 0	4 0 0	5 6 0		3
7 0 5	—	74 3 4	40 8 0	8 8 6	—	8 8 6		4
4 16 9	—	85 8 10	38 7 0	7 10 6	—	7 10 6		5
3 12 0	—	53 0 0	10 14 6	4 18 0	—	4 18 0		6
4 13 1	—	70 13 4	26 15 0	9 7 7	—	9 7 7		7
6 10 8	—	40 0 0	15 18 6	14 0 4	10 8 4	* 24 8 8		8
3 9 11	—	84 0 0	9 6 0	10 3 7	—	10 3 7		9

* Including value of Free Residence and Garden.

List of Schools in operation on the 31st December, 1874.—

Number.	Roll Number of School.	Parish.	District.	School.	Religious Denomination of Manager or Correspondent.		Number and Religious Denomination of Teachers.		Attendance for the Year.			
									Total number of Pupils on Rolls within the Year 1874.			Average daily attendance [illegible]
					Clerical.	Lay.	Principals.	Assistants.	Males.	Fem.	Total.	
10	6601	Balleen,	47	Balleen,	–	R.C.	R.C.	–	32	27	59	31
11	7040	Ballycallan,	–	Ballycallan, m.	R.C.	–	R.C.	–	78	–	78	45
12	7051	Do.	–	Do. f.	R.C.	–	R.C.	–	–	71	71	35
13	7616	Burnchurch,	–	Burnchurch,	–	R.C.	R.C.	–	73	54	126	43
14	10448	Ballyragget,	–	Byrnesgrove, m.	R.C.	–	R.C.	–	84	–	84	44
15	10446	Do.	–	Do. f.	R.C.	–	R.C.	–	–	73	73	35
16	10797	Do.	–	Ballyragget, i.	R.C.	–	R.C.	R.C.	73	59	132	68
17	1115	Castlecomer,	48	Castlecomer, m.	R.C.	–	R.C.	aR.C.	240	–	240	121
18	[illegible]	Do.	–	Do. Convent.	R.C.	–	Nuns		–	271	271	165
19	1796	Do.	–	Clogh, m. day,	R.C.	–	R.C.	–	184	–	184	97
				Do. evg.	R.C.	–	R.C.	–	59	–	59	33
20	1797	Do.	–	Do. f.	R.C.	–	R.C.	aR.C.	–	158	158	63
21	8876	Do.	–	Gazabo, m.	R.C.	–	R.C.	R.C.	204	–	204	75
22	8341	Do.	–	Do. f.	R.C.	–	R.C.	R.C.	–	196	196	79
23	3756	Do.	–	Firoda, m.	R.C.	–	R.C.	–	76	–	76	33
24	3758	Do.	–	Do. f.	R.C.	–	R.C.	–	–	75	75	38
25	3847	Do.	–	Smithstown, m.	R.C.	–	R.C.	–	96	–	96	60
26	5537	Do.	–	Do. f.	R.C.	–	R.C.	–	–	79	79	50
27	6166	Do.	–	Colliery, m.	R.C.	–	R.C.	–	63	–	63	38
28	6162	Do.	–	Do. f.	R.C.	–	R.C.	–	–	61	61	35
29	3456	Do.	–	Chatsworth,	R.C.	–	R.C.	R.C.	89	90	179	96
30	6947	Do.	–	Castlecomer, Workhouse,	P.L.	Gds.	R.C.	–	25	22	47	24
31	1296	Callan,	47	Callan, m.	–	R.C.	R.C.	–	61	–	61	18
32	1602	Do.	–	Do. f.	–	R.C.	R.C.	R.C.	–	57	57	15
33	6162	Do.	–	Do. i.	–	R.C.	R.C.	R.C.	74	50	124	31
34	10214	Do.	–	Callan Lodge, Convent, f.	–	R.C.	Nuns		158	305	463	227
35	8278	Do.	–	Do. Workhouse,	P.L.	Gds.	aR.C.	–	41	59	100	48
36	6618	Clonmore,	48	Clonmore Ord. Agr.	–	R.C.	R.C.	–	69	67	136	60
37	7137	Coolcashin,	47	Crosshill,	R.C.	–	R.C.	–	53	37	90	45
38	3248	Clomantagh,	–	Clomantagh,	R.C.	–	R.C.	R.C.	69	68	137	60
39	4194	Coolcraheen,	–	Clintstown, m.	R.C.	–	R.C.	–	56	–	56	30
40	4194	Do.	–	Do. f.	R.C.	–	R.C.	–	–	60	60	34
41	3022	Coolaghmore,	–	Coolagh,	–	R.C.	R.C.	–	47	27	74	35
42	7247	Clara,	–	Church Clara,	R.C.	–	R.C.	–	63	68	131	65
43	5251	Clonamery,	48	Woodstock, 1st class Agricultural,	–	R.C.	R.C.	–	18	–	18	60
44	7763	Do.	–	Do. f.	–	R.C.	R.C.	–	–	35	35	14
45	795	Dunkitt,	–	Dunkitt, m.	R.C.	–	R.C.	–	104	–	104	35
46	1858	Do.	–	Do. f.	R.C.	–	R.C.	–	–	79	79	38
47	[illegible]	Do.	–	Rigwood,	R.C.	–	R.C.	R.C.	172	12	184	80
48	4677	Do.	–	Ballyhomuck, m.	R.C.	–	R.C.	–	94	–	94	37
49	[illegible]	Do.	–	Do. f.	R.C.	–	R.C.	–	–	87	87	30
50	7014	Derrynahinch,	–	Ballyhale, f.	R.C.	–	R.C.	R.C.	75	74	149	61
51	6876	Do.	–	Castlegannon,	R.C.	–	R.C.	R.C.	84	60	144	65
52	1680	Danesfort,	47	Danesfort,	R.C.	–	R.C.	–	58	31	89	33
53	11207	Do.	–	Ladyswell,	R.C.	–	R.C.	–	42	54	96	42
54	5757	Dysartmoon,	48	Tullagher,	R.C.	–	R.C.	–	52	54	106	61
55	4177	Do.	–	Brownsford, m.	R.C.	–	R.C.	–	128	–	128	65
56	4178	Do.	–	Do. f.	R.C.	–	R.C.	–	–	67	67	37
57	5718	Dysart,	48	Coan, m.	R.C.	–	R.C.	–	69	–	69	45
58	9962	Do.	–	Do. f.	R.C.	–	R.C.	–	–	54	54	31
59	6821	Dunnamaggan,	47	Dunnamaggan,	R.C.	–	R.C.	R.C.	81	74	155	68
60	7673	Dungarvan,	–	Dungarvan, m.	–	R.C.	R.C.	–	89	–	89	38
61	7022	Do.	–	Do. f.	–	R.C.	R.C.	R.C.	–	159	159	85
62	7674	Dunbell,	–	Dunbell,	R.C.	–	R.C.	–	40	49	89	61
63	8213	Erke,	16	Crosspatrick, m.	R.C.	–	R.C.	–	97	–	97	50
64	8213	Do.	–	Do. f.	R.C.	–	R.C.	–	–	105	105	53
65	8022	Do.	–	Moneenroe, m.	R.C.	–	R.C.	–	114	–	114	55
66	3404	Do.	–	Do. f.	R.C.	–	R.C.	–	–	129	129	63
67	5466	Earlstown,	47	Newtown,	–	R.C.	R.C.	–	32	31	63	14
68	1106	Fiddown,	48	Tubbridbritain,	–	R.C.	R.C.	–	35	63	98	45
69	6188	Do.	47	Piltown 1st Class Agr.	–	R.C.	R.C.	–	83	–	83	40
70	6188	Do.	–	Do. f.	–	R.C.	R.C.	–	–	103	103	51

a Including value of Free Residence.

b Including value of Free Residence and Garden.

Province of Leinster : County of Kilkenny—*continued.*

Amount paid for Books, Requisites, and Apparatus, at Reduced Prices.	Aid granted by the Board during the Year 1873. In Free Stock of Books, Requisites, and Apparatus.	In Salaries, Premiums, and other Gratuities.	Results Fees, Financial Year.	Amount of Local Emoluments received in Aid of Teacher's Salary. School Fees.	Subscriptions, Endowments, &c.	Total Local Aid.	Vested or Non-Vested.	Number.
£ s. d.	£ s. d.	£ s. d.	£ s. d.	£ s. d.	£ s. d.	£ s. d.		
0 10 11	—	21 0 0	3 18 6	5 5 0	—	5 5 0		10
8 3 8	—	22 0 0	8 1 6	4 10 0	—	4 10 0		11
8 0 8	—	20 11 0	10 9 0	8 5 8	2 0 0	* 10 5 8		12
—	—	58 8 4	14 7 0	8 14 11	16 0 0	* 24 14 11		13
2 18 8	—	26 0 0	16 9 0	6 2 10	—	6 2 10		14
3 9 10	—	44 0 0	21 18 0	6 6 11	—	6 6 11		15
1 7 8	—	54 6 6	14 2 0	3 5 9	—	3 5 9		16
—	—	93 0 0	24 8 6	10 10 0	12 0 0	22 10 0		17
10 7 7	—	18 9 0	37 0 0	—	—	—		18
8 8 4	—	84 0 0	8 16 0	1 1 5	—	1 1 5		19
			5 16 6	0 15 0	—	0 15 0		
1 16 4	—	63 0 0	10 6 0	3 12 1	—	3 12 1		20
1 11 8	—	61 0 0	14 5 6	3 13 4	—	3 13 4		21
1 12 8	—	64 8 4	18 6 8	0 9 6	—	0 9 6		22
2 8 9	—	24 0 0	12 8 0	4 18 8	—	4 18 8		23
2 16 4	—	25 0 0	12 10 6	2 8 0	5 0 0	* 7 8 0		24
1 14 8	—	24 0 0	4 18 6	4 1 6	1 10 0	* 6 14 6		25
1 5 6	—	27 0 0	6 14 0	1 19 0	1 10 0	* 3 8 0		26
1 15 8	—	30 0 0	11 11 6	—	6 0 0	* 6 0 0		27
1 13 8	—	24 0 0	0 17 0	—	2 10 0	2 10 0		28
1 18 9	—	11 0 0	15 5 6	3 10 6	—	3 10 6		29
3 11 4	—	8 0 0	—	—	—	—		30
0 5 7	—	115 18 4	3 6 10	2 14 2	5 0 0	7 14 2		31
1 15 0	—	111 1 1	6 0 0	0 7 11	5 0 0	5 7 11		32
—	—	90 19 10	4 3 6	1 8 11	—	1 8 11		33
14 7 0	4 0 0	100 18 8	72 4 6	18 4 6	—	18 4 6		34
8 19 7	—	6 0 0	—	—	—	—		35
4 9 11	—	37 0 0	35 6 6	27 17 0	12 0 1	* 40 6 1		36
1 7 0	—	24 0 0	10 14 0	9 0 9	—	9 0 9	N.	37
8 14 1	—	64 0 0	21 15 0	7 11 6	2 0 0	* 9 11 6		38
6 7 0	—	18 0 0	4 8 0	0 10 0	1 0 0	* 1 10 0	V.T.	39
1 19 11	—	20 0 0	7 7 6	0 8 0	1 0 0	* 1 8 0	V.T.	40
1 8 6	—	25 1 8	8 11 0	2 3 2	—	2 3 2		41
1 9 10	—	24 13 4	16 16 0	6 16 9	—	6 16 9		42
2 16 0	—	60 0 0	10 8 1	5 5 9	27 4 8	* 33 10 5	V.C.	43
3 1 4	—	26 0 0	0 6 6	4 0 10	2 10 0	6 10 10	V.C.	44
2 9 10	—	24 0 0	11 0 6	6 18 1	—	6 18 1	V.T.	45
1 6 0	—	24 0 0	12 6 0	7 7 3	—	7 7 3	V.T.	46
1 5 10	—	50 10 0	25 4 8	8 18 0	—	8 18 0		47
5 13 0	—	24 0 0	12 17 0	8 17 11	—	8 17 11		48
1 18 4	—	20 0 0	10 7 0	5 13 5	—	5 13 5		49
3 7 10	—	20 0 0	28 17 0	13 10 1	—	13 10 1		50
4 6 8	—	11 0 0	28 7 0	19 1 10	—	19 1 10		51
0 12 5	—	17 16 4	4 5 0	1 5 3	0 10 0	* 1 15 3	V.T.	52
4 15 11	—	24 0 0	12 7 0	3 15 2	—	3 15 2		53
0 14 7	—	25 10 0	3 15 6	2 3 0	—	2 3 0		54
2 19 4	—	24 0 0	11 10 6	2 16 0	—	2 16 6	V.T.	55
0 14 4	—	20 0 0	10 1 0	6 11 10	—	6 11 10	V.T.	56
4 6 7	—	24 0 0	15 7 0	5 17 0	—	5 17 0		57
5 5 4	—	29 0 0	16 3 6	6 8 0	—	6 8 0		58
2 11 11	—	30 0 0	16 11 6	6 18 6	—	6 18 6		59
4 15 8	—	93 18 4	21 11 6	7 4 6	29 0 0	* 36 4 6		60
6 16 11	—	30 0 0	22 4 0	6 7 6	25 0 0	* 31 7 6		61
1 5 0	—	24 0 0	0 8 6	4 8 8	—	4 8 8		62
5 16 4	—	12 15 1	9 10 0	3 7 1	—	3 7 1		63
2 14 11	—	20 0 0	17 19 0	5 2 0	—	5 2 0		64
1 5 10	—	87 13 4	7 19 0	4 15 9	—	4 15 9		65
4 13 7	—	38 13 4	18 19 0	3 16 6	—	3 16 6		66
3 9 2	—	60 0 5	9 9 0	0 19 5	—	0 19 5		67
1 16 6	—	24 0 0	16 18 0	8 4 1	4 10 0	* 13 14 1	V.T.	68
—	—	45 13 4	6 3 0	5 13 8	63 5 4	* 72 3 7		69
3 3 10	—	20 0 0	13 8 6	11 16 11	4 0 0	15 16 11		70

* Including value of Free garden.

List of Schools in operation on the 31st December, 1874.—

Number.	Roll Number of School.	Parish.	District.	School.		Religious Denomination of Manager or Correspondent. Clerical.	Lay.	Religion and Religious Denomination of Teachers. Principals.	Assistants.	Attendance for the Year. Total number of Pupils on Rolls within the Year 1874. Males.	Fem.	Total.	Average Daily Attendance.
71	6192	Fiddown,	63	Templeorum,	m.	-	R.C.	R.C.	-	88	-	88	41
72	6204	Do.	-	Do.	f.	-	R.C.	R.C.	R.C.	-	108	108	52
73	7107	Freshford,	47	Freshford,	m.	R.C.	-	R.C.	R.C.	156	-	156	60
74	7077	Do.	-	Do.	f.	R.C.	-	R.C.	R.C.	-	170	170	71
75	2916	Fertagh,	43	Johnstown,	m.	R.C.	-	R.C.	-	118	-	118	56
76	2918	Do.	-	Do.	f.	R.C.	-	R.C.	-	-	121	121	63
77	6627	Grange,	47	Churchhill,	.	R.C.	-	R.C.	-	41	58	99	31
78	600	Grange Sylvia,	-	Gowranbridge,	m.	R.C.	-	R.C.	-	125	-	125	57
79	6134	Do.	-	Do.	Conv. f.	R.C.	-	Nuns.		16	165	181	69
80	774	Graiguenamanagh,	39	Graig,	m.	R.C.	-	R.C.	4R.C.	288	-	288	113
81	782	Do.	-	Do.	f.	R.C.	-	R.C.	-	-	283	283	110
82	1146	Do.	47	Coppenagh,	.	R.C.	-	R.C.	-	89	75	164	54
83	1717	Gowran,	-	Gowran,	m.	R.C.	-	R.C.	-	127	-	127	41
84	1781	Do.	-	Do.	f.	R.C.	-	R.C.	2R.C.	-	177	177	79
85	6621	Grangemaccomb,	-	Coneby,	m.	R.C.	-	R.C.	-	117	-	117	61
86	3521	Do.	-	Do.	f.	R.C.	-	R.C.	-	-	85	85	47
87	1916	Inistioge,	-	Inistioge,	m.	-	R.C.	R.C.	R.C.	103	-	103	76
88	3319	Do.	-	Do.	f.	-	R.C.	R.C.	R.C.	-	166	166	73
89	1841	Jerpoint, West,	47	Mullenakill,	.	R.C.	-	R.C.	-	81	25	106	45
90	1201	Kilmakevoge,	-	Rochestown,	m.	R.C.	-	R.C.	R.C.	141	-	141	64
91	4715	Do.	-	Do.	f.	R.C.	-	R.C.	-	-	102	102	34
92	3873	Kilbeacon,	-	Mullinavat,	m.	R.C.	-	R.C.	-	164	-	164	74
93	3173	Do.	-	Do.	f.	R.C.	-	R.C.	R.C.	-	178	178	80
94	6621	Kilmadum,	47	Ballyfoile,	m.	R.C.	-	R.C.	-	101	-	101	41
95	6881	Do.	-	Do.	f.	R.C.	-	R.C.	R.C.	-	113	118	61
96	6536	Killaloe,	-	Desart,	.	-	R.C.	R.C.	-	69	41	79	37
97	5820	Do.	-	Ballyline,	.	R.C.	-	R.C.	-	61	89	150	36
98	5853	Kells,	-	Kells,	.	R.C.	-	R.C.	-	81	43	124	44
99	6811	Kilfane,	-	Mong,	.	R.C.	-	R.C.	-	36	34	69	31
100	7773	Do.	-	Kilfane,	.	-	R.C.	R.C.	-	33	45	78	37
101	5607	Killamery,	53	Windgap,	m.	R.C.	-	R.C.	-	101	-	101	60
102	5608	Do.	-	Do.	f.	R.C.	-	R.C.	R.C.	-	123	123	61
103	4641	Kilcolumb,	49	Bluegills,	m.	R.C.	-	R.C.	-	88	-	88	32
104	6722	Do.	-	Do.	f.	R.C.	-	R.C.	-	-	71	71	29
105	7462	Knocktopher,	47	Knocktopher,	.	R.C.	-	R.C.	R.C.	84	74	158	61
106	7459	Kilmacow	49	Kilmacow,	m.	R.C.	-	R.C.	-	149	-	149	46
107	7460	Do.	-	Do.	f.	R.C.	-	R.C.	R.C.	-	161	161	51
108	7481	Kilmaganny,	63	Kilmaganny,	m.	R.C.	-	R.C.	-	88	-	88	40
109	7523	Do.	-	Do.	f.	R.C.	-	R.C.	-	-	103	103	39
110	6144	Kilmacahill,	47	Paulstown,	m.	R.C.	-	R.C.	-	144	-	144	54
111	6668	Kilmanagh,	-	Kilmanagh,	.	R.C.	-	R.C.	R.C.	57	85	142	61
112	6890	Kilbride,	49	Ballyfasey,	.	R.C.	-	R.C.	R.C.	58	57	115	37
113	6776	Listerlin,	-	Listerlin,	m.	R.C.	-	R.C.	-	93	-	93	37
114	6777	Do.	-	Do.	f.	R.C.	-	R.C.	-	-	73	73	33
115	6298	Muckalee,	47	Muckalee,	m.	R.C.	-	R.C.	-	61	-	61	41
116	7289	Do.	-	Do.	f.	R.C.	-	R.C.	-	-	91	91	39
117	7186	Do.	49	Gorryrane,	.	-	R.C.	R.C.	-	97	84	181	66
118	6776	Mothell,	47	Lisnafunchin,	.	R.C.	-	R.C.	-	38	29	68	27
119	794	Owning,	59	Owning,	.	-	R.C.	R.C.	-	58	48	106	53
120	6374	Outrath,	47	Foulkstown,	.	R.C.	-	R.C.	R.C.	49	79	128	45
121	1164	Powerstown,	63	Skeaghvasteen,	.	R.C.	-	R.C.	R.C.	61	101	162	63
122	6730	Pollrone,	49	Mooncoin,	m.	R.C.	-	R.C.	R.C.	171	-	171	79
123	6457	Do.	-	Do.	Convent, f.	-	R.C.	Nuns.		-	264	264	97
124	7469	Portnascully,	-	Carrigeen,	m.	R.C.	-	R.C.	-	121	-	121	56
125	6370	Do.	-	Do.	f.	R.C.	-	R.C.	-	-	127	127	45
126	872	Rathbeagh,	47	Clone,	.	R.C.	-	R.C.	-	30	34	64	19
127	1802	Rosbercon,	49	Rosbercon,	m.	R.C.	-	R.C.	-	60	-	60	23
128	3360	Do.	-	Do.	f.	R.C.	-	R.C.	-	-	82	82	29
129	2512	Rathpatrick,	-	Slieverue,	m.	R.C.	-	R.C.	-	109	-	109	31
130	2545	Do.	-	Do.	f.	R.C.	-	R.C.	-	-	70	70	25
131	3247	Rathcoole,	47	Johnswell,	m.	R.C.	-	R.C.	-	73	-	73	26
132	4661	Do.	-	Do.	f.	R.C.	-	R.C.	-	-	67	67	33
133	807	Shankill,	-	Boyvanies,	.	R.C.	-	R.C.	-	65	42	107	38

* Including value of Free Residence.

Province of Leinster: County of Kilkenny—*continued.*

Amount paid for Books, Requisites, and Apparatus, at Reduced Prices.	Aid granted by the Board during the Year 1874. In Free Stock of Books, Requisites, and Apparatus.	In Salaries, Premiums, and other Gratuities.	Results Fees, Financial Year.	Amount of Local Contributions received in Aid of Teacher's Salary. School Fees.	Subscriptions, Endowments, &c.	Total Local Aid.	Vested or Non-Vested.	Number.
£ s. d.	£ s. d.	£ s. d.	£ s. d.	£ s. d.	£ s. d.	£ s. d.		
2 4 4	—	34 0 0	11 18 0	11 1 11	4 0 0	b15 1 11		71
2 11 5	—	63 10 0	17 18 0	12 14 4	4 0 0	b17 14 4		72
3 18 5	—	78 0 8	21 0 0	8 14 3	—	8 14 3		73
2 4 5	—	19 10 0	17 0 0	9 0 0	—	9 0 0		74
4 18 8	—	41 0 0	20 17 0	4 4 4	—	4 4 4	V.T.	75
2 14 10	—	60 0 0	18 3 8	8 17 1	—	8 17 1	V.T.	76
8 1 0	—	47 13 4	15 8 0	1 14 0	1 0 0	2 14 0	V.T.	77
2 14 8	—	39 6 8	14 8 0	13 19 2	—	13 19 2		78
5 8 6	—	48 10 0	10 15 0	—	—	—		79
9 14 0	—	123 3 4	43 3 8	18 10 0	8 8 0	26 18 0		80
10 15 5	—	113 10 0	32 10 8	16 0 4	4 4 0	20 1 4		81
—	—	98 0 0	14 5 0	6 10 0	7 10 0	b14 0 0	V.T.	82
8 6 8	—	61 16 8	30 10 0	8 19 4	6 10 0	b16 9 4		83
13 4 9	—	65 6 8	30 16 6	9 8 6	6 10 0	b15 18 6		84
8 8 0	—	65 6 8	28 8 0	11 16 8	—	11 16 8		85
8 17 8	—	87 10 0	16 8 8	6 1 0	0 15 0	b6 16 0		86
8 18 0	—	54 0 0	22 10 8	18 4 8	10 0 0	28 4 8		87
6 8 0	—	63 16 0	24 6 0	14 14 3	14 0 0	b28 14 3		88
—	—	46 0 0	—	1 5 0	4 0 0	b5 5 0	V.T.	89
9 12 3	—	54 0 0	24 10 0	8 19 0	—	8 19 0		90
4 1 0	—	38 0 8	10 0 0	3 0 3	—	3 0 3		91
3 2 11	—	66 0 0	31 6 0	13 2 8	—	13 2 8		92
6 17 10	—	56 10 0	30 5 8	6 10 11	—	6 10 11		93
3 14 0	—	32 8 8	18 10 6	9 9 2	—	9 9 7		94
8 4 11	—	67 8 0	25 11 6	12 8 8	3 0 0	b15 8 8		95
2 15 0	—	21 0 0	0 6 0	4 17 6	3 0 0	b7 17 6		96
4 10 9	—	24 0 0	5 10 6	2 13 10	—	2 13 10		97
1 19 6	—	39 0 0	18 6 5	6 16 11	—	6 16 11		98
2 1 0	—	32 0 0	6 0 8	2 8 0	1 0 0	b3 8 0		99
2 10 6	—	30 0 0	6 19 8	1 10 0	9 10 0	b11 0 0		100
4 8 0	—	82 6 8	18 17 0	12 9 3	2 0 0	b14 9 3		101
5 10 0	—	67 10 0	21 9 0	8 13 11	—	8 13 11		102
2 0 11	—	32 0 0	8 17 0	0 10 8	8 17 6	b6 18 11		103
1 8 10	—	30 0 0	8 8 0	0 17 2	5 17 6	b6 14 8		104
5 4 7	—	44 0 0	24 4 0	11 0 8	—	11 0 8		105
3 1 6	—	41 0 0	18 10 0	11 15 10	—	11 15 10		106
0 0 8	—	61 15 0	21 8 0	0 8 4	—	0 8 4		107
1 11 8	—	78 0 0	14 4 8	3 17 9	17 3 0	b20 14 0		108
8 8 11	—	36 0 0	6 0 6	8 18 9	8 10 0	b17 8 9		109
2 15 0	—	39 10 0	18 12 0	8 13 7	—	8 13 7		110
6 8 1	—	64 8 8	22 15 8	12 15 11	—	12 15 11		111
2 8 1	—	44 0 0	24 10 0	6 16 7	—	6 16 7	V.T.	112
2 10 10	—	44 0 0	11 3 6	7 1 0	1 0 0	b8 1 0		113
1 1 2	—	30 0 0	8 19 7	8 5 0	1 0 0	b9 5 0		114
1 19 3	—	34 0 0	31 5 6	5 4 6	—	5 4 6		115
1 17 3	—	28 18 4	28 11 8	3 10 8	—	3 10 8		116
5 16 9	—	44 0 0	27 8 0	9 19 4	7 0 0	b16 19 4	V.C.	117
0 19 10	—	37 0 0	7 5 6	8 10 0	—	8 10 0		118
8 8 1	—	33 0 0	15 8 8	5 7 1	2 0 0	7 7 1		119
2 3 4	—	45 18 4	20 17 0	0 16 0	—	6 16 8		120
1 11 4	—	49 0 0	23 7 6	10 1 8	6 0 0	b15 1 8	V.T.	121
2 18 5	—	45 0 0	30 7 6	11 11 0	—	11 11 0		122
3 8 6	—	45 0 0	38 8 0	—	30 0 0	b30 0 0		123
2 1 6	—	34 0 0	11 5 0	12 0 0	—	12 0 0		124
2 16 11	—	32 0 0	17 4 0	6 10 0	—	6 10 0		125
2 8 6	—	24 0 0	7 2 0	2 15 8	—	2 15 8		126
1 17 6	—	24 0 0	8 2 0	2 0 4	—	2 0 4	V.T.	127
—	—	30 0 0	5 8 8	0 18 10	—	0 18 10	V.T.	128
2 1 7	—	24 0 0	9 15 0	8 1 0	6 0 0	b6 1 0		129
1 18 0	—	30 0 0	10 11 6	8 1 11	—	8 1 11		130
2 6 0	—	37 0 0	18 4 0	4 0 6	3 0 0	b7 0 6		131
2 17 0	—	28 16 8	17 0 6	4 1 8	—	4 1 8		132
0 11 7	—	24 0 0	7 17 0	4 0 0	—	4 0 0	V.T.	133

b Including value of Free Residence and Garden.

List of Schools in operation on the 31st December, 1874.—

Number.	Roll Number of School.	Parish.	District.	School.		Religious Denomination of Manager or Correspondent: Clerical.	Lay.	Number and Religious Denomination of Teachers: Principals.	Assistants.	Attendance for the Year. Total number of Pupils on Rolls within the Year 1874: Males.	Fem.	Total.	[illegible]
134	1919	Shankill,	47	Paulstown,	f.	R.C.	–	R.C.	R.C.	–	169	169	70
135	6981	St. Patrick's,	–	Kilkenny District Model,	m.	Com.	N.E.	R.C.	Pres.	181	–	181	67
136	6826	Do.	–	Do.	f.	Com.	N.E.	R.C.	E.C.	–	73	73	63
137	6828	Do.	–	Do.	i.	Com.	N.E.	E.C.	–	41	30	71	33
138	10476	Do.	–	St. Patrick's,	f.	R.C.	–	R.C.	2R.C.	–	173	173	82
139	10060	Do.	–	St. Joseph's,	i.	R.C.	–	R.C.	4R.C.	66	163	229	81
140	1301	St. John's,	–	St. John's,	m.	R.C.	–	R.C.	–	136	–	136	84
141	11163	Do.	–	Do.	f.	R.C.	–	R.C.	3R.C.	–	219	213	97
142	11164	Do.	–	Do.	i.	R.C.	–	R.C.	R.C.	102	125	227	82
143	1-828	Do.	–	Do. proper,	m.	R.C.	–	R.C.	–	60	–	60	32
144	8412	Do.	–	Do. [b]	i.	R.C.	–	–	–	–	–	–	–
145	3307	Do.	–	Kilkenny Workh.	.	P.L.	Gds.	4R.C.	R.C.	117	99	216	99
146	4926	Do.	–	Dunmore,	m.	R.C.	–	R.C.	–	65	–	65	36
147	4931	Do.	–	Do.	f.	R.C.	–	R.C.	–	–	69	69	31
148	806	St. Mary's,	–	Kilkenny Conv.,	f.	–	R.C.	Nuns	–	46	657	693	375
149	3129	Stonecarthy,	–	Stoneyford,	m.	R.C.	–	R.C.	–	107	–	107	49
150	3124	Do.	–	Do.	f.	R.C.	–	R.C.	–	–	119	116	46
151	6110	St. Canice,	–	Bennettsbridge,	.	R.C.	–	R.C.	R.C.	49	61	110	43
152	6618	Do.	–	St. Canice,	m.	R.C.	–	R.C.	R.C.	224	–	224	99
153	11174	Do.	–	Do.	i.	R.C.	–	R.C.	R.C.	84	113	207	97
154	9634	Do.	–	Do.	f.	R.C.	–	R.C.	1R.C.	–	241	241	95
155	9546	Do.	–	Thornback,	.	R.C.	–	R.C.	–	37	41	78	41
156	9297	Shanbogh,	49	Shanbogh,	.	–	R.C.	R.C.	–	36	34	69	35
157	3046	The Rower,	–	Rower,	m.	R.C.	–	R.C.	R.C.	159	–	159	65
158	6050	Do.	–	Do.	f.	R.C.	R.C.	R.C.	–	–	140	140	74
159	791	Treadingstown,	47	Bennet's Bridge,	.	R.C.	–	R.C.	R.C.	99	79	178	74
160	1802	Tullaroan,	–	Tullaroan,	m.	R.C.	–	R.C.	–	96	–	96	48
161	6338	Do.	–	Do.	f.	R.C.	–	R.C.	–	–	80	84	36
162	9816	Do.	–	Ballyhaigh,	.	R.C.	–	R.C.	–	42	40	82	35
163	2803	Thomastown,	–	Thomastown,	m.	R.C.	–	R.C.	–	232	–	232	70
164	4161	Do.	–	Do.	f.	R.C.	–	R.C.	–	–	165	169	85
165	11170	Do.	–	Do.	i.	R.C.	–	R.C.	R.C.	49	55	104	63
166	6276	Do.	–	Do. Workhouse,	.	P.L.	Gds.	R.C.	–	41	39	80	68
167	6230	Thornfin,	–	Rivenna,	m.	R.C.	–	R.C.	–	64	–	64	39
168	7867	Do.	–	Do.	f.	R.C.	–	R.C.	–	–	99	99	37
169	6620	Do.	–	Boula,	m.	R.C.	–	R.C.	–	66	–	66	34
170	6502	Do.	–	Do.	f.	R.C.	–	R.C.	–	–	66	66	27
171	1562	Tullahought,	55	Killamoliver,	m.	R.C.	–	R.C.	–	108	–	104	41
172	7530	Do.	–	Do.	f.	R.C.	–	R.C.	–	–	79	79	33
173	8469	Ullard,	59	Ullard,	.	R.C.	–	R.C.	–	32	35	67	35
174	6017	Urlingford,	45	Graine,	.	R.C.	–	R.C.	–	40	47	87	46
175	6124	Do.	–	Urlingford,	m.	R.C.	–	R.C.	–	117	–	117	41
176	7902	Do.	–	Do.	f.	R.C.	–	R.C.	R.C.	–	167	127	47
177	6923	Do.	–	Do. Workhouse,	.	–	–	R.C.	R.C.	80	39	69	32
178	6169	Whitechurch,	53	Whitechurch Ordinary Agricultural,	.	–	R.C.	R.C.	–	69	44	113	33
		Total for County Kilkenny, 178,								10612	11964	21,[illegible]	9,1[illegible]

KING'S

1	5778	Ardnurcher,	33	Horseleap,	m.	R.C.	–	R.C.	–	56	–	56	31
2	5779	Do.	–	Do.	f.	R.C.	–	R.C.	–	–	75	75	32
3	6947	Aghancon,	38	Aghancon,	.	–	R.C.	R.C.	–	39	28	67	30
4	11048	Ballyeaskill,	57	Eskar,	.	R.C.	–	R.C.	R.C.	61	50	111	36
5	809	Ballyboy,	36	Ballyboy,	.	R.C.	–	R.C.	–	44	41	85	23
6	7163	Do.	–	Frankford,	m.	R.C.	–	R.C.	–	63	–	63	31
7	8613	Do.	–	Do.	f.	R.C.	–	R.C.	–	–	74	74	31
8	9720	Do.	–	Drumphal,	.	R.C.	–	R.C.	–	51	74	125	31
9	810	Ballymacwilliam,	37	Trimblestown,	m.	R.C.	–	R.C.	–	63	–	63	25

[a] Inoperative. [b] Including value of Free Residence and Garden.

Province of Leinster: County of Kilkenny—*continued.*

Amounts paid for Books, Requisites, and Apparatus at Reduced Prices.	Aid granted by the Board during the Year 1874: In Free Stock of Books, Requisites, and Apparatus.	In Salaries, Premiums, and other Gratuities.	Results Fees, Financial Year.	Amount of Local Emoluments received in Aid of Teacher's Salary: School Fees.	Subscriptions, Endowments, &c.	Total Local Aid.	Vested or Non-Vested.	Number.
£ s. d.	£ s. d.	£ s. d.	£ s. d.	£ s. d.	£ s. d.	£ s. d.		
11 8 7	—	76 10 0	16 1 0	4 18 6	—	4 18 6		134
25 11 0	21 12 3	}					V.C.	135
9 8 11	15 8 10	} 752 2 1	42 5 6	86 10 1	—	86 10 1	V.C.	136
—	—	}					V.C.	137
8 13 2	—	74 10 0	27 19 5	5 5 11	—	5 5 11		138
0 10 8	—	58 6 5	16 2 0	2 9 10	—	2 9 10		139
5 3 1	—	69 1 5	25 14 0	21 13 1	—	21 13 1	V.T.	140
11 8 9	11 0 9	37 8 4	24 7 0	2 17 11	—	2 17 11		141
2 10 6	10 10 0	92 10 0	21 0 0	8 11 8	—	8 11 8		142
1 6 10	—	41 0 0	—	1 4 5	—	1 4 5	V.T.	143
—	—	57 1 1	—	—	—	—	V.T.	144
14 11 6	—	4 10 0	—	—	—	—		145
5 18 0	—	33 12 4	11 5 0	8 5 0	6 0 0	b [illegible] 5 0		146
2 4 0	—	24 0 0	18 1 5	2 0 8	4 0 0	a 6 0 8		147
85 12 0	—	182 12 4	65 15 0	—	—	—		148
1 15 0	—	24 0 0	14 5 6	6 15 8	—	6 15 8		149
1 16 8	—	47 10 0	24 6 6	4 0 7	—	4 0 7		150
4 6 8	—	25 0 0	15 7 0	10 6 5	—	10 6 5		151
0 1 11	—	67 6 0	41 6 0	9 6 9	—	9 6 9	V.C.	152
6 11 5	4 10 0	14 5 4	—	1 11 1	—	1 11 1	V.C.	153
10 18 9	—	72 10 10	46 6 0	1 8 9	—	1 8 9		154
—	—	80 0 0	9 0 8	4 5 6	—	4 5 6		155
0 14 7	—	24 0 0	1 18 2	0 10 0	1 0 0	1 10 0		156
4 10 2	—	55 10 0	37 8 0	12 5 6	—	12 5 6		157
6 2 1	—	90 0 0	28 2 6	11 6 0	—	11 6 0		158
1 5 8	—	47 10 0	16 8 0	10 4 0	—	10 4 0		159
4 2 1	—	35 10 0	14 7 8	11 19 2	0 10 0	12 9 2	V.T.	160
2 4 4	—	27 10 0	7 12 0	7 14 0	—	7 14 0	V.T.	161
0 15 11	—	25 7 4	11 1 0	8 10 6	—	8 10 6		162
4 3 9	4 0 3	41 0 0	16 17 8	9 4 10	—	9 4 10		163
6 10 11	—	60 2 8	17 4 0	11 8 1	—	11 8 1		164
1 14 4	4 10 0	3 17 9	—	2 0 2	—	2 0 2		165
6 1 4	—	—	—	—	—	—		166
1 17 0	—	24 0 0	9 0 0	5 18 0	—	5 18 0		167
—	—	20 0 0	7 0 6	1 7 6	—	1 7 6		168
1 15 11	—	18 0 0	8 4 9	2 4 6	—	2 4 6		169
1 18 3	—	31 0 0	12 15 0	5 9 0	—	5 9 0		170
2 6 8	—	24 0 0	7 9 0	7 11 8	—	7 11 8		171
2 14 9	—	60 0 0	15 19 0	8 15 0	—	8 15 0		172
2 3 10	—	20 0 0	8 0 8	2 15 0	—	2 15 0		173
5 0 3	—	24 0 0	16 7 0	4 17 0	8 0 0	a 12 17 0	V.C.	174
2 2 1	—	49 18 0	0 10 6	5 10 0	5 10 0	a 11 0 0		175
6 4 10	—	42 6 4	15 18 0	6 1 0	1 10 0	7 11 0		176
4 18 9	—	9 0 0	—	—	—	—		177
5 5 2	—	29 0 0	10 10 0	8 7 5	32 17 5	b 41 3 10	V.C.	178
[illegible] 12 0	73 0 1	7,885 14 10	2,620 17 8	1,149 18 5	470 0 10	1,[illegible] 16 8		

COUNTY—109 Schools.

1 8 8	8 5 0	14 4 5	8 16 0	1 10 0	—	1 10 0		1
4 1 2	—	63 16 4	6 15 0	8 15 0	8 15 0	a 8 10 0		2
1 10 6	—	13 8 6	4 4 0	6 0 0	2 10 0	b 8 10 0		3
—	—	44 0 6	17 11 8	6 8 1	5 0 0	a 21 8 1		4
1 18 5	—	42 10 0	14 6 0	4 0 0	10 0 0	15 0 0		5
1 3 10	—	24 0 0	11 6 6	2 18 1	—	2 18 1		6
1 6 0	—	28 0 0	18 0 0	3 4 10	—	3 4 10		7
2 15 0	—	32 0 0	16 3 0	6 0 0	—	6 0 0		8
2 2 4	—	87 0 0	18 13 0	10 16 1	5 0 0	b 15 16 1		9

a Including value of Free Garden.

b Including value of Free Residence.

List of Schools in operation on the 31st December, 1874.—

Number.	Roll Number of School.	Parish.	District.	School.[a]	Religious Denomination of Managers or Correspondents. Clerical.	Lay.	Principal and Religious Denomination of Teachers. Principals.	Assistants.	Attendance for the Year. Total number of Pupils on Rolls within the Year 1874. Males.	Females.	Total.	Average Daily Attendance for the Year.
10	10515	Ballymacwillm.	37	Ballymacwilliam, f.	R.C.	–	R.C.	–	81	78	97	35
11	9274	Do.	–	Rhode,	R.C.	–	R.C.	R.C.	59	74	133	67
12	1803	Ballycommon,	41	Kilmurry,	R.C.	–	R.C.	R.C.	50	67	120	40
13	1718	Ballykean,	–	Clonygowan,	R.C.	–	R.C.	R.C.	80	90	170	46
14	2481	Do.	–	Raheen,	R.C.	–	R.C.	–	78	83	56	40
15	1046	Birr,	36	Parsonstown, m.	R.C.	–	R.C.	–	181	–	135	60
16	2320	Do.	–	Do. f.	–	R.C.	Nuns		40	473	535	90
17	7912	Do.	–	Do. Model, m.	Com. N. E.		R.C.	E.C.	94	–	94	61
18	7049	Do.	–	Do. do. f.			R.C.	R.C.	–	81	81	40
19	7941	Do.	–	Do. do. i.			R.C.	Pres.	41	41	44	30
20	7049	Do.	–	Do. Workhouse.	P.L.	Gds.	R.C.	–	67	49	73	31
21	5790	Do.	–	Crinkle, m.	R.C.	–	R.C.	–	108	–	109	41
22	6178	Do.	–	Do. f.	R.C.	–	R.C.	–	–	109	108	81
23	8231	Do.	–	Fortel,	R.C.	–	R.C.	–	48	40	84	80
24	10228	Do.	–	Birr,	R.C.	–	R.C.	R.C.	187	–	187	64
25	818	Clonsast,	41	Cloghallock, m.	R.C.	–	R.C.	–	83	–	78	65
26	813	Do.	–	Do. f.	R.C.	–	R.C.	–	–	107	107	65
27	8190	Do.	–	Bracknagh,[a]	–	E.C.	R.C.	–	–	–	–	–
28	9134	Do.	–	Do. m.	R.C.	–	R.C.	–	87	–	87	57
29	1971	Do.	–	Do. f.	R.C.	–	R.C.	–	–	86	86	61
30	811	Croghan,	–	Cannakill,	R.C.	–	R.C.	–	81	–	63	60
31	5491	Clonmacnoise,	35	Clonfanlough,	R.C.	–	R.C.	–	74	78	146	47
32	8176	Do.	–	Shannonbridge, m.	R.C.	–	R.C.	–	100	–	103	47
33	9031	Do.	–	Do. f.	R.C.	–	R.C.	–	–	118	115	41
34	10594	Do.	–	Clonlyon,	R.C.	–	R.C.	–	60	54	117	31
35	7401	Castlejordan,	37	Garr,	R.C.	–	R.C.	–	43	33	76	36
36	[illegible]	Cullenwaine,	8	Cullenwaine,[a]	–	–	–	–	–	–	–	–
37	11038	Clara,	41	Clara,	R.C.	–	R.C.	–	18	30	48	24
38	7871	Cloneyhurke,	–	Portarlington Conv. f.	R.C.	–	Nuns		–	225	225	113
39	10472	Do.	–	Garryhinch,	R.C.	–	R.C.	–	67	53	120	43
40	9437	Dunkerrin,	36	Cangort,	–	E.C.	R.C.	–	60	86	136	4[illegible]
41	4405	Do.	–	[illegible]	R.C.	–	R.C.	R.C.	72	76	143	57
42	3112	Drumcullen,	–	Thomastown,	R.C.	–	R.C.	–	94	34	84	36
43	6891	Do.	–	Killyon,	R.C.	–	R.C.	–	40	59	99	33
44	6816	Durrow,	41	Durrow,	R.C.	–	R.C.	–	56	56	112	41
45	9975	Eglish,	36	Eglish,	R.C.	–	R.C.	R.C.	109	76	185	56
46	[illegible]	Ettagh,	–	Coolderry,	R.C.	–	R.C.	–	–	71	71	32
47	11238	Do.	–	Do. m.	R.C.	–	R.C.	–	–	83	83	37
48	5144	Geashill,	41	Walshisland,	R.C.	–	R.C.	R.C.	58	61	114	50
49	1721	Do.	–	Killeigh,	R.C.	–	R.C.	R.C.	61	63	119	41
50	4794	Do.	–	Killurine,	R.C.	–	R.C.	–	60	40	107	40
51	6267	Do.	–	Meelaghans,	R.C.	–	R.C.	–	47	54	101	31
52	6701	Do.	–	Ballinagar,	R.C.	–	R.C.	–	45	48	91	39
53	9103	Do.	–	Geashill, m.	–	E.C.	R.C.	–	123	–	123	34
54	9492	Do.	–	Do. f.	–	E.C.	R.C.	–	–	77	77	37
55	6771	Gallen,	36	Cloghan, m.	R.C.	–	R.C.	–	138	–	128	41
56	6878	Do.	–	Do. f.	R.C.	–	R.C.	R.C.	–	147	117	57
57	7154	Do.	–	Shannon Harbour,	R.C.	–	R.C.	–	40	40	80	33
58	817	Kilclonfert,	41	Kilclonfert,	R.C.	–	R.C.	–	65	67	122	40
59	821	Killaderry,	–	Philipstown, m.	R.C.	–	R.C.	–	153	–	143	57
60	8448	Do.	–	Do. f.	R.C.	–	R.C.	R.C.	–	109	104	59
61	6079	Killoughy,	–	Mount Bolus, m.	R.C.	–	R.C.	–	115	–	116	31
62	6073	Do.	–	Do. f.	R.C.	–	R.C.	–	19	108	127	40
63	7191	Do.	–	Gorrumore,	R.C.	–	R.C.	–	26	73	58	41
64	9262	Kilbride,	–	Clara Convent, f.	R.C.	–	R.C.	–	–	250	260	125
65	5459	Do.	–	Ballycowan,	R.C.	–	R.C.	–	56	64	60	31
66	2484	Do.	–	Tullamore Convent, f.	–	R.C.	Nuns		617	618	935	374
67	3440	Do.	–	Do. Workhouse,	P.L.	Gds.	R.C.	–	41	58	97	47
68	10235	Do.	–	Charleville,	R.C.	–	R.C.	R.C.	72	45	117	60
69	11214	Do.	–	Clara, prep.	R.C.	–	–	–	–	–	–	–
70	1946	Kilcomin,	39	Clonlisk,	R.C.	–	R.C.	–	75	79	147	46
71	6634	Kinnitty,	–	Kinnitty,	R.C.	–	R.C.	–	54	61	121	43
72	9220	Do.	–	Longford,	R.C.	–	R.C.	–	46	47	93	36

a Including value of Free Residence and Garden.

b Including value of Free Residence.

Province of Leinster: King's County—*continued.*

Amount paid for Books, Requisites, and Apparatus at Reduced Prices.	Aid granted by the Board during the Year 1874. In Free Stock of Books, Requisites, and Apparatus.	In Salaries, Premiums, and other Gratuities.	Results Fees, Principal Teach.	Amount of Local Emoluments received in Aid of Teacher's Salary. School Fees.	Subscriptions, Endowments, &c.	Total Local Aid.	Vested or Non-Vested.	Number.
£ s. d.	£ s. d.	£ s. d.	£ s. d.	£ s. d.	£ s. d.	£ s. d.		
4 4 2	—	23 10 0	14 8 0	7 1 7	—	7 1 7		10
6 7 4	—	55 1 8	11 17 0	0 0 8	—	0 0 8		11
1 19 5	—	10 0 0	18 4 0	6 0 0	4 0 0	*10 0 0	V.F.	12
1 5 8	—	34 13 4	5 8 0	2 7 8	—	0 7 9		13
1 0 10	—	8 0 0	—	3 3 3	—	3 3 3	V.F.	14
1 15 5	—	31 10 0	11 8 0	2 15 1	2 0 0	*4 15 1		15
12 10 2	—	127 0 4	71 15 0	10 3 0	—	10 3 0		16
—	—	}	—	64 14 7	—	63 15 7	V.F.	17
—	—	} 134 19 11	{ 51 13 6	—	—	—	V.F.	18
—	—	}	—	—	—	—	V.F.	19
4 8 11	—	7 10 0	—	—	—	—		20
6 7 6	—	41 8 11	11 14 0	0 19 3	—	0 19 3		21
—	—	85 10 0	0 18 0	7 10 0	—	7 10 0		22
1 5 0	—	24 0 0	1 17 0	6 10 4	2 13 0	*9 11 4		23
8 18 7	—	67 0 0	19 15 8	31 18 2	—	31 18 2		24
2 8 6	—	14 0 0	3 14 0	6 5 0	1 10 0	*6 15 0	V.F.	25
1 7 8	—	20 0 0	10 3 8	1 4 10	—	1 4 10	V.F.	26
2 4 6	—	23 0 0	—	—	—	—		27
1 0 11	—	37 0 0	9 9 0	4 7 6	—	4 7 6		28
0 17 11	—	30 12 4	12 2 0	2 17 8	—	2 17 8		29
1 7 9	—	24 0 0	11 8 0	7 15 0	1 10 0	*14 5 0		30
1 15 8	—	24 0 0	19 17 6	4 4 7	1 0 0	*5 4 7		31
0 10 0	—	88 10 0	16 10 0	0 12 5	—	0 12 5		32
4 3 0	—	43 10 0	11 14 0	0 17 9	—	0 17 9		33
1 5 8	—	30 0 0	9 18 0	5 3 8	—	5 3 0		34
1 15 2	—	24 0 0	6 0 0	2 10 0	—	2 10 0		35
—	—	—	—	—	—	—		36
1 5 3	—	30 0 0	10 8 0	—	22 0 0	*21 11 0		37
12 11 2	6 0 0	81 13 4	20 0 0	7 0 0	—	7 0 0		38
1 5 3	—	24 8 0	9 8 0	6 8 8	7 18 4	*14 0 0		39
4 3 0	—	22 18 4	4 1 6	3 10 7	10 0 0	13 10 7		40
6 6 2	—	54 2 9	15 8 0	13 6 4	—	13 6 4	V.F.	41
1 6 0	—	30 0 0	8 17 0	4 17 1	1 10 0	*6 7 1	V.F.	42
1 12 8	—	31 0 0	16 16 0	6 7 11	4 0 0	*9 7 11		43
2 4 7	—	33 0 0	8 11 0	5 13 2	4 0 0	*9 13 2		44
6 6 5	—	50 0 0	16 10 0	10 14 0	1 0 0	*11 14 0		45
1 0 6	—	20 0 0	11 8 0	8 3 6	—	8 3 6		46
1 12 2	—	—	0 8 0	0 13 8	—	6 13 8		47
—	—	34 0 0	10 13 0	1 11 4	8 0 0	*9 11 4		48
4 3 9	—	44 0 0	10 11 6	2 15 6	5 0 0	7 15 6	V.F.	49
1 8 8	—	44 0 0	4 7 6	6 5 1	3 0 0	9 5 1		50
1 3 10	—	30 0 0	6 5 0	3 10 7	2 0 0	5 10 7		51
6 18 8	—	30 0 0	6 17 0	1 4 0	4 0 0	*5 4 0		52
5 6 4	—	65 15 0	6 16 0	1 11 0	15 0 0	16 11 0		53
—	—	38 0 0	18 9 0	1 10 0	7 10 0	9 0 0		54
9 17 10	—	57 2 4	30 18 0	9 15 0	2 0 0	11 15 0	V.F.	55
1 4 11	—	59 10 8	24 10 0	0 3 5	—	0 3 5	V.F.	56
1 4 11	—	24 0 0	9 15 0	4 12 0	—	4 12 0		57
3 8 6	—	30 0 0	14 18 0	7 8 0	3 0 0	*10 8 0		58
1 6 1	—	30 5 0	13 1 6	8 7 8	3 0 0	*11 7 8	V.F.	59
5 4 8	—	54 0 0	10 6 6	0 3 0	—	0 3 6	V.F.	60
2 17 11	—	24 0 0	8 11 6	1 7 0	—	1 7 8		61
1 14 8	—	35 0 0	11 15 0	3 7 0	—	3 7 9		62
0 10 0	—	20 8 0	8 7 6	1 18 11	5 0 0	6 18 11	V.F.	63
8 14 8	—	37 12 4	42 8 0	61 15 0	—	61 15 0		64
1 10 11	—	24 0 0	19 0 6	3 8 8	4 10 0	*7 18 8		65
21 4 6	—	161 10 0	60 7 8	7 11 10	—	7 11 10	V.F.	66
4 14 10	—	8 10 0	—	—	—	—		67
11 3 0	—	73 10 0	35 19 0	44 5 4	41 0 0	*85 5 4		68
—	—	—	—	—	—	—		69
3 4 8	—	33 13 4	0 4 6	6 1 6	—	6 1 6		70
8 3 1	—	23 0 0	14 1 0	8 8 6	—	8 8 6		71
2 1 10	—	16 0 0	6 10 6	10 0 0	—	10 0 0		72

* No Return. * Incomplete.

List of Schools in operation on the 31st December, 1874.—

Number.	Roll Number of School.	Parish.	District.	School.	Religious Denomination of Members of Correspondence: Clerical.	Lay.	Number and Religious Denomination of Teachers: Principals.	Assistants.	Attendance for the Year. Total number of Pupils on Rolls during the Year 1874: Males.	Fem.	Total.	Average Daily Attendance for the Year.
73	6731	Kilcolman,	36	Ballyegan,	R.C.	–	R.C.	–	73	61	133	[illegible]
74	11368	Do.	–	Cree, [a]	R.C.	–	R.C.	–	–	–	–	–
75	6638	Kilmanaghan,	41	Tubber, m.	R.C.	–	R.C.	–	91	–	91	27
				Do. [b] evg.	–	–	–	–	–	–	–	–
76	8939	Do.	–	Do. f.	R.C.	–	R.C.	–	–	117	117	[illegible]
77	8711	Letterluna,	36	Cadamstown,	R.C.	–	R.C.	–	48	46	94	[illegible]
78	8529	Lynally,	41	Mucklagh,	R.C.	–	R.C.	–	67	[illegible]	76	[illegible]
79	8263	Lemanaghan,	–	Boher, m.	R.C.	–	R.C.	–	105	–	105	[illegible]
80	[illegible]	Do.	–	Do. f.	R.C.	–	R.C.	–	–	133	133	[illegible]
81	10767	Do.	–	Pallas,	R.C.	–	R.C.	R.C.	72	75	147	[illegible]
82	8483	Lusmagh,	36	Ballymacwilliam, m.	–	R.C.	R.C.	–	73	–	73	31
83	8199	Do.	–	Do. f.	–	R.C.	R.C.	–	–	60	60	[illegible]
84	1429	Monasteroris,	37	Edenderry, m.	R.C.	–	R.C.	R.C.	226	–	226	104
85	1402	Do.	–	Do. f.	R.C.	–	R.C.	R.C.	41	235	276	121
86	[illegible]	Do.	–	Do. Workhouse,	P.L.	Gds.	R.C.	R.C.	[illegible]	[illegible]	147	[illegible]
87	5748	Rahan,	41	Island Parish, m.	R.C.	–	R.C.	–	97	–	97	[illegible]
88	5742	Do.	–	Do. f.	R.C.	–	R.C.	–	–	76	76	[illegible]
89	623	Do.	–	Rahan 1st Class Agricultural, m.	R.C.	–	R.C.	–	110	–	110	[illegible]
90	[illegible]	Do.	–	Killina Convent, f.	R.C.	–	Nuns	–	–	219	219	79
91	6127	[illegible]	36	Drumakeenan,	R.C.	–	R.C.	–	71	66	137	63
92	6307	Do.	–	Killeigh,	R.C.	–	R.C.	–	[illegible]	[illegible]	85	[illegible]
93	[illegible]	Roscomroe,	–	Rahanpkeen,	R.C.	–	R.C.	–	70	65	130	[illegible]
94	9106	Reynagh,	–	Garrelly,	R.C.	–	R.C.	–	48	45	93	[illegible]
95	[illegible]	Do.	–	Banagher, m.	R.C.	–	R.C.	–	97	–	97	31
96	[illegible]	Do.	–	Do. Convent, f.	–	R.C.	Nuns	–	–	183	183	[illegible]
97	[illegible]	Do.	–	Do.	R.C.	–	R.C.	–	19	24	43	[illegible]
98	10277	Dunkerrin,	41	Cannakill, f.	R.C.	–	R.C.	–	7	90	97	[illegible]
99	6461	Shinrone,	36	Shinrone, m.	R.C.	–	R.C.	–	114	–	114	67
100	6139	Do.	–	Do. f.	R.C.	–	R.C.	–	–	112	112	37
101	[illegible]	Do.	–	Ballincor,	R.C.	–	R.C.	–	21	[illegible]	[illegible]	[illegible]
102	11092	St. Kieran's,	–	St. Kieran's,	R.C.	–	R.C.	–	58	53	111	73
103	[illegible]	Templeharry,	–	Emmel,	R.C.	–	R.C.	R.C.	78	86	164	[illegible]
104	[illegible]	Do.	–	Moneygall,	R.C.	–	R.C.	R.C.	100	103	203	[illegible]
105	8362	Tisaran,	–	High-street,	R.C.	–	R.C.	–	47	[illegible]	[illegible]	[illegible]
106	[illegible]	Do.	–	Lisheeny,	–	R.C.	R.C.	–	59	[illegible]	[illegible]	[illegible]
107	4408	Wheery,	–	Fortune, m.	R.C.	–	R.C.	–	119	–	119	[illegible]
108	8184	Do.	–	Do. f.	R.C.	–	R.C.	R.C.	–	116	116	[illegible]
109	[illegible]	Do.	–	Leamore,	R.C.	–	R.C.	–	64	48	112	39
		Total for King's County, 109,							6,031	7,828	13,874	5,645

COUNTY OF

Number.	Roll Number of School.	Parish.	District.	School.	Clerical.	Lay.	Principals.	Assistants.	Males.	Fem.	Total.	Average Daily Attendance.
1	11779	Ardagh,	28	Loughill,	R.C.	–	R.C.	R.C.	102	64	166	[illegible]
2	4919	Do.	–	Glynn,	R.C.	–	R.C.	–	78	47	125	[illegible]
3	7076	Do.	–	Ardagh, m.	R.C.	–	R.C.	–	131	–	131	[illegible]
4	7165	Do.	–	Do. f.	R.C.	–	R.C.	–	–	104	104	[illegible]
5	[illegible]	Abbeylara,	–	Abbeylara, m.	R.C.	–	R.C.	–	98	–	98	[illegible]
6	7931	Do.	–	Do. f.	R.C.	–	R.C.	–	–	65	65	27
7	4470	Do.	–	Springtown,	R.C.	–	R.C.	–	52	73	125	[illegible]
8	7577	Ballymacormick,	–	Stonepark, m.	R.C.	–	R.C.	–	106	–	106	[illegible]
9	7578	Do.	–	Do. f.	R.C.	–	R.C.	–	–	98	98	77
10	[illegible]	[illegible]	–	Aghanagh,	R.C.	–	R.C.	–	79	90	169	[illegible]
11	12095	Cashel,	27	Currabeg, m.	R.C.	–	R.C.	–	185	–	185	[illegible]
12	[illegible]	Do.	–	Do. f.	R.C.	–	R.C.	–	–	189	189	[illegible]
13	11368	Columbkille,	28	Gaigue, m.	R.C.	–	R.C.	–	60	–	[illegible]	[illegible]
14	7894	Do.	–	Do. f.	R.C.	–	R.C.	–	–	106	106	[illegible]
15	14200	Do.	–	Clooneen,	R.C.	–	R.C.	R.C.	51	–	51	[illegible]
16	8819	Do.	–	Drumbeggan,	R.C.	–	R.C.	R.C.	127	123	250	[illegible]

[a] No Return.   [b] Inoperative.

Province of Leinster: King's County—*continued.*

Amount paid for Books, &c., and Apparatus at Reduced Prices.	Aid granted by the Board during the Year 1874. In Free Stock of Books, Requisites, and Apparatus.	In Salaries, Premiums, and other Gratuities.	Results Fees, Financial Year.	Amount of Local Endowments received in Aid of Teacher's Salary. School Fees.	Subscriptions, Endowments, &c.	Total Local Aid.	Vested or Non-Vested.	Number.
£ s. d.	£ s. d.	£ s. d.	£ s. d.	£ s. d.	£ s. d.	£ s. d.		
1 5 3	—	27 15 6	6 11 6	8 0 7	—	8 0 7	V.C.	73
1 6 6	4 0 0	—	—	—	—	—		74
1 3 8	—	27 0 0	5 0 0	4 18 6	—	4 18 6		75
—	—	—	—	—	—	—		
—	—	30 0 0	7 10 0	1 11 8	—	1 11 8		76
3 19 9	—	35 0 0	18 0 6	7 15 8	2 0 0	*9 15 8		77
0 13 0	—	24 0 0	0 1 6	7 5 10	4 0 0	*11 5 10		78
—	—	24 0 0	8 17 8	9 5 7	—	9 5 7		79
—	—	30 0 0	11 9 0	8 13 0	—	8 13 0		80
8 17 0	—	37 10 0	13 0 6	8 9 10	6 10 0	*14 19 10		81
4 9 7	—	62 0 0	10 19 6	4 19 0	10 0 0	*14 19 0		82
—	—	25 0 0	9 18 6	3 11 0	6 0 0	9 11 0		83
10 5 2	—	55 5 8	41 10 0	27 1 6	10 0 0	*37 1 6	V.T.	84
10 12 5	—	70 3 4	46 5 5	15 14 5	—	15 14 5	V.T.	85
5 19 5	—	—	—	—	—	—		86
—	—	24 0 0	10 8 0	4 7 0	—	4 7 0		87
1 7 1	—	20 0 0	7 11 6	5 0 11	—	5 0 11		88
4 3 0	1 7 0	43 8 8	9 18 0	4 9 1	5 15 0	*10 4 1	V.C.	89
5 3 4	—	56 5 0	84 12 8	—	—	—		90
3 7 8	—	26 0 0	6 16 0	7 18 7	—	7 18 7		91
1 5 5	—	18 0 0	8 4 0	4 11 6	—	4 11 6		92
2 19 6	—	25 0 0	13 15 0	19 5 0	—	19 5 0		93
2 15 5	—	21 0 0	11 1 0	11 7 7	—	11 7 7		94
2 17 5	—	35 0 0	7 14 0	5 6 2	—	5 6 2		95
17 4 5	—	40 19 4	21 18 0	7 16 1	—	7 16 1		96
0 7 4	—	78 6 8	3 5 0	3 12 7	15 0 0	18 12 7		97
—	—	27 0 0	30 15 6	9 3 9	3 0 0	*12 3 9		98
1 9 6	—	24 0 0	9 17 0	8 4 8	—	8 4 8		99
1 10 7	—	24 0 0	11 0 6	5 8 1	—	5 8 1		100
0 18 2	—	30 0 0	9 14 0	2 3 7	—	2 3 7		101
4 4 8	6 10 0	—	—	5 5 10	4 10 0	9 15 10		102
4 8 8	—	43 1 5	11 3 0	6 7 0	—	6 7 0	V.C.	103
8 9 9	—	57 0 0	28 4 0	17 10 0	—	17 10 0	V.C.	104
7 15 0	—	16 13 4	0 10 0	3 9 6	2 12 0	*5 1 6		105
3 18 0	—	30 6 0	10 15 0	18 10 0	7 10 0	*21 0 0		106
3 7 2	—	23 10 0	6 17 0	8 8 9	—	8 8 9		107
4 6 1	—	39 0 0	12 6 6	13 14 6	—	13 14 6		108
1 15 11	—	26 15 0	15 3 6	1 10 0	—	1 10 0		109
343 11 10	18 8 0	3,082 10 8	1,416 13 9	779 6 8	276 14 4	1,000 3 0		

LONGFORD—108 Schools.

3 18 0	—	56 8 8	15 18 0	12 18 6	—	12 18 6		1
3 3 7	—	24 0 0	10 10 0	4 6 2	2 0 0	*6 6 2		2
1 6 3	—	35 6 8	14 7 0	8 8 10	—	8 8 10		3
2 8 8	—	24 0 0	12 8 7	1 1 0	—	1 1 0		4
—	—	24 0 0	11 3 0	8 14 8	—	8 14 8		5
4 15 8	—	30 0 0	4 15 9	2 10 6	—	2 10 6		6
—	—	30 0 0	3 5 8	1 10 11	—	1 10 11		7
1 5 8	—	25 0 0	10 4 8	0 14 11	6 0 0	*6 14 11		8
1 10 6	—	28 0 0	8 10 6	0 8 5	6 0 0	*6 8 5		9
—	—	24 0 0	6 18 0	0 16 8	—	0 16 8		10
—	—	24 0 0	—	2 5 8	—	2 5 8	V.T.	11
1 18 5	—	43 16 8	9 10 9	1 18 4	—	1 18 4	V.T.	12
2 15 11	—	23 0 0	0 19 0	2 0 0	—	2 0 0		13
1 16 5	—	30 0 0	14 8 8	1 9 0	—	1 9 0		14
1 3 6	—	24 0 0	18 14 6	3 3 6	—	*3 3 6	V.T.	15
5 5 5	—	35 10 0	20 11 6	2 19 5	—	3 19 0		16

* Including value of Free Residence.

† Including value of Free Residence and Garden.

List of Schools in operation on the 31st December, 1874.—

Number.	Roll Number of School.	Parish.	District.	School.	Religious Denomination of Manager or Correspondent: Clerical.	Lay.	Number and Religious Denomination of Teachers: Principals.	Assistants.	Attendance for the Year: Total number of Pupils on Rolls within the Year: Males.	Fem.	Total.	Average Number in Daily Attendance for the Year.
17	[illegible]	Columbcille,	23	Purth,	R.C.	–	R.C.	R.C.	112	60	172	[illegible]
18	6915	Do.	–	Columbcille, m.	R.C.	–	R.C.	R.C.	167	–	[illegible]	[illegible]
19	7071	Do.	–	Do. f.	R.C.	–	R.C.	–	–	[illegible]	[illegible]	[illegible]
20	[illegible]	Do.	–	Cloonback,	R.C.	–	R.C.	R.C.	104	117	221	[illegible]
21	[illegible]	Do.	–	Molly,	R.C.	–	R.C.	R.C.	152	124	276	[illegible]
22	[illegible]	Clonbroney,	–	Clonbroney,	R.C.	–	R.C.	–	80	66	147	[illegible]
23	1174	Do.	–	Ballinalee, m.	R.C.	–	R.C.	–	117	–	117	[illegible]
24	[illegible]	Do.	–	Do. f.	R.C.	–	R.C.	–	–	[illegible]	[illegible]	[illegible]
25	[illegible]	Do.	–	Castlebrock,	R.C.	–	R.C.	–	106	79	185	[illegible]
26	[illegible]	Do.	–	Coolarty,	Pres.	–	Pres.	–	41	55	[illegible]	[illegible]
27	6113	Do.	–	Lisryan, m.	R.C.	–	R.C.	–	[illegible]	–	[illegible]	[illegible]
28	[illegible]	Do.	–	Do. f.	R.C.	–	R.C.	–	–	100	100	[illegible]
29	[illegible]	Do.	–	Ballinamuck,	R.C.	–	R.C.	–	21	[illegible]	[illegible]	[illegible]
30	[illegible]	Clongesh,	–	Newtownforbes, m.	R.C.	–	R.C.	–	[illegible]	–	[illegible]	[illegible]
31	[illegible]	Do.	–	Do. Convent, f.	R.C.	–	Nuns	–	[illegible]	[illegible]	[illegible]	[illegible]
32	[illegible]	Do.	–	Garrowhill, m.	R.C.	–	R.C.	–	148	–	[illegible]	[illegible]
33	[illegible]	Do.	–	Do. f.	R.C.	–	R.C.	–	–	137	137	[illegible]
34	1740	Do.	–	Kilmore,	R.C.	–	R.C.	–	46	[illegible]	135	[illegible]
35	[illegible]	Do.	–	Cloonagh, m.	R.C.	–	R.C.	–	[illegible]	–	[illegible]	[illegible]
36	[illegible]	Do.	–	Do. f.	R.C.	–	R.C.	–	–	114	114	[illegible]
37	[illegible]	Do.	–	Moyne,	R.C.	–	R.C.	R.C.	106	[illegible]	[illegible]	[illegible]
38	[illegible]	Forgney,	23	Forgney,	R.C.	–	R.C.	R.C.	72	[illegible]	144	[illegible]
39	[illegible]	Do.	–	Ballycloghan,	–	R.C.	R.C.	–	[illegible]	[illegible]	[illegible]	[illegible]
40	[illegible]	Granard,	24	Aughnacliffe,	R.C.	–	R.C.	–	74	61	135	[illegible]
41	6310	Do.	–	[illegible]	R.C.	–	R.C.	R.C.	118	73	191	[illegible]
42	1311	Do.	–	Killeen,[a] m.	–	–	–	–	–	–	–	–
43	1457	Do.	–	Do. f.	R.C.	–	R.C.	–	[illegible]	[illegible]	[illegible]	[illegible]
44	1517	Do.	–	Granard, m.	R.C.	–	R.C.	–	[illegible]	–	[illegible]	[illegible]
45	1312	Do.	–	Do.[a] f.	–	–	–	–	–	–	–	–
46	[illegible]	Do.	–	Do. Workhouse,	P.L.	Gds.	R.C.	R.C.	61	[illegible]	116	[illegible]
47	10701	Do.	–	Do. Convent,	R.C.	–	R.C.	–	–	207	207	[illegible]
48	5100	Do.	–	Aughnagarron, m.	R.C.	–	R.C.	–	[illegible]	–	[illegible]	[illegible]
49	[illegible]	Do.	–	Do. f.	R.C.	–	R.C.	–	–	[illegible]	[illegible]	[illegible]
50	5511	Do.	–	[illegible]	R.C.	–	R.C.	–	73	47	[illegible]	47
51	5714	Do.	–	[illegible]	R.C.	–	R.C.	R.C.	[illegible]	–	[illegible]	[illegible]
52	5115	Kilglass,	–	[illegible], m.	R.C.	–	R.C.	–	128	–	[illegible]	[illegible]
53	[illegible]	Do.	–	Do. f.	R.C.	–	R.C.	–	–	[illegible]	105	[illegible]
54	[illegible]	Do.	–	Ballycloghan,[a] m.	–	–	–	–	–	–	–	–
55	[illegible]	Do.	–	Do. f.	R.C.	–	R.C.	R.C.	[illegible]	[illegible]	[illegible]	[illegible]
56	[illegible]	Do.	–	Carrickboy,	Pres.	–	Pres.	–	[illegible]	67	[illegible]	[illegible]
57	[illegible]	Kilglass,	–	Cullyfad,	R.C.	–	R.C.	R.C.	115	[illegible]	[illegible]	[illegible]
58	[illegible]	Do.	–	Drumlish, m.	R.C.	–	R.C.	R.C.	[illegible]	–	[illegible]	[illegible]
59	[illegible]	Do.	–	Do. f.	R.C.	–	R.C.	R.C.	–	221	[illegible]	[illegible]
60	7791	Do.	–	[illegible]	R.C.	–	R.C.	R.C.	101	73	174	[illegible]
61	[illegible]	Do.	–	[illegible]	R.C.	–	R.C.	–	[illegible]	[illegible]	[illegible]	[illegible]
62	[illegible]	Do.	–	[illegible]	R.C.	–	R.C.	–	[illegible]	71	149	[illegible]
63	[illegible]	Do.	–	Glenmore,	R.C.	–	R.C.	R.C.	124	[illegible]	[illegible]	[illegible]
64	[illegible]	Do.	–	[illegible]	R.C.	–	R.C.	R.C.	155	[illegible]	[illegible]	[illegible]
65	[illegible]	Do.	–	[illegible]	R.C.	–	R.C.	R.C.	136	105	241	[illegible]
66	[illegible]	Do.	–	[illegible], m.	R.C.	–	R.C.	R.C.	[illegible]	–	[illegible]	[illegible]
67	[illegible]	Do.	–	Do. f.	R.C.	–	R.C.	R.C.	–	143	143	[illegible]
68	[illegible]	Do.	–	[illegible],[a] m.	–	–	–	–	–	–	–	–
69	[illegible]	Do.	–	Do. f.	R.C.	–	R.C.	–	–	[illegible]	[illegible]	[illegible]
70	[illegible]	Killashee,	–	Cloonagh Ord. Agric.	–	R.C.	R.C.	–	111	–	[illegible]	[illegible]
71	[illegible]	Do.	–	Do. f.	–	R.C.	R.C.	–	–	107	[illegible]	[illegible]
72	[illegible]	Do.	–	Clondara,	R.C.	–	R.C.	–	34	75	109	[illegible]
73	[illegible]	Do.	–	Killashee,	R.C.	–	R.C.	R.C.	110	[illegible]	[illegible]	74
74	[illegible]	Kilcommock,	–	Kenagh, m.	R.C.	–	R.C.	–	[illegible]	–	[illegible]	[illegible]
75	[illegible]	Do.	–	Do. f.	R.C.	–	R.C.	–	–	124	[illegible]	[illegible]
76	[illegible]	Do.	–	Kenagh,	R.C.	–	R.C.	R.C.	[illegible]	61	[illegible]	[illegible]
77	[illegible]	Mostrim,	–	[illegible], m.	R.C.	–	R.C.	–	[illegible]	–	[illegible]	[illegible]
78	[illegible]	Do.	–	Do. f.	R.C.	–	R.C.	–	–	[illegible]	[illegible]	[illegible]
79	[illegible]	Do.	–	Edgeworthstown, m.	R.C.	–	R.C.	–	125	–	[illegible]	47

[a] Including value of Free Garden. [b] Including value of Free Residence.

Province of Leinster: County of Longford—*continued.*

Amount paid for Books, Requisites, and Apparatus at reduced prices.			Aid granted by the Board during the Year 1874. In Free Stock of Books, Requisites, and Apparatus.			In Salaries, Premiums, and other Gratuities.			Results Fees, Financial Year.			Amount of Local Endowments received in Aid of Teacher's Salary. School Fees.			Subscriptions, Endowments, &c.			Total Local Aid.			Vested or Non-Vested.	Number.
£	s.	d.	£	s.	d.	£	s.	d.	£	s.	d.	£	s.	d.	£	s.	d.	£	s.	d.		
8	2	6		—		53	10	0	59	10	0	3	15	3		—		5	15	8		17
8	3	6		—		71	10	0	27	0	0	4	10	0	1	10	0	*5	3	0		18
2	10	0		—		20	0	0	8	18	0	2	1	0		—		2	1	0		19
4	1	0		—		24	14	8	30	3	6	8	7	0		—		8	7	0		20
4	19	0		—		91	15	0	49	16	0	8	15	6		—		8	15	6		21
2	1	3		—		31	16	8	6	18	0	1	11	0		—		1	11	0		22
	—			—		24	6	8	11	5	8	2	12	0		—		2	12	0	V.T.	23
8	1	0		—		31	4	6	11	0	0	0	18	0		—		0	18	0	V.T.	24
1	11	2		—		38	10	0	25	1	6	7	10	0		—		7	10	0	V.T.	25
1	18	2		—		30	12	6	10	12	0		—		8	0	0	8	0	0		26
1	5	5		—		21	0	0	8	3	0	0	12	0	0	12	0	1	4	0		27
1	6	8		—		31	18	6	11	9	6	2	11	0		—		2	11	0		28
	—			—		17	0	8	3	17	4	14	10	6	8	10	0	23	0	6		29
1	8	4		—		61	0	0	11	16	0	2	2	5		—		2	2	5		30
0	1	8		—		31	18	0	9	8	0	4	18	8		—		4	18	8		31
2	10	6		—		30	0	0	11	18	0	6	4	8		—		6	4	8	V.T.	32
1	0	5		—		26	0	0	10	1	6	2	11	10		—		2	11	10	V.T.	33
1	7	8		—		30	0	0	6	5	0	0	15	0		—		0	15	0		34
2	1	8		—		23	0	0	15	17	0	1	5	0		—		2	5	0	V.T.	35
1	7	8		—		20	0	0	8	0	6	0	11	0		—		0	11	6	V.T.	36
3	0	6		—		44	0	0	24	18	0	5	2	0		—		5	0	0		37
3	3	1		—		57	4	8	15	16	6	3	10	1		—		3	10	1		38
1	10	7		—		31	0	0	14	4	6		—		15	0	0	*15	0	0		39
1	14	5		—		27	10	0	16	0	0	2	17	6		—		2	17	6		40
2	17	9		—		45	8	4	17	18	0	3	10	0	1	0	0	*4	16	0		41
1	11	6		—			—			—			—			—			—		V.T.	42
3	4	1		—		18	0	0	2	13	8	1	16	0		—		1	16	0	V.T.	43
2	19	3		—		23	4	5	9	6	0	8	16	0		—		6	16	0	V.T.	44
	—			—			—			—			—			—			—		V.T.	45
6	10	2		—		7	0	0		—			—			—			—			46
6	10	0		—		46	12	4	24	0	0	8	4	10		—		3	4	10		47
1	8	10		—		49	0	0	7	2	6	1	10	6		—		1	10	6		48
1	5	8		—		20	0	0	11	8	6	2	8	0		—		2	8	0		49
	—			—		21	0	0	12	8	8	4	7	0		—		4	7	0		50
8	13	6		—		75	18	4	15	1	0	12	15	0		—		12	15	0		51
4	8	4		—		84	0	0	17	15	6	5	5	6		—		5	5	6	V.T.	52
1	12	6		—		29	0	0	16	6	8	8	11	8		—		8	11	8	V.T.	53
	—			—			—			—			—			—			—			54
1	15	1		—		52	10	0	12	0	0	1	12	1		—		1	12	1		55
2	14	7		—		81	0	0	18	16	8	11	12	6	9	5	0	*20	17	6		56
8	1	10		—		84	0	0	18	1	8	2	14	0		—		2	14	0		57
4	15	2		—		60	0	8	18	16	6		—			—			—			58
3	11	7		—		57	13	4	19	8	6	0	2	6		—		0	2	6		59
1	10	10		—		21	0	0	9	7	6	1	11	0		—		1	11	0		60
1	4	8		—		24	0	0	11	0	6	1	6	5		—		1	6	5		61
0	13	0		—		20	0	0	10	18	6	0	19	6		—		0	19	6		62
7	4	4		—		35	0	0	29	12	0	1	0	0		—		1	0	0		63
3	9	3		—		14	0	0	29	7	0	2	12	0		—		2	12	0		64
4	11	9		—		65	18	4	48	1	8	9	3	8		—		9	3	8		65
2	16	8		—		61	0	0	31	8	6	5	15	0		—		5	15	0		66
3	3	10		—		47	10	0	37	19	6	8	4	10		—		8	4	10		67
	—			—			—			—			—			—			—			68
1	10	10		—		20	0	0	11	14	6	1	11	9		—		1	11	9		69
8	10	6		—		37	8	8	7	0	8		—			—			—		V.T.	70
2	1	8		—		24	15	0	10	16	0		—			—			—		V.T.	71
3	16	6		—		21	0	6	9	10	0	1	9	6		—		1	9	6		72
6	2	0		—		55	15	4	37	16	0	1	8	7		—		1	8	7		73
	—			—		52	10	0	9	0	0	8	7	6		—		8	7	6		74
1	18	6		—		28	0	0	15	0	6	2	8	6		—		2	8	6		75
6	15	1	9	8	3	63	15	0	28	12	6		—		73	0	0	*73	0	0		76
6	4	8		—		24	0	0	6	4	0	1	17	0		—		1	17	0		77
1	12	6		—		30	18	4	23	7	0	2	15	0		—		2	15	0		78
6	15	9		—		50	17	9	11	15	0	1	15	8		—		1	15	8	V.T.	79

* No returns; School closed. † School not in operation. * Including value of Free Residence and Garden.

List of Schools in operation on the 31st December, 1874,—

Number.	Roll Number of School.	Parish.	District.	School.	Religious Denomination of Manager or Correspondent. Clerical.	Lay.	Number and Religious Denomination of Teachers. Principals.	Assistants.	Attendance for the Year. Total number of Pupils on Rolls within the Year. Males.	Fem.	Total.	Average Daily Attendance.
80	2564	Mostrim,	26	Edgeworthstown, f.	R.C.	–	R.C.	–	–	181	184	87
81	4307	Moydow,	–	Moydow, m.	R.C.	–	R.C.	–	123	–	123	66
82	4707	Do.	–	Do. f.	R.C.	–	R.C.	–	–	108	108	59
83	6214	Rathcline,	27	Fermoyle,	R.C.	–	R.C.	–	64	55	119	51
84	5659	Do.	–	Rathcline Ord. Agric.	R.C.	–	R.C.	R.C.	130	130	260	96
85	7224	[illegible],	28	Cooleenbar, [b] m.	–	–	–	–	–	–	–	–
86	5539	Do.	–	Do. f.	–	R.C.	R.C.	–	37	61	98	48
87	1760	Shrule,	–	Ballymahon, m.	R.C.	–	R.C.	R.C.	159	–	171	85
88	3862	Do.	–	Do. Con. f.	–	R.C.	Nuns		–	225	225	75
89	10668	Do.	–	Do. No. 2	R.C.	–	R.C.	–	31	24	55	29
90	6811	Do.	–	Do. Workh.	P.L.	Gds.	R.C.	–	28	20	48	25
91	6828	Do.	–	Gurteen,	R.C.	–	R.C.	R.C.	68	78	136	61
92	6766	Taghsheenod,	–	Carrowroehan,	R.C.	–	R.C.	–	77	58	135	60
93	2318	Taghshinny,	–	Tinelick, m.	R.C.	–	R.C.	–	73	–	73	35
				Do. evg.	–	–	–	–	–	–	–	–
94	2468	Do.	–	Do. f.	R.C.	–	R.C.	–	–	77	77	30
95	12222	Do.	–	Taghshinny,	R.C.	–	R.C.	–	20	31	57	21
96	856	Templemichael,	–	Longford, m.	R.C.	–	R.C.	–	159	–	159	63
97	857	Do.	–	Do. Convt. f.	–	R.C.	Nuns		74	225	299	133
98	6266	Do.	–	Do. Workhs.	P.L.	Gds.	R.C.	–	67	50	117	76
99	10660	Do.	–	Do. Gaol,	Government		R.C.	–	139	–	139	13
100	1419	Do.	–	Cloonahard,	R.C.	–	R.C.	–	66	69	135	64
101	7517	Do.	–	Melview, m.	R.C.	–	R.C.	–	128	–	128	62
102	7518	Do.	–	Do. f.	R.C.	–	R.C.	–	–	169	169	75
103	9803	Do.	–	Bohernameane, m.	R.C.	–	R.C.	–	275	–	274	75
		Total for County Longford, 103 Schools,							7,332	6,631	13,963	4,763

COUNTY OF

Number.	Roll Number of School.	Parish.	District.	School.	Clerical.	Lay.	Principals.	Assistants.	Males.	Fem.	Total.	Average Daily Attendance.
1	8440	Ardee,	23	Ardee Convent,	Nuns		Nuns		–	400	400	150
2	2176	Do.	–	Do. m. l.	R.C.	–	R.C.	–	132	–	132	61
3	[illegible]	Do.	–	Do. Poor,	–	R.C.	R.C.	–	163	23	186	57
4	2144	Do.	–	Do. m.	R.C.	–	R.C.	–	164	–	164	62
5	2392	Do.	–	Do. Workhouse,	P.L.	Gds.	R.C.	–	40	38	78	29
6	2777	Ballybarrack,	–	Dundalk Workhouse,	P.L.	Gds.	R.C.	R.C.	30	40	70	34
7	891	Ballymakenny,	–	Ballymakenny,	R.C.	–	R.C.	–	83	44	127	47
8	2324	Ballymascanlan,	19	[illegible], m.	R.C.	–	R.C.	–	91	–	97	81
9	4562	Do.	–	Do. f.	R.C.	–	R.C.	–	–	101	101	43
10	2447	Do.	–	Aghnaskeagh,	–	R.C.	R.C.	–	65	35	100	50
11	4943	Do.	–	Bellurgan,	R.C.	–	R.C.	–	103	88	191	74
12	5494	Do.	–	Ravensdale, m.	–	R.C.	R.C.	–	143	–	143	63
13	6750	Do.	–	Do. f.	–	R.C.	R.C.	R.C.	–	171	171	66
14	9473	Barronstown,	25	Kilcurry, m.	R.C.	–	R.C.	–	114	–	114	45
15	9966	Do.	–	Do. f.	R.C.	–	R.C.	–	–	108	108	43
16	515	Clogher,	–	[illegible],	R.C.	–	R.C.	R.C.	116	51	167	65
17	9162	Do.	–	Clogher Head, f.	R.C.	–	R.C.	–	80	65	95	44
18	536	Castletown,	–	Castletown,	R.C.	–	R.C.	R.C.	66	99	165	55
19	2222	Carlingford,	19	Carlingford, [c] m.	–	–	–	–	–	–	–	–
20	8577	Do.	–	Do. f.	R.C.	–	R.C.	R.C.	–	159	159	39
21	16384	Do.	–	Do. No. 2,	Pres.	Pres.	Pres.	–	33	40	73	26
22	2791	Do.	–	[illegible], m.	R.C.	–	R.C.	–	90	–	90	38
23	2748	Do.	–	Do. f.	R.C.	–	R.C.	R.C.	–	183	183	62
24	2706	Do.	–	Mullaboy,	R.C.	–	R.C.	–	49	65	114	45
25	3611	Do.	–	Omeath, m.	–	R.C.	R.C.	R.C.	181	–	181	69
26	[illegible]	Do.	–	Do. f.	–	R.C.	R.C.	–	–	185	185	63
27	4732	Do.	–	Rathcor,	R.C.	–	R.C.	–	63	88	151	49
28	10183	Do.	–	[illegible],	R.C.	–	R.C.	R.C.	141	130	271	62
29	2540	Creggan,	–	Annaghvacky,	–	Pres.	R.C.	–	124	105	229	85
30	10116	Do.	–	Courtbane,	–	R.C.	R.C.	R.C.	97	75	172	54
31	4376	Collon,	23	Collon, m.	R.C.	–	R.C.	–	121	–	121	40

a Including value of Free Residence. b School closed. c Including value of Free Residence and Garden.

Province of Leinster: County of Longford—*continued.*

Amount paid for Books, Requisites, and Apparatus, or Published Prices. £ s. d.	Aid granted by the Board during the Year 1874. In Free Stock of Books, Requisites, and Apparatus. £ s. d.	In Salaries, Premiums, and other Gratuities. £ s. d.	Result Fees, Financial Year. £ s. d.	Amount of Local Emoluments received in Aid of Teacher's Salary. School Fees. £ s. d.	Subscriptions, Endowments, &c. £ s. d.	Total Local Aid. £ s. d.	Vested or Non-vested.	Number.
—	—	67 13 4	14 8 0	1 9 0	—	1 9 0	V.T.	80
1 5 3	—	81 0 0	9 3 0	2 12 8	—	2 12 8		81
1 10 3	—	20 0 0	6 16 7	1 6 8	—	1 6 8		82
2 1 4	—	24 0 0	10 13 0	1 0 10	—	1 0 10		83
5 7 8	—	67 5 0	20 14 6	2 4 11	15 0 0	*17 4 11		84
—	—	—	—	—	—	—		85
4 18 10	—	20 0 0	8 11 0	1 13 0	1 10 0	*0 3 0		86
8 15 5	—	51 15 0	11 6 0	6 14 8	—	6 14 8		87
8 10 6	—	33 1 4	20 4 0	11 17 0	—	31 17 0		88
4 9 7	—	16 0 0	7 17 6	—	20 0 0	*20 0 0		89
4 6 0	—	7 10 0	—	—	—	—		90
1 5 7	—	60 0 0	8 0 6	8 17 0	—	8 17 0		91
1 17 2	—	31 0 0	10 10 0	3 13 9	—	5 13 9		92
} —	—	27 10 0	{ 7 16 6	2 13 7	—	2 13 7	V.T.	93
			6 9 5	—	—	—		
1 0 8	—	20 0 0	7 7 0	1 17 0	—	1 17 0	V.T.	94
1 6 9	—	24 14 8	4 8 0	4 0 0	17 9 11	*21 9 11		95
17 8 4	—	123 5 0	30 11 3	7 11 0	—	7 11 0		96
6 5 0	—	107 1 7	35 4 6	17 4 11	—	17 4 11		97
6 4 4	—	5 10 0	—	—	—	—		98
—	—	—	—	—	—	—		99
4 1 0	—	30 0 0	19 3 0	2 13 0	—	2 13 0	N.	100
8 10 4	—	21 0 0	—	6 12 10	2 16 0	*9 3 10		101
1 0 2	—	24 9 0	4 19 8	0 15 0	—	0 15 0		102
2 11 2	—	44 16 8	15 16 2	0 10 10	—	0 19 10		103
379 16 0	8 2 9	3,414 19 8	1,466 1 6	311 7 4	130 12 11	521 0 3		

LOUTH—[illegible] Schools.

1 8 3	—	23 0 0	16 19 6	11 19 11	—	11 19 11		1
—	—	20 0 0	6 18 0	2 6 8	—	2 6 8	V.T.	2
3 16 8	—	24 0 0	15 13 8	—	14 0 0	14 0 0		3
19 15 11	—	16 1 0	45 9 6	18 8 0	—	18 8 0	V.T.	4
4 18 8	—	—	—	—	—	—		5
—	—	4 10 0	—	—	—	—		6
6 5 10	—	24 0 0	7 17 0	10 13 4	—	10 13 4		7
5 17 4	—	24 0 0	6 17 6	4 11 2	10 0 0	14 11 2		8
3 15 6	—	58 5 0	10 1 0	8 6 5	—	8 6 5		9
—	—	23 0 0	7 18 6	8 5 6	10 15 0	*20 0 0		10
5 11 0	—	44 0 0	20 6 5	7 4 4	—	7 4 4		11
4 13 6	—	47 10 0	18 0 0	8 1 6	24 10 0	*33 11 6		12
6 5 7	—	45 0 0	15 10 4	8 1 6	10 0 0	18 1 6		13
4 4 6	—	27 0 0	11 10 6	5 10 0	—	5 10 0		14
3 4 6	—	37 8 4	10 11 6	4 10 10	—	4 19 10		15
1 15 2	—	50 0 0	16 15 0	6 5 8	—	6 6 8		16
1 13 1	—	28 0 0	11 10 0	4 6 1	—	4 6 1		17
0 18 0	—	20 0 0	1 6 0	—	—	—		18
1 13 10	—	—	15 17 0	—	—	—		19
6 11 11	—	47 0 0	14 7 0	6 0 0	—	6 0 0		20
1 6 9	—	24 0 0	8 5 6	5 4 0	14 0 0	19 4 0		21
1 15 6	—	24 0 0	8 4 10	1 5 10	—	1 5 10	V.T.	22
4 9 3	—	51 0 0	15 7 6	5 0 0	—	5 0 0	V.T.	23
5 1 2	—	23 15 0	8 8 6	8 19 10	—	8 19 10	V.T.	24
4 6 5	—	55 0 0	13 6 0	6 0 0	8 10 0	*14 10 0	V.T.	25
1 10 4	—	30 15 0	6 4 10	4 8 6	—	4 8 6	V.T.	26
1 10 7	—	24 0 0	9 7 0	4 5 1	—	4 5 1		27
4 3 0	—	42 8 4	5 0 0	6 0 0	—	6 0 0		28
2 5 8	—	24 0 0	—	4 0 0	—	4 0 0		29
—	—	34 10 0	—	4 10 0	—	4 10 0		30
—	—	25 0 0	13 9 0	5 4 4	—	5 4 4		31

† Including value of Free Grants.

* No Returns.

List of Schools in operation on the 31st December, 1874,—

Number.	Roll Number of School.	Parish.	District.	School.	Religious Denomination of Manager or Correspondent: Clerical.	Lay.	Number and Religious Denomination of Teachers: Principals.	Assistants.	Attendance for the Year. Total number of Pupils on Rolls within the Year 1874: Males.	Fem.	Total.	Average Daily Attendance for the Year.
32	4577	Collon,	26	Collon, f.	R.C.	–	R.C.	–	–	104	104	58
33	10537	Do.	–	Balpatrick,	–	R.C.	R.C.	–	60	30	90	31
34	9371	Clonkeen,	–	Stormanstown, m.	R.C.	–	R.C.	–	108	74	182	63
35	9568	Do.	–	Do.[b] f.	–	–	–	–	–	–	–	–
36	694	Darver,	–	Darver,	R.C.	–	R.C.	–	101	–	101	44
37	10547	Do.	–	Do. f.	R.C.	–	R.C.	–	–	111	111	46
38	847	Dundalk,	–	Dundalk, m.	R.C.	–	R.C.	–	197	–	197	79
39	848	Do.	–	Do. f.	R.C.	–	R.C.	R.C.	–	265	265	161
40	8857	Do.	–	Do. Conv. No. 2, f.	–	R.C.	Nuns		–	488	488	314
41	1176	Do.	–	Mullagharlin, m.	R.C.	–	R.C.	–	127	–	127	59
42	10774	Do.	–	Do. f.	R.C.	–	R.C.	–	–	110	110	44
43	9136	Do.	–	Jocelyn-street,	Pres.	–	Pres.	Pres.	81	91	181	58
44	1802	Dysart,	–	Dysart, m.	R.C.	–	R.C.	–	94	–	94	52
45	1484	Do.	–	Do. f.	R.C.	–	R.C.	–	–	73	73	37
46	1806	Dunleer,	–	Dunleer, m.	R.C.	–	R.C.	–	101	–	101	47
47	1494	Do.	–	Do. f.	R.C.	–	R.C.	–	–	119	119	63
48	8124	Drumshallon,	–	Kellystown,	R.C.	–	R.C.	–	56	48	107	42
49	7686	Do.	–	Fieldstown,	R.C.	–	R.C.	–	67	45	112	44
50	837	Dromiskin,	–	Dromiskin 1st Class Agricultural, m.	R.C.	–	R.C.	–	120	–	120	65
51	9423	Do.	–	Do. f.	R.C.	–	R.C.	–	–	116	116	53
52	6576	Drumin,	–	Drumin,	R.C.	–	R.C.	–	61	57	118	41
53	7597	Drumcar,	–	Williamstown, m.	R.C.	–	R.C.	–	98	–	98	52
54	9510	Do.	–	Do. f.	R.C.	–	R.C.	–	–	78	78	37
55	10418	Dunany,	–	Dunany,	R.C.	–	R.C.	–	11	13	24	17
56	9041	Faughart,	–	Kilcurry, m.	R.C.	–	R.C.	–	114	–	114	56
57	7117	Do.	–	Do. f.	R.C.	–	R.C.	–	–	119	119	56
58	4273	Do.	18	Upper Faughart,	R.C.	–	R.C.	–	71	54	125	56
59	690	Kilsaran,	23	Kilsaran, m.	R.C.	–	R.C.	–	140	–	140	68
60	846	Do.	–	Do. f.	R.C.	–	R.C.	–	–	146	146	41
61	10415	Do.	–	Castlebellingham,	R.C.	–	R.C.	–	30	32	62	31
62	1504	Kildemock,	–	Drakestown,	–	R.C.	R.C.	R.C.	77	58	135	31
63	4084	Killany,	–	Rockdale,	R.C.	–	R.C.	R.C.	101	80	181	78
64	811	Louth,	–	Knockbridge, m.	R.C.	–	R.C.	–	126	–	126	62
65	8904	Do.	–	Do. f.	R.C.	–	R.C.	R.C.	–	177	177	65
66	1358	Do.	–	Louth, m.	R.C.	–	R.C.	R.C.	167	–	167	74
67	8278	Do.	–	Do. f.	R.C.	–	R.C.	R.C.	–	144	144	64
68	7378	Do.	–	Do. No. 2,	R.C.	–	R.C.	–	10	14	24	12
69	8794	Do.	–	Stonetown,	R.C.	–	R.C.	R.C.	96	80	176	51
70	8236	Mullary,	–	Tenure, m.	R.C.	–	R.C.	–	122	–	122	59
71	6007	Do.	–	Do. f.	R.C.	–	R.C.	–	–	102	102	56
72	8356	Mapastown,	–	Dowdstown,	–	R.C.	R.C.	–	37	41	78	39
73	9103	Mosstown,	–	Phillipstown,	R.C.	–	R.C.	–	72	48	120	14
74	842	Port,	–	Boyerstown, or Farrell's Cross, m.	R.C.	–	R.C.	–	87	–	87	38
75	844	Do.	–	Do. f.	R.C.	–	R.C.	R.C.	24	81	105	44
76	9136	Philipstown,	–	Aclint, m.	R.C.	–	R.C.	–	101	–	101	51
77	9135	Do.	–	Do. f.	R.C.	–	R.C.	–	–	104	104	57
78	1576	Roche,	10	Ballinfull, m.	R.C.	–	R.C.	–	134	–	134	74
79	8902	Do.	–	Do. f.	R.C.	–	R.C.	–	–	149	149	53
80	5787	Rathdrumin,	25	Walshestown,	R.C.	–	R.C.	–	81	36	117	48
81	815	St. Mary's,	–	St. Mary's, m.	R.C.	–	R.C.	–	236	–	236	73
82	840	Do.	–	Do. m. I.	R.C.	–	R.C.	–	260	–	260	73
83	6044	Do.	–	Do. Conv. f.	–	R.C.	Nuns		–	410	410	279
84	8340	Do.	–	Drogheda Workhse.	P.L.	Gds.	R.C.	R.C.	73	86	159	71
85	821	St. Peter's,	–	Do. Conv. f.	–	R.C.	Nuns		–	509	509	416
86	10475	Do.	–	Do. do. I.	–	R.C.	Nuns		252	–	252	73
87	9154	Do.	–	Palace-street,	Pres.	–	Pres.	–	18	15	33	20
88	10712	Do.	–	St. Peter's, m.	–	R.C.	R.C.	–	36	11	47	27
89	6437	Stabannon,	–	Stabannon, m.	R.C.	–	R.C.	–	78	–	78	39
90	4088	Do.	–	Do. f.	R.C.	–	R.C.	–	–	84	84	41
91	7858	Termonfeckin,	–	Termonfeckin, m.	R.C.	–	R.C.	–	115	–	115	61
92	7201	Do.	–	Do. f.	R.C.	–	R.C.	–	–	114	114	51

a Including value of Free Residence and Garden.

b Inoperative.

Province of Leinster: County of Louth—*continued.*

Amount paid for Fuel, Repairs, and Improvements, in Previous Years.	Aid granted by the Board during the Year 1874. In Salaries, Premiums, and other Gratuities.	In Free Stock of Books, Requisites, and Apparatus.	Results Fees, Financial Year.	Amount of Local Emoluments received in Aid of Teacher's Salary. School Fees.	Subscriptions, Endowments, &c.	Total Local Aid.	Vested or Non-Vested.	Number.
£ s. d.	£ s. d.	£ s. d.	£ s. d.	£ s. d.	£ s. d.	£ s. d.		
—	—	24 0 0	8 8 6	2 14 8	—	2 14 8		32
4 13 9	—	21 0 0	9 11 0	2 7 6	16 0 0	* 18 7 6		33
0 9 1	—	35 0 0	—	1 17 9	—	1 17 9	V.T.	34
—	—	—	—	—	—	—	V.T.	35
1 3 1	—	41 5 0	10 7 0	7 7 6	—	7 7 6		36
6 3 7	—	24 0 0	18 1 0	13 13 6	6 10 0	19 3 6		37
1 3 1	—	82 0 0	9 10 0	11 8 9	—	11 8 9	V.T.	38
8 10 9	—	61 0 0	20 10 6	10 0 11	—	10 0 11	V.T.	39
18 5 8	—	101 11 6	45 13 6	56 17 1	—	56 17 1		40
2 10 7	—	10 3 4	19 19 6	0 0 0	18 10 0	* 18 10 0		41
3 0 2	—	27 0 0	17 13 0	0 18 0	5 0 0	† 10 18 0		42
12 5 9	—	47 0 0	18 1 0	11 15 0	—	11 15 0		43
2 3 4	—	24 0 0	1 8 0	2 19 4	—	2 19 4	V.T.	44
1 5 0	—	28 0 0	11 1 0	4 7 6	—	4 7 6	V.T.	45
3 19 8	—	80 0 0	8 0 0	5 11 0	—	5 11 0	V.T.	46
1 8 5	—	35 6 8	16 18 0	5 11 8	—	5 11 8	V.T.	47
—	—	32 18 4	2 8 9	1 10 7	4 0 0	* 5 10 7	P.	48
1 14 10	—	81 13 6	19 19 6	6 1 9	—	6 1 9		49
3 17 4	—	27 6 8	11 8 6	14 0 0	3 0 0	17 0 0		50
4 18 5	—	59 0 0	17 15 6	—	—	—		51
4 13 11	—	24 0 0	15 5 6	7 1 9	—	7 1 9		52
4 12 11	—	21 0 0	0 18 6	3 6 9	—	3 6 9		53
—	—	21 0 0	8 0 0	2 2 8	—	2 2 8		54
2 17 3	5 0 0	19 6 0	4 4 6	8 10 6	18 0 0	* 26 10 6		55
3 14 6	—	36 19 8	6 9 9	6 3 11	5 6 0	11 9 11	N.S.A.	56
4 11 8	—	20 10 0	7 11 0	5 4 8	—	5 4 8	N.S.A.	57
3 11 1	—	29 0 0	4 16 0	3 13 6	—	3 13 6		58
0 11 4	—	40 0 6	17 13 0	11 5 9	—	11 5 9		59
8 5 1	—	20 15 0	8 11 0	6 19 5	—	6 19 5		60
2 11 5	—	20 8 0	5 4 0	8 0 4	22 0 0	* 30 0 4		61
5 13 5	—	32 0 0	14 11 0	17 9 6	12 10 0	* 30 19 6		62
9 1 3	—	81 0 0	24 8 0	15 8 7	30 0 0	45 8 7		63
6 7 6	—	29 8 6	22 10 0	15 15 0	—	15 15 0		64
4 0 0	—	47 5 0	20 8 0	10 0 0	—	10 0 0		65
4 17 4	—	57 16 0	11 18 8	0 8 6	3 5 0	† 6 8 8	P.	66
4 13 10	—	51 0 0	84 17 6	0 15 0	5 5 0	* 14 8 0	P.	67
—	—	—	1 4 6	—	—	—		68
3 10 11	—	49 0 0	16 15 6	14 4 6	5 0 0	19 4 9	V.T.	69
1 4 11	—	80 0 0	15 1 0	2 6 6	4 15 0	* 7 18 0		70
2 15 1	—	29 0 6	16 6 0	4 18 4	—	4 18 4		71
2 13 8	—	91 6 4	3 8 0	2 18 6	3 0 0	5 18 6		72
3 15 11	—	65 0 0	26 7 0	2 19 0	20 0 0	22 19 0		73
3 17 4	—	44 0 9	9 9 6	6 6 0	—	6 6 0	V.T.	74
1 7 11	—	17 0 0	10 8 6	8 14 10	—	8 14 10	V.T.	75
—	—	24 0 0	7 6 0	1 6 9	—	1 6 9	V.T.	76
1 17 3	—	20 0 6	11 19 6	9 0 0	—	9 9 0	V.T.	77
8 1 0	—	21 6 0	6 8 6	5 19 0	2 0 0	* 7 19 0	V.T.	78
8 12 7	—	21 0 0	9 9 0	4 1 0	—	4 1 0	V.T.	79
3 9 11	—	22 0 0	14 8 6	6 6 3	—	6 6 3	V.T.	80
7 3 10	—	30 17 0	21 18 0	21 3 0	—	21 3 0	P.	81
8 0 5	—	34 0 0	14 9 0	8 0 6	—	8 0 6	P.	82
31 4 8	—	104 14 0	69 0 0	22 10 6	—	22 10 0		83
0 8 11	—	5 0 0	—	—	—	—		84
12 6 5	—	177 4 8	60 13 5	—	—	—		85
0 15 8	—	25 1 9	6 18 0	—	—	—		86
2 10 4	—	20 0 0	5 0 0	14 18 10	—	14 18 10		87
4 14 10	4 0 0	20 0 0	6 9 0	1 17 6	23 0 0	* 28 17 6		88
2 10 9	—	21 0 0	0 10 9	3 16 6	—	3 16 0		89
1 18 7	—	20 0 0	8 19 6	2 3 5	—	2 3 5		90
1 13 10	—	20 0 0	4 11 6	3 1 8	—	3 1 8		91
3 10 0	—	21 0 0	9 8 0	6 6 6	1 10 0	* 4 18 6		92

* Including value of Free Residence. † Including value of Free Garden.

List of Schools in operation on the 31st December, 1874.—

Number.	Roll Number of School.	Parish.	District.	School.		Religious Denomination of Manager or Correspondent: Clerical.	Lay.	Number and Religious Denomination of Teachers: Principals.	Assistants.	Attendance for the Year — Total number of Pupils on Rolls within the Year: Males.	Fem.	Total.	Average Daily Attendance.
93	1578	Termonfeckin,	20	Carstown,		R.C.	–	R.C.	–	62	57	119	39
94	604	Tullyallen,	–	Tullyallen,	m.	R.C.	–	R.C.	–	86	–	86	37
95	10,426	Do.,	–	Do.	f.	R.C.	–	R.C.	–	–	107	107	63
96	858	Do.	–	Mell,		R.C.	–	R.C.	–	147	–	147	46
97	2745	Tallanstown,	–	Tallanstown,	m.	R.C.	–	R.C.	–	133	–	133	40
98	2746	Do.	–	Do.	f.	R.C.	–	R.C.	–	–	119	119	41
		Total for County Louth, 98,								[illegible]	[illegible]	[illegible]	[illegible]

COUNTY OF

Number.	Roll Number of School.	Parish.	District.	School.		Clerical.	Lay.	Principals.	Assistants.	Males.	Fem.	Total.	Average Daily Attendance.
1	802	Athboy,	22	Fraine,	m.	R.C.	–	R.C.	–	76	–	76	33
2	6291	Do.	–	Do.	f.	R.C.	–	R.C.	–	–	74	74	37
3	1659	Do.	–	Athboy,	m.	R.C.	–	R.C.	R.C.	147	–	147	64
4	1660	Do.	–	Do.	f.	R.C.	–	R.C.	R.C.	–	133	133	64
5	6030	Do.	–	Do.	i.	R.C.	–	R.C.	R.C.	63	86	149	76
6	[illegible]	Do.	–	Balrath,		R.C.	–	R.C.	–	40	33	73	[illegible]
7	4570	Do.	–	Rathcarran,		R.C.	–	R.C.	–	45	41	86	[illegible]
8	1903	Ardcath,	26	Cloghan (or Ardcath),		R.C.	–	R.C.	–	76	–	76	34
9	9750	Do.	–	Ardcath,	f.	R.C.	–	R.C.	–	–	40	40	[illegible]
10	8110	Ardbraccan,	20	Bohermeen,	m.	R.C.	–	R.C.	–	114	–	114	51
11	8364	Do.	–	Do.	f.	R.C.	–	R.C.	–	–	131	131	45
12	8116	Do.	–	Boyerstown,	m.	R.C.	–	R.C.	–	130	–	130	[illegible]
13	11044	Do.	–	Do.	f.	R.C.	–	R.C.	–	–	145	145	[illegible]
14	7160	Ardagh,	21	Meath Hill,	m.	R.C.	–	R.C.	–	107	–	107	[illegible]
15	7161	Do.	–	Do.	f.	R.C.	–	R.C.	–	–	118	118	[illegible]
16	853	Ardsallagh,	22	[illegible],		R.C.	–	R.C.	R.C.	93	61	153	[illegible]
17	8112	Balrathboyne,	–	Cortown,	m.	R.C.	–	R.C.	–	60	–	60	[illegible]
18	8113	Do.	–	Do.	f.	R.C.	–	R.C.	–	–	70	70	[illegible]
19	2380	Ballygarth,	25	Whitecross,		R.C.	–	R.C.	R.C.	101	78	179	[illegible]
20	8783	Bective,	19	Bective,		R.C.	–	R.C.	–	13	12	25	16
21	9039	Do.	–	[illegible],		R.C.	–	R.C.	–	51	42	93	[illegible]
22	[illegible]	Ballivor,	–	Ballivor,	m.	R.C.	–	R.C.	–	133	–	133	49
23	9251	Do.	–	Do.	f.	R.C.	–	R.C.	–	–	123	123	[illegible]
24	863	Clonard,	23	Clonard,	m.	R.C.	–	R.C.	–	101	–	101	[illegible]
25	8975	Do.	–	Do.	f.	R.C.	–	R.C.	–	–	67	67	[illegible]
26	[illegible]	Do.	29	Longwood,	m.	R.C.	–	R.C.	–	94	–	94	[illegible]
27	[illegible]	Do.	–	Do.	f.	R.C.	–	R.C.	–	–	86	86	[illegible]
28	1725	Castletown,	–	Castletown,		R.C.	–	R.C.	–	73	90	163	[illegible]
29	1904	Culmullin,	–	Culmullin,	m.	R.C.	–	R.C.	–	69	–	69	[illegible]
30	6470	Do.	–	Do.	f.	R.C.	–	R.C.	–	–	87	87	[illegible]
31	[illegible]	Colp,	25	Donacarney,	f.	R.C.	–	R.C.	–	–	94	94	[illegible]
32	10850	Do.	–	Do.	m.	R.C.	–	R.C.	–	85	–	85	[illegible]
33	3144	Cushinstown,	–	Cushinstown,		R.C.	–	R.C.	–	40	38	82	[illegible]
34	[illegible]	Crickstown,	22	Curragha,		R.C.	–	R.C.	–	37	36	73	[illegible]
35	[illegible]	[illegible],	–	Tullaghanstown,		R.C.	–	R.C.	–	64	[illegible]	[illegible]	[illegible]
36	[illegible]	[illegible],	–	[illegible],		R.C.	–	R.C.	–	46	41	87	[illegible]
37	[illegible]	Castlejordan,	27	Castlejordan,	m.	R.C.	–	R.C.	–	148	–	148	[illegible]
38	7252	Do.	–	Do.	f.	R.C.	–	R.C.	R.C.	–	161	161	[illegible]
39	[illegible]	Clonalvy,	20	Clonalvy,	m.	R.C.	–	R.C.	–	53	–	53	[illegible]
40	[illegible]	Do.	–	Do.	f.	R.C.	–	R.C.	–	–	44	[illegible]	[illegible]
41	1120	Duleek,	–	Bellewstown,		R.C.	–	R.C.	–	70	49	[illegible]	[illegible]
42	[illegible]	Do.	–	Duleek,	m.	R.C.	–	R.C.	R.C.	137	–	137	[illegible]
43	8114	Do.	–	Do.	f.	R.C.	–	R.C.	R.C.	–	100	100	[illegible]
44	1124	Dowth,	–	Dowth, [a]		–	–	–	–	–	–	–	–
45	[illegible]	Dunboyne,	27	Dunboyne,	m.	R.C.	–	R.C.	–	137	–	[illegible]	[illegible]
46	1494	Do.	–	Do.	f.	R.C.	–	R.C.	R.C.	–	159	159	[illegible]
47	1682	Dunsany,	20	Killeen, or Dunsany,	m.	R.C.	–	R.C.	–	[illegible]	–	[illegible]	[illegible]
48	7941	Do.	–	Dunsany,	f.	R.C.	–	R.C.	–	–	67	67	[illegible]
49	5782	Drumcondra,	26	Drumcondra,	m.	R.C.	–	R.C.	–	[illegible]	–	[illegible]	[illegible]
50	[illegible]	Do.	–	Do.	f.	R.C.	–	R.C.	R.C.	–	147	147	[illegible]

[a] Including value of Free Residence.

[b] Including value of Free Residence and Garden.

Province of Leinster: County of Louth—*continued.*

Amount paid for Books, Requisites, and Apparatus, at Reduced Prices.	Aid granted by the Board during the Year 1874: In Free Stock of Books, Requisites, and Apparatus.	In Salaries, Premiums, and other Gratuities.	Results Fees, Financial Year.	Amount of Local Emoluments received in Aid of Teacher's Salary: School Fees.	Subscriptions, Endowments, &c.	Total Local Aid.	Vested or Non-Vested.	Number.
£ s. d.	£ s. d.	£ s. d.	£ s. d.	£ s. d.	£ s. d.	£ s. d.		
1 5 8	—	21 0 0	9 14 0	5 14 1	—	5 14 1	V.T.	93
—	—	21 0 0	7 9 0	7 13 6	—	7 13 6		94
6 10 5	—	30 0 0	17 2 0	15 9 10	—	15 9 10		95
4 0 8	—	33 15 0	13 18 0	8 10 0	—	8 10 0		96
3 2 11	—	24 0 0	9 11 6	4 18 1	10 0 0	14 18 1		97
3 4 1	—	24 0 0	15 11 0	4 7 0	8 0 0	12 7 0		98
267 15 8	6 0 0	6,837 17 8	1,287 1 4	644 7 10	314 15 0	959 2 10		

MEATH—178 Schools.

Books, &c.	Free Stock	Salaries, &c.	Results Fees	School Fees	Subscriptions, &c.	Total Local Aid	V. or N.V.	No.
8 15 4	—	23 0 0	4 8 6	2 18 10	—	2 18 10	V.S.	1
1 5 8	—	20 0 0	6 8 0	1 5 6	—	1 5 6	V.T.	2
3 10 7	—	78 16 8	16 8 6	4 10 8	—	4 10 8	N.	3
2 7 6	—	54 16 8	18 11 6	4 11 6	—	4 11 6	N.	4
4 6 5	—	53 18 8	6 15 9	3 17 9	—	3 17 9	N.	5
—	—	20 0 0	0 12 0	3 5 10	1 0 0	a 4 5 10		6
—	—	20 0 0	8 10 6	0 19 0	—	0 19 0		7
1 19 4	—	35 0 0	10 17 6	11 0 5	4 0 0	15 0 5		8
2 9 0	—	28 0 0	8 17 6	2 2 6	8 0 0	6 8 6		9
6 14 1	—	29 10 0	13 17 0	4 17 2	6 0 0	b 10 17 2		10
4 1 9	—	39 10 0	16 11 6	6 0 5	5 0 0	a 11 0 5		11
2 12 7	—	57 8 0	15 14 6	6 6 9	6 10 0	a 12 16 9		12
8 14 4	6 0 0	22 10 0	12 15 0	6 13 10	1 10 0	8 3 10		13
—	—	24 0 0	5 13 0	3 14 5	1 10 0	b 5 4 5		14
1 10 3	—	20 0 0	6 10 0	2 11 10	—	2 11 10		15
6 1 10	—	41 0 0	17 19 0	5 8 4	4 10 0	a 9 18 4		16
1 5 0	—	24 0 0	4 6 0	8 15 0	—	8 15 0		17
1 6 11	—	24 0 0	8 18 6	6 15 6	2 10 0	a 5 6 0		18
5 10 1	—	52 0 0	17 18 6	14 7 1	3 0 0	a 17 7 1		19
1 5 8	—	16 0 0	7 5 6	1 12 0	22 10 0	b 23 2 0		20
2 15 3	—	40 18 4	18 18 0	5 10 0	8 0 0	a 13 10 6		21
4 7 10	—	30 0 0	17 7 6	0 4 8	—	0 4 8		22
1 4 10	—	25 10 0	21 15 0	0 17 7	—	0 17 7		23
1 17 10	—	52 8 0	7 7 0	4 14 8	—	4 14 8		24
1 8 3	—	50 0 0	8 18 0	3 11 0	—	3 11 0		25
3 10 4	—	40 16 8	14 8 6	4 7 0	—	4 7 0		26
5 8 2	—	84 13 4	10 11 6	6 16 10	—	6 16 10		27
7 8 10	—	40 0 0	11 18 8	8 10 6	—	8 10 6	V.S.	28
1 10 8	—	15 0 0	2 15 8	4 5 8	3 0 0	a 7 5 8	V.S.	29
1 14 8	—	21 0 0	13 17 0	8 19 6	—	9 15 6		30
2 17 10	—	41 6 0	8 8 0	5 6 7	—	5 6 7	V.S.	31
1 10 1	—	27 8 4	7 19 6	5 1 7	—	5 1 7		32
1 14 6	—	20 0 0	0 11 6	5 8 8	—	5 8 8	V.S.	33
1 1 8	—	24 18 4	8 6 8	7 0 0	0 15 0	a 7 15 0		34
3 0 1	—	20 0 0	0 8 8	2 18 10	7 0 0	a 9 18 10	V.S.	35
1 18 5	—	25 0 0	4 15 0	1 11 8	—	1 11 8		36
7 8 8	—	34 0 0	18 8 0	10 14 6	6 0 0	a 16 14 6		37
0 10 7	—	48 0 0	21 11 0	11 14 1	—	11 14 1		38
1 19 8	—	30 0 0	7 8 0	4 5 5	4 0 0	8 5 5	V.S.	39
1 10 6	—	24 0 0	7 15 0	4 0 8	3 0 0	a 7 0 8	V.S.	40
4 16 8	—	65 8 8	10 16 0	9 6 8	5 0 0	14 6 8	N.	41
5 1 4	—	56 0 0	17 12 6	18 17 6	—	18 17 6		42
1 15 0	—	60 10 0	17 16 0	8 10 11	—	8 10 11		43
—	—	—	—	—	—	—	N.	44
—	—	21 0 0	—	4 16 0	8 0 0	a 6 16 0	V.T.	45
4 7 8	—	40 0 0	6 10 0	5 18 10	2 0 0	7 18 10	V.S.	46
2 8 8	—	91 0 0	8 0 6	8 19 0	7 10 0	b 21 0 0		47
2 12 6	—	20 0 0	7 16 6	8 16 0	5 0 0	8 16 0		48
8 1 0	—	47 0 6	4 0 6	1 8 4	—	1 8 4		49
1 9 7	—	60 0 0	15 14 6	6 18 6	—	6 18 6		50

a Including value of Free Garden. b Inoperative.

List of Schools in operation on the 31st December, 1874.—

Number.	Roll Number of School.	Parish.	District.	School.		Religious Denomination of Manager or Correspondent: Clerical.	Lay.	Number and Religious Denomination of Teachers: Principals.	Assistants.	Attendance for the Year: Total number of Pupils on Rolls within the Year 1874: Males.	Fem.	Total.	Average Daily Attendance for the Year 1874.
51	[illegible]	Donore,	26	Donore,	m.	R.C.	–	R.C.	–	71	–	71	39
52	[illegible]	Do.	–	Do.	f.	R.C.	–	R.C.	–	–	65	65	37
53	8170	Dunshaughlin,	22	Dunshaughlin,	m.	R.C.	–	R.C.	–	87	–	87	39
54	5403	Do.	–	Do.	f.	R.C.	–	R.C.	–	–	85	85	34
55	3118	Do.	–	Do. Workhouse,		P.L.	Gds.	R.C.	–	43	21	64	37
56	8501	Dowdstown,	–	Dillon's Bridge,		–	R.C.	R.C.	–	33	24	57	27
57	9422	Enniskeen,	24	Errey,		Pres.	–	Pres.	–	67	47	114	35
58	[illegible]	Do.	–	Carrickleck,		R.C.	–	R.C.	R.C.	98	74	172	69
59	6351	Grangegeeth,	25	Crewwood,		–	R.C.	R.C.	–	45	40	76	33
60	2539	Do.	–	Grangegeeth,		R.C.	–	R.C.	–	40	38	78	32
61	5497	Girley,	27	Girley,	m.	–	R.C.	R.C.	–	68	–	68	30
62	5106	Do.	–	Do.	f.	–	R.C.	R.C.	–	–	61	61	24
63	7032	Gallow,	27	Gallow,	m.	R.C.	–	R.C.	–	69	–	69	37
64	8301	Do.	–	Do.	f.	R.C.	–	R.C.	–	–	76	76	39
65	871	Johnstown,	28	Johnstown,		R.C.	–	R.C.	–	56	–	80	41
66	865	Kildalkey,	–	Kildalkey,	f.	R.C.	–	R.C.	–	–	84	84	31
67	867	Do.	–	Do.	m.	R.C.	–	R.C.	–	60	–	66	30
68	1814	Do.	–	Carnisle,		R.C.	–	R.C.	–	46	45	84	33
69	[illegible]	Kilbeg,	–	Carlanstown,	m.	–	R.C.	R.C.	–	144	–	144	52
70	6716	Do.	–	Do.	f.	–	R.C.	R.C.	–	–	87	87	36
71	10630	Do.	–	Kilbeg,	m.	R.C.	–	R.C.	–	99	–	99	39
72	10442	Do.	–	Do.	f.	R.C.	–	R.C.	–	–	100	100	36
73	1170	Kilsharvan,	20	Mount Hanover,		–	R.C.	R.C.	–	83	18	61	40
74	1481	Kilskyre,	20	Kilskyre,	m.	R.C.	–	R.C.	–	137	–	137	51
75	1665	Do.	–	Do.	f.	R.C.	–	R.C.	–	–	115	115	56
76	8475	Do.	–	Crossakeel,[a]		R.C.	–	–	–	–	–	–	–
77	9236	Do.	–	Ballinlough,	m.	R.C.	–	R.C.	–	73	–	73	33
78	9091	Do.	–	Do.	f.	–	R.C.	R.C.	–	–	83	83	37
79	1191	Kilmainhamwood	21	Kilmainhamwood,	m.	R.C.	–	R.C.	–	79	–	79	38
80	1681	Do.	–	Do.	f.	R.C.	–	R.C.	–	–	65	65	28
81	9957	Do.	–	Edengora,	m.	R.C.	–	R.C.	–	119	–	119	37
82	[illegible]	Do.	–	Do.	f.	R.C.	–	R.C.	–	–	64	64	29
83	9491	Do.	–	Tyrcork,		R.C.	–	R.C.	–	82	81	163	49
84	1509	Kentstown,	23	Kentstown,	m.	R.C.	–	R.C.	–	100	–	100	43
85	8777	Do.	–	Do.	f.	R.C.	–	R.C.	–	–	71	71	31
86	1771	Kiltale,	28	Kiltale,[b]	m.	–	–	–	–	–	–	–	–
87	3472	Do.	–	Do.	f.	R.C.	–	R.C.	–	–	74	74	35
88	1917	Kilberry,	–	Wilkinstown,	m.	R.C.	–	R.C.	–	107	–	107	46
89	7894	Do.	–	Do.	f.	R.C.	–	R.C.	–	–	83	83	34
90	2521	Do.	–	Kilberry,	m.	R.C.	–	R.C.	–	77	–	77	35
91	7604	Do.	–	Do.	f.	R.C.	–	R.C.	–	–	61	61	35
92	10914	Kilcarn,	–	Johnstown,	f.	R.C.	–	R.C.	–	–	161	161	40
93	9797	Kilalone,	37	Kilalone Ord. Agricul.		R.C.	–	R.C.	–	48	34	82	30
94	8210	Kilmessan,	29	Kilmessan,	m.	R.C.	–	R.C.	–	77	–	77	38
95	6311	Do.	–	Do.	f.	R.C.	–	R.C.	–	–	78	78	31
96	6092	Killary,	28	Heronstown,	m.	R.C.	–	R.C.	–	128	–	128	33
97	10359	Do.	–	Do.	f.	R.C.	–	R.C.	–	–	94	94	61
98	6416	Kells,	20	Kells Workhouse,		P.L.	Gds.	R.C.	R.C.	35	38	73	41
99	8081	Do.	–	Do.		R.C.	–	R.C.	–	58	22	68	77
100	6082	Do.	–	Do. parochial,		R.C.	–	R.C.	–	25	39	64	32
101	10801	Do.	–	Drumbaragh,		R.C.	–	R.C.	–	45	47	92	31
102	5207	Killallon,	–	Killallon,	m.	R.C.	–	R.C.	–	74	–	74	32
103	5721	Do.	–	Do.	f.	R.C.	–	R.C.	–	–	83	83	30
104	6281	Do.	–	Gehanstown,	m.	R.C.	–	R.C.	–	69	–	69	35
105	6733	Do.	–	Do.	f.	R.C.	–	R.C.	–	–	81	81	33
106	7122	Killyon,	–	Killyon,		R.C.	–	R.C.	–	47	69	116	36
107	7767	Kilmore,	–	Moynalvey,	m.	R.C.	–	R.C.	–	79	–	79	28
108	7842	Do.	–	Do.	f.	R.C.	–	R.C.	–	–	47	47	19
109	[illegible]	Killeagh,	33	Ballinacree,		R.C.	–	R.C.	R.C.	84	106	189	75
110	9739	Knockcommon,	10	Rathdrinagh,		–	R.C.	R.C.	–	61	47	108	60
111	876	Laracor,	28	Dangan,	m.	R.C.	–	R.C.	–	108	–	108	43
112	7199	Do.	–	Do.	f.	R.C.	–	R.C.	–	–	98	98	43
113	8602	Loughan,	–	Carnaross,	m.	R.C.	–	R.C.	–	128	–	128	47
114	7918	Do.	–	Do.	f.	R.C.	–	R.C.	–	–	129	129	56

[a] Including value of Free Residence.

[b] Including value of Free Residence and Garden.

Province of Leinster: County of Meath—*continued.*

Amount paid for Books, Requisites, and Apparatus, at Reduced Prices.	Aid granted by the Board during the Year 1874. — In Free Stock of Books, Requisites, and Apparatus.	In Salaries, Premiums, and other Gratuities.	Results Fees, Financial Year.	Amount of Local Emoluments received in Aid of Teacher's Salary. — School Fees.	Subscriptions, Endowments, &c.	Total Local Aid.	Vested or Non-Vested.	Number.
£ s. d.	£ s. d.	£ s. d.	£ s. d.	£ s. d.	£ s. d.	£ s. d.		
1 6 4	—	24 0 0	4 9 6	4 17 0	7 0 0	a11 17 0		51
1 6 0	—	60 0 0	4 3 0	5 4 0	9 10 0	7 14 6		52
2 18 0	—	52 6 4	9 16 6	11 5 8	—	11 5 8		53
3 8 8	—	24 8 0	11 8 0	0 7 4	—	8 7 4		54
—	—	1 10 0	—	—	—	—		55
1 5 8	—	20 0 0	8 14 6	4 14 0	5 0 0	a9 14 0		56
3 5 8	—	27 0 0	8 18 0	2 11 10	1 0 0	b3 11 10		57
5 8 1	—	64 13 4	23 8 0	0 0 0	—	0 0 0		58
2 0 8	—	30 0 0	9 11 0	4 0 0	6 0 0	b10 0 0		59
1 5 0	—	18 0 8	5 10 8	1 9 11	—	1 9 11		60
1 16 8	—	24 0 0	13 19 6	8 18 0	—	8 18 0		61
1 0 3	—	24 0 0	11 14 0	3 16 0	5 0 0	8 16 0		62
5 19 4	—	24 0 0	4 14 6	4 0 10	—	4 0 10		63
1 3 1	—	18 13 4	4 17 7	4 0 1	—	4 0 1		64
4 5 5	0 10 11	27 0 0	18 0 0	5 3 2	2 0 0	7 3 2		65
1 0 0	—	24 0 0	9 11 0	3 0 0	—	3 0 0		66
0 17 0	—	24 0 0	4 18 6	1 11 8	—	1 11 8		67
1 9 11	—	30 0 0	7 1 0	1 15 7	—	1 15 7	V.T.	68
4 4 8	—	48 0 0	11 13 6	6 1 0	5 5 0	b15 6 0	V.T.	69
1 18 8	—	50 10 0	12 8 0	3 15 11	3 5 0	6 17 11	V.T.	70
1 13 0	0 2 2	50 0 0	8 8 6	0 14 5	1 0 0	b1 14 5		71
—	—	24 0 0	12 7 6	4 5 0	4 0 0	b8 5 0		72
1 16 0	—	30 6 8	8 19 6	6 10 0	5 0 0	a7 10 0	V.T.	73
4 7 8	—	55 16 8	16 4 0	8 19 0	5 0 0	a13 19 0	V.T.	74
7 8 8	—	35 16 8	17 13 0	2 7 0	5 0 0	a7 7 0	V.T.	75
1 16 8	0 18 3	—	4 10 6	—	—	—		76
1 5 0	—	24 0 0	7 9 0	2 10 0	4 0 0	a6 10 0		77
3 10 0	—	23 10 0	10 10 6	4 16 6	—	4 16 6		78
1 11 1	—	24 0 0	4 8 0	1 1 5	5 0 0	6 1 5	V.T.	79
2 0 6	—	30 0 0	9 10 6	4 3 0	5 0 0	9 3 0	V.T.	80
4 3 8	—	24 0 0	10 5 6	1 7 0	—	1 7 0		81
7 8 10	—	30 0 0	8 0 0	0 15 6	—	0 15 6		82
1 10 5	—	30 0 0	12 11 0	4 16 10	—	4 16 10		83
3 13 1	—	24 0 0	17 8 0	8 0 0	5 0 0	13 0 0	V.T.	84
1 17 2	—	30 0 0	18 9 0	4 0 0	4 0 0	8 0 0	V.T.	85
—	0 7 0	—	—	—	—	—	V.T.	86
1 0 4	—	30 0 0	6 7 6	4 6 0	1 10 0	b5 16 0	V.T.	87
3 7 1	—	24 0 0	6 1 6	7 15 6	3 0 0	10 18 0		88
1 5 10	—	33 6 8	14 18 6	4 0 0	3 0 0	7 0 0		89
6 7 0	—	24 0 0	9 17 0	6 4 6	0 10 0	6 14 6		90
1 5 0	—	20 0 0	7 11 6	4 5 0	0 10 0	4 15 0		91
5 18 9	—	31 10 0	16 18 0	3 10 11	—	3 10 11		92
1 16 9	—	20 0 0	8 4 0	4 14 2	8 8 0	b13 2 2	V.T.	93
3 3 10	—	30 0 0	15 16 0	7 13 0	5 0 0	b12 13 0		94
1 14 6	—	30 0 0	10 16 6	4 0 0	6 0 0	10 0 0		95
4 18 8	—	26 6 8	15 14 6	5 6 0	0 0 0	a5 6 0		96
—	—	19 0 0	8 6 0	2 13 0	—	2 13 0		97
5 2 3	—	1 10 0	—	—	—	—		98
0 12 0	—	20 0 0	4 1 0	—	6 0 0	6 0 0		99
2 7 7	—	24 0 0	6 2 6	1 10 0	6 0 0	a9 10 0		100
1 12 10	—	27 0 0	6 1 0	2 0 8	—	2 0 8		101
6 3 11	—	24 0 0	8 16 6	4 12 0	—	4 12 0		102
5 5 10	—	24 0 0	11 15 6	1 10 10	1 10 0	a3 0 10		103
1 16 2	—	40 10 0	9 17 6	8 10 0	2 0 0	a4 10 0		104
1 8 4	—	54 10 0	14 18 0	3 11 0	—	3 11 0		105
2 10 1	—	20 0 0	13 9 6	8 15 4	1 0 0	a9 15 4		106
1 6 8	—	24 0 0	12 18 6	5 18 0	—	5 18 0		107
—	—	20 0 0	6 8 6	8 1 2	5 0 0	a5 1 2		108
4 1 8	—	60 1 8	25 1 6	8 9 9	—	8 9 9		109
5 0 1	—	52 0 0	13 18 6	11 7 8	7 0 0	18 7 8		110
1 0 3	—	30 0 0	0 17 6	4 18 8	—	4 18 8		111
2 8 5	—	24 0 0	16 7 0	6 19 0	—	6 19 0		112
4 0 1	—	40 13 4	17 10 0	4 0 0	8 0 0	a7 0 0		113
6 17 0	—	50 10 0	19 18 6	4 18 6	—	4 18 6		114

a No Return. b Incomplete.

List of Schools in operation on the 31st December, 1874.—

Number.	Roll Number of School.	Parish.	District.	School.		Religious Denomination of Manager or Correspondent.		Number and Religious Denomination of Teachers.		Attendance for the Year. Total number of Pupils on Rolls within the Year 1874.			Average Daily Attendance.
						Clerical.	Lay.	Principals.	Assistants.	Males.	Fem.	Total.	
115	6994	Loughan,	25	Woodpole 1st cl. Ag.	m.	–	R.C.	R.C.	–	120	–	120	52
116	7943	Do.	–	Do.	f.	–	R.C.	R.C.	–	–	63	63	30
117	8438	Loughcrew,	–	Loughcrew,		–	R.C.	R.C.	R.C.	82	81	163	71
118	[illegible]	Moynalty,	–	Moynalty,	m.	R.C.	–	R.C.	–	96	–	96	29
119	891	Do.	–	Do.	f.	–	R.C.	R.C.	–	–	107	107	35
120	2099	Do.	24	Carnaross,	m.	–	R.C.	R.C.	–	83	–	83	37
121	[illegible]	Do.	–	Do.[a]	f.	–	–	–	–	–	–	–	–
122	[illegible]	Do.	25	[illegible]		R.C.	–	R.C.	–	17	19	36	19
123	1752	Moybologue,	24	Killagriffe,	m.	R.C.	–	R.C.	–	81	–	81	28
124	3478	Do.	–	Do.	f.	R.C.	–	R.C.	–	–	68	68	24
125	10117	Do.	–	Do.	(2).	R.C.	–	R.C.	–	53	27	80	34
126	4088	Moylagh,	23	Balbrenna,		–	R.C.	R.C.	R.C.	84	76	160	60
127	7478	Do.	–	Gortloney,		R.C.	–	R.C.	R.C.	91	63	154	54
128	4728	Moymet,	23	Kilbride,		R.C.	–	R.C.	–	41	24	65	30
129	7202	Martry,		Castlemartin,		–	R.C.	R.C.	–	33	51	84	17
130	10254	Monktown,	–	Walterstown,		R.C.	–	R.C.	–	30	35	65	24
131	9404	Monknewtown,	24	Monknewtown,		R.C.	–	R.C.	–	47	47	94	31
132	862	Navan,	26	Navan,	m.	R.C.	–	R.C.	R.C.	270	–	270	112
133	863	Do.	–	Do. Convent (1),	f.	R.C.	–	Nuns		90	227	323	173
134	7473	Do.	–	Do. do. (2),	f.	R.C.	–	Nuns		174	370	544	260
135	9751	Do.	–	Do. Commons,		R.C.	–	R.C.	R.C.	78	49	131	55
136	3409	Do.	–	Do. Workhouse,		P.L.	Gds.	[b]R.C.	–	41	20	10	26
137	4284	Nobber,	24	Nobber,	m.	R.C.	–	R.C.	–	125	–	125	47
138	6977	Do.	–	Do.	f.	R.C.	–	R.C.	–	–	111	111	45
139	2544	Oldcastle,	23	Oldcastle Workhouse,		P.L.	Gds.	R.C.	–	36	30	66	26
140	2844	Painestown,	25	Yellow Furze,	m.	R.C.	–	R.C.	–	98	–	98	38
141	8237	Do.	–	Do.	f.	R.C.	–	R.C.	–	–	89	89	41
142	883	Ratoath,	37	Ratoath Ord. Agric.	m.	R.C.	–	R.C.	–	108	–	108	40
143	884	Do.	–	Do.	f.	R.C.	–	R.C.	–	–	60	[illegible]	36
144	9842	Do.	20	Ashbourne,	m.	R.C.	–	R.C.	–	98	–	98	30
145	847	Do.	–	Do.	f.	R.C.	–	R.C.	–	–	90	90	36
146	1425	Rathmolyon,	20	Kill,[a]	m.	R.C.	–	R.C.	–	–	–	–	–
147	1561	Do.	–	Do.	f.	R.C.	–	R.C.	–	44	68	112	23
148	9814	Do.	–	Ardenew,	f.	R.C.	–	R.C.	–	40	67	103	28
149	10919	Do.	–	Rathmolyon,		R.C.	–	R.C.	–	33	14	49	26
150	2382	Rathkenny,	–	Rathkenny,	m.	R.C.	–	[b]R.C.	–	58	–	78	28
151	9281	Do.	–	Do.	f.	R.C.	–	R.C.	–	–	74	74	34
152	8000	Rathcore,	37	Bonnestown,	m.	R.C.	–	R.C.	–	84	–	84	28
153	2976	Do.	–	Do.	f.	R.C.	–	R.C.	–	–	63	63	26
154	8194	Do.	–	Enfield,		R.C.	–	R.C.	–	34	41	75	25
155	10891	Rathfeigh,	23	Rathfeigh,		R.C.	–	R.C.	–	36	80	77	34
156	4362	Rathmore,	–	Moyagher,		–	R.C.	R.C.	–	80	63	143	43
157	9846	Rathregan,	27	Rathregan,		R.C.	–	R.C.	–	34	24	58	21
158	9481	Stamullen,	25	Stamullen,	m.	R.C.	–	R.C.	–	85	–	85	41
159	8926	Do.	–	Do.	f.	R.C.	–	R.C.	–	–	75	75	27
160	10019	Do.	–	Gormanstown,		R.C.	–	R.C.	–	35	31	66	23
161	3473	Siddan,	–	Newtown,		R.C.	–	R.C.	–	77	68	145	47
162	1609	Stackallan,	25	Stackallan,	m.	R.C.	–	R.C.	–	78	–	78	32
163	6922	Do.	–	Do.	f.	R.C.	–	R.C.	–	–	63	63	24
164	1810	Skreen,	–	Skreen,	m.	R.C.	–	R.C.	–	81	–	81	30
165	1482	Do.	–	Do.	f.	R.C.	–	R.C.	–	81	–	81	30
166	1531	Slane,	25	Slane,	m.	R.C.	–	R.C.	–	110	–	110	46
167	1502	Do.	–	Do.	f.	R.C.	–	R.C.	–	–	97	97	46
168	3448	Trim,	23	[illegible]		R.C.	–	R.C.	–	69	50	119	39
169	3037	Do.	–	Trim Dist. Model,	m.	Com.	N.E.	R.C.	–	158	–	158	62
170	5631	Do.	–	Do.	f.	Com.	N.E.	R.C.	R.C.	–	30	30	15
171	5032	Do.	–	Do.	i.	Com.	N.E.	R.C.	R.C.	33	9	42	18
172	3580	Do.	–	Do. Workhouse,		–	R.C.	2R.C.	–	40	38	78	31
173	10913	Do.	–	Do. Convent,		R.C.	–	Nuns		184	320	504	169
174	8771	Teltown,	–	Oristown,	m.	R.C.	–	R.C.	–	68	–	68	24
175	8871	Do.	–	Do.	f.	R.C.	–	R.C.	–	–	67	67	26
		Total for County Meath, 175,								9,102	8,228	17,461	6,505

[a] Including value of Free Garden.

[b] Including value of Free Residence.

Province of Leinster: County of Meath—*continued.*

Amount paid for Books, Requisites, and Apparatus at Reduced Prices.	Aid granted by the Board during the Year 1874. In Free Stock of Books, Requisites, and Apparatus.	In Salaries, Premiums, and other Gratuities.	Results Fees, Provisional Year.	Amount of Local Emoluments received in Aid of Teacher's Salary. School Fees.	Subscriptions, Endowments, &c.	Total Local Aid.	Vested or Non-Vested.	Number.
£ s. d.	£ s. d.	£ s. d.	£ s. d.	£ s. d.	£ s. d.	£ s. d.		
3 15 6	—	17 3 4	26 11 0	5 12 0	20 0 0	a25 11 0		115
3 10 6	—	20 0 0	17 1 6	1 17 9	10 0 0	11 17 9		116
5 0 11	—	64 11 8	40 8 8	—	25 0 0	a25 0 0		117
8 6 6	—	29 0 0	14 18 0	10 5 8	5 0 0	15 5 8		118
1 10 6	—	25 0 0	16 16 0	3 9 0	5 0 0	8 9 0		119
3 10 6	—	30 0 0	13 14 0	1 17 0	—	1 17 0	V.T.	120
—	—	—	—	—	—	—	V.T.	121
2 3 6	—	15 6 4	8 18 6	3 0 0	14 0 0	a17 0 0		122
1 6 6	—	21 0 0	9 0 0	1 0 0	3 10 6	a5 0 0	N.V.—	123
—	—	21 0 0	17 6 8	0 11 0	—	0 11 0	M.N.	124
2 12 8	—	30 0 0	10 3 8	2 18 6	11 0 0	a13 18 6		125
0 5 11	—	43 8 4	23 14 0	5 6 7	—	5 6 7		126
1 5 2	—	40 0 0	0 4 0	0 2 0	2 0 0	a2 2 0		127
2 1 5	—	24 0 0	2 16 0	3 10 0	1 5 0	a4 15 0		128
1 3 8	—	18 0 0	4 0 0	0 12 0	17 0 0	a17 12 0		129
1 16 7	—	20 0 0	10 0 0	3 4 11	6 10 0	b9 14 11		130
1 10 11	—	20 0 0	3 19 6	3 8 6	—	3 8 6		131
17 4 6	—	107 10 0	88 17 0	24 4 0	6 10 0	30 14 6		132
25 4 9	—	112 3 4	51 15 0	6 2 11	—	6 2 11		133
22 5 6	—	124 10 0	110 0 6	49 1 6	—	49 1 6		134
1 9 11	—	64 0 0	13 4 6	1 18 6	4 10 0	6 9 6		135
7 12 10	—	5 10 0	—	—	—	—		136
5 6 6	—	24 0 0	13 15 0	7 4 6	11 10 0	a18 14 6		137
8 8 3	—	28 16 4	13 6 6	5 10 2	11 10 0	a16 9 2		138
2 17 5	—	1 10 0	—	—	—	—		139
6 5 3	—	35 0 0	9 8 6	5 5 0	9 5 0	b14 10 0		140
3 5 0	—	27 6 8	16 0 0	4 8 4	1 8 4	5 16 8		141
1 9 0	—	37 0 0	0 18 6	8 14 1	20 7 9	a29 1 10		142
2 1 8	—	20 0 0	6 3 8	7 4 5	3 0 0	10 4 5		143
0 17 6	—	24 0 0	9 0 6	6 13 8	1 10 0	a8 3 8		144
0 6 7	—	57 0 0	14 17 6	5 17 10	—	5 17 10		145
3 6 0	—	—	—	—	—	—	V.T.	146
2 17 11	—	21 10 0	10 1 6	7 9 9	—	7 9 9	V.T.	147
2 1 2	—	11 4 5	18 13 6	2 8 6	—	2 8 6		148
1 14 6	—	24 0 0	11 10 6	4 0 0	30 10 0	a48 10 0		149
0 11 5	—	24 0 0	8 5 0	2 12 0	—	2 12 0	V.T.	150
1 17 9	—	37 6 8	11 0 6	1 6 0	—	1 6 0	V.T.	151
3 4 8	—	30 0 0	8 1 6	2 16 3	—	2 16 3	V.T.	152
1 0 9	—	24 0 0	13 13 0	2 14 0	—	2 14 0	V.T.	153
3 2 1	—	20 0 0	5 10 6	5 18 11	—	5 18 11		154
—	—	20 0 0	11 10 0	4 5 4	—	4 5 4		155
9 8 8	—	52 0 0	18 9 6	8 7 10	15 0 0	b30 7 10		156
0 7 5	—	16 6 8	8 8 6	2 16 3	—	2 16 3		157
—	—	47 10 0	10 16 6	15 7 2	7 10 0	a30 17 2		158
1 7 1	—	30 0 0	8 5 0	6 15 6	2 10 9	9 3 3		159
2 1 4	—	20 0 0	8 11 0	2 15 9	4 0 0	a6 15 9		160
2 18 6	—	30 15 4	11 19 6	0 8 6	5 5 0	a11 11 6	V.T.	161
3 4 8	—	25 0 0	20 12 6	6 12 9	—	6 12 9	V.T.	162
8 4 11	—	24 0 0	18 6 6	4 14 2	—	4 14 2	V.T.	163
4 0 7	—	24 0 0	9 14 6	0 15 0	10 10 0	b11 5 0	V.T.	164
1 14 3	—	20 0 0	13 18 6	5 0 0	7 15 0	b12 15 0	V.T.	165
3 6 10	—	37 10 6	10 17 6	0 19 11	—	0 19 11	V.C.	166
3 18 0	—	45 0 0	17 4 0	6 5 3	—	6 5 3	V.C.	167
1 6 6	—	28 0 0	11 11 6	3 12 10	—	3 12 10	N.	168
11 12 5	16 18 0	625 18 11 (169–171)	62 3 0	39 19 6 (169–171)	—	39 19 6 (169–171)	V.C.	169
3 12 7	6 19 0		7 13 6				V.C.	170
—	3 0 0		4 6 0				V.C.	171
—	—	3 10 0	—	—	—	—		172
12 3 1	6 6 0	67 14 1	52 19 6	17 4 6	—	17 4 6		173
1 7 0	—	23 0 0	6 9 6	5 2 0	3 0 0	8 2 0	V.T.	174
1 17 5	—	20 0 0	5 5 6	4 0 0	3 0 0	7 0 0	V.T.	175
228 0 1	35 5 4	3,004 16 5	1,130 18 5	320 8 4	367 19 10	1,4[illegible] 8 4		

a Inoperative.

b Including value of Free Residence and Garden.

List of Schools in operation on the 31st December, 1874.—QUEEN'S

No.	Roll Number of School	Parish	District	School		Religious Denomination of Manager or Correspondent: Clerical	Lay	Teachers and Religious Denomination of Teachers: Principals	Assistants	Attendance for the Year: Total number of Pupils on Rolls within the year 1874: Males	Females	Total	Average daily attendance
1	69	Arles,	41	Rock,		R.C.	–	R.C.	–	101	28	129	41
2	4815	Do.,	–	Mountmellick Wkhse.		Official		R.C.	–	30	40	[illegible]	45
3	[illegible]	Aghaboe,	–	Derrinlough (Barry), b	m.	–	–	–	–	–	–	–	–
4	7112	Do.,	–	Do. Convent,	f.	R.C.	–	None		34	128	162	61
5	7718	Do.,	–	Ballacolla,		R.C.	–	R.C.	–	51	58	109	39
6	[illegible]	Do.,	–	Ballygeddy,		R.C.	–	R.C.	–	61	46	107	40
7	[illegible]	Do.,	–	The Manor,		–	E.C.	R.C.	–	37	40	77	41
8	5391	Abbeyleix,	–	Abbeyleix,	m.	R.C.	–	R.C.	–	136	–	136	58
9	[illegible]	Do.,	–	Do. Convent,	f.	R.C.	–	None		–	318	318	135
10	[illegible]	Do.,	–	Do. Workhouse,		Official		R.C.	–	21	20	41	31
11	[illegible]	Aghmacart,	41	Cullahill,		R.C.	–	R.C.	R.C.	–	93	93	41
12	7604	Do.,	–	Gurteen,		R.C.	–	R.C.	R.C.	69	70	139	51
13	9034	Ballyadams,	41	Ballyadams,		R.C.	–	R.C.	R.C.	71	57	128	48
14	[illegible]	Ballyroan,	41	Ballyroan,	m.	R.C.	–	R.C.	–	129	–	129	55
15	[illegible]	Do.,	–	Do.	f.	R.C.	–	R.C.	–	–	121	121	57
16	[illegible]	Borris,	–	Heath,		R.C.	–	R.C.	R.C.	74	44	118	46
17	[illegible]	Do.	–	Maryborough Convent,	f.	R.C.	–	None		34	346	370	[illegible]
18	5402	Bordwell,	–	Paddock,		R.C.	–	R.C.	–	94	63	162	43
19	[illegible]	Coolbanagher,	–	Morette,		R.C.	–	R.C.	R.C.	73	38	110	37
20	911	Do.	–	Emo,	m.	R.C.	–	R.C.	–	63	–	63	27
21	[illegible]	Do.	–	Do.	f.	R.C.	–	R.C.	–	–	60	60	25
22	[illegible]	Do.	–	Coolbanagher,		R.C.	–	R.C.	–	29	31	60	28
23	[illegible]	Clonenagh,	–	Oak,		R.C.	–	R.C.	–	62	48	110	34
24	[illegible]	Do.	–	Ballyfin,		R.C.	–	R.C.	R.C.	80	103	183	55
25	[illegible]	Do.	–	Trumera,		R.C.	–	R.C.	–	43	20	63	28
26	[illegible]	Do.	–	Raheen,		R.C.	–	R.C.	R.C.	82	[illegible]	[illegible]	48
27	[illegible]	Do.	–	Clonad,		R.C.	–	R.C.	–	68	57	125	31
28	[illegible]	Do.	–	Shanahoe,		R.C.	–	R.C.	R.C.	97	91	188	68
29	[illegible]	Do.	–	Camross,		R.C.	–	R.C.	–	67	61	128	39
30	[illegible]	Do.	–	Errill,		R.C.	–	R.C.	–	64	69	133	35
31	[illegible]	Do.	–	Mountrath,	m.	–	E.C.	R.C.	–	65	–	65	27
32	[illegible]	Do.	–	Do.	f.	–	R.C.	R.C.	–	–	63	63	31
33	[illegible]	Do.	–	Kilbricken,	m.	–	R.C.	R.C.	–	140	–	140	47
34	[illegible]	Do.	–	Coolrain,	m.	R.C.	–	R.C.	R.C.	174	–	174	61
35	[illegible]	Do.	–	Do. Convent,	f.	R.C.	–	None		–	270	270	130
36	[illegible]	Do.	–	Rosenallis,		R.C.	–	R.C.	–	[illegible]	63	142	43
37	[illegible]	Castlebrack,	–	Clonaghadoo,		R.C.	–	R.C.	–	66	48	114	27
38	[illegible]	Clonenagh,	–	Kilbricken,	f.	–	R.C.	R.C.	–	–	63	63	24
39	[illegible]	Clonaslee,	–	Tinnahinch,		R.C.	–	R.C.	–	54	30	84	34
40	[illegible]	Dysartgallen,	44	Ballinakill,	m.	R.C.	–	R.C.	R.C.	203	–	[illegible]	101
41	[illegible]	Do.	–	Do.	f.	R.C.	–	R.C.	R.C.	–	186	186	[illegible]
42	[illegible]	Do.	–	Knock,	m.	R.C.	–	R.C.	–	82	–	82	36
43	[illegible]	Do.	–	Do.	f.	R.C.	–	R.C.	–	–	95	95	36
44	1011	Donaghmore,	42	Killasmeestia,		R.C.	–	R.C.	–	84	65	149	45
45	2313	Durrow,	47	Durrow,	m.	–	R.C.	R.C.	–	148	–	148	48
46	[illegible]	Do.	–	Do.	f.	–	R.C.	R.C.	R.C.	–	166	166	48
47	[illegible]	Do.	–	Cullahill,	m.	R.C.	–	R.C.	–	100	–	100	37
48	[illegible]	Dysartenos,	41	Aughnahilla,		R.C.	–	R.C.	R.C.	102	68	170	43
49	[illegible]	Do.	44	Loughanage,		R.C.	–	R.C.	–	49	39	88	38
50	[illegible]	Erke,	41	Urlingford,		–	R.C.	R.C.	R.C.	89	94	183	51
51	687	Kilbeakin,	[illegible]	Do.		R.C.	–	R.C.	R.C.	171	–	171	48
52	[illegible]	Do.	–	Killeshin,		R.C.	–	R.C.	–	40	58	104	30
53	[illegible]	Kilcolmanbane,	41	Cloneslea, a	m.	–	R.C.	–	–	–	–	–	–
54	[illegible]	Do.	–	Do.	f.	–	R.C.	R.C.	–	–	97	97	34
55	[illegible]	Do.	–	Castlecuffe,		R.C.	–	R.C.	R.C.	81	85	166	30
56	[illegible]	Killabban,	44	Rushes,	m.	R.C.	–	R.C.	–	109	–	109	38
57	[illegible]	Do.	–	Do.	f.	R.C.	–	R.C.	–	–	87	87	33
58	[illegible]	Do.	–	Arles,	m.	R.C.	–	R.C.	–	118	–	118	50
59	[illegible]	Do.	–	Do.	f.	R.C.	–	R.C.	R.C.	–	117	117	48
60	1727	Do.	–	Ballylinan,	m.	R.C.	–	R.C.	R.C.	186	–	186	[illegible]
61	[illegible]	Do.	–	Do.	f.	R.C.	–	R.C.	R.C.	–	139	139	[illegible]

a Including value of Free Residence and Garden. b Inoperative. c Including value of Free Garden.

Province of Leinster : Queen's County.

COUNTY—104 Schools.

Amount paid for Books, Requisites, and Apparatus, at Reduced Prices.	Aid granted by the Board during the Year 1874. In Free Stock of Books, Requisites, and Apparatus.	In Salaries, Premiums, and other Gratuities.	Results Fees.	Amount of Local Emoluments received in Aid of Teacher's Salary. School Fees.	Subscriptions, Endowments, &c.	Total Local Aid.	Vested or Non-Vested.	Number.
£ s. d.	£ s. d.	£ s. d.	£ s. d.	£ s. d.	£ s. d.	£ s. d.		
1 14 3	—	21 0 0	11 5 6	10 3 0	1 0 0	*14 2 6		1
1 18 11	—	6 10 0	—	—	—	—		2
—	—	—	—	—	—	—		3
8 18 3	—	18 7 0	11 14 8	4 10 7	—	4 10 1		4
4 8 0	—	24 0 0	5 12 0	3 14 9	—	3 19 8		5
8 10 1	—	26 0 0	5 0 6	4 10 9	3 10 0	*10 8 5		6
0 10 2	—	30 0 0	11 8 0	4 3 8	13 0 0	*17 8 6		7
8 4 6	—	38 0 0	9 15 6	7 18 7	—	7 18 7		8
9 10 8	—	49 17 6	31 17 0	—	—	—		9
4 14 0	4 10 0	—	—	—	—	—		10
1 8 2	—	44 0 0	18 14 6	6 15 4	—	4 15 4		11
8 10 10	—	64 18 4	21 12 6	0 8 3	—	9 8 3		12
1 10 10	—	41 0 0	18 8 6	0 14 8	—	8 14 8		13
1 10 8	—	34 0 0	8 7 0	1 0 6	—	1 0 6		14
8 16 3	—	45 16 8	18 3 6	6 19 9	2 0 0	*8 19 9		15
1 5 8	—	44 0 0	12 14 0	3 4 1	12 0 0	*15 4 1		16
22 18 10	—	60 7 6	24 17 6	—	—	—		17
8 5 7	—	30 0 0	7 17 6	4 0 0	5 0 0	9 0 0		18
—	—	65 0 0	6 11 6	9 8 0	18 0 0	*21 8 0		19
1 11 3	—	24 0 0	6 12 0	1 11 11	17 8 0	*18 11 11		20
6 8 8	4 10 0	18 0 0	11 13 0	1 12 10	14 0 0	15 12 10		21
3 11 6	—	34 0 0	3 8 6	—	—	—		22
9 10 5	—	30 0 0	8 0 6	4 3 7	0 15 0	*4 18 7		23
1 12 0	—	45 0 0	18 13 6	4 13 2	—	4 13 2		24
1 18 1	—	41 10 0	10 4 6	2 11 3	0 15 0	*3 6 3		25
3 17 5	—	46 0 0	19 18 0	2 10 0	—	2 10 0		26
2 0 8	—	44 0 0	0 12 0	4 10 1	4 10 0	*8 0 1		27
2 10 7	—	34 0 0	14 17 6	6 13 6	—	6 13 6		28
1 9 4	—	60 0 0	20 10 6	5 8 0	3 0 0	8 8 0		29
1 6 8	—	21 0 0	8 17 0	5 1 2	1 10 0	*4 11 2		30
1 0 2	—	67 0 0	10 10 6	0 5 0	25 0 0	*25 5 0		31
2 19 9	—	91 0 0	10 13 0	—	20 0 0	*20 0 0		32
—	—	43 6 4	15 8 6	2 13 0	20 0 0	*22 13 0		33
6 8 0	—	71 13 4	20 16 6	—	—	—		34
7 11 0	4 0 8	25 8 0	26 11 6	8 18 0	—	8 18 6	P.	35
—	—	24 0 0	8 11 0	6 5 0	—	6 5 0		36
1 18 8	—	34 0 0	10 16 6	8 10 0	2 0 0	*10 10 8		37
6 12 11	—	44 10 0	12 15 0	0 15 0	18 0 0	18 15 0		38
1 12 10	—	24 0 0	8 0 0	11 1 8	—	11 1 8		39
3 0 0	—	54 0 0	26 11 6	14 10 8	—	14 10 8		40
6 9 6	—	73 6 0	20 10 0	18 3 0	—	18 3 0		41
3 8 11	—	16 0 0	9 15 6	0 0 1	3 0 0	*11 0 1		42
3 8 4	—	45 0 0	14 7 0	0 0 5	—	3 0 5		43
9 11 3	—	39 0 0	0 6 0	5 3 6	—	3 6 6	V.T.	44
8 10 10	—	64 6 8	21 8 0	9 18 4	—	9 10 4		45
8 15 5	—	101 16 8	21 8 0	7 11 8	—	7 11 8		46
—	—	53 0 0	10 4 6	8 8 0	—	8 8 0		47
—	—	61 10 0	8 1 0	3 0 7	6 0 0	41 0 7		48
3 16 10	—	55 8 8	13 7 0	6 14 5	11 0 0	*17 14 5		49
6 1 8	—	36 0 0	17 11 6	7 16 0	15 0 0	*22 16 0		50
3 12 0	—	47 16 8	25 17 6	7 8 3	4 0 0	*11 8 3		51
6 14 8	—	13 11 1	4 16 8	1 8 8	—	1 8 8		52
1 8 0	—	24 0 0	10 11 0	—	—	—	V.T.	53
6 4 10	—	30 0 0	7 0 0	6 12 0	—	6 12 0	V.T.	54
8 17 8	—	61 0 0	15 10 0	12 18 8	—	12 18 8		55
1 8 1	—	30 0 0	10 5 0	7 0 0	—	7 0 0	A.	56
1 7 10	—	30 10 0	12 1 6	3 0 0	—	3 0 0	A.	57
2 8 11	—	34 0 0	14 2 0	4 12 0	—	4 12 0	V.T.	58
1 0 5	—	41 14 6	17 0 0	5 4 0	—	5 4 0	V.T.	59
6 17 11	—	34 0 0	11 18 0	5 8 11	—	5 8 11	V.T.	60
0 10 4	—	48 3 4	16 3 6	3 15 8	—	8 15 8	V.T.	61

¶ Including value of Free Residence.

* No Teacher.

List of Schools in operation on the 31st December, 1874.—

Number.	Roll Number of School.	Parish.	District.	School.	Religious Denomination of Managers or Correspondents. Clerical.	Lay.	Number and Religious Denomination of Teachers. Principals.	Assistants.	Attendance for the Year. Total number of Pupils on Rolls within the Year: Males.	Females.	Total.	
62	11177	Killabban,	44	Mayo,	–	R.C.	R.C.	–	17	14	31	19
63	4774	Do.	–	Killabban, m.	R.C.	–	R.C.	–	90	–	90	49
64	4770	Do.	–	Do. f.	R.C.	–	R.C.	–	–	81	81	39
65	11362	Do.	–	Ballickmoyler,[b]	–	R.C.	R.C.	–	–	–	–	–
66	9181	Do.	39	Ardough,	R.C.	–	R.C.	–	31	30	61	18
67	9700	Kyle,	40	Ballinabanore,	R.C.	–	R.C.	R.C.	92	75	167	82
68	913	Lea,	41	Killeen, m.	R.C.	–	R.C.	–	78	–	78	39
69	916	Do.	–	Do. f.	R.C.	–	R.C.	–	25	116	141	63
70	6265	Do.	–	Rath,	–	R.C.	R.C.	–	78	64	142	47
71	7814	Moyanna,	44	Vicarstown,	R.C.	–	R.C.	–	118	–	118	61
72	8983	Maryboro',	41	Maryboro' Union,[a] m.	Official		–	–	–	–	–	–
73	8994	Do.	–	Do. f.	Official		R.C.	–	–	24	24	8
74	10728	Do.	–	Do. parochial,	R.C.	–	R.C.	–	40	50	90	32
75	918	Offerlane,	–	Castletown, m.	–	R.C.	R.C.	–	77	–	77	27
76	9731	Do.	–	Do. f.	–	R.C.	R.C.	–	–	110	110	40
77	4083	Do.	–	Killinure,	R.C.	–	R.C.	–	40	38	78	30
78	4977	Do.	–	Clonin,	R.C.	–	R.C.	–	97	57	154	41
79	9722	Rosenallis,	–	Mountmellick, m.	R.C.	–	R.C.	R.C.	206	–	206	106
80	7165	Do.	–	Do. Convent, f.	R.C.	–	Nuns		–	319	319	186
81	8764	Do.	–	Derrinaguse,	R.C.	–	R.C.	–	56	37	93	38
82	5182	Do.	–	Rosenallis,	R.C.	–	R.C.	R.C.	53	100	153	56
83	8101	Do.	–	Mountmellick,	R.C.	–	R.C.	–	33	34	67	24
84	914	Kerrymore,	–	Kerry,	R.C.	–	R.C.	–	94	41	135	43
85	894	Rathdowney,	43	Errill,	–	R.C.	R.C.	–	104	107	211	59
86	1154	Do.	–	Rathdowney, m.	R.C.	–	R.C.	–	221	–	221	74
87	1153	Do.	–	Do. f.	R.C.	–	R.C.	R.C.	–	182	182	65
88	11084	Do.	–	Do. No. 2.	R.C.	–	R.C.	–	16	28	43	13
89	9000	Do.	–	Donaghmore Work.[a]	–	–	–	–	–	–	–	–
90	8457	Rathaspick,	44	Wolfhill, m.	R.C.	–	R.C.	R.C.	134	–	134	41
91	8458	Do.	–	Do. f.	R.C.	–	R.C.	R.C.	–	137	137	51
92	4176	Do.	–	Fairymount, m.	–	R.C.	R.C.	–	111	–	111	32
93	4177	Do.	–	Do. f.	–	R.C.	R.C.	–	–	106	106	38
94	7860	Do.	–	Boley,	R.C.	–	R.C.	R.C.	77	46	123	44
95	10221	Scrubbe,	43	Scrubbe,	R.C.	–	R.C.	–	66	40	101	35
96	11044	Do.	44	The Cuddy,	R.C.	–	R.C.	R.C.	63	44	107	41
97	6706	Stradbally,	–	Stradbally, m.	R.C.	–	R.C.	–	177	–	177	78
98	8497	Do.	–	Do. Convent, f.	R.C.	–	Nuns		39	216	255	117
99	10561	Do.	–	Vicarstown, f.	R.C.	–	R.C.	–	–	118	118	64
100	1572	Tankardstown,	–	Shanragh,	R.C.	–	R.C.	R.C.	64	65	129	65
101	1633	Tullomoy,	–	Luggacurren, m.	–	R.C.	R.C.	–	70	–	76	37
102	4749	Do.	–	Do. f.	–	R.C.	R.C.	–	–	68	68	25
103	6611	Timahoe,	–	Timahoe,	R.C.	–	R.C.	R.C.	71	90	161	44
104	8815	Do.	–	Gurrangundrely,	R.C.	–	R.C.	–	49	48	87	44
		Total for Queen's County, 104 Schools,							6,[illegible]	6,[illegible]	12,[illegible]	5,[illegible]

COUNTY OF

1	8705	Ardnurcher,	33	Streamstown, m.	R.C.	–	R.C.	–	78	–	78	22
2	8706	Do.	–	Do. f.	R.C.	–	R.C.	–	–	83	83	33
3	821	Ballyloughloe,	–	Mount Temple, m.	R.C.	–	R.C.	–	101	–	101	41
4	1904	Do.	–	Do. f.	R.C.	–	R.C.	–	–	106	106	43
5	7703	Do.	33	Lower Warren, m.	R.C.	–	R.C.	–	61	–	61	32
6	7704	Do.	–	Do. f.	R.C.	–	R.C.	–	–	56	56	20
7	1640	Ballymorin,	34	Newbristy,	R.C.	–	R.C.	–	62	45	107	33
8	7849	Ballymore,	–	Moyvoughley,	R.C.	–	R.C.	–	59	67	126	63
9	7443	Do.	–	Ballymore, m.	R.C.	–	R.C.	R.C.	187	–	187	77
10	7444	Do.	–	Do. f.	R.C.	–	R.C.	R.C.	–	232	232	70
11	8043	Ballinahown,	33	Ballinahown, m.	R.C.	–	R.C.	–	103	–	103	30
12	8847	Do.	–	Do. f.	R.C.	–	R.C.	R.C.	30	116	146	51

[a] Including value of Free Residence and Garden.

[b] Returns not available.

Province of Leinster: Queen's County—*continued*.

Amount paid for Books, Requisites, and Apparatus of Local Funds	Aid granted by the Board during the Year 1874: In Free Stock of Books, Requisites, and Apparatus	In Salaries, Premiums, and other Gratuities	Results Fees, Financial Year	Amount of Local Emoluments received in Aid of Teacher's Salary: School Fees	Subscriptions, Endowments, &c.	Total Local Aid	Vested or Non-Vested	Number
£ s. d.	£ s. d.	£ s. d.	£ s. d.	£ s. d.	£ s. d.	£ s. d.		
1 10 1	4 0 0	6 0 1	—	—	31 0 0	*31 0 0		62
2 11 6	—	45 0 0	15 10 0	5 10 0	2 10 0	*8 0 0	V.E.	63
1 7 1	—	44 0 0	15 6 6	8 14 5	—	3 14 5	V.E.	64
1 10 0	4 0 0	3 1 0	—	—	—	—		65
1 5 0	—	24 0 0	4 8 8	0 18 6	4 0 0	*5 18 6		66
2 11 9	—	44 0 0	11 10 6	17 12 4	—	17 12 4		67
1 10 1	—	24 0 0	1 10 0	4 6 11	—	4 6 11		68
—	—	81 0 0	3 17 0	8 14 10	2 10 0	*8 0 10		69
1 6 0	—	60 15 8	0 18 0	7 17 1	30 18 11	*47 16 0		70
1 4 6	—	23 0 0	8 1 0	4 7 0	15 0 0	*10 7 0		71
0 4 2	—	—	—	—	—	—		72
—	—	—	—	—	—	—		73
8 18 0	—	45 10 0	10 11 0	4 4 6	40 0 0	*44 4 6		74
1 15 0	—	31 0 0	6 0 0	5 3 9	10 0 0	15 3 9		75
1 10 4	—	41 10 0	14 7 6	3 7 1	10 0 0	13 7 1	V.V.	76
1 8 4	—	20 0 0	6 4 6	3 8 9	3 12 0	*7 18 9		77
1 9 7	—	20 0 0	13 8 0	3 11 4	4 10 0	*8 1 4		78
7 13 4	—	73 16 8	25 11 0	20 13 2	—	20 13 2		79
6 18 0	—	66 17 6	40 9 6	—	—	—		80
0 15 11	—	24 0 0	6 0 0	3 18 3	0 15 0	*4 8 8		81
1 11 0	—	73 10 0	10 0 6	7 2 9	0 0 0	*13 2 9		82
6 17 11	—	34 18 6	16 8 0	8 10 0	30 0 0	*44 10 0		83
1 15 8	—	54 0 0	14 0 0	7 16 0	—	7 16 0		84
6 6 2	—	44 13 4	5 8 0	4 4 3	15 0 0	*19 4 3		85
0 10 0	—	33 0 0	18 16 0	11 2 1	4 10 0	*15 12 1	V.E.	86
0 2 3	—	40 0 0	18 15 8	6 13 1	4 10 0	*13 3 1	N.V.	87
4 15 1	4 0 0	20 0 0	10 1 8	1 15 7	10 0 0	11 15 7		88
—	—	—	—	—	—	—		89
8 1 0	—	49 0 0	11 10 6	8 11 8	—	8 11 8		90
5 17 7	—	68 6 8	18 18 0	6 19 0	—	6 19 0		91
2 8 6	—	24 0 0	8 18 0	8 1 4	—	8 1 4	V.E.	92
1 16 7	—	24 0 0	10 17 6	2 5 4	—	2 5 4	V.E.	93
1 5 8	—	68 0 6	18 3 6	2 14 0	—	2 14 0		94
—	—	21 0 0	6 9 4	5 8 6	15 0 0	*19 8 0		95
4 18 2	—	48 18 4	18 4 0	29 11 0	33 0 0	*61 11 0	V.E.	96
7 6 4	—	31 8 4	17 13 6	9 13 7	—	9 13 7		97
6 8 5	—	97 4 0	33 8 0	—	—	—		98
—	—	46 10 0	12 6 4	7 12 0	6 0 0	*18 12 0		99
4 11 6	—	55 8 8	16 8 0	8 0 11	8 10 0	*16 10 0		100
—	—	58 10 0	15 11 6	0 10 0	33 10 0	*33 0 0	V.E.	101
1 6 0	—	26 0 0	14 4 6	1 12 0	20 0 0	*21 12 0	V.E.	102
4 2 7	—	50 10 0	21 8 0	10 10 2	6 0 0	*16 10 2		103
—	—	29 0 8	13 18 0	5 0 0	3 5 0	*8 5 0	V.V.	104
312 7 6	23 0 6	3,610 18 6	1,041 4 8	548 6 6	563 3 11	1,125 6 7		

WESTMEATH—165 Schools.

Amount paid for Books, Requisites, and Apparatus of Local Funds	In Free Stock of Books, Requisites, and Apparatus	In Salaries, Premiums, and other Gratuities	Results Fees, Financial Year	School Fees	Subscriptions, Endowments, &c.	Total Local Aid	Vested or Non-Vested	Number
2 10 6	—	24 0 0	7 9 6	2 8 0	—	2 8 0		1
1 16 0	—	24 0 0	13 16 6	2 16 10	—	2 16 10		2
—	—	21 0 6	16 4 6	10 15 6	—	10 15 6	V.V.	3
1 15 8	—	28 0 6	15 17 0	6 7 8	—	6 7 8	V.V.	4
1 10 8	—	24 6 0	8 8 6	8 18 7	—	8 18 7		5
1 17 3	—	20 0 0	6 7 8	4 3 2	—	4 3 2		6
2 10 8	—	27 0 0	17 14 6	4 10 0	—	4 10 0	V.V.	7
1 17 11	—	59 6 8	0 7 6	1 1 8	2 0 0	*3 1 8		8
2 10 6	—	58 6 8	24 18 8	2 7 11	6 5 0	*8 12 11		9
3 1 1	—	54 18 4	23 18 6	3 0 0	6 5 0	*9 5 0		10
6 4 0	—	24 0 0	6 6 6	1 11 6	—	1 11 6		11
3 1 6	—	30 18 4	18 10 0	7 15 0	—	7 15 0		12

* Including value of Free Residence. ‡ No Returns. † Including value of Free Garden.

List of Schools in operation on the 31st December, 1874—

No.	Roll Number of School	Parish.	District.	School.	Religious Denomination of Manager or Correspondent: Clerical	Lay.	Number and Religious Denomination of Teachers: Principals.	Assistants.	Attendance for the Year — Total number of Pupils on Rolls within the Year: Male.	Fem.	Total.	Average Daily Attendance
13	931	Castletowndelvin,	69	Ballinavally Ord. Agr.	–	R.C.	R.C.	–	148	–	148	67
14	[illegible]	Do.	–	Do., f.	–	R.C.	R.C.	–	–	116	116	[illegible]
15	[illegible]	Do.	22	Crookedstown, m.	R.C.		R.C.	–	41	–	41	[illegible]
16	[illegible]	Do.	–	Do. f.	R.C.	–	R.C.	–	–	68	[illegible]	[illegible]
17	1212	Do.	–	Rosmead,	R.C.	–	R.C.	–	20	40	[illegible]	[illegible]
18	[illegible]	Do.	83	Delvin Workhouse,	P.L.	Gds.	R.C.	–	14	10	[illegible]	[illegible]
19	[illegible]	Castlelost,	–	Rochfortbridge, m.	R.C.	–	R.C.	–	73	–	73	[illegible]
20	[illegible]	Do.	–	Do. Conv. f.	R.C.	–	Nuns.		59	200	[illegible]	[illegible]
21	[illegible]	Castletown Kindalen.	–	Castletown Geoghegan, m.	R.C.	–	R.C.	–	105	–	[illegible]	[illegible]
22	[illegible]	Do.	–	Do. f.	R.C.	–	R.C.	–	–	[illegible]	[illegible]	[illegible]
23	[illegible]	Do.	–	Ballynagore, m.	R.C.	–	R.C.	–	104	–	[illegible]	[illegible]
24	[illegible]	Do.	–	Do. f.	R.C.	–	R.C.	–	–	104	[illegible]	[illegible]
25	[illegible]	Churchtown,	–	Loughanavally,	R.C.	–	R.C.	R.C.	44	44	[illegible]	[illegible]
26	[illegible]	Drumraney,	–	Ardnagragh, m.	R.C.	–	R.C.	–	127	–	127	[illegible]
27	[illegible]	Do.	–	Do. f.	R.C.	–	R.C.	–	–	[illegible]	[illegible]	[illegible]
28	7171	Do.	–	Drumraney,	R.C.	–	R.C.	–	[illegible]	[illegible]	[illegible]	[illegible]
29	[illegible]	Dysart,	–	Dysart,	R.C.	–	R.C.	R.C.	[illegible]	[illegible]	[illegible]	[illegible]
30	[illegible]	[illegible]	–	[illegible]	R.C.	–	R.C.	R.C.	[illegible]	[illegible]	[illegible]	[illegible]
31	4731	[illegible]	–	Tullystown,	R.C.	–	R.C.	–	51	[illegible]	111	[illegible]
32	[illegible]	Do.	–	[illegible], m.	R.C.	–	R.C.	–	117	–	[illegible]	[illegible]
33	[illegible]	Do.	–	Do. f.	R.C.	–	R.C.	–	–	103	[illegible]	[illegible]
34	[illegible]	Killua,	27	Cloona,	R.C.	–	R.C.	–	[illegible]	[illegible]	[illegible]	[illegible]
35	[illegible]	Killine,	–	Churchillam, No. 1,	R.C.	–	R.C.	–	11	11	[illegible]	[illegible]
36	[illegible]	Do.	–	Do. No. 2, m.	R.C.	–	R.C.	–	[illegible]	–	[illegible]	[illegible]
37	[illegible]	Do.	–	Do. f.	R.C.	–	R.C.	–	–	[illegible]	70	[illegible]
38	[illegible]	Kilbixie,	62	St. Mary's,	R.C.	–	R.C.	–	[illegible]	[illegible]	[illegible]	[illegible]
39	[illegible]	Do.	–	[illegible], m.	R.C.	–	R.C.	–	[illegible]	–	[illegible]	[illegible]
40	[illegible]	Do.	–	Do. f.	R.C.	–	R.C.	–	–	[illegible]	[illegible]	[illegible]
41	[illegible]	Do.	–	[illegible], m.	R.C.	–	R.C.	–	[illegible]	–	[illegible]	[illegible]
42	[illegible]	Do.	–	Do. f.	R.C.	–	R.C.	R.C.	–	[illegible]	[illegible]	[illegible]
43	[illegible]	Do.	–	Knockaville.	R.C.	–	R.C.	R.C.	47	[illegible]	[illegible]	[illegible]
44	[illegible]	Do.	–	[illegible],	R.C.	–	R.C.	–	73	[illegible]	[illegible]	[illegible]
45	[illegible]	Do.	–	Rathwyre, m.	R.C.	–	R.C.	–	102	–	[illegible]	[illegible]
46	[illegible]	Do.	–	Do. f.	R.C.	–	R.C.	R.C.	–	171	[illegible]	[illegible]
47	[illegible]	Do.	–	Downs,	–	R.C.	R.C.	R.C.	[illegible]	111	[illegible]	[illegible]
48	[illegible]	[illegible],	–	[illegible], m.	R.C.	–	R.C.	–	80	–	[illegible]	[illegible]
49	[illegible]	Do.	–	Do. f.	R.C.	–	R.C.	–	–	[illegible]	[illegible]	[illegible]
50	[illegible]	Kilbeggan,	41	Kilbeggan, m.	R.C.	–	R.C.	–	149	–	[illegible]	[illegible]
51	[illegible]	Do.	–	Do. f.	R.C.	–	R.C.	R.C.	–	[illegible]	[illegible]	[illegible]
52	[illegible]	[illegible],	[illegible]	[illegible],	R.C.	–	R.C.	–	[illegible]	[illegible]	[illegible]	[illegible]
53	1781	[illegible],	–	Ballymacmorrigy, m.	–	R.C.	R.C.	–	[illegible]	–	[illegible]	[illegible]
54	[illegible]	Do.	–	Do. f.	R.C.	–	R.C.	–	–	[illegible]	[illegible]	[illegible]
55	[illegible]	Kilkenny, West,	–	[illegible], m.	R.C.	–	R.C.	R.C.	[illegible]	–	[illegible]	[illegible]
56	[illegible]	Do.	–	Do. f.	R.C.	–	R.C.	R.C.	–	[illegible]	[illegible]	[illegible]
57	[illegible]	Killough,	–	Killough, m.	R.C.	–	R.C.	–	70	–	70	[illegible]
58	[illegible]	Do.	–	Do.[a] f.	R.C.	–	R.C.	–	–	–	–	–
59	[illegible]	[illegible],	–	Moate, m.	R.C.	–	R.C.	–	[illegible]	–	[illegible]	[illegible]
60	[illegible]	Do.	–	Do. Convent, f.	–	R.C.	Nuns.		–	[illegible]	[illegible]	[illegible]
61	[illegible]	Kilbride,	–	Kilbride,	R.C.	–	R.C.	–	[illegible]	[illegible]	[illegible]	[illegible]
62	[illegible]	Kilcleagh,	[illegible]	Kilcleagh,	R.C.	–	R.C.	R.C.	[illegible]	[illegible]	[illegible]	[illegible]
63	[illegible]	Do.	62	Moate, (2), m.	R.C.	–	R.C.	R.C.	[illegible]	–	[illegible]	[illegible]
64	[illegible]	Killare,	–	[illegible], m.	R.C.	–	R.C.	–	[illegible]	–	[illegible]	[illegible]
65	[illegible]	Do.	–	Do. f.	R.C.	–	R.C.	–	–	[illegible]	[illegible]	[illegible]
66	[illegible]	Kilcumreragh,	–	Kilcumreragh, m.	R.C.	–	R.C.	–	101	–	101	[illegible]
67	[illegible]	Do.	–	Do. f.	R.C.	–	R.C.	–	–	[illegible]	[illegible]	[illegible]
68	[illegible]	Lackan,	–	Lackan and Leny, m.	R.C.	–	R.C.	–	[illegible]	–	[illegible]	[illegible]
69	[illegible]	Do.	–	Do. f.	R.C.	–	R.C.	–	–	[illegible]	[illegible]	[illegible]
70	[illegible]	Liskish,	–	[illegible],	R.C.	–	R.C.	–	[illegible]	[illegible]	[illegible]	[illegible]
71	[illegible]	Do.	–	[illegible], m.	R.C.	–	R.C.	–	[illegible]	[illegible]	110	[illegible]
72	[illegible]	Do.	–	Do.[a] f.	–	–	–	–	–	–	–	–
73	[illegible]	Lynn,	–	[illegible],	R.C.	–	R.C.	R.C.	[illegible]	70	141	[illegible]
74	[illegible]	Mullingar,	–	Mullingar Convent, f.	R.C.	–	R.C.	–	–	[illegible]	[illegible]	[illegible]
75	[illegible]	Do.	–	[illegible], f.	R.C.	–	R.C.	R.C.	–	[illegible]	[illegible]	[illegible]

[a] Including value of Free Residence and Garden.

[b] Including value of Free Garden.

Province of Leinster: County of Westmeath—*continued*.

Amount paid for Books, Requisites, and Apparatus at Reduced Prices. £ s. d.	Aid granted by the Board during the Year 1873: In Free Stock of Books, Requisites, and Apparatus. £ s. d.	In Salaries, Premiums, and other Gratuities. £ s. d.	Results Fees, Financial Year. £ s. d.	Amount of Local Endowments received in Aid of Teacher's Salary: School Fees. £ s. d.	Subscriptions, Endowments, &c. £ s. d.	Total Local Aid. £ s. d.	Vested or Non-Vested.	Number.
—	—	76 10 0	30 0 0	20 11 10	30 10 0	b 63 1 10	V.S.	13
—	—	29 10 0	10 11 0	8 10 6	14 10 0	b 30 0 0	V.T.	14
0 14 4	—	24 0 0	9 5 0	4 8 0	—	4 8 0	V.T.	15
1 6 3	—	20 0 0	9 8 6	3 3 11	—	3 3 11	V.T.	16
1 10 8	—	24 0 0	9 4 0	0 16 7	2 0 0	b 2 16 7		17
—	—	—	—	—	—	—		18
2 12 10	—	30 10 0	15 16 6	6 1 0	—	6 1 0		19
7 13 8	—	61 5 0	56 0 0	21 6 0	—	21 6 0		20
5 2 10	—	32 0 0	23 10 0	9 7 0	—	9 7 0	V.T.	21
—	—	13 10 0	28 0 6	1 13 4	—	1 13 4	V.T.	22
1 8 3	—	20 10 0	0 6 0	8 10 4	—	8 10 4		23
8 14 11	—	20 0 0	17 1 0	4 14 11	—	4 14 11		24
1 5 6	—	41 0 0	16 17 0	5 2 11	—	5 2 11		25
4 9 9	—	38 0 0	19 15 6	2 3 7	5 0 0	7 3 7		26
3 6 0	—	24 0 0	9 1 0	0 14 6	5 0 0	5 14 6		27
5 15 2	—	26 0 0	8 12 0	2 11 2	3 0 0	b 5 11 2		28
—	—	44 0 0	17 4 6	5 10 10	—	5 10 10		29
4 14 1	—	37 0 0	20 17 6	5 2 6	—	5 2 6		30
2 4 3	—	30 0 0	30 0 0	5 0 10	—	5 0 10		31
2 10 1	—	30 0 0	16 12 0	0 10 4	—	0 10 4		32
1 13 8	—	33 10 0	16 11 0	1 1 0	—	1 1 0		33
2 8 6	—	20 0 0	9 6 0	1 13 7	1 10 0	b 3 3 7		34
3 2 7	—	10 8 4	4 10 6	0 19 0	23 0 0	b 23 19 0		35
1 4 11	—	41 6 8	12 14 6	4 16 0	—	4 16 0		36
2 3 8	—	24 10 0	12 7 0	1 17 4	—	1 17 4		37
4 6 8	—	22 0 0	17 16 6	4 8 6	—	4 8 6		38
2 2 4	—	24 0 0	11 6 6	3 19 10	—	3 19 10	V.T.	39
1 10 5	—	24 0 0	11 3 6	—	—	—	V.T.	40
4 2 1	—	41 10 0	17 1 6	4 8 5	—	4 8 5		41
4 8 5	—	40 0 0	16 14 0	2 19 0	—	2 19 0		42
1 8 1	—	40 0 0	11 7 0	1 10 0	—	1 10 0		43
2 11 1	—	22 0 0	14 10 6	3 0 6	—	3 0 6		44
3 16 1	—	30 8 4	23 1 6	11 13 0	—	11 13 0		45
4 14 9	—	52 0 0	27 17 0	10 0 0	—	10 0 0		46
2 19 6	—	41 0 0	20 3 0	16 5 2	17 4 10	b 33 10 0		47
1 6 3	—	37 0 0	4 3 6	4 0 0	—	4 0 0	V.T.	48
1 6 8	—	28 6 0	18 8 0	8 13 6	—	8 13 6	V.T.	49
6 6 8	—	39 16 8	12 10 6	12 5 10	—	12 5 10	V.T.	50
2 5 6	—	52 0 0	14 1 0	7 6 4	—	7 6 4	V.T.	51
1 11 8	—	20 0 0	9 15 6	4 0 0	—	4 0 0		52
3 0 6	—	40 0 0	17 8 0	7 0 0	5 0 0	b 12 0 0		53
5 2 8	—	18 15 0	21 19 6	5 10 0	5 0 0	b 10 10 0		54
4 17 7	—	69 0 0	27 1 0	5 3 0	—	5 3 0	V.T.	55
7 16 4	—	70 0 0	23 11 6	5 0 1	—	5 0 1	V.T.	56
—	—	26 0 0	—	0 19 0	—	0 19 0		57
1 12 7	—	31 6 8	11 4 0	—	—	—		58
2 7 4	—	45 15 6	12 9 6	7 0 0	—	7 0 0		59
21 8 9	—	88 1 10	30 5 0	17 18 3	—	11 14 8		60
—	—	24 0 0	10 3 6	3 0 0	—	3 0 0		61
2 13 4	—	61 8 8	13 8 6	9 2 8	—	8 8 8	V.T.	62
2 6 5	—	62 6 8	11 11 6	4 15 0	—	4 15 6		63
2 1 8	—	24 0 0	—	3 7 2	—	3 7 2		64
—	—	37 0 0	14 0 10	2 0 0	—	2 0 0		65
1 11 6	—	30 0 0	5 3 0	2 19 5	—	2 19 5		66
2 1 0	—	23 0 0	16 15 0	3 5 7	—	3 5 7		67
1 9 0	—	57 10 0	11 1 0	2 4 0	—	2 4 0		68
2 18 11	—	30 0 0	18 0 0	2 16 8	—	2 16 8		69
1 5 10	—	39 10 0	14 8 0	5 12 0	5 12 0	b 11 4 0		70
2 0 1	—	24 0 0	12 8 0	2 2 0	—	2 2 0		71
—	—	—	—	—	—	—		72
—	—	41 8 8	11 8 8	1 1 0	—	1 1 0		73
19 14 0	—	186 6 4	60 0 6	14 5 6	—	14 5 6		74
1 0 10	—	20 0 0	12 14 0	2 14 0	—	2 14 0	V.T.	75

b Including value of Free Residence. d Returns not available. e Incomplete.

List of Schools in operation on the 31st December, 1874.—

Number.	Roll Number of School.	Parish.	District.	School.	Religious Denomination of Manager or Correspondent. Clerical.	Lay.	Teaching and Religious Denomination of Teachers. Principals.	Assistants.	Attendance for the Year. Total number of Pupils on Rolls within the Year ended. Males.	Fem.	Total.	Average daily attendance.
76	10426	Mullingar,	22	Ballinea, m.	R.C.	–	R.C.	–	104	–	104	45
77	4891	Do.	–	Mullingar Parish,	R.C.	–	R.C.	R.C.	53	46	99	34
78	9234	Do.	–	Glascara, m.	R.C.	–	R.C.	–	51	–	51	23
79	4893	Do.	–	Do. f.	R.C.	–	R.C.	–	–	61	61	31
80	3030	Do.	–	Mullingar, Workho.	P.L.	Gds.	–	–	57	44	101	43
81	6478	Do.	–	Do. Gaol, m.	Governor		–	–	–	–	–	–
82	5016	Do.	–	Do. do. f.	Governor		–	–	–	44	44	8
83	3243	Do.	–	Walshestown,	R.C.	–	R.C.	–	32	42	74	37
				Do. evg.	R.C.	–	–	–	–	–	–	–
84	2462	Multyfarnham,	–	Multyfarnham, m.	–	R.C.	R.C.	–	122	–	122	61
85	[illegible]	Multyfarnham,	–	Multyfarnham, * f.	–	R.C.	R.C.	–	–	–	–	–
86	8834	Mayne,	–	Coole, m.	R.C.	–	R.C.	–	107	–	109	35
87	8031	Do.	–	Do. f.	R.C.	–	R.C.	–	–	78	78	29
88	6016	Newtown,	–	Tyrrellspass, m.	R.C.	–	R.C.	–	168	–	168	66
89	6040	Do.	–	Do. f.	R.C.	–	R.C.	R.C.	–	183	183	64
90	6021	Noughaval,	–	Tang, m.	R.C.	–	R.C.	–	101	–	151	64
91	6032	Do.	–	Do. f.	R.C.	–	R.C.	–	–	129	129	47
92	6433	Portnashangan,	–	Ballynafid, m.	R.C.	–	R.C.	–	55	–	46	24
93	3390	Do.	–	Do. f.	R.C.	–	R.C.	–	–	64	64	21
94	10546	Do.	–	Baltrath, m.	R.C.	–	R.C.	–	69	–	69	27
95	10518	Do.	–	Do. f.	R.C.	–	R.C.	–	–	66	66	25
96	6078	Pass of Kilbride,	–	Milltown, temp. m.	R.C.	–	R.C.	–	108	–	108	34
97	6074	Do.	–	Do. do. f.	R.C.	–	R.C.	–	10	103	113	39
98	97	Rathconrath,	–	Do. m.	R.C.	–	R.C.	–	93	–	93	39
99	9196	Do.	–	Do. f.	R.C.	–	R.C.	–	–	85	85	45
100	1423	Do.	–	Irishtown,	R.C.	–	R.C.	R.C.	60	75	135	53
101	6090	Rahugh,	41	Ardan,	R.C.	–	R.C.	–	65	84	149	46
102	6101	Rathaspick,	83	Rathowen,	R.C.	–	R.C.	R.C.	128	100	228	73
103	6011	Do.	–	Do. * No. 2,	R.C.	–	R.C.	–	–	–	–	–
104	7015	Do.	–	Corry,	R.C.	–	R.C.	–	50	48	98	30
105	6613	Rathgarve,	–	Castlepollard, m.	R.C.	–	R.C.	–	178	–	178	67
106	6614	Do.	–	Do. f.	R.C.	–	R.C.	2 R.C.	–	154	154	66
107	10803	Do.	–	Do. Parochial,	R.C.	–	R.C.	–	29	31	60	29
108	6792	Do.	–	Millcastle,	R.C.	–	R.C.	–	34	31	65	33
109	7946	Do.	–	Ballycomoyle,	R.C.	–	R.C.	–	46	33	79	34
110	6496	Rathconnell,	–	Loughegar,	R.C.	–	R.C.	–	60	74	130	43
111	[illegible]	Do.	–	Turin, m.	R.C.	–	R.C.	–	75	–	75	21
112	[illegible]	Do.	–	Do. f.	R.C.	–	R.C.	–	–	79	79	28
113	[illegible]	Street,	24	Lismacaffry, m.	R.C.	–	R.C.	–	137	–	137	48
114	[illegible]	Do.	–	Do. f.	R.C.	–	R.C.	–	–	160	160	48
115	[illegible]	Do.	–	Bath, m.	R.C.	–	R.C.	–	78	–	78	35
116	[illegible]	Do.	–	Do. f.	R.C.	–	R.C.	–	–	60	60	26
117	1431	St. Mary's,	30	Auburnshower, m.	R.C.	–	R.C.	R.C.	190	–	190	64
118	1494	Do.	–	Do. f.	R.C.	–	R.C.	R.C.	61	213	273	82
119	[illegible]	Do.	–	Coosan, c m.	–	–	–	–	–	–	–	–
120	[illegible]	Do.	–	Do. f.	R.C.	–	R.C.	R.C.	73	91	164	52
121	[illegible]	Do.	–	Athlone Workhouse,	P.L.	Gds.	–	–	57	48	99	57
122	9192	Do.	–	Blackberry Lane,	R.C.	–	R.C.	–	76	56	132	33
123	9132	Do.	–	Climbcorry,	R.C.	–	R.C.	–	59	63	122	33
124	10626	Do.	–	Northgate-street, Athlone,	Pres.	–	Pres.	–	18	29	48	18
125	6416	St. Feighin's,	39	Carpenterstown,	R.C.	–	R.C.	–	93	58	151	46
126	6414	Do.	–	Fore,	R.C.	–	R.C.	–	70	68	138	36
127	6191	Do.	–	Milltown, No. 3, temp.	R.C.	–	R.C.	–	34	33	67	23
128	7128	Do.	–	Collinstown, m.	R.C.	–	R.C.	–	106	–	106	33
129	712	Do.	–	Do. f.	R.C.	–	R.C.	–	–	124	124	46
130	94	Templepatrick,	–	Moyvore, m.	R.C.	–	R.C.	–	109	–	109	32
131	94	Do.	–	Do. f.	R.C.	–	R.C.	–	–	98	98	33
132	147	Templeoran,	–	Sonna, m.	R.C.	–	R.C.	–	68	–	68	21
133	197	Do.	–	Do. f.	R.C.	–	R.C.	–	–	69	69	23
134	6627	Taghmon,	–	Curley, m.	R.C.	–	R.C.	–	106	–	160	37
135	6628	Do.	–	Do. f.	R.C.	–	R.C.	–	–	101	101	38
		Total for County Westmeath, 135,							7,418	7,459	14,897	5,1[illegible]

a Including value of Free Residence. b Including value of Free Garden. c No Teacher.

Province of Leinster: County of Westmeath—*continued.*

Amount paid by Pupils, Local Sources, and Scholarships, or Endowed Funds. £ s. d.	Aid granted by the Board during the Year 1874. In Free Stock of Books, Requisites, and Apparatus. £ s. d.	In Salaries, Premiums, and other Gratuities. £ s. d.	Results Fees, Financial Year. £ s. d.	Amount of Local Contributions received in Aid of Teacher's Salary. School Fees. £ s. d.	Subscriptions, Endowments, &c. £ s. d.	Total Local Aid. £ s. d.	Vested or Non-Vested.	Number.
1 10 2	—	24 0 0	14 14 0	3 8 8	—	3 8 8		76
4 8 4	—	40 4 8	27 11 0	12 14 4	10 0 0	a 22 14 4		77
0 18 10	—	24 0 0	8 1 0	3 14 0	0 10 0	b 4 4 6		78
1 6 6	—	35 5 4	13 0 0	6 0 0	1 0 0	b 6 0 0		79
7 6 3	—	9 10 0	—	—	—	—		80
—	—	—	—	—	—	—		81
—	—	—	—	—	—	—		82
1 8 4	—	23 5 0	12 7 4	1 14 4	1 0 0	a 2 11 8		83
—	—	—	6 18 8	—	—	—		
4 17 6	—	21 0 0	13 13 0	4 5 0	—	4 5 0	V.T.	84
—	—	27 0 0	10 5 6	—	—	—	V.T.	85
1 4 8	—	24 0 0	10 3 6	3 10 6	—	3 10 6	V.T.	86
1 11 1	—	22 0 0	10 8 0	3 0 7	—	3 0 7	V.T.	87
3 5 2	—	29 0 0	27 18 0	3 15 0	—	3 15 0		88
—	—	34 0 0	23 8 0	4 17 6	—	4 17 6		89
4 0 10	—	72 6 8	23 5 0	6 17 2	—	6 17 2		90
2 10 8	—	46 5 4	15 8 0	5 14 11	—	5 14 11		91
1 8 4	—	24 0 0	9 7 0	1 2 6	7 15 0	8 17 6		92
1 0 4	—	30 0 0	10 4 6	0 10 0	8 0 0	a 8 10 0		93
1 5 8	—	37 0 0	10 7 0	1 9 5	—	1 9 5		94
1 1 4	—	20 0 0	8 8 6	2 10 0	2 10 0	a 5 0 0		95
1 17 7	—	31 16 8	12 17 0	4 3 0	—	4 3 0		96
0 10 2	—	28 0 0	19 8 0	4 19 0	—	4 19 0		97
2 2 1	—	34 10 0	24 16 0	3 9 0	1 0 0	a 6 0 0		98
1 8 9	—	35 0 0	19 11 0	6 10 6	—	6 10 6		99
5 19 8	—	24 10 0	28 0 0	1 9 0	—	1 9 0	V.T.	100
1 12 5	—	26 0 0	18 6 0	9 11 0	—	9 11 0		101
7 10 2	—	51 0 0	15 4 0	5 13 1	1 10 0	a 7 3 1		102
1 18 10	—	30 0 0	13 4 6	—	—	—		103
2 7 6	—	30 0 0	7 17 6	2 11 0	—	2 11 0		104
2 19 8	—	54 0 0	20 5 6	10 14 6	—	10 14 6		105
3 4 10	—	30 10 0	24 17 6	7 6 5	—	7 6 5		106
2 18 6	1 0 0	31 10 8	12 9 6	8 10 0	47 0 0	56 10 0		107
—	—	20 0 0	8 8 6	5 0 0	1 0 0	a 6 0 0		108
1 10 6	—	24 0 0	10 15 0	8 8 6	—	8 8 6		109
3 2 6	—	28 0 0	18 3 0	6 6 2	1 0 0	a 4 8 2		110
1 0 0	—	24 0 0	9 1 6	2 12 2	—	2 12 2		111
3 5 8	—	20 0 0	19 11 6	5 18 6	—	5 18 6		112
—	—	24 0 0	6 2 0	5 5 0	—	5 5 0	V.T.	113
—	8 6 6	41 10 0	17 18 0	5 10 8	—	5 10 8	V.T.	114
3 18 11	2 17 11	24 0 0	5 10 6	2 5 0	—	2 5 0		115
—	2 10 4	30 0 0	7 8 0	2 14 4	—	2 14 4		116
5 19 11	—	63 0 0	19 7 6	15 8 0	—	15 8 0	V.T.	117
3 17 11	—	61 0 0	21 12 0	4 0 0	—	4 0 0	V.T.	118
—	—	—	—	—	—	—		119
2 15 7	—	48 0 0	11 18 6	4 14 1	—	4 14 1		120
6 15 11	—	5 0 0	—	—	—	—		121
1 12 10	—	20 0 0	6 14 6	1 11 3	—	1 11 3		122
2 17 8	—	24 0 0	6 11 6	2 17 1	—	2 17 1		123
5 4 4	—	23 0 0	8 6 6	—	17 0 0	17 0 0		124
2 2 6	—	14 10 0	12 19 0	1 1 6	—	1 1 6		125
1 5 4	—	27 6 8	7 8 0	0 16 6	—	0 16 6		126
1 6 0	—	24 0 0	8 4 6	2 0 0	—	2 0 0		127
1 8 4	—	24 0 0	10 8 6	2 7 0	—	2 7 0		128
2 18 6	—	33 0 0	21 18 6	2 16 6	—	2 16 6		129
1 17 6	—	22 0 0	16 16 6	6 7 2	—	6 7 2	V.T.	130
1 5 3	—	30 0 0	19 15 6	2 18 11	—	2 18 11	V.T.	131
1 15 6	—	21 0 0	10 7 6	3 16 0	1 0 0	b 4 16 0	V.T.	132
1 19 6	—	25 0 0	14 11 6	4 1 1	3 0 0	a 7 1 1	V.T.	133
3 4 11	—	24 0 0	16 15 0	1 4 0	—	1 4 0		134
4 13 0	—	25 0 0	17 10 6	5 3 4	—	5 3 4		135
[illegible] 5 4	6 17 9	4,013 17 6	2,[illegible] 7 7	350 6 8	[illegible] 1 10	616 8 8		

a Including value of Free Residence and Garden. b Returns not available. c Inoperative.

List of Schools in operation on the

COUNTY OF

Number.	Roll Number of School.	Parish.	District.	School.		Religious Denomination of Manager or Correspondent. Clerical.	Lay.	Number and Religious Denomination of Teachers. Principals.	Assistants.	Attendance for the Year. Total number of Pupils on Rolls within the Year 1874. Males.	Fem.	Total.	Average Daily Attendance for the Year.
1	1427	Ardcolm,	30	Castlebridge,	m.	R.C.	–	R.C.	–	93	–	93	[illegible]
2	5936	Do.	–	Do.	f.	R.C.	–	R.C.	–	–	86	86	53
3	3756	Adamstown,	–	Adamstown,	m.	R.C.	–	R.C.	–	81	–	81	21
4	3756	Do.	–	Do.	f.	R.C.	–	R.C.	–	–	109	110	29
5	4086	Ardamine,	40	River Chapel,	m.	R.C.	–	R.C.	–	105	–	105	[illegible]
6	4091	Do.	–	Do.	f.	R.C.	–	R.C.	–	–	104	104	[illegible]
7	843	Ballyanne,	60	Rathgarogue,	m.	R.C.	–	R.C.	–	116	–	116	[illegible]
8	6687	Do.	–	Do.	f.	R.C.	–	R.C.	–	–	117	117	[illegible]
9	1615	Ballyhoge,	–	Galbally,		R.C.	–	R.C.	R.C.	64	44	108	[illegible]
10	3084	Ballymitty,	–	Hilltown,		R.C.	–	R.C.	–	53	51	104	[illegible]
11	4028	Ballyhuskard,	–	Ballaghkeen,		R.C.	–	R.C.	–	67	–	67	[illegible]
12	6811	Do.	–	Glenbrien,		R.C.	–	R.C.	R.C.	67	49	116	[illegible]
13	6077	Do.	–	Coolgarrow,		R.C.	–	R.C.	–	43	52	95	[illegible]
14	5910	Bannow,	–	Bannow,		R.C.	–	R.C.	–	[illegible]	57	73	[illegible]
15	7870	Do.	–	Danescastle,		R.C.	–	R.C.	–	71	58	129	[illegible]
16	[illegible]	Ballycanew,	40	Ballycanew,	m.	R.C.	–	R.C.	–	79	–	79	[illegible]
17	6657	Do.	–	Do.	f.	R.C.	–	R.C.	–	–	80	80	[illegible]
18	[illegible]	Ballycarney,	[illegible]	Castledockrell,		R.C.	–	–	–	–	–	–	–
19	[illegible]	Ballynaslaney,	47	Redgate,		R.C.	–	R.C.	–	49	47	96	34
20	[illegible]	Ballybrazil,	40	Aughnalare,		R.C.	–	R.C.	–	61	[illegible]	91	[illegible]
21	10722	Ballyvaldon,	30	Ballyvaldon,		R.C.	–	R.C.	–	60	45	105	44
22	1708	Carnew,	30	Ballyellis,		R.C.	–	R.C.	–	74	64	138	[illegible]
23	2808	Do.	–	Askamore,		R.C.	–	R.C.	–	61	36	70	[illegible]
24	10108	Castle Ellis,	30	Killahurd,		R.C.	–	R.C.	–	61	32	93	[illegible]
25	3100	Clonleigh,	–	Donard,	m.	R.C.	–	R.C.	–	74	–	74	[illegible]
26	2101	Do.	–	Do.	f.	R.C.	–	R.C.	–	–	[illegible]	[illegible]	[illegible]
27	[illegible]	Clonmore,	–	Bree,	m.	R.C.	–	R.C.	–	76	–	76	[illegible]
28	[illegible]	Do.	–	Do.	f.	R.C.	–	R.C.	–	–	60	60	16
29	[illegible]	Clongeen,	–	Clongeen,	m.	R.C.	–	R.C.	–	81	–	81	33
30	6011	Do.	–	Do.	f.	R.C.	–	R.C.	–	–	108	108	[illegible]
31	[illegible]	Clonmines,	40	Clonmines,		R.C.	–	R.C.	–	34	53	87	[illegible]
32	[illegible]	Carnagh,	30	Cushinstown,	m.	R.C.	–	R.C.	–	63	–	63	[illegible]
33	[illegible]	Do.	–	Do.	f.	R.C.	–	R.C.	–	–	[illegible]	[illegible]	[illegible]
34	[illegible]	Chapel,	–	Clonroche,	m.	R.C.	–	R.C.	–	61	–	61	[illegible]
35	[illegible]	Do.	–	Do.	f.	R.C.	–	R.C.	–	–	74	74	[illegible]
36	[illegible]	Clone,	–	Tinnacross,		R.C.	–	–	–	43	34	74	[illegible]
37	[illegible]	Carne,	–	Carne,		R.C.	–	R.C.	–	45	[illegible]	[illegible]	[illegible]
38	[illegible]	Carrick,	–	Barntown,	m.	R.C.	–	R.C.	–	60	–	[illegible]	[illegible]
39	[illegible]	Do.	–	Do.	f.	R.C.	–	R.C.	–	–	77	77	[illegible]
40	[illegible]	Do.	–	Wexford Workhouse,		P.L.	Gds.	aR.C.	–	121	79	200	111
41	[illegible]	Duncormick,	–	Duncormick,		R.C.	–	R.C.	–	54	58	112	[illegible]
42	[illegible]	Donaghmore,	40	Ballygarrett,	m.	R.C.	–	R.C.	–	116	–	116	[illegible]
43	3002	Do.	–	Do.	f.	R.C.	–	R.C.	R.C.	–	141	141	[illegible]
44	[illegible]	Edermine,	60	Oilgate,		R.C.	–	R.C.	R.C.	67	51	118	[illegible]
45	[illegible]	Ferns,	[illegible]	Ferns,	m.	R.C.	–	R.C.	–	161	–	161	[illegible]
46	1761	Do.	–	Do.	f.	R.C.	–	R.C.	–	–	141	141	41
47	[illegible]	Fethard,	49	Poulfur,	m.	R.C.	–	R.C.	–	118	–	118	[illegible]
48	[illegible]	Do.	–	Do.	f.	R.C.	–	R.C.	–	–	[illegible]	[illegible]	[illegible]
49	8764	Horetown,	30	Cullenstown,		R.C.	–	R.C.	–	37	43	80	[illegible]
50	9077	Hook,	43	Loftus Hall,		R.C.	–	R.C.	–	37	37	74	[illegible]
51	9453	Inch,	40	Coolgreany,		R.C.	–	R.C.	R.C.	65	50	115	51
52	919	Kilcavan,	–	Killincooly,	m.	R.C.	–	R.C.	–	[illegible]	–	[illegible]	[illegible]
53	[illegible]	Do.	–	Do.	f.	R.C.	–	R.C.	–	–	[illegible]	[illegible]	[illegible]
54	[illegible]	Kilmannan,	50	Forth,		R.C.	–	R.C.	–	43	[illegible]	84	[illegible]
55	[illegible]	Do.	–	Claristown,		R.C.	–	R.C.	–	[illegible]	18	[illegible]	[illegible]
56	957	Kilmokea,	49	Horeswood,	m.	R.C.	–	R.C.	–	119	–	119	[illegible]
57	[illegible]	Do.	–	Do.	f.	R.C.	–	R.C.	–	–	[illegible]	[illegible]	[illegible]
58	[illegible]	Killinick,	30	Mountfield,		R.C.	–	R.C.	–	67	48	[illegible]	[illegible]
59	[illegible]	Kilmore,	–	Kilmore, No. 1,	m.	R.C.	–	R.C.	–	76	–	76	[illegible]
60	961	Do.	–	Do. No. 2,	m.	R.C.	–	R.C.	–	63	–	63	[illegible]
61	962	Killurin,	–	Glynn,	m.	R.C.	–	R.C.	–	60	–	60	[illegible]
62	[illegible]	Do.	–	Do.	f.	R.C.	–	R.C.	–	65	–	65	57

a Including value of Free Residence.

b Including value of Free Garden.

31st December, 1874.—Province of Leinster.

WEXFORD—131 Schools.

Amount paid for Books, Requisites, and Apparatus, at Reduced Prices.	Aid granted by the Board during the Year 1874: In Free Stock of Books, Requisites, and Apparatus.	In Salaries, Premiums, and other Emoluments.	Results Fees, Financial Year.	Amount of Local Emoluments received in Aid of Teacher's Salary: School Fees.	Subscriptions, Endowments, &c.	Total Local Aid.	Vested or Non-Vested.	Number.
£ s. d.	£ s. d.	£ s. d.	£ s. d.	£ s. d.	£ s. d.	£ s. d.		
7 5 0	—	24 0 0	5 11 6	6 12 0	—	6 12 0	V.T.	1
2 1 5	—	24 0 0	6 8 6	6 18 6	—	6 18 6	V.T.	2
2 5 3	4 8 2	20 11 4	2 10 0	1 10 0	—	1 10 0		3
2 17 10	—	20 0 0	8 11 0	2 14 0	—	2 14 0		4
1 7 6	—	24 0 0	17 8 0	2 19 6	—	2 19 6		5
5 12 11	—	21 13 4	16 7 6	5 17 0	—	5 17 0		6
8 2 8	—	24 0 0	9 14 0	7 8 8	10 10 0	*17 18 8	V.T.	7
2 10 2	—	24 10 0	18 12 0	6 4 9	9 0 0	*15 4 0	V.T.	8
2 10 0	—	32 0 0	11 6 6	4 16 6	—	4 16 6	V.T.	9
1 0 3	—	10 0 0	6 8 6	7 1 1	—	7 1 1		10
2 0 0	—	22 0 0	6 11 0	9 14 6	—	9 14 0		11
3 8 10	—	44 0 0	21 14 0	12 0 0	—	12 0 0		12
1 17 3	—	24 0 0	4 11 6	5 0 11	4 0 0	[a]9 0 11		13
—	—	30 0 0	8 2 0	15 16 0	—	15 16 0		14
4 5 8	—	55 10 0	18 14 6	20 16 0	—	20 16 0		15
3 7 6	—	30 0 0	11 18 0	5 18 7	—	5 18 7		16
5 3 1	—	22 0 0	13 0 0	6 0 0	—	6 0 0		17
6 8 11	—	32 10 0	4 2 0	—	—	—		18
6 10 10	—	31 0 0	16 15 6	6 0 0	5 0 0	11 0 0		19
1 8 8	—	20 0 0	11 7 0	8 6 8	—	8 6 8		20
4 1 10	—	24 0 0	13 8 0	11 6 4	—	11 6 4		21
2 8 7	—	41 10 0	21 17 0	15 4 0	3 0 0	[a]18 4 0		22
—	—	30 0 0	6 10 0	1 2 0	—	1 2 0		23
1 10 0	—	24 0 6	0 18 0	7 7 8	—	7 7 8		24
1 8 3	—	24 0 0	3 4 0	5 16 6	3 0 0	[a]8 16 6	V.T.	25
1 5 3	—	20 0 0	3 15 0	5 0 0	—	5 0 0	V.T.	26
—	—	24 0 0	0 7 0	6 17 0	—	6 17 0		27
1 18 0	—	27 0 0	4 12 0	5 0 3	1 15 0	[a]3 15 8		28
2 11 4	—	17 10 0	6 7 0	1 10 0	—	1 18 0		29
5 8 0	—	24 0 0	7 0 0	5 5 1	4 0 0	*7 5 1		30
1 14 4	—	22 0 0	7 0 0	4 0 6	2 0 0	6 0 6		31
3 18 2	—	24 0 0	9 8 0	5 5 1	1 10 0	[a]6 15 1		32
2 9 0	—	30 0 0	12 0 0	7 0 2	1 0 0	*8 0 2		33
5 6 3	—	72 0 0	8 8 6	4 0 0	0 10 0	[a]4 10 0	V.C.	34
1 1 9	—	21 0 0	7 11 0	5 5 4	0 10 0	[a]5 15 4	V.C.	35
1 7 10	—	22 10 0	6 18 6	1 8 7	—	1 8 7		36
1 11 2	—	34 0 0	14 14 0	20 2 0	—	20 2 0		37
2 16 8	—	24 0 0	10 15 0	16 0 6	—	16 0 6	V.T.	38
3 14 4	—	20 0 0	13 12 0	6 16 10	—	6 16 10	V.T.	39
4 15 0	—	4 10 0	—	—	—	—		40
3 14 5	—	20 0 0	5 18 0	2 10 6	—	2 10 6		41
1 9 0	—	31 15 0	22 0 6	10 2 6	—	10 2 6		42
5 18 6	—	57 10 0	28 17 0	16 8 9	—	16 8 9		43
3 15 5	—	48 13 4	15 8 0	10 0 0	10 0 0	20 0 0		44
4 10 7	—	31 8 4	13 7 6	8 19 9	—	8 19 9		45
4 15 5	—	22 8 8	11 11 0	2 12 3	—	2 12 3		46
0 12 1	—	24 0 0	8 8 8	8 3 0	—	8 3 0	N.V.	47
1 16 3	—	24 0 0	11 15 0	4 14 1	—	4 14 1	...	48
—	—	18 0 8	10 10 8	0 18 7	—	0 18 7		49
0 10 0	—	20 0 0	5 17 6	0 4 8	—	0 4 8		50
2 18 10	—	50 13 4	18 1 0	5 10 0	—	5 10 0		51
1 11 8	—	29 0 0	18 8 0	10 4 1	—	10 4 1		52
0 15 0	—	33 16 8	18 5 6	6 12 7	—	6 12 7		53
1 17 5	—	22 10 0	8 14 0	1 18 4	2 10 0	[a]4 8 4		54
1 6 0	—	24 0 0	6 14 0	5 0 0	—	5 0 0		55
5 0 11	—	47 10 0	10 17 0	11 5 2	1 10 0	*12 15 2		56
0 1 1	—	27 0 0	12 1 0	4 15 0	2 0 0	*6 15 0		57
2 1 5	—	24 0 0	5 8 0	4 14 7	—	4 14 7		58
5 0 11	—	22 0 0	7 18 0	6 12 2	—	6 12 2		59
—	—	36 0 0	8 0 0	9 14 0	—	9 14 0		60
5 12 0	—	18 3 0	—	6 18 0	—	6 12 0		61
5 4 5	—	24 0 0	11 8 5	5 10 0	—	5 10 0		62

* No Teacher.

[a] Including value of Free Residence and Garden.

List of Schools in operation on the 31st December, 1874—

Number.	Roll Number of School.	Parish.	District.	School.	Religious Denomination of Patrons or Correspondents: Clerical.	Lay.	Number and Religious Denomination of Teachers: Principals.	Assistants.	Attendance for the Year: Total number of Pupils on the Rolls within the Year: Males.	Fem.	Total.	Average daily attendance.
63	[illegible]	Killann,	54	Rathnure,	R.C.	–	R.C.	R.C.	161	69	230	94
64	[illegible]	Kilrush,	39	Kingsland,	R.C.	–	R.C.	–	85	76	161	63
65	5176	Killurin,	46	[illegible]	R.C.	–	R.C.	–	65	60	125	52
66	1284	Kilscoran,	39	Ballyduff,	R.C.	–	R.C.	–	46	28	74	29
67	4558	Kilpatrick,	57	Slee,	R.C.	–	R.C.	–	73	55	127	48
68	4587	Kildavin,	–	Murrintown,	R.C.	–	R.C.	–	80	48	128	55
69	[illegible]	Kilmallock,	–	Ballymurn, m.	–	R.C.	R.C.	–	80	–	80	31
70	[illegible]	Do.	–	Do. f.	–	R.C.	R.C.	–	–	65	65	28
71	[illegible]	Kilmuckridge,	–	Kilmuckridge, m.	R.C.	–	R.C.	–	154	–	154	56
72	[illegible]	Do.	–	Do. f.	R.C.	–	R.C.	–	–	116	116	45
73	5168	Kilcowan,	–	Baldwinstown,	R.C.	–	R.C.	–	66	56	121	43
74	6072	[illegible]	46	[illegible]	R.C.	–	R.C.	–	47	39	86	27
75	6436	Kilrane,	50	Kilrane,	R.C.	–	R.C.	–	53	46	99	38
76	6424	Kilturk,	–	Kilturk,	R.C.	–	R.C.	R.C.	38	137	175	75
77	6770	Kilgarvan,	–	Carrowreigh,	R.C.	–	R.C.	R.C.	71	78	149	74
78	7081	Kilnenor,	46	Ballyfad,	R.C.	–	R.C.	–	63	60	123	35
79	7036	Killila,	50	Blackwater, m.	R.C.	–	R.C.	–	116	–	116	48
80	7037	Do.	–	Do. f.	R.C.	–	R.C.	–	–	129	129	61
81	6553	Kilgorman,	46	Castletown, m.	R.C.	–	R.C.	–	129	–	129	46
82	10713	Do.	–	Do. f.	R.C.	–	R.C.	–	–	134	134	61
83	[illegible]	Kilmakilloge,	–	Gorey Convent, f.	R.C.	–	Nuns		80	240	320	130
84	[illegible]	Do.	–	Do. Workhouse,[a]	–	–	–	–	–	–	–	–
85	[illegible]	[illegible]	–	[illegible]	R.C.	–	R.C.	R.C.	67	72	139	51
86	[illegible]	Killinick,	50	Ballycommons,[b]	–	–	–	–	–	–	–	–
87	[illegible]	Do.	–	Killinick,	R.C.	–	R.C.	–	36	41	77	31
88	[illegible]	Lady's Island,	–	Lady's Island,	R.C.	–	R.C.	R.C.	65	56	121	47
89	[illegible]	Mulrankin,	–	Mulrankin,	R.C.	–	R.C.	–	35	46	81	32
90	[illegible]	Mayglass,	–	Mayglass,	R.C.	–	R.C.	–	34	24	58	23
91	[illegible]	Meelnagh,	–	Oulart, m.	R.C.	–	R.C.	–	67	–	67	31
92	[illegible]	Do.	–	Do. f.	R.C.	–	R.C.	–	–	103	140	38
93	2917	Monamolin,	46	Ballinavally,	R.C.	–	R.C.	–	66	44	110	43
94	2207	Newtown,	50	Raheen,	R.C.	–	R.C.	R.C.	75	62	137	50
95	4476	Do.	–	[illegible]	–	R.C.	R.C.	–	54	50	104	37
96	6726	Do.	–	Newtown,	R.C.	–	R.C.	R.C.	86	50	136	41
97	6717	Old Ross,	–	Park,	R.C.	–	R.C.	–	70	59	129	41
98	[illegible]	[illegible]	–	Piercestown, m.	R.C.	–	R.C.	–	80	–	80	34
99	[illegible]	Do.	–	Do. f.	R.C.	–	R.C.	–	–	80	80	39
100	[illegible]	Rossdroit,	–	Courtnacuddy, m.	R.C.	–	R.C.	–	74	–	74	35
101	[illegible]	Do.	–	Do. f.	R.C.	–	R.C.	–	–	80	80	38
102	[illegible]	Do.	–	Davidstown,	R.C.	–	R.C.	R.C.	67	60	127	51
103	[illegible]	Rosslare,	–	Tagoat, m.	R.C.	–	R.C.	–	108	–	108	44
104	[illegible]	Do.	–	Do. f.	R.C.	–	R.C.	–	–	85	85	33
105	[illegible]	Do.	–	Rosslare Fort,	–	R.C.	R.C.	–	37	32	69	29
106	[illegible]	Rossminoge,	46	Craanford, m.	R.C.	–	R.C.	–	91	–	91	37
107	[illegible]	Do.	–	Do. f.	R.C.	–	R.C.	–	–	108	108	44
108	[illegible]	[illegible]	49	Shelbaggan,	R.C.	–	R.C.	–	43	41	84	34
109	[illegible]	St. Peter's,	50	Wexford, No. 1, m.	R.C.	–	R.C.	–	157	–	157	53
110	[illegible]	Do.	–	Do. No. 2, m.	R.C.	–	R.C.	–	285	–	285	78
111	[illegible]	St. Mary's (New Ross)	–	New Ross, Conv., f.	–	R.C.	Nuns		–	477	477	161
112	9047	Do.	–	Do. No. 2, Conv. f.	–	R.C.	Nuns		66	318	376	132
113	[illegible]	Do.	–	Do. Workhouse,	P.L.	Gds.	R.C.	–	68	79	147	45
114	[illegible]	Do. ([illegible])	[illegible]	Kilmyshall,	R.C.	–	R.C.	–	87	114	201	71
115	[illegible]	Do.	–	Newtownbarry, m.	R.C.	–	R.C.	–	134	–	134	57
116	[illegible]	Do.	–	Do. Convent, f.	R.C.	–	Nuns		–	134	134	65
117	[illegible]	Do. (Enniscorthy)	50	Enniscorthy District Model, m.	Com.	N.B.	R.C.	–	45	–	45	31
118	[illegible]	Do.	–	Do. f.	Com.	N.B.	R.C.	–	–	50	50	34
119	[illegible]	Do.	–	Do. i.	Com.	N.B.	R.C.	–	18	26	44	30
120	[illegible]	Do.	–	Do. Convent, f.	R.C.	–	Nuns		100	428	528	224
121	[illegible]	Do.	–	Do. Workhouse,	P.L.	Gds.	R.C.	–	66	68	134	73
122	[illegible]	Do.	–	Templeshannon Con. f.	R.C.	–	Nuns		116	244	360	157
123	[illegible]	St. James and Dunbrody,	49	Ramsgrange, m.	R.C.	–	R.C.	–	136	–	136	47

[a] Including value of Free Residence and Garden.

[b] Including value of Free Residence.

Province of Leinster: County of Wexford—*continued.*

Amount paid for Books, Requisites, and Apparatus, on Sale and Free.	Aid granted by the Board during the Year 1874. In Free Stock of Books, Requisites, and Apparatus.	In Salaries, Premiums, and other Grants, &c.	Results Fees, Financial Year.	Amount of Local Emoluments received in Aid of Teacher's Salary. School Fees.	Subscriptions, Endowments, &c.	Total Local Aid.	Vested or Non-Vested.	Number.
£ s. d.	£ s. d.	£ s. d.	£ s. d.	£ s. d.	£ s. d.	£ s. d.		
3 10 8	—	52 16 8	20 14 6	8 0 0	—	8 0 0		63
3 16 1	—	30 10 0	8 19 6	1 16 6	—	1 16 6		64
—	—	24 5 4	21 11 0	0 0 4	—	0 0 4		65
2 2 10	—	40 0 0	10 10 6	5 1 0	—	5 1 0		66
2 15 6	—	39 0 0	16 1 6	8 17 10	—	8 17 10		67
1 18 0	—	36 0 0	11 7 0	10 17 7	—	10 17 7		68
1 6 0	—	33 0 0	7 13 0	3 13 4	6 0 0	a 9 13 4		69
2 10 8	—	24 0 0	9 16 6	4 14 5	—	4 14 6		70
0 11 6	—	19 0 0	10 9 6	4 1 6	—	4 1 6		71
3 10 4	—	30 0 0	10 13 0	4 3 8	—	4 3 8		72
1 8 5	—	45 6 8	14 0 0	13 14 0	—	13 14 0	V.C.	73
—	—	24 11 0	7 3 6	8 18 0	—	8 18 0		74
2 8 6	—	30 6 8	5 7 6	7 10 1	—	7 10 1		75
7 2 0	—	40 10 0	40 18 0	23 4 11	1 10 0	b 24 14 11		76
2 8 0	—	46 0 0	19 16 6	5 4 8	—	5 4 8		77
6 1 0	—	24 0 0	18 5 0	4 10 0	1 10 0	6 0 0		78
4 0 0	—	38 18 4	18 16 6	18 0 1	—	18 0 1		79
1 5 0	—	30 0 0	81 12 6	10 0 0	—	10 0 0		80
5 17 11	—	20 0 8	26 4 0	10 8 0	3 2 0	b 13 10 0		81
4 6 0	—	29 10 8	32 8 6	10 4 0	—	10 4 0		82
6 16 2	—	38 10 0	28 8 6	3 17 10	8 0 0	11 17 10		83
1 10 0	—	—	—	—	—	—		84
8 17 11	—	45 8 4	13 15 6	8 14 6	—	8 14 6		85
—	—	18 6 7	3 0 0	—	—	—		86
—	—	—	10 0 0	4 8 2	—	4 3 2		87
3 17 1	—	34 0 0	14 9 6	12 0 0	—	12 0 0		88
—	—	32 6 0	7 17 6	6 0 0	9 10 0	a 5 10 0		89
0 18 3	—	21 0 6	3 9 0	8 16 1	—	2 16 1		90
6 16 8	—	21 0 0	9 8 4	3 18 0	—	4 15 4		91
2 16 10	—	30 0 0	0 18 0	7 0 0	—	7 0 0		92
8 18 4	—	34 0 0	17 0 6	18 2 10	—	18 8 10		93
0 14 7	—	44 0 0	30 10 0	7 17 4	—	7 17 4		94
5 13 8	—	40 10 0	27 7 0	6 0 0	10 0 0	a 16 0 0	V.C.	95
6 16 1	—	38 0 0	12 5 0	2 10 0	—	2 10 0		96
1 10 6	—	36 18 4	—	3 0 8	6 0 0	a 8 0 8	V.C.	97
3 16 0	—	33 0 0	7 4 6	5 14 4	6 0 0	b 11 13 4		98
3 2 3	—	21 0 0	7 16 6	4 4 11	3 0 0	b 7 4 11		99
1 6 9	—	10 0 0	5 8 0	5 17 5	—	5 17 5	V.C.	100
1 8 10	—	30 0 0	8 5 0	1 12 0	—	1 12 0	V.C.	101
5 11 4	—	44 0 0	14 2 6	10 8 11	8 0 0	b 18 8 11		102
2 15 10	—	16 0 0	6 11 4	8 11 0	—	8 11 0		103
4 15 1	—	30 0 0	0 3 6	11 16 4	—	11 16 4		104
—	—	30 0 0	6 6 0	9 17 6	3 10 6	b 13 7 6		105
3 1 3	—	24 0 0	13 18 0	7 0 6	—	7 3 6		106
8 9 11	—	30 6 6	16 8 0	0 7 3	—	6 7 3		107
1 0 4	—	30 0 0	4 16 0	8 1 6	—	3 1 0		108
4 15 0	—	33 0 0	8 6 0	—	21 0 0	b 21 0 0		109
2 9 10	—	40 8 4	12 8 0	—	—	—		110
12 10 8	—	70 12 0	60 19 6	0 6 11	—	0 6 11		111
7 8 6	—	63 13 8	60 14 6	4 4 3	15 4 3	24 8 6		112
6 10 0	—	—	—	—	—	—		113
8 1 10	—	35 0 0	20 10 6	5 4 7	—	5 4 7		114
4 2 9	—	32 8 0	17 12 0	8 11 10	—	8 11 10		115
6 7 4	—	28 11 4	16 18 0	8 8 11	—	8 8 11		116
} —	—	247 6 8	33 1 8	30 14 1	—	30 14 1	{ V.C. V.C. V.C.	117 118 119
10 14 11	—	110 0 8	36 17 6	14 15 4	—	14 15 4		120
4 11 10	—	—	—	—	—	—		121
0 17 10	—	78 9 8	81 17 6	5 12 4	32 0 0	37 12 4	N.	122
2 10 0	—	26 0 0	11 8 0	9 1 8	—	9 1 8		123

a No Return. d Inoperative. c Including value of Free Garden.

List of Schools in operation on the 31st December, 1874—

Number.	Roll Number of School.	Parish.	District.	School.	Religious Denomination of Managers or Correspondents: Clerical	Lay	Number and Religious Denominations of Teachers: Principals	Assistants	Attendance for the Year: Total number of Pupils on Rolls within the Year: Males	Fem.	Total	Average number daily present
124	10622	St. James & Dunbrody,	40	Ramsgrange, Conv. f.	R.C.	–	None		–	73	73	52
125	6070	Do. . .	–	Duncannon, . .	R.C.	–	R.C.	–	43	63	104	41
126	8213	Do. . .	–	Ballyhack, . .	R.C.	–	R.C.	–	23	38	61	31
127	6111	Shreen, . .	50	Shreen, . . m.	R.C.	–	R.C.	–	93	–	93	55
128	10479	Do. . .	–	Do. . . f.	R.C.	–	R.C.	–	–	66	66	31
129	10784	St. Selskar, .	–	George's-st., . i. m.	–	R.C.	R.C.	–	177	–	177	73
130	10762	Do. . .	–	Do. . . f.	–	R.C.	R.C.	R.C.	–	279	279	73
131	6185	St. Margaret's, .	–	Curracloe, . .	R.C.	–	R.C.	–	55	36	91	43
132	984	St. John's, .	–	Wexford Convent f.	–	R.C.	None		160	383	543	154
133	4919	Do. . .	–	Do. do. i.	–	R.C.	None		410	–	410	79
134	1792	Taghmon, . .	–	Taghmon, . m.	R.C.	–	R.C.	–	97	–	97	44
135	2311	Do. . .	–	Trinity, . .	R.C.	–	R.C.	–	42	21	63	23
136	5118	Do. . .	–	Coolaw, . . f.	R.C.	–	R.C.	–	–	91	91	39
137	6752	Do. . .	–	Tracystown, . .	R.C.	–	R.C.	–	30	37	63	13
138	1985	Tacumshin, .	–	Tacumshin, . .	R.C.	–	R.C.	–	54	46	100	32
139	1010	Tomhaggard, .	–	Tomhaggard, . .	R.C.	–	R.C.	–	56	53	109	30
140	1930	Tintern, . .	49	Ballycullane, . m.	R.C.	–	R.C.	–	83	–	83	41
141	8258	Do. . .	–	Do. . . f.	R.C.	–	R.C.	–	–	97	97	38
142	6223	Do. . .	50	Danescastle, . .	R.C.	–	R.C.	–	53	70	123	46
143	2096	Templetown, .	49	Templetown, . m.	R.C.	–	R.C.	–	123	–	123	32
144	2727	Do. . .	–	Do. . . f.	R.C.	–	R.C.	–	–	97	97	24
145	2142	Templeshanbo, .	50	Kiltealy, . .	R.C.	–	R.C.	–	104	106	210	33
146	3802	Do. . .	–	Ballindaggan, . day.	R.C.	–	R.C.	–	120	136	256	63
				Do. [a] . . evg.	–	–	–	–	–	–	–	–
147	6352	Toome, . .	50	Carnalin, . m.	R.C.	–	R.C.	–	89	–	89	31
148	6364	Do. . .	–	Do. . . f.	R.C.	–	R.C.	–	–	92	92	27
149	10780	Do. . .	–	Ballyroughter, . .	R.C.	–	R.C.	–	16	89	105	30
150	7304	Templeludigan, .	50	Templeludigan, . .	R.C.	–	R.C.	R.C.	68	72	140	55
151	974	Whitechurch, .	49	Ballykelly, . .	R.C.	–	R.C.	R.C.	46	48	94	34
		Total for County Wexford, 151.							8,800	9,518	18,328	7,[illegible]

COUNTY OF

Number.	Roll Number of School.	Parish.	District.	School.	Clerical	Lay	Principals	Assistants	Males	Fem.	Total	Average
1	2276	Arklow, . .	40	Arklow, . . m.	R.C.	–	R.C.	3 R.C.	438	–	438	177
2	2771	Do. . .	–	Do. . . f.	R.C.	–	R.C.	9 R.C.	56	405	471	182
3	971	Baltinglass, .	44	Baltinglass, . m.	R.C.	–	R.C.	1 R.C.	243	–	243	97
4	972	Do. . .	–	Do. Convent f.	R.C.	–	None		–	261	261	136
5	11190	Do. . .	–	Do. Workhouse, [b]	–	–	–	–	–	–	–	–
6	973	Ballymore, .	–	Grange, . . .	R.C.	–	R.C.	R.C.	90	73	163	73
7	975	Bray, . .	40	Bray, . . m.	R.C.	–	R.C.	R.C.	169	–	169	102
8	976	Do. . .	–	Do. . . f.	R.C.	–	R.C.	R.C.	35	94	129	63
9	7180	Do. . .	–	Do. Conv. (No. 2), f.	–	R.C.	None		97	364	461	200
10	6176	Blessington, .	37	Blessington, . m.	R.C.	–	R.C.	R.C.	135	–	135	50
11	6177	Do. . .	–	Do. . . f.	R.C.	–	R.C.	R.C.	–	141	141	66
12	10111	Do. . .	–	Lacken, . . .	–	R.C.	R.C.	R.C.	92	71	163	61
13	10688	Do. . .	–	Kilbride, . . f.	–	R.C.	R.C.	R.C.	77	65	142	[illegible]
14	9454	Boystown, .	–	Hollywood (Lacken?), . .	R.C.	–	R.C.	–	–	79	79	32
15	10130	Do. . .	–	Do. No. 2, m.	R.C.	–	R.C.	–	116	–	116	46
16	974	Do. . .	–	Baltiboys, . f.	–	R.C.	R.C.	–	47	36	83	26
17	11194	Do. . .	–	Granabeg, . .	R.C.	–	R.C.	R.C.	53	78	131	55
18	8347	Ballintemple, .	40	Ballykillageer, . .	R.C.	–	R.C.	–	81	56	137	44
19	7478	Ballykine, .	–	Macreddin, . m.	R.C.	–	R.C.	–	65	–	65	23
20	2718	Do. . .	–	Do. . . f.	R.C.	–	R.C.	–	–	51	51	18
21	11178	Do. . .	–	Aughrim, . . .	R.C.	–	R.C.	R.C.	50	59	109	44
22	3819	Carnew, . .	39	Shillelagh Workhouse,	P.L.	Gds.	R.C. / E.C.	–	21	43	64	39
23	10106	Do. . .	–	Carnew, . . .	–	R.C.	R.C.	1 R.C.	144	135	279	130
24	977	Crosspatrick(?), .	–	Ballyconnell, . m.	R.C.	–	R.C.	–	58	–	58	31
25	978	Do. . .	–	Do. . . f.	R.C.	–	R.C.	R.C.	–	59	59	33

[a] Inoperative

[b] No returns.

Province of Leinster : County of Wexford—*continued.*

Amount paid for Fuel, Repairs, &c., [illegible]	Aid granted by the Board during the Year 1874. In Free Stock of Books, Requisites, and Apparatus.	In Salaries, Premiums, and other Gratuities.	Results Fees, Financial Year.	Amount of Local Endowments received in Aid of Teacher's Salary. School Fees.	Subscriptions, Endowments, &c.	Total Local Aid.	Vested or Non-Vested.	Number.
£ s. d.	£ s. d.	£ s. d.	£ s. d.	£ s. d.	£ s. d.	£ s. d.		
4 16 0	—	4 6 0	8 7 6	2 14 1	—	2 12 1		124
1 8 8	—	20 0 0	8 13 6	4 11 11	—	4 11 11		125
0 10 0	—	24 0 0	7 8 6	2 9 2	—	2 8 8		126
1 19 1	—	20 0 0	8 16 0	5 14 3	—	5 14 3		127
2 10 6	—	20 0 0	8 12 0	2 0 0	—	2 0 0		128
2 18 4	—	30 10 0	15 18 0	1 17 5	11 8 8	13 1 1		129
2 13 0	—	53 8 8	15 17 0	8 5 11	8 18 6	12 4 7		130
1 5 2	—	78 10 0	30 8 6	6 17 6	—	6 17 6		131
23 10 3	—	194 6 8	147 18 6	—	30 0 0	30 0 0		132
5 11 11	—	60 8 0	10 11 6	6 10 0	9 0 8	15 17 8		133
—	—	46 0 0	19 18 0	9 5 11	—	9 5 11		134
0 11 11	—	20 0 0	5 1 0	4 13 6	—	4 13 0		135
2 10 11	—	32 0 0	10 17 6	7 18 8	—	7 18 8		136
—	—	11 18 4	—	0 13 0	—	0 13 0		137
0 14 6	—	24 0 0	6 10 0	9 10 0	—	9 10 0		138
1 6 7	—	20 0 0	9 8 0	8 10 2	—	8 10 2		139
1 7 0	—	27 0 0	11 8 8	8 0 11	—	8 0 11		140
2 16 11	—	20 0 0	20 8 0	5 6 11	—	5 6 11		141
5 12 1	—	24 0 0	18 18 0	5 10 0	—	5 10 0		142
0 16 2	—	24 0 0	4 18 6	1 2 6	—	1 2 6	N.V.R.	143
1 19 8	—	20 0 0	6 18 0	1 5 2	—	1 5 2	N.V.R.	144
—	—	67 8 0	10 10 6	7 10 0	—	7 10 0	V.T.	145
4 1 11	—	58 10 0	7 4 0	8 6 8	2 0 0	10 6 0	V.T.	146
—	—	—	—	—	—	—		
2 15 6	—	24 0 0	18 14 0	2 18 0	—	2 18 0		147
2 15 0	—	20 0 0	10 4 0	8 16 7	—	8 16 7		148
4 10 7	—	20 0 0	14 15 0	10 5 4	—	10 5 4		149
1 5 4	—	39 0 0	21 5 0	5 10 0	—	5 10 0		150
1 4 11	—	24 0 0	10 14 0	7 0 0	—	7 0 0		151
470 18 8	4 2 2	4,707 18 6	1,947 19 5	910 11 6	230 4 5	1,170 16 0		

WICKLOW—101 Schools.

11 3 1	—	158 18 4	43 1 0	65 11 0	—	65 11 0	P.	1
13 1 6	—	134 3 4	49 10 0	25 5 10	—	25 5 10	P.	2
1 17 0	—	73 15 10	21 1 0	16 18 7	13 0 0	29 18 7		3
12 10 5	—	64 2 4	36 16 6	20 11 1	—	20 11 1		4
1 1 8	—	—	—	—	—	—		5
6 6 2	—	79 18 4	23 4 6	10 8 3	10 0 0	* 22 8 8		6
7 19 11	—	60 8 8	30 8 0	25 4 10	20 0 0	45 4 0		7
8 0 2	—	55 8 4	17 0 0	10 7 8	15 0 0	* 25 7 8		8
20 11 8	—	76 15 0	30 0 8	24 0 1	—	24 0 1		9
4 10 0	—	56 0 0	10 2 0	11 13 0	7 7 0	19 0 0		10
1 9 0	—	49 18 8	16 8 0	7 17 8	14 0 0	* 22 17 8		11
1 9 7	—	57 10 8	4 8 0	9 18 10	15 0 0	* 23 18 10	V.C.	12
—	—	46 5 7	7 13 0	10 5 7	—	10 5 7		13
1 18 5	—	20 0 0	7 2 0	5 10 4	8 8 0	* 8 18 4		14
8 1 4	—	24 0 0	6 17 6	13 13 8	—	13 13 8		15
1 3 5	—	20 0 0	6 15 0	4 5 1	10 0 0	* 14 5 1		16
6 18 6	5 0 0	1 18 4	—	6 0 0	5 0 0	* 11 0 0		17
2 13 7	—	24 0 0	11 10 0	4 13 3	3 10 0	* 7 5 3		18
1 13 7	—	20 0 0	4 18 0	1 2 10	—	1 2 10		19
1 6 11	—	20 0 0	5 14 0	1 10 1	—	1 10 1		20
2 7 6	5 0 0	10 10 10	—	11 0 5	2 10 0	* 11 1 5		21
3 1 11	—	—	—	—	—	—		22
9 8 7	—	56 10 0	46 18 0	13 4 10	25 0 0	* 37 4 10		23
—	—	20 0 0	8 10 0	0 10 0	9 0 0	* 15 10 0	V.C.	24
1 15 0	—	40 0 0	10 4 0	4 14 0	9 0 0	* 13 14 0	V.C.	25

* Including value of Free Residence. * Including value of Free Residence and Garden.

List of Schools in operation on the 31st December, 1874.—

Number.	Roll Number of School.	Parish.	District.	School.	Religious Denomination of Manager or Correspondent. Clerical.	Lay.	Number and Religious Denomination of Teachers. Principals.	Assistants.	Attendance for the Year. Total number of Pupils on Rolls within the Year 1874. Males.	Females.	Total.	Average Daily Attendance.
26	8775	Castle Macadam,	40	Newbridge, m.	R.C.	-	R.C.	-	178	-	178	68
27	8880	Do.	-	Do. f.	R.C.	-	R.C.	R.C.	-	158	158	52
28	8210	Crosspatrick,	39	Coolross,	-	R.C.	R.C.	-	81	15	96	18
29	10062	Do.	-	Coolkenny,	R.C.	-	R.C.	-	74	69	143	64
30	5971	Calary,	40	Calary,	-	R.C.	R.C.	-	74	41	115	37
31	7012	Do.	-	Annamoe,	R.C.	-	R.C.	-	44	31	75	29
32	6587	Delgany,	-	Delgany, Conv. f.	-	R.C.	Nuns		-	198	198	82
33	5220	Do.	-	Blacklion,	R.C.	-	R.C.	-	65	88	153	47
34	283	Derrylossary,	-	St. Kevin's, m.	R.C.	-	R.C.	-	141	-	141	55
35	6651	Do.	-	Do. f.	R.C.	-	R.C.	-	21	153	174	61
36	8221	Do.	-	Roundwood,	R.C.	-	R.C.	R.C.	68	73	141	58
37	10672	Do.	-	Lough Dan,	R.C.	-	R.C.	R.C.	38	71	109	51
38	8118	Donaghmore,	44	Britas,	R.C.	-	R.C.	-	45	49	94	38
39	9425	Do.	-	Davidstown,	R.C.	-	R.C.	R.C.	66	49	115	47
40	1808	Donard,	-	Donard,	R.C.	-	R.C.	R.C.	88	77	165	76
41	11116	Do.	-	Donard Demesne,[a]	-	-	-	-	-	-	-	-
42	4928	Dunganstown,	40	Barrandarrig, m.	R.C.	-	R.C.	-	74	-	74	38
43	4078	Do.	-	Do. f.	R.C.	-	R.C.	-	11	73	84	39
44	7418	Do.	-	Ballinamerig, No. 2,	R.C.	-	R.C.	-	30	27	57	18
45	8161	Do.	-	Newtown, m.	R.C.	-	R.C.	R.C.	70	47	117	77
46	5904	Dunlavin,	44	Dunlavin, m.	R.C.	-	R.C.	-	181	-	181	65
47	6950	Do.	-	Do. f.	R.C.	-	R.C.	R.C.	-	118	118	46
48	10898	Do.	-	Merginstown,	R.C.	-	R.C.	-	47	39	76	31
49	997	Drumkay,	40	Wicklow, m.	R.C.	-	R.C.	R.C.	168	-	168	66
50	8456	Do.	-	Do. i.	R.C.	-	R.C.	-	108	-	108	38
51	10416	Do.	-	Do. Convent,	-	R.C.	Nuns		124	377	501	175
52	9196	Ennereilly,	-	Ballymoyle,	-	R.C.	R.C.	-	18	18	42	13
53	8847	Do.	-	Ardinary,	R.C.	-	R.C.	-	31	23	54	18
54	884	Glenealy,	-	Glenealy,	R.C.	-	R.C.	R.C.	85	71	156	38
55	4248	Hollywood,	41	Hollywood, m.	R.C.	-	R.C.	-	90	-	90	46
56	5027	Do.	-	Do. f.	R.C.	-	R.C.	-	-	103	103	44
57	8196	Hacketstown,	60	Rathnagrue, m.	R.C.	-	R.C.	-	158	-	158	55
58	5097	Do.	-	Do. f.	R.C.	-	R.C.	R.C.	-	184	184	56
59	1778	Inch,	40	Johnstown, m.	R.C.	-	R.C.	-	84	-	84	38
60	1778	Do.	-	Do. f.	R.C.	-	R.C.	-	-	63	63	38
61	2317	Kilcommon,	39	Ballycumber,	-	R.C.	R.C.	-	91	57	148	53
62	4082	Do.	-	Crossbridge, m.	R.C.	-	R.C.	-	61	-	61	18
63	4674	Do.	-	Do. f.	R.C.	-	R.C.	-	-	50	50	17
64	6191	Do.	-	Tinahely,	-	R.C.	R.C.	R.C.	93	100	193	104
65	1155	Kilranelagh,	41	Talbotstown, m.	R.C.	-	R.C.	-	131	-	131	34
66	1176	Do.	-	Do. f.	R.C.	-	R.C.	-	-	151	151	58
67	2424	Kiltegan,	39	Baltroyle, m.	R.C.	-	R.C.	-	110	-	110	61
68	2438	Do.	-	Do. f.	R.C.	-	R.C.	-	-	88	88	29
69	2241	Kilbride,	40	Barranisky,	R.C.	-	R.C.	-	50	41	91	34
70	10715	Do.	-	Templerainey,	R.C.	-	R.C.	-	41	50	91	27
71	7074	Kilcoole,	-	Kilcoole,	R.C.	-	R.C.	-	100	61	161	65
72	7859	Knockrath,	-	Claravale, temp.	R.C.	-	R.C.	-	46	53	99	39
73	1819	Do.	-	Trooperstown,	-	R.C.	R.C.	-	80	61	141	46
74	1922	Do.	-	Glenmalure,	R.C.	-	R.C.	-	28	30	65	19
75	7561	Killiskey,	-	Ballyduff,	R.C.	-	R.C.	-	43	61	104	33
76	981	Kilmacanoge,	-	Kilmacanoge,	R.C.	-	R.C.	-	81	67	148	13
77	1780	Mullinacuff,	39	Kilquiggan, m.	R.C.	-	R.C.	-	68	-	68	32
78	8222	Do.	-	Do. f.	R.C.	-	R.C.	-	-	68	68	17
79	10623	Do.	-	Ballyraheen,	R.C.	-	R.C.	-	41	49	90	27
80	4786	Moyacomb,	-	Parkbridge, f.	R.C.	-	R.C.	-	64	54	118	32
81	8451	Moyne,	40	Askanagap,	R.C.	-	R.C.	-	31	31	62	33
82	5824	Newcastle,	-	Newtownmountkennedy, m.	R.C.	-	R.C.	-	109	-	109	41
83	4801	Do.	-	Do. f.	R.C.	-	R.C.	-	-	96	96	43
84	8023	Do.	-	Newcastle,	R.C.	-	R.C.	-	51	57	108	31
85	11119	Powerscourt,	-	Castletown,	R.C.	-	R.C.	-	88	84	172	69
86	9790	Do.	-	Enniskerry,	R.C.	-	R.C.	-	44	26	70	24
87	10177	Do.	-	Do.[b] No. 2,	-	-	-	-	-	-	-	-

a Including value of Free Residence.

b Including value of Free Residence and Garden.

Province of Leinster: County of Wicklow—*continued.*

Amount paid for Books, Requisites, and Apparatus, at Reduced Prices.	Aid granted by the Board during the Year 1874: In Free Stock of Books, Requisites, and Apparatus.	In Salaries, Premiums, and other Gratuities.	Results Fees, Financial Year.	Amount of Local Contributions received in Aid of Teacher's Salary: School Fees.	Subscriptions, Endowments, &c.	Total Local Aid.	Vested in Board or Trustees.	Number.
£ s. d.	£ s. d.	£ s. d.	£ s. d.	£ s. d.	£ s. d.	£ s. d.		
9 15 3	—	41 0 0	19 0 0	9 9 11	—	9 9 11		26
1 8 2	—	29 17 4	14 8 0	3 0 3	—	8 8 8		27
1 9 8	—	24 0 0	5 8 0	8 6 9	79 0 0	* 88 6 8		28
7 8 7	—	33 0 0	18 14 0	4 6 6	—	4 6 6		29
4 1 3	—	21 0 0	10 1 0	4 8 7	31 0 0	* 35 8 7		30
1 8 7	—	29 0 0	5 8 0	3 12 11	24 5 4	* 27 18 3		31
4 13 11	—	11 1 4	18 7 0	11 9 4	—	11 9 4		32
3 5 0	—	30 0 0	8 4 0	2 15 9	10 0 0	12 15 9		33
1 17 0	—	41 10 0	14 17 0	9 7 4	7 15 0	17 2 4		34
3 5 0	—	70 8 4	21 0 0	11 15 0	17 0 8	* 29 1 5		35
6 15 3	—	63 7 3	10 9 0	10 18 1	4 10 0	* 15 8 1		36
4 4 2	—	75 11 1	25 5 0	19 16 0	11 0 0	* 30 16 0		37
2 18 1	—	30 0 0	6 17 6	6 1 8	—	6 1 8		38
3 9 2	—	47 0 0	14 17 6	4 10 0	—	4 10 6		39
4 15 4	—	44 0 0	17 18 0	7 0 0	—	7 0 0		40
1 9 4	4 0 0	—	—	—	—	—		41
1 5 8	—	30 0 0	11 18 0	3 7 6	—	3 7 6		42
1 11 8	—	24 8 8	11 19 6	5 8 7	—	5 8 7		43
1 11 4	—	30 0 0	4 12 0	2 13 8	—	2 13 8		44
1 17 2	—	44 0 0	5 19 0	1 0 6	4 0 0	* 5 0 6		45
8 1 8	—	63 3 4	13 18 0	5 1 0	—	5 1 0		46
8 11 8	—	46 0 0	15 0 0	5 15 1	—	5 15 1		47
2 1 1	—	30 0 0	11 11 6	4 16 8	2 0 0	* 6 16 8		48
7 8 11	—	32 0 0	7 3 6	8 15 0	3 0 0	11 15 0		49
0 5 0	—	30 0 0	9 11 8	1 16 11	—	1 16 11		50
—	—	111 10 8	41 7 6	18 8 1	—	18 8 1		51
—	—	24 8 8	8 16 0	3 9 10	30 0 0	* 33 9 10		52
1 6 11	—	30 0 0	2 16 0	2 0 8	—	2 0 8		53
8 0 8	—	41 8 0	16 9 0	8 10 7	—	8 10 7		54
8 6 6	—	30 0 0	15 0 6	6 18 4	—	6 18 4		55
3 15 3	—	37 10 0	15 13 8	0 0 6	—	0 0 6		56
8 10 6	—	25 10 0	11 1 0	3 4 0	—	3 4 0		57
4 7 3	—	44 10 0	17 11 0	8 15 0	—	8 15 0		58
1 10 5	—	84 0 0	—	8 18 5	—	8 18 5		59
1 17 8	—	30 0 0	11 6 0	8 18 0	—	8 18 0		60
1 8 0	—	24 0 0	16 8 0	1 16 8	10 0 0	* 11 16 8	T.B.	61
11 18 11	—	24 0 0	2 3 0	0 11 8	—	5 11 6		62
0 10 0	—	30 0 0	8 8 0	1 17 0	—	1 17 0		63
7 8 6	—	80 12 4	40 15 0	16 1 8	24 0 0	* 40 1 8		64
1 9 8	—	24 9 8	8 15 0	4 2 0	—	4 2 0	V.T.	65
8 15 0	—	24 0 0	19 6 0	4 1 8	—	4 1 8	V.T.	66
1 8 0	—	27 0 0	7 9 0	1 10 0	—	1 10 0	B.	67
4 0 0	—	30 0 0	8 1 0	4 6 8	—	4 6 8	B.	68
1 5 10	—	24 0 8	14 16 0	2 15 0	2 0 0	* 4 15 0		69
1 18 7	—	30 0 0	7 12 8	1 14 2	—	1 14 2		70
5 11 10	—	34 8 4	14 7 0	12 14 4	5 0 0	* 17 14 4		71
8 11 10	—	27 0 0	15 14 0	8 13 7	—	8 13 7		72
6 0 8	—	30 0 0	18 13 0	5 4 0	7 18 0	* 13 10 0	V.T.	73
—	—	30 0 0	4 8 8	1 18 4	4 18 0	* 6 7 1		74
3 2 6	—	30 0 0	18 9 8	5 19 5	—	6 15 5		75
4 2 9	—	28 0 0	21 8 0	0 18 5	—	8 16 5		76
2 5 1	—	30 18 4	11 19 0	8 8 8	10 0 0	* 18 8 8	V.T.	77
1 7 8	—	30 0 0	8 14 0	5 19 0	6 0 0	* 11 19 0	V.T.	78
8 10 8	—	27 8 8	14 11 0	2 4 0	8 0 0	* 5 4 0		79
3 13 8	—	24 0 0	11 14 0	5 0 8	—	5 0 8		80
1 0 1	—	10 0 0	8 18 8	1 7 0	—	1 7 0		81
8 13 4	—	30 0 0	11 5 0	9 5 8	—	0 5 9		82
1 8 2	—	29 15 0	18 15 0	8 14 4	—	8 14 4		83
—	—	31 0 0	7 14 0	3 0 0	—	3 0 6		84
8 1 0	—	33 0 0	15 5 0	15 9 8	—	15 9 8		85
8 5 8	—	24 0 0	8 17 0	2 10 7	33 0 0	* 35 10 7		86
—	—	—	—	—	—	—		87

* Complete returns not available.

† Inoperative.

List of Schools in operation on the 31st December, 1874.—

No.	Roll Number of School.	Parish.	District.	School.	Religious Denomination of Managers or Correspondents: Clerical.	Lay.	Name and Religious Denomination of Teachers: Principals.	Assistants.	Total number of Pupils on Rolls within the Year 1874: Males.	Fem.	Total.	Average Daily Attendance
87	[illegible]	Preban,	40	Annaghcarragh, m.	R.C.	–	R.C.	–	80	–	80	[illegible]
[illegible]	[illegible]	Do.	–	Do. f.	R.C.	–	R.C.	–	–	[illegible]	[illegible]	[illegible]
[illegible]	[illegible]	Do.	–	Moneylagh,	R.C.	–	R.C.	–	35	37	72	[illegible]
81	[illegible]	Do.	–	Ballinacarrig,	R.C.	–	R.C.	R.C.	[illegible]	70	[illegible]	[illegible]
[illegible]	[illegible]	Do.	–	Rathdrum, m.	R.C.	–	R.C.	R.C.	[illegible]	–	[illegible]	[illegible]
[illegible]	[illegible]	Do.	–	Do.[a] f.	–	–	–	–	–	–	–	–
[illegible]	[illegible]	Do.	–	Do. Workhouse,	P.L.Gds.		R.C.	–	60	40	100	47
[illegible]	[illegible]	Do.	–	St. Michael's Conv. f.	R.C.	–	Nuns		24	159	[illegible]	[illegible]
[illegible]	[illegible]	Rathdrum,	[illegible]	Baranford-on-Slaney,	R.C.	–	R.C.	R.C.	[illegible]	[illegible]	[illegible]	[illegible]
97	[illegible]	Rathnew,	[illegible]	Killoughter,	R.C.	–	R.C.	–	[illegible]	[illegible]	74	31
[illegible]	[illegible]	Do.	–	Ballybeak,	R.C.	–	R.C.	–	[illegible]	[illegible]	74	[illegible]
[illegible]	[illegible]	Do.	–	Ashford,	R.C.	–	R.C.	R.C.	[illegible]	76	144	87
100	[illegible]	Do.	–	Rathnew,	R.C.	–	R.C.	R.C.	84	[illegible]	[illegible]	[illegible]
101	[illegible]	Redcross,	–	Redcross, No. 2,	R.C.	–	R.C.	–	43	44	87	[illegible]
		Total for County Wicklow, 101 Schools.							[illegible]	8,177	14,767	[illegible]

CONNAUGHT

COUNTY OF

No.	Roll Number of School.	Parish.	District.	School.	Clerical.	Lay.	Principals.	Assistants.	Males.	Fem.	Total.	Average Daily Attendance
1	[illegible]	Arran,	81	Onaght, f.	R.C.	–	R.C.	–	[illegible]	61	135	87
2	[illegible]	Do.	–	Innishmaan Island,[d]	–	–	–	–	–	–	–	–
3	[illegible]	Abbey,	[illegible]	Rivervfield,	R.C.	–	R.C.	–	67	81	[illegible]	[illegible]
4	[illegible]	Abbeygormican,	[illegible]	Mullagh, m.	R.C.	–	R.C.	–	86	–	86	[illegible]
5	[illegible]	Do.	–	Do. f.	R.C.	–	R.C.	–	–	[illegible]	[illegible]	[illegible]
6	[illegible]	Aughrim,	–	Aughrim, m.	R.C.	–	R.C.	–	64	–	64	[illegible]
7	[illegible]	Do.	–	Do. f.	R.C.	–	R.C.	–	–	70	76	[illegible]
8	[illegible]	Abbeyknockmoy,	–	Abbeyknockmoy, m.	R.C.	–	R.C.	–	47	–	57	[illegible]
9	[illegible]	Do.	–	Do. f.	R.C.	–	R.C.	–	–	100	100	84
10	[illegible]	Do.	–	Cloonbrock, m.	–	R.C.	R.C.	–	151	–	151	61
11	[illegible]	Do.	–	Do. f.	–	R.C.	R.C.	R.C.	–	199	199	47
12	[illegible]	Do.	–	Daly's Grove,	–	[illegible]	R.C.	–	40	[illegible]	108	[illegible]
13	[illegible]	Ardrahan,	42	Castle Daly,	–	R.C.	R.C.	–	[illegible]	77	146	[illegible]
14	[illegible]	Do.	–	Ardrahan,	–	R.C.	R.C.	–	103	84	187	[illegible]
15	[illegible]	Do.	–	Ballyglass,[d]	–	–	–	–	–	–	–	–
16	[illegible]	Abbeyknockmoy,	[illegible]	Newtown,[d] m.	–	R.C.	–	–	183	–	[illegible]	[illegible]
17	[illegible]	Do.	–	Do. f.	–	R.C.	R.C.	–	–	215	215	[illegible]
18	[illegible]	Ahascragh,	97	Hollygrove,	R.C.	–	R.C.	–	[illegible]	36	174	[illegible]
19	[illegible]	Athenry,	[illegible]	Newcastle, m.	R.C.	–	R.C.	–	121	–	121	41
20	[illegible]	Do.	–	Do. f.	R.C.	–	R.C.	–	–	104	104	[illegible]
21	[illegible]	Do.	24	Athenry, m.	R.C.	–	R.C.	R.C.	178	–	178	67
22	[illegible]	Do.	–	Do. f.	R.C.	–	R.C.	R.C.	–	178	178	[illegible]
23	[illegible]	Do.	–	Coldwood,	R.C.	–	R.C.	–	[illegible]	41	[illegible]	[illegible]
24	[illegible]	Annaghdown,	–	Carrabeg, f.	R.C.	–	R.C.	–	–	[illegible]	[illegible]	[illegible]
25	[illegible]	Do.	–	Lisnagrath,	R.C.	–	R.C.	R.C.	146	[illegible]	240	[illegible]
26	[illegible]	Do.	[illegible]	Castle Hackett Cat. Agr. m.	–	R.C.	R.C.	–	109	–	109	[illegible]
27	[illegible]	Do.	–	Do. f.	–	R.C.	R.C.	–	–	74	74	[illegible]
28	1331	Ballynakill,	[illegible]	Woodford, m.	R.C.	–	R.C.	–	161	–	161	[illegible]
29	1318	Do.	–	Do. f.	R.C.	–	R.C.	R.C.	5	201	[illegible]	[illegible]
30	[illegible]	Do.	–	Dunlry, m.	R.C.	–	R.C.	–	69	–	[illegible]	[illegible]
31	[illegible]	Do.	–	Do. f.	R.C.	–	R.C.	–	–	87	87	[illegible]
32	[illegible]	Do.	–	Ballynakill 1st Cl. Agr.	–	R.C.	R.C.	–	165	–	[illegible]	51
33	[illegible]	Do.	–	Do. f.	–	R.C.	R.C.	–	–	114	114	[illegible]
34	[illegible]	Do.	27	Tubbercog,	R.C.	–	R.C.	–	116	[illegible]	207	[illegible]
35	4016	Do.	34	Irish Waste Land Society,	R.C.	–	R.C.	R.C.	80	[illegible]	148	[illegible]
36	[illegible]	Do.	27	Ballinacarry,	R.C.	–	R.C.	–	[illegible]	70	[illegible]	34
37	[illegible]	Do.	–	Gurtnaskeave,	R.C.	–	R.C.	R.C.	189	67	209	67
38	6780	Do.	[illegible]	Rossgray,[d]	–	–	–	–	–	–	–	–

[a] Inoperative. [b] Including value of Free Residence and Garden. [c] Including value of Free Residence.

Province of LEINSTER: County of WICKLOW—*continued.*

Amount paid for Books, Requisites, and Apparatus, at Reduced Prices.	Aid granted by the Board during the Year 1874. In Free Stock of Books, Requisites, and Apparatus.	In Salaries, Premiums, and other Gratuities.	Results Fees, Financial Year.	Amount of Local Emoluments received in Aid of Teacher's Salary. School Fees.	Subscriptions, Endowments, &c.	Total Local Aid.	Vested or Non-vested.	Number.
£ s. d.	£ s. d.	£ s. d.	£ s. d.	£ s. d.	£ s. d.	£ s. d.		
—	—	97 0 0	8 19 0	6 12 4	3 7 8	13 0 0		[illegible]
4 5 7	—	20 0 0	6 10 0	6 16 4	—	5 16 6		[illegible]
0 15 3	—	30 0 0	5 1 6	1 13 6	—	1 13 6		[illegible]
6 8 6	—	71 8 4	17 10 6	11 13 2	—	11 19 9	V.F.	91
7 7 7	—	66 16 8	26 11 0	21 13 2	6 0 0	27 13 2	V.F.	92
—	—	—	—	—	—	—	N.C.	93
5 19 8	—	5 10 0	—	—	—	—		[illegible]
14 2 0	—	61 6 8	32 6 6	15 13 9	4 0 0	19 13 9		[illegible]
5 13 10	—	43 0 0	15 11 0	7 18 0	6 15 0	*14 [illegible]		[illegible]
3 4 9	—	30 0 0	0 0 0	5 10 9	—	5 10 0		[illegible]
3 17 3	—	30 0 0	7 6 6	5 9 5	—	5 9 5		[illegible]
5 8 9	—	61 0 0	17 3 0	10 8 1	—	10 8 1		[illegible]
1 19 0	—	44 0 0	10 6 0	8 9 [illegible]	8 0 0	*[illegible]		100
1 13 5	—	20 0 0	0 10 0	1 17 1	—	1 17 1		101
516 19 5	14 0 0	3,902 7 3	1,334 3 0	727 0 1	327 14 8	1,056 3 8		

—1,139 Schools.

GALWAY—302 (?) Schools.

1 10 7	—	11 0 0	7 14 6	4 15 6	—	4 15 0		1
1 6 3	—	—	—	—	—	—		2
1 14 0	—	20 0 0	8 0 6	3 0 0	—	3 0 0	V.F.	3
6 0 6	—	21 0 0	8 7 6	2 4 11	—	2 4 11		4
—	—	20 0 0	5 7 0	2 7 3	—	2 7 3		5
1 12 11	—	24 0 0	4 0 0	0 14 7	—	0 14 7		6
1 9 11	—	20 0 0	4 10 0	2 9 10	—	2 9 10		7
0 10 5	—	—	—	0 6 6	—	0 6 6		8
6 9 9	—	26 10 0	7 14 6	2 6 1	—	2 6 1		9
6 14 0	—	26 0 0	10 8 6	16 17 9	7 0 0	*23 17 9		10
2 6 6	—	30 0 0	14 17 0	10 5 3	—	10 5 3		11
—	—	20 0 0	9 10 0	2 1 6	2 0 0	*4 1 6		12
1 5 8	—	20 0 0	11 6 0	0 18 6	0 10 0	*1 3 6	V.C.	13
5 7 1	—	46 0 0	6 19 0	10 15 1	—	10 15 1	V.C.	14
—	—	—	—	—	—	—		15
0 10 2	—	21 0 0	—	0 6 1	—	0 6 1	V.F.	16
1 10 6	—	24 0 0	8 9 0	1 0 8	6 0 0	7 0 8	V.F.	17
6 6 6	—	43 6 8	6 10 6	1 10 6	—	1 10 6		18
3 0 10	—	24 0 0	14 10 6	3 17 7	—	3 17 7		19
1 8 10	—	24 0 0	7 14 0	3 15 4	—	3 15 4		20
6 17 9	—	62 0 0	14 18 0	6 11 3	—	6 11 3		21
2 19 6	—	53 6 8	9 10 6	0 6 6	—	0 6 6		22
1 11 4	5 0 0	[illegible] 6 8	—	3 7 11	—	3 7 11		23
5 14 0	—	26 0 0	6 13 6	1 8 0	3 1 6	4 9 6		24
5 9 11	—	—	16 14 0	6 2 8	—	6 2 8		25
1 6 6	—	61 10 0	8 10 0	1 16 0	4 0 0	*5 16 0		26
—	—	20 0 0	6 18 6	1 10 0	—	1 10 0		27
1 6 0	—	54 0 0	10 2 0	6 0 4	—	5 0 4	A.	28
2 18 0	—	48 0 0	21 13 0	6 0 0	—	6 0 0	A.	29
1 14 10	—	24 2 8	14 0 6	4 4 0	—	4 4 0	V.F.	30
6 16 9	—	30 0 0	15 18 6	3 3 7	—	3 3 7	V.F.	31
4 6 7	—	24 0 0	9 0 6	0 18 0	—	0 18 0	A.	32
4 0 9	—	20 0 0	6 14 0	0 19 0	—	0 19 0	A.	33
9 2 6	—	62 6 8	15 16 8	6 0 0	7 10 0	*13 10 0		34
9 18 0	—	44 0 0	18 17 0	6 1 10	—	6 1 10	V.F.	35
2 7 6	—	20 0 0	7 0 0	3 8 4	—	3 8 4		36
6 10 9	—	46 15 0	6 11 0	6 13 11	—	6 13 11		37
1 5 6	—	—	—	—	—	—		38

§ No Teacher. * Including value of Free Garden. † Closed.

List of Schools in operation on the 31st December, 1874.—

Number.	Roll Number of School.	Parish.	District.	School.	Religious Denominations of Managers or Correspondents: Clerical	Lay	Number and Religious Denominations of Teachers: Principals	Assistants	Attendance for the Year: Total number of Pupils on Rolls within the Year 1874: Male	Fem.	Total	Average daily attendance
39	7391	Ballynakill,	27	Letterfrack,	R.C.	–	R.C.	–	54	43	97	33
40	8691	Do.	–	Kylemore,[b]	–	–	–	–	–	–	–	–
41	8310	Do.	35	Shrugh, m.	R.C.	–	R.C.	–	108	–	108	40
42	8311	Do.	–	Do. f.	R.C.	–	R.C.	–	–	94	94	41
43	9197	Do.	–	Abbey of Kilnalahan,	R.C.	–	R.C.	R.C.	82	77	159	61
44	9441	Do.	28	Tully,	R.C.	–	R.C.	–	91	115	206	75
45	8695	Do.	–	Lettergesh, m.	–	R.C.	R.C.	–	86	–	86	30
46	8696	Do.	–	Do. f.	–	R.C.	R.C.	–	–	84	84	35
47	9564	Do.	48	Loughaunrick,	R.C.	–	R.C.	–	40	33	73	29
48	1832	Ballymacward,	30	Esker, m.	R.C.	–	R.C.	–	130	–	130	60
49	4224	Do.	–	Do. f.	R.C.	–	R.C.	–	–	118	118	55
50	7925	Do.	–	Lismane, m.	R.C.	–	R.C.	–	190	–	190	55
51	7930	Do.	–	Do. f.	R.C.	–	R.C.	–	–	124	124	47
52	3232	Beagh,	42	Cragg,	–	R.C.	R.C.	–	33	28	61	28
53	6578	Do.	–	Gort Workhouse,	P.L.	Gds.	R.C.	–	33	32	65	34
54	9761	Do.	–	Lough Cutra, f.	–	R.C.	R.C.	R.C.	–	117	117	54
55	9773	Do.	–	Do. m.	–	R.C.	R.C.	–	181	–	181	61
56	6148	Belclare,	32	Sylane,	–	R.C.	R.C.	R.C.	135	112	247	83
57	[illegible]	Do.	–	Belclare,	R.C.	–	R.C.	R.C.	118	100	218	74
58	4617	Boyounagh,	27	Stonetown, m.	R.C.	–	R.C.	–	170	–	170	60
59	[illegible]	Do.	–	Do. f.	R.C.	–	R.C.	R.C.	–	148	148	51
60	9084	Do.	–	Glenamaddy,	R.C.	–	R.C.	R.C.	156	123	279	84
61	6753	Do.	–	Do. Workhouse,	P.L.	Gds.	R.C.	–	24	37	61	22
62	8401	Do.	33	Cashel,	R.C.	–	R.C.	–	152	105	257	45
63	6927	Ballindoon,	34	Derrygimla, m.	R.C.	–	R.C.	–	166	–	166	46
64	6928	Do.	–	Do. f.	R.C.	–	R.C.	–	–	122	122	31
65	9133	Do.	–	Kyleknocka,	R.C.	–	R.C.	–	47	45	92	34
66	9716	Do.	–	Alliebrack,	R.C.	–	R.C.	–	61	50	111	38
67	7107	Ballymacourty,	–	Gurrane, m.	R.C.	–	R.C.	–	88	–	88	35
68	7863	Do.	–	Do. f.	R.C.	–	R.C.	–	–	93	93	34
69	8919	Do.	–	Tonin,	R.C.	–	R.C.	–	18	29	33	16
70	7194	Lower Ballinakill,	36	Derryoober,	R.C.	–	R.C.	R.C.	185	115	300	91
71	7811	Bullaun,	–	Bullaun,	R.C.	–	R.C.	–	66	48	114	39
72	8411	Killererin,	96	Killeelaun,	R.C.	–	R.C.	–	131	98	229	66
73	1400	Clontuskert,	30	Clontuskert, m.	R.C.	–	R.C.	–	160	–	160	31
74	8207	Do.	–	Do. f.	R.C.	–	R.C.	–	–	78	78	32
75	8209	Clonrush,	42	Lakyle,	–	R.C.	R.C.	R.C.	193	98	291	92
76	3657	Clonkeen,	33	Gorteen,[d]	–	–	–	–	–	–	–	–
77	3412	Do.	–	Clonkeen Kerrill, 1st Class Agricultural	R.C.	–	R.C.	–	113	–	113	35
78	10733	Do.	–	Do. f.	R.C.	–	R.C.	–	–	101	101	35
79	7928	Clare Galway,	34	Clare Galway, m.	R.C.	–	R.C.	–	101	–	101	30
80	8167	Do.	–	Do. f.	R.C.	–	R.C.	–	–	181	181	41
81	6860	Cargin,	38	Cloghagh, m.	–	R.C.	R.C.	–	79	–	79	31
82	6924	Do.	–	Do. f.	–	R.C.	R.C.	–	–	117	117	42
83	8173	Clonfert,	35	Clonfert,	R.C.	–	R.C.	–	56	59	115	34
84	8256	Do.	35	Esker, No. 2,	–	R.C.	R.C.	R.C.	95	67	162	57
85	8541	Do.	35	Kylemore,[f]	–	–	–	–	–	–	–	–
86	8558	Do.	–	Lawrencetown, f.	R.C.	–	R.C.	–	–	118	118	46
87	8748	Do.	–	Do. m.	R.C.	–	R.C.	–	97	–	97	33
88	6249	Clonbern,	33	Lorbin,	R.C.	–	R.C.	R.C.	153	165	318	83
89	[illegible]	Do.	–	Mahanagh,	R.C.	–	R.C.	R.C.	115	181	295	73
90	8737	Cummer,	–	Ballinderry,[a] m.	–	–	–	–	–	–	–	–
91	9066	Do.	–	Do. f.	–	R.C.	R.C.	–	11	132	143	46
92	3327	Creg,	–	Ashford,	–	R.C.	R.C.	–	45	42	87	37
93	7213	Donaghpatrick,	–	Cahirallistrane,	–	R.C.	R.C.	–	130	67	207	61
94	10752	Do.	–	Knockroe,	R.C.	–	R.C.	R.C.	137	183	310	69
95	7844	Dunmore,	–	Dunmore, m.	R.C.	–	R.C.	–	227	–	227	76
96	8920	Do.	–	Do. f.	R.C.	–	R.C.	R.C.	–	263	263	97
97	7390	Do.	–	Ballinlass,	–	R.C.	R.C.	–	79	35	114	47
98	9108	Do.	–	Shanballymore,	R.C.	–	R.C.	–	80	73	153	69
99	9120	Do.	–	Fleaka,	R.C.	–	R.C.	R.C.	164	131	295	76
100	9251	Do.	–	Garrafrauns,	R.C.	–	R.C.	–	118	66	184	31

[a] Including value of Free Residence. [b] Closed. [c] Including value of Free Garden.

Province of CONNAUGHT: County of GALWAY—*continued.*

Amount paid for Books, Requisites, and Apparatus at Reduced Prices.	Aid granted by the Board during the Year 1874. In Free Stock of Books, Requisites, and Apparatus.	In Salaries, Premiums, and other Gratuities.	Results Fees, Financial Year.	Amount of Local Emoluments received in Aid of Teacher's Salary. School Fees.	Subscriptions, Endowments, &c.	Total Local Aid.	Vested or Non-Vested.	Number.
£ s. d.	£ s. d.	£ s. d.	£ s. d.	£ s. d.	£ s. d.	£ s. d.		
2 4 4	—	20 9 0	9 9 6	4 10 0	15 0 0	*30 10 0		39
—	—	—	—	—	—	—	N.V.	40
8 0 6	—	21 13 4	16 0 0	6 18 1	—	6 18 1		41
2 5 3	—	24 0 0	14 8 0	4 4 4	—	4 4 4		42
1 11 6	—	44 0 0	13 0 6	5 4 9	—	5 4 9		43
4 1 10	—	24 9 0	16 13 6	—	—	—		44
—	—	—	4 9 0	1 9 8	20 0 0	*21 9 8	V.C.	45
—	—	20 0 0	0 11 0	—	10 0 0	10 0 0	V.C.	46
—	—	20 0 0	4 1 6	5 0 0	—	5 0 0		47
5 10 5	—	21 0 0	7 13 0	3 1 0	—	3 1 0	V.V.	48
1 14 3	—	25 0 0	6 16 6	2 7 10	—	2 7 10	N.V.	49
1 5 9	—	24 0 0	7 16 6	2 2 6	—	2 2 6		50
3 0 1	—	24 10 0	18 7 6	1 13 9	—	1 13 9		51
1 6 11	—	21 0 0	6 8 0	2 14 9	2 0 0	*4 14 9		52
0 8 4	—	—	—	—	—	—		53
4 8 8	—	50 0 0	17 17 0	12 18 3	11 10 0	*24 8 3		54
1 7 6	—	30 0 0	15 0 6	15 0 6	5 0 0	21 0 6		55
2 8 10	—	48 0 0	31 4 0	10 1 11	—	10 1 11	N.V.	56
2 15 9	—	60 0 0	18 19 0	7 3 10	—	7 3 10		57
3 0 0	—	24 0 0	—	2 1 4	—	2 1 4		58
1 4 8	—	34 18 4	—	1 13 9	—	1 13 9		59
5 13 6	—	17 8 0	15 1 0	4 10 4	—	4 10 4		60
1 1 6	—	—	—	—	—	—		61
6 10 1	—	27 6 8	7 18 6	7 10 0	1 0 0	*8 10 0		62
1 4 11	—	20 0 0	10 18 0	3 17 0	1 0 0	*4 17 0		63
1 10 11	—	24 0 0	8 0 0	2 4 11	1 0 0	*3 4 11		64
1 14 9	—	20 0 0	9 14 0	0 8 9	—	0 8 9		65
—	—	20 0 0	8 18 0	0 18 0	—	0 18 0		66
1 11 0	—	24 0 0	7 8 6	1 14 0	—	1 14 0		67
6 9 3	—	20 0 0	8 6 0	1 10 6	—	1 10 6		68
—	—	20 0 6	1 6 0	0 10 0	—	0 10 0		69
4 6 6	—	24 13 4	26 18 8	14 14 4	—	14 14 4	V.C.	70
1 4 10	—	21 0 0	7 2 6	1 8 6	4 0 0	6 0 5		71
—	—	26 10 0	9 18 6	—	—	—		72
1 5 8	—	24 0 0	11 8 0	2 0 1	0 10 0	*3 10 1	V.V.	73
1 3 8	—	24 0 0	8 16 0	1 18 9	—	1 18 9	V.V.	74
2 17 7	—	26 0 0	31 8 0	15 4 0	—	15 4 0	V.V.	75
3 17 4	—	24 0 0	6 10 0	—	—	—		76
—	—	27 0 0	6 9 0	3 4 2	24 18 9	*28 8 11		77
0 10 0	—	28 0 0	8 0 6	1 7 11	—	1 7 11		78
5 18 6	—	27 0 6	15 16 0	9 16 10	—	9 13 10		79
7 14 6	—	45 13 0	11 4 8	8 18 4	—	8 18 4		80
1 11 8	—	21 0 0	11 11 0	4 0 1	6 0 0	*10 0 1		81
1 16 10	—	24 10 0	15 4 0	0 8 6	5 0 0	5 8 6		82
2 0 6	—	20 0 0	10 8 6	6 7 8	1 0 0	*7 7 8		83
5 9 6	—	22 10 0	23 3 6	6 0 8	12 0 0	*18 0 0		84
1 6 2	—	—	2 17 0	—	—	—		85
5 10 3	—	24 16 8	19 15 0	4 17 11	—	4 17 11		86
1 5 2	—	24 0 0	8 18 0	2 5 9	—	2 5 9		87
7 9 1	—	40 0 0	20 8 0	4 0 0	—	4 0 0		88
4 15 0	—	44 0 0	25 1 0	3 8 2	5 0 0	*8 8 2		89
—	—	41 0 0	—	—	—	—		90
2 8 8	—	20 0 0	11 7 6	6 3 0	—	6 3 0		91
9 17 7	—	28 0 0	7 17 0	—	74 0 0	*74 0 0		92
2 0 6	—	28 6 8	16 16 6	4 2 4	—	4 2 4		93
6 15 5	—	54 15 4	24 14 6	6 6 5	—	6 6 5		94
6 19 1	—	65 15 4	36 1 6	12 19 0	—	12 19 0		95
9 16 0	—	40 0 0	33 7 6	12 0 0	—	12 0 0		96
3 0 2	—	74 1 8	6 0 6	5 9 3	4 0 0	9 9 3		97
2 7 10	—	19 3 4	10 10 0	4 14 8	—	4 14 8		98
2 14 10	—	20 13 4	27 8 8	15 2 6	—	15 2 0		99
0 19 3	—	24 0 0	6 11 0	4 19 11	—	4 19 11		100

a Returns not available. b Including value of Free Residence and Garden. c No Returns. d Temporary.

List of Schools in operation on the 31st December, 1874.—

Number.	Roll Number of School.	Parish.	District.	School.	Religious Denomination of Managers or Correspondents: Clerical.	Lay.	Religious Denomination of Teachers: Principals.	Assistants.	Total Number of Pupils on Rolls within the Year 1874: Males.	Fem.	Total.	Average daily attendance
101	10432	Dunmore,	32	Carrakeel,[a]	–	–	–	–	–	–	–	–
102	10475	Do.	–	Sylane, Dunmore, m.	R.C.	–	R.C.	2R.C.	96	80	176	59
103	7246	Donanaghta,	33	Eyrecourt,	R.C.	–	R.C.	–	66	47	105	51
104	7889	Fohanagh,	–	Fohenagh,	R.C.	–	R.C.	–	73	72	145	53
105	10462	[illegible]	34	[illegible]	R.C.	–	R.C.	–	75	71	146	57
106	8757	Inishcaltra,	42	Inishcaltra, m.	–	R.C.	R.C.	–	104	–	102	36
107	8873	Do.	–	Do. f.	–	R.C.	R.C.	–	–	105	105	85
108	4812	[illegible]	34	Kilreenagh,	R.C.	–	R.C.	R.C.	87	84	161	77
109	7914	[illegible]	–	[illegible]	R.C.	–	R.C.	–	41	59	100	57
110	9842	Do.	–	Killeany,	R.C.	–	R.C.	–	40	60	99	45
111	8231	Killallaghtan,	–	Esker,[d] m.	–	–	–	–	–	–	–	–
112	1800	Do.	–	Do. f.	R.C.	–	R.C.	–	57	112	169	60
113	7663	Do.	–	Killallaghtan,	R.C.	–	R.C.	–	90	47	137	34
114	10327	Kilconly,	33	Ironpool,	–	R.C.	R.C.	–	114	96	210	85
115	1009	Kilcoona,	–	Tobberoe,	R.C.	–	R.C.	–	79	87	166	61
116	9804	Do.	–	Lisheen,	R.C.	–	R.C.	R.C.	147	116	263	56
117	10116	Kilcloony,	36	Ballinasloe, m.	R.C.	–	R.C.	–	237	–	237	73
118	8639	Do.	–	Do. Convent, f.	–	R.C.	R.C.	–	110	450	560	160
119	7016	Do.	–	Do. Workhouse,	P.L.	Gds.	2R.C.	–	54	41	95	37
120	11120	Do.	–	Churchill,	Pres.	–	Pres.	–	18	23	41	14
121	10[illegible]	Killian,	–	Woodlawn,	–	R.C.	Pres.	–	65	62	127	62
122	1097	Kilmalinogue,	–	Boley,	R.C.	–	R.C.	–	43	48	91	34
123	1226	Killererin,	27	Trinkill, m.	–	–	R.C.	–	164	–	164	45
124	1921	Do.	–	Do. f.	R.C.	–	R.C.	–	–	149	149	32
125	11124	Killeroran,	–	Killeroran, m.	R.C.	–	R.C.	–	114	–	114	53
126	11187	Do.	–	Do. f.	R.C.	–	R.C.	–	–	103	103	53
127	9173	Do.	32	Barnaderg, m.	R.C.	–	R.C.	–	147	–	147	46
128	2359	Do.	–	Do. f.	R.C.	–	R.C.	–	–	165	165	47
129	7186	Do.	27	Ballygar, m.	–	R.C.	R.C.	–	177	–	177	62
130	7436	Do.	–	Do. f.	–	R.C.	R.C.	–	–	167	167	41
131	10942	Do.	32	Addergoole,	–	R.C.	R.C.	–	78	82	160	38
132	1727	Kilbegnet,	27	Kilbegnet, m.	–	R.C.	R.C.	–	81	–	81	33
133	1566	Do.	–	Do. f.	–	R.C.	R.C.	–	–	89	89	33
134	9905	Do.	–	[illegible], or [illegible] Land,	R.C.	–	R.C.	–	96	64	160	42
135	6702	Do.	–	Creggs,	R.C.	–	R.C.	R.C.	106	77	183	73
136	13[illegible]	Kiltormer,	30	Kiltormer, m.	R.C.	–	R.C.	–	102	–	102	33
137	1502	Do.	–	Do. f.	R.C.	–	R.C.	–	–	90	90	24
138	2108	[illegible]	–	Kingsland, m.	R.C.	–	R.C.	–	100	–	100	33
139	2101	Do.	–	Do. f.	R.C.	–	R.C.	–	–	110	110	41
140	11433	Do.	–	Killosolan, m.	R.C.	–	R.C.	–	117	–	117	38
141	10669	Do.	–	Do. f.	R.C.	–	R.C.	–	–	98	98	31
142	9826	Do.	37	Castlefrench, m.	R.C.	–	R.C.	–	83	–	83	33
143	10844	Do.	–	Do. f.	R.C.	–	R.C.	–	–	86	86	23
144	8051	Kinvarradoorus,	48	Kinvara, f.	–	R.C.	R.C.	R.C.	–	157	131	72
145	8219	Do.	–	Doorus,	R.C.	–	R.C.	–	74	57	131	63
146	3725	Kilreekill,	68	Kilreekill, late Caher-nagarry,	R.C.	–	R.C.	–	83	79	162	32
147	9848	Killimordaly,	36	Attymon, m.	R.C.	–	R.C.	–	124	–	124	38
148	7459	Do.	–	Do. f.	R.C.	–	R.C.	–	–	114	113	43
149	6697	Do.	–	Brackloon,	R.C.	–	R.C.	–	71	91	162	43
150	4401	Killeenadeema,	48	Derrybrien,	R.C.	–	R.C.	–	71	85	156	44
151	5053	Do.	–	Killeenadeema, m.	R.C.	–	R.C.	–	140	–	140	31
152	9256	Do.	–	Do. f.	R.C.	–	R.C.	–	–	103	103	37
153	4404	Kilconierin,	–	Ganty,	–	R.C.	R.C.	–	51	66	117	38
154	4784	Kilcummin,	34	Oughterard, m.	R.C.	–	2R.C.	–	153	–	153	72
155	8828	Do.	–	Do. Convent, f.	–	R.C.	Nuns		–	341	341	155
156	1997	Do.	–	Do. Workhouse,	–	–	R.C.	–	22	20	42	18
157	6014	Do.	–	Gallinasmock,	R.C.	–	R.C.	–	86	45	131	39
158	8773	Do.	–	Glann,	R.C.	–	R.C.	–	53	33	87	17
159	9582	Do.	–	[illegible]	R.C.	–	R.C.	–	87	81	138	53
160	9087	Do.	–	Rosmuck,	R.C.	–	R.C.	R.C.	70	54	124	53
161	10894	Do.	–	Cannus,[f]	–	–	–	–	–	–	–	–
162	8851	Kilquain,	3[illegible]	[illegible]	R.C.	–	R.C.	–	50	58	108	30

[a] No Returns. [b] Including value of Free Residence and Garden. [c] Including value of Free Residence.

Province of CONNAUGHT: County of GALWAY—*continued.*

Amount paid for Books, Requisites, and Apparatus, to Local Funds.	Aid granted by the Board during the Year 1874: In Free Stock of Books, Requisites, and Apparatus.	Aid granted by the Board during the Year 1874: In Salaries, Premiums, and other Gratuities.	Aid granted by the Board during the Year 1874: Results Fees, Financial Year.	Amount of Local Emoluments received in Aid of Teacher's Salary: School Fees.	Amount of Local Emoluments received in Aid of Teacher's Salary: Subscriptions, Endowments, &c.	Amount of Local Emoluments received in Aid of Teacher's Salary: Total Local Aid.	Period of Vacancy	Number.
£ s. d.	£ s. d.	£ s. d.	£ s. d.	£ s. d.	£ s. d.	£ s. d.		
1 8 9	—	—	—	—	—	—		101
8 4 8	—	33 8 8	15 3 0	17 10 8	—	17 16 8		102
3 11 1	—	24 0 0	7 7 0	4 18 0	8 0 0	b 8 18 0		103
8 13 5	—	25 10 0	3 11 6	8 15 1	—	8 15 1		104
2 9 3	—	4 0 0	—	9 0 3	—	9 0 3	V.T.	105
1 3 0	—	24 0 0	10 0 8	4 5 0	—	4 5 8	V.T.	106
3 17 8	—	37 0 0	15 0 0	8 10 0	2 0 0	b 5 10 8	V.T.	107
8 19 8	—	47 2 4	16 18 0	13 3 0	3 0 0	b 16 3 0		108
0 18 7	—	24 0 0	12 8 6	6 11 8	—	6 11 8		109
1 10 11	—	36 0 0	0 14 6	1 7 0	—	1 7 0		110
—	—	—	—	—	—	—		111
9 8 8	—	20 0 0	0 6 6	—	1 10 0	b 1 10 0		112
1 13 0	—	28 0 0	6 13 0	1 16 6	—	1 15 6		113
5 5 5	—	34 0 0	14 9 8	2 6 2	2 5 0	4 11 2		114
5 9 4	—	40 0 0	17 0 0	5 0 0	—	5 0 0		115
4 9 0	—	44 0 0	22 4 0	7 4 8	—	7 4 8		116
11 8 5	—	34 10 0	4 15 6	8 12 4	—	8 12 4		117
29 5 4	12 0 0	149 18 4	60 17 8	8 18 10	—	8 18 10		118
8 17 1	—	4 0 0	—	—	—	—		119
0 1 0	4 10 0	6 0 0	—	22 15 6	—	22 15 6		120
7 1 7	—	37 0 0	14 5 6	—	10 0 0	b 33 0 0		121
1 14 10	—	30 0 0	7 14 0	1 0 1	—	1 0 1	V.T.	122
2 10 6	—	24 16 8	—	1 10 2	—	1 18 2	A.	123
1 5 4	—	25 10 0	4 13 8	1 4 11	—	1 4 11	A.	124
1 16 6	4 10 0	14 10 0	6 10 0	2 7 11	—	2 7 11		125
1 13 11	4 10 0	—	—	1 7 8	—	1 7 8		126
0 14 4	—	24 0 0	4 13 0	4 19 2	—	5 19 2	V.T.	127
1 6 8	—	20 0 0	11 0 8	3 13 1	—	3 13 1	V.T.	128
2 19 6	—	21 0 0	10 18 0	3 18 6	—	3 18 6	V.C.	129
10 8 5	—	34 6 8	18 18 6	8 10 0	—	3 10 0	V.C.	130
—	—	30 0 0	8 16 0	5 14 6	7 1 6	b 13 0 0		131
1 4 8	—	34 0 0	5 8 8	—	—	—	V.T.	132
1 0 4	—	21 0 0	8 16 0	8 10 8	5 0 0	7 12 8		133
1 18 7	—	35 8 0	8 8 0	6 11 0	0 18 0	b 7 9 0		134
7 10 11	—	53 8 4	28 19 6	0 8 0	0 0 0	b 16 8 0		135
0 8 0	—	24 0 0	10 8 0	8 15 1	—	8 15 1	V.T.	136
1 16 8	—	29 0 0	8 1 8	9 16 5	—	9 17 5	V.T.	137
1 8 6	—	24 0 0	8 16 0	6 1 3	—	6 1 3	V.T.	138
0 19 4	—	62 0 0	7 16 0	4 8 0	—	4 8 0	V.T.	139
—	—	37 0 0	15 15 0	11 8 3	25 0 6	b 36 8 9		140
1 18 8	—	34 0 0	10 9 0	5 12 6	—	5 13 6		141
1 4 8	—	18 0 0	8 16 0	1 5 1	—	1 5 1		142
0 4 0	—	20 0 0	6 1 6	0 18 4	—	0 15 4		143
1 12 10	—	38 16 8	28 7 0	7 3 1	—	7 3 1	A.	144
1 5 0	—	32 0 0	18 7 0	6 9 1	1 10 0	7 19 1	V.C.	145
1 1 10	—	18 0 0	4 18 0	3 4 4	—	6 4 6		146
3 0 1	—	25 0 0	8 14 0	1 14 5	—	1 14 5		147
2 1 0	—	27 10 0	8 7 6	8 4 6	—	8 4 6		148
1 16 0	—	24 0 0	8 7 0	9 16 0	—	2 15 0		149
8 8 11	—	23 0 0	19 18 0	8 15 8	1 0 0	7 15 8		150
3 8 11	—	24 0 0	9 11 0	8 0 10	—	2 0 10		151
1 16 6	—	20 0 0	11 9 0	2 11 0	—	8 11 0		152
2 0 6	—	20 0 0	7 7 0	9 3 6	2 10 0	b 4 13 6	V.C.	153
4 3 10	—	42 0 0	21 7 0	8 8 1	—	8 8 1	V.C.	154
8 10 8	—	65 19 4	34 15 8	20 0 0	—	20 0 0		155
—	—	2 10 0	—	—	—	—		156
8 18 4	—	24 0 0	15 0 8	4 0 0	—	4 0 0		157
0 11 0	—	24 0 0	1 1 0	0 15 0	6 0 0	b 6 15 0		158
0 10 2	—	19 17 6	10 17 0	2 14 8	—	2 14 8		159
2 4 5	—	63 0 0	8 15 0	8 0 0	—	8 0 0		160
0 3 0	—	—	—	—	—	—		161
8 0 6	—	60 0 0	8 8 8	8 8 3	—	3 8 8		162

a Inoperative. b Including value of Farm Garden. c No Teacher.

List of Schools in operation on the 31st December, 1874,—

Number.	Roll Number of School.	Parish.	District.	School.		Religious Denomination of Managers or Correspondents: Clerical.	Lay.	Number and Religious Denominations of Teachers: Principals.	Assistants.	Attendance for the Year: Total number of Pupils on Rolls within the Year 1874: Males.	Fem.	Total.	Average Daily Attendance.
163	4789	Kilthomas,	42	Peterswell,		R.C.	–	R.C.	R.C.	129	117	246	78
164	4790	Kilmacduagh,	–	Gort,	m.	R.C.	–	R.C.	R.C.	242	–	242	96
165	4791	Do.	–	Do.[a]	f.	–	–	–	–	–	–	–	–
166	6193	Do.	–	Do. No. 2, Con.	f.	–	R.C.	None		49	269	318	150
167	6810	Do.	–	Kilmacduagh,		R.C.	–	R.C.	–	–	111	111	44
168	6771	Do.	–	Killomoran,		R.C.	–	R.C.	–	60	57	117	44
169	4754	Killora,	–	Craughwell,	m.	R.C.	–	R.C.	–	140	–	140	49
170	4755	Do.	–	Do.	f.	R.C.	–	R.C.	–	–	180	180	84
171	6014	Kilsmoly,	60	Kilsmoly,	m.	R.C.	–	R.C.	–	88	–	88	38
172	6041	Do.	–	Do.	f.	R.C.	–	R.C.	–	–	96	96	50
173	6394	Kinvara,	42	Northampton,		–	R.C.	R.C.	R.C.	115	84	199	61
174	1845	Do.	–	Kinvara Con. Ag.	m.	–	R.C.	R.C.	–	143	–	143	69
175	10709	Killinny,	–	Killiny,		R.C.	–	R.C.	–	53	38	91	37
176	6276	Killalaghtan,	58	Carpaingle,		R.C.	–	R.C.	–	54	65	119	30
177	7295	Do.	–	Killagh,		R.C.	–	R.C.	–	57	42	108	31
178	6348	Do.	–	Killalaghtan,		R.C.	–	R.C.	–	111	58	169	41
179	6851	Killyon,	27	Camanagh,		–	R.C.	R.C.	–	90	25	115	48
180	7921	Do.	–	Killian,	m.	–	R.C.	R.C.	–	161	–	161	47
181	8353	Do.	–	Do.	f.	–	R.C.	R.C.	–	–	124	124	57
182	7172	Killoyes,	32	Ower,		–	R.C.	R.C.	R.C.	62	91	153	47
183	8471	Do.	–	Hamsford,	f.	R.C.	–	R.C.	R.C.	–	158	158	67
184	8504	Do.	–	Do.	f.	R.C.	–	R.C.	–	67	88	155	61
185	8455	Do.	–	Do.	m.	R.C.	–	R.C.	–	161	–	161	86
186	11011	Do.	–	Claran,		R.C.	–	R.C.	R.C.	–	170	170	66
187	11050	Do.	–	Do.	m.	R.C.	–	R.C.	–	148	–	149	64
188	7935	Killannin,	61	Fahy,		R.C.	–	R.C.	R.C.	114	126	240	63
189	6852	Do.	–	Killeen,	m.	R.C.	–	R.C.	–	79	–	79	33
190	8552	Do.	–	Do.	f.	R.C.	–	R.C.	–	–	46	46	22
191	9474	Do.	–	Selerna,		R.C.	–	R.C.	R.C.	104	62	166	76
192	10347	Do.	–	Tully,		R.C.	–	R.C.	–	119	82	201	71
				Do.	evg.	R.C.	–	R.C.	–	39	4	43	22
193	7551	Killererin,	42	Ballinderreen,	m.	R.C.	–	R.C.	–	111	–	111	41
194	7552	Do.	–	Do.	f.	R.C.	–	R.C.	–	–	119	119	47
195	7107	Kilkerrin,	82	Garvandare,	m.	R.C.	–	R.C.	–	208	–	208	90
196	7721	Do.	–	Do.	f.	R.C.	–	R.C.	–	–	162	162	66
197	6810	Do.	–	Shankill,		–	R.C.	R.C.	–	51	60	111	33
198	10611	Do.	–	Kilkerrin,	f.	R.C.	–	R.C.	–	–	129	129	48
199	6512	Killimore,	35	Killimore,	m.	R.C.	–	R.C.	–	237	–	237	76
200	7317	Do.	–	Do.	f.	R.C.	–	R.C.	R.C.	–	196	196	83
201	10880	Kilgerrill,	–	Kilfure,	m.	R.C.	–	R.C.	–	90	–	90	[illegible]
202	10008	Do.	–	Do.	f.	R.C.	–	R.C.	–	–	78	78	[illegible]
203	9575	Kilconnell,	–	Kilconnell,	m.	R.C.	–	R.C.	–	98	–	98	[illegible]
204	9973	Do.	–	Do.	f.	R.C.	–	R.C.	–	–	61	61	[illegible]
205	6306	Kiltartan,	42	Kiltartan,		R.C.	–	R.C.	R.C.	103	76	179	86
206	9848	Kilmeylan,	92	Annagh,	f.	–	R.C.	R.C.	–	49	167	216	97
207	9480	Kilchreest,	42	Kilchreest,		R.C.	–	R.C.	R.C.	145	104	249	73
208	9843	Kilreekill,	33	Aille,		R.C.	–	R.C.	–	90	79	169	60
209	10876	Killogilleen,	42	Ballynamanagh,		R.C.	–	R.C.	R.C.	64	67	155	[illegible]
210	10082	Lickerrig,	85	Lickerrig,		R.C.	–	R.C.	–	77	93	160	44
211	8051	Loughrea,	–	Loughrea,		–	R.C.	R.C.	–	114	61	165	47
212	1010	Do.	–	Do.	m.	R.C.	–	R.C.	R.C.	262	–	262	[illegible]
213	1011	Do.[a]	–	Do.	f.	–	–	–	–	–	–	–	–
214	3306	Do.	–	Loughrea Workhouse,		P.L.	Gds.	R.C.	–	31	18	49	39
215	8082	Do.	–	St. Vincent's Convt.	f.	R.C.	–	None	–	78	439	517	284
216	2174	Lickmolassy,	–	Portumna,	m.	R.C.	–	R.C.	R.C.	161	–	161	70
217	2176	Do.	–	Do.	f.	R.C.	–	R.C.	R.C.	–	115	115	[illegible]
218	6734	Do.	–	Do. Workhouse,		P.L.	Gds.	R.C.	–	28	24	52	[illegible]
219	6379	Do.	–	Gortanumera,		R.C.	–	R.C.	R.C.	179	170	349	112
220	9907	Leitrim,	–	Leitrim,		R.C.	–	R.C.	R.C.	92	92	184	[illegible]
221	7014	Lackagh,	84	Lackagh,		R.C.	–	R.C.	R.C.	130	107	237	[illegible]
222	9050	Do.	–	Rowaunders,	m.	–	R.C.	R.C.	–	119	–	119	[illegible]
223	9070	Do.	–	Do.	f.	–	R.C.	R.C.	–	–	108	108	[illegible]
224	9477	Liskeevy,	32	Belmont,		R.C.	–	R.C.	–	67	84	151	[illegible]

[a] Inoperative. [b] Including value of Free Residence and Garden. [c] Including value of Free Residence.

Province of Connaught: County of Galway—*continued.*

Amount paid for Books, Requisites, and Apparatus or Salaried Prizes	Aid granted by the Board during the Year 1874: In Free Stock of Books, Requisites, and Apparatus	Aid granted by the Board during the Year 1874: In Salaries, Premiums, and other Gratuities	Aid granted by the Board during the Year 1874: Results Fees, Financial Year	Amount of Local Endowments received in Aid of Teacher's Salary: School Fees	Amount of Local Endowments received in Aid of Teacher's Salary: Subscriptions, Endowments, &c.	Amount of Local Endowments received in Aid of Teacher's Salary: Total Local Aid	Vested or Non-Vested	Number
£ s. d.	£ s. d.	£ s. d.	£ s. d.	£ s. d.	£ s. d.	£ s. d.		
5 0 4	—	78 0 0	14 1 8	10 17 11	—	10 17 11	V.C.	163
8 8 0	—	86 18 4	27 6 0	35 11 6	—	35 11 6	V.C.	164
—	—	—	—	—	—	—	V.C.	165
9 11 8	—	83 16 4	19 0 6	—	10 0 0	10 0 0		166
9 14 5	—	24 0 0	17 11 0	6 16 4	—	6 16 4	V.C.	167
—	—	37 10 0	10 14 0	6 17 2	—	6 17 2		168
1 18 4	—	24 0 0	11 14 0	4 4 0	—	4 4 0	V.C.	169
—	—	30 10 0	6 15 0	2 10 8	—	2 10 8	V.C.	170
1 6 0	—	31 15 8	5 18 6	1 10 0	—	1 10 0		171
1 8 1	—	30 0 0	8 8 0	0 14 6	—	0 14 6		172
2 3 4	—	61 15 0	26 10 8	6 18 5	—	6 18 5	V.C.	173
4 10 10	—	68 6 8	23 18 6	8 11 10	—	8 11 10	a.	174
—	—	16 8 4	2 14 0	2 1 8	—	2 1 8		175
2 19 9	—	30 0 0	6 6 0	5 10 2	—	5 10 2		176
1 6 1	—	24 0 0	6 0 6	4 3 0	—	4 3 0		177
1 11 6	—	34 0 0	11 8 0	4 18 6	—	4 18 6		178
4 8 0	—	37 10 0	18 8 0	7 0 0	—	7 0 0	V.C.	179
1 6 8	—	37 0 0	0 15 0	5 0 0	—	5 0 0	V.C.	180
2 15 8	—	50 0 0	8 0 6	4 7 6	—	4 7 6	V.C.	181
2 0 7	—	64 8 4	27 1 6	2 8 0	4 10 0	b6 18 0		182
5 17 10	—	69 0 0	20 10 0	8 10 10	—	8 10 10		183
1 1 11	—	40 8 0	18 18 6	5 8 4	—	5 8 4		184
5 0 9	—	60 6 8	18 0 6	7 10 0	—	7 10 0		185
2 10 6	—	45 18 4	15 7 6	3 6 6	—	3 6 6		186
5 6 8	8 10 0	82 10 0	14 17 0	6 4 11	—	6 4 11		187
7 7 7	—	47 0 8	20 11 0	8 0 0	8 0 0	a16 0 0		188
1 14 4	—	84 15 0	5 11 4	7 1 0	3 0 0	10 1 0		189
—	—	30 0 0	5 18 0	4 10 0	—	4 10 0		190
3 17 4	—	40 18 8	17 15 0	16 12 0	0 8 0	17 0 0		191
}	—		{ 19 10 0	14 7 0	—	14 7 0		192
3 15 0	—	41 6 8	—	—	—	—		
1 7 6	—	24 0 0	14 15 6	0 18 8	—	8 18 8	V.C.	193
1 19 5	—	27 3 4	19 7 0	8 18 3	—	8 18 6	V.C.	194
8 18 3	—	29 0 0	10 10 8	1 5 9	11 4 9	b12 10 6	V.C.	195
—	—	28 10 0	14 9 6	0 15 0	—	0 15 0	V.C.	196
—	—	24 0 0	3 18 0	1 1 7	—	1 1 7		197
4 10 8	—	27 10 0	7 15 6	0 18 0	—	0 18 0		198
6 3 8	—	37 18 4	24 16 6	6 12 0	—	6 12 0		199
3 9 3	—	63 0 0	24 11 0	7 8 4	—	7 8 4		200
6 11 0	—	24 0 0	6 5 6	1 1 0	—	1 1 0		201
0 16 2	—	30 0 0	6 11 0	1 4 7	—	1 4 7		202
2 4 10	—	30 0 0	4 5 6	6 5 7	—	6 5 7		203
0 6 6	—	30 0 0	5 15 6	4 2 7	—	4 2 7		204
2 1 5	—	41 0 0	21 10 0	12 4 8	—	12 4 8		205
1 13 5	—	35 3 4	10 10 0	3 18 8	7 0 0	10 18 8		206
6 9 2	—	41 0 0	19 8 0	7 17 0	—	7 17 0		207
3 1 1	—	30 0 0	6 9 0	1 10 0	—	1 10 0		208
—	—	18 0 0	14 18 0	4 15 6	—	4 15 6	V.T.	209
1 15 9	—	38 10 0	6 7 0	8 16 8	—	8 16 8	V.T.	210
—	—	35 10 0	8 4 0	1 8 8	6 0 0	a6 8 8	V.T.	211
6 3 4	—	68 0 0	17 18 0	7 5 8	8 16 0	a16 1 8	V.T.	212
—	—	—	—	—	—	—	V.T.	213
0 18 8	—	—	—	—	—	—		214
65 8 8	—	130 10 4	50 8 6	18 7 4	—	18 7 4		215
8 16 0	—	74 3 0	26 0 0	15 8 0	—	15 8 0	V.C.	216
5 11 8	—	63 3 4	19 14 6	7 14 8	—	7 14 8	V.C.	217
2 5 0	—	—	—	—	—	—		218
—	—	73 6 4	32 12 0	18 17 6	—	18 17 6	V.C.	219
2 14 10	—	61 0 0	38 12 0	5 8 0	—	5 8 0		220
4 8 6	—	50 6 8	15 4 6	11 11 11	—	11 11 11		221
2 8 8	—	38 0 0	9 8 0	5 8 0	6 0 0	a11 8 0		222
8 4 2	—	30 0 0	7 12 6	6 10 1	4 0 0	10 10 1		223
1 5 9	—	30 0 0	6 18 0	4 14 8	—	4 14 8		224

a Including value of Free Garden.

b No Returns ; [illegible]

List of Schools in operation on the 31st December, 1874.—

Number.	Roll Number of School.	Parish.	District.	School.	Religious Denomination of Manager or Correspondent. Clerical.	Lay.	Number and Religion of Teachers. Principals.	Assistants.	Attendance for the Year. Total number of Pupils on Rolls within the Year 1874. Males.	Fem.	Total.	Average daily attendance.
225	1012	Moyrus,	64	Roundstone,	–	R.C.	R.C.	–	–	77	77	28
226	4941	Do.	–	Kilkerrin,	R.C.	–	R.C.	–	57	25	82	[illegible]
227	7158	Do.	–	Murvey,	R.C.	–	R.C.	–	70	65	135	38
228	8001	Do.	–	Cartna,	R.C.	–	R.C.	–	82	21	103	[illegible]
229	8070	Do.	–	Ballinahinch, [b]	–	–	–	–	–	–	–	–
230	10381	Do.	–	Ardmore,	–	R.C.	R.C.	–	93	30	123	46
231	[illegible]	Do.	–	Ard, [b]	–	–	–	–	–	–	–	–
232	11124	Do.	–	Gorteens, [c]	R.C.	–	R.C.	–	–	–	–	–
233	[illegible]	Do.	–	Mynish Island, [b]	–	–	–	–	–	–	–	–
234	10836	Do.	–	Lettercard, [b]	–	–	–	–	–	–	–	–
235	1219	Moycullen,	–	Moycullen, m.	R.C.	–	R.C.	–	148	–	148	84
236	1681	Do.	–	Do. f.	R.C.	–	R.C.	–	–	113	113	50
237	2319	Do.	–	Knockferry,	R.C.	–	R.C.	R.C.	104	75	179	65
238	8237	Do.	–	Spiddal, m.	–	R.C.	R.C.	R.C.	147	–	147	85
239	4219	Do.	–	Do. f.	R.C.	–	R.C.	–	–	125	125	54
240	8416	Do.	–	Tullokyne,	–	R.C.	R.C.	R.C.	114	96	210	87
241	1778	Monivea,	65	Rye Hill,	–	R.C.	R.C.	R.C.	148	183	280	66
242	2301	Do.	–	Monivea, m.	–	R.C.	R.C.	–	68	64	132	41
243	8384	Do.	–	Do. [b] f.	–	–	–	–	–	–	–	–
244	4974	Meelick,	83	Meelick,	R.C.	–	R.C.	–	48	35	78	39
245	10224	Do.	–	Fahy,	R.C.	–	R.C.	–	47	37	84	[illegible]
246	8249	Moylough,	82	Moylough, m.	R.C.	–	R.C.	–	145	–	145	79
247	6819	Do.	–	Do. f.	R.C.	–	R.C.	R.C.	–	120	128	46
248	8112	Do.	–	Mt. Bellew Bridge, f.	R.C.	–	R.C.	R.C.	38	124	162	40
249	[illegible]	Do.	–	Do. Workhouse,	Official		R.C.	–	22	16	38	16
250	7002	Do.	–	Coolne,	R.C.	–	R.C.	R.C.	95	78	173	61
251	8039	Menlagh and Killascobe,	–	Menlagh, m.	R.C.	–	R.C.	–	158	–	158	39
252	8040	Do.	–	Do. f.	R.C.	–	R.C.	–	–	152	152	39
253	4408	Oranmore,	84	Oranmore, m.	R.C.	–	R.C.	–	134	–	134	45
254	4507	Do.	–	Do. [f] f.	–	–	–	–	–	–	–	–
255	8790	Do.	–	Do. Convent, f.	–	R.C.	Nuns		31	207	238	129
256	9407	Do.	–	Castlegar, m.	R.C.	–	R.C.	–	110	–	112	29
257	9436	Do.	–	Do. f.	R.C.	–	R.C.	–	–	93	93	35
258	8790	Do.	–	Menlough, m.	R.C.	–	R.C.	–	88	–	88	29
259	[illegible]	Do.	–	Do. f.	R.C.	–	R.C.	–	–	60	60	22
260	10187	Do.	–	Briarhill,	R.C.	–	R.C.	–	67	82	149	45
261	[illegible]	Omey,	–	Kingstown,	R.C.	–	R.C.	–	60	66	126	48
262	[illegible]	Do.	–	Claddaghduff, m.	R.C.	–	R.C.	–	161	–	161	61
263	8716	Do.	–	Aughrismore, f.	R.C.	–	R.C.	–	–	150	150	[illegible]
264	8775	Do.	–	Cleggan,	R.C.	–	R.C.	–	80	81	161	[illegible]
265	8870	Do.	–	Omey Island,	R.C.	–	R.C.	–	40	38	78	17
266	[illegible]	Do.	–	Clifden Workhouse,	Official		R.C.	–	40	38	78	30
267	[illegible]	Do.	–	Do. m.	R.C.	–	R.C.	–	109	–	109	44
268	[illegible]	Do.	–	Streamstown,	R.C.	–	R.C.	–	69	57	126	38
269	1160	Rahoon,	–	Bushy Park, m.	R.C.	–	R.C.	–	63	–	63	31
270	8116	Do.	–	Do. f.	R.C.	–	R.C.	–	–	68	68	20
271	1502	Do.	–	Freeport, m.	R.C.	–	R.C.	–	88	–	88	32
272	[illegible]	Do.	–	Furbough,	–	R.C.	R.C.	–	79	74	153	58
273	4001	Do.	–	Claddagh, m.	R.C.	–	R.C.	–	185	–	185	85
274	4407	Do.	–	Do. f.	R.C.	–	R.C.	–	20	120	140	45
275	9077	Do.	–	Barna, f.	R.C.	–	R.C.	–	–	100	100	28
276	1016	Do.	–	Rahoon Convent, f.	–	R.C.	Nuns		103	584	687	301
277	10230	Do.	–	Rahoon,	R.C.	–	R.C.	–	94	64	158	31
278	[illegible]	Do.	–	Galway Workhouse,	Official		R.C.	–	58	72	130	75
279	6012	Do.	–	Do. Dist. Mod. m.	Official		R.C.	Prot.	108	–	108	45
280	6015	Do.	–	Do. f.	Official		R.C.	–	–	60	60	34
281	6014	Do.	–	Do. i.	Official		R.C.	R.C.	37	33	70	30
282	10981	Do.	–	Salthill Industrial,	R.C.	–	–	–	111	–	111	[illegible]
283	5560	Ross,	28	Cornamona,	R.C.	–	R.C.	–	172	110	282	49
284	7340	Do.	28	Clonbur, m.	R.C.	–	R.C.	–	144	–	144	57
285	[illegible]	Do.	–	Do. f.	R.C.	–	R.C.	–	–	146	146	62
286	8361	Do.	29	Tievaleeny, [b]	–	–	–	–	–	–	–	–

[a] Including value of Free Residence and Garden. [b] Closed. [c] Returns not available.

Province of Connaught: County of Galway—continued.

Amount paid for Books, Requisites, and Apparatus, at Reduced Prices.	Aid granted by the Board during the Year 1874: In Free Stock of Books, Requisites, and Apparatus.	Aid granted by the Board during the Year 1874: In Salaries, Premiums, and other Gratuities.	Aid granted by the Board during the Year 1874: Results Fees, Financial Year.	Amount of Local Contributions received in Aid of Teacher's Salary: School Fees.	Amount of Local Contributions received in Aid of Teacher's Salary: Subscriptions, Endowments, &c.	Amount of Local Contributions received in Aid of Teacher's Salary: Total Local Aid.	Vested or Non-Vested.	Number.
£ s. d.	£ s. d.	£ s. d.	£ s. d.	£ s. d.	£ s. d.	£ s. d.		
0 5 7	—	20 6 8	0 16 0	—	—	—	V.T.	225
—	—	21 0 0	8 19 9	17 11 10	—	17 11 10	V.C.	226
2 3 10	—	15 18 4	—	0 6 4	—	0 6 4	V.C.	227
4 0 0	—	20 0 0	8 15 6	1 18 7	1 0 0	*2 18 7		228
—	—	—	—	—	—	—		229
1 19 7	4 10 0	25 18 4	6 6 0	2 5 1	—	2 5 1	V.C.	230
—	—	—	—	—	—	—		231
1 10 4	4 0 0	15 0 0	3 14 0	—	—	—		232
—	—	—	—	—	—	—		233
—	—	—	—	—	—	—		234
7 10 5	—	29 18 4	16 2 6	6 2 8	4 5 0	*19 7 8	V.T.	235
2 0 1	—	22 0 0	14 5 6	5 8 5	0 10 0	*5 18 5	V.T.	236
3 7 9	—	50 0 0	19 14 6	7 2 7	—	7 2 7		237
1 6 8	—	73 10 0	16 4 0	10 3 11	—	10 3 11	V.T.	238
1 16 5	—	50 16 8	14 0 6	7 10 2	—	7 10 2	V.T.	239
3 18 6	—	73 13 4	27 10 0	15 14 4	21 0 0	36 14 4	V.C.	240
4 2 0	—	45 6 8	18 17 0	2 1 0	0 0 0	*5 1 0	V.T.	241
1 14 11	—	38 0 0	10 8 9	1 19 2	11 0 0	*18 19 0		242
—	—	—	—	—	—	—		243
1 16 4	—	20 0 0	8 5 0	8 0 0	—	8 0 0		244
1 17 3	—	18 0 0	8 16 0	4 0 0	—	4 0 0		245
3 4 3	—	27 3 4	20 1 6	7 10 0	—	7 10 0		246
9 14 1	—	48 13 4	14 5 6	4 0 0	5 0 0	9 0 0		247
13 15 4	—	24 10 0	12 3 1	4 15 11	5 0 0	9 15 11		248
1 15 0	—	—	—	—	—	—		249
5 0 7	—	50 0 0	21 4 0	8 8 8	—	8 8 8		250
1 7 4	—	29 3 4	—	1 0 4	2 10 0	3 10 4		251
1 8 6	—	27 0 0	8 10 6	—	2 10 0	2 10 0		252
2 4 0	—	29 3 4	11 11 0	1 14 8	—	1 14 8	V.C.	253
—	—	—	—	—	—	—	V.C.	254
0 19 2	—	63 1 6	21 17 0	—	—	—		255
—	—	24 0 0	2 5 6	7 15 11	—	7 15 11		256
1 8 3	—	21 0 0	4 19 6	4 18 5	—	4 18 5		257
—	—	17 0 0	—	0 7 4	—	0 7 4	V.T.	258
2 18 11	—	31 3 3	3 7 6	0 15 1	—	0 15 1	V.T.	259
5 1 7	—	24 0 0	6 6 0	7 3 5	—	7 3 5		260
1 18 7	—	23 0 0	7 17 0	—	—	—		261
2 3 2	—	24 0 0	11 1 0	0 10 0	—	0 10 0		262
1 14 8	—	20 0 0	8 9 6	0 19 0	—	0 19 0		263
1 5 8	—	24 0 0	4 15 0	0 7 6	—	0 7 6		264
2 0 0	—	17 15 6	1 6 0	0 6 0	—	0 6 0		265
1 16 5	—	—	—	—	—	—		266
2 1 6	—	62 16 8	13 17 6	19 14 5	—	19 14 5		267
—	—	20 0 0	5 6 0	0 9 9	—	0 9 9		268
3 19 1	—	35 16 8	2 12 0	0 18 8	—	0 18 8	V.T.	269
0 15 2	—	20 0 0	8 5 0	1 7 0	—	1 7 0		270
2 15 0	—	27 6 0	8 9 0	2 11 5	—	2 11 5	V.T.	271
2 9 1	—	22 0 0	13 15 6	10 6 0	—	10 6 6	V.T.	272
6 13 8	—	51 0 0	10 9 8	11 18 8	5 0 0	16 18 8	V.T.	273
2 7 8	—	46 0 0	8 14 0	2 6 9	5 0 0	7 6 9	V.T.	274
0 19 10	—	24 0 9	5 10 0	3 5 11	—	3 5 11	V.T.	275
22 6 1	—	127 15 0	67 19 0	—	—	—	V.T.	276
1 10 10	—	30 6 8	7 19 0	2 1 9	—	2 1 9		277
7 1 6	—	—	—	—	—	—		278
21 18 6	—	}					V.C.	279
5 11 8	5 15 11	546 18 7	80 19 0	65 15 10	—	65 15 10	V.C.	280
—	—	}					V.C.	281
0 14 7	4 0 0	—	—	—	55 5 0	55 0 0		282
—	—	20 0 0	0 16 6	—	—	—	V.C.	283
1 5 2	—	0 0 0	—	6 18 7	—	6 18 7		284
1 15 0	—	4 0 0	—	2 0 2	—	2 0 2		285
—	—	—	—	—	—	—		286

* Including value of Free Garden. * Including value of Free Residence. † No Teacher.

List of Schools in operation on the 31st December, 1874—

Number.	Roll Number of School.	Parish.	District.	School.	Religious Denomination of Patrons or Correspondents. Clerical.	Lay.	Number and Religious Denominations of Teachers. Principals.	Assistants.	Attendance for the Year. Total number of Pupils on Rolls within the Year 1874. Males.	Females.	Total.	Average daily Attendance for the Year 1874.
287	1016	St. Nicholas,	34	Galway Monastic, m.	R.C.	–	Monks.		858	–	858	309
288	[illegible]	Do.	–	Do. Mechanics' Institute, evg.	–	–	R.C.	–	210	–	210	23
289	4318	Do.	–	St. Nicholas', f.	R.C.	–	R.C.	–	50	155	205	64
290	4515	Do.	–	Newtownsmith Convt.,	–	R.C.	Nuns		117	807	924	480
291	8419	Do.	–	Bohermore,	R.C.	–	R.C.	–	151	–	151	45
292	4310	Tynagh,	35	Tynagh, m.	R.C.	–	R.C.	–	108	–	108	36
293	4416	Do.	–	Do. f.	R.C.	–	R.C.	–	–	93	93	39
294	[illegible]	Templetogher,	24	Farm,[a]	–	–	–	–	–	–	–	–
295	10733	Do.	–	Do. m.	–	R.C.	R.C.	–	130	106	236	36
296	6960	Do.	–	Williamstown,	R.C.	–	R.C.	–	203	200	403	55
297	8942	Tynagh,	34	Tynagh, m.	R.C.	–	R.C.	–	109	–	109	31
298	8048	Do.	–	Do. f.[b]	R.C.	–	R.C.	–	–	93	93	37
299	3448	Tuam,	32	Tuam Workhouse,	Official.		R.C.	–	33	20	53	33
300	10011	Killascobe,	34	Lecarrowmore,	R.C.	–	R.C.	–	50	0	59	29
301	10012	Do.	–	Drim,	R.C.	–	R.C.	–	64	20	84	33
302	10013	Do.	–	Thomas,	R.C.	–	R.C.	–	30	29	61	34
		Total for County Galway, 302,							21723	21020	42,743	14118

COUNTY OF

Number.	Roll Number of School.	Parish.	District.	School.	Clerical.	Lay.	Principals.	Assistants.	Males.	Females.	Total.	Average daily Attendance.
1	1217	Annaduff,	22	Lisduff, No. 1,[c] m.	–	–	–	–	–	–	–	–
2	8200	Do.	–	Do. f.	R.C.	–	R.C.	–	–	108	108	35
3	1085	Do.	–	Drumsna, m.	R.C.	–	R.C.	–	145	–	145	43
4	8254	Do.	–	Do. f.	R.C.	–	R.C.	–	–	118	118	33
5	3107	Do.	22	Annaduff, m.	R.C.	–	R.C.	–	141	114	255	73
6	4228	Do.	–	Do.[a] f.	–	–	–	–	–	–	–	–
7	8311	Do.	–	Drumad,	R.C.	–	R.C.	–	34	75	109	41
8	1208	Carrigallen,	31	Boughmore,	R.C.	R.C.	–	R.C.	104	101	205	59
9	9637	Do.	–	Drumeela, m.	R.C.	–	R.C.	–	63	–	63	14
10	9222	Do.	–	Do. f.	R.C.	–	R.C.	–	–	103	103	35
11	4318	Do.	–	Carrigallen,	Pres.	–	Pres.	–	71	53	122	51
12	4084	Do.	–	Killygar, m.	–	R.C.	R.C.	R.C.	53	93	118	48
13	8473	Do.	–	Drumshanbo,	–	R.C.	R.C.	–	37	27	64	24
14	7317	Do.	–	Corranagh,	R.C.	–	R.C.	–	27	38	65	31
15	6258	Do.	–	Newtown Gore, No. 1,	–	R.C.	R.C.	–	29	52	78	30
16	10193	Do.	–	Do. No. 2,	R.C.	–	R.C.	–	37	42	79	28
17	10905	Do.	–	Bruslagh, m.	R.C.	–	R.C.	–	130	–	130	43
18	10268	Do.	–	Do. f.	R.C.	–	R.C.	–	–	144	144	41
19	1843	Cloone,	–	Cardiff,	R.C.	–	R.C.	R.C.	170	110	280	88
20	2419	Do.	32	Fenagh, m.	–	R.C.	R.C.	–	110	–	110	32
21	7703	Do.	–	Do. f.	–	R.C.	R.C.	–	–	108	108	43
22	8043	Do.	–	Drumshaloe, f.	R.C.	–	R.C.	–	–	170	170	33
23	8328	Do.	31	Cloone,	R.C.	–	R.C.	–	86	60	146	50
24	6718	Do.	–	Ardlaher,	R.C.	–	R.C.	–	80	57	138	67
25	7132	Do.	–	Drumkeilvy,	R.C.	–	R.C.	–	39	64	130	43
26	8137	Do.	–	Aughamore,	R.C.	–	R.C.	–	102	91	193	59
27	8200	Do.	–	Cloonmorris,	R.C.	–	R.C.	–	37	97	134	74
28	3871	Do.	32	Broom-street,	R.C.	–	R.C.	–	36	61	87	31
29	9006	Do.	31	Drumlowe,	R.C.	–	R.C.	–	40	33	73	17
30	9814	Do.	–	Aughavas,	R.C.	–	R.C.	–	18	29	47	33
31	[illegible]	Do.	–	Drumcoodra,	R.C.	–	R.C.	R.C.	108	81	189	31
32	10398	Do.	–	Sunnaghbeg,	R.C.	–	R.C.	–	271	273	544	35
33	8842	Do.	30	Drumsdore Ord. Agr.	R.C.	–	R.C.	–	150	–	150	35
34	10158	Do.	–	Anna Lloyd,	R.C.	–	R.C.	–	38	40	78	33
35	8018	Do.	–	Mullaghbrack,	R.C.	–	R.C.	–	115	98	213	34
36	6208	Do.	–	Forgnie, m.	R.C.	–	R.C.	–	187	–	187	32
37	8891	Do.	–	Do. f.	R.C.	–	R.C.	–	–	164	161	33
38	10288	Do.	–	Naskira,	R.C.	–	R.C.	–	94	126	220	33

[a] Inoperative. [b] Including value of Free Garden. [c] Closed.

Province of CONNAUGHT: County of GALWAY—*continued.*

Amount paid for Books, Requisites, and Apparatus to National Board.	Aid granted by the Board during the Year 1874. In Free Stock of Books, Requisites, and Apparatus.	In Salaries, Premiums, and other Gratuities.	Results Fees, Financial Year.	Amount of Local Contributions received in Aid of Teacher's Salary. School Fees.	Subscriptions, Endowments, etc.	Total Local Aid.	Vested or Non-Vested.	Number.
£ s. d.	£ s. d.	£ s. d.	£ s. d.	£ s. d.	£ s. d.	£ s. d.		
18 1 1	—	109 16 4	34 15 6	—	—	—		287
—	—	10 0 0	1 4 0	3 10 5	—	6 10 8		288
9 15 1	—	23 14 8	9 14 6	2 17 11	—	2 17 11		289
—	—	231 6 6	84 19 8	—	—	—		290
6 1 4	—	34 4 8	11 10 6	10 9 5	—	10 9 9		291
1 11 6	—	24 0 0	9 1 0	3 4 3	—	3 4 3		292
6 4 0	—	20 0 0	18 14 6	3 13 4	—	3 13 4		293
—	—	—	—	—	—	—		294
3 19 8	—	21 0 0	18 17 0	6 1 0	2 10 0	b8 11 0		295
4 14 7	1 0 6	67 14 0	60 15 0	5 4 4	—	5 4 4		296
1 0 10	—	24 0 0	0 0 6	2 7 0	—	2 7 0		297
8 11 10	—	61 18 8	23 2 6	3 18 10	—	3 18 10		298
8 11 0	—	—	—	—	—	—		299
1 6 3	—	24 0 0	0 10 0	1 15 9	—	1 15 9		300
0 18 9	—	9 0 0	5 3 0	0 16 0	—	0 16 0		301
6 7 0	—	—	—	0 13 6	—	0 13 0		302
681 15 1	64 7 6	8,336 0 8	3,404 10 0	1,361 16 4	338 1 0	1,699 17 4		

LEITRIM—106 Schools.

0 11 7	—	—	—	—	—	—	P.	1
0 17 10	—	25 10 0	17 11 6	1 17 0	—	1 17 0	N.	2
1 7 6	—	54 18 4	10 19 6	0 15 0	6 0 0	12 15 0	V.T.	3
9 9 5	—	84 0 0	18 6 0	2 11 0	—	2 11 8	V.T.	4
—	—	57 0 0	13 8 6	6 0 0	6 0 0	b12 0 0		5
—	—	—	—	—	—	—		6
1 11 6	—	20 0 0	6 9 6	—	—	—		7
5 19 6	—	54 6 8	60 3 0	4 18 0	5 0 0	9 18 0		8
0 10 6	—	24 0 0	7 6 0	1 5 0	—	1 5 0		9
1 6 8	—	20 0 0	9 1 6	1 10 6	—	1 10 6		10
2 0 4	—	57 8 4	14 19 0	6 18 0	—	6 18 0		11
—	—	60 0 0	18 13 0	—	6 10 0	c8 10 0		12
1 6 1	—	24 0 0	4 1 0	—	6 0 0	c6 0 0		13
0 6 1	—	20 6 0	2 5 6	1 1 6	—	1 1 6		14
1 7 0	—	20 7 7	7 4 6	1 6 2	—	1 6 6		15
0 1 1	—	24 0 0	8 13 6	1 1 0	—	1 1 0		16
2 11 3	—	24 18 4	16 13 6	1 5 0	—	1 5 0		17
—	—	20 0 0	17 2 0	0 6 0	—	0 6 0		18
9 19 8	—	78 6 8	41 0 0	0 16 0	0 16 0	b1 12 0	V.T.	19
—	—	24 0 0	11 5 6	4 1 0	—	4 1 0	V.T.	20
0 18 8	—	27 0 0	20 0 0	2 1 6	—	2 1 6		21
1 5 2	—	60 6 4	21 2 6	1 8 1	—	1 8 1	V.E.	22
1 13 9	—	24 0 0	9 6 0	1 1 0	—	1 1 0		23
1 0 10	—	22 0 8	8 0 6	1 0 0	—	1 0 0		24
9 8 1	—	24 0 0	5 7 6	3 3 0	—	3 3 0		25
9 12 10	—	47 6 4	34 7 6	—	—	—		26
6 5 7	—	54 0 0	21 16 6	—	—	—		27
6 7 11	—	30 0 0	11 4 6	—	—	—		28
0 8 0	—	20 0 0	3 18 6	—	—	—		29
1 17 10	—	30 0 0	8 12 0	—	2 0 0	2 0 0		30
1 16 10	—	26 10 0	23 8 6	1 15 6	—	1 10 6		31
1 19 6	—	18 17 9	4 14 0	1 3 0	—	1 5 0		32
1 6 6	—	27 10 0	19 15 0	0 9 0	—	0 0 0	V.T.	33
1 0 4	—	20 0 0	9 17 0	—	—	—		34
9 15 3	—	66 6 4	14 7 0	—	—	—		35
8 10 3	—	82 0 6	10 11 6	1 7 0	4 0 0	c5 7 0		36
8 8 9	—	27 10 0	12 16 0	6 7 0	—	0 7 0		37
1 5 3	—	26 0 0	20 0 0	1 13 6	—	1 13 0		38

b Including value of Free Residence and Garden.   c Including value of Free Residence.

List of Schools in operation on the 31st December, 1874—

Number.	Roll Number of School.	Parish.	District.	School.	Religious Denomination of Manager or Correspondent. Clerical.	Lay.	Number and Religious Denomination of Teachers. Principals.	Assistants.	Attendance for the Year. Total number of Pupils on Rolls within the Year 1874. Males.	Fem.	Total.	Average number daily present.
39	1642	Cloonclare,	12	Kiltyclogher, m.	–	R.C.	R.C.	–	117	–	117	49
40	2354	Do.	–	Do. f.	–	R.C.	R.C.	–	–	124	124	65
41	1751	Do.	–	Loughros,	R.C.	–	R.C.	–	65	36	101	41
42	6127	Do.	–	Manorhamilton, m.	–	R.C.	R.C.	–	147	–	147	61
43	8124	Do.	–	Do. f.	–	R.C.	R.C.	–	–	68	68	39
44	10519	Do.	–	Do. f.	R.C.	–	R.C.	–	13	103	116	46
45	8418	Do.	–	Killea,	–	R.C.	R.C.	–	69	35	104	61
46	6304	Do.	–	Cullentragh,	–	R.C.	R.C.	R.C.	116	93	209	79
				Do.[b] evg.	–	–	–	–	–	–	–	–
47	8788	Do.	–	Mullies, f.	R.C.	–	R.C.	–	35	59	94	41
48	7132	Do.	–	Mossyhara,	R.C.	–	R.C.	–	40	36	76	30
49	7711	Do.	–	Tawnyunshinagh,	–	R.C.	R.C.	–	65	41	106	54
50	8168	Do.	–	Ballaghnabehy,	R.C.	–	R.C.	–	45	61	106	45
51	8166	Do.	–	Castlecarra,	R.C.	–	R.C.	–	69	44	113	31
52	9390	Do.	–	Manorhamilton (Masterson's),	R.C.	–	E.C.	–	31	–	31	12
53	9640	Do.	–	Do. Workhouse,	P.L.	Gds.	R.C.	–	27	13	39	22
54	8617	Do.	–	Gortnalibbert,[b]	–	–	–	–	–	–	–	–
55	9978	Do.	–	Carrigeenagrave,	–	E.C.	R.C.	–	50	50	84	37
56	9832	Do.	–	Corramore,	R.C.	–	R.C.	–	64	48	112	41
57	9657	Do.	–	Mencanaskea,	Diss.	–	Diss.	–	9	16	25	12
58	6554	Do.	–	Brackagh,	–	R.C.	R.C.	–	93	76	169	91
				Do. evg.	–	–	R.C.	–	61	–	61	34
59	7816	Carrowlean,	–	Carrowleane,	–	R.C.	R.C.	R.C.	130	69	199	74
60	4666	Drumreilly,	31	Carrowallen,	–	R.C.	E.C.	–	34	30	64	21
61	4641	Do.	–	Urial, m.	R.C.	–	R.C.	–	73	–	73	61
62	6270	Do.	–	Do. f.	R.C.	–	R.C.	–	–	113	113	49
63	5023	Do.	–	Corraleehan,	R.C.	–	R.C.	–	41	66	80	36
64	6250	Do.	–	Gortahone, m.	R.C.	–	R.C.	R.C.	81	94	175	44
65	6196	Do.	–	Derrahile,	R.C.	–	R.C.	R.C.	71	81	162	41
66	7096	Do.	–	Slievenakilla,	R.C.	–	R.C.	–	36	25	61	25
67	7496	Do.	–	Corraspue,	R.C.	–	R.C.	–	50	46	100	36
68	7476	Do.	–	Allenview,	R.C.	–	R.C.	–	37	16	56	22
69	8166	Do.	–	Ughba & Drumaliffer, m.	R.C.	–	R.C.	–	63	–	63	30
70	9297	Do.	–	Do. f.	R.C.	–	R.C.	–	–	79	79	36
71	8671	Do.	–	Tullynahala,[c]	R.C.	–	–	–	–	–	–	–
72	9195	Do.	–	Tullyvernan,	R.C.	–	R.C.	R.C.	64	65	129	59
73	9256	Do.	–	Aughawillan,	R.C.	–	R.C.	R.C.	91	81	171	61
74	8179	Do.	–	Kilmore, m.	R.C.	–	R.C.	–	86	–	86	32
75	10331	Do.	–	Do. f.	R.C.	–	R.C.	–	–	103	103	42
76	8524	Do.	–	Doburn,	R.C.	–	R.C.	–	94	69	163	43
77	9064	Do.	–	Drumreilly,	R.C.	–	R.C.	–	47	47	94	39
78	9086	Do.	–	Corramahon Agricul.	R.C.	–	R.C.	R.C.	84	67	151	60
79	4968	Drumlane,	16	Newton Manor,	R.C.	–	R.C.	R.C.	102	99	201	80
80	6498	Do.	–	Drumlane,	R.C.	–	R.C.	–	66	32	97	34
81	1476	Do.	–	Gortnaskeagh,	R.C.	–	R.C.	–	38	45	83	31
82	7086	Do.	–	Kilconny,	R.C.	–	R.C.	–	71	62	133	32
83	6925	Do.	–	Moneyduff,	R.C.	–	R.C.	–	62	44	106	41
84	10536	Drumshambo,	–	Drumshambo,	–	E.C.	R.C.	–	30	13	43	23
85	10972	Do.	–	Carrigarnow,	–	E.C.	R.C.	–	46	23	69	31
86	1310	Fenagh,	31	Corrawaun,	R.C.	–	R.C.	–	93	76	169	45
87	6058	Do.	–	Fenagh,	R.C.	–	R.C.	–	21	28	51	18
88	2804	Do.	–	Gloontorvan,	R.C.	–	R.C.	–	61	77	138	43
89	9112	Do.	–	Fenagh,	R.C.	–	R.C.	–	133	101	234	61
90	6136	Do.	–	Drumany,	R.C.	–	R.C.	–	63	60	123	36
91	3338	Inishmagrath,	12	Taroote,	R.C.	–	R.C.	–	70	78	148	31
92	5109	Do.	–	Drumkeeran,	R.C.	–	R.C.	–	93	76	169	63
93	5106	Do.	–	Lisnagroghill,	R.C.	–	R.C.	–	80	65	145	37
94	10188	Do.	–	Greaghnaglough,	R.C.	–	R.C.	–	53	50	103	43
95	3448	Do.	–	Kilmore,	R.C.	–	R.C.	R.C.	93	108	201	63
96	6817	Do.	–	Tullynlevan,	R.C.	–	R.C.	R.C.	91	101	192	89
97	8856	Do.	–	Shannon View,	R.C.	–	R.C.	R.C.	56	57	113	45
98	6153	Do.	–	Mountallen,	R.C.	–	R.C.	R.C.	83	63	146	57

a Including value of Free Garden. b Closed. c Incompetent Teacher in charge.

Province of Connaught : County of Leitrim—*continued.*

Amount paid for Works, Repairs, and Apparatus, of Received Funds			Aid granted by the Board during the Year 1874. In Free Stock of Books, Requisites, and Apparatus			In Salaries, Premiums, and other Gratuities			Results Fees, Parliamentary Vote			Amount of Local Endowment received in aid of Teacher's Salary. School Fees			Subscriptions, Endowments, &c.			Total Local Aid			Vested or Non-Vested	Number
£	s.	d.	£	s.	d.	£	s.	d.	£	s.	d.	£	s.	d.	£	s.	d.	£	s.	d.		
3	4	7	—			24	0	0	17	18	6	6	0	0	0	5	0	*6	5	0	[illegible]	38
—			—			27	10	0	15	8	0	3	12	10	—			3	12	10	[illegible]	39
2	8	0	—			20	10	0	12	3	6	1	13	4	—			1	13	4	V.T.	40
—			—			38	0	0	21	14	0	7	10	0	—			7	10	0		41
3	2	1	—			21	0	0	0	13	0	2	6	0	—			2	6	0		42
5	3	9	—			27	0	0	8	3	6	0	10	0	—			0	10	0		43
2	0	8	—			24	0	0	20	3	6	2	8	0	—			2	8	0	[illegible]	44
6	2	0	—			77	15	0	67	11	0	5	7	0	6	0	6	*11	7	6	V.C.	45
									—			—			—			—				46
0	19	6	—			25	10	0	16	12	0	0	2	0	—			0	2	0		47
2	0	5	—			21	0	0	8	8	8	—			—			—				48
3	0	3	—			35	10	0	21	8	0	1	6	0	6	0	0	[illegible]				49
2	11	0	—			24	0	0	11	11	0	0	12	0	—			0	12	0		50
1	10	8	—			25	0	0	14	4	0	3	8	0	—			3	8	0		51
3	17	0	—			43	8	6	7	14	6	8	11	0	87	0	0	95	11	0		52
8	14	8	—			1	10	0	—			—			—			—				53
—			—			—			—			—			—			—				54
1	7	11	—			45	0	0	18	2	0	1	15	6	7	10	0	*9	5	6		55
—			—			51	0	0	14	6	8	—			—			—				56
0	5	1	—			9	8	10	4	16	0	1	10	0	20	0	0	*21	10	0		57
3	10	9	—			41	6	8	35	11	0	1	4	0	5	10	0	*6	14	0		58
									10	8	0	2	11	0	—			2	11	0		
3	2	10	—			65	18	4	22	14	0	1	19	0	—			1	19	0		59
1	8	0	—			54	0	0	5	16	6	—			5	0	0	*5	0	0		60
—			—			24	0	0	7	0	0	1	0	0	—			1	0	0		61
1	14	11	—			30	0	0	16	4	6	0	14	6	—			0	14	6		62
1	10	7	4	0	0	24	0	0	6	17	0	1	10	0	—			1	10	0		63
4	3	1	—			61	0	0	30	7	8	2	10	0	—			2	10	0		64
1	13	11	—			24	0	0	18	7	0	0	9	6	—			0	9	6		65
2	15	9	—			21	0	0	—			—			—			—				66
2	11	11	—			44	0	0	16	15	6	1	0	0	—			1	0	0		67
1	10	9	—			24	0	0	4	7	6	1	18	0	1	0	0	2	18	0		68
—			—			24	0	0	5	17	8	1	0	0	—			1	0	0		69
1	0	6	—			24	0	0	30	11	6	—			—			—				70
—			—			24	0	0	—			—			—			—				71
1	15	9	—			24	0	0	15	18	6	2	0	0	—			2	0	0		72
0	8	3	—			28	0	0	8	8	6	2	0	0	—			2	0	0		73
—			—			24	0	0	8	15	6	3	8	0	—			3	8	0		74
3	16	6	—			30	8	8	9	15	0	—			—			—				75
1	18	7	—			34	10	0	12	0	0	2	0	0	—			2	0	0		76
0	11	8	—			21	0	0	7	0	0	2	19	6	—			2	19	6		77
2	10	0	—			45	19	4	19	10	0	2	0	0	60	0	0	*62	0	0		78
4	0	0	—			40	0	0	25	15	0	2	0	0	—			2	0	0		79
1	0	11	—			21	0	0	3	3	6	—			—			—				80
1	8	6	—			21	0	0	9	19	6	1	9	6	—			1	9	6		81
0	10	9	—			6	0	0	—			1	3	0	—			1	3	0		82
2	8	8	—			26	0	0	11	0	6	3	3	8	—			3	3	8	V.T.	83
0	7	4	—			24	0	0	9	18	6	0	9	6	16	0	0	16	9	6		84
4	9	6	—			24	0	0	11	17	0	1	11	4	18	0	0	19	11	4		85
2	7	0	—			24	0	0	6	17	6	2	1	6	—			2	1	6	V.T.	86
0	18	10	—			11	5	4	2	18	0	—			23	0	0	*23	0	0		87
5	6	4	—			14	5	4	11	15	0	2	19	0	—			2	19	0		88
4	17	9	—			39	4	5	17	17	0	—			—			—				89
2	18	11	—			21	0	0	7	1	0	1	6	0	—			1	6	0		90
3	7	8	—			37	15	4	29	1	0	0	10	0	—			0	10	0		91
8	16	10	—			61	10	0	17	2	0	5	10	6	—			5	10	6		92
1	6	11	—			65	0	0	21	0	0	2	16	6	14	12	4	*17	8	10		93
1	16	10	—			24	0	0	20	0	8	1	2	6	—			1	2	6		94
0	0	8	—			61	18	8	49	15	0	1	8	6	2	10	6	*3	18	6		95
3	0	11	1	0	6	48	0	0	34	18	0	2	2	0	40	8	8	*42	0	0		96
9	8	0	4	0	0	23	18	4	18	18	6	1	8	0	—			1	8	0		97
8	10	10	—			36	18	4	21	0	0	1	11	6	—			1	11	6		

* Including value of Free Residence and Garden.

† No Returns; School Records destroyed.

List of Schools in operation on the 31st December, 1874.—

Number.	Roll Number of School.	Parish.	District.	School.	Religious Denomination of Managers or Correspondents. Clerical.	Lay.	Religious Denomination of Teachers. Principals.	Assistants.	Total number of Pupils on Rolls within the Year 1874. Males.	Females.	Total.	Average Daily Attendance for the Year.
99	6771	Inishmagrath,	10	Shivdalagh,	R.C.	–	R.C.	R.C.	70	65	135	47
100	8512	Do.	–	Tullycorka,	R.C.	–	R.C.	–	51	65	116	46
101	10694	Do.	–	Dargon, (2)	R.C.	–	R.C.	–	44	47	91	38
102	9183	Do.	–	Clooncown,	R.C.	–	R.C.	–	67	67	171	56
103	10256	Do.	–	Gurteenaille,	–	R.C.	R.C.	R.C.	88	63	151	41
104	10124	Kiltoghert,	22	Jamestown, m.	R.C.	–	R.C.	–	79	–	79	38
105	[illegible]	Do.	–	Do. f.	R.C.	–	R.C.	–	–	76	76	40
106	[illegible]	Do.	31	Crutty,	R.C.	–	R.C.	–	44	44	88	46
107	[illegible]	Do.	22	Drumkeelan More,	R.C.	–	R.C.	–	55	49	104	40
108	[illegible]	Do.	–	Cordarry,	R.C.	–	R.C.	–	67	83	150	49
109	[illegible]	Do.	–	Liscloff, No. 2, m.	R.C.	–	R.C.	–	87	54	141	61
110	8910	Do.	–	Kilmagrane,	R.C.	–	R.C.	–	110	69	178	67
111	8172	Do.	31	Drumshanbo, m.	R.C.	–	R.C.	–	131	–	131	69
112	10301	Do.	–	Do. (6).	Diss.	–	Diss.	–	30	28	64	22
113	[illegible]	Do.	22	Carrick-on-Shannon, m.	–	E.C.	R.C.	R.C.	180	–	180	85
114	[illegible]	Do.	–	Do. f.	–	E.C.	R.C.	R.C.	–	163	163	60
115	[illegible]	Do.	–	Do. Workhouse,	–	E.C.	2R.C.	–	68	60	128	84
116	11012	Do.	–	Do. Convent,	R.C.	–	None		40	209	252	101
117	[illegible]	Do.	–	Leitrim 1st class Agri.	–	E.C.	R.C.	–	110	–	110	37
118	[illegible]	Do.	–	Do.[b] f.	–	–	Pres.	R.C.	–	–	–	–
119	7128	Do.	–	Kiltoghert,	R.C.	–	R.C.	–	104	61	165	61
120	8174	Do.	31	Corrachamangus,	R.C.	–	R.C.	–	71	40	117	42
121	[illegible]	Do.	–	Aughagrane,	R.C.	–	R.C.	–	71	51	122	38
122	[illegible]	Kiltubbrid,	–	Mohercreggagh,	R.C.	–	R.C.	–	33	85	118	62
123	[illegible]	Do.	–	Lisnarban,	R.C.	–	R.C.	–	129	–	129	66
124	7370	Do.	–	Gortagh,[d] m.	–	–	–	–	–	–	–	–
125	[illegible]	Do.	–	Do. f.	R.C.	–	R.C.	–	–	73	73	38
126	[illegible]	Do.	–	Cranny,	R.C.	–	R.C.	–	44	78	122	38
127	[illegible]	Do.	–	Killelars,	R.C.	–	R.C.	R.C.	127	125	252	71
128	[illegible]	Do.	–	Rossy,	R.C.	–	R.C.	–	58	77	135	41
129	7397	Do.	–	Fannamagh,	R.C.	–	R.C.	R.C.	60	97	157	38
130	7632	Do.	–	Mulmaghrain,	R.C.	–	R.C.	–	–	117	117	30
131	[illegible]	Do.	–	Aghacashel,[b]	R.C.	–	R.C.	–	–	–	–	–
132	8178	Killenummery,	12	Killavoggy,	R.C.	–	R.C.	–	80	80	160	38
133	8478	Do.	–	Srecumnas,	R.C.	–	R.C.	–	113	110	223	69
134	9261	Do.	–	Ardvarney,	R.C.	–	R.C.	–	36	37	73	30
135	8724	Killasnet,	–	Drumkeary-bog,	R.C.	–	R.C.	–	59	59	118	44
136	[illegible]	Do.	–	Lackanrainy,	R.C.	–	R.C.	–	86	78	164	54
137	6948	Do.	–	Glenkerrasheen,	R.C.	–	–	R.C.	52	40	92	29
138	6914	Do.	–	Kilgrenak,	R.C.	–	R.C.	–	79	63	142	49
139	[illegible]	Do.	–	Diffreen,	R.C.	–	R.C.	R.C.	107	52	159	58
140	8416	Do.	–	Glenmar,	R.C.	–	R.C.	–	51	45	96	43
141	9633	Do.	–	Killasnet,	R.C.	–	R.C.	R.C.	70	80	150	51
142	10309	Do.	–	Largy,	R.C.	–	R.C.	–	56	44	100	6
143	4452	Killarga,	–	Drumkeel,	R.C.	–	R.C.	R.C.	84	66	150	51
144	[illegible]	Do.	–	Killarga,	R.C.	–	R.C.	–	31	45	76	31
145	6601	Do.	–	Tullynasearna,	R.C.	–	R.C.	R.C.	61	67	128	54
146	[illegible]	Do.	–	Mullaghgarve,	R.C.	–	R.C.	–	117	60	177	77
147	[illegible]	Do.	–	Legnaskeagh,	R.C.	–	R.C.	–	96	74	170	75
148	10222	Do.	–	Cornamorriff,	R.C.	–	R.C.	–	24	29	53	51
149	9199	Do.	–	Coolegan,	R.C.	–	R.C.	–	45	52	97	40
150	[illegible]	Mohill,	29	Eskeragh,[d]	–	–	–	–	–	–	–	–
151	10026	Do.	31	Eslin, m.	R.C.	–	R.C.	R.C.	171	–	171	79
152	10277	Do.	–	Do. f.	R.C.	–	R.C.	R.C.	–	149	143	84
153	7816	Do.	29	Mohill, m.	R.C.	–	R.C.	R.C.	217	–	217	81
154	[illegible]	Do.	–	Do. f.	R.C.	–	R.C.	–	–	153	153	72
155	[illegible]	Do.	–	Do. i.	R.C.	–	R.C.	–	70	68	138	54
156	[illegible]	Do.	–	Do. No. 2, m.	–	E.C.	E.C.	–	168	–	168	83
157	8874	Do.	–	Do. do. f.	–	E.C.	E.C.	–	–	97	97	39
158	8418	Do.	–	Do. Workhouse,	–	E.C.	2R.C.	–	30	40	70	32
159	[illegible]	Do.	–	Cloonmagh, m.	R.C.	–	R.C.	–	285	–	285	87
160	[illegible]	Do.	–	Do. f.	R.C.	–	R.C.	R.C.	–	180	180	69
161	[illegible]	Do.	31	Stracarne, m.	–	E.C.	R.C.	–	120	–	120	57

[a] Including value of Free Residence. [b] No Returns. [d] Including value of Free Garden.

	Aid granted by the Board during the Year 1871.			Amount of Local Emoluments secured in Aid of Teacher's Salary.				
	In Part Stock of Books, Requisites, and Apparatus.	In Salaries, Premiums, and other Gratuities.	Results Fees, Financial Year.	School Fees.	Subscriptions, Endowments, &c.	Total Local Aid.	Vested or Non-Vested.	Number.
d.	£ s. d.	£ s. d.	£ s. d.	£ s. d.	£ s. d.	£ s. d.		
0	—	37 0 0	21 0 0	2 7 5	—	4 7 5		99
1	—	28 16 8	10 3 6	0 13 6	—	0 19 6		100
10	—	21 0 0	15 7 6	1 2 6	—	1 2 6		101
7	—	30 0 0	25 7 0	2 0 0	—	3 0 0		102
6	—	56 0 0	20 19 0	1 0 0	—	1 0 0	V.E.	103
10	—	70 18 4	18 1 0	0 0 0	—	6 0 0		104
1	—	24 16 8	18 1 8	2 5 8	—	2 5 8		105
9	—	44 0 0	11 9 0	6 0 0	—	6 0 0		106
9	—	45 10 0	14 4 0	2 13 0	—	2 13 0	V.T.	107
0	—	56 5 8	13 0 0	3 0 0	3 0 0	6 0 0	V.T.	108
9	—	31 0 0	20 8 0	5 7 6	—	5 7 6		109
1	—	21 0 0	24 3 0	0 10 0	—	0 10 0		110
11	—	51 10 0	11 19 6	8 4 6	—	8 4 6		111
11	—	24 0 0	8 1 0	10 6 3	11 0 0	*21 6 3		112
9	—	57 0 0	20 8 0	6 18 6	15 0 0	21 18 6		113
0	—	63 11 8	25 7 6	3 0 0	15 0 0	18 0 0		114
8	—	9 6 0	—	—	—	—		115
8	—	34 11 8	20 4 0	8 19 6	—	8 19 6		116
0	8 0 6	49 10 0	18 6 6	1 8 0	6 0 0	7 8 0	V.E.	117
	5 14 0	—	13 10 0	—	—	—	V.E.	118
0	—	28 13 4	21 4 6	4 3 6	—	4 3 6		119
	—	24 0 0	8 1 0	4 18 6	—	4 18 6		120
4	—	24 0 0	4 16 0	3 0 0	—	3 0 0		121
6	—	27 0 0	21 0 6	0 18 0	6 0 0	6 18 0		122
7	—	35 7 6	15 1 0	2 0 0	1 0 0	*3 0 0	V.T.	123
	—			—	—			124
	—	25 0 0	8 2 0	4 17 11	1 0 0	5 17 11		125
1	—	32 0 0	18 17 0	2 10 0	—	2 10 0		126
7	—	37 0 0	19 3 0	1 18 0	—	1 18 0		127
0	—	21 0 0	8 15 0	1 5 0	—	1 5 0		128
7	—	44 0 0	15 12 0	3 16 6	—	3 16 6		129
7	—	24 0 0	7 14 0	0 13 0	3 0 0	3 13 0		130
	—	—		—	—	—		131
11	—	52 0 0	10 4 0	3 8 0	—	3 9 0	E.	132
0	—	28 0 0	20 10 6	4 8 0	—	4 8 0		133
9	—	10 0 0		—	—	—		134
5	—	31 10 0	15 18 6	2 0 6	—	2 0 6		135
8	—	29 0 0	22 6 6	0 8 0	—	0 8 0		136
9	—	20 0 0	5 18 0	0 15 6	—	0 15 6		137
	—	17 17 6	—	—	—	—		138
2	—	34 0 0	17 8 6	8 0 0	—	8 0 0		139
11	—	26 2 4	18 10 0	4 2 6	—	4 2 6		140
0	—	24 0 0	16 10 0	2 17 10	—	2 17 10		141
7	4 0 0	15 16 0	—	0 10 0	2 0 0	2 10 0		142
6	—	45 10 0	21 11 0	3 16 0	—	3 16 0		143
5	—	30 0 0	15 4 6	—	—	—		144
9	—	44 0 0	30 18 0	1 11 0	—	1 11 0		145
5	—	21 10 0	22 10 0	2 14 6	—	2 14 6		146
0	—	19 0 0	—	—	—	—		147
9	—	30 0 0	11 0 6	0 18 0	21 10 0	*22 8 0		148
0	—	8 0 0	—	1 0 0	—	1 0 0		149
	—		—		—		E.	150
1	—	35 0 8	24 10 6	6 8 8	—	6 8 8	V.E.	151
7	—	51 8 8	26 0 6	3 16 0	—	3 16 0	V.T.	152
4	—	30 10 0	31 1 6	4 0 0	—	4 0 0		153
1	—	35 8 8	20 14 0	3 0 0	—	3 0 0		154
8	—	27 0 8	11 8 0	1 7 8	—	1 7 8		155
6	—	55 12 4	20 11 8	7 6 0	27 14 0	*35 0 0		156
9	—	45 0 0	25 10 0	6 11 0	16 0 0	*22 0 0		157
0	—	5 10 0		—	—	—		158
10	—	35 18 4	17 16 0	5 10 0	—	5 10 0	V.T.	159
6	—	32 6 4	18 4 0	7 8 5	—	7 8 5	V.T.	160
8	—	24 0 8	9 18 0	2 12 0	3 0 0	5 12 0		161

* Inoperative.

* Including value of Free Residence and Garden.

List of Schools in operation on the 31st December, 1874.—

Number.	Roll Number of School.	Parish.	District.	School.		Religious Denomination of Patrons or Correspondents: Clerical.	Lay.	Number and Religious Denomination of Teachers: Principals.	Assistants.	Total number of Pupils on Rolls within the Year term: Males.	Females.	Total.	Average Number in Daily Attendance.
162	6129	Mohill,	31	Sunaeran,	f.	–	R.C.	R.C.	–	–	109	109	52
163	748[illegible]	Do.	–	Shragane,		R.C.	–	R.C.	R.C.	66	50	116	43
164	817[illegible]	Do.	32	Greaghra,		R.C.	–	R.C.	–	35	48	178	[illegible]
165	[illegible]	Do.	31	Curraun,		R.C.	–	R.C.	–	98	101	199	[illegible]
166	[illegible]	Do.	28	Cloonturk,	m.	R.C.	–	R.C.	–	127	–	127	[illegible]
167	[illegible]	Do.	–	Do.	f.	R.C.	–	R.C.	–	–	130	130	[illegible]
168	140[illegible]	Oughteragh,	31	Fenagh,	m.	R.C.	–	R.C.	–	138	–	138	[illegible]
169	312[illegible]	Do.	–	Do.	f.	R.C.	–	R.C.	–	–	121	121	[illegible]
170	149[illegible]	Do.	–	Derrinkeher,		–	R.C.	R.C.	R.C.	61	78	139	[illegible]
171	[illegible]	Do.	–	Ballinamore,	m.	–	R.C.	R.C.	–	129	–	129	50
172	2921	Do.	–	Do.	f.	–	R.C.	R.C.	–	–	121	121	[illegible]
173	[illegible]	Do.	–	Do.	Convent,	R.C.	–	Nuns		50	60	109	45
174	[illegible]	Do.	–	Drumshiva,	m.	R.C.	–	R.C.	–	101	–	101	[illegible]
175	[illegible]	Do.	–	Do.	f.	R.C.	–	R.C.	R.C.	–	141	141	[illegible]
176	378[illegible]	Do.	–	Cloghar,		–	R.C.	R.C.	R.C.	88	78	160	[illegible]
177	8107	Do.	–	Mayo,		–	R.C.	R.C.	–	70	32	102	31
178	[illegible]	Do.	–	Oughteragh,		–	R.C.	R.C.	–	18	62	80	[illegible]
179	[illegible]	Do.	–	Lisacarn,		R.C.	–	R.C.	–	88	58	146	[illegible]
180	1341	Rossinver,	29	Loughmalrevan,		R.C.	–	R.C.	–	57	52	109	[illegible]
181	[illegible]	Do.	–	Sechude,		–	R.C.	R.C.	–	63	68	131	[illegible]
182	[illegible]	Do.	–	Ballyduffmore,		R.C.	–	R.C.	–	101	–	101	[illegible]
183	[illegible]	Do.	–	Cloonariff,		R.C.	–	R.C.	R.C.	93	66	159	67
184	[illegible]	Do.	–	Edenvella,		R.C.	–	R.C.	R.C.	107	109	216	[illegible]
185	[illegible]	Do.	5	Achill,		–	R.C.	R.C.	–	48	29	77	[illegible]
186	[illegible]	Do.	18	Tawly,		–	–	–	–	–	–	–	–
187	[illegible]	Do.	–	Drummons,		R.C.	–	R.C.	–	78	68	146	[illegible]
188	[illegible]	Do.	–	Aghanlish,		R.C.	–	R.C.	–	64	38	101	[illegible]
189	[illegible]	Do.	5	Boyannagh,		–	R.C.	R.C.	–	8	99	107	107
190	[illegible]	Do.	12	Conray,	f.	R.C.	–	R.C.	R.C.	–	129	129	60
191	[illegible]	Do.	–	Wardhouse,		R.C.	–	R.C.	–	45	54	99	[illegible]
192	7178	Do.	–	Rossinver,		R.C.	–	R.C.	–	86	54	139	[illegible]
193	[illegible]	Do.	–	Uragh,		R.C.	–	R.C.	–	62	48	110	23
194	[illegible]	Do.	–	Glenade,		R.C.	–	R.C.	–	41	36	82	24
195	10097	Do.	–	Tullaghan,		R.C.	–	R.C.	R.C.	80	45	131	[illegible]
		Total for County of Leitrim, 126 Schools,								12803	11676	24,479	[illegible]

COUNTY OF

Number.	Roll Number of School.	Parish.	District.	School.		Clerical.	Lay.	Principals.	Assistants.	Males.	Females.	Total.	Average Number in Daily Attendance.
1	1411	Aglish,	29	Aglish,		R.C.	–	R.C.	–	114	93	207	49
2	[illegible]	Do.	–	Castlebar,	Workho.	P.L. Gdn.		R.C.	–	25	16	41	28
3	[illegible]	Do.	–	Do.	m.	R.C.	–	R.C.	–	178	–	178	75
4	[illegible]	Do.	–	Do.	f.	R.C.	–	R.C.	–	–	104	104	87
5	[illegible]	Addergoole,	29	Rathhall,		R.C.	–	R.C.	R.C.	167	184	351	76
6	1944	Do.	–	Massbrook,		R.C.	–	R.C.	R.C.	62	65	127	[illegible]
7	[illegible]	Do.	–	Laherdane,		R.C.	–	R.C.	–	85	70	155	44
8	[illegible]	Do.	30	Cloondaff,		R.C.	–	R.C.	R.C.	118	122	240	[illegible]
9	[illegible]	Do.	29	Rathbane,		R.C.	–	R.C.	R.C.	178	169	346	76
10	[illegible]	Achill,	30	Slievemore,		–	R.C.	R.C.	–	70	51	121	[illegible]
11	[illegible]	Aughamore,	31	Ballymacleagha,		R.C.	–	R.C.	–	109	117	226	[illegible]
12	[illegible]	Do.	–	Cussard,		R.C.	–	R.C.	R.C.	135	140	275	[illegible]
13	[illegible]	Do.	20	Derrewas,		–	R.C.	R.C.	–	63	94	157	[illegible]
14	[illegible]	Do.	–	Doorgh,		–	R.C.	R.C.	–	50	24	74	[illegible]
15	[illegible]	Do.	–	Tonragee,		R.C.	–	R.C.	–	62	85	97	[illegible]
16	4114	Do.	–	Curvane,		R.C.	–	R.C.	–	100	90	190	[illegible]
17	[illegible]	Do.	–	Dough,		R.C.	–	R.C.	–	94	83	176	57
18	[illegible]	Do.	–	Dunmurry,[b]	f.	R.C.	–	–	–	–	–	–	–
19	[illegible]	Do.	–	Valley,	m.	R.C.	–	R.C.	–	63	26	89	40
20	[illegible]	Do.	–	Doifarned,[a]		R.C.	–	–	–	–	–	–	–
21	[illegible]	Do.	–	Ballasmouth,		R.C.	–	R.C.	–	62	37	99	45

[a] Including value of Free Garden.

[b] Inoperative.

Province of CONNAUGHT: County of LEITRIM—*continued.*

Amount paid for Books, Requisites, and Apparatus at Reduced Prices.	Aid granted by the Board during the Year 1874: In Free Stock of Books, Requisites, and Apparatus.	In Salaries, Premiums, and other Gratuities.	Results Fees, Financial Year.	Amount of Local Emoluments in Aid of Teachers': School Fees.	Subscriptions, Endowments, etc.
£ s. d.	£ s. d.	£ s. d.	£ s. d.	£ s. d.	£ s. d.
1 5 7	—	20 0 0	19 17 0	1 4 6	2 0 0
3 14 0	—	77 6 8	18 17 0	2 12 0	—
0 11 4	—	23 0 0	19 14 0	7 14 0	—
2 2 7	—	24 0 0	23 9 8	8 16 5	—
8 6 8	—	29 0 0	7 11 0	1 7 0	—
1 7 8	—	59 5 0	15 2 4	1 19 0	—
1 10 4	—	21 0 0	4 8 4	1 0 0	—
2 6 9	—	21 0 9	0 8 0	—	—
6 0 9	—	34 8 4	14 15 8	1 13 0	—
3 5 0	—	41 11 0	8 14 8	2 7 0	8 10 0
2 0 8	—	28 0 0	14 4 0	2 14 0	2 10 0
5 17 3	—	0 2 0	0 0 0	0 14 0	—
1 14 0	—	82 13 4	0 8 0	0 10 0	—
1 11 4	—	40 0 0	21 2 0	—	—
3 17 4	—	47 0 0	23 10 8	1 0 0	—
0 19 4	—	24 0 0	7 11 8	1 11 0	—
1 6 6	—	30 0 8	10 10 0	5 3 11	15 0 0
2 14 7	—	25 0 0	10 12 0	1 1 0	—
1 6 8	—	37 0 0	7 16 6	1 16 0	2 6 0
3 11 7	—	38 0 0	37 1 6	5 15 5	5 5 0
1 13 4	—	47 0 0	16 18 0	1 18 11	—
3 14 7	—	34 0 0	21 10 0	6 0 0	—
8 13 10	—	44 18 4	24 1 0	0 11 0	—
1 11 6	—	25 0 0	18 0 0	2 13 6	0 15 0
—	—	—	—	—	—
2 7 8	—	27 10 0	11 8 0	0 17 6	—
2 14 11	—	10 8 10	12 1 6	3 10 0	—
1 8 8	—	28 10 0	14 12 9	2 1 6	5 0 0
4 10 3	—	67 10 0	26 10 6	1 4 8	—
1 6 10	—	20 0 0	13 7 0	—	—
2 16 10	—	24 0 0	12 13 6	1 2 0	—
2 10 6	—	30 0 0	7 9 6	2 16 0	—
1 10 6	—	24 0 0	8 8 0	0 10 0	—
4 10 0	—	29 0 0	16 18 0	4 6 8	—
483 12 6	18 14 10	6,175 8 8	2,915 9 0	498 1 0	168 18 4

MAYO—297 Schools.

1 10 8	—	34 18 4	5 10 0	8 14 11	0 10 0
8 17 7	—	—	—	—	—
6 2 11	—	49 8 8	25 18 6	18 16 11	—
1 17 6	—	23 8 8	5 17 0	1 18 6	—
4 18 6	—	28 18 10	16 7 0	8 6 8	—
—	—	45 0 0	15 13 6	2 6 0	4 0 0
0 7 0	—	61 6 8	8 0 0	8 4 0	3 0 0
2 5 8	—	42 18 4	30 7 0	—	5 0 0
8 13 0	—	54 7 5	14 8 6	3 13 0	—
2 10 8	—	81 0 0	22 4 0	—	—
5 8 10	—	14 0 0	12 5 0	7 5 6	—
5 2 2	—	44 0 0	26 14 6	7 11 2	—
1 6 4	—	20 0 0	2 17 6	—	—
2 0 4	—	20 16 4	2 10 0	—	—
1 8 2	—	44 0 0	4 4 0	—	—
1 18 8	—	23 6 8	8 0 0	—	—
2 8 5	—	81 15 0	11 11 6	2 8 0	—
1 2 0	—	—	—	—	—
1 5 11	—	29 10 0	11 8 0	—	—
—	—	—	—	—	—
1 18 8	—	24 0 0	7 0 8	3 17 6	—

* No Teacher.

List of Schools in operation on the 31st December, 1874—

Number.	Roll Number of School.	Parish.	District.	School.	Religious Denomination of Patrons or Correspondents: Clerical.	Lay.	Teachers' Religious Denomination: Principals.	Assistants.	Total number of Pupils on Rolls within the Year: Males.	Females.	Total.	Average daily attendance.
22	10628	Aughamore,	20	Seale,	R.C.	–	R.C.	–	102	39	140	30
23	4755	Aughagower,	–	Lankill,	–	R.C.	R.C.	–	96	76	170	84
24	4794	Do.	–	Carrabrenedy, [b]	–	R.C.	–	–	–	–	–	–
25	5124	Do.	–	Derrycreeff,	–	R.C.	R.C.	–	67	43	100	46
26	8796	Do.	–	St. Joseph's,	R.C.	–	R.C.	R.C.	113	[illegible]	[illegible]	[illegible]
27	8453	Do.	–	Aughagower,	R.C.	–	R.C.	–	75	60	[illegible]	[illegible]
28	[illegible]	Do.	–	Knappagh,	R.C.	–	R.C.	–	67	17	[illegible]	[illegible]
29	10902	Attymass,	20	Attymass,	R.C.	–	R.C.	R.C.	101	140	241	[illegible]
30	10342	Do.	–	Carrowcrory,	–	–	R.C.	–	143	80	[illegible]	[illegible]
31	8117	Aghamore,	21	Doogary,	–	R.C.	R.C.	R.C.	137	130	[illegible]	[illegible]
32	9210	Do.	–	Aghamore,	R.C.	–	R.C.	R.C.	131	132	[illegible]	[illegible]
33	10619	Do.	–	Cloonfallagh,	R.C.	–	R.C.	R.C.	177	167	[illegible]	[illegible]
34	10613	Do.	–	Carrowrenakan,	R.C.	–	R.C.	R.C.	84	91	175	[illegible]
35	9303	Aughaval,	26	Westport, No. 2,	R.C.	–	R.C.	R.C.	47	[illegible]	[illegible]	[illegible]
36	10581	Ardagh,	24	Rathnamanagh,	R.C.	–	R.C.	–	105	[illegible]	[illegible]	[illegible]
37	10697	Do.	–	Ardagh,	R.C.	–	–	R.C.	109	79	188	[illegible]
38	1657	Annagh,	22	Foxhall or Loghloy,	R.C.	–	R.C.	–	152	114	[illegible]	61
39	9314	Do.	–	Ballyhaunis, m.	–	R.C.	R.C.	R.C.	[illegible]	–	[illegible]	[illegible]
40	7924	Do.	–	Do. f.	–	R.C.	R.C.	R.C.	–	[illegible]	[illegible]	[illegible]
41	9554	Do.	–	Cooladdurna, [b]	–	–	–	–	–	–	–	–
42	10484	Do.	–	Kilkerrin,	R.C.	–	R.C.	–	103	137	[illegible]	[illegible]
43	8928	Ballyovey,	26	Partry,	R.C.	–	R.C.	–	144	–	144	[illegible]
44	10775	Do.	–	Do. f.	R.C.	–	R.C.	–	–	125	125	31
45	1064	Bekan,	22	Brackloon,	R.C.	–	R.C.	–	111	[illegible]	201	[illegible]
46	6815	Do.	–	Bekan, m.	–	R.C.	R.C.	–	[illegible]	–	[illegible]	[illegible]
47	[illegible]	Do.	–	Do. f.	–	R.C.	R.C.	R.C.	–	274	274	[illegible]
48	1967	Breaffy,	26	Breaffy,	R.C.	–	R.C.	R.C.	181	95	[illegible]	[illegible]
49	1146	Balla,	21	Balla, m.	–	R.C.	R.C.	R.C.	[illegible]	–	[illegible]	[illegible]
50	4786	Do.	–	Do. f.	–	R.C.	R.C.	R.C.	–	218	[illegible]	[illegible]
51	1670	Burrishoole,	26	Newport Pratt, m.	–	R.C.	R.C.	–	114	–	114	[illegible]
52	4033	Do.	–	Do. f.	–	R.C.	R.C.	–	–	96	[illegible]	[illegible]
53	1871	Do.	–	Tiernaur,	–	R.C.	R.C.	R.C.	67	75	142	[illegible]
54	1673	Do.	–	Kilmore,	–	R.C.	R.C.	–	84	80	[illegible]	[illegible]
55	1814	Do.	–	Mulranny,	–	R.C.	R.C.	–	99	71	170	51
56	1873	Do.	–	Derrakilla,	–	R.C.	R.C.	R.C.	95	80	[illegible]	[illegible]
57	[illegible]	Do.	–	Shirdagh,	–	R.C.	R.C.	–	72	64	[illegible]	[illegible]
58	6190	Do.	–	Newport, Workho.	P.L.	Gda.	R.C.	–	17	[illegible]	[illegible]	[illegible]
59	7923	Do.	–	Knockavilla,	R.C.	–	R.C.	–	159	109	[illegible]	[illegible]
60	8046	Ballysakeery,	20	Lisglennon,	Pres.	–	Pres.	–	[illegible]	[illegible]	[illegible]	[illegible]
61	9310	Do.	–	Ballysakeery,	R.C.	–	R.C.	–	[illegible]	41	81	[illegible]
62	4416	Do.	–	Cooneal,	R.C.	–	R.C.	R.C.	68	75	161	[illegible]
63	[illegible]	Do.	–	Newtown White, [c]	–	–	–	–	–	–	–	–
64	5128	Ballintober,	26	Ballycarra,	R.C.	–	R.C.	–	46	57	[illegible]	[illegible]
65	[illegible]	Do.	–	Killavally,	–	R.C.	R.C.	R.C.	111	109	[illegible]	[illegible]
66	7374	Do.	–	Ballintober,	R.C.	–	R.C.	R.C.	113	89	[illegible]	[illegible]
67	[illegible]	Ballynahaglish,	20	Lisnalake, Agricul.	R.C.	–	R.C.	R.C.	167	161	[illegible]	[illegible]
68	[illegible]	Do.	–	Carrowgerra, Ord. Agr.	R.C.	–	R.C.	R.C.	97	103	200	74
69	[illegible]	Do.	–	Rahins,	R.C.	–	R.C.	R.C.	[illegible]	[illegible]	[illegible]	[illegible]
70	[illegible]	Do.	–	Strahoon,	R.C.	–	R.C.	–	106	[illegible]	[illegible]	[illegible]
71	5756	Burriscarra,	26	Burriscarra, m.	–	R.C.	R.C.	–	130	–	[illegible]	[illegible]
72	5757	Do.	–	Do. f.	–	R.C.	R.C.	–	–	91	91	[illegible]
73	7967	Ballincholla,	–	Inishmaine, m.	R.C.	–	R.C.	–	199	[illegible]	[illegible]	[illegible]
74	9107	Bohola,	21	Lisnolraine,	R.C.	–	R.C.	R.C.	[illegible]	[illegible]	[illegible]	[illegible]
75	[illegible]	Bohola,	–	Carrowgowan, m.	R.C.	–	R.C.	–	[illegible]	–	[illegible]	[illegible]
76	[illegible]	Do.	–	Do. f.	R.C.	–	R.C.	–	–	184	184	[illegible]
77	[illegible]	Ballyovey,	26	Tristaun, f.	R.C.	–	R.C.	–	[illegible]	186	[illegible]	[illegible]
78	9741	Ballinrobe,	[illegible]	Ballinrobe, m.	–	E.C.	R.C.	R.C.	458	–	[illegible]	[illegible]
79	6117	Do.	–	Do. Workhouse,	P.L.	Gds.	R.C.	–	60	93	[illegible]	[illegible]
80	[illegible]	Do.	–	Creagh,	R.C.	–	R.C.	R.C.	169	[illegible]	[illegible]	[illegible]
81	5797	Ballyhean,	26	Ballyhean,	R.C.	–	R.C.	R.C.	87	75	[illegible]	[illegible]
82	10787	Castlemore,	11	Tonaraugan, m.	R.C.	–	R.C.	–	158	–	[illegible]	[illegible]
83	10788	Do.	–	Do. f.	R.C.	–	R.C.	R.C.	–	143	[illegible]	[illegible]
84	1058	Do.	–	Brusna Ord. Agricul.	R.C.	–	R.C.	R.C.	167	167	334	[illegible]

[a] Including value of Farm Garden. [b] No Returns. [c] Including value of Free Residence and Garden.

	£	s.	d.	£	s.	d.	£	s.	d.	£	s.	d.	£	s.	d.	£	s.	d.	
[illegible]		—		24	0	0	6	7	0		—			—			—		
[illegible]		—		80	0	0	15	6	6	7	4	1	9	0	0	*0	4	1	v.c.
[illegible]		—			—			—			—			—			—		v.c.
[illegible]		—		24	0	0	8	11	8	0	7	0	5	0	0	5	7	8	v.c.
[illegible]		—		29	0	0	4	8	0	5	16	8		—		5	10	3	
[illegible]		—		28	16	6	4	3	6	4	19	4		—		4	19	4	
[illegible]		—		24	0	0	11	15	0	2	18	6	3	6	0	*5	3	0	
[illegible]		—		47	10	0	19	16	8	8	6	0		—		8	6	0	
[illegible]		—		24	0	0	8	4	0	8	8	6		—		8	8	3	
[illegible]		—		48	6	8	15	16	0	4	17	0	3	6	0	*7	8	0	
[illegible]		—		70	0	0	17	16	8	6	14	6		—		6	14	0	
[illegible]		—		40	5	0	19	17	0	0	1	6	1	0	0	*10	1	0	
[illegible]		—		46	6	6	10	6	0	8	12	7		—		8	14	7	
[illegible]		—		47	10	0	15	17	0	8	0	0	30	0	0	*41	0	0	
[illegible]		—		43	0	0	11	7	0	2	18	3		—		4	18	8	
[illegible]		—			—		5	3	0	3	13	8		—		3	13	8	
[illegible]		—		31	18	4	14	18	6	9	14	8		—		9	14	6	v.r.
[illegible]		—		76	10	0	81	17	0	23	3	0	8	0	0	*21	8	0	
[illegible]		—		60	0	0	45	18	6	18	18	0		—		18	10	0	
[illegible]		—		44	0	0		—			—			—			—		
[illegible]		—		24	0	0	9	18	6	9	3	0		—		8	3	0	
[illegible]		—		28	0	0	16	11	0	5	14	0	10	0	0	15	14	0	
[illegible]		—		30	0	0	10	12	6		—			—			—		
[illegible]		—		24	0	0	10	7	0	5	16	0		—		5	16	0	
[illegible]		—		28	0	0	28	7	6	0	8	1	8	4	10	*15	10	11	
[illegible]		—		40	0	6	14	1	6	8	0	0		—		8	0	0	
[illegible]		—		46	10	0	15	8	0	8	16	0	8	0	0	5	18	0	
[illegible]		—		113	0	0	27	12	0		—		19	0	0	10	6	0	v.r.
[illegible]		—		73	17	8	61	9	6		—		10	0	0	10	0	0	v.c.
[illegible]		—		24	0	0	6	3	0	1	0	0	0	15	0	*1	15	0	A.
[illegible]		—		20	0	0	7	12	0	2	6	0		—		2	5	0	A.
[illegible]		—		30	0	0	10	10	6		—		18	0	0	*18	0	0	A.
[illegible]		—		24	0	0	7	10	8		—			—			—		A.
[illegible]		—		24	0	0	6	11	0	8	8	8		—		8	8	8	v.c.
[illegible]		—		47	6	8	19	0	0	3	5	6		—		3	5	6	A.
[illegible]		—		20	0	0	5	6	0	0	6	10		—		0	6	10	v.c.
[illegible]		—		1	10	0		—			—			—			—		
[illegible]		—		80	0	0	1	16	0	2	0	0		—		2	0	0	
[illegible]	1	11	6	18	8	6	2	0	0		—		10	10	0	*12	10	0	
[illegible]		—		24	0	0	6	7	0	0	17	6	7	0	0	*7	17	6	
[illegible]		—		61	0	0	32	6	0	0	10	0		—		0	10	0	
[illegible]		—			—			—			—			—			—		
[illegible]		—		43	0	0	15	6	0	2	6	0	4	5	0	6	11	0	v.c.
[illegible]		—		34	0	0	7	8	0	2	0	0		—		2	0	0	v.c.
[illegible]		—		65	6	8	18	15	6	8	0	0	5	0	0	8	0	0	v.c.
[illegible]		—		74	15	0	27	10	6	4	10	0	5	10	0	*10	0	0	
[illegible]		—		85	6	8	35	19	6	8	17	6	58	19	8	*67	17	2	
[illegible]		—		40	0	0	15	18	6	1	17	6	3	0	0	4	17	6	
[illegible]		—		29	10	0	14	12	6	1	17	6		—		1	17	6	
[illegible]		—		24	0	0	4	19	6	2	11	0	8	0	0	*10	11	0	v.c.
[illegible]		—		20	0	0	4	11	6	0	18	8		—		0	18	8	v.c.
[illegible]		—		45	13	6	10	1	0	3	9	7		—		3	9	7	
[illegible]		—		77	16	0	31	10	6	12	10	6		—		12	10	6	
[illegible]		—		28	10	0	7	13	0	3	0	0		—		3	0	0	
[illegible]		—		48	6	8	9	16	0	2	10	6		—		2	10	6	
[illegible]		—		20	0	0	8	0	0		—			—			—		
[illegible]		—		118	16	8	51	8	0		—		41	10	0	*41	10	0	
[illegible]		—			—			—			—			—			—		
[illegible]		—		48	8	6	14	8	6	4	10	10		—		4	10	10	
[illegible]		—		44	0	0	24	8	0	6	8	6		—		6	8	6	
[illegible]		—		24	0	0	12	10	0	5	1	0		—		5	1	0	
[illegible]		—		54	6	8	60	19	6	7	10	0		—		7	10	0	
16		—		118	3	4	18	19	0	6	4	0	9	0	0	*15	4	0	

* Including value of Free Residence.

* Closed.

List of Schools in operation on the 31st December, 1874,—

Number.	Roll No. of School.	Parish.	District.	School.	Religious Denomination of Managers or Correspondents: Clerical.	Lay.	Number and Religion of Teachers: Principals.	Assistants.	Attendance for the Year: Total number of Pupils on Rolls within the Year 1874: Males.	Fem.	Total.	Average Daily Attendance.
85	1678	Crossboyne,	22	Ballindine, day m.	–	R.C.	R.C.	R.C.	124	–	124	46
				Do. evg.	–	R.C.	R.C.	–	52	–	52	12
86	8925	Do.	–	Do. f.	–	R.C.	R.C.	–	–	125	125	50
87	8948	Do.	–	Crossboyne, day.	–	R.C.	–	R.C.	95	82	177	65
				Do.* evg.	–	–	–	–	–	–	–	–
88	4178	Crossmolina,	20	Lodge,	R.C.	–	R.C.	–	53	48	101	32
89	6409	Do.	–	Letterbrick,	R.C.	–	R.C.	–	61	61	145	23
90	7409	Do.	–	Rathmore,	R.C.	–	R.C.	–	55	51	110	26
91	8578	Do.	–	Crossmolina, m.	R.C.	–	R.C.	–	173	–	173	64
92	10798	Do.	–	Do. f.	R.C.	–	R.C.	R.C.	–	190	190	62
93	9921	Do.	–	Deelbridge,	R.C.	–	R.C.	–	68	42	111	41
94	3158	Cong,	22	Cross, m.	–	R.C.	R.C.	–	230	–	230	81
95	7178	Do.	–	Do. f.	–	R.C.	R.C.	R.C.	–	222	222	57
96	8418	Do.	–	Cong, m.	R.C.	–	R.C.	R.C.	183	–	183	69
97	8418	Do.	–	Do. f.	R.C.	–	R.C.	R.C.	–	168	168	65
98	10875	Do.	–	Barna,	R.C.	–	R.C.	–	69	117	186	50
99	1919	Doonfeeny,	20	Portnahallia,	R.C.	–	R.C.	–	54	40	94	35
100	2881	Do.	–	Ballycastle,	R.C.	–	R.C.	–	87	80	167	60
101	4508	Do.	–	Belderrig,	R.C.	–	R.C.	–	23	50	73	21
102	8737	Do.	–	Palm Hill,	–	R.C.	R.C.	–	55	41	96	31
103	8534	Do.	–	Ballinafad,	Pres.	–	Pres.	–	18	24	42	11
104	6049	Drum,	26	Belcarra, m.	–	R.C.	R.C.	–	105	–	105	63
105	6048	Do.	–	Do. f.	–	R.C.	R.C.	R.C.	–	255	255	78
106	8564	Do.	–	Deerpark,	R.C.	–	R.C.	–	55	40	95	27
107	8765	Do.	–	Cloghans, m.	R.C.	–	R.C.	–	88	–	88	33
108	8721	Do.	–	Do. f.	R.C.	–	R.C.	–	–	80	80	17
109	5191	Islandeady,	–	Cloghervagh,	–	R.C.	R.C.	R.C.	104	80	184	61
110	8464	Do.	–	Glen Island, m.	–	R.C.	R.C.	–	176	–	176	58
111	8899	Do.	–	Do. f.	–	R.C.	R.C.	–	–	153	153	41
112	8854	Do.	–	Curramcale,	R.C.	–	R.C.	–	132	109	241	108
113	10411	Do.	–	Cuagals,	R.C.	–	R.C.	R.C.	119	108	226	36
114	9716	Inishmaine,	–	Innisbark,	R.C.	–	R.C.	–	38	23	61	27
115	1619	Kilcolman,	31	Ballyfarnagh,	–	R.C.	R.C.	R.C.	97	106	203	66
116	1764	Do.	–	[illegible] School Garden	R.C.	–	R.C.	R.C.	298	–	298	71
117	5378	Do.	–	Ballyhaunis, f.	–	R.C.	R.C.	R.C.	–	285	285	80
118	8224	Do.	–	Do. f.	–	R.C.	R.C.	–	88	130	218	69
119	[illegible]	Do.	–	Mornane,*	–	–	–	–	–	–	–	–
120	8909	Do.	–	Cullibee Ord. Agric.	–	R.C.	R.C.	R.C.	137	114	251	84
121	4011	Do.	30	Richmond, f.	R.C.	–	R.C.	–	3,698	318	4,016	81
122	7730	Do.	31	Derrinacarta,	R.C.	–	R.C.	R.C.	140	159	314	104
123	8825	Do.	31	Claremorris, m.	R.C.	–	R.C.	R.C.	250	–	250	100
124	9016	Do.	–	Do. f.	R.C.	–	R.C.	R.C.	–	271	271	95
125	6162	Do.	–	Do. Workh.	P.L.	Gds.	R.C.	–	26	17	43	20
126	7606	Do.	–	Kilmore,	R.C.	–	R.C.	–	73	91	164	53
127	7616	Do.	–	Loughanamona,	–	R.C.	R.C.	R.C.	155	161	316	104
128	8160	Do.	31	Cross, m.	R.C.	–	R.C.	R.C.	189	–	189	51
129	8161	Do.	–	Do. f.	R.C.	–	R.C.	R.C.	–	148	148	49
130	1077	Killasser,	–	Aughamuchugh,	–	R.C.	R.C.	–	134	118	251	61
131	6709	Do.	–	Callow, m.	R.C.	–	R.C.	–	203	–	203	38
132	7218	Do.	–	Do. f.	R.C.	–	R.C.	–	–	186	186	18
133	6904	Do.	–	Knox,	R.C.	–	R.C.	R.C.	181	153	334	56
134	7016	Do.	–	Carramore,	R.C.	–	R.C.	R.C.	153	194	347	70
135	11148	Do.	–	Killasser, m.	R.C.	–	R.C.	–	207	–	207	45
136	11149	Do.	–	Do. f.	R.C.	–	R.C.	–	–	192	192	71
137	1612	Killedan,	–	Kiltimagh, or Newtown Browne, f.	R.C.	–	R.C.	R.C.	–	287	287	81
138	7368	Do.	–	Brackloonagh,	R.C.	–	R.C.	R.C.	258	–	258	73
139	8933	Do.	–	Treenaghleragh,	R.C.	–	R.C.	R.C.	203	167	370	76
140	9769	Do.	–	Cloragh,	R.C.	–	R.C.	R.C.	148	141	289	39
141	1700	Kilmore Moy,	26	Ballina, m.	R.C.	–	R.C.	R.C.	422	–	422	167
142	5818	Do.	–	Do. Convent, f.	–	R.C.	Nuns		136	578	719	173
143	9859	Do.	–	Do. Workhouse,	P.L.	Gds.	R.C.	–	31	28	59	31
144	7064	Do.	–	Culleens, No. 2, f.	R.C.	–	R.C.	–	60	53	113	49

a Including value of Free Residence and Garden. b Including value of Free Residence.

Province of Connaught: County of Mayo—*continued.*

Amount paid for Books, Requisites, and Apparatus at Reduced Prices.	Aid granted by the Board during the Year 1874. In Free Stock of Books, Requisites, and Apparatus.	In Salaries, Premiums, and other Gratuities.	Results Fees, Financial Year.	Amount of Local Emoluments received in Aid of Teacher's Salary. School Fees.	Subscriptions, Endowments, &c.	Total Local Aid.	Vested or Non-Vested.	Number.
£ s. d.	£ s. d.	£ s. d.	£ s. d.	£ s. d.	£ s. d.	£ s. d.		
1 10 5	—	94 0 0	17 3 0	5 4 0	10 5 0	a15 9 0	V.C.	85
—	—		2 10 0	1 10 2	—	1 10 2		
1 5 8	—	36 5 6	0 10 0	6 15 1	14 0 0	a19 15 1	V.C.	86
5 7 4	—	66 13 4	35 8 0	16 1 9	8 0 0	b24 1 9		87
—	—	—	—	—	—	—		
1 7 9	—	20 0 0	6 17 6	—	—	—		88
3 19 7	—	21 0 0	6 15 0	0 13 0	1 0 0	1 13 0		89
0 19 5	—	21 0 0	7 17 0	1 7 6	—	1 7 6		90
6 4 8	—	90 13 4	18 5 6	10 18 6	—	10 18 6		91
4 5 3	—	62 0 0	16 15 0	7 10 6	—	7 10 6		92
2 0 11	—	21 0 0	8 10 6	8 0 10	6 0 0	18 0 10		93
4 11 6	—	76 10 0	36 6 0	—	21 0 0	a22 0 0		94
5 4 4	—	70 0 0	36 10 0	—	12 0 0	12 0 0		95
4 1 2	—	47 10 0	27 4 6	4 10 7	—	4 10 7		96
3 6 7	—	40 0 0	30 3 0	3 12 6	—	3 12 6		97
1 5 8	—	24 0 0	8 13 6	3 1 1	2 0 0	b5 1 1		98
6 18 11	—	60 0 0	11 19 6	—	—	—		99
4 3 10	—	43 10 0	21 18 0	10 0 0	—	10 0 0		100
4 17 5	—	20 0 0	0 8 6	—	5 8 0	5 8 0		101
—	—	70 0 0	14 10 6	2 0 0	1 0 0	b3 0 0		102
1 5 0	—	20 0 0	7 13 0	—	14 0 0	14 0 0		103
2 7 11	—	24 0 0	9 8 0	2 0 10	3 10 0	5 10 10	V.C.	104
1 0 8	—	30 0 0	10 1 0	4 2 10	2 10 0	6 12 10	V.C.	105
4 6 7	—	24 0 0	4 4 0	1 8 0	—	1 8 0		106
1 4 11	—	24 0 0	5 6 0	5 15 5	0 7 0	a5 8 5	V.C.	107
1 9 0	—	20 0 0	4 0 0	0 18 4	—	0 18 4	V.C.	108
—	—	36 0 0	12 12 6	13 1 8	—	13 1 8	V.C.	109
4 2 5	—	32 0 0	12 14 6	3 1 5	12 10 0	a15 11 5	V.C.	110
2 10 8	—	24 0 0	11 3 0	2 11 4	3 10 0	5 1 4	V.C.	111
4 18 0	—	30 0 0	57 1 6	21 5 6	—	21 5 6		112
3 10 0	—	44 0 0	10 7 0	4 9 0	—	4 9 0		113
—	—	24 0 0	2 18 0	—	—	—		114
4 13 4	—	90 13 4	30 18 6	14 15 4	2 1 0	a16 16 4	V.C.	115
6 7 1	—	137 8 4	37 18 4	5 8 7	10 0 0	15 8 7		116
5 4 10	—	103 16 8	33 0 0	8 0 0	17 0 0	a25 0 0	V.C.	117
1 5 8	—	33 10 0	17 3 6	0 18 4	9 12 0	b5 11 4		118
—	—	—	—	—	—	—	V.T.	119
3 14 2	0 16 0	49 0 0	a—	5 3 0	4 0 0	a9 3 0	V.T.	120
1 2 0	—	20 0 0	4 18 6	3 1 11	—	3 1 11	V.T.	121
6 15 2	—	70 3 4	45 19 0	4 7 6	1 10 0	a5 17 6		122
22 6 5	—	64 16 8	23 9 0	24 7 9	—	24 7 9		123
1 18 8	—	64 0 0	21 6 6	20 0 0	13 0 0	b33 0 0		124
—	—	—	—	—	—	—		125
2 10 6	—	30 0 6	11 11 0	5 8 9	—	5 8 9		126
8 14 8	—	60 0 0	45 8 0	—	11 0 0	11 0 0	V.C.	127
1 0 8	—	70 6 0	39 2 6	3 8 6	4 10 0	a7 18 6		128
2 15 3	—	60 13 10	27 17 0	3 3 6	—	3 3 6		129
4 19 0	—	57 10 0	23 8 0	14 13 5	—	14 13 5	V.T.	130
1 6 4	—	43 10 0	7 11 6	3 0 0	3 0 0	a6 0 0		131
2 0 11	—	42 10 0	9 6 6	4 0 0	—	4 0 0		132
6 15 6	—	73 3 4	30 18 0	—	—	—		133
6 16 8	—	45 0 0	28 16 8	0 6 8	—	0 6 8		134
3 0 10	6 0 0	0 0 0	—	0 10 0	—	0 10 0		135
9 16 10	5 0 0	9 0 0	—	—	—	—		136
1 13 8	—	63 10 0	10 10 0	12 10 8	—	12 10 8	V.T.	137
7 19 0	—	65 5 4	20 18 6	10 0 8	—	10 0 8		138
5 4 6	—	70 0 0	18 18 6	7 6 6	—	7 6 6		139
3 0 0	—	46 10 0	5 12 6	2 0 5	—	2 0 5		140
15 16 1	—	164 10 0	45 16 6	19 17 6	—	19 17 6		141
2 8 4	—	101 9 10	57 17 0	—	—	—		142
—	—	2 0 0	—	—	—	—		143
0 15 11	—	20 0 0	4 15 6	3 3 4	—	3 3 4		144

a Inoperative. d Including value of Free Garden. b No Fees paid.

List of Schools in operation on the 31st December, 1874—

Number.	Roll Number of School.	Parish.	District.	School.	Religious Denomination of Managers or Correspondents: Clerical.	Lay.	Principal and Religious Denomination of Teachers: Principals.	Assistants.	Attendance for the Year. Total number of Pupils on Rolls within the Year 1874: Males.	Fem.	Total.	Average daily attendance for the Year 1874.
145	6972	Kilmore Moy,	22	Charles-street, Ballina,	Pres.	–	Pres.	Pres.	103	58	161	73
146	2530	Killconduff,	21	Swineford, m.	R.C.	–	R.C.	–	300	–	308	91
147	7713	Do.	–	Do. Convent, f.	–	R.C.	Nuns		127	443	570	255
148	4810	Do.	–	Do. Workhouse,	P.L.	Gds.	R.C.	–	34	33	67	29
149	6761	Do.	–	Bracklone,	R.C.	–	R.C.	R.C.	212	181	393	99
150	10217	Do.	–	Culmore,	R.C.	–	R.C.	R.C.	148	100	237	66
151	9270	Do.	–	Tumgesh, m.	R.C.	–	R.C.	–	161	–	104	62
152	8277	Do.	–	Do. f.	R.C.	–	R.C.	–	–	165	149	56
153	9871	Do.	–	Curryane,	R.C.	–	R.C.	R.C.	275	153	369	84
154	10946	Do.	–	Kilteff,	R.C.	–	R.C.	R.C.	150	132	273	82
155	3291	Kilbelfad,	27	Cloghans Ord. Agr.	R.C.	–	R.C.	–	87	88	167	83
156	6854	Do.	–	Carracloon, m.	–	R.C.	R.C.	–	123	–	123	57
157	6853	Do.	–	Do. f.	–	R.C.	R.C.	–	–	83	73	41
158	10364	Do.	–	Pontoon,	R.C.	–	R.C.	–	80	80	160	54
159	3027	Kilmore,	–	Corclough, No. 2,	R.C.	–	R.C.	–	78	31	110	45
160	5476	Do.	–	Belmullet Workhouse,	P.L.	Gds.	R.C.	–	54	39	77	30
161	8816	Do.	–	Crosses,	R.C.	–	R.C.	–	80	41	140	63
162	6602	Do.	–	Kilmore Erris,	R.C.	–	R.C.	R.C.	83	53	135	46
163	8765	Do.	–	Shranabro,	R.C.	–	R.C.	–	63	56	120	45
164	6736	Do.	–	Aughleam,	R.C.	–	R.C.	–	73	80	161	35
165	1413	Kilturra,	21	Doocastle Ord. Agr.	–	R.C.	R.C.	R.C.	220	–	220	78
166	2312	Do.	–	Do. f.	–	R.C.	R.C.	–	–	165	158	55
167	10696	Keelogues,	–	Loughkeeran, m.	R.C.	–	R.C.	–	154	–	154	37
168	10961	Do.	–	Do. f.	R.C.	–	R.C.	–	–	153	153	44
169	2262	Kilgarvan,	20	Rooaketaine,	R.C.	–	R.C.	R.C.	209	171	380	81
170	8410	Do.	–	Cairn,	R.C.	–	R.C.	R.C.	123	91	223	68
171	8532	Do.	–	Belfield,	R.C.	–	R.C.	–	109	90	195	68
172	3248	Kilfian,	–	Tonrehown,	R.C.	–	R.C.	–	45	28	74	32
173	8018	Do.	–	Ballykinlettra,	R.C.	–	R.C.	–	49	48	97	32
174	9069	Do.	–	Dooneenarrow,	R.C.	–	R.C.	–	70	48	118	61
175	2276	Kilmovee,	21	Tavrane, m.	–	R.C.	R.C.	–	219	–	212	88
176	2277	Do.	–	Do. f.	–	R.C.	R.C.	–	–	207	207	63
177	3404	Do.	–	Kilmovee, m.	–	R.C.	R.C.	R.C.	308	–	346	181
178	3055	Do.	–	Do. f.	–	R.C.	R.C.	R.C.	–	218	216	76
179	8801	Do.	–	Do. No. 2, m.	R.C.	–	R.C.	–	146	–	146	47
180	8397	Do.	–	Do. f.	R.C.	–	R.C.	R.C.	–	148	148	58
181	1635	Do.	–	Kilkelly, m.	R.C.	–	R.C.	–	231	–	231	88
182	9746	Do.	–	Do. f.	R.C.	–	R.C.	R.C.	–	176	187	61
183	9804	Do.	–	Glassitrum,	R.C.	–	R.C.	R.C.	114	180	276	77
184	1764	Do.	–	Oolar, m.	R.C.	–	R.C.	–	110	–	110	50
185	1037	Do.	–	Do. f.	R.C.	–	R.C.	–	–	106	106	58
186	3219	Kilcommon,	28	Drimnagallagh,	R.C.	–	R.C.	–	87	57	134	43
187	7501	Do.	–	Shraghnamonragh,	R.C.	–	R.C.	–	96	64	169	42
188	8866	Do.	–	Dromadda,	R.C.	–	R.C.	R.C.	89	72	101	50
189	6120	Do.	28	Lahinch,	R.C.	–	R.C.	R.C.	160	119	279	88
190	7847	Do.	20	Ballinrobe, m.	R.C.	–	R.C.	–	139	–	139	52
191	8438	Do.	–	Do. f.	R.C.	–	R.C.	–	–	130	130	65
192	8711	Do.	–	Pollatomish,	–	R.C.	R.C.	–	86	41	167	35
193	7704	Do.	–	Geesala,	R.C.	–	R.C.	–	104	41	145	58
194	7772	Do.	28	Cloghans,	–	R.C.	R.C.	R.C.	138	189	277	105
195	7830	Do.	20	Glencastle,	R.C.	–	R.C.	–	98	63	185	50
196	7878	Do.	–	Dooleeg,	R.C.	–	R.C.	–	78	58	136	45
197	7868	Do.	–	Fishing Station,	R.C.	–	R.C.	–	28	36	63	38
198	8061	Do.	–	Barnatra,	R.C.	–	R.C.	–	104	46	150	45
199	8129	Do.	–	Doohoma,	R.C.	–	R.C.	R.C.	117	73	190	50
200	9381	Do.	–	Ballymonnelly, [a]	–	R.C.	–	–	–	–	–	–
201	9131	Do.	–	Bangor-Erris,	R.C.	–	R.C.	–	93	60	153	58
202	9757	Do.	–	Lavey, [a]	R.C.	–	–	–	–	–	–	–
203	9949	Do.	–	Glenamoy, [a]	R.C.	–	–	–	–	–	–	–
204	11063	Do.	–	Rossport,	R.C.	–	R.C.	–	57	48	107	41
205	10183	Do.	–	Glencullen,	R.C.	–	R.C.	–	72	43	115	32
206	10625	Kilvine,	22	Drymills, m.	R.C.	–	R.C.	–	226	–	226	73
207	10626	Do.	–	Do. f.	R.C.	–	R.C.	–	–	314	314	75

a Including value of Free Garden. b Including value of Free Residence and Garden.

Province of Connaught: County of Mayo—*continued.*

Amount paid for Books, Requisites, and Apparatus at Reduced Prices.	Aid granted by the Board during the Year 1874. In Free Stock of Books, Requisites, and Apparatus.	In Salaries, Premiums, and other Gratuities.	Results Fees, Financial Year.	Amount of Local Emoluments received in Aid of Teacher's Salary. School Fees.	Subscriptions, Endowments, &c.	Total Local Aid.	Vested or Non-Vested.	Number.
£ s. d.	£ s. d.	£ s. d.	£ s. d.	£ s. d.	£ s. d.	£ s. d.		
3 0 1	—	48 3 4	41 11 0	—	38 0 0	68 0 0		145
0 3 0	—	42 14 4	26 6 6	6 18 6	—	6 18 6	V.T.	146
17 1 1	—	80 12 4	24 16 6	12 13 6	—	12 18 6		147
4 6 8	—	—	—	—	—	—		148
5 6 0	—	78 0 0	14 1 6	2 0 0	5 0 0	a 7 0 0		149
3 0 1	—	42 10 0	11 16 0	8 4 3	—	8 4 3		150
3 13 6	—	44 10 0	17 14 0	1 16 6	—	1 16 6		151
3 8 7	—	27 16 8	18 2 6	1 4 0	—	1 4 0		152
5 5 8	—	63 10 0	21 16 8	7 10 0	—	7 10 0		153
8 0 8	—	56 0 0	28 0 0	4 17 3	—	4 17 3		154
3 14 4	—	42 0 0	17 8 0	10 0 0	—	a 10 0 0		155
11 15 8	—	47 10 0	6 7 0	1 6 0	15 3 4	b 19 6 4	V.C.	156
2 0 10	—	24 0 0	8 11 6	—	—	—	V.C.	157
0 16 0	—	20 0 0	0 16 6	1 0 0	—	1 0 0		158
1 10 3	—	87 0 0	13 18 0	7 1 4	—	7 1 4	V.C.	159
4 13 4	—	—	—	—	—	—		160
1 4 11	—	11 19 4	4 1 0	3 10 0	4 0 0	7 10 0		161
1 12 7	—	30 0 0	11 13 0	2 14 6	—	2 14 0		162
1 17 1	—	24 0 0	13 7 6	5 7 6	—	5 7 6		163
—	—	24 0 0	6 0 0	0 11 0	—	0 11 0		164
6 1 7	2 2 0	73 10 0	61 1 6	3 10 0	8 0 0	a 11 10 0	V.T.	165
4 3 7	—	88 18 6	20 14 0	3 0 6	—	3 0 0	V.T.	166
8 12 10	—	35 5 0	11 12 0	4 17 10	—	4 17 10		167
1 15 1	—	27 0 0	14 17 0	6 5 9	—	6 5 9		168
1 6 3	—	28 0 0	15 12 0	2 0 0	—	2 0 0	V.T.	169
2 16 8	—	52 3 4	11 10 0	3 12 0	2 10 0	a 6 2 0		170
1 11 9	—	34 0 0	18 1 0	1 16 0	—	1 16 0		171
—	—	24 0 0	8 6 0	5 2 0	—	5 2 0		172
3 4 6	—	16 0 0	6 11 0	1 10 0	—	1 10 0		173
1 7 3	—	24 0 0	7 6 0	4 0 0	—	4 0 0		174
4 2 2	—	29 13 4	22 17 0	2 18 0	—	2 18 0	V.T.	175
4 7 6	—	47 10 0	22 10 0	5 6 6	—	5 6 6	V.T.	176
4 0 0	—	88 0 10	31 0 11	5 0 6	—	5 0 6	V.C.	177
5 16 7	—	78 13 4	25 16 6	6 2 6	—	6 2 6	V.C.	178
4 10 2	—	27 0 8	5 16 3	2 12 6	—	2 12 6		179
1 10 3	—	71 0 0	25 1 3	2 2 6	—	2 2 6		180
—	—	60 3 4	21 9 6	2 4 0	—	2 4 0		181
3 2 7	—	71 1 6	27 13 0	1 19 0	—	1 19 0		182
8 17 5	—	79 3 4	67 5 8	4 0 0	—	4 0 0		183
8 16 9	4 10 0	22 10 0	14 11 6	1 16 0	—	1 16 0	V.T.	184
8 2 9	4 10 0	20 0 0	21 9 0	3 0 0	—	3 0 0	V.T.	185
3 11 2	—	24 0 0	13 11 6	3 5 0	3 10 0	b 6 15 0	V.C.	186
2 8 9	—	24 0 0	7 18 0	0 5 0	5 0 0	5 5 0	V.C.	187
6 14 8	—	23 0 0	17 7 6	4 5 0	15 0 0	a 19 5 0	V.C.	188
8 8 4	1 0 6	49 0 0	20 9 6	27 2 0	2 0 0	29 2 6	V.C.	189
1 11 8	—	22 0 0	16 7 6	16 3 6	—	16 3 6		190
2 17 2	—	21 0 0	12 14 0	6 13 6	—	6 13 6		191
0 15 2	—	20 0 0	5 10 5	—	—	—		192
—	—	0 0 0	—	—	—	—		193
5 8 0	—	92 0 0	43 8 0	19 6 9	—	19 0 0	V.C.	194
1 17 9	—	24 0 0	4 10 6	—	—	—		195
8 4 4	—	84 0 6	15 0 6	1 0 0	—	1 0 0		196
—	—	0 0 0	—	0 14 2	—	0 14 2	V.C.	197
5 1 0	—	24 0 0	6 18 6	2 0 0	—	2 0 0		198
2 15 6	—	82 18 4	19 7 0	5 16 0	8 0 0	b 14 16 0		199
0 11 2	—	—	—	—	—	—	V.C.	200
2 16 11	—	25 6 6	10 18 0	—	—	—		201
—	—	—	—	—	—	—		202
—	—	—	—	—	—	—		203
1 13 8	—	12 8 8	6 11 6	—	—	—		204
—	—	20 0 0	5 1 0	—	—	—		205
2 14 7	—	85 9 0	15 0 0	16 15 0	—	16 15 0		206
0 8 0	—	85 10 0	19 2 6	6 8 6	—	a 6 8 6		207

a Including value of Free Residence. b No Return. c Closed.

List of Schools in operation on the 31st December, 1874.—

No.	Roll Number of School.	Parish.	District.	School.	Religious Denomination of Managers or Correspondents.		Number and Religious Denomination of Teachers.		Attendance for the Year.			
					Clerical.	Lay.	Principals.	Assistants.	Total number of Pupils on Rolls within the Year 1874. Males.	Females.	Total.	Average Daily Attendance.
208	8787	Kilcommon Erris,	20	Carratigue,	R.C.	–	R.C.	–	52	34	86	55
209	8559	Killala,	–	Killala,	R.C.	–	R.C.	R.C.	101	99	199	73
210	2711	Do.	–	Do. Workhouse,	P.L.	Gds.	R.C.	–	19	17	36	11
211	6476	Do.	–	Rose,	R.C.	–	R.C.	–	64	46	110	50
212	11016	Kilmoiare,	25	The Neale,	–	R.C.	R.C.	–	129	110	239	78
213	3909	Kilmeena,	24	Rossdoane,[b]	–	R.C.	–	–	–	–	–	–
214	4109	Do.	–	Carraholly,	–	R.C.	R.C.	R.C.	85	78	163	45
215	5208	Do.	–	Myna,	R.C.	–	R.C.	R.C.	115	121	236	40
216	5716	Do.	–	Fahy,	R.C.	–	R.C.	–	121	69	190	45
217	7378	Kilmainemore,	21	Keelogues, m.	R.C.	–	R.C.	–	170	–	170	38
218	7497	Do.	–	Do. f.	R.C.	–	R.C.	R.C.	–	216	216	88
219	7327	Kildeagh,	–	Rosahy Ord. Agr.	R.C.	–	R.C.	R.C.	184	156	294	85
				Do. evg.	R.C.	–	R.C.	–	64	–	65	30
220	4783	Do.	–	Lowpark, m.	–	R.C.	R.C.	–	180	–	180	84
221	4784	Do.	–	Do. f.	–	R.C.	R.C.	R.C.	–	241	241	59
222	7914	Do.	–	Cloonsheen, m.	–	R.C.	R.C.	–	164	–	164	44
223	2615	Do.	–	Do. f.	–	R.C.	R.C.	–	–	165	165	64
224	2016	Do.	–	Barnacahogue, m.	–	R.C.	R.C.	–	137	–	137	60
225	2617	Do.	–	Do. f.	–	R.C.	R.C.	–	–	143	143	45
226	7854	Do.	–	Cloonlyon,	R.C.	–	R.C.	R.C.	167	151	318	77
227	7856	Do.	–	Gortkeen,	R.C.	–	R.C.	R.C.	107	180	287	75
228	7858	Do.	–	Glann,	R.C.	–	R.C.	R.C.	150	124	274	68
229	7857	Do.	–	Taunyinagh,	R.C.	–	R.C.	R.C.	118	121	239	64
230	7019	Do.	–	Cloonta, Agr.	R.C.	–	R.C.	R.C.	178	158	336	80
231	8710	Do.	–	Tonaroe,	R.C.	–	R.C.	R.C.	179	162	341	107
232	8856	Do.	–	Lecarrow,	–	R.C.	R.C.	R.C.	90	50	142	55
233	8916	Kilgeever,	23	Carrowkilly,	–	R.C.	R.C.	R.C.	67	85	152	45
234	6315	Do.	–	Inishturk,	–	R.C.	R.C.	–	14	18	32	14
235	3112	Do.	–	Accony,	–	R.C.	R.C.	–	69	65	134	45
236	6187	Do.	–	Killadoon,	–	R.C.	R.C.	R.C.	142	117	259	95
237	6402	Do.	–	Lecarrow,	R.C.	–	R.C.	–	43	62	105	41
238	3128	Do.	–	Louisburgh, m.	–	R.C.	R.C.	R.C.	162	–	162	55
239	3129	Do.	–	Do. f.	–	R.C.	R.C.	R.C.	–	130	130	60
240	9118	Kilmaine,	22	Kilmaine, m.	R.C.	–	R.C.	–	187	–	187	50
241	9119	Do.	–	Do. f.	R.C.	–	R.C.	–	–	160	160	51
242	10817	Knock,	–	Knock, m.	R.C.	–	R.C.	–	191	–	191	55
243	10818	Do.	–	Do. f.	R.C.	–	R.C.	R.C.	–	162	162	54
244	10949	Do.	–	Kenaby,	R.C.	–	R.C.	R.C.	93	90	183	55
245	11033	Do.	–	Shanvaghera,[b]	R.C.	–	R.C.	R.C.	–	–	–	–
246	10772	Do.	21	Coogue,	R.C.	–	R.C.	R.C.	155	118	273	64
247	6826	Kilbride,	24	Kilbride,	R.C.	–	R.C.	–	49	45	94	35
248	9972	Kilmaclasser,	24	Sheagan,	R.C.	–	R.C.	–	38	43	81	35
249	11101	Kilvine,	22	Cullane, m.	R.C.	–	R.C.	–	160	–	160	58
250	11102	Do.	–	Do. f.	R.C.	–	R.C.	–	–	167	167	57
251	6942	Lackan,	20	Carrowmore Palmer,	R.C.	–	R.C.	–	86	80	166	41
252	7170	Do.	–	Rathlackan,	R.C.	–	R.C.	–	64	56	120	42
253	9726	Do.	–	Banagher,	R.C.	–	R.C.	–	78	79	157	47
254	8815	Meelick,	21	Culleens, m.	R.C.	–	R.C.	–	237	–	237	81
255	8816	Do.	–	Do. f.	R.C.	–	R.C.	R.C.	–	240	240	75
256	6867	Manulla,	22	Prizon, Ord. Agr. m.	R.C.	–	R.C.	–	171	–	171	58
257	8291	Do.	–	Do. f.	R.C.	–	R.C.	–	–	142	142	55
258	8706	Mayo,	21	Mayo,	R.C.	–	R.C.	R.C.	108	105	213	58
259	9656	Do.	–	Facefield,	R.C.	–	R.C.	R.C.	185	110	245	55
260	6316	Moygownagh,	20	Cara,	R.C.	–	R.C.	–	14	78	158	35
261	6961	Do.	–	Moygownagh,	R.C.	–	R.C.	–	45	44	89	33
262	2914	Oughaval,	23	Murrisk,	–	R.C.	R.C.	–	67	74	181	44
263	1484	Do.	–	Tievenacroagh,[b]	–	R.C.	–	–	–	–	–	–
264	4787	Do.	–	Westport Workhs.	P.L.	Gds.	R.C.	–	38	25	59	35
265	4796	Do.	–	Brackloon,	–	R.C.	R.C.	–	53	31	80	31
266	4797	Do.	–	Bouris,	–	R.C.	R.C.	R.C.	78	59	137	35
267	4858	Do.	–	Killadangan,	–	R.C.	R.C.	–	61	61	111	33
268	4856	Do.	–	Kilsallagh,	–	R.C.	R.C.	–	80	61	141	31
269	4858	Do.	–	Kilmeena,	–	R.C.	R.C.	–	70	61	131	41

[a] Including value of Free Residence and Garden.

[b] Dismissed Teacher in charge.

Province of Connaught: County of Mayo—*continued*.

Amount paid for Books, Requisites, and Apparatus, at Reduced Prices.	Aid granted by the Board during the Year 1874. In Free Stock of Books, Requisites, and Apparatus.	In Salaries, Premiums, and other Gratuities.	Results Fees, Financial Year.	Amount of Local Emoluments received in Aid of Teacher's Salary. School Fees.	Subscriptions, Endowments, &c.	Total Local Aid.	Vested or Non-Vested.	Number.
£ s. d.	£ s. d.	£ s. d.	£ s. d.	£ s. d.	£ s. d.	£ s. d.		
1 9 3	—	21 0 0	3 2 0	—	—	—		208
6 9 7	—	43 6 0	22 11 0	4 11 0	0 10 0	5 1 0		209
—	—	—	—	—	—	—		210
0 17 0	—	24 17 6	6 16 6	2 8 11	—	2 8 11		211
5 4 5	5 0 0	34 0 0	17 8 0	4 10 6	8 1 6	[a] 12 12 0		212
—	—	—	—	—	—	—	V.C.	213
8 8 1	—	40 0 0	14 6 8	8 10 9	11 10 0	[b] 18 0 9	F.	214
4 6 11	—	40 13 4	12 6 0	4 4 0	—	4 4 0		215
0 6 6	—	21 0 0	6 6 0	8 15 10	—	8 15 10		216
2 6 3	—	24 0 0	2 16 8	2 14 8	—	2 14 8		217
—	—	43 0 0	4 6 0	1 5 10	—	1 5 10		218
12 0 6	—	92 0 0	85 10 0 9 10 0	7 2 0 8 0 0	4 1 7 —	[b] 11 3 7 8 0 0		219
2 12 0	—	82 18 4	22 6 6	3 19 8	0 5 0	[b] 4 4 8	V.C.	220
4 0 1	—	68 11 0	24 8 2	7 11 9	0 10 0	[a] 8 1 9	V.C.	221
3 11 1	—	21 0 0	11 5 0	3 0 0	—	3 0 0	V.C.	222
4 1 2	—	27 6 6	23 5 0	1 0 0	0 15 0	[b] 1 15 0	V.C.	223
1 17 9	—	20 10 0	9 19 0	3 7 6	0 10 0	[b] 3 17 6	V.C.	224
1 0 0	—	16 8 4	14 10 0	6 0 6	—	6 0 6	V.C.	225
4 16 0	—	59 10 0	10 11 11	2 8 0	8 0 0	[b] 4 8 0		226
7 8 4	—	51 10 0	22 0 0	2 6 11	—	2 6 11		227
6 10 1	—	43 10 0	14 0 0	0 11 0	—	0 11 0		228
7 16 7	—	56 10 0	20 5 0	1 5 0	—	1 5 0		229
8 14 0	—	61 10 0	18 15 0	6 1 6	—	6 1 6		230
—	—	76 8 4	64 0 6	5 19 0	—	5 19 0		231
2 0 3	—	49 0 0	8 16 0	2 5 0	—	2 5 0		232
—	—	30 0 0	6 2 6	1 2 6	1 10 0	2 12 6	V.C.	233
1 5 3	—	20 0 0	—	—	—	—		234
2 10 8	—	60 0 0	7 0 0	4 15 0	—	4 15 0	V.C.	235
7 2 1	—	44 0 0	28 12 0	14 8 6	6 0 0	[a] 20 8 6	V.C.	236
1 11 6	—	24 0 0	2 16 8	1 16 0	—	1 16 0		237
0 0 1	—	25 0 0	10 2 6	4 17 1	4 10 0	9 7 1	V.C.	238
2 0 5	—	37 0 0	18 9 6	4 0 0	9 0 0	[a] 13 0 0	V.C.	239
1 19 4	—	34 16 8	22 15 6	5 2 11	—	5 2 11		240
4 8 7	—	20 0 0	26 4 0	9 1 9	—	9 1 9		241
6 6 4	—	29 0 0	16 15 0	6 5 6	—	6 5 6		242
2 0 6	—	20 0 0	14 6 6	5 15 6	—	5 15 6		243
1 15 0	—	22 0 6	19 19 0	6 0 0	—	6 0 0		244
8 6 0	—	42 16 6	14 19 0	—	—	—		245
3 19 11	—	62 18 4	13 16 10	10 11 11	—	10 11 11		246
1 15 0	—	30 0 0	10 18 6	1 0 0	2 0 0	3 0 0		247
0 10 2	—	—	4 8 6	—	7 0 0	[a] 7 0 0		248
3 12 8	5 0 0	61 8 4	7 6 0	9 7 0	—	9 7 0		249
5 10 9	6 10 0	14 6 10	13 2 6	10 8 11	—	10 8 11		250
2 1 4	—	42 0 0	21 0 6	4 0 0	9 14 10	13 14 10		251
1 16 8	—	90 0 0	8 10 0	—	—	—		252
1 8 11	—	91 0 0	11 16 0	2 0 0	—	2 0 0		253
4 18 6	—	76 1 8	27 8 0	8 14 6	—	8 14 6	V.T.	254
3 18 2	—	50 3 4	21 2 6	3 11 1	—	3 11 1	V.T.	255
3 10 8	—	29 0 0	16 12 0	4 0 0	2 15 8	[a] 6 15 8		256
2 10 10	—	23 0 0	8 4 0	2 0 0	—	2 0 0		257
1 8 7	—	44 10 0	17 12 10	5 1 6	4 0 0	9 1 6		258
4 15 0	—	44 0 0	10 1 0	6 10 0	4 0 0	10 10 0		259
2 10 5	—	30 0 0	14 4 6	—	—	—		260
1 17 9	—	29 11 1	9 4 6	1 0 0	—	1 0 0		261
1 16 8	—	20 0 0	6 6 0	—	—	—	L.	262
0 9 0	—	—	—	—	—	—	A.	263
2 4 2	—	5 10 0	—	—	—	—		264
2 10 3	—	37 0 0	8 10 0	1 16 0	5 0 0	6 16 0	V.C.	265
3 7 4	—	41 0 0	15 16 6	4 7 6	28 16 6	[a] 33 4 0	V.C.	266
0 11 6	—	60 0 0	6 8 0	1 17 4	5 0 0	6 17 4	V.C.	267
2 17 8	—	31 18 4	20 1 4	4 10 0	2 10 0	7 0 0	V.C.	268
4 8 4	—	24 0 0	8 17 0	2 4 5	7 0 0	[b] 9 4 5	V.C.	269

[a] Including value of Free Residence. [b] Including value of Free Garden. [c] No Returns. [d] Inoperative.

List of Schools in operation on the 31st December, 1874.—

Number.	Roll Number of School.	Parish.	District.	School.		Religious Denomination of Managers or Correspondents: Clergyman.	Lay.	Number and Religious Denomination of Teachers: Principals.	Assistants.	Attendance for the Year — Total number of Pupils on Rolls within the Year 1874: Males.	Fem.	Total.	Average Daily Attendance.
270	6574	Oughaval,	32	Knappa,		R.C.	–	R.C.	–	41	67	108	50
271	6784	Do.	–	St. Patrick's, a		R.C.	–	R.C.	R.C.	–	–	–	46
272	6941	Do.	–	Letterbrock, b		R.C.	–	–	–	–	–	–	–
273	9114	Do.	–	Derrygorman,		R.C.	–	R.C.	–	45	34	79	32
274	9460	Do.	–	Lenanvey,		R.C.	–	R.C.	R.C.	67	68	135	43
275	7714	Robeen,	32	Ballygarries,		R.C.	–	R.C.	R.C.	160	117	276	68
276	6904	Rathreagh,	34	Towna,		R.C.	–	R.C.	–	47	56	103	38
277	10531	Rosslea,	34	Rosslea,		–	R.C.	R.C.	R.C.	96	95	191	54
278	6475	Shrule,	32	Kilross,		R.C.	–	R.C.	R.C.	94	125	220	54
279	6768	Do.	–	Cloonacurrib,	m.	R.C.	–	R.C.	–	94	–	94	38
280	6769	Do.	–	Do.	f.	R.C.	–	R.C.	–	–	91	91	38
281	7702	Do.	–	Shrule,	m.	R.C.	–	R.C.	R.C.	213	–	213	70
282	7703	Do.	–	Do.	f.	R.C.	–	R.C.	R.C.	–	203	203	69
283	6826	Strade,	21	Strade, a		R.C.	–	–	–	–	–	–	–
284	3170	Toomore,	–	Foxford,	m.	R.C.	–	R.C.	R.C.	183	–	183	76
285	6076	Do.	–	Do.	f.	R.C.	–	R.C.	R.C.	–	201	201	64
286	6304	Do.	–	Toomore,		R.C.	–	R.C.	R.C.	173	150	323	74
287	4107	Turlough,	20	Pheraville,		R.C.	–	R.C.	–	58	64	112	38
288	10246	Do.	–	Turlough, Ord. Ag.	m.	R.C.	–	R.C.	–	103	–	190	41
289	10257	Do.	–	Do.	f.	R.C.	–	R.C.	–	–	183	189	50
290	6966	Do.	–	Oughtamard,		R.C.	–	R.C.	R.C.	101	97	198	48
291	8184	Do.	–	Crimlin,		R.C.	–	R.C.	R.C.	103	91	159	36
292	9117	Do.	–	Park,		R.C.	–	R.C.	R.C.	180	101	240	55
293	6861	Tagheen,	37	Tagheen,	f.	R.C.	–	R.C.	–	–	117	117	46
294	6830	Do.	–	Ahena,	day.	R.C.	–	R.C.	–	133	–	133	57
				Do.	evg.	R.C.	–	R.C.	–	68	–	68	38
295	6836	Templemore,	21	Knockanatan,		R.C.	–	R.C.	R.C.	106	98	204	48
296	9740	Do.	–	Cloongee,	m.	–	R.C.	R.C.	–	115	–	115	32
297	9741	Do.	–	Do.	f.	–	R.C.	R.C.	–	–	101	101	33
		Total for County Mayo, 297 Schools,								31254	24014	55,268	15647

COUNTY OF

Number.	Roll Number of School.	Parish.	District.	School.		Clergyman.	Lay.	Principals.	Assistants.	Males.	Fem.	Total.	Average Daily Attendance.
1	10896	Aughrim,	22	Rodeen,		R.C.	–	R.C.	R.C.	108	162	263	71
2	8121	Do.	–	Creena,		R.C.	–	R.C.	R.C.	86	121	157	40
3	[illegible]	Ardcarn,	–	Woodbrook,		–	R.C.	R.C.	–	94	56	140	42
4	7267	Do.	–	Bridgecurran,	m.	R.C.	–	R.C.	–	125	–	125	48
5	7276	Do.	–	Do.	f.	R.C.	–	R.C.	–	–	104	104	39
6	7399	Do.	–	Woodfield,	m.	R.C.	–	R.C.	–	133	–	133	65
7	7400	Do.	–	Do.	f.	R.C.	–	R.C.	–	–	90	90	38
8	7601	Do.	–	Lisphail, a	m.	R.C.	–	–	–	–	–	–	–
9	7408	Do.	–	Castlehill,	m.	R.C.	–	R.C.	–	170	–	170	68
10	7501	Do.	–	Do.	f.	R.C.	–	R.C.	R.C.	–	141	141	53
11	7787	Do.	–	Kilfinagh,	f.	R.C.	–	R.C.	–	39	63	102	39
12	10438	Do.	–	Cartron (2),		R.C.	–	R.C.	–	115	16	131	43
13	7866	Do.	–	Derrymacarrigan,	m.	R.C.	–	R.C.	–	152	–	152	65
14	8111	Do.	–	Do.	f.	R.C.	–	R.C.	R.C.	–	175	175	11
15	6053	Do.	–	Ardmoyle,		R.C.	–	–	–	57	52	108	41
16	0488	Do.	–	Knale,	f.	R.C.	–	R.C.	–	28	98	124	53
17	8091	Athleague,	37	Athleague,	m.	R.C.	–	R.C.	–	128	–	128	48
18	4568	Do.	–	Do.	f.	R.C.	–	R.C.	R.C.	–	148	148	50
19	5466	Do.	–	Scardane,		R.C.	–	R.C.	R.C.	71	78	149	52
20	16068	Ballintubber,	–	Ballintubber,	m.	R.C.	–	R.C.	–	134	–	134	43
21	10798	Do.	–	Do.	f.	R.C.	–	R.C.	R.C.	–	161	161	52
22	1081	Boyle,	23	Boyle,	m.	R.C.	–	R.C.	R.C.	253	–	253	80
23	1082	Do.	–	Do.	f.	R.C.	–	R.C.	R.C.	–	110	110	43
24	[illegible]	Do.	–	Do. Workhouse,		P.L.	Gds.	R.C.	–	61	49	100	56
25	7664	Do.	–	Deerpark,	m.	R.C.	–	R.C.	–	75	–	75	31
26	6916	Do.	–	Do.	f.	R.C.	–	R.C.	–	–	72	72	27
27	2067	Do.	–	Killyconnighan,		R.C.	–	R.C.	–	69	50	109	44

a Returns not available. b No Teacher. c Including value of Free Residence.

Province of CONNAUGHT: County of MAYO—continued.

Amount paid for Books, Requisites, and Apparatus, at Reduced Prices.	Aid granted by the Board during the Year 1874. In Free Stock of Books, Requisites, and Apparatus.	In Salaries, Premiums, and other Gratuities.	Results Fees, Financial Year.	Amount of Local Emoluments received in Aid of Teacher's Salary. School Fees.	Subscriptions, Endowments, &c.	Total Local Aid.	Vested or Non-Vested.	Number.
£ s. d.	£ s. d.	£ s. d.	£ s. d.	£ s. d.	£ s. d.	£ s. d.		
0 14 10	—	70 0 0	4 18 0	—	—	—		270
5 0 1	—	40 0 0	13 15 0	—	—	—		271
—	—	11 0 0	—	—	—	—		272
—	—	15 0 0	—	0 8 4	—	0 8 4		273
2 0 4	—	40 0 0	9 2 0	1 14 0	0 10 0	*2 4 6		274
8 10 4	—	50 0 0	17 11 0	9 13 4	—	9 13 4		275
1 6 4	—	80 0 0	11 3 6	1 0 0	—	1 0 6		276
1 17 2	—	55 10 0	17 0 6	4 15 2	8 0 0	12 15 2		277
1 13 0	—	44 0 0	24 1 0	1 8 8	1 0 0	*6 9 2	V.C.	278
1 6 11	—	44 0 0	8 8 0	—	—	—	V.T.	279
1 16 10	—	80 0 0	12 8 0	0 10 0	—	0 10 0	V.C.	280
1 18 8	—	62 0 0	61 13 6	2 8 0	15 0 0	*17 3 6		281
4 8 10	—	40 0 0	27 1 6	0 10 0	10 0 0	10 10 0		282
—	—	—	—	—	—	—		283
8 6 11	—	60 10 0	31 13 0	2 18 6	—	2 18 6		284
8 10 1	—	49 0 0	20 4 6	3 2 0	—	3 2 0		285
2 10 6	—	55 6 4	31 2 8	5 8 8	8 0 0	5 8 8		286
1 1 0	—	21 0 0	10 18 0	0 6 11	—	0 6 11	V.T.	287
1 6 3	—	63 18 4	8 14 0	3 15 11	—	3 15 11		288
1 10 3	—	61 6 8	6 15 6	2 8 1	—	2 8 1		289
5 9 7	—	49 0 0	10 14 0	5 14 9	—	5 14 0		290
2 18 0	—	39 0 0	12 15 6	5 3 8	—	5 3 8		291
3 7 8	—	49 0 0	16 3 0	4 10 6	—	4 10 6		292
6 13 2	—	40 0 0	11 18 0	1 2 5	2 0 0	0 2 5		293
6 10 9	—	97 6 0	6 16 0	8 5 6	8 10 0	*0 15 6		294
			—	2 18 6	—	4 16 0		
8 8 10	—	44 17 9	4 10 9	6 9 9	1 0 0	6 9 2		295
2 16 0	—	27 10 6	14 0 6	1 15 0	—	1 15 0	V.C.	296
1 7 8	—	20 0 0	12 19 0	2 6 0	—	2 0 6	V.C.	297
275 18 9	40 0 0	11,324 19 7	4,338 19 6	1,211 17 1	764 11 11	1,970 5 0		

ROSCOMMON—208 Schools.

7 1 2	—	70 16 4	22 18 0	—	—	—		1
6 11 8	—	62 16 8	27 12 0	2 0 0	—	2 0 0		2
0 10 0	—	62 1 9	24 10 0	2 1 0	—	2 1 0	V.C.	3
2 13 4	—	39 10 8	12 12 6	3 5 0	—	3 5 0		4
4 16 8	—	56 10 0	22 13 6	5 5 0	—	5 5 0		5
—	—	60 10 6	16 11 6	4 0 0	—	4 0 0		6
2 14 5	—	78 18 4	17 15 0	0 16 6	—	0 16 6		7
—	—	—	—	—	—	—		8
2 6 10	—	55 0 0	18 0 6	2 0 0	—	2 0 6		9
1 10 11	—	67 11 8	27 4 0	2 2 0	—	2 2 0		10
2 4 9	—	28 11 8	10 6 0	8 10 0	—	8 10 0		11
1 18 11	—	69 10 0	21 15 6	5 0 0	—	5 0 0		12
0 7 11	—	44 3 4	20 19 6	8 15 0	—	8 15 0		13
4 0 6	5 14 0	66 10 0	27 18 0	4 0 6	—	4 6 6		14
3 4 10	—	37 0 0	18 1 6	6 17 6	—	0 17 6		15
—	—	43 10 6	16 4 0	—	—	—		16
1 7 11	—	55 6 8	18 7 0	13 6 0	—	13 6 0		17
4 1 10	—	49 0 0	12 9 6	4 18 8	—	6 15 8		18
3 9 0	—	46 0 0	11 13 0	1 18 4	—	1 18 5		19
3 19 8	—	26 10 0	5 14 4	4 10 6	—	4 10 6		20
5 7 4	—	81 18 4	16 0 0	4 14 9	—	4 14 9		21
7 14 9	—	110 1 4	40 6 0	8 3 0	—	8 3 0		22
6 17 1	—	59 10 0	21 10 0	2 6 0	—	2 5 0		23
0 17 4	—	7 10 0	—	—	—	—		24
2 2 10	—	28 8 10	7 17 6	1 8 8	—	1 8 0		25
5 5 3	—	20 0 0	11 19 0	4 19 6	—	2 16 0		26
2 9 4	—	50 0 0	12 1 0	5 10 0	—	6 10 0		27

* Including value of Free Garden.

* Incomplete.

List of Schools in operation on the 31st December, 1874.—

No.	Roll Number of School	Parish.	District.	School.		Religious Denomination of Manager or Correspondent: Clerical.	Lay.	Religious Denomination of Teachers: Principals.	Assistants.	Attendances for the Year: Total number of Pupils on Rolls within the Year 1874: Males.	Fem.	Total.	[illegible]
28	3770	Boyle,	22	Deerpark,		R.C.	–	R.C.	R.C.	75	89	164	85
29	8561	Do.	–	Carrigeenarue,	m.	R.C.	–	R.C.	–	187	–	187	31
30	3046	Do.	–	Do.	f.	R.C.	–	R.C.	R.C.	–	187	187	41
31	10420	Do.	–	Abbeytown, No. 2,		R.C.	–	R.C.	–	–	159	159	58
32	6040	Do.	–	Tivnagh,		R.C.	–	R.C.	–	46	15	61	25
33	9108	Do.	–	Ardsallagh,		R.C.	–	R.C.	–	59	71	130	41
34	7218	Do.	–	Grange,		R.C.	–	R.C.	R.C.	116	101	217	79
35	10549	Do.	–	Railway Bridge,[a]		Pres.	–	Pres.	–	–	–	–	–
36	4572	Bumlin,	27	Strokestown,[b]	m.	R.C.	–	–	–	–	–	–	–
37	[illegible]	Do.	–	Do.	f.	R.C.	–	R.C.	R.C.	–	160	160	58
38	[illegible]	Do.	–	Do.[c]		R.C.	–	–	–	–	–	–	–
39	6122	Do.	–	Do. Workhouse,		P.L.	Gds.	R.C.	–	28	22	50	28
40	10216	Do.	–	North Yard,	m.	–	E.C.	R.C.	–	140	–	140	45
41	[illegible]	Do.	–	Do.	f.	–	E.C.	R.C.	–	–	115	115	61
42	4158	Baslick,	–	Kilmurry,		–	R.C.	R.C.	R.C.	64	92	156	64
43	2520	Do.	–	Castleplunket,		R.C.	–	R.C.	–	79	71	150	54
44	10442	Do.	–	Caddlebrook,	m.	R.C.	–	R.C.	–	65	–	65	28
45	[illegible]	Do.	–	Do.	f.	R.C.	–	R.C.	–	–	108	108	39
46	[illegible]	Cam,	–	Carrick,		R.C.	–	R.C.	–	93	72	165	58
47	4480	Clonfinlough,	–	Clonfree,	m.	R.C.	–	R.C.	–	229	–	228	64
48	8131	Do.	–	Do.	f.	R.C.	–	R.C.	R.C.	–	181	181	61
49	8450	Do.	–	Aughnasurn,		R.C.	–	R.C.	R.C.	120	96	216	72
50	[illegible]	Do.	–	Cloonagh,		–	E.C.	R.C.	–	140	–	140	38
51	11181	Do.	–	Do.	f.	–	–	R.C.	–	–	203	203	61
52	5107	Cloonygormican,	23	Kinard,		R.C.	–	–	–	127	70	197	60
53	7040	Do.	27	Cuilmore,		–	R.C.	R.C.	R.C.	68	79	147	41
54	8448	Creagh,	23	Creagh,		R.C.	–	R.C.	–	172	64	236	72
55	8254	Do.	–	Newtown,		R.C.	–	R.C.	–	66	69	135	38
56	9018	Do.	–	Attirory,	m.	R.C.	–	R.C.	–	61	–	61	28
57	6018	Do.	–	Do.	f.	R.C.	–	R.C.	–	–	70	70	25
58	5876	Cloonmakert,	27	Ballyleague,		R.C.	–	R.C.	–	110	94	204	62
59	5361	Do.	–	Weakfield,		R.C.	–	R.C.	–	81	[illegible]	163	50
60	[illegible]	Cam,	–	Bridewell,		R.C.	–	R.C.	R.C.	101	88	189	47
61	6104	Creeve,	22	Bolarra,[b]		R.C.	–	–	–	–	–	–	–
62	9287	Do.	27	Cloonshee,	m.	R.C.	–	R.C.	–	154	–	154	64
63	9121	Do.	–	Do.	f.	R.C.	–	R.C.	–	–	137	137	49
64	1318	Dysart,	–	Ballinlava,	m.	R.C.	–	R.C.	–	111	–	111	29
65	1524	Do.	–	Do.	f.	R.C.	–	R.C.	–	–	186	186	31
66	[illegible]	Do.	–	Ballymurray Ord. Ag.		–	R.C.	R.C.	–	142	74	216	43
67	9617	Do.	–	Fearagh,	m.	R.C.	–	R.C.	–	83	–	83	39
68	9516	Do.	–	Do.	f.	R.C.	–	R.C.	–	–	107	107	35
69	1677	Drum,	26	Corrafolia Ord. Agr.		–	R.C.	R.C.	–	164	–	164	38
70	[illegible]	Do.	–	Do.	f.	–	R.C.	R.C.	–	–	137	137	33
71	6648	Do.	–	Drumpark,	m.	R.C.	–	R.C.	–	117	–	117	32
72	6648	Do.	–	Do.	f.	R.C.	–	R.C.	–	–	93	93	38
73	7486	Drumatemple,	27	Drumatemple,	m.	R.C.	–	R.C.	–	176	–	176	67
74	[illegible]	Do.	–	Do.	f.	R.C.	–	R.C.	R.C.	–	166	166	53
75	1765	Elphin,	23	Elphin,	m.	R.C.	–	R.C.	–	149	–	118	64
76	8844	Do.	27	Cloonyquinn,	m.	R.C.	–	R.C.	R.C.	160	–	160	65
77	[illegible]	Do.	–	Do.	f.	R.C.	–	R.C.	–	–	128	128	64
78	8337	Do.	–	Cloonenellaun,		R.C.	–	R.C.	–	80	51	131	36
79	1041	Do.	–	Flaskagh,		R.C.	–	R.C.	R.C.	60	90	150	36
80	[illegible]	Do.	26	Abbey Carton Conv.	f.	–	R.C.	Nuns		–	204	204	152
81	9476	Estersnow,	–	Knockroe,		R.C.	–	R.C.	R.C.	107	89	196	67
82	4104	Fuerty,	27	Fuerty,		R.C.	–	R.C.	R.C.	96	67	163	49
83	6214	Do.	–	Castlecoote,	f.	R.C.	–	R.C.	R.C.	67	89	156	56
84	11051	Do.	–	Cloverhill,		R.C.	–	R.C.	–	98	85	183	67
85	[illegible]	Kilkeevan,	–	Gortaleragh,	m.	R.C.	–	R.C.	–	260	–	260	52
86	6152	Do.	–	Do.	f.	R.C.	–	R.C.	R.C.	–	168	168	67
87	[illegible]	Do.	–	Do.[c] Workhouse,		P.L.	Gds.	–	–	–	–	–	–
88	[illegible]	Do.	–	Turnsa,	m.	R.C.	–	R.C.	–	209	–	209	43
89	[illegible]	Do.	–	Do.	f.	R.C.	–	R.C.	–	–	251	251	84
90	[illegible]	Do.	–	Tarmon,		R.C.	–	R.C.	R.C.	100	71	171	46
91	6626	Do.	–	Cloonmeal,	f.	R.C.	–	R.C.	–	–	124	124	39

[a] No returns. [b] Inoperative. [c] No teacher. [d] Including value of Free Residence and Garden.

Province of Connaught: County of Roscommon—*continued.*

Amount paid for Books, Requisites, and Apparatus at Reduced Prices.	Aid granted by the Board during the Year 1874. In Free Stock of Books, Requisites, and Apparatus.	Aid granted by the Board during the Year 1874. In Salaries, Premiums, and other Gratuities.	Aid granted by the Board during the Year 1874. Results Fees, Financial Year.	Amount of Local Endowments received in Aid of Teacher's Salary. School Fees.	Amount of Local Endowments received in Aid of Teacher's Salary. Subscriptions, Endowments, &c.	Amount of Local Endowments received in Aid of Teacher's Salary. Total Local Aid.	Vested or Non-Vested.	Number.
£ s. d.	£ s. d.	£ s. d.	£ s. d.	£ s. d.	£ s. d.	£ s. d.		
3 2 5	—	38 10 0	14 8 0	1 19 6	—	1 19 0		28
6 3 2	—	30 8 4	23 2 0	7 15 6	—	7 15 6		29
2 10 10	—	59 14 4	76 18 6	9 8 6	—	9 0 6		30
1 6 7	—	45 19 4	11 17 0	—	—	—		31
1 5 5	—	10 6 0	2 6 6	0 10 0	—	0 10 0		32
4 3 8	—	81 10 0	20 11 0	—	—	—		33
4 18 1	—	61 0 0	34 8 6	1 3 6	—	1 3 6		34
3 9 7	—	—	—	—	—	—		35
—	—	—	—	—	—	—		36
7 7 4	—	65 0 0	27 18 6	17 14 4	—	17 14 4		37
1 14 7	—	—	—	—	—	—		38
4 12 11	—	—	—	—	—	—		39
3 0 10	—	43 0 0	11 19 0	4 0 0	11 0 0	*19 0 0	V.C.	40
—	—	19 0 0	9 0 0	—	—	—	V.C.	41
4 10 9	—	40 4 6	24 0 0	1 10 6	4 0 0	*5 10 6		42
3 5 1	—	21 0 0	—	1 6 2	—	1 6 2		43
8 12 7	—	23 0 0	4 18 0	3 0 0	—	3 0 0		44
2 19 3	—	27 0 0	0 0 6	0 4 6	—	0 4 6		45
4 17 8	—	31 6 8	11 13 6	4 3 9	—	4 3 9	V.T.	46
5 1 0	—	37 18 8	22 16 6	4 1 0	—	4 1 6	V.T.	47
1 7 10	—	44 8 8	31 11 6	1 16 6	—	1 16 6	V.T.	48
6 10 10	—	67 10 0	30 0 0	0 9 0	—	0 9 0	V.C.	49
4 5 8	—	62 8 4	8 6 0	1 8 6	—	1 8 4		50
1 18 8	5 10 0	11 18 4	26 11 0	6 6 0	—	6 6 0		51
3 9 6	—	65 18 4	21 15 0	3 11 0	—	3 11 0		52
2 19 8	—	53 0 8	27 19 0	4 0 0	—	4 0 0		53
0 10 2	—	91 0 0	16 0 0	4 17 8	—	4 17 0		54
2 7 0	—	30 0 0	5 10 0	2 0 5	—	2 0 5		55
1 0 8	—	24 0 0	4 6 0	1 10 5	—	1 10 5		56
1 3 11	—	27 0 0	2 10 0	1 5 8	—	1 5 0		57
2 12 0	—	54 3 4	0 18 6	4 5 10	0 10 0	†4 19 10	V.C.	58
1 11 0	—	24 0 0	8 17 11	0 11 0	—	0 11 0		59
0 11 9	—	13 10 0	—	1 5 0	—	1 5 0		60
0 8 11	—	—	—	—	—	—		61
2 11 11	—	46 6 0	24 16 6	4 7 0	—	4 7 0		62
8 0 10	—	44 16 6	28 4 6	5 0 0	—	5 0 0		63
2 4 0	—	84 0 0	6 18 6	1 6 0	—	1 6 0	A.	64
—	—	24 0 0	6 4 6	2 1 6	—	2 1 6	A.	65
3 10 1	—	47 6 8	17 18 0	3 8 0	81 0 0	*83 8 6		66
1 16 5	—	34 10 0	15 4 0	0 10 0	—	0 10 0		67
1 18 4	—	28 0 8	—	1 0 6	—	1 0 0		68
1 15 8	—	20 0 0	6 6 0	4 5 1	—	†6 5 1	A.	69
1 0 7	—	43 16 8	13 0 8	3 17 6	—	3 17 0	A.	70
1 7 4	—	27 0 0	9 10 0	7 10 0	—	7 10 0		71
—	—	20 0 0	6 7 0	5 11 1	—	5 11 1		72
5 6 5	—	27 10 0	10 4 0	6 0 0	—	6 0 0		73
3 15 11	—	26 0 0	21 0 0	2 14 11	—	2 14 11		74
4 18 0	—	53 10 0	20 8 0	3 17 6	—	3 17 6		75
6 9 2	—	77 18 4	27 6 6	10 14 0	5 0 0	15 14 0		76
4 5 4	—	40 16 8	21 11 0	5 6 6	5 0 0	10 6 6		77
4 3 7	—	84 0 0	9 18 0	1 11 6	—	1 11 6		78
4 10 5	—	67 0 8	24 19 0	4 10 8	7 0 0	*11 10 8		79
14 17 6	—	119 3 2	45 11 6	26 17 11	—	26 17 11		80
8 4 2	—	50 10 8	65 11 0	6 8 9	—	6 8 9		81
4 14 8	—	44 0 0	7 14 0	1 0 0	—	1 0 0		82
3 0 5	6 0 0	34 0 0	11 10 0	1 16 6	—	1 16 6		83
4 1 4	4 10 0	31 0 0	15 17 6	4 1 6	—	4 1 6		84
10 14 4	—	65 6 8	14 18 0	15 17 0	—	15 17 0		85
0 9 0	—	40 6 8	20 13 0	12 13 4	—	12 13 4		86
7 6 7	—	—	—	—	—	—		87
3 8 5	—	21 0 0	7 10 0	1 6 6	—	1 6 6		88
9 18 1	—	30 0 0	18 17 6	6 16 11	—	6 16 11		89
8 18 0	—	41 0 0	21 19 6	10 18 6	2 0 0	†12 18 6		90
2 17 1	—	30 0 0	11 1 6	6 8 6	—	3 2 6		91

* Including value of Free Residence.

† Including value of Free Garden.

List of Schools in operation on the 31st December, 1874.—

Number.	Roll Number of School.	Parish.	District.	School.	Religious Denomination of Manager or Correspondent: Clerical.	Lay.	Number and Religious Denomination of Teachers: Principals.	Assistants.	Attendance for the Year. Total number of Pupils on Rolls within the Year 1874: Males.	Fem.	Total.	Average Daily Attendance for Year 1874.
92	11189	Kilmeevan,	27	Cloonfower, m.	R.C.	–	R.C.	–	103	–	103	31
93	11189	Do.	–	Do. f.	R.C.	–	R.C.	–	–	117	117	40
94	2240	Kiltoom,	–	Ballybay,* m.	–	–	R.C.	–	–	–	–	–
95	1843	Do.	–	Do. f.	R.C.	–	R.C.	–	–	104	104	34
96	1464	Do.	–	Famore,	R.C.	–	R.C.	–	74	84	158	32
97	1830	Kiltrustan,	26	Cortober, m.	R.C.	–	R.C.	R.C.	160	–	160	5[illegible]
98	2404	Do.	–	Do. f.	R.C.	–	R.C.	R.C.	–	180	180	61
99	8031	Do.	27	Clongarry,	–	R.C.	R.C.	R.C.	67	103	170	52
100	2347	Kilcolagh,	28	Mantua, m.	R.C.	–	R.C.	–	190	–	190	64
101	2324	Do.	–	Do. f.	R.C.	–	R.C.	–	–	157	157	61
102	6317	Do.	–	Ballinameen, m.	R.C.	–	R.C.	R.C.	216	–	216	8[illegible]
103	8362	Do.	–	Do. f.	R.C.	–	R.C.	R.C.	–	229	229	6[illegible]
104	10721	Do.	–	Bells, m.	R.C.	–	R.C.	–	168	–	168	46
105	10832	Do.	–	Do. f.	R.C.	–	R.C.	–	–	143	143	47
106	2437	Kilteevan,	27	Kilteevan, m.	R.C.	–	R.C.	–	153	–	153	60
107	2611	Do.	–	Do. f.	R.C.	–	R.C.	–	–	182	182	45
108	2861	Kilronan,	28	Greaghnafarna,	R.C.	–	R.C.	R.C.	78	89	167	5[illegible]
109	4609	Do.	–	Ballyfarnon, No. 1,	R.C.	–	R.C.	–	–	100	100	34
110	6635	Do.	–	Do. No. 2,	R.C.	–	R.C.	–	84	83	167	19
111	[illegible]	Do.	–	Keadue, m.	–	R.C.	R.C.	–	187	–	187	54
112	8101	Do.	–	Do. f.	–	R.C.	R.C.	–	–	136	136	56
113	7701	Do.	–	Do. i.	–	R.C.	R.C.	–	54	40	94	40
114	8752	Do.	–	Greaghnaroogh,	–	R.C.	R.C.	R.C.	70	93	163	54
115	7031	Do.	–	Corrtrona,	R.C.	–	R.C.	R.C.	92	77	169	5[illegible]
116	7862	Do.	–	Mount Allen, Ord. Ag.	R.C.	–	R.C.	–	120	–	120	47
117	7861	Do.	–	Do. f.	R.C.	–	R.C.	–	–	136	136	54
118	2298	Kilcorkey,	27	Bellanagare, m.	R.C.	–	R.C.	–	100	–	100	31
119	[illegible]	Do.	–	Do. f.	R.C.	–	R.C.	–	–	137	137	30
120	10830	Do.	–	Tully, m.	–	R.C.	R.C.	–	87	–	87	35
121	10637	Do.	–	Do. f.	–	R.C.	R.C.	–	–	127	127	50
122	7498	Kilmaine,	–	Ballymurray Ord. Agr.	R.C.	–	R.C.	–	84	–	84	25
123	4038	Do.	–	Do. f.	R.C.	–	R.C.	–	–	93	93	30
124	4101	Killummod,	26	Flaxer,	R.C.	–	R.C.	R.C.	88	84	172	61
125	3483	Do.	–	Croghan,	R.C.	–	R.C.	R.C.	129	103	232	80
126	4111	Kiltrustan,	27	Kiltrustan, m.	R.C.	–	R.C.	–	148	–	148	60
127	4112	Do.	–	Do. f.	R.C.	–	R.C.	–	–	114	114	60
128	10171	Do.	–	Rathmagh,	R.C.	–	R.C.	–	76	64	140	41
129	4236	Killinvoy,	–	Knockcroghery, m.	R.C.	–	R.C.	–	133	–	133	43
130	4860	Do.	–	Do. f.	R.C.	–	R.C.	–	–	100	100	30
131	8360	Do.	–	Mount Plunket,	R.C.	–	R.C.	–	44	54	98	24
132	4316	Kilmore,	28	Kilmore,	R.C.	–	R.C.	–	96	90	186	58
133	[illegible]	Do.	–	Dangan, m.	R.C.	–	R.C.	–	169	–	169	51
134	7652	Do.	–	Do. f.	R.C.	–	R.C.	R.C.	–	170	170	67
135	9216	Do.	–	Ballagh,	R.C.	–	R.C.	–	69	107	176	44
136	11901	Do.	–	Scramoge, m.	R.C.	–	R.C.	–	150	–	150	70
137	[illegible]	Do.	–	Do.* f.	–	–	–	–	–	–	–	–
138	6811	Kilgefin,	27	Ballagh,	R.C.	–	R.C.	bR.C.	139	148	288	85
139	6108	Kilbride,	–	Carrowmoneen,	R.C.	–	R.C.	R.C.	76	30	106	50
140	[illegible]	Do.	–	Roxboro', m.	R.C.	–	R.C.	–	68	–	68	43
141	9766	Do.	–	Do. f.	R.C.	–	R.C.	–	–	101	101	30
142	[illegible]	Kilnamanagh,	28	Callow, m.	R.C.	–	R.C.	–	158	–	158	57
143	[illegible]	Do.	–	Do. f.	R.C.	–	R.C.	–	–	141	141	63
144	6777	Kilglass,	27	Kenagh,	R.C.	–	R.C.	–	58	86	144	40
145	7907	Do.	–	Slatta Ord. Agric.,	R.C.	–	R.C.	R.C.	140	153	293	80
146	9498	Do.	–	Ballyfeeny,	–	R.C.	R.C.	–	123	–	124	45
147	[illegible]	Do.	–	Drumlummon,	R.C.	–	R.C.	R.C.	108	100	204	61
148	[illegible]	Kilkeevin,	28	Cloonfad, f.	R.C.	–	R.C.	R.C.	–	248	248	83
149	7744	Do.	–	Do. m.	R.C.	–	R.C.	–	229	–	229	47
150	8091	Do.	–	Granlahan, f.	R.C.	–	R.C.	R.C.	–	236	236	45
151	[illegible]	Do.	–	Carrick, m.	R.C.	–	R.C.	–	173	–	173	56
152	8912	Do.	–	Do. f.	R.C.	–	R.C.	–	–	207	201	60
153	10891	Lisonuffy,	27	Carnisleagh, m.	R.C.	–	R.C.	–	171	–	171	49
154	2078	Do.	–	Do. f.	R.C.	–	R.C.	R.C.	–	165	165	54
155	2915	Do.	–	Curraghroe, m.	R.C.	–	R.C.	–	141	–	141	35

* No Returns.

b Including value of Free Residence.

9	4	10	0	—			—			1	5	0	—			1	5	0		92
0	4	10	0	—			—			8	7	6	—			9	7	6		93
	—			—			—			—			—			—				94
	—			59	0	0	5	4	0	—			—			—			v.r.	95
0	—			94	18	6	9	4	0	9	7	10	—			3	7	10	v.r.	96
2	—			79	16	8	27	8	6	1	3	0	—			1	3	6	v.r.	97
2½	—			60	0	0	31	18	6	2	8	3	—			2	8	3	v.r.	98
1	—			64	0	6	24	8	0	4	6	6	5	0	0	*19	6	6		99
1	2	3	6	41	18	4	30	17	6	4	11	0	2	0	0	*6	11	6		100
9	2	9	5	31	8	7	15	11	6	2	11	0	—			2	11	0		101
7	—			41	9	0	26	1	0	6	13	6	—			6	13	6		102
1	—			19	6	5	60	0	0	4	1	0	—			4	1	0		103
3	1	9	0	30	10	0	23	8	0	0	17	0	—			0	17	0		104
7	1	8	0	28	16	8	24	7	6	1	10	0	—			1	10	0		105
8	—			27	0	4	18	10	6	8	8	6	1	0	0	*8	8	0	v.r.	106
4	—			23	6	6	17	8	6	2	9	0	—			2	9	0	v.r.	107
4	—			14	10	0	27	3	0	5	5	0	—			5	5	6		108
1	—			27	0	0	11	17	0	3	3	4	—			3	3	4		109
3	—			44	1	6	3	16	8	0	6	8	15	16	0	*16	5	8		110
8	—			60	0	0	50	15	0	4	12	0	20	0	0	*24	12	6		111
9	—			61	11	8	21	19	6	4	0	0	15	0	0	*19	0	0		112
6	—			31	0	8	8	13	6	1	15	0	15	0	0	*16	15	0		113
0	3	0	0	58	0	0	29	7	6	2	3	6	5	0	0	7	3	6		114
3	—			62	0	7	29	7	6	3	14	0	—			3	14	0		115
0	—			45	0	0	26	11	0	8	10	8	2	11	6	*5	2	0		116
4	—			41	15	0	31	2	0	1	19	10	—			1	19	10		117
0	—			30	0	0	4	5	0	0	17	0	—			0	17	0		118
6	—			30	0	0	0	10	6	2	1	0	—			2	1	0		119
	—			13	0	0	13	4	0	2	2	6	20	0	0	*22	2	6		120
	—			14	18	8	18	0	0	1	17	8	—			1	17	8		121
1	—			67	0	0	9	10	0	1	19	4	27	16	8	*29	16	0		122
0	—			24	0	0	19	18	6	4	10	0	—			4	10	0		123
0	—			68	0	0	36	8	0	4	8	0	—			4	8	0		124
6	—			77	16	8	20	3	6	7	14	6	—			7	14	0		125
7	—			24	0	0	9	8	6	5	4	0	1	0	0	*6	4	6	v.a.	126
8	—			30	0	0	7	5	0	1	2	6	—			1	2	6	v.a.	127
8	—			33	10	0	13	11	0	4	12	0	—			4	12	6		128
6	—			35	10	8	10	19	0	4	1	0	—			4	1	0	v.a.	129
2	—			20	0	0	10	9	6	2	5	6	—			2	5	4	v.a.	130
11	—			27	18	4	8	1	0	1	0	0	—			1	0	0		131
8	—			32	0	6	17	4	0	—			—			—				132
4	—			45	12	4	25	10	0	2	7	0	—			2	7	0		133
8	—			56	8	6	24	7	0	6	2	3	—			6	2	3		134
3	—			22	10	0	12	13	6	—			—			—				135
8	4	16	0	8	0	0	—			—			—			—				136
	—			—			—			—			—			—				137
10	—			36	0	0	30	1	0	10	8	6	—			10	8	6	v.a.	138
6	—			36	0	9	16	11	6	7	5	0	—			7	5	0	v.a.	139
1	—			39	0	8	19	14	6	10	8	0	—			10	8	0		140
0	—			41	10	0	14	7	0	6	1	6	—			6	1	6		141
7	—			35	8	4	19	7	6	1	13	0	—			1	13	0	v.r.	142
10	—			37	18	4	26	3	0	1	7	6	—			1	7	6	v.a.	143
11	—			20	0	0	6	18	9	1	0	0	—			1	0	0		144
0	—			52	10	0	27	8	6	15	7	0	1	10	0	*16	17	0		145
2	—			55	4	6	10	6	6	3	14	0	10	0	0	13	14	0	v.r.	146
7	—			61	6	8	—			1	0	0	—			1	0	0		147
11	—			40	0	0	11	8	2	4	1	4	—			4	1	4		148
3	—			67	15	4	21	19	6	12	18	0	—			12	18	0		149
4	—			28	0	0	15	15	6	6	1	7	—			6	1	7		150
9	—			34	0	0	17	14	6	—			—			—				151
0	—			60	0	0	16	15	6	6	3	0	—			6	3	0		152
0	—			40	8	4	6	9	6	3	15	0	—			3	15	0	v.r.	153
6	—			63	19	8	25	17	0	4	15	0	—			4	15	0	v.r.	154
4	—			30	0	0	8	14	0	0	19	0	—			0	19	0	v.r.	155

* Including value of Free Residence and Garden.

* Including value of Free Garden.

List of Schools in operation on the 31st December, 1874.—

Number.	Roll Number of School.	Parish.	District.	School.	Religious Denomination of Managers or Correspondents: Clerical	Lay.	Number and Religious Denomination of Teachers: Principals.	Assistants.	Attendance for the Year: Total number of Pupils on Rolls within the Year 1874: Males.	Fem.	Total.	Average number of Pupils daily present during the Year.
156	9016	Lisonuffy,	37	Carrowbrow, f.	R.C.	–	R.C.	–	–	138	169	69
157	7752	Do.	–	Derryhawny,	–	Pres.	R.C.	–	31	30	61	25
158	7195	Moore,	33	Mount Welcome,	–	Pres.	R.C.	R.C.	97	66	163	51
159	7451	Do.	–	Derrylahan,	R.C.	–	R.C.	–	102	65	167	36
160	8903	Do.	–	Harlsepark,	–	Pres.	R.C.	–	74	64	138	46
161	8209	Oran,	37	Cloonycolgan,	R.C.	–	R.C.	R.C.	95	91	186	70
162	9409	Do.	–	Runnamoat,	R.C.	–	R.C.	R.C.	99	120	199	61
163	10849	Do.	–	Ashpark,	–	R.C.	R.C.	–	24	56	84	17
164	11700	Ogulla,	–	Tulsk, f.	–	R.C.	R.C.	–	–	101	104	48
165	8140	Do.	–	Do. m.	–	R.C.	–	–	–	–	–	–
166	8362	Rahara,	–	Rahara,	R.C.	–	R.C.	R.C.	79	75	165	44
167	3450	Roscommon,	–	Roscommon, m.	R.C.	–	R.C.	R.C.	205	–	205	16
168	8918	Do.	–	Do. Workhouse,	P.L.	Gds.	R.C.	–	38	41	80	41
169	[illegible]	Do.	–	Do. Convent, f.	–	R.C.	Nuns		–	298	298	130
170	2011	St. John's,	–	St. John's,	R.C.	–	R.C.	–	67	59	126	33
171	7524	Do.	–	Lloyd,	R.C.	–	R.C.	–	96	45	141	31
172	8769	Do.	–	Glandeff 1st Class Agr.	R.C.	–	R.C.	R.C.	105	113	218	80
173	9780	St. Peter's,	36	Clonown, m.	R.C.	–	R.C.	–	66	–	66	27
174	9240	Do.	–	Do. f.	R.C.	–	R.C.	–	–	95	95	39
175	4195	Do.	–	Deerpark, m.	R.C.	–	R.C.	R.C.	279	–	279	79
176	4196	Do.	–	Do.[a] f.	–	–	–	–	–	–	–	–
177	7728	Do.	–	St. Peter's Convent, f.	–	R.C.	Nuns		18	674	692	162
178	9116	Do.	–	Cloonakilla, m.	R.C.	–	R.C.	–	139	–	139	52
179	9117	Do.	–	Do. f.	R.C.	–	R.C.	–	–	135	133	56
180	7769	Taghboy,	27	Ballyforan Ord. Agric.	R.C.	–	R.C.	R.C.	156	88	244	67
181	2010	Tibohine,	21	Lisdrumneill, m.	R.C.	–	R.C.	–	149	–	149	57
182	5680	Do.	22	Frenchpark, m.	R.C.	–	R.C.	–	146	–	149	47
183	4794	Do.	–	Do. f.	R.C.	–	R.C.	R.C.	–	172	172	61
184	5733	Do.	–	Kingsland,	R.C.	–	R.C.	R.C.	106	99	205	79
185	8100	Do.	21	Loughglynn School Garden, m.	–	R.C.	R.C.	R.C.	164	–	164	72
186	7882	Do.	–	Loughglynn, f.	–	R.C.	R.C.	R.C.	–	158	158	76
187	9376	Do.	21	Cloonarrow, m.	R.C.	–	R.C.	–	154	–	164	39
188	8177	Do.	–	Do. f.	R.C.	–	R.C.	–	–	108	106	26
189	8411	Do.	22	De Freyne, m.	R.C.	–	R.C.	–	154	–	154	47
190	9561	Do.	–	Do. f.	R.C.	–	R.C.	–	–	189	180	41
191	8676	Do.	21	Lisacull, m.	R.C.	–	R.C.	R.C.	294	–	294	75
192	8673	Do.	–	Do. f.	R.C.	–	R.C.	R.C.	–	260	260	79
193	10984	Do.	–	Gorthaganny,	R.C.	–	R.C.	R.C.	199	104	312	80
194	9276	Do.	22	Mullen,	R.C.	–	R.C.	R.C.	116	60	175	61
195	11024	Do.	–	Foragheard,	Pres.	–	Pres.	–	20	17	37	14
196	10118	Do.	21	Mennickaharies,	R.C.	–	R.C.	R.C.	–	222	222	56
197	9740	Do.	–	Ilon, m.	R.C.	–	R.C.	–	209	–	209	56
198	9741	Do.	–	Do. f.	R.C.	–	R.C.	–	–	178	178	47
199	10122	Do.	–	Tibohine, m.	R.C.	–	R.C.	R.C.	184	–	184	98
200	10123	Do.	–	Do. f.	R.C.	–	R.C.	R.C.	–	182	182	94
201	11001	Do.	–	Hasilfalt, m.	R.C.	–	R.C.	R.C.	244	–	241	83
202	11052	Do.	–	Do. f.	R.C.	–	R.C.	R.C.	–	252	252	72
203	[illegible]	Tisrara,	37	Tasawragh,	R.C.	–	R.C.	R.C.	165	101	266	94
204	9041	Do.	–	Mount Talbot,	R.C.	–	R.C.	R.C.	97	101	199	53
205	4900	Termonbarry,	26	Rooskey, m.	R.C.	–	R.C.	–	119	–	140	54
206	4801	Do.	–	Do. f.	R.C.	–	R.C.	R.C.	–	143	143	46
207	8900	Do.	–	Whitehall, m.	R.C.	–	R.C.	–	116	–	114	44
208	4058	Do.	–	Do. f.	R.C.	–	R.C.	–	–	108	101	35
209	9658	Do.	–	Termonbarry,	–	R.C.	R.C.	–	94	70	164	50
210	10758	Do.	–	Cloonfower,	R.C.	–	R.C.	R.C.	118	199	218	45
211	8417	Taghmaconnell	35	Taghmaconnell, m.	R.C.	–	R.C.	–	181	–	181	55
212	4182	Do.	–	Do. f.	R.C.	–	R.C.	–	–	118	118	34
213	7072	Do.	–	Castlesampson,	R.C.	–	R.C.	–	81	72	153	63
214	8117	Taunus,	27	Lephall,	R.C.	–	R.C.	R.C.	59	81	141	65
215	7581	Do.	–	Drumsheghas, m.	R.C.	–	R.C.	–	108	–	108	41
216	8112	Do.	–	Do. f.	R.C.	–	R.C.	–	–	142	148	63
		Total for County Roscommon, 216,							16679	16267	32,159	9716

[a] Including value of Free Residence.

[b] Including value of Free Residence and Garden.

Province of Connaught: County of Roscommon—*continued.*

Amount paid for Books, Requisites, and Apparatus at Reduced Prices.	Aid granted by the Board during the Year 1874: In Free Stock of Books, Requisites, and Apparatus.	In Salaries, Premiums, and other Gratuities.	Results Fees, Financial Year.	Amount of Local Endowments received in Aid of Teacher's Salary: School Fees.	Subscriptions, Endowments, &c.	Total Local Aid.	Vested or Non-Vested.	Number.
£ s. d.	£ s. d.	£ s. d.	£ s. d.	£ s. d.	£ s. d.	£ s. d.		
2 0 9	—	84 18 8	0 9 0	0 15 8	—	0 18 0	V.T.	156
1 8 7	—	32 0 0	7 8 0	0 10 5	1 0 0	*1 10 5		157
1 6 3	—	45 6 8	13 18 0	4 10 0	10 0 0	*14 10 0	V.C.	158
1 10 1	—	20 4 0	15 11 0	3 17 11	—	3 17 11		159
1 11 0	—	25 0 0	9 12 0	2 10 8	10 0 0	*12 10 8	V.C.	160
2 8 3	—	30 10 0	26 7 0	5 8 0	—	5 8 0		161
2 10 1	—	85 10 0	11 11 6	3 17 10	2 10 0	6 7 10		162
0 12 2	—	24 0 0	2 5 6	—	—	—		163
2 8 5	5 0 0	6 18 4	—	0 2 0	—	0 2 0		164
8 0 4	—	45 8 8	22 2 0	—	—	—		165
1 18 8	—	44 0 0	8 0 0	2 19 0	—	2 19 0		166
4 10 1	—	63 15 4	26 18 0	15 0 6	—	15 0 0		167
5 19 1	—	—	—	—	—	—		168
22 14 8	—	111 0 0	60 0 0	61 2 0	—	61 2 0		169
0 18 2	—	24 0 0	5 11 4	2 6 0	—	2 6 0	V.T.	170
1 19 11	—	25 0 0	7 15 0	2 11 2	6 8 0	*8 19 2		171
5 9 4	—	28 5 4	16 6 3	4 8 1	5 17 6	*6 8 1		172
1 5 2	—	24 0 0	5 8 0	2 10 4	—	2 10 4		173
1 7 0	—	21 10 8	8 8 6	1 14 10	—	1 14 10		174
5 18 7	—	55 0 0	10 2 0	13 4 5	—	13 4 5	V.T.	175
—	—	—	—	—	—	—	V.T.	176
11 11 2	—	80 2 0	45 2 0	21 15 8	—	21 15 8		177
3 8 0	—	84 5 0	6 13 0	7 2 10	—	7 2 10		178
2 7 0	—	30 0 0	0 8 0	4 5 10	—	4 5 10		179
8 12 5	—	63 16 8	21 3 0	4 8 7	—	4 8 7	V.C.	180
2 10 8	—	27 0 0	8 0 8	2 0 9	1 10 0	*3 18 0	V.T.	181
1 5 0	—	65 14 5	11 2 8	2 15 0	—	2 15 0	V.T.	182
5 8 10	—	50 8 4	81 6 0	5 11 9	—	5 11 9	V.C.	183
4 9 11	—	58 0 0	27 15 6	4 17 6	—	4 17 6		184
4 4 2	—	96 0 0	23 10 6	1 14 0	25 19 4	*27 4 4		185
3 8 1	—	72 8 0	25 11 0	8 17 10	19 8 8	*18 6 6		186
3 7 8	—	61 0 0	8 5 0	3 6 0	—	3 6 0		187
2 16 0	—	30 0 0	10 0 3	2 14 7	—	2 14 7		188
6 19 1	—	80 10 0	20 8 6	3 9 6	—	3 9 6		189
2 10 4	—	31 10 0	20 5 0	1 11 6	—	1 11 6		190
0 1 0	—	69 13 10	24 10 0	4 10 0	—	4 10 0		191
8 17 8	—	61 8 8	28 11 6	2 9 8	—	2 9 8		192
7 1 7	—	64 4 0	20 14 0	6 2 0	—	6 2 0		193
1 19 0	8 12 0	44 0 0	20 1 0	5 4 6	—	5 4 6		194
1 9 3	4 0 0	14 18 4	4 7 0	—	20 0 0	20 0 0		195
0 18 9	—	52 12 4	13 11 0	0 16 2	1 0 0	*4 16 2		196
8 18 0	—	56 12 4	11 1 5	1 13 6	—	1 13 6		197
9 12 4	—	20 8 8	13 14 0	2 4 0	—	2 4 0		198
4 19 0	—	46 10 0	14 19 0	4 5 6	—	4 5 6		199
2 0 5	—	45 0 8	55 0 0	4 10 8	—	4 10 8		200
9 6 8	6 10 0	60 0 0	30 0 0	1 8 6	—	1 8 6		201
8 11 8	6 0 0	25 16 0	22 16 0	7 8 8	—	7 8 8		202
8 10 4	—	50 18 1	66 11 6	4 8 0	—	4 8 0	V.T.	203
2 14 9	—	56 0 0	13 0 0	1 10 0	—	1 10 0		204
5 19 9	—	61 11 8	16 2 0	0 8 0	—	0 8 0	V.C.	205
2 17 6	—	64 8 8	10 15 6	1 5 8	—	1 5 8	V.C.	206
—	—	80 8 1	9 19 6	4 8 0	—	4 8 0		207
1 0 4	—	28 0 0	19 6 0	0 15 0	—	0 15 0		208
4 8 11	—	48 8 4	11 6 0	6 0 10	10 0 0	16 0 10	V.C.	209
2 17 7	—	25 13 4	18 0 0	6 12 5	—	6 12 5		210
2 5 4	—	84 0 0	4 11 0	0 15 6	—	0 15 6		211
1 15 7	—	30 0 0	10 2 6	1 16 0	—	1 16 0		212
1 10 6	—	20 0 0	15 6 0	2 5 8	—	2 5 8		213
1 18 8	—	60 0 0	20 11 8	1 14 6	—	1 14 6		214
2 11 0	9 12 0	28 8 8	16 15 0	2 2 0	—	2 2 5		215
2 0 6	5 10 0	83 15 4	28 14 6	3 15 0	—	3 15 0		216
203 11 5	77 18 6	8,684 3 10	8,177 11 0	263 16 9	828 8 0	1,120 3 9		

* Including value of Free Grants.

d Closed.

List of Schools in operation on the 31st December, 1874.—

COUNTY OF

Number.	Roll Number of School.	Parish.	District.	School.	Religious Denomination of Manager or Corr. Clerical.	Lay.	Number and Religious Denomination of Teachers. Principals.	Assistants.	Attendance for the Year. Total number of Pupils on Rolls within the Year. Males.	Fem.	Total.	Average Daily Attendance for the Year.
1	1311	Achonry,	18	Carrowmore,	–	R.C.	R.C.	R.C.	98	75	173	61
2	1463	Do.	–	Tubbercurry, m.	R.C.	–	R.C.	R.C.	230	–	230	74
3	[illegible]	Do.	–	Do. f.	R.C.	–	R.C.	R.C.	–	207	207	56
4	8318	Do.	–	Do. Workhouse.	P.L.	Gds.	R.C.	–	20	20	40	24
5	4486	Do.	–	Achonry, m.	–	R.C.	R.C.	–	119	–	119	47
6	4487	Do.	–	Do. f.	–	R.C.	R.C.	–	–	207	207	64
7	4[illegible]	Do.	–	Cloonacool, m.	R.C.	–	R.C.	R.C.	216	–	216	44
8	[illegible]	Do.	–	Do. f.	R.C.	–	R.C.	R.C.	–	231	231	73
9	7787	Do.	–	Bunnacranagh,	R.C.	–	R.C.	2R.C.	237	142	379	130
10	[illegible]	Do.	–	Powellsboro',	R.C.	–	R.C.	R.C.	98	122	219	73
11	8484	Do.	–	Curry Ord. Agricul.	R.C.	–	R.C.	2R.C.	275	225	500	144
12	10457	Do.	–	Cloonagara,	R.C.	–	R.C.	–	97	84	181	56
13	10[illegible]	Do.	–	Carrowvile, m.	R.C.	–	R.C.	–	103	–	103	41
14	10[illegible]	Do.	–	Do. f.	R.C.	–	R.C.	–	–	66	66	36
15	1416	Aghanagh,	26	Ourtalough, f.	R.C.	–	R.C.	R.C.	–	114	114	37
16	10[illegible]	Do.	–	Hollybrook, *	–	–	–	–	–	–	–	–
17	10[illegible]	Do.	–	Cloughogue,	R.C.	–	R.C.	–	70	61	131	44
18	[illegible]	Do.	–	Ballinafad, m.	R.C.	–	R.C.	–	119	–	119	39
19	3[illegible]	Ahamlish,	16	Rantallure, * m.	–	–	–	–	–	–	–	–
20	[illegible]	Do.	–	Do. f.	–	R.C.	R.C.	–	53	150	203	76
21	3736	Do.	–	Grange, m.	R.C.	–	R.C.	R.C.	184	–	184	52
22	10[illegible]	Do.	–	Do. f.	R.C.	–	R.C.	R.C.	–	145	145	56
23	4[illegible]	Do.	–	Cliffoney, m.	–	R.C.	R.C.	–	140	–	140	48
24	3174	Do.	–	Do. f.	–	R.C.	R.C.	–	–	109	109	56
25	[illegible]	Do.	–	Mount Temple,	–	R.C.	R.C.	R.C.	97	96	193	69
26	4618	Do.	–	Castlegal, m.	R.C.	–	R.C.	–	124	–	124	64
27	6108	Do.	–	Do. f.	R.C.	–	R.C.	R.C.	–	143	143	54
28	[illegible]	Do.	–	Inishmurray,	–	R.C.	R.C.	–	25	21	46	26
29	6[illegible]	Do.	–	Mullaghmore,	R.C.	–	R.C.	R.C.	59	78	137	60
30	[illegible]	Do.	–	Breaghwy, f.	R.C.	–	R.C.	–	–	147	147	52
31	11[illegible]	Do.	–	Do. m.	R.C.	–	R.C.	–	100	–	100	46
32	11[illegible]	Do.	–	Cliffoney, i.	–	R.C.	R.C.	–	65	65	130	57
33	1416	Ballysadare,	–	Lisconny, m.	R.C.	–	R.C.	–	125	–	125	47
34	[illegible]	Do.	–	Do. f.	R.C.	–	R.C.	–	–	118	115	44
35	18[illegible]	Do.	–	Camphill Ord. Agr.	R.C.	–	R.C.	–	149	–	143	70
36	[illegible]	Do.	–	Do. f.	R.C.	–	R.C.	–	–	119	119	46
37	7410	Do.	–	Ballysadare, m.	R.C.	–	R.C.	–	139	–	139	54
38	[illegible]	Do.	–	Do. f.	R.C.	–	R.C.	–	–	89	89	41
39	6[illegible]	Ballymacnaghan,	–	Scurry,	R.C.	–	R.C.	R.C.	70	78	148	61
40	10[illegible]	Do.	–	Bloomfield,	R.C.	–	R.C.	R.C.	95	96	191	55
41	[illegible]	Ballynakill,	26	Coolbeck,	R.C.	–	R.C.	R.C.	118	97	215	65
42	[illegible]	Ballymote,	21	Ballymote, f.	R.C.	–	R.C.	R.C.	–	170	171	59
43	[illegible]	Castleconnor,	20	Corballa,	R.C.	–	R.C.	R.C.	134	114	248	75
44	4616	Do.	–	Stokane,	R.C.	–	R.C.	–	103	101	204	79
45	76[illegible]	Do.	–	Carragarry,	R.C.	–	R.C.	–	63	73	136	45
46	10478	Colry,	19	Colry, m.	R.C.	–	R.C.	–	97	–	97	39
47	10476	Do.	–	Do. f.	R.C.	–	R.C.	–	–	95	95	38
48	[illegible]	Do.	–	Drumcondra,	R.C.	–	R.C.	–	32	64	97	36
49	[illegible]	Do.	–	Sligo, Dist. Mod. m.	Com.	N.E.	R.C.	E.C.	173	–	173	63
50	[illegible]	Do.	–	Do. f.	Com.	N.E.	Pres.	Diss.	–	160	160	64
51	[illegible]	Do.	–	Do. i.	Com.	N.E.	E.C.	–	38	35	73	42
52	7251	Cloonoghill,	21	Carrowreagh,	R.C.	–	R.C.	R.C.	69	51	120	49
53	[illegible]	Do.	–	Rosinalday, m.	R.C.	–	R.C.	–	96	–	96	32
54	[illegible]	Do.	–	Do. f.	R.C.	–	R.C.	–	–	76	76	35
55	2761	Drumard,	19	Drumard,	R.C.	–	R.C.	–	36	37	73	36
56	9148	Do.	–	Ballacurragh, m.	R.C.	–	R.C.	–	131	–	131	50
57	10[illegible]	Do.	–	Do. f.	R.C.	–	R.C.	–	–	95	95	38
58	84[illegible]	Drumcliff,	–	Rathcormack, f.	R.C.	–	R.C.	R.C.	73	140	223	77
59	[illegible]	Do.	–	Hollywilliam,	R.C.	–	R.C.	R.C.	114	94	208	68
60	[illegible]	Do.	–	Carney,	R.C.	–	R.C.	R.C.	113	96	209	55
61	[illegible]	Do.	–	Rosses, Lower,	R.C.	–	R.C.	R.C.	76	77	153	49
62	[illegible]	Do.	–	Ballyconnell, m.	R.C.	–	R.C.	–	124	–	124	41

* Including value of Free Residence and Garden. b Including value of Free Garden.

Province of CONNAUGHT: County of SLIGO.

SLIGO—140 Schools.

Amount paid for Books, Requisites, and Apparatus, at Reduced Prices.	Aid granted by the Board during the Year 1874: In Free Stock of Books, Requisites, and Apparatus.	In Salaries, Premiums, and other Gratuities.	Results Fees, Financial Year.	Amounts of Local Emoluments received in Aid of Teacher's Salary: School Fees.	Subscriptions, Endowments, &c.	Total Local Aid.	Vested or Non-Vested.	Number.
£ s. d.	£ s. d.	£ s. d.	£ s. d.	£ s. d.	£ s. d.	£ s. d.		
1 19 6	—	48 10 0	21 16 0	5 0 0	1 10 0	*6 10 0	V.F.	1
8 16 8	—	69 5 4	24 8 0	15 17 2	—	15 17 2	V.F.	2
6 8 0	—	80 0 0	31 17 6	8 13 6	—	8 13 6	V.F.	3
4 8 0	—	—	—	—	—	—		4
4 18 11	—	20 10 0	9 4 8	7 1 6	—	7 1 6	V.F.	5
4 17 0	—	53 11 9	60 5 6	8 13 0	3 10 0	*12 3 6	V.F.	6
3 0 0	—	61 6 8	—	3 10 0	—	3 10 0	V.F.	7
2 18 4	—	48 0 0	—	1 10 0	—	1 10 0	V.F.	8
5 6 11	—	67 5 9	34 14 6	8 17 6	—	8 17 6		9
3 1 10	—	47 0 0	13 9 4	3 2 6	2 15 0	†5 17 6		10
10 2 3	—	61 13 4	72 18 6	6 5 6	—	6 5 6		11
1 19 4	—	24 0 0	—	4 0 0	—	4 0 0		12
2 6 0	—	21 0 0	18 17 0	10 0 0	—	10 0 0		13
2 10 0	—	20 0 0	8 8 0	6 0 0	—	3 0 0		14
—	—	50 0 0	16 18 8	4 3 4	—	4 3 4	A.	15
1 18 6	—	—	—	—	—	—		16
2 5 3	—	68 18 4	16 18 0	2 4 6	—	2 4 0		17
3 4 6	—	40 18 8	13 17 0	4 10 6	—	4 10 0		18
—	—	—	—	—	—	—	V.F.	19
2 14 8	—	65 0 0	21 1 6	6 0 3	25 0 0	*31 0 3	V.F.	20
8 8 2	—	48 0 0	10 7 6	8 8 10	—	8 8 10		21
5 11 3	—	49 10 0	19 4 4	2 14 4	—	2 14 4		22
4 13 3	—	50 0 0	13 18 6	8 17 3	25 0 0	33 17 3		23
—	—	55 0 0	25 11 0	23 0 3	—	23 0 3		24
3 18 6	—	41 0 0	14 19 4	4 14 8	10 0 0	14 14 8	V.F.	25
0 8 4	—	38 10 0	11 9 6	2 4 0	10 0 0	12 4 0		26
3 0 1	—	62 0 0	19 19 0	3 10 0	10 0 0	13 10 0		27
1 10 8	—	20 0 0	2 13 0	—	1 10 0	1 10 0		28
3 8 0	—	67 5 4	14 8 6	8 8 11	—	8 8 11		29
1 8 10	—	26 15 6	14 1 6	6 18 0	—	6 18 0		30
1 17 6	5 0 0	24 0 0	13 19 6	6 13 1	—	6 13 1		31
5 3 9	4 0 0	24 10 0	11 0 0	0 18 3	10 0 0	10 18 3		32
4 7 0	—	27 0 0	18 8 0	4 19 6	—	4 19 6		33
—	—	41 0 0	20 11 0	8 8 8	0 2 6	*8 8 0		34
7 8 7	—	54 0 0	30 11 0	9 8 6	1 6 7	†10 0 1	V.F.	35
—	—	24 10 0	20 1 6	8 9 6	—	8 9 6	V.F.	36
4 0 8	—	68 0 0	17 10 8	5 13 0	—	5 13 0		37
3 7 0	—	26 0 0	10 8 6	4 17 0	—	4 17 0		38
6 1 6	—	53 16 8	10 10 6	2 10 0	—	2 10 0		39
4 17 10	—	58 16 9	20 8 0	3 18 0	—	3 18 0		40
6 15 0	4 15 10	93 3 4	64 17 0	3 1 0	8 0 0	*11 1 0		41
5 0 7	—	45 6 6	30 10 6	7 10 0	—	7 10 0		42
9 10 4	—	52 0 0	26 4 0	9 0 4	—	9 0 4		43
5 6 0	—	65 6 8	21 18 6	4 0 6	—	4 0 0		44
1 18 10	—	—	10 8 6	—	0 13 0	*0 13 0		45
3 10 4	—	35 7 6	9 4 0	8 2 0	—	8 2 0		46
2 0 10	—	30 0 0	7 1 0	1 8 8	—	1 8 8		47
0 10 2	—	6 18 4	1 17 0	1 17 8	—	1 17 8		48
23 1 1	5 4 3							49
—	1 0 11	597 8 11	63 4 10	141 17 6	—	141 17 6		50
—	—							51
5 8 6	—	30 0 0	14 8 6	5 11 6	—	5 11 6		52
8 15 0	—	62 0 0	14 13 0	5 8 8	—	5 8 8		53
1 11 7	—	30 0 0	16 1 6	5 4 0	—	5 4 0		54
1 18 0	—	24 0 0	15 0 6	5 10 0	—	5 10 0		55
4 15 11	—	44 0 0	26 6 6	8 8 0	—	8 8 0		56
5 12 7	—	33 0 0	18 8 0	5 4 0	—	5 4 0		57
6 4 10	5 0 0	50 0 0	62 18 0	0 18 4	—	0 18 4		58
6 15 11	—	42 1 1	40 9 0	5 8 6	—	5 8 6		59
2 18 6	—	60 0 0	36 8 6	6 1 1	—	6 1 1		60
3 12 1	—	44 0 0	16 5 0	4 1 8	—	4 1 0		61
1 7 10	—	24 0 0	14 10 0	2 10 10	—	2 10 10		62

* Inoperative.

† Including value of Free Residence.

List of Schools in operation on the 31st December, 1874.—

Number.	Roll Number of School.	Parish.	District.	School.	Religious Denomination of Managers or Correspondents: Clerical.	Lay.	Number and Religious Denominations of Teachers: Principals.	Assistants.	Attendance for the Year: Total number of Pupils on Rolls within the Year 1874: Males.	Females.	Total.	Average Daily Attendance for Year 1874.
63	12830	Drumcliff,	14	Ballyconnell, f.	R.C.	–	R.C.	–	–	103	103	43
64	10382	Drumrat,	21	Culfadda,	R.C.	–	R.C.	–	89	73	162	60
65	1099	Emlaghfad,	–	Emlaghnaghtan,	R.C.	–	R.C.	R.C.	60	90	175	65
66	3767	Do.	–	Ballymote,	R.C.	–	R.C.	R.C.	156	–	155	69
67	[illegible]	Easky,	20	Cloonacannana,	R.C.	–	R.C.	–	78	105	183	64
68	[illegible]	Do.	–	Owenbeg,	R.C.	–	R.C.	–	72	100	172	41
69	4197	Do.	–	Easky, m.	R.C.	–	R.C.	–	81	–	81	30
70	[illegible]	Do.	–	Do., f.	R.C.	–	R.C.	–	–	75	75	31
71	10479	Do.	–	Rathlee, b m.	–	–	–	–	–	–	–	–
72	[illegible]	Do.	–	Do., f.	R.C.	–	R.C.	–	111	129	238	[illegible]
73	6691	Do.	–	Killandaff, m.	–	R.C.	R.C.	–	80	–	80	31
74	[illegible]	Do.	–	Do., f.	–	R.C.	R.C.	–	–	73	73	[illegible]
75	[illegible]	Kilmactigue,	21	Largan,	R.C.	–	R.C.	–	125	74	199	43
76	[illegible]	Do.	–	Banada,	R.C.	–	R.C.	R.C.	331	80	412	76
77	[illegible]	Do.	–	Kilmactigue, m.	R.C.	–	R.C.	–	190	–	190	31
78	[illegible]	Do.	–	Do., f.	R.C.	–	R.C.	–	–	206	206	61
79	4187	Do.	–	Castlerock,	R.C.	–	R.C.	R.C.	139	147	286	61
80	[illegible]	Kilmacallan,	22	Greyfort,	R.C.	–	R.C.	–	73	101	174	66
81	[illegible]	Do.	–	Annagh,	R.C.	–	R.C.	R.C.	78	100	178	62
82	[illegible]	Do.	–	Ross,	R.C.	–	R.C.	R.C.	100	113	213	67
83	[illegible]	Do.	–	Drumdelany,	R.C.	–	R.C.	–	63	43	106	37
84	[illegible]	Kilross,	–	Cambeen, m.	R.C.	–	R.C.	–	121	–	121	66
85	[illegible]	Do.	–	Do., f.	R.C.	–	R.C.	R.C.	–	164	164	66
86	[illegible]	Do.	–	Clogher,	Pres.	–	Pres.	–	33	29	62	20
87	[illegible]	Do.	–	Tawnylenagh,	R.C.	–	R.C.	R.C.	84	97	181	57
88	1101	Kilmorgan,	–	Kilmorgan,	R.C.	–	R.C.	–	100	90	190	51
89	1172	Kilshalvy,	–	Killavil,	R.C.	–	R.C.	2 R.C.	208	153	361	122
90	6170	Do.	–	Tunnagh,	R.C.	–	R.C.	R.C.	100	73	173	40
91	1213	Kilmactranny,	–	Geevagh Ord. Agri.	R.C.	–	R.C.	R.C.	135	–	135	65
92	[illegible]	Do.	–	Do., f.	R.C.	–	R.C.	–	–	165	165	47
93	[illegible]	Do.	–	Highwood,	R.C.	–	R.C.	–	95	38	133	33
94	[illegible]	Do.	–	Kilmactranny,	R.C.	–	R.C.	–	32	71	103	31
95	[illegible]	Do.	–	Upper Arigna,	R.C.	–	R.C.	–	37	37	71	30
96	[illegible]	Killery,	12	Ballintogher, m.	R.C.	–	R.C.	–	107	–	107	31
97	[illegible]	Do.	–	Do., f.	R.C.	–	R.C.	–	–	86	86	31
98	[illegible]	Do.	–	Cromlagh,	–	R.C.	R.C.	–	99	70	179	36
99	[illegible]	Killaraght,	22	Cloonloogh,	R.C.	–	R.C.	R.C.	103	121	224	78
100	[illegible]	Do.	–	Derryknockeran,	–	R.C.	R.C.	–	80	98	178	61
101	[illegible]	Kilnamanagh,	22	Farranmacfarrell,	R.C.	–	R.C.	R.C.	241	135	376	62
102	10217	Do.	–	Glencarby,	R.C.	–	R.C.	–	44	54	98	30
103	10319	Do.	–	Ralvilla,	R.C.	–	R.C.	–	76	79	155	43
104	6300	Do.	–	Dromore, West, Workhouse,	P.L.	Gds.	R.C.	–	9	15	24	19
105	[illegible]	Killaspugbrone,	12	Strandhill,	R.C.	–	R.C.	–	48	43	91	37
106	9016	Do.	–	Coney Island,	R.C.	–	R.C.	–	27	22	49	22
107	4180	Kilfree,	22	Cara,	R.C.	–	R.C.	M.R.C.	102	109	211	59
108	[illegible]	Do.	–	Mullaghroe, m.	R.C.	–	R.C.	–	108	–	108	65
109	[illegible]	Do.	–	Do., f.	R.C.	–	R.C.	R.C.	–	111	111	49
110	9172	Do.	–	Cloonacagh, f.	R.C.	–	R.C.	R.C.	–	151	151	41
111	4101	Do.	–	Do., m.	R.C.	–	R.C.	–	151	–	151	44
112	4891	Do.	–	Kilfree,	R.C.	–	R.C.	R.C.	100	69	169	61
113	10784	Do.	15	Knockbrack, m.	R.C.	–	R.C.	–	119	–	119	56
114	[illegible]	Do.	–	Do., f.	R.C.	–	R.C.	–	–	119	119	44
115	[illegible]	Kilmacowen,	–	Kilmacowen,	R.C.	–	R.C.	–	41	73	114	35
116	[illegible]	Kilglass,	20	Kilglass,	R.C.	–	R.C.	–	38	57	95	31
117	[illegible]	Do.	–	Inishcrone, m.	R.C.	–	R.C.	–	97	–	97	[illegible]
118	10460	Do.	–	Do., f.	R.C.	–	R.C.	–	28	108	136	37
119	6177	Do.	–	Culleens,	R.C.	–	R.C.	–	120	109	229	50
120	[illegible]	Do.	–	Quigabar,	R.C.	–	R.C.	R.C.	79	41	120	34
121	[illegible]	Killoran,	12	Rockfield,	R.C.	–	R.C.	–	64	66	130	49
122	[illegible]	Do.	–	Coragh,	R.C.	–	R.C.	–	71	72	143	31
123	[illegible]	Do.	–	Killoran,	R.C.	–	R.C.	R.C.	111	[illegible]	[illegible]	78
124	6489	Kilvarnet,	–	Ballynacarrow,	R.C.	–	R.C.	R.C.	51	54	105	45

a Including value of Free Garden.

b Inoperative.

Province of Connaught: County of Sligo—*continued.*

Amount paid for Books, Requisites, and Apparatus at Reduced Prices.	Aid granted by the Board during the Year 1874. In Free Grants of Books, Requisites, and Apparatus.	In Salaries, Premiums, and other Gratuities.	Results Fees, Financial Year.	Amount of Local Contributions received in Aid of Teacher's Salary. School Fees.	Subscriptions, Endowments, &c.	Total Local Aid.	Vested or Non-Vested.	Number.
£ s. d.	£ s. d.	£ s. d.	£ s. d.	£ s. d.	£ s. d.	£ s. d.		
2 6 9	—	20 0 0	14 16 0	0 10 8	—	0 10 8		63
3 0 2	1 5 0	41 0 0	17 5 5	4 0 0	6 13 4	*10 13 4		64
1 6 3	—	46 0 0	10 10 0	3 17 11	—	3 17 11	[illegible]	65
1 10 0	—	52 6 8	26 0 0	8 15 0	—	8 15 0		66
—	—	27 0 0	13 15 0	3 0 0	0 18 0	*3 18 0	A.	67
1 8 3	—	30 5 0	11 13 6	—	—	—	A.	68
1 18 5	—	—	6 10 0	4 10 0	—	4 10 0		69
1 5 3	—	20 0 0	11 10 0	8 2 9	—	8 2 9		70
—	—	—	—	—	—	—		71
1 5 3	—	25 0 0	13 7 6	5 0 0	—	5 0 0		72
1 15 8	—	24 0 0	2 1 0	0 15 0	7 10 0	*8 5 0		73
—	—	20 0 0	6 19 0	0 15 0	8 0 0	*8 15 0		74
5 3 6	—	41 0 0	15 5 6	1 10 0	—	1 10 0	V.T.	75
8 17 10	—	70 6 8	22 5 6	1 10 0	3 14 10	*5 4 10	V.T.	76
6 3 10	—	30 0 0	10 5 0	0 10 0	0 10 0	*1 0 0	V.T.	77
—	—	21 10 0	5 16 0	—	—	—	V.T.	78
6 17 8	—	59 0 0	18 0 0	—	1 0 0	*1 0 0	V.T.	79
3 12 6	2 15 6	31 6 8	20 5 0	4 6 0	—	4 6 0		80
1 6 3	5 10 9	41 0 0	25 13 0	2 8 0	—	2 8 0		81
7 1 2	—	67 10 0	30 15 6	2 18 0	—	2 18 0		82
—	—	60 0 0	21 0 0	2 0 0	—	2 0 0		83
0 17 2	—	24 0 0	7 6 0	2 2 0	6 0 0	*8 2 0		84
—	—	67 16 8	23 0 0	3 0 0	—	3 0 0		85
1 6 11	—	60 0 0	13 1 0	20 0 0	5 0 0	*25 0 0		86
6 13 0	—	60 0 0	31 17 0	5 10 0	—	5 10 0		87
4 8 1	6 10 0	40 3 4	24 5 6	5 0 0	—	5 0 0		88
9 19 7	—	56 6 4	23 0 0	10 12 6	—	10 12 6	A.	89
1 10 1	—	46 13 8	17 5 0	0 17 6	—	0 17 6		90
4 4 1	—	93 0 6	30 0 6	3 7 1	0 15 0	*4 2 1		91
4 5 1	—	97 16 8	60 5 0	6 6 7	1 0 0	*7 6 7		92
8 0 10	—	30 15 6	26 6 0	8 7 6	2 0 0	*8 7 6		93
8 17 3	—	28 10 0	11 7 0	2 0 0	—	2 0 0		94
8 7 11	—	10 6 6	10 7 0	0 4 0	—	0 4 0		95
5 7 8	—	—	6 13 6	2 10 0	—	2 10 0	A.	96
8 8 2	—	—	8 8 0	1 16 4	—	1 16 4	A.	97
5 16 8	—	—	12 16 0	4 10 0	5 0 0	*9 10 0		98
5 17 6	—	64 18 4	40 5 0	10 0 0	10 18 8	*21 18 8		99
5 18 4	3 8 2	65 13 4	17 8 6	8 11 6	—	8 11 6		100
6 16 5	—	49 10 0	12 8 6	0 5 0	—	0 5 0		101
—	—	21 13 4	—	—	—	—		102
8 16 2	—	36 10 0	18 9 6	1 12 6	—	1 12 6		103
3 6 11	—	1 10 0	—	—	—	—		104
1 13 8	—	20 0 0	10 6 6	1 10 6	—	1 10 6		105
1 5 0	—	24 0 0	6 11 5	0 15 6	—	0 15 6		106
7 8 6	—	28 10 0	30 10 6	0 10 0	6 1 6	*6 11 6		107
1 7 6	4 10 0	21 0 0	14 12 0	1 0 0	—	1 0 0	V.T.	108
2 13 11	4 10 0	33 0 0	25 10 6	—	—	—	V.T.	109
4 19 3	—	54 15 0	26 12 0	4 8 10	—	4 8 10		110
6 11 4	—	56 10 0	20 18 0	3 7 0	—	3 7 0		111
1 4 10	—	43 0 0	22 14 6	1 4 0	—	1 4 0		112
1 18 1	—	27 0 0	14 18 6	9 4 0	—	9 4 0		113
6 11 2	—	61 10 0	14 10 6	8 10 0	—	8 10 0		114
1 8 1	—	20 0 0	11 11 0	1 14 6	—	1 14 6		115
4 2 0	—	22 4 0	0 0 6	0 10 8	—	0 10 8		116
5 9 0	—	30 0 0	15 5 6	5 17 8	—	5 17 8		117
3 19 7	—	43 18 4	11 8 6	8 0 0	—	8 0 0		118
3 0 1	—	63 8 4	17 9 0	5 9 0	—	5 9 0		119
4 11 4	—	55 6 4	23 16 6	7 5 0	—	7 5 0		120
1 6 0	—	51 0 0	10 11 0	8 1 0	0 10 0	*8 11 0		121
1 10 1	—	25 16 10	16 16 6	1 6 0	—	1 6 0	V.T.	122
1 9 0	—	33 0 0	22 8 0	4 0 0	—	4 0 0		123
5 5 1	—	50 0 0	23 18 0	4 4 0	—	4 4 0		124

* Including value of Free Residence.

‡ Including value of Free Residence and Garden.

List of Schools in operation on the 31st December, 1874.—

Number.	Roll Number of School.	Parish.	District.	School.	Religious Denomination of Manager or Correspondent.		Number and Religious Denomination of Teachers.		Attendance for the Year.			
									Total number of Pupils on Rolls within the Year 1874.			Average Daily Attendance for the Year.
					Clerical.	Lay.	Principals.	Assistants.	Males.	Fem.	Total.	
125	10456	Kilross,	19	Kilross,	R.C.	–	R.C.	R.C.	109	110	219	81
126	6600	Do.	20	Cronkstown,	R.C.	–	R.C.	R.C.	103	116	219	89
127	10004	Do.	–	Mullanes,	R.C.	–	R.C.	R.C.	127	123	250	73
128	7876	Killaderry,	22	Mount Town,	R.C.	–	R.C.	–	66	64	130	38
129	9486	Do.	–	Cloonagh,	R.C.	–	R.C.	–	66	41	107	41
130	9591	Skreen,	12	Ballinlig,	R.C.	–	R.C.	–	42	43	85	38
131	3217	Do.	20	Tubbercurry,	R.C.	–	R.C.	R.C.	60	101	161	71
132	8455	Do.	12	Carrowcarro,	R.C.	–	R.C.	R.C.	65	52	117	57
133	9805	Do.	–	Dark,	R.C.	–	R.C.	–	61	68	129	43
134	9664	Do.	20	Doonally Ord. Agr.,	–	R.C.	R.C.	R.C.	94	63	157	62
135	4811	Shancough,	22	St. James's Well,	R.C.	–	R.C.	R.C.	186	90	276	72
136	7024	St. John's,	18	Carrowroe,	–	R.C.	R.C.	–	110	75	191	69
137	7201	Do.	–	St. John's, f.	R.C.	–	R.C.	R.C.	73	71	144	60
138	5851	Do.	–	Sligo, Convent, f.	–	R.C.	Nuns		26	645	671	284
139	8239	Do.	–	Do. Workhouse,	P.L. Gdns.		R.C.	–	45	65	110	86
140	8082	Do.	–	Do. Lunatic Asylum, *	Governor		–	–	–	–	–	–
141	10483	Tawnagh,	20	Knockalassa,	R.C.	–	R.C.	R.C.	107	104	211	79
142	2308	Toomour,	–	Kesh,	R.C.	–	R.C.	R.C.	114	71	185	60
143	10280	Do.	–	Carrowcrory, f.	–	E.C.	R.C.	R.C.	59	104	156	48
144	8758	Do.	–	Greenmore,	Pres.	–	Pres.	–	60	50	119	35
145	11096	Do.	–	Carrowcrory, m.	R.C.	–	R.C.	–	86	–	86	29
146	9701	Do.	21	Rathmullen,	R.C.	–	R.C.	–	104	114	218	86
147	4108	Templeboy,	20	Kilrushbiggins,	R.C.	–	R.C.	R.C.	100	110	210	60
148	4308	Do.	–	Ballyweelican,	R.C.	–	R.C.	R.C.	70	85	155	36
149	11218	Do.	–	Augheries, *	–	–	–	–	–	–	–	–
		Total for County Sligo, 149.							11622	11697	23,319	8,015

* Including value of Farm Garden. [b] Including value of Free Residence and Garden.

Province of Connaught: County of Sligo—*continued.*

Amount paid for Books, Requisites, and Apparatus at Reduced Prices.	Aid granted by the Board during the Year 1874. In Free Stock of Books, Requisites, and Apparatus.	In Salaries, Premiums, and other Gratuities.	Results Fees, Financial Year.	Amount of Local Emoluments received in Aid of Teacher's Salary. School Fees.	Appropriations, Endowments, &c.	Total Local Aid.	Vested or Non-Vested.	Number.
£ s. d.	£ s. d.	£ s. d.	£ s. d.	£ s. d.	£ s. d.	£ s. d.		
5 3 11	—	45 13 4	24 10 0	0 5 0	—	0 5 0		125
1 5 9	—	48 16 8	4 8 0	1 19 0	—	1 10 0		126
4 10 9	—	30 10 0	15 14 0	0 14 0	—	6 14 9		127
8 16 0	—	21 0 0	9 15 0	3 5 6	—	3 5 8		128
2 7 11	—	33 13 4	23 11 0	5 12 0	—	5 12 9		129
1 13 8	—	30 10 0	13 17 0	6 7 0	—	6 7 6		130
4 19 5	—	57 10 5	43 9 0	0 12 0	0 15 0	*10 7 0		131
9 1 8	—	44 0 10	27 3 0	7 14 0	—	7 14 0		132
1 11 0	—	21 0 0	15 8 0	7 2 6	—	7 2 0		133
13 7 8	—	64 11 8	34 5 6	12 0 0	23 15 3	*39 0 0		134
9 18 4	—	48 10 0	40 18 0	4 0 0	2 0 0	*8 0 0		135
7 0 4	—	50 5 0	30 5 6	16 0 0	6 0 0	*24 0 0		136
1 12 1	—	41 0 0	11 7 6	1 10 4	6 0 0	7 14 4		137
31 10 6	—	140 2 4	65 13 6	33 16 8	—	38 14 8		138
13 0 0	—	8 10 0	—	—	—	—		139
0 1 0	—	—	—	—	—	—		140
4 1 2	3 4 6	51 13 4	32 16 0	7 16 6	—	7 16 6		141
6 13 3	—	84 0 0	48 17 0	46 12 0	15 0 0	61 12 0		142
8 9 7	—	47 0 0	24 0 0	10 0 0	—	10 0 0		143
2 16 8	3 8 8	23 0 0	11 19 0	—	12 0 0	*12 0 0		144
3 12 1	4 0 0	80 0 0	6 8 0	7 4 6	—	7 4 6		145
2 18 11	1 7 0	17 18 4	17 0 8	7 8 0	6 10 0	*13 18 0		146
2 14 11	—	61 13 4	25 14 0	11 8 6	17 1 3	*28 9 9		147
—	—	56 8 4	20 8 8	3 6 0	—	3 6 0		148
—	—	—	8 15 6	—	—	—		149
225 1 4	59 0 7	6,454 4 11	2,740 10 4	269 13 2	140 16 7	1,118 9 0		

* No returns.

a Including value of Free Residence.

DUBLIN: Printed by ALEXANDER THOM, 87 & 88, Abbey-street,
Printer to the Queen's Most Excellent Majesty.
For Her Majesty's Stationery Office.

www.ingramcontent.com/pod-product-compliance
Lightning Source LLC
Chambersburg PA
CBHW030733230426
43667CB00007B/691
* 9 7 8 3 7 4 1 1 0 4 5 8 9 *